Chelsea Chean

Barb Fellnermayr

437-1211 (ph)

439-1165 (fax)

D0820072

Fourth Canadian Edition
Volume 1

INTERMEDIATE ACCOUNTING

INTERMEDIATE ACCOUNTING

Fourth Canadian Edition
Volume 1

Donald E. Kieso Ph.D., C.P.A.
KPMG Peat Marwick Professor of Accounting
Northern Illinois University
DeKalb, Illinois

Jerry J. Weygandt Ph.D., C.P.A.
Arthur Anderson Alumni Professor of Accounting
University of Wisconsin
Madison, Wisconsin

Canadian Edition prepared by

V. Bruce Irvine Ph.D., C.M.A., F.C.M.A.
University of Saskatchewan
Saskatoon, Saskatchewan

W. Harold Silvester Ph.D., C.P.A., C.A.
University of Saskatchewan
Saskatoon, Saskatchewan

John Wiley & Sons
Toronto New York Chichester Brisbane Singapore

DEDICATED TO

Marilyn	Viola
Lee-Ann	Susan
Cameron	Dianne
Sandra	Daniel

Canadian Cataloguing in Publication Data

Kieso, Donald E.
Intermediate Accounting

4th Canadian ed. / prepared by V. Bruce Irvine,
W. Harold Silvester.
Includes bibliographical references and index.
ISBN 0-471-64094-8 (v. 1)   ISBN 0-471-64095-6 (v. 2)

1. Accounting. I. Weygandt, Jerry J. II. Irvine,
V. Bruce. III. Silvester, W. Harold. IV. Title.

HP5635.K54 1994   657'.044   C94-930183-3

Production Credits

Design: JAQ
Cover Design: Selwyn Simon
Cover Photo Credits: Victor Last
Typesetting: Compeer Typographic Services
Film: Compeer Typographic Services

Printed and bound by Metropole Litho Inc.
10 9 8 7 6 5 4 3 2

ABOUT THE AUTHORS

CANADIAN EDITION

V. Bruce Irvine Ph.D., C.M.A., F.C.M.A., is a professor of Accounting at the University of Saskatchewan. He received his Ph.D. in accounting from the University of Minnesota. Among his publications are articles and reviews in such journals as *C.M.A. "The Management Accounting Magazine,"* *CA Magazine*, *Managerial Planning*, and *The Accounting Review*. Designated "Professor of the Year" several times, Dr. Irvine has extensive teaching experience in financial and managerial accounting and has been instrumental in establishing innovative pedagogical techniques and instructional materials at the University of Saskatchewan. He has had considerable involvement with practising accountants through serving on various local, provincial, national, and international committees and boards of the Society of Management Accountants. Additionally, Dr. Irvine has served in various executive committee positions of the Canadian Academic Accounting Association.

W. Harold Silvester Ph.D., C.P.A., C.A., received his doctorate from the University of Missouri, Columbia, and is Professor of Accounting at the University of Saskatchewan. In his teaching capacity, he has played a key role in introducing pedagogical improvements at the University of Saskatchewan and in developing instructional materials for the Accounting program there. He has been named "Professor of the Year" in recognition of his substantial contributions to the College of Commerce. An important contribution has been the development of materials to integrate computers with accounting instruction. Articles by Professor Silvester have appeared in *CA Magazine* and other academic and professional journals.

U.S. EDITION

Donald E. Kieso, PH.D., C.P.A., received his doctorate in accounting from the University of Illinois. He has served as chairman of the Department of Accountancy and is currently the KPMG Peat Marwick Professor of Accountancy at Northern Illinois University. He has public accounting experience with Price Waterhouse & Co. (San Francisco and Chicago) and Arthur Anderson & Co. (Chicago) and research experience with the Research Division of the American Institute of Certified Public Accountants (New York). He has done postdoctorate work as a Visiting Scholar at the University of California at Berkeley and is a recipient of NIU's Teaching Excellence Award and has twice received the Executive MBA Golden Apple Teaching Award. Professor Kieso is the author of other accounting and business books and is a member of the American Accounting Association, the American Institute of Certified Public Accountants, the Financial Executives Institute, and the Illinois CPA Society. He has served as a member of the Board of Directors of the Illinois CPA Society, the AACSB Accounting Accreditation Committee, the Board of Governors of the American Accounting Association's Administrators of Accounting Programs Group, the State of Illinois Comptroller's Commission, as Secretary-Treasurer of the Federation of Schools of Accountancy, and as Secretary-Treasurer of the American Accounting Association. Professor Kieso is currently serving as a member of the Accounting Education Change Commission, the Board of Directors of Aurora University, as the chair of the Accounting Education Change Liaison Committee of the American Accounting Association, and on committees of the Illinois CPA Society. In 1988 he received the Outstanding Accounting Educator Award from the Illinois CPA Society.

Jerry J. Weygandt, Ph.D., C.P.A., is Arthur Anderson Alumni Professor of Accounting at the University of Wisconsin-Madison. He holds a Ph.D. in accounting from the University of Illinois. Articles by Professor Weygandt have appeared in the *Accounting Review*, *Journal of Accounting Research*, the *Journal of Accountancy*, and other professional journals. These articles have examined such financial reporting issues as accounting for price-level adjustments, pensions, convertible securities, stock option contracts, and interim reports. He is a member of the American Accounting Association, the American Institute of Certified Public Accountants, and the Wisconsin Society of Certified Public Accountants. He has served on numerous committees of the American Accounting Association and as a member of the editorial board of the *Accounting Review*. In addition, he is actively involved with the American Institute of Certified Public Accountants and has been a member of the Accounting Standards Executive Committee (AcSEC) of that organization. He has served as a consultant to a number of businesses and state agencies on financial reporting issues and served on the FASB task force that examined the reporting issues related to "accounting for income taxes." Professor Weygandt has received the Chancellor's Award for Excellence in Teaching; he also served as Secretary-Treasurer of the American Accounting Association. In 1991, he received the Wisconsin Institute of CPA's Outstanding Educator's Award.

PREFACE

The fourth Canadian edition of *Intermediate Accounting* discusses in depth the traditional (intermediate) financial accounting topics as well as the recent developments in accounting recognition, measurement, and disclosure practices promulgated by the leading professional accounting organizations and applied by practitioners in public accounting and industry. Explanations and discussions of financial accounting theory are supported and illustrated by examples taken directly from practice and authoritative pronouncements.

Continuing to keep pace with the complexities of the modern business enterprise, we have included a comprehensive set of topics supported by numerous illustrations and judiciously selected appendices. The appendices are concerned primarily with complex subjects, lesser-used methods, or specialized topics.

The text is organized into six major parts:

1. Financial Accounting Functions and Basic Theory (Chapters 1 to 6)
2. Assets: Recognition, Measurement, and Disclosure (Chapters 7 to 12)
3. Liabilities: Recognition, Measurement, and Disclosure (Chapters 13 to 14)
4. Shareholders' Equity, Dilutive Securities, and Investments (Chapters 15 to 18)
5. Issues Related to Selected Topics (Chapters 19 to 22)
6. Preparation and Analysis of Financial Statements (Chapters 23 to 25)

An Appendix to the book explains and illustrates various time value of money concepts and provides present and future value tables.

After careful consideration and discussion with instructors, we have decided to offer the fourth Canadian edition in two separate volumes. Volume 1 contains Chapters 1-12 (dealing with assets) and Volume 2 contains Chapters 13-25 (dealing with liabilities, shareholders' equity, and other topics). Both volumes contain the Appendix on "Accounting and the Time Value of Money" as well as the table of contents and index for the entire book.

Benefiting from the comments and recommendations of adopters of our third revised edition, we have made significant revisions. Explanations have been expanded where necessary, complicated discussions and illustrations have been simplified, realism has been integrated to heighten interest and relevancy, and new topics and coverage have been added to maintain currency. We have deleted some third revised edition coverage and condensed the coverage of other topics.

We have attempted to balance our coverage so that the discussion of underlying concepts of accounting and their practical application are mutually reinforcing. The study of concepts develops an understanding of procedures, and the performance enriches an understanding of the concepts. Accountants must think as well as act; therefore, we have given equal emphasis to **why** and **how**.

We believe that a full understanding of generally accepted accounting principles (which includes the conceptual framework of financial accounting) is necessary for an individual to appropriately account for transactions and other events affecting a business. From this understanding, and given a comprehension of the economic consequences of transactions and events as well as an appreciation for the behavioural impact of information on users, an individual is likely to exercise more informed judgement when making decisions affecting the financial statements. Additionally, as the preparer of financial statements, an accountant must know how these decisions are incorporated into the accounting record-keeping system.

Within this context, an accountant may face ethical dilemmas. As a new feature in this edition, we have identified this as an aspect of an accountant's life (Chapter 1) and have included some questions, cases, and exercises in various chapters to emphasize that doing accounting requires appropriate consideration for ethical behaviour.

NEW FEATURES

Significant changes in this edition of *Intermediate Accounting* occur as the result of incorporating *CICA Handbook* additions and revisions, recent *Exposure Drafts* of the Accounting Standards Board (AcSB) and Canadian accounting studies. As such, the contents reflect Canadian generally accepted accounting principles and issues to June 1993. Additionally, excerpts from recent financial statements of many Canadian companies are included to illustrate contemporary financial reporting practice.

Numerous new features have been added to the fourth Canadian edition:

1. **The sequence of chapters has changed**. Chapter 19 (Revenue Recognition) in the third revised edition has been moved to Chapter 6 of the fourth edition to reflect the importance of this topic to the entire accounting function. Chapter 6 (Accounting and the Time Value of Money) of the third revised edition has been condensed into an appendix located at the end of the book.
2. A **two-colour presentation** to more clearly distinguish section headings as well as a coloured sidebar to mark the location of end-of-chapter material.
3. A **description of each case, exercise, and problem** is provided for the first time to draw attention to the nature of the issues being addressed.
4. **Financial reporting problems** have been developed and placed as the last item of the homework-assignment material. Most of these financial reporting problems require reference to and analysis and interpretation of Moore Corporation Limited's financial statements and accompanying notes (see Appendix 5A).
5. **Ethical issues** have been addressed in the form of text discussion and assignment material to sensitize students to the ethical considerations, situations, and dilemmas encountered by practising accountants.
6. **"Perspectives . . ."** have been added to stress the relevance of accounting topics to the realities of Canadian business. These interviews occur at the end of each Part. Because these interviews contain considerable accounting content and are relevant to an accountant's professional development, they can serve as a basis for classroom discussion.
7. **Learning objectives** are presented in the side margins throughout the book as aids to readers.

Throughout the book, we have attempted to improve the pedagogy and simplify complex presentations. Also, many new questions, cases, exercises, and problems have been incorporated and those retained have been modified.

Chapter 1 emphasizes that one must be concerned with the "whys" of accounting as well as what is done. This chapter contains a discussion of the nature of financial accounting, the environmental factors influencing and influenced by financial accounting, Canadian generally accepted accounting principles (as defined in the *CICA Handbook*), the nature and importance of judgement, and ethical aspects of making accounting decisions.

In Chapter 2, a conceptual framework for financial accounting is examined based on the contents and definitions in Section 1000 of the *CICA Handbook* and other sources. Chapter 3 is a review of the accounting process. Chapters 4 and 5 concentrate on issues related to the content and presentation of the income statement, statement of retained earnings, balance sheet, and statement of changes in financial position. Chapter 6 examines and illustrates revenue recognition and fully incorporates the *CICA Handbook* material on the topic.

Cash and accounts and notes receivable are examined extensively in Chapter 7. Coverage of inventories in Chapters 8 and 9 emphasize methods most frequently used by businesses in Canada. Such issues as "capitalization of interest cost" and "special sale agreements" are included and implications regarding *CICA Handbook* material on revenue recognition are considered.

CICA Handbook material regarding accounting for capital assets, non-monetary transactions, and captalization of interest cost is included in Chapters 10 and 11, which examine the acquistion, disposition, and amortization of property, plant, and equipment. Issues concerning the determination of acquisition cost, and accounting for expenditures subsequent to acquisition and asset disposal are the focus of Chapter 10. Chapter 11 includes discussion of accounting for natural resources as well as traditional methods of accounting for depreciation, capital cost allowance, and investment tax credits. Chapter 12 covers issues related to intangible assets, incorporating material on amortization drawn from the *Exposure Draft* on capital assets.

Current and contingent liabilities are examined in Chapter 13. Chapter 14 examines bonds and other long-term payables and considers some of the accounting implications of financial mechanisms such as interest rate swaps and in-substance defeasance. A new appendix has been added to Chapter 14 that considers issues related to complex financial instruments. Specifically, issues concerning recognition of substance over form, off-balance-sheet financing, and troubled debt restructuring are discussed, based on material in the AcSB's *Exposure Draft* on "Financial Instruments."

Chapters 15 and 16 on shareholders' equity include a discussion of the related provisions of the Canada Business Corporations Act and current developments regarding the increasing difficulty of distinguishing some financing instruments such as debt or equity. Chapter 17 contains a thorough explanation and illustration of the earnings per share requirements of the *CICA Handbook*. Chapter 18 deals with issues associated with accounting for investments in bonds, shares, and funds and has been organized to provide increased and improved coverage of investments in marketable securities.

Chapter 19 on corporate income tax accounting examines accounting for permanent and timing differences between accounting and taxable income. Alternative approaches are considered with concentration being on the comprehensive deferral method. In addition to interperiod tax allocation, intraperiod tax allocation is addressed.

Coverage of pension costs in Chapter 20 has been written to incorporate an integrated approach. This allows readers to reconcile various account balances in the employer's books with amounts in the pension fund accounts. Chapter 21 on leases provides a complete coverage of Section 3065 of the *Handbook*. Topics in this chapter include "guaranteed and unguaranteed residual values," "bargain purchase options," and "initial direct costs."

Chapter 22 on accounting changes and error analysis has been amended to reflect changes to Section 1506 of the *Handbook*.

Chapter 23 on the statement of changes in financial position presents a work sheet approach to the preparation of this statement. In accordance with Section 1540 of the *Handbook*, this chapter focuses on cash and cash equivalents. An appendix to the chapter illustrates the T-account method for those who prefer this approach.

Basic financial statement analysis is covered in Chapter 24 in which new material regarding aspects of uncertainty and risk have been included. Chapter 25 on "full disclosure" contains numerous examples from the financial statements of influential Canadian firms. The appendix to Chapter 25 contains information on accounting for changing prices that has been appropriately changed to reflect the removal of Section 4510 from the *Handbook*.

The Appendix at the end of the book provides material covering the basics of compound interest, annuities, and present value for those wishing to study or review these topics in preparation for understanding their use in various financial accounting topics covered throughout the book. This material includes compound interest tables.

QUESTIONS, CASES, EXERCISES, AND PROBLEMS

At the end of each chapter, there is a comprehensive set of review and homework material consisting of questions, cases, exercises, and problems.

The questions are designed for review, self-testing, and classroom discussion purposes as well as homework assignments. The cases generally require descriptive as opposed to quantitative solutions; they are intended to confront the reader with situations calling for conceptual analysis and the exercise of judgement. They challenge the reader to identify problems and evaluate alternatives. Typically, an exercise covers a specific topic and requires less time and effort to solve than cases and problems. Problems are more challenging to solve than the exercises. They require a more in-depth understanding of material, are more complex, and often integrate topics in the chapter(s) and necessitate understanding of concepts underlying particular accounting treatments or methods.

Probably no more than one-fourth of the total case, exercise, and problem material need be used to cover the subject matter adequately; consequently, problem assignments may be varied from year to year.

SUPPLEMENTARY MATERIALS

Accompanying this textbook is an expanded package of supplements consisting of instructional aids for students and instructors. The following supplements are available for students: (1) A Student Companion Volume prepared by Irene Wiecek of the University of Toronto and (2) a Checklist of Key Figures.

The Student Companion Volume contains chapter overviews and focus points to give additional insights into the key concepts of the text. As well, review questions and solutions are given to allow the student to gain a better understanding of the material. Problems and worked solutions expose students to the fundamental calculations required for that topic. Finally, cases with full solutions help students develop skills in problem-identification and problem-solving within the context of financial reporting. As well, these cases aid the student in coping with uncertainty and developing sound professional judgement. A special chapter is also included on case analysis.

The following supplements are available exclusively for instructor use: (1) a comprehensive Solutions Manual for the end-of-chapter material, (2) an Instructor's Manual containing lecture outlines, an annotated bibliography, and other enrichment material, and (3) selected solutions on Transparency Masters. New to this edition is a Test Bank (printed and computerized), which contains multiple choice questions, exercises, and problems for class testing.

ACKNOWLEDGEMENTS FOR THE FOURTH CANADIAN EDITION

We thank the many individuals who contributed to the book through their comments and constructive criticism. Special thanks are extended to the primary reviewers of our manuscript:

Jim Allen
Mohawk College

Peter Cunningham
Bishop's University

Brian Duggan
University of Manitoba

David Fleming
George Brown College

Margaret Forbes
Lakehead University

Bruce Hazelton
Sheridan College

Selwyn James
Centennial College

Michelle Pierce
Seneca College

Wendy Roscoe
Concordia University

John Varga
George Brown College

Nora Wilson
Humber College

Walter Woronchak
Sheridan College

Gerry Woudstra
N.A.I.T.

We would also like to thank those who did preliminary reviews in preparation for the writing of this edition:

Dave Carter
University of Waterloo

Ann Clarke-Okah
Carleton University

Peter Cunningham
Bishop's University

Brian Duggan
University of Manitoba

Janet Falk
University College of Fraser Valley

David Ferries
Algonquin College

Leo Gallant
St. Francis Xavier University

Richard Marshall
McGill University

Tom Shoniker
Ryerson Polytechnical University

Ken Sutley
private practice

Irene Wiecek
University of Toronto

Gerry Woudstra
N.A.I.T.

Appreciation is also extended to our colleagues at the University of Saskatchewan who worked on and examined portions of this work and who made valuable suggestions. These include Jack Vicq, Daryl Lindsay, George Murphy, John Brennan, Mardell Vols, Judy Janson, and Maureen Fizzell.

We are most grateful to the staff at John Wiley & Sons Canada Limited: Bill Todd, Edward Ikeda, Diane Wood, Madhu Ranadive, and Karen Bryan. As well, we would like to acknowledge the editorial contributions of Kim Koh, June Trusty, and Claudia Kutchukian.

Sincere appreciation is also extended to the following who provided the authors with excellent services regarding word-processing, research, and proofing: Evadne Merz, Pam Morrell, and Kirsten Jewitt.

We appreciate the cooperation of the Canadian Institute of Chartered Accountants in permitting us to quote from their pronouncements. We also wish to acknowledge the cooperation of the many Canadian companies from whose financial statements we have drawn excerpts.

If this book helps teachers instill in their students an appreciation for the challenges and limitations of accounting, if it encourages students to evaluate critically and understand financial accounting theory and practice, and if it prepares students for advanced study, professional examinations, and the successful pursuit of their careers in accounting and business, then we will have attained our objective.

Suggestions and comments from users of this book will be appreciated. A student reply card has been inserted at the back of the text for this purpose.

Saskatoon, Saskatchewan

V. Bruce Irvine
W. Harold Silvester

TABLE OF CONTENTS

CHAPTER 3

CHAPTER 4

PART 2 ASSETS: RECOGNITION, MEASUREMENT, AND DISCLOSURE 317

CHAPTER 7

CHAPTER 8

CHAPTER 9

CHAPTER 10

CHAPTER 11

CHAPTER 18

CHAPTER 19

PART

1

Financial Accounting Functions and Basic Theory

CHAPTER 1

The Environment of Financial Accounting and the Development of Accounting Standards

Following a dinner, an intense discussion took place between two friends—one studying philosophy and the other studying business who intended to become an accountant. The debate focused on whether or not the discipline of accounting had contributed, or ever could contribute, to the benefit of humanity. The long discussion did not resolve the issue. One reason was that the business student, while having completed an introductory accounting course, had difficulty in identifying and presenting convincing arguments. This student knew what financial statements were, what they looked like, and had a fairly good idea of how debits and credits worked, but could provide only fuzzy or no answers to some fundamental questions: What is accounting? What is the purpose of accounting? Why is accounting important to the social, political, legal, and economic environment of Canada? Is there a fundamental rationale underlying what is done in accounting? If so, what is it? What are the strengths and weaknesses of what accountants do and why? Is accounting simply a product of what governments and pressure groups say it should be? Do accountants ever really exercise judgement in making important decisions, or do they simply carry out procedures that are purely mechanical and will eventually be performed entirely by computers?

Chapters 1 and 2 do not tell the reader how to do accounting. They make no reference to debits and credits. Their purpose is to build a framework for understanding financial accounting in Canada. From this knowledge base, a student of accounting will be in a better position to answer fundamental questions about accounting, such as those raised in the preceding paragraph. With this knowledge the reader will be better able to develop reasonable and justifiable solutions to accounting problems that are encountered (i.e. know why a decision to adopt a particular accounting policy or measurement in a given situation is or is not appropriate).

WHAT IS ACCOUNTING?

Is accounting a service activity, a descriptive/analytical discipline, or an information system?

Objective 1

Define accounting and describe its essential characteristics.

It is all three. As a **service activity**, accounting provides interested parties with quantitative financial information that helps them make decisions about the deployment and use of resources in business as well as nonbusiness entities. As a **descriptive/analytical discipline**, it identifies a great mass of events and transactions that characterize economic activity. Through measurement, classification, and summarization, it reduces those data to relatively few but highly significant and interrelated items that, when appropriately assembled and reported, describe the financial condition, results of operations, and cash flows of a specific economic entity. As an **information system**, it collects and communicates economic information about an entity to various people whose decisions and actions are related to the entity.

Each of these descriptions of accounting—different though they may seem—contains the three essential characteristics of accounting: (1) ***identification, measurement, and communication of financial information about*** (2) ***economic entities to*** (3) ***interested persons***. These characteristics have described accounting for hundreds of years. Yet, in the last 60 years, economic entities have grown so much in size and complexity, and interested persons have increased so greatly in number and diversity, that the responsibility placed on the accounting profession is greater today than ever before.

THE NATURE OF FINANCIAL ACCOUNTING

Financial Accounting

For purposes of study and practice, the discipline of accounting is commonly divided into the following areas or subsets: financial accounting, management accounting, tax accounting, and not-for-profit (public sector) accounting. ***This book concentrates on financial accounting.***

Financial accounting is "that branch of accounting concerned with the classification, recording, analysis, and interpretation of the overall financial position and operating results of an organization."[1] Financial accounting encompasses the processes and decisions that culminate in the preparation of financial statements relative to the enterprise as a whole for use by parties inside and outside the enterprise. **Management accounting** is "that branch of accounting directed towards providing information to assist management in internal decision making, as contrasted with accounting directed towards providing information to outsiders such as shareholders and creditors."[2] Such internal decision making relates to planning, control, and evaluation within an organization.

Typically, an organization employs accountants who are responsible for providing accounting information for internal use by management and for preparing its financial statements. Auditors (public accountants) are responsible for providing an independent assessment of the financial statements in terms of their fairness and conformity with generally accepted accounting principles.

Financial Statements and Financial Reporting

Objective 2

Identify the major financial statements and other means of financial reporting.

Financial statements are a principal means of communicating financial information to those outside an enterprise. **Financial statements** for profit-oriented enterprises normally include (1) a balance sheet, (2) an income statement, (3) a statement of changes in financial position (cash flow statement), and (4) a statement of retained earnings. Notes to financial statements and supporting schedules cross-referenced to these statements are an integral part of such statements.[3]

Some financial information is better provided, or can be provided only, by means of **financial reporting** other than through the formal financial statements. Such information may be available because it is required by authoritative pronouncement, regulatory rule, or custom, or because management wishes to disclose it voluntarily. Financial reporting, other than financial statements, may take various forms and relate to various matters. Examples include the president's letter or supplementary schedules in the corporate annual report, prospectuses, reports filed with government

---

[1] *Terminology for Accountants* (Toronto: Canadian Institute of Chartered Accountants, 1983), p. 65. Financial accounting, as a subset of the discipline of accounting, is generally associated with profit-oriented enterprises. Not-for-profit accounting applies to the provision of financial statements for organizations in which there is no transferable ownership interest and that do not carry on a business with a view to distributing profits. Tax accounting deals with the provision of financial information to tax authorities. We are concerned with financial accounting for profit-oriented enterprises and, as such, do not examine many of the unique aspects of accounting for not-for-profit organizations or tax accounting in this book.

[2] *Ibid.*, p. 90.

[3] *CICA Handbook* (Toronto: CICA), Section 1000, par. .04.

agencies, news releases, management's forecasts, and descriptions of an enterprise's social or environmental impact.[4]

The ***primary focus of this book is on the development of financial information reported in financial statements and related disclosures.***

THE ENVIRONMENT OF FINANCIAL ACCOUNTING

Major Environmental Factors

Objective 3

Describe the environment of financial accounting.

Accounting, like other human activities and disciplines, is largely a product of its environment. The environment of accounting consists of social, economic, political, and legal conditions, restraints, and influences that vary from time to time. As a result, accounting objectives and practices are not the same today as they were in the past. ***Accounting theory and practices have evolved to meet changing demands and influences.*** Modern financial accounting is the product of many influences and conditions, three of which deserve special consideration.

First, ***accounting recognizes that people live in a world of scarce resources.*** Because resources exist in limited supply, people try to conserve them, to use them effectively and efficiently, and to identify and encourage those who can make effective and efficient use of them. Through efficient and effective use of resources, the standard of living increases. Accounting plays a useful role in obtaining a higher standard of living because it helps to identify efficient and inefficient users of resources. For example, by measuring and reporting the assets and net income of a company, information that helps to determine the company's efficiency becomes available (income divided by assets is a measure of return on investment). By comparing the return on investment of various companies, investors and lenders can better assess investment opportunities and thereby channel their scarce resources more effectively.

Second, ***accounting recognizes and accepts society's current legal and ethical concepts of property and other rights*** when determining equity among the varying interests in an economic entity. Accounting looks to its environment for direction with regard to what property rights society protects, what society recognizes as value, and what society acknowledges as equitable and fair.

Third, ***accounting recognizes that in highly developed and complex economic systems, some (owners and investors) entrust the custodianship of and control over property to others (managers).*** The corporate form of organization tends to divorce ownership and management, particularly in large organizations. Thus, the function of measuring and reporting information to absentee owners has emerged as a crucial role for accounting. This role greatly increases the need for **accounting standards**, which are the ***rules of practice governing the contents, measurements, and disclosures in financial statements.*** Absentee investors, unlike the owner-operator, have little opportunity to combine reported information with first-hand knowledge of the conditions and activities of the enterprise. Consequently, existence of standards helps to ensure the relevance, reliability, and comparability of information reported to absentee owners.

The foregoing three influences are impressed on financial accounting by the environment within which it operates and which it is intended to reflect. The following four environmental factors also shape financial accounting to a significant extent:

- The many users and uses that accounting serves.
- The nature of economic activity.
- The economic activity in individual business enterprises.
- The means of measuring economic activity.

---

[4] *Information to be Included in the Annual Report to Shareholders* (Toronto: CICA, 1991). This study provides many suggestions regarding information to be included in a company's annual report beyond the financial statements.

Users and Uses of Financial Accounting Information

Some users of financial accounting information have, or contemplate having, a direct interest in economic entities. **Direct interest users** include present and potential owners, creditors, and suppliers; management; tax authorities; employees; and consumers. Other users have an interest in such entities because their function is to assist or protect persons who have, or contemplate having, a direct interest. These **indirect interest users** include financial analysts, stock exchanges, lawyers, regulatory and registration authorities, financial press and reporting agencies, trade associations, and labour unions.

The recognition of these many potential user groups, each with its unique decision-making process and special needs, can have significant consequences when choices between accounting alternatives are made. Indeed, a research study by the Canadian Institute of Chartered Accountants (CICA) proposed that such a user-oriented perspective form the basis for developing Canadian financial accounting standards.[5] This study built upon the premise that an important objective of financial reporting is the provision of useful information to all potential users in a form and time frame relevant to their various needs. It proceeds to identify 15 user classes (see Table 1-1) and then relates various needs to them (see Table 1-2). From this perspective, a variety of different measurement bases (historical cost, general price-level-adjusted historical cost, current replacement cost, net realizable value) may be relevant to different users, users' needs, and decision processes. Consequently, if financial reports are to provide the most useful information, accountants must be aware of users, their needs, and decision processes.

A user perspective has been an important aspect in the development of accounting reports throughout history. At present, authoritative pronouncements regarding the objectives of financial statements incorporate an emphasis on the perceived needs of the investor and creditor user groups (see later in this chapter). The success, or lack of success, of financial statements in meeting these needs has become an increasingly important issue. For various reasons (e.g., users lack understanding of the assumptions and measurement rules in the accounting model or the accounting model does not adequately reflect economic and environmental realities) even investor and creditor groups have criticized financial statements for not providing the type of information they thought they were getting or expected to receive—a problem referred to as the "**expectations gap**."[6] When we include other groups in the list of users, each with its own distinct needs, it is not difficult to appreciate that the gap can widen between what a single set of financial statements can provide and what is necessary to satisfy all groups. Therefore, while a user orientation is significant to shaping the nature of financial accounting, much remains to be done before the full implications of such an orientation can be incorporated into financial statement reporting.

The Nature of Economic Activity

All societies engage in the fundamental economic activities of production, distribution, exchange, consumption, saving, and investment. In a highly developed economy like that of Canada, these activities become specialized, complex, and intertwined. As economic activities are continuous and interdependent, relationships and accomplishments associated with intervals of time (such as the net income for a year or portion of a year) can be measured only by making allocations based on assumptions (e.g., the allocation of an asset's cost—depreciation expense—to a given year is based on assumed life, benefit pattern, and residual value of the asset). The problems of allocations are intensified in a dynamic economy because the outcome of economic activity is uncertain at the time decisions are made and action is taken. Fortunately, the continuity of enterprise existence and the framework of law, custom, and traditional patterns of action help to stabilize many aspects of the

---

[5] *Corporate Reporting: Its Future Evolution* (Toronto: CICA, 1980).

[6] *Report of the Commission to Study the Public's Expectations of Audits* (Toronto: CICA, 1988).

Table 1-1
User Classes

User Class	Members of Class
(1) Shareholders	Present and Potential
(2) Creditors—Long-term	Present and Potential
(3) Creditors—Short-term	Present and Potential
(4) Analysts and Advisors serving (1), (2), & (3) (e.g., Brokers, Financial Analysts, Journalists)	Present
(5) Employees	Present, Past, and Potential
(6) Nonexecutive Directors	Present and Potential
(7) Customers	Present, Past, and Potential
(8) Suppliers	Present and Potential
(9) Industry Groups	Present
(10) Labour Unions	Present
(11) Government Departments and Ministers (Federal, Provincial, Municipal—e.g., Tax; Statistics; Consumer and Corporate Affairs; Industry, Trade and Commerce)	Present
(12) Public–Political Parties Public Affairs Groups Consumer Groups Environment Groups	Present
(13) Regulatory Agencies (e.g., Stock Exchanges, Securities Commissions)	Present
(14) Other Companies (Domestic and Foreign)	Present
(15) Standard Setters, Academic Researchers	Present

Source: *Corporate Reporting: Its Future Evolution* (Toronto: CICA, 1980), p. 44.

economic environment. The degree of uncertainty is reduced, and the accounting function greatly assisted, when society acts to ensure the protection of property rights, the fulfilment of contracts, and the payment of debts.

Economic Activity in Individual Business Enterprises

Business enterprises are major units that conduct economic activity. They consist of economic resources (assets), economic obligations (liabilities), and residual interests (owners' equity). These elements are increased or decreased by the economic activities of the enterprise. Changes in the resources, obligations, and residual interests (balance sheet items) of an enterprise are the basis for determining the results of operations—revenues, expenses, and net income (income statement items)—and other changes in financial position (e.g., cash flow) with which financial accounting is

Table 1-2
Users' Needs

	Needs	**Classes of Users Having These Needs**
(1)	Assessment of overall performance	
	(a) In absolute terms	(1) to (15)
	(b) Compared to goals	(1) to (15)
	(c) Compared to other entities	(1) to (15)
(2)	Assessment of management quality	
	(a) Profit, overall performance, efficiency	(1) to (11) especially
	(b) Stewardship	(1) (4) (6) (11) (12) (13)
(3)	Estimating future prospects for	
	(a) Profits	(1) to (11) especially
	(b) Dividends and interest	(1) to (4) especially
	(c) Investment and capital needs	(1) to (6), (8) to (14)
	(d) Employment	(5) (10) (11) (12) especially
	(e) Suppliers	(3) (5) (11) (12) (14) especially
	(f) Customers (warranties, etc.)	(7) (9) (11) (12) especially
	(g) Past employees	(5) (10) (11) (12) (13)
(4)	Assessing financial strength and stability	(1) to (15)
(5)	Assessing solvency	(1) to (15)
(6)	Assessing liquidity	(1) to (15)
(7)	Assessing risk and uncertainty	(1) to (15)
(8)	As an aid to resource allocation by	
	(a) Shareholders (present and potential)	(1) (4) (11) (12) (13) (14)
	(b) Creditors (present and potential; long- and short-term)	(2) (3) (4) (8) (11) (12) (13) (14)
	(c) Governments	(11) (12) especially
	(d) Other private sector bodies	(4) (9) (12) (13) (14)
(9)	In making comparisons	
	(a) With past performance	(1) to (15)
	(b) With other entities	(1) to (15)
	(c) With industry and economy as a whole	(1) to (15)
(10)	In valuation of debt and equity holdings in the company	(1) to (4) especially
(11)	In assessing adaptive ability	(1) to (15)
(12)	Determining compliance with laws or regulations	(11) to (13) especially
(13)	Assessing entity's contribution to society, national goals, etc.	(11) (12) especially

Note: The numbers in brackets in Column 2 refer to the user classes in Table 1-1. Some readers may well feel that one or more of the user classes may have additional needs.

Source: *Corporate Reporting: Its Future Evolution* (Toronto: CICA, 1980) pp. 48–49.

concerned. Accounting accumulates and reports economic activity as it affects these aspects of each business enterprise.

Other types of entities (governments, individuals, not-for-profit organizations) also conduct economic activity. While many of the concepts that relate to accounting for business enterprises are appropriate for these entities, some important differences exist. ***This book concentrates on financial accounting and reporting for business entities.***

Measuring Economic Activity

Accounting facilitates the comparison and evaluation of diverse economic activities by the **measurement** (or valuation) of an enterprise's resources and obligations as well as the events that increase or decrease them. As already indicated, the complexity, continuity, and joint nature of economic activity create problems in measuring these activities and associating their economic consequences with relatively short time periods as well as specific segments, processes, and products. Measuring the resources and obligations of an enterprise and measuring the changes in them are two aspects of the same problem. Hence, there is an inseparable connection between the accountant's statement of financial position (balance sheet), the statement indicating the results of operations (income statement), and the statement of changes in financial position (often called the cash flow statement). Money is used as a common standard for purposes of measurement. ***Money permits the measurement of qualitative and quantitative attributes of economic events, resources, and obligations.***[7] Thus, the unit of measurement in accounting is expressed in terms of money or exchange price. Of course, some important activities of enterprises are not measurable in terms of money (e.g., appointing a new president, adopting a tradename or trademark).

Influence of Accounting on the Environment

While accounting is a product of its environment, its importance rests in its capability to shape its environment and play a significant role in the conduct of economic, social, political, legal, and organizational decisions and actions. ***Accounting is a system that feeds back to organizations and individuals information which they can use to reshape their environment.*** It provides information for the re-evaluation of social, political, and economic objectives as well as the relative costs and benefits of the alternative means of achieving these objectives.

Objective 4

Recognize the importance of accounting information and how it can influence decisions.

More specifically, publicly reported accounting numbers can influence the distribution of scarce resources. For example, assume that a gift of art is received by a museum. Should the gift be reported on the museum's financial statements at market value? Doing this could discourage future gifts as prospective donors may perceive the museum as being prosperous and thus not requiring additional donations.

As another example, consider the problems relating to financial institutions' valuation of financial assets (e.g., loans to companies). These loans are generally recorded at their face amount as they are expected to be paid when due. In times of economic downturn, however, some of these loans lose their value because the security offered (e.g., shares in companies, farm land) loses its market value and the borrowers are not able to repay the loan. Despite this, financial institutions may not recognize the loss on a timely basis by making appropriate allowances for bad debts. Many believed that this was a significant factor leading to the collapse of the Canadian Commercial Bank and the Northland Bank in 1985. While recognition of loan losses may not have prevented these collapses,

---

[7] Qualitative attributes, as well as quantitative ones, are measurable or valued in money terms. For instance, at the time of writing, one ounce of gold measured $470 in money terms while one ounce of silver measured $5.49. The difference in price per ounce reflected differences in qualitative attributes. A doubling of the quantity would result in doubling the amount of money measurement. As another example of qualitative attributes being reflected by money measurement, one of Van Gogh's paintings, *Portrait of Dr. Gachet*, was sold at auction for $82,500,000 while an author's brother had difficulty selling one of his paintings for $50 at an art fair. Money measurements reflect both quality and quantity.

perhaps a more timely recognition of loan losses could have resulted in much earlier recognition of problems and the taking of appropriate actions to resolve them. If the crisis had been detected earlier, millions of client and taxpayer dollars might have been saved.[8]

As a final example regarding the potential impact of accounting information, it is clear that nuclear power plants will eventually have to be mothballed and their nuclear cores removed. If accountants report a portion of this expense currently, energy rates will likely be higher today and lower in the future. Conversely, if these costs are charged to operations after these plants are abandoned, energy rates will likely be lower today but higher in the future.

In summary, the accounting information reported by an enterprise affects perceptions of its financial condition and success. These perceptions then lead to changes in economic behaviour. Because behaviour is affected, accounting standard setting is controversial.

THE OBJECTIVES OF FINANCIAL STATEMENTS

Objective 5

Identify the objectives of financial statements and appreciate the importance of having objectives.

The preceding discussion indicates that financial accounting has evolved to reflect the influences and constraints of the environment as well as to influence decisions and actions taken in the environment. This evolution will continue and will likely have an impact on any specific statement regarding the objectives of financial statements. It is important, however, to identify such objectives as they currently exist. Knowledge of objectives is crucial to understanding what is done in financial accounting and why it is done. In addition, it provides a fundamental perspective for deriving acceptable solutions to particular problems faced by an accountant—one should always ask if a particular solution is consistent with the objectives one is trying to achieve.

Surprisingly, a specific statement of the objectives of financial statements had not been developed by the Canadian accounting profession (and those in other countries) until fairly recently. Without doubt, Canadian undertakings in this regard have followed what has been done by the accounting profession in the United States which, in the late 1970s, undertook a conscientious, costly, and time-consuming project to codify a foundation on which financial accounting and reporting standards could be based.[9] Drawing on this work, The Accounting Standards Authority of Canada published, in 1987, a *Conceptual Framework For Financial Reporting* which included statements regarding the objectives of financial reporting, from which the excerpts on page 9 are drawn.[10]

In December 1988, the Accounting Standards Board (AcSB)[11] of the CICA added a section to the *CICA Handbook* (a publication containing recommendations having legal authority regarding

---

[8] While the Canadian Commercial Bank and Northland Bank experiences revealed problems in accounting for loan losses on a timely basis, the fact that most Canadian banks fairly quickly recognized immense losses on loans to Olympia & York Developments Ltd. in response to that company's financial problems revealed in 1992 suggests that lessons have been learned.

[9] "Objectives of Financial Reporting by Business Enterprises," *Statement of Financial Accounting Concepts No. 1* (Stamford, CT: Financial Accounting Standards Board, November, 1978). This was the first of a series of "concepts statements" published by the FASB over an eight-year period. These statements were developed to provide a comprehensive description of a conceptual framework for financial reporting.

[10] *Conceptual Framework for Financial Reporting* (Vancouver: The Accounting Standards Authority of Canada, 1987), pars. 121–123.

[11] The AcSB replaced the Accounting Standards Committee (AcSC) in 1991. The AcSC was called the Accounting Research Committee prior to 1982. For reasons of expediency, we will refer to the AcSB throughout this book as the body responsible for the development of financial accounting recommendations and other material in the *CICA Handbook*, recognizing that the work regarding these standards prior to 1991 was done under the names of the previous Committees. In addition to financial accounting material, the *CICA Handbook* includes recommendations and material on auditing (the responsibility of the Auditing Standards Board or AuSB) and accounting and auditing recommendations applicable to the public sector (the responsibility of the Public Sector Accounting and Auditing Board or PSAAB).

Objectives of Financial Reporting

(The Accounting Standards Authority of Canada perspective)

At the most general level, the objective of financial reporting is to provide information which is useful in making management, investment, credit and similar decisions with regard to an entity. . . .

At the next level, the objective of financial reporting is to present information which will assist users to forecast the probability, amounts and timing of prospective cash flows. Since investing, lending and similar business transactions are undertaken to ultimately increase net assets, investors and creditors require information concerning the risks, timing, returns and rates of return from alternate investment or credit choices. Financial reporting should assist in making choices, since expected cash flows to the entity relate to expected cash flows to the entity's investors and creditors and, in turn, to their wealth and their purchasing power.

At the most specific level, the objective of financial reporting is to provide information regarding an entity with respect to:

- economic resources (assets), claims on resources (liabilities) and the owners' equity, which are summarized in the Statement of Financial Position
- changes in the equity of owners arising from transactions and events during the reporting period (except for dealings with owners), which are summarized in the Statements of Earnings . . .
- changes in the equity of owners arising from all transactions and events during the reporting period, which are summarized in the Statement of Owners' Equity
- all changes in the amounts and composition of the financial position arising from transactions and events in which the entity interacts with and is affected by the external world, which are summarized in the Statement of Changes in Financial Position: Cash Flow.

Canadian financial accounting practices) titled "Financial Statement Concepts." This section included the following statement.[12]

Objective of Financial Statements

(*CICA Handbook* perspective)

The objective of financial statements is to communicate information that is useful to investors, members, contributors, creditors and other users in making resource allocation decisions and/or assessing management stewardship. Consequently, financial statements provide information about:

(a) an entity's economic resources, obligations and equity/net assets;
(b) changes in an entity's economic resources, obligations and equity/net assets; and
(c) the economic performance of the entity.

In discussion of this objective, the *CICA Handbook* states that:

> Investors and creditors of profit oriented enterprises are interested, for the purpose of making resource allocation decisions, in predicting the ability of the entity to earn income and generate cash flows in the future to meet its obligations and to generate a return on investment.[13]

---

[12] *CICA Handbook*, Section 1000, par. .15. The reference to "members" and "contributors" in this quotation pertain to nonprofit organizations.

[13] *Ibid.*, par. .12.

Although these two statements of objectives differ in detail and some specifics, their underlying theme is similar. ***The objectives of financial statements are to provide information that is (1) useful to making investment, credit, and other decisions; (2) helpful for assessing the amounts, timing, and uncertainty of future cash flows; and (3) about enterprise resources, claims to those resources, and changes in them.***

Given these objectives, three observations are important relative to how they are interpreted and their implications on financial accounting. The *first* observation regards the ***orientation as to the use of financial statements.*** Historically, financial statements were used to provide information on the stewardship of management for resources entrusted to it. As such, financial statements served a **stewardship or accountability function**, they were viewed as the means by which management accounted for a company's resources to the suppliers of the resources. This perspective necessarily concentrated on reporting where the resources came from (creditors, debtors, owners), what was done with the resources (invested in assets), how much was involved, and the benefits received from the management of the resources (income generated for a period of time). Within this perspective, it is clear that the historical (actual) cost of assets plays a major role in the measurement of items because it objectively states the dollars spent. The stewardship function continues to be an important aspect. Additionally, however, financial statements are viewed as a source of information that can be ***used to make economic (resource allocation) decisions*** such as investing and granting credit.

The two purposes—reporting on stewardship responsibilities and providing information to make economic decisions—are frequently considered to be interlinked. This relationship is evident if one asks why people want stewardship information, and comes to the answer that it is because such information is useful to making economic decisions (e.g., whether to hold or sell an investment, whether to keep or replace management). There is truth to this line of thinking, yet it also has its dangers and leads to problems in, and criticisms of, financial statements. This is because a stewardship orientation is concerned with what has happened in the past whereas a decision-making orientation is concerned with predicting what will happen in the future. For the person concerned with the latter, measurements based on historical costs may not be viewed as the most useful (compared to current costs or forecasted information, for example).

A *second* observation concerns ***the attention given to the usefulness of information to predict cash flows.*** This might lead to the inference that a cash basis of accounting is advocated over an accrual basis. This is not the case. Accountants believe that information based on accrual accounting generally provides a better indication of an enterprise's present and continuing ability to generate favourable future cash flows than does information limited to the financial effects of cash receipts and payments.[14]

The objective of **accrual accounting** is to ensure that events that change an entity's financial statements are recorded in the periods in which the events occur, rather than only in the periods in which the entity receives or pays cash. Using accrual accounting to determine net income means recognizing revenues when earned rather than when cash is received, and recognizing expenses when incurred rather than when paid. Under accrual accounting, revenues, for the most part, are recognized when sales are made so they can be related to the economic environment of the period in which they occurred. Over the long run, trends in revenues and related expenses are generally more meaningful than trends in cash receipts and payments. They reflect the underlying economic consequences of operating decisions for a time period, not simply the consequences of decisions by management and customers as to when they can or should pay for things.

While an enterprise must be profitable (i.e. generate income on an accrual basis), it must also be able to pay its debts when due. It is possible for an enterprise to be profitable yet not be able to

---

[14] As used here, cash flows means "cash generated and used in operations." The term cash flows is frequently used to also include cash obtained from owners, borrowing, or disposing of assets and cash distributed to owners or used to repay loans and acquire assets. This latter, broader definition is the basis for preparing a cash-based Statement of Changes in Financial Position.

pay bills because of a lack of cash. Therefore, investors, creditors, and others need information regarding cash flows. Such information is provided in the Statement of Changes in Financial Position.

The point is that information helpful for assessing the amounts, timing, and uncertainty of future cash flows is provided in all of the financial statements, not just a cash flow statement.

The *third* observation regarding these objectives of financial statements is that, as they apply to profit-oriented enterprises, they ***emphasize the investor and creditor user groups and combine all remaining groups*** (see Table 1-1) ***into an "other" category***. This reflects a dilemma of contemporary financial accounting and reporting. Traditionally, creditors and investors have been the primary external groups financial accounting has been designed to serve. The growth in size, significance, power, and concerns of other groups has been an important event in our economy. These groups also need financial information when making decisions. At present, the published financial statements of an enterprise represent the only publicly available source of such information. Given the variety of user groups seeking and using them, they are often called "**general purpose financial statements.**"

As suggested previously, however, the various user groups have different needs (decisions to make) and perspectives or viewpoints. Consequently, while these statements may be referred to as "general purpose," the question is whether they provide sufficient information to specific user groups. Perhaps the provision of "**specific purpose statements**" to particular user groups may help resolve the concern.

In summary, the basic objective of financial statements is to provide useful information. The information is designed to report on how an enterprise's resources and obligations have been managed. While other information may be available, financial statement information is considered useful because it can help users:

- Assess overall financial performance.
- Assess management performance.
- Estimate future prospects.
- Assess financial strength and stability.
- Assess solvency.
- Assess liquidity.
- Assess risk and uncertainty.
- Make comparisons when making their decisions.

GENERALLY ACCEPTED ACCOUNTING PRINCIPLES (GAAP)

Given the objectives of financial statements and the proposition that they are established to meet user requirements for information and to satisfy management's fiduciary reporting responsibility, the question is how financial statements are to be prepared to appropriately achieve these objectives.

> **Objective 6**
>
> Know what Generally Accepted Accounting Principles (GAAP) are, what they consist of, and where they are found.

When accountants prepare financial statements, they are faced with the potential dangers of bias, misinterpretation, inexactness, and ambiguity, just like anyone involved in a communication process. In order to minimize these dangers and to produce financial statements that are reasonably fair, understandable, complete, and comparable between enterprises and accounting periods, accountants carry out their work within a framework of generally accepted accounting principles. **Generally accepted accounting principles (GAAP)** ***form the basis on which financial statements are normally prepared.***[15] Without GAAP, accountants or enterprises would have to develop their own theoretical structure and set of practices pertaining to financial accounting. If this happened, financial statements

[15] *CICA Handbook*, Section 1000, par. .59.

Generally Accepted Accounting Principles

Conceptual Framework

- Objectives
- Qualitative Characteristics of Information
- Elements of Financial Statements
- Recognition and Measurement Criteria
- Assumptions
- Principles
- Constraints

Specific Accounting Policies, Practices, Procedures, and Rules

- Recommendations in the *CICA Handbook*

Other Sources (for matters not covered in recommendations of the *CICA Handbook* or when such recommendations are not totally explicit)

- Principles that are generally accepted by virtue of their use in similar circumstances by a significant number of entities in Canada.
- Principles that are consistent with the spirit of the *Handbook* and are developed through the exercise of professional judgement. In exercising professional judgement, principles for analogous situations dealt with in the *Handbook* would be taken into account and reference would be made to:
    - other related or relevant matters dealt with in the *Handbook*
    - practice in similar situations, including consultation with other informed persons
    - Canadian publications, other than the *Handbook*, which would include *Accounting Guidelines*, *Research Studies* by professional organizations, *Abstracts of Issues Discussed* by the CICA's Emerging Issues Committee, and other accounting literature such as textbooks and journals
    - International Accounting Standards
    - standards published by bodies authorized to establish financial accounting standards in other jurisdictions (e.g., countries such as the United States and the United Kingdom).

users would have to familiarize themselves with every company's particular accounting and reporting practices to understand and compare the statements—a virtually impossible task. Consequently, most accountants and members of the financial community recognize GAAP as being useful and necessary even though some aspects of GAAP have provoked debate and criticism.

While GAAP provides the basis on which the financial statements of most profit-seeking enterprises are prepared, ***it is important to realize that following GAAP is not appropriate in all circumstances.*** Regulatory legislation or contractual requirements can justifiably result in an accounting treatment inconsistent with GAAP. Additionally, there can be circumstances where GAAP should not be followed because doing so would result in misleading information. To determine when GAAP is inappropriate, the accountant must be able to adequately assess the situation, exercise judgement, and justify the conclusion reached. For example, in Chapter 2 the basic assumptions under which GAAP is appropriate are examined. One of these assumptions is that the enterprise being accounted for is a going concern. If this is judged not to be the case given the circumstances of a particular enterprise, then measurement of assets and liabilities based on historical costs (the generally accepted approach) would be misleading and using liquidation values (not generally accepted) would be appropriate. Additionally, deviation from GAAP can be acceptable when the purpose of the information to be provided differs from that of fulfilling the previously discussed objectives of financial statements. ***While recognizing that GAAP is not appropriate to all circumstances facing profit-oriented enterprises or adequate to satisfy many specific objectives of users of financial information, this book concentrates on GAAP.***

Generally accepted accounting principles have developed over time.[16] "Generally accepted" means that a given concept or practice has been established by an authoritative accounting body or that it has been accepted as appropriate because of its widespread application.

While "generally accepted accounting principles" had been a phrase used for years by accountants, a common understanding of what it included did not exist. To some it meant only the rules, practices, and procedures that provided guidance for measuring, classifying, communicating, and interpreting information presented in financial statements. To others it included only broad principles (e.g., historical cost, matching), assumptions (e.g., going concern, economic entity), and constraints (e.g., materiality, conservatism) which provided a basis for developing particular rules and practices. Still others, when describing what GAAP included, added to the latter perspective various qualities of information (e.g., relevance, reliability) that accountants should strive to provide in financial statements. To resolve this confusion, the following description of what GAAP includes was incorporated into the *CICA Handbook* in 1988:

> The term generally accepted accounting principles encompasses not only specific rules, practices and procedures relating to particular circumstances but also broad principles and conventions of general application, including underlying concepts.[17]

Based on this broad description and elaborations provided in Section 1000 of the *CICA Handbook* and other sources, the boxed information on page 12 summarizes what is included in Canadian GAAP.

Conceptual Framework

A conceptual framework has been defined as "a coherent system of interrelated objectives and fundamentals that can lead to consistent standards and that prescribes the nature, function, and limits of financial accounting and financial statements."[18] It serves as a general guide in determining procedures, practices, and rules that are stipulated by a standard-setting body and is used by organizations in preparing financial statements. The conceptual framework recognizes that there are various users and uses of financial information, specifies particular objectives of financial statements, identifies qualitative characteristics of information (criteria making information useful) regarding the items (elements) that are to be included in financial statements, and recognizes that there are some underlying recognition and measurement guidelines (assumptions, principles, constraints) which must be adhered to. As such, this framework represents the theoretical base regarding what accounting is and why things are done as they are. The conceptual framework is fairly elaborate and complex, and detailed discussion of it is deferred to Chapter 2.

> *Objective 7*
>
> Identify the purpose of the conceptual framework for financial accounting.

[16] An historical perspective of the interaction between accounting and its environment fosters an appreciation for and understanding of the Canadian accounting heritage and the development of Canadian GAAP. Such a perspective is provided in Appendix 1A at the end of this chapter.

[17] *CICA Handbook*, Section 1000, par. .60.

[18] "Conceptual Framework for Financial Accounting and Reporting: Elements of Financial Statements and Their Measurement," *FASB Discussion Memorandum* (Stamford, CT: FASB, 1976), page 1 of the "Scope and Implications of the Conceptual Framework Project" section.

Specific Accounting Policies, Practices, Procedures, and Rules: The *CICA Handbook*

Objective 8

Appreciate the importance of the *CICA Handbook*, its recommendations, and the issues faced by the AcSB in developing these recommendations.

While a conceptual framework is an important aspect of the financial accounting environment, it does not provide specific answers to the questions of whether and how to account for something in a given circumstance. To find the answers, one must examine the particular policies, practices, procedures, and rules that govern financial accounting in Canada. In this regard, the most important source is the *CICA Handbook* (or simply the *Handbook*).

The development and publication of material governing financial accounting in the *Handbook* is the responsibility of the **Accounting Standards Board (AcSB)**, which was established by the Board of Governors of the Canadian Institute of Chartered Accountants.[19] When the *Handbook* was first published in 1968, it incorporated all CICA accounting and auditing recommendations, previously issued as *Bulletins*, which had been developed since 1946. Since 1968 the *Handbook* has been continuously revised and expanded.

The *Handbook* is divided into various sections and subsections which cover accounting treatments for a multitude of items. Accounting issues are discussed, and acceptable accounting practice is identified in explicit recommendations. These recommendations are set out in italicized type in the *Handbook* so that they are clearly distinguished from the additional material regarding background information and general discussion.[20] The recommendations serve as Canadian **accounting standards**, which are the ***rules of practice governing the content and presentation of financial statements***.[21]

The authority of the *Handbook* is based on the fact that the ***Canada Business Corporations Act and provincial incorporating statutes require that financial statements be prepared in accordance with the Handbook*** (see Appendix 1A for an historical perspective on this and other aspects of standard setting in Canada). A significant consequence of this legislation is that the *Handbook* recommendations effectively become the laws of Canada in terms of financial accounting standards. As these recommendations are determined by the Accounting Standards Board, which consists primarily of accountants, the Canadian accounting profession becomes in effect a self-regulating body (it makes up the laws that govern what it does). This privilege is unique to Canada, as in other countries regulatory agencies and government bodies have a significant impact on, or are totally responsible for, the development of the legally enforceable standards related to financial statement reporting.

PIP Grant Controversy. The legal authority of the recommendations in the *CICA Handbook*, as well as the process of their development by the accounting profession, came under serious challenge in 1982. The challenger was the federal government, which had granted the power in the first place through the Canada Business Corporations Act. The issue concerned the accounting treatment of grants received by Canadian oil companies under the federal government's Petroleum Incentives Program (PIP grants). This program provided for direct incentive payments for exploration and development. The CICA's position, stated in an *Accounting Guideline* issued in February 1982, was to take PIP grants in accordance with the *Handbook* recommendations (Accounting for Government Assistance—issued in 1975). The required accounting was that PIP grants be taken into income as the exploration and development efforts they financed resulted in earnings or were written off. The federal government's preference, supported by the oil companies in general, was to have the grant reflected immediately in income in the year received. Various reasons existed for taking a stance contrary to the *CICA Handbook*, not the least of which was the significantly reduced earnings of oil companies related to other provisions of the National Energy Program. The federal government very seriously considered enacting an Order-in-Council that would have resulted in it legislating

---

[19] *CICA Handbook*, Introduction to Accounting Recommendations, p. 9.

[20] *Ibid.*, p. 10.

[21] *Report of the Commission to Study the Public's Expectations of Audits* (Toronto: CICA, 1988), p. 2.

an accounting standard. This action never took place, as the government eventually backed off.[22]

The PIP grant controversy provided the most serious challenge to the acceptability of the Canadian accounting profession acting as a self-regulating and policy-setting group up to that time in our history. Subsequent events, however, indicated that the authority of the *CICA Handbook* recommendations and the due process for developing the recommendations would not be secure.[23] In this regard, two events—bank failures in 1985 and the growing interest of the Ontario Securities Commission in accounting practices—require special attention.

Bank Failures and the Macdonald Commission. The failure of the Canadian Commercial Bank and the Northland Bank in 1985 and the subsequent judicial inquiry headed by Mr. Justice Estey resulted in considerable concern over the adequacy and/or application of standards for financial reporting by banks in particular and other types of companies by inference. A major response of the CICA was to establish a commission (known as the Macdonald Commission, after its chairman William A. Macdonald) to study the public's expectations of audits. The Commission's report was published in June 1988. Although concerned primarily with auditing, the report included several recommendations regarding the setting of accounting standards.[24] While recognizing that there was a fairly high regard for standards thus far developed, the report noted several problems: there were many important areas not covered by standards; existing standards allowed too many acceptable alternative accounting methods which enabled wide differences in reported results for essentially identical circumstances; and due process, while important, was too slow to deal quickly with fast-emerging accounting problems. To help overcome these problems, the Commission submitted many recommendations including that the Accounting Standards Board:

- Make a comprehensive survey of the existing body of accounting theory, identify important issues for which accounting standards are unstated or unclear, determine priorities, and intensify its efforts to give guidance on those issues, all with a sense of real urgency.

- Move decisively to produce necessary standards expeditiously, without sacrificing due process.

- Sponsor a separate committee or task force to express considered opinions on new accounting issues that are likely to receive divergent or unsatisfactory accounting treatment in practice in the absence of some guidance. These opinions should be developed quickly and be given wide publicity so that members of the profession can give them due weight when dealing with the issues in question.

- Undertake a review of GAAP to identify situations in which alternative accounting methods are accepted and make every effort to eliminate alternatives not justified by substantial differences in circumstances. If justification exists, the criteria for selection of the appropriate policy should be stated clearly.

- In cases where support cannot be mustered for the elimination of alternatives not justified by substantial differences in circumstances, accounting standards should require enterprises to disclose that the choice of policies in this area is arbitrary. This disclosure should indicate the accounting results that would have been obtained by using the alternative. If disclosure of the results in quantitative terms were impractical or excessively costly, the disclosure could be in approximate or general terms (at a minimum stating whether the alternative is more or less conservative than that actually adopted).

---

[22] Robert H. Crandall, "Government Intervention—the PIP Grant Accounting Controversy," *Cost and Management* (now called *CMA Magazine*), September–October 1983, pp. 55–59. This article provides particular insight into the nature of events regarding the controversy and the significance of the Ontario Securities Commission's support for the *CICA Handbook* in the federal government's decision to back off.

[23] A description of the due process for determining *CICA Handbook* contents is presented in Appendix 1B.

[24] *Report of the Commission to Study the Public's Expectations of Audits.*

- Study how to increase the output of its standard-setting activities. As part of this study, it should consider the possibility of obtaining additional financial support from sources other than membership fees without jeopardizing the independence of the standard-setting function.[25]

Carrying out these recommendations will be a tremendous challenge to the AcSB and the accounting profession with the result being considerable activity regarding standard setting in Canada over the next five to ten years.[26] Indeed, since the Macdonald Commission's report, the AcSB has responded to several recommendations. As examples: an Emerging Issues Committee was created to quickly provide guidance as to appropriate treatment for particular and fairly specific accounting issues;[27] the standard-setting structure was changed to enhance the effectiveness and efficiency of the standard-setting process; the AcSB specified a five-year plan which identified issues to be addressed and prioritized them for action. These responses to challenges put forth by the Macdonald Commission are certainly encouraging, but their success is still to be determined.

The Ontario and Other Provincial Securities Commissions. Another important aspect regarding development of financial accounting standards and the self-regulating nature of this task is the role assumed by Canadian regulatory bodies, particularly provincial securities commissions. Each commission is responsible for enforcing the provisions of its respective province's Securities Act, which governs, among other things, the reporting requirements of companies trading on exchanges in its province. With regard to financial statements, these Acts require adherence to *CICA Handbook* recommendations. Generally, until 1989, securities commissions carried out their duties without taking proactive action regarding the provision of financial information. In 1989, however, the Ontario Securities Commission (OSC) and the Quebec Securities Commission released new disclosure requirements for reporting issuers to provide an "Annual Information Form" and "Management Discussion and Analysis of Financial Condition and Results of Operations." Such information was intended to enhance an investor's understanding of the issuer's operations and future prospects.[28] This information was outside the scope of financial statements, but it served to explain items in these statements. In addition, the OSC undertook to survey a sample of the financial statements of companies under its responsibility every year. These surveys revealed that, in the view of the OSC, a substantial number of companies were not complying with *CICA Handbook* recommendations in various parts of their financial statements.[29] While the OSC took a positive stance by consulting with companies and issuing communiqués outlining the OSC's view of appropriate application of GAAP in an attempt to reduce this noncompliance, problems remained. The OSC was concerned that it had insufficient remedies to carry out its mandate effectively. Consequently, proposals were made to change the Ontario Securities Act to increase the OSC's investigative and enforcement powers.[30] These powers raised concern within the accounting profession regarding standard setting as illustrated by the following:

---

[25] *Ibid.*, pp. 139–140.

[26] Within this book, the authors have drawn extensively on recommendations in the *CICA Handbook* and *Exposure Drafts* (preliminary statements that are likely to become formal *Handbook* content within a short time period) as they existed to June 1993. Given that the AcSB's work is ongoing, the reader has to be aware of revisions to standards and development of new standards subsequent to this date.

[27] The Emerging Issues Committee was established by the AcSB. It issues *Abstracts of Issues Discussed*, which report the Committee's discussion and views as to appropriate accounting practice for particular problem areas (e.g., accounting for the GST, gold loans). Over 50 *Abstracts* had been completed by 1993. The guidance in an *Abstract* is important and forceful, but it does not have the legal authority of *CICA Handbook* recommendations.

[28] *Information to be Included in the Annual Report to Shareholders*, p. 268.

[29] See "Listed companies reporting still deficient," by G. Jeffrey in *The Bottom Line*, April 1990, p. 6 or "It's 'OSCkie' time again as OSC metes out financial reporting brickbats," by L. Bellio in *The Bottom Line*, April 1991, p. 7. For an example of the type of deficiencies, examine Case 1-4 at the end of this chapter.

[30] See "OSC enforcement power overhaul triggers vehement CA response," by G. Jeffrey in *The Bottom Line*, July 1990, p. 1. The proposed powers were very controversial and, at the time of writing this book, had not been incorporated into the Ontario Securities Act.

> Price Waterhouse says it is concerned that the OSC might use this expanded authority to "facilitate the introduction of its own requirements in respect of financial statement presentation and disclosure, instead of relying on generally accepted accounting principles as set out in the *CICA Handbook*.
>
> We do not believe that the OSC should itself bring forward accounting and disclosure standards without having those standards subject to the rigorous process of review and judgment now afforded through the CICA process. . . . The emphasis of the OSC should be on enforcement of standards rather than establishing them."[31]

Whether such concern will ever become a reality is very debatable. Indeed, the OSC has been a solid supporter of *CICA Handbook* recommendations and the development process. The past success and acceptance of self-regulation for Canadian standard setting reflects tradition and respect for the accounting profession as well as the significant amounts of time, effort, and dollars devoted to assure that due process takes place. The basic point from our discussion of the PIP grant controversy, the issues and recommendations of the Macdonald Commission related to standard setting, and the interest of regulators in standards and standard setting is that significant problems, concerns, and pressures exist regarding self-regulation. Whether the resources and process devoted to developing accounting standards will be sufficient to prove successful in the future is a critical question facing the accounting profession.

Other Sources of Accounting Practices

While the *CICA Handbook* is the authoritative and primary source to which one looks for answers regarding whether and how to account for something, it may not provide all the answers. The *Handbook* may have no recommendations regarding a particular issue, or the recommendations may not provide an explicit statement of what is acceptable in a given circumstance, or they may permit alternative acceptable ways to account for something. Consequently, the accountant must often look to other sources (which do not have the legal status of the *Handbook*) for guidance and then exercise professional judgement when reaching a decision on particular problems and determining what constitutes acceptable presentation within the context of the conceptual framework.

Objective 9

Appreciate why sources of GAAP other than the *CICA Handbook* must be used, identify what these sources are, and recognize the importance of professional judgement.

There are many such sources of information. These include: generally accepted practices used by a significant number of companies in Canada;[32] consultation with other accountants and informed persons; statements issued by the CICA's Emerging Issues Committee; other publications by Canadian professional accounting organizations;[33] material in Canadian accounting journals and textbooks; International Accounting Standards; and standards published by standard-setting bodies in other countries, particularly the United States.

Even with *Handbook* recommendations and the many other sources for guidance, accountants must rely heavily on **professional judgement** when solving particular financial accounting problems. A CICA research study defined professional judgement as follows:

> The process of reaching a decision on a financial reporting issue can be described as "professional judgment" when it is analytical, based on experience and knowledge (including knowledge of one's

---

[31] *Ibid.*, p. 2.

[32] *Financial Reporting in Canada* (Toronto: CICA) provides information on the reporting practices of 300 Canadian public companies surveyed every two years. Information resulting from surveys of particular industry practices (e.g., oil and gas, real estate) is also published by various accounting firms.

[33] For example, *Accounting Guidelines* are published from time to time by AcSB. These guidelines provide interpretation of some *Handbook* recommendations or offer guidance on particular issues (e.g., presentation and disclosure of financial forecasts) being faced by accountants. Also, the Canadian Institute of Chartered Accountants, the Certified General Accountants Association of Canada (CGAAC), and the Society of Management Accountants of Canada (SMAC) sponsor and publish in-depth *Research Studies* on particular topics. The CGAAC, among its publications, has issued a *GAAP Guide* to assist in understanding accounting standards. While the SMAC's research program is primarily devoted to management accounting concerns, its research studies have included financial reporting aspects (e.g., on leasing and forecasts of earnings).

> own limitations and of relevant standards), objective, prudent and carried out with integrity and recognition of responsibility to those affected by its consequences. Such professional judgment is likely to be most valuable in complex, ill-defined or dynamic situations, especially where standards are incomplete, and should normally involve consultation with other knowledgeable people, identification of potential consequences and documentation of the analytical processes leading to the decision.[34]

Clearly, professional judgement reflects a capacity to make appropriate decisions in unfamiliar and changing situations. While knowledge of GAAP is a necessary requirement of professional judgement, an accountant's experiences, ethics, and ability to recognize the circumstances surrounding a particular situation are additional important components. Professional judgement is not something an accountant has or does not have. Rather, it is a capability of degree reflecting the type and complexity of situations the accountant can deal with and the degree to which skills have been developed in problem identification, analysis, and evaluation to reach logical and justifiable conclusions. To an extent, working through this book can be viewed as an early part of the continuous process of developing professional judgement.

ORGANIZATIONS INFLUENCING FINANCIAL ACCOUNTING IN CANADA

Objective 10

Know the nature of organizations that influence financial accounting.

The discussion of GAAP has identified the framework (theoretical base; legally required and other sources of rules, practices, policies; and significance of professional judgement) within which Canadian financial accounting occurs. From this discussion, it is evident that many organizations have an interest in, and influence on, financial statement reporting. Figure 1-1 depicts some of these.

While the CICA and its Accounting Standards Board have clearly played the dominant role in formulating GAAP (see Appendix 1A), other organizations have also made a significant contribution. These organizations include the Society of Management Accountants of Canada (SMAC), the Certified General Accountants' Association of Canada (CGAAC), the Canadian Academic Accounting Association (CAAA), the International Accounting Standards Committee (IASC), and standard-setting bodies in other countries. The role of domestic organizations varies but includes providing both input and reaction to proposals (Exposure Drafts) developed by the Accounting Standards Board. The input process usually consists of submitting written briefs for consideration by the AcSB when developing standards, and in some cases, membership on the AcSB. Research activities of these organizations have also made an important contribution to accounting in Canada. Foreign organizations influence Canadian GAAP primarily by providing their standards and other documents which serve as a source of information for the AcSB when developing and revising the *Handbook*, and as a guide for exercising professional judgement when an issue arises that is not dealt with in the *Handbook*. A brief description of these organizations is presented in the following paragraphs.

The Society of Management Accountants of Canada

As the name implies, the SMAC is the professional organization of management accountants in Canada. Its professional members (Certified Management Accountants or CMAs) are typically employed by business organizations, although they may work for government organizations or be in public practice.[35] As preparers of management's financial statements and reports, they must be

---

[34] Michael Gibbins and Alister K. Mason, *Professional Judgment in Financial Reporting* (Toronto: CICA, 1988), pp. 132–133.

[35] A common misconception is that CAs (Chartered Accountants) are in public practice (as auditors, tax specialists, etc.), CMAs are accountants in industry, and CGAs are government accountants. While legislation in some provinces and certain stock exchanges may require some audits to be performed by CAs, it is common to find members of all three professional organizations working in industry and government as well as providing services as public accountants.

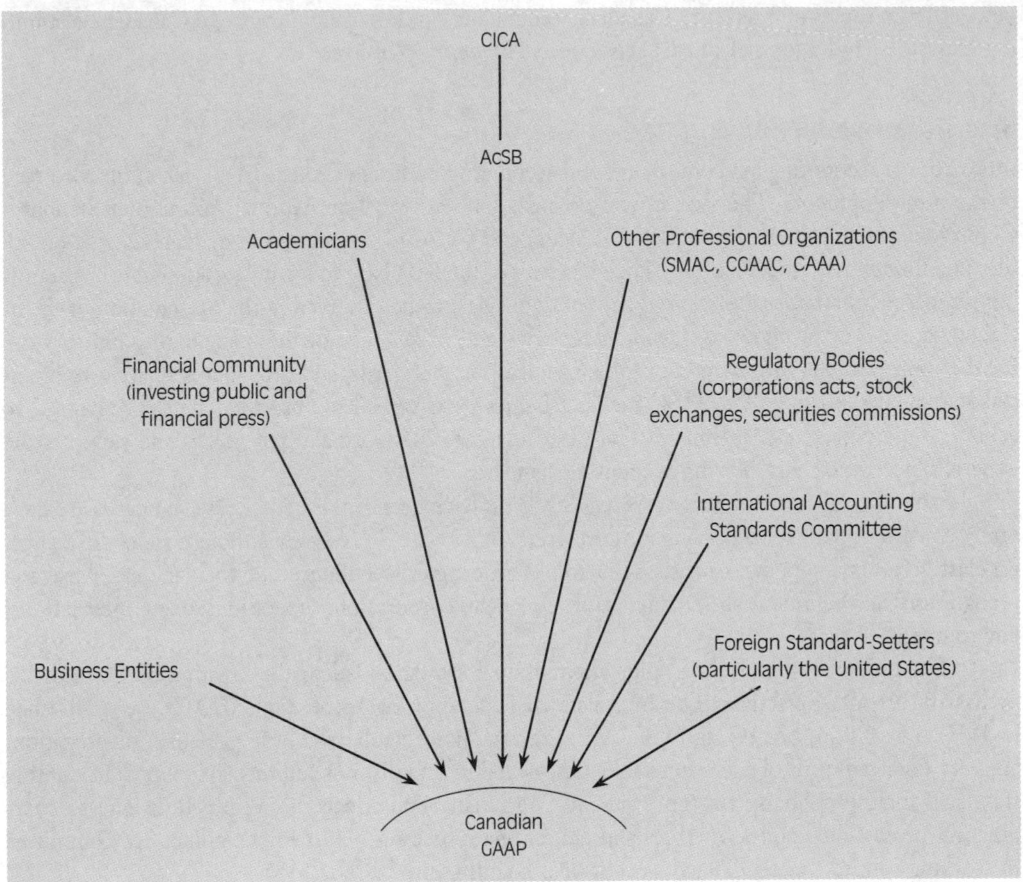

Figure1-1 Organizations Influencing Financial Accounting in Canada

thoroughly familiar with GAAP. In addition, CMAs are responsible for providing information for management decisions. The SMAC has assumed a leadership role in providing direction regarding management accounting practices through its *Management Accounting Guidelines* as well as in conducting research on management accounting topics, as evidenced by the publication of a large number of *Research Studies*. The Society also publishes a journal called *CMA The Management Accounting Magazine*, which includes contemporary articles on issues and topics of concern to management accountants.

The Certified General Accountants' Association of Canada

Professional members of the CGAAC (Certified General Accountants or CGAs) are employed by governments and industry or may be in public practice providing accounting services and audits. The CGAAC publishes a journal called *CGA Magazine* and has established a Research Foundation to promote the study of accounting, auditing, and finance issues. Several *Research Monographs* financed by this foundation have been published. The Association has also published a *GAAP Guide* for use by Canadian professional accountants.

Canadian Academic Accounting Association

Accounting education and research are the primary concerns of the Canadian Academic Accounting Association. Since 1975, it has been active in stimulating examination of accounting education problems and in encouraging increased funding of accounting and auditing research in Canada. Membership includes a good balance of academics and practitioners. This organization publishes a regular newsletter on topics of interest to Canadian accountants, studies of significance to Canadian accounting educators, and a journal titled *Contemporary Accounting Research*.

International Accounting Bodies

International accounting has come of age and accounting bodies in Canada have been at the forefront of these developments. The first formal organization was the International Accounting Standards Committee (IASC). In 1973, the CICA, SMAC, and CGAAC cooperated in making Canada one of the nine founding member nations. The objectives of the IASC are to formulate and publish accounting standards (*International Accounting Standards* or *IASs*) to be observed in the presentation of financial statements, to promote worldwide acceptance and observance of these standards, and to work for the improvement and harmonization of regulations, standards, and procedures relating to financial statement reporting. The IASC member bodies have agreed to "use their best endeavours" to achieve these objectives. Section 1501 of the *CICA Handbook* formally recognizes and supports the general objective of harmonizing accounting standards.

A number of *International Accounting Standards* have been published. These standards are generally consistent with recommendations presented in the *CICA Handbook* although some differences do exist.[36] General support for these standards is growing as is evidenced by their increased use and recognition in the financial statements of Canadian corporations operating in an international environment.

The initial success at developing international standards led to the creation of a worldwide body with broader objectives. The International Federation of Accountants (IFAC) was established in 1977. The CICA, SMAC, and CGAAC were founding members. These Canadian organizations are very involved in the Federation's activities related to establishing auditing guidelines, accounting standards for the public sector (governments), and management accounting practices, and to coordinating professional codes of ethics and educational processes. All member bodies are committed to working toward "a coordinated worldwide accounting profession."

These worldwide bodies are supported by regional organizations. For Canada, the relevant bodies are the Inter-American Accounting Association (IAA) and the Confederation of Asian and Pacific Accountants (CAPA). A primary goal of these organizations is to improve liaison among accountants in the region, promote the objectives and work of the IASC and IFAC, and enhance the professional development and educational activities in the member countries. Conferences and other forms of interaction are organized regularly. The Fédération des Experts Contables Européens (FEE) is the regional organization in Europe.

Standard-Setting Bodies in Other Countries

Financial statement reporting is an activity carried on throughout the world. As such, different countries face similar accounting issues and it is not uncommon for a standard-setting body in one country to look at what standard setters in other countries are doing, or have done, when formulating a standard dealing with the same issue. Also, practising accountants often consider the standards of other countries when making a judgement on how to account for items that are not covered in domestic standards or when domestic standards are not sufficiently precise. When considering standards of other countries, it must be remembered that the nature of these standards (i.e. specific rules oriented for particular problems versus general guidance requiring judgement for particular problems), the due process of their development, the influence of government and regulatory bodies in their formulation, and the general political, legal, economic, and social environment differs between countries. Consequently, while a standard of another country may appear to be applicable to Canada, these differences should be considered before reaching a final conclusion.

---

[36] *Financial Reporting in an International Environment: A Comparison of International Accounting Standards with Canadian Practice* (Toronto: CICA). This material is regularly updated and identifies differences that exist.

As indicated in Appendix 1A, the accounting standards of both Britain and the United States have played a role in the development of Canadian standards and practices. In recent times, the AcSB and Canadian practitioners have particularly and carefully observed developments in the U.S. In many instances, accounting standards and practices developed in the U.S. have been adapted and then included in the *CICA Handbook*. Also, when no Canadian standard or practice is documented, practitioners often rely on U.S. pronouncements for guidance. The similarity of the economic environments of the two countries, the existence of many U.S. subsidiary companies operating in Canada, many Canadian companies having subsidiaries in the U.S., the close relationship between many U.S. and Canadian public accounting firms, and the number of Canadian companies listed on various U.S. stock exchanges are additional reasons for Canadians to be familiar with developments in the U.S. The Canada–U.S. free-trade agreement, particularly as it applies to services such as accounting, suggests that the accounting standards of both countries will be even more closely linked in the future.

There are more standards covering more topics in the United States than in Canada. While Canadian financial reporting standards have a substantial judgemental orientation, those in the U.S. tend to be more rule-oriented and are designed to resolve accounting issues on a problem-by-problem approach. This difference in orientation in part reflects differences in tradition regarding standard development and economic circumstances in the two countries. For example, corporate failures and abuses were more frequent and highly publicized in the U.S. than in Canada. This caused much more public concern and governmental inquiry into the adequacy of U.S. financial statement reporting. Consequently, more accounting standards were developed to "put out the fires" created by such concerns. Additionally, in the U.S., the Securities and Exchange Commission (SEC) acts as a very powerful regulatory body pushing for and influencing the development of accounting standards.

Since 1973, the **Financial Accounting Standards Board (FASB)** has been the private-sector body responsible for establishing and improving standards of financial accounting and reporting in the United States.[37] The work of the FASB, particularly its *Statements of Financial Accounting Standards*, will be used in this book as a reference for guidance on how accounting issues that are not specifically covered by the *CICA Handbook* may be resolved.

ETHICS IN FINANCIAL ACCOUNTING

Objective 11

Understand issues related to ethics and financial accounting.

Robert Sack, a commentator on the subject of accounting ethics, made this observation:

> Based on my experience, new graduates tend to be idealistic . . . thank goodness for that! Still it is very dangerous to think that your armour is all in place and say to yourself "I would have never given in to that." The pressures don't explode on us, they build and we often don't recognize them until they have us.

Sack's comments are particularly appropriate for anyone going into business, or more specifically, accounting. In accounting, as in other areas of business, ethical dilemmas are encountered frequently. Some of these dilemmas are simple and easy to resolve. Many, however, are complex and solutions are not obvious. The focus by business on "maximizing the bottom line," "facing the challenges of competition," and "seeking the quick buck," places accountants in the middle of a self-preservation environment of conflict and pressure. Basic questions such as: Is this way of

---

[37] Prior to the FASB, the American Institute of Certified Public Accountants (AICPA) and its committees had been responsible for developing GAAP in the United States. From 1939 to 1959, the AICPA's Committee on Accounting Procedures issued 51 *Accounting Research Bulletins* and from 1959 to 1973, its Accounting Principles Board issued 31 official pronouncements, called *APB Opinions*. From 1973 through 1990, the FASB issued 106 *Statements of Financial Accounting Standards*, 38 *Interpretations*, 49 *Technical Bulletins*, and 6 *Statements of Financial Accounting Concepts*.

communicating financial information good or bad? Is it right or wrong? What should I do in the circumstance? cannot always be answered by simply adhering to GAAP or following the rules of the profession. Technical competence is not enough when ethical decisions are required.

A practising accountant—either a corporate accountant or a public accountant—must appreciate the importance of recognizing ethical dilemmas, analyse the particular issues, and rationally select the right resolutions. Doing the right thing and making the right decision are not always easy. Being right is not always evident. There are pressures "to bend the rules," "to play the game," or "to just ignore it." Questions such as Will my decision affect my job performance negatively? Will my superiors be upset? Will my colleagues be unhappy with me? often arise when making a tough ethical decision. The decision making is more difficult because a public consensus has not emerged to formulate a comprehensive ethical system that provides guidelines for making ethical judgements.

However, "applied ethics" is still necessary and possible. Accountants should apply the following steps in the process of ethical awareness and decision making:

1. ***Recognize an ethical situation or dilemma***. One's personal ethics, conscience, or sensitivity to others assists in identifying ethical situations and issues. Being sensitive to and aware of the effects (i.e. potential harm or benefit) of one's actions and decisions on individuals or groups (referred to in ethical terms as "stakeholders") is a first step in resolving ethical dilemmas.

2. ***Move toward an ethical resolution by identifying and analysing the principal elements in the situation***. Seek answers to the following questions:

   (a) Which parties (stakeholders) may be harmed or benefited?

   (b) Whose rights or claims may be violated?

   (c) Which specific interests are in conflict?

   (d) What are my responsibilities and obligations?

   This step involves identifying and sorting out the facts.

3. ***Identify the alternatives and weigh the impact of each alternative on various stakeholders***. In financial accounting, consider alternative methods that are available to measure or report the transaction, situation, or event. What is the effect of each alternative on the various stakeholders? Which stakeholders are harmed or benefited most?

4. ***Select the best or most ethical alternative considering all the circumstances and the consequences***. Some ethical issues involve one right answer, and what must be done is to identify the one right answer. Other ethical issues involve more than one right answer; this requires an evaluation of each alternative and the selection of the best or most ethical alternative.

This whole process of ethical sensitivity and selection from alternatives can be complicated by time pressure, job pressure, client pressure, personal pressure, and peer pressure. Throughout this book, some ethical considerations that can be encountered by accountants will be used as examples.

CONCLUSION

The purpose of this chapter is to provide a perspective that can serve as a starting point for understanding financial accounting and as a base for doing it. We have described the nature of financial accounting, the environmental factors influencing its development, the useful role it can play in influencing the environment, the basic objectives of financial statements, the overall framework (generally accepted accounting principles) under which financial statements are prepared, and organizations influencing financial accounting in Canada. From this description, it is evident that ***accounting is a utilitarian function—it is a means to an end rather than an end in itself***. Because the environment within which accounting exists is constantly changing, accounting will continue to evolve in response to these changes. Indeed, continuous evolution has been a constant theme throughout the history of accounting. This evolution is understandable given its utilitarian nature and the fact that generally accepted accounting principles have been developed on a piecemeal basis, and subject to various complex, interacting, and sometimes competing influences.

FUNDAMENTAL CONCEPTS

1. The three essential characteristics of accounting are (1) identification, measurement, and communication of financial information about (2) economic entities to (3) interested persons.

2. Financial statements most frequently provided are (1) the balance sheet, (2) the income statement, (3) the statement of changes in financial position (cash flow statement), and (4) the statement of retained earnings. Notes and schedules cross-referenced to these statements are an integral part of such statements.

3. The objectives of financial statements are to provide information that is (1) useful to making investment, credit, and other decisions; (2) helpful for assessing the amounts, timing, and uncertainty of future cash flows; and (3) about enterprise resources, claims to those resources, and changes in them.

4. Accountants prepare financial statements in accordance with generally accepted accounting principles (GAAP). GAAP encompasses not only specific rules, practices,and procedures but also broad principles of general application, including underlying concepts.

5. Recommendations in the *CICA Handbook* serve as a specific reference point for identifying Canadian GAAP. These recommendations have legal authority conferred by the Canada Business Corporations Act and provincial corporations acts.

6. Responsibility for *CICA Handbook* recommendations on financial accounting rests with the Accounting Standards Board (AcSB) of the Canadian Institute of Chartered Accountants (CICA). While the work of the AcSB is well respected, solving the problems associated with the "expectations gap" and the increasing interest of regulators in accounting standards will provide considerable challenge to the continued success of this work.

7. Determining specific accounting principles to apply in particular situations requires accountants to rely heavily on the exercise of professional judgement.

8. In addition to Canadian literature, the standards and authoritative pronouncements of the International Accounting Standards Committee, the United States, and other countries are an important reference source for guidance when Canadian accountants exercise professional judgement.

9. In addition to the Canadian Institute of Chartered Accountants, other major organizations that are interested in and have influence regarding the Canadian accounting environment are the Society of Management Accountants of Canada (SMAC), the Certified General Accountants Association of Canada (CGAAC), regulators such as the Ontario Securities Commission (OSC), and the Canadian Academic Accounting Association (CAAA).

10. International accounting bodies, primarily the International Accounting Standards Committee (IASC) and the International Federation of Accountants (IFAC), provide organizational means through which harmonization of accounting standards in different countries is evolving. Canada has strongly supported these endeavours, and the standards developed by these groups have closely paralleled Canadian standards.

11. In the performance of their professional duties, accountants are faced with ethical dilemmas. By simply following rules or being technically correct, accountants will not necessarily fulfil their professional responsibility.

APPENDIX 1A

An Historical Perspective on Canadian Financial Accounting and Development of Accounting Standards[38]

Before the twentieth century, partnerships and small corporations formed the commercial and industrial life of Canada. From 1900 to 1920 the economy developed rapidly, and the period witnessed the emergence of large corporations which eventually came to dominate Canadian enterprise. This period marked significant corporate legislation at both the provincial and federal level and the introduction of income taxes during the First World War (1914–1918). Like the stock markets in other Western nations, the Canadian stock market collapsed in 1929 and the country lapsed into the long depression of the 1930s. Significant corporate legislation in 1934 and 1935 attempted to correct various real or imagined abuses. The period following the Second World War witnessed not only the resurgence of commercial and industrial activity but also an increasing awareness by the accounting profession of the role it must play in Canadian life. With considerable help from professional accountants, significant improvement in corporate disclosure legislation was initiated from the mid-1950s to mid-1960s. The importance of the contribution of the Canadian Institute of Chartered Accountants (CICA) in setting accounting standards was reflected in legislation during the 1970s.

Within the context of this overview, major events occurred on the provincial, national, and international scene. They are examined in the following paragraphs and provide an historical perspective on the interaction between accounting and its environment in Canada. Though brief, this discussion should help foster an appreciation for, and understanding of, accounting's heritage and conventions.

To 1920

The Ontario corporate legislation of 1897 and 1907 and the counterpart Canadian legislation of 1917 likely led that of both England and the United States with respect to the extent of financial statement disclosure required. The earlier provincial legislation of 1897 required an "income and expenditure" statement, while the later Act of 1907 required that the balance sheet be audited and that certain assets, liabilities, and equities be distinguished. The federal legislation a decade later virtually copied the Ontario Act. Various influences were at work in those early days. The financial community had been alerted by the abuses in insurance company accounting practices, the rash of bankruptcies at the beginning of the First World War, and the increasing size and frequency of corporate mergers. The Income Tax Acts of 1916 and 1917 greatly influenced corporate legislation, since their application was based on financial statements that not only disclosed a great deal of information but were also attested to by an independent professional accountant.

At the professional organization level, the Association of Accountants in Montreal, in 1880, was the first accounting association chartered in North America.[39] The Institute of Chartered Accountants of Ontario followed in 1883 and the Dominion Association of Chartered Accountants (later named the Canadian Institute of Chartered Accountants) was established in 1902. The strong influence of the Ontario Institute on the early legislation was acknowledged by the assistant provincial secretary at the time. The Dominion Association began publishing its journal, *The Canadian Chartered Accountant* (later changed to the *CA Magazine*), in 1911. In those early years, much of its content consisted of reprints from British and U.S. journals.

The provincially and federally legislated disclosure requirements were probably the chief reason for the relatively high quality of the average public corporation's financial statements in Canada during this period. These requirements, together with the Income Tax Acts, served to alter the emphasis in financial accounting from the balance sheet toward the income statement and to establish the historical cost principle of valuation.

During the last part of the 1920s, England was forced to withdraw much of its financial investment in Canada because of the war and the gap in investment was later filled by the United States. This change in financial influence also

[38] This material is drawn from G.J. Murphy, "The Evolution of Corporate Reporting Practices in Canada," *The Academy of Accounting Historians Working Papers Series Volume 1* (Academy of Accounting Historians, 1979), pp. 329–368; and G.J. Murphy, "Financial Statement Disclosures and Corporate Law: The Canadian Experience," *The International Journal of Accounting*, Spring 1980, pp. 87–99.

[39] Harvey Mann, "CA's in Canada . . . The First Hundred Years," *CA Magazine*, December 1979, pp. 26-30. This article indicates that the Canadian accounting profession has much to be proud of but also that there are some serious problems that require solution.

marked a period of transition in which British influence on Canadian accounting began to wane and the U.S. influence increased.

1920 to 1945

As in most Western countries, the economy of Canada, after experiencing a continuing rise in the 1920s and a stock market crash at the end of the decade, endured a severe and prolonged depression through the 1930s. The concern over abuses in corporate promotion and capitalization, accompanied by a demand for improved financial statement disclosure (much of it coming from the eminent Queen's University Professor R.G.H. Smails) prompted remedial federal legislation in 1934. The same kind of concerns in the United States gave rise to the Securities Acts of 1933 and 1934 and the creation of the Securities and Exchange Commission (SEC). In contrast to the U.S. legislation, the Canadian companies acts did not attempt to set accounting standards beyond disclosure requirements, nor did they set up institutions or procedures to review annual corporate reports. The revolutionary legislation in the United States was mirrored in an evolutionary fashion in Canada.

During the mid-1930s, events in the United States increasingly asserted a strong influence on Canadian accounting. The SEC and the energetic American Institute of Certified Public Accountants (AICPA) began to set forward numerous recommendations on accounting and auditing matters.[40] Most of these were discussed in Canada and many emulated through the Canadian accounting journals and later through the recommendations of the Canadian Institute of Chartered Accountants. The latter, though not prodded by an SEC, began increasingly to undertake the activities and duties of professional accounting leadership by forwarding briefs to governments, commissioning studies, and establishing research organizations. Though the Second World War (1939–1945) dampened much of this activity, the CICA was able to put forward, in 1946, its first recommendations on standards of financial statement disclosure (*Bulletin #1*).

As in the United States, the rise and subsequent fall of prices in the 1920–1940 period lent heavy support to those who argued against the use of any kind of current or appraised value of assets. If value were a function of income, current or appraisal values could be ignored. The emphasis was on the income statement and the objectivity of historical cost for valuation purposes. This emphasis clearly reinforced what had emerged in the first two decades of the century.

1945 to 1965

This period was relatively quiet but effective in that much progress was made at the professional and legislative levels. Though the traditional sources of influence for change continued with steady pressure, there were no important or well-publicized instances of corporate malfeasance or financial reporting inadequacies. In the United States the AICPA and the watchful SEC put forth a profusion of auditing and accounting recommendations, all of which were carefully scrutinized in Canada. Since the British profession and legislation were far less active, events in the United States continued to be much more important to Canadian observers.

At the professional level, the Institutes of Chartered Accountants of Quebec in 1946 and of Ontario in 1962 secured for their members the exclusive auditing right for public corporations. The publication of accounting and auditing recommendations, which began with *Bulletin #1* in 1946, continued as a series through 1968. These recommendations became the common standards for financial reporting in Canada.

The financial statement disclosure provisions of the Ontario Corporations Act of 1953 were a virtual copy of this first Institute *Bulletin* and the briefs of the Institute of Chartered Accountants of Ontario. As in 1907, this provincial legislation became the direct model for federal legislation approximately a decade later, in 1964–65. The Ontario Securities Act of 1965 gave to the Ontario Securities Commission ongoing surveillance responsibilities of the Toronto Stock Exchange. Though this Commission has powers relating to financial statement disclosure and practices not dissimilar to those of the American SEC, it has not promulgated its own set of accounting standards. However, it has set up a process for the review of corporate annual reports and has established annual reporting requirements that are outside the scope of financial statements.

---

[40] Financial accounting standards in the United States tend to be more specific, comprehensive in terms of the number of issues addressed, regulatory, and limiting than those in Canada. As a consequence, a similar item may be accounted for differently in the financial statements of companies in the two countries even if one company is controlled by that in the other country. While understanding these differences is important, there are many other reasons why accountants in Canada need to be aware of U.S. standards and the process and history of their development (as discussed in Chapter 1).

1965 to 1980

Coinciding in time with the legislative approval of the Ontario Securities Act of 1965 and the Canada Corporations Act of 1964–1965—but otherwise unrelated—a major scandal broke upon the Canadian financial scene. The fall of the Atlantic Acceptance Company Limited and, in its wake, several other companies was of grave concern to the investing public, various legislatures, and the accounting profession. This type of concern was of much greater proportions in the United States where instances of corporate scandals and legal suits against auditors abounded and resulted in several Congressional and professional inquiries. These inquiries led to such significant documents as the Metcalf Report, the Moss Report, the Wheat Report, and the Cohen Report. In 1973 the Financial Accounting Standards Board (FASB) was formed as a body independent of the AICPA to establish accounting principles. All of these events in the United States were closely observed by the Canadian profession. Other important influences of the United States on the Canadian scene were the existence of numerous U.S. subsidiary corporations in Canada, the close relationship between many U.S. and Canadian public accounting firms, and the fact that many Canadian corporations were listed on U.S. stock exchanges.

Two important differences between the United States and Canada may help to explain the different responses of the U.S. and Canadian professions during this time period. First, there were many instances of corporate abuse in the United States, while only one (the Atlantic Acceptance debacle) stands out in Canada. Second, the prestige of and long-standing respect for the traditions of the accounting profession were much greater in Canada. By comparison, events in Canada and the responses which they drew were far more subdued.

In 1968, all CICA accounting and auditing recommendations were reorganized into the *CICA Handbook* with revisions being facilitated through continuous updating. In 1969, auditors were required to disclose departure from recommended accounting standards. Of much greater significance, however, was a little-heralded event in 1972 in which *National Policy No. 27* of the Canadian Securities Commission, in its concern for uniformity and disclosure inadequacies, required that the *CICA Handbook* be used to determine generally accepted accounting principles. This requirement was quickly incorporated into the Canada Business Corporations Act of 1975 and the Ontario Securities Act of 1978. Legislative deference to the expertise of the Accounting Research Committee (renamed the Accounting Standards Committee in 1982 and replaced by the Accounting Standards Board in 1991) of the CICA was complete. With this legislation the setting of the laws of the country with regard to financial accounting standards and disclosure became the unique task of this body.

1980 to Present

The discussion in Chapter 1 highlights significant events during this period. These events were the PIP grant controversy, the failure of the Canadian Commercial Bank and the Northland Bank, the Estey judicial inquiry, the Macdonald Commission report, and the growing interest of regulators in financial statement reporting standards. A consequence of these events is an increasing concern for financial statement reporting, standards for reporting, and the process for and self-regulatory nature of setting standards. As stated in the chapter, the AcSB has taken actions to alleviate these concerns. The heavy responsibility placed upon it to meet these challenges demands an ever-increasing devotion of time and resources, and any perceived failure in this regard may well redound to the crippling discredit of the self-regulating nature of the accounting profession.

APPENDIX 1B
The Canadian Standard-Setting Process

The *CICA Handbook*'s content regarding financial accounting is developed by the Accounting Standards Board (AcSB). The structure of this committee and its operating procedures have helped to ensure the exercise of due process when formulating the *Handbook* recommendations. This appendix is to help the reader understand and appreciate the formal process that generates the legal, authoritative policies, practices, procedures, and rules of Canadian GAAP.

The AcSB consists of 13 appointed voting members. These appointees have a broad range of backgrounds and experience in public accounting, industry, commerce, finance, and post-secondary education. Persons in other occupations such as government service, law, and economics may also be appointed. At least two-thirds of the voting members must be members of the Canadian Institute of Chartered Accountants. In addition to Institute appointees, one member can be appointed by each of: the Canadian Council of Financial Analysts; the Financial Executives Institute of Canada; the Canadian Academic Accounting Association; the Certified General Accountants Association of Canada; and the Society of Management Accountants of Canada. Nonvoting members from the CICA staff are the Senior Vice-President, Studies and Standards, and the Accounting Standards Director.

As a matter of philosophy, the AcSB is concerned with the approval of matters of principle and policy when developing recommendations for inclusion in the *CICA Handbook*. As such, it delegates the work regarding the development of standards to task forces or research staff at the CICA.

Given this structure, the various stages in the process of formulating *CICA Handbook* recommendations are illustrated in Figure 1B-1.

To initiate the process, a formal **proposal** must be approved by the AcSB. While suggested projects are primarily identified by the Board or its support staff, any interested party may submit proposals. Once a proposal is approved by the AcSB, it is assigned to a Task Force and/or staff who discuss and debate the issues and then agree on a **Statement of Principles**, which is then presented to the AcSB. The Statement of Principles identifies the issues, analysis, and direction that any recommendations are likely to take. Should approval to continue be given by the AcSB, the Task Force will then be responsible for preparation of an **Exposure Draft**. This document presents the proposed contents of a new section or an amendment to an existing section of the *Handbook*.

After approval by the AcSB, the Exposure Draft is published in the *CA Magazine* and becomes a public document available to all interested persons or organizations. The purpose of issuing an Exposure Draft is to solicit public input on the proposed accounting recommendations. Providing the opportunity for anyone to comment is a crucial part of the due process for determining the recommendations in the *Handbook*. The Task Force considers this input when formulating its submission to the AcSB for revising or adding recommendations to the *Handbook*. If the Task Force's recommendations are approved for inclusion in the *Handbook*, they are distributed to all members of the Institute, other *Handbook* subscribers, and other persons expressing interest. Unless otherwise stated, these recommendations become effective for inclusion in financial statements relating to fiscal years beginning on or after the first of the month that is noted beside the recommendation. The AcSB may determine that the final proposed recommendations are sufficiently different from those in the Exposure Draft and, accordingly, decide that a **Re-exposure Draft** is necessary to obtain additional public feedback. In such cases, the process would revert to the publication in the *CA Magazine* stage as indicated in Figure 1B-1. At any stage in the process, the AcSB could decide to discontinue a project.

While there is oversimplification in Figure 1B-1, it is evident that a very conscientious, thorough, and time-consuming effort is put into the development of *CICA Handbook* recommendations.[41] Indeed, given the complexity of issues addressed by the AcSB and the careful attention paid to the commitment for having a due process, it takes a minimum of two years to develop and approve major recommendations.

---

[41] John Denman, "From committee to board: A review of the AcSC's final years and a look at the future with the new AcSB," *CA Magazine*, February 1992, pp. 66–70. This article provides a more in-depth look at the AcSB and identifies advantages anticipated from its structure and process relative to its predecessor, the AcSC.

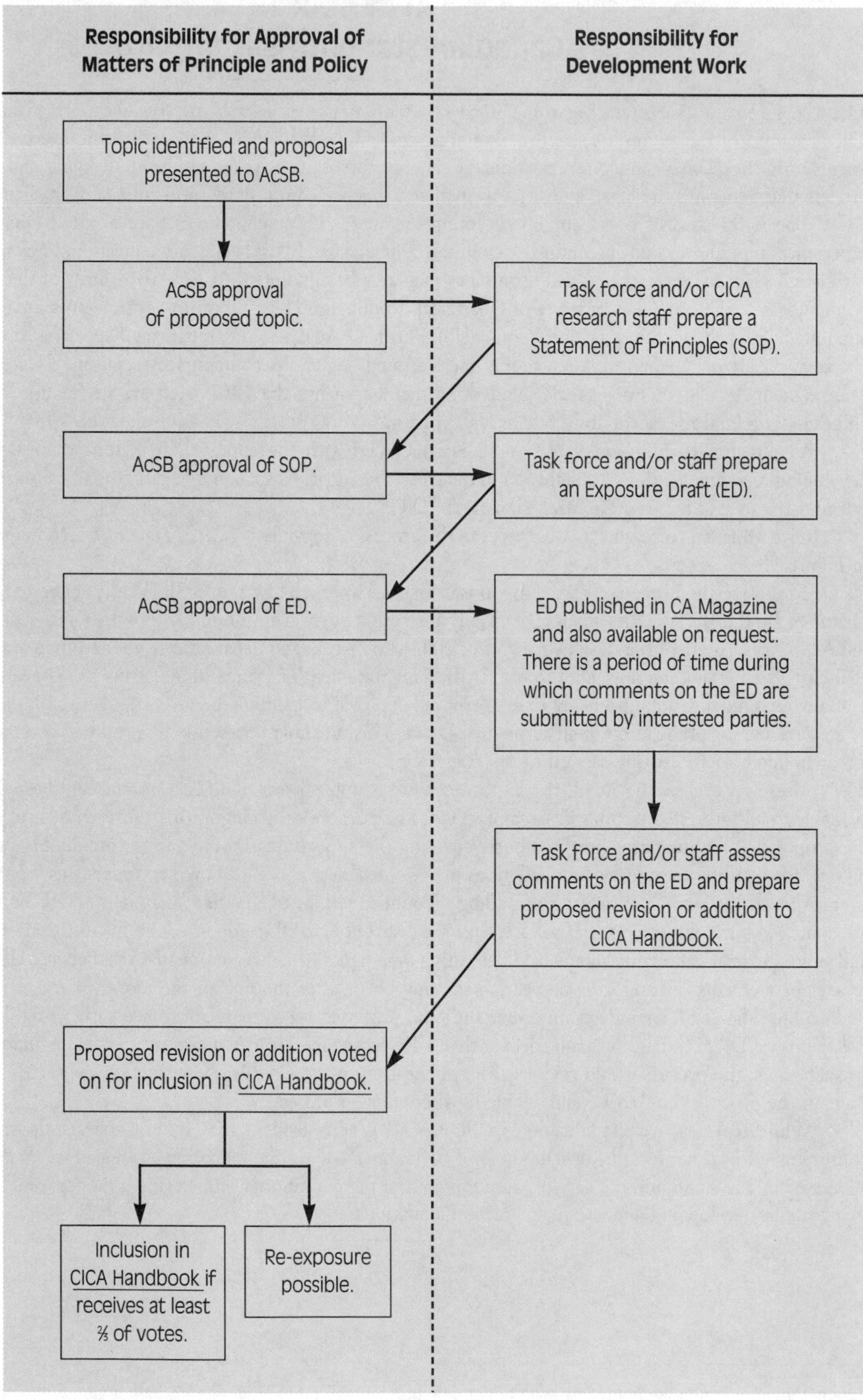

Figure 1B-1 Formulation of *CICA Handbook* Recommendations

Note: All **asterisked** questions, cases, exercises, and problems relate to material covered in an appendix to the chapter.

QUESTIONS

1. What is accounting?
2. Differentiate broadly between financial accounting and managerial accounting.
3. Differentiate between financial statements and financial reporting.
4. Name several environmental conditions that shape financial accounting to a significant extent.
5. Accounting is an unchanging discipline independent of its environment and other influences. Comment.
6. Why is it important to measure performance accurately and fairly when productive resources are privately owned?
7. Provide some examples of how accounting information influences its environment.
8. What are the basic objectives of financial statements?
9. How are current legal and ethical standards related to the basic nature of accounting?
10. In what way does accounting shape its environment and play a role in the conduct of economic, social, political, and legal actions?
11. What is the likely limitation of general-purpose financial statements?
12. If you had to explain or define generally accepted accounting principles to a nonaccountant, what essential characteristics would you include in your explanation? Why are generally accepted accounting principles important?
13. What are the sources of pressure that change and influence the development of Canadian GAAP?
14. Of what value is a common body of theory in financial accounting and reporting?
15. What are the "recommendations" in the *CICA Handbook*? What is the significance of these recommendations to financial accounting?
16. Who has the responsibility for developing *CICA Handbook* recommendations for financial accounting?
17. Why is professional judgement necessary in financial accounting?
18. If you were given complete authority in the matter, how would you propose that accounting principles or standards be developed and enforced?
19. The Canada Business Corporations Act requires that the *CICA Handbook* be used to determine generally accepted accounting principles for financial statement reporting of companies incorporated federally. Explain the significance of this in terms of the apparent role the federal government has delegated to the Accounting Standards Board. How well has the AcSB performed this role? Do you think there is the possibility of having governmental agencies taking over the role of setting accounting standards in Canada? Would such a situation be favourable or unfavourable to the accounting profession?
20. Indicate what is meant by CICA, SMAC, and CGAAC. Identify the differences between these organizations in terms of their role in developing financial accounting standards and in terms of what their professional members do.
21. Explain the role of the Emerging Issues Committee in establishing generally accepted accounting principles.
22. A number of foreign countries have reporting standards different from those in Canada. Give some reasons to explain why reporting standards are often different among countries.
23. Some individuals have indicated that the AcSB must be cognizant of the economic consequences of its pronouncements. What is meant by economic consequences? What dangers will exist if politics play an important role in the development of financial reporting standards?
24. Most incorporated companies prepare financial statements in accordance with GAAP. Why then is there concern about fraudulent financial reporting?
25. How are financial accountants challenged in their work to make ethical decisions? Is not technical mastery of GAAP sufficient in the practice of financial accounting?
26. What significant steps might one apply in the process of moral discernment and ethical decision making?

*27. In 1969 auditors were required to disclose departures from recommended accounting standards. In 1972 the Canadian Securities Commission issued its *National Policy No. 27*, which had significant implications for financial statement reporting. What did *National Policy No. 27* state and what were the implications?

*28. What is an Exposure Draft and what role does it play in developing *CICA Handbook* recommendations?

*29. Under what circumstances may a Re-exposure Draft be issued?

C1-1 **(ENVIRONMENTAL INFLUENCES ON ACCOUNTING)** Prior to its breakup, the Soviet Union had four distinct monetary units, each bearing the name "ruble." The first, sometimes called the "accounting ruble," was employed for budgetary purposes. The second, frequently called the "paper ruble," was used for payroll and for all transactions such as sales in public stores. The third, known as the "Comecon ruble," was used exclusively to account for transactions with the Comecon countries of the Eastern bloc. And the fourth, sometimes called the "gold ruble," was used for foreign trade transactions in hard currencies. The most striking aspect of the currency situation is that these four rubles were not exchangeable or transferable. Yet these rubles could be added together in providing financial information to a total of undefined Soviet rubles.

Instructions

(a) Speculate as to how this type of environment might affect accounting.

(b) How does the environment in Canada influence our accounting and reporting practices?

C1-2 **(NEED FOR ACCOUNTING STANDARDS)** Some argue that having organizations establish accounting principles is wasteful and inefficient. In place of mandatory accounting standards, each company could voluntarily disclose the type of information it considers important. If an investor wants additional information, the investor could contact the company and pay to receive the information desired.

Instructions

Comment on the appropriateness of this viewpoint.

C1-3 **(MEANING OF GENERALLY ACCEPTED ACCOUNTING PRINCIPLES)** At the completion of the Riverdale Co. Ltd.'s audit, the president, Veronica Lodge, asked you about the meaning of the phrase "in conformity with generally accepted accounting principles" that appears in the audit report on the management's financial statements. She observes that the meaning of the phrase must include more than what she thinks of as "principles."

Instructions

(a) Explain what you think is the meaning of the term "generally accepted accounting principles" as used in the audit report. (Do *not* discuss in this part the meaning of "generally accepted," but concentrate on what is meant by accounting principles in the phrase.)

(b) Veronica Lodge wants to know how you determine whether an accounting principle is generally accepted. Discuss the sources of evidence for determining whether an accounting principle has substantial authoritative support. (Do not merely list the titles of publications.)

(c) Veronica Lodge believes that diversity in accounting practice will always exist among independent entities despite continual improvements in comparability. Discuss the arguments that *support* her belief.

(DEFICIENCIES IN FINANCIAL STATEMENTS) The following excerpts are taken from a report in *The Bottom Line* (December 1988, p. 6), which appeared under the headline "OSC appalled at number of deficient financial reports." (While the OSC conducts an annual survey, the following refers to the results of its first survey, which are considered at this stage of the text because they are targeted at a more general level of accounting issues.) **C1-4**

> TORONTO: In its first-ever review of a random sample of 250 financial reports, the Ontario Securities Commission has found 25% of those reports deficient in some way. According to OSC Chief Accountant Michael Meagher, "the frequency and serious nature of some of the problems identified are a cause of concern."
>
> The review, initiated more than a year ago, will now become an annual exercise, with the objective being to "monitor trends in financial reporting," "challenge questionable accounting" and "identify emerging issues and innovative transactions." Companies for the review will be chosen at random, but will generally be public companies listed on the Toronto Stock Exchange. Meagher says the project was launched because the information contained in annual reports and financial statements is so important to the marketplace—for investment decision-making purposes, for example—"that we wanted to have a more detailed look at it to ensure that the financial reporting is of the type we want to have and to challenge presentations that clearly do not adhere to professional standards."

The following were some of the major concerns reported in the story:

- Departures from generally accepted accounting principles because of personal disagreement with the *CICA Handbook* or because of a preference for alternative accounting treatments. According to the OSC, "a departure (from GAAP) is appropriate only where compliance with a particular *Handbook* recommendation would result in misleading financial statements."

- In October 1987, the OSC published a notice encouraging issuers to consult with OSC staff on difficult or unusual financial reporting issues as far in advance of filing as possible. Apparently, this is not always done even though it reduces the risk of uncovering problems late in the process which, in turn, incurs the cost of preparing and distributing revised material to shareholders.

- Selective application of U.S. accounting principles when there is no well-established guidance available in Canada. The problem is that companies are using those parts of U.S. treatment that suit their purposes and rejecting the parts that do not. "However, U.S. GAAP does not automatically become Canadian GAAP and careful judgment is required to determine if use of a particular U.S. GAAP treatment is appropriate," says the report. "This can produce results that would not be acceptable in the U.S. and, therefore, cannot be said to have authoritative support. Furthermore, comparisons with companies that do apply the particular treatment in its entirety may be misleading."

- Defective disclosure in the notes that accompany financial statements. "Ambiguous wording or omission of relevant information makes it difficult to understand the nature of a transaction and the related accounting treatment," says the report. Moreover, "in some cases, a poorly worded note has given the impression that an accounting treatment was inappropriate or contrary to a *Handbook* requirement when such was not the case."

The following are some comments reported in the story:

> Meagher points out that, in all instances where deficiencies or problems were identified, the OSC communicated with the company in question to discuss what kind of corrective action should be taken. This could include greater disclosure in the financial statements, changes in the way information is presented, or accounting differently in the future.
>
> Meagher admits he was surprised at the high percentage of reports found unacceptable in the review. He finds this underscores the need for this review program.
>
> "By identifying problem areas, we should be able to bring about much-needed improvements in financial reporting."

Instructions

(a) Does this report condemn the work of the AcSB and the resulting accounting standards it develops for inclusion in the *CICA Handbook*?

(b) What conclusions and implications do you draw from this report regarding: enforcement of adherence to GAAP; the OSC's offer to help companies resolve difficult issues; exercising professional judgement in the absence of *Handbook* recommendations; and communication skills of accountants and management regarding disclosures?

C1-5 **(MODELS FOR SETTING ACCOUNTING STANDARDS)** Presented below are three models for setting accounting standards:

1. The purely political approach, where national legislative action decrees accounting standards.
2. The private, professional approach, where financial accounting standards are set and enforced by private professional actions only.
3. The public/private mixed approach, where standards are basically set by private sector bodies that behave as though they were public agencies and whose standards to a great extent are enforced through governmental agencies.

Instructions

(a) Which of these three models best describes standard setting in Canada? Comment on your answer.

(b) Why do management and accountants in companies, public accountants, financial analysts, labour unions, industry trade associations, and others take an active interest in standard setting?

(c) In 1982, the federal government came close to legislating an accounting practice (PIP grant controversy). Why would such an action have tremendous consequences regarding Canadian accounting if it had been carried out? Speculate as to why the federal government wished to set its own standard which was contradictory to that of the *CICA Handbook*.

C1-6 **(ACCOUNTING STANDARDS)** The president of Fish Crates Ltd. believes that small companies like his should not have to follow the same accounting standards as large companies.

Instructions

Discuss the president's comment indicating arguments for and against separate standards for small businesses.

(CICA adapted)

C1-7 **(RATIONALIZATION OF THE ACCOUNTING PROFESSIONS)** From time to time, it has been suggested that the various professional accounting bodies in Canada should merge into a single organization.

Instructions

Discuss the advantages and disadvantages of such a merger.

C1-8 **(PROFESSIONAL JUDGEMENT)** Bob Korolischuk recently entered the wholesale business by forming a limited company. He had rented warehouse space, bought inventory, and made sales and deliveries over a period of several months. His inventory management was of significant importance to the likely success of his business and he maintained a record of the purchases made. Because the purchases had been made at varying quantities and unit prices, he became quite confused as to how the inventory should be valued for purposes such as pricing decisions, insurance coverage, renewing a bank loan, preparing financial statements, and determining income tax obligations.

Having taken a basic bookkeeping course, he understood that the *CICA Handbook* was the primary source for generally accepted accounting principles in Canada. He obtained the *Handbook*, expecting it to provide him with clear-cut answers as to how his inventory should be valued in order to satisfy his purposes. He was rather disappointed in what he read. Several methods for inventory valuation were identified as being generally acceptable, but none was recommended as the one to uniquely satisfy his needs.

That evening he met his friend Marilyn, a professional accountant, at a reception. He indicated his dilemma and frustration with the *Handbook* during their conversation. She understood his problem and began her answer by referring to the need for accountants to exercise professional judgement when they are deciding on solutions to particular accounting problems. The discussion continued for the rest of the reception.

Instructions

(a) What, in your opinion, is meant by the phrase "professional judgement"?

(b) Given that GAAP, as expressed in the *CICA Handbook*, is to establish acceptable financial accounting principles and practices, why is professional judgement important?

(c) What factors would you consider to be particularly important if you were to recommend to Bob Korolischuk how the inventory should be valued?

C1-9 **(ADOPTION OF U.S. STANDARDS IN CANADA)** While commenting on the generally high regard for *CICA Handbook* recommendations (standards), the Macdonald Commission Report also noted some sources of dissatisfaction regarding the public's expectations of audits. The areas of dissatisfaction were: Various issues were not covered; there were many acceptable alternatives thus permitting wide differences in reported results for seemingly identical circumstances; the process for developing standards was slow; and there was an inability to deal quickly with fast-emerging issues. To resolve these problems, the Macdonald Commission recommended, among other things, that the AcSB: Undertake a comprehensive survey of accounting theory; identify issues for which standards do not exist or are unclear and then provide guidance on them; expedite the production of standards without sacrificing due process; and review existing standards to pinpoint where there were alternative acceptable methods and eliminate those that are unjustified in general circumstances.

In response to these criticisms and recommendations, some have suggested that the Canadian accounting profession (i.e. through the AcSB) get out of the standard-setting business and that Canadian financial statements simply be prepared by following the standards developed by the Financial Accounting Standards Board in the United States.

Instructions

Provide a list of arguments to support the suggestion that Canadians simply adopt U.S. standards. Provide a list of arguments against this suggestion.

C1-10 **(ETHICAL ISSUE REGARDING EARLY IMPLEMENTATION OF AcSB RECOMMENDATIONS)** When the AcSB issues new recommendations for the *CICA Handbook*, the recommendations are usually effective for inclusion in financial statements relating to fiscal years beginning on or after the first of the month in which the recommendations were published in the *Handbook*. Earlier implementation is encouraged. Becky Hoger, controller, discusses with her financial vice-president the need for early implementation of a recommendation, which would result in a fairer presentation of the company's financial condition and earnings. When the financial vice-president determines that early implementation of the recommendation will adversely affect the reported net income for the year, he discourages Becky from implementing the recommendation until it is required.

Instructions

(a) What, if any, is the ethical issue involved in this case?

(b) Is the financial vice-president acting improperly or immorally?

(c) What does Becky have to gain by advocating early implementation?

(d) Who might be affected by the decision against early implementation?

CHAPTER 2

The Conceptual Framework Underlying Financial Accounting

To many, accounting appears to be primarily procedural in nature. The visible aspects of accounting—keeping records and preparing financial statements—too often suggest the application of a low-level skill in an occupation that offers no challenge and demands no imagination.

In accounting a large body of theory does exist, however. Philosophical objectives, normative theories, interrelated concepts, precise definitions, and rationalized rules constitute a "conceptual framework," which may be unknown to many people but justifies accounting as a truly professional discipline. ***Thus, accountants philosophize, theorize, judge, create, and deliberate as a significant part of their professional activity.*** The subjective aspects that are so critical to current accounting practice, such as searching for truth and fact, judging what is fair presentation, and considering the behaviour induced by presentations, are overshadowed by the appearance of exactitude, precision, and objectivity that accompanies the use of numbers to express the financial results and position of an enterprise.

The conceptual framework for financial accounting is not a description of fundamental truths and axioms as is found in theories regarding the natural sciences, which are derived from and proven by the laws of nature. ***Accounting theory is not something that is discovered; it is created, developed, or decreed based on environmental factors, intuition, authority, and acceptability.*** Because the theoretical framework of accounting is difficult to substantiate with objectivity or by experimentation, arguments concerning it can degenerate into quasi-religious dogmatism. As a result, the sanction for and credibility of accounting theory rests upon its general recognition and acceptance by preparers, auditors, and users of financial statements. Given this, the purpose of this chapter is to examine the nature and usefulness of a conceptual framework for financial accounting, and then progress with an identification and discussion of its components.

THE NATURE OF A CONCEPTUAL FRAMEWORK

Objective 1

Describe what a conceptual framework is and understand its usefulness.

A **conceptual framework** is like a constitution. It is "a coherent system of interrelated objectives and fundamentals that can lead to consistent standards and that prescribes the nature, function, and limits of financial accounting and financial statements."[1]

Why is a conceptual framework necessary? First, to be useful, standard setting should build on and relate to an established body of concepts and objectives. A sound conceptual framework will ***enable the development and issuance of a coherent set of standards and practices*** because they will be built upon the same foundation.

[1] "Conceptual Framework for Financial Accounting and Reporting: Elements of Financial Statements and Their Measurement," *FASB Discussion Memorandum* (Stamford, CT: FASB, 1976), page 1 of the "Scope and Implications of the Conceptual Framework Project" section. This definition is adopted in *Conceptual Framework for Financial Reporting* (Vancouver: The Accounting Standards Authority of Canada, 1987), p. CF–vii.

Second, new and emerging ***practical problems can be more quickly solved by reference to a framework of basic theory***. As an illustration, unique types of financial instruments were issued by companies in the 1980s in response to high interest and inflation rates. Examples are: shared appreciation mortgages (debt in which the lender receives equity participation), deep-discount bonds (debt with no stated interest rate), and commodity-backed bonds (debt that may be repaid in a commodity). For example, Sunshine Mining (a silver mining company) sold two issues of bonds that it would redeem either with $1,000 in cash or 50 ounces of silver, whichever was worth more at maturity. Both bond issues were due in 15 years from issuance and both had a low stated interest rate when they were sold. At what amounts do you think the bonds should be recorded by Sunshine or the buyers of the bonds? If the bond redemption payments may be made in silver, the future value of which is currently unknown, what is the amount of the premium or discount on the bonds and how should it be amortized?

It is difficult, if not impossible, for the Accounting Standards Board (AcSB) to prescribe the appropriate accounting treatment quickly for situations like this. Practising accountants, however, must resolve such problems on a day-to-day basis. Through the exercise of professional judgement and with the help of an accepted conceptual framework, practitioners will be able to dismiss certain alternatives quickly because they fall outside the conceptual framework and then focus on a logical and acceptable treatment.

Third, a conceptual framework should ***increase financial statement users' understanding of and confidence in financial reporting***. Fourth, such a framework should ***enhance comparability among different companies' financial statements***. Similar events and phenomena should be similarly accounted for and reported; dissimilar events should not be.

THE DEVELOPMENT OF A CONCEPTUAL FRAMEWORK

Although a theoretical base for financial accounting has implicitly existed in Canada and has been a part of education and training for some time, it was not formally codified in Canadian literature and professional pronouncements until the 1980s. As such, components of a theory were basically provided through publications in the United States. While many classic studies existed in the United States regarding basic concepts and principles of financial accounting,[2] the work of the Financial Accounting Standards Board (FASB) has been particularly important to developing a contemporary understanding of a comprehensive conceptual framework. This work has been drawn on significantly in developing a Canadian codification of a conceptual framework and a similar endeavour by the International Accounting Standards Committee (IASC).[3]

1. ***Establish the objectives of financial statements***. For what purposes are financial statements intended? To whom should they be directed? What information should be included? What are the limitations of financial statements?

2. ***Determine the essential qualitative characteristics of financial statement information***. What qualities (e.g., relevance, reliability, and comparability) make accounting information

---

[2] Perhaps the most significant U.S. documents in this area were: Maurice Moonitz, *Accounting Research Study No. 1*: "The Basic Postulates of Accounting" (New York: AICPA, 1961); Robert T. Sprouse and Maurice Moonitz, *Accounting Research Study No. 3*: "A Tentative Set of Broad Accounting Principles for Business Enterprises" (New York: AICPA, 1962); *APB Statement No. 4*: "Basic Concepts and Accounting Principles Underlying Financial Statements of Business Enterprises" (New York: AICPA, 1970).

[3] *Framework for the Preparation and Presentation of Financial Statements* (London, England: International Accounting Standards Committee, 1989).

useful to financial statement readers and what are the appropriate trade-offs when conflicts occur between these characteristics (e.g., relevance versus reliability)?

3. ***Define the basic elements of accounting***. What is an asset, liability, revenue, or expense? Are some of these elements more important than others in determining net income? For example, should net income be defined in terms of changes in an enterprise's net assets (excluding capital transactions) over a period of time, or should assets and liabilities be determined only after revenues, expenses, and net income are defined?
4. ***Determine the basis of measurement***. Even after the basic elements are developed, how should they be measured? For example, should historical costs, replacement cost, current selling price, expected cash flows, present value of expected cash flows, or some other valuation system be used to measure an asset?
5. ***Resolve how to treat a change in the measuring unit***. Should the basic measuring unit of accounting be adjusted for changes in the purchasing power of the dollar, should these changes be ignored, or should information on a supplementary basis be presented?

The FASB then devoted considerable financial and human resources in developing five Statements of Financial Accounting Concepts (SFAC) to address these issues.[4] The results served as a foundation to the subsequent development of formal "concepts" or "framework" documents for Canada, other countries, and the IASC.

Objective 2

Appreciate the nature of the development of a conceptual framework in Canada.

In terms of a conceptual framework having a Canadian identity, a CICA research study published in 1980 titled *Corporate Reporting: Its Future Evolution* represented the first major document encompassing the topic.[5] Its contribution to the evolutionary process of deriving a framework for accounting practice resided primarily in its discussion of objectives relating to users and meeting their needs, and suggestions of criteria to be used in developing financial reporting standards. Subsequently, a document titled *Conceptual Framework for Financial Reporting* was published in 1987 to assist in standard setting, provide a basis for academic discussion and student education, and help preparers of financial reports.[6] In December 1988, Section 1000 on "Financial Statement Concepts" was added to the *CICA Handbook* to be used in developing accounting standards and helping financial statement preparers and auditors exercise their professional judgement regarding application of standards and derivation of practices where standards are not yet developed.[7]

While these documents are uniquely Canadian, written with the tradition and environment of Canadian financial accounting in mind, they closely paralleled the various conclusions of the SFACs issued by the FASB. Given the similarities of the two countries in terms of thinking about a conceptual framework, and the fact that the FASB devoted much time, effort, and resources to its work, this consistency is not surprising.

---

[4] *SFAC No. 1*, "Objectives of Financial Reporting by Business Enterprises," presented the goals and purposes of accounting (November 1978). *SFAC No. 2*, "Qualitative Characteristics of Accounting Information," examined the characteristics that make accounting information useful (May 1980). *SFAC No. 3*, "Elements of Financial Statements of Business Enterprises," provided definitions of items that financial statements comprise, such as assets, liabilities, revenues, and expenses (December 1980). *SFAC No. 5*, "Recognition and Measurement in Financial Statements of Business Enterprises," set forth fundamental recognition criteria and guidance on what information should be formally incorporated into financial statements, how the information is to be quantified, and when it should be reported (January 1985). *SFAC No. 6*, "Elements of Financial Statements" replaced *SFAC No. 3* and expanded its scope to include not-for-profit organizations (December 1985). The FASB also issued *SFAC No. 4*, "Objectives of Financial Reporting by Nonbusiness Organizations," that related to nonbusiness organizations (December 1980).

[5] *Corporate Reporting: Its Future Evolution* (Toronto: CICA, 1980).

[6] *Conceptual Framework for Financial Reporting* (Vancouver: The Accounting Standards Authority of Canada, 1987), p. CF–vii.

[7] *CICA Handbook* (Toronto: CICA), Section 1000.

The Canadian, U.S., and IASC developments provide a solid base for defining and understanding current thinking regarding a conceptual framework.[8] As such, these sources have been drawn on extensively when developing the capsule examination of a comprehensive conceptual framework for financial accounting presented in this chapter.

The purpose of presenting this framework is to provide an understanding of the underlying perspective from which accounting standards are, and will be, established. Furthermore, from the point of view of a preparer of financial information, awareness of this framework should provide guidance when choosing what to present in reports, making decisions among alternative ways of representing economic events, and selecting appropriate means of communicating such information. Finally, this framework may be useful to those who use financial statement information by increasing their understanding of both the usefulness and limitations of such information.

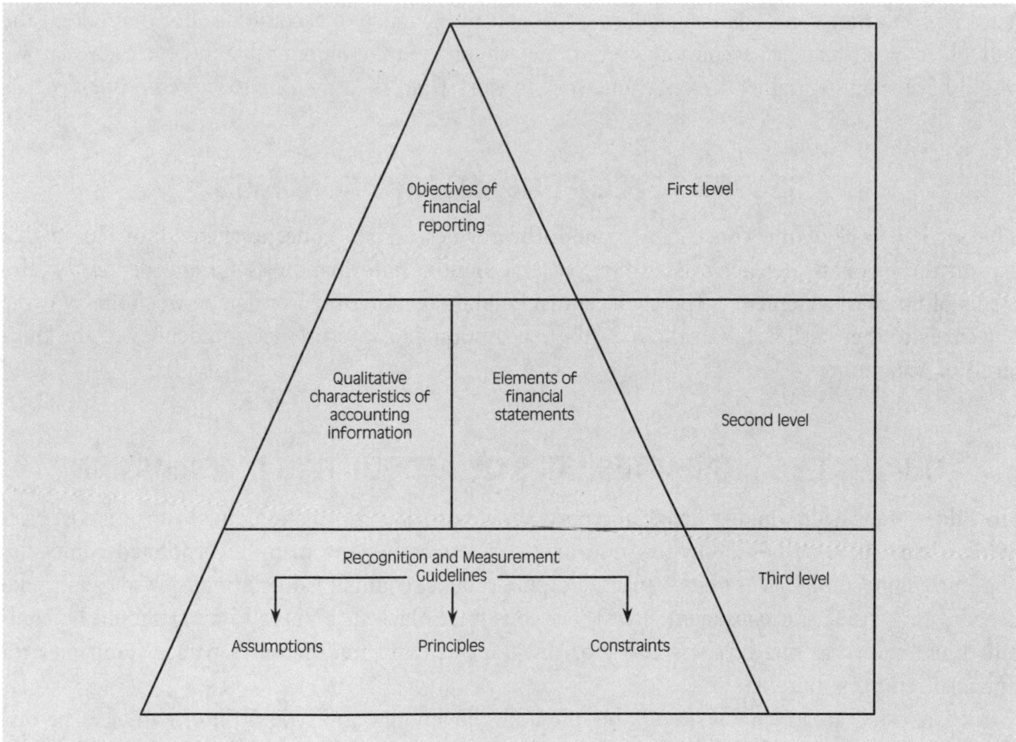

Figure 2-1 A Conceptual Framework for Accounting

Figure 2-1 provides an overview of the conceptual framework.[9] At the first level are the **objectives** that identify the goals and purposes of accounting and are the cornerstones for the conceptual framework. At the second level are the **qualitative characteristics** that make accounting information useful and the **elements** of financial statements (assets, liabilities, and so on). At the third level are the **recognition and measurement guidelines** that accountants use in establishing and applying accounting standards. These recognition and measurement guidelines encompass the **assumptions**, **principles**, and **constraints** that describe the present reporting environment.

---

[8] Canadian documents (including Section 1000 of the *CICA Handbook*, which does not contain any recommendations), SFACs in the United States, and the IASC's framework statement were written with the intent of providing information to standard setters, preparers, auditors, and others which would be useful when carrying out their functions. A conceptual framework does not change existing standards or have the authority of a *Handbook* recommendation.

[9] Adapted from William C. Norby, *The Financial Analysts Journal*, March–April 1982, p. 22.

FIRST LEVEL: BASIC OBJECTIVES

Objective 3

Review the objectives of financial reporting.

As discussed in Chapter 1, the objectives of financial statement reporting are to provide information that is: (1) useful for making investment, credit, and other decisions, (2) helpful for assessing the amounts, timing, and uncertainty of future cash flows, and (3) about enterprise resources, claims to those resources, and changes in them.

While these objectives reflect a broad concern for satisfying information needs of a variety of user groups, tradition has emphasized information that is useful for investor and creditor decisions. This broad concern is further narrowed to the investors' and creditors' interest in their prospects of receiving cash from investments in, or loans to, the business enterprise. Consequently, there is a focus on financial statements that provide information useful for assessing prospective cash flows to the business, on which cash flows to investors and creditors depend.

A statement of objectives is a necessary starting point for developing the framework. Objectives may vary, and they can exert tremendous impact on the practice of accounting. For example, if the only objective of financial accounting were to determine the minimum taxable income each year, we would have a substantially different framework to work from than the one that presently exists.

SECOND LEVEL: FUNDAMENTAL CONCEPTS

The second level of the conceptual framework provides certain conceptual building blocks that explain the qualitative characteristics that make accounting information useful and define the elements of financial statements. These conceptual building blocks form a bridge between the *why* (the objectives of the first level) and the *how* (the recognition and measurement guidelines of the third level) of accounting.

QUALITATIVE CHARACTERISTICS OF ACCOUNTING INFORMATION

How does one decide whether financial reports should provide information on a historical cost basis or on a current value basis? Or how does one decide whether the many incorporated companies (e.g., providing cable TV systems, magazine publications, commercial printing, newspapers, radio broadcasting, trade and consumer shows) that constitute Maclean Hunter Limited should be combined and shown as one business entity or disaggregated and reported as separate companies for financial reporting purposes?

Choosing an acceptable accounting method, the amount and type of information to be disclosed, and the format in which information is presented involves determining which of several alternatives provides the most useful information for decision-making purposes. Therefore, ***the overriding criterion by which an accounting choice can be judged is the usefulness of its consequences for decision making.***

Objective 4

Identify the qualitative characteristics of accounting information.

To help distinguish the more useful from the less useful information, the *CICA Handbook* identifies four qualitative characteristics that make information useful: understandability, relevance, reliability, and comparability.[10] In order to complete this list, we will add the characteristic of consistency, which the *Handbook* recognizes as enhancing comparability.[11] In addition, the *Handbook* identifies certain constraints (benefit versus cost, materiality) as part of the conceptual framework.[12] These are discussed later in the chapter.

Figure 2-2 presents an overview of these notions. The hierarchy in this figure provides a perspective on how these notions fit together and serves as the basis for the following discussion.

---

[10] *CICA Handbook*, Section 1000, par. .18.

[11] *Ibid.*, par. .23.

[12] *Ibid.*, pars. .16 and .17.

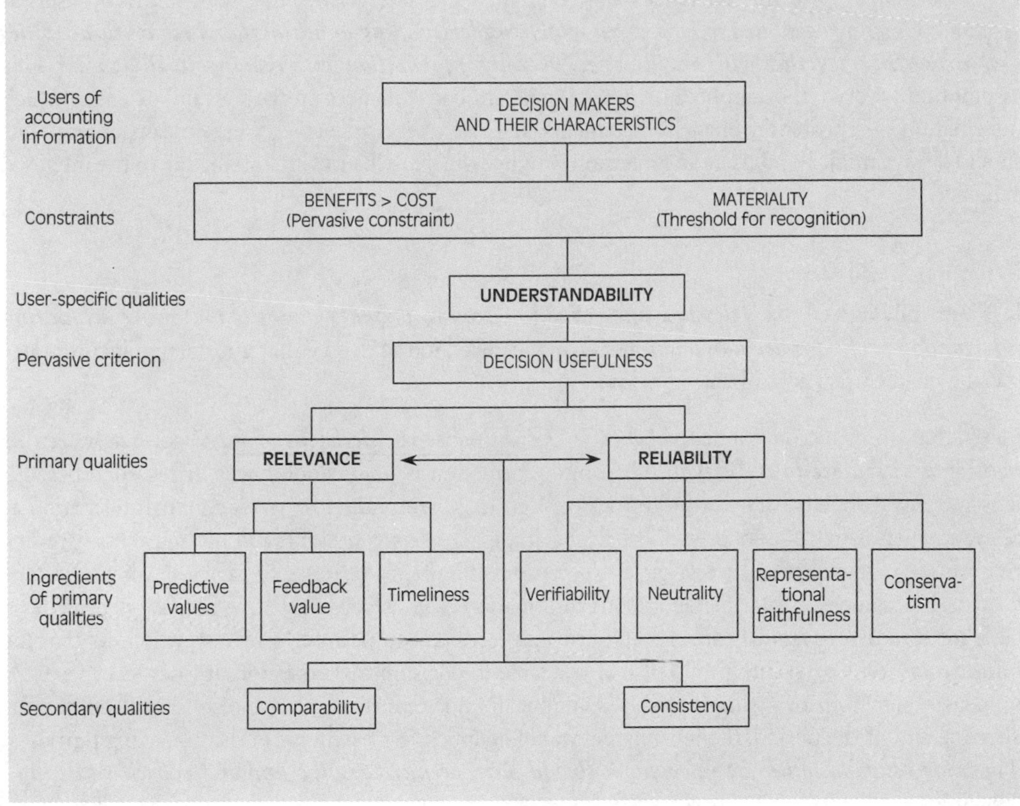

Figure 2-2 A Hierarchy of Qualitative Characteristics for Financial Accounting Information

Decision Usefulness

Without the pervasive criterion of **decision usefulness**, there would be no justification for accounting activity or a basis on which to assess the costs of providing reports. Usefulness is dependent on the extent to which there is an appropriate linking of decision makers and their capability to understand financial information with the primary and secondary qualities of the information, recognizing there are constraints on the information that can be provided.

Understandability

Decision makers vary widely in the types of decisions they make, the methods of decision making they employ, the information they already possess or can obtain from other sources, and their ability to process the information. For information to be useful, there must be a connection between it and the users and the decisions they make. This requires that users be capable of understanding the information as it was intended to be understood by the presenters of the information. Understandability depends not only on the accountant's skills and abilities to provide information that is often complex, but also on the user's ability to comprehend that information. Consequently, **understandability** is viewed as a user-specific qualitative characteristic of information in the conceptual framework.

The range of users' capabilities to understand information creates a dilemma for accountants. For example, assume that Du Pont Canada Inc. issues a three-months' earnings report (interim report) that provides information for decision-making purposes, but some users do not fully understand its content and significance. Although the information may be highly relevant and reliable, it is useless to those who do not understand it, and potentially harmful to those who do use it but do not understand it.

To help resolve this dilemma for accountants, a base level of understandability by users is assumed. ***Users are assumed to have a reasonable understanding of business and economic activities and accounting, together with a willingness to study information with reasonable diligence.***[13] This assumption is very important because it has significant consequences on the way and extent to which information is reported in financial statements. It is also very subjective, which means accountants should always think about users and question whether their disclosures are intelligible to the intended audience.

Primary Qualities

It is generally agreed that ***relevance and reliability are two primary qualities that make accounting information useful for decision making***. Each is achieved to the degree that information incorporates specific characteristics as discussed below.

Relevance. Information is relevant when ***it can influence the decisions of users***[14] (i.e. ***it is seen as making a difference in a decision***). If certain information is understood but is disregarded because it is perceived to have no bearing on a decision, it is irrelevant to that decision. Information is relevant when it helps users predict the financial impact of past, present, and future events (**predictive value**), or confirm or correct prior expectations (**feedback value**). For example, when Du Pont Canada Inc. issues an interim report, this information is considered relevant because it provides a basis for forecasting annual earnings and provides feedback on past performance. It follows that for information to be relevant, it must also be available to decision makers before it loses its capacity to influence their decisions (**timeliness**). If Du Pont did not report its interim results until six months after the end of the period, the information would be much less useful for decision-making purposes. Thus, ***for information to be relevant, it should have predictive value and/or feedback value, and timeliness.***[15]

Reliability. Accounting information is reliable when ***it is in agreement with the actual underlying transactions and events, is capable of independent verification, and is reasonably free from error and bias.***[16] Reliability of accounting information is important to individuals who have neither the time nor the expertise to evaluate the factual content of financial statements. Reliability is achieved through verifiability, representational faithfulness, and neutrality which is affected by the use of conservatism in making judgements under conditions of uncertainty.[17]

Verifiability exists if ***knowledgeable and independent observers concur that the representation of a transaction or event in financial statements is in agreement with the actual underlying transaction or event with a reasonable degree of precision.***[18] When measurements are based on objective evidence, such as invoices, they are highly verifiable. Alternatively, when measurements are based on estimates for which little objective evidence exists (e.g., asset lives or uncollectibility of accounts), the results are less verifiable as they reflect the subjectivity of an accountant's judgement, observation, and experience. Verifiability pertains to the correct application of a measurement basis rather than its appropriateness.

Representational faithfulness means that ***transactions and events affecting an entity are presented in financial statements in a manner that is in agreement with the actual underlying transactions and events.***[19] In other words, do the numbers or other disclosures represent what really happened? For example, if a company's income statement reports sales of $1 billion when it has sales

---

[13] *Ibid.*, par. .19.
[14] *Ibid.*, par. .20.
[15] *Ibid.*
[16] *Ibid.*, par. .21.
[17] *Ibid.*
[18] *Ibid.*
[19] *Ibid.*

of only $800 million, the statement is not representationally faithful. Similarly, if a company reports a source of financing which has all the characteristics of a debt (liability) as a part of shareholders' equity because it was labelled as a special type of share, lack of faithfulness results. To be representationally faithful, ***transactions and events must be accounted for and presented in terms of their economic substance, which is not necessarily their legal or other form.***[20]

Neutrality means that ***information is free from bias that would lead users toward making decisions that are influenced by the way it is measured or presented.***[21] Bias in measurement occurs when an item is consistently overstated or understated. Bias may occur when the choice of an accounting method or disclosure is made with the interests of particular users or particular economic or political objectives in mind.[22] For example, accountants cannot allow a company that produces artificial human body parts to suppress information in financial statement notes about pending lawsuits involving allegations of damage from a product—even though such disclosure could embarrass or harm the company.

Neutrality in standard setting has come under challenge. Some argue that standards should not be issued if they may be economically harmful to an industry or company. We disagree. Standards must be free from bias or there will no longer be credible financial statements. Without credible financial statements, individuals will no longer use this information. An analogy demonstrates this point. In Canada, we have both hockey games and wrestling matches. Many individuals bet on hockey games which they assume are not fixed.But nobody bets on wrestling matches. Why? Because the public assumes that wrestling matches are rigged. If financial information is biased (rigged), the public will lose confidence and no longer use the information.

Conservatism, as an accounting convention, has existed for a long time, but it is often misunderstood. As applied in accounting, conservatism means that ***when there is reasonable doubt about an accounting issue, the solution that will be least likely to overstate net assets and income should be chosen.*** As such, conservatism is a legitimate convention to employ when making judgements under conditions of uncertainty. Although it may affect the neutrality of financial statements, it does so in an acceptable manner.[23] Conservatism, however, does not provide a reason to justify a deliberate understatement of net assets and income.

Secondary Qualities

The use of different acceptable accounting methods by one enterprise in different years or by different companies in a given year would make comparison of financial results difficult. Consequently, to enhance the usefulness of accounting reports, the qualities of comparability and consistency are important parts of the conceptual framework. However, they are considered secondary to the qualities of relevance and reliability. If information is to be useful, it must first be relevant and reliable. Achieving this may require foregoing the secondary qualities.

Comparability. ***Information measured and reported in a similar manner for different enterprises in a given year or for the same enterprise in different years is considered comparable.*** Thus, comparability is a characteristic of the relationship between two pieces of information rather than of a particular piece of information in itself.[24] Comparability enables users to identify similarities and differences in the information provided by two sets of financial statements because the measurements and disclosures are not obscured by the use of noncomparable methods of accounting. For example, if Company A prepares its information on an historical cost basis, but Company B uses a price-level-adjusted basis, it is more difficult to compare and evaluate the two companies. Resource allocation

[20] *Ibid.*
[21] *Ibid.*
[22] *Ibid.*
[23] *Ibid.*
[24] *Ibid.*, par. .22.

decisions involve evaluations of alternatives; a valid evaluation can be made only if comparable information is available.

Consistency. ***Consistency exists when an entity uses the same accounting policies for similar events from period to period.*** Consistency results in enhancing the comparability of financial statements of an enterprise from year to year.[25]

Consistency does not mean that a company cannot switch from one method of accounting to another. Companies can change methods, but the changes are restricted to situations in which it can be demonstrated that the newly adopted method is preferable to the old. Then the nature and effect of the accounting change, as well as the justification for it, must be **fully disclosed** in the financial statements of the period in which the change is made. The meaning of full disclosure is considered later.

While consistency in applying the same methods across different enterprises may improve comparability, such **uniformity** has not become an aspect of practice. The difficulty associated with the notion of uniformity is that dissimilar circumstances may be forced to be reported as being similar.

In summary, accounting reports for any given year are useful in themselves, but they are more useful if they can be compared with reports from other companies and with prior reports of the same entity. For example, if Du Pont Canada Inc. is the only enterprise that prepares interim reports, the information is less useful because the user cannot relate it to interim reports for any other enterprise; that is, it lacks comparability. Similarly, if the measurement methods used to prepare Du Pont's interim report change from one interim period to another, the information is considered less useful because the user cannot relate it to previous interim periods; that is, it lacks consistency.

Trade-offs Between Qualitative Characteristics

The purpose of establishing qualitative characteristics of accounting information is to provide a framework for accountants when they make choices regarding measurements and disclosures. Using such a framework does not provide obvious solutions to accounting problems; rather, it identifies and defines aspects that should be considered when reaching a solution. Many accounting choices require ***trade-offs between the qualitative characteristics.***[26] For example, some believe that financial reports based on current costs provide more relevant information than reports based on historical costs, which are more reliable. There is not, however, any clear-cut consensus on the relative weighting (importance) of relevance and reliability to assist in deciding on such issues. Therefore, while awareness of the qualitative characteristics may help in making choices, the actual decisions typically require the exercise of professional judgement.

THE BASIC ELEMENTS OF FINANCIAL STATEMENTS

Objective 5

Define the basic elements of financial statements.

An important aspect of the theoretical structure is the establishment and definition of the basic categories of items to be included in financial statements. At present, accounting uses many terms that have specific meaning, terms that constitute the language of business or the jargon of accounting.

One such term is "asset." Is it something we own? If the answer is yes, can we assume that any asset leased would never be shown on the balance sheet? Is it something we have the right to use, or is it anything of value used by the enterprise to generate earnings? If the answer is yes, then why should the management of the enterprise not be reported as an asset? It seems necessary, therefore, to develop basic definitions for the elements of accounting. Such definitions provide guidance for identifying what to include and exclude from the financial statements.

---

[25] *Ibid.*, par. .23.

[26] *Ibid.*, par. .24.

With regard to profit-oriented enterprises, the *CICA Handbook* defines the most common elements as shown on page 44.[27] Each of these elements will be explained and examined in more detail in subsequent chapters.

It is useful to think of the elements as two distinct types. The first type—composed of assets, liabilities, and equity—describes resources and claims to resources at a *point in time* and appear in a balance sheet. The second type of elements—net income and its components of revenues, expenses, gains, and losses—describe transactions, events, and circumstances that affect resources, obligations, and equity during a *period of time* and are presented in an income statement. Therefore, elements of the first type are changed by elements of the second type and at any time are the cumulative result of all changes. This interaction is referred to as **articulation**. Thus, the balance sheet (reports elements of the first group) depends on the income statement (reports elements of the second group), and vice versa.

THIRD LEVEL: RECOGNITION AND MEASUREMENT GUIDELINES

Objective 6

Understand the meaning of recognition and measurement.

While an item may meet the definition of an element, it may not be recognized in the financial statements. **Recognition** ***is the process of including an item in the financial statements of an entity.***[28] In order to be recognized, the following criteria must be met:[29]

1. The item has an appropriate basis of measurement and a reasonable estimate can be made of the amount involved; and
2. For items involving obtaining or giving up future economic benefits, it is probable that such benefits will be obtained or given up.

Measurement ***is the process of determining the amount at which an item is recognized in the financial statements.***[30] The first recognition criterion requires that an appropriate (relevant) measurement basis be established for items and that a reasonable (reliable) amount can be determined under that basis before items can be recognized. The second recognition criterion indicates that, even if a measurement can be made, whether an item is recognized and, if so, how it is recognized (i.e. type of element) will be dependent on the probability of future economic consequences.

Recognition and measurement often depend on the exercise of professional judgement, but these criteria are important to making such judgements. For example, suppose a company is being sued for providing faulty service to a defined group of customers. The lawsuit, currently before the court, is for $2 million for damages and compensation. Should the lawsuit be recognized in the financial statements? The $2 million is an appropriate measurement basis. However, it may not be a reasonable estimate of the amount paid in an eventual settlement, which will depend on a judge's ruling or an out-of-court agreement. Consequently, on the grounds that a reasonable amount cannot be determined, the lawsuit will not be recognized in the financial statements. Even if a reasonable amount can be identified, it may not be recognized because its payment is not believed to be probable (the company is fighting the claim in court and its lawyers are advising that the company will win

---

[27] *Ibid.*, pars. .27 and .29 through .40. Notes to financial statements, while providing useful information and being an integral part of the statements, are not an element (par. .25). The *Handbook* also incorporates wording that extends or adjusts these definitions to reflect circumstances pertinent to nonprofit organizations. As our concentration is on financial reporting for profit-oriented enterprises, the provided definitions omit the references to nonprofit organizations. Most of the elements are commonly defined with the exception that for nonprofit organizations: future benefits are linked to the provision of services in the definition of assets; equity is usually called net assets; donations, government grants, and contributions are considered as revenues; and the difference between revenues and expenses has a different significance from net income of a profit-oriented enterprise (i.e. it indicates the extent to which the nonprofit organization has been able to obtain resources to cover the cost of its services).

[28] *Ibid.*, par. .41.

[29] *Ibid.*, par. 44. These criteria assume that an item meets the definition of one of the elements.

[30] *Ibid.*, par. .53.

Elements of Financial Statements

Assets are economic resources controled by an entity as a result of past transactions or events from which future economic benefits may be obtained.

Assets have three essential characteristics:

(a) they embody a future benefit that involves a capacity, singly or in combination with other assets, to contribute directly or indirectly to future net cash flows;
(b) the entity can control access to the benefit; and
(c) the transaction or event giving rise to the entity's right to, or control of, the benefit has already occurred.

It is not essential for control of access to the benefit to be legally enforceable for a resource to be an asset, provided the entity can control its use by other means.

Liabilities are obligations of an entity arising from past transactions or events, the settlement of which may result in the transfer or use of assets, provision of services or other yielding of economic benefits in the future.

Liabilities have three essential characteristics:

(a) they embody a duty or responsibility to others that entails settlement by future transfer or use of assets, provision of services or other yielding of economic benefits, at a specified or determinable date, on occurrence of a specified event, or on demand;
(b) the duty or responsibility obligates the entity leaving it little or no discretion to avoid it; and
(c) the transaction or event obligating the entity has already occurred.

Liabilities do not have to be legally enforceable provided that they otherwise meet the definition of liabilities; they can be based on equitable or constructive obligations. An equitable obligation is a duty based on ethical or moral considerations. A constructive obligation is one that can be inferred from the facts in a particular situation as opposed to a contractually based obligation.

Equity is the ownership interest in the assets of an entity after deducting its liabilities. While equity in total is a residual, it includes specific categories of items, for example, types of share capital, contributed surplus, and retained earnings.

Revenues are increases in economic resources, either by way of inflows or enhancements of assets or reductions of liabilities, resulting from the ordinary activities of an entity. Revenues of entities normally arise from the sale of goods, the rendering of services, or the use by others of entity resources yielding rent, interest, royalties, or dividends.

Expenses are decreases in economic resources, either by way of outflows or reductions of assets or incurrences of liabilities, resulting from an entity's ordinary revenue generating activities.

Gains are increases in equity from peripheral or incidental transactions and events affecting an entity and from all other transactions, events, and circumstances affecting the entity except those that result from revenues or equity contributions.

Losses are decreases in equity from peripheral or incidental transactions and events affecting an entity and from all other transactions, events, and circumstances affecting the entity except those that result from expenses or distributions of equity.

Net Income is the residual amount after expenses and losses are deducted from revenues and gains. Net income generally includes all transactions and events increasing or decreasing the equity of the entity except those that result from equity contributions and distributions.

the case). Although the lawsuit will not be recognized in the financial statements, it may be considered sufficiently important to disclose information about it in the notes to the statements (note disclosure does not constitute recognition as defined).

Recognition and measurement in accounting are influenced by many concepts that have evolved over time and are useful aids in developing rational responses to financial reporting issues. These concepts will be discussed under the categories of basic assumptions, principles, and constraints.

Basic Assumptions

Objective 7

Describe the basic assumptions of accounting.

The basic assumptions of accounting are so apparent that we might ask why they have to be stated at all. They merit special attention, however, because they are critical to understanding accounting and why information is presented in a particular manner. Four basic assumptions underlie financial accounting: (1) the economic entity assumption, (2) the going concern assumption, (3) the monetary unit assumption, and (4) the periodicity assumption.

Economic Entity Assumption. A major assumption in accounting is that ***economic activity can be identified with a particular unit of accountability***. In other words, the activity of any particular business enterprise (the entity for which we wish to account) can be kept separate and distinct from its owners and any other entities.[31] If there were no meaningful way to separate economic events that occur, no basis for accounting would exist.

The economic entity assumption provides a basis which can help the accountant resolve some ethical problems. For example, if a manager uses company funds to pay for personal expenses (e.g., travel during a vacation, gifts for relatives) and requests the accountant to treat these as company expenses, the accountant can refuse to do so, based on the entity assumption. The use of these funds should be recorded as an account receivable from the manager.

The economic entity assumption does not apply solely to the segregation of activities among given business enterprises. An individual, a department or division, or an entire industry can be considered a separate entity if one chooses to define the unit in such a manner. Thus ***an economic entity does not necessarily refer to a legal entity***. A parent company and its subsidiary companies are separate *legal entities*, but merging their activities for accounting and reporting purposes when providing consolidated financial statements does not violate the *economic entity* assumption.

Going Concern Assumption. Most financial statements are prepared on the assumption that ***the business enterprise will continue to operate in the foreseeable future and will be able to realize assets and discharge liabilities in the normal course of operations***.[32] Experience indicates that, in spite of numerous business failures, companies have a fairly high continuance rate. Although accountants do not believe that business firms will last indefinitely, they do expect them to last long enough to fulfil their objectives and commitments.

The implications of this assumption are critical. The historical cost principle would be of limited usefulness if liquidation were assumed. Under a liquidation approach asset values are better stated at net realizable value (sales price less costs of disposal) than at acquisition cost. Amortization policies are justifiable and appropriate only if we assume continuity of an enterprise. If a liquidation approach were adopted, the current-noncurrent classification of assets and liabilities would lose its significance. Labelling anything as a long-term asset or liability would not be justifiable.

---

[31] Surprisingly, such a distinction is not always made in practice. A *Wall Street Journal* article, for example, noted that audit committees of six publicly held companies wanted their chief executive to reimburse the companies an additional $1 million in personal expenses for such items as company yachts, speedboats, refurbishing, and rent money on personal apartments. ("Posners Asked to Repay Firms $1.1 Million More," *The Wall Street Journal*, November 27, 1978, p. 6.)

[32] *CICA Handbook*, Section 1000, par. .58.

The going concern assumption is applicable in most business situations. ***Only where liquidation appears imminent is the assumption inapplicable.*** In these cases a total revaluation of the assets and liabilities can provide information that closely approximates the entity's net realizable value. (Accounting problems related to an enterprise in liquidation are considered in advanced accounting texts.)

Monetary Unit Assumption. Accounting is based on the assumption that ***money is the common denominator by which economic activity is conducted, and that the monetary unit provides an appropriate basis for accounting measurement and analysis.*** This assumption implies that the monetary unit is the most effective means of expressing to interested parties changes in capital and exchanges of goods and services. ***The monetary unit is relevant, simple, universally available, understandable, and useful.*** Application of this assumption is dependent on the even more basic assumption that quantitative data are useful in communicating economic information and in making rational economic decisions.

In general, accountants in Canada have chosen to ignore the phenomenon of price-level changes (inflation and deflation) by assuming that ***the unit of measure—the dollar—remains reasonably stable.*** This is often called the **stable dollar assumption.** It allows accountants to justify adding 1980 dollars to 1994 dollars without any adjustment. Arguments submitted in support of the stable dollar assumption are that the effects of price-level changes are not significant and that presentation of price-level-adjusted data is not easily understood.[33]

Periodicity Assumption. The results of enterprise activity would be most accurately measurable at the time of the enterprise's eventual liquidation. Investors, creditors, managers, governments, and various other user groups, however, cannot wait indefinitely for such information. Consequently, accountants provide financial information periodically.

The periodicity or time period assumption implies that ***the economic activities of an enterprise can be divided into artificial time periods.*** These time periods vary, but the most common are monthly, quarterly, and yearly.

The shorter the time period, the more difficult it is to accurately determine the net income for the period. Problems of allocation mean that a quarter's results are usually less reliable than a year's results. Investors desire and demand that information be quickly processed and disseminated; yet the quicker the information is released, the more it is subject to error. This phenomenon provides an interesting example of the trade-off between reliability (verifiability) and relevance (timeliness) in preparing financial data.

Basic Principles

Objective 8

Explain the application of the basic principles of accounting.

There are four basic principles that accountants use in deciding when and how to measure, record, and report assets, liabilities, revenues, and expenses: (1) the historical cost principle, (2) the revenue realization (recognition) principle, (3) the matching principle, and (4) the full disclosure principle.

Historical Cost Principle. The determination of the measurement base on which an item is to be recognized in financial statements has been one of the most difficult problems in accounting. A number of bases exist on which an amount for a single item can be measured: replacement cost, net realizable value (net amount received from selling an asset), present value of future cash flows, and original cost (less amortization, where appropriate). Which should the accountant use?

Traditionally, preparers and users of financial statements have found that the historical acquisition cost is generally the most useful basis for accounting measurement and reporting. As a result,

[33] In 1982, the *CICA Handbook* did recommend that large, publicly traded enterprises report, as supplementary information, the effects of price changes. This recommendation reflected the need for such information in the high inflation economy at the time. It was withdrawn in 1991 as inflation levels went down. Even when it was recommended that such information was necessary, only a few companies provided it.

under existing GAAP, ***most transactions and events are recognized in financial statements at the amount of cash or cash equivalents paid or received or the fair value ascribed to them when they took place.***[34] This is often referred to as the **historical cost principle**.

Historical cost has an important advantage over other valuations: it is reliable. To illustrate the importance of this advantage, consider the problems that would arise if we adopted some other basis for keeping records. If we were to select net realizable value, for instance, we might have a difficult time establishing a reliable sales value for a given item without selling it. Every member of the accounting department might have a different opinion on the asset's value, and management might desire still another figure. And how often would it be necessary to establish sales value? All companies close their accounts at least annually, and some compute their net income every month. Companies would find it necessary to place a sales value on every asset each time they wished to determine income—a laborious task and one that would result in a figure of net income materially affected by opinion. Similar objections can be levelled against current replacement cost, present value of future cash flows, and other bases of valuation except historical cost.

Historical cost is usually definite and verifiable. Once established, it is fixed as long as the asset remains the property of the company. To rely on the information supplied, both internal and external parties must know that the information is accurate and based on fact. ***By using historical cost as the basis for record keeping, accountants can provide objective and verifiable data in their reports.***

The question "What is cost?" is, however, not always easy to answer. If fixed assets are to be carried in the accounts at cost, are cash discounts to be deducted in determining cost? Does cost include freight and insurance? Does it include cost of installation as well as the price of a machine itself? And what about the cost of reinstallation if the machine is later moved? When land purchased for a building site is already occupied by old structures, is the cost of razing these structures part of the cost of the land?

Furthermore, how do we determine the cost of an item received as a gift? It is not unusual for a developing community to offer a plant site free or at a nominal cost to a company as an inducement to establish operations in the locality. At what price should such an asset be carried? Also, certain assets may be acquired by the issuance of share capital of the acquiring company or perhaps through the issuance of bonds or notes payable. Or, assets may be exchanged for similar or dissimilar assets. If no cash price is stated in the transaction, how is cost to be established? These questions are answered in later chapters; they are raised here only to point out some of the difficulties regularly encountered in accounting for costs.

We ordinarily think of cost as relating only to assets, but liabilities are also accounted for on a cost basis. This becomes evident if we think of cost as "exchange price." Liabilities, such as bonds, notes, and accounts payable, are incurred by a business enterprise in exchange for assets or services on which an agreed price has been placed. This price, established by the exchange transaction, is the "cost" of the liability and provides the amount at which it is recorded in the accounts and reported in financial statements.

Many concerns exist regarding use of the historical cost basis. Criticism is especially strong during a period when prices are changing substantially. At such times historical acquisition cost is said to go "out of date" almost as soon as it is determined. In a period of rising or falling prices, the cost figures of the preceding years are viewed as not comparable with current cost figures. For example, assuming the rate of inflation is 8% per year, a McDonald's quarter-pounder with cheese, which costs $2.75 today (excluding taxes), will cost approximately $55.00 in 39 years if the price directly follows the inflation rate. In a similar manner, financial statements that present the cost of fixed assets acquired 10 or 20 years ago may be misleading because readers of such statements may tend to think in terms of current price levels, not the price levels at the time the assets were purchased. A further complication arises because amortization is based on historical cost. Since

[34] *CICA Handbook*, Section 1000, par. .53.

amortization (e.g., depreciation) expense enters into net income calculations, the net income reported may be suspect because of price changes.

Revenue Realization Principle. The **revenue realization principle**, also called the revenue recognition principle,[35] provides guidance in answering the question of when revenue should be recognized (recorded in the accounts). Revenue is generally recognized when (1) ***performance is achieved*** and (2) ***reasonable assurance regarding the measurability and collectibility of the consideration exists.***[36]

Generally, these two requirements are met when a sale to an independent party occurs. Thus, recognition of revenue takes place at that time. Any basis for revenue recognition short of actual sale opens the door to wide variations in practice. Conservative business individuals may wait until sale of their securities; more optimistic individuals will watch market quotations and take up gains as market prices increase; others may recognize increases that are merely rumoured; and unscrupulous persons will "write up" their investments as they please to suit their own purposes. To give accounting reports uniform meaning, a rule for revenue recognition comparable to the cost rule for asset valuation is essential. ***Recognition through sale provides a uniform and reasonable test in most cases.*** There are, however, exceptions to the rule, and at times the basic rule is difficult to apply, as discussed below:

During Production. Recognition of revenue before a contract is completed is allowed in certain long-term construction contracts. The main feature of this approach (using what is called the percentage-of-completion method) is that revenue and related expenses are recognized periodically based on the percentage of job completion, instead of waiting until the entire job is finished. Although a formal transfer of risks and rewards of ownership has not occurred, performance is considered achieved as construction progresses. Naturally, if it is not possible to obtain dependable estimates of price, cost, and progress, then the accountant should wait and recognize the revenue at the completion date.

End of Production. At times, revenue may be recognized after the production cycle has ended but before a sale takes place. This is the case where the selling price as well as the quantity to be sold is certain. An example is in mining where a ready market at a standard price exists for mineral that has been extracted. The same holds true for some agricultural products with guaranteed price supports set by the government.

Receipt of Cash. Receipt of cash is another basis for revenue recognition. The cash basis approach should be used only when it is impossible to establish the revenue figure at the time of sale because of uncertainty of collection. One form of the cash basis is the **instalment sales method**. This method may be used when payments are made in periodic instalments over a long period of time. Its most frequent use is in the retail industry. Farm and home equipment and furnishings are often sold on an instalment basis. The instalment method is justified on the grounds that the risk of not collecting an account receivable is so great that the sale is not sufficient evidence for revenue recognition to take place. In some instances, this reasoning may be valid. Generally, though, if a sale is completed, revenue should be recognized; if bad debts are expected, they should be recorded as estimates of uncollectible accounts.

Revenue, then, is recognized and recorded in the period in which performance to earn it has been achieved, it is reasonably measurable, and collectibility is reasonably assured. Normally, this is the date of sale, but circumstances may dictate application of the percentage-of-completion approach, the end-of-production approach, or the receipt-of-cash approach.

---

[35] Technically, realization means the process of converting noncash resources and rights into money. Recognition is the process of including an item in the financial statements. Because of this the revenue realization principle is also referred to as the revenue recognition principle.

[36] *CICA Handbook*, Section 1000, par. .47.

Conceptually, the appropriate accounting for revenue recognition should be apparent and should fit nicely into one of the conditions mentioned above, but often it does not. As examples, consider franchises and motion picture sales to television.

Franchising operations have been established for a wide variety of businesses from restaurants to pet-care centres. One need not travel too widely to appreciate the multitude of fast-food chains such as McDonald's or Kentucky Fried Chicken. One of the problems faced by accountants of the franchiser (seller of the franchise) prior to 1984 was when to recognize revenue from the sale of a franchise. In many cases, the entire franchise price was treated as revenue as soon as the franchiser found an individual franchisee (buyer of the franchise) and received a down payment, no matter how small. This revenue recognition practice was faulty because, in many situations, the fees were payable over a period of years, were refundable or uncollectible if the franchises never got started, or were earned only as certain services were performed by the franchiser. In effect the franchisers were counting their fried chickens before they were hatched. Consequently, to more appropriately determine net income for franchises, the basis for revenue recognition was changed from the date the franchise contract was signed to a basis that more closely reflected the requirements of the revenue realization principle.[37]

How should motion picture companies such as the National Film Board of Canada, Metro-Goldwyn-Mayer Inc., Warner Bros., and United Artists account for the sale of rights to show motion picture films on cable television networks and the CBC, CTV, ABC, CBS, or NBC? Should the revenue from the sale of the rights be reported when the contract is signed, when the motion picture film is delivered to the network, when the cash payment is received, or when the film is shown on television? The problem of revenue recognition is complicated because the TV networks are often restricted in the number of times the film may be shown in total and over what time period.

For example, Metro-Goldwyn-Mayer (MGM) sold CBS the rights to show *Gone With the Wind* for $35 million. CBS received the right to show this classic movie once a year over a 20-year period. MGM contended that revenue recognition should coincide with the movie's showings over the 20 years. The accounting profession, on the other hand, argued that all of the revenue should be recognized immediately because (1) the sales price and cost of the film were known, (2) collectibility was assured, and (3) the film was available and accepted by the network. The restriction that the movie be shown only once a year was not considered significant justification for deferring revenue recognition. It is interesting to note that MGM reported the entire $35 million in revenue in the first year.

Matching Principle. In recognizing expenses, accountants attempt to follow the approach of "let the expenses follow the revenues." Expenses are recognized not when wages are paid, or when work is performed, or when a product is produced, but when the work, service, or product actually makes its contribution to revenue. Thus, expense recognition is tied to revenue recognition. This practice is justified by the **matching principle** which dictates ***expenses that are linked to revenue in a cause-and-effect relationship are normally matched with the revenue in the accounting period in which the revenue is recognized.***[38]

For those costs for which it is not reasonable or practicable to reflect a direct cause-and-effect relationship with revenues, some other approach must be adopted so that they are shown as an expense in the appropriate period's income statement. Often, the accountant uses a "systematic and rational" allocation policy in an attempt to approximate the matching principle. This type of expense recognition always involves assumptions about the benefits that are being received as well as the cost associated with those benefits. The cost of a long-lived asset, for example, is allocated over the accounting periods during which the asset is used because the asset contributes to the generation of revenue throughout its useful life.

---

[37] "Franchise Fee Recognition," *Accounting Guideline* (Toronto: CICA, 1984).

[38] *CICA Handbook*, Section 1000, par. .51.

Some costs are charged to the current period as expenses (or losses) simply because no future benefit is anticipated or no apparent connection with future revenue is evident. Examples of these types of costs are officers' salaries and advertising expenses.

In summary, costs are analysed to determine whether a direct relationship exists with revenue. Where this holds true, the costs are expensed and matched against the revenue in the period when the revenue is recognized. If no direct connection appears between costs and revenues, an allocation of cost on some systematic and rational basis may be appropriate. When such an allocation approach is not appropriate, the costs may be expensed immediately.

Costs are generally classified into two categories: product costs and period costs. **Product costs** such as material, labour, and overhead attach to the product and are carried into future periods if the revenue from the product is recognized in subsequent periods. **Period costs** such as officers' salaries and general selling expenses are charged immediately to income because no direct relationship between cost and revenue can be determined.

The problems of expense recognition are as complex as those of revenue recognition. For example, a large oil company spends a considerable amount of money in an advertising campaign. It hopes to attract new customers and develop brand loyalty. Over how many years, if any, should this outlay be expensed? As another example, consider the video rental market. One major company amortizes the cost of all its video tapes over three years: 36% the first year, 36% the second, and 24% the third. Other video rental companies take a more conservative approach, noting that Class A titles (expensive hits) average 28 rentals the first three months, 12 rentals the next three months, 12 more in the next six months, and 18 over the next year. As a result, they charge off these tapes in one year, or two years at most. As an executive of one of the video rental companies noted, "If you ask 12 different people the useful life of a video tape, you get 12 different answers." If so, the result would be 12 different expense recognition patterns, all of them being legitimate attempts to match expenses against revenues.

The conceptual validity of the matching principle has been a subject of debate. A major concern is that matching permits certain costs to be deferred and treated as assets on the balance sheet when in fact these costs may not have future benefits. If abused, this principle permits the balance sheet to become a "dumping ground" for unmatched costs. In addition, there appears to be no objective definition of what is "systematic and rational." Therefore, while the matching principle is an important guideline for determining when expenses are to be recognized, its application requires substantial judgement in many situations.

Full Disclosure Principle. In deciding what information to report, accountants follow the general practice of providing information that is of sufficient importance to influence the judgement and decisions of an informed user. This is often referred to as the **full disclosure principle**. It recognizes that the nature and amount of information included in financial reports reflects a series of judgemental trade-offs. These trade-offs involve striving for (1) sufficient detail to disclose matters that make a difference to users, and (2) sufficient condensation to make the information understandable, keeping in mind costs of preparing and using it. Information about financial position, income, and cash flows can be placed in one of three places: (1) within the main body of financial statements, (2) in the notes and supporting schedules to those statements, or (3) as supplementary information. The following paragraphs provide some broad guidelines for deciding where to place certain kinds of financial information.

The **financial statements** are a formal, structured means of communicating information. To be recognized in the main body of financial statements, ***an item should meet the definition of an element and the recognition criteria***. The item must have been measured, recorded in the books, and passed through the double-entry system of accounting.

The **notes** and **supporting schedules** to financial statements generally amplify or explain the items presented in the main body of the statements. If the information in the main body of the financial statements gives an incomplete picture of the performance and position of the enterprise, additional information that is needed to complete the picture should be included in the notes.

Information in the notes does not have to be quantifiable. Notes can be partially or totally narrative. Examples of notes are: (1) descriptions of the accounting policies and methods used in measuring the elements reported in the statements; (2) explanations of uncertainties and contingencies; and (3) statistics and details too voluminous for inclusion in the statements. The notes are not only helpful but also essential to understanding the enterprise's performance and position.

Supplementary information may include details or amounts that present a different perspective from that adopted in the financial statements. It may be quantifiable information that is high in relevance but low in reliability, or information that is helpful but not essential.

Supplementary information, unless it is cross-referenced in the financial statements, is not considered a part of the financial statements and is not audited.[39] Most companies provide such information, however, on the grounds that it is useful. Examples of supplementary information are financial highlight summaries and historical (5- or 10-year) summaries. A relatively new section in many annual reports, called Management's Discussion and Analysis, is also an important source of information regarding past financial results and, often, strategies and objectives for the future.

The full disclosure principle is not always easy to put into operation because the business environment is complicated and ever-changing. For example, during the past decade many business combinations produced innumerable conglomerate-type organizations and financing arrangements that demanded new and unique accounting and reporting practices and principles. Leases, investment credits, pension funds, franchising, stock options, financial instruments, and mergers had to be studied, and appropriate reporting practices had to be developed. In each of these situations, the accountant was faced with the problem of providing enough information to ensure that the mythical reasonably prudent investor would not be misled.

Basic Constraints

In providing information with the qualitative characteristics that make it useful, two overriding constraints must be considered: (1) the benefit-cost relationship and (2) materiality.[40] An additional constraint is industry practice.

Objective 9

Describe the impact that constraints have on reporting accounting information.

Benefit-Cost Relationship. Too often, users assume that information is a cost-free commodity. Preparers and providers of accounting information know that it is not. The costs of providing information must be weighed against the benefits that can be derived from using it. Obviously, the benefits should exceed the costs. Accountants have traditionally applied this constraint through the notions of "expediency" or "practicality."

The difficulty in benefit-cost analysis is that the costs and especially the benefits are not always evident or measurable. The costs are of several kinds, including costs of collecting, processing, disseminating, auditing, potential litigation, disclosure to competitors, and analysis and interpretation. Benefits accrue both to preparers (e.g., management's control of resources, access to capital) and to users (e.g., allocation of resources, tax assessment), but they are generally more difficult to quantify than are costs.

In addition to considering benefit-cost aspects when preparing an enterprise's financial statements, such analysis is also required by those responsible for developing accounting standards. Among the providers and the users of accounting information, there are those who believe that the costs associated with implementing certain accounting standards are too high when compared with the benefits received. For example, some believe that Canadian GAAP, as represented in the *CICA Handbook*, is too cumbersome and expensive for smaller businesses to adhere to relative to the resulting benefits. Consequently, they have argued that the financial statements of smaller businesses

---

[39] While supplementary information is not audited, *CICA Handbook*, Section 7500, states that the auditor should read the other information in the annual report and consider whether any of it is inconsistent with the financial statements on which the audit report is given. Various actions occur if material inconsistencies are found. However, it is unlikely the auditor would give a report if the inconsistencies were not satisfactorily resolved.

[40] *CICA Handbook*, Section 1000, pars. .16 and .17.

should be governed by less demanding standards. The issues are related to what is called the "big GAAP, little GAAP" controversy (i.e. should there be one GAAP to which all companies adhere, or should GAAP applicable to larger companies differ from that applicable to smaller companies?). While the Accounting Standards Board has generally maintained that its standards are applicable to all companies (an exception existed when it was recommended that only larger companies disclose current cost information), it has recognized that a benefit-cost perspective should be employed when developing standards.[41]

Materiality. ***An item, or an aggregate of items, is material if it is probable that its omission or misstatement would influence or change a decision.***[42] In short, it must make a difference or it need not be disclosed. It is difficult to provide firm guidelines to help judge when an item is or is not material because materiality depends on the *relative size* of the item compared to the size of other items and the *nature* of the item itself. The two sets of numbers presented below illustrate the importance of relative size.

	Company A	Company B
Sales	$10,000,000	$100,000
Costs and expenses	9,000,000	90,000
Income from operations	$ 1,000,000	$ 10,000
Unusual gain	**$ 20,000**	**$ 5,000**

During the period in question, the revenues and expenses and, therefore, the net incomes from operations of Company A and Company B have been proportional. Each had an unusual gain. In looking at the income figure for Company A, it does not appear significant whether the amount of the unusual gain is separated or merged with the regular operating income. It is only 2% of the operating income and, if merged, would not seriously distort the net operating income figure. Company B's unusual gain is only $5,000, but, as this amounts to 50% of its income from operations, it is relatively much more significant than the larger gain realized by A. Obviously, the inclusion of such an item in ordinary operating income would affect the amount of that income materially. Thus we see the importance of the relative size of an item in determining its materiality.

The nature of the item may also be important. For example, if a company violates a statute, the facts and amounts involved should be separately disclosed. Or, a $50,000 misclassification of assets within the noncurrent section may not be considered material in amount, but it is material if it is a misclassification between the noncurrent and current sections.

Materiality is a difficult concept to apply, as the following examples indicate:

1. General Dynamics disclosed that at one time its Resources Group had improved its earnings by $5.8 million at the same time that its Stromberg Datagraphix subsidiary had taken write-offs of $6.7 million. Although both numbers were far larger than the $2.5 million that General Dynamics as a whole earned for the year, neither was disclosed as a separate item in the financial statements. Apparently the effect on net income was not considered material. Perhaps each should have been disclosed separately because the Stromberg write-off appeared to be a one-time charge, whereas the improvement in the Resources Group was ongoing.

2. In the first quarter, GAC's earnings rose from 76 cents to 77 cents a share. Nowhere did the annual report disclose that a favourable on-time tax incentive of 4 cents a share prevented GAC's earnings from sliding to 73 cents a share. The company took the position that this incentive's benefits should not be specifically disclosed because it was not material (6% of net income). As an executive noted, "You know that accountants have a rule of thumb which says that anything under 10% is not material." Of course, the executive's statement seems less than serious. It should have been considered significant that the direction of the company's earnings was completely altered—even though 4 cents a share seems like a small amount.

[41] *Ibid.*, par. .16.
[42] *Ibid.*, par. .17.

These examples illustrate one point: in practice, the answer to what is material is not clear cut, and difficult decisions must be made each period. Only by the exercise of professional judgement can the accountant arrive at answers that are reasonable and appropriate.

Industry Practice. ***The unique nature of some industries and business concerns sometimes requires departure from basic theory.*** For example, banks often report certain investment securities at market value because these securities are traded frequently, and many believe a cash equivalent price provides more useful information than historical cost. In the public utility industry, noncurrent assets may be reported first on the balance sheet to highlight the industry's capital-intensive nature. Agricultural crops are often reported at market value because it is costly to develop accurate cost figures on individual crops. Such variations from basic theory are few; yet they do exist. Therefore, whenever we find what appears to be a violation of basic accounting theory, we should determine whether it is explained by some peculiar feature of the type of business involved before we criticize the procedures followed.

SUMMARY OF THE CONCEPTUAL FRAMEWORK

Figure 2-3 (on page 54) summarizes the essential components of the conceptual framework discussed in this chapter. We cannot overemphasize the usefulness of this framework in helping to understand and resolve many financial accounting problems.

Throughout the remainder of this book, we will examine particular issues of contemporary financial accounting practice. In many cases, clear-cut conclusions as to what one should do regarding identification, measurement, and reporting decisions are not possible. Indeed, it will become obvious that there are many generally accepted accounting alternatives available for measuring and reporting various transactions and events. They are acceptable because of the flexibility provided by the framework and the trade-offs that, by necessity, must be made between its components. The consequence is that professional judgement is a critical aspect of financial reporting. When exercising this judgement, one must relate the framework to the circumstances involved.

The financial statements of a company are those of its management; thus it is really management that selects the generally accepted accounting methods to be used in preparing the financial statements. Senior accounting officers will, however, play a crucial role in determining the policies because of their positions as members of the management team and because of their conceptual and practical expertise.

FUNDAMENTAL CONCEPTS

1. Accounting theory is not discovered; it is created, developed, or decreed and supported and justified by intuition, authority, and acceptability.
2. A conceptual framework is needed to (1) build a coherent set of standards and practices which relate to an established body of objectives and concepts, (2) provide a framework in which new and emerging practical problems may be solved more quickly, (3) increase financial statement users' understanding of and confidence in financial reporting, and (4) enhance comparability among companies' financial statements.
3. The first level of the conceptual framework identifies the basic objectives of financial reporting.
4. The second level of the conceptual framework identifies the qualitative characteristics that make accounting information useful and define the elements of financial statements.
5. The overriding criterion on which accounting choices can be judged is decision usefulness, that is, providing information that is most useful for decision making.
6. To be useful, financial statement information must be understood by users. At a base level, it is assumed that users have a reasonable understanding of business and economic activities and accounting, together with a willingness to study information with reasonable diligence.

(Continued)

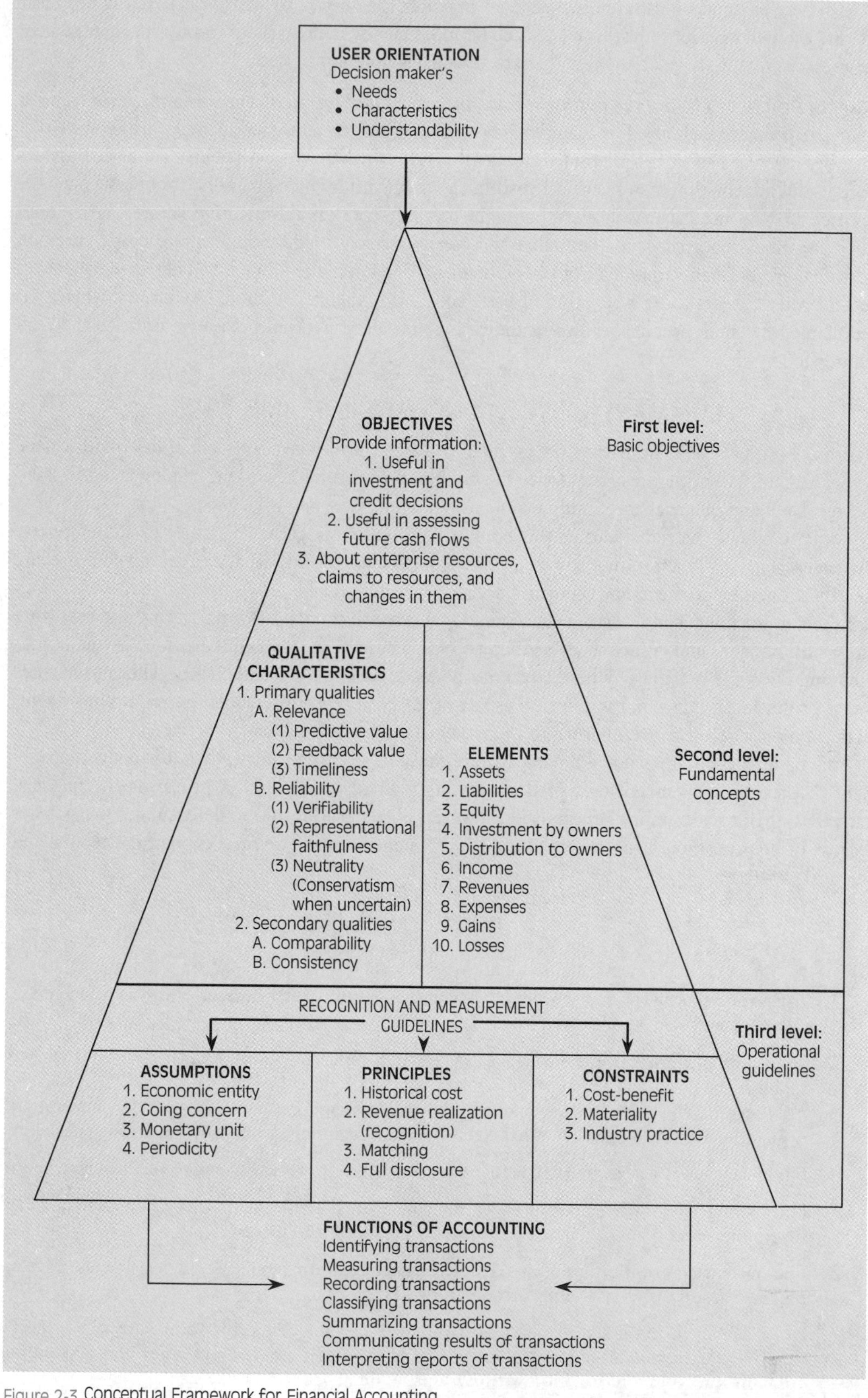

Figure 2-3 Conceptual Framework for Financial Accounting

7. Relevance and reliability are the two primary qualities that make accounting information useful for decision making.
8. Comparability and consistency are the two secondary qualities that make accounting information useful for decision-making purposes.
9. An important aspect of developing any theoretical structure is the establishment of a body of elements and their definitions. Eight interrelated elements that are most directly related to measuring the performance and financial status of an enterprise are identified and defined.
10. The third level of the conceptual framework relates to recognition and measurement guidelines that are used to develop responses to financial reporting issues; they are categorized as basic assumptions, principles, and constraints.
11. The components of this theoretical structure will change to some degree as the environment of accounting changes.

QUESTIONS

1. What is a conceptual framework? Why is a conceptual framework useful in financial accounting?
2. What are the primary objectives of financial reporting?
3. What is meant by the term "qualitative characteristics of accounting information"?
4. Briefly describe the two primary qualities which make accounting information useful.
5. What is the distinction between comparability and consistency?
6. Why is it necessary to develop definitions for the basic elements of financial accounting?
7. Expenses, losses, and distributions to owners are all decreases in net assets. What is the distinction between them?
8. Revenues, gains, and investments by owners are all increases in net assets. What is the distinction between them?
9. What are the four basic assumptions that underlie the financial accounting structure?
10. If the going-concern assumption is not made in accounting, what difference does it make in the amounts shown in the financial statements for the following items?
    (a) Land.
    (b) Unamortized bond premium.
    (c) Depreciation expense on equipment.
    (d) Long-term investments in shares of other companies.
    (e) Merchandise inventory.
    (f) Prepaid insurance.
11. What is the basic accounting problem related to the monetary unit assumption of a stable dollar when there is significant inflation?
12. The chairman of the board of directors of the company for which you are chief accountant has told you that he is entirely out of sympathy with accounting figures based on cost. He believes that replacement values are of far more significance to the board of directors than "out-of-date costs." Present some arguments to convince him that accounting data should still be based on historical acquisition cost.
13. What are the accounting requirements regarding revenue recognition? Why has the date of sale been chosen as the point at which to recognize the revenue resulting from the entire producing and selling process in most cases?
14. What accounting assumption, principle, constraint, or characteristic does Barger Co. Ltd. use in each of the situations below?
    (a) Barger Co. Ltd. uses the lower of cost and market method to value inventories.
    (b) Barger is involved in litigation with Roderick Co. Ltd. over a product malfunction. This litigation is disclosed in the financial statements.
    (c) Barger allocates the cost of its depreciable assets over the life it expects to receive revenue from these assets.
    (d) Barger records the purchase of a new computer at its cash equivalent price.
15. Gurney Co. Ltd. paid $90,000 for a machine in 1992. The Accumulated Depreciation account has a balance of $31,000 at the present time.

The company could sell the machine today for $101,000. The company president believes that the company has a "right to this gain." What does the president mean by this statement? Do you agree?

16. Three expense recognition points (associating cause and effect, systematic and rational allocation, and immediate recognition) were discussed in this chapter under the matching principle. Indicate the basic nature of each of these types of expense recognition and give two examples of each.

17. Explain how you would decide whether to record each of the following expenditures as an asset or an expense:
    (a) Legal fees paid in connection with the purchase of land are $1,000.
    (b) Salem Inc. paves the driveway leading to its office building at a cost of $14,000.
    (c) A meat market purchases a meat-grinding machine at a cost of $230.
    (d) On June 30, Marshall and Jefferson, medical doctors, pay six months' office rent to cover the month of June and the next five months.
    (e) The Buffalo Hardware Company pays $6,000 in wages to labourers for construction on a building to be used in its business.
    (f) Joe's Florists pays wages of $1,400 in November to an employee who drives their delivery truck during that month.

18. Briefly describe the types of information concerning financial position, income, and cash flows that might be provided: (a) within the main body of the financial statements, (b) in the notes to the financial statements, or (c) as supplementary information.

19. In January 1994, Dilley Corp. Ltd. doubled the amount of its outstanding shares by selling on the market an additional 10,000 shares to finance an expansion of the business. As financial statements for 1993 have not yet been completed, you propose that this information be shown by a note on the balance sheet of December 31, 1993. The president objects, claiming that this sale took place after December 31, 1993 and, therefore, should not be shown. Explain your position.

20. Describe the two major constraints inherent in the presentation of accounting information.

21. How is materiality (or immateriality) related to disclosures in financial statements? What factors and measures should an auditor consider in assessing the materiality of a misstatement in the presentation of a financial statement?

22. The president of Uni Enterprises Ltd. has heard that conservatism is a doctrine that is followed in accounting and, therefore, proposes that several policies be followed that are conservative in nature. State your opinion with respect to the acceptability of each of the policies listed below:
    (a) A lawsuit is pending against the company. The president believes there is an even chance that the company will lose the suit and have to pay damages of $140,000 to $190,000. The president recommends that a loss be recorded and a liability created in the amount of $190,000.
    (b) The inventory should be valued at "cost or market, whichever is lower" because the losses from price declines should be recognized in the accounts in the period in which the price decline takes place.
    (c) The company gives a two-year warranty to its customers on all products sold. The estimated warranty costs incurred from this year's sales should be entered as an expense this year instead of an expense in a future period when the warranty costs are actually incurred.
    (d) When sales are made on account, there is always uncertainty about whether the accounts are collectible. Therefore, the president recommends recording the sale when the cash is received from the customers.

CASES

(CONCEPTUAL FRAMEWORK: GENERAL) James Sander has some concerns regarding the theoretical framework in which standards are set. James' supervisors have indicated that theoretical frameworks have little value in the practical sense (i.e. in the real world). James does notice that accounting standards seem to be established after the fact rather than before. He thinks this indicates a lack of theory in establishing the standards, but never really questioned the process at school because he was too busy doing the homework. C2-1

James feels that some of his anxiety about accounting theory and accounting semantics can be alleviated if he identifies the basic concepts and definitions accepted by the profession and considers them in light of his current work. By doing this, he hopes to develop an appropriate connection between theory and practice.

Instructions

Help James recognize the purpose and benefit of a conceptual framework.

(CONCEPTUAL FRAMEWORK: GENERAL) Various attempts have been and are being made to work toward a conceptual framework for financial accounting and reporting. These attempts have met with some success. In Canada, the *CICA Handbook* includes a section on financial statement concepts. In the United States, the FASB issued a series of publications on financial accounting concepts. Internationally, the IASC has issued a statement on a framework for preparing and presenting financial statements. These attempts have helped to clarify the use and application of general accounting concepts for standard-setting bodies and for individual companies when they are making financial accounting decisions. C2-2

Instructions

Identify and discuss the usefulness and limitations of a conceptual framework for financial accounting and reporting, with particular regard to the accounting profession, international harmonization, setting of accounting standards, accounting education, and financial statement users.

(UFE adapted)

(OBJECTIVES OF FINANCIAL REPORTING) After reading the first two chapters of this text, two students were discussing the various aspects of existing statements of financial accounting objectives. One student felt that such statements provide little, if any, guidance to the practicing professional in resolving accounting controversies. He felt that the objectives stated were so broad and general that they were impossible to apply to solve present-day reporting problems. The other student conceded that the objectives were general but indicated that she felt they were needed to provide a starting point for accountants to help them improve financial reporting. C2-3

Instructions

(a) Identify what the basic objectives of financial accounting are.

(b) What do you think is the meaning of the second student's statement that the accounting profession needs objectives as a starting point to resolve accounting controversies?

(QUALITATIVE CHARACTERISTICS) Accounting statements provide useful information about business transactions and events. Those who provide financial reports must often evaluate and select from a set of accounting alternatives. The qualitative characteristics that relate to making accounting information useful for decision making were identified and discussed in Chapter 2. It was also pointed out that trade-offs or sacrifices of one quality for another are often necessary when carrying out the identification, measurement, and communication (reporting) functions of accounting. C2-4

Instructions

(a) Describe briefly what is meant by the following characteristics of accounting information:

1. Understandability.
2. Relevance.
3. Reliability.
4. Comparability.
5. Consistency.

(b) Why is the distinction between primary qualities (relevance and reliability) and secondary qualities (comparability and consistency) made?

(c) For each of the following pairs of information qualities, give an example of a situation in which one may be sacrificed in return for a gain in the other:

1. Relevance and reliability.
2. Relevance and consistency.
3. Comparability and consistency.
4. Relevance and understandability.

(d) What criterion should be used to evaluate trade-offs between information characteristics?

C2-5 **(QUALITATIVE CHARACTERISTICS)** Figure 2-2 provided an identification of qualitative characteristics for financial accounting information. Within this framework are primary qualities of information (and their basic ingredients) and secondary qualities of information. Presented below are a number of questions. If an answer reflects an absence of one of the primary qualities of information, specify which one and the ingredient that is most likely to be missing.

1. What are the two primary qualities that make accounting information useful for decision making?
2. Hurry Inc. does not issue its second quarter report until after the third quarter's results are reported. Which information quality is missing?
3. To which of the two primary qualities that make accounting information useful for decision-making purposes is predictive value an ingredient?
4. Al Ter Nate Co. Ltd. is the only company in its industry to depreciate its plant assets on a straight-line basis. Which quality of accounting information may be absent?
5. Rudnicki Inc. has attempted to determine the replacement cost of its inventory. Three different appraisers arrive at substantially different amounts for this value. The president, nevertheless, decides to report the middle value for external reporting purposes. Which quality of information is lacking in this data?
6. What is the ingredient of information that enables users to confirm or correct prior expectations?
7. Identify the two overall or pervasive constraints.
8. It was once noted that "if it becomes accepted or expected that accounting principles are determined or modified in order to secure purposes other than economic measurement, then we assume a grave risk that confidence in the credibility of our financial information system will be undermined." Which quality of accounting information should ensure that such a situation will not occur?

9. Hydroplane Co. Ltd. switches from FIFO to weighted average to FIFO over a three-year period. Which quality of information is missing?

10. Assume that the profession permits the banking industry to defer losses on investments it sells because immediate recognition of the loss may have adverse economic consequences on the industry. Which quality of information is missing?

(VALUE CHANGE VERSUS INCOME DETERMINATION) The president of the Devo Manufacturing C2-6
Company received an income statement from his controller. The statement covered the calendar year 1994. "Joan," he said to the controller, "this statement indicates that a net income of $3,000,000 was earned last year. You know the value of the company is not that much more than it was a year earlier."

"You're probably right," replied the controller. "You see, there are factors in accounting that sometimes keep reported operating results from reflecting the change in the value of the company."

Instructions

Prepare a detailed explanation of the accounting factors to which the controller referred. Include justification, to the extent possible, for the generally accepted accounting methods.

(ELEMENTS OF FINANCIAL STATEMENTS) Eight interrelated elements that are most directly related C2-7
to measuring the performance and financial status of an enterprise are identified below:

Assets	Net income
Liabilities	Revenues
Equity	Expenses
Gains	Losses

Instructions

State the element or elements associated with each of the following 10 items:

1. Arises from income statement activities that constitute the entity's ongoing major or central operations. Net Income
2. Residual interest in the assets of the enterprise after deducting its liabilities. Equity
3. Increases assets during a period through sale of products. Revenue
4. Decreases assets during the period by the payment of wages. Expenses.
5. Generally includes all changes in equity during the period, except those resulting from investments by owners and distributions to owners. Net Income.
6. Arises from peripheral or incidental transactions. Gain / Losses.
7. Obligation to transfer resources arising from past transaction. liabilities.
8. Increases ownership interest. Equity
9. Decreases net assets in a period from non-owner sources. Losses
10. Items characterized by service potential or future economic benefit. Assets.

(ASSUMPTIONS, PRINCIPLES, AND CONSTRAINTS) Presented below are the assumptions, princi- C2-8
ples, and constraints identified in this chapter:

Economic entity assumption	Full disclosure principle
Going concern assumption	Benefit/cost constraint
Monetary unit assumption	Materiality
Periodicity assumption	Industry practices
Historical cost principle	Matching principle

Instructions

Identify the accounting assumption, principle, or constraint that describes each situation below. Do not use an answer more than once.

1. Allocates expenses to revenues in the appropriate period. Matching Principle.
2. Indicates that market value changes subsequent to purchase are not recorded in the accounts. (Do not use revenue recognition principle.) Historical cost principle
3. Ensures that relevant financial information is reported. Full disclosure principle
4. Rationale that explains why plant assets are not reported at liquidation value. (Do not use historical cost principle.) Going-concern assumption
5. Provides justification to the argument that all standards should not have to be adhered to by small businesses when preparing financial statements. Benefit/cost constraints.
6. Indicates that personal and business record-keeping should be separately maintained. Economic Entity Assumption.
7. Separates financial information into time periods for reporting purposes. Periodicity Assumption.
8. Permits the use of market value valuation in certain specific situations. Industry practices.
9. Requires that information significant enough to affect the decision of reasonably informed users should be disclosed. (Do not use full disclosure principle.) Materiality
10. Assumes that the dollar is the "measuring stick" used to report on financial performance. Monetary Unit Assumption.

C2-9 (ASSUMPTIONS, PRINCIPLES, AND CONSTRAINTS) Presented below are a number of operational guidelines and practices that have developed over time:

1. All important aspects of bond indentures (contracts) are presented in financial statements. full disclosure principle
2. Rationale for accrual accounting is stated. Historical cost principle
3. The preparation of consolidated statements is justified. Periodicity assumption.
4. Reporting must be done at defined time intervals. Periodicity assumption.
5. An allowance for doubtful accounts is established. matching principle
6. Payments out of petty cash are charged to Miscellaneous Expense. Matching Principle
7. Goodwill is recorded only when it is purchased and not when it is built up. Historical cost principle
8. A company charges its sales commission costs to expense when the sales are made. matching principle
9. Price-level changes are not recognized in the accounting records. Monetary unit assumption.

10. Financial information is presented so that reasonably prudent investors will not be misled. Full - disclosure principle

11. Intangibles are capitalized and amortized over the periods that are benefited. Historical cost principle

12. Repair tools are expensed when purchased. Matching principle.

13. Brokerage firms use market value for purposes of valuation of all marketable securities. Materiality

14. Each enterprise is kept as a unit distinct from its owner or owners. Economic entity assumption.

15. All significant subsequent events (i.e. occur after the balance sheet date but before the statements are prepared) are reported. Industry practices.

16. Revenue is recorded at point of sale. Revenue recognition principle.

Instructions

Select the assumption, principle, or constraint that most appropriately justifies each of these procedures and practices. Do not use components of the qualitative characteristics.

(ASSUMPTIONS, PRINCIPLES, AND CONSTRAINTS) A number of accounting procedures and practices are described below: **C2-10**

1. Acid Chemical Corp. "faces possible expropriation (i.e. take-over) of foreign facilities and possible losses on sums owed by various customers on the verge of bankruptcy." The company president has decided that these possibilities should not be noted on the financial statements because Acid still hopes that these events will not take place.

2. Sally Madison, manager of College Bookstore Inc., bought a computer for her own use. She paid for it by writing a cheque on the bookstore's chequing account and charged it to the "Office Equipment" account.

3. Mavis Co. Ltd. recently completed a new 120-storey office building which housed their home offices and many other tenants. All the office equipment for the building that had a per item or per unit cost of $1,000 or less was expensed even though the office equipment has an average life of 10 years. The total cost of such office equipment was approximately $24 million.

4. Borneo Inc. presented its financial statements on the basis of what its assets could be sold for and the amount required to pay off its liabilities on the balance sheet date. When the president was asked why this was done, she stated, "That is what banks are interested in."

5. A large lawsuit has been filed against Crocket Inc. by Miller Co. Ltd. Crocket has recorded a loss and related estimated liability equal to the maximum possible amount it feels it may have to pay. It is confident, however, that either it will not lose the suit or it will owe a much smaller amount.

6. The treasurer of Almaden Co. Ltd. wishes to prepare financial statements only during downturns in their wine production, which occur periodically when the rhubarb crop fails. He states that the statements can be most easily prepared at such times. In no event should more than 30 months pass by without statements being prepared.

7. The RIP Power & Light Corporation has purchased a large amount of property, plant, and equipment over a number of years. Because the general price level has changed materially over the years, it has decided to issue only price-level-adjusted financial statements.

8. Daffodil Manufacturing Co. Ltd. decided to manufacture its own widgets because it would be cheaper to do so than to buy them from an outside supplier. In an attempt to make its statements more comparable with those of its competitors, Daffodil charged its inventory account for what it thought the widgets would cost if they were purchased from an outside supplier.

9. Value Discount Centres Inc. buys its merchandise by the truck- and train-load. Value does not defer any transportation costs in computing the cost of its ending inventory. Such costs, although varying from period to period, are always material in amount.

10. Pizza Bell Inc., a fast-food company, sells franchises for $70,000, accepting a $1,000 down payment and a 50-year note for the remainder. Pizza Bell promises within three years to assist in site selection, building, and management training. Pizza Bell records the $70,000 franchise fee as revenue in the period in which the contract is signed.

Instructions

For each of the foregoing, list the major accounting assumption, principle, or constraint that would be violated. Do not use components of the qualitative characteristics.

C2-11 **(ASSUMPTIONS, PRINCIPLES, AND CONSTRAINTS)** You are engaged to review the accounting records of Homewrecker Corporation prior to the closing of the revenue and expense accounts as of December 31, the end of the current fiscal year. The following information comes to your attention.

1. During the current year, Homewrecker Corporation changed its policy in regard to expensing purchases of small tools. In the past, these purchases were always expensed because they amounted to less than 2% of net income, but the president has decided that capitalization and subsequent depreciation should now be followed. It is expected that purchases of small tools will not fluctuate greatly from year to year.

2. Homewrecker Corporation constructed a warehouse at a cost of $800,000. The company had been depreciating the asset on a straight-line basis over 10 years. In the current year, the controller doubled depreciation expense because the replacement cost of the warehouse had increased significantly.

3. The company decided in October of the current fiscal year to start a massive advertising campaign to enhance the marketability of its product. In November, the company paid $700,000 for advertising time on a major television network to advertise its product during the next 12 months. The controller expensed the $700,000 in the current year on the basis that "once the money is spent, it can never be recovered from the television network."

4. In preparing the balance sheet, detailed information as to the amount of cash on deposit in each of several banks was omitted. Only the total amount of cash under a caption "Cash in Banks" was presented.

5. On July 15 of the current year, Homewrecker Corporation purchased an undeveloped tract of land at a cost of $290,000. The company spent $70,000 in subdividing the land and getting it ready for sale. An appraisal of the property at the end of the year indicated that the land was now worth $450,000. Although none of the lots were sold, the company recognized revenue of $160,000, less related expenses of $70,000, for a net income on the project of $90,000.

6. For a number of years, the company had used the average cost method for inventory valuation purposes. During the current year, the president noted that all the other companies in their industry had switched to the FIFO method. The company decided not to switch to FIFO because net income would decrease $170,000.

Instructions

State whether or not you agree with the decisions made by Homewrecker Corporation. Support your answers with reference, whenever possible, to the appropriate aspects of the conceptual framework developed in this chapter and any assumptions about the circumstances of Homewrecker that you think would be helpful.

C2-12 **(HISTORICAL COST PRINCIPLE)** Presented below is a statement that appeared about Weyerhaeuser Company in a financial magazine:

> The land and timber holdings are now carried on the company's books at a mere $422 million. The value of the timber alone is variously estimated at from $3 billion to $7 billion and is rising all the time. "The understatement of the company is pretty severe," conceded Charles W. Bingham, a senior vice-president. Adds Robert L. Schuyler, another senior vice-president, "We have a whole stream of profit nobody sees and there is no way to show it on our books."

Instructions

(a) What does Schuyler mean when he says that "we have a whole stream of profit nobody sees and there is no way to show it on our books"?

(b) If the understatement of the company's assets is severe, why does accounting not report this information?

(REVENUE RECOGNITION AND MATCHING PRINCIPLE) After listening to the presentation of your report on the financial statements, one of the new directors of Hogan Publishing Co. Ltd. expresses surprise that the income statement assumes that an equal proportion of the revenue is earned with the publication of every issue of the company's magazine. He feels that "performance is achieved" in the process of earning revenue in the magazine business when there is a cash sale for the subscription. He says that he does not understand why most of the revenue cannot be "recognized" in the period of the sale. C2-13

Instructions

(a) List the various accepted methods for recognizing revenue in the accounts and explain when the methods are appropriate.

(b) Discuss the propriety of timing the recognition of revenue in Hogan Publishing Co. Ltd.'s accounts with:

1. The cash sale of the magazine subscription.

2. The publication of the magazine every month.

3. Both events, by realizing a portion of the revenue with cash sale of the magazine subscription and a portion of the revenue with the publication of the magazine every month.

(AICPA adapted)

(REVENUE RECOGNITION AND MATCHING PRINCIPLE) On June 8, 1994, Chet Inc. signed a contract with Nair Associates under which Nair agreed (1) to construct an office building on land owned by Chet, (2) to accept responsibility for procuring financing for the project and finding tenants, and (3) to manage the property for 35 years. The annual net income from the project, after debt service, was to be divided equally between Chet Inc. and Nair Associates. Nair was to accept its share of future net income as full payment for its services in construction, obtaining finances and tenants, and management of the project. C2-14

By May 31, 1995, the project was nearly completed and tenants had signed leases to occupy 90% of the available space at annual rentals aggregating $3,000,000. It is estimated that, after operating expenses and debt service, the annual net income will amount to $1,100,000. The management of Nair Associates believed that the economic benefit derived from the contract with Chet should be reflected on its financial statements for the fiscal year ended May 31, 1995 and directed that revenue be accrued in an amount equal to the commercial value of the services Nair had rendered during the year, that this amount be carried in contracts receivable, and that all related expenditures be charged against the revenue.

Instructions

(a) Explain the main difference between the economic concept of business income as reflected by Nair's management and the measurement of income under generally accepted accounting principles.

(b) Discuss the factors to be considered in determining when revenue has been realized for the purpose of accounting measurement of periodic income.

(c) Is the belief of Nair's management in accord with generally accepted accounting principles for the measurement of revenue and expenses for the year ended May 31,1995? Support your opinion by discussing the application to this case of the factors to be considered for asset measurement and revenue and expense recognition.

(AICPA adapted)

(MATCHING PRINCIPLE) An accountant must be familiar with the concepts involved in determining earnings of a business entity. The amount of earnings reported for a business entity is dependent on the appropriate recognition, in general, of revenues and expenses for a given time period. In some situations, costs are recognized C2-15 as expenses in the time period of the product sale; in other situations, guidelines have been developed for recognizing costs as expenses or losses by other criteria.

Instructions

(a) Explain the rationale for recognizing costs as expenses at the time of product sale.

(b) What is the rationale underlying the appropriateness of treating costs as expenses of a period instead of assigning the costs to an asset? Explain.

(c) In what general circumstances would it be appropriate to treat a cost as an asset instead of as an expense? Explain.

(d) Some expenses are assigned to specific accounting periods on the basis of systematic and rational allocation of asset costs. Explain the underlying rationale for recognizing expenses on the basis of systematic and rational allocation of asset costs.

(e) Identify the conditions in which it would be appropriate to treat a cost as a loss.

(AICPA adapted)

C2-16 (MATCHING PRINCIPLE) Accountants try to prepare income statements that are as accurate as possible. A basic requirement in preparing accurate income statements is to match costs against revenues appropriately. Such matching of costs against revenues requires that costs resulting from typical business operations be recognized in the period in which they expired.

Instructions

(a) List three bases that can be used to determine whether such costs should appear as charges in the income statement for the current period.

(b) As generally presented in financial statements, the following items or procedures have been criticized as improperly matching costs with revenues. Briefly discuss each item from the viewpoint of matching costs with revenues and suggest corrective or alternative means of presenting the financial information.

1. Receiving and handling costs.

2. Valuation of inventories at the lower of cost and market.

3. Cash discounts on purchases.

C2-17 (MATCHING PRINCIPLE) Fine Homes sells and erects shell houses, that is, frame structures that are completely finished on the outside but are unfinished on the inside except for flooring, partition studding, and ceiling joists. Shell houses are sold chiefly to customers who are handy with tools and who have time to do the interior wiring, plumbing, wall completion and finishing, and other work necessary to make the shell houses livable dwellings.

Fine buys shell houses from a manufacturer in unassembled packages consisting of all lumber, roofing, doors, windows, and similar materials necessary to complete a shell house. Upon commencing operations in a new area, Fine buys or leases land as a site for its local warehouse, field office, and display houses. Sample display houses are erected at a total cost of from $20,000 to $29,000 including the cost of the unassembled packages. The chief element of cost of the display houses is the unassembled packages, inasmuch as erection is a short low-cost operation. Old sample models are torn down or altered into new models every three to seven years. Sample display houses have little salvage value because dismantling and moving costs amount to nearly as much as the cost of an unassembled package.

Instructions

(a) A choice must be made between (1) expensing the costs of sample display houses in the periods in which the expenditure is made and (2) spreading the costs over more than one period. Discuss the advantages of each method.

(b) Would it be preferable to amortize (depreciate) the cost of display houses on the basis of (1) the passage of time or (2) the number of shell houses sold? Explain.

(AICPA adapted)

(MATCHING PRINCIPLE) The general ledger of NTV Ltd., a corporation engaged in the development and production of television programs for commercial sponsorship, contains the following asset accounts before amortization at the end of the current year: **C2-18**

	Balance
Rose and Ann	$60,000
Superhero	41,000
Badman	21,500
Spacetrack	9,000
Beverly Bills 90210	4,000

An examination of contracts and records revealed the following information:

1. The first two accounts listed above represent the total cost of completed programs that were televised during the accounting period just ended. Under the terms of an existing contract Rose and Ann will be rerun during the next accounting period, at a fee equal to 50% of the fee for the first televising of the program. The contract for the first run produced $600,000 of revenue. The contract with the sponsor of Superhero provides that he may, at his option, rerun the program during the next season at a fee of 75% of the fee on the first televising of the program.

2. The balance in the Badman account is the cost of a new program that has just been completed and is being considered by several companies for commercial sponsorship.

3. The balance in the Spacetrack account represents the cost of a partially completed program for a projected series that has been abandoned.

4. The balance of the Beverly Bills 90210 account consists of payments made to a firm of engineers that prepared a report relative to the more efficient utilization of existing studio space and equipment.

Instructions

(a) State the general principle (or principles) of accounting that are applicable to the first four accounts.

(b) How would you report each of the first four accounts in the financial statements of NTV Ltd.? Explain.

(c) In what way, if at all, does the Beverly Bills 90210 account differ from the first four? Explain.

(AICPA adapted)

(CONSERVATISM VERSUS CONSISTENCY) You are engaged in the audit of Office Computer Ltd., which opened its first branch office in 1994. During the audit Sharon Babcock, president, raises the question of the accounting treatment of the operating loss of the branch office for its first year, which is material in amount. **C2-19**

The president proposes to capitalize the operating loss as a "start-up" expense to be amortized over a five-year period. She states that branch offices of other firms engaged in the same field generally suffer a first-year operating loss that is invariably capitalized, and you are aware of this practice. She argues, therefore, that the loss should be capitalized so that the accounting will be "conservative"; further, she argues that the accounting must be "consistent" with established industry practice.

Instructions

Discuss the president's use of the words "conservative" and "consistent" from the standpoint of accounting terminology. Discuss the accounting treatment you would recommend.

(AICPA adapted)

C2-20 **(FULL DISCLOSURE PRINCIPLE)** Presented below are a number of facts related to Boxman Inc. Assume that no mention of these facts was made in the financial statements and the related notes.

1. The company decided that, for the sake of conciseness, only net income should be reported on the income statement. Details as to revenues, cost of goods sold, and expenses were omitted.

2. Equipment purchases of $140,000 were partly financed during the year through the issuance of $90,000 in notes payable. The company offset the equipment against the notes payable and reported plant assets at $50,000.

3. The company is a defendant in a patent-infringement suit involving a material amount; you have received assurance from the company's counsel that the possibility of loss is remote.

4. During the year, an assistant controller for the company embezzled $10,000. Boxman's net income for the year was $1,700,000. The assistant controller and the money have not been found.

5. Because of a recent gasoline shortage, it is possible that Boxman may suffer a costly shutdown in the near future similar to those suffered by other companies both within and outside the industry.

6. Boxman has reported its ending inventory at $2,000,000 in the financial statements. No other information related to inventories is presented in the financial statements and related notes.

7. The company changed its method of depreciating equipment from the double-declining balance method to the straight-line method. No mention of this change was made in the financial statements.

Instructions

Assume that you are the auditor of Boxman Inc. and you have been asked to explain the appropriate accounting and related disclosure necessary for each of these items. Provide your explanations.

C2-21 **(MATERIALITY)** The president of a public corporation recently commented, "Our auditor states that our financial statements present fairly our financial position and the results of our operations. I challenged him as to how he determined such fairness. He replied that fairness means that the financial statements are not misstated in amounts that would be considered material.

"I believe that there is some confusion with this materiality concept, since different users of our financial statements may have different ideas as to what is material. For example, bankers, institutional investors, small investors, and tax assessors all have different perceptions of materiality."

Instructions

Discuss the issues raised by the president.

C2-22 **(MATERIALITY CONSTRAINT)** Each of the items below involves the question of materiality to Hickman Co. Ltd.

1. The company purchases several items of equipment each year that cost less than $90 each. Most of them are used for several years, but some of them last for less than a year. The total cost of these purchases is about the same each year.

2. The amount of $1,400 is paid during 1994 for an assessment of additional income taxes for the year 1992. The amount originally paid in 1992 was $26,000, and the amount of this year's income taxes will be $41,000.

3. Land that had originally been purchased for expansion is sold in 1994 at a gain of $9,000. Net income for the year is $72,000, including the gain of $9,000. The company has experienced similar types of gains in the past.

Instructions

State your recommendation as to how each item should be treated in the accounts and in the statements, giving proper consideration to materiality and practicality aspects.

(ACCOUNTING PRINCIPLES: COMPREHENSIVE) Presented below are a number of business transactions that occurred during the current year for McGarva Co. Ltd. **C2-23**

1. Because the general level of prices increased during the current year, the company determined that there was a $14,000 understatement of depreciation expense on its equipment and decided to record it in its accounts. The following entry was made:

Depreciation Expense	14,000	
Accumulated Depreciation		14,000

2. McGarva Co. Ltd. has been concerned about whether intangible assets could generate cash in case of liquidation. As a consequence, goodwill arising from a purchase transaction during the current year and recorded at $900,000 was written off as follows:

Retained Earnings	900,000	
Goodwill		900,000

3. Because of a "fire sale," equipment obviously worth $190,000 was acquired at a cost of $140,000. The following entry was made:

Equipment	190,000	
Cash		140,000
Revenue		50,000

4. The president of the company used his expense account to purchase a new car solely for personal use. The following entry was made:

Miscellaneous Expense	29,000	
Cash		29,000

5. Merchandise inventory which cost $520,000 is reported on the balance sheet at $580,000, the expected selling price less estimated selling costs. The following entry was made to record this increase in value:

Merchandise Inventory	60,000	
Revenue		60,000

6. The company is being sued for $400,000 by a customer who claims damages for personal injury apparently caused by a defective product. Company attorneys feel extremely confident that the company will have no liability for damages resulting from the situation. Nevertheless, the company decides to make the following entry:

Loss from Lawsuit	400,000	
Liability for Lawsuit		400,000

Instructions

In each of the situations above, discuss the appropriateness of the journal entries in light of the components of the conceptual framework.

C2-24 **(ACCOUNTING PRINCIPLES: COMPREHENSIVE)** Presented below is information related to Kibitz Inc.

1. Depreciation expense on the building for the year was $40,000. Because the building was increasing in value during the year, the controller decided to charge the depreciation expense to retained earnings instead of to net income. The following entry was recorded.

Retained Earnings	40,000	
Accumulated Depreciation Buildings		40,000

2. Materials were purchased on January 1, 1994 for $80,000 and this amount was entered in the Materials account. On December 31, 1994, the materials would have cost $94,000, so the following entry is made.

Inventory	14,000	
Gain on Inventories		14,000

3. During the year, the company purchased equipment through the issuance of common shares. The shares had a fair market value of $90,000. The fair market value of the equipment was not easily determinable. The company recorded this transaction as follows:

Equipment	90,000	
Common Shares		90,000

4. During the year, the company sold certain equipment for $190,000, recognizing a gain of $46,000. Because the controller believed that new equipment would be needed in the near future, the controller decided to defer the gain and amortize it over the life of any new equipment purchased.

5. An order for $41,000 has been received from a customer for products on hand. This order was shipped on January 9, 1995. The company made the following entry in 1994:

Accounts Receivable	41,000	
Sales		41,000

Instructions

Comment on the appropriateness of the accounting procedures followed by Kibitz Inc. for the year ended December 31, 1994.

C2-25 **(ACCOUNTING PRINCIPLES: GENERAL)** Each of the following statements represents a decision made by the controller of Siskel Enterprises on which your advice is asked:

1. A building purchased by the company five years ago for $150,000, including the land on which it stands, can now be sold for $200,000. The controller instructs that the new value of $200,000 be entered in the accounts.

2. Material included in the inventory that cost $120,000 has become obsolete. The controller contends that no loss can be realized until the goods are sold, and so the material is included in the inventory at $120,000.

3. Inasmuch as profits for the year appear to be extremely small, no depreciation of fixed assets is to be recorded as an expense this year.

4. The company occupies the building in which it operates under a long-term lease requiring annual rental payments. It sublets certain office space not required for its own purposes. The controller credits rents received against rents paid to get net rent expense.

5. A flood during the year destroyed or damaged a considerable amount of uninsured inventory. No entry was made for this loss because the controller reasons that the ending inventory will, of course, be reduced by the amount of the destroyed or damaged merchandise, and therefore its cost will be included in cost of goods sold and the net income figure will be correct.

6. The company provides housing for certain employees and adjusts their salaries accordingly. The controller contends that the cost to the company of maintaining this housing should be charged to "Wages and Salaries."

7. The entire cost of a new delivery truck is to be charged to an expense account.

8. The company has paid a large sum for an advertising campaign to promote a new product that will not be placed on the market until the following year. The controller has charged this amount to a prepaid expense account.

9. The company operates a cafeteria for the convenience of its employees. Sales made by the cafeteria are credited to the regular sales account for product sales; food purchased and salaries paid for the cafeteria operations are recorded in the regular purchase and payroll accounts.

10. A customer leaving the building slipped on an icy spot on the stairway and wrenched his back. He immediately entered suit against the company for permanent physical injuries and claims damages in the amount of $160,000. The suit has not yet come to trial. The controller has made an entry charging a special loss account and crediting a liability account.

Instructions

You are to state (a) whether you agree with his decision and (b) the reasons supporting your position. Consider each decision independently of all others.

(NONPROFIT ORGANIZATIONS) Nonprofit organizations are organizations in which there is normally no transferable ownership interest and from which the members or contributors do not receive any direct economic benefit, and that are formed for social, educational, religious, health, or philanthropic purposes (Source: "Non-Profit Organizations" *Exposure Draft* of the Accounting Standards Board, January 1992, par. .002). **C2-26**

Nonprofit organizations often rely on donations and volunteers to support the staff in carrying out programs and functions. Financial grants (from governments and other bodies) are subject to uncertainty and, when provided, typically are paid annually or quarterly. These grants may be for operations and/or capital asset purchases. Fundraising programs often take up a substantial amount of time. Cash flow from month to month is frequently a major problem. When there is insufficient cash, programs (i.e. services, projects) are discontinued.

Within this environment, various individuals argue that applying GAAP as specified in the *CICA Handbook* is inappropriate. Others state that nonprofit organizations must be required to follow GAAP so that order can be created out of the chaos that exists due to each organization using its own unique accounting practices.

Instructions

For the following components of the conceptual framework, state (1) why it is not appropriate for nonprofit organizations, and (2) why it is appropriate for nonprofit organizations:

(a) Going concern assumption.

(b) Historical cost principle.

(c) Revenue realization principle.

(d) Matching principle.

(e) Benefits versus costs constraint.

(MATCHING PRINCIPLE: ETHICAL DILEMMA) Sunnyside Nuclear Plant will be mothballed at the end of its useful life (in approximately 20 years) at great expense. The matching principle requires that expenses be matched to revenue. Accountants Iris Stuart and Stanley Smith argue whether it is better to allocate the expense of mothballing over the next 20 years or to ignore it until mothballing occurs. **C2-27**

Instructions

(a) What, if any, is the moral issue underlying the dispute?

(b) What stakeholders should be considered?

(c) What decision would you make?

C2-28 (CONCEPTUAL FRAMEWORK: COMPREHENSIVE) Kathleen Johnson has successfully completed her first accounting course during the winter semester and is now working as a management trainee for National Bank during the summer. One of her fellow management trainees, Doug Stine, is taking the same accounting course this summer and has been having a "lot of trouble." On the second examination, for example, Doug Stine became confused about inventory valuation methods and completely missed all the points on a problem involving LIFO and FIFO.

Doug's instructor recently indicated that the third examination will probably have a number of essay questions dealing with accounting principle issues. Doug is quite concerned about the third examination for two reasons. First, he has never taken an accounting examination where essay questions were required. Second, Doug feels he has to do well on this examination to get an acceptable grade in the course.

Doug has therefore asked Kathleen to help him prepare for the next examination. Kathleen agrees, and suggests that Doug develop a set of possible questions on the accounting principles material that they might discuss.

Instructions

Answer the following questions that were developed by Doug:

1. What is a conceptual framework?

2. Why is there a need for a conceptual framework?

3. What are the objectives of financial reporting?

4. If you had to explain generally accepted accounting principles to a nonaccountant, what essential characteristics would you include in your explanation?

5. What are the qualitative characteristics of accounting? Explain each one.

6. Identify the basic assumptions used in accounting.

7. What are two major constraints involved in financial reporting? Explain both of them.

CHAPTER

3

The Accounting Process

Accounting systems vary widely from one business to another, depending on the *nature of the business* and its *transactions*, the *size of the company*, the *volume of data* to be handled, and the *informational demands* that management and others place on the system.

Broadly defined, an accounting system includes the activities required to provide management with the information needed for planning, controlling, and reporting the financial condition and results of operations of the enterprise. Managers and investors depend on the accounting system to help them answer the following questions:

- How much and what kind of debt is outstanding?
- What is the composition of our asset structure?
- What were our cash inflows and outflows?
- Did we make a profit last period?
- Were our sales higher this period than last?
- Are any of our product lines or divisions operating at a loss?
- Can we safely increase our dividends to shareholders?
- Is our rate of return on net assets increasing?

Many other questions can be answered when there is an effective accounting system to provide the data. A well-devised accounting system is important to every business enterprise. A company that does not keep an accurate record of its business transactions and use such information is likely to lose revenue and operate inefficiently.

Although most companies have satisfactory accounting systems, some companies are inefficient partly because of poor accounting procedures or failure to use or adequately interpret accounting information. Consider, for example, the case of the Canadian Commercial Bank failure in the fall of 1985. Testimony during the judicial inquiry into the failure indicated serious weaknesses in the policies that were used to classify loans—"bad loans" were classified as "good loans." While the financial credibility (liquidity and profitability) of some organizations relative to being able to pay the loans and interest was definitely suspect, this type of information was apparently not a significant criterion in granting the loans or monitoring the realizability of the loans once granted. When one of the largest gold and silver retailers, the International Gold Bullion Exchange (IGBE), was forced to declare bankruptcy, its records were in such a shambles that it was difficult to determine how much money it lost. The company had failed to keep track of its revenues and had written cheques on uncollected funds. IGBE had even allowed its employee health insurance to lapse while it continued to collect premiums from workers.

Even the use of computers provides no assurance of accuracy and efficiency. An example is Maislin Industries Ltd., a Montreal company which was once hailed as one of North America's largest international motor-truck carriers. In anticipation of deregulation in the industry, Maislin pursued a policy of expansion which resulted in a considerable debt position. The following year, many events occurred affecting the company, one of which was a complete breakdown of its integrated computer system which included accounting and other information. Orders were lost, shipments disappeared, billings were incorrect, receivables were not billed for up to six months, and cash flows were a serious problem. Maislin's previously consistent profit performance ended that year with a loss of over $13 million, and the bank called for substantial payment on its loans shortly thereafter.[1] As another example, a BankAmerica spokesman said, "The conversion to a new computer system called MasterNet fouled up data processing records to the extent that BankAmerica was frequently unable to produce or deliver customer statements on a timely basis."[2]

Although these situations are not common, they illustrate the point that accounts and detailed records must be kept by every business enterprise. With this in mind, the objectives of this chapter are to present a concise yet thorough review of the accounting process, to identify and explain basic procedures of the accounting process, and to describe the way in which these procedures are combined in carrying out the accounting cycle. Much of the material serves as a review of what may have been studied in introductory accounting; yet it is of fundamental importance to understanding how and why transactions and other economic events become a part of financial statements, and how and why alternative accounting policies can result in differences in financial position and net income. Even though the procedures are mechanical and are often carried out using computers, one must know what is happening within an accounting system in order to have this understanding.

ACCOUNTING TERMINOLOGY

Financial accounting rests on a framework of concepts (see Chapters 1 and 2) and rules for identifying, recording, classifying, and interpreting transactions and other economic events relating to enterprises. To do accounting, it is important to understand basic terminology employed in collecting accounting data. The terms most commonly used are defined below.

Objective 1

Review basic accounting terminology.

Basic Terminology

Event. A happening of consequence. An event generally is the source or cause of changes in assets, liabilities, and owners' equity. Events may be categorized as external or internal.

Transaction. An **external event** involving the transfer or exchange of something of value between two (or more) entities.

Account. A systematic arrangement that shows the effect of transactions and other events on a specific asset or equity. A separate account is kept for each asset, liability, revenue, expense, and item of capital (owners' equity).

Real and Nominal Accounts. Real (permanent) accounts are asset, liability, and owners' equity accounts which appear on the balance sheet. Nominal (temporary) accounts are revenue and expense accounts; they appear on the income statement. Nominal accounts are periodically closed to proprietor's or partners' capital or to retained earnings; real accounts are not.

Ledger. The book or computer file containing the accounts. Each account usually has a separate page. A **general ledger** is a collection of all asset, liability, owners' equity, revenue, and expense accounts. A **subsidiary ledger** contains the details related to a specific general ledger account.

Journal. The book of original entry where the essential facts and figures regarding all transactions and selected other events are initially recorded. Various amounts are transferred from a journal to accounts in the ledger.

(Continued)

[1] Tony Dimnik and Joseph N. Fry, "Maislin Industries Ltd. (A)" (London: School of Business Administration, The University of Western Ontario, 1986).

[2] "BankAmerica Asks Two Officials to Quit, Sources Assert," *The Wall Street Journal*, October 22, 1987, p. 43.

Posting. The process of transferring the essential facts and figures from the journal to the accounts in the ledger.

Trial Balance. A list of all open accounts in the ledger and their balances. A trial balance taken immediately after all adjustments have been posted is called an **adjusted trial balance.** A trial balance taken immediately after closing entries have been posted is designated an **after-closing** or **post-closing trial balance.**

Adjusting Entries. Entries made at the end of an accounting period to bring all accounts up to date on an accrual accounting basis so that financial statements can be prepared.

Financial Statements. Statements that reflect the collection, tabulation, and final summarization of the accounting data. Four statements are involved: (1) the **balance sheet,** which shows the financial condition of the enterprise at the end of a period, (2) the **income statement,** which measures the results of operations during the period, (3) the **statement of changes in financial position,** which reports the cash and cash equivalents provided and used by operating, investing, and financing activities during the period, and (4) the **statement of retained earnings,** which shows the changes in the retained earnings account from the beginning to the end of the period. **Notes** and **supporting schedules** cross-referenced to the financial statements are an integral part of such statements.

Closing Entries. Entries which reduce all nominal accounts to zero and transfer the resulting net income or net loss to an owners' equity account. The process of making closing entries is known as "closing the ledger," "closing the books," or merely "closing."

DOUBLE-ENTRY ACCOUNTING PROCEDURE

Objective 2

Review double-entry rules.

There are established rules for recording transactions and other events as they occur. These rules are often referred to as double-entry accounting. Debit and credit in accounting simply mean left and right or, depending on the type of account, increase or decrease. The left side of any account is the debit side; the right side, the credit side. In arithmetic, plus and minus signs indicate addition or subtraction; in accounting, addition or subtraction is indicated by the side of the account on which the amount is shown. ***All asset and expense accounts are increased on the left or debit side and decreased on the right or credit side.*** Conversely, ***all liability, revenue, and capital accounts are increased on the right or credit side and decreased on the left or debit side.*** These basic rules of debit and credit for an accounting system are presented below.

Asset Accounts	
Debit + (increase)	Credit – (decrease)

Revenue Accounts	
Debit – (decrease)	Credit + (increase)

Owners' Equity	
Debit – (decrease)	Credit + (increase)

Liability Accounts	
Debit – (decrease)	Credit + (increase)

Expense Accounts	
Debit + (increase)	Credit – (decrease)

Assume a transaction in which service is rendered for cash. Two accounts are affected: both an asset account (Cash) and a revenue account (Sales) are increased. Cash is debited and Sales credited. This reveals the essentials of a **double-entry system**—***for every debit there must be a credit and vice versa.***

This leads, then, to the **basic accounting equation**:

Assets = Liabilities + Owners' Equity

Or simply:

Assets = Equities

Every time a transaction occurs, the elements of the equation change, but the basic equality remains. To illustrate, here are eight different transactions:

1. Owner invests $40,000 for use in the business:

Assets	= Liabilities	+ Owners' equity
+40,000		+40,000

2. Disburse $600 cash for secretarial wages:

Assets	= Liabilities	+ Owners' equity
−600		−600 (expense)

3. Purchase office equipment priced at $5,200, giving a 10% promissory note in exchange:

Assets	= Liabilities	+ Owners' equity
+5,200	+5,200	

4. Receive $4,000 cash for services rendered:

Assets	= Liabilities	+ Owners' equity
+4,000		+4,000 (revenue)

5. Pay off a short-term liability of $7,000:

Assets	= Liabilities	+ Owners' equity
−7,000	−7,000	

6. Declare a cash dividend of $5,000 which will be paid in the future:

Assets	= Liabilities	+ Owners' equity
	+5,000	−5,000

7. Convert a long-term liability of $80,000 into common shares:

Assets	= Liabilities	+ Owners' equity
	−80,000	+80,000

8. Pay cash of $16,000 for a delivery van:

Assets	= Liabilities	+ Owners' equity
−16,000		
+16,000		

Revenue and expense accounts are elements of owners' equity. Revenues are increases (credits) to owners' equity and expenses are decreases (debits). The difference between revenues and expenses for a period of time is the net increase (income) or net decrease (loss) in owners' equity from operations.

The type of ownership structure employed by a business enterprise will dictate the types of accounts that are part of, or affect, the owners' equity section. In a proprietorship or partnership, in addition to revenue and expense accounts, a **Capital** account is used to record the accumulated net investment of an owner. A **Drawing** account is sometimes used to indicate withdrawals by an owner. In a corporation, the owners' equity is divided into at least two categories: **Share Capital** and **Retained Earnings.** The retained earnings section sometimes includes a **Dividends** account to indicate the amount of dividends (distributions to shareholders) declared during the period which is closed to retained earnings at the end of the accounting period.

Figure 3-1 summarizes and relates the transactions affecting owners' equity to the nominal (temporary) and real (permanent) accounts, based on the types of business ownership.

		Ownership Structure			
		Proprietorships and Partnerships		Corporations	
Transactions Affecting Owners' Equity	Impact on Owners' Equity	Nominal (Temporary) Accounts	Real (Permanent) Accounts	Nominal (Temporary) Accounts	Real (Permanent) Accounts
Investment by owner(s)	Increase		Capital		Share Capital and related accounts
Revenues earned	Increase	Revenue		Revenue	
Expenses incurred	Decrease	Expense	Capital	Expense	Retained Earnings
Withdrawal by owner(s)	Decrease	Drawing		Dividends	

Figure 3-1 Transactions Affecting Owner's Equity

THE ACCOUNTING CYCLE

Figure 3-2 (on page 76) identifies the sequential steps in the accounting cycle. These steps incorporate the procedures normally used to ensure that the effects of transactions and selected other events are correctly recorded and included in the financial statements.

Objective 3

Identify steps in the accounting cycle.

IDENTIFICATION AND MEASUREMENT OF TRANSACTIONS AND OTHER EVENTS

The first step in the accounting cycle is analysis of transactions and selected other events. The problem is to determine *what to record*. No simple rules exist that state whether an event should be recorded. Most accountants agree that changes in personnel and managerial policies, and the value of human resources are important. However, none of these are recorded in the accounts. On the other hand, when the company makes a cash sale or purchase, no matter how small, they are always recorded.

What makes the difference? Drawing on the conceptual framework, ***an economic event should be recognized in the financial statements if it affects an element, is reasonably (reliably) measurable, and is relevant.*** When these conditions are met, the consequences of an event should be recognized in the accounting system and reported in the financial statements. To illustrate, consider human resources. R.G. Barry & Co. at one time reported as supplemental data total assets of $14,055,926, including $986,094 for "net investments in human resources." Other companies, including Canadian companies such as Cascades Inc., have experimented with human resource and social responsibility accounting. Should accountants value employees for balance sheet purposes and recognize changes in such value for income statement purposes? Certainly skilled employees are a highly relevant and important asset, but problems of determining their value and reliably measuring changes in it have not yet been solved. Consequently, human resources are not recorded. Perhaps when measurement techniques become more sophisticated and accepted, such information will be presented, if only in supplemental form.

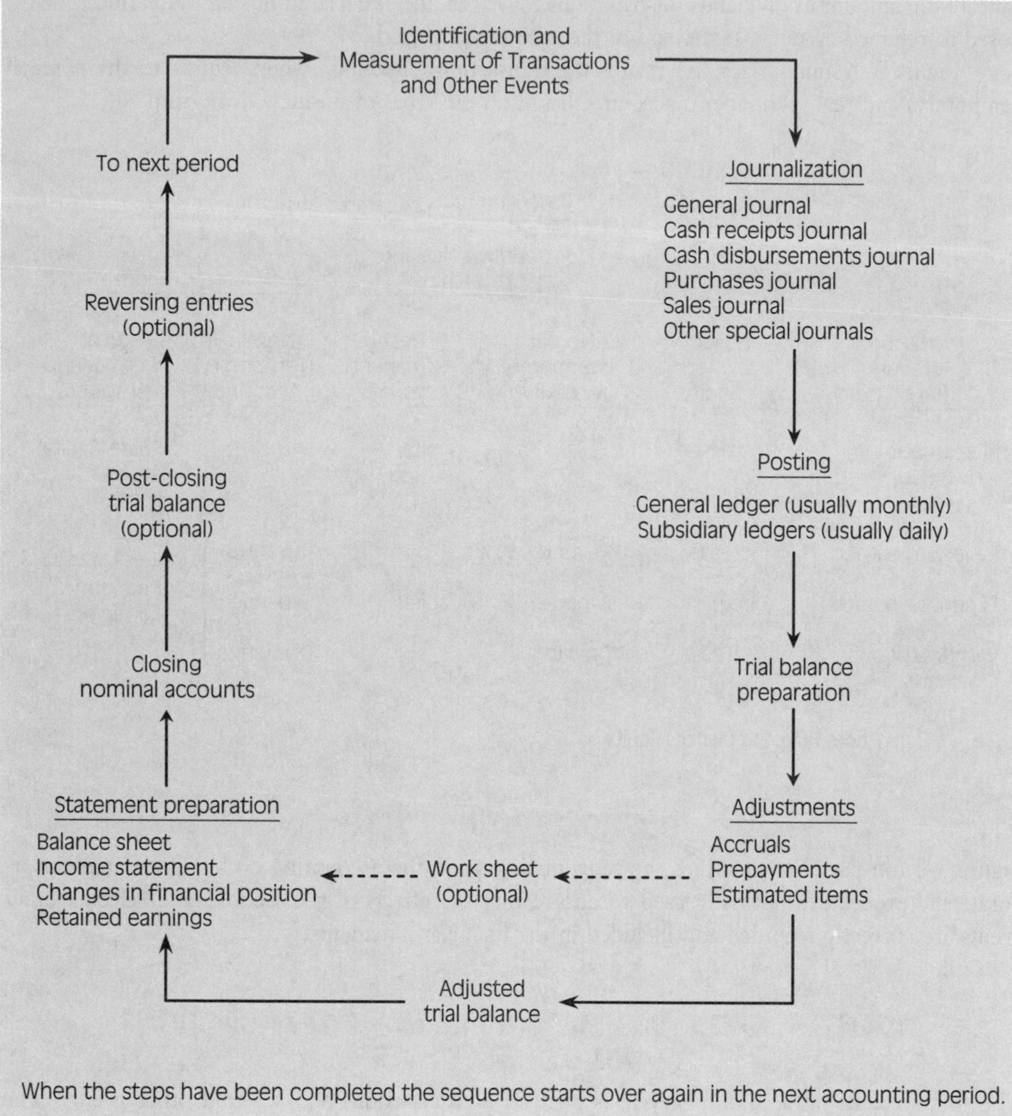

Figure 3-2 The Accounting cycle

The phrase "transactions and other events and circumstances affecting an entity" may be used to describe the sources or causes of changes in an entity's assets, liabilities, and owners' equity. Events are of two types. **External events** involve interaction between an entity and its environment, such as a transaction with another entity, a change in the price of a good or service that an entity buys or sells, a flood or earthquake, or an improvement in technology by a competitor. **Internal events** occur within an entity, such as using buildings and machinery or consuming raw materials in production processes.

Many events have both external and internal aspects. For example, acquiring the services of employees or others involves exchange transactions, which are external events; using those services (labour), often simultaneously with their acquisition, is part of production, which is internal. Events may be initiated and controlled by an entity, such as the purchase of merchandise or the use of a machine, or they may be beyond its control, such as an interest rate change, a theft, vandalism, or the imposition of taxes.

Transactions, as particular kinds of external events, may be an exchange in which each entity both receives and sacrifices value (e.g., making purchases, selling goods or services). Transactions may be nonreciprocal transfers (transfers in one direction) in which an entity incurs a liability, or transfers an asset, to another entity without directly receiving, or giving, value in exchange. Examples include investments by owners, distributions to owners, impositions of taxes, gifts, charitable contributions, and thefts.

In short, accountants record as many events as possible that affect the financial position of the enterprise, but some events are omitted because the problems of measuring them are too complex. The accounting profession, through the efforts of individuals and numerous organizations, as indicated in Chapter 1, is continually working to refine its recognition and measurement techniques.

JOURNALIZATION

The effects of transactions and events on the basic elements of financial statements are categorized and collected in **accounts.** The **general ledger** is a collection of all the asset, liability, owners' equity, revenue, and expense accounts. A **T-account** (illustrated on page 78) is a convenient method for showing the effects of transactions on a particular element.

Objective 4

Record transactions in journals, post to ledger accounts, and prepare a trial balance.

In practice, transactions and selected other events are not originally recorded in the ledger because a transaction affects two or more different accounts, each of which is on a different page in the ledger. To circumvent this problem and to have a complete record of each transaction in one place, a **journal** (book of original entry) is employed. The simplest form of a journal is a chronological listing of transactions and other events expressed in terms of debits and credits to particular accounts. This type of journal is called a **general journal** and is illustrated below for the following transactions.

Nov. 1 Buy a new delivery truck on account from Auto Sales Co., $22,400.

3 Receive an invoice from the *Evening Graphic* for advertising, $280.

4 Return merchandise to Brown Supply for credit, $175.

16 Receive a $95 debit memo from Green Co., indicating that freight on a purchase from Green Co. was prepaid by them, but was our obligation according to the terms of the sale.

GENERAL JOURNAL — Page 12

Date 1994		Acct. No.	Amount Dr.	Amount Cr.
Nov. 1	Delivery Equipment	8	22,400	
	Accounts Payable	34		22,400
	(Purchased delivery truck on account from Auto Sales Co.)			
3	Advertising Expense	65	280	
	Accounts Payable	34		280
	(Received invoice for advertising from *Evening Graphic*)			
4	Accounts Payable	34	175	
	Purchase Returns	53		175
	(Returned merchandise for credit to Brown Supply)			
16	Transportation-In	55	95	
	Accounts Payable	34		95
	(Received debit memo for freight on merchandise purchased from Green Co.)			

Each **general journal entry** consists of four parts: (1) the accounts and amounts to be debited (Dr.); (2) the accounts and amounts to be credited (Cr.); (3) a date; and (4) an explanation. Debits are entered first, followed by the credits, which are slightly indented. The explanation is begun below the name of the last account to be credited. The Acct. No. column is completed at the time the accounts are posted.

Many accounting systems use special journals in addition to the general journal. **Special journals** permit greater division of labour, reduce the time necessary to accomplish the various bookkeeping tasks, and summarize transactions possessing a common characteristic. A special journal may be used to record all cash receipts (Cash Receipts Journal), all cash disbursements (Cash Payments Journal), all sales (Sales Journal), and all purchases (Purchases Journal). While the format of special journals differs from that of a general journal, the basic activity of identifying account titles, increases or decreases in the accounts through appropriate debits and credits, dates, and explanations occurs. As such, working with special journals is more a matter of technique than concept. Consequently, special journals are not examined in this book.

POSTING TO THE LEDGER

The items entered in any journal must be transferred to the general ledger. This procedure is called **posting** and is considered part of the summarizing and classifying activity of the accounting process.

For example, the November 1 entry in the general journal showed a debit to Delivery Equipment of $22,400 and a credit to Accounts Payable of $22,400. This entry requires that the amount in the debit column be posted from the journal to the debit side of the Delivery Equipment account in the ledger, and the amount in the credit column be posted from the journal to the credit side of the ledger's Accounts Payable account.

The numbers in the Acct. No. column in the journal refer to the accounts in the ledger to which the respective items are posted. For example, the "8" to the right of the words "Delivery Equipment" means that Delivery Equipment is account No. 8 in the ledger, to which the $22,400 was posted. Similarly, the "34" placed in the column to the right of "Accounts Payable" indicates that this $22,400 item was posted to account No. 34 in the ledger.

The posting of the general journal is complete when all of the posting reference numbers have been recorded opposite the account titles in the journal. Thus the number in the posting reference column serves two purposes: (1) to indicate the ledger account number of the account involved and (2) to indicate that the posting has been completed for the particular item. Each business enterprise selects its own numbering system for its ledger accounts. One practice is to begin numbering with asset accounts and to follow with liability, owners' equity, revenue, and expense accounts in that order.

The various ledger accounts after the posting process is completed appear below. The source of the data transferred to the ledger account is indicated by the reference GJ12 (General Journal, page 12).

Delivery Equipment No. 8

Nov. 1	GJ12	22,400			

Accounts Payable No. 34

Nov. 4	GJ12	175	Nov. 1	GJ12	22,400
			3	GJ12	280
			16	GJ12	95

(Continued)

Purchase Returns					No. 53
			Nov. 4	GJ12	175

Transportation-In					No. 55
Nov. 16	GJ12	95			

Advertising Expense					No. 65
Nov. 3	GJ12	280			

UNADJUSTED TRIAL BALANCE

An unadjusted trial balance should be prepared at the end of a given period after the entries have been recorded in the journal and posted to the ledger. A **trial balance** is a list of all open accounts in the general ledger and their balances. The trial balance accomplishes two principal purposes:

1. It proves that debits and credits of an equal amount are in the ledger.
2. It supplies a listing of open accounts and their balances which serve as a basis for making adjustments.

The unadjusted trial balance for Victoria's Wholesale is illustrated on the following page.

ADJUSTMENTS

The employment of an accrual accounting system means that numerous adjustments are necessary before financial statements are prepared. If adjustments are not made, certain accounts will not be accurate. For example, if we account for transactions on a cash basis, only cash transactions during the year are recorded. Consequently, if a company's employees are paid every two weeks and the end of an accounting period occurs in the middle of these two weeks, neither a liability nor an expense is shown for the last week.[3] To bring the accounts up to date for the preparation of financial statements, both the wage expense and the wage liability accounts need to be increased. This change is accomplished by means of an **adjusting entry**.

A necessary step in the accounting process, then, is to make adjusting entries and post them to the general ledger so that all accounts are on an accrual basis. Adjusting entries are necessary to achieve an appropriate matching of revenues and expenses in the determination of net income for the current period and to provide a more complete statement of the assets and equities existing at the end of the period. Each adjusting entry affects both a real account (asset, liability, or owners' equity) and a nominal account (revenue or expense).

Objective 5

Explain the reasons for preparing adjusting entries.

[3] See Appendix 3A for a brief discussion of the accrual and cash-based accounting systems. This Appendix also illustrates procedures that may be used to convert from a cash basis to an accrual basis.

Victoria's Wholesale
Trial Balance
December 31, 1994

	Debit	Credit
Cash	$ 13,000	
Accounts Receivable	14,650	
Notes Receivable	8,000	
Inventory, January 1, 1994	89,500	
Office Equipment	16,000	
Furniture and Fixtures	12,300	
Accounts Payable		$ 14,100
Notes Payable		24,000
Victoria's Capital		91,240
Sales		896,000
Sales Returns	3,760	
Sales Allowances	960	
Purchases	713,450	
Purchase Returns		4,140
Transportation-In	6,570	
Sales Salaries Expense	65,700	
Travel Expenses	4,900	
Advertising Expense	21,200	
General Office Salaries	39,800	
Rent Expense	18,000	
Insurance Expense	2,780	
Utilities Expense	4,310	
Telephone Expense	1,260	
Auditing and Legal Expense	2,780	
Miscellaneous Administrative Expense	2,200	
Purchase Discounts		13,500
Sales Discounts	1,860	
	$1,042,980	$1,042,980

Adjustments are necessary whenever the following items exist:

Prepaid (deferred) items:

Prepaid expenses: an expense paid in cash and recorded in an asset or expense account in advance of its use or consumption (e.g., prepaid insurance).

Unearned revenues: cash received which is recorded in a liability or revenue account before it is earned (e.g., rent received in advance).

Accrued items:

Accrued liabilities or expenses: an expense incurred but not yet recognized or paid (e.g., unpaid salaries).

Accrued assets or revenues: a revenue earned but not yet recognized or paid (e.g., interest on notes receivable).

Estimated items: an expense recorded on the basis of subjective estimates because it is a function of unknown future events or developments (e.g., depreciation).

Prepaid Expenses

A **prepaid expense** is an item paid and recorded in advance of its use or consumption. Part of it properly represents expense of the current period and part represents an asset on hand at the end of the period. If a one-year insurance premium is paid in advance on September 1 of the current fiscal year which ends on December 31, one-third of the amount paid represents expense of the current year and two-thirds is an asset at the end of the year, which is properly deferred to and expensed in the following year.

Illustration. A company's year end is December 31. On September 1, 1994 the company purchased a one-year insurance policy for $1,200 which was recorded as follows:

Sept. 1		
Unexpired Insurance	1,200	
Cash		1,200
(Purchase of a one-year insurance policy)		

On December 31, 1994, insurance protection for one-third of the one-year policy has been consumed. Therefore, one-third of the $1,200 paid must be recognized as an expense for 1994, and the asset account must be reduced by the same amount to reflect the future benefits of coverage for eight months in 1995. The adjusting entry required on December 31, 1994 is:

Dec. 31		
Insurance Expense	400	
Unexpired Insurance		400
(To charge one-third of insurance premium to expense)		

After posting this adjusting entry, the ledger accounts show an expense for insurance of $400 and an asset, Unexpired Insurance, of $800.

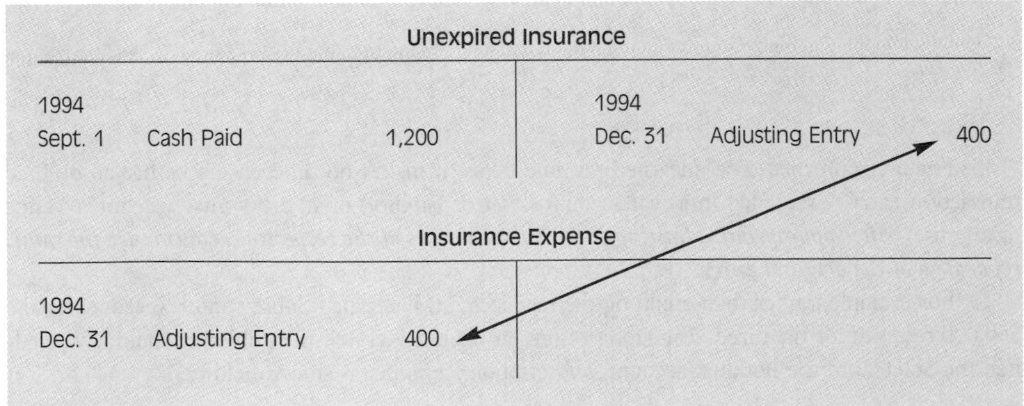

Unearned Revenue

Unearned revenue is cash received and recorded as a liability because it has not yet been earned by providing goods or services to customers. As dictated by the revenue recognition principle, revenue is recorded in the period in which it is realized. When cash is received prior to revenue being realized, the amount applicable to future periods is deferred to the future periods. The amount unearned (received in advance of realization) is considered a liability because it represents an obligation arising from a past transaction to provide a good or service in the future.

Some common unearned revenue items are rent received in advance, interest received in advance on notes receivable, subscriptions and advertising received in advance by publishers, and deposits received from customers prior to delivery of merchandise.

Illustration. Assume that a publisher sells subscriptions to a sports magazine and that it receives $60,000 on January 7, 1994 from customers in payment for a full three years' subscription in advance. The publisher then made the following entry:

Jan. 7		
Cash	60,000	
Unearned Subscription Revenue		60,000
(To record three-year subscriptions revenue received in advance)		

At the end of 1994 one-third of this amount is earned and, therefore, the following adjusting entry is made:

Dec. 31		
Unearned Subscription Revenue	20,000	
Subscription Revenue		20,000
(To recognize as revenue one-third of $60,000)		

The adjusting entry reduces the liability and records $20,000 in the Subscription Revenue account, which represents the amount of revenue earned during the year. These two accounts now show the following balances after adjustment.

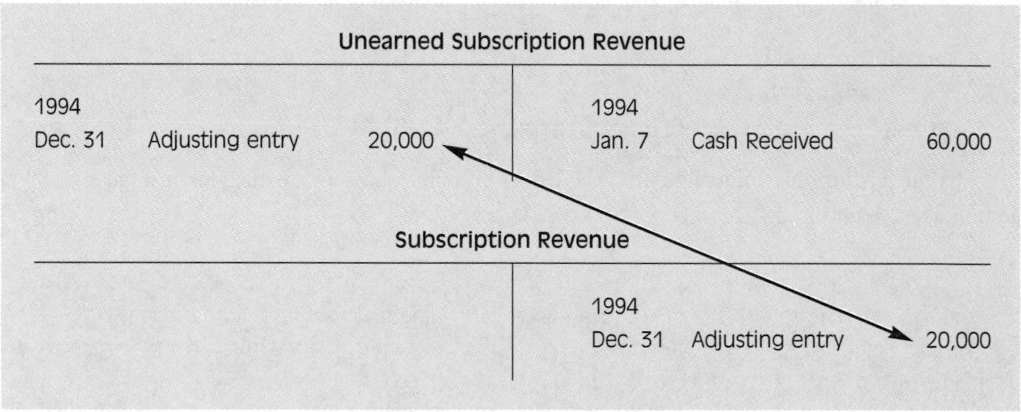

For prepaid expense or unearned revenue items, it makes no difference whether an original transaction entry is recorded in a real account (asset or liability) or in a nominal account (revenue or expense). ***After appropriate adjusting entries, the balances of the respective accounts are the same, regardless of the original entry.***

For example, rather than crediting the real account, Unearned Subscription Revenue, for the $60,000 received for the three-year subscriptions on January 7, 1994, the publisher could have credited the $60,000 to the nominal account, Subscription Revenue, as shown below:

Jan. 7		
Cash	60,000	
Subscription Revenue		60,000

This would necessitate the following adjusting entry:

Dec. 31		
Subscription Revenue	40,000	
Unearned Subscription Revenue		40,000

After the adjusting entry, the Subscription Revenue and the Unearned Subscription Revenue accounts have the same credit balances ($20,000 and $40,000 respectively) as those resulting in the previous illustration in which the $60,000 was originally credited to the real account on January 7.

An important point is that, for prepaid expense and unearned revenue items, ***the nature of original entries must be known in order to make the appropriate adjusting entries.*** The nature of original entries is determined by the accountant when designing the accounting system.

Accrued Liabilities or Expenses

Accrued liabilities or **accrued expenses** are items of expense that have been incurred during the period, but have not yet been recorded or paid. As such, they represent liabilities at the end of the period. The related debits for such items are included in the income statement as expenses. Some common accrued liabilities (accrued expenses) are interest payable, wages and salaries payable, and property taxes payable.

Illustration. When employees are paid on the last day of the month, there are no accrued wages and salaries at the end of the month or year because all employees will have been paid all amounts due. When they are paid on a weekly or biweekly basis, however, it is usually necessary to make an adjusting entry for wages and salaries earned but not paid at the end of the fiscal period. The reason is that the reporting period's last day rarely lands on a payday.

Assume that a business pays its sales staff every Friday for a five-day week, that the total weekly payroll is $8,000, and that December 31 falls on Thursday. On December 31, the end of the fiscal period, the employees have worked four-fifths of a week for which they have not been paid and for which no entry has been made. The adjusting entry on December 31 is:

Dec. 31		
Sales Salaries Expense	6,400	
Salaries Payable		6,400
(To record accrued salaries as of Dec. 31: $\frac{4}{5} \times \$8,000$)		

As a result of this entry, the income statement for the year includes the salaries earned by the sales staff during the last four days in December and the balance sheet shows as a liability salaries payable of $6,400.

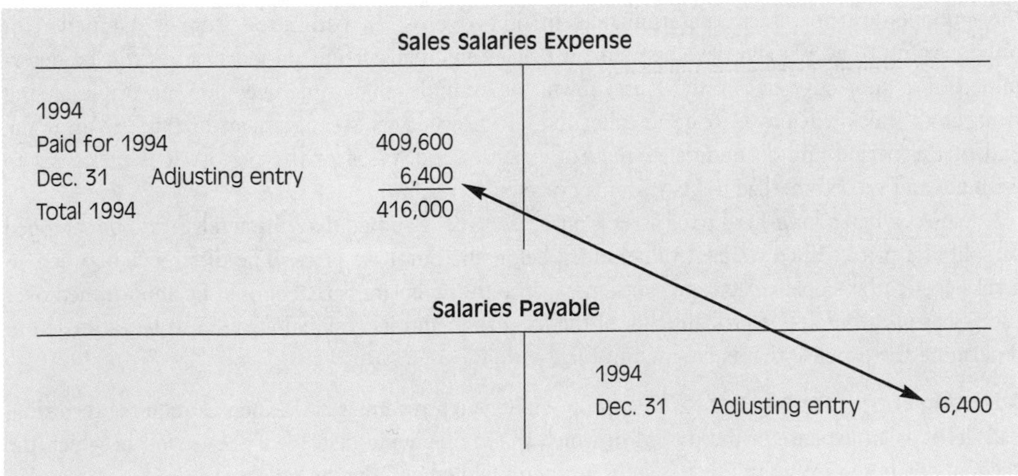

Accrued Assets or Revenues

Items of revenue earned during the period but not yet recorded or collected are called **accrued assets** or **accrued revenues.** Adjusting entries must be made for these items to record the revenue that has been earned but not yet received and to record, as an asset, the amount receivable. Examples of accrued assets are rent receivable and interest receivable.

Illustration. Assume that office space is rented to a tenant at $3,000 per month, that the tenant has paid the rent for the first 11 months of the year, but has paid no rent for December. The adjusting entry on December 31 is:

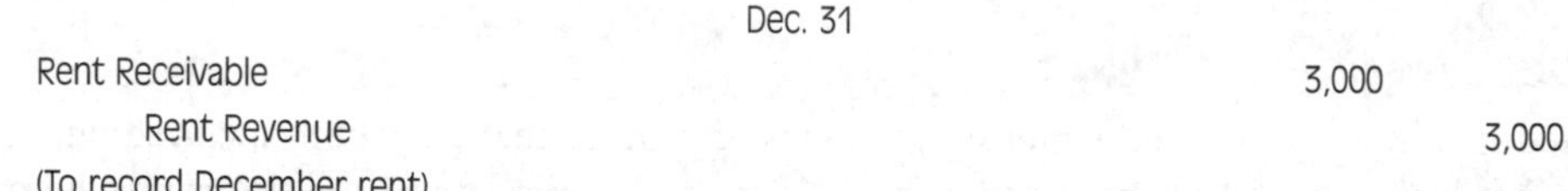

Dec. 31		
Rent Receivable	3,000	
Rent Revenue		3,000
(To record December rent)		

As a result of this entry, an asset of $3,000, Rent Receivable, appears on the balance sheet disclosing the amount due from the tenant as of December 31. The income statement discloses rent revenue of $36,000, the $33,000 received for the first 11 months and the $3,000 for December entered by means of the adjusting entry. After adjustment the accounts appear as follows.

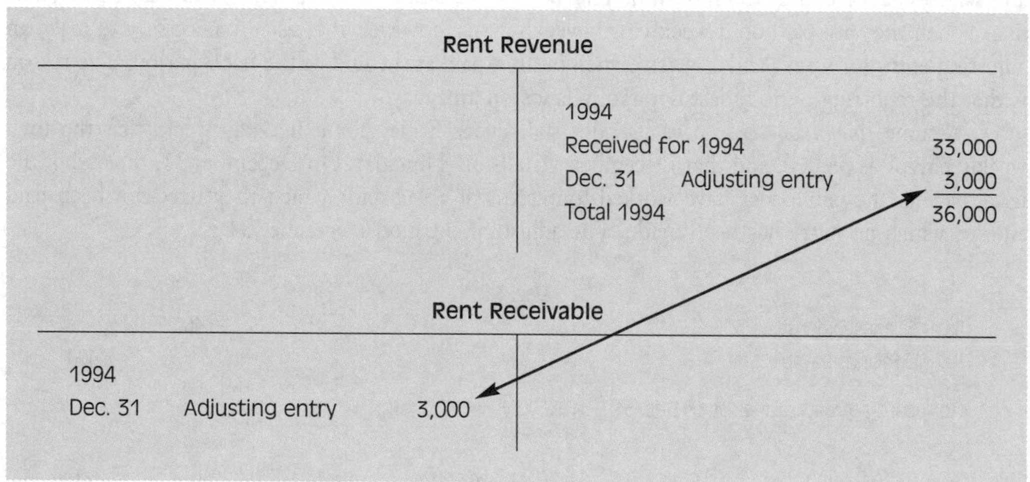

Estimated Items

Uncollectible accounts and depreciation of fixed assets are ordinarily called estimated items because the amounts are not exactly determinable. In other words, an **estimated item** is a function of unknown future events and developments, which means that current period charges can be determined on a subjective basis only. It is known, for example, that some accounts receivable arising from credit sales will prove to be uncollectible. To prevent an overstatement of receivables at the end of the period and an understatement of expenses and losses of the period, it is necessary to estimate and record the bad debts that are expected to result.

Also, when a long-lived fixed asset is purchased, it is assumed that ultimately it will be scrapped or sold at a price (called residual value) much below the purchase price. The difference between an asset's cost and residual value represents an expense to the business that should be apportioned over the asset's useful life. The probable life of the fixed asset and its residual value must be estimated to determine the expense that is charged in each period.

Adjusting Entries for Bad Debts. To appropriately match revenues and expenses requires recording bad debts as an expense of the period in which the sale is made instead of the period in which the accounts or notes are written off. This is accomplished by an adjusting entry.

At the end of each period, an estimate is made of the amount of current period sales on account that will later prove to be uncollectible. The estimate is based on the amount of bad debts experienced in past years, general economic conditions, the age of the receivables, and other factors that indicate uncollectibility of receivables. Usually the amount is determined as a percent of the sales on account for the period, or it is computed by adjusting the Allowance for Doubtful Accounts account to a certain percent of the trade accounts and notes receivable at the end of the period.

Assume, for example, that experience reveals that bad debts usually approximate one-half of 1% of the net sales on account and that net sales on account for the year are $300,000. The adjusting entry for bad debts is:

Dec. 31		
Bad Debts Expense	1,500	
Allowance for Doubtful Accounts		1,500
(To record estimated bad debts for the year: $300,000 × .005)		

Whenever a particular customer's account is determined to be uncollectible, the Allowance for Doubtful Accounts is debited and Accounts Receivable is credited for the amount of the write-off. Methods of determining the amount of the adjusting entry and ways of accounting for a write-off and a write-off reversal are considered in Chapter 7.

Adjusting Entries for Amortization. In accounting, **amortization** is the generic term used to describe the charge to income that recognizes that the life of a tangible or intangible capital asset is finite and that its cost less residual value is to be allocated to the periods of service that it provides.[4] Traditionally, and as is done in this book, the amortization charge for tangible assets other than natural resources is called **depreciation**, and for natural resources it is called **depletion**. Entries for amortization are similar to those made for reducing prepaid expenses in which the original amount was debited to an asset account. The principal difference is that for amortization the credit is usually made to a separate account (e.g., Accumulated Depreciation) instead of to the asset account.

In estimating amortization, the original cost of the asset, its length of useful life, and its estimated residual value are used. Assume that a truck costing $18,000 has an estimated useful life of five years and an estimated residual value of $2,000 at the end of that period. Because the truck is expected to be worth $16,000 less at the time of its disposal than it was at the time of its purchase, the amount of $16,000 represents an expense that is apportioned over the five years of its anticipated use. It is neither logical nor good accounting practice to consider the $16,000 as an expense entirely of the period in which it was acquired or the period in which it was sold, inasmuch as the business benefits from the use of the truck during the entire five-year period.

If the straight-line method is used, each year's depreciation expense is one-fifth of $16,000, or $3,200. Each full year the truck is used the following adjusting entry is made:

Dec. 31		
Depreciation Expense—Delivery Equipment	3,200	
Accumulated Depreciation—Delivery Equipment		3,200
(To record depreciation on truck for the year)		

ADJUSTED TRIAL BALANCE AND PREPARATION OF FINANCIAL STATEMENTS

After adjusting entries have been recorded and posted, another trial balance is prepared. The **adjusted trial balance** is used to prepare the financial statements. The financial statements and their preparation are considered later in the chapter in the section titled "Use of Work Sheets" and in Chapters 4 and 5.

END-OF-PERIOD PROCEDURE FOR INVENTORY AND RELATED ACCOUNTS

When the inventory records are maintained on a **perpetual inventory system,** purchases and issues are recorded directly in the Inventory account as they occur. Therefore, the balance in the Inventory account should represent the ending inventory amount and no adjusting entries are needed. No Purchases account is used because the purchases are debited directly to the Inventory account. However, a Cost of Goods Sold account is used to accumulate the issuances from inventory.

[4] *CICA Handbook* (Toronto: CICA), Section 3060, par. .33. Amortization of tangible capital assets is discussed in depth in Chapter 11. Amortization of intangible capital assets is considered in Chapter 12.

Objective 6

Explain how inventory accounts are adjusted at year end.

When the inventory records are maintained on a **periodic inventory system,** a Purchases account is used and the Inventory account is unchanged during the period. The Inventory account represents the beginning inventory amount throughout the period. At the end of the accounting period, the Inventory account must be adjusted by closing out the *beginning inventory* amount and recording the *ending inventory* amount. The ending inventory is determined by physically counting the items on hand and valuing them at cost or at the lower of cost and market. ***Under the periodic inventory system, cost of goods sold is determined by adding the beginning inventory to the net purchases and then deducting the ending inventory.***

There is more than one way to prepare the entries that update inventory, record cost of goods sold, and close the other related nominal accounts. To illustrate, Collegiate Apparel Shop Ltd. has a beginning inventory of $30,000; Purchases, $200,000; Transportation-In, $6,000; Purchase Returns, $1,200; Purchase Allowances, $800; Purchase Discounts, $2,000; and the ending inventory is $26,000.

One approach is to prepare the following three journal entries to adjust the inventory and then close the accounts related to purchases to the Cost of Goods Sold account:

Adjusting Entries

(1)	Cost of Goods Sold	30,000	
	Inventory (beginning)		30,000
	(To transfer beginning inventory balance to Cost of Goods Sold)		
(2)	Inventory (ending)	26,000	
	Cost of Goods Sold		26,000
	(To record the ending inventory balance)		

Closing Entry

(3)	Purchase Discounts	2,000	
	Purchase Allowances	800	
	Purchase Returns	1,200	
	Cost of Goods Sold	202,000	
	Purchases		200,000
	Transportation-In		6,000
	(To transfer net purchases to Cost of Goods Sold)		

The first two entries adjust the Inventory account and, therefore, are generally viewed as adjusting entries. The third entry transfers net purchases to Cost of Goods Sold and is viewed as a closing entry. Only the Cost of Goods Sold account (which now has a $206,000 balance) remains to be closed.

A second approach is to adjust the inventory and transfer the various merchandise accounts into the Cost of Goods Sold account by preparing a single adjusting/closing entry as shown below. This single entry simply combines the three entries of the first approach.

Adjusting/Closing Entry

Inventory (ending)	26,000	
Purchase Discounts	2,000	
Purchase Allowances	800	
Purchase Returns	1,200	
Cost of Goods Sold	206,000	
Inventory (beginning)		30,000
Purchases		200,000
Transportation-In		6,000
(To transfer beginning inventory and net purchases to Cost of Goods Sold and to record the ending inventory)		

After the foregoing entry, only the Cost of Goods Sold account ($206,000 balance) remains to be closed, as was the case for the first approach.

The following diagram illustrates the first approach. It shows, in T-account form, the process of determining the cost of goods sold through adjusting the inventory balance and closing the accounts related to net purchases on an item-by-item basis. The second approach (single entry) will result in fewer amounts being posted to the Cost of Goods Sold account, but the balance in this account will be the same.

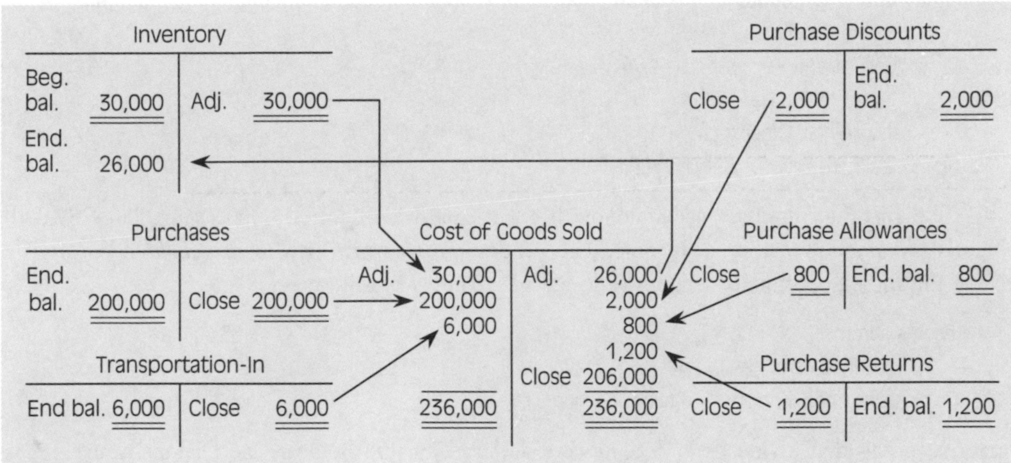

YEAR-END CLOSING

Objective 7

Prepare closing entries.

The procedure generally followed to reduce the balance of nominal (temporary) accounts to zero in order to prepare the accounts for the next period's transactions is known as the **closing process.** In the closing process all of the revenue and expense account balances (income statement items) are transferred to a clearing or suspense account called **Income Summary**, which is used only at the end of each accounting period. Revenues and expenses are merged in the Income Summary account and the resulting balance, the net income or net loss for the period, is then transferred to an owners' equity account (retained earnings for a corporation, and capital accounts for proprietorships and partnerships). Note that all closing entries arc posted to the appropriate general ledger accounts.

For example, assume that revenue accounts of Collegiate Apparel Shop Ltd., a corporation, have the following balances, after adjustments, at the end of the year:

Revenue from Sales	$280,000
Rental Revenue	27,000
Interest Revenue	5,000

These revenue accounts are closed and the balances transferred to the Income Summary through the following closing journal entry:

Revenue from Sales	280,000	
Rental Revenue	27,000	
Interest Revenue	5,000	
Income Summary		312,000
(To close revenue accounts to Income Summary)		

Assume that the expense accounts, including Cost of Goods Sold, have the following balances, after adjustments, at the end of the year:

Cost of Goods Sold	$206,000
Selling Expenses	25,000

(Continued)

General and Administrative Expenses	40,600
Interest Expense	4,400
Income Tax Expense	13,000

These expense accounts are closed and the balances transferred to the Income Summary through the following closing journal entry:

Income Summary	289,000	
Cost of Goods Sold		206,000
Selling Expenses		25,000
General and Administrative Expenses		40,600
Interest Expense		4,400
Income Tax Expense		13,000
(To close expense accounts to Income Summary)		

The Income Summary account now has a credit balance of $23,000 ($312,000-$289,000) which is the amount of the net income. The ***net income is transferred to shareholders' equity*** by closing the Income Summary account to Retained Earnings as follows:

Income Summary	23,000	
Retained Earnings		23,000
(To close Income Summary to Retained Earnings)		

Assuming that dividends of $7,000 were declared during the year, the Dividends account is closed directly to Retained Earnings as follows:

Retained Earnings	7,000	
Dividends		7,000
(To close Dividends to Retained Earnings)		

After the closing process is completed, each income statement (nominal) account will have a zero balance and will be ready for use in the next accounting period. The diagram on page 89 illustrates the closing process in T-account form.

POST-CLOSING TRIAL BALANCE

As mentioned earlier, a trial balance is taken after the regular transactions of the period have been entered, and a second trial balance (adjusted trial balance) is taken after the adjusting entries have been posted. A third trial balance, often called the **post-closing trial balance,** may be taken after posting closing entries. It shows that equal debits and credits have been posted to the Income Summary and that the general ledger remains in balance. The post-closing trial balance consists only of asset, liability, and owners' equity (the real) accounts.

REVERSING ENTRIES

Objective 8

Identify adjusting entries that may be reversed.

After the financial statements have been prepared and the books closed, it is sometimes useful to reverse some of the adjusting entries before entering the regular transactions of the next period. Such entries are called reversing entries.

A **reversing entry** is the exact opposite, both in amount and in account titles, of an adjusting entry made at the end of the previous period. ***Any adjusting entries that create an asset or a liability account can be reversed (i.e. all accruals and some prepaid items).*** Adjustments for depreciation, bad debts, or other such estimated items are not reversed. The recording of reversing entries is an *optional* step in the accounting cycle that may be performed at the beginning of an accounting period. They are made to simplify the recording of a subsequent transaction related to an adjusting entry. The use of reversing entries does not change amounts reported in financial statements.

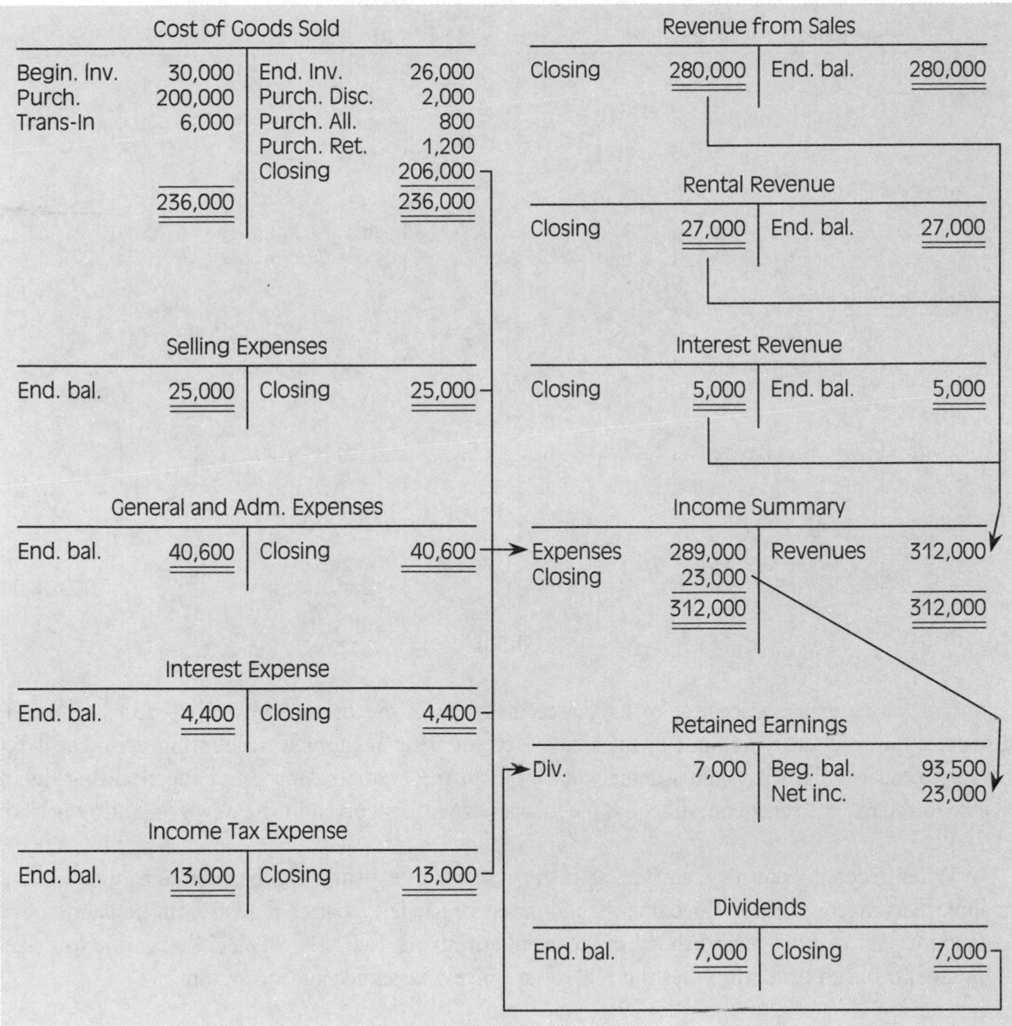

Illustration of Reversing Entries: Accruals

Reversing entries can be used to reverse adjusting entries for accrued revenues and accrued expenses. This reflects the fact that adjusting entries for accruals results in the creation of an asset or liability account. To illustrate the optional use of reversing entries for accrued expenses, see the following transaction and adjustment data:

1. October 24 (initial salary entry): $4,000 of salaries earned between October 1 and October 24 are paid.
2. October 31 (adjusting entry): Salaries earned from October 25 through October 31 are $1,200. These will be paid in the November 8 payroll.
3. November 8 (subsequent salary entry): Salaries paid are $2,500. Of this amount, $1,200 applied to accrued wages payable and $1,300 was earned from November 1 through November 8.

Entries comparing an accounting system that does not use reversing entries to a system that does use reversing entries are shown on page 90.

The comparative entries show that the first three entries are the same whether or not reversing entries are used. The last two entries, however, are different. The November 1 reversing entry eliminates the $1,200 balance in Salaries Payable that was created by the October 31 adjusting entry. The reversing entry also creates a $1,200 credit balance in the Salaries Expense account. While it

Reversing Entries Not Used				Reversing Entries Used			
Initial Salary Entry							
Oct. 24	Salaries Expense	4,000		Oct. 24	Salaries Expense	4,000	
	Cash		4,000		Cash		4,000
Adjusting Entry							
Oct. 31	Salaries Expense	1,200		Oct. 31	Salaries Expense	1,200	
	Salaries Payable		1,200		Salaries Payable		1,200
Closing Entry							
Oct. 31	Income Summary	5,200		Oct. 31	Income Summary	5,200	
	Salaries Expense		5,200		Salaries Expense		5,200
Reversing Entry							
Nov. 1	No entry is made.			Nov. 1	Salaries Payable	1,200	
					Salaries Expense		1,200
Subsequent Salary Entry							
Nov. 8	Salaries Payable	1,200		Nov. 8	Salaries Expense	2,500	
	Salaries Expense	1,300			Cash		2,500
	Cash		2,500				

is unusual for an expense account to have a credit balance, the balance here is correct because it anticipates that the entire amount of the first salary payment in the new accounting period will be debited to Salaries Expense. This debit will eliminate the credit balance, and the resulting debit balance in the expense account will equal the salaries expense incurred in the new accounting period ($1,300).

When reversing entries are made, all cash payments of expenses can be debited to the expense account. This means that on November 8, and on every payday, Salaries Expense can be debited for the amount paid without regard to the existence of any accrued salaries payable. Being able to make the same entry each time simplifies the recording process in an accounting system.

Illustration of Reversing Entries: Prepayments

Adjusting entries for prepayments (i.e. prepaid expenses and unearned revenues) may also be reversed if the initial entry to record the transaction (i.e. payment or receipt of cash) resulted in an increase in an expense or revenue account. This is because any required adjusting entry will result in the creation of an asset or liability account. When the initial transaction is recorded by debiting a prepaid asset or unearned revenue (liability) account, it signals that reversing entries are not used in the accounting system for such a prepayment.

To illustrate the use of reversing entries for prepaid expenses, the following transaction and adjustment data will be used:

1. December 10 (initial entry): $20,000 of office supplies are purchased with cash.
2. December 31 (adjusting entry): $5,000 of office supplies on hand.

Comparison of entries in an accounting system that does not use reversing entries with a system that does use reversing entries is shown on page 91.

After the adjusting entry on December 31 (regardless of whether reversing entries are used), the asset account, Office Supplies Inventory, shows a balance of $5,000 and Office Supplies Expense a balance of $15,000. If Office Supplies Expense was initially debited when the supplies were purchased, a reversing entry is made to return to the expense account the cost of unconsumed supplies. The company then continues to debit Office Supplies Expense for additional purchases of office supplies during the next period.

Reversing Entries Not Used				Reversing Entries Used			
Initial Purchase of Supplies Entry							
Dec. 10	Office Supplies Inventory	20,000		Dec. 10	Office Supplies Expense	20,000	
	Cash		20,000		Cash		20,000
Adjusting Entry							
Dec. 31	Office Supplies Expense	15,000		Dec. 31	Office Supplies Inventory	5,000	
	Office Supplies Inventory		15,000		Office Supplies Expense		5,000
Closing Entry							
Dec. 31	Income Summary	15,000		Dec. 31	Income Summary	15,000	
	Office Supplies Expense		15,000		Office Supplies Expense		15,000
Reversing Entry							
Jan. 1	No entry			Jan. 1	Office Supplies Expense	5,000	
					Office Supplies Inventory		5,000

Why are all prepaid items not entered originally into real accounts (assets and liabilities), thus making reversing entries unnecessary? Sometimes this practice is followed. It is particularly advantageous for items that need to be apportioned over several periods. However, items that do not follow this regular pattern and that may or may not involve two or more periods are ordinarily entered initially in revenue or expense accounts. The revenue and expense accounts may not require adjusting and are systematically closed to Income Summary. Using the nominal accounts adds consistency to the accounting system and makes the recording more efficient, particularly when a large number of such transactions occur during the year. For example, the bookkeeper knows that when an invoice is received for other than a capital asset acquisition, the amount is expensed. At the time an invoice is received, the bookkeeper need not worry whether the item will result in a prepaid expense at the end of the period, because adjustments will be made at the end of the period.

Summary

A summary of guidelines for reversing entries is set out below:

1. All accrued items may be reversed. The adjusting entry will create an asset or liability.
2. All prepaid items for which the original amount was debited or credited to an expense or revenue account may be reversed. The adjusting entry in such cases creates an asset or liability.
3. Adjusting entries for depreciation and bad debts are not reversed.

Recognize that reversing entries do not have to be used; therefore, some companies avoid using them entirely.

SUMMARY OF THE ACCOUNTING CYCLE

A summary of the steps in the accounting cycle shows a logical sequence of the accounting procedures used during a fiscal period. The process begins by making identification and measurement decisions regarding transactions and other selected events to be included in the accounting system. From this the following steps take place:

1. Enter the transactions of the period in appropriate journals.
2. Post from the journals to the ledger(s).
3. Take a trial balance (unadjusted trial balance).
4. Prepare adjusting journal entries and post to the ledger(s).
5. Take a trial balance after adjusting (adjusted trial balance).
6. Prepare the financial statements from the adjusted trial balance.
7. Prepare closing journal entries and post to the ledger(s).
8. Take a trial balance after closing (post-closing trial balance).
9. Prepare reversing entries and post to the ledger (optional step).

This list of procedures constitutes a complete accounting cycle that is normally performed in every fiscal period, regardless of whether it is done manually or with computers.

USE OF WORK SHEETS

Objective 9

Prepare a 10-column work sheet.

To facilitate the end-of-period accounting and reporting process, accountants may use a work sheet. A **work sheet** is a columnar structured document (sheet of paper or computer spreadsheet) used to adjust the account balances and prepare the financial statements. The 10-column work sheet shown on page 93 provides debit and credit columns for the first trial balance, adjustments, adjusted trial balance, income statement, and balance sheet. ***The work sheet does not in any way replace the journalizing, posting, or financial statements.*** Instead, it is the accountant's informal device for accumulating and sorting information needed for the financial statements. Completing the work sheet provides considerable assurance that all of the details related to the end-of-period accounting and statement preparation have been properly brought together.

Adjustments Entered on the Work Sheet

The following information serves as the basis for the entries made in the Adjustments columns of the completed work sheet shown on page 93.

(a) Furniture and equipment is depreciated at the rate of 10% per year based on original cost of $67,000.

(b) Estimated bad debts expense, one-quarter of 1% of sales of $400,000.

(c) Insurance expired during the year, $360.

(d) Interest accrued on notes receivable as of December 31, $800.

(e) The Interest Expense account contains $500 interest paid in advance, which is applicable to next year.

(f) Property taxes accrued December 31, $2,000.

The adjusting entries reflected in the Adjustments columns of the work sheet are:

(a)		
Depreciation Expense—Furniture and Equipment	6,700	
Accumulated Depreciation—Furniture and Equipment		6,700
(b)		
Bad Debts Expense	1,000	
Allowance for Doubtful Accounts		1,000

(Continued)

		Dr.	Cr.
	(c)		
Insurance Expense		360	
Unexpired Insurance			360
	(d)		
Interest Receivable		800	
Interest Revenue			800
	(e)		
Prepaid Interest Expense		500	
Interest Expense			500
	(f)		
Property Tax Expense		2,000	
Property Tax Payable			2,000

The Spencer Co. Ltd.
TEN-COLUMN WORK SHEET
December 31,1994

	Trial Balance		Adjustments		Adjusted Trial Balance		Income Statement		Balance Sheet	
Accounts	Dr.	Cr.	Dr.	Cr.	Dr.	Cr.	Dr.	Cr.	Dr.	Cr.
Cash	1,200				1,200				1,200	
Notes receivable	16,000				16,000				16,000	
Accounts receivable	41,000				41,000				41,000	
Allowance for doubtful accounts		2,000		(b) 1,000		3,000				3,000
Inventory, Jan. 1, 1994	36,000				36,000		36,000			
Unexpired insurance	900			(c) 360	540				540	
Furniture and equipment	67,000				67,000				67,000	
Accumulated depreciation of furniture and equipment		12,000		(a) 6,700		18,700				18,700
Notes payable		20,000				20,000				20,000
Accounts payable		13,500				13,500				13,500
Bonds payable		30,000				30,000				30,000
Common shares		50,000				50,000				50,000
Retained earnings, Jan. 1, 1994		14,200				14,200				14,200
Sales		400,000				400,000		400,000		
Purchases	320,000				320,000		320,000			
Sales salaries expense	20,000				20,000		20,000			
Advertising expense	2,200				2,200		2,200			
Travelling expense	8,000				8,000		8,000			
Salaries, office and general	19,000				19,000		19,000			
Telephone and fax expenses	600				600		600			
Rent expense	4,800				4,800		4,800			
Property tax expense	3,300		(f) 2,000		5,300		5,300			
Interest expense	1,700			(e) 500	1,200		1,200			
Totals	541,700	541,700								
Depreciation expense — furniture and equipment			(a) 6,700		6,700		6,700			
Bad debts expense			(b) 1,000		1,000		1,000			
Insurance expense			(c) 360		360		360			
Interest receivable			(d) 800		800				800	
Interest revenue				(d) 800		800		800		
Prepaid interest expense			(e) 500		500				500	
Property tax payable				(f) 2,000		2,000				2,000
Totals			11,360	11,360	552,200	552,200				
Inventory, Dec. 31, 1994								40,000	40,000	
Totals							425,160	440,800		
Income before income taxes							15,640			
Totals							440,800	440,800		
Income before income taxes								15,640		
Income taxes expense			(g) 3,440				3,440			
Income taxes payable				(g) 3,440						3,440
Net Income							12,200			12,200
							15,640	15,640	167,040	167,040

The adjustments are designated by letter in the work sheet. Any accounts created as a result of the adjustments and that are not already in the trial balance are listed below the totals of the trial balance. The Adjustments columns are then totalled and balanced.

Note that the adjustments for cost of goods sold are not included in the Adjustments columns. Although these adjustments are sometimes included in these columns, this illustration assumes that these entries will be made during the closing process.

Adjusted Trial Balance Columns

The amounts in the Trial Balance columns are combined with amounts in the Adjustments columns and extended to the Adjusted Trial Balance columns. For example, the amount of $2,000, shown opposite the Allowance for Doubtful Accounts in the Trial Balance Cr. column, is added to the $1,000 in the Adjustments Cr. column. The total of $3,000 is extended to the Adjusted Trial Balance Cr. column. Similarly, the $900 debit opposite Unexpired Insurance is reduced by the $360 credit in the Adjustments column, and the resulting $540 is shown in the Adjusted Trial Balance Dr. column. The Adjusted Trial Balance columns are then totalled and determined to be in balance.

Income Statement and Balance Sheet Columns

All the debit items in the Adjusted Trial Balance are extended into the balance sheet or income statement debit columns to the right, depending on the financial statement in which they will appear. Similarly, all the credit items in the Adjusted Trial Balance are extended into one of the two credit columns to the right. Note that the January 1 inventory amount is extended to the Income Statement Dr. column because beginning inventory will appear as an addition in the cost of goods sold section of the income statement.

Ending Inventory

The December 31 inventory, $40,000, is not in either of the trial balances but is listed as a separate item below the accounts already shown. It is in the Balance Sheet Dr. column because it is an asset at the end of the year, and in the Income Statement Cr. column because it will be used as a deduction in the cost of goods sold section of the income statement.

Income Taxes and Net Income

The next step is to total the Income Statement columns; the figure necessary to balance the debit and credit columns is the pretax income or loss for the period. The income before income taxes of $15,640 is shown in the Income Statement Dr. column because the revenues exceeded the expenses by that amount.

The income tax expense and related tax liability are then computed. An effective rate of 22% is applied to arrive at $3,440. Because the Adjustments columns have been balanced, this adjustment is entered in the Income Statement Dr. column as Income Taxes Expense and in the Balance Sheet Cr. column as Income Taxes Payable. The following adjusting journal entry is recorded on December 31, 1994 and posted to the general ledger as well as entered in the work sheet:

(g)		
Income Taxes Expense	3,440	
Income Taxes Payable		3,440

Next, the Income Statement columns are balanced with the income taxes included. The $12,200 difference between the debit and credit columns in this illustration represents net income. The net income of $12,200 is entered in the Income Statement Dr. column to achieve equality and in the Balance Sheet Cr. column as an increase in retained earnings.

Preparation of Financial Statements from Work Sheet

The work sheet provides the information needed for preparation of the financial statements without reference to the ledger or other records. In addition, the data have been sorted into appropriate columns, which facilitates the preparation of the financial statements illustrated on the following pages.

Income Statement. The income statement shown below is that of a trading or merchandising concern. For a manufacturing concern, three inventory accounts (raw materials, work in process, and finished goods) would be involved, and a supplementary statement titled Cost of Goods Manufactured would be prepared.

The Spencer Co. Ltd.
INCOME STATEMENT
For the Year Ended December 31, 1994

Net sales			$ 400,000
Cost of goods sold			
Inventory, Jan. 1, 1994		$ 36,000	
Purchases		320,000	
Cost of goods available for sale		$ 356,000	
Deduct inventory, Dec. 31, 1994		40,000	
Cost of goods sold			316,000
Gross profit on sales			$ 84,000
Selling expenses			
Sales salaries expense		$ 20,000	
Advertising expense		2,200	
Travelling expense		8,000	
Total selling expenses		$ 30,200	
Administrative expenses			
Salaries, office and general	$ 19,000		
Telephone and fax expense	600		
Rent expense	4,800		
Property tax expense	5,300		
Depreciation expense — furniture and equipment	6,700		
Bad debts expense	1,000		
Insurance expense	360		
Total administrative expenses		37,760	
Total selling and administrative expenses			67,960
Income from operations			$ 16,040
Other revenue			
Interest revenue			800
			$ 16,840
Other expense			
Interest expense			1,200
Income before income taxes			$ 15,640
Income taxes			3,440
Net income			$ 12,200

Statement of Retained Earnings. The net income earned by a corporation may be retained in the business or it may be distributed to shareholders by payment of dividends. In the Statement of Retained Earnings shown on page 96, the net income earned during the year was added to the balance of retained earnings on January 1, thereby increasing the balance of retained earnings to $26,400 on December 31. No dividends were declared during the year.

Balance Sheet. The balance sheet prepared from the 10-column work sheet is shown on page 96 and contains items resulting from year-end adjusting entries. Interest receivable, unexpired insurance,

The Spencer Co. Ltd.
STATEMENT OF RETAINED EARNINGS
For the Year Ended December 31, 1994

Retained earnings, Jan. 1, 1994	$14,200
Add: Net income for 1994	12,200
Retained earnings, Dec. 31, 1994	$26,400

and prepaid interest expense are included as current assets, because these assets will be converted into cash or consumed in the ordinary routine of the business within a relatively short period of time. The amount of Allowance for Doubtful Accounts is deducted from the total accounts and notes receivable because it is estimated that only $54,000 of the total of $57,000 will be collected in cash.

The Spencer Co. Ltd.
BALANCE SHEET
as of December 31, 1994

Assets

Current assets			
Cash			$ 1,200
Notes receivable	$16,000		
Accounts receivable	41,000	$57,000	
Less: Allowance for doubtful accounts		3,000	54,000
Interest receivable			800
Merchandise inventory on hand			40,000
Unexpired insurance			540
Prepaid interest expense			500
Total current assets			$ 97,040
Property, plant, and equipment			
Furniture and equipment		$67,000	
Less: Accumulated depreciation		18,700	
Total property, plant, and equipment			48,300
Total assets			$145,340

Liabilities and Shareholders' Equity

Current liabilities		
Notes payable		$ 20,000
Accounts payable		13,500
Property tax payable		2,000
Income taxes payable		3,440
Total current liabilities		$ 38,940
Long-term liabilities		
Bonds payable, due June 30, 1999		30,000
Total liabilities		$ 68,940
Shareholders' equity		
Common shares issued and outstanding, 50,000 shares	$ 50,000	
Retained earnings	26,400	
Total shareholders' equity		76,400
Total liabilities and shareholders' equity		$145,340

In the property, plant, and equipment section, the accumulated depreciation is deducted from the cost of the furniture and equipment; the difference represents the **book value** or **carrying value** of the furniture and equipment.

Property tax payable is shown as a current liability because it is an obligation that is payable within a year. Other short-term accrued liabilities would also be shown as current liabilities.

The bonds payable, due in 1999, are long-term or fixed liabilities and are shown in a separate section. (Interest on the bonds was paid on December 31.)

Because The Spencer Co. Ltd. is a corporation, the owners' capital section of the balance sheet, called Shareholders' Equity, is somewhat different from the capital section for a proprietorship. The total shareholders' equity consists of common shares, which is the original investment by shareholders, and earnings retained in the business.

Closing and Reversing Entries

The entries for the closing process are as follows.

General Journal
December 31, 1994

Account	Debit	Credit
Inventory (December 31)	40,000	
Cost of Goods Sold	316,000	
Inventory (January 1)		36,000
Purchases		320,000
(To record ending inventory balance and to determine cost of goods sold)		
Interest Revenue	800	
Sales	400,000	
Cost of Goods Sold		316,000
Sales Salaries Expense		20,000
Advertising Expense		2,200
Travelling Expense		8,000
Salaries, Office and General		19,000
Telephone and Fax Expense		600
Rent Expense		4,800
Property Tax Expense		5,300
Depreciation Expense—Furniture and Equipment		6,700
Bad Debts Expense		1,000
Insurance Expense		360
Interest Expense		1,200
Income Taxes Expense		3,440
Income Summary		12,200
(To close revenues and expenses to Income Summary)		
Income Summary	12,200	
Retained Earnings		12,200
(To close Income Summary to Retained Earnings)		

After the financial statements have been prepared, the enterprise may use reversing entries to facilitate accounting in the next period. If this were done, the following reversing entries would be made:

January 1, 1995

(a)

Account	Debit	Credit
Interest Revenue	800	
Interest Receivable		800

(Continued)

(b)

Interest Expense	500	
Prepaid Interest Expense		500

(c)

Property Tax Payable	2,000	
Property Tax Expense		2,000

Reversing entries do not appear on the 10-column work sheet because they are recorded in the next year (1995). The main purposes of the work sheet are to obtain the correct balances for preparing the 1994 financial statements and to provide information to facilitate the journalizing of December 31, 1994 adjusting entries.

Monthly Statements, Yearly Closing

The use of a work sheet at the end of each month or quarter permits the preparation of interim financial statements even though the books are closed only at the end of each year. For example, assume that a business closes its books on December 31 but that monthly financial statements are desired. At the end of January, a work sheet can be prepared to supply the information needed for statements for January. At the end of February, a work sheet can be used again. Because the accounts were not closed at the end of January, the income statement taken from the work sheet on February 28 will present the net income for two months. An income statement for the month of February can be obtained by subtracting the items in the January income statement from the corresponding items in the income statement for the two months of January and February.

A statement of retained earnings for February only may also be obtained by adding February's net income and deducting dividends declared in February from the January 31 amount of retained earnings. The balance sheet derived from the February work sheet, however, shows the assets and equities as of February 28, the specific date for which a balance sheet is prepared.

The March work sheet will show the revenues and expenses for three months, and the subtraction of the revenues and expenses for the first two months can be made to supply the amounts needed for an income statement for the month of March only.

COMPUTERS AND ACCOUNTING SOFTWARE

The principles of recording, classifying, and summarizing accounting data described in this chapter are generally applicable to most enterprises. While the activities related to data processing may be done manually, such an approach would be very time-consuming and costly. Consequently, most businesses use relatively low-cost equipment to carry out the data processing in a quick and efficient manner. The nature and type of the equipment that is used varies according to the nature and size of the business, what it does, and the cost.

Processing accounting data has progressed from the use of the quill pen through mechanisms such as large adding machines, small calculators, and posting machines to computers. The computer has revolutionized data processing not only because of its speed and accuracy, but also because it can be programmed to process data in almost any manner desired by management. A significant event has been the development of on-line computer systems which record transactions in the computer as they occur without the use of any source document. The advantages of a computer are that it can do many things with the data collected and it can process data more quickly and efficiently than other types of business equipment.

Currently, nearly every medium- or large-sized business owns or leases computers which, until fairly recently, have been considered too expensive for a small business. Small businesses avoided investing large sums of money but gained the use of computers through EDP service centres or through time-sharing arrangements. However, many small businesses now own computers and obtain the operating and record-keeping efficiencies they provide because of the availability of inexpensive personal computers.

While low-cost and technologically advanced hardware is now available, the related development of low-cost accounting software packages is equally important and significant to the accounting profession. Programs are capable of carrying out most of the mechanical steps in the accounting cycle. Once transactions and events have been identified and analysed according to the accounts affected and the amounts involved, these accounting packages can process the data through all the steps, resulting in the financial statements.

These technological advances have been a great boon to accountants. Accountants no longer need to devote hours to the routine tasks of recording, posting, and summarizing data. They can devote more attention to analysing and interpreting financial information. To an extent, the use of computers and accounting software has taken much of the bookkeeping drudgery out of accounting.

Despite these developments, accountants still have to be expert in knowing and understanding the accounting process. The nature of this process as represented by the procedures in the accounting cycle provides a basic model by which accountants can analyse the effect of various transactions and events on the financial reports. This is particularly important when choosing a method from various generally accepted accounting alternatives. If accountants simply enter transactions or events into a computer without knowing why or what happens afterwards, significant problems (i.e. errors, inability to find information in the system, accepting results without understanding what they mean) are likely to result. With an understanding of the steps in the cycle, such problems are less likely to occur. Also, accountants are responsible for the design of the information system of an enterprise. This requires a complete understanding of the process by which financial statements are derived. While the procedures outlined in this chapter are basic to most accounting systems, it must also be accepted that the accounting system for each enterprise is likely to have its own unique characteristics. To determine and understand these characteristics, accountants must rely heavily on their knowledge of the accounting process.

FUNDAMENTAL CONCEPTS

1. Accounting systems vary widely from one business to another, depending on the nature of the business and the transactions in which it engages, the size of the firm, the volume of data to be handled, and the information demands that management and others place on the system.
2. The established system for recording transactions and other events as they occur is referred to as double-entry accounting.
3. The basic steps in the accounting cycle are (1) identification and measurement of transactions and other events, (2) journalization, (3) posting, (4) unadjusted trial balance, (5) adjustments, (6) adjusted trial balance, (7) statement preparation, and (8) closing. Optional procedures are use of a work sheet, post-closing trial balance, and reversing entries.
4. Events are of two types (1) external and (2) internal. Accountants record as many events as possible that affect the financial position and results of operations of the enterprise. Some events are omitted because of measurement problems.
5. Journalization is the initial recording of transactions and selected other events in chronological order.
6. Posting is the process of transferring the essential facts and figures from the journal to the ledger accounts.
7. A trial balance is a listing of all open ledger accounts and their balances. A trial balance taken immediately after all adjustments have been posted is called an adjusted trial balance. A trial balance taken immediately after closing entries have been posted is called an after-closing or post-closing trial balance.
8. Adjustments are necessary to achieve an appropriate matching of revenues and expenses to determine the net income for the current period and to achieve a proper statement of the assets and equities existing at the end of the period.

(Continued)

9. The closing process reduces the balances of nominal (temporary) accounts to zero in order to prepare the accounts for measuring the next period's transactions.
10. Reversing entries can be used to simplify the accounting process. Accrued items and prepaid items debited or credited to a nominal account can be reversed. Reversing entries, however, are optional.
11. A work sheet may be prepared to facilitate the preparation of financial statements. The work sheet does not in any way replace the financial statements; instead, it is the accountant's informal device for accumulating and sorting the information that is needed for the financial statements.

APPENDIX 3A

Cash Basis Accounting Versus Accrual Basis Accounting

DIFFERENCES BETWEEN CASH BASIS AND ACCRUAL BASIS

Most companies use the **accrual basis of accounting,** recognizing revenue when it is earned and expenses in the period incurred, without regard to the time of receipt or payment of cash. Some small enterprises and the average individual taxpayer, however, use a strict or modified cash basis approach. Under the **strict cash basis of accounting,** revenue is recorded only when the cash is received and expenses are recorded only when the cash is paid. The determination of income on the cash basis rests upon the collection of revenue and the payment of expenses, and the matching principle of accrual accounting is ignored. Consequently, cash basis financial statements are not in conformity with generally accepted accounting principles.

To illustrate and contrast accrual basis accounting and cash basis accounting, assume that Quality Contractor signs an agreement to construct a garage for $22,000. In January, Quality Contractor begins construction, incurs costs of $18,000 on credit, and by the end of January delivers a finished garage to the buyer. In February, Quality Contractor collects $22,000 cash from the customer. In March, Quality Contractor pays the $18,000 due the creditors. The net incomes for each month under cash basis accounting and accrual basis accounting are as follows.

Quality Contractor
INCOME STATEMENT — CASH BASIS ACCOUNTING

	For the Month of			
	January	February	March	Total
Cash Receipts	-0-	$ 22,000	$ -0-	$ 22,000
Cash Payments	-0-	-0-	18,000	18,000
Net income (loss)	-0-	$ 22,000	$(18,000)	$ 4,000

Quality Contractor
INCOME STATEMENT — ACCRUAL BASIS ACCOUNTING

	For the Month of			
	January	February	March	Total
Revenues	$ 22,000	-0-	-0-	$ 22,000
Expenses	18,000	-0-	-0-	18,000
Net income (loss)	$ 4,000	-0-	-0-	$ 4,000

For three months combined, total net income is the same under cash basis accounting and accrual basis accounting; the difference is in the *timing* of net income.

The balance sheet is also affected by the basis of accounting. For instance, if cash basis accounting were used, Quality Contractor's balance sheets at each month end would appear as on page 102. If accrual basis accounting were used, Quality Contractor's balance sheets at each month end would appear as on page 102.

An analysis of the preceding income statements and balance sheets shows why cash basis accounting is inconsistent with basic accounting theory.

1. The cash basis understates revenues and assets from the construction and delivery of the garage in January. The $22,000 accounts receivable, representing a near-term future cash flow, is ignored in cash basis accounting.

Quality Contractor
BALANCE SHEET — CASH BASIS ACCOUNTING

	January 31	As of February 28	March 31
Assets			
Cash	$ -0-	$22,000	$4,000
Total assets	$ -0-	$22,000	$4,000
Liabilities and Owners' Equity			
Owners' equity	$ -0-	$22,000	$4,000
Total liabilities and owners' equity	$ -0-	$22,000	$4,000

Quality Contractor
BALANCE SHEET — ACCRUAL BASIS ACCOUNTING

	January 31	As of February 28	March 31
Assets			
Cash	$ -0-	$22,000	$4,000
Accounts receivable	22,000	-0-	-0-
Total assets	$22,000	$22,000	$4,000
Liabilities and Owners' Equity			
Accounts payable	$18,000	$18,000	$ -0-
Owners' equity	4,000	4,000	4,000
Total liabilities and owners' equity	$22,000	$22,000	$4,000

2. The cash basis understates expenses incurred with the construction of the garage and the liability outstanding at the end of January. The $18,000 accounts payable, representing a near-term future cash outflow, is ignored in cash basis accounting.

3. The cash basis understates owners' equity in January by not recognizing the revenues and the asset until February and overstates owners' equity in February by not recognizing the expenses and the liability until March.

In short, cash basis accounting violates the conceptual theory underlying financial accounting and the consequent definitions of the elements of financial statements.

The **modified cash basis,** a mixture of cash basis and accrual basis, is a method that may be followed by service enterprises (e.g., lawyers, doctors, architects, advertising agencies, public accountants, farming enterprises). Wide variations can exist in the treatment of various items. Generally, capital expenditures having an economic life of more than one year are capitalized as assets and depreciated or amortized over future years. Prepaid expenses, however, may be deferred and expensed in the year to which they apply or they may be fully expensed in the year paid. Expenses paid after the year of incurrence (accrued expenses) may be recognized in the year incurred or only in the year they are paid. Revenue may only be reported in the year of its cash receipt.

CONVERSION FROM CASH BASIS TO ACCRUAL BASIS

Not infrequently an accountant is required to convert a cash basis set of financial statements to the accrual basis for presentation and interpretation to a banker or for audit by an independent public accountant. Figure 3A-1 illustrates how cash basis financial data can be converted to the accrual basis through various types of adjusting items.

In Figure 3A-1 cash receipts are converted to *net sales* by subtracting beginning accounts receivable and adding ending accounts receivable. By expanding the formula to include all of the accounts related to sales, cash receipts can be converted to *gross sales*, as shown at the top of page 103.

As an alternative approach, cash receipts from customers can be converted to net sales by adding or subtracting the change in the balance of accounts receivable from the beginning to the end of the year, as shown below. In essence, if accounts receivable increased during a period (i.e. the beginning balance of accounts receivable was less than the ending

Conversion of Cash Receipts to Gross Sales

Cash receipts from customers		XXX
Plus: Cash discounts	XX	
Sales returns and allowances	XX	
Accounts written off	XX	
Ending accounts receivable	XX	XX
		XXX
Less: Beginning accounts receivable		XX
Gross sales		XXX

balance), it would mean there were more sales on account than cash collected on account during the period. Therefore, adding the increase in accounts receivable to cash received results in the net sales for the period.

Cash receipts from customers { + Increase in accounts receivable or − Decrease in accounts receivable } = Net sales

Similarly cash payments for goods can be converted to cost of goods sold by adding or deducting the change from the beginning to the end of the year in the accounts payable balance and in the inventory balance as shown at the top of page 104.

Figure 3A-1 presents the procedure for the conversion of cash payments for all expenses to the accrual basis operating expenses in the aggregate and, therefore, involves both prepaid and accrued expenses in the conversion. Generally, each expense item is affected by a related accrual or a related prepayment, but not both. For example, the conversion of wages paid to wages expense and the conversion of insurance paid to insurance expense are illustrated separately on page 104.

Cash Basis	⟶	Accrual Basis
Receipts	− Beginning accounts receivable + Ending accounts receivable	= Net sales
Rent receipts	+ Beginning unearned rent revenue − Ending unearned rent revenue − Beginning rent revenue receivable + Ending rent revenue receivable	= Rent revenue
Payments for goods	+ Beginning inventory − Ending inventory − Beginning accounts payable + Ending accrued expenses	= Cost of goods sold
Payments for expenses	+ Beginning prepaid expenses − Ending prepaid expenses − Beginning accrued expenses + Ending accrued expenses	= Operating expenses (except depreciation and similar write-offs)
Payments for property, plant, and equipment	− Cash payments for property, plant, and equipment + Periodic write-off of the asset cost through some formula(s)	= Depreciation or amortization expense

Figure 3A-1 Conversion of Cash Basis to Accrual Basis

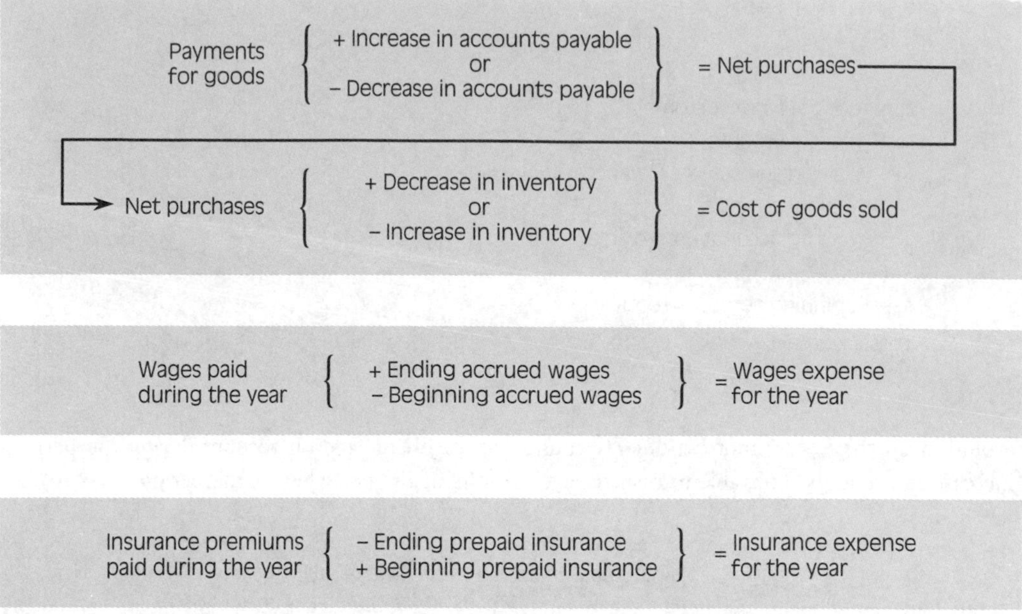

Nonoperating items such as selling common shares or paying off long-term debt are increases and decreases in cash, but they are not revenues or expenses under either the cash basis or the accrual basis.

Illustration. Diana Windsor, D.D.S., keeps her accounting records on a cash basis. During 1994, Dr. Windsor collected \$80,000 from her patients and paid \$30,000 for operating expenses, resulting in a cash basis net income of \$50,000. On January 1 and December 31, 1994, she has fees receivable, unearned fees, accrued expenses, and prepaid expenses as follows.

	January 1, 1994	December 31, 1994
Fees receivable	\$12,000	\$5,000
Unearned fees	–0–	1,000
Accrued expenses	3,800	6,800
Prepaid expenses	2,000	3,000

One approach to restating Diana Windsor's income statement data is presented in work sheet form at the top of page 105. Another approach to converting from the cash basis income statement to the accrual basis is illustrated by the second box on page 105. In the first approach, revenues and expenses are restated on an accrual basis along with net income, whereas only net income is restated in the second approach.

THEORETICAL WEAKNESSES OF THE CASH BASIS

The cash basis does report exactly when cash is received and when cash is disbursed. To many people this is something solid and concrete. Isn't cash what it is all about? Does it make sense to invent something, design it, produce it, market and sell it, if you aren't going to get cash for it in the end? It is frequently said, "Cash is the real bottom line." It is also said, "Cash is the oil that lubricates the economy." If so, then what is the merit of accrual accounting?

Today's economy is considerably more lubricated by credit than by cash. The accrual basis, not the cash basis, recognizes all aspects of the credit phenomenon. Investors, creditors, and other decision makers seek timely information about an enterprise's future cash flows. Accrual basis accounting helps provide this information by reporting the cash inflow and outflow implications associated with earnings activities as soon as they can be estimated with an acceptable degree of reliability. Receivables and payables are forecasters of future cash inflows and outflows. In other words, accrual basis accounting helps in predicting future cash flows by reporting transactions and other events with cash consequences at the time the transactions and events occur, rather than when the cash is received or paid.

Diana Windsor, D.D.S.
Conversion of Income Statement from Cash Basis to Accrual Basis
For the Year ended December 31, 1994

	Cash Basis	Adjustments Add	Adjustments Deduct	Accrual Basis
Revenue from fees:	$80,000			
– Fees receivable, Jan. 1			$12,000	
+ Fees receivable, Dec. 31		$5,000		
– Unearned fees, Dec. 31			1,000	
Restated				$72,000
Operating expenses:	30,000			
– Accrued expenses, Jan. 1			3,800	
+ Accrued expenses, Dec. 31		6,800		
+ Prepaid expenses, Jan. 1		2,000		
– Prepaid expenses, Dec. 31			3,000	
Restated				32,000
Net Income: cash basis	$50,000			
Net Income, accrual basis				$40,000

Diana Windsor, D.D.S.
Conversion of Income Statement from Cash Basis to Accrual Basis
For the year Ended December 31, 1994

Net income on a cash basis	$50,000
–Decrease in fees receivable ($12,000 to $5,000)	(7,000)
–Increase in unearned fees ($0 to $1,000)	(1,000)
–Increase in accrued expenses ($3,800 to $6,800)	(3,000)
+Increase in prepaid expenses ($2,000 to $3,000)	1,000
Net income on an accrual basis	$40,000

Note: All **asterisked** questions, cases, exercises, and problems relate to material contained in the appendix to this chapter.

QUESTIONS

1. Name the accounts debited and credited for each of the following transactions:
   (a) Purchase of 50 litres of gasoline for the delivery truck.
   (b) Purchase of office supplies on account.
   (c) Receipt of cash from customer on account.
   (d) Billing a customer for work done.
2. Give an example of a transaction that results in:
   (a) A decrease in one asset and an increase in another asset.
   (b) A decrease in one liability and an increase in another liability.
   (c) A decrease in an asset and a decrease in a liability.

3. Do the following events represent business transactions? Explain your answer in each case.
   (a) The owner of a business withdraws cash from the business for personal use.
   (b) A computer is purchased on account.
   (c) A contract is signed to have merchandise delivered by a supplier each month.
   (d) A customer returns merchandise and is given credit on account.
   (e) A prospective employee is interviewed.

4. Why are revenue and expense accounts called temporary or nominal accounts?

5. Indicate whether each of the items below is a real or nominal account and whether it appears in the balance sheet or the income statement.
   (a) Office Equipment.
   (b) Income from Services.
   (c) Office Salaries Expense.
   (d) Supplies on Hand.
   (e) Prepaid Rent Expense.
   (f) Salaries and Wages Payable.
   (g) Merchandise Inventory (ending inventory).
   (h) Supplies on Hand.

6. What are the advantages of using the journal in the recording process?

7. Is it necessary that a trial balance be taken periodically? What purpose does it serve?

8. Employees are paid every Saturday. If a balance sheet is prepared on Wednesday, December 31, what does the amount of wages earned during the first three days of the week (December 29, 30, 31) represent? Explain.

9. What is the purpose of the Cost of Goods Sold account (assume a periodic inventory system is being used)?

10. Under a periodic inventory system, is the amount shown for Inventory the same in a trial balance taken before adjusting entries as it is in a trial balance taken after closing entries? Why?

11. Why is the Purchases account debited both when merchandise is purchased for cash and when it is purchased on account? Why is the inventory amount as determined at the end of the fiscal period under a periodic inventory system deducted from the cost of goods available for sale?

12. If the cost of a new microcomputer and printer ($3,460) purchased for office use were recorded as a debit to Purchases, what would be the effect of the error on the balance sheet and income statement in the period in which the error was made?

13. What are adjusting entries and why are they necessary?

14. What are closing entries and why are they necessary?

15. What are reversing entries and why are they made? Are they necessary?

16. What differences are there between the trial balance before closing and the trial balance after closing with respect to the following?
    (a) Cash.
    (b) Retained Earnings account.
    (c) Accounts Payable.
    (d) Expense accounts.
    (e) Revenue accounts.

17. Ontario Enterprises made the following entry on December 31, 1994:

Dec. 31, 1994	Interest Expense	7,000	
	Interest Payable		7,000
	(To record accrued interest expense due on loan from the TD Bank)		

    What entry would the TD Bank make regarding its outstanding loan to Ontario Enterprises? Explain why this must be the case.

18. Jenny Binnie, maintenance supervisor for Hassell Insurance Co., has purchased a riding lawnmower and accessories to be used in maintaining the grounds around corporate headquarters. She has sent the following information to the accounting department:

Cost of mower and accessories	$3,600
Date purchased	7/1/94
Estimated useful life	5 yrs
Estimated residual value	$ 600
Monthly salary of groundskeeper	$1,500
Estimated annual fuel cost	$ 250

    Compute the amount of depreciation expense (related to the mower and accessories) that should be reported on Hassell's December 31, 1994 income statement. Assume straight-line depreciation.

*19. Distinguish between cash basis accounting and accrual basis accounting. Why, for most business enterprises, is accrual basis accounting acceptable and the cash basis unacceptable in the preparation of an income statement and a balance sheet?

*20. List two types of transactions that would receive different accounting treatment using (a) strict cash basis accounting and (b) a modified cash basis.

21. While reviewing the year-end financial statements for Zenith Motors Inc., chief accountant Scott O'Reilly realizes his original estimate of bad debts expense for the current year is too high to permit the bonus payment that is linked to the company's percentage increase in earnings. Both he and his supervisor are in line for the bonus. Scott is contemplating revising downward his bad debts estimate to increase earnings. (a) Should Scott lower his estimate? Who is harmed if he does lower it? (b) If only his supervisor's bonus were affected and not his, should Scott alter his decision?

EXERCISES

(TRANSACTION ANALYSIS: SERVICE COMPANY) Carol Denton is the proprietor of a public accounting firm. During the first month of operations of her business, the following events and transactions occurred. **E3-1**

April 1 Invested $32,000 cash and equipment valued at $13,000 in the business.

2 Hired a secretary/receptionist at a salary of $450 per week payable monthly.

3 Purchased supplies on account $700 (debit an asset account).

7 Paid office rent of $800 for the month.

11 Completed a tax assignment and billed client $1,500 for services rendered. (Use professional fees account.)

12 Received $3,200 advance on a management consulting engagement.

15 Purchased a new computer for $9,000 with personal funds. (The computer will be used exclusively for business purposes.)

17 Received cash of $900 for services completed for Jakarta Co.

21 Paid insurance expense of $110 for the month of April.

30 Paid secretary/receptionist $1,800 for the month.

30 A count of supplies indicated that $120 of supplies had been used.

Instructions

Journalize the transactions in the general journal (omit explanations).

(TRANSACTION ANALYSIS: MERCHANDISING COMPANY) The Real Hardware Store completed the following transactions in the month of May. On May 1, the company had a cash balance of $5,000. **E3-2**

On May 1 Purchased merchandise on account from Ace Wholesale Supply $4,700, terms 2/10, n/30 (i.e. if paid within 10 days a 2% discount can be taken, otherwise the full amount is to be paid by the 30th day).

2 Sold merchandise on account $3,600, terms 2/10, n/30.

5 Received credit from Ace Wholesale Supply for merchandise returned, $100.

9 Received collections in full, less discounts, from customers billed for $2,000 of sales on May 2.

10 Paid Ace Wholesale Supply in full, less discount.

12 Purchased merchandise for cash $2,400.

15 Received refund for poor quality merchandise from supplier on a cash purchase $230.

17 Purchased merchandise from Jackson Distributors $1,900, terms 3/10, n/30, on which Real Hardware is to pay freight costs.

19 Paid freight on May 17 purchase $250.

24 Sold merchandise for cash $6,200.

25 Purchased merchandise for cash $500.

27 Paid Jackson Distributors in full, less discount.

29 Made refunds to cash customers for defective merchandise $80.

31 Sold merchandise on account $1,700, terms n/30.

Real Hardware's chart of accounts includes the following: Cash, Accounts Receivable, Merchandise Inventory, Accounts Payable, Sales, Sales Returns and Allowances, Sales Discounts, Purchases, Purchase Returns and Allowances, Purchase Discounts, Freight-in.

Instructions

(a) Journalize the transactions.

(b) Prepare an income statement through gross profit for the month of May, assuming ending inventory is $2,400 and no beginning inventory.

E3-3 **(CORRECTED TRIAL BALANCE)** The trial balance of Jay Weiseman Company that follows does not balance. Your review of the ledger reveals the following: (a) each account had a normal balance, (b) the debit footings in Prepaid Insurance, Accounts Payable, and Property Tax Expense were each understated $100, (c) transposition errors were made in Accounts Receivable and Fees Earned; the correct balances are $2,750 and $7,690, respectively, (d) a debit posting to Advertising Expense of $300 was omitted, and (e) a $1,000 cash drawing by the owner was debited to Jay Weiseman, Capital, and credited to Cash.

Jay Weiseman Company
Trial Balance
April 30, 1994

	Debit	Credit
Cash	$ 6,400	
Accounts Receivable	2,570	
Prepaid Insurance	700	
Equipment		$ 8,000
Accounts Payable		4,500
Property Tax Payable	560	
Jay Weiseman, Capital		11,800
Fees Earned	7,960	
Salaries Expense	4,200	
Advertising Expense	1,100	
Property Tax Expense		800
	$23,490	$25,100

Instructions

Prepare a corrected trial balance.

E3-4 **(CORRECTED TRIAL BALANCE)** The trial balance of the Sydney Co. Ltd. does not balance. An examination of the ledger shows these errors:

1. Cash received from a customer on account was recorded (both debit and credit) as $1,580 instead of $1,850.

2. The purchase on account of a typewriter costing $900 was recorded as a debit to Office Expenses and a credit to Accounts Payable.

3. Services were performed on account for a client for $2,250; Accounts Receivable was debited $2,250 and Revenue from Fees was credited $225.
4. A payment of $95 for telephone charges was entered as a debit to Office Expenses and a debit to Cash.
5. The Revenue from Fees account was incorrectly totalled at $5,200 instead of $5,280.

Sydney Co. Ltd.
Trial Balance
April 30 , 1994

	Debit	Credit
Cash	$ 5,912	
Accounts Receivable	5,240	
Supplies on Hand	2,967	
Furniture and Equipment	6,100	
Accounts Payable		$ 5,044
Common Shares		8,000
Retained Earnings		2,000
Revenue from Fees		5,200
Office Expenses	2,320	
	$22,539	$20,244

Instructions

From this information prepare a corrected trial balance.

(CORRECTED TRIAL BALANCE) The trial balance of Howard Co. Ltd. shown below does not balance. E3-5

Howard Co. Ltd.
Trial Balance
June 30, 1994

	Debit	Credit
Cash		$ 2,870
Fees Receivable	$ 3,231	
Supplies	800	
Equipment	3,800	
Accounts Payable		2,666
Unearned Fees	1,200	
Common Shares		6,000
Retained Earnings		3,000
Fees Earned		2,380
Wages Expense	3,400	
Office Expense	940	
	$13,371	$16,916

Each of the listed accounts has a normal balance per the general ledger. An examination of the ledger and journal reveals the following errors:

1. Cash received from a customer on account was debited for $570 and Fees Receivable was credited for the same amount. The actual collection was for $750.

2. The purchase of a computer printer on account for $340 was recorded as a debit to Supplies for $340 and a credit to Accounts Payable for $340.
3. Services were performed on account for a client for $890. Fees Receivable was debited for $890 and Fees Earned was credited for $89.
4. A payment of $30 for telephone charges was recorded as a debit to Office Expense for $30 and a debit to Cash for $30.
5. When the Unearned Fees account was reviewed, it was found that $200 of the balance was earned prior to June 30.
6. A debit posting to Wages Expense of $600 was omitted.
7. A payment on account for $206 was credited to Cash for $206 and credited to Accounts Payable for $260.
8. A dividend of $500 was debited to Wages Expense for $500 and credited to Cash for $500.

Instructions

Prepare a correct trial balance. It may be necessary to add one or more accounts to the trial balance.

E3-6 **(ADJUSTING ENTRIES)** Selected accounts of Travis Company as at October 31 are shown below:

Supplies Inventory

Beg. Bal	800	10/31	350

Salaries Expense

10/15	550		
10/31	600		

Unearned Fees

10/31	400	10/20	500

Fees Earned

		10/17	1,200
		10/31	1,488
		10/31	400

Fees Receivable

10/17	1,200		
10/31	1,488		

Salaries Payable

		10/31	600

(Continued)

Supplies Expense		
10/31	350	

Instructions

From an analysis of the T-accounts, reconstruct (a) the October transaction entries and (b) the adjusting journal entries that were made on October 31.

(ADJUSTING ENTRIES) The ledger of Hammond Inc. on March 31 of the current year includes the following selected accounts before adjusting entries have been prepared.

	Debit	Credit
Prepaid Insurance	$ 3,600	
Supplies Inventory	2,800	
Delivery Equipment	25,000	
Accumulated Depreciation		$ 8,400
Notes Payable		20,000
Unearned Rent		9,300
Rent Revenue		60,000
Interest Expense	–0–	
Wage Expense	14,000	

An analysis of the accounts shows the following:

1. The delivery equipment depreciates $400 per month.
2. One-third of the unearned rent was earned during the quarter.
3. Accrued wages at March 31 total $2,100.
4. Interest of $600 is accrued on the notes payable.
5. Supplies on hand total $750.
6. Insurance expires at the rate of $150 per month.

Instructions

Prepare the adjusting entries at March 31, assuming that adjusting entries are made quarterly. Additional accounts are: Depreciation Expense, Insurance Expense, Interest Payable, Supplies Expense, and Wages Payable.

(ADJUSTING ENTRIES) Gertrude's Utopia Resort opened for business on June 1 with eight air-conditioned units. Its trial balance on August 31 is on page 112.

Other data:

1. The balance in prepaid insurance is a two-year premium paid on June 1, 1994.
2. An inventory count on August 31 shows $500 of supplies on hand.
3. Annual depreciation rates are cottages (5%) and furniture (10%). Residual value is estimated to be 10% of cost.

4. Advanced rentals of $4,000 were earned prior to August 31.
5. Salaries of $200 were unpaid at August 31.
6. Rentals of $800 were due from tenants at August 31.
7. The mortgage interest rate is 13% per year.

Gertrude's Utopia Resort
Trial Balance
August 31, 1994

	Debit	Credit
Cash	$ 17,620	
Prepaid Insurance	6,480	
Supplies Inventory	2,600	
Land	20,000	
Cottages	120,000	
Furniture	16,000	
Accounts Payable		$ 4,500
Advanced Rentals		4,600
Mortgage Payable		60,000
Gertrude, Capital		100,000
Gertrude, Drawing	5,000	
Rent Revenue		76,200
Salaries Expense	44,800	
Utilities Expense	9,200	
Repair Expense	3,600	
	$245,300	$245,300

Instructions

(a) Journalize the adjusting entries on August 31 for the three-month period June 1–August 31.

(b) Prepare an adjusted trial balance on August 31.

E3-9 **(ADJUSTING ENTRIES)** A review of the ledger of Grover Company at December 31, 1994 produces the following data pertaining to the preparation of annual adjusting entries:

1. Salaries Payable, $0. There are seven salaried employees. Payday for each month is on the fifth day of the following month. Four employees are paid salaries of $3,500 each per month, and three employees earn $4,000 each per month.

2. Sales Commissions Expense, $17,000. Salespersons are paid commissions equal to 2% of net sales, payable on the tenth day of the month following the sales. Commissions have been paid in full when due. In 1994, commission payments totalled $18,500, which includes commissions payable of $1,500 on December 31, 1993. Net sales were $960,000 in 1994.

3. Unearned Rent, $311,000. The company began subleasing office space in its new building on November 1. Each tenant is required to make a $5,000 security deposit that is refundable when occupancy is terminated. At December 31, the company has the following rental contracts that are paid in full for the entire term of the lease.

Date	Term (in months)	Monthly Rent	Number
Nov. 1	6	$4,000	3
Dec. 1	6	$8,500	4

4. Prepaid Advertising, $13,800. This balance consists of payments on two advertising contracts. The contracts provide for monthly advertising in two trade magazines. The terms of the contracts are as follows:

Contract	Date	Amount	Issues
A650	May 1	$6,600	12
B974	Sept. 1	7,200	24
		13,800	

The first advertisement runs in the month in which the contract is signed.

5. Notes Payable, $81,000. There are two notes outstanding. A $45,000, 12%, one-year note was signed on June 1, and a $36,000, 10%, nine-month note was signed on November 1.

Instructions

Prepare the adjusting entries at December 31, 1994. (Show all computations.)

(ADJUSTING AND REVERSING ENTRIES) When the accounts of G.B. Confections Inc. are examined, the adjusting data listed below are uncovered on December 31, the end of an annual fiscal period. **E3-10**

1. The unexpired insurance account shows a debit of $2,520, representing the cost of a two-year fire insurance policy dated August 1 of the current year.

2. On November 1, Rental Income was credited for $1,800, representing income from a subrental for a three-month period beginning on that date.

3. Purchase of advertising materials for $800 during the year was recorded in the Advertising Expense account. On December 31, advertising materials of $240 are on hand.

4. Interest of $230 has accrued on notes payable.

Instructions

Prepare in general journal form (a) the adjusting entry for each item and (b) the reversing entry for each item where appropriate.

(MISSING AMOUNTS: GROSS PROFIT) Financial information is presented below for four different companies. **E3-11**

	Lena's Cosmetics	Garis Grocery	Pomer Wholesalers	Clark Supply Co.
Sales	$80,000	c	$144,000	$100,000
Sales returns	a	$ 8,000	12,000	10,000
Net sales	74,000	94,000	132,000	g
Beginning inventory	14,000	d	44,000	24,000
Purchases	88,000	100,000	e	85,000
Purchase returns	6,000	10,000	8,000	h
Ending inventory	b	50,000	30,000	28,000
Cost of goods sold	64,000	72,000	f	72,000
Gross profit	12,000	22,000	20,000	i

Instructions

Determine the missing amounts (a–i). Show all computations.

E3-12 (COST OF GOODS SOLD SECTION AND CLOSING ENTRIES) The trial balance of the Derger Co. Ltd. at the end of its fiscal year, August 31, 1994, includes the following accounts: Merchandise Inventory $16,200, Purchases $142,400, Sales $190,000, Freight-in $4,000, Sales Returns and Allowances $3,000, Freight-out $1,000, and Purchase Returns and Allowances $2,000. The ending merchandise inventory is $25,000.

Instructions

(a) Prepare a cost of goods sold section for the year ending August 31.

(b) Prepare the closing entries for the above accounts. Derger Co. Ltd. is a corporation.

E3-13 (ADJUSTING AND REVERSING ENTRIES) On December 31, adjusting information for Hilton Inc. is as follows:

1. Estimated depreciation on equipment $200.
2. Property taxes amounting to $300 have accrued but are unrecorded and unpaid.
3. Employees' wages earned but unpaid and unrecorded $700.
4. Unearned Fee Revenue balance includes $1,200 that has been earned.
5. Interest of $400 on $25,000 note receivable has accrued.

Instructions

(a) Prepare adjusting journal entries.

(b) Prepare reversing journal entries.

E3-14 (CLOSING AND REVERSING ENTRIES) On December 31, the adjusted trial balance of Warren Co. Inc. shows the following selected data:

Commissions Receivable	$5,000	Commissions Earned	$97,000
Interest Expense	7,800	Interest Payable	2,000

Analysis shows that adjusting entries were made for (a) $5,000 of commissions earned but not billed, and (b) $2,000 of accrued but unpaid interest.

Instructions

(a) Prepare the closing entries for the temporary accounts at December 31.

(b) Prepare the reversing entries on January 1.

(c) Enter the adjusted trial balance data in the four accounts. Post the entries in (a) and (b) and balance the accounts. (Use T-accounts.)

(d) Prepare the entries to record (1) the collection of the accrued commissions on January 10 and (2) the payment of all interest due ($2,500) on January 15.

(e) Post the entries in (d) to the temporary accounts.

E3-15 (CLOSING ENTRIES FOR A CORPORATION) Presented below are selected accounts information for Hercules Co. Ltd. as of December 31, 1994:

Merchandise inventory 1/1/94	$ 40,000	Purchases	$205,000
Common shares	75,000	Purchase returns and	
Retained earnings	45,000	allowances	9,000
Dividends	18,000	Purchase discounts	4,000
Sales returns and allowances	12,000	Transportation-in	700
Sales discounts	15,000	Selling expenses	16,000
Sales	410,000	Administrative expenses	38,000
		Income taxes expense	29,000

Instructions

Prepare closing entries for Hercules Co. Ltd. on December 31, 1994. Merchandise inventory was $50,000 on that date.

E3-16 **(WORK SHEET PREPARATION)** The trial balance of Camburn Roofing Inc. at March 31, 1994 is as follows.

Camburn Roofing Inc.
Trial Balance
March 31, 1994

	Debit	Credit
Cash	$ 2,300	
Fees Receivable	2,600	
Roofing Supplies	1,100	
Equipment	6,000	
Accumulated Depreciation—Equipment		$ 1,200
Accounts Payable		1,100
Unearned Fees		300
Common Shares		6,400
Retained Earnings		600
Fees Earned		3,000
Salaries Expense	500	
Miscellaneous Expense	100	
	$12,600	$12,600

Other data:

1. A physical count reveals only $520 of roofing supplies on hand.
2. Equipment is depreciated at a rate of $120 per month.
3. Unearned fees amounted to $100 on March 31.
4. Accrued salaries are $500.

Instructions

Enter the trial balance on a work sheet and complete the work sheet, assuming that the adjustments relate only to the month of March (ignore income taxes).

E3-17 (PARTIAL WORK SHEET PREPARATION) Doell Video Co. prepares monthly financial statements from a work sheet. Selected portions of the January work sheet show the following data.

Doell Video Co.
Work Sheet (Partial)
For Month Ended January 31, 1994

Account Title	Trial Balance Dr.	Trial Balance Cr.	Adjustments Dr.	Adjustments Cr.	Adjusted Trial Balance Dr.	Adjusted Trial Balance Cr.
Supplies inventory	3,256			(a) 1,200	2,056	
Accumulated depreciation	6,760			(b) 260		7,020
Interest payable		100		(c) 50		150
Supplies expense			(a) 1,200		1,200	
Depreciation expense			(b) 260		260	
Interest expense			(c) 50		50	

During February no events occurred that affected these accounts but at the end of February the following information was available:

(a) Supplies on hand $1,110

(b) Monthly depreciation $ 260

(c) Accrued interest $ 50

Instructions

Reproduce the data that would appear in the February work sheet through the Income Statement columns.

***E3-18 (CASH AND ACCRUAL BASIS)** Baker Company maintains its books on the accrual basis. The company reported insurance expense of $20,100 in its 1994 income statement. Prepaid insurance at December 31 amounted to $6,740; cash paid for insurance during the year 1994 totalled $26,250. There was no accrued insurance expense either at the beginning or at the end of 1994.

Instructions

What was the amount, if any, of prepaid insurance at January 1, 1994? Show computations.

***E3-19 (CASH TO ACCRUAL BASIS)** Joan E. Robinson, M.D. maintains the accounting records of Robinson Clinic on a cash basis. During 1994, Dr. Robinson collected $142,600 from her patients and paid $55,470 in expenses. At January 1, 1994 and December 31, 1994 she had fees receivable, unearned fees, accrued expenses, and prepaid expenses as follows (all long-lived assets are rented).

	January 1, 1994	December 31, 1994
Fees receivable	$9,250	$16,100
Unearned fees	2,840	1,620
Accrued expenses	3,435	2,200
Prepaid expenses	2,000	1,775

Instructions

Prepare a schedule that converts Dr. Robinson's "excess of cash collected over cash disbursed" for 1994 to net income on an accrual basis for that year.

(CASH AND ACCRUAL BASIS) Presented below are three independent situations: ***E3-20**

1. Barter Co. had cash purchases of $980,000 during the past year. In addition, it had an increase in trade accounts payable of $9,000 and a decrease in merchandise inventory of $18,000. Determine purchases on an accrual basis.

2. Mark Donovan, M.D., collected $100,000 in fees during 1994. At December 31, 1993, Dr. Donovan had accounts receivable of $15,000. At December 31, 1994, Dr. Donovan had accounts receivable of $28,000 and unearned fees of $4,000. Determine Dr. Donovan's revenue from fees on an accrual basis for 1994.

3. Ronen Company Ltd. reported revenue of $1,400,000 in its accrual basis income statement for the year ended December 31, 1994. Additional information was as follows:

Accounts receivable December 31, 1993	$410,000
Accounts receivable December 31, 1994	520,000
Accounts written off during the year	40,000

Determine how much revenue Ronen should report under the cash basis of accounting.

(CASH AND ACCRUAL BASIS) E. J. Inc. maintains its financial records on the cash basis of accounting. Interested in securing a long-term loan from its regular bank, E. J. Inc. requests you as its accountant to convert its cash basis income statement data to the accrual basis. You are provided with the following summarized data covering 1992, 1993, and 1994. ***E3-21**

	1992	1993	1994
Cash receipts from sales:			
On 1992 sales	$290,000	$150,000	$ 30,000
On 1993 sales	–0–	350,000	100,000
On 1994 sales			408,000
Cash payments for expenses:			
On 1992 expenses	175,000	60,000	25,000
On 1993 expenses	40,000[a]	160,000	55,000
On 1994 expenses		45,000[b]	218,000

[a]Prepayments of 1993 expense.
[b]Prepayments of 1994 expense.

Instructions

(a) Using this data, prepare abbreviated income statements for the years 1992 and 1993 on the cash basis.

(b) Using this data, prepare abbreviated income statements for the years 1992 and 1993 on the accrual basis.

PROBLEMS

(TRANSACTIONS, FINANCIAL STATEMENTS: SERVICE COMPANY) Listed below are the transactions of Yank O'Tooth, D.D.S., for the month of September. **P3-1**

Sept. 1 Yank O'Tooth begins practice as a dentist and invests $15,000 cash.

2 Purchases furniture and dental equipment on account from MOD Co. for $19,200.

4 Pays rent for office space, $800 for the month.

4 Employs a receptionist, Peggy Graham.

5 Purchases dental supplies for cash, $942.

8 Receives cash of $2,100 from patients for services performed.

10 Pays miscellaneous office expenses, $430.

14 Bills patients $5,120 for services performed.

18 Pays MOD Co. on account, $3,600.

19 Withdraws $3,000 cash from the business for personal use.

20 Receives $980 from patients on account.

25 Bills patients $2,110 for services performed.

30 Pays the following expenses in cash: office salaries, $1,600; miscellaneous office expenses, $85.

30 Dental supplies used during September, $350.

Instructions

(a) Enter the transactions shown above in appropriate general ledger T-accounts. Allow 10 lines for the Cash account and 5 lines for each of the other accounts needed. Record depreciation using an eight-year life on the furniture and equipment, the straight-line method, and no residual value. Do not use a Drawing account.

(b) Take a trial balance.

(c) Prepare an income statement, a balance sheet, and a statement of capital.

(d) Close the ledger.

(e) Take a post-closing trial balance.

P3-2 **(TRANSACTIONS, FINANCIAL STATEMENTS: MERCHANDISING COMPANY)** The balance sheet of I.M. Aerosmith Inc., as of December 31, 1993, is presented below.

I.M. Aerosmith Inc.
Balance Sheet
as of December 31, 1993

Assets		Liabilities and Shareholders' Equity		
Cash	$ 3,900	Accounts payable		$ 2,985
Accounts receivable	4,985	Notes payable		5,000
Inventory	3,300	Total liabilities		$ 7,985
Office equipment	4,800			
Accumulated depreciation	(1,440)			
Furniture and fixtures	6,600	Common shares	$10,000	
Accumulated depreciation	(2,200)	Retained earnings	1,960	11,960
Total assets	$19,945	Total liabilities and shareholders' equity		$19,945

The following transactions occurred during the month of January 1994:

Jan. 2 Receives payment of $1,250 on accounts receivable.

3 Purchases merchandise on account from Great North Co. for $1,965, 2/30, n/60, f.o.b. shipping point. (**Note**: 2/30, n/60 means that if paid within 30 days a 2% discount can be taken, otherwise the full amount is to be paid by the 60th day; f.o.b. shipping point means the ownership of the goods passes to the buyer when they leave the seller's premises.)

4 Receives an invoice from *Eagle*, a trade magazine, for advertising, $125.

4 Sells merchandise on account to Doty Co. for $1,034, 2/10, n/30, f.o.b. shipping point.

4 Makes a cash sale to Davis Inc. for $1,886.

6 Sends a letter to Great North Co. regarding a slight defect in one item of merchandise received.

9 Purchases merchandise on account from Nevin's Novelty Company, $651.

11 Pays freight on merchandise received from Great North Co., $90.

11 Receives a credit memo from Great North Co. granting an allowance of $34 on defective merchandise (see transaction of January 6).

15 Receives $600 on account from Doty Co.

19 Sells merchandise on account to Maria Resch, $812, 2/10, n/30.

21 Pays display clerk's salary of $600.

25 Sells merchandise for cash, $2,350.

27 Purchases office equipment on account, $900 (begin depreciating in February).

29 Pays Great North Co. the full amount due.

30 Receives a note from Maria Resch in full amount of her account.

31 A count of the inventory on hand reveals $2,700 of saleable merchandise.

Instructions

(a) Open ledger T-accounts at January 1, 1994.

(b) Enter the transactions into ledger accounts.

(c) Take a trial balance and adjust for depreciation; use 10-year life, straight-line method, and no residual value for all long-term assets. Interest at 12% on the note payable is due every December 31.

(d) Close the ledger for preparation of the monthly financial statements.

(e) Prepare a balance sheet and income statement.

(f) Take a post-closing trial balance.

(ADJUSTING, REVERSING ENTRIES) On January 1, 1994, after reversing entries were made, the trial balance of Varsity Co. contained the account balances shown on page 120, all of which relate to prepaid or unearned items. **P3-3**

Instructions

(a) Give the December 31, 1993 adjusting entry that involved each of the accounts shown.

(b) Which of the adjusting entries in (a) were reversed on January 1, 1994?

	Dr.	Cr.
Interest Expense	$ 200	
Prepaid Insurance ($840 was paid Oct. 1, 1993 for one year's premium)	630	
Subscription Revenue		$2,200
Newsprint on Hand (balance was $9,600 before adjusting)	6,200	
Stationery and Postage Expense	1,860	
Unearned Advertising Revenue (balance was $20,000 before adjusting)		5,000

P3-4 **(ADJUSTING ENTRIES)** The following accounts appeared in the December 31 trial balance of the Turtles Theatre.

Equipment	$192,000	
Accumulated Depreciation of Equipment		$60,000
Notes Payable		80,000
Revenue from Admissions		380,000
Revenue from Concessions		36,000
Advertising Expense	13,680	
Salaries Expense	59,000	
Interest Expense	1,400	

Instructions

(a) From the account balances listed and the information given below prepare the adjusting entries necessary on December 31.

1. The equipment has an estimated life of 20 years and a residual value of $72,000 at the end of that time. (Use straight-line method.)

2. The note payable is a 90-day note given to the bank October 20 and bearing interest at 12%. (Use 360 days for denominator.)

3. In December, 2,000 coupon admission books were sold at $20 each; they could be used for admission any time after January 1. The amount was included in Revenue from Admissions for December.

4. The concession stand is operated by a concessionaire who pays 10% of gross receipts for the privilege of selling popcorn, candy, and soft drinks in the lobby. Sales for December were $35,500, and the 10% due for December has not yet been received or entered.

5. Advertising expense paid in advance and included in Advertising Expense, $1,100.

6. Salaries accrued but unpaid, $4,700.

(b) What amounts should be shown for each of the following on the income statement for the year?

1. Interest expense.
2. Revenue from admissions.
3. Revenue from concessions.
4. Advertising expense.
5. Salaries expense.

(ADJUSTING ENTRIES AND FINANCIAL STATEMENTS) Presented below are the trial balance and the other information related to I.M. Smart, a consulting engineer. P3-5

I.M. Smart, Consulting Engineer
Trial Balance
December 31, 1994

Cash	$31,500	
Accounts Receivable	49,600	
Allowance for Doubtful Accounts		$ 1,750
Engineering Supplies Inventory	1,960	
Unexpired Insurance	1,100	
Furniture and Equipment	25,000	
Accumulated Depreciation of Furniture and Equipment		5,000
Notes Payable		7,200
I.M. Smart, Capital		35,260
Revenue from Consulting Fees		100,000
Rent Expenses	9,750	
Office Salaries Expense	28,500	
Heat, Light, and Water Expense	1,080	
Miscellaneous Office Expense	720	
	$149,210	$149,210

1. Fees received in advance from clients, $7,000.

2. Services performed for clients but not recorded by December 31, $5,500.

3. The Allowance for Doubtful Accounts account should be adjusted to 6% of the accounts receivable balance (adjusted).

4. Insurance expired during the year, $600.

5. Furniture and equipment is being depreciated at 10% per year.

6. I. M. Smart gave the bank a 90-day, 12% note for $7,200 on December 1, 1994. The note was for financing of the business.

7. Rent of the building is $750 per month. The rent for 1994 has been paid, as has that for January, 1995.

8. Office salaries earned but unpaid December 31, 1994, $2,600.

Instructions

(a) From the trial balance and other information given, prepare adjusting entries as of December 31, 1994.

(b) Prepare an income statement for 1994, a balance sheet, and a statement of owner's equity. I.M. Smart withdrew $14,740 cash for personal use during the year.

(ADJUSTING ENTRIES AND FINANCIAL STATEMENTS) Grant Advertising Inc. was founded by Thomas Grant in January of 1990. Presented below are both the adjusted and unadjusted trial balances as of December 31, 1994. P3-6

Grant Advertising Inc.
Trial Balance
December 31, 1994

	Unadjusted		Adjusted	
	Dr.	Cr.	Dr.	Cr.
Cash	$ 7,000		$ 7,000	
Fees Receivable	19,000		20,000	
Art Supplies Inventory	8,500		5,000	
Prepaid Insurance	3,250		2,500	
Printing Equipment	60,000		60,000	
Accumulated Depreciation		$ 28,000		$ 35,000
Accounts Payable		5,000		5,000
Interest Payable		-0-		150
Notes Payable		5,000		5,000
Unearned Advertising Fees		7,000		5,600
Salaries Payable		-0-		1,800
Common Shares		10,000		10,000
Retained Earnings		3,500		3,500
Advertising Fees		58,600		61,000
Salaries Expense	10,000		11,800	
Insurance Expense	-0-		750	
Interest Expense	350		500	
Depreciation Expense	-0-		7,000	
Art Supplies Expense	5,000		8,500	
Rent Expense	4,000		4,000	
	$117,100	$117,100	$127,050	$127,050

Instructions

(a) Journalize the annual adjusting entries that were made.

(b) Prepare an income statement and a statement of retained earnings for the year ending December 31, 1994 and a balance sheet at December 31.

(c) Answer the following questions:

(1) If the estimated useful life of equipment is eight years, what is the expected residual value?

(2) If the note has been outstanding three months, what is the annual interest rate on that note?

(3) If the company paid $12,500 in salaries in 1994, what was the balance in Salaries Payable on December 31, 1993?

P3-7 **(ADJUSTING, CLOSING, REVERSING)** Following on page 123 is the trial balance of the Master Golf Club Inc. as of December 31. The books are closed annually on December 31.

Instructions

(a) Enter the balances in ledger T-accounts. Allow five lines for each account.

(b) From the trial balance and the following information, prepare adjusting entries and post to the ledger accounts:

1. The buildings have an estimated life of 15 years with no residual value (straight-line method).

2. The equipment is depreciated at 10% of cost per year.

3. Insurance expired during the year, $4,000.

4. The rent revenue represents the amount received for 11 months for dining facilities. The December rent has not yet been received.

5. It is estimated that 10% of the dues receivable will be uncollectible.

6. Salaries earned but not paid by December 31, $3,600.

7. Dues paid in advance by members, $8,000, was included in Dues Revenue.

(c) Prepare an adjusted trial balance.

(d) Prepare closing entries and post.

(e) Prepare reversing entries and post.

(f) Prepare a trial balance.

Master Golf Club Inc.
Trial Balance
December 31

Cash	$ 15,000	
Dues Receivable	13,000	
Allowance for Doubtful Accounts		$ 1,100
Land	350,000	
Buildings	120,000	
Accumulated Depreciation of Buildings		48,000
Equipment	150,000	
Accumulated Depreciation of Equipment		75,000
Unexpired Insurance	9,000	
Common Shares		400,000
Retaining Earnings		67,400
Dues Revenue		200,000
Revenue from Greens Fees		8,100
Rent Revenue		15,400
Utilities Expense	54,000	
Salaries Expense	80,000	
Maintenance Expense	24,000	
	$815,000	$815,000

(ADJUSTING AND CLOSING) Presented on page 124 is the December 31 trial balance of Buttercup Boutique. **P3-8**

Instructions

(a) Construct T-accounts and enter the balances shown.

(b) Prepare adjusting journal entries for the following and post to the T-accounts. Open additional T-accounts as necessary. (The books are closed yearly on December 31.)

1. Adjust the Allowance for Doubtful Accounts to 9% of the accounts receivable.

2. Furniture and equipment is depreciated at 20% of cost per year.

3. Insurance expired during the year, $3,400.

4. Interest accrued on notes payable, $3,640.

5. Sales salaries earned but not yet recorded or paid, $2,000.

6. Advertising paid in advance, $700.

7. Office supplies on hand, $1,900, charged to Office Expenses when purchased.

(c) Prepare closing entries and post to the accounts. The inventory on December 31 was $80,000.

Buttercup Boutique
Trial Balance
December 31

Cash	$ 18,500	
Accounts Receivable	42,000	
Allowance for Doubtful Accounts		$ 2,700
Inventory, January	78,000	
Furniture and Equipment	85,000	
Accumulated Depreciation of Furniture and Equipment		34,000
Prepaid Insurance	5,100	
Notes Payable		28,000
Buttercup, Capital		90,600
Sales		600,000
Purchases	400,000	
Sales Salaries	50,000	
Advertising Expense	6,700	
Administrative Salaries	65,000	
Office Expenses	5,000	
	$755,300	$755,300

P3-9 **(ADJUSTING, CLOSING, FINANCIAL STATEMENTS)** The balance sheet of Tony Company as of December 31, 1993 is presented below.

Assets		Liabilities and Capital	
Cash	$ 4,000	Accounts payable	$ 5,000
Accounts receivable	7,500	Notes payable	6,000
Inventory	5,200	Total liabilities	$11,000
Office equipment	7,400		
Accumulated depreciation	(2,220)	Tony, capital	17,880
Furniture and fixtures	10,000		
Accumulated depreciation	(3,000)		
Total	$28,880	Total	$28,880

The following summary transactions occurred during January 1994:

Jan. 1 Sold merchandise on account, $3,800.

2 Collected $3,920 on accounts receivable of $4,000. Sales discounts totalled $80.

3 Sold merchandise for cash, $7,200.

4 Received a $1,500 note from a customer on payment of account.

5 Purchased merchandise on account, $4,600.

6 Paid freight on merchandise purchased, $100.

7 Paid $3,470 on accounts payable of $3,500. Purchase discounts totalled $30.

10 Purchased office equipment on account, $1,300.

28 Paid expenses: advertising, $55; salaries, $840; rent, $400.

At January 31, the following information is available:

(a) Interest on the note payable is paid every December 31. Accrued interest for January is $60. Principal is payable December 31, 1994.

(b) Accrued interest on the note receivable for January is $15.

(c) Accrued salaries at January 31 are $125.

(d) Depreciation expense for January is $70 on office equipment and $80 on furniture and fixtures.

(e) Ending inventory is $4,225.

Instructions

(a) Prepare journal entries in general journal form for the January transactions.

(b) Open ledger accounts, enter the December 31 balances, and post the journal entries from (a).

(c) Prepare a trial balance.

(d) Prepare adjusting entries at January 31 and post.

(e) Prepare an adjusted trial balance.

(f) Prepare an income statement for January and a balance sheet at January 31.

(g) Prepare closing entries at January 31 and post.

(h) Prepare a post-closing trial balance.

(ADJUSTING, REVERSING) The list of accounts and their balances on page 126 represent the unadjusted trial balance of Stardust Inc. at December 31, 1994. **P3-10**

Additional data:

1. On November 1, 1994, Stardust received $12,000 rent from its lessee for a 12-month lease beginning on that date. This was credited to Rent Revenue.

2. Stardust estimates that 4% of the Accounts Receivable balances on December 31, 1994 will be uncollectible. On December 28, 1994, the bookkeeper incorrectly credited Sales for a receipt on account in the amount of $2,000. This error had not yet been corrected on December 31.

3. By a physical count, inventory on hand at December 31, 1994 was $70,000. Record the Cost of Goods Sold amount at the same time as when the inventory adjustment is made.

4. Prepaid insurance contains the premium costs of two policies: Policy A, cost of $1,320, two-year term, taken out on September 1, 1994; Policy B, cost of $1,620, three-year term, taken out on April 1, 1994.

5. The regular rate of depreciation is 10% of cost per year. Acquisitions and retirements during a year are depreciated at half this rate. There were no retirements during the year. On December 31, 1993, the balance of Plant and Equipment was $94,000.

6. On April 1, 1994, Stardust issued 50, $1,000, 6% bonds maturing on April 1, 2004 at 97% of par value. Interest payment dates are April 1 and October 1. No amortization of the bond discount was recorded on October 1, 1994, the first interest payment date.

7. On August 1, 1994, Stardust purchased 18, $1,000, 8% Clark Inc. bonds, maturing on July 31, 1996 at par value. Interest payment dates are July 31 and January 31.

8. On May 30, 1994, Stardust rented a warehouse for $1,100 per month, paying $13,200 in advance, debiting Prepaid Rent.

	Dr.	Cr.
Cash	$ 6,000	
Accounts Receivable	49,000	
Allowance for Doubtful Accounts		$ 750
Inventory	58,000	
Prepaid Insurance	2,940	
Prepaid Rent	13,200	
Investment in Clark Inc. Bonds	18,000	
Land	10,000	
Plant and Equipment	104,000	
Accumulated Depreciation		18,000
Accounts Payable		9,310
Bonds Payable		50,000
Discount on Bonds Payable	1,500	
Common Shares		100,000
Retained Earnings		78,860
Sales		213,310
Rent Revenue		12,000
Purchases	170,000	
Purchase Discounts		2,400
Transportation-Out	9,000	
Transportation-In	3,500	
Salaries and Wages Expense	35,000	
Interest Expense	3,600	
Miscellaneous Expense	890	
	$484,630	$484,630

Instructions

(a) Prepare the year-end adjusting and correcting entries in general journal form using the information given.

(b) Indicate the adjusting entries that could be reversed.

(ADJUSTING, REVERSING) The following list of accounts and their balances represents the unadjusted trial balance of Buckaroos Ltd. at December 31, 1994. **P3-11**

	Dr.	Cr.
Cash	$ 50,770	
Accounts Receivable	98,000	
Allowance for Doubtful Accounts		$ 3,500
Merchandise Inventory	62,000	
Prepaid Insurance	2,620	
Investment in Midnight Oil Co. Bonds (10%)	40,000	
Land	30,000	
Building	115,000	
Accumulated Depreciation—Building		11,500
Equipment	33,600	
Accumulated Depreciation—Equipment		5,600
Goodwill	32,300	
Accounts Payable		106,300
Bonds Payable (20-year; 6%)		210,000
Discount on Bonds Payable	13,440	
Common Shares		121,000
Retained Earnings		20,580
Sales		190,000
Rental Income		6,900
Advertising Expense	27,750	
Supplies Expense	10,800	
Purchases	98,000	
Purchase Discounts		900
Office Salary Expense	17,500	
Sales Salary Expense	36,000	
Interest Expense	8,500	
	$676,280	$676,280

Additional information:

1. Actual advertising costs amounted to $1,850 per month. The company has already paid for advertisements in *People Magazine* for the first quarter of 1995.

2. The building was purchased and occupied January 1, 1992 with an estimated life of 20 years. (The company uses straight-line depreciation.)

3. Prepaid insurance contains the premium costs of two policies: Policy A, cost of $960, one-year term taken out on September 1, 1993; Policy B, cost of $1,980, three-year term taken out on April 1, 1994.

4. A portion of their building has been converted into a snack bar that has been rented to the Yummy Food Corp. since July 1, 1993 at a rate of $4,600 per year payable each July 1.

5. One of the company's customers declared bankruptcy December 30, 1994 and it has been definitely established that the $2,700 due from him will never be collected. This fact has not been recorded. In addition, Buckaroos estimates that 5% of the Accounts Receivable balance on December 31, 1994 (after the write-off) will become uncollectible.

6. Nine hundred dollars given as an advance to a salesperson on December 31, 1994 was charged to Sales Salary Expense. Sales salaries are paid on the 1st and 16th of each month for the following half month.

7. When the company purchased a competing firm on July 1, 1992, it acquired goodwill in the amount of $38,000, which is being amortized.

8. On November 1, 1990, Buckaroos issued 210, $1,000 bonds at 92% of par value. Interest payments are made semi-annually on April 30 and October 31. (Use straight-line method for amortization of the bond discount and presume that amortization is recorded at interest dates and year end.)

9. The equipment was purchased January 1, 1992 with an estimated life of 12 years. (The company uses straight-line depreciation.)

10. On August 1, 1994, Buckaroos purchased 40, $1,000, 10% bonds maturing on August 31, 1999 at par value. Interest payment dates are July 31 and January 31.

11. The inventory on hand at December 31, 1994 was $76,000 per a physical inventory count. Record the adjustment for inventory in the same entry that records the Cost of Goods Sold for the year.

Instructions

(a) Prepare adjusting and correcting entries in general journal form using the information given.

(b) Indicate which of the adjusting entries could be reversed.

P3-12 **(WORK SHEET AND FINANCIAL STATEMENT PREPARATION)** Icebox Company Ltd. closes its books once a year, on December 31, but prepares monthly financial statements by estimating month-end inventories and by using work sheets. The company's trial balance on January 31, 1994 follows.

Icebox Company Ltd.
Trial Balance
January 31, 1994

Cash	$ 11,000	
Accounts Receivable	23,000	
Notes Receivable	3,000	
Allowance for Doubtful Accounts		$ 720
Inventory, Jan. 1, 1994	24,000	
Furniture and Fixtures	30,000	
Accumulated Depreciation of Furniture and Fixtures		7,500
Unexpired Insurance	600	
Supplies on Hand	1,050	
Accounts Payable		6,000
Notes Payable		5,000
Common Shares		20,000
Retained Earnings		27,005
Sales		130,000
Sales Returns and Allowances	1,500	
Purchases	80,000	
Transportation-In	2,000	
Selling Expenses	11,000	
Administrative Expenses	9,000	
Interest Revenue		125
Interest Expense	200	
	$196,350	$196,350

Instructions

(a) Copy the trial balance in the first two columns of an eight-column work sheet.

(b) Prepare adjusting entries in journal form (administrative expenses includes bad debts, depreciation, insurance, supplies, and other office salaries).

1. Estimated bad debts, 0.2% of net sales.
2. Depreciation of furniture and fixtures, 10% of cost per year.
3. Insurance expired in January, $60.
4. Supplies used in January, $240.
5. Office salaries accrued, $700.
6. Interest accrued on notes payable, $240.
7. Interest received but unearned on notes receivable, $75.

(c) Transfer the adjusting entries to the work sheet.

(d) Estimate the January 31 inventory and enter it on the work sheet. The average gross profit earned by the company is 30% of net sales.

(e) Complete the work sheet.

(f) Prepare a balance sheet, an income statement, and a statement of retained earnings. Dividends of $3,000 were paid on the common shares during the month and charged directly against retained earnings.

(WORK SHEET, ADJUSTING, FINANCIAL STATEMENTS) Presented below is the trial balance for Richard Hoffman Company, a proprietorship. **P3-13**

Richard Hoffman Company
Trial Balance
December 31, 1994

Cash	$ 13,600	
Accounts Receivable	64,800	
Allowance for Doubtful Accounts		$ 2,000
Inventory, January 1	74,000	
Land	40,000	
Building	90,000	
Accumulated Depreciation of Building		14,400
Furniture and Fixtures	22,000	
Accumulated Depreciation of Furniture and Fixtures		6,600
Unexpired Insurance	7,800	
Accounts Payable		34,200
Notes Payable		30,000
Mortgage Payable		40,000
Richard Hoffman, Capital		124,730
Sales		720,000
Sales Returns and Allowances	2,800	

(Continued)

Purchases	540,000	
Purchase Returns and Allowances		9,500
Transportation-In	14,800	
Sales Salaries Expense	54,000	
Advertising Expense	9,400	
Salaries, Office and General Expense	31,000	
Heat, Light, and Water Expense	15,100	
Telephone and Fax Expense	1,700	
Miscellaneous Office Expenses	2,000	
Purchase Discounts		9,600
Sales Discounts	5,900	
Interest Expense	2,130	
	$991,030	$991,030

Instructions

(a) Copy the trial balance above in the first two columns of a ten-column work sheet.

(b) Prepare adjusting entries in journal form from the following information. (The fiscal year ends December 31.)

1. Estimated bad debts, one-half of 1% of sales less returns and allowances.
2. Depreciation on building, 4% of cost per year; on furniture and fixtures, 10% of cost per year.
3. Insurance expired during the year, $5,200.
4. Interest at 14% is payable on the mortgage on January 1 of each year.
5. Sales salaries accrued, December 31, $5,000.
6. Advertising expenses paid in advance, $740.
7. Office supplies on hand December 31, $1,400. (Charged to Miscellaneous Office Expenses when purchased.)
8. Interest accrued on notes payable December 31, $3,000.

(c) Transfer the adjusting entries to the work sheet and complete it. Merchandise inventory on hand December 31, $76,000.

(d) Prepare an income statement, a balance sheet, and a statement of proprietor's capital.

(e) Prepare closing journal entries.

(f) Indicate the adjusting entries that could be reversed.

P3-14 **(WORK SHEET, WITHOUT ACCOUNTING RECORDS)** On January 2, 1994, Hofer-James Inc. was organized with two shareholders, Vern Hofer and Malcolm James. Hofer purchased 500 common shares for $50,000 cash; James received 600 common shares in exchange for the assets and liabilities of a men's clothing shop that he had operated as a sole proprietorship. The trial balance immediately after incorporation appears on the work sheet provided. No bookkeeping was done during 1994. The following information was gathered from the chequebooks, deposit slips, and other sources:

1. Most balance sheet account balances at December 31, 1994 were determined and recorded as shown on the work sheet.
2. Cash receipts for the year were as follows:

Advances from customers	$ 2,000
Cash sales and collections on accounts receivable (after sales discounts of $1,600 and sales returns and allowances at $2,300)	132,100
Sale of equipment costing $6,000 on which $1,000 of depreciation had accumulated	5,800
Total cash receipts	$139,900

3. During 1994, the depreciation expense on the building was $2,000; depreciation expense on the equipment was $1,500.
4. Cash disbursements for the year were as follows:

Insurance premiums	$ 1,400
Purchase of equipment	10,000
Addition to building	9,500
Cash purchases and payments on accounts payable (after purchase discounts of $2,200 and purchase returns and allowances of $1,800)	109,000
Salaries paid to employees	38,600
Utilities	3,200
Total cash disbursements	$171,700

5. Bad debts were estimated to be 2% of total sales for the year. The ending accounts receivable balance was $30,000 after eliminating $760 for specific accounts that were written off as uncollectible.

Instructions

Complete the work sheet for the preparation of accrual basis financial statements. Formal financial statements and journal entries are not required. (Prepare your own work sheet because you will need additional accounts.)

Hofer-James Inc.
Work Sheet for Preparation of Accrual Basis
Financial Statements
For the Year 1994

	Balance Sheet January 2, 1994		Adjustments		Income Statement 1994		Balance Sheet December 31, 1994	
	Debit	Credit	Debit	Credit	Debit	Credit	Debit	Credit
Cash	55,000							
Accounts receivable	12,000						30,000	
Merchandise inventory	31,000						51,500	
Unexpired insurance	800						900	
Land	20,000						20,000	
Buildings	30,000							
Accumulated depreciation—buildings		8,000						
Equipment	12,000							

(Continued)

Accumulated depreciation—equipment		3,000						
Accounts payable		36,600						25,600
Advances from customers		1,100						1,700
Salaries payable		2,100						4,600
Common shares		110,000						110,000
	160,800	160,800						

*P3-15 **(CASH AND ACCRUAL BASIS)** On January 1, 1994, Woody Bears and Beckie Howe formed a computer sales and service enterprise in Victoria, British Columbia by investing a total of $90,000 cash. The new company, Microtechnics Sales and Service, had the following transactions during January:

1. Paid $6,000 in advance for three months' rent of office, showroom, and repair space.
2. Purchased 40 microcomputers at a cost of $1,200 each, 6 graphic computers at a cost of $2,500 each, and 25 printers at a cost of $400 each, paying cash upon delivery.
3. Sales, repair, and office employees earned $12,600 in salaries during January, of which $3,000 was still payable at the end of January.
4. Sold 30 microcomputers at $2,100 each, 4 graphic computers for $3,800 each, and 15 printers for $650 each; $65,000 was received in cash in January and $22,950 was sold on a deferred-payment basis.
5. Other operating expenses of $8,400 were incurred and paid for during January; $2,000 of such expenses were incurred but not paid by January 31.

Instructions

(a) Using the transaction data above, prepare (1) a cash basis income statement and (2) an accrual basis income statement for the month of January.

(b) Using the transaction data above, prepare (1) a cash basis balance sheet and (2) an accrual basis balance sheet as of January 31, 1994.

(c) Using examples in the cash basis financial statements, indicate how and why cash basis accounting is inconsistent with the conceptual theory underlying financial statements.

Statement of Income and Retained Earnings

CHAPTER 4

The statement of income, or statement of earnings as it is frequently called,[1] is the report that measures the success of enterprise operations for a given period of time. The business and investment community uses this report to determine profitability, investment value, and credit worthiness. Whether existing confidence in the income statement is well founded is a matter of conjecture. Because the derived income is at best a rough estimate, the reader of the statement should take care not to give it more significance than it deserves. As indicated in Chapter 2, the measurement of income in accounting is a reflection of many assumptions and principles (standards) established over decades by accountants. Examples are the periodicity assumption, the revenue recognition principle, and the matching principle.

IMPORTANCE OF THE STATEMENT OF INCOME

As indicated above, the business and investment community pays close attention to a company's statement of income. *The Globe and Mail*, for example, continually reports the income and earnings per share consequences for Canadian companies. Under the headline "Corby profit on a bender despite drop in drinking," the *Globe* reported a $12.2 million profit ($1.76 per share) over a nine-month period for Corby Distilleries Ltd., compared to $9.8 million ($1.42 per share) for the corresponding period of the previous year. While not usually given such headline status, similar information is reported for many companies (e.g., Moffat Communications Ltd. showed a first quarter profit of $1.7 million [$.35 per share] up from $1.4 million for the corresponding period a year earlier; Orifino Resources Ltd. had a loss of $625,000 [$.03 per share] for one year compared with a profit of $160,000 [$.01 per share] a year earlier).

Objective 1

Identify the uses and limitations of an income statement.

Why is the income statement so important? The main reason is that it provides investors and creditors with information that helps them ***predict the amount, timing, and uncertainty of future cash flows***. Accurate predictions of future cash flows help investors assess the economic value of an enterprise and help creditors determine the probability of repayment of their claims against the enterprise.

The income statement helps users of the financial statements to predict future cash flows in a number of different ways. First, investors and creditors may use the information on the income statement to ***evaluate the past performance of the enterprise***. Although success in the past does not necessarily mean success in the future, some important trends may be determined. It follows that if a reasonable correlation between past and future performance can be assumed, predictions of future cash flows can be made with some confidence.

Second, the income statement can help users ***determine the risk (level of uncertainty) of not achieving particular cash flows***. Information on the various components of income—revenues, expenses, gains, and losses—highlights the relationship of these various components. For example,

[1] *Financial Reporting in Canada—1991* (Toronto: CICA), p. 147, indicated that for the 300 companies surveyed in 1990, the term "earnings" was employed in the titles of 132 income statements. The term "income" was second in acceptance with 128, while the term "operations" was used by 25 companies.

these components allow users to better assess the effect of a change in demand for a company's product on revenues and expenses and, therefore, income. Similarly, segregating operating performance from other aspects of enterprise performance can provide useful insights. As operations are usually the major means by which revenues and, ultimately, cash is generated, results from regular continuing operations usually have greater significance than results from nonrecurring activities and events.

Sometimes even the term "continuing operations" can mislead investors. Consider the case of National Patent Development, a company that specializes in soft contact lenses. It reported $18.6 million in income from continuing operations before taxes. A closer examination of this income, however, revealed that (1) $7.5 million of income came from a gain on the sale of investments by a subsidiary; (2) $2.4 million represented a gain on the granting of a licence to sell its product in exchange for shares in the company it licensed; (3) $3.6 million came from the sale of shares in its investment portfolio; and (4) $3.2 million came from settlement of lawsuits relating to patent infringements. In addition, its largest revenue source, $9.9 million from royalties on its soft contact lenses, might not be continuing because a note indicated that the patent on this process would expire the following year. Therefore, income, "the bottom line," does not tell the whole story. Taken in its entirety the income statement does, nonetheless, provide information on the nature of income and the likelihood that it will continue in the future.

LIMITATIONS OF THE STATEMENT OF INCOME

Economists have often criticized accountants for their definition of income because accountants ***do not include many items*** that contribute to the general growth and well-being of an enterprise. Noted economist J.R. Hicks has defined income as the maximum value an entity can consume during a period and still be as well off at the end as at the beginning.[2] Any effort to measure how well off an individual is at any point in time, however, will prove fruitless unless certain restrictive assumptions are developed and applied.

What was your net income for last year? Let us suppose that you worked during the summer and earned $5,600. Because you paid taxes and incurred tuition and living expenses for school, your income statement may show a loss for the year, if measured in terms of straight dollar amounts. But did you sustain a loss? How do you value the education obtained during the year? One interpretation of Hicks' definition states that you would measure not only monetary income but also "psychic income," the feeling of being well off. Psychic income is defined as a measure of the increase in net wealth arising from qualitative factors, in this case the value of your educational experience.

Accountants know that the recognition of the value of such experiences may be useful, but the problem of measuring it has not been solved. Items that cannot be quantified with any degree of reliability have been excluded in determining accounting income.

That is not to say that income totals are uniform and precise. ***Income numbers are often affected by the accounting methods employed.*** For example, one company may choose to depreciate its plant assets on an accelerated basis; another may choose a straight-line basis. Assuming all other factors are equal, the income of the first company will be lower than that of the second in the first year of operations even though the companies are essentially the same. Thus the ***quality of earnings*** of a given enterprise is important. Companies that use liberal (aggressive) accounting policies report higher income numbers in the short run. In such cases, we say that the quality of the earnings is low.

Other companies generate income in the short run as a result of a nonoperating or nonrecurring event that is not sustainable over a period of time. For example, Chopp Computer Corp.'s share price on the Vancouver Stock Exchange skyrocketed from $1 per share in 1985 to $124 per share in 1986. It was the first share on the VSE to break the $100 per share barrier. The amazing

[2] J.R. Hicks, *Value and Capital* (Oxford: Clarendon Press, 1946), p. 172.

price increase was based on the company's research and development of a prototype for a "super-computer" that would revolutionize the industry and be extremely profitable. The prototype was not completed. The company's shares are no longer listed on the VSE, but were being traded recently for less than $4 per share on the U.S. over-the-counter market.

Capital Maintenance vs. Transaction Approach

Objective 2

Distinguish between the capital maintenance and transaction approach.

Hicks' definition of income subtracts beginning net assets (assets minus liabilities) from ending net assets and adjusts for any additional investments and any distributions (dividends declared or drawings made) during the period. This **capital maintenance approach**, sometimes referred to as the **change in equity approach**, takes the net assets or "capital values" based on some valuation (historical cost, discounted cash flows, current cost, or fair market value) and measures income by the difference in capital values at two points in time.

Suppose that a corporation had beginning net assets of $10,000 and year-end net assets of $18,000, and that during this same period additional owners' investments of $5,000 were made and $1,000 in dividends were declared. Calculation of the net income for the period, employing the capital maintenance approach, is shown below.

Net assets, end of year	$18,000
Net assets, beginning of year	10,000
Increase in net assets	$ 8,000
Add:	
Dividends declared during the year	1,000
Deduct:	
Owners' investments during the year	(5,000)
Net income for year	$ 4,000

The capital maintenance approach has one important drawback: Detailed information concerning the composition of the income is not evident because the revenue and expense amounts are not presented to the financial statement reader.

The alternative procedure measures the basic income-related transactions that occur during a period and summarizes them in an income statement. This method is normally called the **transaction approach**, which focuses on the activities that have occurred during a given period; instead of presenting only a net change, it discloses the components of the change. Income may be classified by customer, product line, or function; by operating and nonoperating, continuing and discontinued, regular and irregular.[3] The transaction approach to income measurement requires the use of revenue, expense, loss, and gain accounts, without which an income statement cannot be prepared.

Elements of the Income Statement

The transaction approach to income measurement is superior to the capital maintenance approach because it provides information on the elements of income. As indicated in Chapter 2, the major elements of the income statement are as follows on page 136.

Revenues take many forms and include sales, fees, interest, dividends, and rents. Expenses also take many forms, such as cost of goods sold, depreciation, interest, rent, salaries and wages, and taxes. Gains and losses also comprise many types, such as those resulting from sale of investments, sale of plant assets, settlement of lawsuits, write-offs of assets due to obsolescence or casualty, and theft.

[3] "Irregular" encompasses transactions and other events that are derived from developments outside the normal operations of the business.

Elements of the Income Statement

Revenues. Increases in economic resources, either by inflows or enhancements of assets or reductions of liabilities, resulting from the ordinary activities of an entity, normally from the sale of goods, the rendering of services, or the use by others of entity resources yielding rent, interest, royalties, or dividends.

Expenses. Decreases in economic resources, either by outflows or reductions of assets or incurrences of liabilities, resulting from the ordinary revenue-earning activities of an entity.

Gains. Increases in equity (net assets) from peripheral or incidental transactions and events affecting an entity and from all other transactions, events, and circumstances affecting the entity except those that result from revenues or equity contributions.

Losses. Decreases in equity (net assets) from peripheral or incidental transactions and events affecting an entity and from all other transactions, events, and circumstances affecting the entity except those that result from expenses or distributions of equity.[4]

The distinction between revenues and gains and between expenses and losses depends to a great extent on the typical activities of the enterprise. For example, the sales price of investments sold by an insurance company may be classified as revenue, whereas the sales price less book value of an investment sold by a manufacturing enterprise will likely be classified as a gain or loss. The different treatment results because the sale of investments by an insurance company is part of its regular operations, whereas in a manufacturing enterprise it is not.

The importance of reporting these elements should not be underestimated. For most decision makers, the parts of a financial statement will often be more useful than the whole. As indicated earlier, investors and creditors are interested in predicting the amounts, timing, and uncertainty of future income and cash flows. Revenues, expenses, gains, and losses occur as a result of numerous events and activities that vary in terms of stability, risk, and predictability. By reporting these income statement elements in some detail and in comparative form with prior years' data, decision makers are better able to assess future income and cash flows.

Single-Step Income Statement

Objective 3

Prepare a single-step income statement.

In reporting revenues, gains, expenses, and losses, many accountants prefer the **single-step income statement**, which comprises just two major groups: revenues and expenses. Expenses are deducted from revenues to arrive at the net income or loss. The expression "single-step" is derived from the single subtraction necessary to arrive at net income. Frequently, however, income taxes are reported separately as the last item to indicate their relationship to income before taxes, as shown on page 137 in the single-step income statement of Dan & Karen Co. Ltd.

The single-step form of income statement is widely used in business reporting today. The primary advantage of this format lies in the ***simplicity of presentation and the absence of any implication that one type of revenue or expense item has priority over another***. Potential classification problems are thus eliminated.

Multiple-Step Income Statement

Objective 4

Prepare a multiple-step income statement.

Some accountants contend that important relationships exist in revenue and expense data and that the income statement becomes more informative and useful when it shows these further classifications, such as the following.

[4] *CICA Handbook*, Section 1000, par. .32–.35.

1. A separation of operating results from those obtained through the subordinate or nonoperating activities of the company. For example, enterprises often present an income from operations figure and then a section entitled Other Revenues and Gains or Other Expenses and Losses that includes interest revenue, interest expense, and dividends received.

2. A classification of expenses by functions, such as merchandising or manufacturing (cost of goods sold), selling, and administration. This permits immediate comparison with costs of previous years and with the costs of other departments during the same year.

Dan & Karen Co. Ltd.
Income Statement
For the Year Ended December 31, 1994

Revenues	
Net sales	$2,972,413
Dividend revenue	98,500
Rental revenue	72,910
Total revenues	$3,143,823
Expenses	
Cost of goods sold	1,982,541
Selling expenses	453,028
Administrative expenses	350,771
Interest expense	126,060
Income tax expense	66,934
Total expenses	$2,979,334
Net income	$ 164,489
Earnings per common share	$1.74

Accountants who show these additional relationships in the operating data favour what is called a **multiple-step income statement**, which recognizes a separation of operating transactions from secondary or ancillary (nonoperating) transactions and matches costs and expenses with related revenues. It highlights certain intermediate components of income that are used for computing ratios to assess the performance of the enterprise. This income statement format has regained its previous popularity. Dan & Karen Co. Ltd.'s multiple-step statement of income is presented on page 138.

For a manufacturing company, the section concerned with the cost of goods manufactured and sold is usually too extensive to include in the income statement. Sometimes, a separate schedule for these data is presented in notes to the financial statements.

Intermediate Components of the Income Statement

The sections and subsections of the income statement are described on page 139. Items 1, 2, 3, and 6 are illustrated in the Dan & Karen Co. Ltd. income statement on page 138.

Although the content of the operating section is always the same, the organization of the material may be different. The breakdown on page 139 uses a **natural expense classification** and is commonly used for manufacturing concerns and for merchandising companies in the wholesale trade. Another classification of operating expenses suitable for retail stores is a **functional expense classification** of administrative, occupancy, publicity, buying, and selling expenses.

Usually, financial statements that are provided to external users have less detail than internal management reports. The latter tend to have more expense categories, usually grouped along the lines of responsibility. This detail allows top management to judge the performance of its staff.

Dan & Karen Co. Ltd.
Income Statement
For the Year Ended December 31, 1994

Sales Revenue			
Sales			$3,053,081
Less: Sales discounts		$ 24,241	
Sales returns and allowances		56,427	80,668
Net sales revenue			2,972,413
Cost of Goods Sold			
Merchandise inventory, Jan. 1, 1994		461,219	
Purchases	$1,989,693		
Less purchase discounts	19,270		
Net purchases	1,970,423		
Freight and transportation-in	40,612	2,011,035	
Total merchandise available for sale		2,472,254	
Less merchandise inventory, Dec. 31, 1994		489,713	
Cost of goods sold			1,982,541
Gross profit on sales			989,872
Operating Expenses			
Selling expenses			
Sales salaries and commissions	202,644		
Sales office salaries	59,200		
Travel and entertainment	48,940		
Advertising expense	38,315		
Freight and transportation-out	41,209		
Shipping supplies and expense	24,712		
Postage and stationery	16,788		
Depreciation of sales equipment	9,005		
Telephone and fax	12,215	453,028	
Administrative expenses			
Officers' salaries	186,000		
Office salaries	61,200		
Legal and professional services	23,721		
Utilities expense	23,275		
Insurance expense	17,029		
Depreciation of building	18,059		
Depreciation of office equipment	16,000		
Stationery, supplies, and postage	2,875		
Miscellaneous office expenses	2,612	350,771	803,799
Income from operations			186,073
Other Revenues and Gains			
Dividend revenue		98,500	
Rental revenue		72,910	171,410
			357,483
Other Expenses and Losses			
Interest on bonds and notes			126,060
Income before taxes			231,423
Income taxes			66,934
Net income for the year			$ 164,489
Earnings per common share			$1.74

Whether a single-step or a multiple-step income statement is used, discontinued operations and extraordinary items, both net of income taxes, are reported separately, following Income from Continuing Operations or Income or Loss Before Discontinued Operations and Extraordinary Items.

Income Statement Sections

1. **Operating Section.** A report of the revenues and expenses of the company's principal operations. (This section may or may not be presented on a departmental basis.)
   (a) **Sales or revenue section.** A subsection presenting sales, discounts, allowances, returns, and other related information, which arrives at the net amount of sales revenue.
   (b) **Cost of goods sold section.** A subsection showing the cost of goods that were sold to produce the sales.
   (c) **Selling expenses.** A subsection listing expenses that result from the company's efforts to make sales.
   (d) **Administrative or general expenses.** A subsection reporting expenses of general administration.
2. **Nonoperating Section.** A report of revenues and expenses resulting from secondary or auxiliary activities of the company. In addition, unusual or infrequent material gains and losses are sometimes reported in this section. Generally, these items break down into two main subsections:
   (a) **Other Revenues and Gains.** A list of revenues earned or gains incurred, generally net of any related expenses, from nonoperating transactions.
   (b) **Other Expenses and Losses.** A list of expenses or losses incurred, generally net of any related incomes, from nonoperating transactions.
3. **Income Taxes.** A short section reporting taxes levied on income from continuing operations.
4. **Discontinued Operations.** Revenues, expenses, and any gain or loss (net of taxes) attributed to a segment of the business that is being discontinued.
5. **Extraordinary Items.** Unusual and infrequent gains and losses of material amounts that did not depend on the decisions of management or owners. These items are shown net of income taxes.
6. **Earnings Per Share.**[5]

Condensed Income Statement

In some cases, it is impossible to present all of the desired expense detail in a single income statement of convenient size. This problem is solved by including only the totals for expense groups in the statement of income and preparing supplementary schedules of expenses to support the totals. When this is done, the income statement itself may be reduced to only a few lines on a single sheet. For this reason, readers who study all the reported data on operations must give their attention to the supporting schedules. The income statement on page 140 for Dan & Karen Co. Ltd. is a condensed version of the detailed multiple-step statement presented earlier and is more representative of income statements available in practice.

An example of a supporting schedule, contained in the notes to the financial statements and detailing the selling expenses, and cross-referenced as Note D, is shown on page 140.

It is always a problem to decide how much detail to include in financial statements. On the one hand, we want to present a simple, summarized statement so that a reader can readily discover the important facts. On the other hand, we want to disclose the results of all activities and to provide more than just a skeletal report.

---

[5] *CICA Handbook*, Section 3500, requires that earnings per share or net loss per share be included on the face of the income statement or in a note cross-referenced to the income statement.

Dan & Karen Co. Ltd.
Income Statement
For the Year Ended December 31, 1994

Net sales		$2,972,413
Cost of goods sold		1,982,541
Gross profit		$ 989,872
Selling expense (see Note D)	$453,028	
Administrative expense	350,771	803,799
Income from operations		$ 186,073
Other revenues and gains		171,410
		$ 357,483
Other expenses and losses		126,060
Income before taxes		$ 231,423
Income taxes		66,934
Net income for the year		$ 164,489
Earnings per share		$1.74

Note D: Selling expenses

Sales salaries and commissions	$202,644
Sales office salaries	59,200
Travel and entertainment	48,940
Advertising expense	38,315
Freight and transportation-out	41,209
Shipping supplies and expense	24,712
Postage and stationery	16,788
Depreciation of sales equipment	9,005
Telephone and fax	12,215
Total selling expenses	$453,028

Professional Pronouncements and the Income Statement

The profession has not taken a position on whether the single-step or the multiple-step income statement should be employed, which has allowed flexibility in the presentation of the components of the income statement data. There are two important areas, however, where some guidelines have been developed. These two areas relate to what should be included in income and how unusual or irregular items should be reported.

Objective 5

Explain how irregular items are reported on the income statement and statement of retained earnings.

What should be included in net income had been a controversy for many years. For example, should irregular gains and losses and corrections of revenues and expenses of prior years be closed directly to Retained Earnings and therefore not reported in the income statement, according to the current operating performance concept? Or should they first be presented in the income statement and then carried to Retained Earnings, along with the net income or loss for the period, according to the all-inclusive concept?

Advocates of the **current operating performance income statement** argue that the net income figure should show only the regular, recurring earnings of the business, based on its normal operations. They feel irregular gains and losses are neither representative nor reflective of an enterprise's future earning power. Therefore, they argue, these gains and losses should not be included in computing net income but should be carried directly to Retained Earnings as special items. These advocates believe that many readers are not trained to differentiate between regular and irregular items and, therefore, they might be confused if such items were included in computing net income.

Advocates of the **all-inclusive income statement** insist that such items be included in net income because they reflect the long-range income-producing ability of the enterprise. They think any gain or loss experienced by the concern, whether directly or indirectly related to operations, contributes to its long-run profitability and should be included in the computation of net income. In addition, they indicate that irregular gains and losses can be separated from the results of regular operations to arrive at income from operations, but net income for the year should include all transactions. These advocates believe that when judgement is allowed to determine irregular items, differences may develop in the treatment of questionable items and, as a result, income data may be manipulated. If permitted, it could be to the advantage of a corporation to run losses through Retained Earnings, but gains through income. Supporters of the all-inclusive concept argue that this flexibility should not be allowed because it leads to poor financial reporting practices. In other words, Gresham's law applies: Poor accounting practices drive out good ones.

The* CICA Handbook *adopted a modified all-inclusive concept and requires application of this approach in practice, as evidenced by Sections 3475, Discontinued Operations and 3480, Extraordinary Items. A number of pronouncements have been issued that require irregular items to be highlighted so that readers of financial statements can better determine the long-run earning power of the enterprise. These irregular items are classified into four general categories:

1. Discontinued operations.
2. Extraordinary items.
3. Certain gains and losses that do not constitute extraordinary items even though they are unusual or infrequent in nature and material in amount.
4. Changes in estimates.

Discontinued Operations. One of the most common irregular items is the disposal of a business or a product line. Because of the increasing importance of this occurrence, a set of classification and disclosure requirements was developed and included in the *CICA Handbook*.[6]

When a business disposes of a segment, the income statement must include a separate category for the gain or loss from ***disposal of a segment***. In addition, the ***results of operations of the segment that has been or will be disposed of*** is reported in conjunction with the gain or loss on disposal, separately from continuing operations. The effects of discontinued operations are shown *net of tax* as a separate category, after continuing operations but before extraordinary items.

To illustrate, Multiplex Products Inc., a highly diversified company, decides to discontinue its electronics division. The electronics division has lost $300,000 (net of tax) during the current year and is sold at the end of the year at a loss of $500,000 (net of tax). The information is shown on the current year's income statement on page 142.

To qualify as discontinued operations, the assets, results of operations, and activities of a segment of a business must be clearly distinguishable from the other assets of the entity. ***Disposals of assets that qualify as disposals of a segment of a business*** include the following:

1. Disposal of a significant product line provided that the assets and results of operations or activities are separately identifiable.
2. Disposal of a subsidiary, operational division, or some other investment that represents the enterprise's only activities in an industry.

---

[6] The reporting requirements for discontinued operations are complex. These complexities are discussed more fully in the appendix to this chapter. Our purpose here is to illustrate the basic presentation of this information on the income statement.

Income from continuing operations (after related taxes)		$20,000,000
Discontinued operations		
Loss from operation of discontinued electronics division (net of tax)	$300,000	
Loss from disposal of electronics division (net of tax)	500,000	800,000
Net income		$19,200,000

3. Disposal of all of the wholesale operations of a firm engaged primarily in retailing.[7]

Examples that do not qualify are (1) discontinuance by a children's wear manufacturer of its operations in Italy but not elsewhere or (2) sale by a diversified company of one but not all of its furniture-manufacturing subsidiaries. Judgement must be exercised in defining a disposal of a segment of a business because the criteria in some cases are difficult to apply.

Extraordinary Items. Extraordinary items are infrequent material transactions or events that are not typical of the normal business activities of the enterprise and are not primarily dependent on decisions of management. All of the following conditions must be satisfied before an item is reported as extraordinary:

1. **Unusual in nature** (not typical of the normal business activities of the enterprise).
2. **Not expected to occur frequently** over several years.
3. **Must not depend primarily on decisions or determinations by management or owners.**[8]

For further clarification, the AcSB specified that the following gains and losses do not constitute extraordinary items:

1. Losses and provisions for losses with respect to bad debts and inventories.
2. Gains and losses from fluctuations in foreign exchange rates.
3. Adjustments with respect to contract prices.
4. Write-down or sale of property, plant, equipment, or other investments.
5. Income tax reductions on utilization of prior period losses or reversal of previously recorded tax benefits.[9]

The items listed above do not constitute extraordinary items in an ongoing business because they result from risks inherent in the enterprise's normal business activities.

Only in rare situations will an event or transaction occur that clearly meets the criteria specified in the *Handbook*, Section 3480, and thus give rise to an extraordinary gain or loss.[10] In some circumstances, gains or losses such as (1) and (4) above could be classified as extraordinary if they were a ***direct result of a major casualty***, such as an earthquake, an ***expropriation***, or a ***prohibition under a newly enacted law or regulation*** that is clearly "unusual, infrequent, and not a result of a management decision."

---

[7] *CICA Handbook*, Section 3475, par. .05.
[8] *Ibid.*, Section 3480, par. .02.
[9] *Ibid.*, Section 3480, par. .04.
[10] Some accountants have concluded that the extraordinary item classification is so restrictive that only such items as a single chemist who knew the secret formula for an enterprise's mixing solution but was eaten by a tiger on a big game hunt or a plant facility that was smashed by a meteor would qualify for extraordinary item treatment.

In determining whether an item is extraordinary, the ***environment in which the entity operates is of primary importance***. The environment includes such factors as industry characteristics, geographic location, and the nature and extent of government regulations. Thus, hail damage to tobacco crops in a location where hailstorms are rare is considered an extraordinary item. On the other hand, frost damage to a fruit orchard in the Okanagan Valley does not qualify as extraordinary because frost damage is normally experienced every three or four years. In this environment, the criterion of infrequency is not met.

Firm guidelines to follow in judging when an item is or is not material have not been established. Some companies have shown items that accounted for less than 1% of income as extraordinary gains or losses. As long as the definition of materiality is not sharply outlined, it will be difficult in some cases to differentiate an ordinary item from an extraordinary item. In making the materiality judgement, extraordinary items should be considered individually and not in the aggregate.

It is generally difficult to determine whether an item is extraordinary, so considerable judgement must be exercised. For example, some paper companies have had their forestry operations curtailed as a result of government action. Is such an event extraordinary or is it part of normal operations? Such determination is not easy; much depends on the frequency of previous actions, the expectation of future events, materiality, and the like.

Extraordinary items are to be shown *net of taxes* in a separate section in the income statement, usually just before net income. After listing the other revenues, costs and expenses, income taxes, and discontinued operations (net of tax), the remainder of the statement shows the following.

Income before extraordinary items
  Extraordinary items (less applicable income taxes of $______)
Net income

Unusual Gains and Losses. Financial statement users must carefully examine the financial statements for items that have some but not all of the characteristics of extraordinary items. As indicated earlier, items such as write-downs of inventories and gains and losses from fluctuations of foreign exchange rates should be reflected in the determination of income before discontinued operations and extraordinary items. Thus, these items are shown with the normal, recurring revenues, costs, and expenses and are shown *before tax*. If they are not material in amount, they are combined with other items in the statement. If they are material, they should be disclosed separately, but shown above Income (Loss) Before Discontinued Operations and Extraordinary Items.

The excerpt on page 144, from the 1991 financial statements of Algonquin Mercantile Corporation, shows how multiple unusual items may be disclosed.

In recent years, there has been a tendency to report unusual items in a separate section just above income from continuing operations before income taxes and discontinued operations and extraordinary items, especially when there are multiple unusual items.

In dealing with items that have some but not all of the characteristics of extraordinary items, the profession attempted to prevent a practice that many accountants believed was misleading. Companies sometimes reported these items on a net-of-tax basis and prominently displayed their earnings-per-share effect. Although not captioned Extraordinary Items, they were presented in the same manner. Some referred to these as "first cousins" to extraordinary items. As a consequence, the *CICA Handbook* stipulates that these items are to be reported in the income statement before Income Before Discontinued Operations and Extraordinary Items.[11]

Change in Estimate. Adjustments that arise as a result of the use of estimates in accounting are not classified as prior period adjustments and, therefore, are used in the determination of income for the

[11] *CICA Handbook*, Section 3480, par. .12 and Section 1520, par. .03 (1).

Algonquin Mercantile Corporation

	1991	1990
Earnings (loss) from continuing operations	$ 321,232	$8,297,276
Unusual and nonrecurring items (Note 11)	(35,232,896)	(2,035,356)
Earnings (Loss) Before Income Taxes and Discontinued Operations	(34,911,664)	6,261,920
Income taxes (Note 15)	541,309	1,986,320
Earnings (Loss) Before Discontinued Operations	(35,452,973)	4,275,600
Loss From Discontinued Operation	(2,000,080)	(10,134,930)
Net Loss for the Period	$(37,453,053)	$(5,859,330)

Notes:

11. Unusual and Non-Recurring Items

The company incurred costs and established provisions for restructuring its continuing operations, including the reduction in carrying values of certain assets and provisions for ongoing losses to the anticipated date of disposition or closure. The company also incurred losses on the write-down and disposal of an investment.

	Ten months ended January 27, 1991	Year ended March 31, 1990
Loss on write-down of investment (note 3)	$32,026,665	—
Loss on disposal of investment (see below)	1,594,363	—
Retail division	357,868	$ 675,850
Food wholesaling division	854,000	359,506
Corporate	400,000	1,000,000
	$35,232,896	$2,035,356

On May 30, 1990 the company declared a special dividend of one common share of The Enfield Corporation Limited for every ten shares of the company. The dividend was paid on June 30, 1990 to shareholders of record on June 12, 1990. This dividend resulted in the distribution of 573,525 pre-consolidation common shares of The Enfield Corporation Limited to shareholders of the company (note 3). The loss of $1,594,363 represents the difference between the book value and market value of the shares.

current period. Items resulting from changes in the estimated lives of fixed assets, adjustment of the costs, realizability of inventories believed to be obsolete in preceding years, and similar items are accounted for in the period of the change if they affect only that period, or in the period of change and future periods if the change affects both.

To illustrate a change in estimate that affects only the period of change, assume that DuPage Materials Limited has consistently estimated its bad debts expense at 1% of credit sales. In 1994, however, DuPage's controller determines that the estimate for the last two years has been too low and that an additional provision for bad debts of $240,000 should be recorded to reduce accounts receivable to net realizable value. The additional provision is recorded at December 31, 1994, as follows:

Bad Debt Expense	240,000	
Allowance for Doubtful Accounts		240,000

The entire change in estimate is included in 1994 income because no future periods are affected by the change. Changes in estimate are *not* handled retroactively, that is, carried back to adjust estimates made in prior years. Changes in estimate that affect both the current period and future periods are examined in greater detail in Chapter 23. ***Changes in estimate are not considered errors (prior period adjustments) or extraordinary items.***

Summary

The public accounting profession now tends to accept a modified all-inclusive income concept instead of the current operating performance concept. Except for a couple of items that are charged or credited directly to Retained Earnings, all other irregular gains or losses or nonrecurring items are closed to Income Summary and are included in the income statement. Of these, discontinued operations of a segment of a business is classified as a separate item in the income statement after continuing operations. The material ***unusual and infrequent items that do not depend primarily on decisions or determinations of management or owners*** are shown in a separate section for *Extraordinary Items* in the income statement, below discontinued operations. Other items of a material amount that are of an ***unusual or nonrecurring*** nature and result from decisions or determinations of management or owners ***are not considered extraordinary*** but should be separately disclosed.

Because of the numerous intermediate income figures that are created by the reporting of these items, careful evaluation of information reported by the financial press is needed. For example, at one time when RCA reported its first quarter results, a *Wall Street Journal* article stated that "RCA earnings climbed by 47% in the first quarter" as compared to the first quarter of the previous year. Conversely, *The New York Times* reported the following regarding RCA's first quarter results: "RCA Slides 46%." Which article was right? Both articles were factually correct. The difference arose because *The New York Times* article, in making its comparison to the same quarter of the previous year, included extraordinary gains in the income of the earlier quarter but *The Wall Street Journal* did not. Such an illustration demonstrates the importance of understanding the intermediate components of net income.

INTRAPERIOD TAX ALLOCATION

Objective 6

Explain intraperiod tax allocation.

Whenever an extraordinary item or discontinued operation occurs, most accountants believe that the resulting income tax effect should be directly associated with that event or item. In other words, the tax for the year should be related, where possible, to *specific* items on the income statement to provide more informative disclosure to statement users. This procedure is called **intraperiod tax allocation**, which is allocation within a period. Its main purpose is to relate the income tax expense of the fiscal period to the following items that affect the amount of the tax provisions: (1) income from continuing operations, (2) discontinued operations, and (3) extraordinary items. The general concept is "Let the tax follow the income."

The income tax expense attributable to income from continuing operations is computed by ascertaining the income tax expense related to revenue and to expense transactions entering into the determination of this income. In this computation, no effect is given to the tax consequences of the items excluded from the determination of income from continuing operations. The income tax expense attributable to other items is determined by the tax consequences of transactions involving these items. Because all of these items are ordinarily material in amount, the applicable tax effect is also material and is disclosed separately and in close association with the related items.

Extraordinary Losses

In applying the concept of intraperiod tax allocation, assume that a company has income before extraordinary items of $250,000 and an extraordinary loss from a major casualty of $100,000. Because the casualty is not expected to occur frequently, has a material effect, is not considered to be usual to the ordinary operating processes of the business, and is beyond the control of management or owners, it is reported as an extraordinary item. The loss is deductible for tax purposes. Therefore, if the income tax rate is assumed to be 48%, the ***income tax payable*** for the year will be determined as follows.

Computation of Income Tax Payable

Income before loss deduction	$250,000
Extraordinary item—loss from casualty	(100,000)
Taxable income	$150,000
Income tax payable at 48%	$ 72,000

The ***income tax expense*** applicable to the $250,000 income before extraordinary items is $120,000, and the *tax reduction applicable to the loss* of $100,000 from the major casualty is $48,000. If the tax reduction of $48,000 is not associated with the extraordinary loss in the income statement, that statement would appear incorrectly as follows.

Incorrect Presentation

Income before tax and extraordinary item	$250,000
Income tax expense	72,000
Income before extraordinary item	$178,000
Extraordinary item—loss from casualty	(100,000)
Net income	$ 78,000

The previous report does not disclose an appropriate relationship between the income tax expense, the income before the extraordinary item, and the "loss." Without the tax benefit of the loss, the $250,000 of operating income would have been taxed at the 48% rate for an income tax expense of $120,000. The income before the extraordinary item would have appeared as $130,000 instead of $178,000. Thus we have the paradoxical situation of a loss of $100,000 making the income before the extraordinary item appear larger by $48,000 instead of smaller. To avoid such a misleading presentation, we may report the tax effect in the income statement along with the loss in the following way.

Correct Presentation

Income before tax and extraordinary item		$250,000
Income tax expense		120,000
Income before extraordinary item		$130,000
Extraordinary item—loss from casualty	$100,000	
Less applicable income tax reduction	48,000	(52,000)
Net income		$ 78,000

Or the extraordinary item may be reported "net of tax" with note disclosure as illustrated on page 147.

Extraordinary Gains

If a company realizes an extraordinary gain, the tax expense is allocated between the gain and the income before the gain. If we assume a $100,000 extraordinary gain, the income statement disclosure is as shown in the second box on page 147.

Correct Presentation with Note

Income before tax and extraordinary item	$250,000
Income tax expense	120,000
Income before extraordinary item	$130,000
Extraordinary item, less applicable income tax (Note 1)	(52,000)
Net income	$ 78,000

Note 1. During the year, the Company suffered a major casualty loss of $52,000, net of an applicable income tax reduction of $48,000.

Extraordinary Gain Less Tax

Income before tax and extraordinary item		$250,000
Income tax expense (48%)		120,000
Income before extraordinary item		$130,000
Extraordinary gain	$100,000	
Less applicable income tax	48,000	52,000
Net income		$182,000

EARNINGS PER SHARE

Objective 7

Explain the reporting of earnings-per-share information.

The results of a company's operations are customarily summed up as net income. The financial world has also accepted another figure as its most significant business indicator—earnings per share.

Earnings per share is determined by dividing net income available to common shareholders (i.e. net income minus preferred dividends) by the weighted-average number of common shares outstanding during the year.[12] To illustrate, assume that Lancer Inc. reports net income of $350,000 and declares and pays preferred dividends of $50,000 for the year; the weighted-average number of shares outstanding during the year is 100,000 shares. The earnings per share is $3.00 as computed below.

$$\frac{\text{Net Income} - \text{Preferred Dividends}}{\text{Weighted-Average Number of Shares Outstanding}} = \text{Earnings Per Share}$$

$$\frac{\$350{,}000 - \$50{,}000}{100{,}000} = \$3.00$$

"Net income per share" or "earnings per share" is a ratio commonly used in prospectuses, proxy material, annual reports to shareholders, and business earnings data for the press and other statistical services. Because of the inherent dangers of focusing attention on earnings per share by itself, the profession concluded that ***earnings per share must be disclosed either on the face of the income statement or in a note to the financial statements.*** In addition to net income per share, per-share amounts should be shown for Income Before Discontinued Operations and Extraordinary Items.[13]

[12] In the calculation of earnings per share, preferred dividends reduce net income if declared and if cumulative even though not declared.

[13] *CICA Handbook*, Section 3500, pars. .09 and .11.

To illustrate comprehensively both the income statement order of presentation and the earnings-per-share data, a comprehensive income statement for Poquito Industries Inc. is presented below. Notice the order in which data are shown. In addition, per-share information is shown at the bottom. Assume that the company had 100,000 shares outstanding for the entire year.

Poquito Industries Inc.
Income Statement
For the Year Ended December 31, 1994

Sales		$1,480,000
Cost of goods sold		600,000
Gross profit		$ 880,000
Selling and administrative expenses		320,000
Income from operations		$ 560,000
Other revenues, expenses, gains, and losses		
Interest revenue	$ 10,000	
Loss on disposal of equipment	(5,000)	
Loss on sale of investments	(45,000)	(40,000)
Income from continuing operations before income taxes		$ 520,000
Income taxes		208,000
Income from continuing operations		**$ 312,000**
Discontinued operations		
Income from operations of Pizza Division, less applicable income taxes of $24,800	**$ 54,000**	
Loss on disposal of Pizza Division, less applicable income taxes of $41,000	**(90,000)**	**(36,000)**
Income before extraordinary item		**$ 276,000**
Extraordinary item		
Loss from earthquake, less applicable income taxes of $23,000		**(45,000)**
Net income		**$ 231,000**
Earnings per common share		
Income from continuing operations		**$3.12**
Income from operations of discontinued division, net of tax		**.54**
Loss on disposal of discontinued division, net of tax		**(.90)**
Income before extraordinary items		**2.76**
Extraordinary loss, net of tax		**(.45)**
Net income		**$2.31**

The earnings-per-share data may also be disclosed parenthetically on an income statement, as illustrated below (this form is especially applicable when only one per-share amount is involved).

Net income **(per share $4.02)**	$804,000

Reporting per-share amounts for gain or loss on discontinued operations or loss on extraordinary items is optional. These per-share amounts can be determined simply by subtraction if they are not specifically reported. For example, if National Sea Products Limited reported earnings per share before extraordinary items of $1.72 and earnings per share on net income of $1.54, it would have had an extraordinary loss of $0.18 per share, net of income tax.

It should be emphasized that the Poquito illustration is highly condensed, and that items such as Unusual Charge, Discontinued Operations, and Extraordinary Item would normally have to be described fully and appropriately in the statement or related notes. The 1991 statement of income of Moore Corporation Limited (see Appendix 5A) presents appropriate earnings-per-share amounts in much the same manner as shown for Poquito. Moore Corporation's Note 16 describes the computation of the earnings per share.

Many corporations have simple capital structures that include only common shares. For these companies, a presentation such as Earnings Per Common Share is appropriate on the income statement. In many instances, however, companies' earnings per share are subject to dilution (reduction) in the future because existing contingencies permit the further issuance of common shares.[14] Examples of such instances are (1) outstanding preferred shares or debt that is convertible into common shares (2) outstanding stock options or warrants, and (3) agreements for the issuance of common shares for little or no consideration in the satisfaction of certain conditions. The computational problems involved in accounting for these dilutive securities in earnings-per-share computations are discussed in Chapter 17.

In summary, the simplicity and availability of figures for per-share earnings lead inevitably to their widespread use. Because of the undue importance that the public, even the well-informed public, attaches to earnings per share, accountants have an obligation to make the earnings-per-share figures as meaningful as possible.

STATEMENT OF RETAINED EARNINGS

Objective 8

Prepare a statement of retained earnings.

A statement of retained earnings is included, together with an income statement, a balance sheet, and a statement of changes in financial position, in the financial statements of an enterprise. Actually, instead of being a statement that reports related data, a **statement of retained earnings** is a reconciliation of the balance of the Retained Earnings account from the beginning to the end of the year. An example of a statement of retained earnings is as follows.

Fieldcrest Corporation
Statement of Retained Earnings
For the Year Ended December 31, 1994
(000 omitted)

Retained earnings January 1, 1994		$ 21,159
Add net income for the year		99,423
		$120,582
Deduct dividends declared on:		
Preferred shares at $5 per share	$15,000	
Common shares at $7 per share	28,000	43,000
Retained earnings December 31, 1994		$ 77,582

Restatement of Beginning Retained Earnings

Retained earnings at the beginning of the year should be the same amount as the preceding year's ending retained earnings. However, in some circumstances the opening balance of Retained Earnings must be restated to reflect changes to the earnings of prior years. These circumstances include prior period adjustments, corrections of errors, and the cumulative effect of changes in accounting policy.

[14] *Ibid.*, par. .30.

Objective 9

Explain how prior period adjustments, accounting changes, and error corrections are reported.

Prior Period Adjustments. Certain gains or losses that should have been included in the income of prior periods are referred to as "prior period adjustments." The *CICA Handbook* requires that items possess all four of the following characteristics to be accounted for and reported as prior period adjustments, which are excluded from the determination of net income for the current period:

(a) specifically identified with and directly related to the business activities of particular prior periods;

(b) not attributed to economic events occurring subsequent to the date of the financial statements for such prior periods;

(c) depend primarily on decisions or determinations by persons other than management or owners; *and*

(d) could not reasonably be estimated prior to such decisions or determinations.[15]

Examples of prior period adjustments are rare. The most common are nonrecurring adjustments or settlements of income taxes and settlements of litigation.

Prior period adjustments should be charged or credited (net of tax) to the opening balance of Retained Earnings and, thus, excluded from the determination of net income for the current period. The following excerpt from the financial statements of Lumonics Inc. serves as an example of how this can be accomplished.

Lumonics Inc.
Consolidated Statement of Retained Earnings
(in thousands of dollars)

	1987	1986
Balance, beginning of year		
As previously reported	$13,575	$17,983
Adjustment of prior year's earnings (Note 11)	(395)	(304)
As restated	13,180	17,679
Net loss for the year	1,697	4,499
Balance, end of year	$11,483	$13,180

Notes:

11. Prior period adjustment

During the year, the Company concluded an out-of-court settlement with Gordon Gould, Refac International Limited, and Patlex Corporation relating to actions against the Company alleging patent infringement in Canada and the United States applicable to the years 1977 to 1986. As a result, the balance of retained earnings at January 1, 1987 has been adjusted by $395,000 (net of income taxes of $295,000) representing the cumulative cost of the settlement as at that date. Of the $395,000, $91,000 (net of income taxes of $69,000) is applicable to 1986 and has been charged to income for that year. The remaining $304,000 is applicable to years prior to January 1, 1986 and the balance of retained earnings at that date has been adjusted accordingly. As at December 31, 1986, deferred income taxes decreased by $295,000 and accounts payable and accrued charges increased by $690,000.

[15] *Ibid.*, Section 3600, par. .03.

Correction of Errors Made in a Prior Period. Items of income or loss related to corrections of errors in the financial statements of a prior period are accounted for and reported in the same way as a prior period adjustment. A mistake or error may occur because of incorrect computation, oversight in considering available information, or misinterpretation of information.[16] For example, depreciation may be incorrectly calculated. When material errors made in a previous period are discovered, the accounts must be corrected in the year of discovery.[17]

To illustrate, assume that in 1994, McCartan Limited determines that it has overstated depreciation expense in 1993 by $187,640 ($114,960 net of tax) owing to an error in computation. The error affected both the income statement and the tax return for 1993. The following journal entry records this retroactive adjustment to correct the error:

Accumulated Depreciation	187,640	
Deferred Income Tax		72,680
Retained Earnings		114,960

Adjustment for this error is presented in the statement of retained earnings for 1994 as follows.

Retained earnings, January 1, 1994, as previously reported	$2,767,890
Correction of an error in depreciation in prior period (net of $72,680 tax)	114,960
Adjusted balance of retained earnings at January 1, 1994	$2,882,850
Net income	697,611
Retained earnings, December 31, 1994	$3,580,461

Changes in Accounting Policy. Changes in accounting policy occur frequently in practice, because important events or conditions may be in dispute or uncertain at the statement date. One example of accounting policy change is the normal recurring corrections and adjustments that are made by every business enterprise. Another accounting policy change results when a company adopts an accounting principle that is different from the one used previously. Changes in accounting policy would include a change in the method of inventory pricing from first-in, first-out (FIFO) to average cost or a change in depreciation from the double-declining to the straight-line method.[18]

These changes are recognized through **retroactive adjustment**, which involves the determination of the effect on the income of the prior periods affected. The financial statements for all prior periods that are presented for comparative purposes should be restated to reflect the new accounting policy, except when the effect is not reasonably determinable for specific prior periods. If this exception is applicable, an adjustment would be made to the beginning retained earnings of the current, or an appropriate earlier, period to show the cumulative effect from all previous periods. Appropriate disclosure relating to a change in an accounting policy should occur.

To illustrate, McCartan Inc. decides at the beginning of 1994 to change from an accelerated depreciation method (double-declining balance) of computing depreciation on its plant assets to the straight-line method. Assume that the depreciation that is calculated using the declining-balance method (40% rate) is the same as that used to determine taxable income. The assets originally cost

---

[16] In accounting, an error is distinguished from a change in an estimate. An error results when information available at the time when the original statements were prepared is either not used or misused. A change in estimate is a result of new information that makes it possible to improve estimates made in prior periods.

[17] *CICA Handbook*, Section 1506, par. .28.

[18] *Ibid.*, Section 1506. Chapter 23 examines in greater detail the problems related to accounting policy changes. Our purpose now is to provide general guidance for the major types of transactions affecting the income statement.

$100,000 and have a service life of five years. The following data are assumed to illustrate the consequences of the change in policy and the manner of reporting the change.

Year	Accelerated Depreciation	Straight-Line Depreciation	Excess of Accelerated Depreciation Over Straight-Line
1992	$40,000	$20,000	$20,000
1993	24,000	20,000	4,000
Total			$24,000

The adjustment for this accounting policy change in the 1994 financial statements could be shown as follows (no comparative statements are shown and the tax rate is 48%).

Retained earnings, January 1, 1994, as previously reported	$250,000
Cumulative effect on prior periods of retroactive application of new depreciation method (net of $11,520 tax)	12,480
Adjusted balance of retained earnings at January 1, 1994	$262,480

In addition to reporting the retroactive adjustment in the statement of retained earnings, a note must be included to describe the change and its effect. The example on page 153 illustrates how this may be accomplished.

As discussed previously, some irregular items appear on the income statement and some on the statement of retained earnings. The chart on page 154 summarizes the *Handbook* recommendations for reporting these transactions and events.

Appropriation of Retained Earnings

Retained earnings are often restricted; they are usually appropriated in accordance with contract requirements, board of directors' policy, or the apparent necessity of the moment. The amounts of retained earnings appropriated are transferred to Appropriated Retained Earnings. The Retained Earnings section may therefore report two separate amounts—retained earnings free (unrestricted) and retained earnings appropriated (restricted). The total of these two amounts equals the total retained earnings balance.

Combined Statement of Income and Retained Earnings

Some accountants believe that the statements of income and retained earnings are so closely related that they present both statements in one combined report. The principal advantage of a combined statement is that all items affecting income and retained earnings appear in one statement. Therefore, the user can assess items such as net income before extraordinary items, prior period adjustments, correction of prior period errors, and changes in accounting policies by examining this single statement. On the other hand, the figure of net income for the year is hidden in the body of the statement, a feature that some find objectionable and the main reason why this method has not gained favour.

When a combined statement is prepared, the income statement is presented as if it were to be issued as an independent report but, instead of closing the statement with the amount of net income, it is extended to include retained earnings, as shown on page 155.

If the company has other capital accounts such as Contributed Surplus, a good practice is to present a statement of these accounts reconciling the beginning and ending balances. The *CICA Handbook* requires that changes in both retained earnings and contributed surplus during a period

Imperial Oil Limited

From the notes to the December 31, 1991 statements:

2. Reporting Changes

In 1991 the company changed its method of accounting for inventories to the last-in, first-out (LIFO) method. Previously the cost of crude oil at refineries and of products was determined using the average-cost method while crude oil in transit was valued at actual cost. During periods of fluctuating crude-oil prices, the LIFO method of inventory valuation reflects these changes in the statement of earnings as they occur. The adoption of the LIFO method has been applied retroactively, and prior periods have been restated.

The effect on 1991 and prior years' inventories, net earnings, and net earnings per share was:

millions of dollars	1991	1990	1989	1988	1987
			increase (decrease)		
Inventories	(389)	(687)	(345)	(275)	(415)
Net earnings	173	(209)	(54)	84	(21)
Net earnings per share (dollars)	0.89	(1.09)	(0.30)	0.51	(0.12)

Also in 1991 the company adopted the new recommendations of the Canadian Institute of Chartered Accountants, requiring that provisions be made for site-restoration costs. For natural resource assets, accruals are made over the useful life of the asset. For other assets, a provision is made at the time management decides either to close or sell a facility or if a contractual obligation exists. Previously, provision was made for cleanup costs where there was a contractual agreement or the site was closed and there was a management approved site-restoration plan. The change in the method of providing for site-restoration costs has been applied retroactively, and prior periods have been restated.

The effect on 1991 and prior years' other long-term obligations, net earnings, and net earnings per share was:

millions of dollars	1991	1990	1989	1988	1987
			increase (decrease)		
Other long-term obligations	304	242	237	160	141
Net earnings	(47)	(28)	(52)	(12)	(8)
Net earnings per share (dollars)	(0.24)	(0.15)	(0.29)	(0.07)	(0.05)

The combined effect on 1991 and prior years' retained earnings at the beginning of the year, net earnings, and net earnings per share for the two reporting changes was:

millions of dollars	1991	1990	1989	1988	1987
			increase (decrease)		
Retained earnings at beginning of year	(586)	(349)	(243)	(315)	(286)
Net earnings	126	(237)	(106)	72	(29)
Net earnings per share (dollars)	0.65	(1.24)	(0.59)	0.44	(0.17)

SUMMARY OF *CICA HANDBOOK* RECOMMENDATIONS*

Type of Situation	Criteria	Examples	Placement on Financial Statements
Extraordinary items	Material, and both unusual and nonrecurring (infrequent). Must also not depend on decisions and determinations by management or owners .	Gains or losses resulting from casualties, an expropriation, or a prohibition under a new law.	Separate section in the income statement entitled Extraordinary Items. (Show net of tax.)
Material gains or losses, not considered extraordinary	Material; character typical of the customary business activities; unusual or infrequent but not both (or unusual and infrequent but the result of decisions or determinations of management or owners).	Write-downs of receivables, inventories; adjustments of contract prices; gains or losses from fluctuations of foreign exchange.	Separately disclosed as a component of net income before extraordinary items or as part of net income from continuing operations if there is a category for discontinued operations in the income statement.
Prior period adjustments	Meet all four characteristics in *CICA Handbook*, Section 3600.	Income tax reassessments for previous years; settlements of litigation.	Adjust the beginning balance of retained earnings. (Show net of tax.)
Correction of an error made in a prior period	Is the result of a mistake in computation, oversight of available information, or misinterpretation of information that is material.	Incorrectly calculated depreciation or allowance for doubtful accounts.	Retroactive adjustment to all financial statements presented for comparative periods and adjustment of beginning retained earnings of earliest period presented. Adjustments are shown net of tax.
Changes in estimates	Result of occurrence of new events, more experience, and new or additional information.	Changes in the realizability of receivables and inventories; changes in estimated lives of equipment, intangible assets; changes in estimated liability for warranty costs, income taxes, and salary payments.	Prospective adjustment by incorporating the change in current and future periods' statements as affected. No retroactive adjustment is made.
Changes in accounting policies	Change from one generally accepted policy to another.	Changing the basis of inventory pricing from FIFO to average cost; change in the method of depreciation from accelerated to straight line.	Retroactive adjustment to all financial statements presented for comparative periods and adjustment of beginning retained earnings of earliest period presented. Adjustments are shown net of tax.
Discontinued operations	Disposal by selling, closing down, or abandoning a segment of the business.	Sale by diversified company of major division that represents only activities in electronics industry. Food distributor that sells wholesale to supermarket chains and through fast-food restaurants decides to discontinue the division that sells to one of two classes of customers.	Results of operations and net gain or loss on discontinued operations are each shown, net of income tax, in a separate category, Discontinued Operations, between the results from continuing operations and extraordinary items. The gain or loss would be shown as an extraordinary item if it resulted from transactions or events that met the criteria for such items.

* This summary provides only the general rules to be followed in accounting for the various situations described above. Exceptions do exist in some of these situations.

be disclosed.[19] This can be accomplished by including separate statements on the changes in these accounts as part of the financial statements, or through disclosure in notes. Examples of income statements, retained earnings statements, and contributed surplus sections are presented in Appendix 5A of Chapter 5 and in Chapter 16.

Magnavox Limited
Combined Statement of Income and Retained Earnings
(lower portion only)

Net income for the year	$ 42,290,385
Retained earnings at beginning of the year	106,734,310
	$149,024,695
Cash dividends paid	15,764,250
Retained earnings at end of year	$133,260,445

FUNDAMENTAL CONCEPTS

1. The statement of income, or statement of earnings, as it is frequently called, is the report that measures the results of enterprise operations for a given period in time.
2. The transaction approach is the method used to report income-related information. This approach focuses on the activities that have occurred during a given period; instead of presenting only a net change, it discloses the components of that change.
3. The distinction between revenues and gains and the distinction between expenses and losses depend on what constitute the enterprise's typical activities.
4. In a single-step income statement, two categories exist: revenues and gains, and expenses and losses. The expenses and losses are deducted from the revenues and gains to arrive at the net income or loss. The expression "single-step" is derived from the single subtraction necessary to arrive at net income.
5. A multiple-step income statement provides a basic division between operating and nonoperating revenues and expenses.
6. Advocates of the current operating performance income statement argue that net income should show only the regular, recurring earnings of the business. Conversely, advocates of the all-inclusive income statement believe that both regular and irregular earnings of the business should be reported as part of net income. The all-inclusive method, with a few exceptions, is the approach used in practice.
7. Special procedures are followed for reporting the following items: discontinued operations, extraordinary items, and unusual or infrequent gains and losses.
8. Intraperiod tax allocation is the procedure where the tax expense for the year is related to specific items on the income statement and in the retained earnings statement.
9. Earnings per share must be disclosed either on the face of the income statement or in a note cross-referenced to the income statement. In addition to net income per share, per-share amounts should be shown for income from continuing operations and income before extraordinary items.
10. The statement of retained earnings discloses prior period adjustments, retroactive effects of error corrections, and any change in accounting policies, net income or loss, dividends, and transfers to and from retained earnings (appropriations).

[19] *Ibid.*, Section 3250, par. .13.

APPENDIX 4A
Accounting for Discontinued Operations

The purpose of the chapter discussion was to provide an understanding of how and where gains and losses related to discontinued operations are reported on the income statement. This appendix discusses the more technical aspects of how this gain or loss is computed, along with related reporting issues.

FIRST ILLUSTRATION: NO PHASE-OUT PERIOD

To illustrate the accounting for a discontinued operation, assume that the Board of Directors of Heartland Ltd. decides to sell the Record Phonograph Division of their company on October 1, 1994. Record Phonograph has provided phonograph records for Heartland's 15 retail stores but management foresee that the compact disc is revolutionizing the stereo industry and will soon render its Record Phonograph Division unprofitable. They find a buyer immediately and sell the division on October 1, 1994.

Heartland Ltd. has income of $2 million for the year 1994, not including a $150,000 loss from operations of the Record Phonograph Division from January 1 to October 1, 1994. Management sell the division at a gain of $400,000. Its tax rate on all items is 30%.

Recall that the assets, results of operations, and activities of a *business segment* must be clearly distinguishable, physically and operationally, to qualify for discontinued operations treatment. The assets and operations of the Record Phonograph Division can be easily identified, and the record business is distinct from Heartland's other lines of business. Accordingly, the ***disposal of the Record Phonograph Division constitutes the disposal of a segment of the business.***

For the period up to the time when management commits to sell the division, the revenues and expenses of the discontinued operations are aggregated and reported as income or loss on discontinued operations, net of tax. The date management formally commits to a formal plan to dispose of a segment of the business is October 1, 1994, the **measurement date**. The plan of disposal should include, as a minimum:

1. Identification of the major assets to be disposed of.
2. The expected method of disposal.
3. The period expected to be required for completion of the disposal.
4. An active program to find a buyer if disposal is to be by sale.
5. Estimated results of operations of the segment from the measurement date to the disposal date.
6. Estimated proceeds or salvage value to be realized by disposal.[20]

Because the segment has actually been sold on October 1, 1994, a gain or loss on disposal is computed. This date is referred to as the ***disposal date***. In this case, the measurement date and the disposal date are the same; consequently, no unusual complications occur. The following diagram illustrates Heartland's situation.

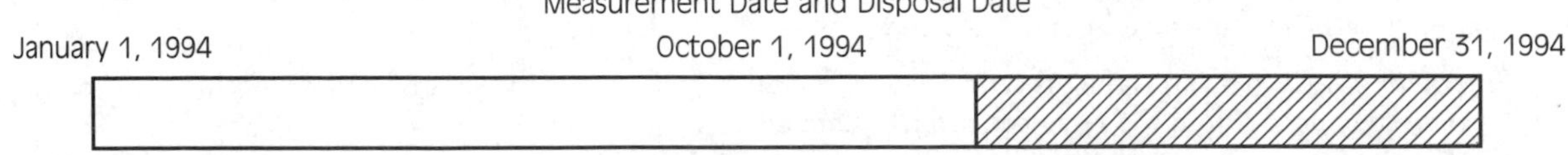

The condensed income statement presentation for Heartland Ltd. for 1994 follows at the top of page 157.

SECOND ILLUSTRATION: PHASE-OUT PERIOD

The first illustration is simplified because the measurement date and the disposal date were exactly the same. Normally, the disposal date would be later than the measurement date. The gain or loss on disposal would be the sum of:

1. Income (loss) from the measurement date to the disposal date (the phase-out period).
2. Gain (loss) on the disposal of the net assets.

---

[20] *Ibid.*, Section 3475, par. .02.

Income from continuing operations before income taxes		$2,000,000
Income taxes		600,000
Income from continuing operations		1,400,000
Discontinued operations		
Loss from operation of Record Phonograph, less income taxes of $45,000	$(105,000)	
Gain on disposal of Record Phonograph, less income taxes of $120,000	280,000	175,000
Net income		$1,575,000

The reason for aggregating the above two items to compute the gain (loss) on disposal is that the selling company needs a reasonable period to phase out its discontinued operations.The income (loss) from operations of the discontinued segment is part of the computation of the gain (loss) on disposal because the phase-out period often enables the seller to obtain a better selling price.

To illustrate the combination of these two components, assume that Heartland's sale of the Record Phonograph Division does not occur until December 1, 1994, at which time it is sold at a gain of $350,000. During the period October 1, 1994 to December 1, 1994, the Record Phonograph Division suffers a loss of $50,000 from operations. The following diagram illustrates Heartland's situation.

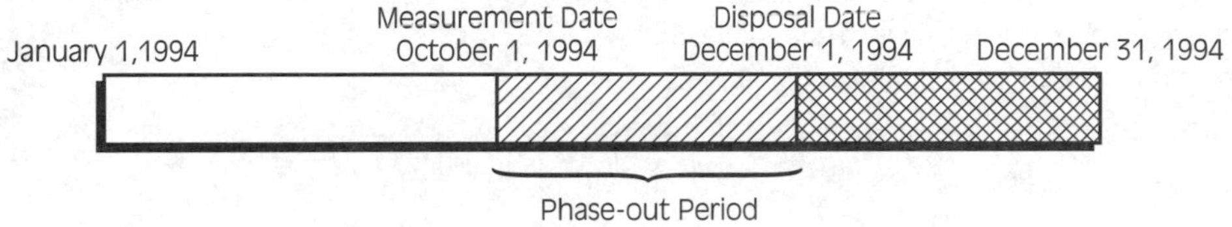

The condensed income statement presentation for Heartland Ltd. for 1994 is as follows.

Income from continuing operations before income taxes		$2,000,000
Income taxes		600,000
Income from continuing operations		1,400,000
Discontinued operations		
Loss from operation of Record Phonograph, less applicable income taxes of $45,000	($105,000)	
Gain on disposal of Record Phonograph, including operating loss of $50,000 and gain on disposal of $350,000, less applicable income taxes of $90,000	210,000	105,000
Net income		$1,505,000

THIRD ILLUSTRATION: EXTENDED PHASE-OUT PERIOD

In the preceding illustration, the disposal of the discontinued operation occurs in the same accounting period as the measurement date. As a result, determining the proper gain or loss on the disposal of the Record Phonograph Division at the end of the year is straightforward. However, the phase-out period often extends into another year. In this case, the profession requires that ***if a loss is expected on disposal, the estimated loss should be reported at the measurement date. If a gain on disposal is expected, it should be recognized when realized, which is ordinarily the disposal date.***[21] In other

[21] *Ibid.*, Section 3475, par. .08.

words, the profession has taken a conservative position by recognizing losses immediately but deferring gains until realized.

Implementing these general rules can be troublesome. To determine the gain or loss on disposal of the segment, the income (loss) from operations must be estimated and then combined with the estimated gain (loss) on sale. If a net loss results, it is recognized at the measurement date. If a net gain arises, it generally is recognized at the date of disposal. ***The major exception is when realized gains exceed estimated unrealized and realized losses. In that special case, realized gains can be recognized in the period of the measurement date***

Net Loss. To illustrate net loss, assume that Heartland Ltd. expects to sell its Record Phonograph Division on May 1, 1995 at a gain of $350,000. In addition, from October 1, 1994 to December 31, 1994, it realizes a loss of $400,000 on operations for this discontinued operation and expects to lose an additional $200,000 on this operation from January 1, 1995 to May 1, 1995. The following diagram illustrates Heartland's situation.

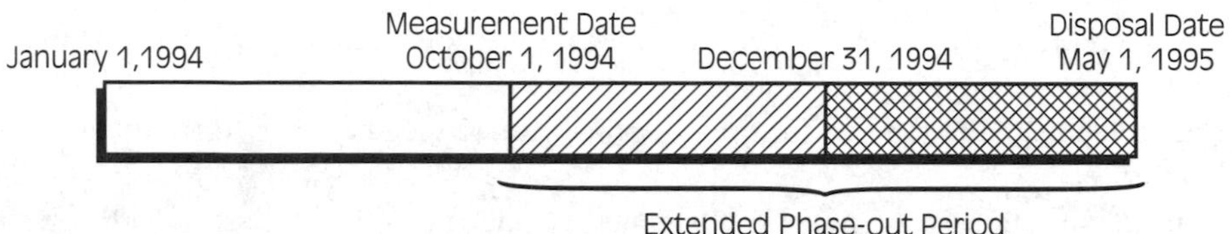

The computation of the net gain or loss on disposal is as follows.

Realized loss on operations October 1–December 31, 1994	$(400,000)
Expected loss on operations January 1–May 1, 1995	(200,000)
Expected gain on sale of assets on May 1, 1995	350,000
Net loss on disposal	$(250,000)

Given that a net loss on disposal is expected, the loss on disposal is recognized in the period of the measurement date. The condensed income statement presentation for Heartland Ltd. for 1994 is therefore reported as shown below.

Income from continuing operations before income taxes		$2,000,000
Income taxes		600,000
Income from continuing operations		1,400,000
Discontinued operations		
Loss from operation of Record Phonograph, net of applicable income taxes of $45,000	**$(105,000)**	
Loss on disposal of Record Phonograph, including provision for losses during phase-out period, $600,000, and estimated gain on sale of assets, $350,000, net of applicable income taxes of $75,000	**$(175,000)**	(280,000)
Net income		$1,120,000

If the estimated amounts of any of the items later prove to be incorrect, the correction should be reported in the later period when the estimate is determined to be incorrect. Prior periods should not be restated.

Net Gain. To illustrate recognition of a realized gain and deferral of an unrealized gain in the same discontinued operation, assume that Heartland Ltd. expects to sell its Record Phonograph Division on May 1, 1995 at a gain of $350,000. In addition, from October 1,1994 to December 31, 1994, it realizes a gain of $200,000 on operations for this discontinued operation and expects to earn an additional profit $100,000 on this operation from January 1, 1995 to May 1, 1995. The computation of the net gain or loss on disposal is shown at the top of page 159.

When a net gain on disposal is expected, the gain should be analysed and classified into realized and unrealized amounts. In this situation, $200,000 of realized gain is recognized in 1994 during October 1 to December 31 operations

Realized gain on operations October 1–December 31, 1994	$200,000
Expected gain on operations January 1–May 1, 1995	100,000
Expected gain on sale of assets on May 1, 1995	350,000
Net gain on disposal	$650,000

and $450,000 ($100,000 + $350,000) of unrealized gain is deferred to 1995. Assuming that the Record Phonograph Division, as before, suffers a loss of $150,000 from operations between January 1 and October 1, 1994, the discontinued operations section of the income statements for 1994 and 1995 would appear as follows.

1994		
Discontinued operations		
Loss from operations of Record Phonograph, less applicable income taxes of $45,000	$(105,000)	
Gain on disposal of Record Phonograph, Less applicable income taxes of $60,000	140,000	35,000

1995	
Discontinued operations	
Gain on disposal of Record Phonograph, less applicable income taxes of $135,000	$315,000

If a net unrealized loss of $150,000 has been expected during the 1995 portion of the extended phase-out period, instead of the $450,000 unrealized gain noted above, a net realized gain on disposal of $50,000 ($200,000−$150,000) before income taxes would be realized in 1994.

Summary

All realized and estimated unrealized gains and losses related to the extended phase-out period are netted as one "event" subsequent to the measurement date. Applying conservatism, if the net amount is a loss, the loss on disposal is recognized in the period of the measurement date. If the net amount is a gain, the gain in part or in full is recognized in the period of the measurement date and the estimated unrealized gain is deferred until the period of realization. Specific treatment is illustrated in the following section.

EXTENDED PHASE-OUT: ADDITIONAL EXAMPLES

As indicated in the preceding discussion, determining the amount to report as the gain or loss on disposal of the segment when the phase-out period extends over two reporting periods can be difficult. Provided in the schedule on page 160 are some additional cases to help you understand how the gain or loss on disposal of a segment of a business is reported for an extended phase-out period. We will use the same measurement and disposal dates as in the previous situations. All situations are reported on a pretax basis.

In Case 2, all three components related to the gain (loss) on disposal were losses; therefore, a ***net loss of $1,400,000 is reported at the measurement date.***

In Case 3, the loss of $600,000 on the sale of the segment assets is greater than the realized $100,000 and expected $400,000 income from operations; therefore, a ***net loss of $100,000 is reported at the measurement date.***

In Case 4, the gain of $900,000 on the sale of the segment assets is greater than the realized $500,000 and expected $300,000 losses from operations; therefore, a ***net gain of $100,000 is reported at the disposal date.***

In Case 5, both components of operations report income and a gain is expected on the sale of the segment assets. As a result, the ***realized income from operations of $400,000 can be reported at the date of measurement*** because there are no realized or estimated losses. ***The remaining estimated gain of $550,000 ($300,000 + $250,000) is deferred and recognized at the disposal date.***

DISPOSALS OF SEGMENTS INVOLVING EXTENDED PHASE-OUT OF DISCONTINUED OPERATIONS

	Realized Income (Loss) on Operations October 1, 1994–December 31, 1994	Expected Income (Loss) on Operations January 1, 1995–May 1, 1995	Expected Gain (Loss) on Sale of Assets	Gain (Loss) on Disposal of Segment	
Case 1	$ (400,000)	$ (200,000)	$350,000	1994	$ (250,000)
				1995	0)
Case 2	(300,000)	(600,000)	(500,000)	1994	$(1,400,000)
				1995	0)
Case 3	100,000	400,000	(600,000)	1994	$ (100,000)
				1995	0)
Case 4	(500,000)	(300,000)	900,000	1994	0)
				1995	$ 100,000)
Case 5	400,000	300,000	250,000	1994	$ 400,000)
				1995	$ 550,000)
Case 6	600,000	(200,000)	(300,000)	1994	$ 100,000)
				1995	0)
Case 7	400,000	(300,000)	350,000	1994	$ 400,000)
				1995	$ 50,000)
Case 8	400,000	(350,000)	300,000	1994	$ 350,000)
				1995	0)

In Case 6, the realized income from operations of $600,000 exceeds the estimated losses from operations ($200,000) and sale ($300,000). As a result, a ***realized gain of $100,000 is reported at the end of 1994, after the gain is realized.***

In Case 7, the net gain on disposal is expected to be $450,000, of which $400,000 is realized and $50,000 is unrealized. ***The realized $400,000 is recognized in 1994 and the net unrealized gain of $50,000*** (the net of a $300,000 expected loss from operations in 1995 and a $350,000 expected gain from disposal in 1995) ***is recognized in 1995.***

In Case 8, the net gain on disposal is expected to be $350,000, all of which is realized and, therefore, recognized in 1994. ***The $400,000 of realized income from operations is reduced by the net expected unrealized loss of $50,000 from 1995*** (the expected loss from operations of $350,000 less the expected gain on sale of $300,000).

DISCLOSURE REQUIREMENTS

Amounts of income taxes applicable to the results of discontinued operations and the gain or loss from disposal of the segment should be disclosed on the face of the income statement or related notes. Revenues applicable to the discontinued operations for the reporting period should be separately disclosed in the related notes.

In addition to the amounts that should be reported in the financial statements, the notes to the financial statements for the period encompassing the measurement date should disclose:

1. The identity of the segment of the business that has been or will be discontinued.
2. The measurement date.
3. Either the disposal date or the period expected to be required for disposal.
4. The expected (or actual) manner of disposition.
5. A description and the carrying value of the remaining assets and liabilities of the segment at the balance sheet date.

An example of the income statement and the note disclosure taken from the annual report of NOVA Corporation is shown on page 161.

Note that companies frequently segregate the assets and liabilities of the segment of the balance sheet into net current and net noncurrent amounts and identify these elements as related to discontinued operations.

As previously stated, if the estimates of income or losses from operations during the phase-out period and of gains or losses on the sale of assets prove incorrect, the correction should be reported in the period when the estimate is determined to be incorrect; prior periods are not restated.

NOVA Corporation of Alberta

Net Income (Loss) from Continuing Operations Before Income Taxes		$(707,000,000)
Income Taxes (Note 17)		78,000,000
Net Income (Loss) from Continuing Operations		(629,000,000)
Discontinued Operation (Note 6)		
Loss from operations	**(35,000,000)**	
Loss on disposal	**(259,000,000)**	**(294,000,000)**
Net Income (Loss)		**$(923,000,000)**

Note 6. Discontinued Operation (millions of dollars)

Effective June 1, 1991, NOVA accounted for its 43% interest in Husky Oil Ltd. ("Husky") as an asset held for sale and accordingly no longer included its share of Husky's earnings or losses in its net income. NOVA's share of earnings or losses from Husky prior to this date has been presented as a discontinued operation. On December 31, 1991, NOVA completed the sale of its interest in Husky for proceeds of $325 million which were used to reduce non-cost-of-service debt. Details of the loss from discontinued operation, including an allocation of interest based on the estimated debt component of the net investment in Husky, are as shown in the chart below:

Year Ended December 31, 1991

NOVA's share of Husky's loss	$ (14,000,000)
Allocation of interest expense	(35,000,000)
Income tax recovery	14,000,000
Loss from operations	(35,000,000)
Loss on disposal of discontinued operation (net of income tax recovery of $30 million)	(259,000,000)
Discontinued operation	$(294,000,000)

Note: All **asterisked** Questions, Cases, Exercises, and Problems relate to material covered in the appendix to each chapter.

QUESTIONS

1. What is the importance of the income statement? What are its major limitations?

2. Why should caution be exercised in the use of the net income figure derived in an income statement? What are the objectives of application of generally accepted accounting principles to the income statement?

3. An article in a prominent magazine noted that if a film company had written off film costs in the first quarter as quickly as some of its competitors, it would have had a loss instead of a profit. A financial analyst noted, therefore, that the company's quality of earnings was low. What does the term "quality of earnings" mean?

4. What is the difference between the capital maintenance approach to income measurement and the transaction approach? Is the final income figure the same under both approaches?

5. What is the major distinction (a) between revenues and gains and (b) between expenses and losses?

6. What are the advantages and disadvantages of the single-step income statement?

7. What are the advantages and disadvantages of a combined statement of income and retained earnings? What is the basis for distinguishing between operating and nonoperating items?

8. Distinguish between the all-inclusive income statement and the current operating performance income statement. According to present generally accepted accounting principles, what form is recommended? Explain.
9. What is the significance of the materiality of a nonrecurring item in deciding the appropriate placement of it in the statement of retained earnings or in the income statement? Explain.
10. How should adjustments to prior years' income be reported in the financial statements? What transactions or events would result in an adjustment to income reported for prior years?
11. Discuss the appropriate treatment in the financial statements of each of the following:
    (a) An amount of $93,000 realized in excess of the cash surrender value of an insurance policy on the life of one of the founders of the company who died during the year.
    (b) A profit-sharing bonus to employees computed as a percentage of net income.
    (c) Additional depreciation on factory machinery because of an error in computing depreciation for the previous year.
    (d) Rent received from subletting a portion of the office space.
    (e) A patent infringement suit, brought two years ago against the company by another company, was settled this year by a cash payment of $685,800.
    (f) A reduction in the Allowance for Doubtful Accounts balance because the account appears to be considerably in excess of the probable loss from uncollectible receivables.
12. Indicate where the following items would ordinarily appear on the financial statements of Wabonnsee Limited for the year 1994:
    (a) The service life of certain equipment was changed from eight to five years. If a five-year life had been used previously, additional depreciation of $362,000 would have been charged in previous years.
    (b) In 1994, a flood destroyed a warehouse that had a book value of $1,475,000. Floods are rare in this locality.
    (c) In 1994, the company wrote off $1 million of inventory that was considered obsolete.
    (d) An income tax refund related to the 1991 tax year was received.
    (e) In 1991, a supply warehouse with an expected useful life of seven years was erroneously expensed.
    (f) Wabonnsee Limited changed its depreciation method from straight-line to double-declining on machinery in 1994. The cumulative effect of the change is $867,000 (net of tax). Assume that the change was not due to changed circumstances, experience, or new information.
13. Give the section of a multiple-step income statement in which each of the following is shown:
    (a) Loss on inventory write-down.
    (b) Loss from a strike.
    (c) Bad debt expense.
    (d) Loss from operations of a segment of the business that was disposed of.
    (e) Gain on sale of machinery.
    (f) Interest revenue.
    (g) Depreciation expense.
    (h) Material write-offs of notes receivable.
14. Larry Graham Land Development Limited purchased land for $70,000 and spent $30,000 developing it. It then sold the land for $150,000. Lorraine Wilcox Manufacturing purchased land for a future plant site for $100,000. Because of a change in plans, Wilcox later sold the land for $150,000. Should these two companies report the land sales, both at gains of $50,000, in a similar manner?
15. You run into Jerry Journal at a party and begin discussing financial statements. Jerry says, "I prefer the single-step income statement because the multiple-step format generally overstates income." How will you respond to Jerry?
16. Howat Corporation has eight expense accounts in its general ledger that could be classified as selling expenses. Should Howat report these eight expenses separately in its income statement or simply report one total amount for selling expenses?
17. Bell Investments reported an unusual gain from the sale of certain assets in its 1994 income statement. How does intraperiod tax allocation affect the reporting of this unusual gain?
18. What effect does intraperiod tax allocation have on reported net income?
19. Diet Right Co. Ltd. computes earnings per share as follows:

$$\frac{\text{Net Income}}{\text{Common Shares Outstanding at Year-End}}$$

    Diet Right has a simple capital structure. What are the possible errors that the company may have made in the computation? Explain.
20. Steeples Corporation reported 1993 earnings per share of $7.21. In 1994, Steeples reported earnings per share as follows:

On income before extraordinary item	$6.40
On extraordinary item	1.88
On net income	$8.28

    Is the increase in earnings per share from $7.21 to $8.28 a favourable trend?
21. What is meant by "tax allocation within a period"? What is the justification for such a practice?

22. When does tax allocation within a period become necessary? How should this allocation be handled?

23. During 1994, Ben Alschuler Company Ltd. earns income of $978,000 before income taxes and realizes a gain of $421,800 on a government-forced expropriation sale of a division plant facility. The income is subject to income taxation at the rate of 34%; the gain on the sale of the plant is taxed at 30%. The gain satisfies the criteria for an extraordinary item. Illustrate an appropriate presentation of these items in the income statement.

24. On January 30, 1993, a suit was filed against Nilo Corporation. On August 6, 1994, Nilo Corporation agreed to settle the action and pay $810,000 in damages to certain current and former employees. How should this settlement be reported in the 1994 financial statements? Discuss.

25. Scott Paper Company decided to close two small pulp mills in Coquitlam, BC. Would these closings be reported in a separate section entitled Discontinued Operations after Income from Continuing Operations? Discuss.

26. What major types of items are reported in the retained earnings statement?

27. The controller for Wil Snyder Limited is discussing the possibility of presenting a combined statement of income and retained earnings for the current year. Indicate a possible advantage and disadvantage of the presentation format.

28. Generally accepted accounting principles usually require the use of accrual accounting to "fairly present" income. If the cash receipts and disbursements method of accounting could "clearly reflect" taxable income, why does this method not usually also "fairly present" income?

29. State some of the more serious problems encountered in seeking to achieve the ideal measurement of periodic net income. Explain what accountants do as a practical alternative.

30. What is meant by the terms "components," "elements," and "items" as they relate to the income statement? Why might items have to be disclosed in the income statement?

*31. How are the measurement and disposal dates defined for the disposal of a segment of a business?

*32. How are gains and losses on disposal of a segment of a business determined?

*33. How should the disposal of a segment of a business be disclosed in the income statement?

CASES

C4-1 **(IDENTIFICATION OF INCOME STATEMENT DEFICIENCIES)** Beatrice Holland Corporation was incorporated and began business on January 1, 1994. It has been successful and now requires a bank loan for additional working capital to finance expansion. The bank has requested an audited income statement for the year 1994. The accountant for Beatrice Holland provides you with the following income statement that the company plans to submit to the bank.

Income Statement

Sales		$760,000
Dividends		32,300
Gain on recovery of insurance proceeds from flood loss (extraordinary)		38,500
		$830,800
Less:		
Selling expenses	$101,100	
Cost of goods sold	510,000	
Advertising expense	13,700	
Loss on obsolescence of inventories	34,000	
Loss on disposal of discontinued operations	48,600	
Administrative expense	73,400	780,800
Income before income taxes		$ 50,000
Income taxes		20,000
Net income		$ 30,000

Instructions

Indicate the deficiencies in the preceding income statement. Assume that the corporation desires a multiple-step income statement.

C4-2 **(ALL-INCLUSIVE VS. CURRENT OPERATING)** Information concerning the operations of a corporation can be presented in an income statement or in a combined statement of income and retained earnings. Income statements could be prepared on either a current operating performance basis or an all-inclusive basis. Proponents of the two types of income statements do not agree on the proper treatment of material nonrecurring and/or unusual charges and credits.

Instructions

(a) Define the terms "current operating performance" and "all-inclusive" as used above.

(b) Explain the differences in content and organization of a current operating performance income statement and an all-inclusive income statement. Include a discussion of the proper treatment of material nonrecurring and/or unusual charges and credits.

(c) Give the principal arguments for the use of each of the three statements: all-inclusive income statement, current operating performance income statement, and a combined statement of income and retained earnings.

(d) What basis is used for preparing the income statement in Canadian practice and how does it differ from the current operating basis and the all-inclusive basis?

(AICPA adapted)

C4-3 **(EXTRAORDINARY ITEMS)** Henry Smits, vice-president of finance for Vanessa Garand Ltd., has recently been asked to discuss with the company's division controllers the proper accounting for extraordinary items. Smits prepared the factual situations presented below as a basis for discussion:

1. An earthquake destroys one of the oil refineries owned by a large multinational oil company. Earthquakes are rare in this geographical location.

2. A publicly held company has incurred a substantial loss in the unsuccessful registration of a bond issue.

3. A large portion of a cigarette manufacturer's tobacco crops are destroyed by a hailstorm. Severe damage from hailstorms is rare in this locality and for the company as a whole.

4. A large diversified company sells a block of shares from its portfolio of securities acquired for investment purposes.

5. A company sells a block of common shares of a publicly traded company. The block of shares, which represents less than 10% of the publicly held company, is the only security investment the company has ever owned.

6. A company that operates a chain of warehouses sells the excess land surrounding one of its warehouses. When the company buys property to establish a new warehouse, it usually buys more land than it expects to use for the warehouse, with the expectation that the land will appreciate in value. Twice during the past five years, the company had sold excess land.

7. A textile manufacturer with only one plant moves to another location and sustains relocation costs of $400,000.

8. A company experiences a material loss in the repurchase of a large bond issue that has been outstanding for three years. The company regularly repurchases bonds of this nature.

9. A railway experiences an unusual flood loss to part of its track system. Flood losses normally occur every three or four years.

10. A machine tool company sells the only land it owns. The land was acquired 10 years ago for future expansion, but the company abandoned all plans for expansion and decided to hold the land for appreciation.

Instructions

Determine whether the foregoing items should be classified as extraordinary items. Present a rationale for your position.

(INCOME REPORTING ITEMS) Russell Franques Limited is a real estate firm that derives approximately 30% of its income from the Gary Logan Division, which manages apartment complexes. As auditor for Russell Franques Limited, you recently overheard the following discussion between that company's controller and financial vice-president. **C4-4**

Vice-President: If we sell the Gary Logan Division, it seems ridiculous to segregate the results of the sale in the income statement. Separate categories tend to be absurd and confusing to the shareholders. I believe that we should simply report the gain on the sale as other revenue or expense, without detail.

Controller: Professional pronouncements require that we disclose this information separately in the income statement. If a sale of this type is considered unusual, infrequent, and not dependent on management decisions, it must be reported as an extraordinary item. Otherwise, it should be reported in a separate section of the income statement labelled Discontinued Operations, which is shown between the income from continuing operations and extraordinary items.

Vice-President: What about the walkout we had last month when our employees were upset about their commission income? Would this situation not also require separate disclosure, perhaps as an extraordinary item?

Controller: I'm not sure whether this item would be reported as extraordinary or not.

Vice-President: Oh well, it doesn't make any difference because the net effect of all these items is immaterial, so no disclosure is necessary.

Instructions

(a) On the basis of the foregoing discussion, answer the following questions: Who is correct about how to handle the sale? What would be in the income statement presentation for the sale of the Gary Logan Division?

(b) How should the walkout by the employees be reported?

(c) What do you think about the vice-president's observation on materiality?

(d) What are the earnings-per-share implications of these topics?

(IDENTIFICATION OF EXTRAORDINARY ITEMS) Eatery Limited is a major manufacturer of food products that are sold in grocery and convenience stores throughout Canada. The company's name is well known and respected because its products have been marketed nationally for over 50 years. **C4-5**

In April 1994, the company was forced to recall one of its major products. A total of 35 people were treated for severe intestinal pain and three eventually died from complications. All of these people had consumed Eatery's product.

The product causing the problem was traced to one specific lot. Eatery keeps samples from all lots of foodstuffs. After thorough testing, Eatery and the legal authorities confirmed that the product had been tampered with after it left the company's plant and was no longer under the company's control.

All of this product was recalled from the market—the only time such an action had ever been required. Anyone who still had this product in their homes, even though it was not from the affected lot, was asked to return the product for credit and refund. A media campaign was designed and implemented by the company to explain what had happened and what the company was doing to minimize any chance of recurrence. Eatery decided to continue the product with the same trade name and same wholesale price. However, the packaging was redesigned completely to be tamper-resistant and safety-sealed, which required the purchase and installation of new equipment.

The corporate accounting staff recommended that the costs associated with the tampered product be treated as an extraordinary charge on the 1994 financial statements. Corporate accounting was asked to identify the various costs that could be associated with the tampered product and related recall. These costs ($000 omitted) are as follows.

1.	Credits and refunds to stores and consumers	$30,000
2.	Insurance to cover lost sales and costs for possible future recalls	5,000
3.	Transportation costs and off-site warehousing of returned product	1,000
4.	Future security measures for other Eatery products	4,000
5.	Testing of returned product and inventory	700
6.	Destroying returned product and inventory	2,400
7.	Public relations program to re-establish brand credibility	4,200
8.	Communication program to inform customers, answer inquiries, prepare press releases, etc.	1,600
9.	Higher cost arising from new packaging	700
10.	Investigation of possible involvement of employees, former employees, competitors, etc.	500
11.	Packaging redesign and testing	2,000
12.	Purchase and installation of new packaging equipment	6,000
13.	Legal costs for defence against liability suits	600
14.	Lost sales revenue due to recall	32,000

Eatery's estimated earnings before income taxes and before consideration of any of the above items for the year ending December 31, 1994 are $230,000,000.

Instructions

(a) Eatery Limited plans to recognize the costs associated with the product tampering and recall as an extraordinary charge.

1. Explain why Eatery could classify this occurrence as an extraordinary charge.

2. Describe the placement and terminology used to present the extraordinary charge in the 1994 income statement.

(b) Refer to the 14 costs identified by the corporate accounting staff of Eatery Limited.

1. Identify the cost items, by number, that should be included in the extraordinary charge for 1994.

2. For any item that is not included in the extraordinary charge, explain why it would not be included and how it would be reported in 1994 financial statements.

(CMA adapted)

(IDENTIFICATION OF INCOME STATEMENT WEAKNESSES) The following financial statement was prepared by employees of Ward Limited. C4-6

Ward Limited
Statement of Income and Retained Earnings
Year Ended December 31, 1994

Revenues	
Gross sales, including sales taxes	$1,044,300
Less returns, allowances, and cash discounts	56,200
Net sales	$ 988,100
Dividends, interest, and purchase discounts	30,250
Recoveries of accounts written off in prior years	13,850
Total revenues	$1,032,200
Costs and expenses	
Cost of goods sold, including sales taxes	$ 425,900
Salaries and related payroll expenses	60,500
Rent	19,100
Freight-in and freight-out	3,400
Bad debts expense	24,000
Addition to reserve for possible inventory losses	3,800
Total costs and expenses	$ 536,700
Income before extraordinary items	$ 495,500
Extraordinary items	
Loss on discontinued styles (Note l)	$ 37,000
Loss on sale of marketable securities (Note 2)	39,050
Loss on sale of warehouse (Note 3)	86,350
Retroactive settlement of income taxes for 1991 and 1992 (Note 4)	34,500
Total extraordinary items	$ 196,900
Net income	$ 298,600
Retained earnings at beginning of year	310,700
Total	$ 609,300
Less: Income taxes	$ 113,468
Cash dividends on common shares	21,900
Total	$ 135,368
Retained earnings at end of year	$ 473,932
Net income per share	$ 1.99

Notes to the Statement of Income and Retained Earnings

1. New styles and rapidly changing consumer preferences resulted in a $37,000 loss on the disposal of discontinued styles and related accessories.
2. The corporation sold an investment in marketable securities at a loss of $39,050. The corporation normally sells securities of this nature.
3. The corporation sold one of its warehouses at an $86,350 loss.
4. The corporation was charged $34,500 retroactively for additional income taxes resulting from a settlement in 1994. Of this amount, $17,000 was applicable to 1992 and the balance was applicable to 1991. Litigation of this nature is recurring for this company.

Instructions

Identify and discuss the weaknesses in classification and disclosure in this single-step statement of income and retained earnings. You should explain why these treatments are weaknesses and what the appropriate presentation of the items is in accordance with professional pronouncements.

C4-7 (CLASSIFICATION OF INCOME STATEMENT ITEMS) As the audit partner for Helpum and Keepem, you are in charge of reviewing the classification of the following items that have occurred during the current year:

1. A merchandising company incorrectly overstated its ending inventory two years ago by a material amount. Inventory for all other periods was correctly computed.
2. An automobile dealer sells for $123,000 an extremely rare 1926 Type 37 Bugatti, which it purchased for $18,000 10 years ago. The Bugatti is the only such display item the dealer owns.
3. A drilling company during the current year extended the estimated useful life of certain drilling equipment from 9 to 15 years. As a result, depreciation for the current year was materially lowered.
4. A retail outlet changed its computation for bad debts expense from 1% to ½ of 1% of sales because of changes in its clientele.
5. A mining concern sells a foreign subsidiary engaged in uranium mining, although it (the seller) continues to engage in uranium mining in other countries.
6. A steel company changes from straight-line depreciation to accelerated depreciation in accounting for its plant assets.
7. A construction company, at great expense, prepares a major proposal for a government loan. The loan is not approved.
8. A water pump manufacturer has suffered big losses resulting from a strike by its employees early in the year.
9. Depreciation for a prior period was incorrectly understated by $900,000. The error was discovered in the current year.
10. A large cattle rancher suffered a major loss because the government required that all cattle in the province be killed to halt the spread of a rare disease. Such a situation has not occurred in the province for 20 years.

Instructions

From the foregoing information, indicate in what section of the income statement or retained earnings statement these items should be classified. Provide a brief explanation of your position.

C4-8 (CAPITAL MAINTENANCE VS. TRANSACTION APPROACH) In early 1979, the Kamal Said Company Ltd. was formed when it issued 10,000 common shares at $20 per share. A few years later, 3,000 additional shares were issued at $35 per share. No other common share transactions occurred until the company was liquidated in 1994. At that time, corporate assets were sold for $1,150,000 and $100,000 of corporate liabilities were paid off. The remaining cash was distributed to shareholders. During the corporation's life, it paid total dividends of $200,000.

Instructions

(a) Discuss the two approaches to calculating income.

(b) If only the facts given above are available, which approach must be used to compute income?

(c) Compute the income of Kamal Said Company Ltd. over its 15-year life.

(DISCONTINUED OPERATIONS) You're the engagement partner on a multidivisional, calendar year-end client with annual sales of $80 million. The company primarily sells electronic transistors to small customers and has one division that deals in sonar devices for naval ships. The Sonar Division has approximately $15 million in sales. *C4-9

It is an evening in February 1994, and the audit work is complete. You are working in the client's office on the report, when you overhear a conversation between the financial vice-president, the treasurer, and the controller. They are discussing the sale of the Sonar Division, expected to take place in June of this year, and the related reporting problems.

The vice-president thinks no segregation of the sale is necessary in the income statement because separate categories tend to be abused and to confuse the shareholders. The treasurer disagrees. He feels that if an item is unusual or infrequent, it should be classified as an extraordinary item, including the sale of the Sonar Division. The controller says an item should be both infrequent and unusual to be extraordinary. He feels that the sale of the Sonar Division should be shown separately, but not as an extraordinary item.

The sale is not new to you because you have read about it in the minutes of the December 16, 1993 board of directors meeting. The minutes indicated plans to sell the sonar plant and equipment by June 30, 1994 to its major competitor, who seems interested. The board estimates that net income and sales will remain constant until the sale, on which the company expects a $700,000 profit.

You also hear the controller disagree with the vice-president that the results of the strike last year and the sale of the old transistor ovens, formerly used in manufacturing, would also be extraordinary items. In addition, the treasurer thinks the government regulation issued last month, which made much of their inventory of raw material useless, should be considered extraordinary. The regulations set beta emission standards at levels lower than those in the raw materials supply, and there is no alternative use for the materials. Finally, the controller claims that the discussion is academic. Since the net effect of all three items is immaterial, no disclosure is required.

Instructions

(a) Does the Sonar Division qualify as a segment of a business in more than one way? If so, why?

(b) Does the Sonar Division qualify as a discontinued operation? Why?

(c) Do the minutes indicate that a formal plan has been established? If not, why?

(d) When should the gain be recognized? What if a loss was anticipated?

(e) Who is correct about reporting the sale? What would the income statement presentation be for the next fiscal year?

(f) Who is right about whether the strike, the sale of fixed assets, and the imposition of a new government regulation constitute extraordinary items?

(g) What do you think about the controller's observation on materiality?

(h) What facts can you give the group about the earnings-per-share ramifications of these topics?

(INFORMATION IN ANNUAL REPORT: ETHICAL DILEMMA) In the financial highlights section of its annual report, Camel Transport Limited declares that its earnings have increased by 10% using an earnings number that includes but gives no hint of a large, unusual, nonrecurring gain that was not determined by management. The financial statements, by contrast, have correctly highlighted and classified the extraordinary items below the operating income. A shareholder who has read the annual report closely asks the chief accountant, Adam Goodfellow, to explain this apparent discrepancy, but Ethan Snake, president of Camel Transport, suggests evading the question by saying that the highlights section is not controlled by GAAP, and anyway it is only for highlights and not details such as extraordinary items. C4-10

Instructions

(a) Is Ethan Snake correct about the highlights section not being controlled by GAAP? Is there an ethical issue involved in this discrepancy?

(b) Who might be affected by this presentation?

(c) What should Adam Goodfellow do?

EXERCISES

E4-1 **(COMPUTATION OF NET INCOME)** Presented below are changes in the account balances of Cajun Furniture Co. Ltd. during the current year, except for retained earnings.

	Increase (Decrease)		Increase (Decrease)
Cash	$ 79,000	Accounts payable	$ (28,000)
Accounts receivable (net)	41,000	Bonds payable	82,000
Inventory	127,000	Common shares	125,000
Investments	(47,000)	Contributed surplus	13,000

Instructions

Compute the net income for the current year, assuming that there were no entries in the retained earnings account except for a dividend declaration of $19,000 which was paid in the current year.

E4-2 **(CAPITAL MAINTENANCE APPROACH)** Presented below is selected information pertaining to the Cathy Graham Company Ltd.:

Cash balance January 1, 1994	$ 13,000
Accounts receivable January 1, 1994	19,000
Collections from customers in 1994	210,000
Capital account balance January 1, 1994	48,000
Total assets January 1, 1994	85,000
Cash investment added July 1, 1994	5,000
Total assets December 31, 1994	103,000
Cash balance December 31, 1994	16,000
Accounts receivable December 31, 1994	36,000
Merchandise taken for personal use during 1994	11,000
Total liabilities December 31, 1994	39,000

Instructions

Compute the net income for 1994.

(INCOME STATEMENT ITEMS) Following are certain account balances of Maritime Products Limited. **E4-3**

Ending inventory	$ 48,000	Sales discounts	$ 21,300
Rental revenue	6,500	Selling expenses	99,400
Interest expense	12,700	Sales	405,000
Purchase allowances	10,500	Income taxes	38,500
Beginning retained earnings	114,400	Beginning inventory	35,300
Ending retained earnings	134,000	Purchases	190,000
Freight-in	10,100	Purchase discounts	17,300
Dividends revenue	71,000	Administrative expenses	82,500
Sales returns	5,800		

Instructions

From the above information, compute the following: (a) total net revenue; (b) cost of goods sold; (c) net income; (d) dividends declared during the current year.

(SINGLE-STEP INCOME STATEMENT) The financial records of Schmidt Ltd. were destroyed by fire at the end of 1994. Fortunately, the controller had kept certain statistical data related to the income statement as presented below. **E4-4**

1. The beginning merchandise inventory was $100,000 and decreased 20% during the current year.
2. Sales discounts amounted to $17,000.
3. 20,000 common shares were outstanding for the entire year.
4. Interest expense was $22,000.
5. The income tax rate was 30%.
6. Cost of goods sold amounted to $495,000.
7. Administrative expenses were 20% of cost of goods sold but only 9% of gross sales.
8. Four-fifths of the operating expenses (total of selling and administrative expenses) related to sales activities.

Instructions

From the foregoing information, prepare a single-step income statement for the year 1994.

(MULTIPLE-STEP AND SINGLE-STEP) Two accountants for the firm of Checkum and Ketchum are arguing about the merits of presenting an income statement in a multiple-step versus a single-step format. The discussion involves the following 1994 information related to Kenneth Kornylo Ltd. ($000 omitted): **E4-5**

Administrative expenses	
Officers' salaries	$ 4,900
Depreciation of office furniture and equipment	3,960
Purchase returns	5,810
Purchases	61,000
Rent revenue	17,230
Selling expenses	
Transportation-out	2,690
Sales commissions	7,980

(Continued)

Depreciation of sales equipment	6,480
Merchandise inventory, beginning inventory	15,400
Merchandise inventory, ending inventory	16,600
Sales	101,000
Transportation-in	2,780
Income taxes	12,790
Interest expense on bonds payable	1,860

Instructions

(a) Prepare a multiple-step income statement for the year 1994. There are 40,000,000 common shares outstanding for the year.

(b) Prepare a single-step income statement for the year 1994.

(c) Which one do you prefer? Discuss.

E4-6 **(MULTIPLE-STEP AND EXTRAORDINARY ITEMS)** The following balances were taken from the books of Shannon Ramage Limited on December 31, 1994:

Interest revenue	$ 86,000
Cash	61,000
Sales	1,380,000
Accounts receivable	150,000
Prepaid insurance	20,000
Sales returns and allowances	150,000
Allowance for doubtful accounts	7,000
Sales discounts	45,000
Land	100,000
Inventory 1/1/94	246,000
Equipment	200,000
Inventory 12/31/94	331,000
Building	140,000
Purchases	830,000
Accumulated depreciation—equipment	40,000
Purchases returns and allowances	125,000
Accumulated depreciation—building	28,000
Purchase discounts	59,000
Notes receivable	155,000
Selling expenses	194,000
Accounts payable	70,000
Bonds payable	100,000
Administrative and general expenses	97,000
Accrued liabilities	32,000
Interest expense	60,000
Notes payable	100,000
Loss from earthquake damage (extraordinary item)	140,000
Common shares	500,000
Retained earnings	21,000

Assume the effective income tax rate on all items is 38%.

Instructions

Prepare a multiple-step income statement; 50,000 common shares were outstanding during the year.

(MULTIPLE-STEP AND SINGLE-STEP) Presented below is a trial balance for Wiens Limited at December 31, 1994. Assume that the loss due to flood damage is an extraordinary item. E4-7

Wiens Limited
Trial Balance
Year Ended December 31, 1994

	Debits	Credits
Administrative expense	$ 15,600	
Equipment	20,000	
Cash	7,000	
Income tax expense	20,800	
Inventory	13,000	
Accounts payable		$ 7,200
Cash dividends	5,000	
Loss due to flood (net of $3,400 taxes)	5,700	
Common shares (22,000 shares)		44,000
Temporary investments	2,000	
Accrued liabilities		3,200
Accounts receivable	15,000	
Appropriation for contingencies		12,000
Notes payable		20,000
Allowance for doubtful accounts		700
Purchases	72,700	
Interest revenue		10,000
Land	9,000	
Notes receivable	17,000	
Selling expense	36,000	
Building	45,000	
Accumulated depreciation—equipment		4,000
Sales		165,000
Transportation-in	1,500	
Accumulated depreciation—building		2,800
Retained earnings		16,400
	$285,300	$285,300

The December 31, 1994, inventory is $19,500.

Instructions

(a) Prepare a multiple-step income statement.

(b) Prepare a single-step income statement.

(c) Which format do you prefer? Discuss.

(MULTIPLE-STEP AND SINGLE-STEP) The accountant of Megan James Shoe Co. Ltd. has compiled the following information from the company's records as a basis for an income statement for the year ended 12/31/94: E4-8

Rental revenues	$ 29,000
Interest on notes payable	18,000
Market appreciation on temporary investments	31,000
Merchandise purchases	449,000
Transportation-in—merchandise	37,000
Wages and salaries—sales	114,800
Materials and supplies—sales	17,600
Common shares outstanding (no. of shares)	10,000*
Income taxes	68,400
Wages and salaries—administrative	135,900
Other administrative expense	51,700
Merchandise inventory January 1, 1994	92,000
Merchandise inventory December 31, 1994	81,000
Purchase returns and allowances	11,000
Net sales	1,040,000
Depreciation on plant assets (70% selling, 30% administrative)	65,000
Dividends declared	16,000

* Remain unchanged all year.

Instructions

(a) Prepare a multiple-step income statement.

(b) Prepare a single-step income statement.

(c) Discuss the relative merits of each of the two income statements.

E4-9 **(MULTIPLE-STEP AND SINGLE-STEP)** Presented below is income statement information related to Valarie Anderson Company Limited for the year 1994:

Administrative expenses	
Officers' salaries	$ 39,000
Depreciation expense—building	28,500
Office supplies expense	9,500
Inventory (ending)	137,000
Flood damage (pretax extraordinary item)	54,000
Purchases	620,000
Sales	970,000
Transportation-in	14,000
Purchase discounts	10,000
Inventory (beginning)	120,000
Sales returns and allowances	5,000
Selling expenses	
Sales salaries	71,000
Depreciation expense—store equipment	18,000
Store supplies expense	9,000

In addition, the company has revenue of $18,000 received from dividends and expense of $9,000 on notes payable. There are 30,000 common shares outstanding for the year. The total effective tax rate on all income is 38%.

Instructions

(a) Prepare a multiple-step income statement for 1994.

(b) Prepare a single-step income statement for 1994.

(c) Discuss the relative merits of each of the two income statements.

(COMBINED STATEMENT) During 1994, David Hefner Co. Ltd. had pretax earnings of $600,000 exclusive of a realized and tax-deductible loss of $130,000 from the expropriation of properties (extraordinary item). In addition, the company discovered that depreciation expense was erroneously overstated by $80,000 in 1990. Retained earnings at January 1, 1994 before error correction was $700,000; dividends of $150,000 were declared on common shares during 1994. One hundred thousand common shares were outstanding during 1994. Assume that a 34% income tax rate applied for both 1990 and 1994. **E4-10**

Instructions

Prepare a combined statement of income and retained earnings beginning with income before taxes and extraordinary items.

(COMBINED SINGLE-STEP) The following information was taken from the records of Duncan Greene Inc. for the year 1994. Income tax applicable to income from continuing operations, $209,000; income tax applicable to loss on discontinuance of Micron Division, $28,500; income tax applicable to extraordinary gain from expropriation, $36,100; income tax applicable to extraordinary loss from a flood, $22,800. Outstanding during 1994 were 25,000 shares. **E4-11**

Extraordinary gain from expropriation	$ 95,000
Loss on discontinuance of Micron Division	75,000
Administrative expenses	240,000
Rent revenue	40,000
Extraordinary loss, flood	60,000
Cash dividends declared	125,000
Retained earnings January 1, 1994	600,000
Cost of goods sold	850,000
Selling expenses	300,000
Sales	1,900,000

Instructions

(a) Prepare a single-step income statement for 1994. Include per-share data.

(b) Prepare a combined single-step income and retained earnings statement.

(c) What are the advantages and disadvantages of the combined statement?

(MULTIPLE-STEP STATEMENT WITH RETAINED EARNINGS) Presented below is information related to Stuart Polon Corp. for the year 1994: **E4-12**

Net sales	$1,350,000
Cost of goods sold	800,000
Selling expenses	65,000
Administrative expenses	48,000
Dividend revenue	20,000
Interest revenue	7,000
Write-off of inventory due to obsolescence	80,000
Depreciation expenses omitted by accident in 1993	40,000
Casualty loss (extraordinary item) before tax	70,000
Dividends declared	105,000
Retained earnings at December 31, 1993	2,200,000

An income tax rate of 34% applies to all items.

Instructions

(a) Prepare a multiple-step income statement for 1994. Assume that 70,000 common shares are outstanding.

(b) Prepare a separate statement of retained earnings for the year ended December 31, 1994.

E4-13 (EARNINGS PER SHARE) The shareholders' equity section of Karl Neufeld Corporation appears below as of December 31, 1994:

Cumulative preferred shares, $4.00 dividend, 100,000 shares authorized, 90,000 shares outstanding		$ 4,500,000
Common shares, authorized and issued 10,000,000 shares		10,000,000
Contributed surplus		20,500,000
Retained earnings Dec. 31, 1993	$132,000,000	
Net income for 1994	34,720,000	166,720,000
		$201,720,000

Net income for 1994 reflects a tax rate of 38%. Included in the net income figure is a loss of $18,000,000 (before tax) as a result of a major casualty (extraordinary item).

Instructions

Compute earnings-per-share data as it should appear on the financial statements of Karl Neufeld Corporation.

E4-14 (CONDENSED INCOME STATEMENT) Presented below are selected ledger accounts of McClure Limited at December 31, 1994:

Cash	$ 185,000	Sales salaries	$284,000
Travel and entertainment	69,000	Telephone—sales	17,000
Merchandise inventory	535,000	Office salaries	346,000
Accounting and legal services	33,000	Utilities—office	32,000
Sales	4,375,000	Purchase returns	15,000
Insurance expense	24,000	Miscellaneous office expenses	8,000
Advances from customers	117,000	Sales returns	79,000
Advertising	54,000	Rental revenue	240,000
Purchases	2,786,000	Transportation-in	72,000
Transportation-out	93,000	Extraordinary loss (before tax)	70,000
Sales discounts	34,000	Accounts receivable	142,500
Depreciation of office equipment	48,000	Interest expense	176,000
Purchase discounts	27,000	Sales commissions	83,000
Depreciation of sales equipment	36,000	Common shares, par value to	950,000

McClure's effective tax rate on all items is 30%. A physical inventory indicates that the ending inventory is $656,000.

Instructions

Prepare a condensed 1994 income statement for McClure Limited.

E4-15 (RETAINED EARNINGS STATEMENT) Trever Dart Corporation began operations on January 1, 1991. During its first three years of operations, Dart reported net income and declared dividends as follows:

	Net Income	Dividends Declared
1991	$ 40,000	$ -0-
1992	125,000	50,000
1993	150,000	50,000

The following information relates to 1994:

Income before taxes	$240,000
Correction of error for understatement of 1992 depreciation expense (before taxes)	30,000
Retroactive (to end of 1993) decrease in income from change in inventory methods (before taxes)	40,000
Dividends declared (of this amount, $25,000 will be paid on January 15, 1995)	100,000
Effective tax rate	40%

Instructions

(a) Prepare a 1994 retained earnings statement for Trever Dart Corporation.

(b) Assume Dart appropriated retained earnings in the amount of $70,000 on December 31, 1994. After this action, what would Dart report as total retained earnings in its December 31, 1994 balance sheet?

E4-16 **(EARNINGS PER SHARE)** At December 31, 1993, Perasalo Corporation had the following shares outstanding:

Cumulative preferred shares, $10 dividend, 110,000 shares issued and outstanding	$11,000,000
Common shares, 4,000,000 shares issued and outstanding	20,000,000

During 1994, Perasalo's only share transaction was the issuance of 400,000 common shares on April 1. During 1994, the following also occurred:

Income from continuing operations before taxes	$23,620,000
Discontinued operations (loss before taxes), not an extraordinary item	3,225,000
Preferred dividends declared	1,100,000
Common dividends declared	2,200,000
Tax rate	40%

Instructions

Compute earnings-per-share data as it should appear in the 1994 income statement of Perasalo Corporation.

***E4-17** **(DISCONTINUED OPERATIONS)** Assume that Roy Mitchell Inc. decides to sell WTVB its television subsidiary in 1993. This sale qualifies for discontinued operations treatment. Pertinent data regarding the operations of the TV subsidiary are as follows:

1. Loss from operations from beginning of year to measurement date, $400,000 (net of tax).
2. Realized loss from operations from measurement date to end of 1993, $600,000 (net of tax).
3. Estimated income from end of year to disposal date of June 1, 1994, $350,000 (net of tax).
4. Estimated gain on sale of net assets on June 1, 1994, $200,000 (net of tax).

Instructions

(a) What is the gain (loss) on the disposal of the segment reported in 1993? In 1994?

(b) Prepare the Discontinued Operations section of the income statement for the year ended 1993.

(c) If the amount reported in 1993 as gain or loss from disposal of a segment by Roy Mitchell Inc. proves to be materially incorrect, when and how should the correction be reported, if at all?

(d) If the TV subsidiary had a realized income of $100,000 (net of tax) instead of a realized loss from the measurement date to the end of 1993, what should be the gain or loss on disposal of the segment reported in 1993? In 1994?

***E4-18 (DISCONTINUED OPERATIONS)** On October 5, 1992, Dave Fior Inc.'s board of directors decides to dispose of the Spic & Span Division. Fior is a real estate firm that derives approximately 25% of its income from the management of apartment complexes. The Spic & Span Division contracts to clean apartments after each tenancy expires for all Fior complexes and several clients. The board decides to dispose of the division because of unfavourable operating results.

Net income for Fior is $84,000 after tax (assume a 30% rate) for the fiscal year ended December 31, 1992. The Spic & Span Division accounts for only $4,200 (after tax) of this amount and only $700 (after tax) in the fourth quarter. Spic & Span accounts for $50,000 inrevenues, of which $8,000 are earned in the last quarter. The average number of common shares outstanding is 20,000 for the year.

Because of unfavourable results and competition, the board believes selling the business intact would be impossible. Their final decision is to complete all current contracts, the last of which expires on May 3, 1994, and then auction off the cleaning equipment on May 10, 1994. This equipment, the only asset of the division, will have a depreciated value of $25,000 at the disposal date. The board believes the sale proceeds will approximate $4,000 after the auction expenses, and estimates Spic & Span's earnings in fiscal year 1993 as $3,000 (before tax), with a loss of $3,500 (before tax) in fiscal year 1994.

Instructions

Prepare the income statement and the appropriate footnotes that relate to the Spic & Span Division for 1992. The income statement should begin with earnings from continuing operations before income taxes. Earnings-per-share computations are not required.

PROBLEMS

P4-1 (COMBINED MULTIPLE-STEP) Presented below is information related to the Cheng Co. Ltd. for 1994:

Retained earnings balance January 1, 1994	$ 880,000
Sales for the year	26,000,000
Cost of goods sold	17,000,000
Interest revenue	70,000
Selling and administrative expenses	4,900,000
Write-off of goodwill (not tax-deductible)	520,000
Income taxes for 1994 excluding discontinued operations and extraordinary items	1,180,000
Assessment for additional 1991 income taxes (normally recurring)	300,000
Gain on the sale of investments (normally recurring)	110,000
Loss due to flood damage—extraordinary item (net of tax)	210,000
Loss on the disposition of the wholesale division (net of tax)	450,000
Loss on operations of the wholesale division (net of tax)	390,000
Dividends declared on common shares	600,000
Dividends declared on preferred shares	90,000

Instructions

Prepare a combined statement of income and retained earnings. Cheng Co. Ltd. decided to discontinue its entire wholesale operations and to retain its manufacturing operations. On September 15, Cheng sold the wholesale operations to Jill Coulter & Company. During 1994, there were 300,000 common shares outstanding all year.

(COMBINED SINGLE-STEP) Presented below is the trial balance of Susan Ruttan Corporation at December 31, 1994. **P4-2**

Susan Ruttan Corporation
Trial Balance
Year Ended December 31, 1994

	Debits	Credits
Purchase discounts		$ 10,000
Cash	$ 210,100	
Accounts receivable	105,000	
Rent revenue		18,000
Retained earnings January 1, 1994		270,000
Salaries payable		18,000
Sales		1,100,000
Notes receivable	110,000	
Accounts payable		49,000
Accumulated depreciation—equipment		28,000
Sales discounts	14,500	
Sales returns	17,500	
Notes payable		70,000
Selling expenses	232,000	
Administrative expenses	99,000	
Common shares		250,000
Income tax expense	38,500	
Dividends	60,000	
Allowance for doubtful accounts		5,000
Supplies	14,000	
Freight-in	20,000	
Land	70,000	
Equipment	140,000	
Bonds payable		100,000
Gain on sale of land		30,000
Accumulated depreciation—building		19,600
Merchandise inventory	89,000	
Building	98,000	
Purchases	650,000	
Totals	$1,967,600	$1,967,600

A physical count of inventory on December 31 resulted in an inventory amount of $100,000.

Instructions

Prepare a combined single-step statement of income and retained earnings. Assume that the only changes in the retained earnings during the current year were from net income and dividends. During the entire year, 10,000 common shares were outstanding.

P4-3 **(IRREGULAR ITEMS)** Joyce Steeves Corporation has 100,000 common shares outstanding. In 1994, the company reported income from continuing operations (before taxes) of $1,210,000. Additional transactions not considered in the $1,210,000 are as follows:

1. In 1994, the company reviewed its accounts receivable and wrote off as an expense of that year $26,000 of accounts receivable that had been carried for years and appeared unlikely to be collected.

2. An internal audit discovered that amortization of intangible assets was understated by $35,000 (net of tax) in a prior period because of a calculation error. The amount was charged against retained earnings.

3. A bank required the company to sell its only investment in common shares during the year at a gain of $145,000. The gain was taxed at a rate of 40%. Assume that the transaction meets the requirements of an extraordinary item.

4. In 1994, Joyce Steeves Corporation sold equipment for $40,000. The equipment had originally cost $80,000 and had accumulated depreciation of $36,000. The gain or loss was considered ordinary.

5. The company discontinued operations of one of its subsidiaries during 1994 at a loss of $190,000 before taxes. Assume that this transaction meets the criteria for discontinued operations. The loss on operations of the discontinued subsidiary prior to the measurement date was $90,000 before taxes; the loss from disposal of the subsidiary (not an extraordinary item) was $100,000 before taxes.

6. The sum of $100,000, applicable to a breached 1990 contract, was received as the result of a lawsuit. Prior to the award, legal counsel was uncertain about the outcome of the suit and had not established a receivable.

Instructions

Prepare an income statement for the year 1994, starting with income from continuing operations before taxes. Compute earnings per share as it should be shown on the face of the income statement. (Assume a tax rate of 38% on all items, unless indicated otherwise.)

P4-4 **(IRREGULAR ITEMS)** The Daum Corporation reported income from continuing operations before taxes during 1994 of $900,000. Additional transactions occurring in 1994 but not considered in the $900,000 are as follows:

1. The corporation experienced an uninsured flood loss (extraordinary) in the amount of $60,000 during the year. The tax rate on this item was 34%.

2. At the beginning of 1992, the corporation purchased a machine for $120,000 (residual value of $30,000) that had a useful life of six years. The bookkeeper used straight-line depreciation for 1992, 1993, and 1994, but failed to deduct the residual value in computing the depreciation base.

3. Sale of a part of its portfolio of securities resulted in a loss of $75,000 (pretax).

4. When its president died, the corporation realized $110,000 from an insurance policy. The cash surrender value of this policy had been carried on the books as an investment in the amount of $46,000 (the gain was nontaxable and not judged to be extraordinary).

5. The corporation disposed of its recreational division at a loss of $115,000 before taxes. Assume that this transaction meets the criteria for discontinued operations.

6. The corporation decided to change its method of inventory pricing from average cost to the FIFO method. The effect of this change on prior years was an increase to 1992 income by $60,000 and a decrease to 1993 income by $20,000 before taxes. The FIFO method has been used for 1994. The tax rate on the retroactive adjustments was 40%.

Instructions

Prepare an income statement for the year 1994, starting with income from continuing operations before taxes and extraordinary items. Compute earnings per share as it should be shown on the face of the income statement.

There were 100,000 common shares outstanding for the year. (Assume a tax rate of 30% on all items, unless indicated otherwise.)

(COMBINED STATEMENT, MULTIPLE- AND SINGLE-STEP) The following account balances were included in the trial balance of the Entwistle Corporation at June 30, 1994: P4-5

Sales	$1,820,000	Depreciation of sales equipment	$ 4,980
Depreciation of office furniture and equipment	7,250	Bad Debt expense—selling	4,850
Sales discounts	31,150	Purchase discounts	21,580
Purchases	1,010,000	Building expense—prorated to administration	9,130
Real estate and other local taxes	7,320	Sales salaries	56,260
Freight-in	31,600	Sales commissions	97,600
Purchase returns	5,150	Miscellaneous office expenses	6,000
Sales returns	62,300	Travel expense—sales	28,930
Dividends received	38,000	Building expense—prorated to sales	6,200
Freight-out	21,400	Dividends declared on preferred shares	14,000
Bond interest expense	18,000	Miscellaneous selling expenses	4,715
Entertainment expense	14,820	Office supplies used	3,450
Income taxes	178,725	Dividends declared on common shares	35,000
Telephone and fax—sales	9,030	Telephone and fax—administration	2,820
Depreciation understatement due to error—1991 (net of tax)	17,700	Merchandise inventory July 1, 1993	250,000

The merchandise inventory at June 30, 1994 amounted to $268,100. The Unappropriated Retained Earnings account had a balance of $187,000 at June 30, 1994 before closing; the only entry in that account during the year was a debit of $41,600 to establish an Appropriation for Bond Indebtedness. There are 70,000 common shares outstanding.

Instructions

(a) Prepare a combined multiple-step statement of income and unappropriated retained earnings for the year ended June 30, 1994.

(b) Prepare a combined single-step statement of income and unappropriated retained earnings for the year ended June 30, 1994.

(COMBINED STATEMENT, MULTIPLE- AND SINGLE STEP) The president of John Rich Corporation provides you with the following selected account balances as of December 31, 1994. P4-6

	Dr.	Cr.
Sales		$2,200,000
Sales office salaries	$ 200,000	
Officers' salaries	220,000	
Building depreciation (50% of building is directly related to sales)	70,000	
Freight-out	46,000	
Cost of goods sold	1,050,000	
Dividends declared and paid	75,000	
Dividends received		45,000
Interest expense—10% bonds	55,000	
Retained earnings—1/1/94		250,000
Expropriation of foreign holdings (extraordinary item)	200,000	
Damages payable from litigation		80,000

The president informs you that the liability for damages payable from litigation arose in 1994 out of a lawsuit initiated in 1990, and the bookkeeper debited retained earnings for $80,000 in 1994. Assume that the company is continually involved in litigation of this nature. The president requests your help in constructing an income statement. She advises you that the corporation had 100,000 common shares outstanding, and was taxed at an effective rate of 35% on all income-related items.

Instructions

(a) Prepare a combined multiple-step statement of income and retained earnings.

(b) Prepare a combined single-step statement of income and retained earnings.

P4-7 **(IRREGULAR ITEMS)** Presented below is a combined single-step statement of income and retained earnings for Joan Currie Co. Ltd. for 1994.

		(000 omitted)
Net sales		$700,000
Cost and expenses		
Cost of goods sold		$500,000
Selling, general, and administrative expenses		66,000
Other, net		17,000
		$583,000
Income before income taxes		$117,000
Income taxes		44,000
Net income		$ 73,000
Retained earnings at beginning of period, as previously reported	$141,000	
Adjustment required for correction of error	(7,000)	
Retained earnings at beginning of period, as restated		134,000
Dividends on common shares		(15,000)
Retained earnings at end of period		$192,000

Additional facts are as follows:

1. "Selling, general, and administrative expenses" for 1994 included a usual but infrequently occurring charge of $10,000,000.

2. Other, Net for 1994 included an extraordinary item (loss) of $12,000,000. If the extraordinary item (loss) had not occurred, income taxes for 1994 would have been $48,500,000 instead of $44,000,000.

3. Adjustment Required for Correction of Error was the result of a change in estimate (useful life of certain assets reduced to eight years and a catch-up adjustment made).

4. Joan Currie Co. Ltd. disclosed earnings per common share for net income in a note cross-referenced to the income statement.

Instructions

Determine from these additional facts whether the presentation of the facts in the Joan Currie Co. Ltd.'s statement of income and retained earnings is appropriate. If the presentation is not appropriate, describe the appropriate presentation and discuss its theoretical rationale.

(STATEMENT OF RETAINED EARNINGS, PRIOR PERIOD ADJUSTMENT) Below is the Retained Earnings account for the year 1994 for Dana Mann Corp. (Assume that the change in depreciation method was not due to changed circumstances, experience, or new information.) P4-8

Retained earnings, January 1, 1994		$370,000
Add:		
Gain on sale of investments (net of tax)	$41,200	
Net income	87,500	
Refund on litigation with government, related to the year 1991 (net of tax)	10,800	
Recognition of income earned in 1993, but omitted from income statement in that year (net of tax)	25,400	164,900
		$534,900
Deduct:		
Loss on discontinued operations (net of tax)	$25,000	
Write-off of goodwill	50,000	
Cumulative effect on income in changing from straight-line depreciation to accelerated depreciation in 1994 (net of tax)	18,200	
Cash dividends	32,000	125,200
Retained earnings December 31, 1994		$409,700

Instructions

(a) Prepare a correct statement of retained earnings. Dana Mann Corp. normally sells investments of the type mentioned above.

(b) State where the items that do not appear in the retained earnings statement would be shown.

(COMBINED STATEMENT AND IRREGULAR ITEMS) A condensed statement of income and retained earnings of the Donna Brockman Co. Ltd. for the year ended December 31, 1994 is presented below. Also presented are three unrelated situations involving accounting changes and classification of certain items as ordinary or extraordinary. Each situation is based on the condensed statement of income and retained earnings of the Donna Brockman Co. Ltd. and requires revisions of the statement. P4-9

Donna Brockman Co. Ltd.
Condensed Statement of Income and Retained Earnings
For the Year Ended December 31, 1994

Sales	$6,000,000
Cost of goods sold	3,500,000
Gross margin	$2,500,000
Selling, general, and administrative expenses	1,800,000
Income before extraordinary item	$ 700,000
Extraordinary item	(500,000)
Net income	$ 200,000
Retained earnings, January 1	800,000
Retained earnings, December 31	$1,000,000

Situation A. During the latter part of 1994, the company discontinued its retail and apparel fabric divisions. The loss on sale of these two discontinued divisions amounted to $620,000. This amount was included as part of selling, general, and administrative expenses. The transaction met the criteria for discontinued operations.

The extraordinary item in the condensed statement of income and retained earnings for 1994 related to a loss sustained as a result of damage to the company's merchandise caused by a tornado that struck its main warehouse in Lethbridge. This natural disaster was considered an unusual and infrequent occurrence for that section of the country.

Situation B. At the end of 1994, Brockman's management decided that the estimated loss rate on uncollectible accounts receivable was too low. The loss rate used for the years 1993 and 1994 was 1.2% of total sales, and owing to an increase in the write-off of uncollectible accounts, the rate was raised to 3% of total sales. The amount recorded in bad debts expense under the heading of Selling, General, and Administrative Expenses for 1994 was $72,000 and for 1993 was $79,000.

The extraordinary item in the condensed statement of income and retained earnings of 1994 related to a loss incurred in the abandonment of outmoded equipment formerly used in the business.

Situation C. On January 1, 1992, Brockman acquired machinery at a cost of $500,000. The company adopted the double-declining balance method of depreciation for this machinery and had been recording depreciation over an estimated life of 10 years, with no residual value. At the beginning of 1994, a decision was made to adopt the straight-line method of depreciation for this machinery. The change was not due to changed circumstances, experience, or new information. Owing to an oversight, however, the double-declining balance method was used for 1994. For financial reporting purposes, depreciation was included in selling, general, and administrative expenses.

The extraordinary item in the condensed statement of income and retained earnings related to shutdown expenses incurred by the company during a major strike by its operating employees during 1994.

Instructions

For each of the three unrelated situations, prepare a revised condensed statement of income and retained earnings of the Donna Brockman Co. Ltd. Ignore income tax considerations and earnings-per-share computations.

(AICPA adapted)

P4-10 **(INCOME STATEMENT AND IRREGULAR ITEMS)** The Windsor Corporation commenced business on January 1, 1991. Recently, the corporation had several accounting problems relating to the presentation of its income statement for financial reporting purposes. You have been asked to examine the following data and information.

Windsor Corporation
Statement of Income
For the Year Ended December 31, 1994

Sales	$10,000,000
Cost of goods sold	5,900,000
Gross profit	$ 4,100,000
Selling and administrative expense	1,300,000
Income before income taxes	$ 2,800,000
Income tax (30%)	840,000
Net income	$1,960,000

1. The controller mentioned that the corporation had difficulty collecting several of its receivables. For this reason, the bad debt write-off was increased from 1% to 2% of sales. The controller estimated that if this rate had been used in past periods, an additional $80,000 worth of expense would have been charged. The bad debts expense for the current period was calculated using the new rate and was part of selling and administrative expense.

2. Common shares outstanding at the end of 1994 totalled 500,000. No shares were purchased or sold during 1994.

3. Windsor management also noted that the following items were not included in the income statement:
   (a) Inventory in the amount of $50,000 that was obsolete had not been written down.
   (b) A major casualty loss suffered by the corporation was partially uninsured and cost $80,000, net of tax (extraordinary item), and was not included in the income statement.

4. Retained earnings as of January 1, 1994 was $2,800,000. Cash dividends of $700,000 were declared and paid in 1994.

5. In January, 1994, although there had been no change in circumstances, experience, or new information, Windsor management changed its method of accounting for plant assets from the straight-line method to the accelerated method (double-declining balance). The controller has prepared a schedule indicating what depreciation expense would have been in previous periods if the double-declining balance method had been used. (The effective tax rate for 1991, 1992, and 1993 was 30%).

	Depreciation Expense Under Straight-Line	Depreciation Expense Under Double-Declining	Difference
1991	$ 75,000	$150,000	$ 75,000
1992	75,000	112,500	37,500
1993	75,000	84,375	9,375
	$225,000	$346,875	$121,875

6. In 1994, Windsor's auditors discovered that two errors were made in previous years. First, when the corporation took a physical inventory at the end of 1991, one of the count sheets was apparently lost. The ending inventory for 1991 was therefore understated by $95,000. The inventory was correctly taken in 1992, 1993, and 1994. Also, the corporation found that in 1993, it had failed to record $20,000 as an expense for sales commissions. The effective tax rate for 1991, 1992, and 1993 was 30%. The sales commissions for 1993 were included in 1994 expenses.

Instructions

Prepare (1) the income statement and (2) the statement of retained earnings for Windsor Corporation for 1994 in accordance with professional pronouncements. Do not prepare notes.

(DISCONTINUED OPERATIONS) Rick Burke Limited management formally decides to discontinue operation of its Electrical Switch Division on November 1, 1993. Rick Burke is a successful corporation with earnings in excess of $38.5 million before taxes for each of the past five years, but the Electrical Switch Division has not contributed to this profitable performance. ***P4-11**

The principal assets of this division are the land, plant, and equipment used to manufacture the switches. The land, plant, and equipment have a net book value of $56 million on November 1, 1993.

Rick Burke's management has entered into negotiations for a cash sale of the facility for $39 million. The expected date of the sale and final disposal of the segment is July 1, 1994.

Rick Burke Limited has a fiscal year ending May 31. The results of operations for the Electrical Switch Division for the 1993–1994 fiscal year and the estimated results for June 1994 are presented below. The before-tax losses after October 31, 1993 are computed without depreciation on the plant and equipment because the net book value as of November 1, 1993 is being used as a basis of negotiation for the sale.

Period	Before-Tax Income (Loss)
June 1, 1993–October 31, 1993	$(3,800,000)
November 1, 1993–May 31, 1994	$(5,900,000)
June 1–30, 1994 (estimated)	$(650,000)

The Electrical Switch Division will be accounted for as a discontinued operation on Burke's 1993–1994 fiscal year financial statements. Burke is subject to a 40% tax rate (federal and provincial income taxes) on operating income and on all gains and losses.

Instructions

(a) Explain how the Electrical Switch Division's assets would be reported on Rick Burke Limited's balance sheet as of May 31, 1994.

(b) Explain how the discontinued operation and pending sale of the Electrical Switch Division would be reported on Rick Burke Limited's income statement for the year ended May 31, 1994.

(c) Explain what information ordinarily should be disclosed in the notes to the financial statements regarding discontinued operations.

(CMA adapted)

FINANCIAL REPORTING PROBLEM

The financial statements of Moore Corporation Limited and accompanying notes, as presented in the company's 1991 annual report, are contained in Appendix 5A. Refer to Moore Corporation Limited's financial statements and notes and answer the following questions.

1. What type of income statement format does Moore Corporation Limited use? Name the possible advantages of this type of format.

2. What is Moore Corporation Limited's primary revenue source?

3. What are the gross profit to net sales ratios for the years 1990 to 1991? Is the trend of the ratios favourable or unfavourable? Explain.

4. What are Moore Corporation Limited's percentages of net income to net sales for the years 1990 to 1991? Is the trend of the percentage comparable to that of gross profit to net sales ratios in the same period? Explain.

Balance Sheet and Statement of Changes in Financial Position

CHAPTER 5

Until recently, investors generally focused on the income statement and earnings per share. They skimmed the balance sheet and all but ignored the statement of changes in financial position. However, investors have learned an important lesson from the high inflation rates in the 1980s as well as the more recent credit crunch: They may have anticipated any surprises in earnings per share if they had not overlooked these financial statements. By carefully analysing balance sheets and statements of changes in financial position, they would have obtained information about liquidity and financial flexibility, which are necessary conditions for any profitable enterprise.

Consider the following situation. A company reports good profits and its shares seem reasonably priced on the basis of its earnings, but the share price keeps dribbling downward, even as the company reports another quarter of improved earnings. Six months later, the income statement shows losses and the company's share price collapses.

Was some information hidden? In many cases the answer is yes. Declining earnings were being hidden by inflated inventory values, overstated accounts receivable, and understated liabilities. A sure sign is a deteriorating balance sheet (i.e. overstated net income in the ending retained earnings balance is counterbalanced by overstated assets and/or understated liabilities). However, just as a deteriorating balance sheet warns of trouble, improving balance sheet quality often foreshadows long-term improvements in earnings. It may be said that earnings are nothing but assumptions filtered through the balance sheet.

SECTION 1: BALANCE SHEET

USEFULNESS OF THE BALANCE SHEET

The **balance sheet**[1] provides information about the nature and amounts of investments in enterprise resources, obligations to enterprise creditors, and the owners' equity in net enterprise resources. The balance sheet contributes to financial reporting by providing a basis for (1) computing rates of return (relationship between assets and income), (2) evaluating the capital structure (relationship of liabilities and owners' equity) of the enterprise, and (3) assessing the liquidity and financial flexibility of the enterprise. In order to make certain judgements about enterprise risk[2] and assessments of future cash flows, one must analyse the balance sheet and determine enterprise liquidity and financial flexibility.

Objective 1

Identify the uses and limitations of a balance sheet.

Liquidity describes "the amount of time that is expected to elapse until an asset is realized or otherwise converted into cash or until a liability has to be paid."[3] Both short-term and long-term

[1] *Financial Reporting in Canada—1991* (Toronto: CICA, 1991) indicated that in 1990, 279 of the 300 companies surveyed used the term "balance sheet." The term "statement of financial position" is used infrequently (20 companies), although it is conceptually appealing. One company used the term "statement of condition."

[2] Risk is an expression of the unpredictability of future events, transactions, circumstances, and results of the enterprise.

[3] "Reporting Income, Cash Flows, and Financial Position of Business Enterprises," *Proposed Statement of Financial Accounting Concepts* (Stamford, CT: FASB, 1981), par. 29.

credit grantors are interested in such short-term ratios as cash or near cash to current liabilities to assess the enterprise's ability to meet current and maturing obligations. Similarly, present and prospective equity holders study the liquidity of an enterprise to assess the likelihood of continuing or increased cash dividends or the possibility of expanded operations. Generally, ***the greater the liquidity, the lower the risk of enterprise failure.***

Financial flexibility is the "ability of an enterprise to take effective actions to alter the amounts and timing of cash flows so it can respond to unexpected needs and opportunities."[4] For example, if a company becomes so loaded with debt that its sources of monies to finance expansion or to pay off maturing debt are limited or nonexistent, that company lacks financial flexibility. An enterprise with a high degree of financial flexibility is better able to survive bad times, to recover from unexpected setbacks, and to take advantage of profitable and unexpected investment opportunities. Generally, ***the greater the financial flexibility, the lower the risk of enterprise failure.***

LIMITATIONS OF THE BALANCE SHEET

As indicated in earlier chapters, the balance sheet ***does not reflect current value*** because accountants have adopted an historical cost basis in valuing and reporting assets and liabilities. When a balance sheet is prepared in accordance with generally accepted accounting principles, most assets are stated at cost; exceptions are receivables at net realizable value; marketable securities at the lower of cost and market; and some long-term investments accounted for under the equity method.

Many accountants believe that all the assets should be restated in terms of current values. There are, however, widely different opinions about the valuation method to be employed. Some contend that historical cost-based statements should be adjusted for constant dollars (general price-level changes) when inflation is significant; others believe that a current cost concept (specific price-level changes) is more useful; still others believe that a net realizable value concept or some variant should be adopted. Regardless of the method favoured, all are significantly different from the historical cost approach. Each approach has the advantage over the historical cost basis of presenting a more accurate assessment of the current value of the enterprise, although the question of whether reliable valuations can be obtained is still unresolved.

Another basic limitation of the balance sheet is that ***judgements and estimates must be used.*** The collectibility of receivables, the salability of inventory, and the useful life of long-term tangible and intangible assets are difficult to determine. Although the process of depreciating long-term assets is a generally accepted practice, the recognition of accretion and enhancement in value is generally ignored by accountants.

Because judgements and estimates used in the preparation of the balance sheet may harm or benefit particular stakeholders, the question of ethics should come into play in the accountant's decision-making process. The accountant needs to be aware of the potential impact of these judgements and estimates on stakeholder interests (i.e. the company vs. the shareholders).

In addition, the balance sheet necessarily ***omits many items that are of financial value to the business*** but cannot be measured objectively. The value of a company's human resources, such as employees, is certainly significant, but such assets are omitted because they are difficult to quantify. Other items of value not reported are customer base, managerial skills, research superiority, and reputation. Such omissions are understandable and excusable. However, many items that are mostly liabilities and could appear on the balance sheet are reported in an "off-balance-sheet" manner, if reported at all.[5] Examples of these omitted items are sales of receivables with recourse, leases, through-put arrangements, and take-or-pay contracts, which are discussed in later chapters.

---

[4] *Ibid.*, par. 25.

[5] For a discussion of various methods that businesses have devised to remove debt from the balance sheet, read "Get It Off the Balance Sheet," Richard Dieter and Arthur R. Wyatt, *Financial Executive*, vol. 48, June 1980, pp. 42, 44–48.

One of the most significant challenges facing the accounting profession is the limitation of financial statements. Financial statement users are turning increasingly to other sources to meet needs that have not been met by the information contained on current GAAP model statements. The accounting profession has been attempting to identify the informational needs of financial statement users and find ways of meeting those needs.[6]

CLASSIFICATION IN THE BALANCE SHEET

Balance sheet accounts are classified so that similar items are grouped together to arrive at significant subtotals. Furthermore, the material is arranged so that important relationships are shown. The three general classes of items included in the balance sheet are assets, liabilities, and owners' equity. Their definitions in the *CICA Handbook*[7] are shown below.

Objective 2

Identify the major classifications of the balance sheet.

Elements of the Balance Sheet

1. **Assets** are resources controlled by an enterprise as a result of past transactions or events from which future economic benefits may be obtained.
2. **Liabilities** are obligations of an enterprise arising from past transactions or events, the settlement of which may result in the transfer of assets, provision of services, or other yielding of economic benefits in the future.
3. **Equity** is the ownership interest in the assets of an entity after deducting its liabilities.

These items are then divided into subclassifications to provide readers with additional information. The following table indicates the general format of balance sheet presentation.

Balance Sheet Classifications

Assets	Liabilities and Shareholders' Equity
Current assets	Current liabilities
Long-term investments	Long-term debt
Property, plant, and equipment	Shareholders' equity
Intangible assets	Share capital
Other assets	Contributed surplus
	Retained earnings

The balance sheet may be classified in some other manner, but these are the major subdivisions and there is very little departure from them in practice. If a proprietorship or partnership is involved, the classifications within the shareholders' equity section are presented differently.

Current Assets

Current assets are cash and other assets that are expected to be converted into cash, sold, or consumed either in one year or in the operating cycle, whichever is longer. The operating cycle is the average time between the acquisition of materials and supplies and the realization of cash through sales of the product for which the materials and supplies have been acquired. The cycle operates from cash through inventory, production, and receivables, and back to cash. When there are several

[6] "The Changing Significance of Financial Statements," Thomas W. Rimerman, *Journal of Accountancy*, April 1990, pp. 79–83.

[7] *CICA Handbook* (Toronto: CICA), Section 1000.

operating cycles within one year, the one-year period is used. If the operating cycle is more than one year, the longer period is used.

Current assets are presented in the balance sheet in the order of their liquidity. The five major items found in the current section are cash, temporary investments in marketable securities, receivables, inventories, and prepayments. Cash is included at its stated value; temporary investments in marketable securities are valued at cost or the lower of cost and market; accounts receivable are stated at the estimated amount collectible; inventories generally are included at cost or the lower of cost and market; and prepaid items are valued at cost.

The above items are not considered current assets if they are not expected to be realized in one year or in the operating cycle, whichever is longer. For example, cash is excluded from the current asset section if it is restricted for purposes other than payment of current obligations or for use in current operations. Generally, the rule is that ***if an asset is to be turned into cash or is to be used to pay a current liability within a year or in the operating cycle, whichever is longer, it is classified as current.*** There are exceptions to this requirement. An investment in common shares, for example, is classified as either a current asset or a noncurrent asset, depending on management's intent. When a company has small holdings of common shares or bonds that are going to be held long term, they should not be classified as current.

Even though a current asset is well defined, certain theoretical problems develop. One problem is justifying the inclusion of prepaid expense in the current asset section. The normal justification is that if these items had not been paid in advance, they would require the use of current assets during the operating cycle. If we follow this logic to its ultimate conclusion, however, any asset purchased previously saves the use of current assets during the operating cycle and is considered current.

Another problem occurs in the current asset definition when fixed assets are consumed during the operating cycle. A literal interpretation of the accounting profession's position on this matter would indicate that an amount equal to the current depreciation and amortization charges on the noncurrent assets should be placed in the current asset section at the beginning of the year, because it will be consumed in the next operating cycle. This conceptual problem is generally ignored, which illustrates that the formal distinction made between current and noncurrent assets is somewhat arbitrary.[8]

Cash. Any restrictions on the general availability of cash or any commitments on its probable disposition must be disclosed. This may be done through notes or in the body of the balance sheet, as exemplified below.

Current assets		
Cash		
Restricted in accordance with terms of the purchase contract	$48,500	
Unrestricted—available for current use	14,928	$63,428

In this example, it was assumed that an amount of cash ($48,500) was restricted to meet an obligation due currently and, therefore, the restricted cash was included under current assets. If cash is restricted for purposes other than current obligations, it is excluded from the current assets, as shown on page 191.

Temporary Investments. The basis of valuation and any differences between cost and current market value should be included in the balance sheet presentation of temporary investments. The

[8] For an interesting discussion of the shortcomings of the current and noncurrent classification framework, see Lloyd Heath, "Financial Reporting and the Evaluation of Solvency," *Accounting Research Monograph No. 3* (New York: AICPA, 1978), pp. 43–69. The principle recommendation is that the current and noncurrent classification be abolished, and that assets and liabilities simply be listed without classification in their present order. This approach is justified on the basis that any classification scheme is arbitrary and that users of the financial statements can assemble the data in the manner they believe most appropriate.

Current assets		
Cash	$78,327	
Less cash restricted for bond redemption	45,000	$33,327
Other assets		
Cash restricted for bond redemption in accordance with the bond indenture		$45,000

generally accepted method for accounting for such investments, often referred to as marketable securities, is cost or market, whichever is lower.[9] The example below is excerpted from the annual report of Inco Limited.

Current assets	
Marketable securities—at cost (market $23,100,000)	$19,796,000

Receivables. The amount and nature of any nontrade receivables, and any amounts pledged or discounted, should be clearly stated. In addition, the anticipated loss due to uncollectibles may be separately disclosed rather than simply reporting a net figure for receivables less the related allowance. Mark's Work Wearhouse reported its receivables as follows.

Mark's Work Wearhouse Ltd.

Current Assets	
Accounts receivable (Note 2)	$10,625,000
Note 2. Accounts Receivable	
Receivable from franchise stores	$ 8,477,000
Other accounts receivable	3,465,000
	11,942,000
Allowance for doubtful accounts	(1,317,000)

Inventories. For a proper presentation of inventories, the basis of valuation (i.e. the lower of cost and market), the method of pricing (FIFO or average cost), and, for a manufacturing concern such as Repap Enterprises Inc., shown in the first box on page 192, the stages of completion of the inventories are disclosed.

Some accountants contend that, in a company that assembles a final product from both purchased and manufactured parts and also sells some of these parts, a distinction of finished goods, work in progress, and raw materials is arbitrary and misleading. They prefer a classification that indicates the source or nature of the inventory amount as shown in the second box on page 192.

Prepaid Expenses. Prepaid expenses included in current assets are expenditures already made for benefits, usually services, to be received within one year or the operating cycle, whichever is longer.[10] These items are current assets because if they had not already been paid, they would require the use of cash during the next year or operating cycle. A common example is the payment in advance for an insurance policy, which is classified as a prepaid expense at the time of the expenditure because the payment precedes the receipt of the benefit of coverage. Prepaid expenses are reported at the

[9] Special rules that apply for both short-term and long term marketable securities are discussed in Chapter 18.
[10] *Financial Reporting in Canada—1991* (Toronto: CICA, 1991) indicated that 226 of the 300 companies in 1990 reported prepaid expenses or prepayments on the balance sheet.

Repap Enterprises Inc.

Current assets	
Inventories	$224,300,000

Note 3. Significant Accounting policies

(c) Inventories

Logs, chips, and supplies are valued at the lower of cost, determined primarily on a weighted-average basis and replacement cost. Paper, pulp, and lumber are valued at the lower of cost, determined on a weighted-average basis, and net realizable value.

Note 4. Inventories

Raw materials and supplies	$107,500,000
Work in process	7,800,000
Finished goods	109,000,000
	$224,300,000

Current assets		
Inventories—at the lower of cost (determined by the FIFO method) and market		
Materials	$195,696	
Direct labour	37,300	
Manufacturing overhead	15,274	$248,270

amount of the unexpired or unconsumed cost. Other common prepaid expenses include prepaid rent, advertising, taxes, and office or operating supplies. Imperial Oil Limited, for example, listed its prepaid expenses in current assets as follows.

Imperial Oil Limited

Current assets	
Inventories of crude oil and products	$604,000,000
Materials, supplies, and prepaid expenses	178,000,000

Companies often include insurance and other prepayments for two or three years in current assets, even though part of the advance payment applies to periods beyond one year or the current operating cycle.

Current Liabilities

Current liabilities are the obligations that are reasonably expected to be liquidated either through the use of current assets or the creation of other current liabilities. This concept includes:

1. Payables resulting from the acquisition of goods and services, such as accounts payable, wages payable, and taxes payable.
2. Collections received in advance for the delivery of goods or performance of services, such as unearned rent revenue or unearned subscriptions revenue.
3. Other liabilities whose liquidation will take place within the operating cycle, such as the portion of long-term bonds to be paid in the current period or short-term obligations arising from purchase of equipment.

At times, even though a liability will be paid in the following year, it is not included in the current liability section. This occurs either when the debt is expected to be refinanced through another long-term issue,[11] or when the debt is retired out of noncurrent assets. This approach is used because liquidation does not result from the use of current assets or the creation of other current liabilities.

Current liabilities are not reported in any consistent order. The items most commonly listed first are notes payable, accounts payable, or "short-term debt"; those most commonly listed last are income taxes payable, current maturities of long-term debt, or "other current liabilities." An example of the Hudson's Bay Company 1992 current liability section is shown below.

Current liabilities	
Short-term borrowings (Note 13)	$ 416,110,000
Trade accounts payable	313,954,000
Other accounts payable and accrued expenses	318,002,000
Income taxes payable	875,000
Long-term debt due within one year (Note 13)	67,909,000
	$1,116,850,000

Current liabilities include such items as trade and nontrade notes and accounts payable, advances received from customers, and current maturities of long-term debt. Income taxes and other accrued items are usually classified separately, if material. Any secured liability, such as investments in shares held as collateral on notes payable, is fully described so that the assets providing the security can be determined.

The excess of total current assets over total current liabilities is referred to as **working capital**, sometimes called net working capital. Working capital represents the net amount of a company's relatively liquid resources; that is, it is the liquid buffer, or margin of safety, available to meet the financial demands during the operating cycle. Working capital as an amount is seldom disclosed on the balance sheet, but it is computed by bankers and other creditors as an indicator of the short-run liquidity of a company. To determine the actual liquidity and availability of working capital to meet current obligations, one must analyse the composition of the current assets and their nearness to cash.

Long-Term Investments

Long-term investments, often referred to simply as investments, normally consist of one of four types:

1. Investments in securities such as bonds, common shares, or long-term notes.
2. Investments in tangible fixed assets not currently used in operations, such as land held for speculation.
3. Investments set aside in special funds such as a sinking fund, pension fund, or plant expansion fund. The cash surrender value of life insurance is included here.
4. Investments in nonconsolidated subsidiaries or affiliated companies.

Long-term investments are to be held for many years and are not acquired with the intention of disposing of them in the near future. They are usually presented on the balance sheet just below Current Assets in a separate section called Investments. Many securities that are rightly shown among the long-term investments are readily marketable, but they should not be included as current assets if they are not held with the intention of converting them into cash in a year or in the operating cycle, whichever is longer.[12]

[11] A detailed discussion of accounting for debt expected to be refinanced is found in Chapter 13.

[12] A discussion of issues related to accounting for long-term investments is presented in Chapter 18.

Canadian Utilities Ltd. reported its investments on the balance sheet and in the notes in the following manner.

Canadian Utilities Ltd.
Balance Sheet

Investments (Note 3)		$94,185,000

Notes to financial statements

3. Investments	Ownership Interest	Amount
Equity Method:		
Operating		
ATCOR Resources Ltd.	50%	$59,953,000
Metscan, Inc.	23.4%	3,977,000
Fort Nelson Transmission Line, a joint venture	50%	8,241,000
Northland Utilities Enterprises Ltd.	33%	2,457,000
Frontec Limited	50%	2,125,000
North Warning System, a joint venture	45%	2,392,000
Under Development:		
Thames Power Limited (a Barking Project)	50%	12,725,000
		91,870,000
Other: at cost		2,315,000
		$94,185,000

Property, Plant, and Equipment and Intangible Assets

Property, plant, and equipment are properties of a durable nature used in the regular operations of the business. These assets consist of physical property such as land, buildings, machinery, furniture, tools, and wasting resources (timberland, minerals). With the exception of land, most assets are either depreciable, such as buildings, or consumable, such as timberlands.

MacMillan Bloedel Limited presented its property, plant, and equipment in its 1991 balance sheet as follows.

MacMillan Bloedel Limited

Property, plant, and equipment: (Note 4)	
Buildings and equipment	$3,068,600,000
Less: Accumulated depreciation	1,383,200,000
	1,685,400,000
Construction in progress	41,800,000
	1,727,200,000
Timber and land less accumulated depletion	203,200,000
Logging roads	12,900,000
	$1,943,300,000

Intangible assets lack physical substance and usually have a high degree of uncertainty concerning their future benefits. They include patents, copyrights, franchises, goodwill, trademarks, trade names, secret processes, and organization costs. Generally, all of these intangibles are written off (amortized) to expense over 5 to 40 years. Intangibles can represent significant economic resources, yet financial analysts often ignore them and accountants write them down or off arbitrarily when future benefits become uncertain and because valuation is difficult.

Maclean Hunter Limited reported intangible assets in its balance sheet and notes as follows.

Maclean Hunter Limited

Intangible assets (Note 8)	$377,200,000
Goodwill	295,200,000

Notes to the financial statements
Note 8. Intangible Assets

	Cost	Accumulated depreciation	Net
Cable television franchises	$312,600,000	$13,500,000	$299,100,000
Broadcast licences	43,700,000	7,000,000	36,700,000
Circulation and subscriber bases	43,900,000	15,500,000	28,400,000
Paging frequencies	7,300,000	600,000	6,700,000
Others	12,800,000	6,500,000	6,300,000
Total	$420,300,000	$43,100,000	$377,200,000

Other Assets

The items included in the Other Assets section vary widely in practice. Some of the items commonly included are deferred charges (long-term prepaid expenses), noncurrent receivables, intangible assets, assets in special funds, and advances to subsidiaries. Such a section unfortunately is too general a classification. Instead, it should be restricted to unusual items sufficiently different from assets included in specific categories. Some deferred costs such as organization costs incurred during the early life of the business are commonly classified here. Even these costs, however, are more properly placed in the intangible asset section.

Long-Term Liabilities

Long-term liabilities are obligations that are not reasonably expected to be liquidated within the normal operating cycle of the business but, instead, are payable at some date beyond that time. Bonds payable, notes payable, deferred income taxes, lease obligations, and pension obligations are the most common long-term liabilities. Generally, a great deal of supplementary disclosure is needed for this section because most long-term debt is subject to various covenants and restrictions for the protection of the lenders. Long-term liabilities that mature within the current operating cycle are classified as current liabilities if their liquidation requires the use of current assets. Generally, long-term liabilities are of three types:

1. Obligations arising from specific financing situations, such as the issuance of bonds, long-term lease obligations, and long-term notes payable.
2. Obligations arising from the ordinary operations of the enterprise, such as pension obligations and deferred income taxes.
3. Obligations extending beyond the coming year that are dependent on the occurrence or non-occurrence of one or more future events to confirm the amount payable, or the payee, or the date payable, such as service or product warranties.

The terms of all long-term liability agreements, including maturity date(s), rates of interest, nature of obligation, and any security pledged to support the debt, should be described in notes to the financial statements. An example of the financial statement and accompanying note presentation is shown below in the excerpt from The Oshawa Group Limited's 1991 financial statements.

The Oshawa Group Limited

Balance Sheet		
Long-term debt (note 4)		$25,300,000
Notes to the Financial Statements		
Note 4. Long-Term Debt		
Mortgages and loans payable	$25,500,000	
Bank indebtedness	1,000,000	
Series A Sinking Fund Debentures	5,000,000	
		31,500,000
Less current portion		6,200,000
		$25,300,000

Shareholders' Equity

The complexity of share capital agreements and the various restrictions on residual equity imposed by federal and provincial corporation laws, liability agreements, and boards of directors make the shareholders' equity section one of the most difficult to prepare and understand. The section is usually divided into three parts.

Shareholders' Equity Section

1. **Share Capital.** Proceeds received from the issue of shares.
2. **Contributed Surplus.** Miscellaneous shareholder equity items.
3. **Retained Earnings.** The corporation's undistributed earnings.

The legal basis for examples and problems presented in this book is the Canada Business Corporations Act (CBCA), which came into force on January 1, 1976. Companies may incorporate under the provincial corporation Acts, which may vary to some extent from the federal Act, although differences are becoming less significant as provinces revise their Acts. For example, prior to the CBCA, federally incorporated companies could have par value shares. Under the CBCA, the concept of par value was abolished, which meant that the entire proceeds from the sale of shares were to be credited to the appropriate share capital account. An amendment to the Ontario Business Corporations Act in 1983 included a similar provision, as do many provincial incorporation Acts. The notion of par value, however, has not disappeared from the Canadian accounting scene.[13] Because

[13] *Financial Reporting in Canada—1991* (Toronto: CICA, 1991) indicated that in 1990 a few of the Canadian companies surveyed still carried a Premium on Shares amount in their Contributed Surplus. Of the 300 companies surveyed, 21 made reference to a par value or stated value in general or as existing for at least one class of their shares. Also, the CBCA permits a restricted use of the notion of par value for reasons having to do with some particular tax issues. Par value shares are allowed under incorporation statutes of British Columbia, Newfoundland, Nova Scotia, Prince Edward Island, Quebec, and the Northwest Territories.

of this, a limited number of examples as well as cases, exercises, and problems in this book will reflect the existence of par value shares.[14] Another point is that the CBCA states that corporations are to issue shares by "classes" and "series of classes." The terms "preferred" and "common" may continue to be used and, as such, will be used throughout this book.

In reporting the share capital account, the amounts authorized, issued, and outstanding are usually disclosed. The contributed surplus is usually presented in one amount; however, breakdowns are informative if the sources of additional capital obtained are varied and material. The retained earnings section may be divided between the unappropriated amount, which is available for dividend declaration, and any amounts legally or voluntarily restricted (called appropriated retained earnings).

The ownership or shareholders' equity accounts in a corporation are considerably different from those in a partnership or proprietorship. Partners' permanent capital accounts and the balance in temporary accounts or drawing accounts are shown separately. Proprietorships ordinarily use a single capital account that summarizes all of the owner's equity transactions. Presented below are illustrations of two shareholders' equity sections.

Fletcher Challenge Canada Limited

Shareholders' equity	
Share capital (Note 9)	
Authorized	
90,000,000 Class "A" common shares without par value	
100,000,000 Class "B" preferred shares without par value	
Issued and outstanding	
60,186,021 Class "A" common shares	$338,953,000
Retained earnings	552,626,000
	$891,579,000

Canadian Occidental Petroleum Limited

Shareholders' equity	
Common shares no par value (Note 8)	
Authorized: unlimited	
Outstanding: 66,696,039	$275,590,000
Contributed surplus	14,038,000
Retained earnings	414,753,000
Cumulative foreign currency translation adjustment	(8,614,000)
Total shareholders' equity	$695,767,000

[14] Most of these examples, cases, exercises, and problems occur in later chapters, particularly in Chapters 15 and 16, where the issue is discussed in greater depth. Some instructors may choose to deal only with no-par value shares. If so, one approach would be to simply assume that all proceeds from the sale of stock are to be credited to the appropriate stock account, even when a par value is given (i.e. there would be no Premium accounts in Contributed Surplus).

CLASSIFIED BALANCE SHEET

Objective 3

Prepare a classified balance sheet using the report and account forms.

One common arrangement followed in the presentation of a classified balance sheet is called the **account form**. It lists assets by sections on the left side and liabilities and shareholders' equity by sections on the right side. The main disadvantage is the need for two facing pages. To avoid the use of facing pages, the **report form**, illustrated below, lists liabilities and shareholders' equity directly after assets on the same page (also see Moore Corporation's balance sheet in Appendix 5A).

Scientific Products, Inc.
Balance Sheet
December 31, 1994

Assets			
Current assets			
Cash		$ 42,485	
Marketable securities—cost that approximates market value		28,250	
Accounts receivable	$165,824		
Less: Allowance for doubtful accounts	1,850	163,974	
Notes receivable		23,000	
Inventories—at average cost		489,713	
Supplies on hand		9,780	
Prepaid expenses		16,252	
Total current assets			$ 773,454
Long-term investments			
Securities at cost (market value $94,000)			87,500
Property, plant, and equipment			
Land—at cost		$125,000	
Buildings—at cost	$975,800		
Less: Accumulated depreciation	341,200	634,600	
Property, plant, and equipment			759,600
Intangible assets			
Goodwill			100,000
Total assets			$1,720,554
Liabilities and Shareholders' Equity			
Current liabilities			
Notes payable to banks		$ 50,000	
Accounts payable		197,532	
Accrued interest on notes payable		500	
Accrued federal income taxes		62,520	
Accrued salaries, wages, and other expenses		9,500	
Deposits received from customers		420	
Total current liabilities			$ 320,472
Long-term debt			
12% debentures due January 1, 2005			500,000
Total liabilities			$ 820,472
Shareholders' equity			
Share capital			
Preferred, $7 cumulative			
Authorized and out-standing, 30,000 shares	$300,000		

(Continued)

Common			
Authorized, 500,000 shares, without par value; issued and outstanding, 400,000 shares	400,000	$700,000	
Contributed surplus		37,500	
Retained earnings			
Appropriated	$ 85,000		
Unappropriated	77,582	162,582	
Total shareholders' equity			900,082
Total liabilities and shareholders' equity			$1,720,554

REPORTING ADDITIONAL INFORMATION

The balance sheet is not complete simply because a listing of the assets, liabilities, and owners' equity accounts has been presented. Great importance is given to supplemental information that is completely new or is an elaboration or qualification of items in the balance sheet. Four types of information that are supplemental to account titles and amounts are normally presented in the balance sheet.

Objective 4

Identify balance sheet information requiring supplemental disclosure.

Supplemental Balance Sheet Information

1. **Contingencies.** Material events that have an uncertain outcome.
2. **Valuations and accounting policies.** Explanations of the valuation methods used or the basic assumptions made concerning inventory valuations, depreciation methods, and investments in subsidiaries, etc.
3. **Contractual situations.** Explanations of certain restrictions or covenants attached either to specific assets or, more likely, to liabilities.
4. **Post-balance sheet disclosures.** Disclosures of certain events that have occurred after the balance sheet date but before the financial statements have been issued.

Contingencies

Gain contingencies are claims or rights to receive assets or have a liability reduced, when existence is uncertain but may become valid eventually. Typical gain contingencies are:

1. Possible receipts of monies from gifts, donations, bonuses, and so on.
2. Possible refunds from the government in tax disputes.
3. Pending court cases where the probable outcome is favourable.

Accountants have adopted a conservative policy in this area. Gain contingencies are not recorded and are disclosed in notes to the financial statements only when the probabilities are high that a gain contingency will become reality. As a result, it is unusual to find information of this type in financial statements and related reports.

Loss contingencies are possible losses that may result when an existing condition or situation involving an uncertainty is resolved, when both of the following conditions are met:

1. It is *likely* that future events will confirm that an asset had been impaired or a liability incurred at the date of the financial statements.
2. The amount of loss can be *reasonably estimated.*

The **CICA Handbook** ***requires that an estimated loss from loss contingencies be accrued by a charge to expense and the recording of a liability.***[15] As indicated earlier, the establishment of a liability for service or product warranties would ordinarily meet the two conditions mentioned above and thus qualify as a loss contingency that should be accrued.

In most loss contingency cases, however, one or both of the conditions are not present. For example, assume that a company is involved in a lawsuit. The company's lawyer indicates that there is a reasonable possibility that they may lose. In such a case, there is only a *reasonable possibility* of loss rather than a *likely* one and, therefore, a liability and the related loss should not be recorded. The nature of the contingency and, where possible, the amount involved, however, should be disclosed in the notes. If a reasonable estimate of the amount is not possible, disclosure is made in general terms, describing the loss contingency and explaining that no estimated amount is determinable. Because these types of contingencies are only possibilities, they should not enter into the determination of net income.

Diversity in accounting practice exists regarding contingencies because varied interpretations are made of the words "likely" and "unlikely." As a result, the contingencies reported and disclosed vary somewhat. This area of practice requires that the accountant use professional judgement because the determination of what constitutes full and proper accounting and disclosure is very subjective.[16]

Some of the more common sources of ***loss contingencies that ordinarily will not be accrued as liabilities*** are:

1. Guarantees of other people's indebtedness.
2. Obligations of commercial banks under standby letters of credit (commitments to finance projects under certain circumstances).
3. Guarantees to repurchase receivables or any related property that has been sold or assigned.
4. Disputes over additional income taxes for prior years.
5. Pending lawsuits whose outcome is uncertain.

General risk contingencies that are inherent in business operations, such as the possibility of war, strike, uninsurable catastrophes, or a business recession, are not reported in the notes to the financial statements. The disclosure of loss contingencies is discussed in greater detail in Chapter 13.

Valuations and Accounting Policies

As indicated in subsequent chapters of this book, accountants utilize many different methods and bases in valuing assets and allocating costs. For instance, inventories can be computed under several cost flow assumptions (LIFO, average cost, FIFO); plant and equipment can be depreciated under several accepted methods of cost allocation (double-declining balance, straight line); and investments can be carried at different valuations (cost, equity, market). Sophisticated users of financial statements know of these possibilities and examine the statements closely to determine the methods used.

The *CICA Handbook* requires disclosure in the financial statements of all significant accounting policies and methods chosen from among alternatives and/or those that are peculiar to a given

---

[15] *CICA Handbook*, Section 3290.

[16] G. Richard Chaley and Heather A. Wier, "The Challenge of Contingencies; Adding Precision to Probability," *CA Magazine*, April 1985, pp. 38–41. The diversity of interpretation of the words "likely," unlikely," "not reasonably estimable," and "possible" among accountants and lawyers is well identified in this article. A solution to improve understanding by assigning a range of probabilities is suggested.

industry.[17] Disclosure is particularly useful if given under a separate heading called "Summary of Significant Accounting Policies" cross-referenced to the financial statement or as the initial note. See Appendix 5A for an example of such a summary. Further discussion of this topic is made in Chapter 25.

Contracts and Negotiations

In addition to contingencies and different methods of valuation disclosed as supplementary data to the financial statements, any contracts and negotiations of significance are disclosed in the notes to the financial statements.

It is mandatory, for example, that the essential provisions of lease contracts, pension obligations, and stock option plans be clearly stated in the notes. The analyst who examines a set of financial statements wants to know not only the amount of the liabilities, but also how the different contractual provisions of these debt obligations affect the company at present and in the future.

Many other items may have an important and significant effect on the enterprise, and this information should be disclosed. The accountant must exercise considerable judgement about whether omission of such information is misleading. "When in doubt, disclose" is an axiom to follow; it is better to disclose a little too much information than not enough.

The accountant's judgement should reflect ethical considerations because the manner of disclosing the accounting principles, methods, and other items that have important and significant effects on the enterprise may subtly represent the interests of a particular stakeholder at the expense of others. A reader, for example, may benefit from highlighting of information in comprehensive notes, while the company that does not wish to emphasize certain information may choose to provide limited, rather than comprehensive, note information.

Post-Balance Sheet Events (Subsequent Events)

Notes to the financial statements should explain any significant financial events taking place after the formal balance sheet date, but before it is finally issued.[18] These events subsequent to the balance sheet are referred to as **post-balance sheet events**, or simply **subsequent events**. The subsequent events period is time-diagrammed below.

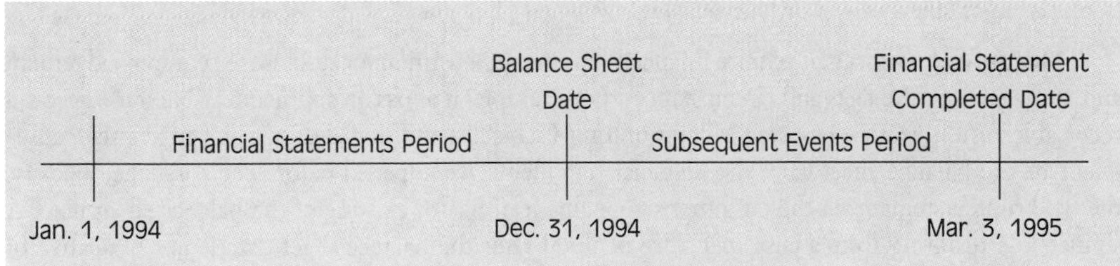

A period of several weeks, and sometimes months, may elapse after the end of the year before the financial statements are issued. Time is required to take and price the inventory, reconcile subsidiary ledgers with controlling accounts, prepare necessary adjusting entries, ensure that all transactions for the period have been entered, obtain an audit of the financial statements, and print the annual report.

Those who read a balance sheet may believe the condition reported to remain constant and project it into the future. However, events or transactions may make this projection inappropriate. Between the date of the balance sheet and its distribution to shareholders and creditors, important transactions or other events that materially affect the company's financial position or operating sit-

---

[17] *CICA Handbook*, Section 1500.

[18] *Ibid.*, Section 3820. The date of completion is a matter of judgement and depends on the particular circumstances and reporting requirements.

uation may occur. Readers must be told if the company has sold one of its plants, acquired a subsidiary, suffered extraordinary losses, settled significant litigation, or experienced any other important event in the post-balance sheet period. Without an explanation in a note, the reader might be misled and draw inaccurate conclusions.

Two types of events or transactions occurring after the balance sheet date may have a material effect on the financial statements or may need to be considered to interpret these statements accurately. First are ***events or transactions that provide additional evidence about conditions existing at the balance sheet date, affect the estimates used in preparing the financial statements, and result in the adjustment of the financial statements.*** The accountant must use all of the information available prior to the issuance of the financial statements to evaluate estimates previously made. To ignore these subsequent events is to pass up an opportunity to improve the accuracy of the financial statements. These events, especially those affecting the realization of assets, such as receivables and inventories or the settlement of estimated liabilities, encompass information that would have been recorded in the accounts had it been available at the balance sheet date. Such subsequent events typically represent the culmination of conditions that have existed for some time.

Second are ***the events that provide evidence about conditions not existing at the balance sheet date but happening subsequent to that date and that do not require adjustment of the financial statements.*** Some of these events may have to be disclosed to keep the financial statements from being misleading. These disclosures take the form of notes, supplemental schedules or, possibly, even pro forma (as if) financial data that make it appear as if the event had occurred on the date of the balance sheet. Below are examples of such events that require disclosure (but do not result in adjustment):

1. A fire or flood that results in a loss.
2. Decline in the market value of investments.
3. Purchase of a business.
4. Commencement of litigation where the cause of action arises subsequent to the date of the financial statements.
5. Changes in foreign currency exchange rates.
6. Issue of share capital or long-term debt.[19]

Identifying events that require financial statement adjustment or disclosure requires judgement and knowledge of the facts and circumstances. For example, if a loss on an uncollectible trade account receivable results from a customer's deteriorating financial condition, leading to bankruptcy subsequent to the balance sheet date, the financial statements are adjusted before their issuance because the bankruptcy stems from the customer's poor financial health existing at the balance sheet date. A similar loss resulting from a customer's fire or flood after the balance sheet date is not indicative of conditions existing at that date, however, and adjustment of the financial statements is not necessary.

The same criterion applies to settlement of litigation. The financial statements must be adjusted if the events that give rise to the litigation, such as personal injury or patent infringement, takes place prior to the balance sheet date. If the event giving rise to the claim takes place subsequent to the balance sheet date, no adjustment is necessary but disclosure is required. Subsequent events, such as changes in the quoted market prices of securities, ordinarily do not result in adjustment of the financial statements because such changes typically reflect a concurrent evaluation of new conditions.

Many subsequent events or developments are not likely to require either adjustment of or disclosure in the financial statements. Typically, these are nonaccounting events or conditions that management normally communicates by other means. These events include legislation, product changes, management changes, strikes, unionization, marketing agreements, and loss of important customers.

---

[19] *Ibid.*, Section 3820, par. .09.

TECHNIQUES OF DISCLOSURE

Objective 5

Identify major disclosure techniques for the balance sheet.

The effect of various contingencies on financial condition, the methods of valuing assets, and the company's contracts and agreements should be disclosed as completely and intelligently as possible. The following methods of disclosing pertinent information are available:

1. Parenthetical explanations.
2. Notes to the financial statements.
3. Cross-reference and contra items.
4. Supporting schedules.

Appendix 5A contains specimen financial statements that illustrate some of these methods.

Parenthetical Explanations

Additional information or description is often given by means of parenthetical explanations following the item. For example, investments in common shares may be presented on the balance sheet under Investments, as shown below.

Investments in common shares at cost (market value, $330,586)—$280,783

This device permits disclosure of additional pertinent balance sheet information that adds clarity and completeness. It has an advantage over a note because it brings the additional information into the body of the statement, where it is less likely to be overlooked. Of course, lengthy parenthetical explanations might distract the reader from the balance sheet information and must be used with care.

Notes

If additional explanations or descriptions cannot be shown conveniently as parenthetical explanations, notes are used. In the following example, inventory costing methods are reported in the balance sheet and accompanying notes.

Imperial Oil Limited

	(000s)	
Under Current Assets:	1991	1990
Inventories (note 3)	$178,241	$190,939

Notes:

3. Inventories

Inventories are carried at the lower of cost, determined on a first-in, first-out basis, and net realizable value and consist of the following:

	(000s)	
	1991	1990
Raw materials	$ 34,965	$ 43,090
Work in process	10,515	10,571
Finished goods	132,761	137,278
	$178,241	$190,939

Notes are commonly used to present other information, such as the existence and amount of any preferred dividends in arrears, the terms of or obligations imposed by purchase commitments, special financial arrangements, depreciation policies, any changes in the application of accounting policies, and the existence of contingencies. The following examples illustrate the use of notes to disclose such information.

Northgate Exploration Limited

Note 13 Commitments and Contingencies

(a) Northgate has guaranteed obligations on behalf of associate Sonora Gold Corp. and has pledged approximately $13,300,000 in short-term deposits to secure the guarantee.

(b) The Corporation, together with four of its senior officers, has been named in a class action suit filed in the United States alleging violations of the Securities Exchange Act of 1934, relating to disclosure concerning the Colomac mine. The Corporation believes the action is not well founded and is being vigorously defended.

Metall Mining Corporation

16. Subsequent Events

(a) During the first quarter of 1992, the Corporation entered into an agreement in principle with Minnove Inc., to form a joint venture to explore, develop, and mine the Izok Lake base metal property in the Northwest Territories. The Corporation will acquire a 40 percent interest in Izok Lake for $15 million, of which $10 million is paid upon the execution of a formal joint venture agreement, $2 million upon the completion of a feasibility study, and $3 million upon the decision being made to put the property into commercial production. As well, the Corporation has agreed to provide $1 million in 1992 for further exploration of the Hood River and Gondor properties.

(b) As part of Bougrine's financing arrangements, effective March 16, 1992, the shareholders of Bougrine formally agreed to accept International Finance Corporation ("IFC"), part of the World Bank, as an additional shareholder. The Corporation and its Tunisian partners agreed to reduce their respective interests by 5 percent to 45 percent each to allow IFC to acquire a 10 percent interest in Bougrine.

Notes must always present all essential facts as completely and succinctly as possible. Careless wording may mislead readers rather than help them. Notes should add to the total information in the financial statements, not raise unanswered questions or contradict other portions of the statements.

Cross-Reference and Contra Items

A direct relationship between an asset and a liability is cross-referenced on the balance sheet. For example, on December 31, 1994, among the current assets the following may be shown.

Cash on deposit with sinking fund trustee for redemption of bonds payable—see Current Liabilities	$800,000

Included among the current liabilities is the amount of bonds payable to be redeemed currently.

Bonds payable to be redeemed in 1995—see Current Assets	$2,300,000

This cross reference points out that $2,300,000 of bonds payable are to be redeemed currently, for which only $800,000 in cash has been set aside. Therefore, the additional cash needed must come from unrestricted cash, from sales of investments, from profits, or from other sources. The same information can be shown parenthetically, if this technique is preferred.

Another procedure is to establish contra or adjunct accounts. A **contra account** is a balance sheet item that reduces either an asset, liability, or shareholders' equity account. Examples include Accumulated Depreciation and Discount on Bonds Payable. Contra accounts provide flexibility in presenting the financial information. With the use of the Accumulated Depreciation account, for example, a reader of the statement can see the original cost of the asset as well as the depreciation to date.

An **adjunct account,** on the other hand, increases either an asset, liability, or shareholders' equity account. An example is Premium on Bonds Payable, which, when added to the Bonds Payable account, provides a picture of the total liability of the enterprise.

Supporting Schedules

Often a separate schedule is needed to present more detailed information about certain assets, liabilities, or shareholders' equity because the balance sheet provides just a single summary item.

Property, plant, and equipment	
Land, building, equipment, and other fixed assets (see Schedule 3)	$643,300

Below is an example of a separate schedule.

Schedule 3
Land, Buildings, Equipment, and Other Assets

	Total	Land	Build-ings	Equip-ment	Other Fixed Assets
Balance Jan. 1, 1994	$740,000	$46,000	$358,000	$260,000	$76,000
Additions in 1994	161,200		120,000	38,000	3,200
	$901,200	$46,000	$478,000	$298,000	$79,200
Assets retired or sold in 1994	31,700			27,000	4,700
Balance Dec. 31, 1994	$869,500	$46,000	$478,000	$271,000	$74,500
Depreciation taken to January 1, 1994	$196,000		$102,000	$ 78,000	$16,000
Depreciation taken in 1994	56,000		28,000	24,000	4,000
	$252,000		$130,000	$102,000	$20,000
Depreciation on assets retired in 1994	25,800			22,000	3,800
Depreciation accumulated December 31, 1994	$226,200		$130,000	$ 80,000	$16,200
Book value of assets	$643,300	$46,000	$348,000	$191,000	$58,300

TERMINOLOGY

The account titles in the general ledger do not always have the best terminology for balance sheet purposes. Account titles are often brief and include technical terms that are understood only by those keeping the records and by accountants. Because balance sheets are examined by other people who are not acquainted with the technical vocabulary of accounting, they should contain descriptions that will be generally understood and not likely to be misinterpreted.

The accounting profession has recommended that the word **"reserve"** be used only to describe an appropriation of retained earnings. This term has been used in several ways: to describe amounts deducted from assets (contra accounts such as accumulated depreciation, and allowance for doubtful accounts), and as part of the title of contingent or estimated liabilities. Because of the different meanings attached to this term, its meaning in the balance sheet is sometimes misinterpreted. The use of "reserve" only to describe appropriated earnings has resulted in a better understanding of its significance when it appears in a balance sheet. Perhaps the use of the word should be discontinued entirely and the term "appropriated" used instead.

Although the word "surplus" may also be misunderstood, it frequently appears in the shareholders' equity section as part of the caption Contributed Surplus. The contributed surplus amount often arises from amounts contributed by shareholders in excess of the amount credited to share capital or other appropriate account. Examples are proceeds from donated shares and credits arising from redemption or conversion of shares, etc. Thus, Contributed Surplus denotes amounts received by contributions from shareholders and sometimes others and is appropriately classified as a part of shareholders' equity. On the other hand, any amounts arising from earnings should be included in Retained Earnings.

The profession's recommendations relating to changes in terminology have been directed primarily to the balance sheet presentation of shareholders' equity, so that the words or phrases used for these unique accounts describe more accurately the nature of the amounts shown.

SECTION 2: STATEMENT OF CHANGES IN FINANCIAL POSITION

One of the three basic objectives of financial reporting was presented in Chapter 2 as assessing the amount, timing, and uncertainty of cash flows. The balance sheet, the income statement, and the statement of retained earnings each present to a limited extent, and in a fragmented manner, information about the cash flows of an enterprise during a period. For instance, comparative balance sheets might show what new assets have been acquired or disposed of and what liabilities have been incurred or liquidated. The income statement provides in a limited manner information about the resources, if not exactly cash, provided by operations. And the statement of retained earnings provides information as to the amount of cash used to pay dividends. But none of these statements presents a detailed summary of all cash inflows and outflows or all the sources and uses of cash during the period. To fill this need, the Accounting Standards Committee of the CICA revised Section 1540 of the *Handbook* in 1985, entitled "Statement of Changes in Financial Position."

PURPOSE OF THE STATEMENT OF CHANGES IN FINANCIAL POSITION

Objective 6

Indicate the purpose of the statement of cash flows.

The primary purpose of the statement of changes in financial position is ***to provide relevant "information about the operating, financing, and investing activities of an enterprise and the effects of those activities on cash resources" during a period.***[20] To achieve this purpose and to aid investors, creditors, and others in their analysis of what is happening to a company's most liquid resources—its cash and cash equivalents—the statement of changes in financial position reports (1) the cash

[20] *Ibid.*, Section 1540, par. .01.

effects of an enterprise' s operations during a period, (2) its investing transactions, (3) its financing transactions, and (4) the net increase or decrease in cash and equivalents during the period.

By reporting the sources, uses, and net increase or decrease in cash, the statement of changes in financial position provides useful information to answer the following important questions:

1. Where did the cash come from during the period?
2. What was the cash used for during the period?
3. What was the change in the balances of cash during the period?

Content and Format of the Statement of Changes in Financial Position

Objective 7

Identify the content of the statement of cash flows.

Cash receipts and cash payments during a period are classified in the statement of changes in financial position under operating, investing, and financing activities. These classifications are defined as follows:

1. **Operating activities** involve the cash effects of transactions that enter into the determination of net income.
2. **Investing activities** include (a) making and collecting loans and (b) acquiring and disposing of debt and equity investments, as well as property, plant, and equipment.
3. **Financing activities** involve liability and shareholders' equity items and include (a) obtaining capital from owners and providing them with a return on, and a return of, their investment and (b) borrowing money from creditors and repaying the amounts borrowed.

With the above three categories of cash and cash equivalents, the statement of changes in financial position has assumed the following basic format.

Format of the Statement of Changes in Financial Position

Cash flows from operating activities	XXX
Cash flows from investing activities	XXX
Cash flows from financing activities	XXX
Net increase (decrease) in cash and equivalents	XXX
Cash and equivalents at beginning of year	XXX
Cash and equivalents at end of year	XXX

The inflows and outflows of cash classified by activity are diagrammed on page 208.

Because most individuals maintain their chequebooks and prepare their tax returns on a cash basis, they can relate to the statement of changes in financial position and comprehend the causes and effects of cash inflows and outflows and the net increase or decrease in cash.

The statement of changes in financial position is valuable in helping users evaluate liquidity, solvency, and financial flexibility. **Liquidity** refers to the nearness to cash of assets and liabilities. **Solvency** refers to the firm's ability to pay its debts as they mature. **Financial flexibility** refers to a firm's ability to respond and adapt to financial adversity and unexpected needs and opportunities.

Preparation of the Statement of Changes in Financial Position

Objective 8

Prepare a statement of cash flows.

The preparation of the statement of changes is presented here as an introduction. A comprehensive coverage of this topic is contained in Chapter 23, which deals entirely with the preparation and the content of the statement of changes. In the intervening chapters, several significant elements and topics that make up the content of the typical statement of changes in financial position will be discussed in detail.

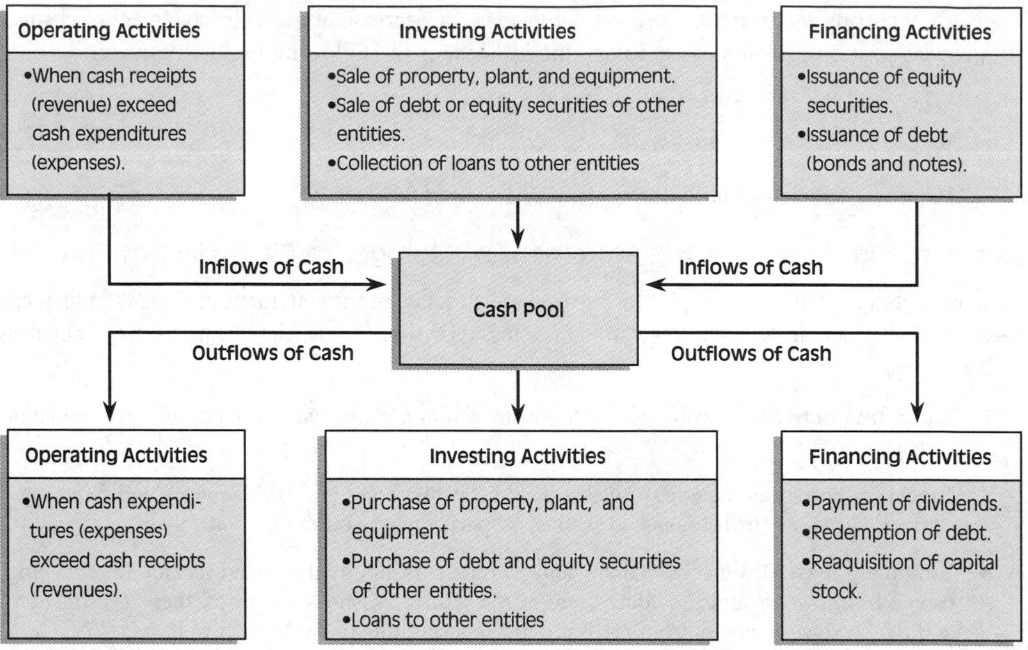

The information that is required to prepare the statement of changes in financial position usually comes from (1) comparative balance sheets, (2) the current income statement, and (3) selected transaction data. Preparing the statement of changes from these sources involves the following steps:

1. Determine the cash provided by operations.
2. Determine the cash provided by or used in investing and financing activities.
3. Determine the change (increase or decrease) in cash during the period.
4. Reconcile the change in cash with the beginning and the ending cash balances.

The following simple illustration demonstrates how these steps are applied in the preparation of the statement of changes in financial position.

In its first year of operations, Telamarketing Inc. issued 50,000 no-par value common shares for $50,000 cash on January 1, 1994. The company rented its office space, furniture, and telecommunications equipment and performed surveys and marketing services throughout the first year. The comparative balance sheets at the beginning and end of the year 1994 appear on page 209. The income statement and additional information for Telamarketing Inc. are also found on page 209.

Cash provided by operations (the excess of cash receipts over cash payments) is determined by converting net income on an accrual basis to a cash basis. This is accomplished by adding to or deducting from net income those items in the income statement not affecting cash. This procedure requires an analysis not only of the current year's income statement but also of the comparative balance sheets and selected transaction data.

Analysis of Telamarketing's comparative balance sheets reveals two items that give rise to noncash credits or charges to the income statement: (1) the increase in accounts receivable caused a noncash credit of $41,000 to revenues and (2) the increase in accounts payable caused a noncash charge of $12,000 to expenses. ***To arrive at cash provided by operations, the increase in accounts receivable must be deducted from net income, and the increase in accounts payable must be added***

Telamarketing Inc.
Balance Sheets

Assets	Dec. 31, 1994	Jan. 1, 1994	Increase/Decrease
Cash	$46,000	$-0-	$46,000 Increase
Accounts receivable (net)	41,000	-0-	41,000 Increase
Total	$87,000	$-0-	
Liabilities and Shareholders' Equity			
Accounts payable	$12,000	$-0-	12,000 Increase
Common shares	50,000	-0-	50,000 Increase
Retained earnings	25,000	-0-	25,000 Increase
Total	$87,000	$-0-	

Telamarketing Inc.
Income Statement
For the Year Ended December 31, 1994

Revenues	$172,000
Operating expenses	120,000
Income before income taxes	52,000
Income tax expense	13,000
Net income	$ 39,000

Additional information:
Dividends of $14,000 were paid during the year.

back to net income. As a result of the accounts receivable and accounts payable adjustments, the cash provided by operations is determined to be $10,000, computed as follows.

Net income		$39,000
Adjustments to reconcile net income to net cash provided by operating activities		
Increase in accounts receivable (net)	$(41,000)	
Increase in accounts payable	12,000	(29,000)
Net cash provided by operating activities		$10,000

The increase of $50,000 in common shares resulting from the issuance of 50,000 shares for cash is classified as a financing activity. Likewise, the payment of $14,000 cash in dividends is a financing activity. Telamarketing Inc. did not engage in any investing activities during the year. The statement of changes in financial position for Telamarketing Inc. for 1994 appears on page 210. The increase in cash of $46,000 reported in the statement of changes in financial position agrees with the increase of $46,000 shown as the change in the cash account in the comparative balance sheets.

An illustration of a more comprehensive statement of changes in financial position is presented for Illustration Company.

Telamarketing Inc.
Statement of Changes in Financial Position
For the Year Ended December 31, 1994

Cash flows from operating activities		
Net income		$39,000
Add (deduct) items not affecting cash		
Increase in accounts receivable (net)	$(41,000)	
Increase in accounts payable	12,000	(29,000)
Net cash provided by operating activities		10,000
Cash flows from financing activities		
Issuance of common shares	50,000	
Payment of cash dividends	(14,000)	
Net cash provided by financing activities		36,000
Net increase in cash		46,000
Cash at beginning of year		-0-
Cash at end of year		$46,000

Illustration Company
Statement of Changes in Financial Position
For the Year Ended December 31, 1994

Operating Activities		
Net income		$320,750
Add (deduct) items not affecting cash		
Depreciation expense	$88,400	
Amortization of intangibles	16,300	
Gain on sale of plant assets	(8,700)	
Increase in accounts receivable (net)	(11,000)	
Decrease in inventory	15,500	
Decrease in notes and accounts payable	(9,500)	91,000
Net cash provided by operating activities		411,750
Investing Activities		
Sale of plant assets	90,500	
Purchase of equipment	(182,500)	
Purchase of land	(70,000)	
Net cash used by investing activities		(162,000)
Financing Activities		
Payment of cash dividend	(19,800)	
Issuance of common shares	100,000	
Redemption of bonds	(50,000)	
Net cash provided by financing activities		30,200
Net increase in cash		279,950
Cash at beginning of year		135,000
Cash at end of year		$414,950

CLASSIFICATION ISSUES IN FINANCIAL STATEMENTS

The accounting profession has stated that "financial reporting is essentially a process of communication of information."[21] Consequently, it is important that similar items be appropriately grouped or classified and that dissimilar items be separated. The reporting of highly summarized accounts (total assets, net assets, total liabilities, etc.) is not encouraged. Individual items should be separately reported and classified in sufficient detail to permit users to assess the "ability of the entity to earn income and generate cash flows in the future to meet its obligations."[22]

Classification in financial statements that groups items with similar characteristics and separates items with different characteristics helps analysts.[23] The following are some considerations for classification:

1. Assets that differ in their ***type or expected function*** in the central operations or other activities of the enterprise should be reported as separate items (e.g., merchandise inventories should be reported separately from property, plant, and equipment).
2. Assets and liabilities with ***different implications for the financial flexibility*** of the enterprise should be reported as separate items (e.g., assets used in operations should be reported separately from assets held for investment and assets subject to restrictions such as leased equipment).
3. Assets and liabilities with ***different general liquidity characteristics*** should be reported as separate items (e.g., cash should be reported separately from inventories).

It is unlikely that the form, content, and classifications of the balance sheet will be changed in the near future. Although some would prefer it, the profession does not appear to be interested in revaluing the elements of the balance sheet to fair values except in certain rare circumstances. However, gradual evolutionary changes may occur in the future as they have in the past.

Fundamental Concepts

1. The balance sheet provides information about the nature and amount of investments in enterprise resources, obligations to enterprise creditors, and the owners' equity in net enterprise resources. This information provides a basis for (1) computing rates of return, (2) evaluating the capital structure of the enterprise, and (3) assessing the liquidity and financial flexibility of the enterprise.
2. Some limitations of the balance sheet are (1) it does not reflect current value, (2) judgements must be used in allocating costs, and (3) it omits many items that are of financial value to the business but cannot be recorded objectively.
3. The three general elements of the balance sheet are assets, liabilities, and owners' equity.
4. The major classifications within the balance sheet on the asset side are current assets; long-term investments; property, plant, and equipment; intangible assets; and other assets.
5. The major classifications of liabilities are current liabilities and long-term liabilities.
6. In a corporation, shareholders' equity is generally classified as share capital, contributed surplus, and retained earnings.

(Continued)

---

[21] *Ibid.*, Section 1500, par. .01.

[22] *Ibid.*, Section 1000, par. .12.

[23] "Reporting Income, Cash Flows, and Financial Positions of Business Enterprises," *Proposed Statement of Financial Accounting Concepts* (Stamford, CT: FASB, 1981), par. 51.

7. Four types of information that are supplemental to assets, liabilities, and owners' equity accounts are normally presented in the balance sheet: (1) contingencies, (2) valuation and accounting policies, (3) contractual situations, and (4) post-balance sheet disclosures.
8. The methods of disclosing pertinent information are (1) parenthetical explanations, (2) notes, (3) cross-reference and contra items, and (4) supporting schedules.
9. Balance sheets may follow either the account form or report form. The most common is the report form.
10. The statement of changes in financial position is now one of the basic financial statements. It reports (1) cash effects of an enterprise's operations during a period, (2) financing transactions, (3) investing transactions, and (4) net increase or decrease in cash (and equivalents) during the period.
11. All cash flows are classified in the statement of changes in financial position as (1) operating activities—the cash effects of transactions that enter into the determination of net income, (2) investing activities—making and collecting loans and acquiring and disposing of debt and equity investments as well as property, plant, and equipment, and (3) financing activities—obtaining capital from owners and paying dividends thereon and assuming and repaying debt.

APPENDIX 5A

Moore Corporation Limited Financial Statements

As at December 31
Expressed in United States currency
in thousands of dollars

Moore Corporation Limited

CONSOLIDATED BALANCE SHEET

ASSETS	1991	1990
CURRENT ASSETS		
Cash	$ 10,236	$ 21,962
Short-term securities, at cost which approximates market value	257,258	257,204
Accounts receivable, less allowance for doubtful accounts $18,038 ($16,780 in 1990)	466,081	476,813
Inventories (Note 2)	319,985	363,833
Prepaid expenses	17,846	21,576
Deferred taxes	23,625	38,825
TOTAL CURRENT ASSETS	1,095,031	1,180,213
PROPERTY, PLANT AND EQUIPMENT		
Land	35,951	36,074
Buildings	274,966	254,464
Machinery and equipment	986,909	930,440
	1,297,826	1,220,978
Less: Accumulated depreciation	601,436	541,703
	696,390	679,275
INVESTMENT IN ASSOCIATED CORPORATIONS (Note 3)	177,163	153,645
OTHER ASSETS (Note 4)	148,389	152,557
	$2,116,973	$2,165,690

LIABILITIES	1991	1990
CURRENT LIABILITIES		
Bank loans (Note 5)	$ 33,192	$ 37,733
Accounts payable and accruals (Note 6)	265,688	331,546
Dividends payable	22,762	22,532
Accrued income taxes	10,306	18,435
TOTAL CURRENT LIABILITIES	331,948	410,246
LONG-TERM DEBT (Note 7)	58,613	56,244
DEFERRED INCOME TAXES AND LIABILITIES (Note 8)	136,713	157,263
EQUITY OF MINORITY SHAREHOLDERS IN SUBSIDIARY CORPORATIONS	4,919	4,266
	532,193	628,019

SHAREHOLDERS' EQUITY	1991	1990
SHARE CAPITAL (Note 9)	301,761	256,893
UNREALIZED FOREIGN CURRENCY TRANSLATION ADJUSTMENTS (Note 10)	30,033	24,651
RETAINED EARNINGS	1,252,986	1,256,127
	1,584,780	1,537,671
	$2,116,973	$2,165,690

Approved by the Board of Directors:

M.K. Goodrich — Director

J. McArthur — Director

For the year ended December 31
Expressed in United States currency and, except earnings per share, in thousands of dollars

Moore Corporation Limited

Consolidated Statement of Earnings

	1991	1990	1989
Sales	$2,492,278	$2,769,596	$2,708,406
Cost of sales	1,663,947	1,780,025	1,737,844
Selling, general and administrative expenses	623,803	678,245	621,110
Depreciation	84,183	77,001	67,868
Interest expense (Note 13)	13,238	17,247	12,787
	2,385,171	2,552,518	2,439,609
Income from operations before provision for restructuring costs	107,107	217,078	268,797
Provision for restructuring costs (Note 14)	10,300	55,000	–
Income from operations	96,807	162,078	268,797
Investment and other income (Note 13)	51,997	84,476	64,169
Earnings before income taxes, minority interests and unrealized exchange adjustments	148,804	246,554	332,966
Income taxes (Note 15)	47,922	74,030	98,269
Minority interests	1,096	1,170	517
Unrealized exchange adjustments	11,712	50,725	32,459
Net earnings	$ 88,074	$ 120,629	$ 201,721
Net earnings per common share (Note 16)	$ 0.91	$ 1.27	$ 2.15
Average shares outstanding *(in thousands)*	97,028	95,245	93,860

For the year ended December 31
Expressed in United States currency
in thousands of dollars

Consolidated Statement of Retained Earnings

	1991	1990	1989
Balance at beginning of year	$1,256,127	$1,226,347	$1,107,235
Net earnings	88,074	120,629	201,721
	1,344,201	1,346,976	1,308,956
Dividends 94¢ per share (94¢ in 1990 and 88¢ in 1989)	91,215	89,539	82,609
Purchase of common shares (Note 9)	–	1,310	–
Balance at end of year	$1,252,986	$1,256,127	$1,226,347

For the year ended December 31
Expressed in United States currency
in thousands of dollars

Moore Corporation Limited

Consolidated Statement of Changes in Cash Resources

	1991	1990	1989
Cash provided by (applied to)			
Operations	**$ 188,471**	$ 258,619	$ 322,594
Investment	**(147,937)**	(186,098)	(190,233)
Financing	**47,128**	52,100	5,766
Dividends	**(91,215)**	(89,539)	(82,609)
Increase (decrease) in cash resources before unrealized exchange adjustments	**(3,553)**	35,082	55,518
Unrealized exchange adjustments	**(3,578)**	(31,345)	(22,961)
Increase (decrease) in cash resources (Note 18(a))	**(7,131)**	3,737	32,557
Cash resources at beginning of year	**241,433**	237,696	205,139
Cash resources at end of year	**$ 234,302**	$ 241,433	$ 237,696
Operations			
Net earnings	**$ 88,074**	$ 120,629	$ 201,721
Items not affecting cash resources (Note 18(b))	**111,478**	144,433	108,765
Decrease (increase) in working capital other than cash resources (Note 18(c))	**(11,081)**	(6,443)	12,108
	$ 188,471	$ 258,619	$ 322,594
Investment			
Expenditure for property, plant and equipment	**$ (120,287)**	$ (166,065)	$ (126,711)
Sale of property, plant and equipment	**8,781**	22,255	3,470
Investment in associated corporations	**(7,962)**	(27,583)	(6,823)
Sale of (addition to) long-term investments	**2,935**	(13,210)	22,650
Reduction in purchase price of Moore Lithorex Direct Marketing Services NV/SA	**–**	12,027	–
Addition to long-term receivables	**(3,433)**	(9,696)	(10,444)
Reduction in long-term receivables	**5,370**	4,322	6,785
Acquisition of businesses	**(4,690)**	(8,133)	(72,758)
Disposal of subsidiaries	**–**	9,501	2,110
Deferred charges	**(28,179)**	(9,734)	(9,795)
Dividends from associated corporations	**3,997**	3,414	2,466
Other	**(4,469)**	(3,196)	(1,183)
	$ (147,937)	$ (186,098)	$ (190,233)
Financing			
Issue of common shares	**$ 44,868**	$ 39,822	$ 34,123
Purchase of common shares (Note 9)	**–**	(1,488)	–
Addition to long-term debt	**12,067**	25,397	1,236
Reduction in long-term debt	**(10,083)**	(11,635)	(29,956)
Other	**276**	4	363
	$ 47,128	$ 52,100	$ 5,766

Notes to Consolidated Financial Statements

1. Summary of accounting policies

Accounting principles:

Moore Corporation Limited is incorporated under the laws of the Province of Ontario, Canada.

The consolidated financial statements are prepared in accordance with accounting principles generally accepted in Canada.

Translation of foreign currencies:

The consolidated financial statements are expressed in United States currency because the greater part of the net assets and earnings are located or originate in the United States. Except for the foreign currency financial statements of subsidiaries in countries with highly inflationary economies, Canadian and other foreign currency financial statements have been translated into United States currency on the following bases: All assets and liabilities at the year-end rates of exchange; income and expenses at average exchange rates during the year.

Net unrealized exchange adjustments arising on translation of foreign currency financial statements are charged or credited directly to shareholders' equity and shown as unrealized foreign currency translation adjustments.

The foreign currency financial statements of subsidiaries in countries with highly inflationary economies are translated into United States currency on the following bases: Current assets, excluding inventory, current liabilities, pension liabilities, long-term receivables and long-term debt, at the year-end rates of exchange; all other assets, liabilities, accumulated depreciation and related charges against earnings and share capital, at historical rates of exchange; income and expenses, other than depreciation and cost of sales, at average exchange rates during the year.

Net unrealized exchange adjustments arising on translation of foreign currency financial statements of subsidiaries in countries with highly inflationary economies are charged to earnings as unrealized exchange adjustments.

Realized exchange losses or gains are included in earnings.

Unrealized exchange losses or gains related to monetary items with a fixed or ascertainable life extending beyond the end of the following fiscal year are deferred and amortized over the remaining life of the asset or liability.

Inventories:

Inventories of raw materials and work in process are valued at the lower of cost and replacement cost and inventories of finished goods at the lower of cost and net realizable value. The cost of the principal raw material inventories and the raw material content of finished goods inventories in Canada and the United States is determined on the last-in, first-out basis. The cost of all other inventories is determined on the first-in, first-out basis.

Property, plant and equipment and depreciation:

Property, plant and equipment are stated at historical cost after deducting investment tax credits and other grants on eligible capital assets. Depreciation is provided on a basis that will amortize the cost of depreciable assets over their estimated useful lives using the straight-line method. All costs for repairs and maintenance are expensed as incurred.

The estimated useful lives of buildings range from 20 to 50 years and of machinery and equipment from 3 to 17 years.

Gains or losses on the disposal of property, plant and equipment are included in earnings and the cost and accumulated depreciation related to these assets are removed from the accounts.

INVESTMENT IN ASSOCIATED CORPORATIONS:

The Corporation accounts for its investment in associated corporations by the equity method.

GOODWILL:

Goodwill is amortized by the straight-line method over periods not exceeding forty years.

AMORTIZATION OF DEFERRED COSTS:

Deferred charges are amortized over periods deemed appropriate to match expenses with the related revenues.

INCOME TAXES:

Income taxes are accounted for on the tax allocation basis which relates income taxes to the accounting income for the year.

No provision has been made for taxes on undistributed earnings of subsidiaries not currently available for paying dividends inasmuch as such earnings have been reinvested in the business.

2. INVENTORIES *(in thousands)*

	1991	1990
Raw materials	$ 93,543	$126,716
Work in process	32,437	34,652
Finished goods	181,060	190,170
Other	12,945	12,295
	$319,985	$363,833

The excess of the current cost over the last-in, first-out of those inventories determined on the latter basis is approximately $51,900,000 at December 31, 1991 (1990–$67,400,000).

3. INVESTMENT IN ASSOCIATED CORPORATIONS

The major investment in associated corporations represents a 45% ownership in Toppan Moore Company, Ltd. in Japan. Dividends received from this corporation in 1991 were $3,697,000 (1990–$2,896,000; 1989–$2,174,000) and its undistributed earnings included in retained earnings are $88,028,000 (1990–$73,313,000; 1989–$61,380,000).

4. OTHER ASSETS *(in thousands)*

	1991	1990
Goodwill, net of accumulated amortization of $18,796 (1990 – $16,066)	$ 36,486	$ 39,719
Long-term receivables	28,997	34,333
Prepaid pension cost	34,702	20,977
Long-term bonds, at cost which approximates market value	17,406	13,993
Computer software	8,621	9,063
Taxes related to a program to restructure the capitalization of and to fund certain subsidiaries, net of amortization of $13,650 (1990 – $11,323)	2,540	5,143
Investment in preferred shares, at market value	4,201	4,201
Other	15,436	25,128
	$148,389	$152,557

5. UNUSED LINES OF CREDIT

The unused lines of credit outstanding at December 31, 1991 for short-term financings are $67,817,000 (1990–$66,154,000).

6. ACCOUNTS PAYABLE AND ACCRUALS *(in thousands)*

	1991	1990
Trade accounts payable	$ 99,727	$130,591
Other payables	34,955	41,870
	134,682	172,461
Accrued payrolls	56,893	50,225
Accrued restructuring costs	8,499	40,151
Accrued employee benefit costs	17,852	16,514
Other accruals	47,762	52,195
	131,006	159,085
	$265,688	$331,546

7. LONG-TERM DEBT *(in thousands)*

	1991	1990
MOORE CORPORATION LIMITED		
Bank loan payable in Japanese yen bearing interest at 7.2% due 1997	**$14,498**	$14,085
6% Subordinated Debentures due 1994 ($1,868 Cdn. in 1991 and 1990)	**1,617**	1,610
Capital lease commitments	**19**	429
MOORE BUSINESS FORMS, INC.		
7.9% Senior Notes due 1996	**8,000**	9,000
Industrial Development Revenue Bonds bearing interest at 6.85% to 9.5% due 2004	**7,350**	7,350
Secured bank loan bearing variable interest to a maximum of 13.5% due 1997	**633**	785
MOORE BUSINESS FORMS DE MEXICO SA		
Bank loan payable in United States dollars bearing variable interest based on the London Interbank Offer Rate plus 1% due 1993	**10,513**	–
MOORE LITHOREX DIRECT MARKETING SERVICES NV/SA		
Secured bank loans payable in Belgian francs bearing interest at 8.05% to 12.96% due 1992 to 1999	**5,916**	8,477
MOORE FRANCE S.A.		
Capital lease commitments	**3,905**	5,595
Bank and other loans payable in French francs bearing interest at 6.5% to 11.75% due 1992 to 2005. Loans amounting to $1,843 (1990 – $2,849) are secured	**2,995**	4,793
OTHER SUBSIDIARIES		
Secured loans	**2,206**	2,288
Capital lease commitments	**766**	1,112
Unsecured loans	**195**	720
	$58,613	$56,244

The sinking fund obligations with respect to the retirement of the 6% Subordinated Debentures for the years 1992 and 1993 were satisfied in prior years.

The long-term debt of other subsidiaries bears interest at rates ranging from 5.0% to 37.0%. This debt matures on various dates to 1998. Loans of other subsidiaries amounting to $2,402,000 (1990–$2,229,000) are payable in currencies other than United States dollars. Loans of $2,206,000 (1990–$2,288,000) are secured by assets of eight subsidiaries.

The net book value of assets subject to lien approximates $43,000,000 (1990 – $50,000,000), the liens being primarily mortgages against property, plant and equipment and the pledge of all assets of a certain subsidiary.

Amounts of $8,678,000 (1990–$10,434,000) on long-term debt due within one year are included in current liabilities. For the years 1993 through 1996 payments required on long-term debt are as follows: 1993–$18,452,000; 1994–$7,477,000; 1995–$6,058,000; and 1996–$11,649,000.

8. DEFERRED INCOME TAXES AND LIABILITIES

Non-current deferred income taxes amount to $106,680,000 (1990–$126,199,000). Deferred liabilities include $16,410,000 (1990–$16,889,000) for pensions under unfunded retirement plans (Note 11).

9. SHARE CAPITAL

The Corporation's articles of incorporation provide that its authorized share capital be divided into an unlimited number of common shares without par value and an unlimited number of preference shares without par value, issuable in one or more series, and non-voting except on arrears of dividends.

CHANGES IN THE ISSUED COMMON SHARE CAPITAL	SHARES ISSUED	AMOUNT *(in thousands)*
Balance, January 1, 1989	93,050,261	$183,126
Dividend Reinvestment Plan	1,191,611	32,177
Exercise of executive stock options	106,795	1,946
Balance, December 31, 1989	94,348,667	217,249
Dividend Reinvestment Plan	1,520,535	39,601
Exercise of executive stock options	11,025	221
Shares purchased and cancelled	(66,500)	(178)
Balance, December 31,1990	95,813,727	256,893
Dividend Reinvestment Plan	1,873,931	43,965
Exercise of executive stock options	54,500	859
Employee awards	1,885	44
Balance, December 31, 1991	97,744,043	$301,761

The Dividend Reinvestment Plan provides for dividend reinvestment whereby the amount of the dividend otherwise receivable by investors in cash (less any applicable withholding tax) is used to acquire shares at a 5% discount from an average market value.

Pursuant to the terms of the 1985 Long-Term Incentive Plan approved by the shareholders of the Corporation on April 4, 1985, 3,000,000 common shares of the Corporation were reserved for issuance. Under the terms of this plan, stock options, stock appreciation rights, restricted stock awards, and performance awards may be granted to certain key employees. The exercise price under all options involving the common shares of the Corporation shall not be less than 100% of fair market value of the shares covered by the option on the date of grant.

Options may be exercised at such times as are determined at the date they are granted and expire not more than ten years from the date granted.

STOCK OPTION ACTIVITY IN 1991

Years granted	**1991**	1989	1988	1987	1985	1983	1981	TOTAL
Number of common shares under option outstanding December 31, 1990	–	391,200	351,500	304,900	237,950	62,300	15,900	1,363,750
Options granted	**443,100**	–	–		–	–	–	443,100
Options lapsed	**(200)**	(2,400)	(3,000)	(2,500)	–	–	–	(8,100)
Options exercised	–	–	–	–	(16,800)	(21,800)	(15,900)	(54,500)
Outstanding December 31, 1991	**442,900**	388,800	348,500	302,400	221,150	40,500	–	1,744,250
Option price per share Canadian currency	**$ 29.31**	$ 34.88	$ 28.56	$ 31.88	$ 25.00*	$ 18.23	$ 11.91	

**Weighted average option price*

Under the terms of the 1985 Long-Term Incentive Plan there were 1,713,200 common shares available for grants as at January 1, 1991 and 1,278,200 at December 31, 1991.

On April 12, 1990, the shareholders of the Corporation approved the Shareholders Rights Plan Agreement (the "Rights Agreement") which provides that each outstanding common share carries one Right to purchase additional common shares. Such Rights may become exercisable in a variety of circumstances, including the announcement of a take-over bid for the common shares of the Corporation or the acquisition by a person or a related group of 15% or more of the Corporation's outstanding common shares. All holders of Rights, with the exception of such acquiring person or group, are entitled to purchase from the Corporation upon payment of an exercise price of $120.00 (Cdn.) the number of additional common shares as can be purchased for twice the exercise price based on the market value of the Corporation's common shares at the time the Rights become exercisable. Also, in the event the Corporation should consolidate or amalgamate with a third party or sell to a third party more than 50% of its assets, the Corporation must ensure that each Right thereafter will entitle the holder to purchase upon payment of the exercise price of $120.00 (Cdn.) common shares of the third party having a market value equal to twice the exercise price. The Rights Agreement must be reconfirmed by the shareholders of the Corporation at a meeting held not earlier than September 30, 1994 and no later than the Corporation's 1995 annual meeting of shareholders in order for the Rights to remain in effect until the January 18, 2000 expiry date. Rights may be redeemed earlier by the Corporation for one cent per Right in certain circumstances. The Rights Agreement provides for a Permitted Bid approved by independent shareholders to proceed without the Rights becoming exercisable.

On October 1, 1990, a Notice of Intention to make a normal course issuer bid to purchase up to 5% of the issued and outstanding common shares of the Corporation was filed with The Toronto Stock Exchange and the Montreal Exchange with an expiry date of October 3, 1991. No shares were purchased in 1991.

In recognition of past services to the Corporation, the Directors awarded 1,885 common shares to Success at Moore project finalists.

As at December 31, 1991, there were no issued preference shares.

10. Unrealized foreign currency translation adjustments *(in thousands)*

	1991	1990	1989
Balance at beginning of year	**$24,651**	$ (2,630)	$ 2,046
Translation adjustment	**5,382**	29,802	(4,676)
Reduction in investment in subsidiaries	–	(2,521)	–
Balance at end of year	**$30,033**	$24,651	$(2,630)

The translation adjustments for each year result from the variation from year to year in rates of exchange at which foreign currency net assets are translated to United States currency.

11. Retirement programs

Defined benefit pension plan

The Corporation and its subsidiaries have several programs covering substantially all of the employees in Canada, the United States, the United Kingdom, Australia, New Zealand, and Puerto Rico.

The following data is based upon reports of independent consulting actuaries as at December 31:

	Canada		United States		International	
Funded Status *(in thousands)*	**1991**	1990	**1991**	1990	**1991**	1990
Actuarial present value of:						
Vested benefit obligation	**$ 58,100**	$ 45,179	**$ 352,906**	$312,012	**$ 63,562**	$ 58,766
Accumulated benefit obligation	**58,463**	45,498	**382,971**	337,016	**66,463**	60,281
Projected benefit obligation	**$ 65,155**	$ 50,647	**$ 471,025**	$414,706	**$ 80,389**	$ 75,503
Plan assets at fair value	**75,152**	60,588	**495,619**	383,143	**104,721**	96,494
Excess of plan assets over projected benefit obligation	**9,997**	9,941	**24,594**	(31,563)	**24,332**	20,991
Unrecognized net loss (gain)	**4,527**	8,760	**(48,943)**	(6,557)	**7,593**	10,564
Unrecognized net obligation (asset)	**(11,863)**	(13,132)	**(27,442)**	(30,490)	**(17,900)**	(21,441)
Unrecognized prior service cost (credit)	**5,120**	509	**60,575**	66,024	**2,948**	3,371
Prepaid (accrued) pension cost included in consolidated balance sheet	**$ 7,781**	$ 6,078	**$ 8,784**	$ (2,586)	**$ 16,973**	$ 13,485
Pension Expense *(in thousands)*						
Service cost	**$ 2,415**	$ 2,347	**$ 14,047**	$ 14,539	**$ 3,206**	$ 3,263
Interest cost	**5,779**	4,283	**35,273**	32,386	**6,117**	5,560
Actual return on assets	**(9,422)**	2,244	**(112,612)**	8,486	**(14,432)**	16,538
Net amortization and deferral	**2,059**	(9,153)	**75,893**	(41,607)	**1,891**	(29,478)
Net pension expense (credit)	**$ 831**	$ (279)	**$ 12,601**	$ 13,804	**$ (3,218)**	$ (4,117)
Other Information						
Assumptions:						
Discount rates						
January 1	**9.5%**	9.0%	**8.8%**	8.5%	**9.1%**	8.7%
December 31	**9.5%**	9.0%	**8.3%**	8.8%	**8.5%**	9.1%
Rate of return on assets	**9.5%**	9.5%	**9.5%**	9.3%	**9.8%**	9.8%
Rate of compensation increase	**6.0%**	7.1%	**6.5%**	6.5%	**7.5%**	7.6%
Amortization period	**15 years**	15 years	**15 years**	15 years	**10 years**	10 years

In 1991, in addition to the net pension expense reported above for the International plans, there was a curtailment gain for Australia of $385,000 attributable to staff reductions.

In some subsidiaries, where either state or funded retirement plans exist, there are certain small supplementary unfunded plans. Pensionable service prior to establishing funded contributory retirement plans in other subsidiaries, covered by former discretionary non-contributory retirement plans, was assumed as a prior service obligation. In addition, the Corporation has entered into retiring allowance and supplemental retirement agreements with certain senior executives. The deferred liability for pensions at December 31, 1991, referred to in note 8, relates primarily to the unfunded portion of this prior service obligation and the supplementary unfunded plans.

All of the retirement plans are non-contributory except for the Reid Dominion Packaging plan in Canada and the New Zealand plan. Retirement benefits are generally based on years of service and employees' compensation during the last years of employment. However, in the United States the retirement benefit accrues each year based upon compensation for that year. At December 31, 1991, approximately 70% of the United States plans' assets, about 60% of the Canadian plans' assets and approximately 85% of the international plans' assets were held in equity securities with the remaining portion of the asset funds being mainly fixed income securities. The Corporation's funding policy is to satisfy the funding standards of the regulatory authorities and to make contributions in order to provide for the accumulated benefit obligation and current service cost. To the extent that pension obligations are fully covered by existing assets, a contribution may not be made in a particular year.

DEFINED CONTRIBUTION PENSION PLAN

Savings plans are maintained in Canada, the United States, the United Kingdom and Australia. Only the savings plan in the United Kingdom requires company contributions for all employees who are eligible to participate in the retirement plans. These annual contributions consist of a retirement savings benefit contribution ranging from 1% to 3% of each year's compensation depending upon age. For all savings plans, if an employee contribution is made, a portion of such contribution is matched by the company. The savings plan expense in 1991 was $4,954,000 (1990 - $9,540,000; 1989 - $12,737,000).

12. POSTRETIREMENT HEALTH CARE AND LIFE INSURANCE BENEFITS

In addition to providing pension benefits, the Corporation and its United States subsidiary provide retired employees with health care and life insurance benefits. The cost of these health care and life insurance benefits is recognized as an expense as claims are incurred. In 1991, the cost for these benefits was approximately $9,663,000 (1990 - $5,720,000; 1989 - $4,640,000).

13. CONSOLIDATED STATEMENT OF EARNINGS INFORMATION *(in thousands)*

INTEREST EXPENSE	**1991**	1990	1989
Interest on long-term debt	**$ 4,889**	$ 4,789	$ 5,936
Other interest	**8,349**	12,458	6,851
	$13,238	$17,247	$12,787
INVESTMENT AND OTHER INCOME			
Interest on short-term investments	**$30,692**	$66,793	$42,224
Equity in earnings of associated corporations	**17,547**	15,361	20,374
Miscellaneous	**3,758**	2,322	1,571
	$51,997	$84,476	$64,169
Rent	**$64,037**	$62,262	$52,309
Repairs and maintenance	**56,259**	59,839	55,128
Communications	**34,357**	35,759	32,924
Taxes other than income and payroll taxes	**20,685**	17,311	13,955
Retirement programs	**19,711**	21,659	12,354
Research and development	**37,193**	35,080	27,812
Amortization of goodwill	**2,730**	2,812	2,303

14. PROVISION FOR RESTRUCTURING COSTS

In the fourth quarter of 1991, a provision of $10.3 million was recorded to cover costs associated with restructuring the Corporation's business in Europe, adding to the provision of $55.0 million established in the second quarter of 1990 to cover the Corporation's worldwide business.

As of December 31, 1991, $56.8 million have been charged against the amounts provided. The balance of the provision is expected to be used in 1992.

15. Income taxes

The components of earnings before income taxes for the three years ended December 31, 1991 are as follows:

Earnings before income taxes *(in thousands)*	1991	1990	1989
Canada	**$ 13,974**	$ 17,767	$ 37,269
United States	**107,657**	87,934	159,232
Other countries	**27,173**	140,853	136,465
	$148,804	$246,554	$332,966

Provision for income taxes *(in thousands)*	1991 Current	1991 Deferred	1990 Current	1990 Deferred	1989 Current	1989 Deferred
Canada (federal and provincial)	**$ 5,066**	**$ 187**	$ 6,318	$ 761	$14,768	$ (14)
United States						
Federal	**30,325**	**2,930**	31,771	(6,910)	45,993	7,140
State	**6,519**	**1,576**	6,523	(656)	10,489	2,048
Other countries	**2,013**	**(3,446)**	38,986	(7,053)	11,174	2,074
Withholding taxes on inter-company dividends	**2,752**	**–**	4,290	–	4,597	–
	$46,675	**$ 1,247**	$87,888	$(13,858)	$87,021	$11,248

Deferred income taxes in each of the three years arose from a number of differences of a timing nature between income for accounting purposes and taxable income in the jurisdictions in which the Corporation and its subsidiaries operate. These timing differences include the variation between tax and accounting depreciation, giving rise to deferred tax debits (credits) of $905,000 in 1991 (1990 - $3,852,000; 1989 - $6,780,000), provision for restructuring costs in 1991 of $(3,380,000), (1990 - $(14,244,000)), pension accruals, and other items.

The effective rates of tax for each year compared with the statutory Canadian rates were as follows:

Effective tax rate	1991	1990	1989
Canadian combined federal and provincial statutory rate	**43.3%**	42.0%	43.0%
Increase (decrease) in the statutory rate resulting from:			
Corporate surtax	**0.9**	0.7	1.0
Manufacturing and processing rate reduction	**(5.5)**	(2.9)	(1.6)
Tax exempt investment income	**(1.1)**	–	(2.8)
Weighted effect of higher (lower) United States tax rate	**0.6**	(1.8)	0.7
Weighted effect of lower tax rate in other countries	**(7.8)**	(9.7)	(12.2)
Withholding taxes	**1.8**	1.7	1.4
Total consolidated effective tax rate	**32.2%**	30.0%	29.5%

The increase in the effective rate of tax in 1991 relative to 1990 reflects the effect on the consolidated results of unrelieved losses and a decline in earnings taxed at low rates.

The increase in the effective rate of tax in 1990 relative to 1989 results from the realization of remaining accumulated tax losses in other countries with the incomes thereafter being subject to full statutory rates.

16. Earnings and fully diluted earnings per common share

The earnings per share calculations are based on the weighted average number of common shares outstanding during the year.

If it were assumed that at the beginning of the year all outstanding stock options had been exercised with the funds derived therefrom yielding an annual return of 3.4% net of tax, the earnings per share for the year would have been $0.91 (1990 - $1.27; 1989 - $2.14).

17. SEGMENTED INFORMATION

The Corporation and its subsidiaries have operated predominantly in one industry segment during the three years ended December 31, 1991, that being the provision of products and services which facilitate the recording, retention, processing, retrieval, and communication of business information. Transfers of product between geographic segments are generally accounted for on a basis that results in a fair profit being earned by each segment. The export of product from Canada is insignificant.

GEOGRAPHIC SEGMENTS *(in thousands)*	CANADA	UNITED STATES	EUROPE	OTHER	CONSOLIDATED
1991					
Total revenue	$273,649	$1,548,728	$391,367	$290,402	$2,504,146
Intergeographical segment sales	(918)	(10,950)	–	–	(11,868)
Sales to customers outside the enterprise	$272,731	$1,537,778	$391,367	$290,402	$2,492,278
Segment operating profit before restructuring costs	$ 16,584	$ 139,381	$ (17,184)	$ (11,482)	$ 127,299
Restructuring costs	–	–	(10,300)	–	(10,300)
Segment operating profit	$ 16,584	$ 139,381	$ (27,484)	$ (11,482)	$ 116,999
Interest expense					(13,238)
General corporate expense					(6,954)
Income from operations					$ 96,807
Identifiable assets	$236,058	$1,075,609	$373,768	$ 90,451	$1,775,886
Intersegment eliminations					(12,000)
Corporate assets including investment in associated corporations					353,087
Total assets					$2,116,973
Depreciation expense	$ 8,003	$ 43,965	$ 20,801	$ 11,414	$ 84,183
Capital expenditures	$ 15,185	$ 79,741	$ 12,229	$ 13,132	$ 120,287
1990					
Total revenue	$267,532	$1,658,641	$444,959	$413,722	$2,784,854
Intergeographical segment sales	(1,267)	(13,991)	–	–	(15,258)
Sales to customers outside the enterprise	$266,265	$1,644,650	$444,959	$413,722	$2,769,596
Segment operating profit before restructuring costs	$ 19,000	$ 155,446	$ (4,747)	$ 70,194	$ 239,893
Restructuring costs	–	(35,094)	(19,906)	–	(55,000)
Segment operating profit	$ 19,000	$ 120,352	$ (24,653)	$ 70,194	$ 184,893
Interest expense					(17,247)
General corporate expense					(5,568)
Income from operations					$ 162,078
Identifiable assets	$268,220	$ 998,135	$401,368	$105,487	$1,773,210
Intersegment eliminations					(8,921)
Corporate assets including investment in associated corporations					401,401
Total assets					$2,165,690
Depreciation expense	$ 6,871	$ 38,661	$ 21,131	$ 10,338	$ 77,001
Capital expenditures	$ 17,096	$ 108,604	$ 23,804	$ 16,561	$ 166,065
1989					
Total revenue	$271,436	$1,675,580	$406,124	$365,509	$2,718,649
Intergeographical segment sales	(209)	(10,034)	–	–	(10,243)
Sales to customers outside the enterprise	$271,227	$1,665,546	$406,124	$365,509	$2,708,406
Segment operating profit	$ 31,922	$ 207,862	$ 8,368	$ 45,205	$ 293,357
Interest expense					(12,787)
General corporate expense					(11,773)
Income from operations					$ 268,797
Identifiable assets	$247,066	$ 973,007	$326,858	$160,477	$1,707,408
Intersegment eliminations					(21,567)
Corporate assets including investment in associated corporations					322,478
Total assets					$2,008,319
Depreciation expense	$ 6,971	$ 36,109	$ 15,342	$ 9,446	$ 67,868
Capital expenditures	$ 6,715	$ 81,214	$ 27,633	$ 11,149	$ 126,711

18. Consolidated Statement of Cash Information *(in thousands)*

(a) Increase (decrease) in cash resources	1991	1990	1989
Cash	**$(11,726)**	$ 5,936	$ 8,979
Short-term securities	**54**	(3,293)	3,598
Bank loans	**4,541**	1,094	19,980
	$ (7,131)	$ 3,737	$ 32,557

(b) Items not affecting cash resources	1991	1990	1989
Depreciation	**$ 84,183**	$ 77,001	$ 67,868
Equity in earnings of associated corporations	**(17,547)**	(15,361)	(20,374)
Minority interests in earnings	**1,096**	1,170	517
Deferred income taxes	**(11,891)**	4,913	5,477
Amortization of goodwill and deferred charges	**26,695**	17,614	15,191
Increase (decrease) in pension reserve	**(1,424)**	11,520	(3,290)
Gain on sale of properties	**–**	(3,151)	(556)
Unrealized exchange adjustments	**11,712**	50,725	32,459
Other	**18,654**	2	11,473
	$111,478	$144,433	$108,765

(c) Decrease (increase) in working capital other than cash resources	1991	1990	1989
Accounts receivable	**$ 10,732**	$ 15,916	$(44,324)
Inventories	**43,848**	(19,297)	17,622
Prepaid expenses	**3,730**	(3,498)	(3,379)
Deferred taxes	**8,725**	(20,405)	(5,595)
Accounts payable and accruals	**(65,858)**	43,686	21,579
Dividends payable	**230**	1,713	2,248
Accrued income taxes	**(8,129)**	(9,640)	21,713
Working capital of acquisitions and disposals	**835**	(6,536)	4,893
Unrealized exchange adjustments	**(6,063)**	(10,226)	(5,501)
Other	**869**	1,844	2,852
	$(11,081)	$ (6,443)	$ 12,108

19. Lease Commitments *(in thousands)*

At December 31, 1991, long-term lease commitments require approximate future rental payments as follows:

Rental payments			
1992	$52,154	1995	$22,340
1993	42,908	1996	18,031
1994	31,322	1997 and thereafter	34,578

20. Contingencies

At December 31, 1991, certain lawsuits and other claims arising in the ordinary course of business were pending against the Corporation. While the outcome of these matters is not determinable, management believes that the ultimate resolution of these matters will not have a material effect on the Corporation's financial position.

21. Differences between Canadian and United States generally accepted accounting principles

The continued registration of the common shares of the Corporation with the Securities and Exchange Commission and listing of the shares on the New York Stock Exchange requires compliance with the integrated disclosure rules of the Securities and Exchange Commission.

The accounting policies in note 1 and accounting principles generally accepted in Canada are consistent in all material aspects with United States generally accepted accounting principles with the following exceptions.

Accounting and Reporting for the effects of income taxes

In February 1992, the Financial Accounting Standards Board in the United States issued a new standard for accounting for income taxes effective for fiscal years beginning after December 15, 1992. The Corporation will adopt the standard effective January 1, 1993 for the purpose of calculating earnings stated in accordance with United States generally accepted accounting principles.

There is no indication that the applicable Canadian accounting standard will be changed.

ACCOUNTING AND REPORTING FOR POSTRETIREMENT BENEFITS OTHER THAN PENSIONS

The Financial Accounting Standards Board in the United States has issued an accounting standard for postretirement benefits other than pensions effective for fiscal years beginning after December 15, 1992, requiring that related costs be accrued over the years eligible employees render service. The Corporation has not quantified the effect of the change on earnings stated in accordance with United States generally accepted accounting principles. The Corporation's accounting for such benefits is described in note 12.

22. COMPARATIVE CONSOLIDATED FINANCIAL STATEMENTS

Comparative figures have been restated where appropriate to conform to the current presentation.

MANAGEMENT REPORT

All of the information in this annual report is the responsibility of management and has been approved by the Board of Directors. The financial information contained herein conforms to the accompanying consolidated financial statements, which have been prepared and presented in accordance with accounting principles generally accepted in Canada and necessarily include amounts that are based on judgements and estimates applied consistently and considered appropriate in the circumstances.

The Corporation maintains a system of internal control which is designed to provide reasonable assurance that assets are safeguarded, that accurate accounting records are maintained, and that reliable financial information is prepared on a timely basis. The Corporation also maintains an internal audit department that evaluates and formally reports to management and the Audit Committee on the adequacy and effectiveness of internal controls.

The consolidated financial statements have been audited by the Corporation's independent auditors, Price Waterhouse, and their report is included below.

The Audit Committee of the Board of Directors is composed entirely of outside directors and meets periodically with the Corporation's independent auditors, management, and the Corporation's Director of Internal Audit to discuss the scope and results of audit examinations with respect to internal controls and financial reporting of the Corporation.

M.K. Goodrich
M.K. GOODRICH
Chairman of the Board, President and
Chief Executive Officer

J.B. McArthur
J.B. MCARTHUR
Vice Chairman of the Board and
Chief Financial Officer

February 19, 1992.

AUDITORS' REPORT

To the Shareholders of Moore Corporation Limited:

We have audited the consolidated balance sheets of Moore Corporation Limited as at December 31, 1991 and 1990 and the consolidated statements of earnings, retained earnings and changes in cash resources for each of the three years in the period ended December 31, 1991. These consolidated financial statements are the responsibility of the Corporation's management. Our responsibility is to express an opinion on these consolidated financial statements based on our audit.

We conducted our audit in accordance with generally accepted auditing standards. Those standards require that we plan and perform an audit to obtain reasonable assurance whether the financial statements are free of material misstatement. An audit includes examining, on a test basis, evidence supporting the amounts and disclosures in the financial statements. An audit also includes assessing the accounting principles used and significant estimates made by management, as well as evaluating the overall financial statement presentation.

In our opinion, these consolidated financial statements present fairly, in all material respects, the financial position of the Corporation as at December 31, 1991 and 1990 and the results of its operations and the changes in its cash resources for each of the three years in the period ended December 31, 1991 in accordance with generally accepted accounting principles.

Price Waterhouse
PRICE WATERHOUSE
Chartered Accountants, Toronto, Canada

February 19, 1992.

QUESTIONS

1. How does information from the balance sheet help users of the financial statements?
2. A recent financial magazine indicated that a drug company had good financial flexibility. What is meant by "financial flexibility" and why is it important?
3. What is meant by "liquidity"? Rank the following assets from one to five in order of liquidity:
   (a) Goodwill. (d) Short-term investments.
   (b) Inventories. (e) Accounts receivable.
   (c) Buildings.
4. What are the major limitations of the balance sheet as a source of information?
5. In its December 31, 1994 balance sheet, Buggert Limited reported as an asset "Net Notes and Accounts Receivable, $6,800,000." What other disclosures are necessary?
6. Should marketable securities always be reported as a current asset? Explain.
7. A stock analyst recently noted that a balance sheet is more critical than the income statement. He stated, "You can show beautiful profits by burying inventories." Explain his comment.
8. What is the relationship between a current asset and a current liability?
9. The Ottawa Senators Ltd. sold 10,000 season tickets at $600 each. By December 31, 1994, 18 of the 40 home games had been played. What amount should be reported as a current liability at December 31, 1994?
10. What is working capital? How does working capital relate to the operating cycle?
11. In what section of the balance sheet should the following items appear, and what balance sheet terminology would you use?
    (a) Chequing account at bank.
    (b) Trade accounts receivable.
    (c) Reserve for sinking fund.
    (d) Unamortized premium on bonds payable.
    (e) Investment in copyrights.
    (f) Long-term investments (pledged against bank loans payable).
12. Where should the following items be shown on the balance sheet, if shown at all?
    (a) Allowance for doubtful accounts receivable.
    (b) Merchandise held on consignment.
    (c) Advances received on sales contract.
    (d) Merchandise out on consignment.
    (e) Franchises.
    (f) Accumulated depreciation of plant and equipment.
    (g) Materials in transit, f.o.b. destination.
13. State the generally accepted accounting principle (standard) applicable to the balance sheet valuation of each of the following assets:
    (a) Trade accounts receivable.
    (b) Land.
    (c) Inventories.
    (d) Marketable securities.
    (e) Prepaid expenses.
14. Refer to the definition of assets. Discuss how a leased building might qualify as an asset of the lessee under this definition.
15. Ann Schmidt says, "Retained earnings should be reported as an asset, since it is earnings that are reinvested in the business." How would you respond to her statement?
16. Cardinal Limited is involved in a lawsuit. Its legal counsel says it is reasonably possible that Cardinal will lose the suit. Should the corporation record a loss and liability on this lawsuit?
17. Sycamore Limited's lawyer says the company will probably prevail in a lawsuit and win damages of $1,000,000. The bookkeeper recorded a receivable and a gain in this amount. Is this correct?
18. What is a gain contingency? A loss contingency? Give two examples of each.
19. The president of your company recently read an article that disturbs him greatly. The author of this article stated that "although the balance sheet and income statement balance to the penny, they are full of estimates and subject to material error." Indicate items found in these statements that are based on estimates and explain why you must resort to "guessing" these amounts.
20. The creditors of MicroTough Limited agree to accept promissory notes for the amount of its indebtedness, with a proviso that two-thirds of the annual profits must be applied to their liquidation. How should these notes be shown on the balance sheet of the issuing company? Give a reason for your answer.
21. What are the major types of subsequent events? Indicate how each of the following subsequent events would be reported:
    (a) Collection of a note written off in a prior period.
    (b) Issuance of a large preferred share offering.
    (c) Acquisition of a company in a different industry.
    (d) Destruction of a major plant in a flood.
    (e) Death of company's chief executive officer (CEO).
    (f) Settlement of a four-week strike at additional wage costs.

(g) Settlement of a federal income tax case at considerably more tax than anticipated at year end.
(h) Change in the product mix from consumer goods to industrial goods.

22. What are some of the techniques of disclosure for the balance sheet?

23. What is the difference between the report form and the account form for the purpose of balance sheet presentation?

24. What are "significant accounting policies"?

25. What types of contractual obligations must be disclosed in great detail in the notes to the balance sheet? Why do you think these detailed provisions should be disclosed?

26. What is the profession's recommendation in regard to the use of the term "reserve"? Explain.

27. What is the purpose of the statement of changes in financial position? How does it differ from a balance sheet and an income statement?

28. The net income for the year for Elgin Ltd. is $750,000, but the statement of changes in financial position reports that the cash provided by operating activities is $890,000. What might account for the difference?

29. Differentiate the meanings of operating activities, investing activities, and financing activities.

30. Each of the following items must be considered in preparing a statement of changes in financial position. Indicate where each item is to be reported in the statement, if at all. Assume that net income is reported as $90,000.
(a) Accounts receivable increased from $32,000 to $37,000 from the beginning to the end of the year.
(b) During the year, 10,000 preferred shares were issued at $110 per share.
(c) Depreciation expense amounted to $15,000 and bond premium amortization amounted to $7,000.

31. The controller is asked by the financial vice-president to include in the supplementary information of the annual report some comments on employee commitment to excellence that distinguishes Zenith Motors Limited from its competitors. The controller knows that such remarks cannot be supported objectively in the balance sheet. Should the controller comply with this request? Might this subjective material mislead some stakeholders?

CASES

C5-1

(REPORTING VARIED TRANSACTIONS) The following items were brought to your attention during the course of the year-end audit:

1. The client expects to recover a substantial amount in connection with a pending refund claim for a prior year's taxes. Although the claim is being contested, counsel for the company has confirmed this expectation.

2. Your client is a defendant in a patent infringement suit involving a material amount. You have received from the client's counsel a statement that the loss can be reasonably estimated and that it is likely to occur.

3. Cash includes a substantial sum set aside specifically for immediate reconstruction of a plant and replacement of machinery.

4. Because of a general increase in the number of labour disputes and strikes, both within and outside the industry, it is very likely that the client will suffer a costly strike in the near future.

5. Trade accounts receivable include a large number of customers' notes, many of which have been renewed several times and may have to be renewed continually for some time in the future. The interest is settled on each maturity date and the manufacturers are in good credit standing.

6. At the beginning of the year the client entered into a 10-year nonrenewable lease agreement. Provisions in the lease require the client to make substantial reconditioning and restoration expenditures at the termination of the lease, if necessary.

7. Inventory includes retired equipment, some at regularly depreciated book value and some at scrap or sale value.

Instructions

For each of the situations above, describe the accounting treatment that you would recommend for the current year. Justify your recommended treatment for each situation.

C5-2 **(POST-BALANCE SHEET EVENTS)** At December 31, 1994, Snap Ltd. has assets of $10,000,000, liabilities of $6,000,000, share capital of $2,000,000 (representing 2,000,000 no-par common shares), and retained earnings of $2,000,000. Net sales for the year 1994 were $18,000,000 and net income was $800,000. As auditors of this company, you are making a review of the company's subsequent events on February 13, 1995, and find the following:

1. On February 3, 1995, one of the Snap Ltd. customers declared bankruptcy. At December 31, 1994, this company owed Snap $300,000, of which $30,000 was paid in January 1995.

2. On January 18, 1995, one of the client's three major plants burned down.

3. On January 23, 1995, a strike was called at one of Snap's largest plants, which halted 30% of its production. As of your renewal date (February 13), the strike has not been settled.

4. A major electronics enterprise has introduced a line of products that will compete directly with Snap's primary line, now being produced in a specially designed new plant. Because of manufacturing innovations, the competitor has been able to achieve quality similar to that of Snap's products, but at a price 50% lower. Snap officials say they will meet the lower prices, which are high enough to cover variable manufacturing and selling costs but which permit recovery of only a portion of fixed costs.

5. Merchandise traded in the open market is recorded in the company's records at $1.40 per unit on December 31, 1994. This price had prevailed for two weeks, after release of an official market report that predicted vastly increased supplies; however, no purchases were made at $1.40. The price throughout the preceding year had been about $2.00, after public disclosure of an error in the official calculations of the prior December resulted in a correction that destroyed the expectations of excessive supplies. Inventory at December 31, 1994 was on a lower of cost and market basis.

6. On February 1, 1995, the board of directors adopted a resolution accepting the offer of an investment banker to guarantee the marketing of $1,000,000 of preferred shares.

Instructions

State in each case how the 1992 financial statements would be affected, if at all.

C5-3 **(REPORTING THE FINANCIAL EFFECTS OF VARIED TRANSACTIONS)** In an examination of Heart Corporation Ltd. as of December 31, 1994, you have learned that the following situations exist. No entries have been made in the accounting records for these items:

1. The corporation erected its present factory building in 1979. Depreciation was calculated by the straight-line method, using an estimated life of 35 years. Early in1994, the board of directors conducted a careful survey and estimated that the factory building had a remaining useful life of 25 years as of January 1, 1994.

2. An additional assessment of 1993 income taxes was levied and paid in 1994.

3. When calculating the accrual for officers' salaries at December 31, 1994, it was discovered that the accrual for officers' salaries for December 31, 1993 had been overstated.

4. On December 15, 1994, Heart Corporation Ltd. declared a stock dividend of 1,000 common shares per 100,000 of its common shares outstanding, payable February 1, 1995, to the common shareholders of record on December 31, 1994.

5. Heart Corporation Ltd., which is on a calendar-year basis, changed its inventory method as of January 1, 1994. The inventory for December 31, 1993 was costed by the average method, and the inventory for December 31, 1994 was costed by the FIFO method.

6. Heart Corporation Ltd. has guaranteed the payment of interest on the 20-year first mortgage bonds of Boss Company, an affiliate. Outstanding bonds of Boss Company amount to $150,000, with interest payable at 10% per annum, due June 1 and December 1 of each year. The bonds were issued by Boss Company on December 1, 1990, and all interest payments have been met by the company with the exception ofthe payment due December 1, 1994. Heart Corporation Ltd. states that it will pay the defaulted interest to the bondholders on January 15, 1995.

7. During the year 1994, Heart Corporation Ltd. was named as a defendant in a suit for damages by Ann Short Company for breach of contract. The case was decided in favour of Ann Short Company and it was awarded $80,000 damages. At the time of the audit, the case was under appeal to a higher court.

Instructions

Describe fully how each of the items above should be reported in the financial statements of Heart Corporation Ltd. for the year 1994.

(CURRENT ASSET AND LIABILITY CLASSIFICATION) Below are the account titles of a number of debit and credit accounts as they might appear on the balance sheet of Jim Langford Inc. as of October 31, 1994. **C5-4**

Debits	Credits
Interest accrued on notes receivable	Preferred shares
Notes receivable	11% first mortgage bonds due in 2001
Petty cash fund	Preferred dividend, payable Nov. 1, 1994
Canadian government securities	Allowance for doubtful accounts
Treasury shares	Estimated income taxes payable
Unamortized bond discount	Customer advances (on contracts to be completed in 1995)
Cash in bank	Appropriation for possible decline in value of raw materials inventory
Land	Premium on bonds redeemable in 1995
Inventory of operating parts and supplies	Officers' 1994 accrued bonus
Inventory of raw materials	Accrued payroll
Patents	Provision for renegotiation of government contracts
Cash and bonds set aside for property additions	Notes payable
Investment in subsidiary	Accrued interest on bonds
Accounts receivable:	Accumulated depreciation
Government contracts	Accounts payable
Regular	Accrued interest on notes payable
Instalments—due next year	Contributed surplus
Instalments—due after next year	8% first mortgage bonds to be redeemed in 1994 out of current assets
Goodwill	
Inventory of finished goods	
Inventory of work in process	
Deficit	

Instructions

Select the current asset and current liability items from among these debits and credits. If there appear to be certain borderline cases that you are unable to classify without further information, mention them and explain your difficulty, or give your reasons for making questionable classifications, if any.

(AICPA adapted)

C5-5 (IDENTIFYING BALANCE SHEET DEFICIENCIES) The assets of John Whitesell Motors Limited are presented below (000s omitted).

John Whitesell Motors Limited
Balance Sheet
December 31, 1994

Assets

Current assets		
Cash		$ 100,000
Unclaimed payroll cheques		27,500
Marketable securities (cost $20,000) at market		34,500
Accounts receivable (less bad debt reserve)		75,000
Inventories—at lower of cost (determined by the next-in, first-out method) and market		220,000
Total current assets		$ 457,000
Tangible assets		
Land (less accumulated depreciation)		$ 80,000
Buildings and equipment	$800,000	
Less: accumulated depreciation	300,000	500,000
Net tangible assets		$ 580,000
Long-term investments		
Shares and bonds		$ 100,000
Sinking fund		50,000
Total long-term investments		$ 150,000
Other assets		
Discount on bonds payable		$ 14,200
Claim against Canadian government (pending)		975,000
Total other assets		$ 989,200
Total assets		$2,176,200

Instructions

Indicate the deficiencies, if any, in the foregoing assets of John Whitesell Motors Limited.

C5-6 (CRITIQUE OF BALANCE SHEET FORMAT AND CONTENT) Presented below is the balance sheet of Craig Eaket Limited (000s omitted).

Craig Eaket Limited
Balance Sheet
December 31, 1994

Assets

Current assets	
Cash	$30,000
Marketable securities	18,000
Accounts receivable	25,000
Merchandise inventory	20,000
Supplies inventory	4,000

(Continued)

Investment in subsidiary company	20,000	$117,000
Investments		
Treasury shares		26,000
Property, plant, and equipment:		
Buildings and land	$91,000	
Less: Reserve for depreciation	30,000	61,000
Other assets		
Cash surrender value of life insurance		18,000
		$222,000
Liabilities and Capital		
Current liabilities		
Accounts payable	$22,000	
Reserve for income taxes	14,000	
Customers' accounts with credit balances	1	$ 36,001
Deferred credits		
Unamortized premium on bonds payable		2,000
Long-term liabilities		
Bonds payable		56,000
Total liabilities		$ 94,001
Share capital		
Capital shares issued	$95,000	
Earned surplus	24,999	
Cash dividends declared	8,000	127,999
		$222,000

Instructions

Criticize the balance sheet presented above. State briefly the proper treatment for the items criticized.

C5-7 **(IDENTIFYING BALANCE SHEET DEFICIENCIES)** The financial statement below was prepared by employees of your client, Susan Bannerman Ltd. The statement is unaccompanied by notes.

Susan Bannerman Ltd.
Balance Sheet
As of November 30, 1994

Current assets		
Cash	$ 100,000	
Accounts receivable (less allowance of $30,000 for doubtful accounts)	419,900	
Inventories	2,554,000	$3,073,900
Less: Current liabilities		
Accounts payable	$ 306,400	
Accrued payroll	8,260	
Accrued interest on mortgage note	12,000	
Estimated taxes payable	66,000	392,660
Net working capital		$2,681,240

(Continued)

Property, plant, and equipment (at cost)	Cost	Depreciation	Value	
Land and buildings	$ 983,300	$310,000	$ 673,300	
Machinery and equipment	1,135,700	568,699	567,001	
	$2,119,000	$878,699		1,240,301
Deferred charges				
Prepaid taxes and other expenses			21,700	
Unamortized discount on mortgage note			10,800	32,500
Total net working capital and noncurrent assets				$3,954,041
Less: Deferred liabilities				
Mortgage note payable			$ 300,000	
Unearned revenue			1,908,000	2,208,000
Total net assets				$1,746,041
Shareholders' equity				
$4 preferred shares				$ 400,000
Common shares				697,000
Contributed surplus				210,000
Retained earnings				483,641
Treasury shares at cost (400 shares)				(44,600)
Total shareholders' equity				$1,746,041

Instructions

Indicate the deficiencies, if any, in the balance sheet above in regard to form, terminology, descriptions, content, and the like.

C5-8 **(ERRORS AND DEFICIENCIES IN THE BALANCE SHEET AND AN INCOME STATEMENT)** The following year-end financial statements were prepared by Mindbenders Limited's bookkeeper. Mindbenders Limited operates a chain of retail stores.

Mindbenders Limited
Balance Sheet
June 30, 1994

Assets

Current assets		
Cash		$ 150,000
Notes receivable		50,000
Accounts receivable, less reserve for doubtful accounts		175,000
Inventories		395,500
Investment securities (at cost)		100,000
Total current assets		$ 870,500
Property, plant, and equipment		
Land (at cost) (Note 1)	$180,000	
Buildings, at cost less accumulated depreciation of $350,000	500,000	
Equipment, at cost less accumulated depreciation of $180,000	400,000	1,080,000
Intangibles		450,000
Other assets		
Prepaid expenses		26,405
Total assets		$2,426,905

(Continued)

Liabilities and Owners' Equity

Current liabilities			
Accounts payable			$ 135,500
Estimated income taxes payable			160,000
Contingent liability on discounted notes receivable			50,000
Total current liabilities			345,500
Long-term liabilities			
15% serial bonds, $50,000 due annually on December 31			
Maturity value		$900,000	
Less: Unamortized discount		35,000	865,000
Total liabilities			$1,210,500
Owners' equity			
Common shares (authorized and issued, 75,000 shares)		$750,000	
Retained earnings			
Appropriated (Note 2)	$120,000		
Free	346,405	466,405	1,216,405
Total liabilities and owners' equity			$2,426,905

Mindbenders Limited

Income Statement

As of June 30, 1994

Sales			$2,500,000
Interest revenue			6,000
Total revenue			2,506,000
Cost of goods sold			1,780,000
Gross margin			726,000
Operating expenses			
Selling expenses			
Salaries	$105,000		
Advertising	75,000		
Sales returns and allowances	50,000	$230,000	
General and administrative expenses			
Wages	84,000		
Property taxes	38,000		
Depreciation and amortization	86,000		
Rent (Note 3)	75,000		
Interest on serial bonds	48,000	331,000	561,000
Income before income taxes			165,000
Income taxes			80,000
Net income			$ 85,000

Notes to financial statements:

Note 1. Includes a future store site acquired during the year at a cost of $90,000.

Note 2. Retained earnings in the amount of $120,000 have been set aside to finance expansion.

Note 3. During the year, the Corporation acquired certain equipment under a long-term lease.

Instructions

Identify and discuss the defects in the financial statements above with respect to terminology, disclosure, and classification. Your discussion should explain why you consider them to be defects. Do not prepare revised statements.

(AICPA adapted)

EXERCISES

E5-1 **(BALANCE SHEET CLASSIFICATIONS)** Presented below are a number of balance sheet accounts of Billy Idol Inc.:

1. Investment in preferred shares
2. Treasury shares
3. Common shares distributable
4. Accumulated depreciation
5. Warehouse in process of construction
6. Petty cash
7. Deficit
8. Marketable securities (short-term)
9. Income taxes payable
10. Accrued interest on notes payable
11. Unearned subscription revenue
12. Work in process
13. Accrued vacation pay
14. Cash dividends payable

Instructions

For each of the accounts above, indicate the proper balance sheet classification. In the case of borderline items, indicate the additional information that would be required to determine the proper classification.

E5-2 **(CLASSIFICATION OF BALANCE SHEET ACCOUNTS)** Presented below are the captions of Depeche Mode Limited's balance sheet:

A. Current assets
B. Investments
C. Property, plant, and equipment
D. Intangible assets
E. Other assets
F. Current liabilities
G. Noncurrent liabilities
H. Share capital
I. Contributed surplus
J. Retained earnings

Instructions

Indicate by letter where each of the following items would be classified:

1. Preferred shares
2. Goodwill
3. Wages payable
4. Trade accounts payable

(Continued)

5. Buildings
6. Marketable securities
7. Current portion of long-term debt
8. Premium on bonds payable
9. Allowance for doubtful accounts
10. Appropriation for contingencies
11. Cash surrender value of life insurance
12. Notes payable (due next year)
13. Common shares
14. Land
15. Bond sinking fund
16. Merchandise inventory
17. Office supplies
18. Prepaid insurance
19. Bonds payable
20. Taxes payable

E5-3 **(CLASSIFICATION OF BALANCE SHEET ACCOUNTS)** Assume that Marilyn Healey Enterprises uses the following headings on its balance sheet:

A. Current assets
B. Investments
C. Property, plant, and equipment
D. Intangible assets
E. Other assets
F. Current liabilities
G. Long-term liabilities
H. Share capital
I. Contributed surplus
J. Retained earnings

Instructions

Indicate by letter where each of the following usually should be classified. If an item should appear in a note to the financial statements, use the letter "N" to indicate this fact. If an item need not be reported at all on the balance sheet, use the letter "X."

1. Advances to suppliers.
2. Unearned rental revenue.
3. Common shares issued.
4. Unexpired insurance.
5. Shares owned in affiliated companies.
6. Unearned subscriptions revenue.
7. Preferred shares issued.
8. Copyrights.
9. Petty cash fund.
10. Sale of large issue of common shares 15 days after balance sheet date.
11. Accrued interest on notes receivable.
12. Twenty-year issue of bonds payable that will mature within the next year. (No sinking fund exists and refunding is not planned.)
13. Machinery retired from use and held for sale.
14. Fully depreciated machine still in use.
15. Organization costs.
16. Salaries that company budget shows will be paid to employees within the next year.
17. Company is a defendant in a lawsuit for $1 million (possibility of loss is reasonably likely).
18. Discount on bonds payable. (Assume related to bonds payable in No. 12.)
19. Accrued interest on bonds payable.
20. Accumulated depreciation.

E5-4 **(PREPARATION OF A CLASSIFIED BALANCE SHEET)** Assume that En Vogue Inc. has the following accounts at the end of the current year:

1. Common shares
2. Discount on bonds payable
3. Treasury shares (at cost)
4. Common shares subscribed
5. Raw materials
6. Investments in preferred shares—long-term
7. Unearned rent revenue
8. Appropriation for plant expansion
9. Work in process
10. Copyrights
11. Buildings
12. Notes receivable (short-term)
13. Cash
14. Accrued salaries payable
15. Accumulated depreciation—buildings
16. Notes receivable discounted
17. Cash restricted for plant expansion
18. Land held for future plant site
19. Allowance for doubtful accounts—accounts receivable
20. Retained earnings—unappropriated
21. Unearned subscription revenue
22. Receivables—officers (due in one year)
23. Finished goods
24. Accounts receivable
25. Bonds payable (due in four years)
26. Share subscriptions receivable

Instructions

Prepare a balance sheet in good form (no monetary amounts are necessary).

E5-5 **(PREPARATION OF A CORRECTED BALANCE SHEET)** John Parkinson Company has decided to expand its operations. The bookkeeper recently completed the balance sheet presented below in order to obtain additional funds for expansion.

John Parkinson Company
Balance Sheet
For the Year Ended 1994

Current assets	
Cash (net of bank overdraft of $40,000)	$200,000
Accounts receivable (net)	330,000
Inventories at lower of average cost and market	395,000
Marketable securities—at market (cost $120,000)	140,000
Property, plant, and equipment	
Building (net)	570,000
Office equipment (net)	160,000
Land held for future use	175,000
Intangible assets	
Goodwill	80,000
Cash surrender value of life insurance	90,000
Prepaid expenses	5,000

(Continued)

Current liabilities	
Accounts payable	95,000
Notes payable (due next year)	125,000
Pension obligation	92,000
Rent payable	55,000
Premium on bonds payable	53,000
Long-term liabilities	
Bond payable	500,000
Appropriation for plant expansion	92,000
Shareholders' equity	
Common shares, no par; authorized 400,000 shares; issued 290,000	290,000
Contributed surplus—donations	160,000
Retained earnings	?

Instructions

Prepare a revised balance sheet given the available information. Assume that the accumulated depreciation balance for the buildings is $140,000 and for the office equipment, $95,000. The allowance for doubtful accounts has a balance of $10,000. The pension obligation is considered a long-term liability.

(CORRECTIONS OF A BALANCE SHEET) The bookkeeper for George Fenton Company has prepared the following balance sheet as of July 31, 1994. E5-6

George Fenton Company
Balance Sheet
As of July 31, 1994

Cash	$ 59,000	Notes and accounts payable	$ 44,000
Accounts receivable (net)	50,500	Long-term liabilities	75,000
Inventories	60,000	Shareholders' equity	155,500
Equipment (net)	84,000		
Patents	21,000		
	$274,500		$274,500

The following additional information is provided.

1. Cash includes $1,200 in a petty cash fund and $9,000 in a bond sinking fund.
2. The net accounts receivable balance comprises the following three items: (a) accounts receivable—debit balances $60,000; (b) accounts receivable—credit balances $6,000; (c) allowance for doubtful accounts—$3,500.
3. Merchandise inventory costing $5,300 is shipped out on consignment on July 31, 1994. The ending inventory balance does not include the consigned goods. Receivables in the amount of $5,300 are recognized on these consigned goods.
4. Equipment has a cost of $100,000 and an accumulated depreciation balance of $16,000.
5. Taxes payable of $7,000 are accrued on July 31. George Fenton Company has set up a cash fund to meet this obligation. This cash fund is not included in the cash balance, but is offset against the taxes payable amount.

Instructions

Prepare a corrected balance sheet as of July 31, 1994 from the available information.

E5-7 **(CURRENT ASSET SECTION OF THE BALANCE SHEET)** Following are selected accounts of Motley Crue Company at December 31, 1994.

Finished goods	$ 52,000
Revenue received in advance	90,000
Bank overdraft	8,000
Equipment	253,000
Work in process	14,000
Cash	37,000
Short-term investments in shares	31,000
Customer advances	36,000
Cash restricted for plant expansion	50,000
Cost of goods sold	2,100,000
Notes receivable	50,000
Accounts receivable	161,000
Raw materials	207,000
Supplies expense	60,000
Allowance for doubtful accounts	10,000
Licences	18,000
Contributed surplus	88,000
Treasury shares	22,000

The following additional information is available:

1. Inventories are valued at the lower of cost and market using FIFO.
2. Equipment is recorded at cost. Accumulated depreciation, computed on a straight-line basis, is $50,600.
3. The short-term investments have a market value of $28,000 (assume marketable).
4. The notes receivable are due June 30, 1997 with interest receivable every June 30. The notes bear interest at 12%. (Hint: Accrue interest due on 12/31/94.)
5. The allowance for doubtful accounts applies to the accounts receivable. Accounts receivable of $50,000 are pledged as collateral on a bank loan.
6. Licences are recorded net of accumulated amortization of $14,000.
7. Treasury shares are recorded at cost.

Instructions

Prepare the current asset section of Motley Crue Company's December 31, 1994 balance sheet, with appropriate disclosures.

E5-8 **(CURRENT VS. LONG-TERM LIABILITIES)** Patricia Corporation Ltd. is preparing its December 31, 1994 balance sheet. The following items may be reported as either a current or long-term liability:

1. On December 15, 1994, Patricia declares a cash dividend of $3.00 per share to shareholders of record on December 31. The dividend is payable on January 15, 1995. Patricia has issued 1,000,000 common shares of which 50,000 shares are held in treasury.
2. Also on December 15, Patricia declares a 10% stock dividend to shareholders of record on December 31. The dividend will be distributed on January 15, 1995. Patricia's no-par value common shares have a market value of $38 per share and an average issuance price of $10.
3. At December 31, bonds payable of $100,000,000 are outstanding. The bonds pay 12% interest every August 31 and mature in instalments of $25,000,000 every August 31, beginning August 31, 1995.

4. At December 31, 1993, customer advances are $12,000,000. During 1994, Patricia collects $30,000,000 of customer advances and earns advances of $27,000,000.

5. At December 31, 1994, retained earnings appropriate for future inventory losses is $15,000,000.

Instructions

For each item above, indicate the dollar amounts to be reported as current liabilities and as long-term liabilities, if any.

(CONTINGENCIES: ENTRIES AND DISCLOSURES) Aerosmith Sound Machines is involved with two contingencies at December 31, 1994: **E5-9**

1. The company is involved in a pending court case. Legal counsel feels it is likely that the company will prevail and be awarded damages of $4,000,000.

2. Aerosmith sells several machines under a one-year warranty. It is likely that a liability of $2,800,000 exists at December 31, 1994 because of this warranty.

Instructions

(a) Prepare all entries necessary at December 31, 1994 to record these contingencies.

(b) What disclosures would Aerosmith make in its December 31, 1994 balance sheet?

(POST-BALANCE SHEET EVENTS) Green Corporation Ltd. issued its financial statements for the year ended December 31, 1994 on March 10, 1995. The following events took place early in 1995: **E5-10**

1. On January 10, 10,000 no-par value common shares were issued at $70 per share.

2. On March 1, Green determined after negotiations with Revenue Canada that income taxes payable for 1994 should be $1,230,000. At December 31, 1994, income taxes payable were recorded at $1,100,000.

Instructions

Discuss how the preceding post-balance sheet events should be reflected in the 1994 financial statements.

(CURRENT ASSETS AND CURRENT LIABILITIES) The current asset and liability sections of the balance sheet of Jorgensen Limited appear as follows. **E5-11**

Jorgensen Limited
Partial Balance Sheet
December 31, 1994

Cash		$ 38,000	Accounts payable	$ 60,000
Accounts receivable	$86,000		Notes payable	64,000
Less allowance for doubtful accounts	7,000	79,000		
Inventories		170,000		
Prepaid expenses		9,000		
		$296,000		$124,000

The following errors in the corporation's accounting have been discovered:

1. January 1995 cash disbursements entered as of December 1994 included payments of accounts payable in the amount of $40,000, on which a cash discount of 2% was taken.

2. The inventory included $27,000 of merchandise that had been received at December 31 but for which no purchase invoices had been received or entered. Of this amount, $12,000 had been received on consignment; the remainder was purchased f.o.b. destination, terms 2/10, n/30.

3. Sales for the first four days of January 1995 in the amount of $30,000 were entered in the sales book as of December 31, 1994. Of these, $21,500 were sales on account and the remainder were cash sales.

4. Cash, not including cash sales, collected in January 1995 and entered as of December 31, 1994, totalled $35,324. Of this amount, $23,324 was received on account after cash discounts of 2% had been deducted; the remainder represented the proceeds of a bank loan.

Instructions

(a) Restate the current asset and liability sections of the balance sheet in accordance with good accounting practice. (Assume that both accounts receivable and accounts payable are recorded gross.)

(b) State the net effect of your adjustments on Jorgensen Limited's retained earnings balance.

E5-12 (POST-BALANCE SHEET EVENTS) For each of the following subsequent (post-balance sheet) events, indicate whether a company should (a) adjust the financial statements, (b) disclose in notes to the financial statements, or (c) neither adjust nor disclose.

1. Sale of a significant portion of the company's assets.
2. Retirement of the company president.
3. Prolonged employee strike.
4. Settlement of federal tax case at a cost considerably in excess of the amount expected at year end.
5. Introduction of a new product line.
6. Loss of assembly plant due to fire.
7. Loss of significant customer.
8. Issuance of a significant number of common shares.
9. Material loss on a year-end receivable because of a customer's bankruptcy.
10. Settlement of prior year's litigation against the company.
11. Merger with another company of comparable size.
12. Hiring of a new president.

E5-13 **(STATEMENT OF CHANGES IN FINANCIAL POSITION: CLASSIFICATIONS)** The major classifications of activities reported in the statement of changes in financial position are operating, investing, and listed financing. Classify each of the transactions that follow according to these five groupings:

1. Operating activity—add to net income.
2. Operating activity—deduct from net income.
3. Investing activity.
4. Financing activity.
5. Reported in two categories of the statement of changes in financial position.

The transactions are as follows:

(a) Issuance of shares.

(b) Purchase of land and building.

(c) Redemption of bonds.

(d) Sale of equipment.

(e) Depreciation of machinery.

(f) Amortization of patent.

(g) Issuance of bonds for plant assets.

(h) Payment of cash dividends.

(i) Purchase of treasury shares.

(j) Increase in accounts receivable during the year.

(k) Decrease in accounts payable during the year.

(l) Exchange of furniture for office equipment.

(m) Loss on sale of equipment.

E5-14 **(PREPARATION OF A STATEMENT OF CHANGES IN FINANCIAL POSITION)** The comparative balance sheets of Patty Loveless Inc. at the beginning and the end of the year 1994 appear below.

Patty Loveless Inc.
Balance Sheets

Assets	Dec. 31, 1994	Jan. 1, 1994	Inc./Dec.
Cash	$ 35,000	$ 13,000	$22,000 Inc.
Accounts receivable (net)	101,000	88,000	13,000 Inc.
Equipment	39,000	22,000	17,000 Inc.
Less accumulated depreciation	(17,000)	(11,000)	6,000 Inc.
Total	$158,000	$112,000	
Liabilities and Shareholders' Equity			
Accounts payable	$ 20,000	$ 15,000	5,000 Inc.
Common shares	100,000	80,000	20,000 Inc.
Retained earnings	38,000	17,000	21,000 Inc.
Total	$158,000	$112,000	

In 1994, net income of $40,000 was reported and dividends of $19,000 were paid. New equipment was purchased and none was sold.

Instructions

Prepare a statement of changes in financial position for the year 1994.

E5-15 (PREPARATION OF A STATEMENT OF CHANGES IN FINANCIAL POSITION) Following is a condensed version of the comparative balance sheets for G. Hammer Limited for the last two years at December 31.

	1994	1993
Cash	$147,000	$ 78,000
Accounts receivable	210,000	185,000
Investments	52,000	74,000
Equipment	298,000	241,000
Less accumulated depreciation	(106,000)	(80,000)
Current liabilities	134,000	161,000
Common shares	160,000	160,000
Retained earnings	307,000	177,000

Additional Information

Investments were sold at a loss (not extraordinary) of $9,000; no equipment was sold; cash dividends paid were $40,000; and net income was $170,000.

Instructions

Prepare a statement of changes in financial position for 1994 for G. Hammer Limited.

E5-16 (PREPARATION OF A STATEMENT OF CHANGES IN FINANCIAL POSITION) A comparative balance sheet for Keith Sweat Limited is presented below.

	December 31	
Assets	1994	1993
Cash	$ 49,000	$ 22,000
Accounts receivable (net)	92,000	66,000
Inventories	180,000	189,000
Land	75,000	110,000
Equipment	270,000	200,000
Accumulated depreciation—equipment	(69,000)	(42,000)
Total	$597,000	$545,000
Liabilities and Shareholders' Equity		
Accounts payable	$ 34,000	$ 47,000
Bonds payable	150,000	200,000
Common stock (no par)	214,000	164,000
Retained earnings	199,000	134,000
Total	$597,000	$545,000

Additional Information

1. Net income for 1994 was $120,000.
2. Cash dividends of $55,000 were declared and paid.
3. Bonds payable amounting to $50,000 were retired through issuance of common shares.

Instructions

Prepare a statement of changes in financial position for 1994 for Keith Sweat Limited.

(PREPARATION OF A BALANCE SHEET) Presented below is the trial balance of Sweet Sensation Limited at December 31, 1994. **E5-17**

	Debits	Credits
Cash	$ 127,000	
Sales		$ 8,000,000
Marketable securities—current	153,000	
Cost of goods sold	4,800,000	
Long-term investments in bonds	269,000	
Long-term investments in shares	327,000	
Short-term notes payable		90,000
Accounts payable		475,000
Selling expenses	2,000,000	
Investment revenue		63,000
Land	310,000	
Buildings	1,040,000	
Dividends payable		150,000
Accrued liabilities		96,000
Accounts receivable	435,000	
Accumulated depreciation—buildings		152,000
Allowance for doubtful accounts		25,000
Administrative expenses	900,000	
Interest expense	211,000	
Inventories	597,000	
Extraordinary gain		80,000
Prior period adjustment—depreciation error	140,000	
Long-term notes payable		900,000
Equipment	600,000	
Bonds payable		1,100,000
Accumulated depreciation—equipment		40,000
Franchise (net of $80,000 amortization)	160,000	
Common shares (no-par value)		1,000,000
Treasury shares	191,000	
Patent (net of $30,000 amortization)	195,000	
Retained earnings		204,000
Contributed surplus		80,000
Totals	$12,455,000	$12,455,000

Instructions

Prepare a balance sheet at December 31, 1994 for Sweet Sensation Limited.

(PREPARATION OF A STATEMENT OF CHANGES IN FINANCIAL POSITION AND A BALANCE SHEET) Randy Travis Limited's balance sheet at the end of 1993 included the following items: **E5-18**

Current assets	$235,000
Land	30,000
Building	120,000
Equipment	90,000

(Continued)

Accumulated depreciation—building		$ 30,000
Accumulated depreciation—equipment		11,000
Patents	40,000	
Current liabilities		150,000
Bonds payable		100,000
Common shares		180,000
Retained earnings		44,000
Totals	$515,000	$515,000

The following information is available for 1994:

1. Net income was $76,000.
2. Equipment (cost, $20,000 and accumulated depreciation, $8,000) was sold for $9,000.
3. Depreciation expense was $3,000 on the building and $9,000 on equipment.
4. Patent amortization was $5,000.
5. Current assets other than cash increased by $19,000. Current liabilities increased by $13,000.
6. An addition to the building was completed at a cost of $20,000.
7. A long-term investment in shares was purchased for $16,000.
8. Bonds payable of $50,000 were issued.
9. Cash dividends of $60,000 were declared and paid.
10. Treasury shares were purchased at a cost of $9,000.

Instructions

(a) Prepare a statement of changes in financial position for 1994.

(b) Prepare a balance sheet at December 31, 1994.

PROBLEMS

P5-1 **(PREPARATION OF A CLASSIFIED BALANCE SHEET)** Presented below is a list of accounts in alphabetical order:

Accounts receivable	Cash in bank
Accrued wages	Cash on hand
Accumulated depreciation—buildings	Cash surrender value of life insurance
Accumulated depreciation—equipment	Commission expense
Advances to employees	Common shares
Advertising expense	Dividends payable
Allowance for doubtful accounts	Equipment
Appropriation for plant expansion	Gain on sale of equipment
Appropriation for possible inventory	Income taxes payable
Bond sinking fund	Interest receivable
Bonds payable	Inventory—beginning
Buildings	Inventory—ending

(Continued)

Land	Price declines
Land for future plant site	Purchases
Loss from flood	Purchase returns and allowances
Notes payable	Retained earnings—unappropriated
Patent (net of amortization)	Sales
Pension obligations	Sales salaries
Petty cash	Temporary investments
Preferred shares	Transportation-in
Premium on bonds payable	Treasury shares (at cost)
Prepaid rent	Unearned subscription revenue

Instructions

Prepare a balance sheet in good form (no monetary amounts are to be shown).

P5-2 **(BALANCE SHEET PREPARATION)** Presented below are a number of balance sheet items for New Kids Inc. for the current year, 1994:

Accumulated depreciation—equipment	$ 292,000	Goodwill	$ 310,000
Inventories	239,800	Payroll taxes payable	177,591
Rent payable—short-term	45,000	Bonds payable	290,000
Taxes payable	98,362	Discount on bonds payable	15,000
Long-term rental obligations	480,000	Cash	160,000
Common shares, no-par value (200,000 shares issued)	200,000	Land	450,000
Preferred shares, no-par value (15,000 shares issued)	150,000	Notes receivable	545,700
Prepaid expenses	87,920	Notes payable to banks	265,000
Equipment	1,470,000	Accounts payable	590,000
Marketable securities (short-term)	81,000	Retained earnings	?
Accumulated depreciation—building	270,200	Refundable income taxes	97,630
Building	1,640,000	Unsecured notes payable (long-term)	1,500,000

Instructions

Prepare a balance sheet in good form. Authorized were 400,000 no-par common shares and 20,000 no-par preferred shares. Assume that notes receivable and notes payable are short term, unless stated otherwise.

P5-3 **(BALANCE SHEET ADJUSTMENT AND PREPARATION)** The trial balance of Baker Company and other related information for the year 1994 is presented below.

Baker Company
Trial Balance
December 31, 1994

Cash	$ 41,000	
Accounts Receivable	163,500	
Allowance for Doubtful Accounts		$ 6,700
Prepaid Expenses	5,900	
Inventory	288,500	
Long-Term Investments	359,000	
Land	85,000	

(Continued)

Construction Work in Progress	134,000	
Patents	26,000	
Equipment	400,000	
Accumulated Depreciation of Equipment		142,000
Unamortized Discount on Bonds Payable	20,000	
Accounts Payable		148,000
Accrued Expenses		48,200
Notes Payable		94,000
Bonds Payable		400,000
Common Shares		535,000
Retained Earnings		75,000
Reserve for Future Plant Expansion		74,000
	$1,522,900	$1,522,900

Additional Information

1. The inventory has a replacement market value of $353,000. The FIFO method of inventory value is used.
2. The market value of the long-term investments that consist of bonds and shares is $380,000.
3. The amount of the Construction Work in Progress account represents the costs expended to date on a building in the process of construction. (The company rents factory space at the present time.) The land on which the building is being constructed cost $85,000, as shown in the trial balance.
4. The patents purchased by the company at a cost of $34,000 are being amortized on a straight-line basis.
5. Of the unamortized discount on bonds payable, $2,000 will be amortized in 1995.
6. The notes payable represent bank loans that are secured by long-term investments carried at $120,000. These bank loans are due in 1995.
7. The bonds payable bear interest at 11% and are due January 1, 2005.
8. Of the 600,000 no-par common shares authorized, 500,000 shares are issued and outstanding.
9. The Reserve for Future Plant Expansion is created by action of the board of directors.

Instructions

Prepare a balance sheet as of December 31, 1994 to fully disclose all important information.

P5-4 **(PREPARATION OF A CORRECTED BALANCE SHEET)** Presented below is the balance sheet of Elton John Corporation Ltd. as of December 31, 1994.

Elton John Corporation Ltd.
Balance Sheet
December 31, 1994

Assets

Goodwill (Note 2)	$ 120,000
Building (Note 1)	1,640,000
Inventories	312,100

(Continued)

Land	750,000
Accounts receivable	170,000
Treasury shares (50,000 shares, no par)	87,000
Cash on hand	93,900
Assets allocated to trustee for plant expansion	
Cash in bank	70,000
Treasury bills, at cost	120,000
	$3,363,000

Equities

Notes payable (Note 3)	$ 600,000
Common shares, authorized and issued, 1,000,000 shares, no-par value	1,120,000
Retained earnings (unappropriated)	453,000
Appreciation capital (Note 1)	500,000
Income taxes payable	75,000
Reserve for depreciation of building	420,000
Reserve for repairs of machinery (Note 4)	68,000
Reserve for contingencies	127,000
	$3,363,000

Note 1
Buildings were stated at cost, except for one building that was recorded at appraised value. The excess of appraisal value over cost was $500,000.

Note 2
Goodwill in the amount of $120,000 was recognized because the Company believed that its book value was not an accurate representation of the fair market value of the Company.

Note 3
Notes payable were long term except for the current instalment of $100,000 that was due.

Note 4
A reserve for repairs was set up by a charge to expense. On consultation with the Company's auditors, it was determined that this contingency did not meet the criteria of a loss contingency. The Company still wished to show this amount in shareholders' equity.

Instructions

Prepare a corrected balance sheet in good form. The notes above are for information only.

P5-5 **(BALANCE SHEET ADJUSTMENT AND PREPARATION)** Presented below is the balance sheet of Roger Taylor Corporation Ltd. for the current year, 1994.

Roger Taylor Corporation
Balance Sheet
December 31, 1994

Current assets	$ 435,000	Current liabilities	$ 380,000
Investments	640,000	Long-term liabilities	1,040,000
Property, plant, and equipment	1,720,000	Shareholders' equity	1,680,000
Intangible assets	305,000		
	$3,100,000		$3,100,000

The following information is presented:

1. The current asset section includes: cash $100,000; accounts receivable $200,000 less $15,000 for allowance for doubtful accounts; inventories $180,000; and prepaid revenue $30,000. The cash balance consists of $116,000 less a bank overdraft of $16,000. Inventories are stated on the lower of FIFO cost and market basis.

2. The investments section includes the cash surrender value of a life insurance contract $40,000; investments in common shares: short-term $80,000 and long-term $140,000; bond sinking fund $180,000; and organization costs $200,000.

3. Property, plant, and equipment includes buildings $1,100,000 less accumulated depreciation $420,000; equipment $420,000 less accumulated depreciation $180,000; land $525,000; and land held for future use $275,000.

4. Intangible assets include a franchise $175,000; goodwill $100,000; and discount on bonds payable $30,000.

5. Current liabilities include accounts payable $90,000; notes payable: short-term $120,000 and long-term $80,000; taxes payable $40,000; and appropriation for short-term contingencies $50,000.

6. Long-term liabilities consist solely of 10% bonds payable due in the year 2002.

7. Shareholders' equity has no-par value preferred shares, authorized 200,000 shares, issued 70,000 shares for $455,000; and no-par value common shares, authorized 400,000 shares, issued 100,000 shares at an average price of $10. In addition, the corporation has unappropriated retained earnings of $225,000.

Instructions

Prepare a balance sheet in good form, adjusting the amounts in each balance sheet classification as affected by the information given above.

P5-6 **(BALANCE SHEET CORRECTION AND PREPARATION)** You have been engaged to examine the financial statements of Exile Limited for the year 1994. The bookkeeper who maintains the financial records has prepared all the unaudited financial statements for the corporation since its organization on January 2, 1988. The client provides you with the information below.

Exile Limited
Balance Sheet
As of December 31, 1994

Assets		**Liabilities**	
Current assets	$1,881,100	Current liabilities	$ 962,400
Other assets	5,171,400	Long-term liabilities	1,439,500
		Capital	4,650,600
	$7,052,500		$7,052,500

An analysis of current assets discloses the following:

Cash (restricted in the amount of $400,000 for plant expansion)	$ 571,000
Investments in land	185,000
Accounts receivable less allowance of $30,000	480,000
Inventories (FIFO flow assumption)	645,100
	$1,881,100

(Continued)

Other assets include:

Prepaid expenses	$ 57,400
Plant and equipment less accumulated depreciation of $1,430,000	4,130,000
Cash surrender value of life insurance policy	74,000
Unamortized bond discount	49,500
Notes receivable (short-term)	165,000
Goodwill, at cost less amortization of $63,000	252,000
Land	443,500
	$5,171,400

Current liabilities include:

Accounts payable	$ 512,400
Notes payable (due 1996)	300,000
Estimated income taxes payable	150,000
	$ 962,400

Long-term liabilities include:

Unearned revenue	$ 459,500
Dividends payable (cash)	230,000
10% bonds payable (due May 1, 1999)	750,000
	$1,439,500

Capital includes:

Retained earnings (unappropriated)	$1,170,600
Common shares, no-par value; authorized 200,000 shares, 184,000 shares issued	1,840,000
Reserve for contingencies	1,640,000
	$4,650,600

The supplementary information below is also provided:

1. On May 1, 1994, the corporation issued at 93.4, $750,000 of bonds to finance plant expansion. The long-term bond agreement provided for the annual payment of interest every May 1. The existing plant was pledged as security for the loan. Use straight-line method for discount amortization.

2. The bookkeeper made the following mistakes:

   (a) In 1992 the ending inventory was overstated by $183,000. The ending inventories for 1993 and 1994 were correctly computed.

   (b) In 1994 accrued wages in the amount of $250,000 were omitted from the balance sheet and these expenses were not charged on the income statement.

   (c) In 1994, a gain of $175,000 (net of tax) on the sale of certain plant assets was credited directly to retained earnings.

3. A major competitor has introduced a line of products that will compete directly with Exile's primary line, now being produced in a specially designed new plant. Because of manufacturing innovations, the competitor's line will be of comparable quality but priced 50% below the client's line. The competitor announced its new line on January 14, 1995. The client indicates that the company will meet the lower prices that are high enough to cover variable manufacturing and selling expenses, but permit recovery of only a portion of fixed costs.

4. You learned on January 28, 1995, prior to completion of the audit, of heavy damage because of a recent fire to one of the client's two plants; the loss will not be reimbursed by insurance. The newspapers described the event in detail.

Instructions

Prepare the corrected classsified balance sheet for Exile Limited in accordance with proper accounting and reporting principles. Describe the nature of any notes that need to be prepared. The books are closed and adjustments to income are to be made through retained earnings.

P5-7 **(PREPARATION OF A STATEMENT OF CHANGES IN FINANCIAL POSITION AND A BALANCE SHEET)** Tony Howard Inc., had the following balance sheet at the end of 1993.

Tony Howard Inc.
Balance Sheet
December 31, 1993

Cash	$ 20,000	Accounts payable	$ 30,000
Accounts receivable	21,200	Long-term notes payable	41,000
Investments	32,000	Share capital	100,000
Plant assets (net)	81,000	Retained earnings	23,200
Land	40,000		
	$194,200		$194,200

During 1994 the following occurred:

1. Tony Howard Inc. sold part of its investment portfolio for $16,000. This transaction resulted in a gain of $3,000 for the firm. The company often sells and buys securities of this nature.
2. A tract of land was purchased for $21,000 cash.
3. Notes payable in the amount of $16,000 were retired before maturity by paying $16,000 cash.
4. An additional $25,000 was received from an issuance of common shares.
5. Dividends totalling $10,000 were declared and paid to shareholders.
6. Net income for 1994 was $30,000 after allowing for depreciation of $11,000.
7. Land was purchased through the issuance of $30,000 in bonds.
8. At December 31, 1994, Cash was $31,200; Accounts Receivable was $42,000; and Accounts Payable remained at $30,000.

Instructions

(a) Prepare a statement of changes in financial position for 1994.

(b) Prepare the balance sheet as it would appear at December 31, 1994.

(c) How would the statement of changes in financial position help the user of the financial statements?

P5-8 **(INCOME STATEMENT AND BALANCE SHEET PREPARATION)** Crystal Schreiber has prepared baked goods for resale since 1986. She started a baking business in her home and has been operating in a rented building with a storefront since 1991. Schreiber incorporated the business as Tasteful Bakery Limited on January 1, 1994, with an initial issue of 2,500 no-par value common shares at $1.00 per share. Crystal Schreiber is the principal shareholder of Tasteful Bakery Limited.

Sales have increased 30% annually since operations began at the present location, and additional equipment is needed to accommodate expected continued growth. Schreiber wishes to purchase some additional baking equipment and to finance the equipment through a long-term note from a commercial bank. Maritime Bank & Trust has asked Schreiber to submit an income statement for Tasteful Bakery Limited for the first five months of 1994 and a balance sheet as of May 31, 1994.

Schreiber assembled the following information from the cash basis records of the corporation for use in preparing the financial statements requested by the bank:

1. The cheque register showed the following 1994 deposits through May 31, 1994:

Issue of common shares	$ 2,500
Cash sales	25,440
Rebates from purchases	130
Collections on credit sales	7,320
Bank loan proceeds	3,000
	$38,390

2. The following amounts were disbursed through May 31, 1994:

Baking materials	$14,300
Rent	3,000
Salaries and wages	5,500
Maintenance	110
Utilities	2,800
Insurance premium	1,680
Equipment	3,000
Principal and interest payment on bank loan	325
Advertising	411
	$31,126

3. Unpaid invoices at May 31, 1994, were as follows:

Baking materials	$356
Utilities	220
	$576

4. Customer records showed uncollected sales of $4,226 at May 31, 1994.
5. Baking materials costing $1,840 were on hand at May 31, 1994. There were no materials in process or finished goods on hand at that date. No materials were on hand or in process and no finished goods were on hand at January 1, 1994.
6. The note evidencing the three-year bank loan was dated January 1, 1994 and stated a simple interest rate of 10%. The loan required quarterly payments on April 1, July 1, October 1, and January 1, consisting of equal principal payments plus accrued interest since the last payment.
7. Schreiber receives a salary of $750 on the last day of each month. The other employees were paid through Friday, May 27, 1994, and an additional $200 was due on May 31, 1994.
8. New display cases and equipment costing $3,000 were purchased on January 2, 1994. They have an estimated useful life of five years. These are the only fixed assets currently used in the business. Straight-line depreciation is to be used for book purposes.
9. Rent was paid for six months in advance on January 2, 1994.
10. A one-year insurance policy was purchased on January 2, 1994.
11. Tasteful Bakery Limited is subject to an income tax rate of 15%.
12. Payments and collections pertaining to the unincorporated business through December 31, 1993 were not included in the records of the corporation, and no cash was transferred from the unincorporated business to the corporation.

Instructions

Using the accrual basis of accounting, prepare for Tasteful Bakery Limited:

(a) An income statement for the five months ended May 31, 1994.

(b) A balance sheet as of May 31, 1994.

FINANCIAL REPORTING PROBLEM

The financial statements of Moore Corporation Limited appear in Appendix 5A. Refer to these financial statements and the accompanying notes to answer the following questions:

(a) What alternative formats could Moore have adopted for its balance sheet? Which format did it adopt?

(b) What alternative formats could Moore have adopted for its income statement? Which format did it adopt?

(c) Which irregular items does Moore report in its financial statements covering the three years 1989 to 1991?

(d) Identify the various techniques of disclosure Moore might have used to disclose additional pertinent financial information. Which technique does it use in its financial statements?

(e) For which items in Moore's balance sheet would you expect to find notes complementing the descriptions and amounts in the balance sheet?

CHAPTER

6

Revenue Recognition

Revenue recognition is one of the most difficult and pressing problems facing the accounting profession. Although the profession has developed general guidelines for revenue recognition, the many methods of marketing and selling products and services can make it extremely difficult to determine when these guidelines are satisfied. In Canada, significant problems involving revenue recognition were linked to the failure of the Canadian Commercial Bank (recognizing revenue before collection was reasonably assured) and Grandma Lee's (recognizing revenue before all significant acts were completed).

Generally, revenue should be recognized (recorded in the accounting system) when performance is achieved, the amount is reasonably measurable and collectible, and all material related expenses can be matched against it. The following examples suggest the difficulty of determining in which accounting period these conditions are met:

> **Frequent-flyer travel awards.** Frequent-flyer programs are so popular that airlines owe participants billions of kilometres of free travel. These travel rewards could cost the airlines millions of dollars. Some airlines have recognized as revenue the full sales price of the ticket at the time the ticket is purchased. The incremental costs expected to be incurred when the free transportation is provided are accrued at the time a free travel award is reached. There is, however, disagreement with this accounting. As one expert noted: "You can no longer say that the entire revenue process is substantially complete when the ticket is sold. Passengers are purchasing tickets with the expectation of a free flight, and we have to account for that liability." Consequently, a portion of the revenue from the tickets sold should be deferred and reported as a liability.

> **Area development rights.** Area development rights are contracts sold by a company granting the developer the exclusive right to open franchises in a particular area. In return, the developer pays the company a nonrefundable fee. In many cases, the company must provide training and advertising support to the franchise and often uses the fee income to service the subsequent costs involved in helping the developer get started. Accountants must determine whether the company has "earned" this revenue when the contract is signed, or when the cash is received, or when the franchises are up and running.

These examples indicate that determining when to recognize revenue is a complex question for which no easy answers exist. The purposes of this chapter are to (1) identify and discuss the general guidelines that exist in GAAP for recognizing revenue and (2) examine and illustrate the application of these guidelines to the recognition of revenue from the sale of goods at the point of delivery (point of sale), before the point of delivery (long-term construction contracts), and after the point of delivery (instalment contracts). In Appendix 6A, the application of the revenue recognition guidelines to service transactions is discussed. In Appendix 6B, special revenue recognition problems related to consignment sales, barter transactions, and franchises are considered.

GUIDELINES FOR REVENUE RECOGNITION

As stated in Chapter 2, revenues are a financial statement element reported in an income statement. **Revenues** are defined as *increases in economic resources, either by way of inflows or enhancements*

of assets or reductions of liabilities, resulting from the ordinary activities of an entity. Revenues of entities normally arise from the sale of goods, the rendering of services, or the use by others of entity resources yielding rent, interest, royalties or dividends.[1]

While this definition tells us what revenues are, it does not tell us when they are to be recognized. In what accounting period will these increases in assets or reductions of liabilities be recorded? To demonstrate why this is a problem, consider the following highly simplified representation of a retailer's ordinary business activities over time.

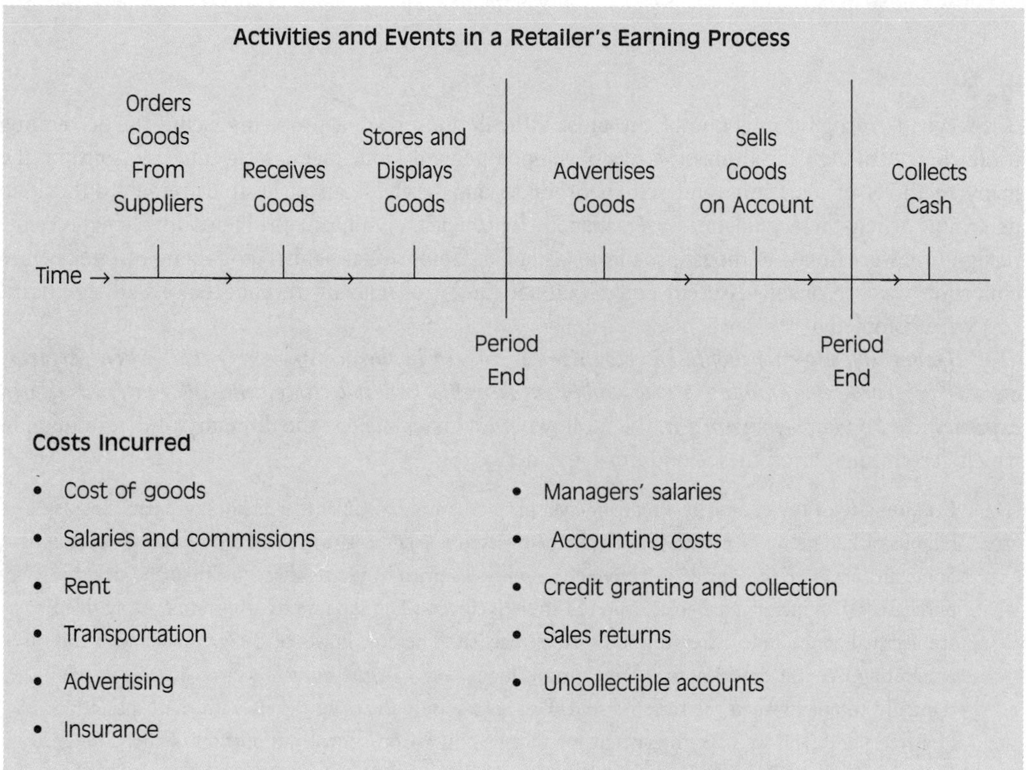

Objective 1

Understand what is included in an earning process, when revenue is earned, and that earning revenue is different from recognizing revenue.

An **earning process** ***consists of all the activities and events a company engages in to earn revenue.*** Given the above representation, when is revenue earned by the retailer? In an economic sense, revenue is earned continuously throughout the earning process—every activity or event in the process contributes to earning revenue. If this were not the case, the retailer would eliminate the unimportant activity, thereby becoming more efficient. Essentially, this reflects a **value-added viewpoint** to earning revenue. ***Each activity or event in the earning process adds value that, when taken together, enables the retailer to sell goods at a price in excess of costs.*** To recognize revenues under a value-added approach would mean that, as each activity or event takes place, an entry would be made to record the portion of the total revenue that is attributable to the activity or event. Therefore, total revenues reported in an income statement prepared under this approach would incorporate the consequences of all activities in the earning process for the given time period. Because of the inability to do this in a sufficiently reliable way, accountants do not recognize revenues in this manner. ***Instead, revenues are recognized at the stage in the earning process when specific criteria in the* CICA**

[1] *CICA Handbook* (Toronto: CICA), Section 1000, par. .37. From this definition, it is evident that solutions to revenue recognition problems clearly have implications for asset and liability valuation—the timing and measurement of a credit to a revenue account results in a corresponding debit to an asset or liability account. Because of this, revenue recognition issues are considered in this book prior to examining accounting for particular assets and liabilities.

Handbook *are judged to have been met.*[2] Therefore, the resulting revenues in an income statement are those from activities or events in the given period that signify the criteria have been met, even though other activities and events associated with the earning process have taken place in prior periods or will take place in future periods.

The *CICA Handbook* provides the following recommendations on revenue recognition.[3]

Objective 2

Know the *CICA Handbook* criteria for revenue recognition and realize that the matching principle also has consequences for revenue recognition.

Revenue Recognition Criteria: *CICA Handbook*

- Revenue from sales and service transactions should be recognized when the requirements as to performance set out [below] are satisfied, provided that at the time of performance ultimate collection is reasonably assured.
- In a transaction involving the sale of goods, performances should be regarded as having been achieved when the following conditions have been fulfilled:
  (a) the seller of the goods has transferred to the buyer the significant risks and rewards of ownership, in that all significant acts have been completed and the seller retains no continuing managerial involvement in, or effective control of, the goods transferred to a degree usually associated with ownership; and
  (b) reasonable assurance exists regarding the measurement of the consideration that will be derived from the sale of goods, and the extent to which goods may be returned.
- In the case of rendering of services and long-term contracts, performance should be determined using either the percentage of completion method or the completed contract method, whichever relates the revenue to the work accomplished. Such performance should be regarded as having been achieved when reasonable assurance exists regarding the measurement of the consideration that will be derived from rendering the service or performing the long-term contract.
- Revenue arising from the use by others of enterprise resources yielding interest, royalties and dividends should be recognized when reasonable assurance exists regarding measurement and collectibility. These revenues should be recognized on the following bases:
  (a) interest: on a time proportion basis;
  (b) royalties: as they accrue, in accordance with the terms of the relevant agreement;
  (c) dividends: when the shareholder's right to receive payment is established.

These criteria reflect the general revenue realization (or recognition) principle of the conceptual framework as discussed in Chapter 2. This principle states that revenue is generally recognized when (1) performance is achieved and (2) reasonable assurance regarding the measurability and collectibility of the consideration exists.[4] The criteria, however, elaborate on when "performance is achieved" as it applies to revenues from the sale of goods, rendering of services, and execution of long-term contracts.

While not stated explicitly in these revenue recognition criteria, the **matching principle** of the conceptual framework ***is also important when deciding if revenue can be recognized.*** This principle states that expenses that are linked to revenues in a cause and effect relationship are normally matched with the revenue in the accounting period in which the revenue is recognized.[5] This means that if the criteria for revenue recognition are met as the result of transactions or events of the

[2] *CICA Handbook*, Section 3400. Recall that "recognition" means recording an item in the accounts and including it in the financial statements.
[3] *Ibid.*, pars. .06–09.
[4] *CICA Handbook*, Section 1000, par. .47.
[5] *Ibid.*, par. .51.

current period but material expenses are to be incurred in a future period, these expenses must be estimated and accrued in the current period so that they are matched with the related revenue. This can usually be done with sufficient reliability (e.g., bad debt expenses). In some cases, however, the future costs may not be reasonably estimable (e.g., some long-term construction or service contracts). Therefore, even if billings have been made and cash has been collected on such a sale, revenue should not be recognized until the future period when related expenses can be determined. The following chart summarizes the key criteria to satisfy in order to recognize revenue from various sources.

Revenue Recognition Criteria: Summary Chart

	Revenue from:		
Criteria	Sale of Goods	Provision of Services and Execution on Long-Term Contracts	Other: Rent, Interest, Royalties, Dividends
Performance is achieved.	X	X	
Amount reasonably measurable.	X	X	X
Collectibility reasonably assured.	X	X	X
Material expenses can be matched.	X	X	

"X" indicates that the criteria must be satisfied in order to recognize revenue.
While the "performance" and "matching" requirements for the Other column are not marked in this summary, events such as the passage of time, fulfilment of terms in an agreement, or being given a right must take place.

Revenue recognition criteria

Objective 3

Realize that determining when the revenue recognition criteria are met requires the exercise of professional judgement.

While these criteria govern revenue recognition, determining when they are met in specific situations requires the exercise of professional judgement. For example, when a real estate company sells some land and receives a 5% down payment, should the entire sales price be recognized as revenue? The answer would depend on the likelihood of being able to collect the full price or the ability to reasonably estimate bad debts. Additionally, the measurement of the sales revenue may be an issue because collections are scheduled far into the future, which raises a concern for separating sales revenue from interest revenue. This is a particular problem if an interest rate is not quoted in the sales contract. The situation can become even more complex if the real estate company is required to develop the land in the future.

There are a variety of ways and conditions under which products and services can be sold. Decisions regarding revenue recognition must be based on an analysis of the underlying substance of the earning process involved. From this, judgement as to when revenue recognition criteria are satisfied can be appropriately justified. This leads to the necessary journal entries to record the revenues so that they are reported in the appropriate period's income statement.

The remainder of this chapter identifies some of the issues involved in revenue recognition and the accounting entries that may be made when the revenue recognition criteria are judged to be met at different points in the earning process. This discussion concentrates on the sale of goods under circumstances where:

1. Revenue recognition criteria are met at the point of delivery (sale).
2. Revenue recognition criteria are met before delivery.
3. Revenue recognition criteria are met after delivery.

REVENUE RECOGNITION CRITERIA MET AT POINT OF DELIVERY (POINT OF SALE)

Many business enterprises market one or more products: retail stores purchase many different articles to sell; manufacturers market the products they have fabricated or processed. In return for the product sold, the enterprise usually receives cash or a promise of cash at some date in the future (credit sales). Thus, sales transactions have two sides: (1) a product for which there are related costs is delivered to a customer and (2) cash or a promise to pay cash in the future is received from the customer.

In the accounts, the revenue and expense consequences of a sales transaction are recorded separately. For the revenue component, the entry is typically to debit Cash or Accounts Receivable and credit the Sales account.

The sales transaction is normally the significant event justifying revenue recognition because all criteria for revenue recognition are typically satisfied at this point in the earning process, as is explained below:

Objective 4

Know when and why revenue recognition criteria are satisfied at the point of delivery (sale) and describe accounting issues related to such revenue recognition.

1. ***Requirements as to performance are satisfied***. The seller, by delivering the goods to the customer, transfers the risks and rewards of ownership to the customer. The seller has no continuing managerial involvement in, or effective control of, the goods to a degree usually associated with ownership.
2. ***The amount of revenue is reasonably measurable***. The amount of revenue is evident from the cash paid or agreed to be paid by the customer. If customers have the right to return products purchased, any material dollar amount of possible returns can be reasonably determined.
3. ***Collectibility is reasonably assured***. If cash is paid, its collectibility is assured. For accounts receivable outstanding at the end of a period, the ability to reasonably estimate bad debts means that this requirement for revenue recognition is satisfied.
4. ***Material expenses can be matched against the revenues***. The cost to acquire or manufacture goods sold has already been incurred and can be assigned to the Cost of Goods Sold expense by an appropriate accounting technique.

For most product sale situations, this typically applies. If, however, any of the criteria were not met at the point of sale or all were satisfied prior to the sale, the revenue would be recognized at some other stage in the earning process.

For example, the seller may retain significant risks of ownership even though the goods are delivered. This would occur when there is a liability for unsatisfactory performance not covered by a warranty, when the buyer has a right to rescind the sale, or when the goods are sent on consignment.[6] Additionally, one must be able to determine whether the buyer or seller has the risks of ownership when goods are in transit between the two (a topic examined in Chapter 8). In essence, determining when risks and rewards of ownership are transferred requires a careful examination of the terms of the sales transaction.[7] Similarly, the ability to reasonably measure the amount of revenue, determine its collectibility, and appropriately match expenses significantly affect being able to justify recognition of revenue at the point of delivery.

Examples Incorporating Issues Related to Recognition at Point of Delivery

To emphasize the importance of professional judgement in determining if revenue should be recognized at the point of delivery, consider the following three examples.

Sales with Buyback Agreements. If a company sells a product in one period and agrees to buy it back in the next accounting period, has the company sold the product? Legal title and possession of

[6] *CICA Handbook*, Section 3400, par. .10. Consignments are examined in Appendix 6B.

[7] *Ibid.*, par. .11.

the product have transferred in this situation, but the economic substance of the transaction is that the seller retains the significant risks and rewards of ownership. In accordance with the revenue recognition criteria, the "selling" company would not be able to record revenue and the inventory and related liability should remain on the seller's books. In other words, no sale.

Revenue Recognition When Right of Return Exists. Whether cash or credit sales are involved, a special problem arises with claims for returns and allowances. In Chapter 7, the accounting treatment for normal returns and allowances is presented. However, certain companies experience such a ***high ratio of returned merchandise to sales*** that they find it necessary to postpone reporting sales until the return privilege has substantially expired. For example, in the publishing industry the rate of return runs up to 25% for hardcover books and 65% for some magazines. Other types of companies that experience high return rates are perishable-food dealers, rack jobbers or distributors who sell to retail outlets, cassette tape and compact disc companies, and some toy and sporting goods manufacturers. Returns in these industries frequently are made either through a right of contract or as a matter of practice involving guaranteed sales agreements or consignments.

Three alternative methods are available when the seller is exposed to continued risks and rewards of ownership through return of the product. These are: (1) not recording a sale until all return privileges have expired; (2) recording the sale, but reducing sales by an estimate of future returns; and (3) recording the sale and accounting for the returns as they occur. Selection of the appropriate method to record sales when right of return exists is made through the exercise of professional judgement based on the revenue recognition criteria. The particularly relevant criteria are: (1) measurability of the consideration to be received, with particular consideration for the reliability of a measure of goods that will be returned, and (2) transfer of risks and rewards of ownership. Specifically, the *CICA Handbook* states:

> Revenues would not be recognized when an enterprise is subject to significant and unpredictable amounts of goods being returned, for example, when the market for a returnable good is untested.[8]

Therefore, when future returns cannot be estimated with reasonable reliability, the revenue would not be recorded when the goods are delivered to buyers. The revenue recognition would be deferred until there is notification from the buyer that only a specific amount of goods will be returned or the return privilege has expired, whichever occurs first. When a reasonable estimate of goods to be returned can be made, the revenue would be recognized when the goods are delivered. Additionally, an allowance for the future returns would be recorded by debiting Sales Returns and crediting Allowance for Sales Returns for the estimated amount. The Sales Returns would be deducted from Sales to determine net sales in an income statement. The Allowance account would be debited when returns occur. Any balance in the Allowance account would be treated as a contra-account to Accounts Receivable in a balance sheet.

Trade Loading and Channel Stuffing. Some companies record revenues at date of delivery with neither buyback nor unlimited return provisions and therefore appear to be following acceptable point of sale revenue recognition, yet they are recognizing revenues and earnings prematurely. The cigarette industry until recently engaged in a distribution practice known as trade loading. "**Trade loading** is a crazy, uneconomic, insidious practice through which manufacturers—trying to show sales, profits, and market share they don't actually have—induce their wholesale customers, known as the trade, to buy more product than they can promptly resell."[9] In total, the cigarette industry appears to have exaggerated operating profits by taking the profits from future years.

In the computer software industry, this same practice is referred to as **channel stuffing**. In 1988 when Ashton-Tate, a software maker, needed to make its financial results look good, it offered deep discounts to its distributors to overbuy and recorded revenue when the software left the loading

---

[8] *Ibid.*, par. .18.

[9] "The $600 Million Cigarette Scam," *Fortune*, December 4, 1989, p. 89.

dock.[10] Of course, the distributors' inventories become bloated and the marketing channel gets stuffed, but the software maker's financial results are improved—only to the detriment of future periods' results, however, unless the process is repeated.

Trade loading and channel stuffing are management and marketing policy decisions and actions that hype sales, distort operating results, and window-dress financial statements. End-of-period accounting adjustments are not made to reduce the impact of these types of sales on operating results. The practices of trade loading and channel stuffing need to be discouraged.

REVENUE RECOGNITION CRITERIA MET BEFORE DELIVERY

Sometimes questions arise as to whether the revenue recognition criteria can be satisfied before the actual delivery of the product. For the most part, recognition at the point of delivery occurs because the uncertainties concerning the earning process are removed and the exchange price provides a reliable basis for measurement. Under certain circumstances, however, revenue recognition is justifiable prior to completion and delivery. The most notable example is when there is work done on a long-term construction contract and the percentage-of-completion method may be applied to appropriately reflect the efforts and accomplishments of each fiscal period.[11]

Long-Term Construction Contracts and Revenue Recognition Issues

Objective 5

Understand why and when revenue can be recognized prior to completion of long-term contracts, and why and when it may not be recognized until completion of such contracts.

Under a long-term contract, a contractor formally agrees to carry out a project for a customer that will take several months or years to complete. Some contracts may consist of constructing several separable units (e.g., buildings or kilometres of roadway) in the context of the entire contracted project (e.g., a neighbourhood development or stretch of highway). Other contracts may be for the design and/or construction of a single unit (e.g., office building, space hardware, ship, golf course). While the specific terms of a particular long-term contract would be unique to the negotiation between the contractor and the customer, it would be expected that a ***contract would specify that the buyer or seller have enforceable rights regarding such things as the price to be paid, performance during the contract period, expected delivery date, and provisions for progress payments. Additionally, the contractor would have budgeted the expected cost of the contract prior to signing it.*** Within this context, the earning process for a contractor who has agreed to complete a project beginning in Year 1 and ending in Year 3 is illustrated below.

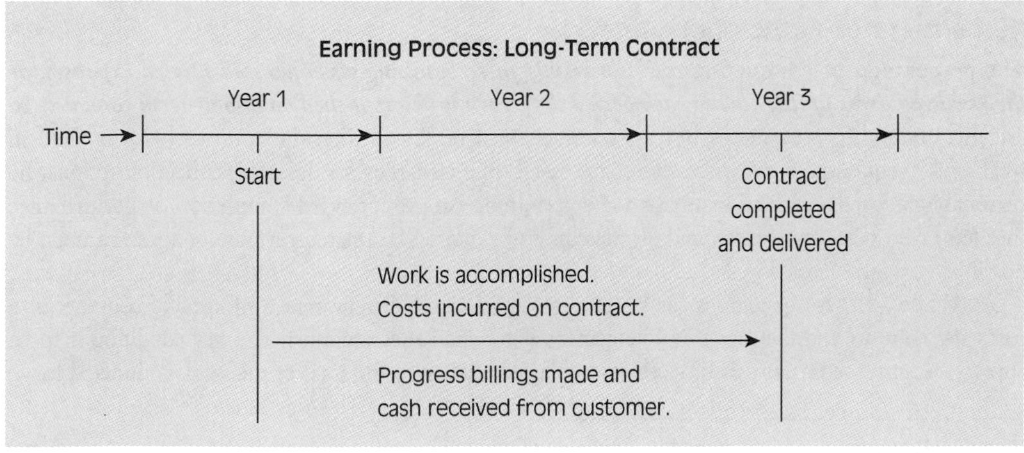

[10] "Software's Dirty Little Secret," *Forbes*, May 15, 1989, p. 128.

[11] While we concentrate on long-term construction contracts to illustrate issues and accounting methods for revenue recognition prior to delivery of a finished "good," similar issues exist for long-term service contracts, as described in Appendix 6A.

Because the project is the result of a contractual agreement and execution of the contract spans more than one accounting period, a basic accounting issue arises: ***In which period or periods should revenue, related expenses, and resulting net income be recognized?*** To be accurate, it can be argued that the recognition should be in Year 3 because it is only then that total actual costs are objectively determinable. Also justifying this conclusion is the fact that the risks and rewards of ownership are transferred to the buyer in Year 3. Such recognition would, however, result in a distortion of the trends in and relationships between reported revenues, expenses, and net income for the three years in which the work was accomplished. Therefore, to better reflect the underlying economic activity, it may be desirable to recognize a portion of the revenue, expenses, and net income in each year of the contract's execution. While the costs incurred each year would be known, the problem with this approach is how to allocate the total contract revenue between the years so that the results reasonably reflect the work accomplished.

In this situation, guidance is provided in the revenue recognition criteria given in the *CICA Handbook* (see page 255). As with the sale of goods, revenue on long-term contracts cannot be recognized until performance is achieved, amounts are reasonably measurable, collection is reasonably assured, and costs can be matched. ***Achieving performance*** is, however, defined quite differently for long-term contracts because a transfer of risks and rewards of ownership to the buyer is not needed, nor is elimination of managerial involvement by the seller. Rather, performance is regarded as being achieved (and, therefore, revenue is recognizable) when reasonable assurance exists regarding the measurement of the consideration that will be derived from the work that has been accomplished on the contract.

Reasonably measuring the amount of revenue would require the contract to specify a fixed-price or a cost-plus formula for revenue. For a fixed-price contract, the ratio of performance completed to total performance required multiplied by the price would yield a measure of revenue earned. For a cost-plus formula contract, the application of the formula to the costs incurred would result in revenue earned, as long as the incurrence of costs reflected the progress toward completion reasonably well. Also, collectibility of the revenue would have to be reasonably assured. When these conditions exist, the contract is accounted for using the ***percentage-of-completion method*** for revenue recognition.[12]

When these conditions do not exist for long-term contracts then revenue recognition would not occur until the contract is completed. In this case, the ***completed-contract method*** of revenue recognition is used.[13]

Percentage-of-Completion Method

Objective 6

Know when the percentage-of-completion method can be used and how to apply it for long-term contracts.

The **percentage-of-completion method** ***results in recognizing revenues and related expenses, or the resulting gross profit, during each period that work is accomplished on a long-term contract.*** To use this method, (1) revenues from the contract must be known (i.e. the contract price is fixed in total or for sequential parts, or revenues are based on a cost-plus formula), (2) collectibility must be reasonably assured, (3) a rational basis for determining progress toward completion or performance that has taken place must exist, and (4) matching of expenses to related revenue of a period must be possible.

While all these conditions for revenue recognition require awareness of specific contents of a particular contract and the exercise of judgement as to when they are satisfied, a key condition is to be able to measure the proportion of work accomplished relative to the total of the work contracted for.

---

12 *CICA Handbook*, Section 3400, par. .14.

13 *Ibid.*, par. .15. For contracts that are short term (e.g., started and completed in the same year), the completed-contract method is appropriate because it relates reported revenues to the work accomplished. From an income tax viewpoint, if a contract is for 24 months or less, the completed-contract method is acceptable to Revenue Canada. Given that a company's income would not be materially distorted over time, and for reasons of expediency, a similar policy may be adopted for financial statement purposes even though the percentage-of-completion method could be used.

Measuring the Progress Toward Completion. As one practising accountant wrote, "The big problem in applying the percentage-of-completion method that cannot be demonstrated in an example has to do with the ability to make reasonably accurate estimates of completion and the final gross profit."[14]

Various methods are used to determine the ***extent of performance or progress toward completion***; the most common are cost-to-cost method, efforts-expended methods, and units-of-work-performed method. All of these methods determine the extent of progress by examining relationships among various measurements of input and/or output pertaining to the contract.

Input measures (costs incurred, labour hours worked) are made in terms of efforts devoted to a contract. **Output measures** (tonnes produced, storeys of a building completed, kilometres of a highway completed) are made in terms of results. Determining what to use for a particular contract requires careful tailoring to the circumstances and the exercise of judgement.

The input measure is based on an established relationship between a unit of input and productivity. If inefficiencies cause the productivity relationship to change, inaccurate measurements of performance achieved result. Another potential problem, **front-end loading**, produces higher estimates of completion by virtue of incurring significant costs up front. For example, costs of uninstalled materials or subcontracts not yet executed should not be considered as costs incurred when using costs to determine the amount of work accomplished.

Output measures can also result in inaccurate measures of performance if the units used are not comparable in time, effort, or cost to complete. For example, using storeys completed can be deceiving: to complete the first storey of an eight-storey building may require more than one-eighth the total cost, due to the foundation and substructure construction.

One of the more popular means used to determine the progress toward completion is the **cost-to-cost method.** Under the cost-to-cost method, the ***percentage of completion is measured by comparing costs incurred to date with the most recent estimate of the total costs to complete the contract*** as shown in the following formula.

$$\frac{\text{Costs incurred to end of current period}}{\text{Most recent estimate of total costs}} = \text{Percentage completed}$$

This percentage is applied to the total revenue or the estimated total gross profit[15] on the contract to determine the revenue or the gross profit amounts ***to be recognized to date***. The amount of revenue or gross profit recognized ***for a particular period*** is computed using the following formula.

$$\left\{\frac{\text{Costs incurred to end of current period}}{\text{Most recent estimate of total costs}} \times \begin{array}{c}\text{Estimated total revenue}\\ \text{(or gross profit)}\\ \text{from the contract}\end{array}\right\} - \begin{array}{c}\text{Total revenue}\\ \text{(or gross profit)}\\ \text{recognized}\\ \text{in prior periods}\end{array} = \begin{array}{c}\text{Current period's}\\ \text{revenue}\\ \text{(or gross profit)}\end{array}$$

Because the cost-to-cost method is used extensively, we have adopted it for use in our illustrations.

Illustration of the Percentage-of-Completion Method (Cost-to-Cost Basis). To illustrate the percentage-of-completion method, assume that Hardhat Construction Company has a contract starting July 1994 to construct a bridge at a fixed price of $4,500,000. The bridge is to be completed in October 1996 at an estimated total cost of $4,000,000. The following data pertain to the construction

[14] Richard S. Hickok, "New Guidance for Construction Contractors: 'A Credit Plus,'" *The Journal of Accountancy*, March 1982, p. 46.

[15] Total gross profit = total revenue on contract − most recent estimate of total costs on contract.

period. Note that by the end of 1995 the estimated total cost has increased from $4,000,000 to $4,050,000 ($2,916,000 actual costs to the end of 1995 plus $1,134,000 estimated yet to be incurred to complete the contract).

	1994	1995	1996
Costs to date	$1,000,000	$2,916,000	$4,050,000
Estimated costs to complete	3,000,000	1,134,000	—
Progress billings during the year	900,000	2,400,000	1,200,000
Cash collected during the year	750,000	1,750,000	2,000,000

Progress billings are invoices sent to the customer throughout the construction period. The amounts billed at various times are determined based on conditions specified in the contract. For example, the billings may be a certain percentage of costs incurred by the contractor or some agreed amount linked to time or stage of completion. Such billings are then paid by the customer. In some cases, the customer, by agreement with the contractor, may hold back on paying a portion of the billings. Through the billing and collection process, the contractor obtains cash to pay for costs during construction. If this did not occur, the contractor would likely run short of cash, which could mean external financing and related interest charges would be incurred or the contract may not be able to be completed. Based on this information, the percentage of the contract completed by the end of each year would be computed as follows.

Hardhat Construction Company
Percentage-of-Completion Method (Cost-to-Cost Basis)

	1994	1995	1996
Contract price	$4,500,000	$4,500,000	$4,500,000
Less estimated cost:			
Costs to date	1,000,000	2,916,000	4,050,000
Estimated costs to complete	3,000,000	1,134,000	—
Estimated total costs	$4,000,000	$4,050,000	$4,050,000
Estimated total gross profit	$ 500,000	$ 450,000	$ 450,000
Percentage completed	**25%**	**72%**	**100%**
	$\left(\frac{\$1,000,000}{\$4,000,000}\right)$	$\left(\frac{\$2,916,000}{\$4,050,000}\right)$	$\left(\frac{\$4,050,000}{\$4,050,000}\right)$

On the basis of the data, the entries below would be prepared (1) to record the costs of construction, (2) to record progress billings, and (3) to record collections (these entries appear as summaries of the many transactions that would be entered individually as they occur during the year).

	1994		1995		1996	
To record cost of construction:						
Construction in Process	1,000,000		1,916,000		1,134,000	
Materials, cash, payables, etc.		1,000,000		1,916,000		1,134,000

(Continued)

To record progress billings:						
Accounts Receivable	900,000		2,400,000		1,200,000	
Billings on Construction in Process		900,000		2,400,000		1,200,000
To record collections:						
Cash	750,000		1,750,000		2,000,000	
Accounts Receivable		750,000		1,750,000		2,000,000

Construction in Process ***is an inventory account, not an expense account.*** The first entry results in all contract costs incurred to the date being included in this account. Note that, ***for the progress billings, the credit is not to a revenue account. The revenue for each year is yet to be determined using the percentage-of-completion method.*** **Billings on Construction in Process** ***is a contra-inventory account***, as will be discussed shortly. Using the previously calculated percentages of the contract completed for each year, the estimated revenue and gross profit to be recognized in each year is determined as follows.

	1994	1995	1996
Revenue recognized in:			
1994 $4,500,000 × 25%	$1,125,000		
1995 $4,500,000 × 72%		$3,240,000	
Less revenue recognized in 1994		1,125,000	
Revenue in 1995		$2,115,000	
1996 $4,500,000 × 100%			$4,500,000
Less revenue recognized in 1994 and 1995			3,240,000
Revenue in 1996			$1,260,000
Gross profit recognized in:			
1994 $500,000 × 25%	$ 125,000		
1995 $450,000 × 72%		$ 324,000	
Less gross profit recognized in 1994		125,000	
Gross profit in 1995		$ 199,000	
1996 $450,000 × 100%			$ 450,000
Less gross profit recognized in 1994 and 1995			324,000
Gross profit in 1996			$ 126,000

The entries to recognize revenue, construction expenses, and gross profit in each year of the contract are shown on the following page.

Note that gross profit as computed ***is debited to the inventory account Construction in Process.*** The Revenue from Long-Term Contract account is credited for amounts as computed previously. The difference between the amounts recognized each year for revenue and gross profit is debited to a nominal account, Construction Expenses (similar to Cost of Goods Sold in a manufacturing enterprise), which is reported in the income statement; this is the actual cost of construction incurred in a period.

	1994		1995		1996	
To recognize revenue, construction expenses, and gross profit:						
Construction in Process (gross profit)	125,000		199,000		126,000	
Construction Expenses	1,000,000		1,916,000		1,134,000	
Revenue from Long-Term Contract		1,125,000		2,115,000		1,260,000

An alternative way to build this entry for each year is to (1) debit Construction Expenses for the actual costs incurred in the year ($1,000,000 in 1994), (2) credit Revenue from Long-Term Contract for the revenue calculated for the year ($1,125,000 in 1994), and (3) debit Construction in Process for the difference, which is the gross profit for the year ($125,000 in 1994).

As a result of these entries, revenue and construction expense amounts for work done on the contract each year are recorded and would be shown in the year's income statement separately or as a net amount (gross profit on long-term contract). Also, under the percentage-of-completion method, the difference between revenue and expenses (i.e. the gross profit) is debited to the Construction in Process inventory account. Therefore, the total of this account at any given time will equal the actual costs incurred to date plus recognized gross profit to date. For our illustration, the Construction in Process account would include the following from entries posted over the term of the project.

Construction in Process		
1994 construction costs	$1,000,000	
1994 recognized gross profit	**125,000**	
1995 construction costs	1,916,000	
1995 recognized gross profit	**199,000**	
1996 construction costs	1,134,000	
1996 recognized gross profit	**126,000**	
Total	$4,500,000	

This inventory account cannot be removed from the contractor's accounts until the construction is completed and ownership is transferred to the buyer. When this occurs, the following entry is made:

Billings on Construction in Process	4,500,000	
Construction in Process		4,500,000

From previous entries to record progress billings, the Billings on Construction in Process account would have a credit balance of $4,500,000 prior to this entry. Therefore, this entry eliminates the balance in the Billings account and the Construction in Process account.

As a concluding point, note that the Hardhat Construction Company illustration contained a change in estimate in the second year, 1995, where the estimated total costs increased from $4,000,000 to $4,050,000. By calculating the percentage completed to the end of 1995 based on the changed estimate of total costs and then deducting from revenues or gross profit computed for progress to the end of 1995 the amount of revenues or gross profit recognized in prior periods, the effect of the change in estimate was accounted for in a catch-up manner. That is, the change in estimate is accounted for in the period of change so that the balance sheet at the end of the period of change and the accounting in subsequent periods are as they would have been if the revised estimate had been the original estimate.

Financial Statement Presentation: Percentage-of-Completion. Generally, when a receivable from a sale is created, a revenue is credited. Also, the Inventory account is reduced by the amount of the expense to be matched against the revenue. This is not the case when accounting for long-term contracts. As shown in the illustration, when Accounts Receivable are recorded, the Billings on Construction in Process account rather than a revenue account is credited. At the same time, the Construction in Process inventory account continues to be carried on the books. This creates a problem because two assets (Accounts Receivable or the Cash collected thereon and Construction in Process) exist in our records but both relate to a single source of benefits (the construction project). Recall, however, that the Billings on Construction in Process account will have a credit balance equal to all amounts billed and set up as Accounts Receivable. Therefore, to avoid reporting two assets when there is really only one (i.e. double-counting), the balance in the Billings on Construction in Process account is subtracted from the Construction in Process account to determine an amount to be reported in the balance sheet.

Hardhat Construction Company

Financial Statement Presentation: Percentage-of-Completion Method

		1994	1995	1996
Income Statement				
Revenue from long-term contracts		$1,125,000	$2,115,000	$1,260,000
Construction expenses		1,000,000	1,916,000	1,134,000
Gross profit		$ 125,000	$ 199,000	$ 126,000
Balance Sheet (Dec. 31)				
Current assets:				
Accounts receivable		$ 150,000	$ 800,000	
Inventories				
Construction in process	$1,125,000			
Less: Billings	900,000			
Costs and recognized profit in excess of billings		$ 225,000		
Current liabilities:				
Billings ($3,300,000) in excess of costs and recognized profit ($3,240,000)			$ 60,000	

Note 1: Summary of significant accounting policies

Long-Term Construction Contracts. The Company recognizes revenues and reports profits from long-term construction contracts, its principal business, under the percentage-of-completion method of accounting. The amounts of revenues and profits recognized each year are based on the ratio of costs incurred to the total estimated costs. Costs included in construction in process include direct material, direct labour, and project-related overhead. Corporate general and administrative expenses are charged to the periods as incurred and are not allocated to construction contracts.

When the costs incurred plus the gross profit recognized to date (the balance in Construction in Process) exceed the billings, this excess is reported as a current asset called "Costs and Recognized

Profit in Excess of Billings." This is classified as a current asset on the grounds that the length of the contract reflects the length of the contractor's operating cycle.

When the billings exceed costs incurred plus gross profit to date, this excess is reported as a current liability called "Billings in Excess of Costs and Recognized Profit." When a company has a number of projects, and costs plus recognized profit exceed billings on some contracts, and billings exceed costs plus recognized profits on others, the contracts should be segregated. The asset side should include only those contracts on which costs plus recognized profit exceed billings, and the liability side should include only those on which billings exceed costs and recognized profit. Separate disclosure of the amounts for billings and costs plus recognized profit is preferable to presenting only the net amount.

Using data from Hardhat Construction Company, its long-term construction activities under the percentage-of-completion method could be reported as on page 265.

While the note in this example satisfies requirements for disclosure of the method for recognizing revenue,[16] additional information may be provided. Such information could include the length of significant contracts, the backlog on uncompleted contracts, the effects of any revisions in estimates, pertinent details about receivables, and significant individual or group concentration of contracts exposing the company to unusual risk.

Completed-Contract Method

Objective 7

Know how to apply the completed-contract method for long-term contracts.

Under the **completed-contract method**, ***revenue, construction expenses, and gross profit are recognized only in the time period when the contract is completed and constructed items are delivered to the buyer.*** Costs of long-term contracts in process and billings are recorded in the period they occur, but there are no interim charges or credits to income statement accounts for revenues, construction expenses, and gross profit.

The annual entries to record costs of construction, progress billings, and collections from customers under the completed-contract method are identical to those illustrated for the percentage-of-completion method. However, when the completed-contract method is used, an entry to recognize revenue, construction expense, and gross profit is not made until the contract is completed. For the bridge project of Hardhat Construction Company, the following entries are made in 1996 under the completed-contract method to recognize revenue and expenses and to close out the inventory and billing accounts:

Billings on Construction in Process	4,500,000	
Revenue from Long-Term Contracts		4,500,000
Construction Expenses	4,050,000	
Construction in Process		4,050,000

The revenue, expenses, and gross profit recognized in each year for the same contract will differ substantially, depending on the method used. This is illustrated by the following summary of recognized gross profits for each year as derived in the Hardhat Construction Company example. The total gross profit on the contract is the same, regardless of the method used.

	Percentage-of-Completion	Completed-Contract
1994	$125,000	$ -0-
1995	199,000	-0-
1996	126,000	450,000
Total	$450,000	$450,000

[16] *CICA Handbook*, Section 1505, par. .04.

Hardhat Construction Company would report its long-term construction activities under the completed-contract method as follows.

Hardhat Construction Company
Financial Statement Presentation: Completed-Contract Method

		1994	1995	1996
Income Statement				
Revenue from long-term contracts		—	—	$4,500,000
Construction expenses		—	—	4,050,000
Gross profit		—	—	$ 450,000
Balance Sheet (Dec. 31)				
Current assets:				
Accounts receivable		$150,000	$800,000	
Inventories				
Construction in process	$1,000,000			
Less: Billings	900,000			
Costs in excess of billings		$100,000		
Current liabilities:				
Billings ($3,300,000) in excess of contract costs ($2,916,000)			$384,000	

Note 1: Summary of significant accounting policies

Long-Term Construction Contracts. The Company recognizes revenues and reports profits from long-term construction contracts, its principal business, under the completed-contract method. Contract costs and billings are accumulated during the periods of construction, but no revenues, construction expenses, or profits are recognized until completion of the contract. Costs included in construction in process include direct material, direct labour, and project-related overhead. Corporate general and administrative expenses are charged to the periods as incurred.

Accounting for Long-Term Contract Losses

Two types of losses may be recognized under long-term contracts:[17]

Objective 8

Identify and apply appropriate accounting for losses on long-term contracts.

1. **Loss in current period on a profitable contract**. Such a loss ***occurs only when the percentage-of-completion method is being used***. It arises when, during construction, there is a significant increase in the estimated total contract costs but the increase does not eliminate all profit on the contract. The estimated cost increase requires a current period adjustment (i.e. recognition of a loss) for the excess gross profit recognized on the project in prior periods. This loss is recorded in the current period because it is the result of a ***change in an accounting estimate*** (discussed in Chapter 4 and expanded on in Chapter 22).
2. **Loss on an unprofitable contract**. ***Under both the percentage-of-completion and the completed-contract methods***, cost estimates at the end of a current period may indicate that a loss will result on completion of the entire contract. When this occurs, the entire expected contract loss must be recognized in the current period.

The treatments described for both types of losses are consistent with accounting's custom of anticipating foreseeable losses in order to avoid overstatement of current and future income (conservatism).

[17] Sak Bhamornsiri, "Losses from Construction Contracts," *The Journal of Accountancy*, April 1982, p. 26.

Losses in Current Period. To illustrate a loss in the current period on a contract originally expected to be profitable on completion, assume that on December 31, 1995, Hardhat Construction Company estimates the costs to complete the bridge contract at \$1,468,962 instead of \$1,134,000 (refer to page 262). Assuming all other data are the same as before and using the percentage-of-completion method, Hardhat would compute the percentage completed and recognize the loss as follows.

Computation of Recognizable Loss: 1995
Percentage-of-Completion Method

Costs to date (Dec. 31, 1995)	\$2,916,000
Estimated costs to complete (revised)	1,468,962
Estimated total costs	\$4,384,962
Percentage completed (\$2,916,000 ÷ \$4,384,962)	66½%
Revenue recognized in 1995 (\$4,500,000 × 66½% − \$1,125,000)	\$1,867,500
Costs incurred in 1995	1,916,000
Loss recognized in 1995	**\$ 48,500**

Hardhat Construction would record the loss in 1995 as follows:

Construction Expenses	1,916,000	
Construction in Process (Loss)		48,500
Revenue from Long-Term Contract		1,867,500

The loss of \$48,500 will be reported on the 1995 income statement as the difference between the reported revenues of \$1,867,500 and the costs of \$1,916,000.

The 1995 loss is a cumulative adjustment of the "excess" of gross profit recognized in prior years (1994, in this case) over the total gross profit that would have been recognized through 1995, based on the revised cost estimates. Total gross profit expected, based on revised cost estimates, is \$115,038 (\$4,500,000 − \$4,384,962). The percentage completed at the end of 1995 is 66½%. Therefore, through 1995, total gross profit that can be recognized is \$76,500 (66½% of \$115,038). Since \$125,000 was recognized in 1994, recognition of a loss of \$48,500 (\$125,000 − \$76,500) is required in 1995 to absorb the overstatement in 1994.

Because the revised total costs to complete the contract are the result of a change in estimate in 1995, the adjustment for the two years is fully absorbed in 1995 rather than retroactively adjusting account balances resulting from prior years' entries. By the end of 1995, however, the Construction in Process and Retained Earnings account balances would be the same as if the new estimates had existed from the start of the contract.

In 1996, Hardhat will recognize the remaining 33½% of revenue (\$1,507,500), given that actual costs in 1996 are as estimated (\$1,468,962). The gross profit in 1996 of \$38,538 plus the \$125,000 in 1994 less the loss of \$48,500 in 1995 will equal the gross profit on the entire contract of \$115,038 (contract price of \$4,500,000 less total contract costs of \$4,384,962). ***Under the completed-contract method, no loss is recognized in 1995 because the contract is still expected to result in a gross profit that will be recognized in full in the year of completion.***

Loss on an Unprofitable Contract. To illustrate the accounting for an overall loss on a long-term contract, assume that at December 31, 1995, Hardhat Construction Company estimates the costs to complete the bridge contract at \$1,640,250 instead of \$1,134,000. Revised estimates relative to the bridge contract appear as follows.

	1994 Original Estimates	1995 Revised Estimates
Contract price	$4,500,000	$4,500,000
Estimated total cost	4,000,000	4,556,250*
Estimated gross profit	$ 500,000	
Estimated loss		$ (56,250)

*($2,916,000 incurred through 1995 + $1,640,250 estimated yet to be incurred in 1996)

Under the percentage-of-completion method, $125,000 of gross profit was already recognized in 1994. This $125,000 must be offset in 1995 because it is now not expected to be realized. In addition, the overall loss of $56,250 must be recognized in 1995 since, under the principle of conservatism, losses must be recognized as soon as estimable. Therefore, a total loss of $181,250 ($125,000 + $56,250) must be recognized in 1995. The revenue recognized in 1995 is computed as follows.

Computation of Revenue Recognized in 1995
Percentage-of-Completion Method

Revenue recognized in 1995:		
Contract price		$4,500,000
Percentage completed		× 64%*
Revenue recognizable to date		$2,880,000
Less revenue recognized prior to 1995		1,125,000
Revenue recognized in 1995		**$1,755,000**
Costs to date (Dec. 31, 1995)	$2,916,000	
Estimated costs to complete	1,640,250	
Estimated total costs	$4,556,250	

*Percentage completed: $2,916,000 ÷ $4,556,250 = 64%

To determine the construction costs to be expensed in 1995, add the total loss to be recognized in 1995 ($125,000 + $56,250) to the revenue to be recognized in 1995. This computation is as follows.

Computation of Construction Expenses: 1995

Revenue recognized in 1995 (computed above)		$1,755,000
Total loss recognized in 1995:		
Reversal of gross profit recognized in 1994	$125,000	
Total estimated loss on the contract	56,250	181,250
Construction expense in 1995		**$1,936,250**

Alternatively, the 1995 construction expenses may be calculated as shown at the top of page 270.

Alternative Computation of Construction Expenses: 1995

Estimated total cost less estimated total loss (equals total revenue)	$4,500,000
Percentage completed, Dec. 31, 1994	64%
Cost to Dec. 31, 1995, before inclusion of total loss	$2,880,000
Add estimated total loss	56,250
Cost to date plus loss	$2,936,250
Deduct cost recognized in prior years (1994)	1,000,000
Construction expense in 1995	**$1,936,250**

Hardhat Construction would record the long-term contract revenues, expenses, and loss in 1995 as follows.

Construction Expenses	1,936,250	
Construction in Process (Loss)		181,250
Revenue from Long-Term Contracts		1,755,000

At the end of 1995, Construction in Process has a balance of $2,859,750, as shown below.[18]

Construction in Process

1994 Construction costs	1,000,000		
1994 Recognized gross profit	125,000		
1995 Construction costs	1,916,000	1995 Recognized loss	181,250
Balance, 2,859,750			

Under the completed-contract method, the total contract loss of $56,250 is recognized in 1995, the year in which it first became evident, through the following entry:

Loss from Long-Term Contracts	56,250	
Construction in Process (Loss)		56,250

The balance in the Construction in Process account after this loss recognition is $2,859,750 ($1,000,000 cost in 1994 + $1,916,000 cost in 1995 − $56,250 loss in 1995), the same as that under the percentage-of-completion method. This is because both methods recognize the full amount of the loss immediately.

Other Possible Situations Where Revenue Recognition May Occur in Advance of Delivery

Objective 9

Identify circumstances, other than for long-term contracts, where revenue recognition might occur prior to delivery.

The *CICA Handbook* specifically states that, when progress on a long-term construction contract can be reasonably determined, revenue recognition can occur prior to delivery of the contracted asset (i.e. the percentage-of-completion method). By not referring explicitly to other unique situations involving the sale of goods, one may conclude that recognizing revenue in these situations can occur only when the risks and rewards of ownership are transferred to a buyer, even though amounts can be reasonably measured, collectibility is assured, and costs can be matched. The following three situations provide examples of circumstances where such a conclusion may be challenged.

[18] If the costs in 1996 are $1,640,250 as projected, at the end of 1996 the Construction in Process account will have a balance of $1,640,250 + $2,859,750, or $4,500,000, equal to the contract price. When the revenue remaining to be recognized in 1996 of $1,620,000 [$4,500,000 (total contract price) − $1,125,000 (1994) − $1,755,000 (1995)] is matched with the construction expense to be recognized in 1996 of $1,620,000 [total costs of $4,556,250 less the total costs recognized in prior years of $2,936,250 ($1,000,000 in 1994 and $1,936,250 in 1995)], a zero profit results. Thus the total loss has been recognized in 1995, the year in which it first became evident.

Completion of Production. In certain cases, revenue has been recognized at the completion of production even though no sale was made. Examples of such situations involve precious metals or agricultural products with assured prices. Revenue was recognized when these metals were mined or agricultural crops harvested because the finished good was available, costs were known, everything could be sold, the sales price was reasonably assured, the units were interchangeable, and no significant future costs were involved in selling and delivering the product.

Today, however, this timing of revenue recognition technically fails to meet all of the criteria for recognizing revenue from the sale of goods. Through retention of ownership, the producer retains a managerial involvement in and effective control of the goods until the point of sale. Despite this, recognition of revenue prior to sale is intuitively justifiable. The critical work associated with the earning process is the extraction of the metal or the harvesting of the crop. Even though there is no formal contract with buyers of the product, the market circumstances are as if there were a contract. Consequently, it may be argued that the spirit of the phrase "performance is achieved" is satisfied even though the letter of the law is not.

Accretion Basis. Accretion is the increase in value resulting from natural growth or the aging process. Farmers experience accretion by growing crops and breeding animals. Timberland and nursery stock increase in value as the trees and plants grow. Some wines improve with age. Is accretion revenue? Should it be recognized as revenue?

Accounting theoreticians are somewhat divided on the issue. Some reject recognition of accretion as revenue. They contend that while there is no doubt that assets have increased in value, the technical process of production remains to be undertaken, followed by conversion into liquid assets.[19] Additionally, even though accretion may occur, determining the amount in any given period would be too subjective. Others conclude that, from a perspective of providing relevant economic information, accretion value should be recognized. In essence, the issue reflected in these viewpoints is whether or not accountants should report revenues on a value-added basis. As stated earlier, this approach has not been adopted in Canada.

Discovery Basis. In the United States, the Security and Exchange Commission's proposal for reserve recognition accounting (RRA) for oil and gas producers revived interest in the use of some form of discovery basis accounting in the extractive industries. As noted above in regard to accretion, there is no doubt that an enterprise's assets may be greatly increased and enhanced by exploration and discovery. Many contend that the financial reporting of companies in the extractive industries would be vastly improved if discovered resources were recognized as assets and changes in oil and gas reserves were included in earnings. Their arguments for the discovery basis are based on the significance of discovery in the earning process and the view that the product's market price can be reasonably estimated.

The arguments against revenue recognition at the time of discovery focus on the uncertainties surrounding the assumptions needed to determine discovery values, the cost of obtaining the necessary data, and the departure from historical cost-based accounting. Except for the SEC's requirement in the United States that RRA be used in supplemental data, the discovery basis of revenue recognition is sanctioned currently neither by current practice nor by official accounting pronouncements.

Objective 10

Understand when circumstances regarding the earning process result in revenue recognition after delivery.

REVENUE RECOGNITION CRITERIA MET AFTER DELIVERY

Recognizing revenue from the sale of goods at the point of delivery (sale) occurs because the revenue recognition criteria are judged to be met at that time in the earning process. When payment is to

[19] W.A. Paton and A.C. Littleton, *An Introduction to Corporate Accounting Standards* (Sarasota, FL: American Accounting Association, 1940), p. 52.

be received after delivery, the criteria require that ultimate collection is reasonably assured.[20] ***If collection in full may not occur, the criteria are still met at delivery, given that a reasonable estimate of bad debts can be made. If such an estimate cannot be made, revenue recognition must be deferred until cash is collected.***[21]

Two accounting methods exist for recognizing revenue or gross profit at the time cash is collected: the ***instalment method*** and the ***cost recovery method.***

The Instalment Method

The expression "**instalment sale**" is generally used to describe any type of sale for which payment is required in periodic instalments over an extended period of time. It has been used in the retail field, where various types of farm and home equipment and furnishings are sold on an instalment basis. It is sometimes used in the heavy equipment industry, where machine installations are paid for over a long period. A more recent application of the method is in land development sales.

Because payment for the products or property sold is spread over a relatively long period, the risk of loss resulting from uncollectible accounts is greater in instalment sales transactions than in ordinary sales. Consequently, various devices are used to protect the seller. In merchandising, the two most common are (1) a conditional sales contract stating that title to the item sold does not pass to the purchaser until all payments have been made and (2) notes secured by a chattel (personal property) mortgage on the article sold. Either of these devices permits the seller to repossess the goods sold if the purchaser defaults on one or more payments. The repossessed merchandise is then resold at whatever price it will bring to compensate the seller for the uncollected instalments and the expense of repossession.

Objective 11

Describe and apply the instalment method of accounting.

Under the **instalment method**, income recognition is deferred until the period of cash collection. Both revenue and cost of sales are recorded in the period of sale but, instead of being closed to the Income Summary account, they are closed to a Deferred Gross Profit account. The deferred gross profit is recognized as realized gross profit and shown in the income statement in the periods cash is collected. The amount of gross profit realized each period depends on the cash collected and the percentage of gross profit on the sale. This is equivalent to deferring both sales revenue and cost of sales to the period of cash collection. Other expenses, such as selling and administrative expenses, are not deferred.

In the remainder of this section, the accounting procedures used when applying the instalment method are examined. Note, however, that this method is used only when bad debts resulting from instalment sales cannot be reasonably estimated. For many instalment sales, reasonable estimates of uncollectible amounts can be made and, therefore, the resulting revenue would be recognized in the period of sale. ***The point is that the instalment method is not a method of accounting for instalment sales in general. Rather, it is a method that is used to account for such sales when collectibility is uncertain and the amount that will be uncollectible in the future is not reasonably determinable.***

Accounting Procedures Under the Instalment Method. From the preceding description of the instalment method, it is apparent that certain information and special accounts are required to determine the deferred (unrealized) gross profit and the realized gross profit in each year of operations. These requirements are as follows:

1. The revenues and costs of instalment sales transactions accounted for using the instalment method must be kept in accounts separate from those pertaining to all other sales transactions.

---

[20] Sometimes cash is received prior to delivery of the goods and is recorded as a deposit (customer advance) because the sale transaction is incomplete. In such cases, the seller has not performed under the contract and has no claim against the purchaser. Cash received represents advances and should be reported as a liability until the contract is performed by delivery of the product.

[21] *CICA Handbook*, Section 3400, par. .16.

2. The gross profit on sales accounted for on the instalment method must be determinable.
3. The amount of cash collected on the current year's instalment sales accounts receivable and on each of the preceding year's receivables must be determinable.
4. Provision must be made for carrying forward each year's deferred gross profit.

Given this, the following describes the journal entries that are made in a given year using the instalment method.

Nature of Journal Entries: Instalment Method

For sales made during the current year:

1. Record the sale by debiting the Instalment Accounts Receivable (noting the year) and crediting Instalment Sales.
2. Record the cost of the sale by debiting Cost of Instalment Sales and crediting Inventory. This assumes use of the perpetual inventory system.[22]
3. Record cash received on this year's sales by debiting Cash and crediting Instalment Accounts Receivable (noting the year).

At year end:

4. Close the revenue and expense accounts to a deferred gross profit account by debiting Instalment Sales, crediting Cost of Instalment Sales, and crediting Deferred Gross Profit on Instalment Sales (noting the year).
5. Record the gross profit realized on cash collected on the current year's receivables by debiting Deferred Gross Profit on Instalment Sales (noting the year) and crediting Realized Gross Profit. The amount is equal to the cash collected multiplied by the gross profit percentage (gross profit ÷ instalment sales revenue) on the current year's sales.

For collections on sales made in prior years:

1. Record cash received by debiting Cash and crediting Instalment Accounts Receivable (noting the year).
2. Record the gross profit realized on the cash collected by debiting Deferred Gross Profit on Instalment Sales (noting the year) and crediting Realized Gross Profit. The amount is the gross profit percentage on the particular prior year's sale multiplied by the cash collected on that year's receivable.

For both:

1. Close the Realized Gross Profit account to the Income Summary.

From this description, it can be seen that the accounting related to the instalment method is fairly complex. The result, however, accomplishes the objective of reporting gross profit in the period when cash is collected.

[22] Under the perpetual inventory system, when a sale is made, the cost of goods sold is recorded and inventory is reduced. For review of the basics of the perpetual method and the periodic method see Chapter 3 (Chapter 8 explains these methods in greater detail). If the periodic method was used, then the Cost of Instalment Sales would be debited at year end, with the credit going to one of several possible accounts, depending on where the item sold came from. For example, if the item sold was from beginning inventory, the Beginning Inventory account would be credited. If it was from purchases of the current year, then Purchases would be credited. If the total beginning inventory and all purchases for the year had been closed to Cost of Goods Sold before the cost of instalment sales had been separated out, then the Cost of Goods Sold account would be credited.

To illustrate the instalment method, assume the following data for the Fesmire Manufacturing Co. Ltd.

Fesmire Manufacturing Co. Ltd: Example Data

	1994	1995	1996
Sales (on instalment)	$200,000	$250,000	$240,000
Cost of sales	150,000	190,000	168,000
Gross profit	$ 50,000	$ 60,000	$ 72,000
Rate of gross profit on sales	**25%[a]**	**24%[b]**	**30%[c]**
Cash receipts from:			
1994 sales	$ 60,000	$100,000	$ 40,000
1995 sales		100,000	125,000
1996 sales			80,000

[a] $\frac{\$50,000}{\$200,000}$ [b] $\frac{\$60,000}{\$250,000}$ [c] $\frac{\$72,000}{\$240,000}$

To simplify the illustration, interest charges have been excluded. The following provides summary entries in general journal form for the transactions in the illustration. As a practical matter, these entries would not appear as summary entries, but would be entered individually as they occur. All transactions not concerned with the instalment method have been omitted.

1994

	Debit	Credit
Instalment Accounts Receivable, 1994	200,000	
Instalment Sales		200,000
(To record sales made on instalment in 1994)		
Cost of Instalment Sales	150,000	
Inventory		150,000
(To record cost of goods sold on instalment in 1994)		
Cash	60,000	
Instalment Accounts Receivable, 1994		60,000
(To record cash collected on instalment receivables)		
Instalment Sales	200,000	
Cost of Instalment Sales		150,000
Deferred Gross Profit, 1994		50,000
(Year-end entry to close instalment sales and cost of instalment sales for the year to deferred gross profit)		
Deferred Gross Profit, 1994	15,000	
Realized Gross Profit on Instalment Sales		15,000
(To remove from deferred gross profit the profit realized through collections)		
Realized Gross Profit on Instalment Sales	15,000	
Income Summary		15,000
(To close profits realized by collections)		

The realized gross profit for 1994 and the deferred gross profit at the end of 1994 are computed as follows.

1994	
Rate of gross profit current year [(sales − cost of sales) ÷ sales] ($200,000 − $150,000) ÷ 200,000	25%
Cash collected on current year's sales	$60,000
Realized gross profit (25% of $60,000)	**15,000**
Deferred gross profit on 1994 sales yet to be realized ($50,000 − $15,000)	**35,000**

1995

Instalment Accounts Receivable, 1995	250,000	
Instalment Sales		250,000
(To record sales made on instalment in 1995)		
Cost of Instalment Sales	190,000	
Inventory		190,000
(To record cost of goods sold on instalment in 1995)		
Cash	200,000	
Instalment Accounts Receivable, 1994		100,000
Instalment Accounts Receivable, 1995		100,000
(To record cash collected on instalment receivables)		
Instalment Sales	250,000	
Cost of Instalment Sales		190,000
Deferred Gross Profit, 1995		60,000
(Year-end entry to close instalment sales and cost of instalment sales for the year to deferred gross profit)		
Deferred Gross Profit, 1994	25,000	
Deferred Gross Profit, 1995	24,000	
Realized Gross Profit on Instalment Sales		49,000
(Year-end entry to remove from deferred gross profit the profit realized through collections)		
Realized Gross Profit on Instalment Sales	49,000	
Income Summary		49,000
(To close profits realized by collections)		

The realized gross profit for 1995 and deferred gross profit at the end of 1995 are computed as follows.

1995	
Current year's sales	
Rate of gross profit [($250,000 − $190,000) ÷ $250,000]	24%
Cash collected on current year's sales	$100,000
Realized gross profit (24% of $100,000)	**24,000**
Deferred gross profit on 1995 sales ($60,000 − $24,000)	**36,000**
Prior years' sales	
Rate of gross profit—1994	25%
Cash collected on 1994 sales in 1995	$100,000
Gross profit realized in 1995 on 1994 sales (25% of $100,000)	**25,000**

(Continued)

Total gross profit realized in 1995	
Realized on collections of 1994 sales	**$ 25,000**
Realized on collections of 1995 sales	**24,000**
Total	$ 49,000

The entries in 1996 would be similar to those of 1995, and the total gross profit realized would be $64,000, as shown by the computations below.

1996	
Current year's sales	
Rate of gross profit [($240,000 − $168,000) ÷ $240,000]	30%
Cash collected on current year's sales	$ 80,000
Gross profit realized on 1996 sales (30% of $80,000)	**24,000**
Deferred gross profit on 1996 sales ($72,000 − $24,000)	**48,000**
Prior years' sales	
1994 sales	
Rate of gross profit—1994	25%
Cash collected on 1994 sales in 1996	$ 40,000
Gross profit realized in 1996 on 1994 sales (25% of $40,000)	**10,000**
1995 sales	
Rate of gross profit—1995	24%
Cash collected on 1995 sales in 1996	$125,000
Gross profit realized in 1996 on 1995 sales (24% of $125,000)	**30,000**
Total gross profit realized in 1996	
Realized on collections of 1994 sales	$ 10,000
Realized on collections of 1995 sales	30,000
Realized on collections of 1996 sales	24,000
Total	$ 64,000

Additional Problems of the Instalment Method. In addition to computing realized and deferred gross profit, other problems are involved in accounting using the instalment method for sales transactions. These problems are related to:

1. Interest on instalment contracts.
2. Defaults and repossessions.

Interest on Instalment Contracts. Because the collection of instalment receivables is spread over a long period, it is customary to charge the buyer interest on the unpaid balance. A schedule of equal payments consisting of interest and principal is set up. Each successive payment has attributed to it a smaller amount of interest and a correspondingly larger amount of principal, as shown in the schedule on page 277. For this example, an item costing $2,400 is sold for $3,000 (gross profit percentage is 20%). Interest at 8% is included in the three equal instalments of $1,164.10.

Interest should be accounted for separately from the gross profit recognized on instalment sales collections during the period. In this example, it is recognized as interest revenue at the time of the cash receipt, given that the year end is December 31.

Defaults and Repossessions. Given appropriate terms in a sales contract and the policy of the credit department, the seller can repossess merchandise sold under an instalment arrangement if the purchaser fails to meet payment requirements. Repossessed merchandise may be reconditioned before it is offered for sale, and then resold for cash or instalment payments.

Instalment Payment Schedule

Date	Cash (Debit)	Interest Revenue (Credit)	Instalment Receivables (Credit)	Instalment Unpaid Balance	Realized Gross Profit (20%)
Dec. 31/94	—	—	—	$3,000.00	—
Dec. 31/95	$1,164.10[a]	$240.00[b]	$ 924.10[c]	2,075.90[d]	$184.82[e]
Dec. 31/96	1,164.10	166.07	998.03	1,077.87	199.61
Dec. 31/97	1,164.10	86.23	1,077.873	-0-	215.57
					$600.00

[a]Periodic payment = Original unpaid balance ÷ PV of an annuity of $1.00 for three periods at 8%:[23] $1,164.10 = $3,000 ÷ 2.57710

[b]$3,000 × .08 = $240.00

[c]$1,164.10 − $240.00 = $924.10

[d]$3,000.00 − $924.10 = $2,075.90

[e]$924.10 × .20 = $184.82

Repossession of merchandise sold is a recognition that the related Instalment Receivable account is not collectible and that it should be written off. Along with this receivable, the applicable deferred gross profit must be removed from the ledger. This is accomplished by the following entry:

Repossessed Merchandise (an inventory account)	XX	
Deferred Gross Profit	XX	
Instalment Accounts Receivable		XX

The entry above assumes that the repossessed merchandise is to be recorded on the books at exactly the amount of the uncollected account less the applicable deferred gross profit. This assumption may or may not be correct. The condition of the merchandise repossessed, the cost of reconditioning, and the market for second-hand merchandise of that particular type must all be considered. ***The objective should be to put any asset acquired on the books at its fair value or, when fair value is not ascertainable, at the best possible approximation of fair value.*** If the fair value of the merchandise repossessed is less than the uncollected balance less the deferred gross profit, a "loss on repossession" should be recorded at the date of repossession.

To illustrate, assume that a refrigerator was sold to Marilyn Hunt for $500 on September 1, 1994. Terms require a down payment of $200 and $20 on the first of every month for 15 months thereafter. It is further assumed that the refrigerator cost $300 and is sold to provide a 40% rate of gross profit on selling price. At the year end, December 31, 1994, a total of $60 would have been collected in addition to the original down payment.

Now if Hunt makes her January and February payments in 1995 and then defaults, the account balances applicable to Hunt at time of default would be:

Instalment Account Receivable	200 (dr.)
Deferred Gross Profit (40% × $240)	96 (cr.)

[23] The appendix at the end of this book entitled "Accounting and the Time Value of Money" explains concepts regarding making measurements that include an interest component. Tables at the end of this appendix provide "factors" (such as the 2.57710 in this example) for present value and future value calculations applicable to a single amount, ordinary annuity, and an annuity due. Generally, those studying intermediate accounting have been previously exposed to this material in other courses. If this is not the case, or a review would help, you may wish to examine this appendix. Many topics considered later in this book require an understanding of time value of money concepts and how they are applied.

The deferred gross profit applicable to the Hunt account still has the December 31, 1994 balance because no entry has been made to take up gross profit realized by cash collections in 1995. The regular entry at the end of 1995, however, will take up the gross profit realized by all cash collections, including amounts received from Hunt. Hence, the balance of deferred gross profit applicable to Hunt's account at the time of default may be computed by applying the gross profit rate for the year of sale to the balance of Hunt's account receivable: 40% of $200, or $80. The account balance should therefore be considered as:

Instalment Account Receivable (Hunt)	200 (dr.)
Deferred Gross Profit (applicable to Hunt after considering $16 of gross profit realized on cash collected in January and February)	80 (cr.)

If the estimated fair value of the article repossessed is $70, the following entry would be made to record the repossession:

Deferred Gross Profit	80	
Repossessed Merchandise	70	
Loss on Repossession	50	
Instalment Account Receivable (Hunt)		200

The amount of the loss is determined by (1) subtracting the deferred gross profit from the amount of the instalment account receivable to determine the unrecovered cost of the merchandise repossessed and (2) subtracting the estimated fair value of the merchandise repossessed from the unrecovered cost to obtain the amount of the loss on repossession.

Balance of account receivable (representing uncollected selling price)	$200
Less deferred gross profit	80
Unrecovered cost	$120
Less estimated fair value of merchandise repossessed	70
Loss on repossession	**$ 50**

If the fair value of the merchandise were $150, then a $30 gain on repossession would be recognized.

Financial Statement Presentation Under the Instalment Method. The previously illustrated entries resulted in only one account, Realized Gross Profit on Instalment Sales, being closed to the Income Summary account each year. Therefore, for a company that has both sales from which revenue is recognized when the sale is made and sales that are accounted for under the instalment method, the ***realized gross profit on instalment sales*** may be reported as illustrated below.

Health Machine Company
Statement of Income
For the Year Ended December 31, 1994

Sales	$620,000
Cost of goods sold	490,000
Gross profit on sales	$130,000
Gross profit realized on instalment sales	**51,000**
Total gross profit on sales	$181,000

If sales accounted for by the instalment method represent a significant part of total sales, disclosure of the current year's instalment sales, cost of those sales, and realized gross profit on cash collections may be desirable. This may be presented in the body of an income statement, as shown below.

Health Machine Company
Statement of Income
For the Year Ended December 31, 1994

	Instalment Method Sales	Other Sales	Total
Sales	**$248,000**	$620,000	$868,000
Cost of goods sold	**182,000**	490,000	672,000
Gross margin on sales	**$ 66,000**	$130,000	$196,000
Less deferred gross profit on instalment sales of this year	**47,000**		47,000
Realized gross profit on this year's sales	**$ 19,000**	$130,000	$149,000
Add gross profit realized on instalment sales of prior years	**32,000**		32,000
Gross profit realized this year	**$ 51,000**	$130,000	$181,000

The year's sales and cost of goods sold amounts in the Instalment Method Sales column are the amounts closed to the Deferred Gross Profit account at year end.

The apparent awkwardness of this presentation is difficult to avoid if full disclosure is to be provided in the income statement. One solution, of course, is to include in the income statement only the gross profit realized during the year and provide a separate schedule showing the details in a note to the statement.

In the balance sheet, it is generally considered desirable to classify ***instalment accounts receivable*** by year of collectibility. There is some question as to whether instalment accounts that are not collectible within the coming year should be included in current assets. If instalment sales are part of normal operations, they may be considered as current assets because they are collectible within the operating cycle of the business. Little confusion should result from this classification if maturity dates are fully disclosed, as illustrated in the following example.

Current assets		
Notes and accounts receivable		
Trade customers	$78,800	
Less allowance for doubtful accounts	3,700	
	$75,100	
Instalment accounts collectible in 1995	22,600	
Instalment accounts collectible in 1996	47,200	$144,900

Repossessed merchandise is a part of inventory and should be included as such in the Current Asset section of the balance sheet. Any ***gain or loss on repossessions*** should be included in the income statement in the Other Revenues and Gains section or Other Expenses and Losses section.

Deferred gross profit on instalment sales is generally treated as unearned revenue and classified as a current liability. *CICA Handbook* Section 1000 permits the inclusion of items on the balance sheet that are not assets or liabilities but items that result from a delay in income statement recognition.[24] Thus, deferred gross profit may be reported with liabilities. An alternative means of disclosure would be to report it as a reduction of instalment accounts receivable. This latter method is conceptually appealing since the reason for the existence of a deferred gross profit is that the seller has retained a significant risk. This position is supported by the argument that "no matter how it is displayed in financial statements, deferred gross profit on instalment sales is conceptually an asset valuation—that is, a reduction of an asset."[25] We favour this position but recognize that until an official standard on this topic is issued, financial statements will probably continue to report such deferred gross profit as a current liability.

The Cost Recovery Method

Objective 12

Explain and apply the cost recovery method of accounting.

The cost recovery method is another method that may be used when the realization criteria are judged not to be met until cash collection takes place. Under the **cost recovery method,** ***no gross profit is recognized until cash payments by the buyer exceed the seller's cost of the merchandise sold.*** After the cost of the merchandise sold has been recovered, additional cash receipts are recognized as realized gross profit.

This method is more conservative than the instalment method. When the recognition criteria are not met until cash is collected, the choice of applying the instalment method or the cost recovery method requires the exercise of professional judgement. The resolution revolves around the extent of the uncertainty associated with the eventual collection of the receivables. The cost recovery method is applicable to situations in which there is a great degree of uncertainty. Such circumstances could exist, for example, when an instalment sale is made to a newly established business engaged in highly speculative activities.

To illustrate the accounting under the cost recovery method and compare it to that of the instalment method, the previously identified data pertaining to Fesmire Manufacturing Co. Ltd.'s 1994 instalment sales and subsequent cash collections will be used. This data and the journal entries associated with the two methods are presented below.

Events:

In 1994: Sales (on instalment contracts)		$200,000
Cost of instalment sales		150,000
Gross profit		$ 50,000
Rate of gross profit		25%
Cash collected on the 1994 instalment sales:		
in 1994,	$ 60,000	
in 1995,	$100,000	
in 1996,	$ 40,000	

For Both Cost Recovery Method and Instalment Method:

	1994		1995		1996	
Instalment Accounts Receivable, 1994	200,000					
Instalment Sales		200,000				
(To record sale made on instalment in 1994)						

(Continued)

[24] *CICA Handbook*, Section 1000, par. .26.

[25] *Statement of Financial Accounting Concepts No. 3* (Stamford, CT: FASB), pars. 156–158.

Cost of Instalment Sales	150,000					
Inventory		150,000				
(To record cost of goods sold on instalment in 1994)						
Cash	60,000		100,000		40,000	
Instalment Accounts Receivable, 1994		60,000		100,000		40,000
(To record cash collections on instalment during year)						
Instalment Sales	200,000					
Cost of Instalment Sales		150,000				
Deferred Gross Profit, 1994		50,000				
(Year-end entry to close instalment sales and cost of instalment sales for 1994 to deferred gross profit)						
For Cost Recovery Method:						
Deferred Gross Profit, 1994	—		10,000		40,000	
Realized Gross Profit on Instalment Sales		—		10,000		40,000
(Year-end entry to remove from deferred gross profit the profit realized from cash collected during the year after full cost of the goods sold has been collected)						
For Instalment Method:						
Deferred Gross Profit, 1994	15,000		25,000		10,000	
Realized Gross Profit		15,000		25,000		10,000
(Year-end entry to remove from deferred gross profit the profit realized from cash collected during the year. Equals gross profit rate of 25% multiplied by cash collected each year)						

For both the cost recovery method and the instalment method, Realized Gross Profit for each year would be closed to the Income Summary account.

As this example shows, the entries to record the instalment sales, cost of instalment sales, cash collections, and closing a year's instalment sales and cost of these sales to deferred gross profit are the same under both methods. ***The difference between the methods occurs with regard to the timing of recognizing realized gross profit.***

Realized gross profit is reported in the appropriate year's income statement in the same manner as illustrated under the instalment method. Any balance in the Deferred Gross Profit account is, preferably, reported as a contra-account deducted from the related receivables in the balance sheet. Alternatively, the Deferred Gross Profit account may be reported as a current liability, as is the common case when the instalment method is used.

CONCLUDING REMARKS

As stated in the opening sentence of this chapter, revenue recognition is one of the most difficult and pressing problems facing the accounting profession. The difficulties arise because companies earn revenues in different ways. Any particular company's earning process and specific circumstances may result in the revenue recognition criteria established in the *CICA Handbook* being met at a time different than that for another company. Clearly, judgement is required regarding any decision to recognize revenue, and that judgement must be based on justifiable reasons. To help in making such judgements the following may be useful:

1. Know the criteria for revenue recognition as presented in the *CICA Handbook*.
2. Know the earning process associated with a particular situation. Such understanding may be helped by identifying on a time-line the major transactions and events that occur in the earning process.
3. Examine the earning process with the objective of determining when all the criteria for revenue recognition are met. It is at this time revenue can be recognized.

FUNDAMENTAL CONCEPTS

1. The *CICA Handbook*, Section 3400, states, generally, that revenue can be recognized at the time in the earning process when (1) performance is achieved, (2) the amount is reasonably measurable, and (3) collectibility is reasonably assured. It provides specific definitions of when performance is achieved regarding the sale of goods, rendering of services, and executing long-term contracts. Also, in Section 1000, the *Handbook* states that (4) matching expenses with related revenue is necessary. Consequently, we add this as a fourth criterion for revenue recognition to occur.
2. In many situations, the criteria for revenue recognition are met at the date of sale (delivery). In other situations, however, the criteria may be met prior to delivery or after delivery.
3. Companies that experience a high rate of return of their goods, which cannot be reasonably estimated when the goods are delivered, would postpone reporting revenue until the return privilege has expired.
4. For long-term construction contracts, revenue may be recognized during construction when the amount of revenue is measurable, estimates of the costs to complete are reasonably determinable, the extent of progress toward completion is reasonably estimable, and collectibility is reasonably assured. When these conditions are met, the percentage-of-completion method is applied.
5. The completed-contract method, which defers the recognition of revenue until the completion of the long-term contract, should be used when the conditions for using the percentage-of-completion method do not apply.
6. Expected losses resulting from long-term contracts should be recognized entirely in the earliest period in which they are estimable, regardless of whether the percentage-of-completion method or the completed-contract method is used.
7. The instalment and cost recovery methods of accounting are used when the revenue recognition criteria, specifically the collectibility requirement, are not satisfied until cash is collected. Under the instalment method, a proportion of gross profit on the sale is realized with each cash collection. Under the cost recovery method, gross profit is not recognized until the cost of the item sold is recovered. These cash collection methods are applicable when collection of the sale price is uncertain and the uncollectibles are not reasonably estimable.

APPENDIX 6A
Accounting for Service Sales Transactions

SERVICE INDUSTRIES AND SERVICE TRANSACTIONS

The number and variety of businesses that offer services to the public are increasing and the range of services they offer are broadening. Examples of the types of industries that offer services are listed below.

- Accounting
- Advertising agencies
- Architects
- Cemetery associations
- Computer service organizations
- Correspondence schools
- Electronic security
- Employment agencies
- Engineering firms
- Entertainers
- Extended care organizations
- Fitness centres
- Garbage and waste removal firms
- Interior design or decoration firms
- Legal services
- Management consultants
- Medical practitioners
- Modelling agencies
- Mortgage banking
- Moving and storage firms
- Placement agencies
- Private and social clubs
- Public relations firms
- Real estate brokerages
- Research and development labs
- Retirement homes
- Transport firms
- Travel agencies

This list is representative only of service industries; an all-inclusive list cannot be provided because the range of services is so wide. The common ground of all organizations that provide services is that they engage in **service transactions.**

> Service transactions are defined as transactions between a seller and a purchaser in which, for a mutually agreed price, the seller performs, agrees to perform at a later date, or agrees to maintain readiness to perform an act or acts, including permitting others to use enterprise resources that do not alone produce a tangible commodity or product as the principal intended result.[26]

Although this definition does not require that the act or acts to be performed be specified by a contract, in practice most service transactions performed over a period of time or requiring performance in the future are formalized by a contract. However, agreements to perform at a later date and agreements to maintain a readiness to perform an act are typically only commitments or executory contracts. As such, they are not recorded in accrual-based, transaction-oriented financial statements.

Some transactions may involve both services and products. ***When provision of a product is incidental to the rendering of a service, the transaction is accounted for as a service transaction.*** For example, a fixed-price equipment maintenance contract that includes parts is considered a service transaction. Conversely, ***if a service is incidental to the sale of a product, the transaction is accounted for as a product transaction.*** For example, the inclusion of a warranty or guarantee in the sale of a product is considered incidental to the sale of the product.

Determining when a service or a product is incidental to a transaction can be difficult. An incidental nature may be indicated, however, in either of the following two ways:

1. The inclusion of a product or a service does not result in a variance in the total transaction price from what would be charged excluding the product or service.
2. A product is not sold or a service is not rendered separately in the seller's normal business.[27]

When both the product and the service are stated separately and the total transaction price varies because the product or the service is included, the transaction is accounted for as both a product and a service transaction. For example,

[26] *Accounting for Certain Service Transactions* (Stamford, CT: FASB, 1978), p. 1.
[27] *Ibid.*, pp. 10–11.

equipment maintenance contracts in which parts are charged separately qualifies for separable product and service transaction accounting.

REVENUE AND EXPENSE RECOGNITION FOR SERVICE TRANSACTIONS

A major accounting issue regarding service transactions concerns when revenue should be recognized. Solutions depend on when all the revenue recognition criteria are met in the earning process. The criteria for service transactions are the same as exist for product sales: performance is achieved, measurement is reasonably determinable, collectibility is reasonably assured or uncollectible amounts can be estimated, and expenses can be matched against the revenue.

Within the context of the specific *CICA Handbook* recommendations on revenue recognition criteria (see page 255), the following explanatory statements are made:

> Revenue from service transactions . . . is usually recognized as the service . . . activity is performed, using either the percentage of completion method or the completed contract method.
>
> The percentage of completion method is used when performance consists of the execution of more than one act, and revenue would be recognized proportionately by reference to the performance of each act. Revenue recognized under this method would be determined on a rational and consistent basis, such as on the basis of sales value associated costs, extent of progress, or number of acts. For practical purposes, when services are provided by an indeterminate number of acts over a specific period of time, revenue would be recognized on a straight line basis over the period unless there is evidence that some other method better reflects the pattern of performance.
>
> The completed contract method would only be appropriate when performance consists of the execution of a single act or when the enterprise cannot reasonably estimate the extent of progress toward completion.[28]

Consequently, performance is linked to the execution of a defined act or acts. Given that measurement of revenue and expenses can be related to such execution and that collection is reasonably assured, then revenue can be recognized.

The matching principle specifies that costs should be charged to expense in the period in which the revenue with which they are associated is recognized as earned. Costs should not be deferred unless they are expected to be recoverable from future revenue. Costs to be incurred in periods subsequent to the period of related revenue recognition should be accrued (i.e. debit an expense and credit a liability). If such future costs exist and are material but cannot be reasonably estimable, then revenue recognition must be deferred.

For service transactions, costs incurred to earn revenue may be categorized as follows:

1. **Initial direct costs** are costs that are directly associated with negotiating and consummating service agreements. They include, but are not necessarily limited to, commissions, legal fees, and costs of credit investigations. No portion of supervisory and administration expenses or other indirect expenses, such as rent and facilities costs, is included in initial direct costs.
2. **Direct costs** are costs that have a clearly identifiable beneficial or causal relationship (i) to the services performed or (ii) to the level of services performed for a group of customers (e.g., labour costs and repair parts included as part of a service agreement).
3. **Indirect costs** are all costs other than initial direct costs and direct costs. They include general and administrative expenses, advertising expenses, and general selling expenses.[29]

Indirect costs would be charged to expense as incurred, regardless of the revenue recognition method applied to the transaction. The method of accounting for initial direct costs and direct costs is dependent on the revenue recognition method applied to the transactions.

---

[28] *CICA Handbook*, Section 3400, pars. .13–15.

[29] *Accounting for Certain Service Transactions*, pp. 13 and 14.

METHODS OF SERVICE REVENUE RECOGNITION

Depending on when the criteria for revenue recognition for service transactions are satisfied, one of the four following methods of accounting would be used:

1. Specific performance method.
2. Proportional performance method.
3. Completed performance method.
4. Collection method.

Specific Performance Method

The **specific performance method** is appropriate when a service transaction consists of a *single act*. Revenue should be recognized at the time the act is completed. Initial direct costs and direct costs should be charged to expense at the time revenues are recognized. Thus, initial direct costs and direct costs incurred before the service is performed should be deferred until the revenue is recognized. In essence, this method of recognizing revenue from service transactions is akin to recognizing revenue from the sale of goods at the time of delivery.

This method could be used by a real estate broker who would record sales commissions as revenue when a real estate transaction is closed. It might also be applicable to an employment agency. Because the agency has rendered its services in locating and placing an employee for its client, the fee would be recorded at the time the employee is placed. However, if experience shows that there is a reasonable possibility of having to refund the fee because an employment period contingency is built into the arrangement, it is appropriate to record an allowance based on estimates of fees that will never be collected.

Proportional Performance Method

The **proportional performance method** is appropriate when services are performed in ***more than one act over more than one time period and the extent of performance achieved in any one period relative to total required performance can be reasonably determined.*** Revenue would be recognized as the various acts that make up the entire service contract occur. The proportional performance method is another name for the percentage-of-completion method. This method can be applied in a slightly different manner depending on the particular set of circumstances:

1. ***Specified number of identical or similar acts***. An equal amount of revenue would be recorded for each act performed. The processing of monthly mortgage payments by a mortgage banker is an appropriate situation in which this method could be applied.
2. ***Specified number of defined but not identical acts***. Revenue is recognized in the ratio that the direct costs of performing each act have to the total estimated direct cost of the entire transaction. A correspondence school that provides progress evaluations, lessons, examinations, and grading might appropriately use this method. If the direct cost ratio is impractical or not objectively determinable as a measurement basis, a systematic and rational basis that reasonably relates revenue recognition to performance should be used. As a last resort, the straight-line method could be used.
3. ***Unspecified number of identical or similar acts with a fixed period of performance***. Revenue is recognized on the straight-line method over the specified period unless there is evidence that another method is more representative of the pattern of performance. A two-year club membership in which the club's facilities are available for the member's usage throughout that period is an example of appropriate application of the straight-line method.

Under the proportional performance method, *initial direct costs* are recorded as expenses in the period the related revenue is recognized. When there is a close correlation between the incurrence of *direct costs* and the extent of performance achieved, direct costs may be recorded as expenses as they are incurred. Otherwise, the accounting system must be set up so that the direct costs are matched against the related revenue.

Completed Performance Method

The **completed performance method** is appropriate when the service contract requires the performance of ***more than one act and the proportional performance method cannot be employed or the last of a series of acts is so significant in***

relation to the entire service transaction that performance cannot be deemed to have been achieved until the last act occurs. For example, for a moving company that packs, loads, and delivers goods to various locations, the act of delivery is so significant to its performance completion that revenue should not be recognized until delivery occurs. The completed performance method is equivalent to the completed-contract method.

Under the completed performance method, initial direct costs and direct costs would be expensed when revenue is recognized. Costs incurred before performance is completed should be deferred until the revenue is recognized.

Collection Method

If there is a significant degree of uncertainty surrounding the collectibility of service revenue and a reasonable estimate of uncollectible amounts cannot be made, then revenue or related gross profit should not be recognized until cash is collected. The collection method may be similar to the instalment method or the cost recovery method of accounting for the sale of goods, depending on the degree of uncertainty associated with cash collection.

APPENDIX 6B

Revenue Recognition for Special Sales Transactions

To supplement and illustrate our presentation of revenue recognition, we have chosen to cover three common yet unique types of sales transactions—consignment sales, bartering, and franchise sales.

CONSIGNMENT SALES ACCOUNTING

A specialized method of marketing certain types of products makes use of a device known as a consignment. In **consignment sales arrangements** ***the delivery of the goods by the manufacturer (or wholesaler) to the dealer (or retailer) does not constitute achievement of performance because the manufacturer retains title to the goods.*** Under this arrangement, the **consignor** (manufacturer) ships merchandise to the **consignee** (dealer), who acts as an agent for the consignor in selling the merchandise. However, the risks and rewards of ownership remain with the consignor. Both consignor and consignee are interested in selling—the former to make a profit or develop a market, the latter to make a commission on the sales.

The consignee accepts the merchandise and agrees to exercise due diligence in caring for and selling it. Cash received from customers is remitted to the consignor by the consignee, after deducting a sales commission and any chargeable expenses. The consignor recognizes revenue only after receiving notification of sale, which is usually accompanied by a cash remittance from the consignee. The merchandise is carried throughout the consignment as the inventory of the consignor, separately classified as Merchandise on Consignment. It is not recorded as an asset on the consignee's books. On sale of the merchandise, the consignee has a liability for the net amount due the consignor. The consignor periodically receives from the consignee an **account sales report** that shows the merchandise received, merchandise sold, expenses chargeable to the consignment, and the cash remitted.

To illustrate consignment accounting entries, assume that Nelba Manufacturing Ltd. ships merchandise costing $36,000 on consignment to Best Value Stores. Nelba pays $3,750 of freight costs and Best Value pays $2,250 for local advertising costs that are reimbursable from Nelba. By the end of the period, two-thirds of the consigned merchandise has been sold for $40,000 cash. Best Value notifies Nelba of the sales, retains a 10% commission, and remits the cash due Nelba. The following journal entries would be made by the consignor (Nelba) and the consignee (Best Value).

Transaction	Nelba Manufacturing Ltd. (Consignor)			Best Value Stores (Consignee)		
Shipment of consigned merchandise	Inventory on Consignment	36,000		No entry (record memo of merchandise received)		
	Finished Goods Inventory		36,000			
Payment of freight costs by consignor	Inventory on Consignment	3,750		No entry		
	Cash		3,750			
Payment of advertising by consignee	No entry until notified			Receivable from Consignor	2,250	
				Cash		2,250
Sales of consigned merchandise	No entry until notified			Cash	40,000	
				Payable to Consignor		40,000
Notification of sales and expenses and remittance of amount due	Cash	33,750		Payable to Consignor	40,000	
	Advertising Expense	2,250		Receivable from Consignor		2,250
	Commission Expense	4,000		Commission Revenue		4,000
	Revenue from Consignment Sales		40,000	Cash		33,750

(Continued)

Adjustment of inventory on consignment and recording cost of sales	Cost of Goods Sold 26,500 Inventory on Consignment 26,500 [2/3 ($36,000 + $3,750) = $26,500]		No entry

Under the consignment arrangement, the manufacturer (consignor) accepts the risk that the merchandise might not sell and relieves the dealer (consignee) of the need to commit part of its working capital to inventory. A variety of different systems and account titles are used to record consignments, but they all share the common goal of postponing the recognition of revenue until it is known that a sale to a third party has occurred.

REVENUE RECOGNITION AND BARTER TRANSACTIONS

Due to a variety of economic and tax circumstances, companies may engage in **barter transactions.** For example, radio and television stations often barter advertising time for scripts, tapes, programs, or space in newspapers. A plumber may trade services with an electrician, an attorney may arrange for a house painter to paint the attorney's home in exchange for legal services, or an automobile dealer may barter a truck to a cleaning service company in exchange for a cleaning service contract.

The issue of concern is whether revenue and related expenses should be recognized as the result of barter transactions. Because no cash or claim to cash is involved, one may argue that there would be no revenue. However, an exchange of economic substance does occur and to ignore this fact would significantly detract from the relevancy of financial statements.

The *CICA Handbook* addresses barter transactions when discussing the accounting consequences of nonmonetary transactions.[30] The basic requirement is that the fair value of the asset or services received or given up, whichever is more readily determinable, is to be recorded as revenue when the criteria for revenue recognition are met. **Fair value** is the amount that would be agreed on by informed parties dealing at arm's length in an open and unrestricted market.[31] The cost of the service or book value of the asset given up would be the related expense.[32]

FRANCHISES

Accounting for franchise sales provides an excellent focus for exemplifying various revenue recognition issues related to special sales transactions. Franchise sales are a common event in our business environment. They provide a variety of situations necessitating considerable professional judgement in deciding when revenue recognition criteria are met. In accounting for franchise sales, the accountant must fully understand the terms and conditions specified in a particular franchise sales contract when deciding on the revenue recognition consequences of various transactions and events.

Franchises and Accounting Abuses

A **franchise** is defined as:

> . . . a contractual privilege, often exclusive, granted by one party (the franchiser) to another (the franchisee) permitting the sale of a product, use of a trade name or rendering of a service in a single outlet at a specified location (individual franchise) or in a number of outlets within a specified territory (area franchise). The rights and responsibilities of each party are usually set out in a franchise agreement which normally outlines specific marketing practices to be followed, specifies the contribution of each party to the operation of the business, and sets forth certain operating procedures.[33]

---

[30] *CICA Handbook*, Section 3830. The material in this Section is considered in detail in Chapter 10 where exchanges (e.g., trade-ins) involving property, plant, and equipment are examined.

[31] *Ibid.*, par. .04.

[32] Under Canadian income tax requirements, the difference between the fair value of what is received and the cost of what is given up in a barter transaction is considered to be a part of taxable income.

[33] "Franchise Fee Revenue," *Accounting Guideline* (Toronto: CICA, 1984), par. 1.

Four types of franchising arrangements have evolved: (1) manufacturer–retailer, (2) manufacturer–wholesaler, (3) service sponsor–retailer, and (4) wholesaler–retailer. The fastest-growing category, and the one that causes particular revenue recognition problems, has been the **service sponsor–retailer** arrangement. Included in this category are such industries and businesses as:

Soft ice cream drive-ins (Tastee Freez, Dairy Queen)
Food drive-ins (McDonald's, Kentucky Fried Chicken, Wendy's)
Restaurants (Perkins, Pizza Hut, Denny's)
Motels (Holiday Inn, Howard Johnson, Best Western)
Auto rentals (Avis, Hertz, Tilden)
Part-time help (Kelly Services)
Others (H & R Block, Arthur Murray Studios, Seven-Eleven Stores)

Franchise companies derive their revenue from one or both of two sources: (1) from the sale of initial franchises and related assets or services and (2) from continuing fees based on the operations of franchises. The **franchiser** (the party who grants business rights under the franchise) normally provides the **franchisee** (the party who operates the franchised business) with services such as the following:

1. Assistance in site selection:
   (a) Analysing location.
   (b) Negotiating leases.
2. Evaluation of potential income.
3. Supervision of construction activity:
   (a) Obtaining financing.
   (b) Designing the building.
   (c) Supervising contractor while building.
4. Assistance in the acquisition of signs, fixtures, and equipment.
5. Provision of bookkeeping and advisory services and supplies:
   (a) Setting up franchisee's records.
   (b) Advising on income, real estate, and other taxes.
   (c) Advising on local regulations of the franchisee's business.
6. Provision of employee and management training.
7. Provision of quality control.
8. Provision of advertising and promotion.[34]

Prior to the mid-1980s, it was common practice for franchisers to recognize the entire franchise fee at the date of sale, whether the fee was received then or was collectible over a long period of time as represented by a long-term note. Frequently, franchisers recorded the entire amount as revenue in the year of sale, even though many of the services were yet to be performed and uncertainty existed regarding the collection of the entire fee. In effect, the franchisers were counting their fried chickens before they were hatched.

A **franchise agreement** may provide for refunds to the franchisee if certain conditions are not met, and the franchise fee profit can be reduced sharply by future costs of obligations and services to be rendered by the franchiser. To curb the abuses of premature revenue recognition and to help accountants make appropriate judgements as to when revenue is

[34] Archibald E. MacKay, "Accounting for Initial Franchise Fee Revenue," *The Journal of Accountancy*, January 1970, pp. 66–67.

recognizable, an *Accounting Guideline* titled "Franchise Fee Revenue" was issued in 1984.[35] The criteria for revenue recognition provided in Section 3400 of the *CICA Handbook* issued in 1986 codified the basic principles inherent in the *Guideline*. Drawing on these sources, the following material provides an impression of the issues involved in accounting for franchise transactions and then gives some examples of the accounting entries that could be made in different circumstances.

Initial Franchise Fees

The **initial franchise fee** is consideration for establishing the franchise relationship and providing some initial services. Initial franchise fees are to be recorded as revenue only when and as the franchiser makes "substantial performance" of the services it is obligated to perform and collection of the fee is reasonably assured. **Substantial performance** occurs when the franchiser has no remaining obligation to refund any cash received or excuse any nonpayment of a note and has performed all the significant initial services required under the contract. Generally, the conditions for substantial performance are not met until the commencement of operations by the franchisee.

Illustration of Entries for Initial Franchise Fees

To illustrate, assume that Tum's Pizza Ltd. charges an initial franchise fee of $50,000 for the right to operate a Tum's Pizza franchise. Of this amount, $10,000 is payable when the agreement is signed and the balance is payable in five annual payments of $8,000 each. In return for the initial franchise fee, the franchiser will help in locating the site, negotiate the lease or purchase of the site, supervise the construction activity, and provide the bookkeeping services. The credit rating of the franchisee indicates that money can be borrowed at 8%. The present value of an ordinary annuity of five annual receipts of $8,000 each discounted at 8% is $31,941.60, which is the "principal" amount of the note. The discount of $8,058.40 represents the interest revenue to be earned by the franchiser over the payment period. The above facts could, depending on the specific circumstances, give rise to any of the entries shown below. The revenue recognized in each entry reflects judgement that the facts presented for each circumstance justify that the revenue recognition criteria have been met regarding the amount involved.

1. If there is reasonable expectation that the down payment may be refunded and if substantial future services remain to be performed by Tum's Pizza Ltd., the entry would be:

Cash	10,000.00	
Notes Receivable	40,000.00	
Discount on Notes Receivable		8,058.40
Unearned Franchise Fees		41,941.60

2. If the probability of refunding the initial franchise fee is extremely low, the amount of future services to be provided to the franchisee is minimal, collectibility of the note is reasonably assured, and substantial performance has occurred, the entry would be:

Cash	10,000.00	
Notes Receivable	40,000.00	
Discount on Notes Receivable		8,058.40
Revenue from Franchise Fees		41,941.60

3. If the initial down payment is not refundable and represents a fair measure of the services already provided, a significant amount of services is still to be performed by the franchiser in future periods, and collectibility of the note is reasonably assured, the entry would be:

---

[35] *Ibid. An Accounting Guideline* was a document issued by the Steering Committee of the CICA's Accounting Standards Committee (now the Accounting Standards Board). Essentially, such *Guidelines* were the predecessor of *Abstracts of Issues Discussed*, issued currently by the CICA's Emerging Issues Committee. The *Guidelines* provided interpretation of *CICA Handbook* recommendations and opinions on particular issues of concern. They did not have the authority of *Handbook* recommendations.

Cash	10,000.00	
Notes Receivable	40,000.00	
Discount on Notes Receivable		8,058.40
Revenue from Franchise Fees		10,000.00
Unearned Franchise Fees		31,941.60

4. If the initial down payment is not refundable and no future services are required of the franchiser, but collection of the note is so uncertain that recognition of the note as an asset is unwarranted, the entry would be:

Cash	10,000.00	
Revenue from Franchise Fees		10,000.00

5. Under the same conditions as stated under case 4 except that the down payment is refundable or substantial services are yet to be performed, the entry would be:

Cash	10,000.00	
Unearned Franchise Fees		10,000.00

In cases 4 and 5, where collection of the note is extremely uncertain, cash collections may be recognized using the instalment method or the cost recovery method.

Continuing Franchise Fees

Continuing franchise fees are received in return for the continuing rights granted by the franchise agreement. They may be linked to providing such services as management training, advertising and promotion, legal assistance, and other support. Continuing fees should be recognized as revenue when they are earned and receivable from the franchisee, unless a portion of them has been designated for a particular future purpose, such as providing a specified amount for building maintenance or local advertising. In that case, a portion of the continuing fee should be deferred until the designated purpose has occurred. The amount deferred should be sufficient to cover the estimated cost and provide a reasonable profit on the particular requirement.

Bargain Purchases

In addition to paying continuing franchise fees, franchisees frequently purchase some or all of their equipment and supplies from the franchiser. The franchiser would account for these sales as it would for any other product sales. Sometimes, however, the franchise agreement grants the franchisee the right to make **bargain purchases** of equipment or supplies after the initial franchise fee is paid. If the bargain price is lower than the normal selling price of the same product, or if it does not provide the franchiser a reasonable profit, then a portion of the *initial* franchise fee should be deferred. When the franchisee subsequently purchases the equipment or supplies, the deferred portion of the initial franchise fee would be transferred to a revenue account (i.e. added to the bargain price-based revenue). This treatment reflects the fact that the franchisee is really paying the normal price through two types of payments: the bargain purchase price and part of the initial franchise fee.

Options to Purchase

A franchise agreement may give the franchiser an **option to purchase** the franchisee's business. For example, as a matter of management policy, the franchiser may reserve the right to purchase a profitable franchised outlet or to purchase one that is in financial difficulty. If it is probable at the time the option is given that the franchiser will ultimately purchase the outlet, then the initial franchise fee should not be recognized as revenue but should be recorded as a Deferred Franchise Purchase Option (a liability). When the option is exercised, the liability would reduce the franchiser's investment in the outlet.

Illustration of Entries for Continuing Fees, Bargain Purchases, and Options

To illustrate these concepts, assume the facts given on page 290 for the Tum's Pizza Ltd. example. In addition, assume that Tum's Pizza Ltd. charges a continuing franchise fee of $4,200 annually for services rendered during the year.

1. ***Continuing franchise fee with a portion designated for a particular purpose.*** If 20% of the continuing franchise fee is designated specifically for future building maintenance to be provided by the franchiser, the entry to record receipt of the franchise fee would be:

Cash	4,200.00	
Revenue from Continuing Franchise Fees		3,360.00
Unearned Franchise Fees ($4,200 × .20)		840.00

When maintenance is provided, assuming that the franchiser will receive a 25% markup on the selling price, the entries are:

Unearned Franchise Fees	840.00	
Revenue from Continuing Franchise Fees		840.00
Maintenance Expense [$840 − (840 × .25)]	630.00	
Cash (or Accounts Payable)		630.00

2. ***Sales to franchisee on a normal basis***. If during the year Tum's Pizza Ltd. sells supplies costing $3,000 to the franchisee at the normal $4,000 price, the entries are:

Cash (or Accounts Receivable)	4,000.00	
Franchise Product Sales		4,000.00
Cost of Franchise Product Sales	3,000.00	
Supplies Inventory		3,000.00

3. ***Bargain purchase***. Collectibility of the note for the initial franchise fee is reasonably assured and substantial performance by the franchiser has occurred (see entry 2, page 290). If after the initial franchise fee is paid, the franchisee has the right to purchase up to $20,000 fair value of supplies at their cost of $15,000, the entry to record the initial franchise fee would be:

Cash	10,000.00	
Notes Receivable	40,000.00	
Discount on Notes Receivable		8,058.40
Revenue from Franchise Fees		36,941.60
Unearned Franchise Fees		5,000.00

When the franchisee subsequently purchases the supplies, the entries are:

Cash (or Accounts Receivable)	15,000.00	
Unearned Franchise Fees	5,000.00	
Franchise Product Sales		20,000.00
Cost of Franchise Product Sales	15,000.00	
Supplies Inventory		15,000.00

4. ***Option to purchase***. Collectibility of the note for the initial franchise fee is reasonably assured and substantial performance by the franchiser has occurred (see entry 2, page 290.) The franchise agreement contains an option allowing Tum's Pizza Ltd. to purchase the outlet at any time during the next five years. If it is likely that this option will ultimately be exercised, the entry to record the initial franchise fee would be:

Cash	10,000.00	
Notes Receivable	40,000.00	
Discount on Notes Receivable		8,058.40
Deferred Franchise Purchase Option (liability)		41,941.60

Assume that the franchiser exercised the option at the beginning of the second year and paid the franchisee $40,000. The following entries would have been made by the franchiser at the end of the first year to record the $8,000 collection on the note and the interest earned on the principal of the note outstanding for the year (8% × $31,941.60 = $2,555.33; see page 290 regarding the determination of the $31,941.60).

Cash	8,000.00	
Notes Receivable		8,000.00
Discount on Notes Receivable	2,555.33	
Interest Revenue		2,555.33

Therefore, the balance in Notes Receivable would be $32,000 (dr.), in Discount on Notes Receivable, $5,503.07 (cr.), and Deferred Franchise Purchase Option, $41,941.60 (cr.). These accounts would be eliminated when the option is exercised and the $40,000 is paid to the franchisee as shown in the following entry:

Investment in Franchise Operation	24,555.33	
Deferred Franchise Purchase Option	41,941.60	
Discount on Notes Receivable	5,503.07	
Notes Receivable		32,000.00
Cash		40,000.00

Franchiser's Costs

Franchise accounting also involves appropriate accounting for the **franchiser's costs**. The objective is to match related costs and revenues by reporting them as components of income in the same accounting period. Franchisers should defer **direct costs** (usually incremental costs) relating to specific franchise sales for which revenue has not yet been recognized. Costs should not be deferred, however, without reference to anticipated revenue and its realizability. **Indirect costs** of a regular and recurring nature such as selling and administrative expenses would be expensed as incurred.

Disclosures by Franchisers

The method of accounting for revenue from franchise fees must be disclosed in the notes to the financial statements.[36] Disclosure of all significant commitments and obligations resulting from franchise agreements, including a description of services that have not yet been substantially performed, is desirable. Initial franchise fees should be segregated from other franchise fee revenue if they are significant. Where possible, revenues and costs related to franchiser-owned outlets should be distinguished from those related to franchised outlets.

Note: All **asterisked** questions, cases, exercises, and problems relate to material contained in an appendix to the chapter.

QUESTIONS

1. What are the criteria for revenue recognition?
2. What conditions need to exist in order to recognize revenue at the point of delivery (sale) for goods sold on an instalment contract?
3. What is an earning process?
4. What is a "value-added" viewpoint to earning revenue? Why do accountants not recognize revenue to reflect this viewpoint?
5. Under what conditions may a seller who is exposed to continued risks of a high rate of return of the product sold recognize revenue when the sale (delivery) occurs?
6. What are the two basic methods of accounting for long-term construction contracts? Indicate the circumstances that determine when one or the other of these methods should be used.
7. Leigh's Construction Co. has a $100-million contract to construct a highway overpass and cloverleaf. The total estimated cost for the project is $85 million. Costs incurred in the first year of the project are $17 million. Leigh's Construction Co. appropriately uses the percentage-of-completion method. How much revenue and gross profit should Leigh's recognize in the first year of the project?
8. For what reasons should the percentage-of-completion method be used over the completed-contract method whenever possible?
9. What are the two types of losses that can become evident in accounting for long-term contracts? What is the nature of each type of loss? How is each type accounted for?
10. What is accretion? Why is accretion not generally recognized as revenue?
11. What is the nature of an instalment sale? How do instalment sales differ from ordinary credit sales?
12. Describe the instalment method of accounting.
13. How are operating expenses (not included in cost of goods sold) handled under the instalment method of accounting? What is the justification for such treatment?

[36] *CICA Handbook*, Section 1505, par. .10.

14. B. Bonds sold his condominium for $500,000 on September 14, 1994; he had paid $350,000 for it in 1986. Bonds collected the selling price as follows: 1994, $80,000; 1995, $320,000; and 1996, $100,000. Bonds appropriately uses the instalment method. Prepare a schedule to determine the realized gross profit for 1994, 1995, and 1996 from the instalment sale. Ignore any interest aspects in answering.

15. When the instalment method is used and interest is involved, how should it be treated for accounting purposes?

16. How should the results of sales accounted for by the instalment method be reported on the income statement?

17. At what time is it appropriate to recognize revenue or gross profit in the following cases: (a) instalment sales with no reasonable basis for estimating the degree of collectibility; (b) merchandise shipped on consignment; (c) profit on incomplete construction contracts; and (d) cash collected on subscriptions to future publications?

18. When is revenue recorded under the cost recovery method? When is gross profit realized?

*19. When should revenue from service sales transactions be recognized?

*20. What are four methods of accounting for service revenue recognition? Which product sales revenue recognition methods are these methods similar to in terms of the timing of revenue recognition?

*21. What is the nature of a sale on consignment? When is revenue recognized from a consignment sale?

*22. Why, in franchise arrangements, may it not be appropriate to recognize the entire initial franchise fee as revenue at the date of sale?

*23. How should a franchiser account for continuing franchise fees and routine sales of equipment and supplies to franchisees?

*24. What consequences are there for the franchiser's recording of the initial franchise fee when the franchise agreement:
(a) Contains an option allowing the franchiser to purchase the franchised outlet and it is likely that the option will be exercised?
(b) Allows the franchisee to purchase equipment and supplies from the franchiser at bargain prices?

CASES

C6-1 **(RECOGNITION OF REVENUE FROM SUBSCRIPTIONS)** *Physical Fitness* is a monthly magazine that has been on the market for 18 months. Its current circulation is 1.2 million copies. Negotiations are now under way to obtain a bank loan to update their facilities. They are producing close to capacity and expect to grow at an average of 20% per year over the next three years.

After reviewing the financial statements of *Physical Fitness*, Cher Green, the bank loan officer, has indicated that a loan would be offered to *Physical Fitness* only if it could increase the current ratio (current assets ÷ current liabilities) to a specified level.

Ronold Schwartz, the marketing manager of *Physical Fitness*, has devised a plan to meet these requirements. Schwartz indicates that an advertising campaign can be initiated to immediately increase their circulation. The potential customers would be contacted after the purchase of another magazine's mailing list. The campaign would include:

1. An offer to subscribe to *Physical Fitness* at three-quarters of the normal price.
2. A special offer to all subscribers to receive the most current world atlas whenever requested at a guaranteed price of $1.00.
3. An unconditional guarantee that any subscriber will receive a full refund if dissatisfied with the magazine.

Although the offer of a full refund is risky, Schwartz claims that few people will ask for a refund after receiving half of their subscription issues. Schwartz notes that other magazine companies have tried this sales promotion technique and experienced great success. Their average cancellation rate was 25%. On the average, each company increased their initial circulation threefold and in the long run had increased circulation to twice that before the promotion. In addition, 70% of the new subscribers are expected to take advantage of the atlas premium. Schwartz feels confident that the increased subscriptions from the advertising campaign will increase the current ratio.

You are the controller of *Physical Fitness* and must give your opinion of the proposed plan.

Instructions

(a) When should revenue from the new subscriptions be recognized, given the cancellation guarantee?

(b) How would you classify the estimated reduced revenue from cancellations stemming from the unconditional guarantee for the new subscriptions?

(c) How should the atlas premium be recorded? Are the estimated premium claims a liability? Explain.

(d) Does the proposed plan achieve the goals of increasing the current ratio?

(REVENUE RECOGNITION: LAW FIRM) Craik, Jones & Integrity is a law firm engaged in the general practice of law. Client services are billed either on an hourly charge basis or on a contingency fee (percentage of the judgement received) basis, depending on the nature of the engagement. The timing of cash receipts is subject to wide variation, depending on the nature of the engagement, possible court approval of fees, and the ability of the client to pay. The firm recognizes revenue on the cash basis. C6-2

Mr. Craik, one of the partners, believes the cash basis is too conservative a basis for general revenue recognition. He proposes that work charged on an hourly basis to financially capable clients should be recognized as performed. On the basis of past experience, the amount and timing of receipt of income from certain contingency fee cases can be estimated. As Mr. Craik observes, "It may take four years to get to trial or a reasonable settlement offer. But we know the odds and expected payoff pretty well when we accept the case. There are not that many surprises." The cash basis should be limited to those engagements that have considerable uncertainty regarding timing and collection. Fee revenue recognized and not billed would be charged to the Work in Progress account.

Instructions

Discuss the problems of revenue recognition for the law firm and give recommendations.

(RECOGNITION OF REVENUE: TRADING STAMPS) Lick & Stick Stamps Inc. was formed early this year to sell trading stamps throughout the West to retailers who distribute the stamps free to their customers. Books for accumulating the stamps and catalogues illustrating the merchandise for which the stamps may be exchanged are given free to retailers for distribution to stamp recipients. Centres with inventories of merchandise premiums have been established for redemption of the stamps. Retailers may not return unused stamps to Lick & Stick. C6-3

The following schedule expresses Lick & Stick's expectations as to percentages of a normal month's activity that will be attained. For this purpose, a "normal month's activity" is defined as the level of operations expected when expansion of activities ceases or tapers off to a stable rate. The company expects that this level will be attained in the third year and that sales of stamps will average $5,000,000 per month throughout the third year.

Month	Actual Stamp Sales (%)	Merchandise Premium Purchases (%)	Stamp Redemptions %
6th	30	40	10
12th	60	60	45
18th	80	80	70
24th	90	90	80
30th	100	100	95

Lick & Stick plans to adopt an annual closing date at the end of each 12 months of operation.

Instructions

(a) Discuss the factors to be considered in determining when revenue should be recognized in measuring the income of a business enterprise.

(b) Discuss the accounting alternatives that should be considered by Lick & Stick for the recognition of its revenues and related expenses.

(c) For each accounting alternative discussed in (b), give balance sheet accounts that would be used and indicate how each should be classified.

(AICPA adapted)

C6-4 **(RECOGNITION OF REVENUE: FUTURE COLLECTION AND COST INCURRENCE)** Digger O'Dell Ltd. operates a chain of funeral parlours in Ontario. In 1994, the company introduces a new "pre-need" plan. The plan is offered to individuals who wish to arrange for their funerals and burials in advance. The plan sells for $5,500 and may be purchased by paying $1,000 down and the balance in nine equal annual instalments of $500 each. Interest at 10% per annum is charged only on late payments. Items included in the package and an item price breakdown associated with each are listed below:

Cemetery lot	$2,000
Burial vault and memorial plaque	2,500
Funeral service	1,000
Total	$5,500

The cemetery lot location and the burial vault and memorial plaque are chosen by the customer when the contract is signed and guaranteed by O'Dell. The actual cost for funeral services can, for obvious reasons, be determined only at some unknown future time.

During 1994, 50 contracts are signed and the down payments are received.

Instructions

Provide a report to the owner, Mr. O'Dell, regarding the issues and problems in this situation concerning when and how revenue may be recognized. Identify at least three distinct alternative ways that O'Dell may use to recognize revenue from sale of "pre-need" plans. Assess each alternative identified by arguing how or why it may or may not be consistent with Canadian GAAP. Conclude by indicating which alternative you would recommend to O'Dell.

C6-5 **(REVENUE RECOGNITION: REAL ESTATE DEVELOPMENT)** Holiday Lakes is a new recreational real estate development that consists of 500 lakefront and lake-view lots. As a special incentive to the first 100 buyers of lake-view lots, the developer is offering three years of free financing on 10-year, 12% notes, no down payment, and one week at a nearby established resort—"a $1,200 value." The normal price per lot is $10,000. The cost per lake-view lot to the developer is an estimated average of $2,000. Development costs continue to be incurred and the actual average cost per lot is not known at this time. The resort promotion cost is $700 per lot. The notes are held by Resort Acceptance Corp., a wholly owned subsidiary of Holiday Lakes.

Instructions

(a) Discuss the revenue recognition and gross profit measurement issues in this situation.

(b) How would the developer's past financial and business experience influence your decision concerning the recording of sales transactions?

(c) Assume that 50 people have accepted the offer, signed 10-year notes, and have stayed at the local resort. Prepare the journal entries that you believe are appropriate.

(d) What should be disclosed in the notes to the financial statements?

(REVENUE RECOGNITION: LONG-TERM CONTRACT) Gargantuan Inc. is a large conglomerate consisting of 44 subsidiary companies with plants and offices throughout Canada and the world. Dunlop & Co. is the international public accounting firm engaged to design and install a computerized information, accounting, and cost control system in each of Gargantuan's subsidiaries. The accounting firm is given three years to complete the engagement; it intends to work continuously on the project but will assign the largest number of its staff to the project during its least busy period each year (May to October). Dunlop & Co. obtained this consulting engagement at a fixed price of $5,200,000 after much study, planning, and an elaborate presentation. C6-6

Instructions

Identify, discuss, and provide recommendations regarding revenue recognition issues faced by Dunlop & Co. in this case.

(FRANCHISE REVENUE) Calorie Counter Inc. sells franchises to independent operators throughout eastern *C6-7
Canada. The contract with the franchisee includes the following provisions:

1. The franchisee is charged an initial fee of $70,000. Of this amount, $20,000 is payable when the agreement is signed and a $50,000 noninterest-bearing note is payable in instalments of $10,000 at the end of each of the five subsequent years.

2. All of the initial franchise fee collected by Calorie Counter Inc. is to be refunded and the remaining obligation cancelled if, for any reason, the franchisee fails to open the franchise.

3. In return for the initial franchise fee, Calorie Counter Inc. agrees to (a) assist the franchisee in selecting the location for the business, (b) negotiate the lease for the land, (c) obtain financing and assist with building design, (d) supervise construction, (e) establish accounting and tax records, and (f) provide expert advice over a five-year period, relating to such matters as employee and management training, quality control, and promotion.

4. In addition to the initial franchise fee, the franchisee is required to pay to Calorie Counter Inc. a monthly fee of 2% of the franchisee's sales. This fee is for menu planning, recipe innovations, and the privilege of purchasing ingredients from Calorie Counter Inc. at or below prevailing market prices.

Management of Calorie Counter Inc. estimates that the value of the services rendered to the franchisee at the time the contract is signed amounts to at least $20,000. All franchisees to date have opened their locations at the scheduled time and none have defaulted on any of the notes receivable.

The credit ratings of all franchisees would entitle them to borrow at an interest rate of 10%. The present value of an ordinary annuity of five annual receipts of $10,000 discounted at 10% is $37,908.

Instructions

(a) Discuss the alternatives that Calorie Counter Inc. might use to account for the initial franchise fee, evaluate each by applying generally accepted accounting principles, and give illustrative entries for each alternative.

(b) Given the nature of Calorie Counter Inc.'s agreement with its franchisees, when should revenue be recognized? Discuss the question of revenue recognition for both the initial franchise fee and the additional monthly fee of 2% of the franchisee's sales. Give illustrative entries for both types of revenue.

(c) Assume that Calorie Counter Inc. sells some franchises for $90,000 (which includes a charge of $20,000 for the rental of equipment for its useful life of 10 years), that $40,000 of the fee is payable immediately and the balance on noninterest-bearing notes at $10,000 per year, that no portion of the $20,000 rental payment is refundable in case the franchisee goes out of business, and that title to the equipment remains with the franchiser. What would be the preferable method of accounting for the rental portion of the initial franchise fee? Explain.

(AICPA adapted)

C6-8 **(ETHICAL ISSUE, CHANNEL STUFFING)** In order to increase revenue at the end of the year, MicroWord Incorporated, a manufacturer of computer software, discounts its major lines to dealers with the condition that the dealers increase purchases by 40% before year end. In the early stages of the discount program, Anthony DiFore, the controller, complains to his financial vice-president, Anna Cragg, that recording this revenue would be misleading and premature. Cragg says that the company must increase revenue to meet the requirements of its debt contracts, and adds: "Because the sales will come in the near future, why should it matter that we record them this year?"

Instructions

(a) Is the discount program a way to increase revenue?

(b) What moral dilemma does DiFore recognize? Who is harmed by the discount program?

(c) Should DiFore vigorously argue against the discount policy?

(d) If dealers returned a large number of software packages in the succeeding calendar year, do you think the discount program and its reporting policy are reasonable and ethical from an accountant's perspective?

EXERCISES

E6-1 **(REVENUE RECOGNITION ON BOOK SALES WITH HIGH RETURNS)** Mercury Publishing Co. publishes college textbooks that are sold to bookstores on the following terms. Each title has a fixed wholesale price, terms f.o.b. shipping point (i.e. transfer of legal title occurs when shipments leave seller's premises), and payment is due 60 days after shipment. The retailer may return a maximum of 30% of an order at the retailer's expense. Sales are made only to retailers who have good credit ratings. Past experience indicates that the normal return rate is 12% and the average collection period is 72 days.

Instructions

(a) Identify alternative revenue recognition times in the earning process that Mercury could employ concerning textbook sales.

(b) Briefly discuss which alternative in (a) is the appropriate treatment.

(c) In late July, Mercury shipped books invoiced at $16,000,000. Prepare the journal entry to record this event that best conforms to your answer to (b).

(d) In October, $2 million of the invoiced July sales were returned according to the return policy, and the remaining $14 million was paid. Prepare the entry recording the return and payment.

E6-2 **(REVENUE RECOGNITION ON MARINA SALES WITH DISCOUNTS)** Waskesiu Marina has 300 available slips that rent for $2,500 per season. Payments must be made in full at the start of the boating season, April 1. Slips may be reserved if paid for by the prior December 31. Under a new policy, if payment is made by the prior December 31, a 5% discount is allowed. The boating season ends October 31 and the marina has a December 31 year end. To provide cash flow for major dock repairs, the marina operator is also offering a 25% discount to slip renters who pay for the second season following the current December 31.

For the fiscal year ended December 31, 1994, all 300 slips were rented at full price. There were 200 slips reserved and paid for the 1995 boating season, and 60 slips reserved and paid for the 1996 boating season.

Instructions

(a) Prepare the appropriate journal entries for fiscal 1994.

(b) Assume the marina operator knows little about accounting. Explain the significance of the above accounting to him.

E6-3 **(RECOGNITION OF PROFIT, PERCENTAGE-OF-COMPLETION)** In 1994, Skyscraper Construction Company agreed to construct an apartment building at a price of $1,000,000. The information relating to the costs and billings for this contract is as follows.

	1994	1995	1996
Costs incurred to date	$320,000	$600,000	$ 790,000
Estimated costs yet to be incurred	480,000	200,000	–0–
Customer billings to date	150,000	410,000	1,000,000
Collection of billings to date	120,000	340,000	950,000

Instructions

(a) Assuming that the percentage-of-completion method is used, (1) compute the amount of gross profit recognized in 1994 and 1995 and (2) prepare journal entries for 1995.

(b) For 1995, show how the details related to this construction contract would be disclosed on the balance sheet and on the income statement.

(GROSS PROFIT ON UNCOMPLETED CONTRACT) On April 1, 1994, J.P. Fertakis Inc. entered into a cost-plus, fixed-fee contract to construct an electric generator for Pullman Corporation. At the contract date, Fertakis estimated that it would take two years to complete the project at a cost of $2,000,000. The fixed fee stipulated in the contract is $300,000. Fertakis appropriately accounts for this contract under the percentage-of-completion method. During 1994, Fertakis incurred costs of $700,000 related to the project, and the estimated costs yet to be incurred from December 31, 1994 to complete the contract is $1,300,000. Pullman was billed $600,000 under the contract.

Instructions

Prepare a schedule to compute the amount of gross profit to be recognized by Fertakis under the contract for the year ended December 31, 1994. Show supporting computations in good form.

(AICPA adapted)

(ANALYSIS OF PERCENTAGE-OF-COMPLETION FINANCIAL STATEMENTS) In 1994, Big Jobs Construction Corp. began work on a three-year contract. The contract price was $3,000,000. Big Jobs uses the percentage-of-completion method for financial accounting purposes. The income to be recognized each year is based on the proportion of cost incurred to total estimated costs for completing the contract. The financial statement presentation relating to this contract at December 31, 1994 is as follows:

Balance Sheet

Accounts receivable—construction contract billings		$64,500
Construction in progress	$195,000	
Less contract billings	184,500	
Cost of uncompleted contract in excess of billings		10,500

Income Statement

Gross profit (before tax) on the contract recognized in 1994	$58,500

Instructions

(a) How much cash was collected in 1994 on this contract?

(b) What was the initial estimated total gross profit before tax on this contract?

(AICPA adapted)

E6-6 **(RECOGNITION OF REVENUE ON LONG-TERM CONTRACT AND ENTRIES)** Giant Construction Company uses the percentage-of-completion method of accounting. In 1994, Giant began work under contract #R2-D2, which had a contract price of $2,300,000. Other details follow.

	1994	1995
Costs incurred during the year	$ 400,000	$1,425,000
Estimated costs to complete, as of December 31	1,200,000	-0-
Billings during the year	420,000	1,680,000
Collections during the year	350,000	1,500,000

Instructions

(a) What portion of the total contract price would be recognized as revenue in 1994? In 1995?

(b) Assuming the same facts as those above except that Giant used the completed-contract method of accounting, what portion of the total contract price would be recognized as revenue in 1995?

(c) Prepare a complete set of journal entries for 1994 using the percentage-of-completion method.

E6-7 **(RECOGNITION OF PROFIT AND BALANCE SHEET AMOUNTS FOR LONG-TERM CONTRACTS)** Factory Construction Company began operations January 1, 1994. During the year, Factory Construction entered into a contract with Cam Corp. to construct a manufacturing facility. At that time, Factory estimated that it would take five years to complete the facility at a total cost of $4,500,000. The total contract price for construction of the facility was $6,300,000. During 1994, Factory incurred $950,000 in construction costs related to this project. The estimated cost to complete the contract was $4,050,000. Cam Corp. was billed and paid 25% of the contract price.

Instructions

Prepare schedules to compute the amount of gross profit to be recognized for the year ended December 31, 1994, and the amount to be shown as "Construction in process in excess of related billings" or "Billings on uncompleted contract in excess of construction in process" at December 31, 1994, under each of the following methods:

(a) Completed-contract method.

(b) Percentage-of-completion method.

Show supporting computations in good form.

(AICPA adapted)

E6-8 **(LONG-TERM CONTRACT REPORTING: COMPLETED-CONTRACT METHOD)** Monument Construction Company began operations in 1994. Construction activity for the first year is shown on page 301. All contracts are with different customers, and any work remaining at December 31, 1994 is expected to be completed in 1995.

Instructions

Prepare a partial income statement and balance sheet to indicate how the above information would be reported for financial statement purposes. Monument Construction Company uses the completed-contract method.

Project	Total Contract Price	Billings through 12/31/94	Cash Collections through 12/31/94	Contract Costs Incurred through 12/31/94	Estimated Additional Costs to Complete
1	$ 560,000	$ 360,000	$340,000	$450,000	$140,000
2	670,000	220,000	210,000	126,000	504,000
3	490,000	490,000	440,000	340,000	-0-
	$1,720,000	$1,070,000	$990,000	$916,000	$644,000

E6-9 **(ANALYSIS OF INSTALMENT SALES ACCOUNTS)** Bit-Buy Co. appropriately uses the instalment method of accounting. On December 31, 1995, prior to adjusting entries to recognize realized gross profit for the year, the ledger shows balances in the Instalment Receivables and Deferred Gross Profit accounts as indicated below. The gross profit on sales for the various years is also identified below.

Instalment Receivables		Deferred Gross Profit		Gross Profit on Sales	
from 1993	$12,000	from 1993	$ 7,000	1993	35%
from 1994	40,000	from 1994	26,000	1994	34%
from 1995	130,000	from 1995	96,000	1995	32%
Bal. 12/31/95	$182,000 dr.	Bal. 12/31/95	$129,000 cr.		

Instructions

(a) Prepare the adjusting entry or entries required on December 31, 1995 to recognize 1995 realized gross profit. (Cash receipts entries have already been made.)

(b) Compute the amount of cash collected in 1995 on accounts receivable of each year.

E6-10 **(INTEREST REVENUE FROM INSTALMENT SALE)** MF Co. Ltd. sells farm machinery on the instalment plan. On July 1, 1994, MF enters into an instalment sales contract with Agriculture Inc. for a 10-year period. Equal annual payments under the instalment sale are $100,000 and are due on July 1. The first payment is made on July 1, 1994.

Additional Information

1. The amount that would be realized on an outright sale of similar farm machinery is $676,000.
2. The cost of the farm machinery sold to Agriculture is $473,000.
3. The finance charges relating to the instalment period are $324,000, based on a stated interest rate of 10%, which is appropriate.
4. Circumstances are such that the collection of the instalments due under the contract is reasonably assured.

Instructions

What income or loss before income taxes should MF Co. Ltd. record for the year ended December 31, 1994 as a result of the above transactions?

(AICPA adapted)

E6-11 **(INSTALMENT METHOD AND COST RECOVERY METHOD)** A capital goods manufacturing business that started on January 4, 1993 and operates on a calendar-year basis uses the instalment method in accounting for all its sales. The following data were taken from the 1993 and 1994 records.

	1993	1994
Instalment sale	$480,000	$620,000
Gross profit as a percentage of sales	20%	16⅔%
Cash collections on sales of 1993	$130,000	$240,000
Cash collections on sales of 1994	-0-	$160,000

The amounts given for cash collections exclude amounts collected for interest charges.

Instructions

(a) Compute the amount of realized gross profit to be recognized on the 1994 income statement, prepared using the instalment method.

(b) State where the balance of Deferred Gross Profit would be reported on the financial statements for 1994.

(c) Compute the amount of realized gross profit to be recognized on the 1994 income statement, prepared using the cost recovery method.

(CICA adapted)

E6-12 **(GROSS PROFIT CALCULATIONS AND REPOSSESSED MERCHANDISE)** Smith Corporation, which began business on January 1, 1994, appropriately uses the instalment method of accounting. The following data were obtained for the years 1994 and 1995.

	1994	1995
Instalment sales	$750,000	$840,000
Cost of instalment sales	585,000	630,000
General and administrative expenses	70,000	84,000
Cash collections on sales of 1994	310,000	300,000
Cash collections on sales of 1995	-0-	400,000

Instructions

(a) Compute the balance in the Deferred Gross Profit accounts on December 31, 1994 and on December 31, 1995.

(b) A 1994 sale resulted in default in 1996. At the date of default, the balance on the instalment receivable was $12,000 and the repossessed merchandise had a fair value of $8,000. Prepare the entry to record the repossession.

(AICPA adapted)

E6-13 **(INSTALMENT SALES: DEFAULT AND REPOSSESSION)** Ettredge Company uses the instalment method in accounting for its instalment sales. On January 1, 1994, Ettredge Company had an instalment account receivable from Robert Greenberg with a balance of $1,600. During 1994, $200 was collected from Greenberg. When no further collection could be made, the merchandise sold to Greenberg was repossessed. The merchandise had a fair market value of $550 after the company spent $60 for reconditioning of the merchandise. The merchandise was originally sold with a gross profit of 40%.

Instructions

Prepare the entries on the books of Ettredge Company to record all transactions related to Greenberg during 1994 (ignore interest charges).

E6-14 **(INSTALMENT METHOD: DEFAULT AND REPOSSESSION)** Fine Buys Inc. was involved in two default and repossession cases during the year. It had been using the instalment method of accounting for both cases.

1. A refrigerator was sold to D. Sanders for $1,800, including a 30% gross profit. Sanders made a down payment of 20%, four of the remaining 16 equal payments, and then defaulted on further payments. The refrigerator was repossessed, at which time the fair value was determined to be $820.

2. An oven that cost $1,200 was sold to W. Jones for $1,500 on the instalment basis. Jones made a down payment of $225 and paid $75 per month for six months, after which he defaulted. The oven was repossessed; the estimated value at time of repossession was determined to be $600.

Instructions

Prepare the journal entries to record the repossessions (ignore interest charges).

***E6-15** **(CONSIGNMENT ACCOUNTING)** On May 3, 1994, Dunn Company consigned 70 freezers, costing $350 each, to Crane Company. The cost of shipping the freezers amounted to $840 and was paid by Dunn Company. On December 30, 1994, an account of sales was received from the consignee, reporting that 40 freezers had been sold for $600 each. Remittance was made by the consignee for the amounts due, after deducting a commission of 6%, advertising of $200, and total installation costs of $600 on the freezers sold.

Instructions

(a) Compute the inventory value for the consignor on the unsold units in the hands of the consignee.

(b) Compute the profit for the consignor for the units sold.

(c) Compute the amount of cash that was remitted by the consignee.

***E6-16** **(FRANCHISE FEE, INITIAL DOWN PAYMENT)** On January 1, 1994, Jody Neet signed an agreement to operate as a franchisee of Sickbay Hospital Supplies, Inc., for an initial franchise fee of $70,000. The amount of $40,000 was paid when the agreement was signed, and the balance is payable in five annual payments of $6,000 each, beginning January 1, 1995. The agreement provides that the down payment is not refundable and that no future services are required of the franchiser. Jody Neet's credit rating indicates that she can borrow money at 11% for a loan of this type.

Instructions

(a) How much should Sickbay record as revenue from franchise fees on January 1, 1994? At what amount should Neet record the acquisition cost of the franchise on January 1, 1994?

(b) What entry would be made by Sickbay on January 1, 1994, if the down payment were refundable and substantial future services remain to be performed by Sickbay?

(c) How much revenue from franchise fees would be recorded by Sickbay on January 1, 1994 in each of the following situations?

1. The initial down payment was not refundable, it represented a fair measure of the services already provided, with a significant amount of services still to be performed by Sickbay in future periods, and collectibility of the note is reasonably assured.

2. The initial down payment is not refundable and no future services are required by the franchiser, but collection of the note is so uncertain that recognition of the note as an asset is unwarranted.

3. The initial down payment has not been earned and collection of the note is so uncertain that recognition of the note as an asset is unwarranted.

***E6-17 (FRANCHISE ENTRIES)** Tasty Steak House Inc. charges an initial franchise fee of $100,000. On the signing of the agreement, a payment of $40,000 is due; thereafter, three annual payments of $20,000 are required. The credit rating of the franchisee is such that it would have to pay interest at 10% to borrow money.

Instructions

Prepare the entries to record the initial franchise fee on the books of the franchiser under the following assumptions:

(a) The down payment is not refundable, no future services are required by the franchiser, and collection of the note is reasonably assured.

(b) The franchiser has substantial services to perform and the collection of the note is very uncertain.

(c) The down payment is not refundable, collection of the note is reasonably certain, the franchiser has yet to perform a substantial amount of services, and the down payment represents a fair measure of the services already performed.

PROBLEMS

P6-1 (THREE-PART REVENUE RECOGNITION) Caddy Industries Ltd. has three operating divisions—Book Publishing Division, Protection Securities Division, and Construction Division. Each division maintains its own accounting system and method of revenue recognition.

Book Publishing Division
The Book Publishing Division sells large volumes of novels to a few book distributors, which in turn sell to several national chains of bookstores. Book Publishing allows distributors to return up to 30% of sales, and distributors give the same terms to bookstores. While returns from individual titles fluctuate greatly, the returns from distributors have averaged 20% in each of the past five years. A total of $8,000,000 of novel sales were made to distributors during fiscal 1994. On November 30, 1994, $3,000,000 of fiscal 1994 sales were still subject to return privileges over the next six months. The remaining $5,000,000 of fiscal 1994 sales had actual returns of 21%. Sales from fiscal 1993 totalling $2,000,000 were collected in fiscal 1994, less 18% returns. This Division records revenue according to the revenue recognition criteria when the right of return exists.

Protection Securities Division
Protection Securities Division works through manufacturers' agents in various cities. Orders for alarm systems and down payments are forwarded from agents, and the Division ships the goods from the factory directly to customers (usually police departments and security guard companies). Although Protection Securities Division pays the shipping costs for convenience, sales agreements require the buyer to reimburse the Division for such costs. Customers are billed directly for the balance due plus actual shipping costs. The firm received orders for $7,000,000 of goods during the fiscal year ended November 30, 1994. Down payments of $700,000 were received and $6,000,000 of goods were billed and shipped. Actual freight costs of $110,000 were also billed. Commissions of 10% on product price are paid to manufacturing agents after goods are shipped to customers. Such goods are warranted for 90 days after shipment, and warranty returns have been about 1% of sales. Revenue is recognized at the point of sale by this Division.

Construction Division
During the fiscal year ended November 30, 1994, Construction Division had one construction project in process. A $30,000,000 contract for construction of a civic centre was signed on June 19, 1994, and construction began

on August 1, 1994. Estimated costs of completion at the contract date were $25,000,000 over a two-year time period from the date of the contract. On November 30, 1994, construction costs of $8,000,000 had been incurred and progress billings of $9,500,000 had been made. The construction costs to complete the remainder of the project were reviewed on November 30, 1994, and were estimated to amount to only $16,000,000 because of an expected decline in raw materials costs. Revenue recognition is based on the percentage-of-completion method.

Instructions

Compute the revenue to be recognized in fiscal year 1994 for each of the three operating divisions of Caddy Industries Ltd. in accordance with generally accepted accounting principles.

P6-2 **(RECOGNITION OF PROFIT AND ENTRIES, PERCENTAGE-OF-COMPLETION AND COMPLETED-CONTRACT METHODS)** Steeltoe Construction Company has contracted to build an office building. The construction is scheduled to begin on January 1, 1994 and the estimated time of completion is July 1, 1997. The building cost is estimated to be $40,000,000 and will be billed at $49,000,000, the fixed price. The following data relate to the construction period.

	1994	1995	1996	1997
Costs to date	$12,000,000	$20,000,000	$28,000,000	$40,000,000
Estimated cost to complete	28,000,000	20,000,000	12,000,000	-0-
Progress billings to date	6,000,000	18,000,000	28,000,000	49,000,000
Cash collected to date	6,000,000	15,000,000	25,000,000	49,000,000

Instructions

(a) Compute the estimated gross profit for 1994, 1995, 1996, and 1997, assuming that the percentage-of-completion method is used. Ignore income taxes.

(b) Prepare the necessary journal entries for Steeltoe Construction Company for the years 1996 and 1997, using the percentage-of-completion method.

(c) Prepare the necessary journal entries for the years 1996 and 1997, using the completed-contract method.

P6-3 **(RECOGNITION OF PROFIT AND BALANCE SHEET PRESENTATION, PERCENTAGE-OF-COMPLETION)** On February 1, 1994, Mamoth Construction Company obtained a contract to build an athletic stadium. The stadium was to be built at a total cost of $5,400,000 and was scheduled for completion by September 1, 1996. One clause of the contract stated that Mamoth was to deduct $20,000 from the $6,900,000 contract billing price for each week that completion was delayed. Completion was delayed six weeks, which resulted in a $120,000 penalty. This delay was not predictable prior to 1996. Below are the data pertaining to the construction period.

	1994	1995	1996
Costs to date	$1,800,000	$3,850,000	$5,500,000
Estimated cost to complete	3,600,000	1,650,000	-0-
Progress billings to date	1,200,000	3,500,000	6,780,000
Cash collected to date	1,000,000	2,800,000	6,780,000

Instructions

(a) Using the percentage-of-completion method, complete the gross profit recognized in the years 1994–1996.

(b) Prepare a partial balance sheet for December 31, 1995, showing how the account balances would be presented.

P6-4 **(LONG-TERM CONTRACT WITH AN OVERALL LOSS)** On July 1, 1994, Cherub Construction Inc. contracted to build an office building for Heavenly Corp. for a total contract price of $1,900,000. On July 1, Cherub estimated that it would take between two and three years to complete the building. On December 31, 1996, the building was deemed substantially completed. Following are accumulated contract costs incurred, estimated costs to complete the contract, and accumulated billings to Heavenly for 1994, 1995, and 1996.

	At Dec. 31/94	At Dec. 31/95	At Dec. 31/96
Contract costs incurred to date	$ 150,000	$1,200,000	$2,070,000
Estimated costs to complete the contract	1,350,000	800,000	-0-
Billings to Heavenly	300,000	1,100,000	1,800,000

Instructions

(a) Using the percentage-of-completion method, prepare schedules to compute the profit or loss to be recognized as a result of this contract for the years ended December 31, 1994, 1995, and 1996. Ignore income taxes.

(b) Using the completed-contract method, prepare schedules to compute the profit or loss to be recognized as a result of this contract for the years ended December 1994, 1995, and 1996. Ignore income taxes.

P6-5 **(LONG-TERM CONTRACT WITH INTERIM LOSS)** On March 1, 1994, Darwin Construction Company contracted to construct a factory building for Grace Manufacturing Inc. for a total contract price of $8,400,000. The building was completed by October 31, 1996. The annual contract costs incurred, estimated costs to complete the contract, and accumulated billings to Grace for 1994, 1995, and 1996 are given below.

	1994	1995	1996
Contract costs incurred during the year	$3,200,000	$2,600,000	$1,450,000
Estimated additional costs to complete the contract determined at year end	3,200,000	1,450,000	-0-
Billings to Grace during the year	3,200,000	3,500,000	1,700,000

Instructions

(a) Using the percentage-of-completion method, prepare schedules to complete the profit or loss to be recognized as a result of this contract for the years ended December 31, 1994, 1995, and 1996. Ignore income taxes.

(b) Using the completed-contract method, prepare schedules to compute the profit or loss to be recognized as a result of this contract for the years ended December 31 1994, 1995, and 1996. Ignore income taxes.

P6-6 **(LONG-TERM CONTRACTS, THREE PROFITABLE AND TWO LOSSES)** Wishful Construction Company commenced business on January 1, 1994. Construction activities for the first year of operations are shown in the table on page 307. All projects are with different customers, and any work remaining at December 31, 1994 is expected to be completed in 1995. The percentage-of-completion method is used by the company.

Instructions

(a) Prepare a schedule to compute the gross profit (loss) in 1994 for each project.

(b) Prepare a 1994 partial income statement to show the aggregate total revenues, construction expenses including provision for losses, and gross profit for the year from all projects.

(c) Prepare a schedule to determine the appropriate amounts to be shown in the December 31, 1994 balance sheet for "Construction in process in excess of billings" and "Billings in excess of construction in process." Prepare a partial balance sheet showing how items related to the projects would be reported.

Project	Total Contract Price	Billings through 12/31/94	Cash Collections through 12/31/94	Contract Costs Incurred through 12/31/94	Estimated Additional Costs to Complete
A	$300,000	$200,000	$180,000	$248,000	$ 67,000
B	350,000	110,000	105,000	67,800	271,200
C	280,000	280,000	255,000	186,000	–0–
D	200,000	35,000	25,000	123,000	87,000
E	240,000	205,000	200,000	185,000	15,000
	$1,370,000	$830,000	$765,000	$809,800	$440,200

(COMPLETED-CONTRACT METHOD) Tough Construction Company Inc. entered into a fixed-price contract with City Clinic on July 1, 1992 to construct a four-storey office building. At that time, Tough estimated that it would take between two and three years to complete the project. The total contract price for construction of the building is $4,500,000. Tough appropriately accounted for this contract under the completed-contract method in its financial statements. The building was deemed completed on December 31, 1994. Estimated percentage of completion, accumulated contract costs incurred, estimated costs to complete the contract, and accumulated billings to City Clinic under the contract were as follows. **P6-7**

	At December 31, 1992	At December 31, 1993	At December 31, 1994
Percentage of completion	30%	60%	100%
Contract costs incurred	$1,140,000	$2,820,000	$4,800,000
Estimated costs to complete the contract	$2,660,000	$1,880,000	–0–
Billings to City Clinic	$1,600,000	$2,700,000	$4,500,000

Instructions

(a) Prepare schedules to compute the amount to be shown as "Cost of uncompleted contract in excess of related billings" or "Billings on uncompleted contract in excess of related costs" at December 31, 1992, 1993, and 1994. Ignore income taxes. Show supporting computations in good form.

(b) Prepare schedules to compute the profit or loss to be recognized as a result of this contract for the years ended December 31, 1992, 1993, and 1994. Ignore income taxes. Show supporting computations in good form.

(AICPA adapted)

(INSTALMENT METHOD AND REPOSSESSION ENTRIES) Selected transactions of Hirez TV Sales Company are presented below: **P6-8**

1. A television set costing $560 is sold to G. Murphy on November 1, 1994 for $800. Murphy makes a down payment of $200 and agrees to pay $30 on the first of each month for 20 months thereafter. The instalment method is used to account for this sale.

2. Murphy pays the $30 instalment due December 1, 1994.

3. On December 31, 1994, the appropriate entries are made to record profit realized on the instalment sales.

4. The first seven 1995 instalments of $30 each are paid by Murphy. (Make one entry.)

5. In August 1995, the set is repossessed, after Murphy fails to pay the August 1 instalment and indicates that he will be unable to continue the payments. The estimated fair value of the repossessed set is $100.

Instructions

Prepare journal entries to record these transactions and events on the books of Hirez TV Sales Company.

P6-9 **(INSTALMENT METHOD COMPUTATIONS AND ENTRIES)** Presented below is summarized information for Aardvark Co., which sells merchandise on the instalment basis and uses the instalment method to account for such sales.

	1994	1995	1996
Sales (on instalment plan)	$250,000	$260,000	$280,000
Cost of sales	150,000	169,000	179,200
Gross profit	$100,000	$ 91,000	$100,800
Collections from customers on:			
1994 instalment sales	$ 80,000	$100,000	$ 70,000
1995 instalment sales		90,000	120,000
1996 instalment sales			110,000

Instructions

(a) Compute the realized gross profit for each of the years 1994, 1995, and 1996.

(b) Prepare journal entries required in 1996.

P6-10 **(INSTALMENT METHOD AND INCOME STATEMENTS)** GW Stores sells merchandise on open account as well as on instalment terms. The instalment method is used to account for the instalment sales. Information for the years 1994, 1995, and 1996 is as follows.

	1994	1995	1996
Sales on account	$385,000	$426,000	$525,000
Instalment sales	350,000	275,000	380,000
Collections on instalment sales			
Made in 1994	110,000	120,000	120,000
Made in 1995		110,000	140,000
Made in 1996			125,000
Cost of sales			
Sold on account	264,000	297,000	399,600
Sold on instalment	234,500	165,000	235,600
Selling expenses	77,000	87,000	92,000
Administrative expenses	50,000	51,000	52,000

Instructions

From the data above, which cover the three years since GW Stores commenced operations, determine the net income for each year.

(INSTALMENT METHOD COMPUTATIONS AND ENTRIES) Castle Stores sells appliances for cash and also on the instalment plan. For sales on instalment plans, the instalment method is used. Entries to record cost of sales are made monthly. **P6-11**

Castle Stores
Trial Balance
December 31, 1995

Cash	$153,000	
Instalment Accounts Receivable, 1994	48,000	
Instalment Accounts Receivable, 1995	91,000	
Inventory—New Merchandise	131,200	
Inventory—Repossessed Merchandise	24,000	
Accounts Payable		$ 98,500
Deferred Gross Profit, 1994		45,600
Common Shares		170,000
Retained Earnings		93,900
Sales		353,000
Instalment Sales		200,000
Cost of Sales	255,000	
Cost of Instalment Sales	130,000	
Gain or Loss on Repossessions	800	
Selling and Administrative Expenses	128,000	
	$961,000	$961,000

The accounting department has prepared the following analysis of cash receipts for the year:

Cash sales (including sale of repossessed merchandise)	$353,000
Instalment accounts receivable, 1994	104,000
Instalment accounts receivable, 1995	109,000
Other	36,000
Total	$602,000

Repossessions recorded during 1995 on instalment sales in 1994 are summarized as follows:

Uncollected balance	$8,000
Loss on repossession	800
Repossessed merchandise (realizable value)	4,800

Instructions

From the trial balance and accompanying information:

(a) Compute the rate of gross profit for 1994 and 1995.

(b) Prepare closing entries as of December 31, 1995 under the instalment method of accounting.

(c) Prepare an income statement for the year ended December 31, 1995. Include only the realized gross profit in the income statement when reporting the results regarding instalment sales.

(INSTALMENT METHOD COMPUTATION AND ENTRIES) Tufasnails Inc. sells merchandise for cash and also on the instalment plan. For instalment plan sales, the instalment method is used. Entries to record cost of goods sold are made at the end of each year. **P6-12**

Repossessions of merchandise sold in 1994 were made in 1995 and were recorded correctly as follows:

Deferred Gross Profit, 1994	7,200	
Repossessed Merchandise	8,000	
Loss on Repossessions	2,800	
Instalment Accounts Receivable, 1994		18,000

Part of this repossessed merchandise was sold for cash during 1995, and the sale was recorded by a debit to Cash and a credit to Sales.

The inventory of repossessed merchandise on hand December 31, 1995 is $4,000; of new merchandise, $160,000. There was no repossessed merchandise on hand January 1, 1995.

Collections on accounts receivable during 1995 were:

on Instalment Accounts Receivable, 1994	$80,000
on Instalment Accounts Receivable, 1995	50,000

The cost of the merchandise sold under the instalment plan during 1995 was $115,200.

Tufasnails Inc.
Trial Balance
December 31, 1995

	Dr.	Cr.
Cash	$ 98,400	
Instalment Accounts Receivable, 1994	80,000	
Instalment Accounts Receivable, 1995	110,000	
Inventory Jan. 1, 1995	120,000	
Repossessed Merchandise	8,000	
Accounts Payable		$ 47,200
Deferred Gross Profit, 1994		64,000
Common Shares		200,000
Retained Earnings		40,000
Sales		380,000
Instalment Sales		180,000
Purchases	380,000	
Loss on Repossessions	2,800	
Operating Expenses	112,000	
	$911,200	$911,200

Note: The rate of gross profit on instalment sales for 1994 and 1995 can be determined from the information provided.

Instructions

(a) From the trial balance and other information given, prepare adjusting and closing entries as of December 31, 1995.

(b) Prepare an income statement for the year ended December 31, 1995. Include only the realized gross profit in the income statement when reporting the results regarding instalment sales.

***P6-13 (FRANCHISE: INITIAL FEE, CONTINUING FEE, BARGAIN PURCHASE)** On January 1, 1994, William's Photo Inc. entered into a franchise agreement with a local business, allowing the business (franchisee) to open an outlet under the William's Photo name. The franchisee paid 40% of the initial $40,000 franchise fee, and gave a $24,000, two-year, 12% note payable for the difference. Interest on the note is due annually on December 31. In return for the initial franchise fee, William's Photo located a site in a shopping mall, negotiated the lease, and installed photo-processing equipment. According to the franchise agreement, the franchisee is to pay a $10,000 continuing annual franchise fee, of which 10% must be spent by William's Photo on local advertising. When the full initial franchise fee is paid, the franchisee has an option to purchase the photo-processing equipment at 50% of its fair market value. It is estimated that the equipment will be worth $10,000 on January 1, 1996. At January 1, 1994, collectibility of the franchisee's note was reasonably assured, and William's Photo had substantially performed all contracted services. During 1994 and 1995, William's Photo fulfilled its obligations to provide local advertising services and incurred other annual costs of $5,000. On January 1, 1996, the franchisee paid the note and exercised its bargain purchase option on the equipment.

Instructions

Prepare the journal entries needed on the books of William's Photo Inc. to record each of the following:

(a) January 1, 1994: receipt of the initial franchise fee.

(b) During 1994: receipt of the continuing franchise fee and incurrence of advertising and other costs.

(c) December 31, 1994: receipt of annual interest on the note.

(d) During 1995: receipt of the continuing franchise fee and incurrence of advertising and other costs.

(e) December 31, 1995: receipt of annual interest on the note.

(f) January 1, 1996: collection of the note and sale of the photo-processing equipment.

(FRANCHISE: INITIAL FEE, CONTINUING FEE, SALES, PURCHASE OPTION) On January 1, 1994, Herbie's Restaurants Inc. entered into a franchise agreement granting the franchisee the right to do business under Herbie's name. According to the terms of the franchise agreement, Herbie's has an option to purchase the restaurant at any time within the next five years. It is probable that this option will be exercised. The initial franchise fee is $90,000. The franchisee paid $30,000 down and gave a $60,000 note to be paid in four years on which interest should be imputed at 8%. Collectibility of the note is reasonably assured and Herbie's had substantially performed all requirements by January 1, 1994. Terms of the franchise agreement provide that the franchisee must pay a continuing annual fee of $30,000. Half of this is for the purchase of food and supplies from Herbie's at the normal sales price. During 1994, Herbie's provided services costing $8,000 to the franchisee and provided food and supplies costing $10,000. At December 31, 1994, Herbie's purchased the restaurant from the franchisee, paying $80,000 and cancelling the franchisee's note. *P6-14

Instructions

Prepare the journal entries needed on the books of Herbie's Restaurants Inc. to record each of the following:

(a) January 1, 1994: receipt of the initial franchise fee.

(b) During 1994: receipt of the continuing franchise fee and provision of food, supplies, and services to the franchisee.

(c) December 31, 1994: amortization of discount on the note and the purchase of the restaurant. The straight-line method of discount amortization is used.

PERSPECTIVES

FROM TEN YEARS OUT

Joyce Carter
Wayne Crawley
Gerard McInnis

Joyce Carter, Wayne Crawley, and Gerard McInnis were classmates at Saint Mary's University where they took Intermediate Accounting 10 years ago. Since earning their CA designations in 1986, they have pursued different career paths. All three are excited by the challenges presented by their current occupations.

Joyce became V.P. of Finance with one of her audit clients, an owner-managed company in the commercial and residential real estate development, real estate brokerage, and property management business. Wayne is a Manager, Internal Audit Function, with Nova Scotia Power Inc., the provincial power utility which was recently privatized by the government of the Province of Nova Scotia, and recently was named Facilitator for the corporation's Effectiveness Program, a re-engineering initiative. He reports to the President and CEO and to the Audit Committee. Gerard continues to work for Peat Marwick Thorne, where he shares responsibility for a growing forensic accounting practice—litigation accounting, business valuation, civil litigation work, and fraud investigation.

What do you remember about your Intermediate Accounting course, and what role did it play in your education?

Joyce: I must admit that I had to go back to my course notes to review what topics were included. It's hard to believe that I covered each of these topics, but I must have. I think at that point we had nothing to relate the elements and issues to—they were covered in a vacuum. Looking back, I can see that Intermediate really set the foundation for everything that was yet to come, but at the time I had no idea.

Everything that is on the financial statements—there it is in Intermediate! I had to resolve an issue related to debt forgiveness last year. I knew there was no clear Canadian standard on it so I had to reason it out based on what I knew about principles in general. When I went back to my course notes, there it was in the Intermediate text. I was relieved, I had handled it correctly!

Wayne: I agree that it was a base. If you are going on in accounting, you have to take Intermediate. Actually, the most important thing I took away from Intermediate Accounting wasn't the technical component, that is, how to account for debt forgiveness or for discounted bonds, but it was the approach to learning that material in a condensed amount of time with all the other pressures. That was the most beneficial thing I learned, and I still use that everyday.

I was faced with a problem last week where we had to get certain things done in a limited amount of time. It was the approach to studying for Intermediate Accounting, not just to pass it but to do well, that helped me get through the CA program and everything else I had done. I don't think I knew that at the time. I experimented with different approaches, and knew I was building confidence. Intermediate was the big course.

Gerard: We were exposed to a lot in terms of the technical aspects of accounting. Whether you learn it all or not, you learn that there is a body of knowledge. I think that is the biggest thing I learned. You can't know everything. The biggest problem in public accounting is recognizing the issues. You don't have to know the answer, but you do have to be able to recognize that there is a problem and then you can research it further. That's a good thing about Intermediate Accounting—everything gets thrown in there, you get exposed to everything at least once, then in later courses you come back and revisit some of these areas.

What approach did you take to the study of the material?

Wayne: I'd pick and choose what was important in the chapter and then I'd try to connect or link that material with other topics covered and other things I knew. I'd do a lot of problems, even making up my own! I tried to be organized, to anticipate, and be prepared beforehand. And I took good notes.

I had a rule. I wouldn't let a full week go by if I didn't understand the previous topic. First, I'd try it on my own. Failing that, I'd seek out someone else in the class who was a good student and try to work it out with him or her. If I still wasn't satisfied, I would make sure I went to the professor.

I think it's important to team up with someone else in the class, someone who you expect will do well. I remember picking out Joyce. I wanted to learn from her. It's got be 50/50, not 90/10. I'd change if it wasn't working out. She learned differently from the way I learned, so we learned from each other. Everyone learns differently.

Joyce: Organization was the key for me, even though it was very time-consuming. The need for organization and taking good notes and never letting myself get behind has continued with me and has extended into other areas of my life as well.

Gerard: I wasn't as organized as Wayne and Joyce. I didn't spend much time going over practice questions, but really studied to understand everything I took—then I didn't care what they would ask me, the numbers would follow. I still use this approach today.

Because I was working so many hours, I found I had to be disciplined and always tried to make effective use of the hours I had. Working to understand the concepts is key. A "memorize the formula" approach is a frustrating way to learn. It's too easy to get bogged down.

Many of the Intermediate topics apply to large companies. Do you think the course is equally relevant to small business?

Gerard: The Intermediate material definitely relates more to big business, there's no doubt about that. But is that bad? I think the basics of revenue recognition, accrual accounting, and asset and liability issues are there and they are relevant, even though some other chapters are less relevant for small business. It depends on how you define "small," too.

Joyce: Whether your business is large or small, you still have reporting requirements, you still have to prepare financial statements and you may or may not have complicated issues to deal with. You're reporting internally, and to banks and other investors. It doesn't matter if you are an Esso or the small company I work for, you still need that base. I think it is very important.

Wayne: The major problem I have is not whether the topics apply to both large and small business, but that too often the topics get taught in isolation. No one tells the students why they are there. They come to class, and bang, Chapter 1!

Accounting provides information needed for decision making. Everyone uses it. The university uses it. The church uses it. Manufacturers use it. Everyone uses accounting information. And if they don't have good information, they may not make good decisions.

What do you think needs to be done?

Gerard: To enhance the course, you need to go beyond the straight lecture and the textbook.

Wayne: We need to "close the loop," to put accounting in perspective as just one part of the system. We are not in "accounting" or "marketing," we are in "business," and we need to work together.

I heard a speaker at a luncheon recently and he said something that I really believe is the key. Strong management is why companies are successful. It is strong management which attracts capital; management are people—people attract capital. Banks don't lend money to companies, they lend it to people. And capital employs labour.

How do you get capital? This is the finance side. You need labour? This is the human resources side. You need marketing. You need accounting because you need information. This is the "loop." The material in the course should stay the same. It's the perspective that has to be added.

Gerard: I think you recognize this more when you're working in industry. Accounting can't be dealt with in isolation.

In my job, I work in the valuation area, trying to determine values for goodwill and other assets, and in financing their acquisition. Valuation issues aren't black and white. We relate everything to cash flow. That's the investor's perspective.

From the business' perspective, often it is optics—optics in terms of financial reporting. We have an issue here; how can we best represent this to our shareholders? To our banker?

Wayne: There is no one right answer in many situations. It's a question of how can we approach this? What options do we have? What's best for the company? What's the downside? Accounting is a business tool to provide information for making decisions.

Too often people get pigeonholed. There is a perception that accountants are bean counters. In business you have to get past this. You have to recognize that individuals have sets of skills. Intermediate Accounting doesn't make you an "accountant"; it provides you with basic skills to fit with those of other disciplines.

PART

2

Assets: Recognition, Measurement, and Disclosure

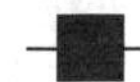

CHAPTER

7 Cash and Receivables

Assets are the heart of an enterprise. Assets generate revenues that turn into cash inflows to pay creditors, compensate employees, reward owners, provide for asset replacement, and provide for growth.

One characteristic of assets is their **liquidity**, that is, the amount of time expected to elapse until an asset is realized or otherwise converted into cash. An asset that is available for conversion into cash quickly is a liquid asset. Liquidity is one indication of an enterprise's ability to meet its obligations as they come due. A liquid enterprise is likely to have a lower risk of failure than an illiquid enterprise and generally has greater financial flexibility to accept unexpected new investment opportunities. Severe illiquidity is a cause of bankruptcy: consider White Farm, Braniff Airlines, Atlantic Acceptance, and numerous other industry leaders that have gone under because of lack of liquidity. Thus, the accountants must provide information that allows management, creditors, and investors to assess the enterprise's current liquidity and prospective cash flows.

The primary liquid assets of most enterprises are cash, temporary investments, and receivables. This chapter covers cash and cash equivalents, accounts receivable, and notes receivable. Temporary investments (marketable securities) are discussed in Chapter 18, along with long-term investments.

SECTION 1: CASH AND CASH EQUIVALENTS

NATURE AND COMPOSITION OF CASH

Objective 1

Identify items considered to be cash.

Cash, the most liquid of assets, is the standard medium of exchange and provides the basis for measuring and accounting for all other items. It is generally classified as a current asset. To be reported as **cash,** an asset must be readily available for the payment of current obligations and it must be free from any contractual restriction that limits its use in satisfying debts.

Cash consists of coin, currency, and available funds on deposit at the bank. Negotiable instruments such as money orders, certified cheques, cashiers' cheques, personal cheques, and bank drafts are also viewed as cash. Savings accounts are usually classified as cash, although the bank has a legal right to demand notice before withdrawal. Because the privilege of prior notice is rarely exercised, savings accounts are considered to be cash.

Certificates of deposit (CDs), deposit receipts, treasury bills, commercial and finance company paper, similar types of deposits and "short-term paper"[1] that provide small investors with an

[1] A variety of "short-term paper" is available for investment. **Certificates of deposit** (CDs) represent formal evidence of indebtedness, issued by a bank, subject to withdrawal under the specific terms of the instrument. Issued in $10,000 and $100,000 denominations, they mature in 30 to 360 days and generally pay interest at the short-term interest rate in effect at date of issuance. **Savings certificates** are issued by banks and trust companies in various denominations. The interest rate is tied to current savings rates. **Treasury bills** are government obligations generally having 91- and 182-day maturities; they are sold on a discount basis in $10,000 denominations at weekly government auctions. **Commercial paper** is a short-term note (30 to 270 days) issued by corporations with good credit ratings. Issued in $5,000 and $10,000 denominations, these notes generally yield a higher rate than treasury bills.

opportunity to earn high rates of interest are more appropriately classified as temporary investments than as cash. The logic for this classification is that these situations usually contain restrictions or penalties on their conversion into cash.

Items that present classification problems are postdated cheques, IOUs, travel advances, postage stamps, and special cash funds. **Postdated cheques and IOUs** are treated as receivables. **Travel advances** are properly treated as receivables if the advances are to be collected from the employees or deducted from their salaries. Otherwise, classification of the travel advance as a prepaid expense is more appropriate. **Postage stamps on hand** are classified as part of the office supplies inventory or as a prepaid expense. **Petty cash funds and change funds** are included in current assets as cash because these funds are used to meet current operating expenses and to liquidate current liabilities.

MANAGEMENT AND CONTROL OF CASH

Objective 2

Explain common techniques employed to control cash.

The accounting department faces two problems in accounting for cash transactions: (1) proper controls must be established to ensure that no unauthorized transactions are entered into by officers or employees; and (2) information necessary for the proper management of cash on hand and cash transactions must be provided. Most companies place the responsibility for proper record control of cash transactions on the accounting department. Record control, of course, is not possible without adequate physical control; therefore, the accounting department must take an interest in preventing intentional or unintentional mistakes in cash transactions. It should be emphasized that even with sophisticated control devices, errors can and do happen. *The Wall Street Journal* ran a story entitled "A $7.8 Million Error Has a Happy Ending for a Horrified Bank," which described how Manufacturers Hanover Trust Co., one of the largest banks in the United States, mailed about $7.8 million too much in cash dividends to its shareholders. Happily, most of the monies were subsequently returned.

Regulating the amount of cash on hand is primarily a management problem, but accountants must be able to provide the information required by management for regulating cash on hand through the special transactions of borrowing or investing.

Using Bank Accounts

A company can vary the number and location of banks and the types of bank accounts used to obtain desired control objectives. For large companies operating in multiple locations, the location of bank accounts can be important. Establishing collection accounts in strategic locations can accelerate the flow of cash into the company by shortening the time between the mailing of a payment by a customer and the use of the cash by the company. Multiple collection centres are generally used to reduce the size of a company's **collection float**, which is the difference between the amount on deposit according to the company's records and the amount of collected cash according to the bank record.

The **general chequing account** is the principal bank account used by most companies and frequently the only type of bank account maintained by small businesses. Cash is deposited into and disbursed from this account as all transactions are cycled through it. Deposits from and disbursements to all other bank accounts are made through the general chequing account.

Imprest bank accounts are used to make a specific amount of cash available for a limited purpose. The account acts as a clearing account for a large volume of cheques or for a specific type of cheque. The specific and intended amount to be cleared through the imprest account is deposited therein by transferring that amount from the general chequing account or other source. Imprest bank accounts are often used for disbursing payroll cheques, dividends, commissions, bonuses, confidential expenses (for example, officers' salaries), and travel expenses.

Lockbox accounts are frequently used by large, multilocation companies to make collections in cities within areas of heaviest customer billing. The company rents a local post office box and authorizes a local bank to pick up the remittances mailed to that box number. The bank empties the box at least once a day and immediately credits the company's account for collections. The greatest advantage of a lockbox is that it accelerates the availability of collected cash. Generally, in a lockbox arrangement the bank microfilms the cheques for record purposes and provides the company with a deposit slip, a list of collections, and any customer correspondence. If the control over cash is improved and if the income generated from accelerating the receipt of funds exceeds the cost of the lockbox system, it is considered to be worth undertaking.

Electronic Funds Transfer (EFT)

Business and individuals use about 1.5 billion cheques annually to pay their bills. This process is not without cost. Preparing, issuing, receiving, and clearing a cheque through the banking system is estimated to cost between 55 cents and $1.00. It is not surprising, therefore, that in this electronic age new methods are being developed to transfer funds among parties without the use and movement of paper. We are entering the age of **electronic funds transfer (EFT)**, a process that uses wire, telephone, telegraph, computer, (maybe even satellite), or other electronic device rather than paper to make instantaneous transfers of funds.

Canada's major banks spent the 1980s developing national automated teller machine (ATM) networks. The pace of development has been hectic. It is expected that most banks will be affiliated with a few national electronic banking networks that consolidate most retail banking services in much the same way that VISA and MasterCard have unified consumer credit services.

But the new ATM electronic networks will be far more powerful than the credit card networks of VISA and MasterCard because they will operate with the **debit card,** which can give access to all of a customer's accounts within a bank. Using an ATM, customers are able to withdraw cash and make deposits to both their chequing and savings accounts, as well as to transfer funds between accounts and make balance inquiries. By linking ATMs nationally, the networks are building the first electronic funds transfer system capable of processing large-volume retail fund transfers between computers at different banks.

Already the use of cheques has disappeared for certain fund transfers. For example, many employers send banks a magnetic tape that transfers payroll funds from the firm's account to each employee's account. Very soon the services provided by these ATM networks will accommodate electronic transfers from home and retail point-of-sale terminals. The banks will have the power to replace with electronic transactions many of those 1.5 billion cheques that are issued annually.

The Imprest Petty Cash System

Almost every company finds it necessary to pay small amounts for many expenses, such as employees' lunches and taxi fares, minor office supply items, and small expense payments. It is frequently impractical to require that such disbursements be made by cheque, yet some control over them is important. A simple method of obtaining reasonable control, while adhering to the rule of disbursement by cheque, is the **imprest system** for petty cash disbursements. This is how the system works:

1. Some individual is designated petty cash custodian and given a small amount of currency from which to make small payments.

Petty Cash Fund	300	
Cash		300

2. As disbursements are made, the petty cash custodian obtains signed receipts from each individual to whom cash is paid. If possible, evidence of the disbursements should be attached to the petty cash receipt. (Petty cash transactions are not recorded until the fund is reimbursed and then such entries are recorded by someone in accounting, other than the petty cash custodian.)
3. When the supply of cash runs low, the custodian presents to the general cashier a request for reimbursement supported by the petty cash receipts and other disbursement evidence. The custodian receives a company cheque to replenish the fund.

Office Supplies Expense	42	
Postage Expense	53	
Entertainment Expense	76	
Cash Over and Short	2	
Cash		173

4. If it is decided that the amount of cash in the petty cash fund is excessive, an adjustment may be made as follows (lowering the fund balance from $300 to $250):

Cash	50	
Petty Cash		50

Entries are made to the Petty Cash account only to increase or decrease the size of the fund.

There are usually expense items in the fund, except immediately after reimbursement; therefore, if accurate financial statements are desired, the funds must be reimbursed at the end of each accounting period and also when nearly depleted.

Under the imprest system, the petty cash custodian is responsible at all times for the amount of the fund on hand either as cash or in the form of signed receipts. These receipts provide the evidence required by the disbursing officer to issue a reimbursement cheque. Two additional procedures are followed to obtain more complete control over the petty cash fund:

1. Surprise counts of the funds are made from time to time by a superior of the petty cash custodian to determine that the fund is being accounted for satisfactorily.
2. Petty cash vouchers are cancelled or mutilated after they have been submitted for reimbursement, so that they cannot be used to secure a second and improper reimbursement.

Physical Protection of Cash Balances

Not only must cash receipts and cash disbursements be safeguarded through internal control measures, but also the cash on hand and in banks must be protected. Because receipts become cash on hand and cash disbursements are made from cash in banks, adequate control of receipts and disbursements is a part of the protection of cash balances. Certain other procedures, however, should be given some consideration.

Physical protection of cash is so elementary a necessity that it requires little discussion. Every effort should be made to minimize cash on hand in the office. A petty cash fund, perhaps change funds, and the current day's receipts should be all that is on hand at any one time, and these funds should be kept, insofar as possible, in a vault, safe, or locked cash drawer. Each day's receipts should be transmitted intact to the bank as soon as practicable. Accurately stating the amount of available cash both in internal management reports and in external financial statements is also extremely important.

Every company has a record of cash received, disbursed, and the balance. Because of the many cash transactions, however, errors or omissions may be made in keeping this record. Therefore, it is necessary to periodically prove the balance shown in the general ledger. Cash actually present in the office—petty cash, change funds, and undeposited receipts—can be counted and compared with the company records. Cash on deposit is not available for count and is proved by preparing a **bank reconciliation**—a reconciliation of the company's record with the bank's record of the company's cash.

Reconciliation of Bank Balances

At the end of each calendar month, the bank supplies each customer with a **bank statement** (a copy of the bank's account with the customer) together with the customer's cheques that have been paid by the bank during the month. If no errors were made by the bank or the customer, if all deposits made and all cheques drawn by the customer reached the bank within the same month, and if no unusual transactions occurred that could affect either the company's or the bank's record of cash, the balance of cash reported by the bank to the customer should be the same as that shown in the customer's own records as of the same point in time. This condition seldom occurs, for one or more of the following reasons.

Reconciling Items

1. **Deposits in transit.** End-of-month deposits of cash recorded on the depositor's books in one month are received and recorded by the bank in the following month.
2. **Outstanding cheques.** Cheques written by the depositor are recorded when written but may not be recorded by, or "clear," the bank until the next month.
3. **Bank charges.** Charges recorded by the bank against the depositor's balance for such items as bank services, printing cheques, not-sufficient-funds (NSF) cheques, and safe-deposit box rentals. The depositor may not be aware of these charges until receipt of the bank statement.
4. **Bank credits.** Collections or deposits by the bank for the benefit of the depositor that may be unknown to the depositor until receipt of the bank statement. Examples are note collection for the depositor as well as interest earned on CDs or interest-bearing chequing accounts.
5. **Bank or depositor errors.** Errors on the part of the bank or the depositor cause the bank balance to disagree with the depositor's book balance.

Hence, differences between the depositor's record of cash and the bank's record are usual and expected. Therefore, the two must be reconciled to determine the nature and amount of the differences between the two amounts.

A **bank reconciliation** is a schedule explaining any differences between the bank's and the company's records of cash. If the difference results only from transactions not yet recorded by the bank, the company's record of cash is considered correct. But if part of the difference arises from other items, either the bank's records or the company's records must be adjusted.

There are two methods of bank reconciliation. One reconciles from the bank statement balance to the book balance, or vice versa. The other, which is more widely used, reconciles from both the bank balance and the book balance to a correct cash balance. This latter form and its common reconciling items are shown on page 323.

This form of reconciliation consists of two sections: (1) "balance per bank statement" and (2) "balance per depositor's books." Both sections end with the same "correct cash balance." The correct cash balance is the amount to which the books must be adjusted and is the amount reported on the balance sheet. Adjusting journal entries are prepared from the addition and deduction items appearing in the "Balance per depositor's books." Any errors attributable to the bank should be called to the bank's attention immediately.

REPORTING CASH

Objective 3

Indicate how cash and related items are reported.

Although the reporting of cash is relatively straightforward, a number of issues merit special attention. These issues relate to the reporting of:

1. Restricted cash.
2. Bank overdrafts.
3. Cash equivalents.

Bank Reconciliation Form and Content

Balance per bank statement (end of period)		$$$
Add: Deposits in transit	$$	
Undeposited receipts (cash on hand)	$$	
Bank errors that understate the bank statement balance	$$	$$
		$$$
Deduct: Outstanding cheques	$$	
Bank errors that overstate the bank statement balance	$$	$$
Correct cash balance		$$$
Balance per depositor's books		$$$
Add: Bank credits and collections not yet recorded in the books	$$	
Book errors that understate the book balance	$$	$$
		$$$
Deduct: Bank charges not yet recorded in the books	$$	
Book errors that overstate the book balance	$$	$$
Correct cash balance		$$$

Restricted Cash

Compensating Balances. Occasionally banks and other lending institutions require customers to whom they lend money to maintain minimum cash balances. These minimum balances, called **compensating balances,** are defined as "that portion of any demand deposit (or any time deposit or certificate of deposit) maintained by a corporation which constitutes support for existing borrowing arrangements of the corporation with a lending institution. Such arrangements would include both outstanding borrowings and the assurance of future credit availability."

Compensating balances may be payment for bank services rendered to the company for which there is no direct fee (e.g., cheque processing and lockbox management). By requiring a compensating balance, the bank achieves an effective interest rate on a loan that is higher than the stated rate because it has the use of the restricted amount that must remain on deposit.

The need for the disclosure of compensating balances was highlighted in the 1970s when a number of companies were involved in a liquidity crisis. Many investors believed that the cash reported on the balance sheet was fully available to meet recurring obligations, but these funds were restricted because of the need for these companies to maintain minimum cash balances at various lending institutions.

Disclosure of compensating balances depends on the classification of the related loan or borrowing arrangement. If the balances are required for short-term borrowing, then the compensating amount could be separately disclosed under Current Assets. Restricted balances held as compensating balances against long-term borrowing arrangements should be separately classified as noncurrent assets in either the Investments or Other Assets sections, using a caption such as Cash on Deposit Maintained as Compensating Balance. In addition, a note to the financial statements should indicate the nature of the arrangement and cash restriction.

Central Guaranty Trustco Limited reported the note on page 324 regarding compensating balances.

Other Types of Restrictions. Petty cash, payroll, and dividend funds are examples of cash set aside for a particular purpose. In most situations, these fund balances are not material and therefore are not segregated from cash when it is reported in the financial statements. When material in amount, restricted cash is segregated from "regular" cash for reporting purposes. The **restricted cash** is classified either in the Current Asset or in the Long-Term Asset section, depending on the date

Central Guaranty Trustco Limited

Note: Restricted Assets
In February 1992, the Trust Company agreed to maintain deposits with a Canadian chartered bank amounting to $300,000,000 in connection with its daily clearing arrangements. In addition, the Trust Company agreed to pledge securities to the bank amounting to at least $90,000,000.

of availability or disbursement. If the cash is to be used (within a year or the operating cycle, whichever is longer) for payment of existing or maturing obligations, classification in the Current Asset section is appropriate. On the other hand, if the cash is to be held for a longer period, the restricted cash is shown in the Long-Term Asset section of the balance sheet.[2]

Bank Overdrafts

Bank overdrafts occur when a cheque is written for more than the amount in the cash account. Bank overdrafts should be reported in the Current Liabilities section and are usually added to the amount reported as accounts payable. If material, these items should be separately disclosed, either on the face of the balance sheet or in the related notes.

Bank overdrafts are generally not offset against the cash account. A major exception is when available cash is present in another account in the same bank on which the overdraft occurred. Offsetting in this case is permitted.

Cash Equivalents

A current classification that has become popular is Cash and Cash Equivalents. Cash equivalents are short-term, highly liquid investments that are both (a) readily convertible to known amounts of cash and (b) so near their maturity that they present insignificant risk of changes in interest rates. Generally, only investments with original maturities of three months or less qualify under this definition. Examples of cash equivalents are treasury bills and commercial paper purchased with cash that is in excess of immediate needs. Some companies combine cash with temporary investments on the balance sheet. In these cases, the amount of the temporary investments is either described parenthetically or in the notes.

SUMMARY

Cash and cash equivalents include the medium of exchange and most negotiable instruments. If the item cannot be converted to coin or currency on short notice, it is separately classified as an investment, a receivable, or a prepaid expense. Cash that is not available for payment of currently maturing liabilities is segregated and classified in the Long-Term Assets section. The schedule on the following page summarizes the classification of cash-related items.

SECTION 2: RECEIVABLES

Objective 4

Define "receivables" and identify the different types of receivables.

Receivables are claims held against customers and others for money, goods, or services. For financial statement purposes, receivables are classified as either *current* (short term) or *noncurrent* (long term). **Current receivables** are expected to be collected within a year or during the current operating cycle, whichever is longer. All other receivables are classified as **noncurrent**. Receivables are further classified in the balance sheet as either trade receivables or nontrade receivables.

---

[2] *CICA Handbook* (Toronto: CICA), Section 3000, par. .01.

Classification of Cash, Cash Equivalent, and Noncash Items

Item	Classification	Comment
Cash	Cash	If unrestricted, report as cash. If restricted, identify and classify as current and noncurrent assets.
Petty cash and change funds	Cash	Report as cash.
Short-term paper	Cash equivalents	Investments with maturity of less than three months, often combined with cash.
Short-term paper	Temporary investments	Investments with maturity of 3 to 12 months.
Postdated cheques and IOUs	Receivables	Assumed to be collectible.
Travel advances	Receivables	Assumed to be collected from employees or deducted from their salaries.
Postage on hand (as stamps or in postage meters)	Prepaid expenses	May also be classified as office supplies inventory.
Bank overdrafts	Current liability	If right of offset exists, reduce cash.
Compensating balances:		
1. Legally restricted	Cash separately classified as a deposit maintained as compensating balance	Classify as current or noncurrent in the balance sheet.
2. Arrangement without legal restriction	Cash with note disclosure	Disclose details of the arrangement separately in notes.

Trade receivables are amounts owed by customers for goods sold and services rendered as part of normal business operations. Trade receivables, usually the most significant receivable of an enterprise, may be subclassified into accounts receivable and notes receivable. **Accounts receivable**, which are oral promises of the purchaser to pay for goods and services sold, are normally collectible within 30 to 60 days and are represented by "open accounts" resulting from short-term extensions of credit. **Notes receivable** are written promises of the maker to pay a certain sum of money on a specified future date and may arise from sales, financing, or other transactions. Notes may be short term or long term.

Nontrade receivables arise from a variety of transactions and are oral or written promises to pay or deliver. Some examples of nontrade receivables are:

1. Advances to officers and employees.
2. Advances to subsidiaries.
3. Deposits to cover potential damages or losses.
4. Deposits as a guarantee of performance or payment.
5. Dividends and interest receivable.
6. Claims against:
   (a) Insurance companies for casualties sustained.
   (b) Defendants under suit.
   (c) Governmental bodies for tax refunds.

(d) Common carriers for damaged or lost goods.

(e) Creditors for returned, damaged, or lost goods.

(f) Customers for returnable items (crates, containers, etc.).

Because of the peculiar nature of nontrade receivables, they are generally classified and reported as separate items in the balance sheet.

The remainder of this chapter is divided into two parts—accounts receivable and notes receivable. In our coverage of accounts receivable, emphasis is given to trade accounts receivable because of their importance. Our coverage of notes receivable includes both short-term and long-term notes.

ACCOUNTS RECEIVABLE

The three primary accounting problems associated with accounts receivable are:

1. **Recognition** of accounts receivable.
2. **Valuation** of accounts receivable.
3. **Disposition** of accounts receivable

Recognition of Accounts Receivable

Objective 5

Explain accounting issues related to recognition of accounts receivable.

In most receivables transactions, the amount to be recognized is the exchange price between the two parties. The ***exchange price is the amount due from the debtor*** (a customer or borrower) and is generally evidenced by some type of business document, often an invoice. Two factors that may complicate the measurement of the exchange price are (1) the availability of discounts (trade and cash discounts) and (2) the length of time between the sale and the due date of payments (the interest element).

Trade Discounts. Customers are often quoted prices on the basis of list or catalogue prices that may be subject to a trade or quantity discount. Trade discounts are used to avoid frequent changes in catalogues, to quote different prices for different quantities purchased, or to hide the true invoice price from competitors.

Trade discounts are commonly quoted in percentages. For example, if your textbook has a list price of $60 and the publisher sells it to college bookstores for list less a 30% trade discount, the receivable recorded by the publisher is $42 per textbook. The normal price practice is simply to deduct the trade discount from the list price and bill the customer net.

As another example, the producers of Nabob recently sold a 285-g jar of its instant coffee that had a list price of $4.65 to various supermarkets for $3.90, a trade discount of approximately 16%. The supermarkets in turn sold the instant coffee for $3.99 per jar. Nabob would record the receivable and related sales revenue at $3.90 per jar, not $4.65.

Cash Discounts (Sales Discounts). Cash discounts (sales discounts) are offered as an inducement for prompt payment and communicated in terms that read 2/10, n/30 (2% if paid within 10 days, gross amount due in 30 days), or 2/10, E.O.M. (2% if paid within 10 days of the end of the month).

Companies that fail to take sales discounts are usually not managing their money wisely. An enterprise that receives a 1% reduction in sales prices for payment within 10 days, total payment due within 30 days, is effectively earning 18.25% (.01 divided by 20/365) or at least avoiding that rate of interest cost. For this reason, it is usual for companies to take the discount unless their cash is severely limited.

The easiest and most commonly used method of recording sales and related sales discount transactions is to enter the receivable and sale at the gross amount. Under this method, sales discounts are recognized in the accounts only when payment is received within the discount period. Sales discounts would then be shown in the income statement as a deduction from sales, to arrive at net sales.

Some accountants contend that sales discounts not taken reflect penalties added to an established price to encourage prompt payment. That is, the seller offers sales on account at a slightly higher price than if selling for cash, and the increase is offset by the cash discount offered. Thus, customers who pay within the discount period purchase at the cash price; those who pay after expiration of the discount period are penalized because they must pay an amount in excess of the cash price. If this approach is adopted, sales and receivables are recorded net, and any discounts not taken are subsequently debited to Accounts Receivable and credited to Sales Discounts Forfeited. The following entries illustrate the difference between the gross and net methods.

Entries Under Gross and Net Methods

Gross Method			Net Method		
Sale of $10,000, terms 2/10, n/30:					
Accounts Receivable	10,000		Accounts Receivable	9,800	
Sales		10,000	Sales		9,800
Payment of $4,000 received within discount period:					
Cash	3,920		Cash	3,920	
Sales Discount	80		Accounts receivable		3,920
Accounts Receivable		4,000			
Payment of $6,000 received after discount period:					
Cash	6,000		Accounts Receivable	120	
Accounts Receivable		6,000	Sales Discounts Forfeited		120
			Cash	6,000	
			Accounts Receivable		6,000

If the gross method is employed, sales discounts should be reported as a deduction from sales in the income statement. If the net method is used, Sales Discounts Forfeited should be considered as an Other Revenue item. Theoretically, the recognition of Sales Discounts Forfeited is correct because the receivable is stated closer to its realizable value and the net sale figure measures the revenue earned from the sale.

As a practical matter, the net method is seldom used because it requires additional analysis and bookkeeping. For example, the net method requires adjusting entries to record sales discounts forfeited on accounts receivable that have passed the discount period.

Nonrecognition of Interest Element. Ideally, receivables should be measured in terms of their present value: the discounted value of the cash to be received in the future. When expected cash receipts require a waiting period, the receivable face amount is not worth the amount that is ultimately received.

To illustrate, assume that a company makes a sale on account for $1,000, with payment due in four months. The applicable rate of interest is 12% and payment is made at the end of the four months. The present value of that receivable is not $1,000 but $961.54 ($1,000 × .96154, Table A-2; n = 1, i = 4%). In other words, $1,000 to be received four months from now is not the same as $1,000 received today.

Theoretically, any revenue after the period of sale is interest revenue. In practice, accountants have chosen to ignore this generally for accounts receivable because the amount of the discount is not usually material in relation to the net income for the period. Generally, receivables arising from transactions with customers in the normal course of business that are due in customary trade terms not exceeding approximately one year are excluded from present value considerations.[3]

Valuation of Accounts Receivable

Objective 6

Explain accounting issues related to valuation of accounts receivable.

Having recorded the receivables at their face value (the amount due), the accountant then faces the problem of financial statement presentation. Reporting of receivables involves (1) their classification and (2) their valuation on the balance sheet.

Classification, as already discussed, involves a determination of the length of time the receivable will be outstanding. Receivables intended to be collected within a year or the operating cycle, whichever is longer, are classified as current; all other receivables are classified as long term.

The valuation of receivables is slightly more complex. Short-term receivables are valued and reported at **net realizable value**—the net amount *expected* to be received in cash, which is not necessarily the amount legally receivable. Determining net realizable value requires an estimation of uncollectible receivables and any returns or allowances to be granted.

Uncollectible Accounts Receivable. As one accountant so aptly noted: "The credit manager's idea of heaven probably would envisage a situation in which everybody (eventually) paid his debts."[4] Sales on any basis other than for cash make subsequent failure to collect the account a real possibility. An uncollectible account receivable is a loss of revenue that requires, through proper entry in the accounts, a decrease in the asset accounts receivable and a related decrease in income and shareholders' equity.

The chief problem in recording uncollectible accounts receivable is establishing the time at which to record the loss. Two general procedures are in use.

Methods for Recording Uncollectibles

1. **Direct write-off method**. No entry is made until a specific account has definitely been established as uncollectible. Then the loss is recorded by crediting Accounts Receivable and debiting Bad Debt Expense.
2. **Allowance method**. An estimate is made of the expected uncollectible accounts from all sales made on account or from the total of outstanding receivables. This estimate is entered as an expense and a reduction in accounts receivable (via an increase in the allowance account) in the period in which the sale is recorded.

The direct write-off method records the bad debt in the year it is determined that a specific receivable cannot be collected; the allowance method enters the expense on an estimated basis in the accounting period that the sales on account are made.

Supporters of the **direct write-off method** contend that facts, not estimates, are recorded. It assumes that a good account receivable resulted from each sale, and that later events proved certain accounts to be uncollectible and worthless. From a practical standpoint this method is simple and convenient to apply, although we must recognize that receivables do not generally become worthless at an identifiable moment of time. The direct write-off is theoretically deficient because it usually

---

[3] In the United States, *APB Opinion No. 21*, "Interest on Receivables and Payables," provides that all receivables are subject to present value measurement techniques and interest imputation, if necessary, except for the following specifically excluded types:
(a) Normal accounts receivable due within one year.
(b) Security deposits, retainages, advances, or progress payments.
(c) Transactions between parent and subsidiary.
(d) Receivables due at some determinable future date.

[4] William J. Vatter, *Managerial Accounting* (Englewood Cliffs, N.J.: Prentice-Hall, 1950), p. 60.

does not match costs with revenues of the period, nor does it result in receivables being stated at estimated realizable value on the balance sheet. ***As a result, its use is not considered appropriate, except when the amount uncollectible is immaterial.***

Advocates of the **allowance method** believe that bad debt expense should be recorded in the same period as the sale to obtain a proper matching of expenses and revenues and to achieve a proper carrying value for accounts receivable. They support the position that although estimates are involved, the percentage of receivables that will not be collected can be predicted from past experiences, present market conditions, and an analysis of the outstanding balances. Many companies set their credit policies to provide for a certain percentage of uncollectible accounts. Failure to attain that percentage means that sales are being lost by credit policies that are too restrictive.

Because the collectibility of receivables is considered a loss contingency, the allowance method is appropriate only in situations where it is likely that an asset has been impaired and that the amount of the loss can be reasonably estimated. A receivable is a prospective cash inflow and the probability of its collection must be considered in valuing this inflow. These estimates normally are made either (1) on the basis of percentage of sales or (2) on the basis of outstanding receivables.

Percentage-of-Sales (Income Statement) Approach. If there is a fairly stable relationship between previous years' credit sales and bad debts, then that relationship can be turned into a percentage and used to determine this year's bad debt expense.

The percentage-of-sales method matches costs with revenues because it relates the charge to the period in which the sale is recorded. To illustrate, assume that E.T. Morgan, Inc. estimates from past experience that about 2% of credit sales become uncollectible. If E.T. Morgan, Inc. had charge sales of $400,000 in 1994, the entry to record bad debt expense using the percentage-of-sales method is as follows:

Bad Debt Expense	8,000	
Allowance for Doubtful Accounts		8,000

The Allowance for Doubtful Accounts is a valuation account (i.e. contra asset) and is subtracted from the trade receivables on the balance sheet. The amount of bad debt expense and the related credit to the allowance account are unaffected by any balance currently existing in the allowance account. Because the bad debt expense is related to a nominal account (Sales), and any balance in the allowance is ignored, this method is frequently referred to as the **income statement approach.** A proper matching of costs and revenues is therefore achieved.

Percentage-of-Receivables (Balance Sheet) Approach. Using past experience, a company can estimate the percentage of its outstanding receivables that will become uncollectible, without identifying specific accounts. This procedure provides a reasonably accurate estimate of the receivables' realizable value, but does not fit the concept of matching cost and revenue. Rather, its objective is to report receivables in the balance sheet at net realizable values; hence, it is referred to as the **balance sheet approach.**

The percentage of receivables may be applied using one **composite rate** that reflects an estimate of the uncollectible receivables. Another approach that is more sensitive to the actual status of the accounts receivable is achieved by setting up an **aging schedule** and applying a different percentage based on past experience to the various age categories. An aging schedule is frequently used in practice. It indicates which accounts require special attention by providing the age of such accounts receivable. The following schedule of Wilson & Co. on page 330 is an example.

The amount $37,650 would be the bad debt expense to be reported for this year, assuming that no balance existed in the Allowance account. To change the illustration slightly, assume that the Allowance account had a credit balance of $800 before adjustment. In this case, the amount to be added to the Allowance account is $36,850 ($37,650 − $800), and the following entry is made:

Bad Debt Expense	36,850	
Allowance for Doubtful Accounts		36,850

Wilson & Co.
Aging Schedule

Name of Customer	Balance Dec. 31	Under 60 days	60–90 days	91–120 days	Over 120 days
Western Stainless Steel Ltd.	$ 98,000	$ 80,000	$18,000	$	$
Brockway Steel Ltd.	320,000	320,000			
Freeport Sheet & Tube Co.	55,000				55,000
Allegheny Iron Works	74,000	60,000		14,000	
	$547,000	**$460,000**	**$18,000**	**$14,000**	**$55,000**

Summary

Age	Amount	Percentage Estimated to be Uncollectible	**Required Balance in Allowance**
Under 60 days old	$460,000	4	**$18,400**
61–90 days old	18,000	15	**2,700**
91–120 days old	14,000	20	**2,800**
Over 120 days	55,000	25	**13,750**
Year-end balance of allowance for doubtful accounts			$37,650

The balance in the Allowance account after this entry is therefore correctly stated as $37,650. ***If the Allowance balance before adjustment had a debit balance of $200***, then the amount to be recorded for bad debt expense would be $37,850 ($37,650 desired balance + $200 debit balance). In the percentage-of-receivables method, the balance in the Allowance account *cannot be ignored* because the percentage is related to a real account (Accounts Receivable).

An aging schedule is usually not prepared to determine the bad debt expense but rather as a control device to determine the composition of receivables and to identify delinquent accounts. The estimated loss percentage developed for each category is based on previous loss experience and the advice of credit department personnel. Regardless of whether a composite rate or an aging schedule is employed, the primary objective of the percentage-of-receivables method for financial statement purposes is to report receivables in the balance sheet at net realizable value. However, it is deficient in that it may not match the bad debt expense to the period in which the sale takes place.

The allowance for doubtful accounts as a percentage of receivables will vary, depending on the industry and the economic climate. Normally, bad debt expense will rise during recessions.

In summary, the percentage-of-receivables method results in a more accurate valuation of receivables on the balance sheet. From a matching viewpoint, the percentage-of-sales approach provides the best results. The following diagram relates these methods to the basic theory.

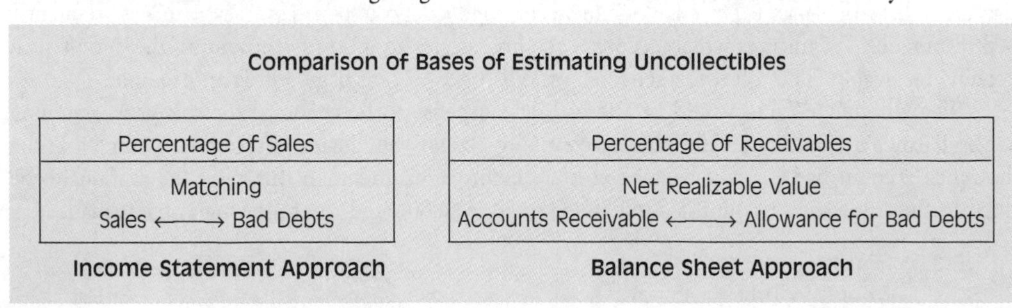

The account title employed for the allowance account is usually Allowance for Doubtful Accounts or simply Allowance.

Collection of Accounts Receivable Written Off. When a particular account receivable is determined to be uncollectible, the balance is removed from the books by debiting Allowance for Doubtful Accounts and crediting Accounts Receivable. If a collection is made on a receivable that was previously written off, the procedure to be followed is first to re-establish the receivable by debiting Accounts Receivable and crediting Allowance for Doubtful Accounts. An entry is then made to debit Cash and credit the customer's account in the amount of the remittance received.

If the direct write-off approach is employed, the amount collected is debited to Cash and credited to a revenue account entitled Uncollectible Amounts Recovered, with proper notation in the customer's account.

Special Allowance Accounts. To properly match expenses to sales revenues, it is sometimes necessary to establish additional allowance accounts. These allowance accounts are reported as contra accounts to accounts receivable and establish the receivables at net realizable value. The most common allowances are:

1. Allowance for sales returns and allowances.
2. Allowance for collection expenses.

Sales Returns and Allowances. Many accountants question the soundness of recording returns and allowances in the current period when they are derived from sales made in the preceding period. Normally, however, the amount of mismatched returns and allowances is not material, if such items are handled consistently from year to year. Yet, if a company completes a few special orders involving large amounts near the end of the accounting period, returns and allowances should be anticipated in the period of the sale to avoid distorting the income statement of the current period.

As an example, Astro Turf Limited recognizes that approximately 5% of its $1,000,000 trade receivables outstanding are returned or some adjustment made to the sale price. Omission of a $50,000 charge could have a material effect on net income for the period. The entry to reflect this anticipated sales return and allowance is:

Sales Returns and Allowances	50,000	
Allowance for Sales Returns and Allowances		50,000

Sales returns and allowances are reported as an offset to sales revenue in the income statement. Returns and allowances are accumulated separately instead of debited directly to the Sales account, simply to let the business manager and the statement reader know their magnitude. The allowance is an asset valuation account (contra asset) and is deducted from total accounts receivable.

In most cases, the inclusion in the income statement of all returns and allowances made during the period, whether or not they resulted from the current period's sales, is an acceptable accounting procedure justified on the basis of practicality and immateriality.[5]

Collection Expenses. A similar concept holds true for collection expenses. If a significant handling and service charge is incurred to collect the open accounts receivables at the end of the year, an allowance for collection expenses should be recorded. For example, Sears, Roebuck & Company reports its receivables net, with an attached schedule indicating the types of receivables outstanding. Sears' contra account is entitled Allowance for Collection Expenses and Losses on Customer Accounts, as follows.

---

[5] An interesting side light to the entire problem of returns and allowances has developed in recent years. Determination of when a sale *is* a sale has become difficult, because in certain circumstances the seller is exposed to such a high risk of ownership through possible return of the property that the entire transaction is nullified and the sale not recognized. Such situations have developed particularly in sales to related parties. This subject is discussed in more detail in Chapters 8 and 19.

Sears, Roebuck & Company

Receivables	
Customer instalment accounts receivable	
Easy payment accounts	$2,221,017,167
Revolving charge accounts	1,372,874,725
	3,593,891,892
Other customer accounts	101,904,882
Miscellaneous accounts and notes receivable	96,446,334
	3,792,243,108
Less: Allowance for collection expenses and losses on customer accounts	236,826,866
	$3,555,416,242

Disposition of Accounts Receivable

Objective 7

Explain accounting issues related to disposition of accounts receivable.

In the normal course of events, accounts receivable are collected when due and removed from the books. However, as credit sales and receivables have grown in size and significance, the "normal course of events" has evolved. ***In order to accelerate the receipt of cash from receivables, the owner may transfer the receivables to another company for cash.***

There are various reasons for this early transfer. First, for competitive reasons, providing sales financing for customers is virtually mandatory in many industries. In the sale of durable goods, such as automobiles, trucks, industrial and farm equipment, computers, and appliances, a large majority of the sales are on an instalment contract basis. Many major companies in these industries have therefore created wholly owned subsidiaries with responsibility for accounts receivable financing. General Motors of Canada Ltd. has its General Motors Acceptance Corp. of Canada (GMAC); Sears has its Sears Acceptance Corp.; and Chrysler Corporation of Canada has its Chrysler Finance Corporation.

Second, the holder of receivables may sell them because money is tight and access to normal credit is not available or is prohibitively expensive. Also, a firm may sell its receivables, instead of having to borrow, to avoid violating existing lending agreements.

Finally, billing and collection are often time-consuming and costly. Credit card companies such as MasterCard, VISA, and others provide merchants with immediate cash.

Conversely, some purchasers of receivables buy them to obtain the legal protection of ownership rights afforded a purchaser of assets as opposed to the lesser rights afforded a secured creditor. In addition, banks and other lending institutions may be forced to purchase receivables because of legal lending limits; that is, they cannot make any additional loans but they can buy receivables and charge a fee for this service.

The transfer of accounts receivable to a third party for cash is generally accomplished in one of two ways:

1. Assignment of accounts receivable (pledging a security interest).
2. Sale (factoring) of accounts receivable.

Assignment of Accounts Receivable. The owner of the receivables (the assignor) borrows cash from a lender (the assignee) by writing a promissory note designating or pledging the accounts receivable as collateral. If the note is not paid when due, the assignee has the right to convert the collateral to cash, that is, to collect the receivables.

General Assignment. If the assignment is general, all the receivables serve as collateral for the note. New receivables can be substituted for the ones collected. To illustrate, Machlin Motor Company assigns its accounts receivable to First City Finance Company as collateral for a loan of $946,000. The entry to record this transaction is as follows:

Cash	946,000	
Notes Payable		946,000

No special entries are made to the receivable accounts to record the assignment. Information concerning the assigned receivables is disclosed in a note or in a parenthetical explanation. To illustrate, Methanex Corporation reported its general assignment in the following manner.

Methanex Corporation

Note 7 (a) The term bank loan bears interest at a certain bank's U.S. base rate plus 1½% per annum, is repayable in quarterly instalments and is secured, together with the operating bank loan of the ammonia operations by a $70 million fixed and floating charge demand debenture on the ammonia plant and a general assignment of ammonia accounts receivable and inventory.

Specific Assignment. In a specific assignment, the borrower and lender enter into an agreement as to (1) who is to receive the collections, (2) the finance charges (which are in addition to the interest on the note), (3) the specific accounts that serve as security, and (4) notification or nonnotification of account debtors. Collections on the assigned accounts are generally made by the assignor.

To illustrate, on March 1, 1994, Howat Mills Ltd. assigns $700,000 of its accounts receivable to the Royal Bank as collateral for a $500,000 note. Howat Mills will continue to collect the accounts receivable; the account debtors are not notified of the assignment. The Royal Bank assesses a finance charge of 1% of the accounts receivable assigned and interest on the note of 12%. Settlement by Howat Mills to the bank is made monthly for all cash collected on the assigned receivables. (See page 334.)

Receivables assigned are identified by recording them in an Assigned Accounts Receivable account. An alternative is to indicate in the notes to the financial statements the accounts receivable assigned. In addition to recording the collection of receivables, all discounts, returns and allowances, and bad debts must be recognized. Each month, the proceeds from the collection of the assigned accounts receivable are used to retire the note obligation. In addition, interest on the note is paid.

Specifically assigned accounts receivable should be reported in Howat Mills' financial statements as a separate asset account if material. Its equity in the assigned accounts should be disclosed. For instance, Howat Mills Ltd. has equity of $200,000 ($700,000 − $500,000) in its assigned receivables at March 1.

Sales (Transfers) of Accounts Receivable. Sales of receivables have increased substantially in recent years. A common example is a sale to a factor. **Factors** are finance companies or banks that buy receivables from businesses for a fee and then collect the remittances directly from the customers. Factoring, traditionally associated with the textiles, apparel, footwear, furniture, and home furnishing industries, has now spread to many other types of businesses and represents a billion-dollar business. As an illustration, Sears, Roebuck & Co. recently arranged to sell $550 million of customer accounts receivable at 99.015% of face value. Credit cards such as MasterCard and VISA are a type of factoring arrangement.

Factoring arrangements vary widely, but typically the purchaser charges a ¾ to 1½% commission of the receivables purchased (4% to 5% for credit card factoring). The diagram on page 335 illustrates in sequential process the basic procedures in factoring.

Entries for Assignment of Specific Accounts Receivable

Assignment of accounts receivable and issuance of note on March 1, 1994:

Howat Mills Ltd.			Royal Bank		
Cash	493,000		Notes Receivable	500,000	
Finance Charge	7,000*		Finance Revenue		7,000*
Accounts Receivable Assigned	700,000		Cash		493,000
Notes Payable		500,000			
Accounts Receivable		700,000			
*(1% × $700,000)					

Collection in March of $440,000 of assigned accounts less cash discounts of $6,000. In addition sales returns of $14,000 were received:

Howat Mills Ltd.			Royal Bank		
Cash	434,000				
Sales Discounts	6,000				
Sales Returns	14,000		(no entry)		
Accts. Receivable Assigned		454,000			
($440,000 + $14,000 = $454,000)					

Remitted March collections plus accrued interest to the bank on April 1:

Howat Mills Ltd.			Royal Bank		
Interest Expense	5,000*		Cash	439,000	
Notes Payable	434,000		Interest Revenue		5,000*
Cash		439,000	Notes Receivable		434,000
*($500,000 × .12 × 1/12)					

Collection in April of the balance of assigned accounts less $2,000 written off as uncollectible:

Howat Mills Ltd.			Royal Bank		
Cash	244,000				
Allowance for Doubtful Accounts	2,000		(No entry)		
Accts Receivable Assigned		246,000*			
*($700,000 − $454,000)					

Remitted the balance due of $66,000 ($500,000 − $434,000) on the note plus interest on May 1:

Howat Mills Ltd.			Royal Bank		
Interest Expense	660*		Cash	66,660	
Notes Payable	66,000		Interest Revenue		660*
Cash		66,660	Notes Receivable		66,000
*($66,000 × .12 × 1/12)					

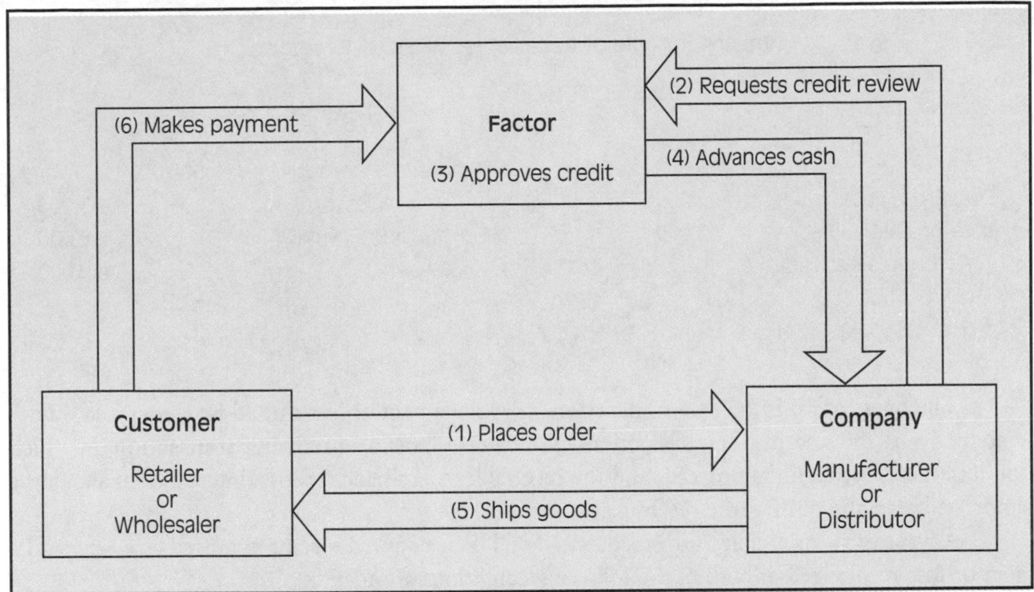

In factoring transactions, receivables are sold on either a without recourse or with recourse basis.[6]

Transfer Without Recourse. When receivables are sold **without recourse,** the purchaser assumes the risk of collectibility and absorbs any credit losses. The transfer of accounts receivable in a nonrecourse transaction is an outright sale of receivables both in form (transfer of title) and substance (transfer of risk and reward). In nonrecourse transactions, as in any sale of assets, Cash is debited for the proceeds. Accounts Receivable is credited for the face value of the receivables. The difference, reduced by any provision for probable adjustments (discounts, returns, allowances, etc.), is recognized as a Loss on the Sale of Receivables. The seller uses a Due From Factor account to explain the amount of proceeds retained by the factor to cover the probable adjustments in the form of sales discounts, sales returns, and sales allowances.

To illustrate, Crest Textiles Ltd. factors $500,000 of accounts receivable with Commercial Factors Ltd. on a *without recourse* basis. The receivable records are transferred to Commercial Factors Ltd., which will receive the collections. Commercial Factors assesses a finance charge of 3% of the amount of accounts receivable and retains an amount equal to 5% of the accounts receivable. The journal entries for both Crest Textiles and Commercial Factors for the receivables transferred without recourse are shown on page 336.

In recognition of the sale of receivables, Crest Textiles records a loss of $15,000. The factor's income will be the difference between the financing revenue of $15,000 and the amount of any uncollectible receivables.

A comprehensive illustration of all the entries involved in the sale, collection, and final settlement of these receivables for both Crest Textiles and Commercial Factors is presented in Appendix 7B, page 352.

Transfer With Recourse. If receivables are sold **with recourse**, the seller guarantees payment to the purchaser in the event the debtor fails to pay. Many contend that a sale has not occurred because the transferor retains the same risk of collection after the deal as before. Others disagree, noting that most of the risks and benefits have transferred and therefore a sale should be recorded.

---

[6] **Recourse** is the right of a transferee of receivables to receive payment from the transfer of those receivables for (a) failure of the debtors to pay when due, (b) the effects of prepayments, or (c) adjustments resulting from defects in the eligibility of the transferred receivables. In EIC-9, the Emerging Issues Committee of the CICA point out that there are degrees of recourse in transfers of receivables. It is necessary to assess the degree to which risks and rewards are transferred when accounting for transfer of receivables.

Entries for Sale of Receivables Without Recourse

Crest Textiles Ltd.			Commercial Factors Ltd.		
Cash	460,000		Accounts Receivable	500,000	
Due From Factor	25,000*		Due to Crest		25,000
Loss on Sale of Rec.	15,000**		Financing Revenue		15,000
Accounts Receivable		500,000	Cash		460,000
*(5% × $500,000)					
**(3% × $500,000)					

The question is: Is it a **sale transaction**, in which a gain or loss should be recognized immediately? Or is the sale of receivables on a with-recourse basis a **borrowing transaction**, in which the difference between the proceeds and the receivables is a financing cost (interest) that should be amortized over the term of the receivables?

A transfer of receivables with recourse should be accounted for and reported as a sale, and a gain or loss recognized, if both of the following conditions are met:[7]

1. The transferor has transferred the significant risks and rewards of ownership of the receivables.

2. The consideration received from the transfer may be measured with reasonable precision.

If the transfer with recourse does not meet these conditions, the proceeds from the transfer of the receivables is accounted for as a borrowing. That is, instead of crediting receivables a current liability titled Liability on Transferred Accounts Receivable is credited.

The journal entries for Crest Textiles and Commercial Factors for the transfer of receivables both as a sale and as a borrowing are as follows.

Entries by Crest Textiles Ltd. for Receivables Transferred With Recourse

Treated as a Sale by Crest			Treated as a Borrowing by Crest		
Cash	460,000		Cash	460,000	
Due From Factor	25,000*		Due From Factor	25,000	
Loss on Sale of Rec.	15,000**		Discount on Transferred Accts. Rec.	15,000	
Accounts Receivable		500,000	Liability on Transferred Accts. Rec.		500,000
*(5% × $500,000)					
**(3% × $500,000)					

Note two differences: First, when the transaction is classified as a borrowing, Crest Textiles recognizes a liability instead of crediting Accounts Receivable. Second, instead of recording a loss of $15,000 on the transfer, Crest Textiles records a discount under the borrowing of $15,000, which is amortized to interest expense over the borrowing period.

The rules for determining an acceptable practice for accounting for sales of receivables with and without recourse are illustrated on page 337.

A comprehensive illustration of all the entries involved in the sale, collection, and final settlement of these receivables for both Crest Textiles and Commercial Factors is presented in Appendix 7B, page 353.

[7] CICA Emerging Issues Committee, EIC-9, *Transfer of Receivables*, p. 9-2.

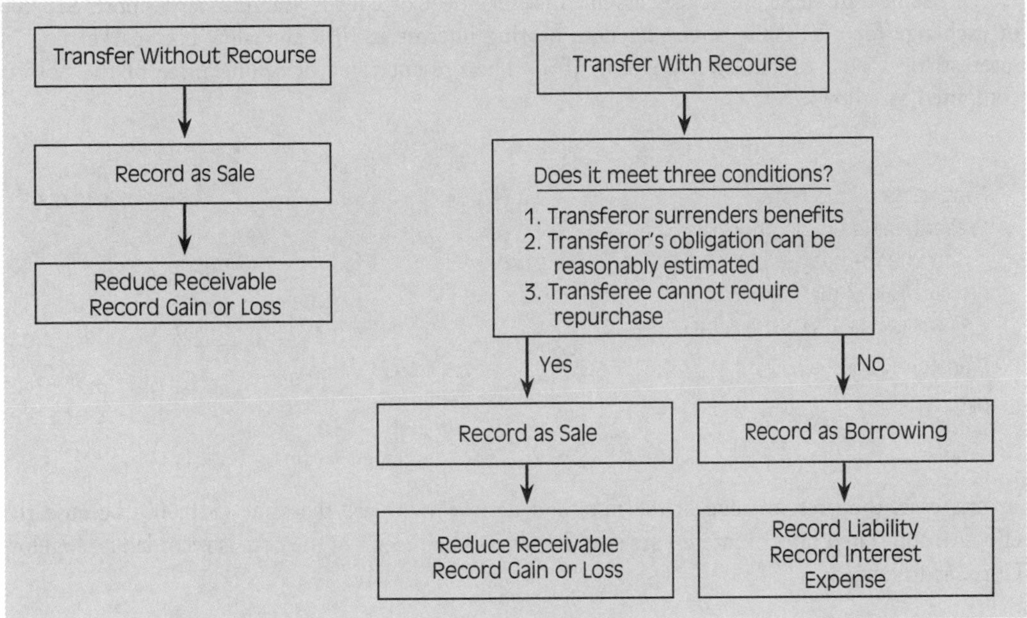

NOTES RECEIVABLE

A note receivable is supported by a formal **promissory note**, which is a written promise to pay a certain sum of money at a specific future date. Such a note is a negotiable instrument that is signed by a **maker** in favour of a designated **payee**, who may legally and readily sell or otherwise transfer the note to others. Although notes contain an interest element because of the time value of money, notes are classified as interest bearing or noninterest bearing. **Interest-bearing notes** have a stated rate of interest, whereas **noninterest-bearing notes** include the interest as part of their face amount instead of stating it explicitly. Notes receivable are considered fairly liquid, even if long term, because they may be easily converted into cash.

Notes receivable are frequently accepted from customers who need to extend the payment period on an outstanding receivable. Notes are sometimes required of high risk or new customers. In addition, notes are often used in loans to employees and subsidiaries and in the sales of property, plant, and equipment. In some industries (e.g., the pleasure and sport boat industry), all credit sales are supported by signed notes. The majority of notes, however, originate from lending transactions. The basic issues in accounting for notes receivable are the same as those for accounts receivable:

1. Recognition.
2. Valuation.
3. Disposition

Recognition of Notes Receivable

> *Objective 8*
>
> Distinguish between accounting for interest-bearing versus noninterest-bearing notes receivable.

The proper amount to record for these notes is the present value of the future cash flows. Determining this amount can become complicated, however, particularly when a noninterest-bearing note or a note bearing an unreasonable interest rate is issued.

Notes Bearing Reasonable Interest. Short-term notes, as already mentioned, are recorded at face value (less allowances) because the interest inherent in the maturity value is immaterial. Long-term notes receivable, however, should be recorded and reported at the ***present value of the cash expected to be collected.*** When the interest stated on an interest-bearing note is equal to the effective (market) rate of interest, the note sells at face value. When the stated rate is different from the market rate, the cash exchanged (present value) will be different from the face value of the note. The difference between the face value and the cash exchanged, either a discount or a premium, is then recorded and amortized over the life of a note to approximate the effective (market) interest rate.

To illustrate these differences, assume that Bigelow Corp. lends Scandinavian Imports $10,000 in exchange for a $10,000, three-year note bearing interest at 10% annually. The market rate of interest for a note of similar risk is also 10%. The present value or selling price of the note is computed as follows.

Face value of the note		$10,000
Present value of the principal:		
$10,000 ($p_{\overline{3}\rceil 10\%}$) = $10,000 (.75132)	$7,513	
Present value of the interest:		
$1,000 ($P_{\overline{3}\rceil 10\%}$) = $1,000 (2.48685)	2,487	
Present value of the note		10,000
Difference		$ -0-

In this case, the present value of the note and its face value are the same ($10,000) because the effective and stated rates of interest are also the same. The receipt of the note is recorded by Bigelow Corp. as follows:

Notes Receivable	10,000	
Cash		10,000

Bigelow Corp. would recognize the interest earned each year as follows:

Cash	1,000	
Interest Revenue		1,000

If the market rate of interest for Scandinavian Imports' note for $10,000 at 10% had been 12%, the present value would have been computed as shown below.

Face value of the note		$10,000
Present value of the principal:		
$10,000 ($p_{\overline{3}\rceil 12\%}$) = $10,000 (.71178)	$7,118	
Present value of the interest:		
$1,000 ($P_{\overline{3}\rceil 12\%}$) = $1,000 (2.40183)	2,402	
Present value of note		9,520
Difference (Discount)		$ 480

In this case, because the effective rate of interest (12%) is greater than the stated rate (10%), the present value of the note is less than the face value; that is, the note was exchanged at a discount. The receipt of the note at a discount is recorded by Bigelow as follows:

Notes Receivable	10,000	
Discount on Notes Receivable		480
Cash		9,520

The discount on notes receivable is a valuation account and is reported on the balance sheet as a contra-asset account to notes receivable. The discount is amortized and interest revenue is recognized annually by the **effective interest method**. The three-year discount amortization and interest revenue schedule is shown on page 339.

On the date of issue, the note has a present value of $9,520. Its unamortized discount—additional interest income to be spread over the three-year life of the note—is $480.

Schedule of Note Discount Amortization
Effective Interest Method
10% Note Discounted at 12%

	Cash Interest 10%	Effective Interest 12%	Discount Amortized	Unamortized Discount Balance	Present Value of Note
Date of issue				**$480**	**$9,520**
End of Year 1	**$1,000**[a]	**$1,142**[b]	**$142**[c]	338[d]	9,662[e]
End of Year 2	1,000	1,159	159	179	9,821
End of Year 3	1,000	1,179	179	–0–	10,000
	$3,000	$3,480	$480		

[a]$10,000 × 10% = $1,000
[b]$9,520 × 12% = $1,142
[c]$1,142 – $1,000 = $142
[d]$480 – $142 = $338
[e]$9,520 + $142 = $9,662

At the end of Year 1, Bigelow receives $1,000 in cash. But its effective interest income is $1,142 ($9,520 × 12%). The difference between $1,000 and $1,142 is the amortized discount, $142. By subtracting $142 from $480, we get $338, the unamortized discount at the end of Year 1. The carrying amount of the note is now $9,662 ($9520 + 142). This process is repeated until the end of Year 3.

Receipt of the annual interest and amortization of the discount for the first year is recorded by Bigelow as follows (amounts per amortization schedule):

Cash	1,000	
Discount on Notes Receivable	142	
Interest Revenue		1,142

When the present value exceeds the face value, the note is exchanged at a premium. The premium is recorded as a debit and amortized using the effective interest method over the life of the note as annual reductions in the amount of interest revenue recognized.

Noninterest-Bearing or Unreasonable Interest-Bearing Notes. Interest is an inherent and natural ingredient of notes receivable, particularly when the note is long term. Yet during the sixties and seventies, numerous business transactions that were material in amount were consummated either with no apparent interest or with a very low stated interest rate.

The accounting profession responded to this practice by issuing a standard that ensures proper accounting for transactions where the form does not reflect the economic substance because it does not provide a realistic interest rate.[8]

The three important categories in the accounting for notes receivable that have an unrealistic interest rate are:

1. Notes received solely for cash.
2. Notes received for cash, but with some right or privilege also being exchanged. For example, a corporation may lend a supplier cash that is receivable five years hence with no stated interest, in exchange for which the supplier agrees to make products available to the lender at lower than prevailing market prices.
3. Notes received in a noncash exchange for property, goods, or services.

[8] "Interest on Receivables and Payables," *Opinions of the Accounting Principles Board No. 21* (New York: AICPA, 1971), par. 12.

Notes Received Solely for Cash. If a noninterest-bearing note (zero coupon) or a note with an unrealistic interest rate is received solely for cash, its present value is the cash paid to the issuer. The interest rate (implicit) is the rate that equates the cash paid with the amounts received in the future. The difference between the future (face) amount and the present value (cash paid) is recorded as a discount or premium and amortized to interest revenue over the life of the note.

To illustrate, assume Jeremiah Company receives a three-year, $10,000, noninterest-bearing note, the present value of which is $7,721.80. The implicit rate that equates the total cash to be received ($10,000 at maturity) to the present value of the future cash flows ($7,721.80) is 9% (the present value of $1 for three periods is $0.77218). The entry to record the transaction is as follows:

Notes Receivable	10,000.00	
Discount on Notes Receivable ($10,000 − $7,721.80)		2,278.20
Cash		7,721.80

Interest revenue at the end of the first year using the effective interest method is recorded as follows:

Discount on Notes Receivable	694.96	
Interest Revenue ($7,721.80 × 9%)		694.96

If a note with an unrealistic interest rate is received, the same procedure is followed. In this case, though, the interest rate is the rate that equates the cash paid to the amounts (principal and interest) to be received in the future.

Note Received for Cash and Other Rights. The lender may also accept a ***note in exchange for cash and other rights and privileges.*** For example, Ideal Equipment Ltd. accepts a five-year, $100,000, noninterest-bearing note from Outland Steel Corp., plus the right to purchase 10,000 tonnes of steel at a bargain price in exchange for $100,000 in cash. Assume that the current rate of interest that would be charged on another note without the right to purchase at a bargain price is 10%. The acceptance of the note is recorded and the present value of the note is computed as follows:

Notes Receivable	100,000	
Prepaid Purchases	37,908	
Discount on Notes Receivable		37,908*
Cash		100,000

*Present value = $100,000 × $p_{\overline{5}|10\%}$ = $100,000 × .62092 = $62,092;
Discount = $100,000 − $62,092 = $37,908.

The difference between the $62,092 present value of the note and its maturity value of $100,000 represents interest of $37,908. It is amortized to interest revenue over the five-year life of the note, using the effective interest method. The excess of the $100,000 over the $62,092 represents an asset, Prepaid Purchases. Prepaid Purchases is allocated to purchases or inventory in proportion to the number of tonnes of steel purchased each year relative to the total 10,000 tonnes for which a bargain price is available. For example, if 3,000 tonnes of steel were purchased during the first year of the five-year bargain period, the following entry would be recorded by Ideal Equipment:

Purchases (Inventory)	11,372	
Prepaid Purchases (3,000/10,000 × $37,908)		11,372

Note that although Prepaid Purchases and the Discount on Notes Receivable are both recorded initially as $37,908, they are written off differently. Prepaid Purchases are written off in the ratio of the tonnes purchased, while the discount is amortized using the effective interest method. The value of the right or privilege, in this case the price reduction, aids in determining the interest implicit in the transaction.

Notes Received for Property, Goods, or Services. When a ***note is received in exchange for property, goods, or services*** in a bargained transaction entered into at arm's length, the stated interest rate is presumed to be fair except for these conditions:

1. No interest rate is stated.
2. The stated interest rate is unreasonable.
3. The face amount of the note is materially different from the current cash sales price for the same or similar items or from the current market value of the debt instrument.

In these circumstances, the present value of the note is measured by the fair value of the property, goods, or services or by an amount that reasonably approximates the market value of the note. To illustrate, Oasis Development Ltd. sold a corner lot to Rusty Pelican as a restaurant site and accepted in exchange a five-year note having a maturity value of $35,247 and no stated interest rate. The land originally cost Oasis $14,000 and had an appraised fair value of $20,000. Given the criterion above, it is acceptable to use the fair market value of the land, $20,000, as the present value of the note. The entry to record the sale is as follows:

Notes Receivable	35,247	
Discount on Notes Receivable ($35,247 − $20,000)		15,247
Land		14,000
Gain on Sale of Land ($20,000 − $14,000)		6,000

The discount is amortized to interest revenue over the five-year life of the note, under the effective interest method.

Imputing an Interest Rate. In each of the previous situations, the effective or real interest rate was evident or determinable by other factors involved in the exchange, such as the fair market value of what was either given or received. But if the fair value of the property, goods, services, or other rights is not determinable and if the note has no ready market, the problem of determining the present value of the note is more difficult. To estimate the present value of a note under such circumstances, an applicable interest rate that may differ from the stated interest rate is approximated. This process of interest rate approximation is called **imputation** and the resulting interest rate is called an **imputed interest rate.** The imputed interest rate is used to establish the present value of the note by discounting, at that rate, all future receipts (interest and principal) on the note.

> The objective for computing the appropriate interest rate is to approximate the rate which would have resulted if an independent borrower and an independent lender had negotiated a similar transaction under comparable terms and conditions with the option to pay the cash price upon purchase or to give a note for the amount of the purchase which bears the prevailing rate of interest to maturity. The rate used for valuation purposes will normally be at least equal to the rate at which the debtor can obtain financing of a similar nature from other sources at the date of the transaction.[9]

The choice of a rate is affected by the prevailing rates for similar instruments of issuers with similar credit ratings. It is also affected specifically by restrictive covenants, collateral, payment schedule, the existing prime interest rate, etc. Determination of the imputed interest rate is made when the note is received; any subsequent changes in prevailing interest rates are ignored.

Accounting for Imputed Interest. On December 31, 1994, Brown Interiors Limited rendered architectural services and accepted in exchange a long-term promissory note with a face value of $550,000, a due date of December 31, 1999, and a stated interest rate of 2%, receivable at the end of each year. The fair value of the services is not readily determinable and the note is not readily marketable.

---

[9] *Ibid.*, par. 13.

Under the circumstances—the maker's credit rating, the absence of collateral, the prime interest rate at that date, and the prevailing interest on the maker's outstanding debt—an 8% interest rate is determined to be appropriate. The present value of the note and the imputed fair value of the architectural services are determined as follows.

Face value of the note		$550,000
Present value of $550,000 due in 5 years		
at 8%: $550,000 × $p_{\overline{5}\rceil 8\%}$ = $550,000 × .68058	$374,319	
Present value of $11,000 ($550,000 × 2%) payable		
annually for 5 years at 8% =		
$11,000 × $P_{\overline{5}\rceil 8\%}$ = $11,000 × 3.99271	43,920	
Present value of the note		418,239
Discount		$131,761

The receipt of the note in exchange for the services is recorded as follows:

December 31, 1994

Notes Receivable	550,000	
Discount on Notes Receivable		131,761
Revenue from Services		418,239

The five-year amortization schedule appears below.

Schedule of Note Discount Amortization

Effective Interest Method

2% Note Discounted at 8% (Imputed)

Date	Cash Interest (2%)	Effective Interest (8%)	Discount Amortized	Unamortized Discount Balance	Present Value of Note
12/31/94				**$131,761**	**$418,239**
12/31/95	**$11,000**[a]	**$ 33,459**[b]	**$ 22,459**[c]	109,302[d]	440,698[e]
12/31/96	11,000	35,256	24,256	85,046	464,954
12/31/97	11,000	37,196	26,196	58,850	491,150
12/31/98	11,000	39,292	28,292	30,558	519,442
12/31/99	11,000	41,558[f]	30,558	-0-	550,000
	$55,000	$186,761	$131,761		

[a]$550,000 × 2% = $11,000
[b]$418,239 × 8% = $33,459
[c]$33,459 − $11,000 = $22,459
[d]$131,761 − $22,459 = $109,302
[e]$418,239 + $22,459 = $440,689
[f]$3 adjustment to compensate for rounding

On December 31, 1994, the date of issue, the 2% coupon note has a present value of $418,239 and an unamortized discount balance of $131,761. The cash interest payment is $11,000 ($550,000 × 2%) for all years. Interest expense is $33,459 ($418,239 × 8%) and the amortized discount is $22,459 ($33,459 − $11,000) for 1995. At the end of 1995, the unamortized discount balance is $109,302 ($131,761 − $22,459) and the carrying amount of the note is $440,698 ($418,239 + $22,459). This process is repeated until December 31, 1999.

Valuation of Notes Receivable

Like accounts receivable, short-term notes receivable are recorded and reported at their net realizable value; that is, at their face amount less all necessary allowances. The primary notes receivable allowance account is Allowance for Doubtful Accounts. The computations and estimations involved in valuing short-term notes receivable and recording bad debt expense and the related allowance are exactly the same as for trade accounts receivable. Either a percentage of sales revenue or an analysis of the receivables can be used to estimate the amount of uncollectibles.

Long-term notes receivable can pose additional estimation problems. We need only look at the problems our financial institutions, most notably our largest banks, are having in collecting their receivables from energy loans, agricultural loans, and loans to less developed countries.

Disposition of Notes Receivable

Notes are usually held to maturity date, at which time the face value plus any accrued interest is collected and the note is removed from the accounts. Frequently, however, the holder of the note speeds up the conversion to cash by transferring the receivable to another party. These transfers are usually referred to as "discounting the note before maturity date."

Objective 9

Explain the accounting procedures in transferring or selling notes receivable.

Discounting Notes Receivable. Notes receivable may be converted to cash through discounting at a bank. The bank accepts the note and pays the holder cash equal to the note's maturity value less a discount that represents the bank's financing (interest) charge. At maturity, the bank collects the face value of the note plus interest from the maker.

Notes may be discounted with or without recourse. In those instances when a note is discounted *without recourse*, the Notes Receivable account is credited as in an outright sale. The transferor no longer has an asset, having conveyed all the risks and benefits of ownership to the transferee. In a nonrecourse transfer, the difference between the book carrying value of the note and the cash proceeds is recorded as a gain or loss on sale.

The more common transaction is discounting a note at a bank *with recourse*. If the maker fails to pay at maturity, the bank presents the note to the transferor, who is then liable for payment. Is the discounting of a note a sale with a gain or loss to be recognized and a contingent liability to be disclosed? Or is it a borrowing transaction that is accounted for by retaining the notes receivable in the accounts, reporting the endorser's obligation among the current liabilities, and recognizing interest expense or interest revenue? As discussed in connection with accounts receivable factored with recourse, if two conditions are met (see page 336), good accounting practice requires that the transfer (discounting) of notes receivable with recourse be reported as a sale and a gain or loss recognized. Likewise, if the transfer with recourse does not meet those two conditions, the transaction is accounted for as a borrowing with a liability recorded and reported along with interest expense.

When notes are transferred, the purchaser of the note uses traditional concepts of present value to determine the amount to pay. Payment is based on the present value of the face value plus the present value of the interest payments discounted at the rate the purchaser desires to earn.

The discounting of short-term notes that have only one interest payment date remaining sometimes disregards present value computations and uses a special procedure. This procedure, often referred to as "discounting notes receivable" is a misnomer because present value measurement is not used. To illustrate this procedure, accounting for a discounted note receivable becomes a six-step process:

1. Compute the maturity value of the note (face value plus interest to maturity).
2. Compute the discount (the bank's discount rate times the maturity value times the time to maturity).
3. Compute the proceeds (maturity value minus the bank's discount).

4. Compute the book carrying value of the note (face value plus interest accrued to date of discounting).
5. Compute the gain or loss, if a sale, or the interest revenue or expense, if a borrowing (proceeds minus the book carrying value).
6. Record the journal entry.

To illustrate, on July 30, Reliable Appliance Ltd. discounts at the bank a customer's three-month, $10,000 note receivable dated June 30 and bearing interest at 12%. The bank accepts the note *with recourse* and discounts it at 15%. The maturity value, discount, proceeds, book carrying value, and interest element are computed as follows.

Discounting With Recourse

	Face value of note	$10,000.00
	Plus interest ($10,000 × .12 × 3/12)	300.00
Step 1.	**Maturity value**	**10,300.00**
Step 2.	Less discount ($10,300 × .15 × 2/12)	257.50
Step 3.	**Proceeds**	**10,042.50**
Step 4.	Book carrying value ($10,000 + [$10,000 × .12 × 1/12])	10,100.00
Step 5.	**Interest expense or loss on sale**	**$ 57.50**

When recorded as a sale (see the example on page 345), the transferor would disclose its contingent liability on the discounted notes with recourse by reporting the contingency in a note. Alternatively, the endorser could credit Notes Receivable Discounted, instead of Notes Receivable, for $10,000 and report it as a contra asset deducted from Notes Receivable in the Current Asset section. This would serve to disclose the endorser's contingent liability for default by the maker of the note.

Notice that the first two journal entries are the same for a note treated as a sale and a note treated as a borrowing. In the third entry, however, the borrowing assumes that a new liability is created—Liability on Discounted Notes Receivable. This assumes that if the borrower defaults, then the endorser pays the note (as reflected in the last journal entry).

Dishonoured Notes. Notes receivable that are not paid at maturity (whether discounted or not) remain notes receivable and are considered notes receivable past due. Defaulted notes should be separately classified on the balance sheet. If all efforts to collect fail, the note is written off as a loss. Whether the loss is charged to the Allowance for Doubtful Accounts or directly to a loss account depends on (1) whether the company has an Allowance for Doubtful Accounts and (2) whether the periodic provisions cover losses only on accounts receivable or on both accounts and notes receivable.

CONCEPTUAL ISSUES RELATED TO THE TRANSFER OF RECEIVABLES

As indicated in the above discussion, the transfer of receivables to a third party for cash takes one of three forms:[10]

1. One form is to borrow from a third party and ***assign or pledge the receivables*** as collateral. Both the form of this transaction and its substance suggest that it be accounted for and reported as a borrowing.

[10] Understanding these transactions is made more difficult by the inconsistent use of terms to describe these transactions in practice. When you encounter such transactions, classify them in accordance with their basic nature as one of the three forms presented here.

Entries for Sale or Borrowing

Discounting a Sale			Discounting a Borrowing		
Receipt of a 3-month note from an overdue customer, June 30:					
Notes Receivable	10,000.00		Notes Receivable	10,000.00	
Accounts Receivable		10,000.00	Accounts Receivable		10,000.00
Interest accrued (June 30–July 30) at date of discounting, July 30:					
Interest Receivable	100.00		Interest Receivable	100.00	
Interest Revenue		100.00	Interest Revenue		100.00
Discounting of notes receivable with recourse, July 30:					
Cash	10,042.50		Cash	10,042.50	
Loss on Sale of Note	57.50		Interest Expense	57.50	
Notes Receivable		10,000.00	Liability on Discounted		
Interest Receivable		100.00	Notes Receivable		10,000.00
			Interest Receivable		100.00
If payment of note by the maker at maturity date, September 30:					
			Liability on Discounted		
(No entry)			Notes Receivable	10,000.00	
			Notes Receivable		10,000.00
If maker defaults and endorser pays note the following day with interest of $300 plus the bank protest fee of $25, October 1:					
Notes Receivable			Notes Receivable		
Past Due*	10,325.00		Past Due*	10,325.00	
Cash		10,325.00	Cash		10,325.00
			Liability on Discounted		
			Notes Receivable	10,000.00	
			Notes Receivable		10,000.00

* Accounts Receivable is frequently used as the account to reinstate the default.

2. A second form is to ***transfer the receivables without recourse*** to a third party in exchange for cash. Both the form of this transaction and its substance suggest that it be accounted for and reported as a *sale*.

3. A third form is to ***transfer the receivables with recourse*** to a third party in exchange for cash. In this case, the form of the transaction may be either a sale or a borrowing, depending on the facts.

At one extreme are outright sales of assets and at the other are borrowings collateralized by assets (pledges). In between are sales of assets with recourse. The transactions at the two extremes are easy to account for—the ones in the middle create accounting problems.

Regarding the in-between situation, the authors believe that the proceeds from the transfer of receivables with recourse should be reported initially as a liability. The transfer should not be treated as a sale of the receivables unless and until both the future economic benefits embodied in the receivables and the related inherent risks of collectibility are transferred. The transferor's retention of credit risk through the recourse provisions generally leaves the transferor in a position undistinguishable from that of any other borrower.

ACCOUNTS AND NOTES RECEIVABLE: BALANCE SHEET PRESENTATION

The general rules in classifying the typical transactions in the receivable section are (1) segregate the different receivables that an enterprise possesses, if material; (2) ensure that the valuation accounts are appropriately offset against the proper receivable accounts; (3) determine that receivables classified in the Current Asset section will be converted into cash within the year or the operating cycle, whichever is longer; (4) disclose any loss contingencies that exist on the receivables; and (5) disclose any receivables assigned or pledged as collateral.

Any discount or premium resulting from the determination of present value in notes receivable transactions is not an asset or a liability separable from the note that gives rise to it. Therefore, the discount or premium is reported in the balance sheet as a direct deduction from or addition to the note's face amount. It is not classified as a deferred charge or deferred credit. However, the face amount of the note and its effective interest rate may be disclosed in the balance sheet or in the notes. If several notes are involved, the principal amount and the balance of total unamortized discount may be presented in the balance sheet, with the details of each note disclosed individually in a note or a separate schedule to the balance sheet. The following asset sections of Colton Corporation's balance sheet illustrate many of the disclosures of receivables.

Colton Corporation
Partial Balance Sheet
As of December 31, 1994

Current assets		
Cash and cash equivalent		$ 1,870,250
Accounts receivable (Note 2)	$8,977,673	
Less allowance for doubtful accounts[11]	500,226	
	8,477,447	
Advances to subsidiaries due 9/30/95	2,090,000	
Notes receivable—trade (Note 2)	1,532,000	
Dividends and interest receivable	75,500	
Federal income taxes refundable	146,704	
Other receivables and claims (including debit balances in accounts payable)	174,620	12,496,271
Total current assets		14,366,521
Noncurrent receivables		
Notes receivable from officers and key employees		376,090
Claims receivable (litigation settlement to be collected over four years)		585,000

Note 2: Accounts and notes receivable

In November 1994, the Company arranged with a finance company to refinance a part of its indebtedness. The loan is evidenced by a 12% note payable. The note is payable on demand and is secured by substantially all the accounts receivable.

In May 1994, the Company entered into an agreement with a financial institution whereby the Company had the right to sell designated receivables, with recourse, not to exceed $3,000,000 at any time. During the period May 1 through September 20, 1994, proceeds totaling $2,480,000 were received from such sales. Losses totaling $202,640 were recognized on these sales during 1994. As of December 31, 1994, $171,500 of transferred receivables remains uncollected.

In several countries outside Canada, notes receivable are discounted with banks. The contingent liability under such arrangements amounted to $751,000 at December 31, 1994.

---

[11] Although disclosure of the Allowance for Doubtful Accounts is not mandatory in Canada, some firms do so on a voluntary basis. *Financial Reporting in Canada, 1991* indicates that about 6% of the sample firms choose to refer to the Allowance for Doubtful Accounts in their annual financial statements.

FUNDAMENTAL CONCEPTS

1. To be reported as cash, an item must be readily available for the payment of current obligations and it must be free from any contractual restrictions.
2. Cash presents special management and control problems. It is the asset most readily convertible into other types of assets (i.e. most subject to embezzlement). Its amount must also be managed carefully so that neither too much nor too little is available at any one time.
3. An imprest petty cash system is frequently used to pay small amounts of money for items such as postage, minor office supplies, taxi fares, and other small expense payments.
4. Cash on deposit with a bank is not available for count and must therefore be verified. A bank reconciliation is a schedule explaining the differences between the depositor's record of cash in the bank and the bank's record (bank statement) of cash on deposit.
5. A current asset classification that has become popular is Cash and Cash Equivalents.
6. Restricted cash is classified separately either in the Current Asset or in the Long-Term Asset section, depending on the date of availability or disbursement.
7. A compensating balance is that portion of a deposit maintained by a depositor as support for existing borrowing arrangements or future credit availability with a lending institution.
8. Current (short-term) receivables are claims against others for money, goods, or services collectible within one year or the operating cycle, whichever is longer.
9. Although the net method of recording credit sales is theoretically correct, the gross method is used almost universally because of bookkeeping convenience and lack of materiality.
10. In accounting for uncollectible receivables, the allowance method, which conforms to the accrual accounting principles, should be used over the direct write-off method, which violates such principles.
11. The percentage-of-sales approach (income statement approach) emphasizes the matching principle by relating the bad debt expense to the current period's credit sales.
12. The percentage-of-receivables approach (balance sheet approach) reports accounts receivable at net realizable value by adjusting the allowance account.
13. To accelerate the receipt of cash from accounts receivable, many companies assign (pledge as security for a loan) or factor (sell) them.
14. Receivables may be transferred or discounted with or without recourse. Transfers without recourse are accounted for as sales, whereas transfers with recourse may be accounted for as sales or a borrowing, depending on the circumstances.
15. The sale of receivables results in the recognition of a loss on sale and removal of the receivables from the transferor's books. Borrowing against receivables results in the recognition of a liability and interest expense.
16. Interest is inherent in all borrowing transactions, even though some commercial notes have no stated interest rate. In the absence of an explicit interest rate, or if an unreasonably low rate is stated, a reasonable amount of interest must be imputed.

APPENDIX 7A

Four-Column Bank Reconciliation

To illustrate a bank reconciliation, Nugget Mining Company's books show a cash balance at the Bank of Montreal on November 30, 1994, of $20,502. The bank statement covering the month of November showed an ending balance of $22,190. An examination of Nugget's accounting records and November bank statement identified the following reconciling items:

1. A deposit of $3,680 was mailed November 30 but does not appear on the bank statement.
2. Cheques written in November but not charged to the November bank statement are:

Cheque 7327	$ 150
7348	4,820
7349	31

3. Nugget has not yet recorded the $600 interest collected by the bank on November 20 on Quebec Hydro bonds held by the bank for Nugget.
4. Bank service charges of $18 are not yet recorded on Nugget's books.
5. One of Nugget's customer's cheques for $220 was returned with the bank statement and marked NSF. The bank treated this bad cheque as a disbursement.
6. Nugget discovered that cheque 7322, written in November for $131 in payment of an account payable, was recorded in their books as $311.
7. A cheque of Nugent Oil Co. Ltd. in the amount of $175 accompanied the bank statement and was incorrectly charged to Nugget Mining.

The reconciliation of bank and book balances to the correct cash balance of $21,044 would appear as follows.

Nugget Mining Company
Bank Reconciliation
Bank of Montreal, November 30, 1994

Balance per bank statement (end of period)		$22,190
Add: Deposit in transit	$3,680	
Bank error—incorrect cheque charged to account by bank	175	3,855
		$26,045
Deduct: Outstanding cheques:		
#7327	$ 150	
#7348	4,820	
#7349	31	5,001
Correct cash balance		**$21,044**
Balance per books		$20,502
Add: Interest collected by the bank	$ 600	
Error in recording cheque #7322	180	780
		$21,282
Deduct: Bank service charges	$ 18	
NSF cheque returned	220	238
Corrected cash balance		**$21,044**

The journal entries required to adjust and correct Nugget Mining's books in early December 1994 are taken from the items in the Balance Per Books section and are as follows:

Cash	600	
Interest Revenue		600
(To record interest on Quebec Hydro bonds, collected by bank)		
Cash	180	
Accounts Payable		180
(To correct error in recording amount of cheque #7322)		
Office Expense—Bank Charges	18	
Cash		18
(To record bank service charges for November)		
Accounts Receivable	220	
Cash		220
(To record customer's cheque returned NSF)		

When the entries are posted, Nugget's cash account will have a balance of $21,044. Nugget should return the Nugent Oil Co. Ltd. cheque to the Bank of Montreal and inform the bank of the error.

FOUR-COLUMN BANK RECONCILIATION

In addition to the method presented above, another form of reconciliation, frequently used by auditors and typically illustrated in auditing textbooks, is the so-called **proof-of-cash** or **four-column bank reconciliation.** It is an expanded version of the bank reconciliation illustrated previously in this appendix. The proof-of-cash form of reconciliation is actually four reconciliations in one:

1. Reconciliation of the **beginning-of-the-period cash balances** per the bank statement and the books (first column).
2. Reconciliation of the **current period cash receipts** (deposits) per the bank statement to receipts recorded in the books (second column).
3. Reconciliation of the **current period cash disbursements** per the bank statement to disbursements recorded in the books (third column).
4. Reconciliation of the **end-of-the-period cash balances** per the bank statement and the books (fourth column).

The top row (Per bank statement; see page 350) is a summary of the transactions for the period as taken from the bank statement. The beginning and ending bank balances are shown on the bank statement, as are the bank receipts (as shown in the Deposits column) and the bank disbursements (as shown in the Charges or Cheques cashed column).

The "per books" line is a summary of the cash transactions as recorded in the books. These totals should be taken directly from the books, preferably from the Cash account itself, which should, of course, show receipts and disbursements as debit and credit entries and the beginning and ending cash balances.

The left-hand and right-hand columns are simply *end-of-the-prior-period and end-of-the-current-period* reconciliations, the preparation of which is illustrated on page 350. The two centre columns, receipts and disbursements, tie the left-hand column and right-hand column reconciliations together. With few exceptions, the amounts needed to complete these centre columns may be found in the figures included in either the top or bottom rows or in the left- and right-hand columns; no new data need be added.[12]

---

[12] An exception would be a customer's cheque deposited, returned NSF, and redeposited without entry in the same period. In this situation, receipts and disbursements per bank would be higher than the receipts and disbursements per books. Deposits would have been reported twice in the bank statement but only recorded once for the books' purposes. Also, the bank would have shown a disbursement when the cheque bounced. No disbursement has been recorded in the accounting records.

The four-column proof of cash is preferred by auditors as a means of identifying all differences between the books and the bank statement during the period covered by the reconciliation. It is generally prepared by auditors when a company has weak internal control over cash; it assists in identifying unauthorized and unrecorded transfers of cash.

To illustrate the four-column reconciliation, the data provided for the Nugget Mining Company at November 30 on this page will be used, along with the following information:

1. The cash balance as of October 31, 1994, per the bank statement (the beginning of November balance) was $17,520.
2. The cash balance as of October 31, 1994, per Nugget's books was $18,020.
3. The total cash receipts (deposits) per the November bank statement are $96,450. These receipts include a deposit in transit of $4,200 at October 31.
4. The total cash receipts per Nugget's books during November are $95,330.
5. The total cash disbursements per the bank statement for November are $91,780. These disbursements include $3,700 of cheques outstanding at October 31.
6. The total cash disbursements per the books during November are $92,848.

The completed reconciliation would appear as follows.

Nugget Mining Company
Proof of Cash for November 1994
Bank of Montreal: Chequing Account

	Balance October 31	November Receipts	November Disbursements	Balance November 30
Per bank statement	$17,520	$96,450	$91,780	$22,190
Deposits in transit:				
at October 31	4,200	(4,200)		
at November 30		3,680		3,680
Outstanding cheques:				
at October 31	(3,700)		(3,700)	
at November 30			5,001	(5,001)
Bank error—incorrect cheque charged by bank			(175)	175
Correct amounts	**$18,020**	**$95,930**	**$92,906**	**$21,044**
Per books	$18,020	$95,330	$92,848	$20,502
Interest collected by bank		600		600
Error in recording cheque #7322			(180)	180
Unrecorded service charges at November 30			18	(18)
NSF cheque returned			220	(220)
Correct amounts	$18,020	$95,930	$92,906	$21,044

An alternative procedure for preparing a proof-of-cash reconciliation involves reconciling from the bank balance to the book balance, rather than reconciling both amounts to a correct cash balance. This alternative follows on page 351.

(Bank to Book Form)
Nugget Mining Company
Proof of Cash for November 1994
Bank of Montreal: Chequing Account

	Balance October 31	November Receipts	November Disbursements	Balance November 30
Per bank statement	**$17,520**	**$96,450**	**$91,780**	**$22,190**
Deposits in transit:				
at October 31	4,200	(4,200)		
at November 30		3,680		3,680
Outstanding cheques:				
at October 31	(3,700)		(3,700)	
at November 30			5,001	(5,001)
Bank error—incorrect cheque			(175)	175
Interest collected by bank		(600)		(600)
Error per books—cheque #7322			180	(180)
Unrecorded service charges				
at November 30			(18)	18
NSF cheque returned by bank			(220)	220
Per books	**$18,020**	**$95,330**	**$92,848**	**$20,502**

The preceding bank to book reconciliation method is generally illustrated in auditing textbooks. The auditors frequently use this form because their main objective is to identify all of the items that make up the difference between the bank's records and the depositor's records. Preparation of the adjusting entries is secondary. This form is usually more difficult because each of the reconciling items must be analysed carefully to determine whether an addition or subtraction from the top-of-the-column "Per bank" amount is the correct reconciliation treatment.

APPENDIX 7B

Comprehensive Illustrations of Transfers of Receivables

The complexities and details of recording journal entries related to the transfer, collection, and final settlement of transferred receivables are discussed in this appendix. Discussed first is the transfer of receivables *without recourse* and then the transfer of receivables *with recourse*, (a) as a *sale* transaction and (b) as a *borrowing* transaction.

TRANSFER OF RECEIVABLES WITHOUT RECOURSE

Crest Textiles Ltd. factors $500,000 of accounts receivable with Commercial Factors Ltd., on a *without recourse* basis. On May 1, the receivable records are transferred to Commercial Factors Ltd., which will receive the collections. Commercial Factors assesses a finance charge of 3% and retains an amount equal to 5% of the accounts receivable. Crest Textiles handles returned goods, claims for defective goods (allowances), and disputes concerning shipments. Crest has not recorded any bad debts expense relative to these receivables. In the process of collecting the cash, Commercial Factors acknowledges sales discounts but charges the cost of such discounts to Crest Textiles by debiting the Due to Crest Textiles account. Credit losses (uncollectible accounts) are absorbed by Commercial Factors, and on the basis of an analysis of the accounts purchased, Commercial Factors allows $4,100 for uncollectible accounts.

Entries for Factored Receivables Without Recourse

Crest Textiles Ltd.			Commercial Factors Ltd.		
Sale of accounts receivable without recourse on May 1:					
Cash	460,000		Accounts Receivable	500,000	
Due From Factor	25,000*		Due to Crest Textiles		25,000
Loss on Sale of Rec.	15,000**		Financing Revenue		15,000
Accounts Receivable		500,000	Cash		460,000
			Bad Debt Expense	4,100	
			Allow. for Doubtful Accounts		4,100
*(5% × $500,000)					
**(3% × $500,000)					
Transactions in May and June: Collections of $483,800 by factor; sales returns and allowances of $9,500; sales discounts taken of $2,600; and uncollectibles of $4,100 are written off by the factor.					
Sales Ret. and Allow.	9,500		Cash	483,800	
Sales Discounts	2,600		Due to Crest Textiles	12,100	
Due From Factor		12,100	Accounts Receivable		495,900
			Allow. for Doubtful Accounts	4,100	
			Accounts Receivable		4,100
Final settlement between Crest Textiles and Commercial Factors:					
Cash	12,900		Due to Crest Textiles	12,900	
Due From Factor ($25,000 − $9,500 − $2,600)		12,900	Cash		12,900

Note from the entries above that the factor's income is the difference between the financing revenue of $15,000 and the bad debt expense of $4,100. As indicated earlier, in a without-recourse transfer of receivables, the factor absorbs the loss from uncollectibles. Crest Textiles absorbs the cost of sales discounts and sales returns and allowances.

TRANSFER OF RECEIVABLES WITH RECOURSE

To illustrate the differences between the two methods of accounting for a transfer of receivables with recourse—in one case, a sale, and in another case, a borrowing—the same data previously used in the Crest Textiles/Commercial Factors illustration will be used. (The same data was chosen for purposes of comparability, even though the situations in real life would dictate different rates, risks, etc.) One different piece of information is Crest's estimate that $4,100 of the accounts transferred to Commercial Factors will not be paid by the debtors. The entries for both a sale and a borrowing by Crest Textiles appears below.

Entries for Factored Receivables With Recourse

Crest Textiles, Inc.

Treated as a **Sale** by Crest			Treated as a **Borrowing** by Crest		
Transfer of accounts receivable on May 1:					
Cash	460,000		Cash	460,000	
Due From Factor	25,000*		Due From Factor	25,000*	
Loss on Sale of Rec.	15,000**		Discount on Transferred Accts. Rec.	15,000**	
Accounts Receivable		500,000	Liability on Transferred Accts. Rec.		500,000
*(5% × $500,000)					
**(3% × $500,000)					
Recognition of doubtful accounts on May 1:					
Bad Debt Expense	4,100		Bad Debt Expense	4,100	
Due from Factor		4,100	Allow. for Doubtful Accounts		4,100
Transactions in May and June: Collections of $483,800 by the factor; sales returns and allowances of $9,500; sales discounts taken of $2,600; and uncollectibles of $4,100 materialize:					
Sales Ret. and Allow.	9,500		Same entry		
Sales Discounts	2,600				
Due From Factor		12,100			
			Allow. for Doubtful Accts.	4,100	
			Due From Factor		4,100
			Liability on Transferred Accts. Rec.	500,000*	
			Accounts Receivable		500,000*
			*($483,800 + $9,500 + $2,600 + $4,100)		
			Interest Expense	15,000	
			Discount on Transferred Accts. Rec.		15,000
Final settlement between Crest Textiles and the factor:					
Cash	8,800		Same entry		
Due From Factor		8,800*			
*($25,000 – $9,500 $2,600 – $4,100)					

First, note that in the borrowing-with-recourse example, Crest Textiles credited a liability on May 1 instead of crediting Accounts Receivable. Second, in both with-recourse cases, Crest Textiles reimburses the factor for the $4,100 of uncollectible accounts and records the bad debt expense on its books, whereas in the without-recourse illustration shown on page 352, Commercial Factors absorbed the loss due to uncollectibility. However, because accounts receivable are removed from the books when the transfer is treated as a sale, it is meaningless to credit an allowance account when recognizing the bad debt expense. Therefore, Crest immediately credited Due From Factor for the $4,100, thereby crediting the factor for the bad debts anticipated. Third, Crest recognized interest expense of $15,000 over the two months the receivables were outstanding (borrowing situation) instead of recording the loss on sale of $15,000 at May 1.

Note: All **asterisked** questions, cases, exercises, and problems relate to material contained in the appendices to this chapter.

QUESTIONS

1. What may be included under the heading of "cash"?

2. In what accounts should the following items be classified?
   (a) Coins and currency.
   (b) Treasury (government) bonds.
   (c) Certificate of deposit.
   (d) Cash in a bank that is in receivership.
   (e) NSF cheque (returned with bank statement).
   (f) Deposit in foreign bank (exchangeability limited).
   (g) Postdated cheques.
   (h) Cash (to be used for retirement of long-term bonds).
   (i) Deposits in transit.
   (j) Three shares of General Motors stock (intention is to sell in one year or less).
   (k) Savings and chequing account balances.
   (l) Petty cash.
   (m) Stamps.
   (n) Travel advances.

3. Distinguish among the following: (1) a general chequing account, (2) an imprest bank account, and (3) a lockbox account.

4. What is electronic funds transfer and what is the effect of its widespread use likely to have on record-keeping and accounting?

5. Define a "compensating balance." How should a compensating balance be reported?

6. DMI reported in a recent annual report "Restricted cash for debt redemption." In which section of the balance sheet would this item be reported?

7. What are the reasons for a company to give trade discounts? Why are trade discounts not recorded in the accounts like cash discounts?

8. What are two methods of recording accounts receivable transactions when a cash discount situation is involved? Which is the most theoretically correct? Which is used in practice most of the time? Why?

9. What are the basic problems that occur in the valuation of accounts receivable?

10. Why is the account Allowance for Sales Returns and Allowances sometimes used? What other similar types of allowance accounts are employed? What is their purpose?

11. What is the theoretical justification of the allowance method as contrasted with the direct write-off method of accounting for bad debts?

12. Indicate how well the percentage-of-sales method and the aging method accomplish the objectives of the allowance method of accounting for bad debts.

13. Of what merit is the contention that the allowance method lacks the objectivity of the direct write-off method? Discuss in terms of accounting's measurement function.

14. Because of calamitous earthquake losses, Tritt Ltd., one of your client's oldest and largest customers, suddenly and unexpectedly became bankrupt. Approximately 30% of your client's total sales have been made to Tritt Ltd. during each of the past several years. The amount due from Tritt Ltd.—none of which is collectible—equals 22% of total accounts receivable, an amount that is considerably in excess of what was determined to be an adequate provision for doubtful accounts at the close of the preceding year. How would your client record the write-off of the Tritt Ltd. receivable if it is using the allowance method of accounting for bad debts? Justify your suggested treatment.

15. What is the normal procedure for handling the collection of accounts receivable previously written off using the direct write-off method? The allowance method?

16. Leopard Inc. shows a balance of $300,000 in Accounts Receivable on December 31, 1994. Of this amount, $100,000 is assigned to the Canadian Finance Co. Ltd. as security for a loan of $82,000. Illustrate three satisfactory methods for showing this information on the balance sheet for December 31, 1994.

17. Identify three forms by which receivables can be transferred to a third party for cash. Conceptually, what is the nature or substance of each form?

18. Identify the different methods of disclosing the loss contingency for notes receivable discounted with recourse.

19. What is imputed interest? In what situations is it necessary to impute an interest rate for notes receivable? What are the considerations involved when imputing an appropriate interest rate?

20. On January 1, 1994, Porter Ltd. sells property for which it had paid $490,000 to Williams Limited, receiving in return William's noninterest-bearing note for $800,000, payable in five years. What entry would Porter make to record the sale, assuming that Porter frequently sells similar items of property for a cash sales price of $655,000?

21. Walker Inc. includes in its trial balance for December 31 an item for "Accounts Receivable, $700,000." This balance consists of the following items:

Due from regular customers	$523,000
Refund receivable on prior year's income taxes (an established claim)	10,000
Loans to officers	22,000
Loan to wholly owned subsidiary	45,500
Advances to creditors for goods ordered	61,000
Accounts receivable assigned as security for loans payable	21,500
Notes receivable past due plus interest on these notes	17,000
Total	$700,000

Illustrate how these items should be shown in the balance sheet as of December 31.

CASES

C7-1 **(CASH REPORTING)** Presented below are two financial statement excerpts. Answer the question(s) that follow each of these excerpts:

1. Penn Central Limited reported the following information.

	Current Year	Prior Year
	(in thousands)	
Current Assets:		
Cash and short-term investments (Note 2)	$9,123	$5,227

Note 2: Cash and short-term investments consisted of the following:

	Current Year	Prior Year
	(in thousands)	
Cash on hand and demand deposits	$ 554	$1,809
Temporary cash investments	8,569	3,418
	$9,123	$5,227

Short-term investments are stated at cost that approximates market value.

Penn Central Limited does not maintain any significant formal or informal compensating balance arrangements with financial institutions.

Instructions

(a) Why does the company report the amount of the short-term investments in the notes to the financial statements?

This item should be separately disclosed details of the arrangement in the notes.

(b) What are compensating balance arrangements and how should they be reported in the financial statements?

(c) Indicate the possible differences between cash equivalents and short-term investments.

2. Manville Corporation Ltd. presented the following information.

	Current Year	Prior Year
	($000)	
Cash (including time deposits of $3,799 in the current year and $2,846 in the prior year) (Note 3)	$7,957	$6,588

Note 3: In connection with bankruptcy proceedings, the Company has placed certain funds in escrowed accounts and segregated other accounts on the books and records of the company. These funds totalled approximately $278,379,000 in the current period and $220,358,000 in the preceding period.

Instructions

(a) What is the difference between a demand deposit and a time deposit?

(b) Why are the amounts of time deposits reported separately?

(c) Why are the funds in escrow not reported as part of cash? Provide examples of why cash might be restricted.

(d) Why is petty cash not reported separately in the financial statements?

C7-2 **(BAD DEBT ACCOUNTING)** Bucky Bob Inc. has significant amounts of trade accounts receivable. Bucky Bob uses the allowance method to estimate bad debts instead of the direct write-off method. During the year, some specific accounts were written off as uncollectible, and some that were previously written off as uncollectible were collected.

Instructions

(a) What are the deficiencies of the direct write-off method?

(b) What are the two basic allowance methods used to estimate bad debts, and what is the theoretical justification for each?

(c) How should Bucky Bob account for the collection of the specific accounts previously written off as uncollectible?

C7-3 **(VARIOUS RECEIVABLE ACCOUNTING ISSUES)** Davis Company Ltd. uses the net method of accounting for sales discounts. Davis also offers trade discounts to various groups of buyers.

On August 1, 1994, Davis factored some accounts receivable on a without recourse basis, incurring a finance charge. Davis also has some notes receivable bearing an appropriate rate of interest. The principal and total interest are due at maturity. The notes were received on October 1, 1994, and they will mature on September 30, 1996. Davis's operating cycle is less than one year.

Instructions

(a) 1. Using the net method, how should Davis account for the sales discounts at the date of sale? What is the rationale for the amount recorded as sales under the net method?

2. Using the net method, what is the effect on Davis's sales revenues and net income when customers do not take the sales discounts?

(b) What is the effect of trade discounts on sales revenues and accounts receivable? Why?

(c) How should Davis account for the accounts receivable factored on August 1, 1994? Why?

(d) How should Davis account for the notes receivable and the related interest on December 31, 1994? Why?

(BAD DEBT REPORTING ISSUES) Roebuck Inc. conducts a wholesale merchandising business that sells approximately 5,000 items per month with a total monthly average sales value of $200,000. Its annual bad debt ratio has been approximately 1½% of sales. In recent discussions with his bookkeeper, Mr. Roebuck has become confused by all the alternatives apparently available in handling the Allowance for Doubtful Accounts balance. The following information has been shown: C7-4

1. An allowance can be set up (a) on the basis of a percentage of sales or (b) on the basis of a valuation of all past due or otherwise questionable accounts receivable—those considered uncollectible being charged to such allowance at the close of the accounting period—or specific items are charged off directly against (c) gross sales or to (d) bad debt expense in the year in which they are determined to be uncollectible.

2. Collection agency and legal fees, and so on, incurred in connection with the attempted recovery of bad debts, can be charged to (a) bad debt expense, (b) allowance for doubtful accounts, (c) legal expense, or (d) general expense.

3. Debts previously written off in whole or in part but currently recovered can be credited to (a) other revenue, (b) bad debt expenses, or (c) allowance for doubtful accounts.

Instructions

Which of the foregoing methods would you recommend to Mr. Roebuck in regard to (1) allowances and charge-offs, (2) collection expenses, and (3) recoveries? State briefly and clearly the reasons supporting your recommendations.

(BASIC NOTE AND ACCOUNTS RECEIVABLE TRANSACTIONS) C7-5

Part 1. On July 1, 1994, Sunchi Ltd., using a calendar-year accounting period, sells special order merchandise on credit and receives in return an interest-bearing note receivable from the customer. Sunchi Ltd. will receive interest at the prevailing rate for a note of this type. Both the principal and interest are due in one lump sum on June 30, 1995.

Instructions

(a) When should Sunchi Ltd. report interest income from the note receivable? Discuss the rationale for your answer.

(b) Assume that the note receivable was discounted without recourse at a bank on December 31, 1994. How would Sunchi Ltd. determine the amount of the discount and what would be the appropriate accounting for the discounting transaction?

Part 2. On December 31, 1994, Sunchi Ltd. has significant amounts of accounts receivable as a result of credit sales to its customers. The company uses the allowance method based on credit sales to estimate bad debts. Based on past experience, 2% of credit sales are normally not collected. This pattern is expected to continue.

Instructions

(a) Discuss the rationale for using the allowance method based on credit sales to estimate bad debts. Contrast this method with the allowance method based on the balance in the trade receivables accounts.

(b) How should Sunchi Ltd. report the allowance for bad debts account on its balance sheet at December 31, 1994? Also, describe the alternatives, if any, for presentation of bad debt expense in Sunchi Ltd.'s 1994 income statement.

(AICPA adapted)

(BAD DEBT REPORTING ISSUES) Shellack Ltd. sells office equipment and supplies to many organizations in the city and surrounding area on contract terms of 2/10, n/30. In the past, over 75% of credit customers have taken advantage of the discount by paying within 10 days of the invoice date. C7-6

The number of customers taking the full 30 days to pay has increased within the last year. Current indications are that less than 60% of the customers are now taking the discount. Bad debts as a percentage of gross credit sales have risen from 1.5% provided in the past years, to about 4% in the current year.

The controller has responded to a request for more information on the deterioration in accounts receivable collections with the report reproduced below.

Shellack Ltd.
Finance Committee Report
Accounts Receivable Collections
May 31, 1994

The fact that some credit accounts will prove uncollectible is normal. Annual bad debt write-offs have been 1.5% of gross credit sales over the past five years. During the last fiscal year, this percentage increased to slightly less than 4%. The current Accounts Receivable balance is $1,600,000. The condition of this balance in terms of probability of collection is as follows:

Proportion of Total	Age Categories	Probability of Collection
68%	Not yet due	99%
15%	Less than 30 days past due	96½%
8%	31 to 60 days past due	95%
5%	61 to 120 days past due	91%
2½%	121 to 180 days past due	75%
1½%	Over 181 days past due	20%

The Allowance for Doubtful Accounts had a credit balance of $40,300 on June 1, 1993. Shellack has provided for a monthly bad debt expense accrual during the fiscal year based on the assumption that 4% of gross credit sales will be uncollectible. Total gross credit sales for the 1993–1994 fiscal year amounted to $4,000,000. Write-offs of bad accounts during the year totalled $145,000.

Instructions

(a) Using the age categories identified in the controller's report to the Finance Committee, prepare an accounts receivable aging schedule for Shellack Ltd. showing:

1. The amount of accounts receivable outstanding for each age category and in total.

2. The estimated amount that is uncollectible for each category and in total.

(b) Compute the amount of the year-end adjustment necessary to bring Allowance for Doubtful Accounts to the balance indicated by the age analysis. Then prepare the necessary journal entry to adjust the accounting records.

(c) In a recessionary environment with tight credit and high interest rates:

1. Identify steps Shellack Ltd. might consider to improve the accounts receivable situation.

2. Evaluate each step identified in terms of the risks and costs involved.

C7-7 **(REPORTING OF NOTES RECEIVABLE, INTEREST, AND SALE OF RECEIVABLES)** On July 1, 1994, Nakane Inc. sold special-order merchandise on credit and received in return an interest-bearing note receivable from the customer. Nakane will receive interest at the prevailing rate for a note of this type. Both the principal and interest are due in one lump sum on June 30, 1995.

On September 1, 1994, Nakane sold special-order merchandise on credit and received a noninterest-bearing note receivable from the customer. The prevailing rate of interest for a note of this type is determinable. The note receivable is due in one lump sum on August 31, 1996.

Nakane also has significant amounts of trade accounts receivable as a result of credit sales to its customers. On October 1, 1994, some trade accounts receivable were assigned to Lendyou Finance Company on a with-recourse, nonnotification basis (Nakane handles collections) for an advance of 75% of their amount at an interest charge of 20% on the balance outstanding.

On November 1, 1994, other trade accounts receivable were factored on a without-recourse basis. The factor withheld 5% of the trade accounts receivable factored as protection against sales returns and allowances and charged a finance charge of 3%.

Instructions

(a) How should Nakane determine the interest income for 1994 on the:

1. Interest-bearing note receivable? Why?

2. Noninterest-bearing note receivable? Why?

(b) How should Nakane report the interest-bearing note receivable and the noninterest-bearing note receivable on its balance sheet at December 31, 1994?

(c) How should Nakane account for subsequent collections on the trade accounts receivable assigned on October 1, 1994, and the payments to Lendyou Finance? Why?

(d) How should Nakane account for the trade accounts receivable factored on November 1, 1994? Why?

(AICPA adapted)

(ACCOUNTING FOR NONINTEREST-BEARING NOTE) Soon after beginning the year-end audit work on March 10 at Tuffy Co. Ltd., the auditor has the following conversation with the controller. C7-8

Controller: The year ended March 31 should be our most profitable in history, and as a consequence, the Board of Directors has just awarded the officers generous bonuses.

Auditor: I thought profits were down this year in the industry, according to your latest interim report.

Controller: Well, they *were* down, but 10 days ago we closed a deal that will give us a substantial increase for the year.

Auditor: Oh, what was it?

Controller: Well, you remember a few years ago our former president bought shares in Pearson Enterprises because he had those grandiose ideas about becoming a conglomerate? For six years, we haven't been able to sell the shares, which cost us $3,000,000 and haven't been paid a nickel in dividends. Thursday, we sold the shares to Gambler Ltd. for $4,000,000. So, we'll have a gain of $700,000 ($1,000,000 pretax), which will increase our net income for the year to $4,000,000 compared with last year's $3,800,000. As far as I know, we'll be the only company in the industry to register an increase in net income this year. That should help the market value of the company's shares!

Auditor: Do you expect to receive the $4,000,000 in cash by March 31, your fiscal year end?

Controller: No. Although Gambler Ltd. is an excellent company, it's a little tight on cash because of its rapid growth. Consequently, Gambler is going to give us a $4,000,000 noninterest-bearing note, with $400,000 due each year for the next 10 years. The first payment is due on March 31 of next year.

Auditor: Why is the note noninterest-bearing?

Controller: Because that's what everybody agreed to. Since we don't have any interest-bearing debt, the funds invested in the note don't cost us anything and besides, we weren't getting any dividends on the Pearson Enterprises shares.

Instructions

Do you agree with the way the controller has accounted for the transaction? If not, how should the transaction be accounted for?

C7-9 **(FINANCIAL AND ACCOUNTING IMPACTS OF CREDIT CARDS)** Household Inc. operates a full-line department store that is dominant in its market area, is easily accessible to public and private transportation, has adequate parking facilities, and is near a large permanent military base. The president of the company, Susan Denson, seeks your advice on a recently received proposal.

A local credit union, in which your client has an account, recently affiliated with a popular national credit card plan and has extended an invitation to your client to participate in the plan. Under the plan, affiliated banks and credit unions mail credit card applications to people who have good credit ratings, regardless of whether they are customers of the credit union. If the recipients wish to receive a credit card, they complete, sign, and return the application and instalment credit agreement. Holders of the credit cards may charge merchandise or services at any participating establishment throughout the nation.

The credit union guarantees payment to all participating merchants on all invoices that are properly completed, signed, and validated with the impression of credit cards that are not expired or reported stolen or cancelled. Local merchants including your client may turn in all card-validated sales tickets or invoices to their affiliated local credit union at any time and receive immediate credits to their chequing accounts at 96.5% of the face value of the invoices. If card users pay the credit union or bank in full within 30 days for amounts billed, the credit union levies no added charges against the customer. If they elect to make their payments under a deferred payment plan, the credit union adds a service charge that amounts to an effective interest rate of 18% per annum on unpaid balances. Only the local affiliated credit unions, banks, and the franchiser of the credit card plan share in these revenues.

The 18% service charge approximates what your client has been billing customers who pay their accounts over an extended period on a schedule similar to that offered under the credit card plan. Participation in the plan does not prevent your client from carrying on credit business as in the past.

Instructions

(a) What are (1) the positive and (2) the negative financial- and accounting-related factors that Household Inc. should consider in deciding whether to participate in the described credit card plan? Explain.

(b) If Household Inc. does participate in the plan, which income statement and balance sheet accounts may change materially as the plan becomes fully operative? (Such factors as market position, sales mix, prices, markup, etc., are expected to remain the same as in the past.) Explain.

(AICPA adapted)

C7-10 **(ETHICAL ISSUES: BAD DEBT REPORTING)** Little Burger Co. Ltd. is a subsidiary of Big Burger Co. Ltd. The controller believes that the yearly allowance for doubtful accounts for Little Burger should be 2% of net credit sales. The president, nervous that the parent company might expect the subsidiary to sustain its 10% growth rate, suggests that the controller increase the allowance for doubtful accounts to 3% yearly. The supervisor thinks that the lower net income, which reflects a 6% growth rate, will be a more sustainable rate for Little Burger.

Instructions

(a) Should the controller be concerned with Little Burger Co. Ltd.'s growth rate in estimating the allowance? Explain your answer.

(b) Does the president's request pose an ethical dilemma for the controller? Give your reasons.

(ETHICAL ISSUES: CLASSIFICATION OF NOTES RECEIVABLE) Zenith Limited has several current notes receivable on its year-end balance sheet. While collection seems certain, it may be delayed beyond one year. Because of this, the controller wants to reclassify these notes as noncurrent. The treasurer of Zenith also thinks that collection will be delayed but does not favor reclassification because this will reduce the current ratio from 1.5:1 to .8:1. This reduction in current ratio is detrimental to company prospects for securing a major loan. C7-11

Instructions

(a) Should the controller reclassify the notes? Give your reasons.

(b) Considering the possible harm to stakeholders, what is the ethical dilemma for the controller and the treasurer?

EXERCISES

(DETERMINING CASH BALANCE) The controller for Salty Co. Ltd. is attempting to determine the amount of cash to be reported on its December 31, 1994, balance sheet. The following information is provided: E7-1

1. Commercial savings account of $1,000,000 and a commercial chequing account of $600,000 held at First Canada Trust.
2. Special savings account held at Corporate Credit Union (a savings and loan organization) permits Salty to write cheques on the $6,000,000 balance.
3. Travel advances of $180,000 for executive travel for the first quarter of next year (employee to reimburse through salary reduction).
4. Cash restricted in the amount of $1,500,000 for the retirement of long-term debt.
5. Petty cash fund of $1,000.
6. An IOU from David Castle, a company officer, in the amount of $190,000.
7. A bank overdraft of $110,000 has occurred at one of the banks the company uses to deposit its cash receipts. At the present time, the company has no deposits at this bank.
8. The company has two certificates of deposit, each totalling $500,000. These certificates of deposit have a maturity of 120 days.
9. Salty has received a cheque that is dated January 12, 1995, in the amount of $125,000.
10. Salty has agreed to maintain a cash balance of $500,000 at all times at the Ontario National Bank to ensure future credit availability.
11. Salty has purchased $2,100,000 of commercial paper of Kennedy Co. Ltd., which is due in 60 days.
12. Currency and coin on hand amount to $6,200.

Instructions

(a) Compute the amount of cash to be reported on Salty Co. Ltd.'s balance sheet at December 31, 1994.

(b) Indicate the proper reporting for items that are not reported as cash on the December 31, 1994, balance sheet.

(DETERMINE CASH BALANCE) Presented below are a number of independent situations. For each situation, determine the amount that should be reported as cash. If the item(s) are not reported as cash, explain the rationale. E7-2

1. Chequing account balance, $750,000; certificate of deposit, $1,400,000; cash advance to subsidiary, $980,000; utility deposit paid to gas company, $250.

2. Chequing account balance, $500,000; an overdraft of $10,000 in special chequing account at same bank as normal chequing account; cash held in a bond sinking fund, $200,000; petty cash fund, $300; coins and currency on hand, $1,350.

3. Chequing account balance, $490,000; postdated cheque from customer, $11,000; cash restricted due to maintaining compensating balance requirement, $100,000; certified cheque from customer, $9,800; postage stamps on hand, $620.

4. Chequing account balance at bank, $29,000; balance at Royal Trust (has chequing privileges), $48,000; NSF cheque received from customer, $800.

5. Chequing account balance, $600,000; cash restricted for future plant expansion, $500,000; short-term treasury bills, $180,000; cash advance received from customer, $900 (not included in chequing account balance); cash advance of $7,000 to company executive, payable on demand; refundable deposit of $26,000 paid to federal government to guarantee performance on construction contract.

E7-3 **(PETTY CASH)** Metro Inc. decided to establish a petty cash fund to help ensure internal control over its small cash expenditures. The following information is available for the month of April:

1. On April 1, it established a petty cash fund in the amount of $200.

2. A summary of the petty cash expenditures made by the petty cash custodian as of April 10 is as follows:

Delivery charges paid on merchandise purchased	$70.00
Supplies purchased and used	15.00
Postage expense	33.00
IOUs from employees	17.00
Miscellaneous expense	36.00

The petty cash fund was replenished on April 10.

3. The petty cash fund balance was increased $50 to $250 on April 20.

Instructions

Prepare the journal entries to record transactions related to petty cash for the month of April.

E7-4 **(PETTY CASH)** The petty cash fund of Rene's Repair Service, a sole proprietorship, contains the following:

1. Coins and currency		$ 9.20
2. Postage stamps		3.00
3. An IOU from Mary Mechanic, an employee, for cash advance		40.00
4. Cheque payable to Rene's Repair Service from John Brakeshoe, an employee, marked NSF		34.00
5. Vouchers for the following:		
Stamps	$20.00	
Two Grey Cup tickets for Mary Lou Rene	70.00	
Typewriter repairs	21.35	111.35
		$197.55

The general ledger account Petty Cash has a balance of $200.

Instructions

Prepare the journal entry to record the reimbursement of the petty cash fund.

(BANK RECONCILIATION AND ADJUSTING ENTRIES) Boli Limited deposits all receipts and makes all payments by cheque. The following information is available from the cash records. E7-5

June 30 Bank Reconciliation

Balance per bank	$7,000
Add: Deposits in transit	1,540
Deduct: Outstanding cheques	(2,000)
Balance per books	$6,540

Month of July Results

	Per Bank	Per Books
Balance July 31	$8,550	$9,250
July deposits	5,000	5,910
July cheques	4,100	3,200
July notes collected (not included in July deposits)	900	-0-
July bank service charge	15	-0-
July NSF cheque of a customer returned by the bank (recorded by bank as a charge)	235	-0-

Instructions

(a) Prepare a bank reconciliation going from balance per bank and balance per book to corrected Cash account.

(b) Prepare the general journal entry to correct the Cash account.

(BANK RECONCILIATION AND ADJUSTING ENTRIES) Flintstone Inc. has just received the August 31, 1994 bank statement, which is summarized below. E7-6

Toronto Dominion Bank	Disbursements	Receipts	Balance
Balance August 1			$ 9,369
Deposits during August		$32,000	41,369
Note collected for depositor, including $72 interest		1,272	42,641
Cheques cleared during August	$34,400		8,241
Bank service charges	20		8,221
Balance August 31			8,221

The general ledger Cash account contained the following entries for the month of August:

Cash

Balance, August 1	10,050	Disbursements in August	34,903
Receipts during August	35,000		

Deposits in transit at August 31 are $4,000 and cheques outstanding at August 31 total $1,150. Cash on hand at August 31 is $310. The bookkeeper improperly entered one cheque in the books at $146.50 that was written for $164.50 for supplies; it cleared the bank during the month of August.

Instructions

(a) Prepare a bank reconciliation dated August 31, 1994, proceeding to a corrected balance.

(b) Prepare any entries necessary to make the books correct and complete.

(c) What amount of cash should be reported in the August 31 balance sheet?

E7-7 **(FINANCIAL STATEMENT PRESENTATION OF RECEIVABLES)** Andretti Limited shows a balance of $181,140 in the Accounts Receivable account on December 31, 1994. The balance consists of the following:

Instalment accounts due in 1995	$20,000
Instalment accounts due after 1995	27,000
Overpayment to creditors	2,640
Due from regular customers, of which $40,000 represents accounts pledged as security for a bank loan	79,000
Advances to employees	2,500
Advance to subsidiary company (made in 1989)	50,000
	$ 181,140

Instructions

Illustrate how the information above should be shown on the balance sheet of Andretti Limited on December 31, 1994.

E7-8 **(DETERMINE ENDING ACCOUNTS RECEIVABLE)** Your accounts receivable clerk, Mr. Ray Martin, to whom you pay a salary of $1,100 per month, has just purchased a new Cadillac. You decided to test the accuracy of the accounts receivable balance of $132,000 as shown in the ledger. The following information is available for your **first year** in business:

1. Collections from customers	$198,000
2. Merchandise purchased	360,000
3. Ending merchandise inventory	90,000
4. Goods are marked to sell at 40% above cost	

Instructions

Compute an estimate of the ending balance of accounts receivable from customers that should appear in the ledger and any apparent shortages. Assume that all sales are made on account.

E7-9 **(RECORD SALES GROSS AND NET)** On June 3, Joffrey Co. Ltd. sold to Ken Stene merchandise having a sale price of $3,000, with terms of 2/10, n/60, f.o.b. shipping point. An invoice totalling $90, terms n/30, was received by Ken Stene on June 8 from the Barton Transport Service for the freight cost. On receipt of the goods on June 5, Ken Stene notified Joffrey Co. Ltd. that merchandise costing $400 contained flaws that rendered it worthless; the same day, Joffrey Co. Ltd. issued a credit memo covering the worthless merchandise and asked that it be returned at company expense. The freight on the returned merchandise was $25, paid by Joffrey Co. Ltd. on June 7. On June 12, the company received a cheque for the balance due from Ken Stene.

Instructions

(a) Prepare journal entries on Joffrey Co. Ltd.'s books to record all the events noted above on the following bases:

1. Sales and receivables are entered at gross selling price.

2. Sales and receivables are entered at net of cash discounts.

(b) Prepare the journal entry under basis 2, assuming that Ken Stene did not remit payment until July 29.

E7-10 **(COMPUTING BAD DEBTS)** At January 1, 1994, the credit balance in the Allowance for Doubtful Accounts of the Spencer Company Ltd. was $400,000. For 1994, the provision for doubtful accounts is based on a percentage of net sales. Net sales for 1994 were $70,000,000. On the basis of the latest available facts, the 1994 provision for doubtful accounts is estimated to be 0.8% of net sales. During 1994, uncollectible receivables amounting to $490,000 were written off against the allowance for doubtful accounts.

Instructions

Prepare a schedule computing the balance in Spencer's Allowance for Doubtful Accounts at December 31, 1994.

(COMPUTING BAD DEBTS AND PREPARING JOURNAL ENTRIES) The trial balance before adjustment of Beacon Enterprises shows the following balances. **E7-11**

	Dr.	Cr.
Accounts Receivable	$90,000	
Allowance for Doubtful Accounts	1,750	
Sales (all on credit)		$680,000
Sales Returns and Allowances	30,000	

Instructions

Give the entry for estimated bad debts assuming that the allowance is to provide for doubtful accounts on the bases of (a) 8% of gross accounts receivable and (b) 1.5% of net sales.

(BAD DEBT REPORTING) The chief accountant for Coppola Corporation Ltd. provides you with the following list of accounts receivable written off in the current year. **E7-12**

Date	Customer	Amount
Mar. 31	Creative Designs	$7,800
June 30	Gene Associates	6,700
Sept. 30	Susan's Dress Shop	7,000
Dec. 31	Foremost Corporation Ltd.	8,730

Coppola Corporation Ltd. follows the policy of debiting Bad Debt Expense as accounts are written off. The chief accountant maintains that this procedure is appropriate for financial statement purposes.

All of Coppola Corporation Ltd.'s sales are on a 30-day credit basis. Sales for the current year total $2,100,000 and research has determined that bad debt losses approximate 2% of sales.

Instructions

(a) Do you agree or disagree with the Coppola policy concerning recognition of bad debt expense? Why or why not?

(b) By what amount would net income differ if bad debt expense was computed using the percentage-of-sales approach?

(BAD DEBTS: AGING) Paul Dornstauder Inc. includes the following account among its trade receivables. **E7-13**

Avery Brooks

1/1	Balance forward	700	1/28	Cash (#1710)	1,100
1/20	Invoice #1710	1,100	4/2	Cash (#2116)	1,350
3/14	Invoice #2116	1,350	4/10	Cash	150
4/12	Invoice #2412	1,780	4/30	Cash (#2412)	1,000
9/5	Invoice #3614	490	9/20	Cash (#3614 and part of #2412)	790
10/17	Invoice #4912	860	10/31	Cash (#4912)	860
11/18	Invoice #5681	2,000	12/1	Cash (#5681)	1,350
12/20	Invoice #6347	800	12/29	Cash (#6347)	800

Instructions

Age the balance and specify any items that apparently require particular attention.

E7-14 **(JOURNALIZING VARIOUS RECEIVABLE TRANSACTIONS)** Presented below is information related to Renny Inc.:

July 1 Renny Inc. sells to Higgins Co. Ltd. merchandise having a sales price of $8,000, with terms 2/10, net/60. Renny records its sales and receivables net.

July 3 Higgins Co. Ltd. returns defective merchandise having a sales price of $700.

July 5 Accounts receivable of $9,000 are factored with Kelly Credit without recourse at a financing charge of 10%. Cash is received for the proceeds; collections are handled by the finance company. (These accounts are all past the discount period.)

July 9 Specific accounts receivable of $10,000 (gross) are assigned to Tultex Credit as security for a loan of $6,000 at a finance charge of 6% of the amount of the loan. The finance company will make the collections. (All the accounts receivable are past the discount period.)

Dec. 29 Higgins Co. Ltd. notifies Renny that it is bankrupt and will pay only 10% of its account. Give the entry to write off the uncollectible balance using the allowance method. (**Note**: First record the increase in the receivable on June 11 when the discount period has passed.)

Instructions

Prepare all necessary entries in general journal form for Renny Inc.

E7-15 **(ASSIGNED ACCOUNTS RECEIVABLE)** Presented below is information related to Frechette Inc.:

1. Customers' accounts in the amount of $40,000 are assigned to the Speedy Finance Company as security for a loan of $30,000. The finance charge is 3% of the amount borrowed.
2. Cash collections on assigned accounts amount to $19,000.
3. Collections on assigned accounts to date, plus a $400 cheque for interest on the loan, are forwarded to Speedy Finance Company.
4. Additional collections on assigned accounts amount to $15,200.
5. The loan is paid in full plus additional interest of $150.
6. Uncollected balances of the assigned accounts are returned to the regular customers' ledger.

Instructions

Prepare entries in journal form for Frechette Inc.

E7-16 **(JOURNALIZING VARIOUS RECEIVABLE TRANSACTIONS)** The trial balance before adjustment for Vision Enterprises Inc. shows the following balances.

	Dr.	Cr.
Accounts Receivable	$92,000	
Allowance for Doubtful Accounts	2,120	
Sales		$430,000
Sales Returns and Allowances	7,600	

Instructions

Using the data above, give the journal entries required to record each of the following cases (each situation is independent):

1. To obtain additional cash, Vision factors, without recourse, $24,000 of accounts receivable with Shifty Finance. The finance charge is 10% of the amount factored.
2. To obtain a one-year loan of $54,000, Vision assigns $70,000 of specific receivable accounts to Fandango Financial. The finance charge is 8% of the loan. The cash is received and the accounts turned over to Fandango.
3. The company wants to maintain the Allowance for Doubtful Accounts at 4% of gross accounts receivable.
4. The company wishes to increase the allowance by 1½% of net sales.

(TRANSFER OF RECEIVABLES WITH RECOURSE) Barnell Inc. factors receivables with a carrying amount of $195,000 to Antonelli Company for $160,000 on a with-recourse basis. **E7-17**

Instructions

(a) Assuming that this transaction should be reported as a sale, prepare the appropriate journal entry.

(b) Assuming that this transaction should be reported as a borrowing, prepare the appropriate journal entry.

(TRANSFER OF RECEIVABLES WITH RECOURSE) Tillis Inc. factors $110,000 of accounts receivable with BN Financing Inc. on a with-recourse basis. BN Financing will collect the receivables. The receivables records are transferred to BN Financing on August 15, 1994. BN Financing assesses a finance charge of 2% of the amount of accounts receivable and also reserves an amount equal to 4% of accounts receivable to cover probable adjustments. **E7-18**

Instructions

(a) What conditions must be met for a transfer of receivables with recourse to be accounted for as a sale?

(b) Assume that the conditions in (a) are met. Prepare the journal entry on August 15, 1994 for Tillis to record the sale of receivables.

(c) Assume that not all of the conditions in (a) are met. Prepare the journal entry on August 15, 1994 for Tillis to record the transfer of receivables.

(TRANSFER OF RECEIVABLES WITHOUT RECOURSE) Lexia Inc. factors $200,000 of accounts receivable with Mooney Finance on a without-recourse basis. On July 1, 1994, the receivable records are transferred to Mooney Finance, which will receive the collections. Mooney Finance assesses a finance charge of 1½% of the amount of accounts receivable and retains an amount equal to 4% of accounts receivable to cover sales discounts, returns, and allowances. **E7-19**

Instructions

(a) Prepare the journal entry on July 1, 1994 for Lexia Inc. to record the sale of receivables without recourse.

(b) Prepare the journal entry on July 1, 1994 for Mooney Finance to record the purchase of receivables without recourse.

(COMPUTE INCOME EFFECT OF VARIOUS TRANSFERS OF RECEIVABLES) Stoefel Company Ltd. requires additional cash for its business. Stoefel has decided to use its accounts receivable to raise the additional cash as follows: **E7-20**

1. On July 4, 1994, Stoefel assigned $400,000 of accounts receivable to Stickum Finance. Stoefel received an advance from Stickum of 85% of the assigned accounts receivable, less a commission on the advance of 3%. Prior to December 31, 1994, Stoefel collected $220,000 on the assigned accounts receivable and remitted $232,720 to Stickum, $12,720 of which represented interest on the advance from Stickum.

2. On December 1, 1994, Stoefel sold $300,000 of net accounts receivable to Wunsch Co. Ltd. for $250,000. The receivables were sold outright on a nonrecourse basis.

3. On December 31, 1994, an advance of $120,000 was received from the First Bank by pledging $160,000 of Stoefel's accounts receivable. Stoefel's first payment to First Bank is due on January 30, 1995.

Instructions

Prepare a schedule showing the income statement effect for the year ended December 31, 1994, as a result of the above facts. Show supporting computations in good form.

(AICPA adapted)

E7-21 (NOTE TRANSACTIONS AT UNREALISTIC INTEREST RATES) On July 1, 1994, Goodness Company Ltd. made two sales:

1. It sold land having a fair market value of $700,000 in exchange for a four-year noninterest-bearing promissory note in the face amount of $1,101,460. The land is carried on Goodness Company Ltd.'s books at a cost of $585,000.

2. It rendered services in exchange for a 4%, eight-year promissory note having a maturity value of $300,000 (interest payable annually).

Goodness Company Ltd. recently had to pay 8% interest for money that it borrowed from Western National Bank. The customers in these two transactions have credit ratings that require them to borrow money at 12% interest.

Instructions

Record the two journal entries that should be recorded by Goodness Company Ltd. for the sales transactions above that took place on July 1, 1994.

E7-22 (NOTE RECEIVABLE AT UNREALISTIC INTEREST RATES) On December 31, 1994, Jodie Company Ltd. sold some of its product to Foster Inc., accepting a $350,000 noninterest-bearing note receivable in full on December 31, 1997. Jodie Company Ltd. enjoys a high credit rating and, therefore, borrows funds from its several lines of credit at 9%. Foster Inc., however, pays 12% for its borrowed funds. The product sold is carried on the books of Jodie Company Ltd. based on a manufactured cost of $190,000. Assume that the effective interest method is used for discount amortization.

Instructions

(a) Prepare the journal entry to record the sale on December 31, 1994 by Jodie Company Ltd. Assume that a perpetual inventory system is used.

(b) Prepare the journal entries on the books of Jodie Company Ltd. for the year 1995 that are necessitated by the sales transaction of December 31, 1994.

(c) Prepare the journal entries on the books of Jodie Company Ltd. for the year 1996 that are necessitated by the sale on December 31, 1994.

E7-23 (DISCOUNTING OF NOTE; DEFAULT) Following is information related to Gemini Co. Ltd. and Dennis Inc.:

May 1 Gemini Co. Ltd. gave Dennis Inc. an $8,400, 60-day, 10% note in payment of its account of the same amount.

16 Dennis Inc. discounted the note at the bank at a 12% discount rate.

June 30 On the maturity date of the note, Gemini Co. Ltd. paid the amount due.

Instructions

(a) Record the transactions above on both the books of Gemini Co. Ltd. and the books of Dennis Inc. (Assume it is a borrowing transaction.)

(b) Assume that Gemini Co. Ltd. dishonoured its note and the bank notified Dennis Inc. that it had charged the maturity value plus a protest fee of $30 to the Dennis Inc. bank account. What entry or entries should Dennis Inc. make on receiving this notification?

(PROOF OF CASH) Following is the general format of a four-column bank reconciliation with the various categories and operations numbered (1) through (8). ***E7-24**

	Balance 10/31	November Receipts	November Disbursements	Balance 11/30
Per Bank Statement	$XXXXX	$XXXXX	$XXXXX	$XXXXX
Items to be added:	(1)	(3)	(5)	(7)
Items to be deducted:	(2)	(4)	(6)	(8)
Per Books	$XXXXX	$XXXXX	$XXXXX	$XXXXX

Instructions

(a) For each of the following items indicate in which columns the reconciling items would appear. Question 1 is answered as an example.

6 7 1. November service charge of $25 was included on bank statement.

__ 2. The bank collected a $500 note receivable for the firm in November, plus $30 interest. The firm had not yet recorded this receipt.

__ 3. An NSF cheque in the amount of $375 was returned with the November bank statement. This cheque would be redeposited in December. The firm had not yet made an entry for this NSF cheque.

__ 4. All $9,000 of cheques written in October, which had not cleared the bank at October 31, cleared the bank in November.

__ 5. October service charge of $20 was included in book disbursements for November.

__ 6. A $5,000 deposit in transit was included in book disbursements for November.

__ 7. The bank, in error, credited the firm's account for $400 in November for another firm's deposit.

__ 8. A cheque written November for $680 was written in the cheque register in error in the amount of $860. This cheque cleared the bank in November for $680. Both the debit to Utilities Expense and the credit were overstated as a result of this error in the books.

__ 9. The initial $4,500 deposit shown on the November bank statement was included in October's book receipts.

__ 10. $8,000 of cheques written in November had not cleared the bank by November 30.

(b) Prepare the entries that should be recorded to make the books complete and accurate at November 30.

PROBLEMS

P7-1 (CASH RELATED ISSUES) Presented below are five independent situations:

1. The bank reconciliation for April 1994 of Slimfast Co. Ltd. was as follows:

Balance per bank statement 4/30/94	$80,000
Add deposits in transit	6,000
	86,000
Less outstanding cheques	15,000
Balance per books 4/30/94	$71,000

During May 1994, the bank recorded $74,000 of cash receipts and $35,900 of cash disbursements. All deposits in transit and outstanding cheques from April cleared the bank in May. Outstanding cheques at May 31, 1994 totalled $13,300. Determine the cash balance per books as of May 31, 1994.

2. Ultra Enterprises owns the following assets at December 31, 1994:

Cash in bank—savings account	79,000
Cash on hand	9,300
Cash refund due from Revenue Canada	31,400
Chequing account balance	17,000
Postdated cheques	750
Certificates of deposit (180-day)	90,000

What amount should be reported as cash?

3. The June 30 bank reconciliation of Amherst Inc. indicated that deposits in transit totalled $375. During July, the general ledger account Cash in Bank showed deposits of $15,250, but the bank statement indicated that only $15,100 in deposits were received during the month. What were the deposits in transit at July 31?

4. In September, cash disbursements per books for Katrina Co. Ltd. were $22,900, cheques clearing the bank were $24,000, and outstanding cheques at September 30 were $1,500. What were the outstanding cheques at August 31?

5. Chopin Corporation Ltd. on July 1, 1994 obtained a $4,000,000, six-month loan at an annual rate of 12% from the Royal Bank. As part of the loan agreement, Chopin was required to maintain a $500,000 compensating balance in a chequing account at the Royal Bank. Normally, Chopin would maintain a balance of only $200,000 in this chequing account. The chequing account pays 5% interest. Determine the effective interest rate paid by Chopin for this loan.

Instructions

Answer the questions relating to each of the five independent situations as requested.

P7-2 (DETERMINE PROPER CASH BALANCE) Orion Equipment Inc. closes its books regularly on December 31, but at the end of 1994 it held its cash book open so that a more favourable balance sheet could be prepared for credit purposes. Cash receipts and disbursements for the first 10 days of January were recorded as December transactions. The following information is given:

1. January cash receipts recorded in the December cash book totalled $38,640, of which $21,000 represented cash sales and $17,640 represented collections on account for which cash discounts of $360 were given.

2. January cash disbursements recorded in the December cheque register liquidated accounts payable of $26,450, on which discounts of $159 were taken.

3. The ledger has not been closed for 1994.

4. The amount shown as inventory was determined by physical count on December 31, 1994.

Instructions

(a) Prepare any entries you consider necessary to correct Orion's accounts at December 31.

(b) To what extent was Orion Equipment Inc. able to show a more favourable balance sheet at December 31 by holding its cash book open? Assume that the balance sheet that was prepared by the company showed the following amounts.

	Dr.	Cr.
Cash	$35,000	
Receivables	42,000	
Inventories	67,000	
Accounts payable		$45,000
Other current liabilities		13,200

(BANK RECONCILIATION AND ADJUSTING ENTRIES) The cash account of Orbison Inc. showed a ledger balance of $5,589 on June 30, 1994. The bank statement as of that date showed a balance of $4,100. On comparing the statement with the cash records, the following facts were determined: **P7-3**

(a) Bank service charges for June were $25.

(b) A bank memo stated that Trudy Mumm's note for $800 and interest of $36 had been collected on June 29, and the bank had made a charge of $6 on the collection. (No entry had been made on Orbison's books when Mumm's note was sent to the bank for collection.)

(c) Receipts for June 30 of $2,738 were not deposited until July 2.

(d) Cheques outstanding on June 30 totalled $1,936.

(e) The bank had charged Orbinson Inc.'s account for a customer's uncollectible cheque for $452 on June 29.

(f) A 60-day, 6%, $1,500 customer's note dated April 25 and discounted by Orbison on June 12 remained unpaid by the customer on the due date. On June 28, the bank charged Orbison for $1,520, which included a protest fee of $5 (Orbison disclosed discounted notes receivable by use of a note to the financial statements.)

(g) A customer's cheque for $90 had been entered as $60 in the cash receipts journal by Orbison on June 15.

(h) Cheque 742 in the amount of $491 had been entered in the cashbook as $419, and cheque 747 in the amount of $58 had been entered as $580. Both cheques had been issued to pay for purchases of equipment.

Instructions

(a) Prepare a bank reconciliation dated June 30, 1994 and proceed to a corrected cash balance.

(b) Prepare any entries necessary to make the books correct and complete.

(BANK RECONCILIATION AND ADJUSTING ENTRIES) Presented below is information related to Crusher Inc.: **P7-4**

1. Balance per books at October 31, $41,847.85; receipts, $173,523.91; disbursements, $166,213.54. Balance per bank statement November 30, $56,574.20.

2. The following cheques were outstanding at November 30:

1224	$1,635.29
1230	2,468.30
1232	3,625.15
1233	502.17

3. Included with the November bank statement and not recorded by the company were a bank debit ticket for $27.40 covering bank charges for the month, a debit ticket for $372.13 for a customer's NSF cheque returned, and a credit ticket for $1,500 representing bond interest collected by the bank in the name of Crusher Inc. Cash on hand at November 30 recorded and awaiting deposit amounted to $1,915.40.

Instructions

(a) Prepare a bank reconciliation (bank balance to book balance) at November 30, 1994 for Crusher Inc. from the above information.

(b) Prepare any journal entries required to adjust the Cash account at November 30.

P7-5 **(BANK RECONCILIATION)** Presented below is information related to Iona Industries.

Iona Industries
Bank Reconciliation
May 31, 1994

Balance per bank statement		$30,928.46
Less outstanding cheques:		
1224	$2,125.00	
1230	932.65	
6139	960.57	
6140	1,420.00	5,438.22
		25,490.24
Add deposit in transit		4,710.56
Balance per books (correct balance)		$30,200.80

Cheque Register: June

Date	Payee	Cq. No.	V. Pay	Discount	Cash
June 1	Dan Collins Mfg.	6141	$ 237.50		$ 237.50
1	Riley Construction	6142	915.00	$ 9.15	905.85
8	Office Supply Co. Inc.	6143	122.90	2.45	120.45
9	Dan Collins Mfg.	6144	306.40		306.40
10	Petty Cash	6145	89.93		89.93
17	Allservice Photo	6146	706.00	14.12	691.88
22	Linda Elbert Publishing	6147	447.50		447.50
23	Payroll Account	6148	4,130.00		4,130.00
25	Barnes Tools Inc.	6149	390.75	3.91	386.84
28	American Insurance Agency	6150	1,050.00		1,050.00
28	Lembke Bros.	6151	2,250.00		2,250.00
29	R. Petersen, Inc.	6152	750.00		750.00
30	Geo. Bates Mfg.	6153	300.00	6.00	294.00
			$11,695.98	$35.63	$11,660.35

Statement
Bank of Montreal
General Chequing Account of Iona Industries: June 1994

Debits			Date	Credits	Balance
					$30,928.46
$2,125.00	$ 237.50	$ 905.85	June 1	$4,710.56	32,370.67
932.65	120.45		12	1,507.06	32,824.63
1,420.00	447.50	306.40	23	1,458.55	32,109.28
4,130.00		11.05 (SC)	26		27,968.23
89.93	2,250.00	1,050.00	28	4,157.48	28,735.78

Cash received June 29 and 30 and deposited in the mail for the general chequing account June 30 amounted to $4,501.05. Because the cash account balance at June 30 is not given, it must be calculated from other information in the problem.

Instructions

From the information above, prepare a bank reconciliation (to the correct balance) as of June 30, 1994 for Iona Industries.

P7-6 **(BAD DEBT REPORTING)** Presented below are a series of unrelated situations.

1. Herrera's unadjusted trial balance at December 31, 1994 includes the following accounts.

	Debit	Credit
Allowance for doubtful accounts	$ 4,000	
Sales		$1,550,000
Sales returns and allowances	100,000	

Herrera estimates its bad debt expense to be 1½% of net sales. Determine its bad debt expense for 1994.

2. An analysis and aging of Sunshine Inc. accounts receivable at December 31, 1994 disclose the following:

Amounts estimated to be uncollectible	$ 170,000
Accounts receivable	1,700,000
Allowance for doubtful accounts (per books)	150,000

What is the net realizable value of Sundstrom's receivables at December 31, 1994?

3. Cajun Co. Ltd. provides for doubtful accounts based on 3% of credit sales. The following data are available for 1994:

Credit sales during 1994	$2,100,000
Allowance for doubtful accounts 1/1/94	17,000
Collection of accounts written off in prior years (customer credit was re-established)	9,000
Customer accounts written off as uncollectible during 1994	32,000

What is the balance in the Allowance for Doubtful Accounts at December 31, 1994?

4. At the end of its first year of operations, December 31, 1994, Jergens Inc. reports the following information:

Accounts receivable, net of allowance for doubtful accounts	$950,000
Customer accounts written off as uncollectible during 1994	24,000
Bad debt expense for 1994	79,000

What should be the balance in accounts receivable at December 31, 1994 before subtracting the allowance for doubtful accounts?

5. The following accounts are taken from Joyner Inc.'s balance sheet at December 31, 1994.

	Debit	Credit
Net credit sales		$750,000
Allowance for doubtful accounts	$ 16,000	
Accounts receivable	430,000	

If doubtful accounts are 3% of accounts receivable, determine the bad debt expense to be reported for 1994.

Instructions

Answer the questions relating to each of the five independent situations as requested.

P7-7 **(BAD DEBT REPORTING: AGING)** Snake Corporation Ltd. operates in an industry that has a high rate of bad debts. On December 31, 1994, before any year-end adjustments, the balance in Snake's Accounts Receivable account was $555,000 and the Allowance for Doubtful Accounts had a balance of $25,000. The year-end balance reported in the statement of financial position for the Allowance for Doubtful Accounts will be based on the aging schedule shown below.

Days Account Outstanding	Amount	Probability of Collection
Less than 15 days	$300,000	.98
Between 16 and 30 days	100,000	.90
Between 31 and 45 days	80,000	.80
Between 46 and 60 days	40,000	.70
Between 61 and 75 days	20,000	.60
Over 75 days	15,000	.00

Instructions

(a) What is the appropriate balance for the Allowance for Doubtful Accounts on December 31, 1994?

(b) Show how accounts receivable would be presented on the balance sheet prepared on December 31, 1994.

(c) What is the dollar effect of the year-end bad debt adjustment on the before-tax income for 1994?

(CMA adapted)

P7-8 **(BAD DEBT REPORTING)** From inception of operations to December 31, 1993, Mackenzie Corporation Ltd. provided for uncollectible accounts receivable under the allowance method: provisions were made monthly at 3% of credit sales; bad debts written off were charged to the Allowance account; recoveries of bad debts previously written off were credited to the Allowance account; and no year-end adjustments to the Allowance account were made. Mackenzie's usual credit terms are net 30 days.

The balance in the Allowance for Doubtful Accounts was $110,000 at January 1, 1994. During 1994, credit sales totalled $9,000,000; interim provisions for doubtful accounts were made at 3% of credit sales; $90,000 of bad debts were written off; and recoveries of accounts previously written off amounted to $15,000. Mackenzie installed a computer facility in November 1994 and an aging of accounts receivable was prepared for the first time as of December 31, 1994. A summary of the aging is as follows.

Classification Month of Sale	Balance in Each Category	Estimated % Uncollectible
November–December 1994	$1,080,000	2
July–October	650,000	10
January–June	420,000	25
Prior to 1/1/94	150,000	80
	$2,300,000	

Based on the review of collectibility of the account balances in the "Prior to 1/1/94" aging category, additional receivables totalling $60,000 were written off as of December 31, 1994. The 80% uncollectible estimate applied to the remaining $90,000 in the category. Effective with the year ended December 31, 1994, Mackenzie adopted a new accounting method for estimating the allowance for doubtful accounts at the amount indicated by the year-end aging analysis of accounts receivable.

Instructions

(a) Prepare a schedule analysing the changes in the Allowance for Doubtful Accounts for the year ended December 31, 1994. Show supporting computations in good form. (**Hint:** In computing the 12/31/94 allowance, subtract the $60,000 write-off.)

(b) Prepare the journal entry for the year-end adjustment to the Allowance for Doubtful Accounts balance as of December 31, 1994.

(AICPA adapted)

P7-9 **(BAD DEBT REPORTING)** Presented below is information related to the Accounts Receivable accounts of Kawaiso Inc. during the current year 1994:

1. An aging schedule of the accounts receivable as of December 31, 1994 is as follows.

Age	Net Debit Balance	% to Be Applied After Correction Made
Under 60 days	$173,500	1
61–90 days	137,000	3
91–120 days	40,900*	6
Over 120 days	23,640	$4,200 definitely uncollectible; estimated remainder collectible is 25%
	$375,040	

*The $2,500 write-off of receivables is related to the 91–120 days category.

2. The Accounts Receivable control account has a debit balance of $375,040 on December 31, 1994.

3. Two entries are made in the Bad Debt Expense account during the year: (1) a debit on December 31 for the amount credited to Allowance for Doubtful Accounts and (2) a credit for $2,500 on November 3, 1994, and a debit to Allowance for Doubtful Accounts because of a bankruptcy.

4. The Allowance for Doubtful Accounts is as follows for 1994.

Allowance for Doubtful Accounts

Date	Item	Amount	Date	Item	Amount
Nov. 3	Uncollectible accounts written off	2,500	Jan. 1	Beginning balance	8,750
			Dec. 31	5% of $375,040	18,752

5. A credit balance exists in Accounts Receivable (61–90 days) of $4,800, which represents an advance on a sales contract.

Instructions

Assuming that the books have not been closed for 1994, make the necessary correcting entries.

***P7-10 (JOURNALIZE VARIOUS ACCOUNTS RECEIVABLE AND NOTES RECEIVABLE TRANSACTIONS)** The balance sheet of Gisele Inc. at December 31, 1993 includes the following:

Notes receivable	$ 52,000	
Less: Notes receivable discounted	16,000	$ 36,000
Accounts receivable	$182,100	
Less: Allowance for doubtful accounts	17,300	164,800

Transactions in 1994 include the following:

1. Notes receivable discounted at 12/31/93 matured and were paid, with the exception of a $5,000 note for which the company had to pay $5,070, which included $70 of interest and protest fees. Recovery was expected in 1994. (Use Notes Receivable Past Due account.)
2. Accounts receivable of $139,000 were collected, including accounts of $40,000 on which 2% sales discount were allowed.
3. $6,400 was received in payment of an account that was written off the books as worthless in 1991. (**Hint**: Re-establish the receivable account.)
4. Customer accounts of $19,500 were written off during the year.
5. At year end, the Allowance for Doubtful Accounts was estimated to need a balance of $20,000. This estimate was based on an analysis of aged accounts receivable.
6. Gisele Inc. discounted a $15,000, 90-day note dated November 1, 1994 on December 1, 1994. The note had a 12% interest rate and was discounted at 15%. (Treat as a sale.)

Instructions

Prepare all journal entries necessary to reflect the transactions above.

P7-11 (ASSIGNED ACCOUNTS RECEIVABLE: JOURNAL ENTRIES) Scott Jordan Ltd. financed some of its current operations by assigning accounts receivable to a finance company. On July 1, 1994, it assigned, under guarantee, specific accounts amounting to $70,000. The finance company advanced to Scott Jordan Ltd. 80% of the accounts assigned (20% of the total to be withheld until the finance company has made a full recovery), less a finance charge of ½% of the total accounts assigned.

On July 31, Scott Jordan Ltd. received a statement that the finance company had collected $40,000 of these accounts and had made an additional charge of ½% of the total accounts outstanding as of July 31, this charge to be deducted at the time of the first remittance due to Scott Jordan Ltd. from the finance company. (**Hint**: Make entries at this time.)

On August 31, 1994, Scott Jordan Ltd. received a second statement from the finance company, together with a cheque for the amount due. The statement indicated that the finance company had collected an additional $18,000 and had made a further charge of ½% of the balance outstanding as of August 31.

Instructions

(a) Make all entries on the books of Scott Jordan Ltd. that were involved in the transactions above.

(b) Explain how these accounts should be presented in the balance sheet of Scott Jordan Ltd. at July 31 and at August 31.

(AICPA adapted)

(NOTES RECEIVABLE JOURNAL ENTRIES) Kereluk Sports produces soccer, football, and track shoes. The treasurer recently completed negotiations in which Kereluk Sports agrees to loan Muskoday Inc., a leather supplier, $500,000. Muskoday Inc. will issue a noninterest-bearing note due in five years (a 12% interest rate is appropriate), and has agreed to furnish Kereluk Sports with leather at prices that are 10% lower than those usually charged. **P7-12**

Instructions

(a) Prepare the accounting entry to record this transaction on Kereluk Sports' books.

(b) Determine the alances at the end of each year for which the note is outstanding for the following accounts for Kereluk Sports:

Notes receivable
Unamortized discount
Interest revenue

(NOTES RECEIVABLE JOURNAL ENTRIES) On December 31, 1994, Carbuncle Inc. rendered services to Dalman Limited at an agreed price of $100,000, accepting $28,000 down and agreeing to accept the balance in four equal instalments of $18,000 receivable each December 31. An assumed interest rate of 11% is implicit in the agreed price. **P7-13**

Instructions

Prepare the journal entries to be recorded by Carbuncle Inc. for the sale and for the receipts and interest on the following dates (assuming that the effective interest method is used for amortization purposes):

(a) December 31, 1994.

(b) December 31, 1995.

(c) December 31, 1996.

(d) December 31, 1997.

(e) December 31, 1998.

(DISCOUNTING OF NOTES RECEIVABLE) Riley Inc. accepts Smiley Inc.'s $30,000, six-month note receivable, dated July 31, 1994, payable on January 31, 1995, and bearing interest at 10% for services rendered. On October 31, Riley discounts with recourse Smiley's note at 12% at the Toronto Dominion Bank. **P7-14**

Instructions

(a) Prepare journal entries on Riley's books on the following dates, treating the discounting as a sale transaction:

1. July 31, 1994: Receipt of the note.

2. October 31, 1994: Discounted note with recourse.

3. January 31, 1994: Smiley pays principal and interest to the Toronto Dominion Bank.

4. Assume that, instead of paying off the note on January 31, 1995, Smiley defaults and Riley pays the note, interest, and a bank protest fee of $50.

(b) Prepare journal entries on Riley's books for each of the four events listed in (a), treating the discounting as a borrowing transaction.

P7-15 (COMPREHENSIVE RECEIVABLES PROBLEM) You are engaged in your fifth annual examination of the financial statements of Lester Limited. Your examination is for the year ended December 31, 1994. The client prepared the following schedules of Trade Notes Receivable and Interest Receivable for you at December 31, 1994. You have agreed the opening balances with your prior year's audit workpapers.

Lester Limited
Trade Notes Receivable and Related Interest Receivable
Trade Notes Receivable

	Issue Date	Terms	Interest Rate (%)	Bal. Dec. 31, 1993	1994 Debits	1994 Credits	Bal. Dec. 31, 1994
Morley Co.	4/1/93	One year	14	$50,000		$ 50,000	
Ekberg Co.	5/1/94	90 days after date	—		$ 30,000	29,375	$ 625
Kennedy Ind.	7/1/94	60 days after date	12		6,000		6,000
J. Schmidt	8/3/94	Demand	12		15,000		15,000
					50,000	50,000	
Minerva Corp.	10/2/94	60 days after date	12		50,000		50,000
Slezak Inc.	11/1/94	90 days after date	10		42,000	30,000	12,000
Peaches Ltd.	11/1/94	90 days after date	12		32,000		32,000
Totals				$50,000	$225,000	$159,375	$115,625

Interest Receivable

Due From	Bal. Dec. 31 1993	1994 Debits	1994 Credits	Bal. Dec. 31, 1994
Morley Co.	$5,250	$1,750	$7,000	
Kennedy Ind.		120		$ 120
J. Schmidt		400		400
Minerva Corp.		1,000	575	425
Slezak Inc.		700		700
Peaches Ltd.		640		640
Totals	$5,250	$4,610	$7,575	$2,285

Your examination reveals this information:

1. Interest was computed on a 360-day basis. In computing interest, it was the corporation's practice to exclude the first day of the note's term and to include the due date.

2. The Ekberg Company's 90-day noninterest-bearing note was discounted on May 16 at 10%, and the proceeds were credited to the Trade Notes Receivable account. The note was paid at maturity.

3. Kennedy Industries became bankrupt on August 31, and the corporation would recover 60 cents on the dollar. The corporation used the allowance method for recording bad debt expense.

4. Jeannie Schmidt, president of Lester Limited, confirmed that she owed Lester Limited $15,000 and that she expected to pay the note within six months. You are satisfied that the note is collectible.

5. Minerva Corporation's 60-day note was discounted on November 1 at 10% and the proceeds were credited to the Trade Notes Receivable and Interest Receivable accounts. On December 2, Lester Limited received notice from the

bank that Minerva Corporation's note was not paid at maturity and that it had been charged against Lester's chequing account by the bank. On receiving the notice from the bank, the bookkeeper recorded the note and the accrued interest in the Trade Notes Receivable and Interest Receivable accounts. Minerva Corporation paid Lester Limited the full amount due in January 1995.

6. Slezak Inc.'s 90-day note was pledged as collateral for a $30,000, 60-day, 10% loan from the Royal Bank on December 1.

7. On November 1, the corporation received four, $8,000, 90-day notes from Peaches Ltd. On December 1, the corporation received payment from Peaches Ltd. for one of the $8,000 notes, with accrued interest. Prepayment of the notes was allowed without penalty. The bookkeeper credited the Peaches Ltd. Accounts Receivable account for the cash received.

Instructions

Prepare the adjusting journal entries that you would suggest at December 31, 1994 for the transactions above. Reclassify all past due notes and related carrying costs to accounts receivable.

(AICPA adapted)

(COMPREHENSIVE RECEIVABLES PROBLEM) Ascot Inc. had the following long-term receivable account balances at December 31, 1994: **P7-16**

Note receivable from sale of division	$1,500,000
Note receivable from officer	400,000

Transactions during 1995 and other information relating to Ascot's long-term receivables are as follows:

1. The $1,500,000 note receivable is dated May 1, 1994, bears interest at 10%, and represents the balance of the consideration received from the sale of Ascot's electronics division to Pitt Limited. Principal payments of $500,000 plus appropriate interest are due on May 1, 1995, 1996 and 1997. The first principal and interest payment is made on May 1, 1995. Collection of the note instalments is reasonably assured.

2. The $400,000 note receivable is dated December 31, 1994, bears interest at 9%, and is due on December 31, 1996. The note is due from Bob Doyle, president of Ascot Inc. and is collateralized by 10,000 of Ascot's common shares. Interest is payable annually on December 31 and all interest payments are paid on their due dates through December 31, 1996. The quoted market price of Ascot's common shares is $46 each on December 31, 1995.

3. On April 1, 1995, Ascot sells a patent to Carr Co. Ltd. in exchange for a $100,000 noninterest-bearing note due on April 1, 1997. There is no established exchange price for the patent, and the note has no ready market. The prevailing rate of interest for a note of this type at April 1, 1995 is 12%. The present value of $1 for two periods at 12% is 0.797. The patent has a carrying value of $50,000 at January 1, 1995, and the amortization for the year ended December 31, 1995 will be $10,000. The collection of the note receivable from Carr is reasonably assured.

4. On July 1, 1995, Ascot sells a parcel of land to Denver Limited for $200,000 under an instalment sale contract. Denver makes a $60,000 cash down payment on July 1, 1995, and signs a four-year, 11% note for the $140,000 balance. The equal annual payments of principal and interest on the note will be $45,125, payable on July 1, 1996, through July 1, 1999. The land could have been sold at an established cash price of $200,000. The cost of the land to Ascot is $140,000. Circumstances are such that the collection of the instalments on the note is reasonably assured.

Instructions

(a) Prepare the long-term receivable section of Ascot's balance sheet at December 31, 1995.

(b) Prepare a schedule showing the current portion of the long-term receivables and accrued interest receivable that will appear in Ascot's balance sheet at December 31, 1995.

(c) Prepare a schedule showing interest revenue from the long-term receivables that will appear on Ascot's income statement for the year ended December 31, 1995.

(AICPA adapted)

***P7-17 (PROOF OF CASH)** You have been hired as the new assistant controller of Davidson Inc. and are assigned the task of proving the Cash account balance. As of December 31, 1994, you have obtained the following information relative to the December cash operations:

1. Balance per bank:

11/30/94	$137,600
12/31/94	115,666

2. Balance per books:

11/30/94	101,162
12/31/94	105,439

3. Receipts for the month of December, 1994:

per bank	714,280
per books	742,400

4. Outstanding cheques:

11/30/94	37,258
12/31/94	45,297

5. Dishonoured cheques returned by the bank and recorded by Davidson Inc. amounted to $3,125 during the month of December 1994; according to the books, $2,500 was redeposited. Dishonoured cheques, recorded on the bank statement but not on the books until the following months, amounted to $820 at November 30, 1994 and $1,150 at December 31, 1994.
6. On December 31, 1994, a $1,300 cheque of Northridge Construction was charged to the Davidson Inc. account by the bank in error.
7. Proceeds of a Bryant Company note collected by the bank for Davidson on December 10, 1994 were not entered on the books:

Principal	$2,000
Interest	40
	2,040
Less collection charge	10
	$2,030

8. Interest on a bank loan for the month of December charged by the bank but not recorded on the books amounted to $4,500.
9. Deposit in transit:

12/31/94	$30,150

Instructions

Prepare bank reconciliations as of November 30, 1994 and December 31, 1994 using a four-column "proof of cash" with the following column headings for amounts.

11/30/94 Beginning Reconciliation	Receipts	Disbursements	12/31/94 Ending Reconciliation

Proceed from Balance Per Bank Statement to Balance Per Books.

(PROOF OF CASH) Using the data given in Problem 7-17, prepare (a) a four-column bank reconciliation proceeding from Balance Per Bank Statement to Correct Balance and Balance Per Books to Corrected Balance and (b) accompanying entries to adjust the books at December 31. ***P7-18**

(PROOF OF CASH) You have been hired by Judd Hirsch Manufacturing as an internal auditor. One of your first assignments is to reconcile the bank account for the Manitoba Division. The bank statement shows the following: ***P7-19**

Beginning balance August 1, 1994	$ 90,125
Deposits: (20)	915,376
Cheques: (64) plus debit memos	(851,515)
Service charges: New cheques	(45)
Ending balance August 31, 1994	$ 153,941

The cash account on the books of the Manitoba Division is as follows:

Cash

July 1	64,192	July 31 Cash Disbursements	665,441
July 31 Cash Receipts	682,429	Aug. 1 Bank Reconciliation	375
Aug. 31 Cash Receipts	919,872	Aug. 31 Cash Disbursements	856,456

Your review of last month's bank reconciliation and the current bank statement reveals the following:

1. Outstanding cheques:

July 31, 1994	$25,742
August 31, 1994	33,561

2. Deposits in transit:

July 31, 1994	16,422
August 31, 1994	20,918

3. Cheque 216 for office furniture was written for $795 but recorded in the cash disbursements journal as $975. The bank deducted the cheque as $795.

4. A cheque written on the account of Judd Hirsch Manufacturing for $583 was deducted by the bank from the Manitoba Division account.

5. Included with the bank statement was a debit memorandum dated August 31 for $2,475 for interest on a note taken out by the Manitoba Division on July 30.

6. The service charge for new cheques had not been recorded.

7. The July 31, 1994 bank reconciliation showed as reconciling items a service charge of $25 and an NSF cheque for $350.

Instructions

(a) Prepare a four-column proof of cash reconciling the balance per bank to the balance per book.

(b) Prepare a four-column proof of cash reconciling balance per bank to the Correct Balance and balance per books to the Correct Balance.

(c) Prepare any adjusting journal entries necessary to correct the cash account per the books of the Manitoba Division.

***P7-20 (COMPREHENSIVE JOURNAL ENTRIES FOR SELLER AND FACTOR)** Joan Robinson Ltd. factors $400,000 of accounts receivable with Augustana Factors Inc. on a without-recourse basis. The finance charge is 3% of the amount of receivables and an additional 4% is retained to cover probable adjustments. Per the terms of the factoring agreement, Robinson handles returned goods, allowances, and shipping disputes. Augustana collects the cash and acknowledges sales discounts, but such discounts are charged to Robinson. Credit losses are absorbed by Augustana. Robinson has not recorded any bad debt expense related to the factored receivables. The following transactions pertain to this factoring:

Aug. 1 The receivable records are transferred to Augustana Factors. Augustana estimates that $3,200 of the accounts will prove to be uncollectible.

Aug. 31 Augustana collects $234,000 during August after allowing for $9,000 of sales discounts. Sales returns and allowances during August totalled $2,400.

Sept. 20 Augustana writes off a $2,000 account after learning of the company's bankruptcy.

Sept. 30 Augustana collects $151,720 during September. Sales returns and allowances during September totalled $880.

Oct. 10 Robinson and Augustana make a final cash settlement.

Instructions

(a) Prepare all journal entries for both companies on the above dates.

(b) Compute the net cash proceeds Robinson ultimately realizes from the factoring.

(c) Compute the factor's net income from the factoring.

***P7-21 (COMPREHENSIVE JOURNAL ENTRIES FOR SELLER AND FACTOR)** Bargain Furnishings Inc. factors $700,000 of accounts receivable with Melba Financing on a with-recourse basis. The situation indicates that Bargain should account for the factoring as a borrowing activity. The finance charge is 3% of the amount of accounts receivable; an additional 4% is withheld to cover sales discounts, returns, and allowances. Bargain handles returns, allowances, and shipping disputes. Melba handles cash collections, acknowledging sales discounts that are charged to Bargain. The receivable records are transferred to Melba on February 2, at which time uncollectible accounts are estimated to be $10,000. During February and March, Melba collects $672,400; sales returns and allowances are $9,500; sales discounts are $8,100; and bad debts of $10,000 materialize. On April 7, Bargain and Melba make a final cash settlement.

Instructions

(a) Prepare all journal entries for Bargain Furnishings Inc. that result from the above transactions.

(b) Indicate how the above transactions would be reflected on Bargain's February 2 balance sheet.

***P7-22 (COMPREHENSIVE JOURNAL ENTRIES: FACTORING)** Woolens Inc. factors $1,000,000 of accounts receivable with Wolverine Credit on a without-recourse basis. On June 1, the receivable records are transferred to Wolverine Credit, which will make the collections. Wolverine Credit assesses a finance charge of 4% of the total accounts receivable factored and retains an amount equal to 6% of the total receivables to cover sales discounts, returns, and allowances. Woolens handles any returned goods, claims and allowances for defective goods, and disputes concerning shipments. Wolverine handles the sale discounts and absorbs the credit losses.

During the month of June, the factor collects $650,000; merchandise totalling $14,300 is returned; sales discounts of $12,500 are taken; and allowances of $8,600 are granted.

During the month of July, the factor collects $237,000; merchandise totalling $5,300 is returned; no sales discounts are allowed; and allowances of $3,800 for defective goods are granted.

On August 1, Woolens Inc. and Wolverine Credit agree that any further returns, discounts, and allowances will be absorbed by Woolens; Wolverine therefore returns the balance of the retainer held for such events. Uncollectibles are estimated to be $7,000.

Instructions

(a) Prepare the entries on Woolens' books at June 1, for the June transactions, for the July transactions, and at August 1.

(b) Prepare the entries on Wolverine Credit's books at June 1, for the June transactions, for the July transactions, and at August 1.

FINANCIAL REPORTING PROBLEM

In the Financial Strategy section of a corporate annual report, management stated that "We believe it is more important to focus on the cash flow generated by our business than on net income." Do you agree with management's comment? Explain.

CHAPTER

8 Valuation of Inventories: Cost Flow Methods

Identification, measurement, and disclosure of inventory require careful attention because inventories are one of the most significant assets of many enterprises. The sale of inventory at a price greater than total cost is the primary source of income for manufacturing and retail businesses. Inventories are particularly significant because they may materially affect both the income statement and the balance sheet.

Inventories ***are asset items held for sale in the ordinary course of business or goods that will be used or consumed in the production of goods to be sold.*** Assets that are specifically excluded from inventory because they are not normally sold in the course of business include plant and equipment awaiting final disposition and securities being held for sale.

The accounting problems associated with inventory valuation are complex. Chapters 8 and 9 discuss the basic issues involved in identifying, measuring, and reporting inventoriable items. In Chapter 8, the concentration is on determining the items and costs to be included in inventory, analysing the effect of inventory errors, and describing and comparing cost flow methods applicable to inventory valuation. In Chapter 9, the lower of cost and market rule and inventory estimation methods are examined.

MAJOR CLASSIFICATIONS OF INVENTORY

Objective 1

Identify major classifications of inventory.

A **merchandising business** ordinarily purchases its merchandise in a form ready for sale. It reports the cost assigned to unsold units at the end of the period as merchandise inventory. Only one inventory account, Merchandise Inventory, appears in the financial statements.

A **manufacturing business** produces goods to be sold to merchandising firms. A manufacturing company normally has three inventory accounts—Raw Materials, Work in Process, and Finished Goods. The cost assigned to goods and materials on hand but not yet placed into production is reported as **raw materials inventory.** Raw materials include the wood to make baseball bats or the steel to make cars. These materials ultimately can be traced directly to the end product. In a continuous production process, some units are not completely processed at a given point in time. The cost of the raw material on which production has started, but not completed, plus the direct labour cost applied specifically to this material and an applicable share of manufacturing overhead costs constitute the **work-in-process inventory.** The costs identified with the completed but unsold units on hand at the end of the fiscal period are reported as **finished goods inventory.** The relationship of these inventory accounts and the flow of costs through these accounts in a merchandising company are illustrated and contrasted to that of a manufacturing firm as shown on the following page.

The *CICA Handbook* states that it is desirable to disclose the amounts of the major categories that make up total inventory.[1] It is common, therefore, to see three inventory accounts on the balance

[1] *CICA Handbook* (Toronto: CICA), Section 3030, par. .10.

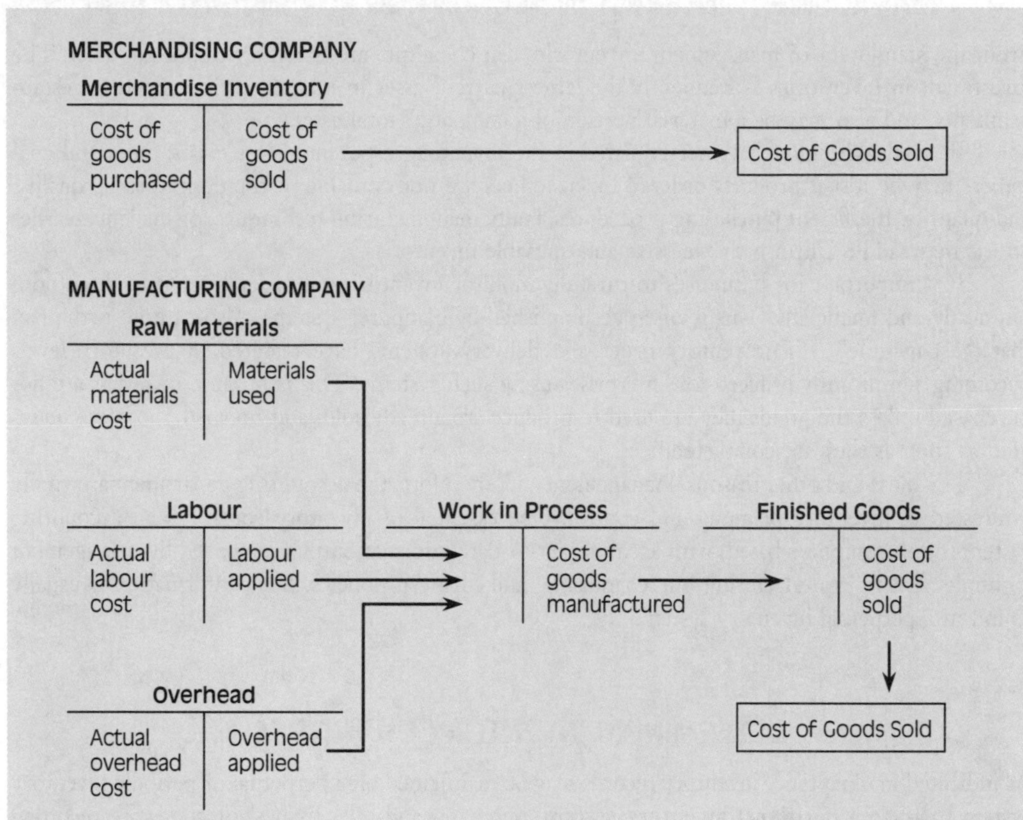

sheet (or in notes cross-referenced to them) of a manufacturer: (1) raw materials, (2) work in process, and (3) finished goods.[2] A **Manufacturing** or **Factory Supplies Inventory** account might also exist for a manufacturing company. This account includes such items as machine oil, nails, and cleaning materials that are used in production but are not the primary materials being processed. As an illustration, an annual report of NOVA Corporation of Alberta reported inventories in the current asset section of its balance sheet at the amount of $291 million, cross-referenced to Note 3 shown below.

NOVA Corporation of Alberta
From the notes to the financial statements

3. Inventories (millions of dollars)

December 31	1991	1990	1989
Materials and supplies	$ 88	$ 75	$ 87
Raw materials	119	161	148
Work in process	7	6	10
Finished goods	77	113	200
	$291	$355	$445

[2] *Financial Reporting in Canada—1991* (Toronto: CICA, 1991), indicated that all components of inventory were set out by approximately 41% of the companies which were surveyed and which had inventory. Lack of such segregation by the remaining companies would, in part, be because they had only one category (for example, they were merchandising companies). For example, Mark's Work Wearhouse Ltd. showed only the amount of $30,606,000 for inventory in the current asset section of its January 25, 1992 balance sheet.

MANAGEMENT INTEREST IN ACCOUNTING FOR INVENTORIES

From the standpoint of management, inventories can constitute an extremely important asset. The investment in inventories is frequently the largest current asset in manufacturing and retail establishments, and also may be a material portion of a company's total assets.

If unsaleable items have accumulated in the inventory, a potential loss exists. Sales and customers may be lost if products ordered by customers are not available in the desired style, quality, and quantity. Inefficient purchasing procedures, faulty manufacturing techniques, or inadequate sales efforts may saddle a firm with excessive and unusable inventories.

It is important for businesses to carefully monitor inventories in order to control them both physically and financially. This is often accomplished by computer systems. Also of note is the fact that "just-in-time" (JIT) inventory order and delivery systems have resulted in inventory levels becoming significantly reduced for enterprises using such systems. This is because materials are not purchased unless the goods they are used to produce are already sold, and finished goods are delivered as soon as they are completed.[3]

For these and other reasons, management and, therefore, the accounting department are vitally interested in inventory planning and control. One essential of inventory control is an accounting system (often computer-based) with accurate, up-to-date information that is needed by management to implement its manufacturing, merchandising, and financial policies. Such information is usually found in a perpetual inventory system.

DETERMINING INVENTORY QUANTITIES

Objective 2

Distinguish between the perpetual and periodic inventory systems.

As indicated in Chapter 3, inventory records may be maintained on a perpetual or periodic inventory system basis. In a **perpetual inventory system,** purchases and sales (issues) of goods are recorded directly in the Inventory account as they occur. No Purchases account is used because the purchases are debited directly to Inventory. A Cost of Goods Sold account is used to accumulate the cost of issuances from inventory as they occur. The balance in the Inventory account at the end of the year should represent the ending inventory amount.

When the inventory records are maintained on a **periodic inventory system,** a Purchases account is used to record acquisitions. The balance in the Inventory account (which represents the beginning inventory) is unchanged during the period. At the end of the accounting period, a closing entry is made which debits the Inventory account for the ending inventory amount and credits the Inventory account for the beginning inventory amount. Costof goods sold is determined by using the following calculation: Beginning Inventory + Net Purchases − Ending Inventory.

To illustrate the difference between a perpetual and a periodic system, assume that Katt Ltd. had the following transactions during the current year.

Beginning inventory	100 units at \$ 6 = \$ 600
Purchases	900 units at \$ 6 = \$5,400
Sales	600 units at \$12 = \$7,200
Ending inventory	400 units at \$ 6 = \$2,400

[3] Ideally, use of a JIT inventory order and delivery system would mean that a manufacturing company would have no, or only a small amount of, work in process inventory at any given time. Some accountants suggest that the flow of costs in a JIT system could, therefore, be described as Last-In-Right-Out. More significantly, however, is the fact that accountants would not have to be concerned with the flow of costs between inventory and cost of goods sold in such a situation because there would be no inventory or only an immaterial amount.

The entries to record these transactions during the current year are as follows.

Entries Under Perpetual and Periodic Inventory Systems

Perpetual Inventory System			Periodic Inventory System		
Purchase merchandise for resale:					
Inventory (900 at $6)	5,400		Purchases (900 at $6)	5,400	
Accounts Payable		5,400	Accounts Payable		5,400
Record sale:					
Accounts Receivable	7,200		Accounts Receivable	7,200	
Sales (600 at $12)		7,200	Sales (600 at $12)		7,200
Cost of Goods Sold					
(600 at $6)	3,600		(No entry necessary)		
Inventory		3,600			
Closing entries:					
			Inventory (ending)	2,400	
(No entry necessary)			Cost of Goods Sold	3,600	
			Purchases		5,400
			Inventory (beginning)		600

When a periodic system is employed, how is the ending inventory determined? One method is to take a **physical inventory count** once a year. However, most companies need more current information regarding their inventory levels to protect against stockouts or overpurchasing and to aid in the preparation of monthly or quarterly financial reports. As a consequence, many companies use a **modified perpetual inventory system** in which increases and decreases in quantities only—not dollar amounts—are kept in a detailed inventory record. It is merely a memorandum device outside the double-entry system which helps in determining the level of inventory at any point in time.

While a physical inventory count is necessary to determine the ending inventory under a periodic system, a count would also be taken at least once a year under a perpetual inventory system. No matter what type of inventory records are in use or how well organized the procedures for recording purchases and issuances, the danger of error is always present. Waste, breakage, theft, improper entry, failure to prepare or record requisitions, and any number of similar possibilities may cause the inventory records to differ from the actual inventory on hand. This requires periodic verification of the inventory records by actual count, weight, or other measurement. When a difference exists between the count and the perpetual inventory account amount, an entry is needed to correct the perpetual inventory account. To illustrate, assume that at the end of the reporting period the perpetual inventory account had a balance of $2,600, but a physical count indicated $2,400 was actually on hand. The entry to record the necessary write-down is as follows:

Inventory Over and Short	200	
Inventory		200

Perpetual inventory overages and shortages generally represent a misstatement of cost of goods sold. The difference is a result of normal and expected shrinkage, breakage, shoplifting, incorrect record-keeping, and the like. Inventory Over and Short would therefore be an adjustment of cost of goods sold. In practice, the account Inventory Over and Short is sometimes reported in the Other

Revenues and Gains or Other Expenses and Losses section, depending on its balance. Note that in a periodic inventory system the Inventory Over and Short account does not exist because there are no accounting records available against which to compare the physical count. Thus, inventory overages and shortages are buried in cost of goods sold.

As indicated previously, most companies take a physical inventory count only once a year.[4] More frequent counts are desirable in businesses that deal in extremely costly merchandise, but in general an annual physical inventory is sufficient to ensure reasonable accuracy of the records.

The physical inventory count should be taken near to the end of the concern's fiscal year. Because this is not always possible, physical inventories taken within two or three months of the year's end are satisfactory if detailed inventory records are maintained with a fair degree of accuracy.

BASIC ISSUES IN INVENTORY VALUATION

When goods sold or used during an accounting period do not correspond exactly to the goods bought or produced during that period, the quantity of physical inventory held either increases or decreases. In addition, the cost of the items could increase or decrease during a period. Accounting for these increases or decreases requires that the cost of all the goods available for sale or use be allocated between the goods that were sold or used and those that are still on hand. The **cost of goods available for sale or use** is the sum of (1) the cost of the goods on hand at the beginning of the period and (2) the cost of the goods acquired or produced during the period. The **cost of goods sold** is the difference between the cost of goods available for sale during the period and the cost of goods on hand at the end of the period as shown below.

Beginning inventory, Jan. 1	$100,000
Cost of goods acquired or produced during the year	800,000
Total cost of goods available for sale	$900,000
Ending inventory, Dec. 31	200,000
Cost of goods sold during the year	$700,000

Within this calculation, the valuation (measurement) of the ending inventory is a major accounting issue. The resulting amount is a significant determinant of the current and following years' cost of goods sold and net income (i.e. ending inventory of the current year is the beginning inventory of the next year). Also, the ending inventory amount is reported in the current year's balance sheet as a current asset.

The valuation of inventories can be a complex process that requires determination of:

1. ***The physical goods or items to be included in inventory*** (who owns the goods?—goods in transit, consigned goods, special sales agreements).
2. ***The cost to be included in inventory*** (product vs. period costs, variable costing vs. absorption costing).
3. ***The cost flow assumption to be adopted*** (specific identification, average cost, FIFO, LIFO).

PHYSICAL GOODS TO BE INCLUDED IN INVENTORY

Technically, purchases should be recorded when legal title to the goods passes to the buyer (i.e. the risks and rewards of ownership are transferred to the buyer). General practice, however, is to record

[4] Some companies have developed inventory controls or methods of verifying inventories, including statistical sampling, that are highly effective and sufficiently reliable to make unnecessary an annual physical count of each item of inventory.

acquisitions when the goods are received, because it is difficult for the buyer to determine the exact time of legal passage of title for every purchase and because no material error is likely to result from such a practice if it is consistently applied.

Goods in Transit

Purchased merchandise that is in transit—not yet received—at the end of a fiscal period may or may not be the property of the buyer. To determine who (seller or buyer) owns goods in transit, the "transfer of risks and rewards" rule must be applied. To do this requires knowledge of the terms of the purchase-sale contract which stipulates when legal title for the goods passes from the seller to the buyer.

If the goods are shipped **f.o.b. shipping point** (f.o.b. means free on board), risks and rewards of ownership (i.e. legal title) pass to the buyer when the seller delivers the goods to the common carrier (transporter) who acts as an agent for the buyer. If the goods are shipped **f.o.b. destination,** risks and rewards do not pass until the goods reach the destination. "Shipping point" and "destination" are designated by a particular location, for example, f.o.b. Montreal.[5]

Therefore, goods in transit at the end of a fiscal period that were sent f.o.b. shipping point should be recorded by the buyer as purchases of the period and be included in ending inventory. To disregard such purchases would result in an understatement of inventories and accounts payable in the balance sheet and an understatement of purchases and ending inventories in the calculation of cost of goods sold for the income statement. If the goods were shipped f.o.b. destination, they would not be recorded as purchases until the following period when they are received. To ensure that goods in transit at the end of a period are correctly accounted for in the appropriate time period, the accountant normally prepares a purchase cut-off schedule for the end of the period. Because goods in transit sent f.o.b. shipping point on or before the period's end would not be received until after the end of the period, the cut-off schedule would not be completed until these goods were received.

When a purchase-sale contract makes no reference to the freight charges, it is assumed that (1) the buyer pays the freight when the terms are f.o.b. shipping point and (2) the seller pays the freight when the terms are f.o.b. destination. In cases where there is some question as to whether title has passed, the accountant exercises judgement based on industry practices, the intent of the sales agreement, the policies of the parties involved, and any other available evidence of intent.

Consigned Goods

In Appendix 6B, the nature of consignment shipments and accounting for consignment sales was discussed. In terms of accounting for inventory, it is important to recognize that goods out on consignment remain the property of the consignor and must be included in the consignor's inventory at purchase price or production cost plus the cost of handling and shipping involved in the transfer to the consignee. Occasionally, the inventory out on consignment is shown as a separate item or reported in notes, but unless the amount is large there is little need for this.

No entry is made by the consignee to adjust the inventory account for goods received because they are the property of the consignor. The consignee should be extremely careful not to include any of the goods consigned as a part of inventory.

No entry is made by consignee to adjust Inventory account for goods rec'd

Special Sale Agreements

While the transfer of legal title is a general guideline used to determine whether the risks and rewards of ownership have passed from a seller to a buyer, transfer of legal title and the underlying economic

[5] Terms other than f.o.b. shipping point or f.o.b. destination may be used to identify when legal title passes. These terms are used in the text to reflect that an agreement as to when title passes must be reached between the buyer and seller in the purchase-sale contract.

substance of the situation (passage of risks and rewards) may not match. For example, it is possible that legal title has passed to the purchaser but the seller of the goods retains the risks of ownership. Conversely, transfer of legal title may not occur, but the economic substance of the transaction is that the seller no longer retains the risks and rewards of ownership. Three special sale situations, discussed in Chapter 6 from a revenue recognition perspective, are considered below in terms of inventory implications.

Sales with Buyback Agreement. Sometimes an enterprise finances its inventory without reporting either the liability or the inventory on its balance sheet. Such an approach usually involves the "sale" of a good with either an implicit or explicit "buyback" agreement. These arrangements are often referred to as **product financing arrangements** or described as **parking transactions** (because the seller simply parks the inventory on another enterprise's balance sheet for a short period of time).

To illustrate, Hill Enterprises transfers ("sells") inventory to Chase Inc. and simultaneously agrees to repurchase this merchandise at a specified price over a specified period in the future. Chase Inc. then uses the inventory as collateral and borrows against it, using the loan proceeds to pay Hill Enterprises. Hill Enterprises repurchases the inventory in the future and Chase Inc. employs the proceeds from repayment to meet its loan obligation.

The essence of this transaction is that Hill Enterprises is financing its inventory—and retaining risks of ownership—even though technical title to the merchandise was transferred to Chase Inc. The advantage to Hill Enterprises for structuring a transaction in this manner is the removal of the current liability from its balance sheet and the ability to manipulate income. The advantages to Chase Inc. are that the purchase of the goods may solve a LIFO liquidation problem (discussed later), or that it may be interested in a reciprocal agreement at a later date.

The *CICA Handbook*, section 3400 (regarding revenue recognition), has implications that will tend to curtail this practice, at least in terms of enabling a "selling company" to remove the inventory and liability from its balance sheet. This is because the *Handbook* requires the seller to transfer the risks and rewards of ownership before a sale can be recognized.[6] By implication, a "buying company" should not recognize the goods received as its inventory. Canadian practitioners, however, will have to continue to exercise judgement regarding substance over form in such situations.

Sales with High Rates of Return. Quality Publishing Co. Ltd. delivers (sells) textbooks to University Bookstores with an agreement that any books not sold may be returned for full credit. In the past, approximately 25% of the textbooks delivered were returned. Should Quality Publishing report its deliveries to University Bookstores as sales transactions or should it treat the delivered books as inventory until being notified of how many were sold? An acceptable accounting treatment is that, if a reasonable prediction of the returns can be established, then the goods should be considered sold. Conversely, if returns are unpredictable, removal of these goods from the inventory is inappropriate. Essentially, the choice of an appropriate treatment depends on whether there is reasonable assurance of the measurement of the ultimate consideration to be derived from the sale given that goods may be returned.[7] If not, only the items actually sold by the purchaser could be accounted for as revenue, with all remaining items being part of the seller's inventory.

Sales on Instalment. Because the risk of loss from uncollectibles is higher in instalment sale situations than in other sale transactions, the seller often withholds legal title to the merchandise until all the payments have been made. The question is whether the inventory should be considered sold, even though legal title has not passed. The economic substance of the transaction is that the goods should be excluded from the seller's inventory if the percentage of bad debts can be reasonably estimated.

---

[6] *CICA Handbook*, Section 3400, par. .07.

[7] *Ibid.*

EFFECT OF INVENTORY ERRORS

If items are incorrectly included in or excluded from inventory, there will be errors in the financial statements.

Objective 3

Identify the effects of inventory errors on the financial statements.

Ending Inventory Misstated. What would happen if the beginning inventory and purchases are recorded correctly, but some items on hand are not included in ending inventory? In this situation we would have the following effects on the financial statements at the end of the period.

Balance Sheet		Income Statement	
Inventory	Understated	Cost of goods sold (ending inventory is understated)	Overstated
Working capital (current assets less current liabilities)	Understated	Net income	Understated
Current ratio (current assets divided by current liabilities)	Understated		
Retained earnings	Understated		

Net income and, therefore, retained earnings are understated because cost of goods sold is overstated; the current ratio and working capital are understated because a portion of ending inventory is omitted.

To illustrate the effect on net income over a two-year period, assume that, for the current year, the ending inventory of Weiseman Inc. is understated by $10,000 and that all other items are correct. The effect of this error will be an understatement of net income in the current year and an overstatement of net income in the following year relative to the correct net income amounts. The error will affect the following year because the beginning inventory will be understated, thereby causing net income to be overstated. Both net income figures are misstated, but the total for the two years is correct as the two errors will be counterbalanced (offset) as illustrated in the first box on page 392.

If ending inventory is overstated, the reverse effect occurs. Inventory, working capital, current ratio, net income, and retained earnings are all overstated and cost of goods sold is understated. The effect of the error on the net income will be counterbalanced in the next year, but both years' net income will be misstated, thereby destroying the usefulness of any analysis of a trend in earnings.

Purchases and Inventory Misstated. Suppose that certain goods that we own are not recorded as a purchase and were not counted in ending inventory. The effect on the financial statements (assuming this purchase is on account) is shown in the second box on page 392.

To omit goods from purchases and inventory results in an understatement of inventory and accounts payable in the balance sheet and an understatement of purchases and ending inventory in the calculation of cost of goods sold in the income statement. Net income for the period and, therefore, retained earnings are not affected by the omission because purchases and ending inventory are both understated by the same amount—the error offsets itself in cost of goods sold. Total working capital is unchanged, but the current ratio is overstated (given it was greater than 1 to 1) because of the omission of equal amounts from inventory and accounts payable.

To illustrate the effect on the current ratio, Relias Company understated accounts payable and ending inventory by $40,000. The understated and correct data are shown in the third box on page 392. The correct ratio is 2 to 1 instead of 3 to 1. Thus, understatement of accounts payable and ending inventory can lead to a "window dressing" of the current ratio (make it appear better than it is).

If both purchases (on account) and ending inventory are overstated, then the effects on the balance sheet are exactly the reverse. Inventory and accounts payable are overstated and the current ratio is understated—working capital and retained earnings are not affected. Cost of goods sold and net income are not affected because the errors offset one another.

Weiseman Inc.
Effect of Inventory Error on Two Periods
(All figures assumed)

	Incorrect		Correct	
	1993	1994	1993	1994
Revenues	$100,000	$100,000	$100,000	$100,000
Cost of goods sold				
Beginning inventory	$ 25,000	$ 20,000	$ 25,000	$ 30,000
Purchased or produced	45,000	60,000	45,000	60,000
Goods available for sale	$ 70,000	$ 80,000	$ 70,000	$ 90,000
Less: Ending inventory	20,000*	40,000	30,000	40,000
Cost of goods sold	$ 50,000	$ 40,000	$ 40,000	$ 50,000
Gross profit	$ 50,000	$ 60,000	$ 60,000	$ 50,000
Administrative and selling expenses	40,000	40,000	40,000	40,000
Net income	$ 10,000	$ 20,000	$ 20,000	$ 10,000
	Total income for 2 years = $30,000		Total income for 2 years = $30,000	

*Ending inventory understated by $10,000 in 1993.

Balance Sheet		Income Statement	
Inventory	Understated	Purchases	Understated
Accounts payable	Understated	Ending inventory in cost of goods sold calculation	Understated
Working capital	No effect	Cost of goods sold	No effect
Current ratio	Overstated	Net income	No effect
Retained earnings	No effect		

Purchases and Ending Inventory Understated		Purchases and Ending Inventory Correct	
Current assets	$120,000	Current assets	$160,000
Current liabilities	$ 40,000	Current liabilities	$ 80,000
Current ratio	3 to 1	Current ratio	2 to 1

The importance of accurate computation of purchases and inventory to ensure that appropriate amounts are presented in financial statements cannot be overemphasized. One only has to read the financial press to learn how the misstatement of inventory can generate high income numbers. For example, Anixter Bros. Inc. once had to restate its income by $1.7 million because an accountant in the antenna manufacturing division overstated the ending inventory thereby reducing its cost of sales. The practice of some Canadian farm equipment manufacturers of treating deliveries to dealers as sales of the company (with concurrent reductions in inventory) can also result in significantly inflating reported income when sales to the ultimate consumer do not keep pace with the deliveries.

COSTS TO BE INCLUDED IN INVENTORY

One of the most important problems in dealing with inventories concerns the amount at which the inventory should be stated in the accounting reports. Inventories, like other assets, are generally accounted for on a basis of cost (other bases are discussed in Chapter 9).

Objective 4

Identify the items that are included as inventory cost.

Product Costs

Product costs are those costs that "attach" to the inventory. These costs are directly connected with the bringing of goods to the place of business of the buyer and converting such goods to a saleable condition. Such charges would include the purchase price of the items and related freight, hauling and other direct costs of acquisition, as well as labour and other production costs incurred in processing the goods up to the time of sale.

It would be theoretically correct to allocate to inventories a share of any buying costs or expenses of a purchasing department, storage costs, and other costs incurred in handling the goods before they are sold. Because of the practical difficulties involved in allocating such costs and expenses, however, these items are not ordinarily included in valuing inventories.

Period Costs

Selling expenses and, under ordinary circumstances, **general and administration expenses** are not considered to be directly related to the acquisition or production of goods and, therefore, are not considered to be a part of the cost of inventories. Such costs are **period costs** rather than product costs.

Conceptually, these expenses are as much a cost of the product as the initial purchase price and related freight charges attached to the product. Why then are these costs not considered inventoriable? In some cases, these charges are not material and no real purpose is served by making an allocation of these costs to inventory. In other situations, especially where selling expenses are significant, the cost is more directly related to the cost of goods sold than to the unsold inventory. In most cases, the costs are so unrelated or indirectly related to the inventory acquisition process that any allocation is purely arbitrary. One guideline that may be followed is to charge to inventory those costs that bear a fairly direct relationship to the quantity produced or purchased. If, for example, an increase in administrative expenses occurs without a subsequent increase in inventories, justification exists for treating the cost as a period charge on the basis that the inventory quantities were not affected.

Interest costs associated with getting inventories ready for sale usually are expensed as incurred. A major argument for this approach is that interest costs are a cost of financing and not a cost of the asset. Additionally, it may be argued that the informational benefit of capitalizing interest costs to inventory does not justify the cost of doing it. Others have argued, however, that interest costs incurred to finance activities associated with bringing inventories to a location and condition ready for sale are as much a cost of the asset as materials, labour, and overhead and, therefore, should be capitalized.[8] If interest is capitalized, this policy and the amount capitalized in the current period should be disclosed.[9]

Treatment of Purchase Discounts

Purchase discounts are sometimes reported in the income statement as a financial revenue (similar to interest revenue). However, purchase discounts should really be recorded as a reduction of purchases. Otherwise, a company is recognizing revenue before the goods have been sold (to the extent

[8] The reporting rules related to interest cost capitalization have their greatest impact in accounting for long-term assets and, therefore, are discussed in detail in Chapter 11. This brief overview provides the basic issues when inventories are involved.

[9] *CICA Handbook*, Section 3850, par. .03.

that such purchases are still in inventory at the end of the period). It is generally held that a business does not realize revenue by buying goods and paying bills; it realizes revenue by selling the goods.

The use of a Purchase Discounts account indicates that the company is reporting its purchases and accounts payable at the gross amount. An alternative approach is to record the purchases and accounts payable at an amount net of the cash discounts. This treatment is often considered more theoretically appropriate because it (1) provides a correct reporting of the cost of the asset and related liability and (2) presents the opportunity to measure the inefficiency of financial management if the discount is not taken. In the net approach, the failure to take a purchase discount within the discount period is recorded in a Purchase Discounts Lost account (for which someone is held responsible). The following example serves to illustrate the differences between the gross and net methods.

Entries Under Gross and Net Methods

Gross Method			Net Method		
Purchase cost $10,000, terms 2/10, net 30:					
Purchases	10,000		Purchases	9,800	
Accounts Payable		10,000	Accounts Payable		9,800
Invoices of $4,000 are paid within discount period:					
Accounts Payable	4,000		Accounts Payable	3,920	
Purchase Discounts		80	Cash		3,920
Cash		3,920			
Invoices of $6,000 are paid after discount period:					
Accounts Payable	6,000		Accounts Payable	5,880	
Cash		6,000	Purchase Discounts Lost	120	
			Cash		6,000

If the **gross method** is employed, purchase discounts should be deducted from purchases in determining cost of goods sold. If the **net method** is used, purchase discounts lost should be considered a financial expense and reported in the Other Expense section of the income statement. Many believe that the difficulty involved in using the somewhat more complicated net method is not justified by the resulting benefits. Also, some contend that management is reluctant to report the amount of purchase discounts lost in the financial statements. These reasons may account for the widespread use of the less logical but simpler gross method.

Manufacturing Costs

As previously indicated, a business that manufactures goods utilizes three inventory accounts—Raw Materials, Work in Process, and Finished Goods. Work in process and finished goods include raw materials, direct labour, and manufacturing overhead costs. Manufacturing overhead costs include indirect material, indirect labour, and such items as depreciation, insurance, heat, and electricity incurred in the manufacturing process. The raw materials and work in process inventories are incorporated into a **Statement of Cost of Goods Manufactured** as illustrated in the first box on page 395.

Cost of goods manufactured statements are prepared primarily for internal use; such details are rarely disclosed in published financial statements. The cost of goods sold reported in the income statement of a manufacturing firm is determined in a manner similar to that for a merchandising concern except that the cost of goods manufactured during the year is substituted for the cost of goods purchased. For example, if the inventory of finished goods was $16,000 at the beginning of the year and $10,000 at the end of the year, the calculation of Cost of Goods Sold for the income statement of Leonard Inc. would be as shown in the second box on page 395.

Leonard Inc.
Statement of Cost of Goods Manufactured
For the Year Ended December 31, 1994

Raw materials consumed			
Raw materials inventory, Jan. 1, 1994			$ 14,000
Add net purchases:			
Purchases		$126,000	
Less: Purchase returns and allowances	$1,800		
Purchase discounts	1,200	3,000	123,000
Raw materials available for use			$137,000
Less **raw materials inventory, Dec. 31, 1994**			17,000
Cost of raw materials consumed			$120,000
Direct labour			200,000
Manufacturing overhead			
Supervisors' salaries		$ 63,000	
Indirect labour		20,000	
Factory supplies used		18,000	
Heat, light, power, and water		13,000	
Depreciation on building and equipment		27,000	
Tools expense		2,000	
Patent expense		1,000	
Miscellaneous factory expenses		6,000	150,000
Total manufacturing costs for the period			$470,000
Work in process inventory, Jan. 1, 1994			33,000
Total manufacturing costs			$503,000
Less **work in process inventory, Dec. 31, 1994**			28,000
Cost of goods manufactured during the year			**$475,000**

Cost of goods sold	
Finished goods inventory, Jan. 1, 1994	$ 16,000
Cost of goods manufactured during 1994	475,000
Cost of goods available for sale	$491,000
Finished goods inventory, Dec. 31, 1994	10,000
Cost of goods sold	$481,000

The principles applied in classifying inventory amounts on the income statement and on the balance sheet are the same for a manufacturing firm as for a merchandising concern.

One issue of importance for costing inventory of a manufacturing company is whether or not fixed manufacturing overhead costs should be included in inventory (absorption or full costing) or charged to expenses of the period (variable or direct costing). This issue is briefly discussed in Appendix 8A.

METHODS OF INVENTORY VALUATION

When the number of units of ending inventory and the costs to be included have been determined, inventory valuation requires that a choice be made from several acceptable methods to determine the dollar amount assigned to inventory. The methods available include the following:

Cost Flow Methods:
- Specific Identification
- First-In, First-Out (FIFO)
- Average Cost (weighted average or moving average)
- Last-In, First-Out (LIFO)
- Standard Cost

Cost Modified for Market Value Changes Methods:
- Lower of Cost and Market
- Current Replacement Cost

Cost Approximation (Estimation) Methods:
- Gross Profit
- Retail Inventory

Long-Term Construction Contract Methods:
- Completed Contract
- Percentage of Completion

The method chosen depends on several factors. The remainder of this chapter considers these factors regarding the cost flow methods identified above. The lower of cost and market, gross profit, and retail inventory methods are examined in Chapter 9. The selection of the appropriate method to account for a long-term construction contract was examined in Chapter 6. The current replacement cost method is discussed in Chapter 25.

COST FLOW ASSUMPTIONS: A FRAMEWORK FOR ANALYSIS

Objective 5

Understand the difference between physical flow of inventory and cost flow assigned to inventory.

During any given fiscal period it is likely that merchandise will be purchased at several different prices. If inventories are to be priced at cost and numerous purchases have been made at different unit costs, the question arises as to which of the various costs should be assigned to Inventory on the balance sheet and which costs should be charged to Cost of Goods Sold on the income statement? Conceptually (to match actual costs with the physical flow of goods), a specific identification of the cost of items sold and unsold seems appropriate, but this is often not only difficult but impossible to do. Consequently, the accountant must turn to the consistent application of one of several other cost methods that are based on differing but systematic inventory cost flow assumptions. Indeed, the actual physical flow of goods and the cost flow assumption are often quite different. ***There is no requirement that the cost flow assumption adopted be consistent with the physical movement of goods.***

Issues regarding the various cost flow methods will be illustrated and discussed using the following data which summarizes inventory related activities of Call-Mart Inc. during its ***first month of operations***. It is important to note that the company experienced ***increasing unit costs for its purchases throughout the month.***

Call-Mart Inc.

Inventory Related Activities (Basic Data)

Date	Purchases	Sold or Issued	Balance
Mar. 2	2,000 @ $4.00		2,000 units
Mar. 15	6,000 @ 4.40		8,000 units
Mar. 19		4,000 units	4,000 units
Mar. 30	2,000 @ 4.50		6,000 units

The ending inventory consisted of 6,000 units. Also, the 4,000 units were sold for $10.00 each for a total sales revenue of $40,000. As there was no beginning inventory, there were 10,000 units available for sale at a total cost of $43,400.

The problem is which cost or costs should be assigned to the 6,000 units of ending inventory and to the 4,000 units sold. The solution depends on what one wishes to accomplish. There are, as previously indicated, several acceptable alternative cost flow methods that may be chosen. These methods are based on different assumptions and accomplish different objectives. A suggested approach to selecting a method is as follows:

1. Identify possible objectives to be accomplished.
2. Know the different acceptable methods, their assumptions, and how they work.
3. Evaluate the advantages and disadvantages of the different methods for achieving the objectives.
4. Choose the method appropriate to the situation and the objective(s) to be accomplished.

OBJECTIVES OF INVENTORY VALUATION

Objective 6

Recognize there are various objectives to accomplish when assigning costs to inventories.

The following general objectives are often associated with making a decision as to which inventory cost flow method to choose:

1. To match expenses (cost of goods sold) realistically against revenue.
2. To report inventory on the balance sheet at a realistic amount.
3. To minimize income taxes.

While the first two are legitimate objectives of financial statements, the third should not be relevant to financial statement accounting; however, it sometimes enters into financial accounting systems for reasons of expediency.

The financial statement objectives of inventory valuation are inherently logical and useful when assessing the merits and limitations of the various cost flow methods within the framework of generally accepted accounting principles. They do, however, beg the question of "what is realistic?" The answer will depend on the purpose of preparing the financial statements. More will be said of this later in this chapter under the heading "Which Method to Select?"

COST FLOW METHODS OF INVENTORY VALUATION: THEIR ASSUMPTIONS AND HOW THEY WORK

Specific Identification

Objective 7

Describe and compare the cost flow assumptions used in accounting for inventories.

Specific identification requires identifying each item sold and each item in inventory. The costs of the specific items sold are included in the cost of goods sold, while the costs of specific items on hand are included in the inventory. This method may be used only in instances where it is practical to identify specific items and their costs from the different purchases made. Any goods on hand may then be identified as quantities remaining from specific purchases, and the invoice cost of each lot or item may be separately determined.

This method has limited application in most companies because of the impossibility or impracticability of segregating specific items as coming from separate purchases. It can be successfully applied, however, in situations where a relatively small number of costly, easily distinguishable (e.g., by physical characteristics, serial numbers, or special markings) items are handled. In the retail trade this includes some types of jewellery, fur coats, automobiles, and some furniture and appliances. In manufacturing it includes special orders and products manufactured under a job cost system.

Given the data for Call-Mart Inc., suppose it was determined that the 6,000 units of inventory consisted of 1,000 from the March 2 purchase, 3,000 from the March 15 purchase, and 2,000 from the March 30 purchase. Ending inventory and cost of goods sold would be determined as shown on page 398.

Conceptually, this method is appealing because actual costs are matched against actual revenues and ending inventory is at actual cost. The cost flow matches the physical flow of the goods.

Specific Identification Method

Date Purchased	Units	Unit Cost	Total
Mar. 2	1,000	$4.00	$ 4,000
Mar. 15	3,000	4.40	13,200
Mar. 30	2,000	4.50	9,000
Ending inventory	6,000		$26,200

Goods available for sale (total of beginning inventory and purchases)	$43,400
Deduct ending inventory	26,200
Cost of goods sold	$17,200

On closer observation, however, deficiencies can be found in using this method as a basis for inventory valuation and income measurement.

One argument against specific identification is that it enables manipulation of net income. For example, assume that a wholesaler purchases plywood early in the year at three different prices. When the plywood is sold, the wholesaler can, if desired, select either the lowest or the highest cost to charge to expense simply by selecting the plywood from a specific lot for delivery to the customer. A business manager, therefore, can manipulate net income by delivering to the customer the higher or lower cost item, depending on whether a lower or higher reported income is desired for the period.

Another problem relates to the arbitrary allocation of costs that sometimes occurs with specific inventory items. In certain circumstances, it is difficult to relate adequately, for example, shipping charges and discounts directly to a given inventory item. The alternative, then, is to allocate these costs somewhat arbitrarily, which leads to a breakdown in the precision of the specific identification method.[10]

First-In, First-Out (FIFO)

The **FIFO method** assigns costs to goods sold in the order in which costs were incurred; that is, the cost of the first good purchased is assumed to be the cost of the first sold (in a merchandising concern) or first used (in a manufacturing concern). The cost assigned to the inventory remaining would therefore come from the most recent purchases (i.e. "last-in, still-here").

Using the data for Call-Mart Inc., and assuming that the company is using the FIFO method and the periodic system (amount of inventory computed only at the end of the month), the cost of the ending inventory is computed by starting with the most recent purchase and working back until all units in the inventory are accounted for. The ending inventory and cost of goods sold are determined on the following page.

[10] A good illustration of the cost allocation problem arises in the motion picture industry. Often actors and actresses receive a percentage of net income for a given movie or television program. Some actors who have these arrangements have alleged that their programs have been extremely profitable to the studios but they have received little in the way of profit sharing. Actors contend that the studios allocate additional costs to successful films (specifically identifiable inventory items) to ensure that there will be no profits to share. Such contentions illustrate the type of problems that can emerge when contracts are based on accounting numbers which can incorporate arbitrary allocations. One way to help overcome such problems is to establish specific measurement rules regarding how the accounting numbers are to be determined, rather than just stating the numbers to be used. This should be done before the contract is signed so that all parties clearly understand what they are getting into.

Periodic Inventory System: FIFO Method

Date of Invoice	No. Units	Unit Cost	Total Cost
Mar. 30	2,000	$4.50	$ 9,000
Mar. 15	4,000	4.40	17,600
Ending inventory	**6,000**		**$26,600**

Cost of goods available for sale	$43,400
Deduct ending inventory	26,600
Cost of goods sold	**$16,800**

If a perpetual inventory system in quantities and dollars is used, a cost figure is attached to each withdrawal when it is made. In the example below, the cost of the 4,000 units removed on March 19 would be made up of the items purchased on March 2 and March 15. The inventory on a FIFO basis perpetual system for Call-Mart Inc. as shown discloses the ending inventory cost ($26,600) and a cost of goods sold of $16,800 (2,000 @ $4.00 + 2,000 @ $4.40).

Perpetual Inventory System: FIFO Method

Date	Purchased	Sold or Issued	Balance	
Mar. 2	(2,000 @ $4.00) $ 8,000		2,000 @ $4.00	$ 8,000
Mar. 15	(6,000 @ 4.40) 26,400		2,000 @ 4.00 6,000 @ 4.40	34,400
Mar. 19		2,000 @ $4.00 2,000 @ $4.40 } $16,800	4,000 @ 4.40	17,600
Mar. 30	(2,000 @ 4.50) 9,000		4,000 @ 4.40 2,000 @ 4.50	**26,600**

When FIFO is used, the ending inventory and cost of goods sold for a period would be the same whether a periodic or perpetual system is employed. This is true because the same costs will always be first-in and, therefore, first-out, whether cost of goods sold is recorded as goods are sold throughout the accounting period (the perpetual system) or as a residual at the end of the period (the periodic system).

One objective of FIFO is to approximate the physical flow of goods. When the physical flow of goods is actually first-in, first-out, the FIFO method very nearly represents specific identification. At the same time, it does not permit manipulation of income because the enterprise is not free to pick a certain cost to be charged as an expense.

Another advantage of the FIFO method is that the ending inventory amount is close to its current cost. Because the cost of the first goods in are the cost of the first goods out, the ending inventory amount will be composed of the cost of the most recent purchases. This approach generally provides an approximation of replacement cost for inventory on the balance sheet when the inventory turnover is rapid and/or price changes have not occurred since the most recent purchases.

The basic disadvantage of this method is that current costs are likely not matched against current revenues on the income statement. The oldest costs are charged against the more current revenue, which can lead to distortions in gross profit and net income.

Average Cost

As the name implies, the **average-cost method** prices items in the inventory on the basis of the average cost of the goods available for sale during the period.

When the periodic inventory system is used, the average cost is computed at the end of the period using the **weighted-average cost method.** Using the data for Call-Mart Inc., the application of the weighted-average cost method for a periodic inventory system is as follows.

Periodic Inventory System: Weighted-Average Cost Method

	Date	No. Units	Unit Cost	Total Cost
Inventory	Mar. 1	—	—	—
Purchases	Mar. 2	2,000	$4.00	$ 8,000
Purchases	Mar. 15	6,000	4.40	26,400
Purchases	Mar. 30	2,000	4.50	9,000
Total goods available		10,000		$43,400

Weighted-average cost per unit $\frac{\$43{,}400}{10{,}000} = \$4.34$

Inventory in units 6,000

Ending inventory **6,000 x $4.34 = $26,040**

Cost of goods available for sale	$43,400	
Deduct ending inventory	26,040	
Cost of goods sold	**$17,360**	(= 4,000 × $4.34)

As implied in this example, any beginning inventory is included both in the total units available and in the total cost of goods available in computing the average cost per unit.

Another average-cost method is the **moving-average cost method,** which is used with perpetual inventory systems. The application of the moving-average cost method for a perpetual inventory system is shown below.

Perpetual Inventory System: Moving-Average Cost Method

Date	Purchased	Sold or Issued	Balance
Mar. 2	(2,000 @ $4.00) $ 8,000		(2,000 @ $4.00) $ 8,000
Mar. 15	(6,000 @ 4.40) 26,400		(8,000 @ 4.30) 34,400
Mar. 19		(4,000 @ $4.30) **$17,200**	(4,000 @ 4.30) 17,200
Mar. 30	(2,000 @ 4.50) 9,000		(6,000 @ 4.367) **26,200**

Calculation of moving-average cost per unit:

After March 15 purchase
= Cost of units available / Units available
= [($2,000 × $4.00) + (6,000 × $4.40)] / (2,000 + 6,000)
= ($8,000 + $26,400) / 8,000
= $34,400 / 8,000
= $4.30

After March 30 purchase
= [(4,000 × $4.30) + (2,000 × $4.50)] / (4,000 + 2,000)
= $26,200 / 6,000
= $4.367

As indicated above, a new average unit cost is computed each time a purchase is made. After the March 15 purchase, this cost is $4.30 per unit. This unit cost is used in costing withdrawals until another purchase is made, when a new average unit cost is computed. Accordingly, the unit cost of the 4,000 units withdrawn on March 19 is $4.30, for a total cost of goods sold of $17,200. On March 30 a new unit cost of $4.367 (rounded to three decimals) is determined, given the purchase of 2,000 units for $9,000.

The use of the average-cost methods is usually justified on the basis of practical rather than conceptual reasons. They are simple to apply, objective, and not as subject to income manipulation as some of the other inventory costing methods. In addition, proponents of the average-cost methods argue that it is often impossible to measure a specific physical flow of inventory and therefore it is better to cost items on an average-cost basis. This argument is particularly persuasive when the inventory involved is relatively homogeneous in nature.

In terms of achieving financial statement objectives, an average-cost method results in an average of costs being employed to determine the cost of goods sold in the income statement and ending inventory in the balance sheet. In comparison to the FIFO method, an average-cost method results in more recent costs being reflected in the cost of goods sold, but older costs in ending inventory. Relative to the LIFO method (discussed below) an average-cost method reflects more recent costs in ending inventory, but older costs in the cost of goods sold. Therefore, the average-cost methods may be viewed as a compromise between the FIFO and LIFO methods. Some would argue that, as a compromise, an average-cost method has the advantages of neither and the disadvantages of both of these other methods. In terms of the objective of income tax minimization, an average-cost method can be used in Canada and it may provide some income tax advantages during periods of rising prices.

Last-In, First-Out (LIFO)

The **LIFO method** assigns costs on the assumption that the cost of the most recent purchase is the first cost to be charged to cost of goods sold. The cost assigned to the inventory remaining would therefore come from the earliest acquisitions (i.e. "first-in, still-here").

If the periodic inventory system is used, then it would be assumed that the total quantity sold or issued during the period would have come from the most recent purchases, even though such purchases may have taken place after the actual date of sale. Conversely, the ending inventory costs would consist first of costs from the beginning inventory and then of costs from purchases early in the period. Using the data for Call-Mart Inc., the assumption would be made that the 4,000 units withdrawn consisted of the 2,000 units purchased on March 30 and 2,000 of the 6,000 units purchased on March 15. Therefore, the cost of the ending inventory of 6,000 units would be assumed to come from the cost of any beginning inventory (none in this example) and then the earliest purchases in the period (2,000 units on March 2 and 4,000 units on March 15). The inventory and cost of goods sold would then be computed as shown below.

Periodic Inventory System: LIFO Method

Date of Invoice	No. Units	Unit Cost	Total Cost
Mar. 2	2,000	$4.00	$ 8,000
Mar. 15	4,000	4.40	17,600
Ending inventory	**6,000**		**$25,600**

Cost of goods available for sale	$43,400
Deduct ending inventory	25,600
Cost of goods sold	**$17,800**

If a perpetual inventory system is kept in quantities and dollars, application of the last-in, first-out method will result in an ending inventory of $25,800 and cost of goods sold of $17,600 as shown below.

Perpetual Inventory System: LIFO Method

Date	Purchased	Sold or Issued	Balance	
Mar. 2	(2,000 @ $4.00) $ 8,000		2,000 @ $4.00	$ 8,000
Mar. 15	(6,000 @ 4.40) 26,400		2,000 @ 4.00 6,000 @ 4.40	34,400
Mar. 19		(4,000 @ $4.40) **$17,600**	2,000 @ 4.00 2,000 @ 4.40	16,800
Mar. 30	(2,000 @ 4.50) 9,000		2,000 @ 4.00 2,000 @ 4.40 2,000 @ 4.50	**25,800**

When using the LIFO method, the month-end periodic inventory computation illustrated previously (inventory $25,600 and cost of goods sold $17,800) shows different amounts from the perpetual inventory computation shown above (inventory $25,800 and cost of goods sold $17,600). This is because the former matches the total withdrawals for the month with the total purchases for the month, whereas the latter matches each withdrawal with the immediately preceding purchases. In effect, the periodic computation assumed that goods that were not purchased until March 30 were included in the sale or issue of March 19.While this is not physically possible, remember that it is not necessary to match physical item flows with cost flows when measuring cost of goods sold. The perspective to be taken is that of determining which costs will be matched against the revenues.

EVALUATION OF LIFO RELATIVE TO OTHER COST FLOW METHODS

Objective 8

Evaluate LIFO as a basis for understanding the differences between the cost flow methods.

Use of the LIFO cost flow approach is controversial. Some do not believe it to be appropriate for conceptual reasons while others believe it to be conceptually superior to other approaches, given that financial statements are prepared on an historical cost basis. Arguments for and against the use of LIFO necessarily reflect a perception regarding many fundamental issues about financial accounting: What is relevant? Is the income statement or the balance sheet more important? Should income tax requirements dictate methods to be selected for preparing financial statements?

While reaching a conclusion regarding the acceptability of LIFO is a matter of individual judgement, the following identification of the major advantages and disadvantages of LIFO should be considered. Careful reflection on this listing will indicate that, for most points, the advantages of LIFO become the disadvantages of other cost flow methods (FIFO and Average Cost) and vice versa.

Major Advantages of LIFO

Matching. In LIFO, the more recent costs are matched against current revenues to provide what may be viewed as a more realistic measure of current earnings.[11] During periods of inflation, many

[11] Imperial Oil Limited in 1991, and Petro Canada in 1992, changed to the LIFO method. The explanation given in Petro Canada's financial report for the first quarter of 1992 was: "The change was made to more closely match current costs with current revenues in determination of the results of the Company's operations." While this matching represents the strongest financial reporting advantage of the LIFO method, many are of the opinion that this advantage is outweighed by its disadvantages. For example, at the time of writing this book, the International Accounting Standards Committee had issued an exposure draft which excluded the LIFO method as being a permissible approach for assigning costs to inventories.

challenge the quality of non-LIFO historical cost-based earnings, noting that by failing to match current costs against current revenues ***transitory "paper" or "inventory" profits are created.*** Inventory profits occur when the inventory costs matched against sales are less than the replacement cost of the inventory. The cost of goods sold therefore is perceived to be understated and profit is overstated. By using LIFO (rather than FIFO or average cost), more recent costs are matched against revenues and inventory profits are thereby reduced. Although LIFO has this advantage over other historical cost-based methods, it should be realized that LIFO falls short of measuring current cost (replacement cost) income. In order to measure current cost income, the cost of goods sold should consist of the cost that will be incurred to replace the goods that have been sold (a next-in, first-out approach, which is not currently acceptable).

Future Earnings Hedge. With LIFO, a company's future reported earnings will not be affected substantially by future price declines. LIFO eliminates or substantially minimizes write-downs to market as a result of price decreases because the inventory value ordinarily will be lower than net realizable value. In contrast, inventory costed under FIFO is more vulnerable to price declines, which can reduce net income substantially.

Major Disadvantages of LIFO

Reduced Earnings. Many corporate managers view the lower profits reported under the LIFO method, relative to other methods, as a distinct disadvantage. This view assumes that prices are increasing; when prices are declining, the opposite effect may occur. Some fear that the implications on net income from using LIFO may be misunderstood and that, as a result of the lower profits, the price of the company's shares will fall. In fact, there is some evidence to refute this contention. Studies have indicated that users of financial data exhibit a sophistication that enables them to recognize the impact on reported income from using LIFO compared to other methods and, as a consequence, reflect this in their assessment of a company's share price.

Inventory Understated. Under LIFO, the inventory valuation on the balance sheet is normally outdated because the oldest costs remain in inventory. This understatement presents several problems, but manifests itself most directly in evaluating the working capital position of the company. The magnitude and direction of the variation in the carrying amount of inventory and its current price depend on the degree and direction of the changes in price and the amount of inventory turnover.

Physical Flow. LIFO does not approximate the physical flow of the items except in a few situations (e.g., for sales from a coal pile, the last coal bought is the first coal out as the coal remover is not going to take coal from the inside of the pile). However, matching more recent costs against revenues may be viewed as a higher priority objective than reflecting the physical flow of goods when choosing an inventory valuation method.

Involuntary Liquidation. Use of LIFO raises the problem of involuntary inventory liquidation. If the base or layers of old costs are eliminated (e.g., when units sold exceed the units purchased for a period), strange results can occur because old, irrelevant costs can be matched against current revenues. A severe distortion in reported income for a given period is likely to result.

Poor Buying Habits. Because of the liquidation problem, LIFO may cause poor buying habits. A company may simply purchase more goods and match these costs against revenue to ensure that old costs are not charged to expense. Furthermore, the possibility always exists with LIFO that a company will attempt to manipulate its net income at the end of the year simply by altering its pattern of purchases.

Not Acceptable for Tax Purposes. Because of definitions in the Income Tax Act as to how inventory amounts may be determined, LIFO inventory valuation is not accepted by Revenue Canada for purposes of determining taxable income except in a few special circumstances.

SUMMARY ANALYSIS OF FIFO, WEIGHTED-AVERAGE, AND LIFO METHODS

A summary of the differing effects of the three major cost flow methods on the financial statements is shown on page 405. The numbers were derived in the discussion of each method using the data for Call-Mart Inc. to illustrate the use of the periodic system for the month of March. The sales revenue reflects that the 4,000 units were sold for $10 each. Since there was no beginning inventory, the cost of goods available for sale is the same for all methods. (The continuation of this example for the month of April, which incorporates beginning inventory, is presented in Appendix 8B.) The difference in gross profit and, therefore, net income (other expenses would be the same) is due to the differing cost flow assumptions associated with each method. Since the example incorporated a period of rising prices, the gross profit (and, therefore, net income) is highest under FIFO and lowest under LIFO.

At the bottom of the comparative results is a listing of the three objectives previously identified as being most commonly associated with choosing an inventory method. As developed in the prior discussion, the strongest argument favouring LIFO for financial statement reporting purposes is that it matches more current costs against current revenue. FIFO results in a more current cost for inventory on the balance sheet.

In terms of income tax minimization or deferral of tax payments, the method resulting in the lowest taxable income for the period would be preferred. While LIFO results in the lowest income in periods of rising prices (assuming there is little or no liquidation of old layers), it is not permitted for calculating taxable income in Canada for most businesses. Consequently, the average-cost method, which is permitted by Revenue Canada, would more effectively accomplish this objective in a period of rising prices.

The fact that LIFO is generally not allowed for determining taxable income in Canada is in direct contrast to the situation in the United States, where it is accepted for tax purposes. The Internal Revenue Service in the U.S. requires that if LIFO is used for income tax purposes, it must also be used for financial reporting purposes (this is known as the LIFO conformity rule). While one may argue the merits of LIFO for financial reporting purposes on a more conceptual level, the IRS ruling is likely primarily responsible for the much higher use of the LIFO method in financial statements in the U.S. as compared to Canada.[12]

WHICH METHOD TO SELECT?

Objective 9

Understand the importance of judgement in selecting an inventory cost flow method.

The *CICA Handbook* indicates that Specific Identification, FIFO, Average Cost, and LIFO are generally acceptable and commonly used methods for determining the cost of inventory for financial reporting purposes.[13] The *Handbook* also states:

> The method selected for determining cost should be one which results in the fairest matching of costs against revenues regardless of whether or not the method corresponds to the physical flow of goods.[14]

---

[12] *Financial Reporting in Canada—1991* reported that of 258 inventory cost method disclosures, 121 (47%) used FIFO, 6 (2%) used LIFO, 95 (37%) used average cost, 8 (3%) used specific identification, 2 (1%) used standard cost, 13 (5%) used the retail method, and 13 (5%) used other methods. For comparison, a similar U.S. study, *Accounting Trends and Techniques—1990*, reported that of 1,015 method disclosures, 366 (36%) used LIFO, 401 (39%) used FIFO, 200 (20%) used average cost, and 48 (5%) used other methods. Data from the United States indicate a significant shift from FIFO to LIFO took place during the 1970s and early 1980s. The high rate of inflation and tax advantages of LIFO in such circumstances were, no doubt, at least partially responsible for the shift. Although inflation was also significant in Canada, a shift to LIFO was not evident.

[13] *CICA Handbook*, Section 3030, par. .07. Noteworthy about the *Handbook's* section dealing with inventory is that it does not explicitly identify these methods as the only ones that are acceptable. At the time of writing this book, the Accounting Standards Board's agenda included plans to review and expand the *Handbook's* coverage of inventories.

[14] *Ibid.*, Section 3030, par. .09.

Comparative Results of FIFO, Weighted-Average and LIFO Inventory Methods: Periodic System

	Method					
	FIFO		Weighted-Average		LIFO	
Partial Income Statement:						
Sales Revenue		$40,000		$40,000		$40,000
Cost of Goods Sold:						
Beginning inventory	$ -0-		$ -0-		$ -0-	
Purchases	43,400		43,400		43,400	
Goods Available	$43,400		$43,400		$43,400	
Deduct:						
Ending Inventory	26,600		26,040		25,600	
Cost of Goods Sold		16,800		17,360		17,800
Gross Profit		$23,200		$22,640		$22,200
Balance Sheet:						
Inventory		$26,600		$26,040		$25,600
Objectives:						
1. Matching	Old costs against current revenue		Average cost against current revenue		"Current" costs against current revenue*	
2. Balance Sheet Valuation	"Current" costs*		Average cost		Old costs	
3. Income Tax Minimization	Results in higher taxable income in periods of rising prices.		Best in Canada in periods of rising prices as results in highest cost of goods sold next to LIFO.*		Not allowed in Canada in most situations. If it were, it would be best in periods of rising prices.	

*Results in a realistic accomplishment of objective relative to other methods.

What method will provide the fairest matching? The answer can be derived only by exercising professional judgement, given knowledge of the particular circumstances and the consequences desired in terms of the objectives of the financial statements. As indicated in Chapter 1, a primary objective of financial reporting is to communicate information that is useful to investors, creditors, and others in making their resource allocation decisions and/or assessing management stewardship. Therefore, the inventory valuation method which leads to the accomplishment of this objective would certainly be the fairest (more relevant) one to choose. Making the appropriate choice, however, depends on awareness of a number of things such as who the users are, the decisions being made, and what information fits their decision models. If one method was the fairest for all situations, then the accounting profession would certainly not have acceptable alternative methods. Consequently, in our present state of understanding, professional judgement is the basis for determining the method to use.

An important point is that a company can use one method (FIFO, for example) for financial statement reporting and another method (Average Cost) for tax purposes. This is legal and reasonable as the objectives of financial reporting are different from those of income tax determination. Having "two sets of books" may, however, be inefficient—a judgement requiring the accountant to be fully cognizant of the circumstances.

STANDARD COST METHOD

A manufacturing company that uses a **standard cost system** predetermines the unit costs for material, labour, and manufacturing overhead. Usually the standard costs are determined on the basis of the costs that should be incurred per unit of finished goods when the plant is operating at normal capacity. Deviations from actual costs are recorded in variance accounts that are examined by management so that appropriate action can be taken to achieve greater control over costs.

For financial statement purposes, reporting inventories at standard costs is acceptable if there is no significant difference between actual and standard. If there is a significant difference, the inventory amounts should be adjusted to estimated actual cost.[15] Otherwise the net income, assets, and retained earnings would be misstated. A detailed examination of standard costing is available in most managerial and cost accounting texts, but is beyond the scope of this book.

CONCLUDING COMMENT

All of the inventory valuation methods described in this chapter are used to some extent. Indeed, a company may use different methods for different types of inventory.

It can be seen that freedom to shift from one inventory costing method to another at will would permit a wide range of possible net income figures for a given company for any given period. This would make financial statements less comparable. The variety of methods has been devised to assist appropriate financial reporting rather than to permit manipulation. Hence, it is necessary that the costing method most suitable to a company be selected and, once selected, be applied consistently thereafter. If conditions indicate that the inventory costing method in use may be unsuitable, serious consideration should be given to all other possibilities before selecting another method. If a change is made, it should be clearly explained and its effect disclosed in the financial statements.[16] The following note in the December 31, 1991 financial statements of Imperial Oil Limited provides an example of such disclosure.

[15] *Ibid.*, Section 3030, par. .04.

[16] *Ibid.*, Section 1000, pars. .22 and .23.

Imperial Oil Limited
Excerpt from Note 1 of the
December 31, 1991 Financial Statements

1. REPORTING CHANGES

In 1991 the company changed its method of accounting for inventories to the last-in, first-out (LIFO) method. Previously the cost of crude oil at refineries and of products was determined using the average-cost method while crude oil in transit was valued at actual cost. During periods of fluctuating crude-oil prices, the LIFO method of inventory valuation reflects these changes in the statement of earnings as they occur. The adoption of the LIFO method has been applied retroactively, and prior periods have been restated.

The effect on 1991 and prior years' inventories, net earnings and net earnings per share was:

millions of dollars	*1991*	*1990*	*1989*	*1988*	*1987*
			increase (decrease)		
Inventories	(389)	(687)	(345)	(275)	(415)
Net earnings	173	(209)	(54)	84	(21)
Net earnings per share (dollars)	0.89	(1.09)	(0.30)	0.51	(0.12)

FUNDAMENTAL CONCEPTS

1. Inventories are items held for sale in the ordinary course of business or goods that will be used or consumed in the production of goods to be sold. Inventories are among the most significant assets of manufacturing and merchandising enterprises in terms of size and importance to management.

2. Raw materials, work in process, and finished goods are the major categories of inventory for manufacturing companies. Factory or manufacturing supplies inventory may also exist. Since merchandising companies ordinarily purchase goods in a form ready for sale, only one inventory account—Merchandise Inventory—appears in their financial statements.

3. Two inventory systems are common—perpetual and periodic. The perpetual system results in keeping an up-to-date record of units and cost of inventory items in the accounting records. In this system, additions to and reductions of inventory are recorded as they occur. No such record is kept under the periodic system. Under the periodic system, year-end inventory must be determined by a physical count upon which the amount of ending inventory and cost of goods sold is based. Even under the perpetual system, an annual count is needed to test the accuracy of the records.

4. The valuation (assigning a dollar amount) of inventory affects balance sheet and income statement (through cost of goods sold) amounts.

5. Inventory errors can occur for many reasons throughout the valuation process and, when they occur, can have important consequences regarding financial statement information.

6. Valuation of inventory requires determination of (a) the physical goods to be included, (b) the costs to be included, and (c) the cost flow assumption to be adopted.

7. Items for which there is possession of the risks and rewards of ownership make up the inventory. Ownership regarding goods in transit, consignments, and special sale agreements must be carefully determined by examining contracts and the economic substance of the transactions.

(Continued)

8. Determining the cost to assign to quantities of inventory requires specification of which costs should be included. Basically, the cost should be the laid-down cost (those incurred to get the inventory to its current condition and location). Application of this definition is fairly straightforward for some costs (purchase price, freight, discounts) but difficult for other costs (interest charges, storage costs, fixed manufacturing costs). Consequently, for practical reasons, allocating the latter type of costs to inventory may not be done.
9. If the unit cost is different for various purchases, the question is which costs will be assigned to ending inventory and, as a consequence, to cost of goods sold. The primary cost flow methods for making such an assignment are FIFO, Average Cost, LIFO, and Specific Identification.
10. Determining which cost flow method to use requires (a) identifying the objectives to be accomplished, (b) knowing the various methods, their assumptions, and how they work, (c) evaluating the methods relative to the objectives, and (d) choosing the method that most satisfies the objectives. Inevitably, trade-offs exist between methods and objectives such that no one method satisfies all objectives.
11. The only guidance provided by the *CICA Handbook* is that the method chosen should result in "the fairest matching of costs against revenues regardless of whether or not the method corresponds to the physical flow of goods." Consequently, exercise of judgement is required when choosing a cost flow method.

APPENDIX 8A
Variable Costing Versus Absorption Costing

Fixed manufacturing overhead costs present a special problem in costing inventories because two concepts exist relative to the costs that attach to the product as it flows through the manufacturing process. These two concepts are (1) **variable costing,** frequently called **direct costing,** and (2) **absorption costing,** also called **full costing.**

In a variable costing system, all costs must be classified as variable or fixed. **Variable costs** are those that fluctuate in direct proportion to changes in output, and **fixed costs** are those that remain constant in spite of changes in output. Under variable costing, only costs that vary directly with the production volume are charged to products as manufacturing takes place. Direct material, direct labour, and the variable costs in manufacturing overhead are charged to work-in-process and finished goods inventories and subsequently become part of cost of goods sold. Fixed overhead costs such as property taxes, insurance, depreciation on plant building, and salaries of supervisors are considered to be **period costs** and are not viewed as costs of the products being manufactured. Instead all fixed costs are charged as expenses to the current period under variable costing.

Under an absorption costing system, all manufacturing costs (variable and fixed, direct and indirect) incurred in the factory or production process attach to the product. Direct material, direct labour, and all manufacturing overhead—fixed as well as variable—are charged to output and allocated to cost of goods sold and inventories.

Proponents of the variable costing system believe that it provides information that is more useful to management in formulating pricing policies and in controlling costs than is in reports prepared under an absorption costing system. Also, because fixed costs are included in inventory under the absorption costing system, it may be argued that such a system would result in distorting net income from period to period when production volume fluctuates each period. If such is the case, variable costing may be a more appropriate basis for reporting income. Absorption costing, however, is the dominantly used basis for external financial reporting. Its supporters believe it provides a more reasonable representation of a firm's investment in inventories.

The *CICA Handbook* states:

> In the case of inventories of work in process and finished goods, cost should include the laid-down cost of materials plus the cost of direct labour applied to the product and the applicable share of overhead expense properly chargeable to production.[17]

This statement leaves to one's judgement the issue of how fixed overhead costs are to be treated in terms of whether or not they are "properly chargeable to production." The *Handbook* also states that "in some cases, a portion of fixed overhead is excluded where its inclusion would distort the net income for the period by reason of fluctuating volume of production."[18] This guideline certainly reflects that variable costing is acceptable but suggests that it would be considered more the exception than the rule for external financial reporting. Clearly, however, judgement is called for when making a decision in particular circumstances.

---

[17] *Ibid.*, Section 3030, par. .06.

[18] *Ibid.*, par. .03.

APPENDIX 8B

Inventory Valuation Methods: An Extension of the Example

The example used in the chapter to illustrate the mechanics of the FIFO, Average-Cost, and LIFO methods assumed a situation of no beginning inventory and a period of rising prices. In this appendix, the example is extended for one more month. As such, the ending inventory on March 31 as calculated in the chapter illustrations becomes the beginning inventory for April. The material in this appendix assumes the use of the periodic system and continuing rising prices. If the perpetual system were used, the purchases and sales of April would be recorded in the perpetual inventory record on a basis consistent with the procedures illustrated in the chapter.

The following schedules should be studied carefully to understand how each financial statement figure is calculated and why the results differ among inventory methods. Because the weighted-average cost method will result in the lowest taxable income and, therefore, taxes paid (LIFO is not acceptable for tax purposes), it has been used to determine the amount of cash paid for income taxes when determining cash balances at the end of April. It is assumed that taxes are paid at the end of each month. It should be noted, however, that the calculation of income tax expense when determining net income for each inventory method was based on multiplying the respective income before taxes by 40% (the assumed tax rate). Consequently, this results in a difference between the tax expense and the tax paid for the FIFO and LIFO methods. The difference is because the financial statements are being prepared using an inventory method different from that used for preparing tax returns. The amount of the difference between the tax expense and tax paid is accounted for as an interperiod tax allocation, a complex topic examined in Chapter 19. Also, while recognizing that the March 31 retained earnings would be different under each inventory method, the given $10,000 balance is assumed for all the methods.

Selected Data for April

Beginning cash balance	$ 7,000
Beginning retained earnings	10,000
Beginning inventory (from March 31),	
6,000 units:	
FIFO cost	26,600
Weighted-average cost	26,040
LIFO cost	25,600
Operating expenses for April	10,000
40% tax rate	

Inventory-related activities in April:

Date	Purchases	Sales	Balance in Units
Beginning			6,000
April 5		4,000 @ $11.00	2,000
April 10	3,000 @ $5.00		5,000
April 20	4,000 @ $5.20		9,000
April 25		3,000 @ $11.50	6,000
April 30	1,000 @ $5.25		7,000

The comparative results of using FIFO, Weighted-Average Cost, and LIFO on net income are shown below.

Comparative Results of FIFO, Weighted-Average Cost, LIFO

	FIFO	Weighted-Average	LIFO
Sales	$78,500	$78,500	$78,500
Cost of goods sold	31,600	33,545	36,050
Gross profit	$46,900	$44,955	$42,450
Operating expenses	10,000	10,000	10,000
Income before taxes	$36,900	$34,955	$32,450
Income tax expense	14,760	13,982	12,980
Net income	$22,140	$20,973	$19,470
Cost of Goods Sold:			
Beginning inventory	$26,600	$26,040	$25,600
Purchases	41,050	41,050	41,050
Goods available	$67,650	$67,090	$66,650
Deduct: Ending inventory	36,050	33,545	30,600
Cost of goods sold	$31,600	$33,545	$36,050

The following schedule shows the final balances of selected items at the end of April.

Balance of Selected Items, April 30

Method	Inventory	Gross Profit	Tax Expense	Net Income	Retained Earnings	Cash*
FIFO	$36,050 (1,000 @ $5.25) (4,000 @ $5.20) (2,000 @ $5.00)	$46,900	$14,760 (0.40 × $36,900)	$22,140	$32,140 ($10,000 + $22,140)	$20,468
Weighted-Average	$33,545 $\left(\frac{\$67,090}{14,000} \times 7,000\right)$	$44,955	$13,982 (0.40 × $34,955)	$20,973	$30,973 ($10,000 + $20,973)	$20,468
LIFO	$30,600 (6,000 of Beginning Inventory for $25,600 plus 1,000 @ $5.00)	$42,450	$12,980 (0.40 × $32,450)	$19,470	$29,470 ($10,000 + $19,470)	$20,468

(Continued)

*Cash at month end		= Beginning Balance	+ Sales	– Purchases	– Operating Expenses	– Taxes Paid**
FIFO:	$20,468	= $7,000	+ $78,500	– $41,050	– $10,000	– $13,982
Weighted-Average:	$20,468	= $7,000	+ $78,500	– $41,050	– $10,000	– $13,982
LIFO:	$20,468	= $7,000	+ $78,500	– $41,050	– $10,000	– $13,982

**Taxes paid in all cases are based on weighted-average method calculations which result in the lowest amount under Canadian tax reporting in this situation. Any difference between tax expense and tax paid would result in adjusting Deferred Income Taxes as discussed in Chapter 19.

Note: All **asterisked** questions, cases, exercises, or problems relate to material contained in the appendices.

QUESTIONS

1. Why should inventories be included (a) in the balance sheet and (b) in the computation of net income?
2. In what ways are the inventory accounts of a merchandising business different from those of a manufacturing enterprise?
3. What is the difference between a perpetual inventory system and a periodic inventory system? If a company maintains a perpetual inventory, should its physical inventory at any date be equal to the amount indicated by the perpetual inventory records? Why?
4. Where, if at all, should the following items be classified on a balance sheet?
   (a) Manufacturing supplies.
   (b) Goods received on consignment.
   (c) Raw materials.
   (d) Land held by a realty firm for sale.
   (e) Goods in transit that were recently purchased f.o.b. destination.
   (f) Goods out on approval to customers.
5. Clayton Inc. indicated in a recent annual report that approximately $8 million of merchandise was received on consignment. Should Clayton Inc. report this amount on its balance sheet? Explain.
6. What is a "sales with buyback" agreement? How should such an arrangement be reported in the financial statements of the "seller"?
7. At a balance sheet date Doberville Ltd. held title to goods in transit amounting to $110,100. This amount was omitted from the purchases figure for the year and also from the ending inventory. What is the effect of this omission on the net income for the year as calculated when the books are closed? On the company's financial position as shown in its balance sheet? Is materiality a factor in determining whether an adjustment for this item should be made?
8. Define "cost" as applied to the valuation of inventories.
9. Herbie Co. Ltd. purchases 100 units of an item at a total invoice cost of $30,000. What is the cost per unit? If the goods are shipped f.o.b. shipping point and the freight bill was $3,000, what is the cost per unit if Herbie pays the freight charges? If these items were bought on 2/10, n/30 terms and the invoice and the freight bill were paid within the discount period, what would be the cost per unit?
10. Havasi Corp. is considering alternative methods of accounting for the cash discounts it takes when paying suppliers promptly. One method suggested was to report these discounts as financial revenue (like interest revenue) when payments are made. Comment on the propriety of this approach.
11. Specific identification is sometimes said to be the ideal method of assigning cost to inventory and to cost of goods sold. Briefly indicate the arguments for and against this method of inventory valuation.
12. As compared with the FIFO method of costing inventories, does the LIFO method result in a larger or smaller net income in a period of rising prices? What is the comparative effect on net income in a period of falling prices?
13. First-in, first-out; weighted-average cost; and last-in, first-out methods are often used instead of specific identification for inventory valuation purposes. Compare these methods with the specific identification method, discussing the theo-

retical propriety of each method regarding the determination of income and asset valuation.

14. In an article which appeared in *The Wall Street Journal*, the phrases "phantom (paper) profits" and "high LIFO profits through involuntary liquidation of inventory" were used. Explain what was likely meant by these phrases.

15. Define standard costs. What are the advantages of a standard cost system? Present arguments in support of each of the following three methods of treating standard cost variances (actual costs—standard costs) for purposes of financial reporting:
    (a) They may be carried as deferred charges or credits on the balance sheet.
    (b) They may appear as charges or credits on the income statement.
    (c) They may be allocated between inventories and cost of goods sold.

*16. Briefly indicate the arguments for and against variable costing. Indicate how each of the following conditions would affect the amounts of net income reported under conventional absorption and variable costing.
    (a) Sales and production are in balance at a standard volume.
    (b) Sales exceed production.
    (c) Production exceeds sales.

*17. What is the difference between variable costing and conventional absorption costing? Is variable costing acceptable for external financial reporting? Explain.

CASES

(INVENTORIABLE COSTS) Peter Packrat, an inventory control specialist, is interested in better understanding the accounting for inventories. Although Peter understands the more sophisticated computer inventory control systems, he has little knowledge of how inventory cost is determined. In studying the records of Eastwood Enterprises which sells normal brand-name goods from its own store and on consignment through Sherie Inc., he asks you to answer the following questions. C8-1

Instructions

(a) Should Eastwood Enterprises include in its inventory normal brand-name goods purchased from, and sent by, its suppliers but not yet received if the terms of purchase are f.o.b. shipping point (manufacturer's plant)? Why?

(b) Should Eastwood Enterprises include freight-in expenditures for the goods in (a) as an inventory cost? Why?

(c) Eastwood Enterprises purchased cooking utensils for sale in the ordinary course of business three times during the current year, each time at a higher price than the previous purchase. What would have been the effect on ending inventory and cost of goods sold had Eastwood used the weighted-average cost method instead of the FIFO method?

(d) What are products on consignment? How should they be treated in the financial records of the consignor (Eastwood Enterprises) and the consignee (Sherie Inc.)?

(AICPA adapted)

(INVENTORIABLE COSTS) You are asked to travel to Calgary to observe and verify the inventory of the Calgary branch of one of your clients. You arrive on Thursday, December 30, and find that the inventory procedures have just been started. You see a railway car on the sidetrack at the unloading door and ask the warehouse superintendent how she plans to inventory the contents of the car. She responds: "We are not going to include the contents in the inventory." C8-2

Later in the day, you ask the bookkeeper for the invoice on the carload and the related freight bill. The invoice lists the various items, prices, and extensions of the goods in the car. You note that the carload was shipped December 24 from Montreal, f.o.b. Montreal, and that the total invoice price of the goods in the car was $34,200. The freight bill called for a payment of $1,200. Terms were net 30 days. The bookkeeper affirms the fact that this invoice is to be held for recording in January.

Instructions

(a) Does your client have a liability which should be recorded at December 31? Discuss.

(b) Prepare the journal entry or entries required to reflect any adjustment.

(c) For what possible reason(s) might your client wish to postpone recording the transaction?

C8-3 **(EVALUATION OF ACCOUNTING POLICIES USING GAAP)** "Accounting Change Aids White Farm" was the headline for a report in the Saskatoon *Star-Phoenix*. This report contained the following comments from White Farm Manufacturing Canada Ltd.'s vice-president of marketing with regard to the company's attempts to recover under new ownership after being placed in receivership the previous year:

> In the past, most manufacturers, including the old White, treated a sale as a sale when a piece of equipment was put on a dealer's lot. Once we had a wholesale order for a combine or tractor, most companies booked it as a sale. Whatever the invoice read as revenue was revenue, and whatever costs were incurred up to that point were expenses. And then they'd book a profit. Until that piece of equipment was actually sold to a farmer, the company in most cases finances that equipment on the dealer's lot.

The report went on to state that the practice of booking a profit before it is realized led to a series of problems. Consequently, the company changed its accounting policy so that it did not book profits until a unit was sold at the retail level. At that point, all the firm's costs were behind it and it was recording real profits.

Instructions

(a) Within the framework of GAAP, discuss the appropriateness or lack thereof of the original accounting policy of White and other farm equipment manufacturers in terms of recognizing revenue and cost of goods sold (i.e. inventory reductions).

(b) What type of "problems" could such an accounting policy have led to?

(c) Given this practice, how would one account for the equipment that remained on a dealer's lot at a fiscal year end?

(d) How could the new policy "aid" the company?

C8-4 **(INVENTORIABLE COSTS: COMPLEX)** The controller for Gurney Enterprises Ltd. has recently hired you and wishes to determine your expertise in the area of inventory accounting. She therefore requests that you answer the following unrelated situations:

(a) A company is involved in the wholesaling and retailing of automobile tires for foreign cars. Most of the inventory is imported, and it is valued on the company's records at the actual purchase cost plus freight-in. At year end, the warehousing costs are allocated to the cost of goods sold and the ending inventory. Should warehousing costs be considered a product cost or a period cost? (**Note:** Consider various reasons for warehousing items when developing your answer.)

(b) A certain portion of a company's "inventory" is composed of obsolete items. Should obsolete items that are not currently consumed in the production of "goods or services to be available for sale" be classified as part of inventory?

(c) A company purchases airplanes for sale to others. However, until they are sold, the company charters and services the planes. What is the appropriate way to report these airplanes in the company's financial statements?

(d) A competitor uses standard costs for valuing inventory. Is this permissible?

(e) A company wants to buy coal deposits but does not want the financing for the purchase to be reported on its financial statements. The company therefore establishes a trust to acquire the coal deposits. The company agrees to buy the coal over a certain period of time at specified prices. The trust is able to finance the coal purchase and pay off the loan as it is paid by the company for the minerals. How should this transaction be reported?

C8-5 **(FIFO, LIFO, AND MOVING-AVERAGE COST)** Local Drilling Inc. is a Canadian drilling site company. All of the company's drilling material is purchased by the head office and stored at a local warehouse before being shipped to the drilling sites. The price of drilling material has been steadily decreasing over the past few years. The drilling material is sent to various sites, when requested by the site manager, where it is stored and then used in drilling. Managers are charged the cost of the inventory when it is sent based on the cost assigned to the item in the head office records. At any given time, it is estimated that about one-half of the company's drilling material inventory will be at the local warehouse. A site manager's performance is partially evaluated on the net income reported for the site.

Instructions

Given the options of choosing the FIFO, moving-average cost, or LIFO inventory costing methods and use of a perpetual inventory system:

(a) Which costing method would you, as a site manager, want to be used? Why?

(b) As a site manager, what might you do regarding the requesting of inventory if FIFO were used? Why and what might the implications be for the company as a whole?

(c) As the decision maker at head office, which method would you recommend if you wanted the results to be "fair" for all site managers? Why?

(d) Which method would you recommend be used in determining taxable income of the company? Why?

(e) Which method would you recommend be used for financial statement purposes? Why?

(UFE of CICA adapted)

C8-6 **(COST DETERMINATION)** Teng Company has been growing rapidly, but during this period the accounting records have not been properly maintained. You were recently employed to correct the accounting records and to assist in the preparation of the financial statements for the fiscal year ended February 28, 1994. One of the accounts you have been analysing is entitled "Merchandise." That account in summary form follows. Numbers in parentheses following each entry correspond to related numbered explanations and additional information that you have accumulated during your analysis.

Merchandise

Balance, March 1, 1993	(1)	Merchandise sold	(5)
Purchases	(2)	Consigned merchandise	(6)
Freight-in	(3)		
Insurance	(4)		
Freight-out on consigned merchandise	(7)		
Freight-out on merchandise sold	(8)		

Explanations and Additional Information

(1) You have satisfied yourself that the March 1, 1993 inventory balance represents the appropriate cost of the few units in inventory at the beginning of the year. Teng employs the FIFO method of accounting for inventories.

(2) The merchandise purchased was recorded in the account at the sellers' catalogue list price, which is the price appearing on the face of each vendor's invoice. All purchased merchandise is subject to a trade (chain) discount of 20%—10%. These discounts have been accounted for as revenue when the merchandise was paid for.

All merchandise purchased was also subject to cash terms of 2/15, n/30. During the fiscal year Teng recorded $4,000 in purchase discounts as revenue when the merchandise was paid for. Some purchase discounts were lost because payment was made after the discount period ended. All purchases of merchandise were paid for in the fiscal year they were recorded as purchased.

(3) All merchandise is purchased f.o.b. sellers' business locations. The freight-in amount is the cost of transporting the merchandise from the sellers' business locations to Teng.

(4) The insurance charge is for an all-perils policy to cover merchandise in transit to Teng from sellers.

(5) The credit to this account for merchandise sold represents the supplier's catalogue list price of merchandise sold by Teng plus the cost of the beginning inventory; the debit side of the entry was made to the cost of goods sold account.

(6) Consigned merchandise represents goods that were shipped to Simard Company during February 1994 priced at the seller's catalogue list price. The offsetting debit was made to accounts receivable when the merchandise was shipped to Simard. None of these goods had yet been sold by Simard Company.

(7) The freight-out on consigned goods is the cost of trucking the consigned goods to Simard from Teng.

(8) Freight-out on merchandise sold is the amount paid trucking companies to deliver merchandise sold to Teng's customers.

Instructions

Consider each of the eight numbered items independently and explain specifically how and why each item, if correctly accounted for, should have affected:

(a) The amount of cost of goods sold to be included in Teng's income statement.

(b) The amount of any other account to be included in Teng's February 28, 1994 financial statements.

Organize your answer in the following format:

Item Number	How and Why the Amount of Cost of Goods Sold Should Have Been Affected	How and Why the Amount of Any Other Account Should Have Been Affected

C8-7 **(LIFO INVENTORY ADVANTAGES)** Paul Wiebe, president of Dovetail Inc., a Canadian company merchandising trophies, recently read an article in a U.S. trade magazine which claimed that many U.S. businesses similar to his had adopted or were considering adopting the LIFO method for costing inventories. The article stated that these companies were switching to LIFO to (1) neutralize the effect of inflation in their financial statements, (2) eliminate inventory profits, and (3) reduce income taxes. Mr. Wiebe wonders if the switch would benefit his company.

Dovetail Inc. currently uses the FIFO method of inventory valuation in its periodic inventory system. The company has a high inventory turnover rate and inventories represent a significant proportion of the assets.

Mr. Wiebe wishes to use an inventory method that is best for the company in the long run rather than select a method because it is a current fad.

Instructions

(a) Explain to Mr. Wiebe what "inventory profits" are and how the LIFO method of inventory valuation could reduce them.

(b) Explain to Mr. Wiebe how the choice of an inventory method may affect the income taxes paid with particular reference to what he read in the article regarding LIFO.

(c) Would Mr. Wiebe have to use the same inventory method for financial reporting as is used for income tax determination? Explain why.

C8-8 **(ETHICAL ISSUES: YEAR-END INVENTORY PURCHASE)** Yorkville Motors Company uses the LIFO method for inventory costing. In an effort to lower net income, the president tells the plant accountant to take the unusual step of recommending to the purchasing department a large purchase of inventory at year end. The price of the item has nearly doubled during the year, and the item represents a major portion of inventory value.

Instructions

(a) Should the plant accountant recommend the inventory purchase to lower income? Who will benefit?

(b) If Yorkville Motors had been using the FIFO method of inventory costing, would the president give the same order? Why?

(ETHICAL ISSUES: MANIPULATION OF INVENTORY AMOUNTS) Nason Co. Ltd. manufactures **C8-9** and distributes a line of toys for adolescents, preschool children, and infants. As a consequence, the corporation has large seasonal variations in sales. The company issues quarterly financial statements, and first-quarter earnings were down from the same period last year.

During a visit to the Preschool and Infant Division, Nason's president expressed dissatisfaction with the division's first-quarter performance. As a result, John Kraft, division manager, felt pressure to report higher earnings in the second quarter. Kraft was aware that Nason uses the LIFO inventory method so he had the purchasing manager postpone several large inventory orders scheduled for delivery in the second quarter. Kraft knew that the use of older inventory costs during the second quarter would cause a decline in the cost of goods sold and thus increase earnings.

During a review of the preliminary second-quarter income statement, Donna Jensen, division controller, noticed that the cost of goods sold was low relative to sales. Jensen analysed the inventory account and discovered that the scheduled second-quarter material purchases had been delayed until the third quarter. Jensen prepared a revised income statement using current replacement costs to calculate cost of goods sold and submitted the income statement to John Kraft, her superior, for review. Kraft was not pleased with these results and insisted that the second-quarter income statement remain unchanged. Jensen tried to explain to Kraft that the interim inventory should reflect the expected cost of the replacement of the liquidated inventory when the inventory is expected to be replaced before the end of the year. Kraft did not relent and told Jensen to issue the income statement using the LIFO costs. Jensen is concerned about Kraft's response, and is contemplating what her next action should be.

Instructions

(a) Determine whether or not the actions of John Kraft, division manager, are ethical and explain why.

(b) Recommend a course of action that Donna Jensen should take in proceeding to resolve this situation.

(CMA adapted)

(VARIABLE COSTING AND FINANCIAL STATEMENT PRESENTATION) You have a client ***C8-10** engaged in a manufacturing business with relatively heavy fixed costs and large inventories of finished goods. These inventories constitute a very material item on the balance sheet. The company has a cost accounting system that assigns all manufacturing costs to the product each period.

The controller of the company has informed you that the management is giving serious consideration to the adoption of direct costing as a method of accounting for plant operations and inventory valuation. The management wishes to have your opinion of the effect, if any, that such a change would have on:

(1) The year-end financial position.

(2) The net income for the year.

Instructions

State your reply to the request and the reasons for your conclusions.

EXERCISES

(INVENTORIABLE COSTS) Presented below is a list of items which may or may not be reported as inven- **E8-1** tory in a company's December 31 balance sheet:

1. Goods out on consignment at another company's store.
2. Goods purchased f.o.b. destination that are in transit at December 31.
3. Goods sold to another company, for which our company has signed an agreement to repurchase at a set price that covers all costs related to the inventory.

4. Goods sold where returns are unpredictable.
5. Goods sold f.o.b. shipping point that are in transit at December 31.
6. Freight charges on goods purchased, but not sold.
7. Factory labour costs incurred on goods still unsold.
8. Goods sold on an instalment basis.
9. Interest costs incurred for inventories that are routinely manufactured.
10. Costs incurred to advertise goods held for resale.
11. Materials on hand not yet placed into production by a manufacturing firm.
12. Office supplies.
13. Goods purchased f.o.b. shipping point that are in transit at December 31.
14. Raw materials on which a manufacturing firm has started production, but which are not completely processed.
15. Goods held on consignment from another company.
16. Costs identified with units completed by a manufacturing firm, but not yet sold.
17. Goods sold f.o.b. destination that are in transit at December 31.
18. Factory supplies.
19. Temporary investments in shares and bonds that will be resold in the near future.

Instructions

Indicate which of these items would typically be reported as inventory in the financial statements. If an item should *not* be reported as inventory, indicate how it should be reported in the financial statements.

E8-2 **(INVENTORY CUTOFF ERRORS)** In an annual audit at December 31, 1994, you find the following transactions near the closing date.

1. Merchandise received on January 6, 1995 costing $510 was entered in the purchase journal on January 7, 1995. The invoice showed the shipment was made f.o.b. supplier's warehouse on December 31, 1994. Because it was not on hand at December 31, it was not included in inventory.
2. A special machine, made to order for a customer, was finished and, at the customer's request, was held in the back part of the shipping room on December 31, 1994 to be delivered within the next week. The customer was billed on December 31 as the customer agreed to bear responsibility for the machine while it was being held.
3. Merchandise costing $2,300 was received on January 3, 1995 and the related purchase invoice recorded January 5. The invoice showed the shipment was made on December 29, 1994 f.o.b. destination.
4. Merchandise costing $720 was received on December 28, 1994 and the invoice was not recorded. You located it in the hands of the purchasing agent; it was marked on consignment.
5. A packing case containing a product costing $1,100 was standing in the shipping room when the physical inventory was taken. It was not included in the inventory because it was marked "Hold for shipping instructions." Your investigation revealed that the customer's order was dated December 18, 1994, but that the case was shipped and the customer billed on January 10, 1995. The product was a stock item of your client.

Instructions

Assuming that each of the amounts is material, state whether the merchandise should be included in the client's inventory and give the reason for your decision on each item.

(INVENTORIABLE COSTS) The Sun-Dog Manufacturing Company maintains a general ledger account for each class of inventory, debiting such accounts for increases during the period, and crediting them for decreases. The transactions below relate to the Raw Materials inventory account, which is debited for materials purchased and credited for materials requisitioned for use: E8-3

1. An invoice for $7,500, terms f.o.b. destination, was received and entered January 2, 1995. The receiving report shows that they were received December 28, 1994.
2. Materials costing $29,000, shipped f.o.b. destination, were not entered by December 31, 1994 "because they were in a railroad car on the company's siding on that date and had not been unloaded."
3. Materials costing $7,300 were returned on December 29, 1994 to the creditor and were shipped f.o.b. shipping point. They were entered on that date, even though they were not expected to reach the creditor's place of business until January 6, 1995.
4. An invoice for $10,100, terms f.o.b. shipping point, was received and entered December 30, 1994. The receiving report shows that the materials were received January 4, 1995 and the bill of lading shows that they were shipped January 2, 1995.
5. Materials costing $20,525 were received December 30, 1994 but no entry was made for them because "they were ordered with a specified delivery of no earlier than January 10, 1995."

Instructions

Prepare correcting general journal entries required on December 31, 1994, assuming that the books have not been closed.

(INVENTORIABLE COSTS: ERROR ADJUSTMENTS) The following purchase transactions occurred during the last few days of the Alco Company's business year, which ends October 31, or in the first few days after that date. A periodic inventory system is used. E8-4

1. An invoice for $4,000, terms f.o.b. shipping point, was received and entered November 1. The invoice shows that the material was shipped October 29, but the receiving report indicates receipt of goods on November 3.
2. An invoice for $2,800, terms f.o.b. destination, was received and entered November 2. The receiving report indicates that the goods were received October 29.
3. An invoice for $3,375, terms f.o.b. shipping point, was received October 15 but never entered. Attached to it is a receiving report indicating that the goods were received October 18. Across the face of the receiving report is the following notation: "Merchandise not of same quality as ordered—returned for credit October 19."
4. An invoice for $3,250, terms f.o.b. shipping point, was received and entered October 27. The receiving report attached to the invoice indicates that the shipment was received October 27 in satisfactory condition.
5. An invoice for $5,400, terms f.o.b. destination, was received and entered October 28. The receiving report indicates that the merchandise was received November 2.

Before preparing financial statements for the year, you are instructed to review these transactions and to determine whether any correcting entries are required and whether the inventory of $74,200 determined by physical count should be changed.

Instructions

Complete the following schedule and state the correct inventory at October 31. Assume that the books have not been closed. Also, given your correcting entries, identify entries that must be made after closing in order for the accounts of November to be correct.

Transaction	Purchase and Related Payable Should Be Recognized in (month)	Purchase and Related Payable Were Recognized in (month)	Correcting Journal Entries Needed	Should Inventory Be Included in October Ending Inventory?	Was Inventory Included in October Ending Inventory?	Dollar Adjustments Needed to October Ending Inventory?

E8-5 (DETERMINING MISSING AMOUNTS) Two or more items are omitted in each of the following tabulations of income statement data. Fill in the amounts that are missing.

	1993	1994	1995
Sales	$290,000	$	$400,000
Sales Returns	9,000	12,000	
Net Sales		347,000	
Beginning Inventory	20,000	30,000	
Ending Inventory			
Purchases		260,000	298,000
Purchase Returns and Allowances	5,000	8,000	10,000
Transportation-In	8,000	9,000	12,000
Cost of Goods Sold	235,000		293,000
Gross Profit on Sales	46,000	91,000	97,000

E8-6 (FINANCIAL STATEMENT PRESENTATION OF MANUFACTURING AMOUNTS) Schmidt Company is a manufacturing firm. Presented below is selected information from its 1994 accounting records:

Raw materials inventory, 1/1/94	$ 30,800	Transportation-out	8,000
Raw materials inventory, 12/31/94	41,400	Selling expenses	300,000
Work-in-process inventory, 1/1/94	72,600	Administrative expenses	180,000
Work-in-process inventory, 12/31/94	51,600	Purchase discounts	10,640
Finished goods inventory, 1/1/94	35,200	Purchase returns and allowances	3,960
Finished goods inventory, 12/31/94	42,000	Interest expense	15,000
Purchases	278,600	Direct labour	440,000
Transportation-in	6,600	Manufacturing overhead	330,000

Instructions

(a) Compute the cost of raw materials used.

(b) Compute the cost of goods manufactured.

(c) Compute cost of goods sold.

(d) Indicate how inventories would be reported in the 12/31/94 balance sheet.

E8-7 (PURCHASES RECORDED NET) Presented below are the transactions related to Truffles Inc.

May 10 Purchased goods billed at $14,500 subject to cash discount terms of 2/10, n/60.

11 Purchased goods billed at $13,000 subject to terms of 1/15, n/30.

19 Paid invoice of May 10.

24 Purchased goods billed at $11,500 subject to cash discount terms of 2/10, n/30.

Instructions

(a) Prepare general journal entries for the transactions above under the assumption that purchases are to be recorded at net amounts after cash discounts and that discounts lost are to be treated as a financial expense.

(b) Assuming no purchase or payment transactions other than those given above, prepare the adjusting entry required on May 31 if financial statements are to be prepared as of that date.

(PERIODIC VERSUS PERPETUAL ENTRIES) The Phoenix Company sells one product, the Wipplesnip. Presented below is information for January for the Phoenix Company:

Jan. 1	Inventory	100 units at $5 each
Jan. 4	Sale	70 units at $8 each
Jan. 11	Purchase	150 units at $6 each
Jan. 13	Sale	130 units at $8.50 each
Jan. 20	Purchase	150 units at $7 each
Jan. 27	Sale	110 units at $9 each

Phoenix uses the FIFO cost flow assumption. All purchases and sales are on account.

Instructions

(a) Assume Phoenix uses a periodic system. Prepare all necessary journal entries, including the end-of-month adjusting/closing entry to record cost of goods sold. A physical count indicates that the ending inventory for January is 90 units.

(b) Compute gross profit using the periodic system.

(c) Assume Phoenix uses a perpetual system. Prepare all necessary journal entries.

(d) Compute gross profit using the perpetual system.

(INVENTORY ERRORS) Miller Company makes the following errors during the current year: **E8-9**

1. Ending inventory is correct, but a purchase on account was not recorded. (Assume this purchase was recorded in the following year.)

2. Ending inventory is overstated, but purchases are recorded correctly.

3. Both ending inventory and purchases on account are understated. (Assume this purchase was recorded in the following year.)

Instructions

Indicate the effect of each of these errors on working capital, current ratio (assume that the current ratio is positive), retained earnings, and net income for the current year and the subsequent year.

(INVENTORY ERRORS) Sprocket Company has a calendar-year accounting period. The following errors have been discovered in 1994: **E8-10**

1. The December 31, 1992 merchandise inventory had been understated by $13,000.

2. Merchandise purchased on account during 1993 was recorded on the books for the first time in February 1994, when the original invoice for the correct amount of $5,430 arrived. The merchandise had arrived December 28, 1993 and was included in the December 31, 1993 merchandise inventory. The invoice arrived late because of a mixup on the wholesaler's part.

3. Accrued interest of $1,250 at December 31, 1993 on notes receivable had not been recorded until the cash for the interest was received in March 1994.

Instructions

(a) Compute the effect of each error on the 1993 net income.

(b) Compute the effect, if any, of each error on the December 31, 1993 balance sheet items.

E8-11 **(INVENTORY ERRORS)** At December 31, 1994 Sanford Inc. reported current assets of $300,000 and current liabilities of $200,000. The following items may have been recorded incorrectly:

1. Goods purchased costing $43,000 were shipped f.o.b. shipping point by a supplier on December 28. Sanford received and recorded the invoice on December 29, but the goods were not included in Sanford's physical count of inventory because they were not received until January 4.
2. Goods purchased costing $15,000 were shipped f.o.b. destination by a supplier on December 26. Sanford received and recorded the invoice on December 31, but the goods were not included in Sanford's physical count of inventory because they were not received until January 2.
3. Goods held on consignment from Number One Company were included in Sanford's physical count of inventory at $13,000.
4. Freight-in of $3,000 for items on hand was debited to advertising expense on December 28.

Instructions

(a) Compute the current ratio based on Sanford's balance sheet.

(b) Recompute the current ratio after corrections are made.

(c) By what amount will income (before taxes) be adjusted up or down as a result of the corrections?

E8-12 **(INVENTORY ERRORS)** The net income per books was determined without knowledge of the errors indicated.

Year	Net Income per Books	Error in Ending Inventory	
1989	$50,000	Overstated	$ 3,000
1990	52,000	Overstated	9,000
1991	54,000	Understated	11,000
1992	56,000	No error	
1993	58,000	Understated	6,000
1994	60,000	Overstated	8,000

Instructions

(a) Prepare a work sheet to show the adjusted net income figure for each of the six years after taking into account the inventory errors.

(b) Would the differences in reported income per the books and the corrected income be of significance? Why?

E8-13 **(LIFO, FIFO, AND AVERAGE COST: PERIODIC AND PERPETUAL)** Inventory information for Part 321 discloses the following for the month of June:

June	1: Balance	300 units @ $10
	11: Purchased	800 units @ $12
	20: Purchased	500 units @ $15
June	10: Sold	200 units @ $24
	15: Sold	500 units @ $25
	27: Sold	300 units @ $27

Instructions

(a) Assuming that the periodic inventory method is used, compute the cost of goods sold and ending inventory under (1) LIFO, (2) FIFO, and (3) weighted-average cost.

(b) Assuming that the perpetual inventory record is kept in units and dollars, determine the cost of the ending inventory under (1) LIFO, (2) FIFO, and (3) moving-average cost. Support your answers for LIFO and moving-average cost by preparing the perpetual inventory card.

(c) When does LIFO produce a lower gross profit than FIFO?

E8-14 **(LIFO, FIFO, AND AVERAGE-COST DETERMINATION)** El Speedo Co. Ltd.'s record of transactions for the month of April was as follows:

Purchases

April	1	(balance on hand)	600 @ $6.26
	4		1,500 @ 6.00
	8		800 @ 6.40
	13		1,200 @ 6.50
	21		700 @ 6.60
	29		800 @ 6.79
			5,600

Sales

April	3	500 @ $10.00
	9	1,400 @ 10.50
	11	600 @ 11.00
	23	1,200 @ 11.50
	27	900 @ 12.00
		4,600

Instructions

(a) Assuming that the periodic system is used, compute the inventory at April 30 using (1) LIFO and (2) average cost.

(b) Assuming that perpetual inventory records are kept in units and dollars, determine the inventory using (1) FIFO and (2) LIFO, supporting your answer with perpetual inventory cards.

(c) Compute cost of goods sold assuming periodic inventory procedures and inventory priced at FIFO.

(d) In an inflationary period, which of the inventory methods (LIFO, FIFO, average cost) will show the highest net income?

E8-15 **(COMPUTE FIFO, LIFO, AVERAGE COST: PERIODIC)** Presented on page 424 is information related to Product A of Roberto Inc. for the month of July.

Instructions

(a) Assuming that the periodic inventory method is used, compute the inventory cost at July 31 under each of the following cost flow assumptions:

1. FIFO.

2. LIFO.

3. Weighted-average cost (round the weighted-average unit cost to the nearest one-tenth of one cent).

(b) Answer the following questions:

1. Which of the methods will yield the lowest figure for gross profit in the income statement? Explain why.

2. Which of the methods will yield the lowest figure for ending inventory in the balance sheet? Explain why.

Date	Transaction	Units In	Unit Cost	Total	Units Sold	Selling Price	Total
July 1	Balance	100	$4.10	$ 410.00			
6	Purchase	800	4.21	3,368.00			
7	Sale				300	$7.00	$ 2,100.00
10	Sale				300	7.30	2,190.00
12	Purchase	400	4.54	1,816.00			
15	Sale				200	7.40	1,480.00
18	Purchase	300	4.60	1,380.00			
22	Sale				400	7.40	2,960.00
25	Purchase	500	4.70	2,350.00			
30	Sale				200	7.50	1,500.00
	Totals	2,100		$9,324.00	1,400		$10,230.00

E8-16 **(FIFO AND LIFO; PERIODIC AND PERPETUAL)** The following is a record of transactions for transistor radios for the month of May.

May 1	Balance	400 units @ $20.00	May 10	Sale 300 units @ $40.00
12	Purchase	600 units @ $25.00	20	Sale 560 units @ $42.00
28	Purchase	400 units @ $30.00		

Instructions

(a) Assuming that perpetual inventories are *not* maintained and that a physical count at the end of the month shows 540 units to be on hand, what is the cost of the ending inventory using (1) FIFO, (2) LIFO, and (3) weighted-average cost?

(b) Assuming that perpetual records are maintained, calculate the ending inventory using (1) FIFO, (2) LIFO, and (3) moving-average cost.

E8-17 **(FIFO AND LIFO; INCOME STATEMENT PRESENTATION)** The board of directors of Wayward Corporation Ltd. is considering whether or not it should instruct the accounting department to shift from a first-in, first-out (FIFO) basis of pricing inventories to a last-in, first-out (LIFO) basis. The following information is available:

Sales	20,000 units @ $45
Inventory Jan. 1	6,000 units @ 20
Purchases	6,000 units @ 22
	10,000 units @ 25
	7,000 units @ 30
Inventory Dec. 31	9,000 units @ ?
Operating expenses	$240,000

Instructions

Prepare a condensed income statement for the year on both bases for comparative purposes.

(FIFO AND LIFO EFFECTS) You are the vice-president of finance of Ski Galore Ltd., a retail company that prepared two different schedules of gross profit for the first quarter ended March 31, 1994. These schedules appear below. **E8-18**

	Sales ($5 per unit)	Cost of Goods Sold	Gross Profit
Schedule 1	$150,000	$124,900	$25,100
Schedule 2	150,000	126,000	24,000

The computation of cost of goods sold in each schedule is based on the following data.

	Units	Cost per Unit	Total Cost
Beginning inventory, January 1	10,000	$4.00	$40,000
Purchase, January 10	8,000	4.20	33,600
Purchase, January 30	6,000	4.25	25,500
Purchase, February 11	9,000	4.30	38,700
Purchase, March 17	12,000	4.10	49,200

W. Goldblum, the president of the corporation, cannot understand how two different gross profits can be computed from the same set of data. As the vice-president of finance you have explained to Ms. Goldblum that the two schedules are based on different assumptions concerning the flow of inventory costs: first-in, first-out, and last-in, first-out. Schedules 1 and 2 were not necessarily prepared in this sequence of cost flow assumptions.

Instructions

Prepare two separate schedules computing cost of goods sold and supporting schedules showing the composition of the ending inventory under both cost flow assumptions.

(FIFO AND LIFO: PERIODIC) The Sports Shop began operations on January 1, 1994. The following stock record card for tennis racquets existed at the end of the year. **E8-19**

Date	Terms	Units Received	Unit Invoice Cost	Gross Invoice Amount
1/15	Net 30	50	$20.00	$1,000.00
3/15	1/5, net 30	65	16.00	1,040.00
6/20	1/10, net 30	90	15.00	1,350.00
9/12	1/10, net 30	84	12.00	1,008.00
11/24	1/10, net 30	76	11.00	836.00
Totals		365		$5,234.00

A physical inventory on December 31, 1994 reveals that 110 tennis racquets were in stock. The bookkeeper informs you that all the discounts were taken. Assume that The Sports Shop uses the invoice price less discount for recording purchases and uses the periodic system.

Instructions

(a) Compute the 12/31/94 inventory using the FIFO method.

(b) Compute the 1994 cost of goods sold using the LIFO method.

(c) Compute the 12/31/94 inventory using the weighted-average cost method (round unit cost to nearest cent).

(d) What method would you recommend in order to minimize income in 1994? Explain.

E8-20 **(ALTERNATIVE INVENTORY METHODS: COMPREHENSIVE)** Dold Corporation Ltd. began operations on December 1, 1994. The only inventory transaction in 1994 was the purchase of inventory on December 10, 1994 at a cost of $20 per unit. None of this inventory was sold in 1994. Relevant information is as follows:

Ending inventory units		
December 31, 1994		100
December 31, 1995 from purchases on:		
December 2, 1995	100	
July 20, 1995	50	150

During 1995 the following purchases and sales were made.

	Purchases	Sales	
March 15	300 units at $24	April 10	200
July 20	300 units at $25	August 20	300
September 4	200 units at $28	November 18	150
December 2	100 units at $30	December 12	200

The company uses the periodic inventory method.

Instructions

Determine ending inventory under (1) specific identification, (2) FIFO, (3) LIFO, and (4) average cost.

PROBLEMS

P8-1 **(INVENTORY ADJUSTMENTS)** Midi Co. Ltd., a manufacturer of small tools, provided the following information from its accounting records for the year ended December 31, 1994:

Inventory at December 31, 1994 (based on physical count of goods in Midi's plant at cost on December 31, 1994)	$1,610,000
Accounts payable at December 31, 1994	1,340,000
Net sales (sales less sales returns)	8,230,000

Additional information is as follows:

1. Included in the physical count were tools billed to a customer f.o.b. shipping point on December 31, 1994. These tools had a cost of $31,000 and were billed at $45,000. The shipment was on Midi's loading dock waiting to be picked up by the common carrier.

2. Goods were in transit from a vendor to Midi on December 31, 1994. The invoice cost was $85,000 and the goods were shipped f.o.b. shipping point on December 29, 1994.

3. Work-in-process inventory costing $25,000 was sent to an outside processor for plating on December 30, 1994.

4. Tools returned by customers and held pending inspection in the returned goods area on December 31, 1994 were not included in the physical count. On January 8, 1995, the tools costing $31,000 were inspected and returned to inventory. Credit memos totalling $42,000 were issued to the customers on the same date.

5. Tools shipped to a customer f.o.b. destination on December 26, 1994 were in transit at December 31, 1994 and had a cost of $40,000. Upon notification of receipt by the customer on January 2, 1995, Midi issued a sales invoice for $52,000.

6. Goods, with an invoice cost of $33,000, received from a vendor at 5:00 p.m. on December 31, 1994 were recorded on a receiving report dated January 2, 1995. The goods were not included in the physical count, but the invoice was included in accounts payable at December 31, 1994.

7. Goods received from a vendor on December 26, 1994 were included in the physical count. However, the related $54,000 vendor invoice was not included in accounts payable at December 31, 1994 because the accounts payable copy of the receiving report was lost.

8. On January 3, 1995 a monthly freight bill in the amount of $5,000 was received. The bill specifically related to merchandise purchased in December 1994, one-half of which was still in the inventory at December 31, 1994. The freight charges were not included in either the inventory or in accounts payable at December 31, 1994.

Instructions

Using the format shown below, prepare a schedule of adjustments as of December 31, 1994 to the initial amounts per Midi's accounting records. Show separately the effect, if any, of each of the eight transactions on the December 31, 1994 amounts. If the transactions do not have an effect on the initial amount shown, state *NONE*.

	Inventory	Accounts Payable	Net Sales
Initial amounts	$1,610,000	$1,340,000	$8,230,000
Adjustments—increase (decrease)			
1			
2			
3			
4			
5			
6			
7			
8			
Total adjustments			
Adjusted amounts	$	$	$

(AICPA adapted)

P8-2 **(INVENTORY ADJUSTMENTS)** Straf Ltd. is a wholesale distributor of automotive replacement parts. Initial amounts taken from Straf's accounting records are as follows:

Inventory at December 31, 1994 (based on physical count of goods in Straf's warehouse on December 31, 1994)	$1,320,000

Accounts payable at December 31, 1994.

Vendor	Terms	Amount
Rask Company Ltd.	2%, 10 days, net 30	$ 260,000
Savage Corporation	Net 30	300,000
McConnell Company	Net 30	215,000
Marion Enterprises	Net 30	220,000
Tiffany Products	Net 30	—
Tucson Company	Net 30	—
		$ 995,000
Sales in 1994		$8,540,000

Additional information is as follows:

1. Parts received on consignment from Savage Corporation by Straf, the consignee, amounting to $170,000, were included in the physical count of goods in Straf's warehouse on December 31, 1994 and in accounts payable at December 31, 1994.
2. Parts costing $24,000 were purchased from Tiffany and paid for in December 1994. These parts were sold in the last week of 1994 and appropriately recorded as sales of $32,000. The parts were included in the physical count of goods in Straf's warehouse on December 31, 1994 because the parts were on the loading dock waiting to be picked up by customers who had been informed the parts were ready and had stated they would pick them up as soon as possible.
3. Parts in transit on December 31, 1994 to customers, shipped f.o.b. shipping point on December 28, 1994, amounted to $34,000. The customers received the parts on January 6, 1995. Sales of $55,000 to the customers for the parts were recorded by Straf on January 2, 1995.
4. Retailers were holding $220,000 at cost ($280,000 at retail), of goods on consignment from Straf, the consignor, at their stores on December 31, 1994.
5. Goods were in transit from Tucson to Straf on December 31, 1994. The cost of the goods was $37,500 and they were shipped f.o.b. shipping point on December 29, 1994.
6. A quarterly freight bill in the amount of $5,200 specifically relating to merchandise purchased in December 1994, all of which was still in the inventory at December 31, 1994, was received on January 3, 1995. The freight bill was not included in the inventory or in accounts payable at December 31, 1994.
7. All of the purchases from Rask occurred during the last seven days of the year. These items have been recorded in accounts payable and accounted for in the physical inventory at cost before discount. Straf's policy is to pay invoices in time to take advantage of all cash discounts, adjust inventory accordingly, and record accounts payable, net of cash discounts.

	Inventory	Accounts Payable	Net Sales
Initial amounts	$1,320,000	$ 995,000	$8,540,000
Adjustments—increase (decrease)			
1	(170,000)	(170,000)	
2	(24,000)		
3			55,000
4	220,000		
5	37,500	37,500	
6	5,200	5,200	
7	(254,800)	(254,800)	
Total adjustments			
Adjusted amounts	$	$	$

Instructions

Prepare a schedule of adjustments to the initial amounts using the format shown on the previous page. Show the effect, if any, of each of the transactions separately and if the transactions would have no effect on the amount shown, state *NONE*.

(AICPA adapted)

(PURCHASES RECORDED GROSS AND NET) Some of the transactions of Wendland Inc. during August are listed below: P8-3

August 10 Purchased merchandise on account, $8,000, terms 2/10, n/30.

13 Returned part of the purchase of August 10, $1,200, and received credit on account.

15 Purchased merchandise on account, $10,000, terms 1/10, n/60.

25 Purchased merchandise on account, $12,000, terms 2/10, n/30.

28 Paid amount due on the invoice of August 15.

Instructions

(a) Assuming that purchases are recorded at gross amounts and that discounts are to be recorded when taken:
1. Prepare general journal entries to record the transactions.
2. Describe how the various items would be shown in the financial statements.

(b) Assuming that purchases are recorded at net amounts and that discounts lost are treated as financial expenses:
1. Prepare general journal entries to enter the transactions.
2. Prepare the adjusting entry necessary on August 31 if financial statements are to be prepared at that time.
3. Describe how the various items would be shown in the financial statements.

(c) Which of the two methods do you prefer and why?

(VARIOUS INVENTORY ISSUES) The following independent situations relate to inventory accounting:

1. Sandstone Inc.'s inventory of $1,100,000 at December 31, 1994 was based on a physical count of goods priced at cost and before any year-end adjustments relating to the following items

   a. Goods shipped f.o.b. shipping point on December 24, 1994 from a vendor at an invoice cost of $90,000 to Sandstone Inc. were received on January 4, 1995.

   b. The physical count included $29,000 of goods billed to Doogie Co. Ltd. f.o.b. shipping point on December 31, 1994. The carrier picked up these goods on January 3, 1995.

   What amount should Sandstone report as inventory on its December 31, 1994 balance sheet?

2. Aerosmith Inc. had 1,500 units of Part INXS on hand May 1, 1994 costing $21 each. Purchases of Part INXS during May were as follows.

	Units	Unit Cost
May 9	2,000	$22.00
17	3,500	23.00
26	2,000	25.50

A physical count on May 31, 1994 shows 2,500 units of Part INXS on hand. Using the FIFO method, what is the cost of Part INXS inventory at May 31, 1994? Using the LIFO method, what is the inventory cost? Using the weighted-average cost method, what is the inventory cost?

3. Patsy Inc., a retail store chain, had the following information in its general ledger for the year 1994:

Merchandise purchased for resale	$817,200
Interest on notes payable to vendors	8,700
Purchase returns	16,500
Freight-in	21,000
Freight-out	17,100
Cash discounts on purchases	6,800

What is Patsy's inventoriable cost for 1994?

4. Varsity Co. Ltd. purchased goods with a list price of $120,000, subject to trade discounts of 20% and 10% (applied consecutively), with no cash discounts allowable. How much should Varsity Co. Ltd. record as the cost of these goods?

Instructions

Answer each of the questions and explain your answer.

P8-5 **(COMPUTE FIFO, LIFO, AND AVERAGE COST: PERIODIC)** As the controller of Hall Inc., a merchandising company, you made three different schedules of gross profit for the third quarter ended September 30. These schedules appear below.

	Sales ($10 per Unit)	Cost of Goods Sold	Gross Profit
Schedule A	$570,000	$321,280	$248,720
Schedule B	570,000	308,960	261,040
Schedule C	570,000	314,640	255,360

The computation of cost of goods sold in each schedule is based on the following data.

	Units	Cost per Unit	Total Cost
Beginning inventory, July 1	11,000	$5.00	$ 55,000
Purchase, July 25	18,000	5.46	98,280
Purchase, August 15	32,000	5.56	177,920
Purchase, September 5	13,000	5.60	72,800
Purchase, September 25	16,000	5.80	92,800

Tim Martin, president of the corporation, cannot understand how three different gross margins can be computed from the same set of data. As controller, you have explained that the three schedules are based on three different assumptions concerning the flow of inventory costs: first-in, first-out; last-in, first-out; and weighted-average cost. Schedules A, B, and C were not necessarily prepared in this sequence of cost flow assumptions.

Instructions

Prepare three separate schedules computing cost of goods sold and supporting schedules showing the composition of the ending inventory under each of the three cost flow assumptions.

(COMPUTE FIFO, LIFO, AND AVERAGE COST: PERIODIC AND PERPETUAL) The J.T. Kirk Company is a multi-product firm. Presented below is information concerning one of their products, Dilithium-48. **P8-6**

Date	Transaction	Quantity	Price/Cost
1/1	Beginning inventory	1,500	$10
2/4	Purchase	2,000	16
2/20	Sale	2,500	31
4/2	Purchase	3,000	23
11/4	Sale	2,000	34

Instructions

Compute cost of goods sold, assuming Kirk uses:

(a) Periodic system, FIFO cost flow.

(b) Perpetual system, FIFO cost flow.

(c) Periodic system, LIFO cost flow.

(d) Perpetual system, LIFO cost flow.

(e) Periodic system, weighted-average cost flow.

(f) Perpetual system, moving-average cost flow.

(COMPUTE FIFO, LIFO, AND AVERAGE COST: PERIODIC AND PERPETUAL) Apollo Co. Ltd.'s record of transactions concerning Part XS for the month of April was as follows: **P8-7**

Purchases

April 1	(balance on hand)	100 @ $5.00
4		400 @ 5.10
11		300 @ 5.20
18		200 @ 5.35
26		600 @ 5.60
30		200 @ 5.80

Sales

April 5	300
12	200
27	800
28	200

Instructions

(a) Compute the inventory at April 30 on each of the following bases. Assume that the periodic system is used for inventory valuation. Carry unit costs to the nearest cent.

1. First-in, first-out (FIFO).

2. Last-in, first-out (LIFO).

3. Weighted-average cost.

(b) If the perpetual inventory system is used, would the amounts be the same for ending inventory in 1, 2, and 3 of part (a)? Explain and calculate by preparing perpetual inventory cards for LIFO and moving-average cost methods. Carry unit costs to four decimal places.

P8-8 **(COMPUTE FIFO, LIFO, AND AVERAGE COST: PERIODIC AND PERPETUAL)** Here is some of the information found on a detail inventory card for Kerri Inc. for the first month of operations.

	Received		Issued,	Balance,
Date	No. of Units	Unit Cost	No. of Units	No. of Units
Jan. 2	1,200	$3.00		1,200
7			700	500
10	600	3.20		1,100
13			500	600
18	1,000	3.30	300	1,300
20			1,100	200
23	1,300	3.40		1,500
26			800	700
28	1,900	3.50		2,600
31			1,300	1,300

Instructions

(a) From this information compute the ending inventory on each of the following bases. Assume that perpetual inventory records are kept in units only and, therefore, ending inventory costs are determined using a periodic method. Carry unit costs to the nearest cent.

1. First-in, first-out (FIFO).

2. Last-in, first-out (LIFO).

3. Weighted-average cost.

(b) If the perpetual inventory record were kept in units and dollars, would the amounts shown as ending inventory for part (a) be the same? Explain and support your answer by preparing a perpetual inventory card for LIFO and moving-average cost (use unit cost to four decimal places).

P8-9 **(LIFO EFFECT ON INCOME)** Kid Toys Inc. manufactures two products: Rocket Robin and Batman. At December 31, 1994 the company used the first-in, first-out (FIFO) inventory method. Effective January 1, 1995 Kid Toys changed to the last-in, first-out (LIFO) inventory method. The cumulative effect of this change is not determinable and, as a result, the ending inventory of 1994 for which the FIFO method was used is also the beginning inventory for 1995 for the LIFO method. Any layers added during 1995 should be costed by reference to the first acquisitions of 1995 and any layers liquidated during 1995 should be considered a permanent liquidation. The information on page 431 was available from Kid Toys' inventory records for the two most recent years.

Instructions

Compute the effect on income before income taxes for the year ended December 31, 1995 resulting from the change from the FIFO to the LIFO inventory method.

	Rocket Robin		Batman	
	Units	Unit Cost	Units	Unit Cost
1994 purchases				
January 7	7,000	$4.10	22,000	$2.00
April 16	12,000	4.50		
November 8	17,000	5.30	18,500	3.20
December 13	9,000	6.40		
1995 purchases				
February 11	3,000	6.70	23,000	3.60
May 20	8,000	7.50		
October 15	20,000	8.10		
December 23			15,500	4.30
Units on hand				
December 31, 1994	15,100		15,000	
December 31, 1995	18,000		13,200	

(AICPA adapted)

P8-10 **(FINANCIAL STATEMENT EFFECTS OF FIFO AND LIFO)** The management of Mucklow Co. Ltd. has asked its accounting department to describe the effect upon the company's financial position and its income statement of accounting for inventories on the LIFO rather than the FIFO basis during 1994 and 1995. The accounting department is to assume that the change to LIFO would have been effective on January 1, 1994 and that the initial LIFO base would have been the inventory value on December 31, 1993. Presented below are the company's financial statements and other data for the years 1994 and 1995 when the FIFO method was in fact employed.

Financial Position as of	12/31/93	12/31/94	12/31/95
Cash	$ 90,000	$119,400	$ 145,000
Accounts receivable	80,000	100,000	120,000
Inventory	120,000	144,000	176,000
Other assets	160,000	170,000	200,000
Total assets	$450,000	$533,400	$ 641,000
Accounts payable	$ 40,000	$ 60,000	$ 80,000
Other liabilities	70,000	80,000	110,000
Common shares	200,000	200,000	200,000
Retained earnings	140,000	193,400	251,000
Total equities	$450,000	$533,400	$ 641,000

Income for Year Ended	12/31/94	12/31/95
Sales	$900,000	$1,350,000
Less: Cost of goods sold	$516,000	$ 760,000
Other expenses	205,000	304,000
	$721,000	$1,064,000
Net income before income taxes	$179,000	$ 286,000
Income taxes (40%)	71,600	114,400
Net income	$107,400	$ 171,600

Other data:

1. Inventory on hand at 12/31/93 consisted of 40,000 units valued at $3.00 each.
2. Sales (all units sold at the same price in a given year):

   1994: 150,000 units @ $6.00 each
   1995: 180,000 units @ $7.50 each

3. Purchases (all units purchased at the same price in given year):

   1994: 150,000 units @ $3.60 each
   1995: 180,000 units @ $4.40 each

4. Dividends declared and paid in 1994 were $54,000 and in 1995 were $114,000.
5. Income taxes at the effective rate of 40 percent are paid on December 31 each year.

Instructions

Name the account(s) presented in the financial statement that would have different amounts for 1995 if LIFO rather than FIFO had been used and state the new amount for each account that is named. The income tax expense is based on the net income before taxes amount. For purposes of determining taxes paid, assume that the FIFO method continues to be used for determining taxable income. The difference between tax expense and taxes paid is charged to a Deferred Income Taxes account, and this account incorporates the effect of the different methods in the financial statements for only the two-year period.

(CMA adapted)

P8-11 (ERRORS AFFECTING BALANCE SHEET AND NET INCOME) The books of Bobby Co. Ltd. on December 31, 1994 are in agreement with the following balance sheet:

Bobby Co. Ltd.

Balance Sheet as of December 31, 1994

Assets	
Cash	$ 26,000
Accounts and notes receivable	43,000
Inventory	80,000
	$149,000
Liabilities and Shareholders' Equity	
Accounts and notes payable	$ 25,000
Common shares	100,000
Retained earnings	24,000
	$149,000

The following errors were made by the corporation on December 31, 1993 and were not corrected: the inventory was overstated by $7,000, prepaid expense of $1,200 was omitted, and accrued revenue of $1,500 was omitted. On December 31, 1994 the inventory was understated by $10,000, prepaid expense of $1,500 was omitted, accrued expense of $1,200 was omitted, and unearned income of $1,400 was omitted.

The net income shown by the books for 1994 was $16,000.

Instructions

(a) Compute the corrected net income for 1994.

(b) Prepare a corrected balance sheet for December 31, 1994.

(COMPREHENSIVE INVENTORY ADJUSTMENT PROBLEM) Brody Inc. cans two food commodities that it stores at various warehouses. The company employs a perpetual inventory accounting system under which the finished goods inventory is charged with production and credited for sales at standard cost. The detail of the finished goods inventory is maintained by the computing department in units and dollars for the various warehouses. **P8-12**

Company procedures call for the accounting department to receive copies of daily production reports and sales invoices. Units are then extended at standard cost and a summary of the day's activity is posted to the Finished Goods Inventory general ledger control account. Next the sales invoices and production reports are sent to the computing department for processing. Every month the control account and detailed records are reconciled and adjustments recorded. The last reconciliation and adjustments were made at November 30, 1994.

Your audit firm observed the taking of the physical inventory at all locations on December 31, 1994. The inventory count began at 1:00 p.m. and was completed at 5:00 p.m. The company's figure for the physical inventory is $421,700. The general ledger control account balance at December 31 was $487,800, and the final computer run of the inventory showed a total of $487,100.

Unit cost data for the company's two products are as follows.

Product	Standard Cost
A	$4.00
B	5.00

A review of December transactions disclosed the following:

1. Sales invoice #1603, 12/2/94, was priced at standard cost for $17,400 but was listed on the accounting department's daily summary at $14,700.

2. A production report for $13,600, 12/15/94, was processed twice in error by the computing department.

3. Sales invoice #1481, 12/9/94, for 1,400 units of product A, was priced at a standard cost of $2.00 per unit by the accounting department. The computing department noticed and corrected the error but did not notify the accounting department of the error.

4. A shipment of 2,500 units of product A was invoiced by the billing department as 2,000 units on sales invoice #1703, 12/27/94. The error was discovered in your review of transactions.

5. On December 27 the Toronto warehouse notified the computing department to remove 2,200 unsaleable units of product A from the finished goods inventory, which it did without receiving a special invoice from the accounting department. The accounting department received a copy of the Toronto warehouse notification on December 29 and made up a special invoice that was processed in the normal manner (it went through the computing department again). The units were not included in the physical inventory.

6. A production report for the production on January 3 of 3,100 units of product B was incorrectly processed (through accounting and computing) for the Oshawa plant as of December 31.

7. A shipment of 600 units of product B was made from the Sudbury warehouse to Fresh Markets Inc. at 5:30 p.m. on December 31 as an emergency service. The sales invoice was processed as of December 31. The client prefers to treat the transaction as a sale in 1994 and, therefore, it was processed through accounting and computing for 1994.

8. The working papers of the auditor observing the physical count at the Winnipeg warehouse revealed that 600 units of product B were omitted from the client's physical count. The client concurred that the units were omitted in error.

9. A sales invoice for 450 units of product A shipped from the Halifax warehouse was mislaid and was not processed until January 5. The units involved were shipped on December 30.

10. The physical inventory of the Victoria warehouse excluded 325 units of product A that were marked "reserved." Upon investigation it was ascertained that this merchandise was being stored for Bill's Markets Inc., a customer. This merchandise, which has not been recorded as a sale, is billed as it is shipped which reflects industry practice.

11. A shipment of 8,000 units of product B was made on December 27 from the Halifax warehouse to the Winnipeg warehouse. The shipment arrived on January 6, but had been excluded from the physical inventory count.

Instructions

Prepare a work sheet to reconcile the balances for the physical inventory, Finished Goods Inventory general ledger control account, and computing department's detail of finished goods inventory. The following format is suggested for the work sheet:

	Physical Inventory	General Ledger Control Account	Computing Department's Detail of Inventory
Balance per client	$421,700	$487,800	$487,100

(AICPA adapted)

CHAPTER 9

Inventories: Additional Valuation Problems

In Chapter 8, different methods for computing the cost of inventories were explained by examining the various cost flow assumptions used in accounting. In addition to being able to rationally choose from and apply these methods, other concerns regarding inventory valuation exist and are examined in this chapter.

For example, what happens if the value of the inventory increases or decreases after the initial purchase date? Does the financial reporting system recognize these increases and decreases in the valuation of inventory? The answers, in terms of financial statement preparation, lie in the lower of cost and market rule.

What happens if there is a fire and a physical count of lost inventory cannot be made? How is the amount of the destroyed inventory determined so that an insurance claim can be justified? What happens in large department stores where monthly inventory figures are needed, but monthly counts are not feasible? These questions involve the development and use of estimation techniques to value the ending inventory without a physical count. The gross profit method and the retail inventory method are widely used estimation methods and are discussed in this chapter.

Our examination of inventory concludes with a consideration of some additional issues related to inventory valuation (relative sales value method, valuation at net realizable value regardless of cost, and accounting for purchase commitments) and then identifying and illustrating requirements regarding disclosure of inventories in financial statements.

LOWER OF COST AND MARKET

Objective 1

Recognize that the lower of cost and market basis for inventory valuation is a departure from the historical cost principle and why this is acceptable.

A major departure from adherence to the historical cost rinciple is made in the area of inventory valuation. If inventory declines in value below its original cost for whatever reason (e.g., obsolescence, price-level changes, damaged goods), the inventory should be written down to reflect this loss. Applying conservatism in accounting means that known losses are to be recognized in the period of occurrence. In contrast, known gains are not recognized until realized. ***The general rule is that the historical cost principle is abandoned when the future utility (revenue-producing ability) of the asset is no longer as great as its original cost.*** A departure from cost is justified since a loss of utility should be charged against revenues in the period in which it occurs. Inventories are valued therefore on the basis of the lower of cost and market instead of on an original cost basis.

Cost is the acquisition price of inventory determined by one of the cost-based methods. The term "**market**" in the phrase "the lower of cost and market" (cost or market, whichever is lower) requires a specific definition. As the *CICA Handbook* notes:

> In view of the lack of precision in meaning, it is desirable that the term "market" not be used in describing the basis of valuation. A term more descriptive of the method of determining market, such as "replacement cost", "net realizable value" or "net realizable value less normal profit margin" would be preferable.[1]

---

[1] *CICA Handbook* (Toronto: CICA), Section 3030, par. .11.

Objective 2

Understand various definitions of possible market amounts that may be used when applying lower of cost and market.

Replacement cost generally means the amount that would be needed to acquire an equivalent item, by purchase or production, as it would be incurred in the normal course of business operations (i.e. buying or manufacturing from usual sources in normal quantities). **Net realizable value** is the estimated selling price of the item in the ordinary course of business less reasonably predictable future costs to complete and dispose of the item. **Net realizable value less normal profit margin** is determined by deducting a normal profit margin from the previously defined net realizable value amount. For example, a retailer may have in inventory calculator wristwatches that had cost $30.00 each. If their purchase cost is presently $28.00, that would be their replacement cost. If their selling price today is $50.00, and there were no additional costs to sell them, then this amount would be their net realizable value. If a normal profit margin is 35% of selling price, the net realizable value less normal profit margin would be $32.50. Consequently, in this example, the inventory would be valued at $30.00 per unit (its historical cost) under the lower of cost and market rule if market were either net realizable value or net realizable value less normal profit margin, but would be valued at $28.00 per unit if market were replacement cost.

Given different interpretations as to what market can be, the question becomes: What definition of market should be used when applying the lower of cost and market rule? The *CICA Handbook* recognizes several possibilities, all of which are generally accepted (see the previous quotation), but is silent on which is appropriate in particular circumstances. This is understandable, given various practical problems associated with implementing any definition of market in particular situations for various types of inventories. (Some of these considerations are identified later under the heading "Evaluation of Lower of Cost and Market Rule.") However, ***net realizable value is the most frequently used method of determining "market" in Canada.***[2] This is likely due to the conclusions reached by a CICA research study which stated that:

> . . . selling prices do not necessarily fluctuate with costs and that, as a result, a decline in the cost of replacement or reproduction, in itself, is not conclusive evidence that a loss will be incurred. It is only if selling prices vary directly with changes in costs that replacement cost provides an accurate measure of the anticipated loss of gross profits and, under such conditions, exactly the same result can be accomplished by using net realizable value less normal profits. Due to its obvious limitations and because consistent use may produce unreasonable results, the lower of cost and replacement cost can hardly be classified as a practical interpretation of the lower of cost and market basis of valuing inventories.
>
> The only reasonable choice of interpretation seems to be between net realizable value and net realizable value less normal profit. Both of these interpretations have the desired quality of being capable of consistent application. The choice between the two reduces itself to the question of which interpretation provides the more accurate measurement of the loss which will actually be experienced. Under the net realization theory, the loss charged against the income of the current period is limited to irrecoverable cost which is, in effect, the true loss (cost incurred without return or benefit) that is expected to be suffered. Under the net realizable value less normal profit theory, all or part of the charge against income does not represent a true loss.
>
> Since any departure from cost disrupts the normal process of matching costs with related revenues and is an arbitrary shifting of income from one period to another, it would seem most logical to insist on that interpretation of market which causes the lesser disruption of or shift away from the normal matching process. Net realizable value wins over net realizable value less a normal profit because the latter interpretation results in a larger inventory adjustment and, therefore, unnecessarily accentuates the shift in income. . . . If the lower of cost and market basis of inventory valuation in the ordinary course of business operations is to be used, market should be limited to

---

[2] *Financial Reporting in Canada—1991* (Toronto: CICA, 1991) reports that, of the interpretations of market disclosed in 1990 financial statements of the surveyed companies, net realizable value was used 237 times, replacement cost 68 times, net realizable value less normal profit margin 12 times, and other definitions 23 times.

net realizable value since this is the most reasonable interpretation from the point of view of both income measurement and balance sheet presentation.[3]

The accounting profession in the United States has adopted a different approach for determining "market" in the application of the lower of cost and market rule.[4] Generally, market is the replacement cost of the item. When applying the lower of cost and market rule, however, "market" cannot exceed net realizable value (the ceiling) or be less than net realizable value less a normal profit margin (the floor).[5] Therefore, the value used for "market" is the middle value of these three possibilities. Once the designated market has been determined, it is compared to the cost and the lower amount is used for the inventory valuation.

The U.S. approach is based on the premise that declines in replacement cost are reflective of or predict a decline in selling price (realizable value). The ceiling and floor limits are introduced to protect against situations where this premise is in serious error. Consequently, while the underlying objective of reflecting a decline in utility of inventory is common to both Canada and the United States, each has reached a different conclusion as to how this is to be accomplished.

How Lower of Cost and Market Works

Objective 3

Explain how lower of cost and market works and how it is applied.

The lower of cost and market rule requires that the inventory be valued at cost unless "market" is lower than cost, in which case the inventory is valued at "market." To apply this rule (regardless of using a Canadian definition of market or determining market under the U.S. rules): (1) determine the cost using an acceptable historical cost flow method; (2) determine the market value to be used; then (3) compare the cost to the market. The cost or market figure, whichever is lower, is then used for inventory valuation on the financial statements.

To illustrate, assume the following information.

The Lower of Cost and Market Approach

		Market		
Case	Cost	Net Realizable Value	Replacement Cost	Net Realizable Value Less Normal Profit Margin
1	$1.00	$1.50	$1.10	$1.20
2	1.00	1.10	.90	.70
3	1.00	.80	.95	.56
4	1.00	.80	.40	.56
5	1.00	.95	1.05	.80

[3] Gertrude Mulcahy, *Use and Meaning of "Market" in Inventory Valuation* (Toronto: CICA, 1963), p. 19.

[4] Generally, we do not identify U.S. financial reporting standards in this Canadian text, particularly when a specific Canadian position exists. We do so in this particular case because awareness of the U.S. standard may help to better understand the rationale of Canadian practice. Also, the comparison serves to illustrate that different countries can come to different conclusions when trying to account for the same phenomenona problem which is faced head on by the International Accounting Standards Committee when it is trying to develop international accounting standards, or by international financial people when they are assessing financial statements of companies from different countries.

[5] "Restatement and Revision of Accounting Research Bulletins," *Accounting Research Bulletin No. 43* (New York: AICPA, 1953), Ch. 4, par. 8. It should be noted that a literal interpretation of the U.S. rules is frequently not applied in practice. Rather, *ARB No. 43* is considered a guide, and professional judgement is often exercised. Indeed, *Accounting Research Study No. 13 "The Accounting Basis of Inventories"* (New York: AICPA, 1973) recommends that net realizable value be adopted.

In the illustration, cost is given. Therefore, to apply the lower of cost and market rule, the next step is to determine the market amount to be used. Under Canadian GAAP, this would be accomplished by a company's management specifying which of the three definitions of market it will adopt. If net realizable value is designated as the "market" value, as is commonly the case for Canadian companies, the application of a "lower of cost and net realizable value" approach will result in inventory being shown at cost in Cases 1 and 2 (because cost is lower than net realizable value) and net realizable value in Cases 3, 4, and 5 (net realizable value is less than cost). If, however, net realizable value less normal profit margin is the designated "market" value, inventory will be shown at cost in Case 1 and net realizable value less normal profit margin in Cases 2, 3, 4, and 5 because the net realizable value less normal profit is lower than cost except for Case 1. Use of replacement cost as market would result in using cost in Cases 1 and 5 and replacement cost in Cases 2, 3, and 4.

To determine market under the U.S. rules, the first step is to determine amounts for all three of the possible market values. Given this, the next step is to identify which of these three amounts will be the designated market value to be compared to the cost. As previously noted, the market value used will be the middle value of the three. For Case 2, this is the $.90 replacement cost. It is less than the $1.10 net realizable value (the ceiling) and higher than the $.70 net realizable value less normal profit margin (the floor). Because the determined market value (replacement cost of $.90) is less than the cost ($1.00), ending inventory in this case is valued at $.90. For Case 1, replacement cost is $1.10. Since market cannot be less than the net realizable value less a normal profit margin of $1.20, this latter amount is the designated market value. It is the middle value of the three possible market amounts in Case 1. Since the $1.00 cost is less than the $1.10 market value in Case 1, the ending inventory is valued at $1.00. With this explanation as a base, the following summarizes the amount that is used in each of Cases 1 through 5 to value inventory under the U.S. rules for determining the lower of cost and market:

Case 1. Cost. It is lower than any of the possible market values.

Case 2. Replacement cost. It is the designated market as it is the middle value of the three market possibilities and it is lower than cost.

Case 3. Net realizable value (ceiling). It is the designated market as it is the middle value of the three market possibilities (market cannot exceed this amount) and is lower than cost.

Case 4. Net realizable value less a normal profit margin (floor). It is the designated market as it is the middle value of the three market possibilities (market cannot be less than this amount) and is lower than cost.

Case 5. Net realizable value (ceiling). For the same reasons as Case 3.

Methods of Applying the Lower of Cost and Market Rule

The lower of cost and market rule may be applied to inventory on an item-by-item basis, to the total of the components of each major category of inventory, or to the total of the entire inventory.

To illustrate, consider the example on page 441, for a business which has two categories of inventory (radios and TVs) and different types in each category. If the lower of cost and market rule is applied to individual items, the amount of inventory is $12,250. It is $12,650 when applied to major categories and $12,700 when applied to the total inventory.

Relative to the other methods, applying the rule to the total of the inventory results in a smaller reduction of inventory to market when market is less than cost. This is because market values higher than cost are offset against market values lower than cost when only totals are considered. This also applies to a lesser extent when the categories approach is used, but not at all when the item-by-item approach is applied. Therefore, the item-by-item approach is more conservative than the others because the likelihood of having to reduce cost to market is greater and the amount of any reduction is larger.

Methods of Applying Lower of Cost and Market

	Cost	Market	Lower of Cost and Market by: Individual Items	Major Categories	Total Inventory
Radios					
Type A	$ 800	$ 750	$ 750		
B	1,500	1,600	1,500		
C	900	800	800		
Total Radios	$ 3,200	$ 3,150		$ 3,150	
TV Sets					
Type X	$ 3,000	$ 3,400	3,000		
Y	4,500	4,300	4,300		
Z	2,000	1,900	1,900		
Total TVs	$ 9,500	$ 9,600		$ 9,500	
Total Inventory	$12,700	$12,750	$12,250	$12,650	$12,700

In Canada ***the most common practice is to apply lower of cost and market to the inventory on a total basis***. Companies likely favour this application because it is required by Canadian income tax rules. The tax rules in the United States require the application of the lower of cost and market to individual items and, consequently, that method is more common in the United States. Whichever method is selected for financial reporting, it should be applied consistently from period to period.

Recording "Market" Instead of Cost

Objective 4

Know how to account for inventory on the lower of cost and market basis.

Two methods are used for recording inventory at market, when market is lower than cost. One method, referred to as the **direct method**, simply records the ending inventory at the market figure at the year end. As a result, no loss is separately reported in the income statement; the loss is buried in cost of goods sold. The second method, referred to as the **indirect** or **allowance method**, records ending inventory at the cost amount and then establishes a separate contra-asset account and a loss account to reduce the inventory to market.

The following illustration, using a *periodic* inventory system, shows the entries under both approaches assuming an ending inventory cost of $82,000 and a determined market value of $70,000.

Accounting for the Reduction of Inventory to Market: Periodic Inventory System

Direct Method (Ending Inventory Recorded at Market)			Indirect or Allowance Method (Ending Inventory Recorded at Cost and a Loss and Allowance Separately Recorded)		
To record ending inventory:					
Inventory	70,000		Inventory	82,000	
Cost of Goods Sold		70,000	Cost of Goods Sold		82,000

(Continued)

To write down inventory to market:					
No entry.			Loss Due to Market Decline of Inventory	12,000	
			Allowance to Reduce Inventory to Market		12,000

If the company had used a *perpetual* inventory system, the entries would be as follows.

Accounting for the Reduction of Inventory to Market: Perpetual Inventory System

(No inventory closing entries are necessary under the perpetual method; only the reduction to market is recorded.)

To reduce inventory from cost to market:

Cost of Goods Sold	12,000		Loss Due to Market Decline of Inventory	12,000	
Inventory		12,000	Allowance to Reduce Inventory to Market		12,000

The advantage of separately recording the loss is that it may then be reported as a separate item in the income statement, thereby not distorting the cost of the sales for the year. Therefore, the trend in the rate of gross profit is not affected by gains or losses due to market fluctuations. The following illustrates how the two methods result in differing amounts being reported in the income statement (although the net income will be the same under either method).

Direct Method

Sales		$200,000
Cost of goods sold		
Inventory Jan. 1	$ 65,000	
Purchases	125,000	
Goods available	$190,000	
Inventory Dec. 31 (at market which is less than cost)	**70,000**	
Cost of goods sold *(the loss is buried in cost of goods sold).		120,000
Gross profit on sales		$ 80,000

Indirect or Allowance Method

Sales		$200,000
Cost of goods sold		
Inventory Jan. 1	$ 65,000	
Purchases	125,000	
Goods available	$190,000	
Inventory Dec. 31 (at cost)	**82,000**	
Cost of goods sold		108,000

(Continued)

Gross profit on sales	$ 92,000
Loss due to market decline of inventory	12,000
(shown in other expenses and losses)	
	$ 80,000

The second presentation is preferable because it clearly discloses the loss resulting from the market decline of inventory prices. The first presentation buries the loss in the cost of goods sold.

The Allowance to Reduce Inventory to Market (contra asset) is shown on the balance sheet as a $12,000 deduction from the inventory cost of $82,000 resulting in the net inventory amount of $70,000 being the lower of cost and market figure. Use of the Allowance account has the benefit of keeping the total of subsidiary inventory accounts in agreement with the control account for total inventory because both will be based on cost.

Although use of an Allowance account permits balance sheet disclosure of the amount of inventory at cost and the lower of cost and market, it raises the problem of how to dispose of the account's balance in subsequent periods. If the merchandise to which the allowance applies is still on hand, the account may be retained. But if the goods that suffered the decline (from cost to market) have been sold, this account should be removed from the books. A "new" allowance account is then established to record any reduction from cost to market for the ending inventory of the current period.

Some accountants leave the Allowance account on the books and merely adjust the balance at the next year end to agree with the discrepancy between cost and the lower of cost and market at that balance sheet date. Thus, if prices are falling, a loss is recorded and, if prices are increasing, a loss recorded in prior years is recovered and a gain (recovery of a previously recognized loss) is recorded. The following example provides an illustration.

Date	Inventory at Cost	Inventory at Market	Amount Required in Allowance Account	Adjustment of Allowance Account Balance	Effect on Net Income
Dec. 31/91	$188,000	$176,000	$12,000 cr.	$12,000 inc.	Loss
Dec. 31/92	194,000	187,000	7,000 cr.	5,000 dec.	Gain
Dec. 31/93	173,000	174,000	-0-	7,000 dec.	Gain
Dec. 31/94	182,000	180,000	2,000 cr.	2,000 inc.	Loss

Recognition of a gain or loss in this manner has the same effect on net income as closing any beginning balance in the Allowance account and recording any reduction from cost to market for the year's ending inventory. Note that the ***Allowance account can never have a debit balance.*** If such were the case, it would result in the inventory net of the allowance exceeding the cost of the inventory, a situation not permitted under generally accepted accounting principles.

Evaluation of Lower of Cost and Market Rule

Objective 5

Evaluate conceptual difficulties regarding the lower of cost and market basis.

Conceptually, the lower of cost and market rule has some deficiencies. First, if inventory can be written down because of a loss in utility, does it not seem appropriate to be able to write inventory up when the utility of the asset increases? Decreases in the value of the asset and the charge to income are recognized in the period in which the loss in utility occurs—not in the period of sale. On the other hand, increases in the value of the asset are recognized only at the point of sale. This situation is inconsistent and can lead to distortions in the presentation of income data.

Even if we accept this inconsistency, another problem arises in defining market. Basically, any of three concepts of market can be used in Canada: replacement cost, net realizable value, and net realizable value less a normal profit.[6] Replacement cost could be chosen because changes in replacement cost are easily identified and may reflect a corresponding decline in sales value. Frequently, however, a reduction in the replacement cost of an item does not indicate a corresponding reduction in the utility of the item. To illustrate, assume that a retailer has several shirts that were bought for $15.00 each. The replacement cost of these shirts falls to $14.50, but the selling price remains the same. Has the retailer suffered a loss? To recognize a loss now misstates this period's income and also that of future periods because, upon sale of the shirts in future periods, the full price is received.

Net realizable value reflects the future revenue-producing potential of the asset and, for that reason, is the most conceptually sound concept of market. Unfortunately, net realizable value may be difficult to measure with a sufficient degree of reliability and, therefore, replacement cost may be the only available option. For example, replacement cost may be the most reasonable and practical definition of "market" for raw materials and work-in-process inventories given that they do not have a selling price per se.

Using net realizable value less a normal profit as the definition of market requires dealing with the difficult problems of determining both the net realizable value and a normal profit. In addition, under this approach, a loss recognized in one period is offset by the recognition of profit in a future period. To illustrate, assume that an item costing $10 has a net realizable value of $8 and that the normal profit is $3. Companies using net realizable value will recognize a loss of only $2 ($10 – $8); companies using net realizable value less a normal profit margin will show a loss of $5 ($10 – $2 – $3) and then, when the item is sold, recognize a profit of $3. The purpose of the latter approach is to show a normal profit margin in the period of sale.

From the standpoint of accounting theory there is little to justify the lower of cost and market rule. Despite this, lower of cost and market is, by far, the most commonly used basis for valuation of inventories in Canada.[7] Its acceptance is based on tradition and the practical desire to provide conservatism in financial statement reporting. The rule does result in conservatism because a loss is recognized in the period in which it is deemed to occur. However, the amount carried forward as inventory is matched against the revenue of the periods in which it is sold. Therefore, despite the conservatism in the current period, the result is a higher income in future periods than would be the case if costs were carried forward. Since the total income over several periods will be the same whether or not the lower of cost and market rule is applied, the real issue regarding its acceptability lies in determining in which period the loss should be recognized.

THE GROSS PROFIT METHOD OF ESTIMATING INVENTORY

The basic purpose of taking a physical inventory is to verify the accuracy of the perpetual inventory records or, if no records exist, to arrive at an inventory amount. Sometimes, taking a physical inventory is impractical. Then, estimation methods are used to approximate inventory on hand. One such method is called the gross profit method. This method is used in situations where only an estimate of inventory is needed (e.g., preparing interim reports or testing the reasonableness of the cost derived by some other method). It is also used where both inventory and inventory records have been destroyed by fire or other catastrophe.

Objective 6

Determine inventory by applying the gross profit method.

The **gross profit method** is based on the assumptions that (1) the beginning inventory plus net purchases equal total goods to be accounted for; (2) goods not sold must be on hand; and (3) if the net sales, reduced to cost, are deducted from the sum of the opening inventory plus net purchases, the result is the ending inventory.

---

[6] As previously mentioned, market is usually defined as net realizable value in Canadian practice, but the other definitions are recognized as being acceptable in the *CICA Handbook* (Section 3030, par. .11) and are used (see footnote 2 of this chapter).

[7] *Financial Reporting in Canada—1991* reported that lower of cost and market, or a variation of it, was used by 256 companies, cost by 20 companies, market by 16 companies, and various other approaches by 5 companies.

To illustrate, assume that Gizmo Co. has a beginning inventory of $60,000 and net purchases of $200,000. Net sales amount to $280,000. The average gross profit rate (margin) on selling price for the company is 30%. The calculation of inventory on hand would be as follows:[8]

Beginning inventory		$ 60,000
Net purchases		200,000
Goods available (at cost)		$260,000
Net sales (at selling price)	$280,000	
Less: Gross profit (30% of $280,000)	84,000	
Sales (at cost)		196,000
Approximate inventory (at cost)		**$ 64,000**

All the information needed to compute the inventory at cost, except for the gross profit percentage, is available in the current period's accounting records. The gross profit percentage is determined by reviewing company policies and prior period amounts. Prior periods' percentages must be adjusted if they are not considered representative of the current period.

Gross Profit Percent Versus Percent of Markup

The gross profit percent is the most commonly used number to convey the profitability associated with items sold. A stated percentage may, however, be determined by dividing gross profit by either selling price or cost, as shown below.

$$\frac{\text{Gross Profit}}{\text{Selling Price}} = \frac{\$5.00}{\$20.00} = 25\% \text{ of selling price} \qquad \frac{\text{Gross Profit}}{\text{Cost}} = \frac{\$5.00}{\$15.00} = 33\tfrac{1}{3}\% \text{ of cost}$$

While the amount of gross profit ($5.00) is the same for each calculation, the resulting rates are different. If one simply called the result the gross profit percent there may be confusion: is it a percent of selling price (25%) or a percent of cost (33⅓%)? To overcome this problem, the usual interpretation is that the **gross profit percent *is based on selling price. When the***

---

[8] An alternative method of estimating inventory using the gross profit percent, considered by some to be less complicated than the traditional method illustrated, uses the standard income statement format as follows (assume the same data as in the Gizmo Co. illustration):

Sales		$280,000		$ 280,000
Cost of sales				
Beginning inventory	$ 60,000		$ 60,000	
Purchases	200,000		200,000	
Goods available for sale	260,000		260,000	
Ending inventory	(3) ?		(3) **64,000** Est.	
Cost of goods sold		(2) ?		(2) **196,000** Est.
Gross profit on sales (30%)		(1) ?		(1) **84,000** Est.

Compute the unknowns as follows: first the gross profit amount, then cost of goods sold, and then the ending inventory.

(1) $280,000 × 30% = $84,000 (gross profit on sales).
(2) $280,000 − $84,000 = $196,000 (cost of goods sold).
(3) $260,000 − $196,000 = $64,000 (ending inventory).

***relationship is based on cost, it is called the* percent of markup on cost** (the gross profit amount would be called the markup).[9]

Because a gross profit percent based on selling price is used in the gross profit method to estimate inventory, it is necessary to know whether a stated percentage is based on selling price or cost. If the percent of markup is given, it must be converted to a gross profit percent of selling price. The following formulas can be used to convert a given percent of markup on cost to a gross profit percent on selling price and vice versa.

1. **Percent gross profit** on selling price $= \dfrac{\text{percent markup on cost}}{100\% + \text{percent markup on cost}}$

2. **Percent of markup** on cost $= \dfrac{\text{percent gross profit on selling price}}{100\% - \text{percent gross profit on selling price}}$

Appraisal of Gross Profit Method

Objective 7

Know when the gross profit method can be used and appreciate its limitations.

The gross profit method is not normally acceptable for annual financial reporting purposes because it provides only an estimate. A physical inventory is needed to verify that the inventory indicated in the records is actually on hand. Nevertheless, the gross profit method is used whenever an estimate of the ending inventory is needed (e.g., fire loss) or permitted (e.g., for interim reporting). Note that the gross profit method will follow closely the inventory method used (FIFO, LIFO, average cost) because the gross profit percentage is based on amounts in historical records.

One major disadvantage of the gross profit method is that ***it is an estimate***; as a result, a physical inventory must be taken once a year to verify that the inventory is actually on hand.

A second disadvantage is that the method ***uses past percentages*** to determine current inventory amounts. Although the past can often provide expectations about the future, a current rate is more appropriate. Whenever significant fluctuations occur, a past percentage should be appropriately adjusted.

Third, ***care must be taken when applying a blanket gross profit rate.*** A blanket rate is an average of the gross profit rates for several different items. Frequently a manufacturer, wholesaler, or retailer handles merchandise with widely varying rates of gross profit. In these situations, the gross profit method may have to be applied by subsections, lines of merchandise, or a similar basis that classifies merchandise according to rates of gross profit.

RETAIL INVENTORY METHOD

Objective 8

Appreciate when the retail inventory method can be used, know what information is required to apply it, and how the information is used to determine ending inventory.

Retailers with certain types of inventory may use the specific identification method to value their inventories. Such an approach makes sense when individual inventory units are significant (e.g., automobiles, pianos, or fur coats). However, imagine attempting to use such an approach for Canadian Tire or Sears—high-volume retailers that have many different types of merchandise at low unit costs.

Some retailers have installed computers and point-of-sale terminals which enable them to keep excellent perpetual inventory records for the multitude of items and sales. From these inventory systems, information regarding units on hand and their cost may be readily available.

Many retailers, however, do not have such systems or their computer systems may not be sufficiently sophisticated to provide all the necessary information. For these retailers, any type of unit cost inventory method will be unsatisfactory. Consequently, they may use what is called the

[9] The terms "gross profit percentage," "gross margin percentage," "rate of gross profit," and "rate of gross margin" are synonymous, reflecting the relationship of gross profit to selling price. The terms "percentage markup" or "rate of markup" are used to describe the relationship of markup (equals gross margin) to cost, although some continue to refer to this as a gross profit percentage.

retail inventory method. Given that appropriate information is kept in the accounting records, this method enables the retailer to estimate inventory when necessary and take a physical inventory at retail prices. Because an observable pattern between cost and price usually exists, an inventory taken at retail can be converted to inventory at cost through formula.

Retail inventory method enables retailer to estimate inventory & take physical inv. at retail price.

The retail inventory method requires that a record be kept of (1) the total cost and retail value of goods purchased, (2) the total cost and retail value of the goods available for sale, and (3) the sales for the period. Sales for the period are deducted from the retail value of the goods available for sale to produce an estimated ending inventory at retail. The ratio of cost to retail for all goods passing through a department or company is determined by dividing the total goods available for sale at cost by the total goods available at retail. The inventory valued at retail is converted to approximate cost by applying the cost to retail ratio. The retail inventory method is illustrated for Simon's Inc. below.

Simon's Inc.
Retail Inventory Method
(current period)

	Cost	Retail
Beginning inventory	$14,000	$ 20,000
Purchases	63,000	90,000
Goods available	$77,000	$110,000
Deduct: Sales		85,000
Ending inventory, at retail		$ 25,000
Ratio of cost to retail ($77,000/$110,000)		**70%**
Ending inventory at cost (70% of $25,000)		**$ 17,500**

The total goods available for sale (at retail) less the goods sold (at retail) equals the goods on hand (at retail). The goods on hand at retail are then converted to goods on hand at cost by applying the cost to retail ratio. To avoid a potential misstatement of the inventory, periodic inventory counts are made, especially in retail operations where loss due to shoplifting and breakage is common. When a physical count at retail is taken, the inventory cost is determined by multiplying the resulting amount at retail by the cost to retail ratio. Discrepancy between the records and the physical count will require an adjustment to make the records agree with the count.

The retail method is sanctioned by various retail associations and the accounting profession, and is allowed (except for methods approximating a LIFO valuation) by Revenue Canada. One advantage of the retail inventory method is that the inventory balance ***can be approximated without a physical count.*** This makes the method particularly useful for the preparation of interim reports. Insurance adjusters use this approach to estimate losses from a fire, flood, or other type of casualty. This method also acts as a ***control device*** because any deviations from a physical count at the end of the year have to be explained. In addition, the retail method ***expedites the physical inventory count*** at the end of the year. The inventory-taking crew need only record the retail prices of each item. There is no need to look up each item's invoice cost, thus saving time and expense.

Retail Method Terminology

Objective 9

Understand retail method terminology.

The amounts shown in the Retail column of the preceding illustration represent the **original retail prices** (***cost plus an original markup or markon***), assuming no other price changes up or down. Sales prices, however, are frequently changed from the original retail prices. For retailers, the term

markup means an additional markup on original selling price (i.e. an increase in the price above the original sales price). **Markup cancellations** are decreases in prices of merchandise that had been marked up above the original retail price. Markup cancellations cannot be greater than markups. **Net markups** refer to markups less markup cancellations.

Markdowns are decreases in price below the original selling price. Markdowns are a common phenomenon and occur because of special sales, soiled and damaged goods, overstocking, or competition. **Markdown cancellations** are increases in prices of merchandise that had been marked down below the original selling price. Markdown cancellations cannot exceed markdowns. Markdowns less markdown cancellations equal **net markdowns.**

To illustrate these different terms, assume that Designer Clothing Store recently purchased 100 high-fashion shirts from Marroway Ltd. The cost for these shirts was $1,500, or $15 a shirt. Designer Clothing established the selling price on these shirts at $30 each. Therefore, there was an original markup or markon of $15 per shirt. The manager noted that the shirts were selling quickly, so she added $5 to the price of each shirt. This markup made the price too high and sales lagged. Consequently, the manager reduced the price to $32. To this point there has been a markup of $5 and a markup cancellation of $3 on the original selling price of a shirt. When the major marketing season ended, the manager marked the remaining shirts down to a price of $23. This price change constitutes a markup cancellation of $2 and a $7 markdown. If the shirts are later priced at $24, a markdown cancellation of $1 occurs.

Retail Inventory Method with Markups and Markdowns

To determine the ending inventory figures using the retail inventory method, one must decide on the treatment to be given to markups, markup cancellations, markdowns, and markdown cancellations in the calculation of the ratio of cost to retail. To illustrate the different possibilities, assume the following conditions for In-Fashion Stores Inc.

	Cost	Retail
Beginning inventory	$ 500	$ 1,000
Purchases (net)	20,000	35,000
Markups		3,000
Markup cancellations		1,000
Markdowns		2,500
Markdown cancellations		2,000
Sales (net)		25,000

In-Fashion Stores Inc.
Retail Inventory Method

	Cost		Retail
Beginning inventory	$ 500		$ 1,000
Purchases (net)	20,000		35,000
Merchandise available for sale	$20,500		$36,000
Add:			
Markups		$ 3,000	
Less markup cancellations		(1,000)	
Net markup			2,000
	$20,500		$38,000

(Continued)

Cost ratio $\frac{\$20,500}{\$38,000}$ = 53.9%				(A)
Deduct:				
Markdowns		$ 2,500		
Less markdown cancellations		(2,000)		
Net markdowns			500	
	$20,500		$37,500	
Cost ratio $\frac{\$20,500}{\$37,500}$ = 54.7%				(B)
Deduct sales (net)			25,000	
Ending inventory at retail			$12,500	

The computations of ending inventory under the two identified cost to retail ratios are:

(A) 12,500 × 53.9% = 6,737.50
(B) 12,500 × 54.7% = 6,837.50

(A) reflects a cost percentage after net markups but before net markdowns. The second percentage (B) is computed after both the net markups and net markdowns. Which percentage should be employed to compute the ending inventory valuation? The answer depends on what the ending inventory amount is to reflect.

Objective 10

Determine ending inventory using the conventional retail inventory method and understand why it results in ending inventory approximating the lower of average cost and market.

The **conventional retail inventory method** ***uses the cost to retail ratio incorporating net markups (markups less markup cancellations) but excluding net markdowns (markdowns less markdown cancellations)*** as shown in the calculation of ratio (A). ***It is designed to approximate the lower of average cost and market***, with market being net realizable value less normal profit margin. To understand why net markups but not net markdowns are included in the cost to retail ratio, it is necessary to understand how a retail outlet operates. When a company has a net markup on an item, it normally indicates that the market value of that item has increased. On the other hand, if the item has a net markdown, it means that a decline in the utility of that item has occurred. Therefore, to approximate the lower of average cost and market, net markdowns are considered a current loss and are not involved in the calculation of the cost to retail ratio. Thus, the cost to retail ratio is lower, which leads to an approximate lower of cost and market amount for ending inventory.

For example, assume two different items were purchased for $5 each, and the original sales price was established at $10 each. One item was subsequently marked down to a selling price of $2. Assuming no sales for the period, if markdowns are included in the cost to retail ratio the ending inventory is computed in the following manner.

Average Cost Method
Markdowns Considered in Cost to Retail Ratio

	Cost	Retail
Purchases	$10.00	$20.00
Deduct: Markdowns		8.00
Ending inventory, at retail		$12.00

Cost to retail ratio $\frac{\$10.00}{\$12.00}$ = 83.3%

Ending inventory, at average cost ($12.00 × .833) = $10.00

This approach results in ending inventory at the average cost of the two items on hand without considering the loss on the one item. If markdowns are not considered, the result is ending inventory at the lower of average cost and market. The calculation is as shown below.

Conventional Retail Inventory Method (Lower of Average Cost and Market)
Markdowns Not Included in Cost to Retail Ratio

	Cost	Retail
Purchases	$10.00	$20.00
Cost to retail ratio $\frac{\$10.00}{\$20.00} = 50\%$		
Deduct: Markdowns		8.00
Ending inventory at retail		$12.00
Ending inventory, at lower of average cost and market ($12.00 × .50) = $6.00		

Under the conventional retail inventory method the cost to retail ratio is 50% ($10/$20) and ending inventory is $6 ($12 × .50), the same as lower of average cost and market.

The $6 inventory valuation includes the two inventory items, one inventoried at $5 and the other at $1. Basically, for the item with the decline in market, the sale price was reduced from $10 to $2 and the cost reduced from $5 to $1.[10] Therefore to ***approximate the lower of average cost and market, the cost to retail ratio must be established by dividing the cost of goods available by the sum of the original retail price of these goods plus the net markups; the net markdowns are excluded from the ratio.*** The basic format for the retail inventory method using the conventional approach is illustrated below using the In-Fashion Stores Inc. information.

In-Fashion Stores Inc.
Conventional Retail Inventory Method (Lower of Average Cost and Market)

	Cost		Retail
Beginning inventory	$ 500		$ 1,000
Purchases (net)	20,000		35,000
Totals	$20,500		$36,000
Add net markups:			
Markups		$ 3,000	
Markup cancellations		(1,000)	2,000
Totals	$20,500		$38,000
Deduct net markdowns:			
Markdowns		$ 2,500	
Markdown cancellations		(2,000)	500
Sales price of goods available			$37,500
Deduct: Sales			25,000
Ending inventory, at retail			$12,500

(Continued)

[10] The conventional method defines market as net realizable value less the normal profit. In other words, the sale price of the item written down is $2.00, but after subtracting a normal profit of 50% of selling price (or 100% of cost) the inventoriable amount becomes $1.00.

$$\text{Cost to retail ratio} = \frac{\text{cost of goods available}}{\text{original retail price of goods available} + \text{net markups}}$$

$$= \frac{\$20{,}500}{\$38{,}000} = 53.9\%$$

Ending inventory at lower of average cost and market (53.9% × $12,500.00) $ 6,737.50

Because an averaging effect occurs, an exact lower of average cost and market inventory valuation is ordinarily not obtained, but an adequate approximation is achieved. Also, as indicated previously, net realizable value less normal profit margin is the interpretation of market that results. Using a cost ratio based on totals after adding net markups *and* deducting net markdowns results in ending inventory at *approximate average cost* instead of approximate lower of average cost and market.

Many possible cost to retail ratios could be calculated, depending upon whether or not the beginning inventory, net markups, and net markdowns are included. The following schedule summarizes some of the methods of inventory valuation approximated by the inclusion or exclusion of various items in the cost to retail ratio, given that net purchases are always included in the ratio.

Retail Inventory Method: Identification of Inventory Valuation Method Approximated by Including Various Items in the Cost to Retail Ratio

Beginning Inventory	Net Markups	Net Markdowns	Inventory Valuation Method Approximated
Include	Include	Include	Average Cost
Include	Include	Exclude	Lower of Average Cost and Market (Conventional Method)
Exclude	Include	Include	FIFO Cost
Exclude	Include	Exclude	Lower of FIFO Cost and Market

It is also possible to utilize the retail method to approximate a LIFO cost flow. Because this is seldom used in Canada, the complexities involved are not considered in this book.[11]

Special Items Relating to the Retail Method

The retail inventory method becomes more complicated when items such as freight-in, purchase returns and allowances, and purchase discounts are involved. **Freight costs** are treated as a part of the cost of the purchase; **purchase returns and allowances** are ordinarily considered as a reduction of the cost price and the retail price; **purchase discounts** usually are considered as a reduction of the cost of purchases. In short, the treatment for the items affecting the cost column of the retail inventory approach follows the computation for cost of goods available for sale. Note also that **sales returns and allowances** are considered as proper adjustments to gross sales; **sales discounts to customers**, however, are not recognized when sales are recorded gross. To adjust for the Sales Discount account in such a situation would provide an ending inventory figure at retail that would be overvalued.

[11] The U.S. edition of this text is a useful reference for those interested in LIFO retail concepts and calculations.

In addition, a number of special items require careful analysis. **Transfers-in** from another department, for example, should be reported in the same way as purchases from an outside enterprise. **Normal shortages** (breakage, damage, theft) should reduce the retail column because these goods are no longer available for sale. These costs are reflected in the selling price because a certain amount of shortage is considered normal in a retail enterprise. As a result, this amount is not considered in computing the cost to retail percentage but is shown as a deduction similar to sales to arrive at ending inventory at retail. **Abnormal shortages** should be deducted from both the cost and retail columns prior to calculating the cost to retail ratio and reported as a special inventory amount or as a loss. To do otherwise distorts the cost to retail ratio and overstates ending inventory. Finally, companies often provide their employees with special discounts to encourage loyalty, better performance, and so on. **Employee discounts** should be deducted from the retail column in the same way as sales. These discounts should not be considered in the cost to retail percentage because they do not reflect an overall change in the selling price.

To illustrate some of these treatments in more detail, assume that Executive Apparel Co. Ltd. determines its inventory using the conventional retail inventory method as shown below.

Executive Apparel Co. Ltd.
Conventional Retail Inventory Method: Lower of Average Cost and Market

	Cost		Retail
Beginning inventory	$ 1,000		$ 1,800
Purchases	30,000		60,000
Freight-in	**600**		—
Purchase returns	**(1,500)**		**(3,000)**
Totals	$30,100		$58,800
Net markups			9,000
Abnormal shrinkage	**(1,200)**		**(2,000)**
Totals	**$28,900**		**$65,800**
Deduct:			
Net markdowns			1,400
Sales		**$36,000**	
Less sales returns and allowances		**(900)**	**35,100**
Employee discounts			**800**
Normal shrinkage			**1,300**
Ending inventory at retail			$27,200

Cost-to-retail ratio $= \dfrac{\$28,900}{\$65,800} = 43.9\%$

Ending inventory at lower of average cost and market (43.9% × $27,200) = $11,940.80

Appraisal of Retail Inventory Method

The retail inventory method is used (1) to permit the computation of net income without the necessity of a physical count of the inventory, (2) as a control measure in determining inventory shortages, (3) in controlling quantities of merchandise on hand, and (4) as a source of information for insurance and tax purposes.

One characteristic of the retail inventory method is that it ***has an averaging effect for varying rates of gross profit.*** When applied to an entire business where rates of gross profit vary among departments, no allowance is made for possible distortion of results because of these differences. Many businesses refine the retail method under such conditions by computing inventory separately by departments or by classes of merchandise with similar rates of gross profit. In addition, the reliability of this method rests on the assumption that the distribution of items in the inventory is similar to the "mix" in the total goods available for sale.

ADDITIONAL ISSUES RELATED TO INVENTORY VALUATION

While this and the previous chapter have addressed many important issues, three additional concerns require discussion in order to complete our consideration of inventory determination and valuation for financial reporting purposes. These are valuation of inventory using the relative sales value method, valuation of inventory at net realizable value (regardless of its cost), and accounting for purchase commitments.

Valuation Using Relative Sales Value

Objective 11

Explain when and why the relative sales value method is used to value inventories.

A special inventory valuation problem arises when a group of varying units is purchased at a single **lump sum price**, a so-called **basket purchase**. Assume that Woodland Developers purchases land for $3 million that can be subdivided into 400 lots. These lots are of different sizes and shapes but can be sorted into three groups graded A, B, and C. As lots are sold, the purchase cost of $3 million must be apportioned among the lots sold and the lots remaining.

It is inappropriate to divide the total cost of $3 million by 400 lots to get a cost of $7,500 for each lot because they vary in size, shape, and attractiveness. When such a situation is encountered—and it is not at all unusual—the common practice is to allocate the total cost among the various units on the basis of their relative sales value. For the example given, the allocation works out as follows.

Allocation of Cost

Lots	Number of Lots	Sales Price per Lot	Total Sales Price	Relative Sales Price	Total Cost	Cost Allocated to Lots	Cost per Lot
A	100	$30,000	$3,000,000	300/750	$3,000,000	$1,200,000	$12,000
B	100	18,000	1,800,000	180/750	3,000,000	720,000	7,200
C	200	13,500	2,700,000	270/750	3,000,000	1,080,000	5,400
			$7,500,000			$3,000,000	

The cost of lots sold (using the amounts given in the column for Cost per Lot) and the gross profit can be determined as follows.

Determination of Gross Profit

Lots	Number of Lots Sold	Cost per Lot	Cost of Lots Sold	Sales	Gross Profit
A	77	$12,000	$ 924,000	$2,310,000	$1,386,000
B	80	7,200	576,000	1,440,000	864,000
C	100	5,400	540,000	1,350,000	810,000
			$2,040,000	$5,100,000	$3,060,000

This information may be analysed in a slightly different way. The ratio of the cost to the selling price of all the lots is 40% ($3,000,000 ÷ $7,500,000). Accordingly, given the total sales price of lots sold is $5,100,000, then the cost of the lots sold is 40% of $5,100,000, or $2,040,000. The ending inventory is $960,000 ($3,000,000 – $2,040,000).

Valuation of Inventory at Net Realizable Value

Objective 12

Identify when and why inventory can be valued at net realizable value, regardless of its cost.

For the most part, inventory is recorded at cost or the lower of cost and market. Under certain circumstances, however, support exists for ***recording inventory at net realizable value regardless of its cost.*** As such, inventory is reported at market, defined as net realizable value, regardless of its cost. When the net realizable value is greater than cost, a net revenue is recognized even though the inventory has not been sold. This exception to normal revenue recognition being at the point of sale is permitted when (1) there is a controlled market with a fixed price applicable to all quantities and (2) no significant costs of disposal are involved. As such, it is argued that the criteria for revenue recognition are met at the time of production rather than when goods are sold.

Recording inventory at net realizable value occurs in companies having inventories of certain metals (especially rare ones) or agricultural products for which there is a controlled market (fixed price) and costs of disposal are estimable or immaterial. For example, Rio Algom Limited states in the notes to its financial statements: "Concentrates awaiting shipment under firm contracts and coal inventories are valued at estimated realizable prices and therefore revenue is recorded at the time of production."

Another reason for allowing this method of valuation is that sometimes the cost figures are too difficult to obtain. In a typical manufacturing plant, various raw materials are used and labour costs incurred to create a finished product. Because the cost of each individual component part is known, the various items in inventory, whether completely or partially finished, can be accounted for on a cost basis. In a meat-packing house, however, a different situation prevails. The "raw material" consists of cattle, hogs, or sheep, each unit of which is purchased as a whole and then divided into parts that are the products. Instead of one product out of many raw materials, many products are made from one "unit" of raw material. To accurately assign the cost of an animal "on the hoof" into the cost of ribs, chucks, and shoulders, for instance, is a practical impossibility. It is much easier and more useful to determine the market price of the various products and value them in the inventory at selling price less the various costs, such as shipping and handling, necessary to get them to market. Hence, because of a peculiarity of the meat-packing industry, inventories are sometimes carried at sales price less distribution costs.

Purchase Commitments: A Special Problem

Objective 13

Explain accounting issues related to purchase commitments.

In many lines of business the survival and continued profitability of an enterprise is dependent upon having a sufficient supply of merchandise to meet customer demands. Consequently, it is quite common for a company to contract for the purchase of inventory weeks, months, or even years in advance. This is particularly critical for companies using just-in-time (JIT) ordering and delivery systems. Generally, title to the merchandise or materials described in these purchase commitments has not passed to the buyer. Indeed, the goods may exist only as work in process, natural resources, or unplanted seeds.

Usually it is neither necessary nor proper for the buyer to make any entries to reflect commitments for purchases of goods that have not been shipped by the seller. Ordinary orders, for which the prices are determined at the time of shipment and that are *subject to cancellation* by the buyer or seller, represent neither an asset nor a liability to the buyer and need not be recorded in the books or reported in the financial statements.

Even with formal *noncancellable* purchase contracts, no asset or liability is recognized at the date of inception because the contract is "executory" in nature; neither party has fulfilled its part of the contract. However, if material, the existence of such contracts and some details should be disclosed in the notes to the financial statements.[12] The following is such a note.

---

[12] *CICA Handbook*, Section 3280, par. .01.

Note 4. Contracts for the purchase of raw materials in 1995 have been executed in the amount of $600,000. The market price of such raw materials on December 31, 1994 is $640,000.

In the foregoing illustration it was assumed that the contracted price was less than, or equal to, the market price at the balance sheet date. ***If the contracted price exceeds the market price and losses are reasonably determinable and likely to occur at the time of purchase, losses should be recognized in the period during which such declines in prices take place.***[13] For example, if purchase contracts for delivery in 1995 have been executed at a firm price of $640,000 and the market price of the materials on the company's year end of December 31, 1994 is $600,000, the following entry is made on December 31, 1994:

Loss on Purchase Contracts	40,000	
Accrued Loss on Purchase Contracts		40,000

This loss is shown on the income statement under Other Expenses and Losses. The Accrued Loss on Purchase Contracts is reported in the liability section of the balance sheet. When the goods are delivered in 1995, the entry is:

Purchases	600,000	
Accrued Loss on Purchase Contracts	40,000	
Accounts Payable		640,000

If the price has partially or fully recovered before the inventory is received, the Accrued Loss on Purchase Contracts could be reduced. A resulting gain (Recovery of Loss) is then reported in the period of the price increase for the amount of the partial or full recovery.

Accounting for purchase commitments (and, for that matter, all commitments) is unsettled and controversial. Some argue that these contracts should be reported as assets and liabilities at the time the contract is signed; others believe that recognition at the delivery date is most appropriate.[14] Clearly, the treatment of such contracts in practice is far from being uniform. What is done for particular contracts in particular situations rests on judgement being exercised within the context of generally accepted accounting principles and experience.

FINANCIAL STATEMENT PRESENTATION OF INVENTORIES

Objective 14

Know requirements regarding disclosure of inventory in financial statements and how these requirements can be met.

Inventories are one of the most significant assets of manufacturing and merchandising enterprises. The *CICA Handbook* requires disclosure of the basis of inventory valuation, any change in the basis from that used in the previous period, and the effect of such change on the net income for the period. It is also desirable that the amounts of the major categories making up the total inventory be disclosed (e.g., finished goods, work in process, and raw materials).[15]

The examples shown on pages 456 and 457 illustrate presentations of inventory in financial statements.

---

[13] *Ibid.*, Section 3290, par. .12.

[14] See, for example, Yuji Ijiri, *Recognition of Contractual Rights and Obligations, Research Report* (Stamford, CT: FASB, 1980), who argues that firm purchase commitments might be capitalized. "Firm" means it is unlikely that performance under the contract can be avoided without severe penalty. Also, Mahendra R. Gujarathi and Stanley F. Biggs, "Accounting for Purchase Commitments: Some Issues and Recommendations," *Accounting Horizons*, September 1988, pages 75–82, conclude that "recording an asset and liability on the date of inception for noncancelable purchase commitments is suggested as the first significant step towards alleviating the accounting problems associated with the issue. At year end, the potential gains and losses should be treated as contingencies [for which accounting standards provide] a coherent structure for the accounting and informative disclosure for such gains and losses."

[15] At the time of writing, the Accounting Standards Board's work program included a project to review and expand the *Handbook*'s coverage regarding inventories.

The Oshawa Group Limited

(From the year ended January 25, 1992 financial statements)

Balance Sheet—in current assets	1992	1991
Inventories (in millions of dollars)	$285.5	$286.5

From the summary of significant accounting policies:

Inventories

Warehouse inventories are valued at the lower of cost and net realizable value with cost being determined on a first-in, first-out basis. Retail inventories are valued at the lower of cost and net realizable value less normal profit margins as determined by the retail method of inventory valuation.

MacMillan Bloedel Limited

(From the December 31, 1991 financial statements, in millions of dollars)

Balance Sheet—in current assets	1991	1990
Inventories (note 2)	$483.6	$531.3

From the Notes:

1. **Accounting policies:**
   (c) Valuation of inventories
   Inventories of operating and maintenance supplies and raw materials are valued at the lower of average cost and replacement cost or net realizable value. Inventories of manufactured products are valued at the lower of average cost and net realizable value.

2. **Inventories:**

	December 31	
	1991	1990
Operating and maintenance supplies	$ 78.8	$ 80.2
Logs, pulp chips and pulpwood*	124.9	154.0
Lumber, panelboards and other building materials	198.6	210.0
Pulp and paper products*	50.7	56.3
Containerboard and packaging products	30.6	30.8
	$483.6	$531.3

*At December 31, 1991 these inventories are valued at net realizable value, which is lower than cost.

These examples show disclosure of the basis for inventory valuation (e.g., lower of cost and market), the cost flow method used, and the definition of market used for the major categories making up the total inventory. It is quite acceptable, as shown in the illustrations, for a company to use different valuation methods for different components of its inventory. The use of notes is the basic means for disclosing such information.

Celanese Canada Inc.
(From the year ended December 31, 1991 financial statements)

	(thousands)		
Balance Sheet—in current assets	1991	1990	1989
Inventories (note 4)	$40,503	$37,321	$38,790

From the Notes:

(4) **Inventories**
Substantially all inventories are valued using the last-in, first-out (LIFO) method of determining cost. Other inventories are valued at current cost. Inventory values are not in excess of net realizable value and do not include depreciation of property, plant and equipment. Inventories at December 31 were:

	1991	1990	1989
Raw materials	$ 5,978	$ 6,099	$ 9,272
Work in process	2,474	1,855	1,772
Finished goods	17,314	21,048	20,366
Stores and supplies	14,737	8,319	7,380
Total	$40,503	$37,321	$38,790

If inventories had been valued using the first-in, first-out (FIFO) method of determining cost, total inventories would have been $15,549 higher at December 31, 1991.

The *CICA Handbook* (Section 3030, par. .12) states that "reserves for future decline in inventory values, or any similar reserves, should not be deducted in arriving at inventory valuation." This requirement does not preclude an enterprise from appropriating a portion of retained earnings for an anticipated decline.

Prior to 1990, the *CICA Handbook* contained a section which recommended that large, publicly owned Canadian companies report the effects of changing prices as supplementary information in the financial statements. The current cost amounts for inventory and cost of goods sold were part of this supplementary information. Considerable controversy existed regarding this requirement. Many contended that the high cost of preparing this information was not warranted by the benefits received. Others disagreed, noting that historical cost income numbers were misleading in a period of rising prices (as was experienced in the 1980s) because profits based on such costs were illusory—a company had to replace inventory sold at a higher price than existed when it was purchased. Thus, it was argued, disclosure of changing price information was useful for a better assessment of the quality of enterprise income. The debates ended and the *Handbook*'s recommendations were withdrawn, however, when inflation was no longer at high levels. Concepts regarding reporting the effects of changing prices are considered in Chapter 25.

FUNDAMENTAL CONCEPTS

1. In addition to having different methods for assigning cost to inventories as explained in Chapter 8, there are other means for determining a valuation for inventories. Primary among these are lower of cost and market, gross profit, and retail inventory valuation approaches.

(Continued)

2. The lower of cost and market approach is a departure from historical cost justified on the basis that any loss of future utility (revenue-producing ability) should be recognized in the period of occurrence (i.e. conservatism).
3. Under the lower of cost and market approach, the cost (FIFO, average cost, LIFO) and market (replacement cost, net realizable value, or net realizable value less normal profit margin) of inventory are separately determined. The inventory valuation is then the lower of the two amounts.
4. Net realizable value is, by far, the most frequently used definition of market employed by Canadian companies, although the other interpretations are recognized as being acceptable in the *CICA Handbook* and are used to some extent.
5. The lower of cost and market amount may be determined on an item-by-item basis, major category basis, or total inventory basis. The total inventory basis is most commonly used in Canada.
6. The gross profit method of estimating inventory is based on reducing net sales to their cost and deducting that amount from cost of goods available for sale to get ending inventory at cost. To apply this method, a gross profit on sales percentage must be determined. This percentage may be determined from examining prior periods' accounting records and current policies regarding a company's gross profit on selling price or markup on cost.
7. Because the gross profit method results in an estimate of the cost of ending inventory (i.e. it is not based on a physical count), it is unacceptable for annual financial reporting purposes. It is acceptable for interim reporting, determining amounts for insurance claims regarding inventory destroyed by fire or other catastrophes, or for testing the reasonableness of inventory cost derived by other methods.
8. The retail inventory method is based on multiplying a cost to retail percentage (derived from information in the accounting records) by the retail price of ending inventory (determined by a count or from accounting records).
9. To apply the retail inventory method, records must be kept of the costs and retail prices for beginning inventory, net purchases, and abnormal spoilage, as well as the retail amount of net markups, net markdowns, and net sales. Determination of the items going into the numerator and denominator of the cost to retail ratio depend on the type of inventory valuation estimate desired.
10. The conventional retail method includes net markups but excludes net markdowns in the calculation of the cost to retail ratio. This is the most commonly used retail inventory method and it results in an approximation of inventory at the lower of average cost and market, market being defined as net realizable value less a normal profit margin.
11. Other issues related to inventory valuation include using the relative sales value method, valuation of inventory at net realizable value regardless of its cost, and accounting for purchase commitments.
12. Disclosure of the basis of inventory valuation and any change in the basis are required by the *CICA Handbook*. Also, it is desirable to disclose major categories of inventory, the method used to determine cost, and the definition of market applied under the lower of cost and market method.

QUESTIONS

1. Where there is evidence that the "market value" of inventory is less than cost, what is the appropriate accounting treatment under the lower of cost and market rule?
2. Why are inventories valued at the lower of cost and market? What are the arguments against the use of the lower of cost and market method of valuing inventories?
3. What methods may the accountant employ in applying the lower of cost and market procedure when there are several items and major categories in the total inventory? Which method is normally used in Canada and why?

4. Given the use of the lower of cost and market basis for valuing inventory, determine the amount that will be used to value a unit of inventory in the following cases assuming (a) use of the most frequently used definition of market in Canadian practice and (b) U.S. rules are applied.

	Cases				
	1	2	3	4	5
Cost	$15.90	$15.90	$15.90	$15.90	$15.90
Net realizable value	14.40	19.20	15.30	10.20	16.20
Net realizable value less normal profit	12.70	17.40	13.50	8.60	14.80
Replacement cost	14.60	17.10	12.60	9.50	16.50

5. What method(s) may be used in the accounts to record a loss when the "market" value of inventory is less than cost? Describe each method.

6. What factors justify inventory being valued at net realizable value, regardless of its cost?

7. Under what circumstances is relative sales value an appropriate basis for determining the price assigned to inventory?

8. At December 31, 1994, Pepper Co. Ltd. has outstanding contracts for the purchase of 450,000 L, at $0.55/L, of a raw material to be used in their manufacturing process. The company prices its raw material inventory at cost or market, whichever is lower. Assuming that the market price as of December 31, 1994 is $0.51/L, how will you treat this situation in the accounts under each of the following circumstances?
   (a) The contracts are significant in relation to current financial position and future operations, are not subject to cancellation, and the price is firm.
   (b) The contracts can be cancelled by Pepper Co. Ltd. on payment of a cancellation fee of $10,000.
   (c) The contracts may be cancelled by either party without penalty.
   (d) How would the contracts be accounted for in the above situations if the market price on December 31, 1994 was $0.56/L?

9. List the major uses of the gross profit method.

10. Will the percent of markup on cost or the percent of gross profit based on selling price be the higher amount for a given item? Convert the following percentages of markup on cost to percentages of gross profit based on selling price: 20% and 33⅓%. Convert the following gross profit percentages based on selling price to percentages of markup based on cost: 33⅓% and 60%.

11. Tulle Inc. with annual net sales of $5 million maintains a markup of 25% based on cost. Tulle's expenses average 15% of net sales. What is Tulle's gross profit and net profit in dollars?

12. A fire destroys all of the merchandise of Macadamia Company on February 10, 1994. Presented below is information compiled up to the date of the fire:

Inventory January 1, 1994	$ 300,000
Sales to February 10, 1994	1,600,000
Purchases to February 10, 1994	1,130,000
Freight-in to February 10, 1994	65,000
Rate of gross profit on selling price	40%

What was the approximate inventory on February 10, 1994 prior to the fire?

13. What conditions must exist for the retail inventory method to provide valid results?

14. Explain and give a numerical example of how the conventional retail method provides an inventory valuation that approximates the lower of average cost and market amount. What is the definition of market that results from using this method?

15. (a) Determine the ending inventory for the furniture department of the Buster Department Store from the following data using the conventional retail inventory method:

	Cost	Retail
Inventory Jan. 1	$ 146,000	$ 280,500
Purchases	1,400,000	2,163,000
Freight-in	73,000	
Markups, net		92,000
Markdowns, net		46,000
Sales		2,246,000

(b) If the results of a physical inventory indicate an inventory at retail of $240,000, what are the possible explanations for the difference between this amount and your answer to (a)?

16. Twister Ltd. provides the following information with respect to its inventories:

Inventories	$140,800,506

What additional disclosure is necessary to present the inventory in accordance with generally accepted accounting practices?

CASES

C9-1 **(LOWER OF COST AND MARKET)** You are in charge of the audit of Holmes Inc. The following items were in Holmes' inventory at November 30, 1994 (fiscal year end).

Product Number	075936	078310	079104	081111
Selling price per unit November 30, 1994	$16.00	$22.00	$28.00	$14.00
Standard cost per unit, as included in inventory at November 30, 1994	$ 9.00	$11.00	$14.26	$ 7.80

In discussion with Holmes' marketing and sales personnel you were told that there will be a general 9% (rounded to the next highest five cents) increase in selling prices, effective December 1, 1994. This increase will affect all products except those having 081 as the first three digits of the product code. The 081 codes are assigned to new product introductions, and for product code 081111, the selling price will be $9.00 effective December 1, 1994.

In addition, you were told by the controller that Holmes attempts to earn a 40% gross profit on selling price on all their products.

From the cost department you obtained the following standard costs, which will be used for fiscal 1995.

Product Number	1995 Standard
075936	$ 8.23
078310	$10.78
079104	$14.74
081111	$ 7.52

Sales commissions and estimates of other costs of disposal approximate 25% of standard costs to manufacture. Assume that standard costs provide a reasonable approximation of the replacement cost of the product.

Instructions

(a) Determine the net realizable value of each item expected for fiscal 1995.

(b) Assuming the net realizable values for (a) are to be used to determine the lower of cost and market valuation for the November 30, 1994 inventory, and that there were 5,000 units of each item on hand, how and at what amount would the inventory be shown on the balance sheet using an item-by-item approach? A total inventory approach?

(c) When market is lower than cost, why should inventories be reported at market? Why are inventories reported at cost when market is greater than cost?

C9-2 **(RETAIL INVENTORY METHOD)** Stay-on Company, your client, manufactures paint. The company's president, Ms. Stay, has decided to open a retail store to sell Stay-on paint as well as wallpaper and other supplies that would be purchased from suppliers. She has asked you for information about the conventional retail method of valuing inventories at the retail store.

Instructions

Prepare a report to the president explaining the conventional retail method. Your report should include these points:

(a) Description and accounting features of the method.

(b) The conditions that may distort the results under the method.

(c) A list of the advantages of using the retail method relative to using cost methods of inventory pricing.

(d) The accounting theory underlying the treatment of net markdowns and net markups under the method.

(RETAIL INVENTORY METHOD) Presented below are a number of items that may be encountered in computing the cost to retail percentage when using the conventional retail method or the average-cost retail method: C9-3

1. Sales discounts
2. Markdowns
3. Markdown cancellations
4. Cost of items transferred in from other departments
5. Retail value of items transferred in from other departments
6. Purchase discounts (purchases recorded gross)
7. Estimated retail value of goods broken or stolen
8. Cost of beginning inventory
9. Retail value of beginning inventory
10. Cost of purchases
11. Retail value of purchases
12. Markups
13. Markup cancellations
14. Employee discounts (sales recorded net)

Instructions

For each of the items listed above, indicate whether it is included in the cost-to-retail percentage (1) under conventional retail and (2) under average-cost retail.

(GENERAL INVENTORY ESTIMATION ISSUES) You have just been hired as a new accountant for the accounting firm of Ponder and Wonder. The manager of the office wants to test your formal education and provides you with the following factual situations that were encountered by the firm: C9-4

1. In December 1994, one of the clients underwent a major management change and a new president was hired. After reviewing the various policies of the company, the president's opinion was that prior systems employed by the company did not allow for adequate testing of obsolescence (including discontinued products) and overstocks in inventories. Accordingly, the president changed the mechanics of the procedures for reviewing obsolete and excess inventory and for determining the amount. These reviews resulted in a significant increase in the amount of inventory that was written off in 1994 relative to previous years. You are satisfied that these procedures are appropriate and provide reliable results. The amount charged against operations for excess and obsolete inventory for 1994 would be $500,000. Had the 1994 methods been employed in the previous two years, the additional expense for 1993 would have been $120,000 and for 1992, $115,000. The amounts for the obsolescence expensed in 1992 and 1993 were $200,000 and $180,000 respectively. Net income for 1994 before adjustment for the obsolescence charge was $900,000.

Instructions

How should these charges be reported in the 1994 financial statements, if at all?

2. Another client, Sunburst Foods, was upset because it was requested by Ponder and Wonder to write down its inventory on an item-by-item basis. The item-by-item computation resulted in a write-down of approximately $380,000 as follows.

Product	Product Lines	
	Frozen	Cans
Cut beans	—	$ 30,000

(Continued)

Peas	—	46,000
Mixed vegetables	$ 74,000	34,000
Spinach	182,000	—
Carrots	14,000	—
	$270,000	$110,000

The company stated that the products are sold on a line basis (frozen or canned) with customers taking all varieties, and only rarely are sales made on an individual product basis. Therefore, it was argued, the application of the lower of cost and market rule to the product lines would result in an appropriate determination of income (loss). A pricing of the inventory on this basis would result in a $150,000 write-down as the reductions to market on the item-by-item basis as shown above would be partially offset in each product line by some products having a market in excess of cost.

Instructions

Why do you believe Ponder and Wonder argued for the item-by-item approach? Which method should be used, given the information in this case?

3. A client's major business activities are the purchase and resale of used heavy mining and construction equipment, including trucks, cranes, shovels, conveyors, crushers, etc. The company was organized in 1979. In its earlier years, it purchased individual items of heavy equipment and resold them to customers throughout Canada. In the mid-1980s, the company began negotiating the "package" purchase of all the existing equipment at mine sites, concurrent with the closing down of several of the large iron mines in Ontario and exhausted coal mines in Saskatchewan. The mine operators preferred to liquidate their mine assets on that basis rather than hold auctions or leave the mine site open until all of the equipment could be liquidated. As there were numerous pieces of equipment in these package purchases, the client found it difficult to assign costs to each item individually. As a result, the company followed the policy of valuing these "package" purchases by the cost recovery method. Under this method, the company recognized no income until the entire cost had been recovered through sales revenues. This produced the effect of deferring income to later periods and represented, for financial reporting purposes, a "conservative" valuation of inventories in what was essentially a new field for the company where its level of experience had not been demonstrated.

Instructions

Comment on the propriety of this approach.

C9-5 **(ETHICAL ISSUES: LOWER OF COST AND MARKET—DIRECT OR ALLOWANCE)** The market value of Zenith Co. Ltd.'s inventory has declined significantly below its cost. Chris Stuart, the controller, wants to use the direct method to write down inventory without calling attention to the decline in market value. Her supervisor, financial vice-president Hal Smith, prefers the allowance method because it more clearly discloses the decline in market value and it does not distort the cost of goods sold.

Instructions

(a) What, if any, is the ethical issue involved in making this decision?

(b) Is any stakeholder harmed if Stuart's direct method is used?

(c) What should Chris Stuart do?

C9-6 **(ETHICAL ISSUES: PURCHASE COMMITMENTS)** Bluff Cascade had signed a long-term purchase contract to buy 20,000 board feet of timber from the British Columbia Forest Service at $250 per thousand board feet. Under the contract, Bluff Cascade must cut and pay $5,000,000 for this timber during the next year. Currently, the market value is $200 per thousand board feet. Samuel Allen, the controller, wants to recognize a $1,000,000 loss on the contract in the year-end financial statements; but the financial vice-president, Dave Weiseman, argues that the loss is temporary and it should be ignored. Allen notes, however, that market value has remained near $200 for many months, and he sees no sign of significant change.

Instructions

(a) What are the ethical issues, if any?

(b) Is any particular stakeholder harmed by the financial vice-president's solution?

(c) What would you do if you were the controller?

EXERCISES

(LOWER OF COST AND MARKET: JOURNAL ENTRIES) Cougar Company Ltd. determined its ending inventory at cost and at lower of cost and market at December 31, 1993 and December 31, 1994. This information is presented below. E9-1

	Cost	Lower of Cost and Market	
12/31/93	$356,000	$325,000	31,000
12/31/94	415,000	395,000	

Instructions

(a) Prepare the journal entries required at 12/31/93 and 12/31/94, assuming that the inventory is recorded directly at market and a periodic inventory system is used.

(b) Prepare journal entries required at 12/31/93 and 12/31/94, assuming that the inventory is recorded at cost and an allowance account is adjusted at each year end under a periodic system.

(c) Which of the two methods provides the highest net income in each year? Both methods have the same effect on net income.

(LOWER OF COST AND MARKET) The inventory of Panther Inc. on December 31, 1994 consists of these items. E9-2

Part No.	Quantity	Cost per Unit	Net Realizable Value per Unit
110	1,000	$ 92	$100
111	600	65	54
112	400	80	76
113	200	180	195
120	400	205	208
121[a]	1,500	16	?
122	200	230	225

[a]Part No. 121 is obsolete and each unit has a realizable value of $.20 as scrap. This part had sold previously for $14.

Instructions

(a) Determine the inventory as of December 31, 1994 by the method of cost or market, whichever is lower, and apply the method directly to each item.

(b) Determine the inventory by cost or market, whichever is lower, and apply the method to the total of the inventory.

E9-3 (LOWER OF COST AND MARKET) Simms Company uses the lower of cost and market method, on an individual-item basis, in pricing its inventory items. The inventory at December 31, 1994 consists of products D, E, F, G, H, and I. Relevant per-unit data for these products appear below.

	Item D	Item E	Item F	Item G	Item H	Item I
Estimated selling price	$120	$110	$180	$90	$110	$135
Cost	80	80	160	80	50	54
Replacement cost	120	70	140	30	70	45
Estimated selling expense	30	30	60	30	30	45
Normal profit	20	20	40	20	20	30

Instructions

Using the lower of cost and market rule, determine the unit value for balance sheet reporting purposes at December 31, 1994 for each of the inventory items above using (1) the most commonly used Canadian definition of market and (2) the U.S. rules to determine market.

E9-4 (LOWER OF COST AND MARKET) Trump Company Ltd. follows the practice of pricing its inventory at the lower of cost and market, on an individual-item basis.

Item No.	Quantity	Cost per Unit	Cost to Replace	Estimated Selling Price	Cost of Completion and Disposal	Normal Profit
1320	1,300	$3.30	$3.10	$4.60	$.35	$1.25
1333	1,200	2.70	2.30	3.50	.50	.50
1426	800	4.40	3.80	5.00	.40	1.00
1437	1,000	3.50	3.00	3.10	.25	.90
1510	1,400	2.25	2.00	3.25	.80	.60
1522	500	3.10	2.90	3.90	.50	.60
1573	3,000	1.90	1.60	2.50	.75	.50
1626	1,000	4.70	5.30	6.00	.50	1.00

Instructions

From the information above, determine the amount of Trump Company Ltd.'s inventory assuming use of (1) the most commonly used definition of "market" in Canadian practice and (2) U.S. rules to determine market.

E9-5 (INVENTORY VALUATION METHOD COMPARISON) Wintermint Co. Ltd. began business on January 1, 1994. Information about its inventories under different valuation methods follows.

	Inventory		
	LIFO Cost	FIFO Cost	Lower of FIFO Cost and Market
December 31, 1994	$18,500	$26,000	$19,500
December 31, 1995	14,400	20,000	16,000

Instructions

(a) Indicate the inventory basis that will show the highest net income in (1) 1994 and (2) 1995.

(b) Indicate whether the FIFO cost basis will provide a higher or lower profit than the lower of cost and market basis in 1995 and indicate by how much.

(LOWER OF COST AND MARKET: VALUATION ACCOUNT) Presented below is information related to Vanilla Enterprises. E9-6

	Jan. 31	Feb. 28	Mar. 31	Apr. 30
Inventory at cost	$15,000	$15,100	$16,000	$13,000
Inventory at the lower of cost and market	14,300	13,600	15,600	12,800
Purchases for the month		22,000	26,000	28,000
Sales for the month		33,200	36,800	50,000

Instructions

(a) From the information prepare (as far as the data permit) monthly income statements in columnar form for February, March, and April. The inventory is to be shown in the statement at cost, the gain or loss due to market fluctuations is to be shown separately, and a valuation account is to be set up for the difference between cost and the lower of cost and market.

(b) Prepare the journal entry required to establish the valuation account at January 31 and entries to adjust it monthly thereafter.

(RELATIVE SALES VALUE METHOD) Buy and Sell Inc. purchased a tract of land for $86,000. This land was improved and subdivided into building lots at an additional cost of $44,000. These building lots were all of the same size but owing to differences in location were offered for sale at different prices as follows. E9-7

Group	No. of Lots	Price per Lot
1	9	$7,000
2	15	4,600
3	17	4,000

Operating expenses for the year allocated to this project totalled $21,000. Lots unsold at year end were as follows:

Group 1	5 lots
Group 2	7 lots
Group 3	2 lots

Instructions

Determine the year-end inventory and net income from these operations.

(RELATIVE SALES VALUE METHOD) Finesse Furniture Company purchases, during 1994, a carload of wicker chairs. The manufacturer sells the chairs to Finesse for a lump sum of $125,000 because it is discontinuing manufacturing operations and wishes to dispose of its entire stock. Three types of chairs are included in the carload. The three types and the estimated selling price for each are listed below. E9-8

Type	No. of Chairs	Estimated Selling Price for Each
Lounge chairs	400	$200
Armchairs	300	150
Straight chairs	750	100

During 1994 Finesse sells 200 lounge chairs, 100 armchairs, and 120 straight chairs.

Instructions

What is the amount of gross profit realized during 1994? What is the amount of inventory of unsold wicker chairs on December 31, 1994?

E9-9 **(PURCHASE COMMITMENTS)** Quality Company was having difficulty obtaining key raw materials for its manufacturing process. The company therefore signs a long-term noncancellable purchase commitment with its largest supplier of this raw material on November 30, 1994 at an agreed price of $500,000. At December 31, 1994 the raw material has declined in price to $465,000, and it is further anticipated that the price will drop another $15,000, so that at the date of delivery the value of the inventory will be $450,000.

Instructions

What entries will you make on December 31, 1994 to recognize these facts?

E9-10 **(PURCHASE COMMITMENTS)** At December 31, 1994 Alberta Wine Company has outstanding noncancellable purchase commitments for 50,000 litres, at $3 per litre, of raw material to be used in its manufacturing process. The company prices its raw material inventory at cost or market, whichever is lower.

Instructions

(a) Assuming that the market price as of December 31, 1994 is $3.40 per litre, how will this commitment be treated in the accounts and statements? Explain.

(b) Assuming that the market price as of December 31, 1994 is $2.60, how will you treat this commitment in the accounts and statements?

(c) Give the entry in January 1995 when the 50,000 litre shipment is received, assuming that the situation given in (b) existed at December 31, 1994. Give an explanation of your entry.

E9-11 **(GROSS PROFIT METHOD)** Arden Inc. uses the gross profit method to estimate inventory for monthly reporting purposes. Presented below is information for the month of May:

Inventory May 1	$ 160,000
Purchases (gross)	640,000
Freight-in	30,000
Sales	1,000,000
Sales returns	30,000
Purchase discounts	12,000

Instructions

(a) Compute the estimated inventory at May 31, assuming that the gross profit is 25% of sales.

(b) Compute the estimated inventory at May 31, assuming that the markup is 25% of cost.

(GROSS PROFIT METHOD) Craig Campbell requires an estimate of the cost of goods lost by fire on March 9. Merchandise on hand on January 1 was $38,000. Purchases since January 1 were $75,000; freight-in, $3,400; purchase returns and allowances, $2,400. Sales were made at a markup of 33⅓% on cost and totalled $102,000 to March 9. Goods costing $7,700 were left undamaged by the fire; remaining goods were destroyed. **E9-12**

Instructions

(a) Compute the cost of goods destroyed.

(b) Compute the cost of goods destroyed, assuming that the gross profit is 33⅓% of sales.

(GROSS PROFIT METHOD) You are called by Bill Sullivan of Gremlin Co. on July 16 and asked to prepare a claim for insurance as a result of a theft that took place the night before. You suggest that an inventory be taken immediately. The following data are available: **E9-13**

Inventory July 1	$ 38,000
Purchases—goods placed in stock July 1–15	100,000
Sales—goods delivered to customers (gross)	123,000
Sales returns—goods returned to stock	4,000

Your client reports that the goods on hand on July 16 cost $29,000, but you determine that this figure includes goods of $6,000 received on a consignment basis. Your past records show that sales prices are set at approximately 40% over cost.

Instructions

Compute the claim against the insurance company.

(GROSS PROFIT METHOD) Nottingham Forest Inc. handles three principal lines of merchandise with these varying rates of gross profit on cost: **E9-14**

Lumber	35%
Millwork	30%
Hardware and fittings	45%

On August 18 a fire destroyed the office, lumber shed, and a considerable portion of the lumber stacked in the yard. To file a report of loss for insurance purposes, the company must know what the inventories were immediately prior to the fire. The only pertinent information you are able to obtain are the following facts from the general ledger, which was kept in a fireproof vault and thus escaped destruction.

	Lumber	Millwork	Hardware
Inventory Jan. 1	$ 250,000	$ 90,000	$ 45,000
Purchases to Aug. 18	1,500,000	376,000	164,000
Sales to Aug. 18	2,079,000	500,500	210,250

Instructions

Submit your estimate of the inventory amounts immediately prior to the fire.

E9-15 (GROSS PROFIT METHOD) Presented below is information related to Lakehead Co. Ltd. for the current year:

Beginning inventory	$ 600,000
Purchases	1,500,000
Total goods available for sale	2,100,000
Sales	2,500,000

Instructions

Compute the ending inventory, assuming that (1) gross profit is 30% of sales; (2) markup is 25% of cost; (3) markup is 50% of cost; and (4) gross profit is 40% of sales.

E9-16 (RETAIL INVENTORY METHOD) Presented below is information related to Splinter Company.

	Cost	Retail
Beginning inventory	$ 58,000	$100,000
Purchases (net)	122,000	200,000
Net markups		10,345
Net markdowns		26,135
Sales		209,710

Instructions

(a) Compute the ending inventory at retail.

(b) Compute a cost-to-retail percentage (round to two decimals):

1. Excluding both markups and markdowns.
2. Excluding markups but including markdowns.
3. Excluding markdowns but including markups.
4. Including both markdowns and markups.

(c) Which of the methods in (b) above (1, 2, 3, or 4):

1. Provides the most conservative estimate of ending inventory?
2. Provides an approximation of lower of cost and market?
3. Is used in the conventional retail method?

(d) Compute ending inventory at lower of cost and market (round to nearest dollar).

(e) Compute cost of goods sold based on (d).

(f) Compute gross profit based on (d).

(RETAIL INVENTORY METHOD) The records of Wayne's World Inc. report the following data for the **E9-17**
month of September:

Sales	$99,000
Sales returns	1,000
Markups	10,000
Markup cancellations	1,500
Markdowns	9,300
Markdown cancellations	2,800
Freight on purchases	2,400
Purchases (at cost)	48,400
Purchases (at sales price)	88,000
Purchase returns (at cost)	1,000
Purchase returns (at sales price)	3,000
Beginning inventory (at cost)	30,000
Beginning inventory (at sales price)	46,500

Instructions

Compute the ending inventory by the conventional retail inventory method.

(RETAIL INVENTORY METHOD: CONVENTIONAL AND AVERAGE-COST) Friar Tuck Company **E9-18**
began operations on January 1, 1993, adopting the conventional retail inventory system. None of its merchandise was marked down in 1993 and, because there was no beginning inventory, its ending inventory for 1993 of $38,500 would have been the same under either the conventional system or the average-cost system. All pertinent data regarding purchases, sales, markups, and markdowns for 1994 are shown below.

	Cost	Retail
Inventory Jan. 1, 1994	$ 38,500	$ 62,000
Markdowns (net)		13,000
Markups (net)		20,000
Purchases (net)	127,900	178,000
Sales (net)		181,000

Instructions

Determine the cost of the 1994 ending inventory under (1) the conventional retail method and (2) the average-cost retail method.

PROBLEMS

(LOWER OF COST AND MARKET) Renata Ltd. manufactures desks. Most of the company's desks are **P9-1**
standard models and are sold on the basis of catalogue prices. At December 31, 1994, the following per-unit information for four types of finished desks appears in the company's records.

Finished Desks	A	B	C	D
1994 catalogue selling price	$450	$480	$880	$1,050
FIFO cost per inventory list 12/31/94	460	450	820	960
Estimated current cost to manufacture (at December 31, 1994 and early 1995)	460	370	720	1,000
Sales commissions and estimated other costs of disposal	50	60	90	120
1995 catalogue selling price	520	550	920	1,200

The 1994 catalogue is in effect through November 1994 and the 1995 catalogue is effective as of December 1, 1994. Generally, the company attempts to obtain a 20% gross profit on selling price and has usually been successful in doing so.

Instructions

At what per-unit amount should each of the four types of desks appear in the company's December 31, 1994 inventory, assuming that the company has adopted a lower of FIFO cost and market approach for valuation of inventories? Use net realizable value as the definition of market.

P9-2 **(LOWER OF COST AND MARKET)** Shafer's Inc. follows the practice of valuing its inventory at the lower of cost and market. The following information is available from the company's inventory records as of December 31, the company's year end.

Item	On-Hand Quantity	Unit Cost	Replacement Cost/Unit	Estimated Unit Selling Price	Completion & Disposal Costs/Unit	Normal Unit Profit
A	1,100	$7.50	$8.40	$10.50	$1.50	$1.80
B	800	8.20	8.40	9.40	.90	1.20
C	1,000	5.60	5.40	7.20	1.10	.40
D	1,000	3.80	4.20	6.30	.80	1.50
E	1,200	6.50	6.30	6.80	.70	1.00

Instructions

(a) Indicate the inventory amount that should be used for each item under the lower of cost and market rule assuming (1) the most commonly used Canadian practice and (2) U.S. rules.

(b) Shafer's Inc. applies the lower of cost and market rule directly to each item in the inventory but maintains its inventory account at cost to account for the items above. Give the adjusting entry, if one is necessary, to write down the ending inventory from cost to market assuming (1) the common Canadian interpretation of market and (2) U.S. rules.

(c) Shafer's Inc. applies the lower of cost and market rule to the total of the inventory. What is the dollar amount for inventory as of 12/31 assuming (1) the most common Canadian interpretation of market and (2) U.S. rules?

P9-3 **(LOWER OF COST AND MARKET: ERRORS)** Oakbrook Ltd., which began operations in 1991, always values its inventories at the current replacement cost. Its annual inventory figure is arrived at by taking a physical count and then pricing each item in the physical inventory at current prices determined from recent vendors' invoices or catalogues. Here is the condensed income statement for this company for the last four years.

	1991	1992	1993	1994
Sales	$850,000	$880,000	$950,000	$990,000
Cost of goods sold	560,000	590,000	630,000	650,000
Gross profit	$290,000	$290,000	$320,000	$340,000
Operating expenses	190,000	180,000	200,000	210,000
Income before income taxes	$100,000	$110,000	$120,000	$130,000

Instructions

(a) Do you see any objections to the procedure for valuing inventories? Explain.

(b) Assuming that the inventory at cost and as determined by the corporation (using replacement cost) at the end of each of the four years is as follows, restate the condensed income statements using cost for inventories.

Ending Inventory	At Cost	Replacement Cost as Determined by Company
1991	$130,000	$154,000
1992	140,000	168,000
1993	135,000	167,000
1994	150,000	167,000

(LOWER OF COST AND MARKET) Lester Inc. is a food wholesaler that supplies independent grocery stores in the immediate region. The first-in, first-out (FIFO) method of inventory valuation is used to determine the cost of the inventory at the end of each month. Transactions and other related information regarding two of the items (instant coffee and sugar) carried by Lester are given below for October, the last month of Lester's fiscal year. **P9-4**

	Instant Coffee	Sugar
Standard unit of packaging:	Case containing 24, one-kg jars	Baler containing 12, five-kg bags
Inventory, 10/1:	1,000 cases @ $70.00 per case	500 balers @ $11.00 per baler
Purchases:	1. 10/10—1,600 cases @ $72.00 per case plus freight of $480.00 2. 10/20—2,400 cases @ $74.00 per case plus freight of $480.00	1. 10/5—850 balers @ $11.75 per baler plus freight of $420.00 2. 10/16—640 balers @ $12.00 per baler plus freight of $420.00 3. 10/24—600 balers @ $12.20 per baler plus freight of $420.00
Purchase terms:	2/10, net/30, f.o.b. shipping point	Net 30 days, f.o.b. shipping point
October sales:	3,700 cases @ $88.00 per case	2,000 balers @ $14.50 per baler
Returns and allowances:	A customer returned 50 cases that had been shipped by error. The customer's account was credited for $4,400.00.	As the October 16 purchase was unloaded, 20 balers were discovered as damaged. A representative of the trucking firm confirmed the damage and the balers were discarded. Credit of $240.00 for the merchandise and $13.00 for the freight was received by Lester.
Inventory values including freight and net of purchase discounts—10/31:		
• Most recent quoted price	$74.50 per case	$13.80 per baler
• Net realizable value	$76.00 per case	$13.20 per baler
• Net realizable value less a normal profit	$61.00 per case	$10.70 per baler

Lester's sales terms are 1/10, net/30, f.o.b. shipping point. Lester records all purchases net of purchase discounts and takes all purchase discounts.

Instructions

(a) Calculate the number of units in inventory and the FIFO unit cost for instant coffee and sugar as of October 31.

(b) Lester Inc. applies the lower of cost and market (net realizable value) rule in valuing its year-end inventory. Calculate the total dollar amount of the inventory for instant coffee and sugar, applying the lower of cost and market rule on an individual-product basis.

(c) Can Lester Inc. apply the lower of cost and market rule to groups of products or the inventory as a whole rather than on an individual product basis? Explain your answer.

(CMA adapted)

P9-5 **(ENTRIES FOR LOWER OF COST AND MARKET: DIRECT AND ALLOWANCE)** Murphy Music Ltd. determined its ending inventory at cost and at lower of cost and market at December 31, 1993, 1994, and 1995, as shown below.

	Cost	Lower of Cost or Market
12/31/93	$650,000	$650,000
12/31/94	780,000	720,000
12/31/95	900,000	815,000

Instructions

(a) Prepare the journal entries required at 12/31/94 and 12/31/95, assuming that a periodic inventory system and the direct method of adjusting to market is used.

(b) Prepare the journal entries required at 12/31/94 and 12/31/95, assuming that a periodic inventory is recorded at cost and reduced to market through the use of an allowance account.

P9-6 **(GROSS PROFIT METHOD)** Hustler Inc. lost most of its inventory in a fire in December just before the year-end physical inventory was taken. Corporate records disclose the following:

Inventory (beginning)	$ 80,000	Sales	$415,000
Purchases	300,000	Sales returns	21,000
Purchase returns	28,000	Gross profit % based on selling price	35%

Merchandise with a selling price of $30,000 remained undamaged after the fire, and damaged merchandise has a salvage value of $7,150. The company does not carry fire insurance on its inventory. It is estimated that the year-end inventory would have been subject to a normal 10% write-down for obsolescence.

Instructions

Prepare a schedule computing the fire loss incurred by Hustler Inc. (Do not use the retail inventory method.)

P9-7 **(GROSS PROFIT METHOD)** On June 30, 1994 a flash flood damaged the warehouse and factory of Unlucky Inc., completely destroying the work-in-process inventory. There was no damage to either the raw materials or finished goods inventories. A physical inventory taken after the flood revealed the following valuations:

Raw materials	$ 60,000
Work in process	-0-
Finished goods	150,000

The inventory on January 1, 1994 consisted of the following:

Raw materials	$ 50,000
Work in process	160,000
Finished goods	164,000
	$374,000

A review of the records disclosed that the gross profit historically approximated 40% of sales. The sales for the first six months of 1994 were $420,000. Raw material purchases were $140,000. Direct labour costs for this period were $95,000 and manufacturing overhead was applied at 52% of direct labour.

Instructions

Compute the value of the work-in-process inventory lost at June 30, 1994.

(GROSS PROFIT METHOD) Wilton Co. Ltd. is an importer and wholesaler. Its merchandise is purchased from several suppliers and is warehoused until sold. P9-8

In conducting his audit for the year ended June 30, 1994, the corporation's auditor determined that the system of internal control was good. Accordingly, he observed the physical inventory at an interim date, May 31, 1994, instead of at year end.

The following information was obtained from the general ledger:

Inventory July 1, 1993	$ 120,000
Physical inventory May 31, 1994	147,000
Sales for 11 months ended May 31, 1994	970,000
Sales for year ended June 30, 1994	1,060,000
Purchases for 11 months ended May 31, 1994 (before audit adjustments)	650,000
Purchases for year ended June 30, 1994 (before audit adjustments)	755,000

The audit disclosed the following information:

Shipments received in May and included in the physical inventory but recorded as June purchases	$ 12,000
Shipments received in unsaleable condition and excluded from physical inventory; credit memos had not been received nor had chargebacks to vendors been recorded:	
Total at May 31, 1994	1,500
Total at June 30, 1994 (including the May unrecorded chargebacks)	2,000
Deposit made with vendor and charged to purchases in April 1994	
Product was shipped in July 1994	3,000
Deposit made with vendor and charged to purchases in May 1994	
Product was shipped, f.o.b. destination, on May 29, 1994 and was included in May 31, 1994 physical inventory as goods in transit	6,500
Through the carelessness of the receiving department, a June shipment was damaged by rain. This shipment was later sold in June at its cost of $8,000.	

Instructions

In audit engagements in which interim physical inventories are observed, a frequently used auditing procedure is to test the reasonableness of the year-end inventory by the application of gross profit ratios. Given this, you are asked to prepare schedules which show the determination of:

(a) The gross profit ratio for the 11 months ended May 31, 1994.

(b) The cost of goods sold during June 1994.

(c) The June 30, 1994 inventory.

(AICPA adapted)

P9-9 **(GROSS PROFIT METHOD)** On April 15, 1994 a fire damaged the office and warehouse of Nevin Inc. The only accounting record saved was the general ledger, from which the trial balance below was prepared.

Nevin Inc.
Trial Balance
March 31, 1994

Cash	$ 20,000	
Accounts receivable	40,000	
Inventory December 31, 1993	80,200	
Land	35,000	
Building and equipment	110,000	
Accumulated depreciation		$ 41,300
Other assets	3,600	
Accounts payable		23,700
Other expense accruals		10,200
Common shares		100,000
Retained earnings		52,000
Sales		140,200
Purchases	52,000	
Other expenses	26,600	
	$367,400	$367,400

The following data and information have been gathered:

1. The fiscal year of the corporation ends on December 31.

2. An examination of the April bank statement and cancelled cheques revealed that cheques written during the period April 1–15 totalled $13,000: $5,700 paid to accounts payable as of March 31, $3,400 for April merchandise shipments, and $3,900 paid for other expenses. Deposits during the same period amounted to $12,950, which consisted of receipts on account from customers with the exception of a $950 refund from a vendor for merchandise returned in April.

3. Correspondence with suppliers revealed unrecorded obligations at April 15 of $10,600 for April merchandise shipments, including $2,300 for shipments in transit on that date.

4. Customers acknowledged indebtedness of $36,000 at April 15, 1994. It was also estimated that customers owed another $8,000 that will never be acknowledged or recovered. Of the acknowledged indebtedness, $600 will probably be uncollectible.

5. The companies insuring the inventory agreed that the corporation's fire-loss claim should be based on the assumption that the overall gross profit ratio for the past two years was in effect during the current year. The corporation's audited financial statements disclosed the following information.

	Year Ended December 31	
	1993	1992
Net sales	$525,000	$395,000
Net purchases	215,000	208,000
Beginning inventory	50,000	62,000
Ending inventory	80,200	50,000

6. Inventory with a cost of $8,000 was salvaged and sold for $4,400. The balance of the inventory was a total loss.

Instructions

Prepare a schedule computing the amount of inventory fire loss. The supporting schedule of the computation of the gross profit ratio should be in good form.

(AICPA adapted)

(RETAIL INVENTORY METHOD) The records for the Appliance Department of the Homeware Store are summarized below for the month of January: **P9-10**

Inventory January 1, at retail, $30,000; at cost, $17,000
Purchases in January, at retail, $142,000; at cost, $86,500
Freight-in, $7,000
Purchase returns, at retail, $3,000; at cost, $2,300
Purchase allowances, $2,200
Transfers in from Suburb Branch, at retail, $18,000; at cost, $11,000
Net markups, $8,000
Net markdowns, $4,000
Inventory losses due to normal breakage, etc., at retail, $400
Sales at retail, $86,000
Sales returns, $3,400

Instructions

Compute the inventory for this department as of January 31 at (1) sales price and (2) lower of average cost and market.

(RETAIL INVENTORY METHOD) Presented below is information related to Claven Inc. for 1994. **P9-11**

	Cost	Retail
Inventory 12/31/93	$240,000	$ 390,000
Purchases	930,000	1,460,000
Purchase returns	55,500	80,000
Purchase discounts	18,000	—
Gross sales (after employee discounts)	—	1,450,000
Sales returns	—	97,500
Markups	—	120,000
Markup cancellations	—	40,000
Markdowns	—	45,000
Markdown cancellations	—	20,000
Freight-in	69,000	—
Employee discounts granted	—	8,000
Loss from breakage (normal)	—	2,500

Instructions

Assuming that Claven uses the conventional retail inventory method, compute the amount of its ending inventory at December 31, 1994.

P9-12 (RETAIL INVENTORY METHOD) Calypso Department Store Inc. uses the retail inventory method to estimate ending inventory for its monthly financial statements. The following data pertain to a single department for the month of October:

Inventory October 1	
At cost	$ 52,000
At retail	100,000
Purchases (exclusive of freight and returns):	
At cost	272,000
At retail	515,000
Freight-in	16,600
Purchase returns	
At cost	5,600
At retail	8,000
Markups	9,000
Markup cancellations	2,000
Markdowns (net)	8,000
Normal spoilage and breakage	12,000
Sales	480,000

Instructions

(a) Using the conventional retail method, prepare a schedule computing estimated lower of average cost and market inventory for October 31.

(b) A department store using the conventional retail inventory method estimates the ending inventory as $72,000. An accurate physical count reveals only $64,000 of inventory at lower of average cost and market. List the factors that may have caused the difference between the estimated inventory and the physical count.

P9-13 (STATEMENT AND NOTE DISCLOSURE, AND LCM) Coleman Specialty Company, a division of Reichenbacher Inc., manufactures three models of gear shift components for bicycles that are sold to bicycle manufacturers, retailers, and catalogue outlets. Since beginning operations in 1976, Coleman has used normal absorption costing and has assumed a first-in, first-out cost flow in its perpetual inventory system. Except for overhead, manufacturing costs are accumulated using actual costs. Overhead is applied to production using predetermined overhead rates. The balances of the inventory accounts at the end of Coleman's fiscal year, November 30, 1994, follow. The inventories are stated at cost before any year-end adjustments.

Finished goods	$645,000
Work in process	112,500
Raw materials	240,000
Factory supplies	67,500

The following information relates to Coleman's inventory and operations:

1. The finished goods inventory consists of the items below.

	Cost	Market
Down tube shifter		
Standard model	$ 67,500	$ 66,400
Click adjustment model	94,500	86,600
Deluxe model	108,000	110,000
Total down tube shifters	$270,000	$263,000

(Continued)

Bar end shifter		
Standard model	$ 81,000	$ 90,050
Click adjustment model	99,000	97,550
Total bar end shifters	$180,000	$187,600
Head tube shifter		
Standard model	$ 78,000	$ 77,650
Click adjustment model	117,000	119,300
Total head tube shifters	$195,000	$196,950
Total finished goods	$645,000	$647,550

2. One-half of the head tube shifter finished goods inventory is held by catalogue outlets on consignment.

3. Three-quarters of the bar end shifter finished goods inventory has been pledged as collateral for a bank loan.

4. One-half of the raw materials balance represents derailleurs acquired at a contracted price 20% above the current market price. The market value of the rest of the raw materials is $127,400.

5. The total market value of the work-in-process inventory is $108,700.

6. Included in the cost of factory supplies are obsolete items with an historical cost of $4,200. The market value of the remaining factory supplies is $65,900.

7. Coleman applies the lower of cost and market method to each of the three types of shifters in finished goods inventory. For each of the other three inventory accounts, Coleman applies the lower of cost and market method to the total of each inventory account.

8. Consider all amounts presented above to be material in relation to Coleman's financial statements taken as a whole.

Instructions

(a) Prepare the inventory section of Coleman's balance sheet as of November 30, 1994, including any required note(s).

(b) Without prejudice to your answer to (a), assume that the market value of Coleman's inventories is less than cost. Explain how this decline would be presented in Coleman's income statement for the fiscal year ended November 30, 1994.

(CMA adapted)

CHAPTER

10 Acquisition and Disposition of Property, Plant, and Equipment

Objective 1

Describe the major characteristics of property, plant, and equipment.

Almost every business enterprise of any size or activity uses assets of a durable nature in its operations. Such assets are commonly referred to as (1) **property, plant, and equipment**, (2) **plant assets**, or (3) **fixed assets**, and they include land, building structures (offices, factories, warehouses), and equipment (machinery, furniture, tools). The three terms describing these assets are used interchangeably throughout this textbook. Property, plant, and equipment display the following characteristics:

1. ***They are acquired for use in operations and not for sale***. Only assets used in the normal operations of the business should be classified as property, plant, and equipment. An idle building held for sale is more appropriately classified separately as an investment; land held by land developers or subdividers is classified as inventory.

2. ***They are long term in nature and usually subject to depreciation***. Property, plant, and equipment yield services over a number of years. The investment in these assets is assigned to future periods through periodic depreciation charges. The exception is land, which is not depreciated.

3. ***They possess physical substance***. Property, plant, and equipment are characterized by physical existence or substance and thus are differentiated from intangible assets, such as patents or goodwill. Unlike raw material, however, property, plant, and equipment do not physically become part of the product held for resale.

This chapter discusses the basic accounting problems associated with (1) the incurrence and types of costs related to property, plant, and equipment and (2) the accounting methods used to record the retirement or disposal of these costs. Depreciation—allocating costs of property, plant, and equipment to accounting periods—is presented in Chapter 11 (Depreciation and Depletion).

ACQUISITION OF PROPERTY, PLANT, AND EQUIPMENT

Objective 2

Identify the costs included in the initial valuation of land, building, and equipment.

Historical cost is the usual basis for valuing property, plant, and equipment. ***Historical cost is measured by the cash or cash equivalent price of obtaining the asset and bringing it to the location and condition necessary for its intended use***. The purchase price, freight costs, and installation costs of a productive asset are considered part of the asset's cost. These costs are allocated to future periods through depreciation. Any costs related to the asset that are incurred after its acquisition, such as additions, improvements, or replacements, are added to the asset's cost if they provide future service potential; otherwise, they are expensed immediately.

Cost at the date of acquisition should be the basis used because the cash or cash equivalent price best measures the asset's value at that time. Disagreement does exist concerning differences between historical cost and other valuation methods such as replacement cost or fair market value arising after acquisition. Writing up of fixed asset values is not considered appropriate in ordinary circumstances. Although minor exceptions are noted (e.g., reorganizations), current standards indicate that departures from historical cost are rare.

The main reasons for this position are (1) at the date of acquisition, cost reflects fair value; (2) historical cost involves actual, not hypothetical transactions, and as a result is the most reliable;

anticipated but should be recognized when the asset is sold.
; have been considered, such as (1) constant dollar accounting
hanges), (2) current cost accounting (adjustments for specific
value, or (4) a combination of constant dollar accounting and
These alternative valuation concepts are discussed in Appendix
;).

ıd and to ready it for use should be considered as part of the
de (1) the purchase price; (2) closing costs, such as title to the
fees; (3) costs incurred in getting the land in condition for its
g, draining, and clearing; (4) assumption of any liens, such as
ımbrances on the property; and (5) any additional land improve-

ed for the purpose of constructing a building, all costs incurred
buildings are considered land costs. ***Removal of old buildings,***
:onsidered costs of the land because these costs are necessary to
ended purpose. Any proceeds obtained in the process of getting
such as salvage receipts on the demolition of an old building or
:ared, are treated as reductions in the price of the land.
cal improvements, such as pavements, street lights, sewers, and
ged to the Land account because they are relatively permanent in
laced by the local government body. In addition, if the improve-
permanent in nature, such as landscaping, then the item is properly
nprovements with limited lives, such as private driveways, walks,
recorded separately as Land Improvements so that they can be
ives.
ed part of property, plant, and equipment. If the major purpose of
land is speculative, however, it is more appropriately classified as an invest-
... the land is held by a real estate concern for resale, it should be classified as part of inventory.

In cases where land is held as an investment, the accounting treatment given taxes, insurance, and other direct costs incurred while holding the land is a controversial problem. Many believe these costs should be capitalized because the revenue from the investment still has not been received. This approach is reasonable and seems justified except in cases where the asset is currently producing revenue (such as rental property).

Cost of Buildings

The cost of buildings should include all expenditures related directly to their acquisition or construction. These costs include (1) materials, labour, and overhead costs incurred during construction and (2) professional fees and building permits. Generally, companies contract to have their buildings constructed. All costs incurred, from excavation to completion, are considered part of the building costs.

One accounting problem is deciding what to do about an old building that is on the site of a newly proposed building. Is the cost of removal of the old building a cost of the land or a cost of the building? The answer is that if land is purchased with an old building on it, then the cost of demolition less its salvage value is a cost of getting the land ready for the intended use and relates to the land rather than to the new building. As indicated earlier, all costs of getting the asset ready for its intended use are costs of that asset.

Cost of Equipment

The term "equipment" in accounting includes delivery equipment, office equipment, machinery, furniture and fixtures, furnishings, factory equipment, and similar fixed assets. The cost of such assets includes the purchase price, freight and handling charges incurred, insurance on the equipment while in transit, cost of special foundations if required, assembling and installation costs, and costs of conducting trial runs. Costs thus include all expenditures incurred in acquiring the equipment and preparing it for use. The goods and services tax (GST) is an exception to this rule. GST paid on assets acquired is treated as a reduction of the GST due to the Receiver General for Canada.

Self-Constructed Assets

Objective 3

Describe the accounting problems associated with overhead application.

Determining the cost of machinery and equipment is a problem when companies (particularly in the railway and utility industries) construct their own assets. Without a purchase price or contract price, the company must allocate costs and expenses to arrive at the construction cost to be entered in the property records. Materials and direct labour used in construction pose no problem because these costs can be traced directly to work and material orders related to the fixed assets constructed.

The assignment of indirect costs of manufacturing creates special problems, however. These indirect costs, called overhead, include power, heat, light, insurance, property taxes on factory buildings and equipment, factory supervisory labour, depreciation of fixed assets, and supplies. These costs may be handled in three ways:

1. ***Assign no fixed overhead to the cost of the constructed asset.*** The major reason for this treatment is that indirect overhead is generally fixed in nature and does not increase as a result of constructing one's own plant or equipment. This approach assumes that the company will have the same costs regardless of whether the company constructs the asset or not, so to charge a portion of the overhead costs to the equipment will normally relieve current expenses and consequently overstate income of the current period. In contrast, variable overhead costs that increase as a result of the construction should be assigned to the cost of the asset.

2. ***Assign a portion of all overhead to the construction process.*** This approach, a full costing concept, is appropriate if one believes that costs attach to all products and assets manufactured or constructed. This procedure assigns overhead costs to construction as it would to normal production. It is employed extensively because most accountants believe a better matching of costs with revenues is obtained. Advocates of this approach indicate that failure to allocate overhead costs understates the initial cost of the asset and results in an inaccurate allocation in the future.

3. ***Allocate on basis of lost production.*** A third alternative is to allocate to the construction project the cost of any curtailed production that occurs because the asset is built instead of purchased. This method is conceptually appealing, but is based on "what might have occurred." This is an opportunity cost concept and is difficult to measure.

Overhead costs directly attributed to construction of an asset should be assigned to obtain the cost. If the allocated overhead results in recording the construction costs in excess of the costs that would be charged by an outside independent producer, the excess overhead should be recorded as a period loss rather than capitalized to avoid capitalizing the asset at more than its probable market value.

Interest Costs During Construction

Objective 4

Describe the accounting problems associated with interest capitalization.

The proper accounting for interest costs has been a long-standing controversy in accounting. Three approaches have been suggested to account for the interest incurred in financing the construction or acquisition of property, plant, and equipment:

1. ***Capitalize no interest charges during construction.*** Under this approach, interest is considered a cost of financing and not a cost of construction. It is argued that if the company uses equity financing rather than debt financing, this expense will not exist. The major arguments against this approach are that an implicit interest cost is associated with the use of cash regardless of its source; if equity financing is employed, a real cost exists to the shareholders although a contractual claim does not develop.

2. ***Capitalize only the actual interest costs incurred during construction.*** This approach relies on the historical cost concept that only actual transactions are recorded. It is argued that interest incurred is as much a cost of acquiring the asset as the cost of the materials, labour, and other resources used. As a result, a company that uses debt financing will have an asset of higher cost than an enterprise that uses equity financing. The results achieved by this approach are held to be unsatisfactory by some because the cost of an asset should be the same whether cash, debt financing, or equity financing is employed.

3. ***Charge construction with all costs of funds employed, whether identifiable or not.*** This method is an economic cost approach that maintains that one part of the cost of construction is the cost of financing, whether by debt, cash, or equity financing. An asset should be charged with all costs necessary to get it ready for its intended use. Interest, whether actual or imputed, is a cost of building, just as labour, materials, and overhead are costs. A major criticism of this approach is that imputation of a cost of equity capital is subjective and outside the framework of an historical cost system.

The profession generally adopts the second approach discussed above. Actual interest may be capitalized in accordance with the concept that the historical cost of acquiring an asset includes all costs (including interest costs) incurred to bring the asset to the condition and location necessary for its intended use. As a result, capitalization of interest is permitted.[1] Implementing this general approach requires that three items be considered:

1. Qualifying assets.
2. Capitalization period.
3. Amount to capitalize.

Qualifying Assets. ***To qualify for interest capitalization, assets must require a period of time to get ready for their intended use.*** Interest costs may be capitalized starting with the first expenditure related to the asset, and continue until the asset is substantially completed and ready for its intended use.

Assets that qualify for interest cost capitalization include assets under construction for an enterprise's own use (including buildings, plants, and large machinery) and assets intended for sale or lease that are constructed or otherwise produced as discrete projects (ships or real estate developments). Examples of assets that do not qualify for interest capitalization are (1) assets that are in use or ready for their intended use, and (2) assets that are not used in the earnings activities of the enterprise or that are not undergoing the activities necessary to get them ready for use (such as land that is not being developed and assets not being used because of obsolescence, excess capacity, or need for repair).

Capitalization Period. The capitalization period (i.e. the period of time during which interest may be capitalized) begins when three conditions are present:

1. Expenditures for the asset have been made.
2. Activities that are necessary to get the asset ready for its intended use are in progress.
3. Interest cost is being incurred.

Interest capitalization continues as long as these three conditions are present. The capitalization period should end when the asset is substantially complete and ready for its intended use.

Amount to Capitalize. The amount of interest capitalized is subject to professional judgement.[2] To be capitalized, interest should be directly attributable to the project. This, in many cases, is difficult

---

[1] *CICA Handbook* (Toronto: CICA), Section 3060, par. .26.

[2] In accordance with *CICA Handbook*, par. 1000.49 (b), professional judgement may be based on such factors as analogous situations in the *Handbook, Accounting Guidelines*; International Accounting Standards; accounting standards established in other jurisdictions; and CICA research studies. Since the *Handbook* does not provide any guidelines for the measurement of interest to be capitalized, FASB No. 34 is used in this discussion. There may be other appropriate methods of measuring capitalizable interest.

to measure. One method of identifying the amount "directly attributable" uses the lower of actual interest cost incurred during the period and avoidable interest. **Avoidable interest** is the amount of interest cost incurred during the period that theoretically could have been avoided if expenditures for the asset had not been made.

To apply the avoidable interest concept, the potential amount of interest to be capitalized during an accounting period may be determined by multiplying the interest rate(s) by the weighted-average amount of accumulated expenditures for qualifying assets during the period.

Weighted-Average Accumulated Expenditures. In computing weighted-average accumulated expenditures, the construction expenditures are weighted by the amount of time (fraction of a year or accounting period) that interest cost could be incurred on the expenditure. To illustrate, assume a 17-month bridge construction project with expenditures for the current year of $240,000 on March 1; $480,000 on July 1; and $360,000 on November 1. The weighted-average accumulated expenditure for the year ended December 31 is computed as follows.

Computation of Weighted-Average Accumulated Expenditures

Date	Expenditures	×	Capitalization Period*	=	Average Accumulated Expenditures
March 1	240,000		10/12		200,000
July 1	480,000		6/12		240,000
Nov 1	360,000		2/12		60,000
	$1,080,000				$500,000

*Months between the date of expenditures and the date interest capitalization stops or end of year, whichever comes first (in this case December 31).

In computing the weighted-average accumulated expenditures, the expenditures are weighted by the amount of time that interest cost could be incurred on the expenditure. For the March 1 expenditure, a ten months' interest cost can be associated with the expenditure; for the expenditure on July 1, only six months' interest cost can be incurred; and for the expenditure made on November 1, only two months of interest cost incurred.

Interest Rates. The principles that may be used in selecting the appropriate interest rates to be applied to the weighted-average accumulated expenditures are:

1. For the portion of weighted-average accumulated expenditures that is less than or equal to any amounts borrowed specifically to finance construction of the assets, ***use the interest rate incurred on the specific borrowings.***

2. For the portion of weighted-average accumulated expenditures that is greater than any debt incurred specifically to finance construction of the assets, ***use a weighted-average of interest rates incurred on all outstanding debt during the period.***[3]

An illustration of the computation of a weighted-average interest rate for debt greater than the amount incurred specifically to finance construction of the assets follows.

[3] Various interest rates may be used. For our purposes, we will use the specific borrowing rate followed by the average interest rate because we believe it to be more conceptually consistent. For a discussion of this issue and others related to interest capitalization see Kathryn M. Means and Paul M. Kazenski, "SFAS 34: Receipt for Diversity," *Accounting Horizons*, September 1988.

Computation of Weighted-Average Interest Rate

	Principal	Interest
12%, two-year note	$ 600,000	$ 72,000
9%, ten-year bonds	2,000,000	180,000
7.5%, twenty-year bonds	5,000,000	375,000
	$7,600,000	$627,000

$$\text{Weighted-average interest rate} = \frac{\text{Total interest}}{\text{Total principal}} = \frac{\$627{,}000}{\$7{,}600{,}000} = 8.25\%$$

Special Issues Related to Interest Capitalization. Three issues related to interest capitalization that merit special attention are:

1. Expenditures for land.
2. Interest revenue.
3. Significance of interest capitalization.

Expenditures for Land. When land is purchased with the intention of developing it for a particular use, interest costs associated with those expenditures qualify for interest capitalization. If the land is purchased as a site for a structure (such as a plant site), interest costs capitalized during the period of construction are part of the cost of the plant, not the land. Conversely, if land is being developed for lot sales, any capitalized interest cost should be part of the acquisition cost of the developed land. However, interest costs involved in purchasing land that is held for speculation should *not* be capitalized because the asset is ready for its intended use.

Interest Revenue. Companies frequently borrow money to finance construction of assets and temporarily invest the excess borrowed funds in interest-bearing securities until the funds are needed to pay for construction. During the early states of construction, interest revenue earned may exceed the interest cost incurred on the borrowed funds. The question is whether it is appropriate to offset interest revenue against interest cost when determining the amount of interest to be capitalized as part of the construction cost of assets. If it is assumed that short-term investment decisions are not related to the interest incurred as part of the acquisition cost of assets, then interest revenue should *not* be netted with capitalized interest. Some accountants are critical of this because a company may defer the interest cost but report the interest revenue in the current period.

Many Canadian companies have adopted the method of capitalizing interest described above; some use different methods of determining the amount to be capitalized while others refuse to capitalize interest.[4] Many believe that "interest should be capitalized on all pre-earning assets"[5] while others argue that no interest cost should be capitalized. An example showing the calculation, recording, and reporting of capitalized interest is presented in Appendix 10A.

ACQUISITION AND VALUATION

Objective 5

Identify the various means of acquiring and valuing plant assets.

An asset should be recorded at the fair market value of what is given up to acquire it or at its own fair market value, whichever is more clearly evident. Fair market value, however, is sometimes

[4] See John M. Boersema and Mark van Helden, "The Case Against Interest Capitalization," *CA Magazine*, December 1986, pp. 58–60.

[5] J. Alex Milburn, *Incorporating the Time Value of Money Within Financial Accounting* (Toronto: CICA, 1988).

obscured by the process through which the asset is acquired. As an example, assume that land and buildings are bought together for one price. How are separate values for the land and buildings determined? A number of accounting problems of this nature are examined in the following sections.

Cash Discounts

When plant assets are purchased subject to cash discounts for prompt payment, there is the question of how the discount should be reported. If the discount is taken, it should be considered a reduction in the purchase price of the asset. What is not clear, however, is whether a reduction in the asset cost should occur if the discount is not taken.

Two points of view exist on this matter. Under one approach, the discount, whether taken or not, is considered a reduction in the cost of the asset. The rationale for this approach is that the real cost of the asset is the cash or cash equivalent price of the asset. In addition, some argue that the terms of cash discounts are so attractive that failure to take them indicates management error or inefficiency. On the other hand, some argue that the discount should not always be considered a loss because the terms may be unfavourable or because it may not be prudent for the company to take the discount. At present, both methods are employed in practice. The former method is generally preferred.

Deferred Payment Contracts

Plant assets are purchased frequently on long-term credit contracts through the use of notes, mortgages, bonds, or equipment obligations. ***To properly reflect cost, assets purchased on long-term credit contracts should be accounted for at the present value of the consideration exchanged between the contracting parties at the date of the transaction.*** An asset purchased today, therefore, in exchange for a $10,000 noninterest-bearing note payable four years from now, should not be recorded at $10,000. The present value of the $10,000 note establishes the exchange price of the transaction (the purchase price of the asset). Assuming an appropriate interest rate of 12% at which to discount this single payment of $10,000 due four years from now, this asset should be recorded at $6,355.20 [$10,000 × .63552; see Table A-2 for the present value of an amount, $p = \$10,000 \times P_{\overline{4|}12\%}$].

When no interest rate is stated or if the specified rate is unreasonable, an appropriate interest rate must be imputed. The objective is to approximate the interest rate that the buyer and seller would negotiate at arm's length in a similar borrowing transaction. Such factors to be considered in imputing an interest rate are the borrower's credit rating, the amount and maturity date of the note, and prevailing interest rates. If determinable, the cash exchange price of the asset acquired should be used as the basis for recording the asset and for measuring the interest element.

To illustrate, Sutter Company purchases a specially built robot spray painter for its production line. The company issues a $100,000, five-year, noninterest-bearing note to Wrigley Robotics, Ltd. for the new equipment when the prevailing market rate of interest for obligations of this nature is 10%. Sutter is to pay off the note in five $20,000 instalments at the end of each year. The fair market value of this particular specially built robot is not readily determinable and must therefore be approximated by establishing the market value (present value) of the note. Computation of the present value of the note and entries at the date of purchase and the dates of payment are as follows:

At Date of Purchase

Equipment	75,816	
Discount on Notes Payable	24,184	
Notes Payable		100,000

*Present value of note = $20,000 ($P_{\overline{5|}10\%}$)
= $20,000 (3.79079) (Table A-4)
= $75,816

(Continued)

At End of First Year

Interest Expense	7,582	
Notes Payable	20,000	
Cash		20,000
Discount on Notes Payable		7,582

Interest expense under the effective interest approach is $7,582 [($100,000 − $24,184) × 10%]. The entry at the end of the second year to record interest and to pay off a portion of the note is as follows:

At End of Second Year

Interest Expense	6,340	
Notes Payable	20,000	
Cash		20,000
Discount on Notes Payable		6,340

Interest expense in the second year under the effective interest approach is $6,340 [($100,000 − $24,184) − ($20,000 − $7,582)] × 10%.

If an interest rate is not imputed in such deferred payment contracts, the asset will be recorded at an amount different than its fair value. In addition, interest expense will be understated in the income statement in all periods involved.

Lump Sum Purchase

A special problem of pricing fixed assets arises when a group of plant assets is purchased at a single lump sum price. When such a situation occurs, and it is not at all unusual, the practice is to allocate the total cost among the various assets on the basis of their relative fair market values. The assumption is that costs will vary in direct proportion to sales value. This is the same principle that was applied to allocate a lump sum cost among different inventory items.

To determine fair market value, an appraisal for insurance purposes, the assessed valuation for property taxes, or simply an independent appraisal by an engineer or other appraiser may be used.

To illustrate, Norduct Heating Ltd. decides to purchase several assets of a small heating concern, Comfort Heating, for $80,000. Comfort Heating is in the process of liquidation and its assets sold are as below.

	Book Value	Fair Market Value
Inventory	$30,000	$ 25,000
Land	20,000	25,000
Building	35,000	50,000
	$85,000	$100,000

The $80,000 purchase price would be allocated on the basis of the relative fair market values in the manner shown on page 486.

Issuance of Shares

When property is acquired by issuance of securities, such as common shares, the cost of the property is not properly measured by the average issuance price of such shares. If the shares are being actively traded, ***the market value of the shares issued is a fair indication of the cost of the property acquired because this value is a good measure of the current cash equivalent price.***

Inventory	$\frac{\$25,000}{\$100,000} \times \$80,000 = \$20,000$
Land	$\frac{\$25,000}{\$100,000} \times \$80,000 = \$20,000$
Building	$\frac{\$50,000}{\$100,000} \times \$80,000 = \$40,000$

For example, Upgrade Living Co. decides to purchase some adjacent land for expansion of its carpeting and cabinet operation. In lieu of paying cash for the land, the company issues to Deedland Company 5,000 no-par value common shares that have a fair market value of $12 per share. Upgrade Living Co. would make the following entry:

Land (5,000 × $12)	60,000	
Common Shares		60,000

If the market value of common shares exchanged is not determinable, the market value of the property should be established and used as a basis for recording the asset and issuance of the common shares.[6]

Exchanges of Property, Plant, and Equipment (Nonmonetary Assets)

The proper accounting for exchanges of nonmonetary assets (such as inventories and property, plant, and equipment) is controversial.[7] Some accountants argue that the accounting for these types of exchanges should be based on the fair value of the asset given up or the fair value of the asset received with a gain or loss recognized; others believe that the accounting should be based on the recorded amount (book value) of the asset given up with no gain or loss recognized; and still others favour an approach that recognizes losses in all cases, but defers gains in special situations.

Ordinarily, accounting for exchange of nonmonetary assets should be based on ***the fair value of the asset given up or the fair value of the asset received, whichever is clearly more evident.***[8] Thus, any gains or losses on the exchange should be recognized immediately. The rationale for this approach is that ***the earnings process related to these assets is completed*** and, therefore, gains or losses should be recognized. This approach is always employed when ***the assets exchanged are dissimilar in nature***, such as the exchange of land for a building, or the exchange of equipment for inventory. If the fair value of either asset is not reasonably determinable, the book value of the asset given up is usually used as the basis for recording the nonmonetary exchange.

The general rule is modified when an exchange involves ***similar nonmonetary assets and little or no monetary consideration is given or received.*** For example, when a company exchanges inventory items for inventory of another company because of colour, size, etc. to facilitate sale to an outside customer, the earnings process is not considered culminated and a gain or loss should not be recognized. Likewise, if a company trades similar productive assets (assets held for or used in the production of goods or services) such as land for land or equipment for equipment, the enterprise

[6] When the fair market value of the shares is used as the basis of valuation, careful consideration must be given to the effect that the issuance of additional shares will have on the existing market price. Where the effect on market price appears significant, an independent appraisal of the asset received should be made. This valuation should be employed as the basis for valuation of the asset as well as for the shares issued. In the unusual case where the fair market value of the shares or the fair market value of the asset cannot be determined objectively, the board of directors of the corporation may set the value.

[7] Nonmonetary assets are items whose price in terms of the monetary unit may change over time, whereas monetary assets are fixed in terms of units of currency by contract or otherwise (e.g., cash and short- or long-term accounts and notes receivable).

[8] *CICA Handbook*, Section 3830, par. .05.

is not considered to have completed the earnings process and, therefore, a gain or loss should not be recognized.[9]

Gains on exchange of similar nonmonetary assets should be recognized when the ***amount of monetary consideration received or given is not minimal*** (i.e. greater than 10% of the fair value of the total consideration received or given). In these instances, exchanges of similar nonmonetary assets are accounted for in the same way as exchanges of dissimilar assets.

In summary, gains or losses on nonmonetary transactions are always recognized when the exchange involves dissimilar assets. When similar assets are exchanged and cash is received or given up, gains or losses are recognized unless the amount of cash involved is less than 10% of the estimated fair value of the total consideration given or received.[10] When the cash or some other form of monetary consideration involved is minimal, the cost of the asset received is equal to the book value of the asset(s) given up plus the cash given or minus any cash received.

To illustrate the accounting for these different types of transactions, the discussion is divided into three sections as follows:

1. Accounting for dissimilar assets.
2. Accounting for similar assets.
3. Accounting for similar assets when little or no cash is received or given up.

Dissimilar Assets. The cost of a nonmonetary asset acquired in exchange for a dissimilar nonmonetary asset is usually recorded at the **fair value of the asset given up**, and a gain or loss is recognized. The **fair value of the asset received** should be used only if it is more clearly evident than the fair value of the asset given up.

To illustrate, Neufeld Transportation Limited exchanges a number of used trucks plus cash for vacant land that may be used for a future plant site. The trucks have a combined book value of $42,000 (cost $64,000 less $22,000 accumulated depreciation). Neufeld's purchasing agent, who has previous dealings in the second-hand market, indicates that the trucks have a fair market value of $49,000. In addition to the trucks, Neufeld must pay $17,000 cash for the land. The cost of the land is $66,000, computed as follows.

	Computation of Land Cost
Fair value of trucks exchanged	$49,000
Cash paid	17,000
Cost of land	$66,000

The journal entry to record the exchange transaction is:

Land	66,000	
Accumulated Depreciation—Trucks	22,000	
Trucks		64,000
Gain on Disposal of Trucks		7,000
Cash		17,000

The gain is the difference between the fair value of the trucks and their book value. It is verified as follows.

[9] *CICA Handbook*, Section 3830, par. .08.
[10] *Ibid.*

		Computation of Gain
Fair value of trucks		$49,000
Cost of trucks	$64,000	
Less accumulated depreciation	22,000	
Book value of trucks		42,000
Gain on disposal of used trucks		$ 7,000

It follows that if the fair value of the trucks is $39,000 instead of $49,000, a loss on the exchange of $3,000 ($42,000 − $39,000) will be reported. In either case, as a result of the exchange of dissimilar assets, the earnings process on the used trucks has been completed and ***a gain or loss should be recognized.***

Similar Assets. Similar nonmonetary assets are those of the same general type, that perform the same function, or are employed in the same line of business. Generally, when similar nonmonetary assets are exchanged and a gain or loss results, the gain or loss should be recognized. For example, Information Processing, Inc. trades its used accounting machine for a new model. The accounting machine given up has a book value of $8,000 (original cost $12,000 less $4,000 accumulated depreciation) and an estimated fair value of $6,000. It is traded for a new model that has a list price of $16,000. In negotiations with the seller, a trade-in allowance of $9,000 is finally agreed on for the used machine. The cash payment that must be made for the new asset and the cost of the new machine are computed as follows.

	Cost of New Machine
List price of new machine	$16,000
Less trade-in allowance for used machine	9,000
Cash payment due	7,000
Fair value of used machine	6,000
Cost of new machine	$13,000

The journal entry to record this transaction is:

Equipment	13,000	
Accumulated Depreciation—Equipment	4,000	
Loss on Disposal of Equipment	2,000	
Equipment		12,000
Cash		7,000

The loss on the disposal of the used machine can be computed as follows.

	Computation of Loss
Fair value of used machine	$6,000
Book value of used machine	8,000
Loss on disposal of used machine	$2,000

Why is the trade-in allowance for the old asset not used as a basis for the new equipment? The trade-in allowance is not employed because it includes a price concession (similar to a price discount) to the purchaser. For example, few individuals pay list price for a new car. Trade-in allowances on the used car are often so inflated that actual selling prices are below list prices. In short, the list price of a new car is usually inflated and to record the car at list price will state it at an amount in excess of its cash equivalent price. Use of fair value in this situation is highly subjective and not as reliable (verifiable) as carrying value. Normally, assets should not be valued at more than their cash equivalent price. However, when the cash equivalent price is not sufficiently reliable, the gain or loss should not be recognized immediately but added or deducted from the cost of the newly acquired asset.

Similar Assets: Little or No Cash Received or Given. The accounting treatment for exchanges of similar nonmonetary assets when little or no cash is received or given is more complex. In these instances, if the exchange does not complete the earnings process, then any gain or loss is not recognized. The real estate industry provides a good example of why the profession decided not to recognize gains on exchanges of similar nonmonetary assets. In the early 1970s when the real estate business was booming, it was common practice for companies to "swap" estate holdings. To illustrate, Landmark Company and Hillfarm, Inc. each had undeveloped land on which they intended to build shopping centres. Appraisals indicated that the land of both companies had increased significantly in value. The companies decided to exchange (swap) their undeveloped land, record a gain, and report their new parcels of land at current fair value. But, should income be recognized at this point? The profession's position was that the earnings process is not completed because the companies remain in the same economic position after the swap as before; therefore, the asset acquired should be recorded at book value with no gain or loss recognized.

To illustrate, Davis Rent-A-Car has a rental fleet of automobiles that are primarily Ford Motor Company products. Davis's management is interested in increasing the variety of automobiles in its rental fleet by adding numerous models of General Motors products. During a long delay in delivery from the manufacturer, Davis arranges with Nertz Rent-A-Car to exchange a group of Ford Escorts and Tempos with a fair value of $160,000 and a book value of $135,000 (cost $150,000 less accumulated depreciation $15,000) for a number of Chevy Novas and Pontiac Phoenixes. The fair value of the automobiles received from Nertz is $170,000; Davis, therefore, pays $10,000 in cash in addition to the Ford automobiles exchanged. The total gain to Davis Rent-A-Car is computed as follows.

	Computation of Gain
Fair value of Ford automobiles exchanged	$160,000
Book value of Ford automobiles exchanged	135,000
Total gain (unrecognized)	$ 25,000

Because the earnings process is not considered completed in this transaction, the total gain is deferred and the basis of the General Motors automobiles is reduced via two different but acceptable computations, as shown below.

Basis of New Automobiles to Davis

Fair value of GM automobiles	$170,000		Book value of Ford automobiles	$135,000
Less gain deferred	(25,000)	OR	Cash paid	10,000
Basis of GM automobiles	$145,000		Basis of GM automobiles	$145,000

The entry by Davis to record this transaction is as follows:

Automobiles (GM)	145,000	
Accumulated Depreciation—Automobiles	15,000	
Automobiles (Ford)		150,000
Cash		10,000

The gain that reduces the basis of the new automobiles will be recognized when those automobiles are sold to an outside party. If these automobiles are held for an extended period of time, depreciation charges will be lower and net income higher in subsequent periods because of the reduced basis.

Presented below in summary form are the accounting requirements for recognizing gains and losses on exchanges of nonmonetary assets:

1. Compute the total gain or loss on the transaction, which is equal to the difference between the fair value of the asset given up and the book value of the asset given up.
2. If a gain or loss is computed in 1,

   (a) and the earnings process is considered completed, the entire gain or loss is recognized (dissimilar assets).

   (b) and the earnings process is not considered complete (similar assets) and monetary consideration given or received is greater than 10% of the total consideration received or given, the entire gain or loss is recognized.

   (c) and the earnings process is not considered complete (similar assets) and little or no monetary consideration is involved, no gain or loss is recognized. The asset received is recorded at the carrying value of the asset adjusted by the amount of monetary consideration received or given in the exchange.

Acquisition and Disposition by Donation or Gift

An enterprise may be both the recipient and the maker of donations. Such exchanges are referred to as **nonreciprocal transfers** because they are transfers of assets in one direction. Many agricultural and transportation enterprises, for example, have received substantial donations (in the form of rebates and subsidies) from the federal government.

When assets are acquired in this manner, a strict cost concept dictates that the valuation of the asset should be zero. A departure from the cost principle seems justified because the only costs incurred are legal fees and other relatively minor expenditures, which do not constitute a reasonable basis of accounting for the assets acquired. To record nothing, we believe, is to ignore the economic realities of an increase in wealth and asset utility. Therefore, ***the appraisal or fair market value of the asset should be used to establish a proper basis of asset valuation for purposes of enterprise accountability.***

Acquisition by Donation: Capital Approach. The classification of the offsetting credit to the asset received, however, is controversial. Some believe that the credit should be to Donated Capital (a contributed surplus account) because these donations increase the amount of assets and, therefore, shareholders' equity available to the enterprise. To illustrate, Max Wayer Meat Packing, Inc. has recently accepted a donation of land with a fair value of $150,000 from the City of Burlington in return for a promise to build a packing plant in Burlington. Max Wayer's entry is:

Land	150,000	
Donated Capital		150,000

Acquisition by Donation: Deferred Revenue Approach. Others argue that capital is contributed only by the owners of the business and that donations are benefits to the enterprise and should be reported as revenue. An issue related to the revenue approach is whether the revenue should be reported immediately or over the period that the asset is employed. If the asset is donated by a government organization, the purpose of the donation will determine how the credit should be recorded. For example, to attract new industry a city may offer land; but the receiving enterprise may incur additional costs in the future (transportation, higher taxes, etc.) because the location is not the most desirable. As a consequence, the revenue should be deferred and recognized as these costs are incurred. If known additional costs are to be incurred, an Unrealized Government Grant account could be established in the liability section and written off over the term during which the additional costs are incurred.

Regardless of whether assets or funds to acquire assets are received from federal, provincial, or municipal governments, Section 3800 of the *Handbook* requires that recipients follow the prescribed accounting methods. These methods are based on a "revenue approach" which requires that the amount received should be deferred and recognized over the period that the related assets are employed. This is accomplished by either reducing the cost of the asset by the amount of government assistance received, or recording the amount of assistance received from the various governmental sources as a deferred credit and amortizing it to revenue over the life of the related asset. To illustrate, Max Wayer Meat Packing, Inc. has recently received a grant of $225,000 from the federal government to upgrade its sewage treatment facility. The entry to record receipt of the grant, if Max Wayer wishes to use the cost reduction method, will be as follows:

Cash	225,000	
Equipment		225,000

This results in the equipment being carried on the books at cost minus the related government assistance. As a result, the annual depreciation charge for the equipment will be reduced over its useful life and net income will be increased.

Alternatively, an unrealized revenue account can be credited with the amount of the grant. This unrealized revenue account will then be amortized periodically to income over a term equal to the useful life of the equipment. The entries to record receipt of the grant and amortization for the first year (assuming a 10-year term) will be as follows:

Cash	225,000	
Deferred Revenue—Government Grants		225,000
Deferred Revenue—Government Grants	22,500	
Revenue—Government Grants		22,500

It should be emphasized that whether the capital approach or the unrealized revenue approach is used, if the donation is contingent upon some performance (such as building a plant), this contingency should be reported in the notes to the financial statements.

In practice, enterprises record cash from governments (grants) related to current expenses and revenues to flow through the income statement, while cash and noncash donations from shareholders and other nongovernment entities or individuals are generally credited to an appropriate contributed surplus account.

Disposition by Donation. When a nonmonetary asset is donated, that is, given away, the amount of the donation should be recorded at the fair market value of the donated asset. If a difference exists between the fair market value of the asset and its book value, a gain or loss should be recognized.[11] To illustrate, Kline Industries donates land which cost $80,000 and has a fair market value of $110,000 to the City of Vancouver for a city park. The entry to record this donation will be:

Donation	110,000	
Land		80,000
Gain on Disposition of Land		30,000

The donation cost will ordinarily be classified in the Other Expense section of the income statement. Sometimes a real estate developer will donate certain property in a development to a municipality

[11] "Accounting for Nonmonetary Transactions," *op. cit.*, par. 18.

to enhance the value of the development. In this case, the donation will be added to the cost of development rather than treated as an expense.

COSTS SUBSEQUENT TO ACQUISITION

Objective 6

Describe the accounting treatment for costs subsequent to acquisition.

After plant assets are installed and ready for use, additional costs are incurred that range from ordinary repair costs to significant additions. The major problem is allocating these costs subsequent to acquisition to the proper time periods. In general, costs incurred to achieve greater future benefits should be capitalized, whereas expenditures that simply maintain a given level of services should be expensed. In order for costs to be capitalized, one of three conditions must be present:

1. The useful life of the asset must be increased.
2. The quantity of units produced from the asset must be increased.
3. The quality of the units produced must be enhanced.

Expenditures that do not increase an asset's future benefits should be expensed. Ordinary repairs are expenditures that maintain the existing condition of the asset or restore it to normal operating efficiency and should be expensed immediately.

In addition, most expenditures below an established arbitrary minimum amount are expensed rather than capitalized. Many enterprises have adopted the rule that expenditures below, say, $100 or $500, should always be expensed. Although conceptually this treatment may not be correct, expediency demands it. Otherwise, accountants will have to set up depreciation schedules for such things as wastepaper baskets and ashtrays.

The distinction between a **capital (asset)** and **revenue (expense)** expenditure is not always clear cut. For example, determination of the property unit with which costs should be associated is critical. If a fully equipped steamship is considered a property unit, then replacement of the engine will be considered an expense, whereas if the ship's engine is considered a property unit, then its replacement will be capitalized. It follows that the disposition and treatment of many items require considerable analysis and judgement before the proper distinction can be made. In most cases, consistent application of a capital/expense policy is justified as more important than attempting to provide general theoretical guidelines for each entry.

Generally, four major types of expenditures are incurred relative to existing assets.

Major Types of Expenditures

1. **Additions**. Increase or extension of existing assets.
2. **Improvements and replacements**. Substitution of an improved asset for an existing one.
3. **Rearrangement and reinstallation**. Movement of assets from one location to another.
4. **Repairs**. Expenditures that maintain assets in condition for operation.

Additions

Additions should present no major accounting problems. By definition, ***any addition to plant assets is capitalized*** because a new asset has been created. The addition of a wing to a hospital or the addition of an air-conditioning system to an office, for example, increases the service potential of that facility and should be capitalized and matched against the revenues that will result in future periods.

The most difficult problem that develops in this area is accounting for any changes related to the existing structure as a result of the addition. Is the cost that is incurred to tear down a wall of the old structure to make room for the addition a cost of the addition or an expense or loss of the period? The answer is that it depends on the original intent. If the company had anticipated that an addition was going to be added later, then this cost of removal is a proper cost of the addition. But if the company had not anticipated this development, it should properly be reported as a loss in the current period on the basis that the company was inefficient in its planning. Normally, the carrying amount of the old wall remains in the accounts, although theoretically it should be removed.

Improvements and Replacements

Improvements (often referred to as betterments) and replacements are substitutions of one asset for another. The distinguishing feature between an improvement and a replacement is that an improvement is the substitution of a better asset for the one currently used (say, a concrete floor for a wooden floor). A replacement, on the other hand, is the substitution of a similar asset (a wooden floor for a wooden floor).

Many times improvements and replacements occur as a result of a general policy to modernize or rehabilitate an older building or piece of equipment. The problem is differentiating these types of expenditures from normal repairs. Does the expenditure increase the future service potential of the asset, or does it merely maintain the existing level of service? Frequently the answer is not clear cut, and good judgement must be used in order to classify these expenditures properly.

If it is determined that the expenditure increases the future service potential of the asset and, therefore, should be capitalized, this capitalization is handled in one of three ways, depending on the circumstances.

1. **Substitution approach**. Conceptually, the substitution approach is the correct procedure if the carrying amount of the old asset is available. If the carrying amount of the old asset can be determined, it is a simple matter to remove the cost of the old asset and replace it with the cost of the new asset.

   To illustrate, Instinct Enterprises decides to replace the pipes in its plumbing system. A plumber suggests that in place of the cast iron pipes and copper tubing, a newly developed plastic tubing be used. The old pipe and tubing has a book value of $15,000 (cost of $150,000 less accumulated depreciation of $135,000), and a fair market value of $1,000. The plastic tubing system has a market value of $125,000. Assuming that Instinct has to pay $124,000 for the new tubing after exchanging the old tubing, the entry is:

Plumbing System	125,000	
Accumulated Depreciation	135,000	
Loss on Disposal of Plant Assets	14,000	
Plumbing System		150,000
Cash		124,000

   The problem with this approach is determining the book value of the old asset. Generally, the components of a given asset depreciate at different rates, but no separate accounting is made. As an example, the tires, motor, and body of a truck depreciate at different rates, but most concerns use only one depreciation rate for the truck. Separate depreciation rates could be set for each component, but practicality precludes the use of this approach. If the carrying amount of the old asset cannot be determined, one of two other approaches is adopted.

2. **Capitalizing the new cost**. The justification for capitalizing the cost of the improvement or replacement is that even though the carrying amount of the old asset is not removed from the accounts, sufficient depreciation was taken on the item to reduce the carrying amount almost to zero. Although this assumption may not be true in every case, in many situations the differences would not be significant. Improvements especially are handled in this manner.

3. **Charging to accumulated depreciation**. There are times when the quantity or quality of the asset itself has not been improved, but its useful life has been extended. Replacements, particularly, may extend the useful life of the asset, yet they may not improve the quality or quantity of service or product produced. In these circumstances, the expenditure may be debited to Accumulated Depreciation rather than to the Asset account on the theory that the replacement extends the useful life of the asset and thereby recaptures some or all of the past depreciation. The carrying amount of the asset is the same whether the asset is charged or the accumulated depreciation is charged.

Rearrangement and Reinstallation

Rearrangement and reinstallation costs, which are expenditures intended to benefit future periods, are different from additions, replacements, and improvements. An example is the rearrangement or reinstallation of a group of machines to facilitate future production. If the original installation cost can be estimated along with the accumulated depreciation taken to date, the rearrangement and reinstallation cost may properly be handled as a replacement. If not, which is generally the case, the new costs (if material in amount) should be capitalized as an asset to be amortized over those future periods expected to benefit.[12] If these costs are not material, or if they cannot be separated from other operating expenses, or if their future benefit is questionable, they should be immediately expensed.

Repairs

Ordinary repairs are expenditures made to maintain plant assets in operating condition; they are charged to an Expense account in the period in which they are incurred on the basis that it is the only period benefited. Replacement of minor parts, lubricating and adjusting of equipment, repainting, and cleaning are examples of maintenance charges that occur regularly and are treated as ordinary operating expenses.

It is often difficult to distinguish a repair from an improvement or replacement. The major consideration is whether the expenditure benefits more than one year or one operating cycle, whichever is longer. If a **major repair**, such as an overhaul, occurs, several periods will benefit and the cost should be handled as an addition, improvement, or replacement.

If income statements are prepared for short periods of time, say, monthly or quarterly, the same principles must still apply. Ordinary repairs and other regular maintenance charges for an annual period may benefit several quarters, and allocation of the cost among periods concerned may be required. A concern will often find it advantageous to concentrate its repair program at a certain time of the year, perhaps during the period of least activity or when the plant is shut down for vacation. Short-term comparative statements may be misleading if such expenditures are shown as expenses of the quarter in which they are incurred. To give comparability to monthly or quarterly income statements, an account such as Allowance for Repairs may be used so that repair costs are better assigned to periods benefited.

To illustrate, Cricket Tractor Company estimated that its total repair expense for the year will be $720,000. It decides to charge each quarter for a portion of the repair cost even though the total cost for the year will occur only in two quarters.

End of First Quarter (zero repair costs incurred)

Repair Expense	180,000	
Allowance for Repairs (1/4 × $720,000)		180,000

End of Second Quarter ($344,000 repair costs incurred)

Allowance for Repairs	344,000	
Cash, Wages Payable, Inventory, etc.		344,000
Repair Expense	180,000	
Allowance for Repairs (1/4 × $720,000)		180,000

(Continued)

[12] Another cost of this nature is relocation costs. For example, when Shell Oil moved its world headquarters from New York to Houston, it amortized the cost of relocating over four years. Conversely, relocation costs necessitated by the company's move to Calgary were charged to revenue. The point is that no definitive guidelines have been established in this area, and generally costs are deferred over some arbitrary period in the future. Some writers have argued that these costs should generally be expensed as incurred. See, for example, Charles W. Lamden, Dale L. Gerboth, and Thomas W. McRae, "Accounting for Depreciable Assets," *Accounting Research Monograph No. 1* (New York: AICPA, 1975), pp. 54–61.

End of Third Quarter (zero repair costs incurred)

Repair Expense	180,000	
Allowance for Repairs (1/4 × $720,000)		180,000

End of Fourth Quarter ($380,800 repair costs incurred)

Allowance for Repairs	380,800	
Cash, Wages Payable, Inventory, etc.		380,800
Repair Expense	184,800	
Allowance for Repairs ($344,000 + $380,800 − $180,000 − $180,000 − 180,000)		184,800

Ordinarily, no balance in the Allowance for Repairs account should be carried over to the following year. The fourth quarter will normally absorb the variation from estimates. If balance sheets are prepared during the year, the allowance account should be added to or subtracted from the property, plant, and equipment section to obtain a proper valuation.

Some accountants advocate accruing estimated repair costs beyond one year. This approach is based on the assumption that depreciation does not take into consideration the incurrence of repair costs. For example, in aircraft overhaul and open hearth furnace rebuilding, an allowance for repairs is sometimes established because the amount of repairs can be estimated with a high degree of certainty. Although conceptually appealing, it is difficult to justify the Allowance for Repairs account as a liability because one may ask, Whom do you owe? Placement in the shareholders' equity section is also illogical because no addition to the shareholders' investment has taken place. One possibility is to treat allowance for repairs as an addition to or subtraction from the asset on the basis that the value has changed. In general, expenses should not be anticipated before they arise unless estimates of the future costs are reasonably accurate.

Summary

The schedule summarizing the accounting treatment for costs incurred subsequent to the acquisition of capitalized assets discussed in this section is presented on page 496.

DISPOSITIONS OF PLANT ASSETS

Objective 7

Describe the accounting treatment for the disposal of property, plant, and equipment.

Plant assets may be retired voluntarily or disposed of by sale, exchange, involuntary conversion, or abandonment. Regardless of the time of disposal, depreciation should be taken up to the date of disposition, and all accounts related to the retired asset should be removed. Ideally, the book value of the specific plant asset will be equal to its disposal value. But this is generally not the case. As a result, a gain or loss develops. The reason: depreciation is an estimate of cost allocation and not a process of valuation. The gain or loss is really a correction of net income for the years during which the fixed asset is used. If it is possible at the time of acquisition to forecast the exact date of disposal and the amount to be realized at disposition, then a more accurate estimate of depreciation will be recorded and no gain or loss will have been incurred.

Gains and losses on the retirement of plant assets should be shown in the income statement along with other items that arise from customary business activities. If, however, the "operations of a segment of a business" are sold, abandoned, spun off, or otherwise disposed of, then the results of "continuing operations" should be reported separately from "discontinued operations." Any gain or loss from disposal of a segment of a business should be reported with related results of discontinued operations and not as an extraordinary item. These reporting requirements were discussed in Chapter 4.

Sale of Plant Assets

Depreciation must be recorded for the period of time between the date of the last depreciation entry and the date of sale. To illustrate, assume that depreciation on a machine costing $18,000 has been

Summary of Costs Subsequent to Acquisition of Property, Plant, and Equipment

Type of Expenditure	Normal Accounting Treatment
Additions	Capitalize cost to asset account.
Improvements and Replacements	(a) **Carrying value known:** Remove cost of and accumulated depreciation on old asset, recognizing any gain or loss. Capitalize cost of improvement/replacement. (b) **Carrying value unknown:** 1. If the asset's useful life is extended, debit accumulated depreciation for cost of improvement/replacement. 2. If the quantity or quality of the assets' productivity is increased, capitalize cost of improvement/replacement to asset account.
Rearrangement and Reinstallation	(a) If original installation cost is *known*, account for cost of rearrangement/reinstallation as a replacement (carrying value known). (b) If original installation cost is *unknown* and rearrangement/replacement cost is *material* in amount and benefits future periods, capitalize as an asset. (c) If original installation cost is *unknown* and rearrangement/reinstallation cost is *not material or future benefit is questionable,* expense the cost when incurred.
Repairs	(a) **Ordinary:** Expense cost of repairs when incurred. (b) **Major:** As appropriate, treat as an addition, improvement, or replacement.

recorded for nine years at the rate of $1,200 per year. If the machine is sold in the middle of the tenth year for $7,000, the entry to record depreciation to the date of sale is:

Depreciation Expense	600	
Accumulated Depreciation of Machinery		600

This separate entry ordinarily is not made because most companies enter all depreciation, including this amount, in one entry at the end of the year. In either case the entry for the sale of the asset is:

Cash	7,000	
Accumulated Depreciation of Machinery ($1,200 × 9 plus $600)	11,400	
Machinery		18,000
Gain on Disposal of Machinery		400

The book value of the machinery at the time of the sale is $6,600 ($18,000 − $11,400); because it is sold for $7,000, the amount of the gain on the sale is $400.

Involuntary Conversion

Sometimes, an asset's service is terminated through some type of involuntary conversion such as fire, flood, theft, or expropriation. The gains and losses are treated no differently from those in any other type of disposition except that they are often reported in the extraordinary items section of the income statement.

To illustrate, Camel Transport Corp. was forced to sell a plant located on company property that stood directly in the path of a proposed highway. For a number of years the province had sought to purchase the land on which the plant stood but the company resisted. The province ultimately exercised its right of eminent domain and was upheld by the courts. In settlement, Camel received \$500,000, which was substantially in excess of the \$200,000 book value of the plant and land (cost of \$400,000 less accumulated depreciation of \$200,000). The following entry was made:

Cash	500,000	
Accumulated Depreciation of Plant Assets	200,000	
Plant Assets		400,000
Gain on Disposal of Plant Assets		300,000

The gain or loss that develops on these types of unusual, nonrecurring transactions that are not a result of management actions should normally be shown as an extraordinary item in the income statement. Similar treatment would be given to other types of involuntary conversions such as those resulting from a major casualty (such as an earthquake) or an expropriation, assuming that it meets the conditions for extraordinary item treatment. The difference between the amount recovered (expropriation award or insurance recovery), if any, and the book value of the asset would be reflected as a gain or loss.

Abandonment of Assets

If an asset is scrapped or abandoned without any cash recovery, a loss should be recognized in the amount of the asset's book value. If scrap value exists, the gain or loss that occurs is the difference between the asset's scrap value and its book value. If an asset still can be used even though it is fully depreciated, either the asset may be kept on the books at historical cost less its related depreciation or the asset may be carried at scrap value.

OTHER ASSET VALUATION METHODS

We have assumed that cost is the appropriate basis for valuing assets at acquisition. The major exception has been the acquisition of plant assets through donation. Another approach that is sometimes allowed and not considered a violation of historical cost is a concept often referred to as **prudent cost**. This concept states that if for some reason you are ignorant about a certain price and pay too much for the asset originally, it is theoretically preferable to charge a loss immediately.

As an example, assume that a company constructs an asset at a cost substantially in excess of its present economic usefulness. In this case, an appropriate procedure is to charge these excess costs as a loss to the current period, rather than capitalize them as part of the cost of the asset. This problem seldom develops because at the outset individuals either use good reasoning in paying a given price or fail to recognize any such errors.

On the other hand, a purchase that is obtained at a bargain, or a piece of equipment internally constructed at what amounts to a cost savings, should not result in immediate recognition of a gain under any circumstances. Although immediate recognition of a gain is conceptually appealing, the implications of such a treatment will completely change the entire basis of accounting.

The general accounting standard of ***lower of cost and market does not apply to property, plant, and equipment.*** And even when property, plant, and equipment has suffered partial obsolescence, accountants are reluctant to write it down to net realizable value. The reason is that, unlike inventories, it is difficult to arrive at a net realizable value that is not subjective and arbitrary for property, plant, and equipment. In addition, many argue that depreciation is a method of cost allocation and, therefore, should not be concerned with valuation.

There is some concern that permitting write-offs of this type may lead companies to make unreasonable write-offs in bad years to ensure that future periods will be relieved of these costs (the "big bath" phenomenon). We are not sympathetic with these arguments and believe that whenever a **permanent impairment** in the revenue-producing ability of property, plant, and equipment occurs, a loss should be recognized.

FUNDAMENTAL CONCEPTS

1. The usual basis for valuing property, plant, and equipment is historical cost, as measured by the cash or cash equivalent price of obtaining an asset and bringing it to the location and condition necessary for its intended use.
2. Recording an asset at the fair market value of what is given up to acquire it or at its own fair value is complicated by cash discounts, deferred payment plans, lump sum purchases, issuance of securities, interest capitalization, acquisition by gift, self-construction, and nonmonetary exchanges.
3. Interest may be capitalized as part of certain assets under construction, starting with the first expenditure related to the asset and continuing until the asset is substantially complete and ready for use.
4. The general rule in accounting for exchanges of nonmonetary assets is to record the fair value inherent in the exchange. Exceptions to this general policy occur if fair value is not determinable or if the exchange is not the completion of the earning process.
5. The exchange of nonmonetary assets is generally viewed as a completion of the earning process requiring measurement and recognition of either a gain or a loss. In exchanges of similar nonmonetary assets, the earnings process is not considered complete when a minimal amount of cash is given or received. In these cases, gains and losses are not recognized.
6. Nonreciprocal transfers of assets are one-sided transactions, either receipts of gifts or donations of assets. The appraisal or fair market value of the asset should be used to establish a reasonable basis of valuation.
7. Costs subsequent to acquisition are either capitalized or expensed, depending on whether the costs are incurred to achieve greater future benefits (capitalize) or to maintain a given level of services (expense). In order for such costs to be capitalized, one of three conditions must be present: (1) the useful life of the asset must be increased; (2) the quantity of units produced must be increased; or (3) the quality of the units produced must be enhanced.
8. At the time of disposal of plant assets, depreciation should be taken up to the date of disposition, all accounts related to the retired assets should be removed from the accounts, and any gain or loss should be recognized.
9. Disposals of plant assets may result from sale, involuntary conversion, abandonment, or exchange and may result in gains or losses includable in income determination.

APPENDIX 10A
Illustration of Interest Capitalization

To illustrate the issues related to interest capitalization, assume that on November 1, 1993, Shalla Company contracted with Pfeifer Construction Co. to have a building constructed for $1,400,000 on land costing $100,000 (purchased from the contractor and included in the first payment). Shalla made the following payments to the construction company during 1994.

January 1	March 1	May 1	December 31	Total
$210,000	$300,000	$540,000	$450,000	$1,500,000

Construction was completed and the building was ready for occupancy on December 31, 1994. Shalla Company had the following debt outstanding at December 31, 1994.

Specific Construction Debt

1. 15% three-year note to finance construction of the building, dated December 31, 1993, with interest payable annually on December 31.	$750,000

Other Debt

2. 10% five-year note payable, dated December 31, 1990 with interest payable annually on December 31.	$550,000
3. 12% ten-year bonds issued December 31, 1989, with interest payable annually on December 31.	$600,000

The weighted-average accumulated expenditures during 1994 are computed as follows.

Computation of Weighted-Average Accumulated Expenditures

Date	Expenditures	×	Capitalization Period	=	Average Accumulated Expenditures
January 1	$ 210,000		12/12		$210,000
March 1	300,000		10/12		250,000
May 1	540,000		8/12		360,000
December 31	450,000		-0-		-0-
	$1,500,000				$820,000

Note that the expenditure made on December 31, the last day of the year, does not have any interest cost. The avoidable interest can be computed as follows.

Computation of Avoidable Interest

Weighted-Average Accumulated Expenditures	×	Interest Rate	=	Avoidable Interest
$750,000		15% (construction note)		$112,500
70,000		11.04% (weighted average of other debt)*		7,728
$820,000				$120,228

(Continued)

*Weighted-average interest rate computation:

	Principal	Interest
10%, five-year note	$ 550,000	$ 55,000
12%, ten-year bonds	600,000	72,000
	$1,150,000	$127,000

$$\frac{\text{Total interest}}{\text{Total principal}} = \frac{\$\ 127,000}{\$1,150,000} = 11.04\%$$

Avoidable interest: $120,228

The actual interest cost, representing the maximum amount of interest that may be capitalized during 1994, is computed as follows.

Construction note	$750,000 × .15	=	$112,500
Five-year note	$550,000 × .10	=	55,000
Ten-year bonds	$600,000 × .12	=	72,000
Actual interest			$239,500

The interest cost to be capitalized is the lesser of $120,228 (avoidable interest) and $239,500 (actual interest), which is $120,228.

The journal entries to be made by Shalla Company during 1994 would be as follows:

January 1		
Land	100,000	
Building (or Construction in Process)	110,000	
Cash		210,000
March 1		
Building	300,000	
Cash		300,000
May 1		
Building	540,000	
Cash		540,000
December 31		
Building	450,000	
Cash		450,000
Building	120,228	
Interest Expense ($239,500 – $120,228)	119,272	
Cash ($112,500 + $55,000 + $72,000)		239,500

Capitalized interest should be written off over the useful life of the assets involved as part of depreciation and not over the term of the debt. The total interest cost incurred during the period should be disclosed; the portion charged to expense and the portion capitalized should be indicated.

At December 31, 1994, Shalla should report the amount of interest capitalized either as part of the nonoperating section of the income statement or in the notes accompanying the financial statements. Both forms of disclosure are illustrated below.

Capitalized Interest Reported in the Income Statement

Income from operations		XXX
Other expenses and losses:		
Interest expense	$239,500	
Less capitalized interest	120,228	119,272
Income before income taxes		XXXXX
Income tax expense		XXX
Net income		XXXX

Capitalized Interest Disclosed in a Note

Note 1: Accounting Policies

Capitalized interest. During 1994 total interest cost was $239,500 of which $120,228 was capitalized and $119,272 was charged to expense.

APPENDIX 10B
Casualty Insurance

Business enterprises constantly face the risk of loss of assets by fire, storm, theft, accident, or other casualties. Generally companies shift the burden of such losses by entering into a casualty insurance contract whereby an insurance company in consideration for a premium payment assumes the risk of all or a portion of these losses. The premium, a charge per $100 of insurance carried, is paid in advance. When a premium discount is given when the term of the policy exceeds one year, companies pay insurance premiums in advance, creating the asset (deferred charge) **prepaid insurance.**

When an insured asset is damaged, destroyed, or lost, the relevant accounts must be adjusted and settlement with the insurance company must be completed. The maximum amount recoverable is the *fair market value* of the property at the date of loss and is referred to as the **insurable value.** Although the book value is irrelevant in determining the amount recoverable from the insurance company, it is used for accounting purposes to measure the loss (or gain) resulting from the casualty and any insurance settlement. For example, if $40,000 is recovered under an insurance policy after the complete destruction of an asset having a book value of $34,000, a gain of $6,000 would be recognized. In some instances the amount recoverable is limited by some special feature such as a **deductible clause** in the case of automobile insurance ($50 or $100 deductible) or a **co-insurance clause** in the case of fire insurance.

Co-insurance

Because most assets are only partially destroyed by any casualty, companies would take out only enough insurance to cover a fraction of the value of the asset and receive full reimbursement of most losses if they were not encouraged through a co-insurance clause to do otherwise. Most casualty insurance policies therefore contain a **co-insurance clause** which provides that if the property is insured for less than a certain percentage (frequently 80%) of its fair market value (insurable value) at the time of the loss, the insurance company will be liable for only a portion of any loss; that is, the owner becomes a **co-insurer** with the insurance company.

Stated proportionately, co-insurance means that the amount recoverable is to the loss as the face value of the policy (amount of insurance carried) is to the co-insurance requirement (amount of insurance that should be carried). As a formula, co-insurance may be stated as follows.

$$\frac{\text{Face value of policy}}{\text{Co-insurance requirement}} \times \text{Loss} = \text{Amount Recoverable}$$

The following example illustrates the use of the formula in determining the amount recoverable using an 80% co-insurance clause.

Amount Recoverable Under Co-insurance

	Case 1	Case 2	Case 3	Case 4
Fair market value	$10,000	$10,000	$10,000	$10,000
Face value of policy	7,000	5,000	9,000	8,000
Co-insurance requirement	8,000	8,000	8,000	8,000
Amount of loss	6,000	6,000	6,000	9,000
Amount recoverable	5,250[a]	3,750[b]	6,000[c]	8,000[d]

[a] $\frac{\$7,000}{\$8,000} \times \$6,000 = \$5,250$

[b] $\frac{\$5,000}{\$8,000} \times \$6,000 = \$3,750$

[c] $\frac{\$9,000}{\$8,000} \times \$6,000 = \$6,750$*

[d] $\frac{\$8,000}{\$8,000} \times \$9,000 = \$9,000$**

*Amount recoverable limited to amount of loss.

**Amount recoverable limited to face value of policy.

As shown above, ***the amount recoverable from the insurance company is the lowest of (1) the amount of the loss, (2) the face value of the policy, or (3) the co-insurance formula amount.***

Recovery from Multiple Policies

If an asset is insured under two or more insurance policies, recovery of a loss is obtained from the different policies in proportion to the face value of each policy. If the policies have **co-insurance** requirements, the amount recoverable under each of the policies is computed by multiplying the loss by a fraction, the numerator of which is the face value of the individual policy, and ***the denominator of which is the higher of (1) the total face value of all policies, or (2) the amount required under the co-insurance requirement of the particular policy.*** The formula is shown below:

$$\text{Amount Recoverable Under Each Policy} = \text{Fair Market Value of Asset Destroyed (Total Loss)} \times \frac{\text{Face Value of Individual Policy}}{\text{Total Face Value of All Policies OR Co-insurance Requirements*}}$$

*whichever is higher

To illustrate, assume that an asset having a fair market value of $100,000 is insured under policies presented below, and that a fire loss of $72,000 is suffered. The policies contain different co-insurance requirements of 70%, 85%, and 90%. The recovery from each policy would be as follows.

Amount Recoverable Under Multiple Co-insurance Policies

Policy	Face Value	Requirement	Fraction*	Loss	Amount Collectible
A	$30,000	$70,000	30/80	$72,000	$27,000
B	40,000	85,000	40/85	72,000	33,882
C	10,000	90,000	10/90	72,000	8,000
	$80,000				$68,882

*Note that the denominator in each fraction is the higher of the face value of all policies or the co-insurance requirement.

ACCOUNTING FOR CASUALTY LOSSES

In the event of a casualty loss the accounting records as maintained or as reconstructed (if destroyed in the casualty) must be adjusted as of the date of the casualty. The loss may be summarized in a casualty loss account, charging such account for the book value of the assets destroyed or damaged and crediting it for amounts recoverable from salvage and from insurance companies. The total amount recoverable (receivable) from the insurance companies would be classified as a current asset if current settlement is anticipated. If the casualty loss is material and the consequence of an unusual and infrequent event or circumstance, it would be classified as an extraordinary item.

Because the amount recovered under insurance policies is based upon fair market and appraised values, the insurance proceeds may exceed the book value of the assets destroyed or damaged. The excess of insurance proceeds over the book value should be presented as a book gain.

Note: All **asterisked** questions, cases, exercises, and problems relate to material contained in the appendix to the chapter.

QUESTIONS

1. What are the major characteristics of plant assets?

2. Broussard Inc. owns land that it purchased on January 1, 1986 for $400,000. At December 31, 1994 its current value is $750,000 as determined by appraisal. At what amount should Broussard report this asset on its December 31, 1994 balance sheet? Explain.

3. Name the items, in addition to the amount paid to the former owner or contractor, that may be properly included as part of the acquisition cost of the following plant assets:
   (a) Land.
   (b) Machinery and equipment.
   (c) Buildings.

4. Indicate where the following items would be shown on a balance sheet:
   (a) A lien that was attached to the land when purchased.
   (b) Landscaping costs.
   (c) Attorney's fees and recording fees related to purchasing land.
   (d) Variable overhead related to construction of machinery.
   (e) A parking lot servicing employees in the building.
   (f) Cost of temporary building for workers during construction of a building.
   (g) Interest expense on bonds payable incurred during construction of a building.
   (h) Sidewalks that are maintained by the city.
   (i) The cost of demolishing an old building that was on the land when purchased.

5. Three positions have normally been taken with respect to the recording of fixed manufacturing overhead as an element of the cost of plant assets constructed by a company for its own use:
   (a) It should be excluded completely.
   (b) It should be included at the same rate as is charged to normal operations.
   (c) It should be allocated on the basis of the lost production that occurs from normal operations.

   What are the circumstances or rationale that support or deny the application of these methods?

6. The Buildings account of Moseby Inc. includes the following items that were used in determining cost for depreciation of a building:
   (a) Organization and promotion expenses.
   (b) Architect's fees.
   (c) Interest and taxes during construction.
   (d) Commission paid on the sale of common shares.
   (e) Bond discount and expenses.

   Do you agree with these charges? If not, how would you deal with each of the items above in the corporation's books and in its annual financial statements?

7. One financial accounting issue encountered when a company constructs its own plant is whether the interest cost on funds borrowed to finance construction should be capitalized and then amortized over the life of the assets constructed. What is a common accounting justification for capitalizing such interest?

8. What interest rates should be used in determining the amount of interest to be capitalized? How should the amount of interest to be capitalized be determined?

9. How should the amount of interest capitalized be disclosed in the footnotes to the financial statements? How should interest revenue from temporarily invested excess funds borrowed to finance the construction of assets be accounted for?

10. Discuss the basic accounting problem that arises in handling each of the following situations:
    (a) Assets purchased by issuance of share capital.
    (b) Acquisition of plant assets by gift or donation.
    (c) Purchase of a plant asset subject to a cash discount.
    (d) Assets purchased on a long-term credit basis.
    (e) A group of assets acquired for a lump sum.
    (f) An asset traded in or exchanged for another asset.

11. Kirkland Industries acquired equipment this year to be used in its operations. The equipment was delivered by the suppliers, installed by Kirkland, and placed into operation. Some of it was purchased for cash with discounts available for prompt payment. Some of it was purchased under long-term payment plans for which the interest charges approximated prevailing rates. What costs should Kirkland capitalize for the new equipment purchased this year? Explain.

12. Adamson Co. Ltd. purchased for $1,000,000, property that included both land and a building to be used in operations. The seller's book value was $300,000 for the land and $900,000 for the building. By appraisal, the fair market value was estimated to be $500,000 for the land and $2,000,000 for the building. At what amount should Adamson report the land and the building at the end of the year?

13. Barney Black is studying for an accounting examination. He is having difficulty with the topic of exchanging plant assets. Explain to Barney what steps should be followed when accounting for an exchange of plant assets.

14. Fiona Company purchased a heavy-duty truck on July 1, 1990 for $30,000. It was estimated that it would have a useful life of 10 years and then would have a trade-in value of $6,000. It was traded on October 1, 1994 for a similar truck costing $39,000; $13,000 was allowed as trade-in value (also fair value) on the old truck

and $26,000 was paid in cash. What is the entry to record the trade-in? The company uses the straight-line method.

15. Once equipment has been installed and placed in operation, subsequent expenditures relating to this equipment are frequently thought of as being in the nature of repairs or general maintenance and, hence, chargeable to operations in the period in which the expenditure is made. Actually, determination of whether such an expenditure should be charged to operations or capitalized involves a much more careful analysis of the character of the expenditure. What are the factors that should be considered in making such a decision? Discuss fully.

16. What accounting treatment is normally given to the following items in accounting for plant assets?
    (a) Additions.
    (b) Major repairs.
    (c) Improvements and replacements.

17. New machinery, which replaced a number of employees, was installed and put in operation in the last month of the fiscal year. The employees had been dismissed after payment of an extra month's wages and this amount was added to the cost of the machinery. Discuss the propriety of the charge and, if it was improper, describe the proper treatment.

18. To what extent do you consider the following items to be proper costs of the fixed asset? Give reasons for your opinions.
    (a) Overhead of a business that builds its own equipment.
    (b) Cost of constructing new models of machinery.
    (c) Cash discounts on purchases of equipment.
    (d) Interest paid during construction of a building.
    (e) Cost of a safety device installed on a machine.
    (f) Freight on equipment returned before installation, for replacement by other equipment of greater capacity.
    (g) Cost of moving machinery to a new location.
    (h) Cost of plywood partitions erected as part of the remodeling of the office.
    (i) Replastering of a section of the building.
    (j) Cost of a new motor for one of the trucks.

19. Recently, Capital Manufacturing presented the account Allowance for Repairs in the long-term liability section. Evaluate this procedure.

20. Arbor Enterprises has a number of fully depreciated assets that are still being used in the main operations of the business. Because the assets are fully depreciated, the president of the company decides not to show them on the balance sheet or disclose this information in the footnotes. Evaluate this procedure.

21. Recently, Moonbeam Inc. decided to discontinue production of one of its product lines because demand for it had fallen substantially. Although it is highly unlikely that the plant may be used for this type of production in the future, the controller is reluctant to write the plant down to its net realizable value. Why might the controller be reluctant to write the asset down?

*22. Is any interest capitalized relative to noninterest-bearing debts and accrued liabilities? Explain. Identify three noninterest-bearing liabilities.

*23. Guillory Limited began the month of March with accumulated expenditures of $280,000 on its construction project and made $120,000 additional expenditures during March. Guillory's debt outstanding during March consisted of a $100,000, 12% construction bank loan and $500,000 of 9.6% bonds. Its trade payables and accrued liabilities (noninterest-bearing) on March 1 were $50,000 and on March 31 were $40,000. What is the amount of interest capitalized by Guillory Limited for March?

CASES

(OPTIONS TO PURCHASE PROPERTY) Your client, Quaid Plastics, found three suitable sites, each having certain unique advantages, for a new plant facility. In order to thoroughly investigate the advantages and disadvantages of each site, one-year options were purchased for an amount equal to 6% of the contract price of each site. The costs of the options cannot be applied against the contracts. Before the options expired, one of the sites was purchased at the contract price of $300,000. The option on this site had cost $18,000. The two options not exercised had cost $12,000 each. **C10-1**

Instructions

Present arguments in support of recording the cost of the land at each of the following amounts: (a) $300,000; (b) $318,000; (c) $342,000.

(AICPA adapted)

C10-2 (ACQUISITION, IMPROVEMENTS, AND SALE OF REALTY) Laumann Company purchased land for use as its corporate headquarters. A small factory that was on the land when it was purchased was torn down before construction of the office building began. Furthermore, a substantial amount of rock blasting and removal had to be done to the site before construction of the building foundation began. Because the office building was set back on the land far from the public road, Laumann Company had the contractor construct a paved road which led from the public road to the parking lot of the office building.

Three years after the office building was occupied, Laumann Company added four stories to the office building. The four stories had an estimated useful life of five years more than the remaining useful life of the original office building.

Ten years later the land and building were sold at an amount more than their book value and Laumann Company had a new office building constructed in another province for use as its new corporate headquarters.

Instructions

(a) Which of the above expenditures should be capitalized? How should each be depreciated or amortized? Discuss the rationale for your answer.

(b) How would the sale of the land and building be accounted for? Include in your answer how to determine the net book value at the date of sale. Discuss the rationale for your answer.

C10-3 (ACCOUNTING FOR SELF-CONSTRUCTED ASSETS) Silicon Labs, Inc. began operations five years ago producing stetrics, a new type of instrument it hoped to sell to doctors, dentists, and hospitals. The demand for stetrics far exceeded initial expectations, and the company was unable to produce enough stetrics to meet demand.

The company was manufacturing its product on equipment that it built at the start of its operations. To meet demand, more efficient equipment was needed. The company decided to design and build the equipment since the equipment currently available on the market was unsuitable for producing stetrics.

In 1986, a section of the plant was devoted to development of the new equipment and a special staff of personnel was hired. Within six months a machine was developed at a cost of $510,000 which successfully increased production and reduced labour costs substantially. Sparked by the success of the new machine, the company built three more machines of the same type at a cost of $315,000 each.

Instructions

(a) In general, what costs should be capitalized for self-constructed equipment?

(b) Discuss the propriety of including in the capitalized cost of self-constructed assets:

1. The increase in overhead caused by the self-construction of fixed assets.

2. A proportionate share of overhead on the same basis as that applied to goods manufactured for sale.

(c) Discuss the proper accounting treatment of the $195,000 ($510,000 − $315,000) by which the cost of the first machine exceeded the cost of the subsequent machines. This additional cost should not be considered research and development costs.

C10-4 (CAPITALIZATION OF INTEREST) Cardboard Airline is converting from piston-type planes to jets. Delivery time for the jets is three years, during which period substantial progress payments must be made. The multimillion-dollar cost of the planes cannot be financed from working capital; Cardboard must borrow funds for the payments.

Because of high interest rates and the large sum to be borrowed, management estimates that interest costs in the second year of the period will be equal to one-third of income before interest and taxes, and one-half of such income in the third year.

After conversion, Cardboard's passenger-carrying capacity will be doubled with no increase in the number of planes, although the investment in planes would be substantially increased. The jet planes have a seven-year service life.

Instructions

Give your recommendation concerning the proper accounting for interest during the conversion period. Support your recommendation with reasons and suggested accounting treatment. (Disregard income tax implications.)

(AICPA adapted)

(ASSETS ACQUIRED THROUGH ISSUANCE OF SHARES) You have been engaged to examine the financial statements of McGarva Corporation Ltd. for the year ending December 31, 1994, by Messrs. Berger and Dixon, original owners of options to acquire oil leases on 5,000 hectares of land for $900,000. They expected that (1) the oil leases would be acquired by the corporation and (2) subsequently 180,000 of the corporation's common shares would be sold to the public at $15 per share. In February 1994, they exchanged their options, $300,000 cash, and $125,000 of other assets for 75,000 of the corporation's common shares. The corporation's board of directors appraised the leases at $1,600,000, basing its appraisal on the price of other parcels recently leased in the same area. The options were therefore recorded at $700,000 ($1,600,000 − $900,000 option price). **C10-5**

The options were exercised by the corporation in March 1994, prior to the sale of common shares to the public in April 1994. Leases on approximately 500 hectares of land were abandoned as worthless during the year.

Instructions

(a) Why is the valuation of assets acquired by a corporation in exchange for its own common shares sometimes difficult?

(b) 1. What reasoning might McGarva Corporation Ltd. use to support valuing the leases at $1,600,000, the amount of the appraisal by the board of directors?

2. Assuming that the board's appraisal was sincere, what steps might McGarva Corporation Ltd. have taken to strengthen its position to use the $1,600,000 valuc and to provide additional information if questions were raised about possible overvaluation of the leases?

(c) Discuss the propriety of charging one-tenth of the recorded value of the leases to expense at December 31, 1994 because leases on 500 hectares of land were abandoned during the year.

(AICPA adapted)

(COSTS OF ACQUISITION) The invoice price of a machine is $40,000. Various other costs relating to the acquisition and installation of the machine including transportation, electrical wiring, special base, and so on amount to $7,000. The machine has an estimated life of 10 years, with no residual value at the end of that period. **C10-6**

The owner of the business suggests that the incidental costs of $7,000 be charged to expense immediately for the following reasons:

1. If the machine should be sold, these costs cannot be recovered in the sales price.
2. The inclusion of the $7,000 in the machinery account on the books will not necessarily result in a closer approximation of the market price of this asset over the years, because of the possibility of changing demand and supply levels.
3. Charging the $7,000 to expense immediately will reduce income taxes.

Instructions

Discuss *each* of the points raised by the owner of the business.

(AICPA adapted)

C10-7 (ACQUISITION COSTS OF LONG-TERM ASSETS) You have recently been hired as a junior accountant in the firm of Check and Doublecheck. Mr. Check is an alumnus of the same school from which you graduated and, therefore, is quite interested in your accounting training. He therefore presents the following situations and asks for your response.

Situation I. Every few years one of our clients publishes a new catalogue for distribution to its sales outlets and customers. The latest catalogue was published in 1993. Periodically, current price lists and new product brochures are issued. The company is now contemplating the issue of a new catalogue during the latter part of 1996. The cost of the new catalogue has been accounted for as follows:

(a) Estimated total cost of the catalogue is accounted for over a period beginning with the initial planning (1994) and is expected to end at time of publication.

(b) Estimated costs are accumulated in an accrued liability account through monthly charges to selling expenses.

(c) Monthly charges were based upon the estimated total cost of the guide and the estimated number of months remaining before publication; periodic revisions were made to the estimates as current information became available.

(d) Actual costs were recorded as charges to the accrued liability account as they were accrued.

In summary, the company accrues the entire estimated cost (including anticipated costs to be incurred) of a contemplated catalogue through charges to operations prior to the expected publication date.

Instructions

Comment on the propriety of this treatment.

Situation II. Recently a construction company agreed to construct a new hospital for its client at the construction company's cost; that is, the contractor was to realize no profit. The construction company was interested in performing this service because it had substantial interests in the community and wanted to make the community more attractive. The building was completed in 1994 at a cost of $24,000,000. An appraisal firm indicated, however, that the fair market value of the property was $26,000,000, the difference due to the $2,000,000 that the company did not charge the hospital.

Instructions

At what amount should the hospital value the asset? A related question is whether the donated profit on the hospital should be reported as revenue or as a capital contribution. What is your answer to this question?

Situation III. Recently, one of our clients asked whether it would be appropriate to capitalize a portion of the salaries of the corporate officers for time spent on construction activities. During construction, one of the officers devotes full time to the supervision of construction projects. His activities are similar to those of a construction superintendent for a general contractor. During periods of heavy construction activity, this officer also employs several assistants to help with administrative matters related to construction. All other officers are general corporate officers.

The compensation and other costs related to the construction officer are not dependent upon the level of construction activity in a particular period (except to the extent that additional assistants are employed on a short-term basis). These expenses would continue to be incurred even if there was no construction activity unless the company decided to discontinue permanently, or for the foreseeable future, all construction activity. In that case, it could well reach the decision to terminate the construction officer. The company has, however, aggressive expansion plans which anticipate continuing construction of shopping centre properties.

Instructions

What salary costs, if any, should be capitalized to the cost of properties?

(ETHICAL ISSUES: CLASSIFICATION OF LAND AND BUILDING COSTS) Tasty Cola Bottling Company purchased a warehouse in a downtown district where land values are rapidly increasing. Tom Scott, Controller, and Maria Valdez, Financial Vice-President, are trying to allocate the cost of the purchase between the land and the building. The Controller, noting that depreciation can only be taken on the building, favours undervaluing the land and placing a very high proportion of the cost on the warehouse itself, thus reducing taxable income and income taxes. Valdez, his supervisor, argues that the allocation should recognize the increasing value of the land, regardless of the depreciation potential of the warehouse. Besides, she says, net income is negatively impacted by additional depreciation and the company's stock price goes down. **C10-8**

Instructions

(a) What are the ethical issues, if any?

(b) What stakeholder interests are in conflict?

(c) How should these costs be allocated? Why?

EXERCISES

(ACQUISITION COSTS OF REALTY) The following expenditures and receipts are related to land, land improvements, and buildings acquired for use in a business enterprise. The receipts are enclosed in parentheses. **E10-1**

(a) Cost of real estate purchased as a plant site (land $200,000 and building $50,000)	$250,000
(b) Commission fee paid to real estate agency	5,000
(c) Installation of fences around property	6,000
(d) Cost of razing and removing building	13,000
(e) Proceeds from salvage of demolished building	(5,000)
(f) Interest paid during construction on money borrowed for construction	13,000
(g) Cost of parking lots and driveways	24,000
(h) Money borrowed to pay building contractor (signed note)	(300,000)
(i) Payment for construction from note proceeds	300,000
(j) Cost of land fill and clearing	8,000
(k) Delinquent real estate taxes on property assumed by purchaser	7,000
(l) Premium on six-month insurance policy during construction	12,000
(m) Refund of one-month insurance premium because construction completed early	(2,000)
(n) Architect's fee on building	22,000
(o) Cost of trees and shrubbery planted (permanent in nature)	12,000
(p) Excavation costs for new building	4,000

Instructions

Identify each item by letter and list the items in columnar form, as shown below. All receipt amounts should be reported in parentheses. For any amounts entered in the Other Accounts column also indicate the account title.

Item	Land	Land Improvements	Building	Other Accounts

E10-2 **(ACQUISITION COSTS OF REALTY)** Gifford Inc. purchased land as a factory site for $600,000. The process of tearing down two old buildings on the site and constructing the factory required six months.

The company paid $42,000 to raze the old buildings and sold salvaged lumber and brick for $4,300. Legal fees of $2,900 were paid for title registration and drawing the purchase contract. Payment to an engineering firm was made for a land survey, $2,200, and for drawing the factory plans, $68,000. The land survey had to be made before definitive plans could be drawn. A liability insurance premium paid during construction cost $6,000. The contractor's charge for construction was $2,840,000. The company paid the contractor in two instalments; $1,200,000 at the end of three months and $1,640,000 upon completion. Interest costs of $135,000 were incurred to finance the construction.

Instructions

Determine the cost of the land and the cost of the building as they should be recorded on the books of Gifford Inc. Assume that the land survey was for the building.

E10-3 **(ACQUISITION COSTS OF TRUCKS)** Cory Company operates a retail computer store. To improve delivery services to customers, the company purchases four new trucks on April 1, 1994. The terms of acquisition for each truck are described below:

1. Truck #1 has a list price of $30,000 and is acquired for a cash payment of $28,400.
2. Truck #2 has a list price of $32,000 and is acquired for a down payment of $6,000 cash and noninterest-bearing note with a face amount of $26,000. The note is due April 1, 1995. Cory would normally have to pay interest at a rate of 10% for such a borrowing, and the dealership has an incremental borrowing rate of 8%.
3. Truck #3 has a list price of $32,000. It is acquired in exchange for a computer system that Cory carries in inventory. The computer system cost $24,000 and is normally sold by Cory for $31,000. Cory uses a perpetual inventory system.
4. Truck #4 has a list of $28,000. It is acquired in exchange for 1,000 of Cory's no-par value common shares. The shares have a market value of $26 per share.

Instructions

Prepare the appropriate journal entries for the foregoing transactions for Cory Company.

E10-4 **(PURCHASE AND SELF-CONSTRUCTED COST OF ASSETS)** Woodward Distribution both purchases and constructs various equipment it uses in its operation. The following items for two different types of equipment were recorded in random order during the calendar year 1994:

Purchase	
Cash paid for equipment, including sales tax of $6,000	$126,000
Freight and insurance cost while in transit	2,000
Cost of moving equipment into place at factory	3,100
Wage cost for technicians to test equipment	4,000
Insurance premium paid during first year of operation on this equipment	1,500
Special plumbing fixtures required for new equipment	8,000
Repair cost incurred in first year of operations related to this equipment	2,300

(Continued)

Construction	
Material and purchased parts (gross cost $200,000; failed to take 3% cash discount)	$200,000
Imputed interest on funds used during construction (share financing)	14,000
Labour costs	190,000
Overhead costs (fixed—$38,000; variable—$95,000)	133,000
Profit on self-construction	30,000
Cost of installing equipment	4,400

Instructions

Compute the total cost for each of these two pieces of equipment. If an item is not capitalized as a cost of the equipment, indicate how it should be reported.

(TREATMENT OF VARIOUS COSTS) Tritt Supply Company, a newly formed corporation, incurred the following expenditures related to Land, to Buildings, and to Machinery and Equipment: **E10-5**

Legal fees for title search		$ 800
Architect's fees		5,100
Cash paid for land and dilapidated building thereon		100,000
Removal of old building	$20,000	
Less salvage	5,500	14,500
Surveying before construction		650
Interest on short-term loans during construction		21,000
Excavation before construction for basement		19,000
Machinery purchased (subject to 3% cash discount, which was not taken); record net		60,000
Freight on machinery purchased		1,340
Storage charges on machinery, necessitated by noncompletion of building when machinery was delivered		2,180
New building constructed (building construction took 6 months from date of purchase of land and old building)		490,000
Assessment by city for drainage project		8,600
Hauling charges for delivery of machinery from storage to new building		720
Trees, shrubs, and other landscaping after completion of building (permanent in nature)		9,400
Installation of machinery		2,000

Instructions

Determine the amounts that should be debited to Land, to Buildings, and to Machinery and Equipment accounts. Assume the benefits of capitalizing interest during construction exceed the cost of implementation.

(CORRECTION OF IMPROPER COST ENTRIES) Plant acquisitions for selected companies are as follows: **E10-6**

1. Collins Company purchased office equipment for $40,000, terms 2/10, n/30. Because the company intended to take the discount, it made no entry until it paid for the acquisition. The entry was:

Office Equipment	40,000	
Cash		39,200
Purchase Discounts		800

2. Arsenio Inc. recently received at zero cost land from the Village of Paradise Hills as an inducement to locate their business in the Village. The appraised value of the land is $35,000. The company made no entry to record the land because it had no cost basis.

3. Beatty Company built a warehouse for $700,000. It could have purchased the building for $850,000. The controller made the following entry:

Warehouse	850,000	
Cash		700,000
Profit on Construction		150,000

4. Crystal Clear Inc. acquired land, buildings, and equipment from a bankrupt company, Winger Co., for a lump sum price of $600,000. At the time of purchase, Winger's assets had the following book and appraisal values.

	Book Values	Appraisal Values
Land	$200,000	$150,000
Buildings	250,000	350,000
Equipment	200,000	300,000

To be conservative, the company decided to take the lowest of the two values for each asset acquired. The following entry was made:

Land	150,000	
Buildings	250,000	
Equipment	200,000	
Cash		600,000

5. Colonial Enterprises purchased store equipment by making a $3,000 cash down payment and signing a one-year, $23,000, 12% note payable. The purchase was recorded as follows:

Store Equipment	28,760	
Cash		3,000
Note Payable		23,000
Interest Payable		2,760

Instructions

Prepare the entry that should have been made at the date of each acquisition.

***E10-7 (CAPITALIZATION OF INTEREST)** Brown Furniture Company started construction of a combination office and warehouse building for their own use at an estimated cost of $6,000,000 on January 1, 1994. Brown expects to complete the building by December 31, 1994. Brown has the following debt obligations during the construction period:

Construction loan—12%, interest payable semiannually, issued December 31, 1993	$2,000,000
Short-term loan—10%, interest, payable monthly, principal payable at maturity on May 30, 1995	1,400,000
Long-term loan—11%, interest payable on January 1 of each year. Principal payable on January 1, 1998	2,000,000

Instructions

(Carry all computations to two decimal places.)

(a) Assume that Brown completed the office and warehouse building on December 31, 1994 as planned at a total cost of $6,200,000 and the weighted average of accumulated expenditures was $4,000,000. Compute the avoidable interest on this project.

(b) Compute the depreciation expense for the year ended December 31, 1995. Brown elected to depreciate the building on a straight-line basis and determined that the asset has a useful life of 10 years.

(CAPITALIZATION OF INTEREST) On December 31, 1993, Hope Inc. borrowed $3,000,000 at 13% payable annually to finance the construction of a new building. In 1994, the company made the following expenditures related to this building: March 1, $480,000; June 1, $600,000; July 1, $1,500,000; December 1, $1,200,000. Additional information is provided as follows: ***E10-8**

1. Other debt outstanding:

Ten-year, 13% bond, December 31, 1987 interest payable annually	$4,000,000
Six-year, 10% note, dated June 30, 1991 interest payable annually	$1,600,000

2. March 1, 1994 expenditure included land costs of $150,000.

3. Interest revenue earned in 1994 $49,000

Instructions

(a) Determine the amount of interest to be capitalized in 1994 in relation to the construction of the building.

(b) Prepare the journal entry to record the capitalization of interest and the recognition of interest expense, if any, at December 31, 1994. Assume that Interest Expense was debited on June 30, 1994 for interest related to the six-year, 10% note.

(CAPITALIZATION OF INTEREST) On July 31, 1994, Matlock Company engaged Cheers Tooling to construct a special-purpose piece of factory machinery. Construction was begun immediately and was completed on November 1, 1994. To help finance construction, on July 31 Matlock discounted a $300,000, 3-year, 12% note payable on which interest is due annually at the Bank of Montreal. $200,000 of the proceeds of the note was paid to Cheers on July 31. The remainder of the proceeds was temporarily invested in short-term marketable securities at 9% until November 1. On November 1, Matlock made a final $100,000 payment to Cheers. Other than the note to the Bank of Montreal, Matlock's only outstanding liability at December 31, 1994 is a $30,000, 10%, 6-year note payable, dated January 1, 1991, on which interest is payable each December 31. ***E10-9**

Instructions

(a) Calculate the interest revenue, weighted-average accumulated expenditures, avoidable interest, and total interest cost to be capitalized during 1994. Round all computations to the nearest dollar.

(b) Prepare the journal entries needed on the books of Matlock Company at each of the following dates:

1. July 31, 1994.

2. November 1, 1994.

3. December 31, 1994.

(CAPITALIZATION OF INTEREST) The following three situations involve the capitalization of interest: ***E10-10**

Situation I. On January 1, 1994, Moore Inc. signed a fixed-price contract to have Builder Associates construct a major plant facility at a cost of $6,000,000. It was estimated that it would take three years to complete the project. Also on January 1, 1994, to finance the construction cost, Moore borrowed $6,000,000 payable in 10 annual instalments of $600,000, plus interest at the rate of 12%. During 1994, Moore made deposit and progress payments totalling $2,500,000 under the contract; the weighted-average amount of accumulated expenditures was $1,100,000 for the year. The excess borrowed funds were invested in short-term securities, from which Moore realized investment income of $367,500.

Instructions

What amount should Moore report as capitalized interest at December 31, 1994?

Situation II. During 1994, Leno Construction constructed and manufactured certain assets and incurred the following interest costs in connection with those activities:

	Interest Costs Incurred
Warehouse constructed for Leno's own use	$41,000
Special-order machine for sale to unrelated customer, produced according to customer's specifications	12,000
Inventories routinely manufactured, produced on a repetitive basis	11,000

All of these assets required an extended period of time for completion.

Instructions

Assuming the effect of interest capitalization is material, what is the total amount of interest cost to be capitalized?

Situation III. Bordeaux Inc. has a fiscal year ending April 30. On May 1, 1994 Bordeaux borrowed $10,000,000 at 11% to finance construction of its own building. Repayments of the loan are to commence the month following completion of the building. During the year ended April 30, 1995, expenditures for the partially completed structure totalled $7,000,000. These expenditures were incurred evenly throughout the year. Interest earned on the unexpended portion of the loan amounted to $455,000 for the year.

Instructions

How much should be shown as capitalized interest on Bordeaux's financial statements at April 30, 1995?

(CPA adapted)

E10-11 (ENTRIES FOR EQUIPMENT ACQUISITIONS) Busby Engineering Company purchased conveyor equipment with a list price of $21,000. The vendor's credit terms were 2/10, n/30. Presented below are three independent cases related to the equipment. Assume that the purchases of equipment are recorded gross.

(a) Busby paid cash for the equipment eight days after the purchase.

(b) Busby traded in equipment with a book value of $1,600 (initial cost, $3,500), and paid $18,700 in cash one month after the purchase. The old equipment could have been sold for $2,000 at the date of trade.

(c) Busby gave the vendor a $22,300 noninterest-bearing note for the equipment on the date of purchase. The note was due in one year and was paid on time. Assume that the effective interest rate in the market was 9%. (Round to the nearest dollar.)

Instructions

Prepare the general journal entries required to record the acquisition and payment in each of the independent cases above.

E10-12 (ENTRIES FOR ASSET ACQUISITION, INCLUDING SELF-CONSTRUCTION) Below are transactions related to Douglas Company:

(a) The City of Saskatoon gives the company five hectares of land as a plant site. The market value of this land is determined to be $63,000.

(b) 13,000 no-par value common shares are issued in exchange for land and buildings. The property has been appraised at a fair market value of $820,000, of which $190,000 has been allocated to land and $630,000 to buildings. The Douglas Company shares are not listed on any exchange, but a block of 100 shares was sold by a shareholder 12 months ago at $65 per share, and a block of 200 shares was sold by another shareholder 18 months ago at $58 per share.

(c) No entry has been made to remove from the accounts for Materials, Factory Supplies, Direct Labour, and Overhead the amounts properly chargeable to plant asset accounts for machinery constructed during the year. The following information is given relative to costs of the machinery constructed:

Materials used	$12,500
Factory supplies used	900
Direct labour incurred	15,000
Additional overhead (over regular) caused by adaptation of equipment to construct special machine	3,000
Fixed overhead rate applied to regular manufacturing operations	60% of direct labour cost
Cost of similar machinery if it had been purchased from outside suppliers	44,000

Instructions

Prepare journal entries on the books of Douglas Company to record these transactions.

(ENTRIES FOR ACQUISITION OF ASSETS) Presented below is information related to Gepetto Ltd. Company: **E10-13**

1. On July 6, Gepetto Ltd. acquired the plant assets of Al Bundy Company, which had discontinued operations. The appraised value of the property is:

Land	$ 400,000
Building	1,200,000
Machinery and Equipment	800,000
Total	$2,400,000

Gepetto Ltd. gave 12,500 of its no-par value common shares in exchange. The shares had a market value of $153 each on the date of the purchase of the property.

2. Gepetto Ltd. expended the following amounts in cash between July 6 and December 15, the date when it first occupied the building:

Repairs to building	$125,000
Construction of bases for machinery to be installed later	135,000
Driveways and parking lots	122,000
Remodeling of office space in building, including new partitions and walls	130,000
Special assessment by city	18,000

3. On December 20, the company paid cash for machinery, $250,000, subject to a 2% cash discount, and freight on machinery of $11,500.

Instructions

Prepare entries on the books of Gepetto Ltd. for these transactions.

E10-14 (PURCHASE OF EQUIPMENT WITH NONINTEREST-BEARING DEBT) Phoebe Inc. has decided to purchase equipment from Jason Industries on January 2, 1994 to expand its production capacity to meet customers' demand for its product. Phoebe issues an $800,000, five-year, noninterest-bearing note to Jason for the new equipment when the prevailing market rate of interest for obligations of this nature is 12%. The company will pay off the note in five $160,000 instalments due at the end of each year over the life of the note.

Instructions

(a) Prepare the journal entry(ies) at the date of purchase. (Round to nearest dollar in all computations.)

(b) Prepare the journal entry(ies) at the end of the first year to record the payment and interest, assuming that the company employs the effective interest method.

(c) Prepare the journal entry(ies) at the end of the second year to record the payment and interest.

(d) Assuming that the equipment had a 10-year life and no residual value, prepare the journal entry necessary to record depreciation in the first year. (Straight-line depreciation is employed.)

E10-15 (PURCHASE OF COMPUTER WITH NONINTEREST-BEARING DEBT) Dave Stieb Inc. purchased a computer on December 31, 1993 for $100,000, paying $25,000 down and agreeing to pay the balance in five equal instalments of $15,000 payable each December 31 beginning in 1994. An assumed interest of 10% is implicit in the purchase price.

Instructions

(a) Prepare the journal entry(ies) at the date of purchase. (Round to two decimal places.)

(b) Prepare the journal entry(ies) at December 31, 1994 to record the payment and interest (effective interest method employed).

(c) Prepare the journal entry(ies) at December 31, 1995, to record the payment and interest (effective interest method employed).

E10-16 (NONMONETARY EXCHANGE WITH BOOT) Goliath Footware Ltd., which manufactures shoes, hired a recent college graduate to work in the accounting department. On the first day of work, the accountant was assigned to total a batch of invoices with the use of an adding machine. Before long, the accountant, who had never before seen such a machine, managed to break the machine. Goliath Footware Ltd. gave the machine plus $700 to Wallace Business Machine Company in exchange for a new machine. Assume the following information about the machines.

	Goliath Footware (Old Machine)	Wallace Co. (New Machine)
Machine cost	$580	$540
Accumulated depreciation	270	-0-
Fair value	170	870

Instructions

For each company, prepare the necessary journal entry to record the exchange.

(NONMONETARY EXCHANGE WITH BOOT) Rogers Company purchased an electric wax melter on 6/30/94 by trading in their old gas model and paying the balance in cash. The following data relate to the purchase: **E10-17**

List price of new melter	$15,800
Cash paid	10,000
Cost of old melter (five-year life, $1,200 residual value)	11,200
Accumulated depreciation—old melter (straight-line)	6,000
Second-hand market value of old melter	5,100

Instructions

Prepare the journal entry(ies) necessary to record this exchange, assuming that the melters exchanged are (1) similar in nature; (2) dissimilar in nature. Rogers' fiscal year ends on 12/31 and depreciation has been recorded through 12/31/93.

(NONMONETARY EXCHANGE WITH BOOT) Peking Inc. exchanged equipment used in its manufacturing operations plus $5,500 in cash for similar equipment used in the operations of Nathaniel Company. The following information pertains to the exchange. **E10-18**

	Peking Inc.	Nathaniel Co.
Equipment (cost)	$28,000	$29,000
Accumulated depreciation	22,000	10,000
Fair value of equipment	10,000	15,500
Cash given up	5,500	

Instructions

Prepare the journal entries to record the exchange on the books of both companies.

(NONMONETARY EXCHANGE WITH BOOT) Diablo Inc. has negotiated the purchase of a new piece of automatic equipment at a price of $48,000 plus trade-in, f.o.b. factory. Diablo Inc. paid $8,000 cash, gave an instalment note calling for monthly payments of $4,000 for 10 months plus interest at 12% on the unpaid balance, and traded in used equipment. The used equipment had originally cost $32,000; it had a book value of $13,000 and a second-hand market value of $6,800, as indicated by recent transactions involving similar equipment. Freight and installation charges for the new equipment amounted to $1,300. **E10-19**

Instructions

(a) Prepare the general journal entry to record this transaction, assuming that the assets Diablo Inc. exchanged are similar in nature.

(b) Assuming the same facts as in (a) except that the asset traded in has a fair market value of $15,000, prepare the general journal entry to record this transaction.

(ANALYSIS OF SUBSEQUENT EXPENDITURES) Columbia Resources Group has been in its plant facility for 15 years. Although the plant is quite functional, numerous repair costs are incurred to maintain it in sound working order. The company plant asset book value is currently $800,000, as indicated below: **E10-20**

Original cost	$1,200,000
Accumulated depreciation	400,000
	$ 800,000

During the current year, the following expenditures were made to the plant facility:

(a) Because of increased demands for its product, the company increased its plant capacity by building a new addition at a cost of $310,000.

(b) The entire plant was repainted at a cost of $23,000.

(c) The roof was an asbestos cement slate; for safety purposes it was removed and replaced with a wood shingle roof at a cost of $62,000. Book value of the old roof was $39,000.

(d) The electrical system was completely updated at a cost of $24,000. The cost of the old electrical system was not known. It is estimated that the useful life of the building will not change as a result of this updating.

(e) A series of major repairs were made at a cost of $60,000, because parts of the wood structure were rotting. The cost of the old wood structure was not known. These extensive repairs are estimated to increase the useful life of the building.

Instructions

Indicate how each of these transactions would be recorded in the accounting records.

E10-21 (ANALYSIS OF SUBSEQUENT EXPENDITURES) The following transactions occurred during 1994. Assume that depreciation of 10% per year is charged on all machinery and 4% per year on buildings, on a straight-line basis, with no estimated residual value. Depreciation is charged for a full year on all fixed assets acquired during the year, and no depreciation is charged on fixed assets disposed of during the year.

Jan. 30 A building that cost $92,000 in 1977 is torn down to make room for a new building. The wrecking contractor was paid $5,100 and was permitted to keep all materials salvaged.

Mar. 10 Machinery that was purchased in 1987 for $16,000 is sold for $2,600 cash, f.o.b. purchaser's plant. Freight of $300 is paid on this machinery.

Mar. 20 A gear breaks on a machine that cost $9,000 in 1989 and the gear is replaced at a cost of $420.

May 18 A special base installed for a machine in 1988 when the machine was purchased has to be replaced at a cost of $5,400 because of defective workmanship on the original base. The cost of the machinery was $14,200 in 1988; the cost of the base was $3,500, and this amount was charged to the Machinery account in 1988.

June 23 One of the buildings is repainted at a cost of $7,300. It had not been painted since it was constructed in 1990.

Instructions

Prepare general journal entries for the transactions. (Round to nearest dollar.)

E10-22 (ANALYSIS OF SUBSEQUENT EXPENDITURES) Plant assets often require expenditures subsequent to acquisition. It is important that they be accounted for properly. Any errors will affect both the balance sheets and income statements for a number of years.

Instructions

For each of the following items, indicate whether the expenditure should be capitalized (C) or expensed (E) in the period incurred.

______ 1. Betterment.

______ 2. Replacement of a broken part on a machine.

______ 3. Expenditure that increases the useful life of an existing asset.

______ 4. Expenditure that increases the efficiency and effectiveness of a productive asset but does not increase the asset's residual value.

(Continued)

C 5. Expenditure that increases the efficiency and effectiveness of a productive asset and increases the asset's residual value.

C 6. Expenditure that increases the quality of the output of the productive asset.

C 7. Improvement to a machine that increases its fair market value and its production capacity by 30% without extending the machine's useful life.

E 8. Ordinary repairs.

C 9. Improvement.

C 10. Interest on borrowing necessary to finance a major overhaul of machinery. The overhaul extended the life of the machinery.

E10-23

(ENTRIES FOR DEPRECIATION OF ASSETS) On December 31, 1993, Jocelyn Inc. has a machine with a book value of $940,000. The original cost and related accumulated depreciation at this date are as follows:

Machine	$1,300,000
Accumulated depreciation	360,000
	$ 940,000

Depreciation is computed at $60,000 per year on a straight-line basis.

Instructions

Following are a set of independent situations. For each independent situation, indicate the journal entry to be made to record the transaction. Make sure that depreciation entries are made to update the book value of the machine prior to its disposal.

(a) A fire completely destroys the machine on June 30, 1994. An insurance settlement of $630,000 was received for this casualty. Assume the settlement was received immediately.

(b) On March 1, 1994, Jocelyn sold the machine for $990,000 to Spade Company.

(c) On July 31, 1994, Jocelyn donated this machine to the Bluebird City Council. The fair market value of the machine at the time of the donation was estimated to be $980,000.

E10-24

(DISPOSITION OF ASSETS) On April 1, 1994, Alba Company received an award of $400,000 cash as compensation for the forced sale of the company's land and building, which stood in the path of a new provincial highway. The land and building cost $60,000 and $280,000, respectively, when they were acquired. At April 1, 1994, the accumulated depreciation relating to the building amounted to $170,000. On August 1, 1994, Alba purchased a piece of replacement property for cash. The new land cost $90,000 and new building cost $320,000.

Instructions

Prepare the journal entries to record the transactions on April 1 and August 1, 1994.

***E10-25 (CAPITALIZATION OF INTEREST)** Brunettin Inc. is in the process of starting construction on a new machine it intends to use in its operations. Its expenditures to date and related debt outstanding for the month of May are as follows:

Accumulated expenditures (May 1)		$600,000
Expenditures during May		100,000
Trade payables (noninterest-bearing)		
Outstanding May 1	$ 60,000	
May 31	30,000	
Bank loan at 12%	700,000	

Instructions

Determine the amount of interest to capitalize on Brunettin's machine for the month of May.

***E10-26 (CAPITALIZATION OF INTEREST)** Bernadine Company is constructing an asset for its own use and has been capitalizing interest on expenditures for the asset since development activities began. The following details are necessary for the current month's entry:

Expenditures	
Accumulated expenditures (July 1)	$2,000,000
Accumulated expenditures (July 31)	2,400,000

Debt (Outstanding during July)

A short-term, 15% note payable of $1,500,000

A note of $900,000, bearing interest at 12%, specifically for financing construction of the asset

A 9% mortgage note of $700,000

Instructions

(a) Compute the weighted-average accumulated expenditures, avoidable interest, and interest to be capitalized for the month of July.

(b) Determine the accumulated expenditure balance at the start of the next month (August 1).

***E10-27 (CO-INSURANCE)** Presented below are data for three independent cases involving co-insurance coverage.

	Case 1	Case 2	Case 3
Fair market value at date of loss	$68,000	$82,000	$50,000
Face value of policy	40,800	68,880	36,860
Co-insurance requirement (80%)	54,400	65,600	40,000
Amount of loss	45,000	51,000	42,000

Instructions

For each of the cases above compute the amount recoverable.

PROBLEMS

P10-1 (CLASSIFICATION OF ACQUISITION AND OTHER ASSET COSTS) At December 31, 1993, certain accounts included in the Property, Plant, and Equipment section of Fowler Limited's balance sheet had the following balances:

Land	$230,000
Buildings	890,000
Leasehold improvements	660,000
Machinery and equipment	875,000

During 1994 the following transactions occurred:

Land site number 621 was acquired for $850,000. In addition, to acquire the land Fowler paid a $40,000 commission to a real estate agent. Costs of $35,000 were incurred to clear the land. During the course of clearing the land, timber and gravel were recovered and sold for $13,000.

A second tract of land (site number 622) with a building was acquired for $520,000. The closing statement indicated that the land value was $400,000 and the building value was $120,000. Shortly after acquisition, the building was demolished at a cost of $45,000. A new building was constructed for $230,000 plus the following costs:

Excavation fees	$38,000
Architectural design fees	12,000
Building permit fee	2,500
Imputed interest on funds used during construction (share financing)	8,500

The building was completed and occupied on September 30, 1994.

A third tract of land (site number 623) was acquired for $650,000 and was put on the market for resale.

During December 1994 costs of $92,000 were incurred to improve leased office space. The related lease will terminate on December 31, 1996 and it is not expected to be renewed. (**Hint**: Leasehold improvements should be handled in the same manner as land improvements.)

A group of new machines was purchased under a royalty agreement which provides for payment of royalties based on units of production for the machines. The invoice price of the machines was $87,000, freight costs were $3,800, unloading charges were $2,200, and royalty payments for 1994 were $17,500.

Instructions

(a) Prepare a detailed analysis of the changes in each of the following balance sheet accounts for 1994:

Land	Leasehold improvements
Buildings	Machinery and equipment

Disregard the related accumulated depreciation accounts.

(b) List the items in the problem that were not used to determine the answer to (a) and indicate where, or if, these items should be included in Fowler's financial statements.

(AICPA adapted)

(CLASSIFICATION OF ACQUISITION COSTS) Selected accounts included in the property, plant, and equipment section of Travis Inc.'s balance sheet at December 31, 1993 had the following balances: **P10-2**

Land	$350,000
Land improvements	175,000
Buildings	1,200,000
Machinery and equipment	1,100,000

During 1994 the following transactions occurred:

1. A tract of land was acquired for $150,000 as a potential future building site.
2. A plant facility consisting of land and building was acquired from Stein Ltd. in exchange for 20,000 of Travis's common shares. On the acquisition date, Travis's shares had a closing market price of $40 each on the Toronto stock exchange. The plant facility was carried on Stein's books at $110,000 for land and $320,000 for the building at the exchange date. Current appraised values for the land and building, respectively, are $230,000 and $690,000.

3. Items of machinery and equipment were purchased at a total cost of $400,000. Additional costs were incurred as follows:

Freight and unloading	$17,000
Sales taxes	20,000
Installation	26,000

4. Expenditures totalling $100,000 were made for new parking lots and sidewalks at the corporation's various plant locations. These expenditures had an estimated useful life of 15 years.

5. A machine costing $80,000 on January 1, 1986 was scrapped on June 30, 1994. Double-declining balance depreciation has been recorded on the basis of a 10-year life.

6. A machine was sold for $20,000 on July 1, 1994. Original cost of the machine was $45,000 on January 1, 1991, and it was depreciated on the straight-line basis over an estimated useful life of seven years and a residual value of $3,000.

Instructions

(a) Prepare a detailed analysis of the changes in each of the following balance sheet accounts for 1994:

Land	Buildings
Land improvements	Machinery and equipment

(**Hint**: Disregard the related accumulated depreciation accounts.)

(b) List the items in the problem that were not used to determine the answer to (a), showing the pertinent amounts and supporting computations in good form for each item. In addition, indicate where, or if, these items should be included in Travis's financial statements.

(AICPA adapted)

P10-3 **(CLASSIFICATION OF LAND AND BUILDING COSTS)** Smidge Co. Ltd. was incorporated on January 2, 1994, but was unable to begin manufacturing activities until July 1, 1994 because new factory facilities were not completed until that date.

The Land and Building account at December 31, 1994 was as follows:

January 31, 1994	Land and building	$160,000
February 28, 1994	Cost of removal of building	4,800
May 1, 1994	Partial payment of new construction	60,000
May 1, 1994	Legal fees paid	3,770
June 1, 1994	Second payment on new construction	40,000
June 1, 1994	Insurance premium	2,280
June 1, 1994	Special tax assessment	4,000
June 30, 1994	General expenses	16,300
July 1, 1994	Final payment on new construction	40,000
December 31, 1994	Asset write-up	18,850
		$350,000
December 31, 1994	Depreciation—1994 at 1%	3,500
	Account balance	$346,500

The following additional information is to be considered:

1. To acquire land and building the company paid $80,000 cash and 800 shares of its $8 cumulative no-par value preferred shares. Fair market value is $106 per share.

2. Cost of removal of old buildings amounted to $4,800 and the demolition company retained all materials of the building.

3. Legal fees covered the following:

Cost of organization	$1,610
Examination of title covering purchase of land	1,300
Legal work in connection with construction contract	860
	$3,770

4. Insurance premium covered the building for a one-year term beginning May 1, 1994.

5. The special tax assessment covered street improvements that are permanent in nature.

6. General expenses covered the following for the period from January 2, 1994 to June 30, 1994.

President's salary	$ 8,500
Plant superintendent covering supervision of new building	4,200
Office salaries	3,600
	$16,300

7. Because of a general increase in construction costs after entering into the building contract, the board of directors increased the value of the building $18,850, believing that such an increase was justified to reflect the current market at the time the building was completed. Retained earnings was credited for this amount.

8. Estimated life of building—50 years.
Write-off for 1994—1% of asset value (1% of $350,000, or $3,500).

Instructions

(a) Prepare entries to reflect correct land, building, and accumulated depreciation allowance accounts at December 31, 1994.

(b) Show the proper presentation of land, building, and accumulated depreciation accounts on the balance sheet at December 31, 1994.

(AICPA adapted)

P10-4 **(ANALYSIS OF MACHINERY COSTS)** During 1994, Stonehedge Company manufactured a machine for its own use. At December 31, 1994, the account related to that machine is as follows:

Machinery

Old machine cost	$ 9,200	Old machine cost	$9,200
Cost of dismantling old machine	1,500	Cash proceeds from sale of old machine	800
Raw materials used in construction of new machine	27,000	Depreciation for 1994, 10% of $85,700	8,570
Labour in construction of new machine	39,000		
Cost of installation	2,600		
Materials used in trial runs	1,500		
Profit on construction	14,900		

An analysis of the details in the account discloses the following:

1. The old machine, which was removed during installation of the new one, has been fully depreciated.

2. Cash discounts received on the payments for materials used in construction totalled $540 and were reported in the Purchases Discount account.

3. The Factory Overhead account shows a balance of $300,000, which includes variable overhead and total fixed overhead, for the year ended December 31, 1994. The production of the machine accounts for $12,000 of the variable overhead. Fixed overhead is normally priced to operations at $5 per hour of labour; 3,000 hours of labour were consumed in the production of the machine.

4. A profit was recognized on construction for the difference between costs incurred and the price at which the machine could have been purchased. The profit was credited to "self-construction gains."

5. Machinery has an estimated life of 10 years with no residual value. The new machine was used for production beginning July 1, 1994.

Instructions

Prepare the entries necessary to correct the Machinery account as of December 31, 1994 and to record depreciation expense for the year 1994.

P10-5 **(DISPOSITION, INCLUDING CONDEMNATION, DEMOLITION, AND TRADE-IN)** Presented below is a schedule of property dispositions for Genetics Co. Ltd.

Schedule of Property Dispositions

	Cost	Accumulation Depreciation	Cash Proceeds	Fair Market Value	Nature of Disposition
Land	$40,000	—	$34,000	$34,000	Expropriation
Building	15,000	—	4,700	—	Demolition
Warehouse	65,000	$11,000	75,000	75,000	Destruction by fire
Machine	8,000	3,000	1,800	7,200	Trade-in
Furniture	10,000	7,850	—	3,000	Contribution
Automobile	8,000	3,460	2,900	2,900	Sale

The following additional information is available:

Land. On February 15, land held primarily as an investment was expropriated by the city, and on March 31, another parcel of unimproved land to be held as an investment was purchased at a cost of $36,000.

Building. On April 2, land and building were purchased at a total cost of $75,000, of which 20% was allocated to the building on the corporate books. The real estate was acquired with the intention of demolishing the building, and this was accomplished during the month of November. Cash proceeds received in November represent the net proceeds from demolition of the building.

Warehouse. On June 30, the warehouse was destroyed by fire. The warehouse was purchased January 2, 1980 and had depreciated $11,000. On December 27, part of the insurance proceeds was used to purchase a replacement warehouse at a cost of $71,000.

Machine. On December 26, the machine was exchanged for another machine having a fair market value of $5,400 and cash of $1,800 was received. (Round to nearest dollar.)

Furniture. On August 15, furniture was donated to a qualified charitable organization. No other donations were made or pledged during the year.

Automobile. On November 3, the automobile was sold to Dini Petty, a shareholder.

Instructions

Indicate how these items would be reported on the income statement of Genetics Co. Ltd.

(AICPA adapted)

(CAPITALIZATION OF INTEREST) Vantage Unlimited is a book distributor that had been operating in its original facility since 1968. The increase in certification programs and continuing education requirements in several professions has contributed to an annual growth rate of 15% for Vantage since 1988. Vantage's original facility became obsolete by early 1993 because of the increased sales volume and the fact that Vantage now carries tapes and discs in addition to books. *P10-6

On June 1, 1993, Vantage contracted with Dern Construction to have a new building constructed for $5,000,000 on land owned by Vantage. The payments made by Vantage to Dern Construction are shown in the schedule below.

Date	Amount
July 30, 1993	$1,200,000
January 30, 1994	2,400,000
May 30, 1994	1,400,000
Total payments	$5,000,000

Construction was completed and the building was ready for occupancy on May 27, 1994. Vantage had no new borrowing directly associated with the new building but had the following debt outstanding at May 31, 1994, the end of its fiscal year:

- 15½%, five-year note payable of $2,000,000, dated April 1, 1992, with interest payable annually on April 1.
- 12%, ten-year bond issue of $4,000,000 sold at par on June 30, 1986, with interest payable annually on June 30.

Management wishes to capitalize interest on the new building. The effect of capitalizing the interest on the new building, compared with the effect of expensing the interest, is material.

Instructions

(a) Compute the weighted-average accumulated expenditures on Vantage's new building during the capitalization period.

(b) Using the weighted-average method, compute the avoidable interest on Vantage's new building.

(c) Some interest cost of Vantage Unlimited is capitalized for the year ended May 31, 1994.

1. Identify the items relating to interest cost that should be disclosed in Vantage's financial statements.

2. Compute the amount of each of the items that should be disclosed.

(CMA adapted)

(CLASSIFICATION OF COSTS AND INTEREST CAPITALIZATION) On January 1, 1993, Glessner Inc. purchased a tract of land (site number 101) with a building for $600,000. Glessner paid a real estate broker's commission of $30,000, legal fees of $6,000, and title guarantee insurance of $18,000. The closing statement indicated that the land value was $500,000 and the building value was $100,000. Shortly after acquisition, the building was razed at a cost of $70,000. P10-7

Glessner entered into a $4,000,000 fixed-price contract with Tyler Builders Inc. on March 1, 1993 for the construction of an office building on land site number 101. The building was completed and occupied on September 30, 1994. Additional construction costs were incurred as follows:

Plans, specifications, and blueprints	$21,000
Architects' fees for design and supervision	82,000

The building is estimated to have a 40-year life from date of completion and will be depreciated using the 150% declining balance method.

To finance the construction cost, Glessner borrowed $4,000,000 on March 1, 1993. The loan is payable in ten annual instalments of $400,000 plus interest at the rate of 10%. Glessner's weighted-average amounts of accumulated building construction expenditures were as follows:

For the period March 1 to December 31, 1993	$1,600,000
For the period January 1 to September 30, 1994	2,200,000

Instructions

(a) Prepare a schedule that discloses the individual costs making up the balance in the land account in respect of land site number 101 as of September 30, 1994.

(b) Prepare a schedule that discloses the individual costs that should be capitalized in the office building account as of September 30, 1994. Show supporting computations in good form.

(AICPA adapted)

P10-8 **(NONMONETARY EXCHANGES WITH BOOT)** Stallman Co. Ltd. wishes to exchange a machine used in its operations. Stallman has received the following offers from other companies in the industry:

1. Morton Company offered to exchange a similar machine plus $22,000.
2. Pelzer Company offered to exchange a similar machine.
3. Ekdahl Company offered to exchange a similar machine, but wanted $18,000 in addition to Stallman's machine.

In addition, Stallman contacted Braver Inc., a dealer in machines. To obtain a new machine, Stallman must pay $93,000 in addition to trading in its old machine.

	Stallman	Morton	Pelzer	Ekdahl	Braver
Machine cost	$160,000	$120,000	$147,000	$160,000	$130,000
Accumulated depreciation	50,000	45,000	70,000	72,000	-0-
Fair value	92,000	70,000	92,000	110,000	185,000

Instructions

For each of the four independent situations, prepare the journal entries to record the exchange on the books of each company. (Round to nearest dollar.)

P10-9 **(NONMONETARY EXCHANGES WITH BOOT)** On August 1, 1994, Swenson Inc. exchanged productive assets with Wallace Inc. Swenson's asset is referred to below as "Asset A" and Wallace's is referred to as "Asset B." The following facts pertain to these assets.

	Asset A	Asset B
Original cost	$96,000	$110,000
Accumulated depreciation (to date of exchange)	40,000	52,000
Fair market value at date of exchange	60,000	62,000
Cash paid by Swenson Inc.	2,000	
Cash received by Wallace Inc.		2,000

Instructions

(a) Assume that Assets A and B are dissimilar, and record the exchange for both Swenson Inc. and Wallace Inc. in accordance with generally accepted accounting principles.

(b) Assume that Assets A and B are similar, and record the exchange for both Swenson Inc. and Wallace Inc.

P10-10 **(NONMONETARY EXCHANGES WITH BOOT)** Presented below are unrelated transactions related to the acquisition of plant assets for Soft Scent Spray Ltd. for the current year:

1. Soft Scent acquired a machine with a list price of $230,000 on May 1 of the current year. To acquire this machine, Soft Scent exchanged 7,000 no-par common shares, and paid cash of $60,000. The Soft Scent shares were selling for $21 per share on May 1.

2. A used truck costing $25,000 with a book value of $7,000 is exchanged for a new truck with a fair market value of $13,500 and $9,000 cash is given. Assume that the assets exchanged are similar productive assets.

3. Used machinery having a fair market value of $28,000 and cash of $2,000 is received in exchange for a newer piece of machinery having a book value of $24,000 (original cost $37,000 less accumulated depreciation of $13,000). Assume that the assets exchanged are similar productive assets.

4. Soft Scent purchased plant assets which included land and building for cash of $150,000. Soft Scent borrowed $100,000 in cash at 12% interest (principal and interest are due in one year) to finance part of the purchase. The property was appraised for tax purposes as follows: land, $36,000, and building, $90,000. It is decided to use the tax appraisals to allocate cost between the land and the building because the relative tax values appear reasonable.

5. An old computer has a book value of $53,000 (original cost $90,000 less $37,000 accumulated depreciation), and a fair market value of $75,000. A new computer having a fair market value of $135,000 is obtained by paying $60,000 cash and trading in the old computer. Assume that the assets exchanged are considered similar in nature.

Instructions

(a) Prepare the general journal entries necessary to record these transactions during the current year.

(b) Assume that the assets exchanged in the foregoing transactions were dissimilar in nature, and prepare the general journal entries necessary to record these transactions during the current year.

P10-11 **(NONMONETARY EXCHANGES WITH BOOT)** During the current year, Pasture Construction trades an old crane that has a book value of $86,000 (original cost $140,000 less accumulated depreciation $54,000) for a new crane from Sheldon Manufacturing Ltd. The new crane cost Sheldon $170,000 to manufacture. The following information is also available.

	Pasture Const.	Sheldon Mfg. Ltd.
Fair market value of old crane	$ 72,000	
Fair market value of new crane		$200,000
Cash paid	128,000	
Cash received		128,000

Instructions

(a) Assume that this exchange is considered to involve dissimilar assets (culmination of the earnings process), and prepare the journal entries on the books of (1) Pasture Construction and (2) Sheldon Manufacturing.

(b) Assume that this exchange is considered to involve similar assets (no culmination of the earnings process), and prepare the journal entries on the books of (1) Pasture Construction and (2) Sheldon Manufacturing.

(c) Assuming the same facts as those in (a), except that the fair market value of the old crane is $98,000 and the cash paid $102,000, prepare the journal entries on the books of (1) Pasture Construction and (2) Sheldon Manufacturing.

(d) Assuming the same facts as those in (b), except that the fair market value of the old crane is $90,000 and the cash paid $110,000, prepare the journal entries on the books of (1) Pasture Construction and (2) Sheldon Manufacturing.

P10-12 (COSTS OF SELF-CONSTRUCTED ASSETS) Curtin Mining Inc. received a $760,000 low bid from a reputable manufacturer for the construction of special production equipment needed by Curtin in an expansion program. Because the company's own plant was not operating at capacity, Curtin decided to construct the equipment there and recorded the following production costs related to the construction.

Services of consulting engineer	$ 32,000
Work subcontracted	28,000
Materials	300,000
Plant labour normally assigned to production	130,000
Plant labour normally assigned to maintenance	160,000
Total	$650,000

Management prefers to record the cost of the equipment under the incremental cost method. Approximately 40% of the corporation's production is devoted to government supply contracts that are all based in some way on cost. The contracts require that any self-constructed equipment be allocated its full share of all costs related to the construction. The following information is also available:

1. The production labour was for partial fabrication of the equipment in the plant. Skilled personnel were required and were assigned from other projects. The maintenance labour would have been idle time of nonproduction plant employees who would have been retained on the payroll whether or not their services were utilized.

2. Payroll taxes and employee fringe benefits are approximately 35% of labour cost and are included in manufacturing overhead cost. Total manufacturing overhead for the year was $6,096,000, including the $160,000 maintenance labour used to construct the equipment.

3. Manufacturing overhead is approximately 60% variable and is applied on the basis of production labour cost. Production labour cost for the year for the corporation's normal products totalled $8,270,000.

4. General and administrative expenses include $27,000 of allocated executive salary cost and $13,750 of postage, telephone, supplies, and miscellaneous expenses identifiable with this equipment construction.

Instructions

(a) Prepare a schedule computing the amount that should be reported as the full cost of the constructed equipment to meet the requirements of the government contracts. Any supporting computations should be in good form.

(b) Prepare a schedule computing the incremental cost of the constructed equipment.

(c) What is the greatest amount that should be capitalized as the cost of the equipment? Why?

(AICPA adapted)

P10-13 (PURCHASES BY DEFERRED PAYMENT, LUMP SUM, AND NONMONETARY EXCHANGES) Prima Company is a manufacturer of ballet shoes and is experiencing a period of sustained growth. In an effort to expand its production capacity to meet the increased demand for its product, the company recently made several acquisitions of plant and equipment. Josh Wolfson, newly hired in the position of Fixed Asset Accountant, requested that Frank Navas, Prima's Controller, review the following transactions:

Transaction 1. On June 1, 1994, Prima Company purchased equipment from Diana Limited. Prima issued a $10,000 four-year noninterest-bearing note to Diana for the new equipment. Prima will pay off the note in four equal instalments due at the end of each of the next four years. At the date of the transaction, the prevailing market rate of interest for obligations of this nature was 10%. Freight costs of $200 and installation costs of $300 were incurred in completing this transaction. The appropriate factors for the time value of money at a 10% rate of interest are given below:

Future value of $1 for four (4) periods	1.46
Future value of an ordinary annuity for four (4) periods	4.64
Present value of $1 for four (4) periods	0.68
Present value of an ordinary annuity for four (4) periods	3.17

Transaction 2. On December 1, 1994, Prima Company purchased several assets of Anya Shoes Inc., a small shoe manufacturer whose owner was retiring. The purchase amounted to $180,000 and included the assets listed below. Prima Company engaged the services of Morgan Appraisal Inc., an independent appraiser, to determine the fair market values of the assets which are also presented below.

	Anya Book Value	Fair Market Value
Inventory	$ 60,000	$ 50,000
Land	40,000	50,000
Building	70,000	100,000
	$170,000	$200,000

During its fiscal year ended May 31, 1995, Prima incurred $8,000 for interest expense in connection with the financing of these assets.

Transaction 3. On March 1, 1995, Prima Company exchanged a number of used trucks plus cash for vacant land adjacent to its plant site. Prima intends to use the land for a parking lot. The trucks had a combined book value of $30,000, as Prima had recorded $20,000 of accumulated depreciation against these assets. Prima's purchasing agent, who has had previous dealings in the second-hand market, indicated that the trucks had a fair market value of $40,000 at the time of the transaction. In addition to the trucks, Prima Company paid $15,000 cash for the land.

Instructions

(a) Plant assets such as land, buildings, and equipment receive special accounting treatment. Describe the major characteristics of these assets that differentiate them from other types of assets.

(b) For each of the three transactions described previously, determine the value at which Prima Company should record the acquired assets. Support your calculations with an explanation of the underlying rationale.

(c) The books of Prima Company show the following additional transactions for the fiscal year ended May 31, 1994:

1. Acquisition of a building for speculative purposes.

2. Purchase of a two-year insurance policy covering plant equipment.

3. Purchase of the rights for the exclusive use of a process used in the manufacture of ballet shoes.

For each of these transactions, indicate whether the asset should be classified as a plant asset. If it is

i. a plant asset, explain why.

ii. not a plant asset, explain why and identify the proper classification.

(CMA adapted)

FINANCIAL REPORTING PROBLEM

Refer to the financial statements and other documents of Moore Corporation Limited presented in Appendix 5A and answer the following questions:

(a) What changes have occurred in Moore's property, plant, and equipment account?

(b) How does Moore report the net gain or loss on disposal of property, plant and equipment?

Depreciation and Depletion

CHAPTER

11

Accountants, engineers, lawyers, and economists all define depreciation differently, and probably will continue to do so because each group uses depreciation in a different context. All agree, however, that most assets are on an inevitable "march to the rubbish heap," and some type of write-down or write-off of costs is needed to indicate that the usefulness of an asset has declined.[1]

For accounting, the word ***"amortization" is used in a generic sense to describe the charge to income which recognizes that the life of a capital asset is finite and that its cost less residual value is to be allocated to the periods of service provided by the asset.***[2] Traditionally, however, **depreciation** is the term most often employed to indicate that tangible assets (other than natural resources) have declined in service potential. Where natural resources such as timber, oil, and coal are involved, the term **depletion** is employed. The expiration of intangible assets, such as patents or goodwill, is called **amortization** (the specific rather than the generic meaning of the term).

The allocation of the costs of various assets to time periods is a consequence of the periodicity (time period) assumption and accrual requirements of financial accounting. To provide timely (relevant) information about a company, the results of operations for a particular time period and the financial position at a point in time are measured. Businesses, however, purchase or otherwise acquire assets which are used to provide benefits over several periods. Therefore, in addition to determining the appropriate cost of such an asset (applying the cost principle as examined in Chapter 10), it is necessary to make decisions which will allocate the cost to particular periods so that the recognized expense in each period is appropriately matched to the benefits derived from the asset's use. Determining how this may be accomplished is the purpose of this chapter. We will consider the nature of depreciation and depletion (amortization of intangibles is examined in Chapter 12) and then describe, illustrate, and assess various methods that are available to allocate costs to time periods. Some special accounting problems associated with depreciation (partial periods, revision of estimates, and investment tax credit consequences) and depletion (determining the cost of natural resources, difficulties in estimation, and dealing with discovery value) will also be addressed.

DEPRECIATION: A PROCESS OF COST ALLOCATION

Most people at one time or another purchase or trade in an automobile. In discussions with the automobile dealer, depreciation is a consideration on two points. First, how much has the old car

[1] But not all agree when it comes to certain assets. For example, the idea that churches depreciate the cost of houses of worship, monuments, and historical treasures has met with considerable opposition: "Depreciating cathedrals and churches is stupid. . . . It would be like trying to compare the cost per soul saved among the churches." Another opponent wrote that "depreciating churches would be like depreciating the Pyramids and the Sphinx of Egypt, and the Sistine Chapel at the Vatican. Figuring such depreciation is the acme of futility." However, a defender of the concept replied, "The Parthenon may still be there, but its roof has fallen in. Physical assets that are exhaustible should be depreciated." *The Wall Street Journal*, April 10, 1987, pp. 1 and 10. Another point of view is that for cathedrals, churches, and other not-for-profit organizations, cash flow is far more significant than income. Consequently, since depreciation is a noncash expense, the issue of whether or not it is recorded is not particularly crucial.

[2] *CICA Handbook* (Toronto: CICA), Section 3060, par. .33. In order to differentiate the application of the concept of amortization among tangible assets, natural resources, and intangibles, we will use the terms depreciation, depletion, and amortization, respectively.

Depreciation is an allocation process, not a valuation process

Objective 1

Explain the concept of depreciation.

"depreciated"? That is, what is the trade-in value? Second, how fast will the new car depreciate? That is, what will its trade-in value be? In both cases depreciation is thought of as a loss in value.

To accountants, ***depreciation is not a matter of valuation but a means of cost allocation.*** Assets are not depreciated on the basis of a decline in their fair market value, but on the basis of systematic charges of a determined cost to expense. **Depreciation** ***is the accounting process of allocating the cost of a tangible asset to expense in a systematic and rational manner to those periods expected to benefit from the use of the asset.***

write-off to expense in a "systematic & rational" manner

It is undeniably true that between the time an asset is purchased and the time it is sold or scrapped the value of the asset will fluctuate. Attempts to measure these interim value changes have not been well received by accountants because values are difficult to measure objectively. Therefore, the asset's depreciable cost is charged to depreciation expense over its estimated life; there is no attempt to value the asset at fair market value between acquisition and disposition. The cost allocation approach is used because a matching of costs with benefits (revenues) occurs and because fluctuations in market value are tenuous and difficult to measure. Further, because of the going concern assumption and the fact that a depreciable asset is generally expected to be held to the end of its useful life, interim market value changes are not considered to be relevant to the determination of income or financial position.[3]

FACTORS INVOLVED IN THE DEPRECIATION PROCESS

Objective 2

Identify and describe the factors that must be considered when determining depreciation charges.

Before a pattern of charges to revenue can be established, three basic questions must be answered:

1. What depreciable base (amortizable amount) is to be used for the asset?
2. What is the asset's useful life?
3. What method of cost apportionment is best for the asset?

The answers to these questions involve the distillation of several estimates into the resulting depreciation charge. A perfect measure of depreciation for each period cannot be expected since the estimates on which depreciation is based assume perfect knowledge of the future, which is never attainable. Nevertheless, the accountant and management must exercise their collective judgement when deriving answers to these questions in order to achieve a rational matching of expenses against revenues in the income statement.

Depreciable Base for the Asset

Depreciable base = "cost - residual value"

The **depreciable base** or **amortizable amount** is a function of two factors: the original cost of the asset and its residual value. While historical cost was discussed in Chapter 10, little attention was given to residual value. **Residual value** is defined as the ***estimated net realizable value of a capital asset at the end of its useful life to an enterprise.***[4] It is the amount to which the asset is to be written

---

[3] These arguments support the historical cost assumption. Alternatively, many would argue the merits of using current values (costs) as an alternative to historical acquisition costs, particularly in periods of significant price changes. This viewpoint is addressed in Chapter 25.

[4] *CICA Handbook*, Section 3060, par. .14. Technically, the total amortization that should be charged to income over an asset's useful life is the greater of (a) the cost less *salvage value* over the *life* of the asset, and (b) the cost less *residual value* over the *useful life* of the asset (par. .31). Salvage value is defined as the estimated net realizable value of a capital asset at the end of its life and is normally negligible (par. .15). While cost less salvage value will be equal to or greater than cost less residual value, the life of the asset will typically be equal to or longer than the useful life of the asset. Consequently, the general result is that the allocation of cost less residual value over useful life is likely to result in the same or a greater total amortization charge to income over that life than is the total of the charge to amortization over the useful life based on cost less salvage value over the asset's life. Accepting this, and to avoid complexity, our discussion and illustrations will consider cost less residual value as the amortizable amount.

down or depreciated during its useful life. To illustrate, if an asset has a cost of $10,000 and a residual value of $1,000, the depreciable base is $9,000.

Original cost	$10,000
Less residual value	1,000
Depreciable base	$ 9,000

Companies differ as to their estimate of residual value. For example, many companies depreciate their computer equipment on a straight-line basis, but estimated residual values vary considerably. Differences in residual value result because it is an estimate. Even though one may attempt to derive a residual value based on information about prevailing net realizable value of similar assets that have reached the end of their useful lives, such information may be difficult to find, of a conflicting nature, or nonexistent. Consequently, although companies have similar assets and may depreciate them using the same method and estimated life, differences in estimated residual value would result in different amounts being charged to depreciation expense each year by each company.

From a practical standpoint, residual value is often considered to be zero because the amount is immaterial. Some long-lived assets, however, have substantial residual values which should be considered in determining the depreciable base. Examples presented in this chapter include residual value to illustrate how it has an impact on the calculation of depreciation expense under the various methods.

Estimation of Useful Life

The **useful life** of a capital asset is ***the estimate of either the period over which it is expected to be used by the enterprise or the number of production or similar units that can be obtained from the asset by the enterprise.***[5]

There is often a basic difference between the useful life of an asset and its physical life. A piece of machinery may be physically capable of producing a given product for many years beyond its service life, but the equipment is not used for all of those years because the cost of producing the product in later years may be too high. For example, many tractors in the Western Development Museum at Saskatoon are preserved in remarkable physical condition as an historic reminder of Canadian farming development, although their service lives were terminated many years ago.

Assets are retired for two reasons: **physical factors** (e.g., casualty or expiration of physical life) and **economic factors** (e.g., technological or commercial obsolescence).

Physical factors relate to such things as decay or wear and tear that result from use and the passage of time. Physical factors set the outside limit for the useful service life of an asset.

The reasons an asset is scrapped before its physical life expires are varied. Economic or functional factors shorten the asset's service life. New processes or techniques, or improved machines, for example, may provide the same service at lower cost and with higher quality. Changes in the product may shorten the service life of an asset. Environmental factors can also influence a decision to retire a given asset.

The economic or functional factors can be classified into three categories: inadequacy, supersession, and obsolescence. **Inadequacy** results when an asset ceases to be useful to a given enterprise because the demands of the firm have changed. For example, a company may require a larger building

[5] *Ibid.*, par. .16. The life of any capital asset, other than land, is finite and is normally the shortest of the physical, technological, commercial, and legal life (par. .16). When the useful life for a capital asset other than land is expected to exceed 40 years, but cannot be estimated and clearly demonstrated, the amortization period should be limited to 40 years (par. .32).

to handle increased production. Although the old building may still be sound, it has become inadequate for the enterprise's purposes. **Supersession** is the replacement of one asset with another more efficient and economical asset; for example, the replacement of an 8088 computer processor with a pentium processor or the replacement of a Boeing 727 with a Boeing 767. **Obsolescence** is the catch-all term for situations not involving inadequacy and supersession. Because the distinction between these categories appears artificial, it is probably best to consider economic factors totally instead of trying to make distinctions that are not clear cut.

To illustrate these concepts, consider a new nuclear power plant. What do you think would be the most important factors in determining its useful life: physical factors or economic factors? The limiting factors seem to be: (1) ecological considerations, (2) competition from other power sources (non-nuclear), and (3) safety concerns. Physical life does not appear to be the primary factor affecting useful life. Although the plant's physical life may be far from over, the plant may become obsolete in 10 years.

For a house, physical factors undoubtedly supersede economic or functional factors relative to useful life. Whenever the physical nature of the asset is the primary determinant of useful life, maintenance plays a vital role. The better the maintenance, the longer the life of the asset.[6]

The problem of estimating service life is difficult; experience and judgement are the primary means of determining service lives. In some cases, arbitrary lives are selected; in others, sophisticated statistical methods are employed to establish a useful life for accounting purposes. In many cases, the primary basis for estimating the useful life of an asset is the enterprise's past experience with the same or similar assets. In a highly industrial economy such as that of Canada, where research and innovation are so prominent, economic and technological factors have as much effect, if not more, on service lives of tangible assets as do physical factors. As residual value normally declines with usage and the passage of time, determination of the useful service life of an asset can have significant implications regarding estimation of a residual value and the resulting depreciable base for the asset.

METHODS OF COST ALLOCATION (DEPRECIATION)

Given that the depreciable base and useful life of an asset are determined, the depreciation charge depends on the method selected to calculate the depreciation. The accounting profession requires that the depreciation method employed be "systematic and rational."[7] The arbitrary assignment of cost to accounting periods without regard to the probable pattern of losses in an asset's services is not acceptable.

Depreciation methods may be classified as follows:[8]

1. Straight-line method.
2. Activity methods (units of use or production).

---

[6] The airline industry also illustrates the type of problem involved in estimation. In the past, aircraft were assumed not to wear out—they just became obsolete. However, some jets have been in service as long as 20 years, and maintenance of these aircraft has become increasingly expensive. In addition, the public's concern about worn-out aircraft has been heightened by recent disasters and near disasters in which jetliners suddenly began peeling themselves open. As a result, some airlines are finding it necessary to replace aircraft not because of obsolescence but because of their physical deterioration. The oil tanker industry provides a similar example.

[7] *CICA Handbook*, Section 3060, par. .31.

[8] *Financial Reporting in Canada—1991* (Toronto: CICA, 1991) reports that, of the companies surveyed, there were 262 disclosing use of the straight-line method, 89 using a decreasing charge method, 69 using the units of production (activity) method, and 4 using the sinking fund method (primarily in connection with real estate development operations). In the United States, *Accounting Trends and Techniques—1990* reported that there were 562 cases of straight-line, 135 cases of a decreasing charge method, and 50 cases of the units-of-production method.

3. Decreasing charge (accelerated depreciation) methods:
   (a) Declining balance.
   (b) Sum-of-the-years'-digits.

4. Special depreciation methods:
   (a) Inventory method.
   (b) Retirement and replacement methods.
   (c) Group and composite-life methods.
   (d) Compound interest methods.

To illustrate, assume Cando Co. Ltd. recently purchased a crane for construction purposes. Pertinent data concerning the purchase of the crane are as follows.

Cost of crane	$500,000
Estimated useful life in years	5 years
Estimated residual value	$ 50,000
Productive life in hours	30,000 hours

Straight-Line Method

Under the **straight-line method**, ***depreciation is considered a function of the passage of time.*** This method is widely used because of its simplicity. The straight-line method is often justified on a more theoretical basis as well. When creeping obsolescence is the primary reason for a limited service life, a decline in usefulness may be constant from period to period. The depreciation charge for the crane is computed as follows.

Objective 3

Know how to determine depreciation charges using the straight-line, activity, and decreasing charge methods.

$$\frac{\text{Cost less residual value}}{\text{Estimated service life}} = \text{Depreciation charge}$$

$$\frac{\$500{,}000 - \$50{,}000}{5} = \$90{,}000$$

The major objection to the straight-line approach is that it rests on two tenuous assumptions: (1) the asset's economic usefulness is the same each year, and (2) maintenance expense is about the same each period (given constant revenue flows). If such is not the case, a rational matching of expense with revenues will not result from application of this method.

Another problem of this method is that distortions in the rate of return analysis (income ÷ assets) can develop. Table 11-1 (on page 536) indicates how the rate of return increases, given constant revenue flows, as the asset's book value decreases. Relying on the increasing trend of the rate of return in such circumstances can be very misleading as a basis for evaluating the success of operations.[9] The increase in the rate of return is the result of an accounting method and does not

[9] Table 11-1 indicates the nature of the problem by considering consequences on rate of return analysis for a single asset situation. There are, of course, usually many depreciable assets reported in financial statements and these assets are replaced as they wear out. Also, the asset "portfolio" often is increasing. As a result, some may argue that, because the cost of new assets is continuously added, the undepreciated book value of the asset portfolio would, in reality, not decline over the years as indicated in the illustration and, therefore, the rate of return would not dramatically increase. While this argument has some practical merit in the circumstances in which it is framed, other circumstances may exist. The point is that anyone looking at a rate of return analysis should be aware of this potential problem within the context of the particular situation.

reflect significant improvement in the underlying economic performance. ***With the exception of the compound interest methods, the rate of return trend can be similarly distorted by other depreciation methods.***

Table 11-1
Depreciation and Rate of Return Analysis: Crane Example

Year	Depreciation Expense	Undepreciated Asset Balance (book value)	Income Flow (after depreciation expense)	Rate of Return (income ÷ book value)
0		$500,000		
1	$90,000	410,000	$100,000	24.4%
2	90,000	320,000	100,000	31.2%
3	90,000	230,000	100,000	43.5%
4	90,000	140,000	100,000	71.4%
5	90,000	50,000	100,000	200.0%

Activity Method

An **activity method** (sometimes called a variable charge approach) ***determines depreciation as a function of use or productivity instead of the passage of time.*** It results in a good matching of costs and revenues when benefits received from an asset are a function of fluctuating activity or productivity. The life of the asset is considered in terms of either the output it provides (units it produces) or the input required to produce the output (number of hours it works). Conceptually, a cost/benefit association is best established in terms of an **output measure**, but often the output is not homogeneous and/or is difficult to measure. In such cases, an **input measure** such as machine hours is an appropriate basis for determining the amount of depreciation charge for a given accounting period.

The crane poses no particular problem because the usage (hours) is relatively easy to measure. If we assume that the crane is used 4,000 hours the first year, the depreciation charge is calculated as follows.

$$\frac{\text{(Cost less residual)} \times \text{Hours this year}}{\text{Total estimated hours}} = \text{Depreciation charge}$$

$$\frac{(\$500{,}000 - \$50{,}000) \times \mathbf{4{,}000}}{30{,}000} = \mathbf{\$60{,}000}$$

The major limitation of this method is that it is not appropriate in situations in which depreciation is a function of time instead of activity. For example, a building is subject to a great deal of steady deterioration from the elements (a function of time) regardless of its use. In addition, where an asset's useful life is subject to economic or functional factors, independent of its use, the activity method loses much of its significance. For example, if a company is expanding rapidly, a particular building may soon become obsolete for its intended purposes, without activity playing any role in its loss of utility. Another problem in using an activity method is that the total units of output or service hours to be received over the useful life is often difficult to determine.

Decreasing Charge Methods

The **decreasing charge methods** (often called accelerated depreciation methods) ***provide for a higher depreciation expense charge in the earlier years and lower charges in later periods.*** The main justification for this approach is that more depreciation should be charged in earlier years when the asset suffers the greatest loss of its services. Another argument is that repair and maintenance costs are often higher in the later periods, and the accelerated methods thus provide a fairly constant total cost (for depreciation plus repairs and maintenance) because the depreciation charge is lower in the later periods. Two decreasing charge methods (the declining balance method and the sum-of-the-years'-digits method) are considered in the following paragraphs.

Declining Balance Method. The **declining balance method** ***uses a depreciation rate*** (expressed as a percentage and called the declining balance rate) ***which remains constant throughout the asset's life*** (assuming no change in estimates occur). ***This rate is applied to the reducing book value each year to determine the depreciation expense.*** The declining balance rate may be determined in a variety of ways, but this book will use a multiple of the straight-line rate.[10] For example, the *double*-declining balance rate for a 10-year-life asset would be 20% (double or multiply by 2 the straight-line rate which is 1/10 or 10%; or divide the multiple of the straight-line rate which is 2 in this case by the estimated life, 2/10 is 20%). For an asset with a 20-year life, the *triple*-declining balance rate would be 15% (3 × 1/20, or 3/20) while the *double*-declining balance rate would be 10% (2 × 1/20, or 2/20).

Unlike other methods, ***in the declining balance method the residual value is not deducted in computing the depreciable base.*** The declining balance rate is multiplied by the book value of the asset at the beginning of each period. Since the book value of the asset is reduced each period by the depreciation charge, the constant rate is applied to a successively lower book value. The result is a lower depreciation charge each year. This process continues until the book value of the asset is reduced to its estimated residual value at which time depreciation is discontinued. Using a double-declining balance rate, the depreciation charges for the crane example of Cando Co. Ltd. are presented in Table 11-2.

Table 11-2
Double-Declining Depreciation Schedule: Crane Example

Year	Book Value of Asset, Start of Year	Rate on Declining Balance[a]	**Debit Depreciation Expense**	Balance of Accumulated Depreciation	Book Value, End of Year
1	$500,000	40%	**$200,000**	$200,000	$300,000
2	300,000	40%	**120,000**	320,000	180,000
3	180,000	40%	**72,000**	392,000	108,000
4	108,000	40%	**43,200**	435,200	64,800
5	64,800	40%	**14,800**[b]	450,000	50,000

[a] 2 × 1/5 = 40%, or 2/5 = 40%.
[b] Limited to $14,800 as it is assumed the book value will not be less than residual value.

---

[10] A pure form of the declining balance method (sometimes called the "fixed percentage of book-value method") has also been suggested as a possibility, but is not used extensively in practice. This approach finds a rate that depreciates the asset exactly to residual value at the end of its expected useful (*n* years) life. The formula for determining this rate is as follows:

$$\text{Depreciation rate} = 1 - \sqrt[n]{\frac{\text{Residual Value}}{\text{Acquisition Cost}}}$$

Enterprises sometimes switch from the declining balance to the straight-line method near the end of an asset's useful life to ensure that the asset is depreciated only to residual value. This may be done on practical grounds and, because amounts involved are not material, a retroactive adjustment for a change in an accounting policy is not made.

Sum-of-the-Years'-Digits Method. The **sum-of-the-years'-digits method** ***results in a decreasing annual depreciation charge because a decreasing fraction for each year is multiplied by a constant depreciable cost*** (original cost less residual value). Each fraction uses the sum of the years of the asset's life as a denominator (5 + 4 + 3 + 2 + 1 = 15, for a 5-year life)[11] and the number of years of estimated life remaining as of the beginning of the year as a numerator. In this method, the numerator decreases year by year although the denominator remains constant (5/15, 4/15, 3/15, 2/15, and 1/15). At the end of the asset's useful life, the balance remaining would be equal to the residual value. This method is illustrated in Table 11-3 regarding the crane example. The sum-of-the-years'-digits method has not been used much in Canadian practice.

Table 11-3

Sum-of-the-Years'-Digits Depreciation Schedule: Crane Example

Year	Depreciation Base	Remaining Life in Years	Depreciation Fraction	**Depreciation Expense**	Book Value, End of Year
1	$450,000	5	5/15	**$150,000**	$350,000
2	450,000	4	4/15	**120,000**	230,000
3	450,000	3	3/15	**90,000**	140,000
4	450,000	2	2/15	**60,000**	80,000
5	450,000	1	1/15	**30,000**	50,000[a]
		15	15/15	**$450,000**	

[a]Residual value.

SPECIAL DEPRECIATION METHODS

Objective 4

Know various special depreciation methods and understand how they work.

Sometimes an enterprise does not select one of the more popular depreciation methods because the assets involved have unique characteristics, or the nature of the industry dictates that a special depreciation method be adopted. Generally, these methods can be classified as follows:

1. Inventory method.
2. Retirement and replacement methods.
3. Group and composite methods.
4. Compound interest methods.

[11] What happens if the estimated service life of the asset is, let us say, 35 years? How would you calculate the sum-of-the-years'-digits? Fortunately, mathematicians have developed a formula that permits easy computation (n is the years of an asset's life):

$$\frac{n(n+1)}{2} = \frac{35(35+1)}{2} = 630$$

Inventory Method

The **inventory method** (often called the appraisal system) is used to value small tangible assets such as hand tools or utensils. A tool inventory, for example, might be taken at the beginning and end of the year; ***the value of the beginning inventory plus the cost of tools acquired for the year less the value of the ending inventory provides the amount of depreciation expense for the year***. This method is appealing because separate depreciation schedules for the assets in use are impractical.

The major objection to this depreciation method is that it is not "systematic and rational." No set formula exists, and a great deal of subjectivity may be involved in arriving at the valuations presented. In some situations, a market or liquidation value is used, a practice that is criticized as a violation of the historical cost principle.

Retirement and Replacement Methods

The retirement and replacement methods are used principally by public utilities and railways that own many similar units of small value such as poles, ties, conductors, and telephones. The purpose of these approaches is to avoid elaborate depreciation schedules for individual assets. The distinction between the two methods is that the **retirement method** ***charges the cost of the retired asset (less residual value) to depreciation expense***; the **replacement method** ***charges the cost of units purchased as replacements less residual value from the units replaced to depreciation expense***. In the replacement method the original cost of the old assets is maintained in the accounts indefinitely.

To illustrate these two methods, assume that the transmission lines of Hi-Test Utility Ltd. originally cost $1,000,000 and that eight years later lines costing $150,000 are replaced with lines having a cost of $200,000. Any residual value from the old transmission lines (assume $5,000 for the example) is considered a reduction of the depreciation expense in the period of retirement or replacement under both methods. Note that neither makes use of an Accumulated Depreciation account.

Entries Under Retirement and Replacement Methods

Retirement Method			Replacement Method		
Record installation of line—1986					
Plant assets—Lines	1,000,000		Plant Assets—Lines	1,000,000	
Cash		1,000,000	Cash		1,000,000
Record retirement of old asset as depreciation expense net of residual—1994					
Depreciation expense	150,000		(no entry)		
Plant Assets—Lines		150,000			
Cash	5,000				
Depreciation expense		5,000			
Record cost of new asset as depreciation expense net of residual value—1994					
(no entry)			Depreciation Expense	200,000	
			Cash		200,000
			Cash	5,000	
			Depreciation expense		5,000
Record cost of new asset—1994					
Plant assets—Lines	200,000		(no entry)		
Cash		200,000			

Both methods are subject to the criticism that a proper allocation of costs to all periods does not occur, particularly in the early years. To overcome this objection, a special allowance account may be established in the earlier years so that an assumed depreciation charge can be provided. The probability of retirements or replacements being fairly constant is essential to the validity of these methods; otherwise, depreciation is simply a function of when retirement and replacement occur.

Group and Composite Methods

Depreciation methods are usually applied to a single asset. In some circumstances, however, many assets may be depreciated by a single calculation using one rate. For example, a company may place all of its computers (regardless of type, use, life) into a single, multiple-asset account. A similar accounting for office furnishings or other office equipment may occur.

Two methods of depreciating multiple-asset accounts can be employed: the group method and the composite method. ***The two methods are not different in the type of computations involved: find an average and depreciate on that basis.*** The different names for the methods are used to reflect the degree of similarity of the assets subject to the calculations. The term ***"group" refers to a collection of assets that are similar in nature; "composite" refers to a collection of assets that are dissimilar in nature.*** The **group method** is used when the assets are fairly homogeneous and have approximately the same useful lives. The **composite method** is used when the assets are heterogeneous and have different lives. The group method more closely approximates a single-unit cost procedure because the dispersion from the average is not great.

To illustrate, Smart Motors depreciates its fleet of cars, trucks, and campers on a composite basis. The depreciation rate is established in the following manner.

Asset	Original Cost	Residual Value	Depreciable Cost	Estimated Life (yrs)	Depreciation per Year (straight line)
Cars	$145,000	$25,000	$120,000	3	**$40,000**
Trucks	44,000	4,000	40,000	4	**10,000**
Campers	35,000	5,000	30,000	5	**6,000**
	$224,000	$34,000	$190,000		**$56,000**

Depreciation or composite rate on original cost $= \frac{\$56,000}{\$224,000} = 25\%$

Composite life = 3.39 years (the depreciable cost of $190,000 divided by $56,000)

The depreciation or composite rate is determined by dividing the depreciation per year by the total original cost of all the assets. If there are no changes in the assets, they will be depreciated to the residual value in the amount of $56,000 per year (the original cost of $224,000 × the composite rate of 25%). As a result, it will take Smart Motors 3.39 years (composite life as indicated in the illustration) to depreciate these assets.

The differences between the group or composite method and the single-unit depreciation approach become accentuated when examining asset retirements. If an asset is retired before, or after, the average service life of the group is reached, the resulting gain or loss is buried in the Accumulated Depreciation account. This practice is justified because some assets will be retired before the average service life and others after the average life. For this reason, ***the debit to Accumulated Depreciation is the difference between original cost and cash received. No gain or loss on disposition is recorded.*** To illustrate, suppose that one of the campers with a cost of $5,000 was sold for $2,600 at the end of the third year. The entry is:

Accumulated Depreciation	2,400	
Cash	2,600	
Cars, Trucks, and Campers		5,000

If a new type of asset is purchased (mopeds, for example), a new depreciation rate must be computed and applied in subsequent periods.

Cominco Ltd. uses a composite basis for depreciating some of its assets and reports this fact as follows [italics provided by authors].

Cominco Ltd.
From the summary of significant accounting policies
for the year ended December 31, 1992

Land, Buildings and Equipment

Land, buildings and equipment are recorded at cost and include the cost of renewals and betterments. When assets are sold or abandoned, the recorded costs and related accumulated depreciation are removed from the accounts and any gains or losses are included in earnings. Repairs and maintenance are charged against earnings as incurred.

Depreciation is calculated on the straight-line method using rates based on the estimated service lives of the respective assets. *In some integrated mining and manufacturing operations, assets are pooled and depreciated at composite rates.* Depreciation is not provided on major additions until commencement of commercial operation.

The group or composite method simplifies the bookkeeping process and tends to average out or offset errors caused by over- or under-depreciation. As a result, periodic income is not distorted by gains or losses on disposals of assets.

On the other hand, the single asset approach (1) simplifies the computation mathematically; (2) identifies gains and losses on disposal; (3) isolates depreciation on idle equipment; and (4) represents the best estimate of the depreciation of each asset, not the result of averaging the cost over a longer period of time.

Compound Interest Methods

The calculations for the compound interest methods are not illustrated in this book.[12] Conceptually, the interest methods have much to offer, but they have found limited acceptance. At the present time, their use in Canada is limited primarily to companies with real estate development operations. Unlike most depreciation methods, the compound interest methods (sinking fund method and annuity method) are **increasing charge methods** ***that result in lower depreciation charges in the early years and higher depreciation charges in the later years.***

The excerpt from the financial statements of CT Financial Services Inc. on page 542 illustrates how this company discloses its use of a compound interest method.

SELECTION OF A DEPRECIATION METHOD

Objective 5

Identify and understand the reasons for selecting a depreciation method.

Which depreciation method should be selected and why? Conceptually, the selection of a depreciation method (as with the selection of any accounting method) should be determined on the basis of which method best meets the objectives of financial reporting in the particular circumstances. To

[12] These calculations are generally considered in more advanced texts or courses and, as such, are beyond the scope intended for this book.

CT Financial Services Inc.
From the summary of significant accounting policies
for the year ended December 31, 1991

(iv) **Real estate investment properties**

. . . .

Depreciation on buildings is provided on a 5%, sinking fund basis over periods of 30 and 50 years. The depreciation charge increases annually and consists of a fixed annual amount together with an amount equivalent to interest compounded at the rate of 5% so as to fully depreciate the buildings over the specified period. The depreciation charged on buildings in the thirtieth year will be approximately four times the amount charged in the first year, while that charged in the fiftieth year will be approximately eleven times.

achieve these objectives, many believe that ***matching of expenses rationally against benefits (revenues) should occur.***[13]

If the method to be chosen is the one which rationally matches depreciation expense against the benefits to be received from the asset, it is first necessary to identify the pattern of benefits to be received. Possible benefit patterns (net revenues before depreciation) are indicated in the following graph.

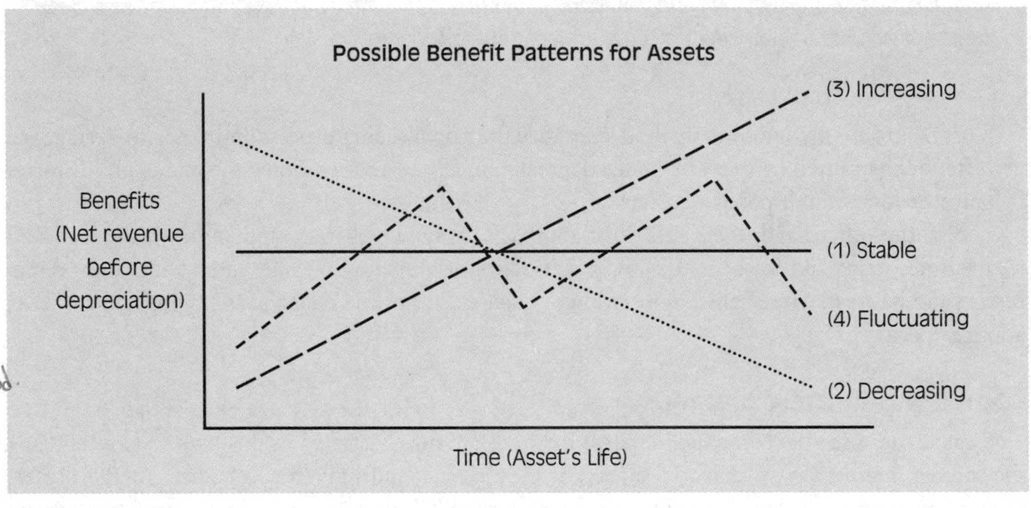

Pattern (1) would represent an asset providing roughly the same level of benefits for each year of its life. A warehouse could be an example. For such assets, the straight-line depreciation method would be rational because it gives a constant depreciation expense each period. An airplane may be an example of an asset with a decreasing benefit pattern (2). When it is new, it is constantly in service on major routes but, as it gets older, it may be repaired more frequently and used for more peripheral routes. Therefore, depreciation expense should decline each year (which is what occurs under decreasing charge methods) if expense is rationally to match benefits. The use of a truck (in terms of kilometres driven) may fluctuate considerably from period to period, yielding a benefit pattern which varies (4). An activity method would rationally match depreciation expense against such a benefit pattern. An increasing benefit pattern (3) may result from ownership of a computer. When bought, it is likely that few and less complicated programs are used and many "bugs" have to be ironed out. As time passes, more complex programs may be added, providing increased benefits.

---

[13] *CICA Handbook*, Section 3060, par. .35, states that, when selecting a method, the objective is to provide a rational and systematic basis for allocating the amortizable amount of a capital asset over its estimated useful life.

While appropriate matching is important in selecting a depreciation method, it may be difficult in many cases to develop projections of future revenues and therefore *simplicity* may govern. In such cases, it might be argued that the straight-line method of depreciation should be used. However, others might argue that whatever is used for tax purposes should be used for book purposes because it *eliminates some record-keeping costs*. Because Canadian companies must use the capital cost allowance approach for income tax purposes (discussed later in this chapter), they may be tempted to use the same for financial reporting purposes. The objectives of financial reporting differ, however, from those of income tax determination. Therefore, for many companies, it is not uncommon to have "two sets of records" when accounting for depreciation: one for financial reporting and another for income tax determination. While this is legal and acceptable given the differences in objectives, a consequence is that financial statement income before taxes will differ from taxable income in any given year. Consequently, income tax expense (based on financial statement income before taxes) will differ from income taxes paid (based on taxable income). The financial accounting consequences of this difference are examined in Chapter 19.

The *perceived economic consequence* of the resulting financial reporting may also be a factor influencing selection of a depreciation method. For example, at one time, U.S. Steel (now U.S.X.) changed its method of depreciation from an accelerated to a straight-line method for financial reporting purposes. Many observers noted that the reason for the change was to report higher income so that it would be less susceptible to takeover by another enterprise. In effect, the company wanted to report higher income so that the market value of its shares would rise.[14]

As another illustration, in the 1980s the real estate industry in the United States was frustrated with depreciation accounting based on the position that real estate often does not decline in value. In addition, because real estate was highly leveraged, most U.S. real estate concerns reported losses in earlier years when the sum of depreciation and interest charges exceeded the revenues from the real estate project. The industry argued for some form of increasing charge method of depreciation (lower depreciation at the beginning and higher depreciation at the end) so that higher total assets and net income would be reported in the earlier years of the project. Some even used an economic consequences argument that Canadian real estate companies (which could and did use an increasing charge method) had a competitive edge over U.S. real estate companies. In support of this view, they pointed to the increasing number of acquisitions by Canadian real estate companies of U.S. real estate companies and properties.

SPECIAL DEPRECIATION ISSUES

Objective 6

Understand and know how to resolve and account for special issues related to depreciation.

Several special issues related to depreciation remain to be discussed. The major issues are:[15]

1. How should depreciation be computed for partial periods?
2. Does depreciation provide for the replacement of assets?
3. How are revisions in depreciation rates handled?

---

[14] This assumption is highly tenuous. It is based on the belief that stock market analysts will not be able to recognize that the change in depreciation methods is purely cosmetic and therefore will give more value to the shares after the change. In fact, research in this area reports just the opposite. One study showed that companies that switched from accelerated to straight-line (which increased income) experienced declines in share value after the change; see Robert J. Kaplan and Richard Roll, "Investors' Evaluation of Accounting Information: Some Empirical Evidence," *The Journal of Business*, April 1972, pp. 225–257. Others have noted that switches to more liberal accounting policies (generating higher income numbers) have resulted in lower stock market performance. One rationale is that such changes signal the market that the company is in trouble and leads to scepticism about managements' attitudes and behaviour.

[15] *CICA Handbook*, Section 3060, pars. .39–.41, deal with accounting for future removal and site restoration costs that are likely to be incurred as the result of environmental law, contract, or company policy. These provisions are to be recorded as liabilities and are not classified with, or linked to, accumulated depreciation. As such, accounting for these responsibilities is examined in Chapter 13.

4. How should an impairment in value be accounted for?
5. How is "depreciation" determined for tax purposes (the tax method of capital cost allowance determination)?

Depreciation and Partial Periods

Plant assets are seldom purchased on the first day of a fiscal period or disposed of on the last day of a fiscal period. A practical question is: How much depreciation should be charged for the partial period involved?

Assume, for example, that an automated drill machine with a five-year life is purchased by Athabaska Steel Inc. for $45,000 (no residual value) on June 10. The company's fiscal year ends December 31 and depreciation is charged for 6⅔ months during that year. The total depreciation for a full year (assuming straight-line depreciation) is $9,000 ($45,000/5), and the depreciation for the partial year is as follows.

$$\frac{6\frac{2}{3}}{12} \times \$9{,}000 = \$5{,}000$$

Rather than making a precise allocation of cost for a partial period as shown above, many companies establish a policy to simplify the calculation of depreciation for partial periods. For example, depreciation may be computed for the full period on the opening balance in the asset account and no depreciation charged on acquisitions during the year. Other policies may be to charge a full year's depreciation on assets used for a full year and one-half year's depreciation in the years of acquisition and of disposal, or to charge a full year's depreciation in the year of acquisition and none in the year of disposal.

The following schedule shows the amounts of depreciation allocated under five different policies using straight-line depreciation on the $45,000 automated drill machine purchased by Athabaska Steel Inc.

Fractional-Year Depreciation Policies

Fractional-Year Policy	Depreciation Year 1	Recognized Each Fiscal Year Year 2–5	Depreciation Year 6
1. Nearest fraction of a year	$5,000[a]	$9,000	$4,000[b]
2. Nearest full month	5,250[c]	9,000	3,750[d]
3. Half year in period of acquisition and disposal	4,500	9,000	4,500
4. Full year in period of acquisition, none in period of disposal	9,000	9,000	-0-
5. None in period of acquisition, full year in period of disposal	-0-	9,000	9,000

[a]6.667/12 ($9,000)
[b]5.333/12 ($9,000)
[c]7/12 ($9,000)
[d]5/12 ($9,000)

590

A company is at liberty to adopt any of several fractional-year policies in allocating cost to the first and last years of an asset's life so long as the method is applied consistently. For illustrations in this book, depreciation is computed on the basis of the nearest full month unless otherwise stated.

What happens when an accelerated method such as double-declining balance is used and partial periods are involved? As an illustration, assume that an asset was purchased for $10,000 on July 1, 1992 with an estimated useful life of five years. The depreciation figures for 1992, 1993, and 1994 are as below.

Exhibit 12-12

	Double-Declining Balance		
1st Full Year	(40% × 10,000)	=	$4,000
2nd Full Year	(40% × 6,000)	=	2,400
3rd Full Year	(40% × 3,600)	=	1,440

Depreciation from July 1, 1992 to December 31, 1992 (1/2 year)

0.5 × $4,000	=	$2,000

Depreciation for 1993

0.5 × $4,000	=	$2,000
0.5 × 2,400	=	1,200
		$3,200
or ($10,000 – $2,000) × 40%	=	$3,200

Depreciation for 1994

0.5 × 2,400	=	$1,200
0.5 × 1,440	=	720
		$1,920
or ($10,000 – $5,200) × 40%	=	$1,920

In computing depreciation expense for partial periods in this example, the depreciation charge for a full year was first determined and this amount was then prorated on a straight-line basis to depreciation expense between the two accounting periods involved. A simpler approach when using the declining balance method is to calculate the partial year depreciation expense for the year of acquisition (e.g., the $2,000 for 1992 as shown in the example) and then apply the depreciation rate (40%) to the book value at the beginning of each successive year. This is shown in the illustration as the "or" calculations. The charge for each year is the same regardless of the alternative mathematics employed.

Depreciation and Replacement of Assets

A common misconception about depreciation is that it provides funds (cash) for the replacement of assets. Depreciation is similar to any other expense in that it reduces net income, but it differs in that ***it does not involve a current cash outflow***.

To illustrate why depreciation does not provide funds for replacement of plant assets, assume that a business starts operating with plant assets of $500,000, which have a useful life of five years. The company's balance sheet at the beginning of the period is as follows.

Plant assets	$500,000	Owner's equity	$500,000

Now if we assume that the enterprise earned no revenue over the five years, the income statements are as below.

	Year 1	Year 2	Year 3	Year 4	Year 5
Revenue	-0-	-0-	-0-	-0-	-0-
Depreciation	(100,000)	(100,000)	(100,000)	(100,000)	(100,000)
Loss	**$(100,000)**	**$(100,000)**	**$(100,000)**	**$(100,000)**	**$(100,000)**

The balance sheet at the end of the five years is as follows.

Plant assets	-0-	Owner's equity	-0-

This extreme illustration points out that depreciation in no way provides funds for the replacement of assets. Funds for the replacement of assets come from revenues; without revenues no income materializes, and no cash inflow results. A separate decision must be made by management to set aside cash to accumulate asset replacement funds.

Revision of Depreciation Rates

When a depreciable asset is purchased, depreciation rates are carefully determined based on past experience with similar assets and all other available pertinent information. The provisions for depreciation are only estimates, however, and it may be necessary to revise them during the life of the asset. Unexpected physical deterioration, unforeseen obsolescence, or a change in the law or environment may indicate that the useful life of the asset is less than originally estimated. Improved maintenance procedures, revision of operating procedures, or similar developments may prolong the life of the asset beyond the expected period.[16]

For example, assume that machinery costing $90,000 originally is estimated to have a life of 20 years with no residual value and has been depreciated for five years. In the sixth year it is estimated that it will be used an additional 25 years (including the sixth year). Depreciation has been recorded at the rate of 1/20 of $90,000, or $4,500 per year by the straight-line method. On the basis of a 30-year life, depreciation should have been 1/30 of $90,000, or $3,000 per year. Depreciation has, therefore, been overstated, and net income has been understated by $1,500 for each of the past five years, or a total amount of $7,500. The amount of the difference can be computed as follows.

	Per Year	For Five Years
Depreciation charged per books (1/20 × $90,000)	$4,500	$22,500
Depreciation based on a 30-year life (1/30 × $90,000)	3,000	15,000
Excess depreciation charged	**$1,500**	**$ 7,500**

[16] *CICA Handbook*, Section 3060, par. 37, states that the amortization method and estimates of the life and useful life of a capital asset should be reviewed on a regular basis.

The *CICA Handbook*, Section 1506, requires that the ***effects of changes in estimates be accounted for in the period of change and applicable future periods***; that is, no changes are to be made in previously reported results. Opening balances are not adjusted and no attempt is made to "catch up" for prior periods. The reason is that changes in estimates are a continual and inherent part of any estimation process. As new information becomes available, it is incorporated into current and future reports. Therefore, no entry is made at the time the change in estimate occurs, and ***charges for depreciation in the current and subsequent periods are based on allocating the remaining book value less any residual value over the remaining estimated life***. The book value to be depreciated over the remaining 25 years is determined as follows.

Machinery	$90,000
Less: Accumulated depreciation	22,500
Book value of machinery at end of fifth year	**$67,500**

If we assume the machinery will have a residual value of $1,000 at the end of the revised life, the entry to record depreciation for the current and remaining years is:

Depreciation Expense	2,660	
Accumulated Depreciation—Machinery		2,660
($67,500 − $1,000)/25		

If the double-declining balance method were used, the change in estimated life would result in a changed depreciation rate to be applied to the book value in the current (sixth) and subsequent years. As this method ignores residual value in determining depreciation expense, a change in residual value is ignored in the revised calculation. Using the information regarding the machine costing $90,000, the change in estimated life would be handled as indicated below.

1. For years 1–5

Depreciation rate = 2/20 = 10%

Year	Depreciation Expense	Accumulated Depreciation	Book Value
1	$9,000	$ 9,000	$81,000
2	8,100	17,100	72,900
3	7,290	24,390	65,610
4	6,561	30,951	59,049
5	5,905	36,856	53,144*

*To determine the book value when using the double-declining balance method, one may use the following formula rather than make the annual calculations:

Book value = $(1 - r)^n c$

Where r = depreciation rate

n = number of full years from the date of acquisition of the asset

c = cost of asset

For the above example:

Book value = $(1 - r)^n c$

= $(1 - .1)^5$ $90,000

= .59049 × $90,000

= $53,144

2. Determine the new depreciation rate to be applied in the sixth and subsequent years.

Revised depreciation rate = 2 (1/remaining years of life)
= 2 (1/25)
= 2/25
= .08 or 8%

3. Using the revised rate, determine the depreciation expense in the normal manner of multiplying the book value at the beginning of the period by the new rate.

For year 6 = .08 ($53,144) = $4,252
For year 7 = .08 ($53,144 − $4,252) = $3,911
etc.

Impairment in Value

An impairment in value occurs when the revenue-producing ability of property, plant, and equipment falls below expectations. Reasons for a decline in value include significant technological developments, physical damage, changes in external economic conditions, a substantial decline in the market for the product produced, and a change in laws or general environmental conditions. When a decline results in an asset's "value" being less than its book value or **net carrying amount** (cost less accumulated depreciation), the questions become whether or not the asset should be written down and, if so, how the amount of the write-down should be determined.

The *CICA Handbook* states that ***when the net carrying amount of a capital asset***, less any related accumulated provision for future site removal and restoration costs and deferred income taxes, ***exceeds the net recoverable amount, the excess should be charged to income.***[17] The **net recoverable amount** is the estimated *undiscounted* future net cash flow from the use of an asset during its remaining useful life together with its residual value.[18]

To write down the carrying value of an asset, there would be a charge (debit) to an income statement account (e.g., Loss Due to Obsolescence) and the Accumulated Depreciation account would be increased (credited). (While crediting the asset account directly would accomplish the objective of reducing the asset's carrying or book value, crediting the Accumulated Depreciation account has the benefit of preserving the original cost of the asset.) ***Once an asset's carrying value has been written down, it would not be reversed if there were a subsequent increase in the net recoverable value.***[19]

In some situations, both a write-down and a revision in estimates of the asset's remaining useful life and residual value may simultaneously occur. When this happens, the write-down is first recorded and the depreciation charge is then determined on a prospective basis using the revised carrying value, remaining useful life, and residual value.

To illustrate, in 1989, Hi-Tech Industries purchased equipment for producing high speed chain-drive contact printers. The equipment cost $1,000,000, had an expected life of eight years, and an estimated residual value of $200,000. Two years later, with the emergence of the laser printer

---

[17] *Ibid.*, par. .39. Provisions for future removal and site restoration costs and for deferred income taxes are considered in Chapters 13 and 19 respectively.

[18] *Ibid.*, par. .10. The future cash flow is not discounted because the purpose of the calculation is to determine recovery, not valuation (par. .52). Projecting the net recoverable amount is based on assumptions reflecting the enterprise's planned course of action and management's judgement of the most probable set of economic conditions for the remaining useful life of the asset. An asset write-down occurs when the long-term expectation is that the net carrying amount will not be recovered (par. .46); that is, the loss is of a permanent nature.

[19] *Ibid.*, par. .43.

as a faster, higher quality printer than the chain-drive contact type, it became apparent to Hi-Tech's management that its production equipment had suddenly suffered an impairment in value. In early 1991 when the carrying value of the equipment was $800,000, management determined that (1) its net recoverable value was only $300,000, (2) the life should be reduced from six to two remaining years, and (3) the residual value should be reduced to $50,000.

The entry to record the write-down could be as follows:

Loss Due to Equipment Obsolescence	500,000	
Accumulated Depreciation—Equipment ($800,000 – $300,000)		500,000

The loss of $500,000 is not extraordinary but, because it occurs infrequently and is material in amount, it could be reported as a separate item in the income statement. Future depreciation would be $125,000 a year based on the new carrying value of $300,000, a remaining life of two years, and a residual value of $50,000.

Tax Method of Capital Cost Allowance Determination

Objective 7

Describe the income tax method of determining capital cost allowance.

For the most part, issues related to tax accounting are not discussed in a financial accounting text. However, because the concepts of tax "depreciation" are similar to those of book depreciation, a short overview of this subject is presented.

The **capital cost allowance method** is ***used for purposes of determining "depreciation" in calculating taxable income by Canadian corporations regardless of the method used for financial reporting purposes.*** Because companies use it for tax purposes, some also use it for financial reporting rather than keep two sets of records. Such an action, while expedient, may not provide a rational allocation of costs in the financial reports. Therefore, many companies keep a record of capital cost allowance for tax purposes and use another method to determine depreciation for financial statements.

The mechanics of this method are the same as for the declining balance method except that:

1. The government, through the Income Tax Act (Income Tax Regulations, Schedule II), specifies the rate to be used for an asset class. This rate is called the Capital Cost Allowance (CCA) rate. The Income Tax Act identifies several different classes of assets and the maximum CCA rate for each class. Examination of the definition of each asset class and the examples given in the Income Tax Act is necessary to determine the class into which a particular asset falls.

2. CCA is determined for each asset class and can be claimed only on year-end amounts for each class. Assuming no net additions (purchases less disposals, if any) to a class during a year, the maximum CCA allowed is the CCA rate for the class multiplied by the undepreciated capital cost (UCC) at year end, before the CCA deduction is taken for the year. In a year when there is a net addition (regardless of when it occurs) the maximum CCA on the net addition is one-half of the allowed CCA rate multiplied by the amount of the net addition. The CCA for the net addition plus the CCA on the remaining UCC would be the total CCA for the asset class. If there were only one asset in a class, the maximum CCA allowed in the year of its acquisition would be one-half of the CCA rate multiplied by the acquisition cost, even if the asset was purchased one week before year end. Thereafter, the maximum CCA per year would be the allowed rate multiplied by the UCC at year end, before the CCA deduction. No CCA would be allowed in the year of disposal for this single asset, even if it was sold just before year end.

3. CCA is taken even if it results in an undepreciated capital cost (book value) less than estimated residual value.

4. It is not required that the maximum rate be taken in any given year, although that would be the normal case as long as a company had taxable income after taking the maximum.

5. Instead of being labelled depreciation expense, it is called capital cost allowance in tax returns.

Assuming that the crane of Cando Co. Ltd. was a Class 8 asset for which the CCA rate allowed is 20%, Table 11-4 shows the calculations required to determine CCA for the first three years. This example also assumes that no other assets were in the class. If there were other Class 8 assets owned prior to purchase of the crane, or purchased or sold during the three years, Table 11-4 indicates how they would be incorporated. See Appendix 11A for a discussion of the tax treatment for additions, retirements, and asset class eliminations.

Exhibit 12.19

Table 11-4

Capital Cost Allowance Schedule: Crane Example

UCC beginning of year 1	$ -0-
Additions during year	500,000
Deduct the lower of the proceeds from or cost of assets in class disposed of during the year	-0-
UCC before CCA	$500,000
CCA for year 1 = (20% × $500,000) × .5	50,000
UCC beginning of year 2	$450,000
Additions	-0-
Deduct disposals	-0-
UCC before CCA	$450,000
CCA for year 2 = (20% × $450,000)	90,000
UCC beginning of year 3	$360,000
Additions	-0-
Deduct disposals	-0-
UCC before CCA	$360,000
CCA for year 3 = (20% × $360,000)	72,000
UCC beginning of year 4	$288,000

(Continued in Appendix 11A)

It should be noted that determination of CCA is subject to rules set by government legislation and, as such, is subject to alteration from time to time. Furthermore, various provincial governments can have different rules with regard to determining CCA for purposes of calculating the income on which provincial taxes are based. This example is based on the Federal Income Tax Act for 1993.

DISCLOSURE OF PROPERTY, PLANT, AND EQUIPMENT, AND DEPRECIATION[20]

Objective 8

Describe financial statement disclosures for property, plant, and equipment, and depreciation.

Financial statement disclosure of property, plant, and equipment should be by major category (e.g., land, buildings, machinery). Disclosure may be in the body of the financial statement or related notes. For each category there should be disclosure of the cost, accumulated depreciation, amount of any write-downs, depreciation method or methods used, and the amortization period or rate being used. The amount of depreciation expense and any write-downs for the period should also be disclosed. The net carrying amount of any plant and equipment that is not being depreciated should be disclosed along with an explanation as to why (e.g., it was in the process of being constructed). Pledges, liens, and other commitments related to property, plant, and equipment should be identified. Any liability secured by these assets should not be offset against the assets, but should be reported in the liability section of the balance sheet.

[20] *Ibid.*, pars. 58 through .63 provide the basis for this identification of disclosures.

The financial report of Andres Wines Ltd. illustrates an acceptable disclosure (also see Moore Corporation Limited's financials in Appendix 5A).

Andres Wines Ltd.

From the Balance Sheet

	1991	1990
Fixed Assets (note 2)	$10,942,219	$11,472,294

From the Notes to financial statements

1. *Accounting policies* (in part)

(c) *Fixed Assets*

Fixed assets are carried at cost less accumulated depreciation. Depreciation of fixed assets is calculated on the straight-line basis in amounts sufficient to amortize the cost of fixed assets over their estimated useful lives as follows:

Buildings	2.5% per year
Manufacturing machinery and equipment	7.5% per year
Other equipment	10% to 20% per year

2. *Fixed Assets*

	1991			1990
	Cost	Accumulated Depreciation	Net	Net
	$	$	$	$
Land	864,109	—	864,109	864,109
Buildings	7,714,823	3,017,101	4,697,722	4,878,609
Machinery and equipment	19,214,313	13,833,925	5,380,388	5,729,576
	27,793,245	16,851,026	10,942,219	11,472,294

From the Income Statement

	1991	1992
Depreciation	$1,220,717	$1,248,906

INVESTMENT TAX CREDIT

Objective 9

Explain the investment tax credit and know how it is accounted for.

From time to time, the federal government and certain provincial governments have attempted to stimulate the economy by permitting special tax advantages to enterprises that invest in capital assets. One such advantage is the investment tax credit. An **investment tax credit** allows an enterprise to reduce its ***taxes payable by a stipulated percentage of the cost of qualified depreciable assets purchased.*** The capital cost to depreciate for tax purposes is reduced by the amount of the tax credit in the year it is claimed.

To illustrate, suppose that an enterprise purchases an asset for $100,000 in 1994 that qualifies for a 10% investment tax credit. If the company has a tax liability of $30,000 before the credit, the company's final tax liability is as follows:

Taxes payable for 1994 prior to investment credit	$30,000
Less: Investment tax credit ($100,000 × 10%)	10,000
Final tax liability	$20,000

The Accounting Issue

A vigorous controversy existed within the accounting profession regarding how the investment tax credit should be accounted for in financial statements. Many believed the investment tax credit was a government reduction in the cost of qualified property similar to a purchase discount, and that it should be accounted for over the same period as that of the related asset (cost reduction or deferral approach). Others believed the investment tax credit was a selective reduction in tax expense in the year of the purchase, and that it should be handled as such for financial reporting purposes (tax reduction or flow-through approach). The arguments for the two approaches are presented below.

Cost Reduction or Deferral Method. Advocates for this position argue that earnings (or reduction in tax expense) do not arise from the purchase of qualified property. Instead, the use of the asset creates the benefits to be received from the investment tax credit. Additional support is given to this argument if part of the investment tax credit must be refunded; for example, if the asset is not kept for a given number of years.

Another position taken is that the true cost of the asset is not the invoice cost, but the invoice cost less the investment tax credit. Many believe that a company would not buy the property unless the credit were available, and the invoice cost of the asset should be reduced accordingly.

Tax Reduction or Flow-Through Method. In this method the investment tax credit is considered to be a selective tax reduction in the period of the purchase and, therefore, tax expense for that period is reduced by the full amount of the credit. Advocates of this approach indicate that realization of the credit does not depend on future use of the asset. Therefore, the benefits of the credit should not be deferred. The investment tax credit isearned by the act of investment and is not affected by the use or nonuse, retention or nonretention, of the asset.

Resolution of the Accounting Issue

The key point regarding the appropriateness of a method is how one views the economic substance of an investment tax credit. Is the government providing part of the cost of acquiring the asset, or is the government reducing the current taxes of companies which invest in new assets?[21] Investment tax credits appear to possess the characteristics of both perspectives.

Recognizing the arguments for each approach, the Accounting Standards Board concluded that those favouring the cost reduction approach were more persuasive. Consequently, the *CICA Handbook* states that ***investment tax credits should be accounted for using the cost reduction approach.***[22] ***Such credits would be either (1) deducted from the asset's cost with depreciation or amortization calculated on the net amount, or (2) deferred and amortized to income on the same basis as the related asset.***[23] ***These two ways of applying the cost reduction method result in the same net income each year*** although amounts of particular accounts used to derive the net income are different as is shown in the following illustration.

Illustration. The cost reduction method may be applied by deducting the investment tax credit from the asset's cost with depreciation calculated on the net amount, or the investment tax credit may be deferred and amortized to income on the same basis as the asset to which it relates is depreciated.

To illustrate the accounting under these treatments, assume that Chris Corp. purchases machinery on January 1, 1994 for $100,000 which qualifies for a 10% investment tax credit. The

---

[21] Jonathan M. Kligman, "Investment Tax Credits: Some Key Issues," *CA Magazine*, October 1983, pp. 78–80. This article provides a good perspective on the controversy over which approach is appropriate and the type of input the Accounting Standards Board dealt with when resolving the issue.

[22] *CICA Handbook*, Section 3805, par. .12.

[23] *Financial Reporting in Canada—1991* showed that of 68 companies accounting for an investment tax credit in 1990, 66 used a cost reduction approach exclusively while 2 used both the cost reduction and flow-through approaches. Of the companies using the cost reduction method, it was reported that 52 deducted the tax credit from the asset's cost and 9 deferred it and amortized it to income.

machinery has a useful life of 10 years and no residual value. Assume that the company uses the straight-line depreciation method for both financial reporting and tax purposes.[24] For income tax purposes, the depreciable base is deemed to be $90,000 (the $100,000 acquisition cost less the investment tax credit of $10,000) as is required under tax legislation. Therefore, $9,000 is deductible each year when determining taxable income. Furthermore, assume that the company's net income before depreciation and income taxes is $35,000 and that the tax rate is 50%.

EX. 12-22

Entries Under Cost Reduction Method Approaches for Investment Tax Credits

Investment Tax Credit Treated as a Reduction of Asset's Cost			Investment Tax Credit Deferred and Amortized		
At time of purchase, 1/1/94:					
Machinery	100,000		Machinery	100,000	
Cash		100,000	Cash		100,000
Recognition and payment of taxes in 1994:					
Income Tax Expense	13,000		Income Tax Expense	13,000	
Cash		3,000	Cash		3,000
Machinery		10,000	Deferred Investment Tax Credit		10,000
			Deferred Investment Tax Credit	1,000	
			Income Tax Expense		1,000
Recognition of depreciation in 1994:					
Depreciation Expense	9,000		Depreciation Expense	10,000	
Accumulated Depreciation		9,000	Accumulated Depreciation		10,000
Annual entries in subsequent periods assuming income before depreciation and income taxes of $35,000:					
Income Tax Expense	13,000		Income Tax Expense	13,000	
Cash		13,000	Cash		13,000
			Deferred Investment Tax Credit	1,000	
			Income Tax Expense		1,000
Depreciation Expense	9,000		Depreciation Expense	10,000	
Accumulated Depreciation		9,000	Accumulated Depreciation		10,000

The predominantly used approach of treating the investment tax credit as a reduction of the asset's cost with depreciation calculated on the net amount ($90,000/10 years = $9,000 per year) is somewhat easier to understand. It also avoids problems associated with having an additional account (Deferred Investment Tax Credit) to deal with and the fact that, when the deferral and amortization

[24] While the CCA method would normally be used for tax purposes, this assumption has been made to avoid the complexities of dealing with differences between income tax expense in financial statements and income tax paid based on tax returns. The differences result from different methods being used for financial reporting and tax determination (to be examined in Chapter 19). Assuming there are no differences simplifies the illustration, allowing concentration on the cost reduction approaches regarding investment tax credits. The principles illustrated would apply even if straight-line were used for financial statements and CCA for tax purposes.

approach is used, there is a difference between the tax expense each year ($12,000) and the tax rate (50%) multiplied by the financial statement income before tax ($35,000 less depreciation expense of $10,000).[25] However, it can be seen that the net income for each year under both approaches would be $13,000 ($35,000 − $9,000 − $13,000 under the reduction of asset cost approach; $35,000 − $10,000 − $12,000 under the deferral and amortization approach).

DEPLETION

Natural resources, sometimes called wasting assets, include petroleum, minerals, and timber. They are characterized by two main features: (1) complete removal (consumption) of the asset and (2) replacement of the asset only by an act of nature. Unlike buildings and machinery, natural resources are consumed physically over the period of use and do not maintain their physical characteristics. Still, the accounting problems associated with natural resources are similar to those encountered with other capital assets. The questions to be answered are:

1. How is the depletion base (amortizable amount) established?
2. What pattern of allocation should be employed?

Establishment of Depletion Base

Objective 10

Understand the issues and know how to account for depletion of natural resources.

How is the cost for an oil well determined? Sizeable expenditures are needed to find the natural resource, and for every successful discovery there are many "dry holes." Furthermore, long delays are encountered between the time costs are incurred and benefits are obtained from the extracted resources. As a result, a conservative policy frequently is adopted in accounting for the expenditures incurred in finding and extracting natural resources.

The **costs of natural resources** can be divided into three categories: (1) acquisition cost of property, (2) exploration costs, and (3) development costs. The **acquisition cost** of the property is the price paid to obtain the property right to search and find an undiscovered natural resource or the price paid for an already discovered resource. In some cases, property is leased and special royalty payments paid to the lessor if a productive natural resource is found and is commercially profitable. Generally, the acquisition cost is placed in an account titled Undeveloped or Unproved Property and held in that account pending the results of exploration efforts.

As soon as the enterprise has the right to use the property, considerable **exploration costs** are likely to be incurred in finding the resource. The accounting treatment for these costs varies: some firms expense all exploration costs; others capitalize only those costs that are directly related to successful projects (**successful efforts approach**); and others adopt a **full-cost approach** (capitalization of all costs whether related to successful or unsuccessful projects).

Proponents of the full-cost approach believe that unsuccessful ventures are a cost of those that are successful, because the cost of drilling a dry hole is a cost that is needed to find the commercially profitable wells. Those who believe that only the costs of successful projects should be capitalized contend that unsuccessful companies will end up capitalizing many costs that will make them, over a short period of time, show no less income than does a company that is successful. In addition, it is contended that to accurately measure cost and effort for a single property unit, the only relevant measure is the cost directly related to that unit. The remainder of the costs should be allocated as period charges (like advertising).

---

[25] The discrepancy is due to what is called a **permanent difference** between tax accounting and financial accounting (considered in Chapter 19). It is created because of the consequences of how the investment tax credit and depreciation expense amounts are arrived at in the amortization and deferral approach. Essentially, for tax purposes, the additional $1,000 depreciation taken over the depreciation under the asset cost reduction approach has no impact on the determination of the amount of taxes paid each year.

Canadian practice is mixed in terms of these two approaches.[26] Larger companies such as Imperial Oil Limited and Petro Canada use the successful efforts approach. The smaller- to medium-sized companies favour the full-cost approach. Exceptions to this generality regarding size include Norcen Energy Resources Ltd. and PanCanadian Petroleum Ltd., which are fairly large companies that use the full-cost method; Total Canada Oil and Gas Ltd. and Paramount Resources Ltd., while being relatively small, use the successful efforts method. The differences in net income figures under the two methods can be staggering as indicated by the following:

> Regina-based Saskoil piled up a loss of $39 million in 1992 despite more revenue and a lighter debt load, . . .
>
> By the magic of changed accounting methods, it's not the worst year ever for the mid-sized producer of oil and natural gas. Saskoil a year ago reported a loss of $23.8 million in 1991—but it has revised the figure to a whopping $74.9 million loss. The dramatic change in 1991 financial results was triggered by Saskoil replacing its former accounting method with one used generally by major companies in the oil and gas business. . . . Taking on the so-called successful efforts accounting method starting in 1993 also forced Saskoil to reduce its historical retained earnings by $223.6 million. Under its old accounting method Saskoil would have registered a loss of $37 million from its 1992 operations.[27]

The final category of costs incurred in finding natural resources are **development costs**. These costs are incurred to obtain access to proven reserves and to provide facilities for extracting, treating, gathering, and storing the resource. Such costs include depreciation and operating costs of support equipment (e.g., moveable heavy machinery) used in the development activities. The depreciation on these tangible assets would be calculated using an appropriate method but, instead of charging the amount to Depreciation Expense, it would be capitalized to the Natural Resource asset account and become part of the depletion base.

Depletion of Resource Cost

When the depletion base is established, the next problem is determining how the natural resource cost will be allocated to accounting periods. Normally, depletion for a time period is computed using an activity base approach (e.g., units of production method). In this approach, the total cost of the natural resource is divided by the number of units estimated to be in the resource deposit to obtain a cost per unit of product. This cost per unit is multiplied by the number of units extracted during a period to determine the period's depletion.

For example, suppose MacClede Oil Co. Ltd. acquired the right to use 400 hectares of land in northern Alberta to explore for oil. The lease cost is $50,000; the related exploration costs for a discovered oil deposit on the property are $100,000; and development costs incurred in erecting and drilling the well are $850,000. Total costs related to the oil deposit before the first barrel is extracted are, therefore, $1,000,000. It is estimated that the well will provide approximately 1 million barrels of oil. The depletion rate established is computed as shown at the top of page 556.

If 250,000 barrels are withdrawn in the first year, then the depletion charge for the year is $250,000 (250,000 barrels at $1.00). The entry to record the depletion is:

Depletion	250,000	
Accumulated Depletion		250,000

[26] *Oil and Gas Survey, 1992* (Toronto: Price Waterhouse, 1992) reported that of the 36 companies in the survey, 12 used the successful efforts method and 24 used the full-cost approach. This document and others published by various accounting firms (e.g., KPMG Peat Marwick Thorne) provide a very informative description of issues involved and accounting practices used by Canadian oil and gas companies, and would be of use to those with a specific interest in the topic.

[27] *The Star Phoenix*, Saskatoon, February 25, 1993.

$$\frac{\text{Total cost}}{\text{Total estimated units available}} = \textbf{Depletion cost per unit}$$

$$\frac{\$1{,}000{,}000}{1{,}000{,}000} = \textbf{\$1.00 per barrel}$$

In some instances an Accumulated Depletion account is not used, and the credit goes directly to the Natural Resources asset account. ***The depletion charge would initially become part of the cost of the resource extracted (in addition to labour and other direct costs) and then be charged against revenue as the resource is sold.*** This cost flow would be similar to that of depreciation on a factory of a manufacturing company, which is initially part of the cost of goods manufactured and is then charged to the income statement in the period in which the goods are sold. The following balance sheet presents the cost of the property and the amount of depletion entered to date.

Oil deposit (at cost)	$1,000,000	
Less: Accumulated depletion	250,000	$750,000

The tangible equipment used in extracting the oil may also be depreciated on a units-of-production basis, especially if the useful lives of the equipment can be directly assigned to the given resource deposit. If the equipment is used in more than one job, other cost allocation methods such as the straight-line method or accelerated depreciation methods may be more appropriate.

Status of Oil and Gas Accounting

As indicated, either the successful efforts or the full-cost method is acceptable in accounting for costs in the oil and gas industry. The descriptions provided in the preceding comments were very simplified. The actual application of either method is complex and constitutes a significant amount of detailed study, which is beyond the scope of this book. As there are a multitude of judgmental and definitional factors associated with each method, one major accounting problem concerns the wide range of interpretations that may be employed when applying a method. Consequently, even though a company states it is following one or the other of the methods, assuming comparability of financial statements with other companies using the same method can be misleading.

The problem is overcome, to some extent, because companies using the *successful efforts* method (generally large integrated companies, many of which are foreign owned) follow a fairly common set of accounting policies based on a standard established in the United States.[28] Limiting the diversity of interpretations used in the *full-cost* accounting method was the purpose of a *Guideline* (not a recommendation) issued by the Accounting Standards Board in 1986 and revised in 1990.[29] Additionally, some basic aspects of accounting for oil and gas properties were addressed in Section 3060 of the *CICA Handbook* on capital assets.

Special Problems in Depletion Accounting

Accounting for natural resources has some interesting problems that are uncommon to most other types of assets. For purposes of discussion we have divided these problems into three categories:

[28] "Financial Accounting and Reporting by Oil and Gas Producing Companies," *Statement of the Financial Accounting Standards Board No. 19* (Stamford, CT: FASB).

[29] "Full Cost Accounting in the Oil and Gas Industry," *Accounting Guideline* (Toronto: CICA, 1990).

1. Difficulty of estimating recoverable reserves.
2. Problems of discovery value.
3. Accounting for liquidating dividends.

Estimating Recoverable Reserves. Not infrequently the estimate of recoverable (proven) reserves has to be changed either because new information becomes available or because production processes become more sophisticated. Natural resources such as oil and gas deposits and some rare metals have recently provided the greatest challenges. Estimates of these reserves are, in large measure, "knowledgeable guesses."

This problem is the same as that faced in accounting for changes in estimates of the useful lives of plant and equipment. The procedure is to revise the depletion rate on a prospective basis by dividing the remaining cost by the estimate of the new recoverable reserves. This approach has much merit because the required estimates are so tenuous.

Discovery Value. Discovery value accounting and reserve recognition accounting (RRA) are similar. RRA is specifically related to the oil and gas industry, whereas discovery value is a broader term associated with the whole natural resource area. Essentially, application of these approaches means that, when a company finds a resource, its value would be reported on the balance sheet. In general practice, discovery values are not recognized under generally accepted accounting principles. If discovery value were recorded, an asset account would be debited and an Unrealized Appreciation account would be credited. Unrealized Appreciation would be part of shareholders' equity and would be transferred to revenue (realized income) as the natural resource is sold.

A similar issue arises with resources such as growing timber, aging liquor, and maturing livestock which increase in value over time. One could record the increase in value as the accretion occurs by a debit to an asset account and a credit to an income or to an unrealized income account. These increases can be substantial. For example, the timber resources of a large lumber company were at one time valued at $1.7 billion whereas the book value was approximately $289 million. Accountants have resisted recording these increases because of the uncertainty regarding the final sales price and the problem of estimating the costs involved in getting the resources ready for sale. The trade-offs that exist between the desired qualities of relevancy and reliability of information are particularly evident regarding the possibilities of reporting discovery values.

Liquidating Dividends. A company may own as its only major asset a certain property from which it intends to extract natural resources. If the company does not expect to purchase additional properties, it may distribute gradually to shareholders their capital investment by paying dividends equal to the accumulated amount of net income (after depletion) plus the amount of depletion charged. The major accounting problem is to distinguish between dividends that are a return of capital and those that are not. A company issuing a liquidating dividend should debit the appropriate Share Capital account for that portion related to the original investment instead of Retained Earnings, because the dividend is a return of part of the investor's original contribution. Shareholders must be informed that the total dividend consists of a liquidation of capital as well as a distribution of income.

To illustrate, at December 31, 1994, Callahan Mining has a retained earnings balance of $1,650,000, accumulated depletion on mineral properties of $2,100,000, and common share capital of $5,435,493. Callahan's board declares and pays a dividend of $3.00 a share on the 1,000,000 shares outstanding. The entry to record the $3,000,000 dividend is as follows:

Retained Earnings	1,650,000	
Common Shares	1,350,000	
Cash		3,000,000

The $3.00 dividend per share represents a $1.65 ($1,650,000 ÷ 1,000,000 shares) per share return on investment and a $1.35 ($1,350,000 ÷ 1,000,000) per share liquidating dividend.

FINANCIAL REPORTING OF NATURAL RESOURCES AND DEPLETION

Objective 11

Know how to disclose natural resources and related depletion in financial statements.

Disclosure requirements for natural resources and depletion are of the same nature as for property, plant, equipment, and depreciation as previously discussed.[30] As such, proper classification is necessary along with appropriate disclosure of the cost, accumulated depletion, depletion charged during the reporting period, any write-downs, and method used to determine depletion. Also, guidance for reporting has come from the AcSB's *Guideline* on full-cost accounting and U.S. standards. These latter documents indicate that both publicly traded and privately held companies engaged in significant oil and gas producing activities should disclose (1) the basic method of accounting for costs incurred in these activities (e.g., full-cost or successful efforts) and (2) the manner of determining and disposing of costs relating to these activities (e.g., expensing immediately, or capitalizing followed by depreciation and depletion). Public companies, in addition to these disclosures, may report as supplementary information numerous schedules disclosing such things as reserve quantities; capitalized costs; acquisition, exploration, and development activities and costs; operating results by business segment and geographic area (countries); and present value of future net cash flows from proven oil and gas reserves.

The following excerpt from the 1992 financial statements of Imperial Oil Limited provides an example of disclosures regarding accounting policies applied to its property, plant, and equipment.

Imperial Oil Limited
(from the Summary of Significant Accounting Policies)

Property, Plant and Equipment

Property, plant and equipment, including related preoperational and design costs of major projects, are recorded at cost. Cost for property, plant and equipment of acquired companies is the fair market value to the company at the date of acquisition.

The company follows the successful-efforts method of accounting for its exploration and development activities. Under this method, costs of exploration acreage are capitalized and amortized over the period of exploration or until a discovery is made. Costs of exploration wells are capitalized until their success can be determined. If the well is successful, the costs remain capitalized; otherwise they are expensed. Capitalized exploration costs are reevaluated annually. All other exploration costs are expensed as incurred. Development costs, including the cost of natural gas and natural-gas liquids used as injectants in enhanced (tertiary) oil-recovery projects, are capitalized.

Maintenance and repair costs are expensed as incurred. Improvements that increase or prolong the service life or capacity of an asset are capitalized.

Investment tax credits and other similar grants are treated as a reduction of the capitalized cost of the asset to which they apply.

Depreciation and depletion (the allocation of the cost of assets to expense over the period of their useful lives) are calculated using the unit-of-production method for producing properties. Depreciation of other plant and equipment is calculated using the straight-line method, based on the estimated service life of the asset. In general, refineries are depreciated over 25 years; other major assets, including chemical plants and service stations, are depreciated over 20 years.

Gains or losses on assets sold or otherwise disposed of are included in the consolidated statement of earnings.

[30] *CICA Handbook*, Section 3060 recommendations cover all capital assets of profit-oriented enterprises, except for goodwill (discussed in Chapter 12).

FUNDAMENTAL CONCEPTS

1. Amortization is the generic term used to describe the charge to income which recognizes that the life of a capital asset is finite and that its cost less residual value is to be allocated to the periods of service provided by the asset. Traditionally, amortization of tangible capital assets (other than natural resources) is called depreciation, and for natural resources it is called depletion. In the specific rather than generic use of the word, amortization refers to the allocation of the cost of intangible assets.
2. Depreciation is the result of a cost allocation process to match expenses against revenues systematically and rationally, and it is not intended to result in financial statement amounts that reflect period to period values or value changes in the related assets.
3. Determining the amount of depreciation for a period requires determination of (a) the base amount (amortizable amount) to be depreciated (cost less residual value), (b) the estimated useful life, and (c) the method of cost allocation to be used.
4. Various depreciation methods are generally acceptable. The accountant must exercise appropriate judgement when selecting and implementing the method that is most appropriate for the circumstances. Rational matching, tax reporting, simplicity, and perceived economic consequences are factors that have an impact on such judgements.
5. Special problems are encountered in determining depreciation for partial periods, overcoming the misconception that depreciation accounting results in providing funds for asset replacement, accounting for revisions in estimates that constitute components of the depreciation expense calculation (treat as a prospective adjustment), accounting for an impairment in value (write-down of the carrying or book value), and determining depreciation (capital cost allowance) for income tax purposes.
6. The basis of valuation (usually historical cost) for property, plant, and equipment, major categories of assets, related accumulated depreciation, pledges related to these assets, current period's expense, and the methods and rates used to calculate depreciation, and any write-downs are among the things that should be disclosed in financial statements.
7. Investment tax credits are provided by the government to promote investment in certain assets. The *CICA Handbook* requires use of the cost reduction approach to account for these tax credits.
8. The costs of natural resources consist of expenditures related to acquisition, exploration, and development. The amount of the costs which are capitalized and then allocated to production (rather than expensed directly) depends on whether the successful efforts or full-cost approach is used. Capitalized resource costs are usually charged to depletion using an activity approach (units-of-production method).
9. Particular issues related to accounting for natural resource industries include the difficulty of estimating recoverable reserves, determining discovery value, and appropriately determining and reporting a liquidating dividend.
10. Disclosure in financial statements of natural resource companies would include proper classification, identifying the method used for establishing cost and depletion charges, and possibly additional supplementary information regarding reserve quantities, operating results by geographic area, and acquisition, exploration, and development activity.

APPENDIX 11A

Tax Method of Capital Cost Allowance: Extension of Example to Include Additions, Retirements, and Asset Class Elimination

The chapter provided a basic illustration of the tax method of capital cost allowance determination. While the mechanics of this method were described, several complexities remain. The purpose of this appendix is to illustrate some of these complexities—namely, how to account for additions, retirements, and asset class elimination for purposes of determining taxable income.

Table 11A-1 presents a Capital Cost Allowance Schedule incorporating information to illustrate these complexities. The schedule is a continuation of that shown in Table 11-4 (page 550) dealing with the determination of capital cost allowance for a crane (No. 1) purchased by Cando Co. Ltd. which had a cost of $500,000 and on which capital cost allowance had been taken for three years resulting in undepreciated capital cost of $288,000 at the beginning of year 4 for Class 8 assets. The continuation of this schedule is based on the occurrence of the following transactions:

1. In year 4, the company bought another crane (or any other Class 8 asset) for $700,000.
2. In year 5, the company sold the first crane for $300,000.
3. In year 6, the company sold the second crane for $500,000. This resulted in no assets remaining in Class 8.

Table 11A-1

Capital Cost Allowance Schedule: Continuation of Table 11-4

UCC beginning of year 4	$288,000
Additions during year 4—crane No. 2	700,000
UCC before CCA	$988,000
CCA for year 4 = [(20% × $288,000) + (.5 × 20% × $700,000)]	127,600
UCC beginning of year 5	$860,400
Deduct the lower of the proceeds from ($300,000) or cost of ($500,000) crane No. 1 disposed of during the year	300,000
UCC before CCA	$560,400
CCA for year 5 = (20% × $560,400)	112,080
UCC beginning of year 6	$448,320
Deduct the lower of the proceeds from ($500,000) or cost of ($700,000) crane No. 2 disposed of during the year	500,000
Note: This disposal eliminates all Class 8 assets of the company.	
Recaptured capital cost allowance	$ 51,680

Additions to Asset Class

The purchase of another crane (No. 2) in year 4 resulted in a net addition of $700,000 to the undepreciated capital cost at the end of year 4. Consequently, the balance of undepreciated capital cost at the end of year 4 is made up of this $700,000 plus the $288,000 undepreciated capital cost of crane No. 1. The capital cost allowance for year 4 is, therefore, 20% of $288,000 ($57,600) plus one-half of 20% of the net addition of $700,000 ($70,000) for a total of $127,600.

Retirements from an Asset Class

Continuation of Class. When there is more than one asset in a class from which an asset is disposed of, and when the proceeds from or cost of the asset disposed of (whichever is lower) is less than the undepreciated capital cost balance, then the proceeds or cost (whichever is lower) is deducted from the undepreciated capital cost balance for the class. This is what happened in year 5 when the company sold crane No. 1 for $300,000. Since the proceeds were less than the $500,000 original cost, the $300,000 amount was deducted from the $860,400 undepreciated capital cost balance before determining the capital cost allowance for year 5.

Elimination of Class. When the disposal of an asset results in the elimination of an asset class (either because there are no more assets remaining in the class or because the disposal results in the elimination of the undepreciated capital cost balance of the class), the following may result:

(a) A recapture of capital cost allowance.

(b) A recapture of capital cost allowance and a capital gain.

(c) A terminal loss (only when the last asset in the class is disposed of and a balance still exists in the UCC of that class after deducting proceeds or cost of the disposed asset, whichever is lower).

The amount of proceeds, original cost of the asset, and balance of the undepreciated capital cost for the class must be examined to determine which of these results occur.

A **recapture of capital cost allowance** occurs when the lower of the proceeds from or cost of the asset disposed of is greater than the balance of undepreciated capital cost. The difference represents the amount of recaptured capital cost. This recapture would be included in calculating taxable income and is subject to income tax at the normal rates. The events of year 6 reflected in Table 11A-1 illustrate this situation. Since the $500,000 proceeds are lower than the cost of crane No. 2, they are deducted from the $448,320 balance of undepreciated capital cost resulting in the $51,680 recaptured capital cost allowance.

If an asset of a class is sold for more than its cost, a **capital gain** results, regardless of whether or not the asset class is eliminated. For tax purposes, a capital gain (difference between proceeds and cost when proceeds exceed cost) is treated differently from a recapture of capital cost. Essentially, the taxable capital gain (amount subject to tax) is a specified portion of the capital gain as defined above (generally three-quarters in 1994). The taxable capital gain is then included with other taxable income and is taxed at the normal rates. As indicated previously, the full amount of the recaptured capital cost allowance is included in taxable income and is subject to the normal tax rate applicable to the taxable income being reported. If crane No. 1 had been sold in year 5 for $575,000 the capital gain would be $75,000, and the taxable capital gain would be $56,250. The amount of $500,000 would have been deducted from the UCC. If crane No. 2 had been sold for $750,000 in year 6, a capital gain and a recapture of capital cost allowance would result. The capital gain would be $50,000 and, therefore, a taxable capital gain of $37,500 would occur. The recaptured capital cost allowance would be $251,680 (the $700,000 cost less the $448,320 undepreciated capital cost balance for the asset class being eliminated).

While this example illustrates the basic calculations related to the determination of capital gains, taxable capital gains, and recaptured capital cost allowance, it has necessarily been oversimplified. In essence, the tax rate on taxable capital gains is specified by tax law, which may change from time to time and have implications in terms of other considerations (e.g., refundable dividend tax on hand). Similarly, the tax rate applicable to recaptured capital cost allowance is subject to the particular circumstances of the nature of taxable income being reported (of which the recaptured amount is a component). For example, the recapture will be "active" income provided the business is "active" and, thus, may be subject to a reduced tax rate on the first $200,000 of active income earned. These and other technical and definitional aspects are beyond the scope of this text. The reader is warned that determining income taxes payable requires specialist knowledge regarding tax laws.

A **terminal loss** occurs when the proceeds from the disposal of the last asset in a class are less than the undepreciated capital cost balance. A terminal loss is deducted in full when determining taxable income. If crane No. 2 had been sold in year 6 for $300,000, a terminal loss of $148,320 would result (the $448,320 undepreciated capital cost less the $300,000 proceeds).

Note: All **asterisked** questions, cases, exercises, and problems relate to material contained in the appendix to the chapter.

QUESTIONS

1. Define amortization as the word is used generically in accounting. Distinguish between depreciation, depletion, and amortization (in the specific sense).

2. What is accounting for depreciation, and what is its objective? Are the decreasing charge methods of depreciation consistent with this objective? Discuss.

3. Identify the factors that are relevant in determining the annual depreciation charge and explain whether these factors are determined objectively or whether they are based on judgement.

4. Recently, a governor of a university noted that "depreciation of assets for any university or college is nonsensical. We're not public companies. Forcing such institutions to depreciate would only boost our bookkeeping costs for no good reason." Do you agree? Discuss.

5. The plant manager of a manufacturing firm suggested that accountants should speed up depreciation on the machinery in the finishing department because improvements were rapidly making those machines obsolete and a depreciation fund big enough to cover their replacement is needed. Discuss the accounting concept of depreciation and the effect on a business concern of the depreciation recorded for plant assets, paying particular attention to the issues raised by the plant manager.

6. For what reasons are plant assets retired? Define inadequacy, supersession, and obsolescence.

7. Atrium Inc. purchased machinery for $120,000 on January 4, 1994. It is estimated that the machinery will have a useful life of 20 years, residual value of $20,000, production of 84,000 units, and working hours of 42,000. During 1994 the company uses the machinery for 14,600 hours, and the machinery produces 22,000 units. Compute depreciation expense for 1994 under the straight-line, units-of-output, working-hours, sum-of-the-years'-digits, and double-declining balance methods.

8. What are the major factors to consider when determining the depreciation method to use?

9. Under what conditions is it appropriate for a business to use the composite method of depreciation for its assets? What are the advantages and disadvantages of this method?

10. If a company uses the composite method and its composite rate is 7.5% per year, what entry should it make when assets that originally cost $50,000 and have been used for 10 years are sold for $13,000?

11. Under what conditions is it appropriate for a concern to use the retirement method of depreciation for assets? What is the major advantage and disadvantage of this method?

12. If a business that uses the retirement method sells for $17,000 assets that cost $36,000 five years ago, what entry should be made? The assets sold consist of 500 small motors, which usually last about seven years.

13. A building that was purchased December 31, 1969 for $1,500,000 was originally estimated to have a life of 50 years with no residual value at the end of that time. Depreciation has been recorded through 1993. During 1994 an examination of the building by an engineering firm discloses that its remaining estimated useful life is 15 years including 1994. What should be the amount of depreciation for 1994?

14. Marilyn Mueller purchases a computer for $5,000 on July 1, 1994. She intends to depreciate it over four years using the double-declining balance method. Residual value is $1,000. Compute depreciation for 1995, given the year end is December 31.

15. It has been suggested that plant and equipment could be replaced more quickly if depreciation rates for income tax and accounting purposes were substantially increased. As a result, business operations would receive the benefit of more modern and more efficient plant facilities. Discuss the merits of this proposition.

16. The net recoverable amount of certain equipment is determined to be less than its net carrying (book) value. Explain how this impairment in value should be recorded and reported.

17. List (a) the similarities and (b) the differences in the accounting for depreciation and depletion.

18. In the extractive industries, businesses may pay dividends in excess of net income. What is the maximum permissible? How can this practice be justified?

19. The following statement appeared in a financial magazine: "RRA—or Rah-Rah, as it's sometimes dubbed—is subject to controversy. Oil companies, for example, are convinced that the approach is misleading. Major accounting firms agree." What is RRA? Why might oil companies and accountants believe that this approach is misleading?

20. Pride Oil uses successful efforts accounting and provides full-cost results as well. Under successful efforts, retained earnings were $29 million and net income was $4 million. Under full cost, Pride Oil would have reported retained earnings of $42 million and net income of $4 million. Explain the difference between successful efforts and full-cost accounting.

*21. A capital gain may occur whenever an asset is disposed of, whereas a terminal loss may occur only when an asset class is eliminated. Explain why this is so.

CASES

C11-1 **(DEPRECIATION: STRIKE, UNITS-OF-PRODUCTION, OBSOLESCENCE)** Presented below are three different and unrelated situations involving depreciation accounting. Answer the question(s) at the end of each situation.

Situation I. Mixit Inc. manufactures electrical appliances, most of which are used in homes. Company engineers have designed a new type of blender which, through the use of a few attachments, will perform more functions than any blender currently on the market. Demand for the new blender can be projected with reasonable probability. In order to make the blenders, Mixit needs a specialized machine that is not available from outside sources. It has been decided to make such a machine in Mixit's own plant.

Instructions

(a) Discuss the effect of projected demand in units for the new blenders (which may be steady, decreasing, or increasing) on the determination of a depreciation method for the machine.

(b) What other matters should be considered in determining the depreciation method? Ignore income tax considerations.

Situation II. Douglas Paper Co. Ltd., a subsidiary of Forrester Inc., operates a 300-tonne-per-day pulp mill and four sawmills in British Columbia. The company is in the process of expanding its pulp mill facilities to a capacity of 1,000 tonnes per day and plans to replace three of its older, less efficient sawmills with an expanded facility. One of the mills to bereplaced did not operate for most of 1994 (current year), and there are no plans to reopen it before the new sawmill facility becomes operational.

In reviewing the depreciation rates and in discussing the residual values of the sawmills that were to be replaced, it was noted that if present depreciation rates were not adjusted, substantial amounts of plant costs on these three mills would not be depreciated by the time the new mill came on stream.

Instructions

What is the appropriate accounting for the four sawmills at the end of 1994?

Situation III. Recently, Hansen Ltd. experienced a strike that affected a number of its operating plants. The president of the company suggested that it was not appropriate to report depreciation expense during this period because the equipment did not depreciate and an improper matching of costs and revenues would result. He based his position on the following points:

1. It is inappropriate to charge the period with costs for which there are no related revenues arising from production.

2. The basic factor of depreciation in this instance is wear and tear; and because equipment was idle, no wear and tear occurred.

Instructions

Comment on the appropriateness of the president's comments.

C11-2 **(DEPRECIATION: CHANGE IN USE)** In 1992, a large corporation decided to construct a large new processing building at one of its mine sites. A smaller building capable of handling one-third of the capacity of the new building had been used for several years. The new building was completed and ready for operation in the spring of 1994. Much of the equipment used in the processing activities of the old building was transferred to the new one.

At the time the new building began operations, the old building had a book value of $500,000. The auditors assessed the circumstances for this major client and indicated that they thought this amount should be written off as a loss in 1994. Management of the corporation protested this accounting treatment. Their argument against such a write-off was that the old building had not been torn down and was still capable of handling processing activities should the need arise. Indeed, they had left the building standing in order to protect against the possibility that things might go wrong with the new building or that the new building's capacity might be insufficient to handle all processing at some time in the future. When the decision to construct the new building was made, management had attempted to forecast product demand and allowed an additional 20% capacity to the new building but they recognized that, in such a business, forecasts could be off considerably. Indeed, in 1994, demand for the processed ore had fallen to two-thirds of that which had been expected, leaving the new processing building operating at considerably below its capacity. These circumstances led the auditors to conclude that the old building, while capable of being used in operations, was not likely to be used in the foreseeable future.

Instructions

Analyse this situation and make recommendations regarding the accounting for the old building in 1994.

C11-3 **(UNIT VERSUS GROUP OR COMPOSITE DEPRECIATION)** The independent public accountant is frequently called upon by management for advice regarding methods of computing depreciation. Of comparable importance, although it arises less frequently, is the question of whether depreciation should be based on consideration of an asset as a unit or as part of a group of assets.

Instructions

(a) Briefly describe the accounting for depreciation based on approaches to treating assets as (1) units and (2) a group.

(b) Present the arguments for and against each of the two approaches.

(c) Describe how retirements are recorded under each of the two approaches.

(AICPA adapted)

C11-4 **(DEPRECIATION: BASIC CONCEPTS)** Lendsay Manufacturing Co. Ltd. was organized January 1, 1994. During 1994, the straight-line method of depreciating plant assets has been used in preparing reports for management.

On November 8, 1994 you are having a conference with Lendsay's officers to discuss the depreciation method to be used for financial statement reporting. The president has suggested the use of a new method, which he feels is more suitable than the straight-line method for the needs of the company during the period of rapid expansion of production and capacity that he foresees. Following is an example in which the proposed method is applied to a fixed asset with an original cost of $248,000, an estimated useful life of five years, and a residual value of $8,000.

Year	Years of Life Used	Fraction Rate	Depreciation Expense	Accumulated Depreciation at End of Year	Book Value at End of Year
1	1	1/15	$16,000	$ 16,000	$232,000
2	2	2/15	32,000	48,000	200,000
3	3	3/15	48,000	96,000	152,000
4	4	4/15	64,000	160,000	88,000
5	5	5/15	80,000	240,000	8,000

The president favours the new method because he has heard that:

1. It will increase the funds recovered during the years near the end of the assets' useful lives when maintenance and replacement disbursements are high.

2. It will result in increased depreciation charges in later years when the company is likely to be in a better operating position.

Instructions

(a) What is the purpose of accounting for depreciation?

(b) Is the president's proposal within the scope of generally accepted accounting principles? In making your decision discuss the circumstances, if any, under which use of the method would be reasonable and those, if any, under which it would not be reasonable.

(c) Do depreciation charges recover or create funds? Explain.

(DEPRECIATION: COMPUTER SOFTWARE) Various companies are in the business of developing and marketing computer software packages (e.g., word processing, spreadsheets, business graphics, accounting packages). Several important accounting issues exist regarding how to classify, measure, and report the costs related to such operations. Specifically, issues include where the line should be drawn between expensing and capitalizing costs, whether or not the costs expensed should be shown as research and development costs or not, how capitalized costs should be amortized, and how the various items should be disclosed in the financial statements. **C11-5**

Generally, computer software costs may be categorized into four types as follows (categories basically follow the stages of incurrence, although these stages can be overlapping):

1. Idea formulation and feasibility: these include costs of study and documentation related to market feasibility (potential market, duration of market, expected selling price, etc.), financial feasibility (determining if future revenues will exceed future costs), and assessing managements' commitment and ability (the company must have or be able to obtain the necessary resources and commitment).

2. Determining technological feasibility and design of the product: these costs relate to the detailed product design, and coding and testing that are required to determine that the product can be produced to meet design specifications. Completion of this stage occurs when the product is sufficiently defined so that the costs of production can be reliably estimated.

3. Preparation for production: presuming that the previous stages have been successful in terms of developing a product that has technological market and financial feasibility as well as commitment and ability to produce, the next step would be preparing for mass production and distribution. Cost at this level relates to producing product masters and related coding and testing as well as completion of documentation and training materials for the customer.

4. Production of software packages: the costs incurred at this stage are for duplicating the software, documentation, and training materials as well as packaging the product for customers.

Instructions

(a) Throughout this process there are various ways to account for the costs incurred: Treat as an operating expense of the period, treat as research and development costs, capitalize to a fixed asset account and amortize on a systematic and rational basis, or capitalize to an inventory account and charge to cost of sales when realization takes place. Analyse each of the four categories, considering they are part of a total process related to the ongoing operations of a company and reach conclusions as to how the costs should be accounted for. Also, for any costs you believe should be capitalized, indicate how they should be amortized, depreciated, or otherwise charged to expense.

(b) Because of the rapid technological and product changes related to the software industry, it is proposed by some that an "ongoing recoverability test" be carried out regarding any costs which have been capitalized. What would be the accounting purpose of such tests and what type of things do you think such tests would investigate?

EXERCISES

(DEPRECIATION: CONCEPTUAL UNDERSTANDING) Schuler Ltd. acquired a plant asset at the beginning of Year 1. The asset has an estimated service life of five years. An employee has correctly prepared the following depreciation schedules for this asset using (1) the straight-line method and (2) the double-declining balance method. **E11-1**

Year	Straight-Line	Double-Declining Balance
1	$ 6,000	$13,200
2	6,000	7,920
3	6,000	4,752
4	6,000	2,851
5	6,000	1,277
Total	$30,000	$30,000

Instructions

Answer the following questions:

(a) What is the cost of the asset being depreciated?

(b) What amount, if any, was used in the depreciation calculations for the residual value for this asset?

(c) Which method will produce the lowest net income in Year 1?

(d) Which method will produce the highest charge to income in Year 4?

(e) Which method will produce the highest book value for the asset at the end of Year 3?

(f) If the asset is sold at the end of Year 3, which method would yield the highest gain (or lowest loss) on disposal of the asset?

E11-2 **(DEPRECIATION COMPUTATIONS: SIX METHODS, PARTIAL PERIOD)** Monroe Co. Ltd. purchased machinery for $240,000 on May 1, 1994. It is estimated to have a useful life of 10 years, residual value of $15,000, production of 240,000 units, and working hours of 25,000. During 1995 Monroe Co. Ltd. uses the machinery for 2,650 hours, and the machinery produces 26,000 units.

Instructions

Given depreciation or CCA has been correctly recognized for the year ended December 31, 1994, compute the depreciation charge for the year ended December 31, 1995 under each of the following methods (round to nearest cent):

(a) Straight-line.

(b) Units-of-output.

(c) Working hours.

(d) Sum-of-the-years'-digits.

(e) Declining-balance (use 20% as the annual rate).

(f) Capital cost allowance (tax method) assuming a CCA rate of 20%.

E11-3 **(DEPRECIATION COMPUTATIONS: FIVE METHODS, PARTIAL PERIODS)** Wester Inc. purchased equipment for $228,000 on April 1, 1994. It was estimated that the equipment would have a useful life of eight years and a residual value of $12,000. Estimated production was 40,000 units and estimated working hours were 20,000. During 1994 the company used the equipment for 1,400 hours and the equipment produced 2,500 units.

Instructions

Compute depreciation expense under each of the following methods. Wester Inc. is on a calendar-year basis ending December 31.

(a) Straight-line method for 1994.

(b) Activity method (units-of-output) for 1994.

(c) Activity method (working hours) for 1994.

(d) Double-declining balance method for 1995.

(e) What is the capital cost allowance for 1994 and 1995 assuming a CCA rate of 30% and that the equipment was the only item in the asset class?

(DEPRECIATION COMPUTATIONS: FIVE METHODS, PARTIAL PERIODS) Corky Co. Ltd. purchased a new machine for its assembly process on October 1, 1994. The cost of this machine was $150,000. The company estimated that the machine would have a residual value of $24,000. Its useful life was estimated at five years and its working hours were estimated at 21,000 hours. Year end is December 31. **E11-4**

Instructions

Compute the depreciation expense under the following methods: (1) straight-line depreciation for 1994, (2) activity method for 1994 assuming that machine usage was 800 hours, (3) sum-of-the-years'-digits for 1995, (4) double-declining balance for 1995, and (5) capital cost allowance for 1994 and 1995 using a CCA rate of 25%.

(DEPRECIATION COMPUTATION: REPLACEMENT, NONMONETARY EXCHANGE) Burke Inc. bought a machine on June 1, 1991 for $42,000, f.o.b. the place of manufacture. Freight costs were $300, and $500 was expended to install it. The machine's useful life was estimated at 10 years, with a residual value of $2,500. In June 1992 an essential part of the machine was replaced, at a cost of $2,430, with one designed to reduce the cost of operating the machine. **E11-5**

On June 1, 1995 the company bought a new machine of greater capacity for $39,000, delivered, being allowed a trade-in value (assume equals fair market value) on the old machine of $24,000. Removing the old machine from the plant cost $125 and installing the new one cost $1,200. It was estimated that the new machine would have a useful life of 10 years, with a residual value of $3,000 at the end of that time.

Instructions

Assuming that depreciation is to be computed on the straight-line basis, determine the amount of gain or loss on the disposal of the first machine on June 1, 1995 and the amount of depreciation that should be provided during the company's fiscal year which begins on June 1, 1995.

(RETIREMENT AND REPLACEMENT METHODS) The following transactions and events occurred during Hadley Power Corporation's initial year of operations regarding meters which it owns and installs in houses. The life of a meter varies from 1 to 15 years, with the average being about 11 years. **E11-6**

Jan. 10 Purchases 13,000 meters at $150 each.

Apr. 15 Discards 40 of the meters purchased January 10, 1994 as worthless.

June 20 Sells 80 of the meters purchased January 10, 1994 for $2,000.

Dec. 12 Replaces 1,200 meters at $160 each.

Instructions

Prepare entries to record these transactions using (a) the retirement method and (b) the replacement method.

E11-7 (COMPOSITE DEPRECIATION) Presented below is information related to Simpson Ltd.

Asset	Cost	Estimated Residual	Estimated Life (in years)
A	$40,500	$6,500	10
B	40,260	5,700	9
C	36,000	3,600	8
D	19,000	2,200	7
E	23,500	3,100	6

Instructions

(a) Compute the rate of depreciation per year to be applied to the cost of the assets under the composite method.

(b) Prepare the adjusting entry necessary at the end of the year to record depreciation for a year.

(c) Prepare the entry to record the sale of fixed asset D for cash of $5,200. It was used for six years, and depreciation was entered under the composite method.

E11-8 (DEPRECIATING SMALL TOOLS) Carter Manufacturing Ltd. has approximately 3,000 hand tools, which it uses in its operations. Each is of relatively small value and is frequently replaced. The total cost of such tools is approximately $27,000.

Because of the characteristics of this asset, the company prefers not to keep detailed records of each tool and depreciate it. You are asked to suggest some reasonably simple method of accounting for these tools so that the asset is carried at a fair amount and operating expenses are charged with a fair amount. What do you suggest?

Instructions

Describe and illustrate your suggested method with pro forma entries for the various types of transactions that might occur.

E11-9 (DEPRECIATION: CHANGE IN ESTIMATE) Machinery purchased in 1989 for $60,000 was originally estimated to have a life of eight years with a residual value of $4,000 at the end of that time. Depreciation has been entered for five years on this basis. In 1994, it is determined that the total estimated life (including 1994) should have been 10 years with a residual value of $3,000 at the end of that time. Assume straight-line depreciation.

Instructions

(a) Prepare the entry required to correct the prior years' depreciation.

(b) Prepare the entry to record depreciation for 1994.

E11-10 (DEPRECIATION: REPLACEMENT, CHANGE IN ESTIMATE) Canseco Ltd. constructed a building at a cost of $2,800,000 and has occupied it since January 1974. It was estimated at that time that its life would be 40 years, with no residual value.

In January 1994, a new roof was installed at a cost of $400,000, and it was estimated then that the building would have a useful life of 25 years from that date. The cost of the old roof was $200,000.

Instructions

(a) What amount of depreciation should have been charged annually from the years 1974 through 1993? (Assume straight-line depreciation.)

(b) What entry should be made in 1994 to record the replacement of the roof?

(c) Prepare the entry in January 1994 to record the revision in the estimated life of the building, if necessary.

(d) What amount of depreciation should be charged for the year 1994?

E11-11 (DEPRECIATION COMPUTATION: ADDITION, CHANGE IN ESTIMATE) In 1966, Winston Inc. completed the construction of a building at a cost of $2,100,000 and first occupied it in January 1967. It was estimated that the building would have a useful life of 40 years, and a residual value of $100,000 at the end of that time.

Early in 1977, an addition to the building was constructed at a cost of $595,000. At that time it was reaffirmed that the remaining life of the building would be as originally estimated, and that the addition would have a life of 30 years and a residual value of $25,000.

In 1995 it is determined that the probable life of the building will extend to the end of 2026, or 20 years beyond the original estimate.

The straight-line method is used.

Instructions

(a) Compute the annual depreciation that would have been charged from 1967 through 1976.

(b) Compute the annual depreciation that would have been charged from 1977 to 1994.

(c) Prepare the entry to adjust the account balances because of the revision of the estimated life in 1995.

(d) Compute the annual depreciation to be charged beginning with 1995.

E11-12 (ERROR ANALYSIS AND DEPRECIATION COMPUTATIONS) Carter Ltd. shows the following entries in its Equipment account for 1994; all amounts are based on historical cost.

Equipment

Jan. 1	Balance	136,750	June 30	Cost of equipment sold (purchased prior to 1994)	24,000
Aug. 10	Purchases	33,850			
12	Freight on equipment purchased	900			
25	Installation costs	2,500			
Nov. 10	Repairs	500			

Instructions

(a) Prepare any correcting entries necessary.

(b) Assuming that depreciation is to be charged for a full year on the ending balance in the asset account, compute the depreciation charge for 1994 under each of the methods listed below. Assume an estimated life of 10 years, with no residual value. The machinery included in the January 1, 1994 balance was purchased in 1992.

1. Straight-line.

2. Sum-of-the-years'-digits.

3. Declining balance (assume twice the straight-line rate).

E11-13 (DEPRECIATION FOR PARTIAL PERIODS) On April 10, 1994, Schuettler Inc. sold equipment that it purchased for $203,960 on August 20, 1987. It was originally estimated that the equipment would have a life of 12 years and a residual value of $20,000 at the end of that time, and depreciation has been computed on that basis. The company uses the straight-line method of depreciation.

Instructions

(a) Compute the depreciation charge on this equipment for 1987, for 1994, and the total charge for the period from 1987 to 1994, inclusive, under each of the following six assumptions with respect to partial periods:

1. Depreciation is computed for the exact period of time during which the asset is owned (use 365 days for base).
2. Depreciation is computed for the full year on the January 1 balance in the asset account.
3. Depreciation is computed for the full year on the December 31 balance in the asset account.
4. Depreciation for one-half year is charged on plant assets acquired or disposed of during the year.
5. Depreciation is computed on additions from the beginning of the month following acquisition and on disposals to the beginning of the month following disposal.
6. Depreciation is computed for a full period on all assets in use for over one-half year, and no depreciation is charged on assets in use for less than one-half year.

(b) Briefly evaluate the methods above, considering them from the point of view of basic accounting theory as well as simplicity of application.

E11-14 (IMPAIRMENT OF VALUE AND CHANGE IN ESTIMATE) The management of Wheeler Inc. was discussing whether certain equipment should be written down as a charge to current operations because of obsolescence. The assets in question had a cost of $900,000 with depreciation taken to date of $400,000. Management determined that the net recoverable amount for these assets was only $200,000 and that this amount should be appropriately recorded in the accounts. Further, the asset's remaining useful life was reduced from eight to five years. It is now estimated that the equipment has a residual value of $25,000.

Instructions

(a) Prepare the journal entry to record the write-down of the equipment.

(b) If no future use is expected of the asset, prepare the journal entry to record the write-down of the equipment to its net realizable value of $25,000.

(c) Where should the loss on the write-down be reported in the income statement?

(d) What accounting issues did management face in accounting for this write-down?

E11-15 (INVESTMENT TAX CREDIT: COST REDUCTION METHOD, ALTERNATIVE APPROACHES) Ebert Inc. purchased machinery and equipment in January 1994 amounting to $196,000. All of these acquisitions qualified for a 10% investment tax credit. The productive life of the acquired equipment was estimated to be seven years. The company's income before depreciation and taxes was $480,000 (tax rate 45%). Assume depreciation is based on the straight-line method and the "depreciation" to calculate taxable income is based on the straight-line method applied to the equipment cost net of the investment tax credit.

Instructions

(a) Prepare the entry(ies) required at December 31, 1994 to account for the income tax expense, investment credit, and depreciation, assuming that the investment tax credit is treated as a reduction of the assets' cost.

(b) Prepare the entry(ies) required at December 31, 1994 to account for the income tax expense, investment credit, and depreciation, assuming that investment tax credit is deferred and amortized.

(c) Does the net income under these two approaches of applying the cost reduction method differ for 1994? Show calculations.

(INVESTMENT TAX CREDIT: COST REDUCTION METHOD, ALTERNATIVE APPROACHES) **E11-16** Farthing Inc. bought a number of machines at a total cost of $100,000 on January 10, 1994. All of them qualified for a 10% investment tax credit. Farthing Inc. had income before depreciation and taxes of $540,000 (tax rate 35%) and depreciates the machines over a six-year period using the straight-line method. Also, assume that "depreciation" for tax purposes is for a six-year period using straight-line amounts based on the machines' cost less the investment credit.

Instructions

(a) Prepare the entry(ies) for 1994 to account for the machine purchase, income taxes, the investment tax credit, and depreciation. Assume that the investment tax credit is treated as a reduction of the asset's cost under the cost reduction method.

(b) Assuming that the investment tax credit is deferred and amortized under the cost reduction method, what would the entries asked for in (a) be?

(INVESTMENT TAX CREDIT, COST REDUCTION METHOD: ERROR ANALYSIS AND CORRECTION) **E11-17** You are the assistant controller for Horseshoe Enterprises Inc. On January 1, 1994, Horseshoe purchased heavy machinery with an estimated service life of 20 years. The machinery cost $450,000. This machinery qualified for a 10% investment tax credit. The bookkeeper stated that, to follow the *CICA Handbook* recommendations, the cost reduction method would be used for handling this transaction. Accordingly, the following entry was made:

Machinery	405,000	
Reserve for Investment Credit	45,000	
Accounts Payable		450,000

Income tax expense for the year before any allowable credits was correctly determined to be $116,000. The controller therefore made the following entry on December 31, 1994:

Dec. 31	Income Tax Expense	71,000	
	Deferred Investment Tax Credit	45,000	
	Income Taxes Payable		71,000
	Reserve for Investment Credit		45,000

The bookkeeper, however, is unsure of the entries above and asks your opinion.

Instructions

If you believe that the cost reduction method has not been applied correctly, prepare the entry(ies) that will correct the books and bring them into proper balance for 1994. (Ignore any depreciation considerations and assume the application of the cost reduction method is to be applied by treating the tax credit as a reduction of the asset's cost).

(DEPLETION COMPUTATIONS: MINING) Goldcap Mining Inc. purchased land on February 1, 1994 **E11-18** at a cost of $1,270,000. It estimated that a total of 60,000 tonnes of mineral was available for mining. After it has removed all the natural resources, the company will be required to restore the property to its previous state because of strict environmental protection laws. It estimates the cost of this restoration at $90,000. It believes it will be able to sell the property afterwards for $120,000. It incurred developmental costs of $160,000 before it was able to do any mining. In 1994, resources removed totalled 30,000 tonnes, of which 22,000 tonnes were sold.

Instructions

Compute the following information for 1994: (1) per unit material cost; (2) total material cost of 12/31/94 inventory; and (3) total material cost in cost of goods sold for 1994.

E11-19 **(DEPLETION COMPUTATIONS: TIMBER)** National Lumber Ltd. owns a 7,000-hectare tract of timber purchased in 1987 at a cost of $1,600 per hectare. At the time of purchase the land was estimated to have a value of $400 per hectare without the timber. National Lumber Ltd. has not logged this tract since it was purchased. In 1994, National had the timber cruised. The cruise (appraiser) estimated that each hectare contained 8,000 cubic metres of timber. In 1994, National built 20 kilometres of roads at a cost of $4,500 per kilometre. After the roads were completed, National logged 3,500 trees containing 850,000 cubic metres.

Instructions

(a) Determine the depletion expense for 1994.

(b) If National depreciates the logging roads on the basis of timber cut, determine the depreciation for 1994.

(c) If National plants five seedlings at a cost of $5 per seedling for each tree cut, how should National account for this reforestation?

E11-20 **(ETHICAL ISSUE: DEPRECIATION—CHANGE IN ESTIMATE)** Brewster Manufacturing Inc. faces a decline in sales of their principal product, an automatic sprinkler system for highrise buildings. The financial vice-president, John MacDonald, suggests lengthening asset lives to reduce depreciation expense. Machinery purchased for $860,000 in January 1991 was originally estimated to have a life of 9 years with a residual value of $50,000 at the end of the period. Depreciation has been recorded for 3 years on this basis. MacDonald wants to change the estimated life of the machinery to 12 years (assume straight-line depreciation). The controller, Anne Jablonski, disagrees with MacDonald and says it would be unethical to increase net income in this manner.

Instructions

(a) Is the change in asset lives unethical, or simply a good business practice by a far-sighted vice-president?

(b) Assume that the change in asset lives is made according to MacDonald's suggestion. Prepare the entry to record depreciation for 1994, assuming no change in residual value.

***E11-21** **(CAPITAL COST ALLOWANCE, RETIREMENTS)** During 1994, Spartan Co. Ltd. sold its only Class 3 asset. At the time of sale, the balance of the undepreciated capital cost for this class was $48,000. The asset had originally cost $162,000. Indicate what the resulting amounts would be for any recaptured capital cost, capital gain, and terminal loss assuming that the asset was sold for: (a) $28,000; (b) $75,000; (c) $180,000.

PROBLEMS

P11-1 **(DEPRECIATION FOR PARTIAL PERIODS: VARIOUS METHODS AND CCA)** The cost of equipment purchased by Skarpinsky Inc. on April 1, 1993 was $70,000. It was estimated that the machine would have a $6,000 residual value at the end of its service life. Its service life was estimated at seven years; its total working hours were estimated at 40,000 and its total production was estimated at 500,000 units. During 1993, the machine was used for 6,000 hours and produced 55,000 units. During 1994, the machine was used for 5,500 hours and produced 48,000 units. (Round per hour and unit costs to three decimal places.)

Instructions

Compute depreciation expense on the machine for the year ending December 31, 1993 and the year ending December 31, 1994 using the following methods: (1) straight-line; (2) units-of-output; (3) working hours; (4) sum-of-the-years'-digits; and (5) declining balance (twice the straight-line rate). Also compute the capital cost allowance for 1993 and 1994 assuming a CCA rate of 30%.

(ACQUISITION COST, DEPRECIATION, PARTIAL PERIODS) Oheto Inc. purchased Machine #201 on May 1, 1993. The following information regarding this machine was gathered at the end of May: **P11-2**

Price	$78,500
Credit terms	2/10, n/30
Freight-in costs	$ 1,130
Preparation and installation costs	$ 1,940
Labour costs during regular production operations	$10,500

It was expected that the machine could be used for 10 years, after which the residual value would be zero. Oheto Inc. intended to use the machine for only eight years, however, after which it expected to sell it for $4,400. The invoice for Machine #201 was paid May 5, 1993. Oheto prepares financial statements on a calendar year basis.

Instructions

(a) Compute the depreciation expense for the years indicated using the following methods. (Round to the nearest cent.)

1. Straight-line method for 1993 and 1994.

2. Double-declining balance method for 1993 and 1994.

(b) Calculate the capital cost allowance for 1993 and 1994 assuming a CCA rate of 25%.

(c) Suppose the president of Oheto Inc. tells you that because the company is a new organization, she expects it will be several years before production and sales are at optimum levels. She asks you to recommend a depreciation method that will allocate less of the company's depreciation expense to the early years and more to later years of the assets' lives. What method would you recommend?

(DEPRECIATION: PARTIAL PERIODS, MACHINERY) Kirby Tools Inc. records depreciation annually at the end of the year. Its policy is to take a full year's depreciation on all assets used throughout the year and depreciation for half a year on all machines acquired or disposed of during the year. The depreciation rate for the machinery is 10% applied on a straight-line basis, with no estimated residual value. **P11-3**

The balance of the Machinery account at the beginning of 1994 was $172,300; the Accumulated Depreciation on Machinery account had a balance of $72,900. The following transactions affecting the machinery accounts took place during 1994:

Jan. 15 Machine No. 38, which cost $9,600 when acquired June 3, 1987, was retired and sold as scrap metal for $600.

Feb. 27 Machine No. 81 was purchased. The fair market value of this machine was $12,500. It replaced Machines No. 12 and No. 27, which were traded in on the new machine. Machine No. 12 was acquired Feb. 4, 1982 at a cost of $5,500 and was still carried in the accounts although fully depreciated and not in use; Machine No. 27 was acquired June 11, 1987 at a cost of $8,200. In addition to these two used machines, $9,200 was paid in cash.

Apr. 7 Machine No. 54 was equipped with electric control equipment at a cost of $940. This machine, originally equipped with simple hand controls, was purchased Dec. 11, 1990 for $1,800. The new electric controls can be attached to any one of several machines in the shop.

12 Machine No. 24 was repaired at a cost of $700 after a fire caused by a short circuit in the wiring burned out the motor and damaged certain essential parts.

July 22 Machines No. 25, 26, and 41 are sold for $2,900 cash. The purchase dates and cost of these machines are:

No. 25	$4,000	May 8, 1986
No. 26	3,200	May 8, 1986
No. 41	2,800	June 1, 1988

Nov. 17 Rearrangement and reinstallation of several machines to facilitate material handling and to speed up production are completed at a cost of $13,000.

Instructions

(a) Record each transaction in general journal entry form.

(b) Compute and record depreciation for the year. No machines now included in the balance of the account were acquired before January 1, 1985.

P11-4 (DEPRECIATION COMPUTATIONS, NET OF INVESTMENT TAX CREDIT AS BASE) On January 1, 1992, Hadyn Ltd., a small machine-tool manufacturer, acquired new industrial equipment for $1,100,000. This new equipment was eligible for a 2% investment tax credit. Hadyn took full advantage of the credit and accounted for the amount using the cost reduction method by treating the investment tax credit as a reduction in the equipment's cost. The new equipment had a useful life of five years and the residual value was estimated to be $125,000. Hadyn estimated that the new equipment could produce 12,000 machine tools in its first year. It estimated that production would decline by 1,000 units per year over the remaining useful life of the equipment.

The following depreciation methods may be used: double-declining balance, straight-line, or units-of-output.

Instructions

Which depreciation method would maximize net income for financial statement reporting for the three-year period ending December 31, 1994? Prepare a schedule showing the amount of accumulated depreciation at December 31, 1994 under the method selected.

(AICPA adapted)

P11-5 (DEPRECIATION: PARTIAL PERIODS, ERROR ANALYSIS) The following data relate to the Plant Asset account of Craven Co. Ltd. at December 31, 1993.

	Plant Asset			
	A	B	C	D
Original cost	$36,000	$54,000	$84,000	$78,000
Year purchased	1988	1989	1990	1992
Useful life	10 years	15,000 hours	15 years	10 years
Residual value	$ 3,000	$ 3,000	$ 4,500	$ 5,000
depreciation method	Sum-of-the-years'-digits	Activity	Straight-line	Double-declining balance
Accumulated depreciation through 1993[a]	$24,000	$35,200	$15,900	$15,600

[a]In the year an asset is purchased, Craven Co. Ltd. does not record any depreciation expense on the asset. In the year an asset is retired or traded in, the company takes a full year's depreciation on the asset.

The following transactions occurred during 1994:

(a) On May 5, Asset A was sold for $12,000 cash. The company's bookkeeper recorded this retirement in the following manner:

Cash	12,000	
Asset A		12,000

(b) On December 31, it was determined that Asset B had been used 2,000 hours during 1994.

(c) On December 31, before computing depreciation expense on Asset C, management decided the useful life remaining from 1/1/94 was 10 years.

(d) On December 31, it was discovered that a plant asset purchased in 1993 had been expensed completely in that year. This asset cost $35,000 and has a useful life of 10 years and no residual value. Management decided to use the double-declining balance method for this asset, referred to as "Asset E."

Instructions

Prepare the necessary correcting entries for the year 1994 and any additional entries necessary to record the appropriate depreciation expense on the above-mentioned assets.

(DEPRECIATION AND ERROR ANALYSIS) A depreciation schedule for semitrucks of Alomar Manufacturing Inc. was requested by your auditor soon after December 31, 1994, showing the additions, retirements, depreciation, and other data affecting the income of the company in the four-year period 1991 to 1994, inclusive. The following data were obtained: **P11-6**

Balance of Semitrucks accounts, Jan. 1, 1991:	
Truck No. 1 purchased Jan. 1, 1988, cost	$18,000
Truck No. 2 purchased July 1, 1988, cost	22,000
Truck No. 3 purchased Jan. 1, 1990, cost	30,000
Truck No. 4 purchased July 1, 1990, cost	24,000
Balance, Jan. 1, 1991	$94,000

The Semitrucks—Accumulated Depreciation account had a balance of $30,200 on January 1, 1991 (depreciation on the four trucks from the respective dates of purchase, based on a five-year life). No debit charges had been made against the account before January 1, 1991.

Transactions between January 1, 1991 and December 31, 1994 and their record in the ledger were as follows:

July 1, 1991 Truck No. 3 was traded for a larger one (No. 5), the agreed purchase price (fair market value) of which was $32,000. Alomar Manufacturing Inc. paid the automobile dealer $14,000 cash on the transaction. The entry was a debit to Semitrucks and a credit to Cash, $14,000.

Jan. 1, 1992 Truck No. 1 was sold for $3,000 cash; the entry debited Cash and credited Semitrucks, $3,000.

July 1, 1993 Truck No. 4 was damaged in an accident to such an extent that it was sold as junk for $700 cash. Alomar received $2,500 from the insurance company. The entry made by the bookkeeper was a debit to Cash, $3,200 and credits to Miscellaneous Income, $700, and Semitrucks, $2,500.

July 1, 1993 A new truck (No. 6) was acquired for $23,000 cash and was charged at that amount to the Semitrucks account. (Assume truck No. 2 was not retired.)

Entries for depreciation had been made at the close of each year as follows: 1991, $20,200; 1992, $21,000; 1993, $23,050; 1994, $25,100.

Instructions

(a) For each of the four years compute separately the increase or decrease in net income arising from the company's errors in determining or entering depreciation or in recording transactions affecting trucks, ignoring income tax considerations.

(b) Prepare one compound journal entry as of December 31, 1994 for adjustment of the Semitrucks account to reflect the correct balances as revealed by your schedule, assuming that the books have not been closed for 1994.

P11-7 (DEPLETION, TIMBER, AND EXTRAORDINARY LOSS) In 1968, Silver Logging and Lumber Company purchased 3,000 hectares of timberland on the north side of Mount St. Helens, at a cost of $800 per hectare. In 1980, Silver began selectively logging this timber tract. In May of 1980, Mt. St. Helens erupted, burying the timberland of Silver under a metre of ash. All of the timber on the Silver tract was downed. In addition, logging roads built at a cost of $150,000 were destroyed, as was logging equipment which had a net book value of $300,000.

To the time of the eruption, Silver had logged 20% of the estimated 500,000 cubic metres of timber. Prior to the eruption, Silver estimated the land to have a value of $200 per hectare after the timber was harvested. Silver depreciates logging roads on the basis of timber harvested.

Silver estimated it would take three years to salvage the downed timber at a cost of $700,000. The timber can be sold for pulp wood at an estimated price of $4 per cubic metre. The value of the land is unknown, but until it will grow vegetation again, which scientists say may be as long as 50 to 100 years, the value is nominal.

Instructions

(a) Determine the depletion cost per cubic metre for the timber harvested prior to the eruption of Mt. St. Helens.

(b) Prepare the journal entry to record the depletion prior to the eruption.

(c) If this tract represents approximately half of the timber holdings of Silver, determine the amount of the estimated loss and show how the losses of roads, machinery, and timber and the salvage of the timber should be reported in the financial statements of Silver for the year ended December 31, 1980.

P11-8 (DEPLETION AND DEPRECIATION: MINING) Nexus Mining Ltd. purchased a tract of mineral land for $606,000. It estimated that this tract will yield 120,000 tonnes of ore with sufficient mineral content to make mining and processing profitable. It further estimated that 6,000 tonnes of ore will be mined the first year and 12,000 tonnes each year thereafter. The land will have a residual value of $30,000.

The company built structures and sheds on the site at a cost of $36,000. It is estimated that these structures had a physical life of 15 years but, because they must be dismantled if they are to be moved, they have no residual value. The company does not intend to use the buildings elsewhere. Mining machinery installed at the mine was purchased second-hand at a cost of $60,000. This machinery cost the former owner $96,000 and was 50% depreciated when purchased. Nexus Mining Ltd. estimated that about half of this machinery would still be useful when the present mineral resources are exhausted but that dismantling and removal costs would just about offset its value at that time. The company does not intend to use the machinery elsewhere. The remaining machinery would last until about one-half of the present estimated mineral ore has been removed and would then be worthless. Cost is to be allocated equally between these two classes of machinery.

Instructions

(a) As chief accountant for the company, you are to prepare a schedule showing estimated depletion and depreciation costs for each year of the expected life of the mine.

(b) Draft entries in general journal entry form to record depreciation and depletion for the first year assuming actual production of 7,000 tonnes. Nothing occurred during the year to cause the company engineers to change their estimates of either the mineral resources or the life of the structures and equipment.

P11-9 (COMPREHENSIVE, DEPRECIATION COMPUTATIONS) Kumaki Ltd., a manufacturer of steel products, began operations on October 1, 1992. The accounting department of Kumaki has started the fixed-asset and depreciation schedule presented below. You have been asked to assist in completing this schedule. In addition to ascertaining that the data already on the schedule are correct, you have obtained the following information from the company's records and personnel:

1. Depreciation is computed from the first of the month of acquisition to the first of the month of disposition.

2. Land A and Building A were acquired from a predecessor corporation. Kumaki paid $800,000 for the land and building together. At the time of acquisition, the land had an appraised value of $180,000, and the building had an appraised value of $720,000.

3. Land B was acquired on October 2, 1992 in exchange for 2,500 of Kumaki's newly issued common shares. At the date of acquisition, the shares had a fair value of $30 each. During October 1992, Kumaki paid $16,000 to demolish an existing building on this land so it could construct a new building.

4. Construction of Building B on the newly acquired land began on October 1, 1993. By September 30, 1994, Kumaki had paid $320,000 of the estimated total construction costs of $450,000. It was estimated that the building would be completed and occupied by July 1995.

5. Certain equipment was donated to the corporation by a local university. An independent appraisal of the equipment when donated placed the fair value at $50,000 and the residual value at $3,000.

6. Machinery A's total cost of $175,000 includes installation expense of $1,000 and normal repairs and maintenance of $15,000. Residual value is estimated as $16,000. Machinery A was sold on February 1, 1994.

7. On October 1, 1993, Machinery B was acquired with a down payment of $7,900 and the remaining payments to be made in 11 annual instalments of $10,000 each, beginning October 1, 1993. The prevailing interest rate was 8%. The following data were abstracted from present-value tables (rounded).

	Present Value of $1.00 at 8%	Present Value of an Annuity of $1.00 at 8%
10 years	.463	6.710
11 years	.429	7.139
15 years	.315	8.559

Kumaki Ltd.
Fixed Asset and Depreciation Schedule
For Fiscal Years Ended September 30, 1993 and September 30, 1994

Assets	Acquisition Date	Cost	Residual Value	Depreciation Method	Estimated Life in Years	Depreciation Expense Year Ended September 30 1993	1994
Land A	Oct. 1, 1992	$ (1)	N/A	N/A	N/A	N/A	N/A
Building A	Oct. 1, 1992	(2)	$40,000	Straight-line	(3)	$15,000	(4)
Land B	Oct. 2, 1992	(5)	N/A	N/A	N/A	N/A	N/A
Building B	Under construction	320,000 to date	—	Straight-line	30	—	(6)
Donated equipment	Oct. 2, 1992	(7)	3,000	Declining balance, 15% rate	10	(8)	(9)
Machinery A	Oct. 2, 1992	(10)	16,000	Sum-of-the-years' digits	8	(11)	(12)
Machinery B	Oct. 1, 1993	(13)	—	Straight-line	20	—	(14)

N/A—Not applicable

Instructions

For each numbered item on the foregoing schedule, supply the correct amount. Round each answer to the nearest dollar.

(AICPA adapted)

P11-10 (COMPREHENSIVE DEPRECIATION COMPUTATIONS) Information pertaining to Kennedy Inc.'s property, plant, and equipment for 1994 is presented below.

Account balances at January 1, 1994	Debit	Credit
Land	$ 200,000	
Building	1,500,000	
Accumulated depreciation—building		$328,877
Machinery and equipment	1,080,000	
Accumulated depreciation—machinery and equipment		300,000
Automotive equipment	115,000	
Accumulated depreciation—automotive equipment		84,600

Depreciation method and useful life

Building—declining balance method, rate of 1.5 times straight-line rate, 25-year life.
Machinery and equipment—Straight-line; 10 years.
Automotive equipment—Sum-of-the-years'-digits; 4 years.
The residual value of the depreciable assets is immaterial.
Depreciation is computed to the nearest month.

Transactions during 1994 and other information

On January 2, 1994, Kennedy purchased a new car for $10,500 cash and a trade-in of a two-year-old car with a cost of $9,000 and a book value of $2,700. The new car had a cash price of $13,000; the market value of the trade-in was not known.

On April 1, 1994, a machine purchased for $24,500 on April 1, 1989 was destroyed by fire. Kennedy recovered $16,000 from its insurance company.

On July 1, 1994, machinery and equipment were purchased at a total invoice cost of $275,000; additional costs of $4,000 for freight and $22,000 for installation were incurred.

Kennedy determined that the automotive equipment comprising the $115,000 balance at January 1, 1994 would have been depreciated at a total amount of $18,000 for the year ended December 31, 1994 had there been no changes in the amount during the year.

Instructions

(a) For each depreciable asset classification, prepare schedules showing depreciation expense and accumulated depreciation that would appear on Kennedy's income statement for the year ended December 31, 1994 and balance sheet at December 31, 1994, respectively.

(b) Prepare a schedule showing gain or loss from disposal of assets that would appear in Kennedy's income statement for the year ended December 31, 1994.

(c) Prepare the property, plant, and equipment section of Kennedy's December 31, 1994 balance sheet.

P11-11 (COMPREHENSIVE DEPRECIATION AND ERROR ANALYSIS) You are engaged in the examination of the financial statements of Shand Ltd. for the year ended December 31, 1994. The schedules that follow for the property, plant, and equipment and related accumulated depreciation accounts have been prepared by the client. You have verified the opening balances to your prior year's audit workpapers. Your examination reveals the following information:

1. All plant and equipment was depreciated on the straight-line basis (no residual value taken into consideration) using the following estimated lives: buildings, 25 years; all other items, 10 years. The company's policy was to take one-half year's depreciation on all asset acquisitions and disposals during the year.

2. On April 1, the company entered into a 10-year lease contract for a die-casting machine with annual rentals of $8,000 payable in advance every April 1. The lease could be cancelled by either party (60 days written notice is required) and there was no option to renew the lease or buy the equipment at the end of the lease. The estimated useful life of the machine was 10 years with no residual value. The company recorded the die-casting machine in the Machinery and Equipment account at $55,962, the present discounted value at the date of the lease, and $2,798, applicable to the machine, was included in depreciation expense for the year. (**Hint**: Leases with these conditions should not be capitalized nor should a liability be recognized.)

3. The company completed the construction of a wing on the plant building on June 30. The useful life of the building was not extended by this addition. The lowest construction bid received was $72,000, the amount recorded in the Buildings account. Company personnel constructed the addition at a cost of $63,000 (materials, $33,000; labour, $15,000; and overhead, $15,000).

4. On August 18, $20,000 was paid for paving and fencing a portion of land owned by the company and used as a parking lot for employees. The expenditure was charged to the Land account.

5. The amount shown in the machinery and equipment asset retirement column represented cash received on September 5 upon disposal of a machine purchased in July 1990 for $60,000. The bookkeeper recorded depreciation expense of $4,500 on this machine in 1994.

6. Quebec City donated land and a building appraised at $30,000 and $70,000, respectively, to Shand Ltd. for a plant. On September 1, the company began operating the plant. Because no costs were involved, the bookkeeper made no entry to record the transaction.

Shand Ltd.
Analysis of Property, Plant, and Equipment, and
Related Accumulated Depreciation Accounts
Year Ended December 31, 1994

Assets

Description	Final 12/31/93	Additions	Retirements	Per Books 12/31/94
Land	$ 80,000	$ 20,000		$100,000
Buildings	160,000	72,000		232,000
Machinery and equipment	400,000	55,962	$30,000	425,962
	$640,000	$147,962	$30,000	$757,962

Accumulated Depreciation

Description	Final 12/31/93	Additions[a]	Retirements	Per Books 12/31/94
Buildings	$ 80,000	$ 7,840		$ 87,840
Machinery and equipment	160,000	41,298		201,298
	$240,000	$ 49,138		$289,138

[a]Depreciation expense for the year.

Instructions

Prepare the journal entries at December 31, 1994 to adjust the accounts for the transactions noted above. Disregard income tax implications. The books have not been closed. Computations should be rounded to the nearest dollar.

(AICPA adapted)

P11-12 (COMPREHENSIVE, ASSETS AND INTEREST CAPITALIZATION WITH DEPRECIATION COMPUTATIONS) Universal Sporting Goods Inc. was experiencing growth in the demand for its products over the last several years. The last two Olympic Games greatly increased the popularity of basketball around the world. As a result, a European sports retailing consortium entered into an agreement with Universal's Roundball Division to purchase basketballs and other accessories on an increasing basis over the next five years.

To be able to meet the quantity commitments of this agreement, Universal had to obtain additional manufacturing capacity. A real estate firm located an available factory in close proximity to Universal's Roundball manufacturing facility, and Universal agreed to purchase the factory and used machinery from Eastern Athletic Equipment Ltd. on October 1, 1993. Renovations were necessary to convert the factory for Universal's manufacturing use.

The terms of the agreement required Universal to pay Eastern $50,000 when renovations started on January 1, 1994, with the balance to be paid as renovations were completed. The overall purchase price for the factory and machinery was $400,000. The building renovations were contracted to Burke Construction at $100,000. The payments made, as renovations progressed during 1994, are shown below. The factory was placed in service on January 1, 1995.

	1/1	4/1	10/1	12/31
Eastern	$50,000	$100,000	$100,000	$150,000
Burke		30,000	30,000	40,000

On January 1, 1994, Universal secured a $500,000 line-of-credit with a 12% interest rate to finance the purchase cost of the factory and machinery, and the renovation costs. Universal drew down on the line-of-credit to meet the payment schedule shown above; this was Universal's only outstanding loan during 1994.

Walter Noble, Universal's controller, capitalized the interest costs for this project to the Building account. Universal's policy regarding purchases of this nature was to use the appraisal value of the land for book purposes and prorate the balance of the purchase price over the remaining items. The building had originally cost Eastern $300,000 and had a net book value of $50,000, while the machinery originally cost $125,000 and had a net book value of $40,000 on the date of sale. The land was recorded on Eastern's books at $40,000. An appraisal, conducted by independent appraisers at the time of acquisition, valued the land at $240,000, the building at $84,000, and the machinery at $36,000.

Charles Jerrold, chief engineer, estimated that the renovated plant would be used for 15 years, with an estimated residual value of $30,000. Jerrold estimated that the productive machinery would have a remaining useful life of five years and a residual value of $3,000. Universal's depreciation policy specified the declining balance method be used for both machinery (at twice the straight-line rate) and building (at one and one-half times the straight-line rate), and that one-half year's depreciation be taken in the year an asset is placed in service and in the year in which it is disposed of or retired.

Instructions

(a) Determine the amounts to be recorded on the books of Universal Sporting Goods Inc. as of December 31, 1994 for each of the following properties acquired from Eastern Athletic Equipment Ltd.:

1. Land.

2. Building.

3. Machinery.

(b) Calculate Universal Sporting Goods Inc.'s 1995 depreciation expense, for book purposes, for each of the properties acquired from Eastern Athletic Equipment Ltd.

(c) Discuss the arguments for and against the capitalization of interest costs.

(CMA adapted)

(CAPITAL COST ALLOWANCE: PURCHASES AND RETIREMENTS) Winger Co. Ltd. engaged in the following transactions regarding Class 10 assets (30% CCA rate): ***P11-13**

1988—Purchased asset No. 1 for $150,000.
1990—Purchased asset No. 2 for $108,000.
1991—Sold asset No. 1 for $13,175.
1992—Purchased asset No. 3 for $200,000.
1994—Sold asset No. 2 for $96,000.

Instructions

(a) Prepare a capital cost allowance schedule for Class 10 assets covering the years ended December 31, 1990 through 1994.

(b) Indicate the amounts of any capital gains, recaptured capital cost, or terminal loss that would result if, during 1995, asset No. 3 was sold (thereby eliminating Class 10 assets for the company) for (1) $230,000, (2) $100,000, (3) $20,000.

CHAPTER 12

Intangible Assets

Intangible assets are generally characterized by a lack of physical existence and a high degree of uncertainty concerning future benefits. These criteria are not so clear cut as they may seem. The following dialogue with a well-known accountant typifies some of the major problems encountered in attempting to define intangibles.[1]

Q. I infer, Mr. May, from your experience that you know what in ordinary speech the word "tangible" means, don't you?

A. Yes.

Q. Well, what do you understand it to mean in ordinary speech?

A. Something that can be touched, I imagine.

Q. Like merchandise?

A. Yes.

Q. You can touch merchandise or horses?

A. Yes.

Q. Can you touch an account receivable?

A. You can touch the debtor.

Q. Is that the basis on which you include the debtor's debt as tangible?

A. It had not occurred to me before, but possibly it is.

Objective 1

Describe the characteristics of intangible assets.

This dialogue indicates that the ***lack of physical existence*** is not by itself a satisfactory criterion for distinguishing a tangible from an intangible asset. Such assets as bank deposits, accounts receivable, and long-term investments lack physical substance, yet accountants classify them as tangible assets.

Some accountants believe that intangible assets' major characteristic is the ***high degree of uncertainty concerning the future benefits*** that are to be received from its employment. For example, many intangibles (1) have value only to a given enterprise, (2) have indeterminate lives, and (3) are subject to large fluctuations in value because their benefits are based on a competitive advantage. The determination and timing of future benefits are extremely difficult and pose serious valuation problems. Some tangible assets possess similar characteristics but they are not so pronounced.

Other accountants, finding the problem of defining intangibles insurmountable, prefer simply to present them in financial statements on the basis of tradition. The more common types of intangibles are patents, copyrights, franchises, goodwill, organization costs, and trademarks or trade names. These intangibles may be further subdivided on the basis of the following characteristics:

1. **Identifiability.** Separately identifiable or lacking specific identification.
2. **Manner of acquisition.** Either acquired singly, in groups, or in business combinations or developed internally.

---

[1] From testimony given to referee, *In the Matter of the Estate of E.P. Hatch Deceased (1912)*. Reprinted in Bishop Carleton Hunt, ed., *Twenty-Five Years of Accounting Responsibility. 1911–1936* (New York: Price Waterhouse and Company, 1936), I, p. 246. Selected essays and discussions of George O. May.

3. **Expected period of benefit.** Either limited by law or contract or related to human or economic factors, or indefinite or undetermined duration.

4. **Separability from an entire enterprise.** Rights that are transferable without title, salable, or inseparable from the enterprise or a substantial part of it.[2]

VALUATION OF PURCHASED INTANGIBLES

Objective 2

Explain the procedure for valuing and amortizing intangible assets.

Intangibles, like tangible assets, are ***recorded at cost.*** Cost includes all costs of acquisition and expenditures necessary to make the intangible asset ready for its intended use—for example, purchase price, legal fees, and other incidental expenses.

If intangibles are acquired for shares or in exchange for other assets, ***the cost of the intangible is the fair market value of the consideration given or the fair market value of the intangible received, whichever is more clearly evident.*** When several intangibles, or a combination of intangibles and tangibles, are bought in a "basket purchase," the cost should be allocated on the basis of fair market value or on the basis of relative sales value. Essentially the accounting treatment for intangibles closely parallels that followed for tangible assets.

The profession has resisted employment of some other basis of valuation, such as current replacement costs or appraisal value for intangible assets. The basic attributes of intangibles—their uncertainty as to future benefits and their uniqueness—have discouraged valuation in excess of cost.[3]

AMORTIZATION OF INTANGIBLE ASSETS

Intangible assets should be amortized by systematic charges to revenue over their useful lives. In determining useful life, a number of factors should be considered. These include:

1. Legal, regulatory, or contractual provisions.

2. Provisions for renewal or extension.

3. Effects of obsolescence, demand, competition, and other economic factors.

4. A useful life may parallel the service life expectancies of individuals or groups of employees.

5. Expected actions of competitors and others may restrict present competitive advantages.

6. An apparently unlimited useful life may in fact be indefinite and benefits cannot be reasonably projected.

7. An intangible asset may be a composite of many individual factors with varying economic lives.[4]

One problem relating to the amortization of intangibles is that some intangibles have indeterminable useful lives. In this case, ***intangible assets must be amortized over a period not exceeding 40 years.***[5] The 40-year requirement is based on the premise that only a few intangibles, if any, last for a lifetime. In exceptional cases when it is possible to estimate and clearly demonstrate a life longer than 40 years, it is permissible to use an appropriate longer amortization period. These instances rarely occur. Therefore, when it is difficult to determine useful life, a 40-year term is practical, although admittedly it is an arbitrary solution. Another reason for this 40-year limitation is simply that it ensures that companies start to write off their intangibles. Prior to the 40-year rule, there was evidence that

[2] "Intangible Assets," *Opinions of the Accounting Principles Board No. 17* (New York: AICPA, 1970), par. 10.

[3] For example, Sprouse and Moonitz in *AICPA Accounting Research Study No. 3*, "A Tentative Set of Broad Accounting Principles for a Business Enterprise," advocate abandonment of historical cost in favour of replacement cost for most asset items, but suggest that intangibles should normally be carried at acquisition cost less amortization because valuation problems are so difficult.

[4] *APB Opinion No. 17, op. cit.*, par. 27.

[5] *CICA Handbook* (Toronto: CICA), Section 3060, par. .32.

some companies retained their intangibles (notably goodwill) indefinitely on their balance sheet for only one reason—to avoid the charge against income that occurs when goodwill is written off.

Intangible assets acquired from other enterprises (notably goodwill) should not be written off at acquisition. Some accountants contend that certain intangibles should not be carried as assets on the balance sheet under any circumstances but should be written off directly to Retained Earnings or Contributed Surplus. However, the immediate write-off to Retained Earnings and Contributed Surplus is not acceptable because this approach denies the existence of an asset that has just been purchased.

Intangible assets are generally amortized on a straight-line basis, although there is no reason why another systematic approach might not be employed if the firm demonstrates that another method is appropriate. In any case, the method and period of amortization should be disclosed. When intangible assets are amortized, the charges should be included in expenses and the credits should be made either to the appropriate intangible asset accounts or to separate accumulated amortization accounts.

SPECIFICALLY IDENTIFIABLE INTANGIBLE ASSETS

Objective 3

Identify the types of specifically identifiable intangible assets.

Originally, the accounting profession recognized two types of classification for intangibles: (1) intangibles that have a limited life and (2) intangibles that have an unlimited life. The classification framework was changed to intangibles that are specifically identifiable as contrasted to "goodwill type" intangible assets (unidentifiable values). **Specifically identifiable** means that costs associated with obtaining a given intangible asset can be identified as a part of the cost of that intangible asset. In contrast, **goodwill type intangibles** may create some right or privilege, but they are not specifically identifiable, and they have an indeterminable life. The major identifiable assets and goodwill are discussed below.

Patents

Patents are granted by the federal government. The two principal kinds of patents are **product patents**, which cover actual physical products, and **process patents**, which govern the process by which products are made. A patent gives the holder exclusive right to use, manufacture, and sell a product or process ***for a period of 17 years*** without interference or infringement by others. If a patent is purchased from an inventor (or other owner), the purchase price represents its cost. Other costs incurred in securing a patent, attorneys' fees, and other unrecovered costs of a successful legal suit to protect the patent can be capitalized as part of the patent cost. Research and development costs related to the *development* of the product, process, or idea that is subsequently patented are usually expensed as incurred, however. See pages 597–602 for a more complete presentation of accounting for research and development costs.

The cost of a patent should be amortized over its legal life or its useful life (the period benefits are expected to be received), whichever is shorter. If a patent is owned from the date it is granted and is expected to be useful during its entire legal life, it should be amortized over 17 years. If it appears that the patent will be useful for a shorter period of time, say, for five years, its cost should be amortized to expense over five years. Changing demand, new inventions superceding old ones, inadequacy, and other factors often limit the useful life of a patent to less than the legal life.

Legal fees and other costs incurred in successfully defending a patent suit are debited to the Patents account, an asset account, because such a suit establishes the legal rights of the holder of the patent. Such costs should be amortized along with acquisition cost over the remaining useful life of the patent. In the event that the firm is unsuccessful in defending the patent infringement suit, the cost of litigation should be expensed. In addition, any capitalized costs should be written off since the company no longer has a valid patent.

Amortization of patents may be computed on a time basis or on a basis of units produced and may be credited directly to the Patents account. It is acceptable also, although less common in practice, to credit an Accumulated Patent Amortization account. To illustrate, assume Harcott incurs $170,000 on January 1, 1994 to successfully defend a patent. The patent has a useful life of 17 years and is amortized on a straight-line basis. The entries to record the legal fees and amortization at the end of each year are as follows:

January 1, 1994

Patents	170,000	
Cash		170,000
(To record legal fees related to patent)		

December 31, 1994

Patent Amortization Expense	10,000	
Patents (or Accumulated Patent Amortization)		10,000
(To record amortization of patent)		

Amortization based on units of production would be computed in a manner similar to that described for depreciation on property, plant, and equipment.

Although a patent's useful life should not extend beyond its legal life of 17 years, small modifications or additions may lead to a new patent. The effect may be to extend the life of the old patent, in which case it is permissible to apply the unamortized costs of the old patent to the new patent if the new patent provides essentially the same benefits. Alternatively, if a patent becomes worthless because demand drops for the product produced, the asset should be written off immediately to expenses.

Copyrights

A **copyright** is a federally granted right that all authors, painters, musicians, sculptors, and other artists have in their creations and expressions. A copyright is granted for the ***life of the creator plus 50 years***, and gives the owner, or heirs, the exclusive right to reproduce and sell artistic or published work. Copyrights are not renewable. Like patents, they may be assigned or sold to other individuals. The costs of acquiring and defending a copyright may be capitalized, but the research costs involved must be expensed as incurred.

Generally, the useful life of a copyright is less than its legal life. The costs of the copyright should be allocated to the years in which the benefits are expected to be received, not exceeding 40 years. The difficulty of determining the number of years over which benefits will be received normally encourages the company to write these costs off over a fairly short period of time.

Trademarks and Trade Names

A **trademark** or **trade name** is a word, phrase, or symbol that distinguishes or identifies a particular enterprise or product. The right to use a trademark or trade name is granted by the federal government. In order to obtain and maintain a protected trademark or trade name, the owner must have made prior and continuing use of it. Trade names like Kleenex, Pepsi-Cola, Oldsmobile, Excedrin, Shreddies, and Sunkist create immediate product identification in our minds, thereby enhancing the marketability.

The capitalizable cost of a trademark or trade name is the purchase price if it is acquired. If a trademark or trade name is developed by the enterprise itself, the capitalizable cost includes attorney fees, registration fees, design costs, successful legal defence costs, and other expenditures directly related to securing it (excluding research costs). When the total cost of a trademark or trade name is insignificant, it can be expensed rather than capitalized.

Although the life of a trademark, trade name, or company name may be unlimited, for accounting purposes the cost should be amortized over the periods benefited. However, because of the uncertainty involved in estimating their useful life, the cost of trademarks and trade names is frequently amortized over a much shorter period of time.[6]

Leaseholds

A **leasehold** is a contractual understanding between a lessor (owner of property) and a lessee (renter of property) that grants the lessee ***the right to use specific property, owned by the lessor, for a specific period of time in return for stipulated, and generally periodic, cash payments.*** Most lease agreements provide simply for the right of the lessee to use property of the lessor for stipulated periods. In such a case, the rent is included as an expense on the books of the lessee. Special problems, however, develop in the following situations.

Lease Prepayments. If the rent for the period of the lease is paid in advance, or if a lump sum payment is made in advance in addition to periodic rental payments, it is necessary to allocate this prepaid rent to the proper periods. The lessee, by payment of the amount agreed upon, has purchased the exclusive right to use the property for an extended period of time. These prepayments should be reported as a prepaid expense and not as an intangible asset.

Capitalization of Leases. In some cases, the lease agreement transfers substantially all of the benefits and risks incident to ownership of the property so that the economic effect on the parties is similar to that of an instalment purchase. As a result, the asset value recognized when a lease is capitalized is classified as a tangible rather than an intangible asset. Such a lease is referred to as a **capital lease.** According to *CICA Handbook* Section 3065, the lessee must record a capital lease as an asset and an obligation at an amount equal to the present value of the minimum lease payments required during the lease term, excluding that portion of the payments representing executory costs such as insurance, maintenance, and taxes to be paid by the lessor.[7] Further, in such cases, it is appropriate for the lessee to depreciate the capitalized asset in a manner consistent with the lessee's normal depreciation policy for owned assets.

The CICA requires that if the lessee is party to a lease that meets one or more of the four criteria below, the lessee must classify the transaction as a capital lease and record an asset and a liability at an amount equal to the present value of the future lease payments:

1. There is reasonable assurance that the lessee will obtain ownership of the leased property at the end of the lease term.
2. The lease contains a bargain purchase option.
3. The lease term is equal to a major portion (usually 75% or more) of the economic life of the leased property.
4. The present value of the lease payments (excluding executory costs) equals or exceeds 90% of the fair value of the leased property.[8]

Significant provisions of material leases should be disclosed in the financial statements or in notes to the financial statements, to acquaint the reader with the financial effect of lease commitments. Chapter 21 is devoted entirely to accounting for leases.

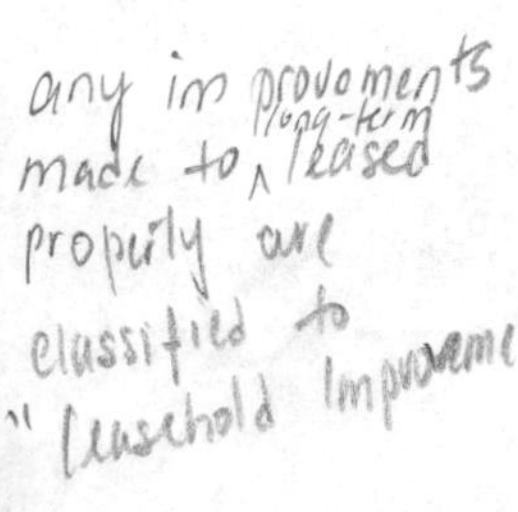

Leasehold Improvements. Long-term leases ordinarily provide that any improvements made to the leased property revert to the lessor at the end of the life of the lease. If the lessee constructs new buildings on leased land or reconstructs and improves existing buildings, the lessee has ***the right to***

[6] To illustrate how various intangibles might arise from a given product, consider what the creators of the highly successful game *Trivial Pursuit* did to protect their creation. First, the creators *copyrighted* the 6,000 questions that are at the heart of the fun. Then they shielded the *Trivial Pursuit* name by applying for a registered *trademark.* As a third mode of protection, the creators obtained a *design patent* on the playing board's design since it represents a unique graphic creation.

[7] *CICA Handbook*, Section 3065, par. .16.

[8] *Ibid.*, Section 3065, par. .06.

use such facilities during the life of the lease, but they become the property of the lessor when the lease expires.

The lessee should charge the cost of the facilities to the Leasehold Improvements account and ***depreciate the cost as operating expense over the remaining life of the lease, or the useful life of the improvements, whichever is shorter.*** If a building with an estimated useful life of 25 years is constructed on land leased for 35 years, the cost of the building should be depreciated over 25 years. On the other hand, if the building has an estimated life of 50 years, it should be depreciated over 35 years, the life of the lease.

If the lease contains an option to renew for a period of additional years and the likelihood of renewal is too uncertain to warrant apportioning the cost over the longer period of time, the leasehold improvements are generally written off over the original term of the lease (assuming that the life of the lease is shorter than the useful life of the improvements). Leasehold improvements are generally shown in the property, plant, and equipment section, although some accountants classify them as intangible assets. The rationale for intangible asset treatment is that the improvements revert to the lessor at the end of the lease and are therefore more of a right than a tangible asset.

Organization Costs

Costs incurred in the formation of a corporation such as fees to underwriters for handling issues of shares or bonds, legal fees, provincial and federal fees of various sorts, and promotional expenditures involving the organization of a business are classified as **organization costs.**

These items are usually charged to an account called Organization Costs or Organization Expense, and may be carried as an asset on the balance sheet as expenditures that will benefit the company over its life. These costs are amortized over an arbitrary period (maximum 40 years), since the life of the corporation is indeterminable. However, the amortization period is frequently short (5–10 years) because of the assumption that the early years of a business benefit most from organization costs and that these costs lose their significance once the business becomes fully established.

It is sometimes difficult to draw a line between organization costs, normal operating expenses, and losses. Some accountants contend that ***operating losses incurred in the start-up of a business*** should be capitalized, since they are unavoidable and are a cost of starting a business. This approach seems unsound, however, since losses have no future service potential and thus cannot be considered an asset.

The position that operating losses should not be capitalized during the early years is supported by accounting standards in other countries. For example, in the United States the FASB concluded that the accounting practices and reporting standards should be no different for a development stage enterprise trying to establish a new business than they are for other enterprises. Some unique notations and disclosures explaining the start-up situation may be useful. However, the same "generally accepted accounting principles that apply to established operating enterprises shall govern the recognition of revenue by a development stage enterprise and shall determine whether a cost incurred by a development stage enterprise is to be charged to expense when incurred or is to be capitalized or deferred."[9]

In Canada an exception is made for certain expenditures incurred by companies during the pre-operating period (prior to commencement of commercial operations). The CICA's Emerging

---

[9] "Accounting and Reporting by Development Stage Enterprises," *Statement of Financial Accounting Standards No. 7* (Stamford, CT: FASB, 1975), par. 10. A company is considered to be in the developing stages when its efforts are directed toward establishing a new business and either the principal operations have not started or no significant revenue has been earned. The FASB, in evaluating the economic impact of applying to development stage enterprises the same accounting principles that apply to established operating enterprises, interviewed officers of 15 venture capital companies. The consensus of those officers was that whether a development stage enterprise defers or expenses pre-operating costs has little effect on the amount of or the terms under which venture capital is provided. According to those officers, the venture capital investor relies on an evaluation of potential cash flows resulting from an investigation of the technological, marketing, management, and financial aspects of the enterprise.

Issues Committee recommends deferral of pre-operating expenditures that satisfy the following criteria:[10]

1. The expenditure is related directly to placing the new business into service.
2. It is incremental in nature.
3. It is probable that the expenditure is recoverable from future operations.

Losses occurring after the commencement of commercial operations should not be capitalized.

Franchises and Licences

When you drive down the street in an automobile purchased from a Chrysler dealer, fill your tank at the corner Esso station, eat lunch at McDonald's, work at a Coca-Cola bottling plant, live in a home purchased through a Century 21 real estate broker, and vacation at a Holiday Inn resort, you are dealing with franchises. A **franchise** is a contractual arrangement under which the franchisor grants the franchisee the right to sell certain products or services, to use certain trademarks or trade names, or perform certain functions, usually within a designated geographical area.

The franchisor, having developed a unique concept or product, protects its concept or product through a patent, copyright, trademark, or trade name. The franchisee acquires the right to exploit the franchisor's idea or product by signing a franchise agreement.

Another type of franchise is the arrangement commonly entered into by a municipality (or other governmental body) and a business enterprise that uses public property. In such cases, a privately owned enterprise is permitted to use public property in performing its services. Examples are the use of public waterways for a ferry service, the use of public land for telephones or electric lines, the use of phone lines for cable TV, the use of city streets for a bus line, or the use of the airwaves for radio or TV broadcasting. Operating rights obtained through agreements with governmental units or agencies are frequently referred to as **licences** or **permits**.

Franchises or licences may be for a definite period of time, an indefinite period of time, or perpetual. The enterprise securing the franchise or licence carries an intangible asset account entitled Franchise or Licence on its books only when there are costs (i.e. a lump sum payment in advance or legal fees and other expenditures) that are identified with the acquisition of the operating right. ***The cost of a franchise (or licence) with a limited life should be amortized as operating expense over the life of the franchise***. A franchise with an indefinite life or a perpetual franchise should be carried at cost and amortized over a reasonable period not to exceed 40 years. If a franchise is deemed to be worthless, it should be written off immediately.

Annual payments made under a franchise agreement should be entered as operating expenses in the period in which they are incurred. They do not represent an asset to the concern since they do not relate to future rights to use public property.

Property Rights

Most of the intangibles discussed above represent **rights**—rights to use, produce, sell, or operate something. Other rights appear to be growing in significance and value—water, mineral, solar and wind (the legal right to free flow of light and air across one's property), and other types of property rights. Although these rights have a value of their own, they are generally attached to a particular parcel of property. Therefore, the value of such property rights, if *inseparable* from the property, is accounted for as part of the capitalized land cost.

If the right is separable from the property, as in the case of mineral rights, its cost may be capitalized separately. If minerals are later discovered or developed, the cost of the rights should be reclassified and capitalized as part of the cost of the minerals and written off as the mineral deposit is depleted.

---

[10] CICA Emerging Issues Committee, EIC-27, "Revenues and Expenditures During the Pre-Operating Period."

GOODWILL

Objective 4

Explain the conceptual issues related to goodwill.

Goodwill is undoubtedly one of the most complex and controversial assets presented in financial statements. It is often referred to as the most "intangible" of the intangibles. Goodwill is unique because unlike receivables, inventories, and patents that can be sold or exchanged individually in the marketplace, goodwill can be identified only with the business as a whole. For example, a substantial list of regular customers and an established reputation are unrecorded assets that give the enterprise a valuation greater than the sum of the fair market value of the individual identifiable assets. Goodwill is comprised of many advantageous factors and conditions that might contribute to the value and the earning power of an enterprise.[11]

1. Superior management team.
2. Outstanding sales organization.
3. Weakness in management of a competitor.
4. Effective advertising.
5. Secret process or formula.
6. Good labour relations.
7. Outstanding credit rating.
8. Top-flight training program.
9. High standing in the community.
10. Discovery of talents or resources.
11. Favorable tax conditions.
12. Favorable government regulation.
13. Favorable association with another company.
14. Strategic location.
15. Unfavorable developments in the operations of a competitor.[12]

Goodwill is recorded only when an entire business is purchased because goodwill is a "going-concern" valuation and cannot be separated from the business as a whole.[13] Goodwill generated internally should not be capitalized in the accounts because measuring the components of goodwill

---

[11] George R. Catlett and Norman O. Olson, "Accounting for Goodwill," *Accounting Research Study No. 10* (New York: AICPA, 1968), pp. 17–18.

[12] Another study clustered 17 specific characteristics of goodwill into four more general categories as follows:

Increasing Short-Run Cash Flows
Production economics
Raise more funds
Cash reserves
Low cost of funds
Reduce inventory holding cost
Avoiding transaction cost
Tax benefits

Exclusiveness
Access to technology
Brand name

Human Factor
Managerial talent
Good labour relations
Good training programs
Organizational structure
Good public relations

Stability
Assurance of supply
Reducing fluctuations
Good government relations

See Haim Falk and L. A. Gordon, "Imperfect Markets and the Nature of Goodwill," *Journal of Business Finance and Accounting* (April 1977), pp. 443–463.

[13] *CICA Handbook*, Section 1580, par. .54.

(as listed previously) is simply too complex and associating any costs with future benefits is too difficult. The future benefits of goodwill may have no relationship to the costs incurred in the development of that goodwill. To add to the mystery, goodwill may exist in the absence of specific costs to develop it. In addition, because no objective transaction with outside parties has taken place, a great deal of subjectivity—even misrepresentation—might be involved.

Recording Goodwill

Objective 5

Describe the accounting procedures for valuing and recording goodwill.

To record goodwill, the fair market value of the net tangible and identifiable intangible assets is compared with the purchase price of the acquired business. The difference is considered goodwill, which is why goodwill is sometimes referred to as a "plug" or "gap filler" or "master valuation" account. ***Goodwill is the residual or the excess of the cost over the fair value of the identifiable net assets acquired.***

To illustrate, Multi-Diversified, Inc. decides that it needs a parts division to supplement its existing tractor distributorship. The president of Multi-Diversified is interested in a small concern near Toronto (Tractorling Company) that has an established reputation and is seeking a merger candidate. The balance sheet of Tractorling Company is presented below.

Tractorling Co.
Balance Sheet
as of Dec. 31, 1994

Assets		Equities	
Cash	$ 25,000	Current liabilities	$ 55,000
Receivables	35,000	Share capital	100,000
Inventories	42,000	Retained earnings	100,000
Property, plant, and equipment (net)	153,000		
Total assets	$255,000	Total equities	$255,000

After considerable negotiation, Tractorling Company decides to accept Multi-Diversified's offer of $400,000. What then is the value of the goodwill, if any?

The answer is not obvious. The fair market value of Tractorling's identifiable assets are not disclosed in the cost-based balance sheet. Suppose that as the negotiations progress, Multi-Diversified conducts an investigation of the underlying assets of Tractorling to determine the fair market value of the assets. Such an investigation may be accomplished either through a purchase audit undertaken by Multi-Diversified's auditors in order to estimate the values of the seller's assets, or an independent appraisal from some other source. The following valuations are determined.

Fair Market Values

Cash	$ 25,000
Receivables	35,000
Inventories	122,000
Property, plant, and equipment	205,000
Patents	18,000
Liabilities	(55,000)
Fair market value of net assets	$350,000

Normally, differences between current fair value and book value are more common among the long-term assets, although significant differences can also develop in the current asset category. Cash obviously poses no problems, and receivables normally are fairly close to current valuation, although at times certain adjustments need to be made because of inadequate bad debt provisions. Liabilities usually are stated at their book value, although if interest rates have changed since incurring the liabilities, a different valuation may be appropriate. Careful analysis must be made in this area to determine that no unrecorded liabilities are present.

The $80,000 difference in inventories ($122,000 – $42,000) could result from a number of factors, the most likely being that Tractorling Company used LIFO. Recall that during periods of inflation, LIFO better matches expenses against revenues, but in doing so creates a balance sheet distortion. Ending inventory is comprised of older layers costed at lower valuation.

In many cases, the values of long-term assets such as property, plant, and equipment, and intangibles may have increased substantially over the years. This difference could be due to inaccurate estimates of useful lives; continual expensing of small expenditures (less than $300); inaccurate estimates of residual values; the discovery of some unrecorded assets (as in Tractorling's case where Patents are discovered to have a fair value of $18,000); or substantial increase in replacement costs.

Since the fair market value of the net assets is now determined to be $350,000, why does Multi-Diversified pay $400,000? Undoubtedly, the seller points to an established reputation, good credit rating, top management team, well-trained employees, and so on, as factors that make the value of the business greater than $350,000. At the same time, Multi-Diversified places a premium on the future earning power of these attributes as well as the basic asset structure of the enterprise today. At this point in the negotiations, price can be a function of many factors: the most important is probably sheer skill at the bargaining table. The difference between the purchase price of $400,000 and the fair market value of $350,000 is labelled goodwill. Goodwill is viewed as a value or a group of unidentifiable values (intangible assets), the cost of which "is measured by the excess of the cost of the group of assets or enterprise acquired less liabilities assumed.[14] This procedure for valuation is referred to as a master valuation approach because goodwill is assumed to cover all the values that cannot be specifically identified with any identifiable tangible or intangible asset. This approach is shown below.

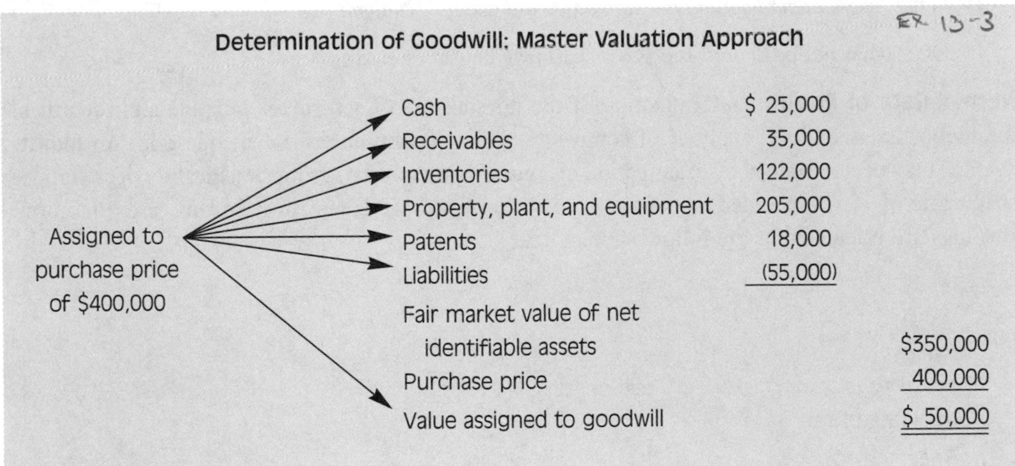

[14] *CICA Handbook*, Section 1580, par. .44(b).

The entry to record this transaction would be as follows:

Cash	25,000	
Receivables	35,000	
Inventories	122,000	
Property, plant, and equipment	205,000	
Patents	18,000	
Goodwill	50,000	
Liabilities		55,000
Cash		400,000

Goodwill is often identified on the balance sheet as the ***excess of cost over the fair value*** of the net assets acquired.

Valuing Goodwill

To determine the purchase price for a business and the resulting goodwill is a difficult and inexact process. As indicated, it is often possible to determine the fair value of identifiable assets, but how does a buyer value intangible factors like good management, good credit rating, and so on?

One method is called the **excess earnings approach.** Using this approach, the total earning power that a company commands is computed. The next step is to calculate "normal earnings" by determining the normal rate of return on assets in that industry. ***The difference between what the firm earns and what is normal in the industry is referred to as the excess earning power.*** This extra earning power indicates that there are unidentifiable values (intangible assets) that provide this increased earning power. Finding the value of goodwill then is a matter of discounting these excess earnings to the present.

This approach appears to be a systematic and logical way of determining goodwill. However, each factor necessary to compute a value under this approach is subject to question. Generally, the problems relate to getting answers to the following questions:

1. What is a normal rate of return?
2. How does one determine the future earnings?
3. What discount rate should be applied to the excess earnings?
4. Over what period should the excess earnings be discounted?

Normal Rate of Return. Determination of the normal rate of return for tangible and identifiable intangible assets requires analyses of companies similar to the enterprise in question. An industry average may be determined by examination of annual reports or data from statistical services. Suppose that a rate of 15% is decided as normal for a concern such as Tractorling. In this case, the normal earnings are calculated in the following manner.[15]

Fair market value of Tractorling's net identifiable assets	$350,000
Normal rate of return	15%
Normal earnings	$ 52,500

[15] The fair value of Tractorling's assets (rather than historical cost) is used to compute the normal profit, because fair value is closer to the true value of the company's assets exclusive of goodwill.

Determination of Future Earnings. The starting point for this type of analysis is normally the past earnings of the enterprise. Although estimates of future earnings are needed, the past often provides useful information concerning the future earnings potential of a concern. Past earnings—generally three to six years—are also useful because estimates of the future are usually overly optimistic and the hard facts of previous periods bring a sobering sense of reality to the negotiations.

Tractorling's net earnings for the last five years are as follows.

Earnings History: Tractorling

1990	$ 60,000	
1991	55,000	Average Earnings
1992	110,000[a]	$\frac{\$375,000}{5 \text{ years}} = \$75,000$
1993	70,000	
1994	80,000	
	$375,000	

[a]Includes extraordinary gain of $25,000.

The average net earnings for the last five years is $75,000 or a rate of return of approximately 21.4% on the current value of the assets, excluding goodwill ($75,000 divided by $350,000). A question that needs answering is whether $75,000 is representative of the future earnings of this enterprise.

Often, past earnings of a company to be acquired need to be adjusted because the acquirer tends to evaluate the average earnings on the basis of its own accounting procedures. Suppose that in determining earning power, Multi-Diversified measures earnings in relation to a FIFO inventory valuation figure rather than LIFO, which Tractorling employs, and that the use of LIFO reduces Tractorling's net income by $2,000 per year. In addition, Tractorling uses accelerated depreciation although Multi-Diversified uses straight-line. As a result Tractorling's earnings are lower by $3,000.

Also, assets discovered on examination that may affect the earning flow should be considered. Patent costs not previously recorded should be amortized, say, at the rate of $1,000 per period. Finally, because the estimate of future earnings is what is to be determined, some items like the extraordinary gain of $25,000 should probably be excluded. An analysis can now be made as shown at the top of page 594. The excess earnings would be determined to be $21,500, ($74,000 − $52,500).

Choosing a Discount Rate to Apply to Excess Earnings. Determination of the discount rate is a fairly subjective estimate.[16] The lower the discount rate, the higher the value of the goodwill. To

[16] The following illustration shows how the capitalization rate might be computed for a small business:

A Method of Selecting a Capitalization Rate

Long-term Canadian government bond rate	10%
Plus: Average premium return on small company shares over government bonds	10
Expected total rate of return on small publicly held shares	20
Plus: Premium for greater risk and illiquidity	6
Total required expected rate of return, including inflation component	26
Less: Consensus long-term inflation expectation	6
Capitalization rate to apply to current earnings	20%

From Warren Kissin and Ronald Zulli, "Valuation of a Closely Held Business," *The Journal of Accountancy* (June 1988), p. 42.

Average net earnings per Tractorling computation		$75,000
Add		
Adjustment for switch from LIFO to FIFO	$2,000	
Adjustment for change from accelerated to straight-line approach	3,000	5,000
		80,000
Deduct		
Extraordinary gain ($25,000/5)	5,000	
Patent amortization on straight-line basis	1,000	6,000
Adjusted average net earnings		$74,000

illustrate, assume that the excess earnings are $21,500 and that these earnings will continue indefinitely. If the excess earnings are capitalized at a rate of 25% in perpetuity[17] the results are as follows.

Capitalization at 25%

$$\frac{\text{Excess earnings}}{\text{Capitalization rate}} \quad \frac{\$21{,}500}{.25} = \$86{,}000$$

If the excess earnings are capitalized in perpetuity at a somewhat lower rate of 15%, a much higher goodwill figure results.

Capitalization at 15%

$$\frac{\text{Excess earnings}}{\text{Capitalization rate}} \quad \frac{\$21{,}500}{.15} = \$143{,}333$$

Because the continuance of excess profits is uncertain, a conservative rate (higher than normal rate) is usually employed. Factors that are considered in determining the rate are the stability of past earnings, the speculative nature of the business, and general economic conditions.

Discounting Period for Excess Earnings. Determination of the period over which the excess earnings will exist is perhaps the most difficult problem associated with computing goodwill. If it is assumed that the excess earnings will last indefinitely, then goodwill is $143,333 as computed in the previous section (assuming a rate of 15%).

Another method of computing goodwill that gives the same answer, using the normal return of 15%, is to discount the total average earnings of the company and subtract the fair market value of the net identifiable assets as follows.

---

[17] Why do we divide by the capitalization rate to arrive at the goodwill amount? Recall that the present value of an ordinary annuity is equal to

$$P_{\overline{n}|i} = \frac{1 - \dfrac{1}{(1+i)^n}}{i}$$

When a number is capitalized into perpetuity, $(1 + i)^n$ becomes so large that $1/(1 + i)^n$ essentially equals zero, which leaves $1/i$ or, as in the case above, $21,500/.25.

Average earnings capitalized at 15% in perpetuity	
($74,000/.15)	$493,333
Less fair market value of assets	350,000
Present value of estimated earnings (goodwill)	$143,333

Frequently, however, the excess earnings are assumed to last a limited number of years (e.g., 10) and then it is necessary to discount these earnings only over that time. Assume that Multi-Diversified believes that the excess earnings of Tractorling will last 10 years and, because of the uncertainty surrounding this earning power, 25% is considered an appropriate rate of return. The present value of an annuity of $21,500 ($74,000 − $52,500) discounted at 25% for ten years is $76,765.75.[18] This is the amount that Multi-Diversified should be willing to pay above the fair value of net identifiable assets.

Other Methods of Valuation[19]

Some accountants fail to discount but simply multiply the excess earnings by the number of years they believe the excess earnings will continue. This approach, often referred to as the **number of years method**, is used to provide a rough measure for what the goodwill factor should be. The approach has only the advantage of simplicity; it is more accurate to recognize the discount factor.

An even simpler method is one that relies on multiples of average yearly earnings that are paid for other companies in the same industry. If Nocturnal Airlines were recently acquired for five times its average yearly earnings of $50 million, or $250 million, then Canadian Northern Airways, a close competitor with $80 million in average yearly earnings, would be worth $400 million.

Another method (somewhat similar to discounting excess earnings) is the **discounted free cash flow method**, which involves a projection of the acquired company's free cash flow over a long period, typically 10 or 20 years. The method first projects into the future a dozen or so important financial variables, including production, prices, noncash expenses (such as depreciation and amortization), taxes, and capital outlays, all adjusted for inflation. The objective is to determine the amount of cash that will accumulate over a specified number of years. The present value of the free cash flows is then computed. This amount represents the price to be paid for the business.[20]

For example, if Magnaputer Computer Company is expected to generate $1 million a year for 20 years and the buyer's rate-of-return objective is 15%, the buyer would be willing to pay about $6.26 million for Magnaputer Company. (The present value of $1 million to be received for 20 years discounted at 15% is $6,259,330.)

In practice, prospective buyers use a variety of methods to produce a "valuation curve" or range of prices. But the actual price paid may be more a factor of the buyer's or seller's ego and horse-trading acumen.

Valuation of goodwill is at best a highly uncertain process. The estimated value of goodwill depends on a number of factors, all of which are extremely tenuous and subject to bargaining.

---

[18] The present value of an annuity of one dollar received in a steady stream for 10 years in the future discounted at 25% is 3.57050 (3.57050 × $21,500 = $76,765.75).

[19] A recent article lists three "asset-based approaches" (tangible net worth, adjusted book value, and price–book value ratio methods) and three "earnings-based approaches" (capitalization of earnings, capitalization of excess earnings, and discounted cash flow methods) as the popular methods for valuing closely held businesses. See Warren Rissin and Ronald Zulli, "Valuation of a Closely Held Business," *The Journal of Accountancy* (June 1988), pp. 38–44.

[20] Tim Metz, "Deciding How Much a Company Is Worth Often Depends on Whose Side You're On," *The Wall Street Journal*, March 18, 1981.

Amortization of Goodwill

Once goodwill has been recognized in the accounts, the next question is: What is the proper accounting at this point? Three basic approaches have been suggested.

1. **Charge goodwill off immediately to shareholders' equity**. *Accounting Research Study No. 10*, "Accounting for Goodwill," identifies a position that goodwill differs from other types of assets and demands special attention.[21] Unlike other assets, goodwill is not separable and distinct from the business as a whole and therefore is not an asset in the same sense as cash, receivables, or plant assets. In other words, goodwill cannot be sold when the business is not sold. Furthermore, the accounting treatment for purchased goodwill and goodwill internally created should be consistent. Goodwill created internally is immediately expensed and does not appear as an asset; the same treatment should be accorded purchased goodwill. Amortization of purchased goodwill leads to double counting, because net income is reduced by amortization of the purchased goodwill as well as by the internal expenditure made to maintain or enhance the value of the assets. Perhaps the best rationale for direct write-off is that determination of the periods over which the future benefits are to be received is so difficult that immediate charging to shareholders' equity is justified.

2. **Retain goodwill indefinitely unless reduction in value occurs**. Many accountants believe that goodwill can have an indefinite life and should be maintained as an asset until a decline in value occurs. They contend that inasmuch as internal goodwill is being expensed to maintain or enhance the purchased goodwill, some form of goodwill should always be an asset. In addition, without sufficient evidence that a decline in value has occurred, a write-off of goodwill is both arbitrary and capricious and will lead to distortions in net income.

3. **Amortize goodwill over its estimated life**. Still other accountants believe that goodwill's value eventually disappears and it is proper that the asset be charged to expense over the periods affected. This procedure provides a better matching of costs and revenues.

CICA Handbook Section 1580 takes the position that goodwill should be written off over its useful life, which is dependent on a number of factors such as regulatory restrictions, demand, competition, and obsolescence. ***The profession did note that goodwill should never be written off immediately or amortized over more than 40 years.***

Immediate write-off was not considered proper, because it would lead to the untenable conclusion that goodwill has no future potential. The profession merely prohibits the writing off of goodwill in the period of purchase and over a period exceeding 40 years; no other mention is made regarding another period. Some believe that a five-year period for amortization would be appropriate unless a shorter period is obviously justified.[22] Such circumstances would include continuous losses or an exodus of managerial talent. A single loss year or a combination of loss years does not automatically necessitate a charge-off of the goodwill.

The amortization of goodwill should be computed using the straight-line method unless another method is deemed more appropriate, and it should be treated as a regular operating expense. Where the amortization is material, a disclosure of the charge is necessary, as well as the method and period of amortization.

Negative Goodwill: Badwill

Negative goodwill, often appropriately dubbed badwill, or bargain purchase, arises when the fair market value of the assets acquired is higher than the purchase price of the assets. This situation is a result of market imperfections because the seller would be better off to sell the assets individually than in total. Situations do occur in which the purchase price is less than the value of the net

---

[21] Catlett and Olson, *op. cit.*, pp. 89–95.

[22] A recent study of goodwill reached the following conclusion: "Thus, the 40-year amortization period used in current practice is too long and cannot be supported on either theoretical or technical grounds. Consequently, a rapid amortization of capitalized goodwill over a relatively short period of time should occur." J. Ron Colley and Ara G. Volkan, "Accounting for Goodwill," *Accounting Horizons* (March 1988), p. 40.

identifiable assets and therefore a credit develops; the credit is referred to as negative goodwill or ***excess of fair value over the cost of the assets acquired.***

CICA Handbook ***Section 1580 takes the position that an excess of fair value over purchase price should be allocated to reduce proportionately the values assigned to nonmonetary assets.*** The possibility that this allocation might reduce all nonmonetary assets to zero without utilizing the full amount of the excess of fair value acquired over the purchase price is not contemplated. In the rare occasions when this condition does develop, the unallocated excess should be classified as a deferred credit and amortized systematically to income over the period estimated to be benefited.[23]

Negative goodwill most frequently develops in a depressed securities market when the market value of a company's shares is less than book value. For example, Emhart Corp. offered $23 a share (a premium over market) for U.S.M. Corp. shares which had a per-share book value of $43. Emhart Corp. (in consolidation) was able to write down its newly acquired plant assets by more than $49 million and thereby effect a reduction in annual depreciation charges of $5.8 million and add 50 cents annually to its earnings per share. (On top of the $2 a share it would gain from consolidating U.S.M.'s reported profits, this extra $2.50 per share represented a 90% increase over Emhart's prior year earnings.)

Reporting of Intangibles

The reporting of intangibles differs from the reporting of property, plant, and equipment in that the contra accounts are not normally shown. The amortization of intangibles is frequently credited directly to the intangible asset.[24]

The financial statements should disclose the method and period of amortization. Intangible assets shown net of amortization might appear on the balance sheet as follows.

Intangible assets (Note 3)		
Patents	$ 98,000	
Franchises	115,000	
Goodwill	342,000	$555,000

Note 3. The patents are amortized on a unit-of-production approach over a period of six years. The franchises are perpetual in nature, but in accordance with *CICA Handbook* Section 3060 they are being written off over the maximum period allowable (40 years) on a straight-line basis. The goodwill arises from the purchase of Multi-Media and is being amortized over a 10-year period on a straight-line basis.

The example at the top of page 598, taken from the 1991 annual report of Mitel Corporation, illustrates reporting of intangibles using contra-valuation accounts.

Some companies follow the practice of writing their intangibles down to $1.00 to indicate that they have intangibles of uncertain value. This practice is not in accord with good accounting. It would be much better to disclose the nature of the intangible, its original cost, and other relevant information such as competition, danger of obsolescence, and so on.

Research and Development Costs

Objective 6

Identify the conceptual issues related to research and development costs.

Research and development (R & D) costs are not in themselves intangible assets but, because research and development activities frequently result in the development of something that is patented or

[23] *CICA Handbook*, Section 1580, par. .44.

[24] *Financial Reporting in Canada—1991* (Toronto: CICA, 1991) reports that the most common type of intangible is goodwill, followed by licences, trademarks, patents, and customer lists.

Mitel Corporation

	1991	1990
Other assets (Notes 5 and 16)	$ 7,100,000	$2,900,000
Note 5. Other assets		
Cost:		
Assets held for resale	$ 5,000,000	$ 300,000
Goodwill	2,800,000	2,200,000
Patents, trademarks, and other	4,800,000	3,700,000
	12,600,000	6,200,000
Less accumulated amortization:		
Goodwill	2,800,000	1,300,000
Patents, trademarks, and other	2,700,000	2,000,000
	5,500,000	3,300,000
	$ 7,100,000	$2,900,000

copyrighted (such as a new product, process, idea, formula, composition, or literary work), R & D costs are presented here.

Many businesses expend considerable sums of money on research and development to create new products or processes, to improve present products, and to discover new knowledge that may be valuable at some future date. The following schedule shows the outlays for R & D made by selected Canadian companies.

Reported Research and Development Expense: 1991

Company	Dollars	% of Sales	% of Profits
Northern Telecom Limited	$948,300,000	21.0	128.0
Imperial Oil Limited	109,000,000	1.2	67.3
Mitel Corporation	51,700,000	12.0	53.4
Falconbridge Ltd.	11,500,000	0.7	8.8
Epic Data Inc.	2,802,000	11.0	162.0

The difficulties in accounting for these R & D expenditures are (1) identifying the costs associated with particular activities, projects, or achievements and (2) determining the magnitude of the future benefits and the length of time over which such benefits may be realized. Because of these latter uncertainties, the accounting profession (through *Handbook* Section 3450) has standardized and simplified accounting practice in this area by requiring that ***all research costs be charged to expense when incurred. Development costs should also be expensed when incurred except in certain narrowly defined circumstances.***

To differentiate research and development costs from each other and from other similar costs, the CICA adopted the following definitions:

> **Research** is planned investigation undertaken with the hope of gaining new scientific or technical knowledge and understanding. Such investigation may or may not be directed towards a specific practical aim or application.

Development is the translation of research findings or other knowledge into a plan or design for new or substantially improved material devices, products, processes, systems or services prior to the commencement of commercial production or use.[25]

Many costs have characteristics similar to those of research and development costs, for instance, costs of relocation and rearrangement of facilities, start-up costs for a new plant or new retail outlet, marketing research costs, promotion costs of a new product or service, and costs of training new personnel. To further distinguish between research, development, and these other similar costs, the following schedule provides examples of activities that typically would be excluded from both research and development.[26]

1. **Research Activities**

   (a) Laboratory research aimed at discovery of new knowledge.

   (b) Searching for applications of new research findings or other knowledge.

   (c) Conceptual formulation and design of possible product or process alternatives.

2. **Development Activities**

   (a) Testing in search for or evaluation of product or process alternatives.

   (b) Design, construction, and testing of pre-production prototypes and models.

   (c) Design of tools, jigs, moulds, and dies involving new technology.

3. **Activities Not Considered Either Research or Development**

   (a) Engineering follow-through in an early phase of commercial production.

   (b) Quality control during commercial production, including routine testing of products.

   (c) Trouble-shooting in connection with breakdowns during commercial production.

   (d) Routine or periodic alterations to existing products, production lines, manufacturing processes, and other ongoing operations.

   (e) Adaptation of an existing capability to a particular requirement or customer's need as part of a continuing commercial activity.

   (f) Routine design of tools, jigs, moulds, and dies.

   (g) Activity, including design and construction engineering, related to the construction, relocation, rearrangement, or start-up of facilities or equipment other than facilities or equipment whose sole use is for a particular research and development project.

Elements of Research and Development Costs

The costs associated with R & D activities are as follows:[27]

Objective 7

Describe the accounting procedures for research and development costs.

(a) Materials and services devoted to research and/or development activities.

(b) Direct costs of personnel engaged in R & D activities (salaries, wages, payroll taxes, etc.).

(c) Depreciation of plant assets used in the R & D activity.

(d) Amortization of any intangible assets that are directly associated with the R & D activities.

(e) Overhead allocated on a reasonable basis.

---

[25] *CICA Handbook*, Section 3450, par. .02.

[26] *Ibid.*, Section 3450, pars. .04, .05, .06.

[27] *Ibid.*, Section 3450, par. .13.

Consistent with (c), if an enterprise conducts R & D activities using its own research facility consisting of buildings, laboratories, and equipment that has alternative future uses, the facility should be accounted for as a capitalized operational asset. The depreciation and other costs related to such research facilities are accounted for as R & D expenses.

Sometimes enterprises conduct R & D activities for other entities under a **contractual arrangement**. In this case, the contract usually specifies that all direct costs, certain specific indirect costs, plus a profit element, should be reimbursed to the enterprise performing the R & D work. Because reimbursement is expected, such R & D costs should be recorded as receivables. It is the company for whom the work has been performed that reports these costs as R & D activities.

A special problem arises in distinguishing R & D costs from selling and administrative activities. Except for "routine" market research costs, research and development costs may include those associated with any product or process regardless of whether they are related to production, marketing, or administrative activities. For example, the costs of software incurred by an airline in acquiring, developing, or improving its computerized reservation system or for developing a general management information system would be considered development costs.

As previously emphasized, Canadian firms must write off all development costs as expenses of the period incurred except when all the following criteria for deferral are met:

(a) The product or process is clearly defined and the costs attributable to it can be identified.

(b) The technical feasibility of the product or process has been established.

(c) The management of the enterprise has indicated its intention to produce and market or use the product or process.

(d) The future market for the product or process is clearly defined or, if it is used internally rather than sold, its usefulness to the enterprise has been established.

(e) Adequate resources exist or are expected to be available to complete the project. Furthermore, the total amount of development costs deferred must be limited to the extent that their recovery can reasonably be regarded as assured.[28]

To illustrate the identification of R & D activities and the accounting treatment of related costs, assume that Next Century Ltd. conducts research and produces and markets laser machines for medical, industrial, and defence uses. The types of expenditures related to its laser machine activities are listed below along with the recommended accounting treatment.

Next Century Ltd.

Type of Expenditure	Accounting Treatment
1. Construction of long-range research facility (three-storey, 100,000 square metre building) for use in current and future projects.	Capitalize and depreciate as R & D expense.
2. Acquisition of R & D equipment for use on current project only.	Capitalize and depreciate as R & D expense.
3. Purchase of materials to be used on current and future R & D projects.	Inventory and allocate to R & D projects as consumed.
4. Salaries of research staff designing new laser bone scanner.	Expense immediately as research.
5. Research costs incurred under contract for New Horizon Ltd. and billable monthly.	Expense as operating expense in period of related revenue recognition.

(Continued)

[28] *Ibid.*, Section 3450, par. .13.

6.	Material, labour, and overhead of prototype laser scanner.	Capitalize as development cost if all criteria are met.
7.	Cost of testing prototype and design modifications.	Capitalize as development cost if all criteria are met.
8.	Legal fees to obtain patent on new laser scanner.	Capitalize as patent and amortize to cost of goods manufactured.
9.	Executive salaries.	Expense as operating expense (general and administrative).
10.	Cost of marketing research related to promotion of new laser scanner.	Expense as operating expense (selling).
11.	Engineering costs incurred to advance the laser scanner to full production stage.	Capitalize as development cost if all criteria (*CICA Handbook* Section 3450.21 (a) – (e)) are met.
12.	Costs of successfully defending patent on laser scanner.	Capitalize as patent and amortize to cost of goods manufactured.
13.	Commissions to sales staff marketing new laser scanner.	Expense as operating expense (selling).

Acceptable accounting practice requires that disclosure be made in the financial statements (generally in the notes) of the total R & D costs charged to expense in each period for which an income statement is presented.

An example of an R & D disclosure is the following excerpt from the 1987 annual report of Leigh Instruments Ltd.

Notes to Financial Statements

Note 1. Accounting Policies

(c) Development projects:

Development projects include labour, depreciation and other specific project associated costs. These projects have a clearly defined future market which will create value at least in an amount equal to the costs incurred. Investments in these projects are amortized over their estimated useful lives, usually a three- to ten-year period, commencing on the date, in management's opinion, that the project becomes operational. In most cases, a project becomes operational when it reaches the accounting breakeven level.

Note 5

Complete projects—cost	$14,208,078
Accumulated amortization	5,737,719
Net book value	$ 8,470,359

Costs of research and development activities that are unique to companies in the **extractive industries** (prospecting, acquisition of mineral rights, exploration, drilling, mining, and related mineral development) and those costs discussed above which are similar to but not classified as R & D may be: (1) expensed as incurred, (2) capitalized and either depreciated or amortized over an appropriate period of time, or (3) accumulated as part of inventoriable costs. Choice of the appropriate accounting treatment for such costs should be guided by the degree of certainty of future benefits and the principle of matching revenues and expenses.

An example of reported exploration and development costs for an extractive industry company follows as excerpted from the 1991 annual report of Rio Algom Limited.

Notes to the Financial Statements

Accounting Policies

Mineral Exploration and Development Costs

Exploration costs are written off as incurred. Expenditures on development projects are capitalized while the projects are considered to be of value to the Corporation.

Note 8. Mining Properties and Preproduction Expenditures

	1991	1990
Preproduction expenditures, at cost	$387,765,000	$385,819,000
Less accumulated amortization	181,446,000	176,367,000
	$206,319,000	$209,452,000

Conceptual Questions

The requirement that all research costs and most development costs incurred internally be expensed immediately is a conservative, practical solution which ensures consistency in practice and uniformity among companies. But the practice of immediately writing off expenditures made in the expectation of benefiting future periods cannot be justified on the grounds that it is good accounting theory.[29]

Defendants of immediate expensing contend that from an income statement standpoint, long-run application of this standard makes little difference. The amount of R & D costs charged against income during each accounting period would be about the same whether there is immediate expensing or capitalization and subsequent amortization because of the ongoing nature of many companies' R & D activities. Critics of this practice argue that the balance sheet should report an intangible asset related to expenditures that have future benefit. To preclude capitalization of all R & D expenditures removes from the balance sheet what may be a company's most valuable asset. This standard represents one of the many trade-offs made among relevance, reliability, and cost–benefit considerations.[30]

DEFERRED CHARGES AND LONG-TERM PREPAYMENTS

Deferred charges is a classification often used to describe a number of different items that have debit balances, among them certain types of intangibles. Intangibles sometimes classified as deferred charges include plant rearrangement costs, pre-operating and start-up costs, and organization costs. How do these items happen to be classified in this section and not in a separate intangible section? Probably the major reason is that the deferred charge section often serves as a "dumping ground" for a number of small items.

Deferred charges also include such items as long-term prepayments for insurance, rent, taxes, and other down payments. The deferred charge classification probably should be abolished because it cannot be clearly differentiated from other amortizable and depreciable assets (which are also deferred charges) and a more informative disclosure could be made of the smaller items often found in this section of the balance sheet. Such a classification has even less relevance today because the conceptual framework project establishes a definition for assets that seems to exclude deferred charges.

---

[29] The International Accounting Standards Committee issued a standard that is in agreement with the CICA. The International Committee identified certain circumstances that justify the capitalization and deferral of development costs. See "Accounting for Research and Development Activities," *International Accounting Standard No. 9* (London, England: International Accounting Standards Committee, 1978), par. 17.

[30] For a discussion of the position that R & D should be capitalized in certain situations, see Harold Bierman, Jr. and Roland E. Dukes, "Accounting for Research and Development Costs, *The Journal of Accountancy* (April 1975).

FUNDAMENTAL CONCEPTS

1. Intangible assets are generally characterized by a lack of physical existence and a high degree of uncertainty concerning future benefits. Intangibles may be categorized according to their separate identity, manner of acquisition, expected periods of benefit, and separability from the enterprise.
2. The valuation of purchased intangibles is the acquisition cost (the fair market value of the consideration given or the fair value of the intangible received, whichever is more clearly evident).
3. Intangible assets should be amortized by systematic charges to expense over their estimated useful lives. The straight-line method of amortization is most commonly used.
4. Costs of specifically identifiable intangible assets having determinable lives are capitalized and amortized. Costs related to intangibles not specifically identifiable and developed internally are usually expensed as incurred.
5. Specifically identifiable intangibles that typically have determinable lives include patents, copyrights, trademarks and trade names, leaseholds, franchises, and licences and permits. The capitalized cost of such intangibles is amortized over their legal, contractual, or useful life, whichever is shorter. Generally, the maximum amortization period would not exceed 40 years.
6. Goodwill is recorded only when an entire business is purchased because goodwill is the "going-concern" valuation and cannot be separated from the business as a whole. Costs incurred to generate goodwill internally are not capitalized. Goodwill is recorded at cost and amortized over the estimated useful life, not to exceed 40 years.
7. Goodwill may be measured as the excess of the cost over the fair value of the identifiable net assets acquired in the purchase of a whole business or as the discounted present value of expected earnings in excess of anticipated normal earnings from the tangible and identifiable intangible assets.
8. All research costs are expensed when incurred. Generally, development costs are expensed when incurred. However, when certain criteria are met, development costs may be capitalized and amortized over the period benefiting. The accounting problem is one of differentiating between research, development costs, and other similar costs. Fixed assets used in research and development activities should be capitalized and depreciated.

QUESTIONS

1. What are the major accounting problems related to accounting for intangibles?
2. Accounting authors and practitioners have proposed various solutions to the problems of accounting in terms of historical cost for goodwill and similar intangibles. What problems of accounting for goodwill and similar intangibles are comparable to those of accounting for plant assets? What problems are different?
3. Many accountants advocate the abandonment of historical cost for plant assets but argue that historical cost should be used in accounting for intangible assets. Are the two viewpoints inconsistent?
4. Intangible assets may be classified on a number of different bases. Indicate three different bases and illustrate how intangibles could be subdivided into these groupings.
5. What are some examples of internally created intangibles? Why does the accounting profession make a distinction between internally created "goodwill type" intangibles and other intangibles?
6. In 1994, Weatherman Inc. spent $400,000 for "goodwill" visits by sales personnel to key customers. The purpose of these visits was to build a solid, friendly relationship for the future and to gain insight into the problems and needs of the companies served. How should this expenditure be reported?
7. State the generally accepted accounting procedures for the amortization and write-down or write-off of capitalized intangible assets.
8. It has been argued, on the grounds of conservatism, that all intangible assets should be written off immediately after acquisition. Give the accounting arguments against this treatment.
9. Innovative Company spent $175,000 developing a new process, $40,000 in legal fees to obtain a patent, and $87,000 to market the process that was patented, all in the year 1994. How should these costs be accounted for in 1994?
10. Indicate the period of time over which each of the following should be amortized:
    (a) Development costs.
    (b) Trademarks.

(c) Goodwill.
(d) A 25-year lease with payments of $75,000 per year on property with an estimated useful life of 50 years. The lessee has the option to renew the lease for 25 additional years at $5,000 per year.
(e) Franchises.
(f) Patents.
(g) Leasehold improvements.
(h) Copyrights.

11. What is a lease prepayment? What are property rights capitalized by the lessee? What are leasehold improvements? Should any of these items be classified as an intangible asset?

12. On January 1, 1989 an intangible asset with a 35-year estimated useful life was acquired. On January 1, 1994 a review was made of the estimated useful life, and it was determined that the intangible asset had an estimated useful life of 45 more years. Assuming that the company wants to amortize this intangible over the maximum period possible, how many more years may this intangible be amortized?

13. Recently Pergold Limited entered into a lease agreement with Shady Developers Inc. to lease some land for 25 years in southwest Alberta. Pergold Limited as lessee then built on this site a number of apartment buildings having a useful life of 35 years. The lease agreement states that the lessee has the option to renew the lease for another 20 years. Over what period should the apartments be depreciated?

14. Recently, a group of university students decided to incorporate for the purposes of selling a process to recycle the waste products from manufacturing cheese. Some of the initial costs involved were legal fees and office expense incurred in starting the business, and incorporation fees. One student wishes to charge these costs against income in the current period; another wishes to defer these costs and amortize them in the future; and another believes these costs should be netted against contributed surplus. Which student is correct?

15. What is goodwill? What is negative goodwill?

16. Under what circumstances is it appropriate to record goodwill in the accounts? How should goodwill, properly recorded on the books, be amortized in order to conform with generally accepted accounting principles?

17. Explain how "average excess earnings" are determined. What is the justification for the use of this method of estimated goodwill?

18. In examining financial statements, financial analysts often write off goodwill immediately. Evaluate this procedure.

19. Discuss two methods for estimating the value of goodwill in determining the amount that should properly be paid for it.

20. What is the nature of research and development costs? What other costs have similar characteristics?

21. Research and development activities may include (a) personnel costs, (b) materials and equipment costs, and (c) indirect costs. What is the recommended accounting treatment for these three types of R & D costs?

22. Which of the following activities should be expensed currently as R & D costs?
(a) Testing in search or evaluation of product or process alternatives.
(b) Engineering follow-through in an early phase of commercial production.
(c) Legal work in connection with patent applications or litigation, and the sale or licensing of patents.
(d) Adaptation of an existing capability to a particular requirement or customer's need as a part of continuing commercial activity.

23. During the current year, Bassett Railroad spends $600,000 to develop a computer program that will assist in identifying and locating all of its rolling equipment. How should Bassett account for this expenditure?

24. In 1992, Odie Inc. developed a new product to be marketed in 1995. In connection with the development of this product, the following costs were incurred in 1994: development costs, $400,000; materials and supplies consumed, $50,000; compensation paid to research consultants, $80,000. It was anticipated that these costs would be recovered in 1995. What was the amount of development costs that Odie should record in 1994 as a charge to income?

25. An intangible asset with an estimated useful life of 30 years was acquired on January 1, 1984 for $360,000. On January 1, 1994, a review was made of intangible assets and their expected service lives and it was determined that this asset had an estimated useful life of 35 more years from the date of the review. What was the amount of amortization for this intangible asset for 1994?

CASES

(PATENT COST) In examining the books of Vogel Mfg. Company, you find on the December 31, 1994 balance sheet the item "Cost of Patents, $822,000." Referring to the ledger accounts, you note the following items regarding one patent acquired in 1991: **C12-1**

1991	Legal costs incurred in defending the validity of the patent	$ 35,000
1992	Legal costs in prosecuting an infringement suit	74,000
1993	Legal costs (additional expenses) in the infringement suit	24,500
1993	Cost of improvements (unpatented) on the patented device	131,200

There are no credits in the account, and no allowance for amortization has been set up on the books for any of the patents. Three other patents issued in 1988, 1990, and 1991 were developed by the staff of the client. The patented articles are currently very marketable, but it is estimated that they will be in demand only for the next few years.

Instructions

Discuss the items included in the Patent account from an accounting standpoint.

(AICPA adapted)

(ACCOUNTING FOR INTANGIBLE-TYPE EXPENDITURES) Wadge Inc. is a large publicly held corporation. Listed below are six selected expenditures made by the company during the current fiscal year ended April 30, 1994. The proper accounting treatment of these transactions must be determined in order that Wadge's annual financial statements be prepared in accordance with generally accepted accounting principles. **C12-2**

(a) Wadge Inc. spent $3,000,000 on a program designed to improve relations with its dealers. This project was favourably received by the dealers and Wadge's management believed that significant future benefits should be received from this program. The program was conducted during the fourth quarter of the current fiscal year.

(b) A pilot plant would be constructed during 1993–94 at a cost of $5,000,000 to test a new production process. The plant would be operated for approximately five years. At that time, the company would make a decision regarding the economic value of the process. The pilot plant was too small for commercial production, so it would be dismantled when the test was over.

(c) A new product will be introduced next year. The company spent $4,000,000 during the current year for design of tools, jigs, moulds, and dies for this product.

(d) Wadge Inc. purchased Mariah Company for $6,000,000 in cash in early August 1994. The fair market value of the identifiable assets of Mariah was $5,000,000.

(e) A large advertising campaign was conducted during April 1994 to introduce a new product to be released during the first quarter of the 1994–95 fiscal year. The advertising campaign cost $3,500,000.

(f) During the first six months of the 1993–94 fiscal year, $500,000 was expended for legal work in connection with a successful patent application. The patent became effective November 1, 1993. The legal life of the patent was 17 years while the economic life of the patent was expected to be approximately 10 years.

Instructions

For each of the six expenditures presented, determine and justify:

(a) The amount, if any, that should be capitalized and be included on Wadge's Statement of Financial Position prepared as of April 30, 1994.

(b) The amount that should be included in Wadge's Statement of Income for the year ended April 30, 1994.

(CMA adapted)

C12-3 (ACCOUNTING FOR POLLUTION EXPENDITURE) Acker Company operates several plants at which limestone is processed into quicklime and hydrated lime. The Batavia Plant, where most of the equipment was installed many years ago, continually deposits a dusty white substance over the surrounding countryside. Citing the unsanitary condition of the neighbouring community of Geneva, the pollution of the Fox River, and the high incidence of lung disease among workers at Batavia, the area's Pollution Control Agency has ordered the installation of air pollution control equipment. Also, the Agency has assessed a substantial penalty, which will be used to clean up Geneva. After considering the costs involved (which could not have been reasonably estimated prior to the Agency's action), management decides to comply with the Agency's orders, the alternative being to cease operations at Batavia at the end of the current fiscal year. The officers of Acker Company agree that the air pollution control equipment should be capitalized and depreciated over its useful life, but they disagree over the period(s) to which the penalty should be charged.

Instructions

Discuss the conceptual merits and reporting requirements of accounting for the penalty as a:

(a) Charge to the current period.

(b) Correction of prior periods.

(c) Capitalizable item to be amortized over future periods.

(AICPA adapted)

C12-4 (ACCOUNTING FOR PRE-OPENING COSTS) After securing lease commitments from several major stores, Red River Shopping Centre Inc. built a shopping centre in a growing suburb.

The shopping centre would have opened on schedule on January 1, 1994 if it had not been struck by a severe tornado in December; it opened for business on October 1, 1994. All of the additional construction costs that were incurred as a result of the tornado were covered by insurance.

In July 1993, in anticipation of the scheduled January opening, a permanent staff was hired to promote the shopping centre, obtain tenants for the uncommitted space, and manage the property.

A summary of some of the costs incurred in 1993 and the first nine months of 1994 follows.

	1993	January 1, 1994 through September 30, 1994
Interest on mortgage bonds	$360,000	$270,000
Cost of obtaining tenants	150,000	180,000
Promotional advertising	270,000	278,500

The promotional advertising campaign was designed to familiarize shoppers with the centre. Had it been known in time that the centre would not open until October 1994, the 1993 expenditure for promotional advertising would not have been made. The advertising had to be repeated in 1994.

All of the tenants who had leased space in the shopping centre at the time of the tornado accepted the October occupancy date on condition that the monthly rental charges for the first nine months of 1994 be cancelled.

Instructions

Explain how each of the costs for 1993 and the first nine months of 1994 should be treated in the accounts of Red River Shopping Centre Inc. Give the reasons for each treatment.

(AICPA adapted)

(ACCOUNTING FOR PATENTS) On June 30, 1994, your client, Joiner Limited, is granted two patents covering plastic cartons that it has been producing and marketing profitably for the past three years. One patent covers the manufacturing process and the other covers the related products. C12-5

Joiner executives tell you that these patents represent the most significant breakthrough in the industry in the past 30 years. The products have been marketed under the registered trademarks Safetainer, Duratainer, and Sealrite. Licences under the patents have already been granted by your client to other manufacturers in Canada and abroad and are producing substantial royalties.

On July 1, Joiner commences patent infringement actions against several companies whose names you recognize as those of substantial and prominent competitors. Joiner's management is optimistic that these suits will result in a permanent injunction against the manufacture and sale of the infringing products and collection of damages for loss of profits caused by the alleged infringement.

The financial vice-president has suggested that the patents be recorded at the discounted value of expected net royalty receipts.

Instructions

(a) What is the meaning of "discounted value of expected net royalty receipts"? Explain.

(b) How would such a value be calculated for net royalty receipts?

(c) What basis of valuation for Joiner's patents would be generally accepted in accounting? Give supporting reasons for this basis.

(d) Assuming no practical problems of implementation and ignoring generally accepted accounting principles, what is the preferable basis of valuation for patents? Explain.

(e) What would be the preferable theoretical basis of amortization? Explain.

(f) What recognition, if any, should be made of the infringement litigation in the financial statements for the year ending September 30, 1994? Discuss.

(AICPA adapted)

(ACCOUNTING FOR GOODWILL) After extended negotiations, Flynn Corporation Ltd. bought from Inez Company most of the latter's assets on June 30, 1994. At the time of the sale Inez's accounts (adjusted to June 30, 1994) reflected the following descriptions and amounts for the assets transferred. C12-6

	Cost	Contra (Valuation) Account	Book Value
Receivables	$ 86,600	$ 2,500	$ 84,100
Inventory	107,000	5,400	101,600
Land	18,000	—	18,000
Buildings	208,600	73,000	135,600
Fixtures and equipment	203,900	42,000	161,900
Goodwill	50,000	—	50,000
	$674,100	$122,900	$551,200

You ascertain that the contra (valuation) accounts were allowance for doubtful accounts, allowance to reduce inventory to market, and accumulated depreciation.

During the extended negotiations, Inez held out for a consideration of approximately $700,000 (depending on the level of the receivables and inventory). As of June 30, 1994, however, Inez agreed to accept Flynn's offer of $500,000 cash plus 1% of the net sales (as defined in the contract) of the next five years with payments at the end of each year. Inez expected that Flynn's total net sales during this period would exceed $15,000,000.

Instructions

(a) How should Flynn Corporation Ltd. record this transaction? Explain.

(b) Discuss the propriety of recording goodwill in the accounts of Flynn Corporation Ltd. for this transaction.

(AICPA adapted)

C12-7 (ACCOUNTING FOR GOODWILL) Oily Co. Ltd., a retail fuel oil distributor, has increased its annual sales volume to a level three times greater than the annual sales of a dealer it purchased in 1992 in order to begin operations.

The board of directors of Oily Co. Ltd. has recently received an offer to negotiate the sale of Oily Co. Ltd. to a large competitor. As a result, the majority of the board wants to increase the stated value of goodwill on the balance sheet to reflect the larger sales volume developed through intensive promotion and the current market price of sales gallonage. A few of the board members, however, prefer to eliminate goodwill altogether from the balance sheet in order to prevent "possible misinterpretations." Goodwill has been accounted for in accordance with *Handbook* requirements during 1994.

Instructions

(a) Discuss the meaning of the term "goodwill."

(b) List the techniques used to calculate the tentative value of goodwill in negotiations to purchase a going concern.

(c) Why are the book and market values of the goodwill of Oily Co. Ltd. different?

(d) Discuss the propriety of the following actions:

1. Increasing the stated value of goodwill prior to the negotiations.

2. Eliminating goodwill completely from the balance sheet prior to negotiations.

(AICPA adapted)

C12-8 (ACCOUNTING FOR RESEARCH AND DEVELOPMENT COSTS) Enviro Inc. is in the process of developing a revolutionary new product. A new division of the company is formed to develop, manufacture, and market this new product. As of year end (December 31, 1994), the new product has not been manufactured for resale; however, a prototype unit is built and is in operation.

Throughout 1994 the new division incurred certain costs. These costs included design and engineering studies, prototype manufacturing costs, administrative expenses (including salaries of administrative personnel), and market research costs. In addition, approximately $800,000 in equipment (with an estimated useful life of 10 years) was purchased for use in developing and manufacturing the new product. Approximately $300,000 of this equipment was built specifically for the design development of the new product; the remaining $500,000 of equipment was used to manufacture the pre-production prototype and will be used to manufacture the new product once it is in commercial production.

Instructions

(a) How are "research" and "development" defined in the *CICA Handbook*?

(b) Briefly indicate the practical and conceptual reasons for the conclusion reached by the Accounting Standards Board on accounting and reporting practices for research and development costs.

(c) In accordance with the *CICA Handbook*, how should the various costs of Enviro described above be recorded on the financial statements for the year ended December 31, 1994?

(AICPA adapted)

EXERCISES

(CLASSIFICATION ISSUES: INTANGIBLES) Presented below is a list of items that could be included in the intangible asset section of the balance sheet: **E12-1**

1. Investment in a subsidiary company.
2. Timberland.
3. Cost of engineering activity required to advance the design of a product to the manufacturing stage.
4. Lease prepayment (six months' rent paid in advance).
5. Cost of equipment obtained under a capital lease.
6. Retained earnings appropriation.
7. Costs incurred in the formation of a corporation.
8. Operating losses incurred in the start-up of a business.
9. Sinking fund for repayment of bonds.
10. Cost of a franchise.
11. Goodwill generated internally.
12. Goodwill acquired in the purchase of a business.
13. Cost of testing in search for product alternatives.
14. Cost of developing computer software for internal use.
15. Cost of developing a patent.
16. Cost of purchasing a patent from an inventor.
17. Legal costs incurred in securing a patent.
18. Unrecovered costs of a successful legal suit to protect the patent.
19. Research and development costs.
20. Long-term receivables.
21. Cost of modifying the design of a product or process.
22. Cost of acquiring a copyright.
23. Cost of developing a trademark.
24. Cost of securing a trademark.

Instructions

(a) Indicate which items on the list above would generally be reported as intangible assets in the balance sheet.

(b) Indicate how, if at all, the items not reportable as intangible assets would be reported in the financial statements.

E12-2 (CLASSIFICATION ISSUES: INTANGIBLES) Presented below is selected account information related to Erma Bombeck Inc. as of December 31, 1994. All these accounts have debit balances.

Cable television franchises	Film contract rights
Music copyrights	Customer lists
Research and development costs	Prepaid expenses
Goodwill	Covenants not to compete
Cash	Brand names
Discount on notes payable	Notes receivable
Accounts receivable	Investments in affiliated companies
Property, plant, and equipment	Organization cost
Leasehold improvements	Land

Instructions

Identify which items should be classified as an intangible asset. For those items not classified as an intangible asset, indicate where they would be reported in the financial statements.

E12-3 (CLASSIFICATION ISSUES: INTANGIBLE ASSET) Orcim Inc. has the following amounts included in its general ledger at December 31, 1994:

Organization costs	$11,000
Trademarks	15,000
Discount on bonds payable	40,000
Deposits with advertising agency for ads to promote goodwill of company	10,000
Excess of cost over book value of net assets of acquired subsidiary	60,000
Cost of equipment acquired for research and development projects	90,000
Costs of developing a secret formula for a product that is expected to be marketed for at least 20 years	80,000

Instructions

(a) On the basis of the information above, compute the total amount to be reported by Orcim for intangible assets on its balance sheet at December 31, 1994. Equipment has alternative future use.

(b) If an item is not to be included in intangible assets, explain its proper treatment for reporting purposes.

E12-4 (INTANGIBLE AMORTIZATION) Presented below is selected information for Blackwell Company. Answer each of the factual situations.

1. Blackwell purchased a patent from Pryor Co. Ltd. for $800,000 on January 1, 1992. The patent is being amortized over its remaining legal life of 10 years, expiring on January 1, 2002. During 1994, Blackwell determined that the economic benefits of the patent would not last longer than five years from the date of acquisition. What amount should be reported in the balance sheet for the patent, net of accumulated amortization, at December 31, 1994?

2. Blackwell bought a franchise from Taylor Co. Ltd. on January 1, 1993 for $300,000. It was estimated that the franchise had a useful life of 60 years. Its carrying amount on Taylor Co. Ltd.'s books at January 1, 1993 was $400,000. Blackwell decided to amortize the franchise over the maximum period permitted. What amount should be amortized for the year ended December 31, 1994?

3. On January 1, 1990, Blackwell incurred organization costs of $350,000. Blackwell amortized these costs over an arbitrary period of five years. What amount should be reported as unamortized organization costs as of December 31, 1994?

E12-5 (CORRECT INTANGIBLE ASSET ACCOUNT) As the recently appointed auditor for Heartland Limited, you have been asked to examine selected accounts before the six-month financial statements of June 30, 1994 are prepared. The controller for Heartland Limited mentions that only one account (shown below) is kept for Intangible Assets.

Intangible Assets

		Debit	Credit	Balance
January 4	Research and development	920,000		920,000
January 5	Legal costs to obtain patent	80,000		1,000,000
January 31	Payment of seven months' rent on property leased by Heartland	84,000		1,084,000
February 1	Share issue costs	49,200		1,133,200
February 11	Proceeds from issue of common shares		250,000	883,200
March 31	Unamortized bond discount on bonds due March 31, 2014	84,000		967,200
April 30	Promotional expenses related to start-up of business	207,000		1,174,200
June 30	Operating losses for first six months	241,000		1,415,200

Instructions

Prepare the entry or entries necessary to correct this account. Assume that the patent has a useful life of 10 years, and organization costs are being amortized over a five-year period.

(RECORDING AND AMORTIZATION OF INTANGIBLES) Sanborn Company, organized in 1994, has set up a single account for all intangible assets. The following summary discloses the debit entries that have been recorded during 1995: **E12-6**

1/2/95	Purchased patent (seven-year life)	$ 280,000
4/1/95	Goodwill purchased (indefinite life)	360,000
7/1/95	10-year franchise, expiration date 7/1/2005	450,000
8/1/95	Payment for copyright (four-year life)	144,000
9/1/95	Research and development costs	185,000
		$1,419,000

Instructions

Prepare the necessary entries to clear the Intangible Asset account and to set up separate accounts for distinct types of intangibles. Make the entries as of December 31, 1995, recording any necessary amortization and reflecting all balances accurately as of that date.

(ACCOUNTING FOR TRADE NAME) In early January of 1993, Bright N Shine applied for a trade name, incurring legal costs of $18,000. In January of 1994, Bright N Shine incurred $7,800 of legal fees in a successful defence of its trade name. **E12-7**

Instructions

(a) Compute 1993 amortization, 12/31/93 book value, 1994 amortization, and 12/31/94 book value if the company amortizes the trade name over its expected economic life of 40 years.

(b) Repeat part (a), assuming a useful life of five years.

(ACCOUNTING FOR LEASE TRANSACTION) Prairie Grains Inc. leases an old building which it intends to improve and use as a warehouse. To obtain the lease, the company pays a bonus of $45,000. Annual rental for the six-year lease period is $120,000. No option to renew the lease or right to purchase the property is given. After the lease is obtained, improvements costing $180,000 are made. The building has an estimated remaining useful life of 17 years. **E12-8**

Instructions

(a) What is the annual cost of this lease to Prairie Grains Inc.?

(b) What amount of annual depreciation, if any, on a straight-line basis should Prairie Grains record?

(c) How would the annual charges stated above be changed if Prairie Grains had been granted as part of the lease agreement the right to purchase the building for a nominal sum at the end of the lease period?

E12-9 (ACCOUNTING FOR ORGANIZATION COSTS) Richmond Corporation Ltd. was organized in 1993 and began operations at the beginning of 1994. The company was involved in interior design consulting services. The following costs were incurred prior to the start of operations:

Attorney's fees in connection with organization of the company	$15,000
Improvements to leased offices prior to occupancy	25,000
Fees to underwriters for handling share issue	4,000
Costs of meetings of incorporators to discuss organizational activities	9,000
Filing fees to incorporate	2,000
	$55,000

Instructions

(a) Compute the total amount of organization costs incurred by Richmond.

(b) Assuming Richmond Corporation Ltd. is amortizing costs for financial reporting purposes over a five-year term, prepare the journal entry to amortize organization costs for 1994.

E12-10 (ACCOUNTING FOR PATENTS, FRANCHISES, AND R & D) Leedown Company has provided information on intangible assets as follows:

A patent was purchased from Spademan Company for $1,800,000 on January 1, 1993. Leedown estimated the remaining useful life of the patent to be nine years. The patent was carried in Spademan's accounting records at a net book value of $2,000,000 when Spademan sold it to Leedown.

During 1994, a franchise was purchased from York Limited for $480,000. In addition, 5% of revenue from the franchise must be paid to York. Revenue from the franchise for 1994 was $2,500,000. Leedown estimated the useful life of the franchise to be 12 years and took a full year's amortization in the year of purchase.

Leedown incurred research and development costs in 1994 as follows:

Materials and equipment	$142,000
Personnel	176,000
Indirect costs	102,000
	$420,000

Leedown estimated that these costs would be recouped by December 31, 1997.

On January 1, 1994, Leedown, because of recent events in the field, estimated that the remaining life of the patent purchased on January 1, 1993 was only five years from January 1, 1994.

Instructions

(a) Prepare a schedule showing the intangibles section of Leedown's balance sheet at December 31, 1994. Show supporting computations in good form.

(b) Prepare a schedule showing the income statement effect for the year ended December 31, 1994 as a result of the facts above. Show supporting computations in good form.

(AICPA adapted)

E12-11 **(ACCOUNTING FOR PATENTS)** Shoreline Inc. has its own research department. In addition, the company purchases patents from time to time. The following statements summarize the transactions involving all patents now owned by the company.

During 1988 and 1989, $153,000 was spent developing a new process that was patented (No. 1) on March 18, 1990 at additional legal and other costs of $18,700. A patent (No. 2) developed by Al Einstein, an inventor, was purchased for $60,000 on November 30, 1991, on which date it had 12½ years yet to run.

During 1990, 1991, and 1992, research and development activities cost $170,000. No additional patents resulted from these activities.

A patent infringement suit brought by the company against a competitor because of the manufacture of articles infringing on Patent No. 2 was successfully prosecuted at a cost of $14,200. A decision in the case was rendered in July 1992.

A competing patent (No. 3) was purchased for $64,000 in August 1993. This patent still had 16 years to run. During 1994, $60,000 was expended on patent development: $20,000 of this amount represented the cost of a device for which a patent application had been filed, but no notification of acceptance or rejection by the Patent Office had been received. The other $40,000 represented costs incurred on uncompleted development projects.

Instructions

(a) Compute the carrying value of these patents as of December 31, 1994, assuming that the legal and useful life of each patent is the same and that each patent is to be amortized from the first day of the month following its acquisition.

(b) Prepare a journal entry to record amortization for 1994.

E12-12 **(ACCOUNTING FOR PATENTS)** During 1990, Rainbow Technology spent $180,000 in research and development costs. As a result, a new product called the Crusher was patented at additional legal and other costs of $30,000. The patent was obtained on October 1, 1990, and had a legal life of 17 years and a useful life of 10 years.

Instructions

(a) Prepare all journal entries required in 1990 and 1991 as a result of the transactions above.

(b) On June 1, 1992, Rainbow spent $32,600 to successfully prosecute a patent infringement. As a result, the estimate of useful life was extended to 12 years from June 1, 1992. Prepare all journal entries required in 1992 and 1993.

(c) In 1994, Rainbow determined that a competitor's product would make the Crusher obsolete and the patent worthless by December 31, 1995. Prepare all journal entries required in 1994 and 1995.

E12-13 **(ACCOUNTING FOR GOODWILL)** On July 1, 1994, Windsor Inc. purchased Conner Company by paying $300,000 cash and issuing a $100,000 note payable to John Conner. At July 1, 1994, the balance sheet of Conner Company was as follows:

Cash	$ 50,000	Accounts payable	$190,000
Receivables	90,000	Conner, capital	245,000
Inventory	100,000		$435,000
Land	40,000		
Buildings (net)	75,000		
Equipment (net)	70,000		
Trademarks	10,000		
	$435,000		

The recorded amounts all approximated current values except for land (worth $60,000), inventory (worth $125,000), and trademarks (worthless).

Instructions

(a) Prepare the July 1 entry for Windsor Inc. to record the purchase.

(b) Prepare the December 31 entry for Windsor Inc. to record amortization of goodwill. The goodwill is estimated to have a useful life of 50 years.

E12-14 (COMPUTE GOODWILL) The net worth of Imagesetter Company excluding goodwill totals $800,000 and earnings for the last five years total $890,000. Included in the latter figure are extraordinary gains of $80,000, nonrecurring losses of $40,000, and sales commissions of $30,000. In developing a sales price for the business, a 14% return on net worth is considered normal for the industry, and annual excess earnings are to be capitalized at 20% in arriving at goodwill.

Instructions

Compute estimated goodwill.

E12-15 (COMPUTE NORMAL EARNINGS) Omni Petroleum Inc.'s pretax accounting income for the year 1994 is $850,000 and included the following items:

Extraordinary losses	$ 44,000
Extraordinary gains	135,000
Profit-sharing payments to employees	65,000
Amortization of goodwill	50,000
Amortization of identifiable intangibles	57,000
Depreciation on building	80,000

Webster Oil Industries is seeking to purchase Omni Petroleum Inc. In attempting to measure Omni's normal earnings for 1994, Webster determines that the fair value of the building is triple the book value and that the remaining economic life is double that used by Omni. Webster will continue the profit-sharing payments to employees; such payments are based on income before depreciation and amortization.

Instructions

Compute the normal earnings (for the purposes of computing goodwill) of Omni Petroleum Inc. for the year 1994.

E12-16 (COMPUTE GOODWILL) Fast Track News Inc. is considering acquiring Ahran Company in total as a going concern. Fast Track makes the following computations and conclusions:

The fair value of the individual assets of Ahran Company is	$720,000
The liabilities of Ahran Company are	410,000
A fair estimate of annual earnings for the indefinite future is	90,000 per year

Considering the risk and potential of Ahran Company, Fast Track feels that it must earn a 24% return on its investment.

Instructions

(a) How much should Fast Track be willing to pay for Ahran Company?

(b) How much of the purchase price will be goodwill?

(COMPUTE GOODWILL) As the president of Starr Records Inc., you are considering purchasing Ace Tape Company, whose balance sheet is summarized as follows: E12-17

Current assets	$ 300,000	Current liabilities	$ 300,000
Investments	700,000	Long-term debt	500,000
Other assets	300,000	Common shares	400,000
		Retained earnings	100,000
Total	$1,300,000	Total	$1,300,000

The fair market value of current assets is $600,000 because of the undervaluation of inventory. The normal rate of return on net assets for the industry is 15%. The average expected annual earnings projected for Ace Tape Company is $145,000.

Instructions

Assuming that the excess earnings continue for five years, how much would you be willing to pay for goodwill? (Estimate goodwill by the present value method.)

(COMPUTE GOODWILL) Net income figures for Balloon Bunch Company are as follows: E12-18

1989—$64,000 1990—$50,000
1991—$81,000 1992—$80,000
1993—$70,000

Tangible net assets of this company are appraised at $400,000 on December 31, 1993. This business is to be acquired by Dane Co. Ltd. early in 1994.

Instructions

What amount should be paid for goodwill if:

(a) 13% is assumed to be a normal rate of return on net tangible assets, and average excess earnings for the last five years are to be capitalized at 25%?

(b) 11% is assumed to be a normal rate of return on net tangible assets, and payment is to be made for excess earnings for the last four years?

(COMPUTE GOODWILL) Jaspar Corporation Ltd. is interested in acquiring Byron Plastics Company. It has determined that Byron Company's excess earnings have averaged approximately $100,000 annually over the last six years. Byron Company agrees with the computation of $100,000 as the approximate excess earnings and feels that such amount should be capitalized over an unlimited period at a 20% rate. Jaspar Corporation Ltd. feels that because of increased competition the excess earnings of Byron Company will continue for seven more years at best and that a 15% discount rate is appropriate. E12-19

Instructions

(a) How far apart are the positions of these two parties?

(b) Is there really any difference in the two approaches used by two parties in evaluating Byron Company's goodwill? Explain.

(COMPUTE GOODWILL) Ernie Corporation Ltd. is contemplating the purchase of Mastodon Industries and evaluating the amount of goodwill to be recognized in the purchase. Mastodon reports the following net incomes: E12-20

1988—$170,000
1989—$200,000
1990—$240,000
1991—$250,000
1992—$400,000

Mastodon has indicated that 1992 net income included the sale of one of its warehouses at a gain of $140,000 (net of tax). Net identifiable assets of Mastodon have a total fair market value of $850,000.

Instructions

Calculate goodwill in the following cases, assuming that expected income is to be a simple average of normal income for the past five years.

(a) Goodwill is determined by capitalizing average net earnings at 16%.

(b) Goodwill is determined by presuming a 16% return on identifiable net assets and capitalizing excess earnings at 25%.

E12-21 (COMPUTE FAIR VALUE OF IDENTIFIABLE ASSETS) Clarabelle Company bought a business that would yield exactly a 20% annual rate of return on its investment. Of the total amount paid for the business, $70,000 was deemed to be goodwill, and the remaining value was attributable to the identifiable net assets.

Clarabelle Company projected that the estimated annual future earnings of the new business would be equal to its average annual ordinary earnings over the past four years. The total net income over the past four years was $380,000, which included an extraordinary loss of $35,000 in one year and an extraordinary gain of $95,000 in one of the other three years.

Instructions

Compute the fair market value of the identifiable net assets that Clarabelle Company purchased in this transaction.

E12-22 (ACCOUNTING FOR R & D COSTS) Sabrina Company from time to time embarks on a research program when a special project seems to offer possibilities. In 1993 the company expends $300,000 on a research project, but by the end of 1993 it is impossible to determine whether any benefit will be derived from it.

Instructions

(a) What account should be charged for the $300,000, and how should it be shown in the financial statements?

(b) The project is completed in 1994, and a successful patent is obtained. The development costs to complete the project are $100,000. The administrative and legal expenses incurred in obtaining patent number 472-1001-84 in 1994 total $21,000. The patent has an expected useful life of five years. Record these costs in journal entry form. Also, record development cost and patent amortization (full year) in 1994.

(c) In 1995 the company successfully defends the patent in extended litigation at a cost of $44,000, thereby extending the economic life of the patent to 12/31/02. What is the proper way to account for this cost? Also, record patent amortization (full year) in 1995.

(d) Additional engineering and consulting costs incurred in 1995 required to advance the design of a product to the manufacturing stage total $60,000. These costs enhance the design of the product considerably. Discuss the proper accounting treatment for this cost.

E12-23 (ACCOUNTING FOR R & D COSTS) The Loogman Company incurred the following costs during 1994:

Quality control during commercial production, including routine testing of products	$52,000
Laboratory research aimed at discovery of new knowledge	70,000

(Continued)

Testing for evaluation of new products	24,000
Modification of the formulation of a plastics product	9,000
Engineering follow-through in an early phase of commercial production	14,000
Adaptation of an existing capability to a particular requirement or customer's need as a part of continuing commercial activity	13,000
Troubleshooting in connection with breakdowns during commercial production	27,000
Searching for applications of new research findings	17,000

Instructions

Compute the total amount Loogman should classify and expense as research and development costs for 1994.

E12-24 **(ACCOUNTING FOR R & D COSTS)** Filly Company incurred the following costs during 1994 in connection with its research and development activities:

Cost of equipment acquired that will have alternative uses in future research and development projects over the next five years (uses straight-line depreciation)	$300,000
Materials consumed in research and development projects	63,000
Consulting fees paid to outsiders for research and development projects	100,000
Personnel costs of persons involved in research and development projects	96,000
Indirect costs reasonably allocable to research and development projects	55,000
Materials purchased for future research and development projects	42,000

Instructions

Compute the amount to be reported as research and development expense by Filly on its income statement for 1994. Assume equipment purchased at beginning of year.

E12-25 **(ACCOUNTING FOR R & D COSTS)** Listed below are four independent situations involving research and development costs:

1. During 1994 Morton Co. Ltd. incurred the following costs:

Research and development services performed by Nehls Company for Morton	$325,000
Testing for evaluation of new products	300,000
Laboratory research aimed at discovery of new knowledge	400,000

For the year ended December 31, 1994, how much research and development expense should Morton report?

2. Penner Ltd. incurred the following costs during the year ended December 31, 1994:

Design, construction, and testing of pre-production prototypes and models	$270,000
Routine, ongoing efforts to refine, enrich, or otherwise improve upon the qualities of an existing product	250,000
Quality control during commercial production including routine testing of products	300,000
Laboratory research aimed at discovery of new knowledge	360,000

What is the total amount to be classified and expensed as research and development for 1994?

3. Hazelton Company incurred costs in 1994 as follows:

Equipment acquired for use in various research and development projects	$900,000
Depreciation on the equipment above	150,000
Materials used in R & D	300,000

(Continued)

Compensation costs of personnel in R & D	400,000
Outside consulting fees for R & D work	150,000
Indirect costs appropriately allocated to R & D	260,000

What is the total amount of research and development that should be reported in Hazelton's 1994 income statement?

4. Stein Inc. incurred the following costs during the year ended December 31, 1994:

Laboratory research aimed at discovery of new knowledge	$200,000
Radical modification to the formulation of a chemical product	125,000
Research and development costs reimbursable under a contract to perform research and development for Houck, Inc.	350,000
Testing for evaluation of new products	275,000

What is the total amount to be classified and expensed as research and development for 1994?

Instructions

Provide the correct answer to each of the four situations.

PROBLEMS

P12-1 **(CORRECT INTANGIBLE ASSET ACCOUNT)** Theresa Flagg Inc., organized in 1993, has set up a single account for all intangible assets. The following summary discloses the debit entries that have been recorded during 1993 and 1994.

Intangible Assets

07/1/93	Five-year franchise; expiration date 6/30/98	$ 42,000
10/1/93	Advance payment on leasehold (four-year lease)	28,000
12/31/93	Net loss for 1993 including incorporation fees, $1,000 and related legal fees of organizing, $5,000 (all fees incurred in 1993)	16,000
01/2/94	Patent purchased (eight-year life)	74,000
03/1/94	Cost of developing a secret formula (indeterminate life)	75,000
04/1/94	Goodwill purchased (indefinite life)	280,000
06/1/94	Legal fee for successful defence of patent	13,000
09/1/94	Research and development costs	160,000

Instructions

Prepare the necessary entries to clear the Intangible Assets account and to set up separate accounts for distinct types of intangibles. Make the entries as of December 31, 1994, recording any necessary amortization and reflecting all balances accurately as of that date. (Assume a 40-year amortization for intangibles unless specified.)

P12-2 **(ACCOUNTING FOR PATENTS)** Brady Laboratories holds a valuable patent (No. 758-6002-1A) on a precipitator that prevents certain types of air pollution. Brady does not manufacture or sell the products and processes it develops; it conducts research and develops products and processes which it patents, and then assigns the patents to manufacturers on a royalty basis. Occasionally it sells a patent. The history of Brady patent number 758-6002-1A is as follows.

Date	Activity	Cost
1984–1985	Research conducted to develop precipitator	$384,000
Jan. 1986	Design and construction of a prototype	87,600
March 1986	Testing of models	42,000
Jan. 1987	Fees paid to engineers and lawyers to prepare patent application; patent granted July 1, 1987	64,600
Nov. 1988	Engineering activity necessary to advance the design of the precipitator to the manufacturing stage	81,500
Dec. 1989	Legal fees paid to successfully defend precipitator patent	35,000
April 1991	Research aimed at modifying the design of the patented precipitator	43,000
July 1994	Legal fees paid in unsuccessful patent infringement suit against a competitor	34,000

Brady assumed a useful life of 17 years when it received the initial precipitator patent. On January 1, 1992 it revised its useful life estimate downward to five remaining years. Amortization was computed for a full year if the cost was incurred prior to July 1, and there was no amortization for the year if the cost was incurred after June 30. The company's year end was December 31.

Instructions

Compute the carrying value of patent No. 758-6002-1A on each of the following dates: (a) December 31, 1987, (b) December 31, 1991, (c) December 31, 1994.

(ACCOUNTING FOR FRANCHISE, PATENTS, AND TRADE NAME) Information concerning Crawford Co. Ltd.'s intangible assets is as follows: **P12-3**

1. On January 1, 1994, Crawford signed an agreement to operate as a franchisee of Thomson Service Inc., for an initial franchise fee of $75,000. Of this amount, $15,000 was paid when the agreement was signed and the balance was payable in four annual payments of $15,000 each beginning January 1, 1995. The agreement provided that the down payment was not refundable and no future services were required of the franchisor. The present value at January 1, 1994 of the four annual payments discounted at 14% (the implicit rate for a loan of this type) was $43,700. The agreement also provided that 5% of the revenue from the franchise must be paid to the franchisor annually. Crawford's revenue from the franchise for 1994 was $900,000. Crawford estimated the useful life of the franchise to be 10 years.

2. Crawford incurred $65,000 of experimental and development costs in its laboratory to develop a patent which was granted on January 2, 1994. Legal fees and other costs associated with registration of the patent totalled $13,600. Crawford estimated that the useful life of the patent would be eight years.

3. A trademark was purchased from Brewster Company for $40,000 on July 2, 1991. Expenditures for successful litigation in defence of the trademark totalling $8,500 were paid on July 1, 1994. Crawford estimated that the useful life of the trademark would be 20 years from the date of acquisition.

Instructions

(a) Prepare a schedule showing the intangibles section of Crawford's balance sheet at December 31, 1994. Show supporting computations in good form.

(b) Prepare a schedule showing all expenses resulting from the transactions that will appear on Crawford's income statement for the year ended December 31, 1994. Show supporting computations in good form.

(AICPA adapted)

P12-4 **(AMORTIZATION OF VARIOUS INTANGIBLES)** The following information relates to the intangible assets of Contraption Company.

	Organization Costs	Goodwill	Purchased Patent Costs
Original cost at 1/1/1994	$84,000	$300,000	$48,000
Useful life at 1/1/1994 (estimated)	Indefinite[a]	50 years	6 years

[a]Management has decided to write off the organization costs over five years.

Instructions

(a) Assuming straight-line amortization, compute the amount of the amortization of *each* item for 1994 in accordance with generally accepted accounting principles.

(b) Prepare the journal entries for the amortization of organization costs and goodwill for 1994.

(c) Assume that at January 1, 1995, Contraption Company incurred $10,000 of legal fees in defending the rights to the patents. Prepare the entry for the year 1995 to amortize the patents.

(d) Assume that at the beginning of year 1996, the company decided that the patent costs would be applicable only for the years 1996 and 1997. (A competitor had developed a product that would eventually make Contraption's obsolete.) Record the amortization of the patent costs at the end of 1996.

P12-5 **(COMPUTE GOODWILL)** Presented below are financial forecasts related to Bensman Limited for the next 10 years.

Forecasted average earnings (per year)	$ 65,000
Forecasted market value of net assets, exclusive of goodwill (average over 10 years)	360,000

Instructions

You have been asked to compute goodwill under the following methods. The normal rate of return on net assets for the industry is 15%.

(a) Goodwill is equal to five years' excess earnings.

(b) Goodwill is equal to the present value of five years' excess earnings discounted at 12%.

(c) Goodwill is equal to the average excess earnings capitalized at 16%.

(d) Goodwill is equal to average earnings capitalized at the normal rate of return for the industry of 15%.

(COMPUTE GOODWILL) Following is information related to Benton Inc. for 1994, its first year of operation. **P12-6**

Income Summary

Raw Material Purchased	$145,900	Sales	$550,000
Productive Labour	41,250	Closing Inventories	
Factory Overhead	29,750	Raw Material	32,400
Selling Expenses	39,400	Goods in Process	32,000
Administrative Expenses	24,950	Finished Goods	39,000
Interest Expense	8,650	Appreciation of Land	4,500
Opening Inventories		Profit on Sale of	
Raw Material	34,500	Forfeited Shares	7,200
Goods in Process	20,000		
Finished Goods	35,000		
Extraordinary Loss (net)	9,700		
Income Taxes	85,000		
Net Income	191,000		
	$665,100		$665,100

Instructions

Benton is negotiating to sell the business after one full year of operation. Compute the amount of goodwill as 200% of the income before extraordinary items and before taxes that is in excess of $150,000; $150,000 is considered to be a normal return on investment.

(COMPUTE GOODWILL) Penner Inc., a high-flying conglomerate, has recently been involved in discussions with Fox Inc. As its accountant, you have been instructed by Penner to conduct a purchase audit of Fox's books to determine a possible purchase price for Fox's net assets. The following information is found: **P12-7**

Total identifiable assets of Fox's (fair market value)	$260,000
Liabilities	60,000
Average rate of return on net assets for Fox's industry	15%
Forecasted earnings per year based on past earnings figures	40,000

Instructions

(a) Penner asks you to determine the purchase price on the basis of the following assumptions:

1. Goodwill is equal to three years' excess earnings.

2. Goodwill is equal to the present value of excess earnings discounted at 15% for three years.

3. Goodwill is equal to the capitalization of excess earnings at 15%.

4. Goodwill is equal to the capitalization of excess earnings at 25%.

(b) Penner asks you which of the methods above is the most theoretically sound. Justify your answer. Any assumptions made should be clearly indicated.

P12-8 **(ACCOUNTING FOR PURCHASE OF A BUSINESS)** Monona Ltd. has recently become interested in acquiring an Eastern Canadian plant to handle many of its production functions in that market. One possible candidate is Kapulet Inc., a closely held corporation, whose owners have decided to sell their business if a proper settlement can be obtained. Kapulet's balance sheet appears as follows.

Current assets	$150,000	Current liabilities	$ 80,000
Investments	50,000	Long-term debt	100,000
Plant assets (net)	400,000	Share capital	220,000
Total assets	$600,000	Retained earnings	200,000
		Total equities	$600,000

Monona has hired Canadian Appraisal Corporation to determine the proper price to pay for Kapulet Inc. The appraisal firm finds that the investments have a fair market value of $150,000 and that inventory is understated by $60,000. All other assets and equities are properly stated. An examination of the company's income for the last four years indicates that the net income has steadily increased. In 1994 the company has a net operating income of $100,000, and this income should increase 20% each year over the next four years. Monona believes that a normal return in this type of business is 18% on net assets. The asset investment in the Eastern Canadian plant is expected to stay the same for the next four years.

Instructions

(a) Canadian Appraisal Corporation has indicated that the fair value of the company can be estimated in a number of ways. Prepare an estimate of the value of the firm, assuming that any goodwill will be computed as:

1. The capitalization of the average excess earnings of Kapulet Inc. at 18%.
2. The purchase of average excess earnings over the next four years.
3. The capitalization of average excess earnings of Kapulet Inc. at 24%.
4. The present value of the average excess earnings over the next four years discounted at 15%.

(b) Kapulet Inc. is willing to sell the business for $1,000,000. How do you believe Canadian Appraisal should advise Monona?

(c) If Monona were to pay $770,000 to purchase the assets and assume the liabilities of Kapulet Inc., how would this transaction be reflected on Monona's books?

P12-9 **(COMPUTE GOODWILL)** Hawkeye Law Inc. has contracted to purchase Ellis Motor Company including the goodwill of the latter company. The agreement between purchaser and seller on the price to be paid for goodwill is as follows: "The value of the goodwill to be paid for is to be determined by capitalizing at 18% the average annual earnings from ordinary operations for the last five years in excess of 16% on the net worth, which, for purposes of this computation, is to be considered to be $306,250."

The net income per books for the last five years is:

1990	$43,150
1991	49,680
1992	64,320
1993	51,250
1994	78,080

As assistant to the treasurer of Hawkeye Law, you are instructed to review the accounts of Ellis Motors and determine the amount to be paid for goodwill in accordance with the terms of the contract. In your review of the accounts you discover the following:

1. An additional assessment of federal income taxes in the amount of $10,120 for the year 1992 was made and paid in 1994. The amount was charged against Retained Earnings.

2. In 1990 the company reviewed its accounts receivable and wrote off as an expense of that year $18,180 of accounts receivable that had been carried for years and appeared very unlikely to be collected.

3. In 1991 an account for $2,100 included in the 1990 write-off was collected and credited to Miscellaneous Income.

4. A fire in 1993 caused a loss, charged to income, as follows:

Book value of property destroyed	$29,400
Recovery from insurance company	10,000
Net loss	$19,400

5. Expropriation of property in 1993 resulted in a gain of $9,080 credited to income.

6. Amounts paid out under the company's product guarantee plan and charged to expense in each of the five years were as follows:

1990	$1,000
1991	1,300
1992	950
1993	1,100
1994	1,400

7. In 1994 the president of the company died, and the company realized $75,000 on an insurance policy on his life. The cash surrender value of this policy had been carried on the books as an investment in the amount of $62,240. The excess of proceeds over cash surrender value was credited to income.

Instructions

What is the price to be paid for the goodwill in accordance with the contract agreement? Prepare your computations in good form so that you can answer any questions asked by the treasurer in regard to your conclusions.

P12-10 **(ACCOUNTING FOR VARIOUS INTANGIBLE ASSETS AND R & D COSTS)** The following situations relate to accounting for intangible assets and research and development costs:

1. Wilde Corporation, a development stage company, deferred all its pre-operating research costs. Its 1993 financial statements consisted only of statements of cash receipts and disbursements, capital shares, and assets and unrecovered pre-operating costs and liabilities. The officers indicated that operations would start on June 30, 1994 and complete financials would be issued on December 31, 1994.

2. Hanson Inc. developed computer software to be used internally for its management information systems. The corporation incurred $290,000 in developing this new software package.

3. Williams Research is developing a new space station under contract for Star Search Inc. The contract, signed January 4, requires payments to Williams Research of $600,000 on December 31, and $1,000,000 at the completion of the project. On December 31 Williams Research recorded an account receivable of $600,000 and deferred development costs of $400,000.

4. Warfield Co. Ltd. purchased two patents directly from the inventors. Patent No. 1 could be used only in its listening device research project. Patent No. 2 could be used in many different projects and was currently being used in a research project.

5. Green Golf Company deferred all of its 1993 research costs, which totalled $360,000. In November 1994, you were hired as controller and were informed that an additional $450,000 had been deferred thus far in 1994. The company wanted to issue comparative financial statements in accordance with generally accepted accounting principles for the first time this year.

Instructions

For each of the situations above discuss the accounting treatment you would recommend.

P12-11 (ACCOUNTING FOR R & D COSTS) During 1992, Chaucer Tool Company purchased a building site for its proposed product development laboratory at a cost of $60,000. Construction of the building was started in 1992. The building was completed on December 31, 1993 at a cost of $380,000 and was placed in service on January 2, 1994. The estimated useful life of the building for depreciation purposes was 20 years, the straight-line method of depreciation was to be employed, and there was no estimated residual value.

Management estimated that about 50% of the development projects would result in long-term benefits (that is, at least 10 years) to the corporation. The remaining projects either benefited the current period or were abandoned before completion. Below is a summary of the number of projects and the direct costs incurred in conjunction with the development activities for 1994.

Upon recommendations of the development group, Chaucer acquired a patent for manufacturing rights at a cost of $90,000. The patent was acquired on April 1, 1993 and had an economic life of 10 years.

	Number of Projects	Salaries and Employee Benefits	Other Expenses (excluding Building Depreciation Charges)
Development of viable products (management intent and capability criteria are met)	15	$ 90,000	$50,000
Abandoned projects or projects that benefit the current period	10	60,000	15,000
Projects in process—results indeterminate	5	40,000	12,000
Total	30	$190,000	$77,000

Instructions

If generally accepted accounting principles were followed, how would the items above relating to product development activities be reported on the company's (a) income statement for 1994 and (b) balance sheet as of December 31, 1994?

(CMA adapted)

P12-12 (COMPREHENSIVE PROBLEM ON INTANGIBLES) Patricia Schmalz Ltd. was incorporated on January 3, 1993. The corporation's financial statements for its first year's operations were not examined by a public accountant. You have been engaged to examine the financial statements for the year ended December 31, 1994 and your examination is substantially completed. The corporation's trial balance appears below.

Patricia Schmalz Corporation
Trial Balance
December 31, 1994

	Debit	Credit
Cash	$ 15,000	
Accounts Receivable	73,000	
Allowance for Doubtful Accounts		$ 1,460
Inventories	50,200	

(Continued)

Machinery	82,000	
Equipment	37,000	
Accumulated Depreciation		26,200
Patents	135,000	
Leasehold Improvements	36,100	
Prepaid Expenses	13,000	
Organization Expenses	32,000	
Goodwill	30,000	
Licencing Agreement No. 1	60,000	
Licencing Agreement No. 2	57,000	
Accounts Payable		79,800
Unearned Revenue		17,280
Share Capital		300,000
Retained Earnings, January 1, 1994		159,060
Sales		720,000
Cost of Goods Sold	475,000	
Selling and General Expenses	180,000	
Interest Expense	8,500	
Extraordinary Losses	20,000	
Totals	$1,303,800	$1,303,800

The following information relates to accounts that may yet require adjustment:

1. Patents for Patricia Schmalz's manufacturing process were acquired January 2, 1994 at a cost of $102,000. An additional $33,000 was spent in December 1994 to improve machinery covered by the patents and charged to the Patents account. Depreciation on fixed assets was properly recorded for 1994 in accordance with Patricia Schmalz's practice, which provided a full year's depreciation for property on hand June 30 and no depreciation otherwise. Schmalz used the straight-line method for all depreciation and amortization and the legal life on its patents.

2. On January 2, 1993, Schmalz purchased Licencing Agreement No. 1, which was believed to have an unlimited useful life. The balance in the Licencing Agreement No. 1 account included its purchase price of $57,000 and expenses of $3,000 related to the acquisition. On January 1, 1994, Schmalz purchased Licencing Agreement No. 2, which had a life expectancy of 10 years. The balance in the Licencing Agreement No. 2 account included its $54,000 purchase price and $6,000 in acquisition expenses, but it had been reduced by a credit of $3,000 for the advance collection of 1995 revenue from the agreement.

   In late December 1993 an explosion caused a permanent 70% reduction in the expected revenue-producing value of Licencing Agreement No. 1 and in January 1995 a flood caused additional damage that rendered the agreement worthless.

3. The balance in the Goodwill account included (a) $14,000 paid December 30, 1993 for an advertising program that would assist in increasing Schmalz's sales over a period of four years following the disbursement and (b) legal expenses of $16,000 incurred for Schmalz's incorporation on January 3, 1993.

4. The Leasehold Improvements account includes (a) $15,000 cost of improvements with a total estimated useful life of 12 years, which Schmalz, as tenant, made to leased premises in January 1993, (b) moveable assembly line equipment costing $15,000 that was installed in the leased premises in December 1994, and (c) real estate taxes of $6,100 paid by Schmalz in 1994, which under the terms of the lease should have been paid by the landlord. Schmalz paid its rent in full during 1994. A 10-year nonrenewable lease was signed January 3, 1994 for the leased building that Schmalz used in manufacturing operations.

5. The balance in Organization Expenses account properly included costs incurred during the organizational period. The corporation had exercised its option to amortize 50% of its organization costs over a 10-year period for federal income tax purposes and wished to amortize these for accounting purposes on the same basis.

Instructions

Prepare an eight-column worksheet to adjust accounts that require adjustment and include columns for an income statement and a balance sheet.

A separate account should be used for the accumulation of each type of amortization and for each prior period adjustment. Formal adjusting journal entries and financial statements are *not* required. (**Hint**: Amortize Licencing Agreement No. 1 over 40 years before the explosion damage loss is determined.)

(AICPA adapted)

P12-13 (COMPUTATION OF R & D EXPENSE) Following are four independent situations involving research and development costs.

1. During 1994 Babycakes Inc. incurred the following costs:

Research services performed by Misty Company for Babycakes	$325,000
Testing and evaluation of possible new products	300,000
Laboratory research aimed at discovery of new knowledge	375,000

For the year ended December 31, 1994, how much research and development expense should Babycakes report?

2. Anderson Ltd. incurred the following costs during the year ended December 31, 1994:

Design, construction, and testing of pre-production prototypes and models*	$220,000
Routine, ongoing efforts to refine, enrich, or otherwise improve upon the qualities of an existing product*	250,000
Quality control during commercial production including routine testing of products	300,000
Laboratory research aimed at discovery of new knowledge	360,000

*Assume that *Handbook* Section 3450 criteria for capitalization are met and that the economic life of the related product(s) is 10 years.

What is the total amount to be expensed as research and development cost for 1994?

3. Zelensky Company incurred costs in 1994 as follows:

Equipment acquired for use in various research and development projects	$890,000
Depreciation of the equipment above	135,000
Materials used in R & D	300,000
Compensation costs of personnel in R & D	400,000
Outside consulting fees for R & D work	150,000
Indirect costs appropriately allocated to R & D	260,000

What is the total amount of research and development that should be reported in Zelensky's 1994 income statement?

4. Crown Inc. incurred the following costs during the year ended December 31, 1994:

Laboratory research aimed at discovery of new knowledge	$175,000
Radical modification to the formulation of a potential chemical product	125,000
Research and development costs reimbursable under a contract to perform research and development for Jeff King Inc.	350,000
Testing for evaluation of a new product	275,000

What is the total amount to be classified and expensed as research and development for 1994?

Instructions

Provide the correct answer to each of the four situations.

FINANCIAL REPORTING PROBLEM

Refer to the financial statements and other documents of Moore Corporation Limited presented in Appendix 5A and answer the following questions:

1. What is the amount of goodwill reported in Moore's financial statements in 1991? How does Moore amortize its goodwill?

2. Can you estimate the age or remaining life of Moore's property, plant, and equipment from the information provided for 1991 in the financial statements or accompanying notes? Was there any significant change in this regard from the previous year?

PERSPECTIVES

CANADIAN ACCOUNTING IN AN INTERNATIONAL ENVIRONMENT

Ron Charow

Ron Charow, 33, is the Corporate Controller for United Westburne Inc., North America's largest distributor of electrical, plumbing, and other construction materials with over $2 billion in annual sales. United Westburne has locations in both Canada and the United States, with its head office in Montreal. Prior to joining United Westburne, Ron worked at Deloitte & Touche for 8 years, where he specialized in financial instruments and derivative products. In addition to his responsibilities at United Westburne, Ron teaches Advanced Accounting Theory in the Graduate Diploma Program for Chartered Accountancy and in the Graduate Taxation Progam at McGill University, as well as courses in their UFE preparatory school.

Why did you become a CA?

I felt it important to have a professional designation that would lead to a variety of career choices with challenging and exciting opportunities. I believe that a CA designation opens many doors and also helps an individual build a foundation of personal skills that are useful regardless of career choice.

As Corporate Controller, are there particular Intermediate Accounting issues that you encounter more frequently than others?

In fact, almost every Intermediate Accounting subject occurs regularly, particularly issues concerning revenue recognition, asset valuation, capital transactions, financial statement disclosure, earnings per share, as well as commitments including off-balance-sheet financing. Just the other day, I was dealing with diverse issues such as volume rebates and interest rate swaps.

Your work and teaching responsibilities have exposed you to an area of accounting that is receiving an increasingly large amount of attention, namely international accounting. Why is this area becoming so important?

Clearly, the impact of the internationalization of trade, represented by trade agreements such as NAFTA, the FTA, and the European Economic Community, is being felt. They affect business in a number of ways, from capital markets to sourcing of labour. The impact of the communications superhighway is also being felt. Accounting standards will need to respond to these important changing environments.

How do you see the internationalization of trade affecting accounting in Canada?

This movement should promote further harmonization of Canada's accounting standards with international standards and those in other countries. The standards developed in Canada need to promote Canada's competitiveness in the international environment and promote a level playing field for Canadian companies amongst the international players.

Generally, with the globalization of capital markets, international investors can invest in companies around the world. In making their investment decisions, investors will analyse financial statements which are not necessarily comparable due to differing accounting standards between countries. It is important that Canada's accounting standards do not place Canadian companies at a competitive disadvantage.

How does Canada's current accounting standard-setting process compare with those of other countries?

Canada compares quite favourably. We have a structured standard-setting process that ensures high quality. These standards generally provide for the application of judgement in both financial accounting and reporting, more so than in the United States and elsewhere.

Looking ahead, how do you expect the global economy will affect Canada's accounting standards?

There are some areas that will require attention, for example, the amortization period of goodwill, accounting for foreign currency, including timing of recognition of gains and losses, and the use of purchase accounting versus pooling for business acquisitions.

There are also likely to be further joint standard-setting processes between Canada and international standard setters, like the one followed for the financial instruments *Exposure Draft* released in recent years.

What opportunities do you see the global market presenting for today's accounting students?

There will be a demand for Canadian accountants throughout the world due to the reputation our Canadian designation has achieved internationally. There will be opportunities in the areas of taxation dealing with cross-border transactions, transfer pricing, the restatement of earnings on a comparative basis, and converting financial results from one set of accounting standards to another. Other opportunities will present themselves in the financial services sector and in the area of derivative products.

How would you recommend interested accounting students prepare to take advantage of the opportunities presented by an increasingly international market?

It is important that Canadian students develop an appreciation of the global economy and that they continue to supplement their education as they advance through their careers by acquiring a second or third language, gaining exposure to foreign cultures, and reading business journals and magazines from other countries, for example, *The Wall Street Journal*.

Depending on where students work, many CA firms and other organizations have exchange programs between their international offices. I'd recommend that students take advantage of these opportunities when they arise. Additionally, when working with international clients it is important to pick up on differences in accounting standards between countries and to gain an appreciation of the differences and why they exist.

Students should also develop skills in the use of technology and be able to function within a hi-tech environment. An appreciation of finance is also critical in understanding the role of global capital markets and their impact on doing business.

Most importantly, though, students should actively seek out those opportunities that are of interest to them and pursue careers in international environments.

Appendix: Accounting and the Time Value of Money

A prime purpose of financial accounting is to provide information that is useful in making business and economic decisions. Certainly the relationship between time and money is central to economic decision making. It would seem reasonable, then, to expect that any accounting system that has decision usefulness as a primary goal should have a rational basis for reflecting the time value of money in the values it assigns to assets and liabilities—that is, should provide monetary measurements that are interpretable in present value terms.[1]

Would you like to be a millionaire? If you are 20 years old now, can save $100 every month and can invest those savings to earn an after-tax rate of return of 1% per month (over 12% per year), you could be a millionaire before you are 59 years old. Or if you could invest just $10,000 today at that same interest rate, you would have over a million dollars by age 59. Such is the power of *interest*, especially when it is energized with a generous dosage of *time*.[2]

Business enterprises both invest and borrow large sums of money. The common characteristic in these two types of transactions is the **time value of the money** (i.e. the interest factor involved). The timing of the returns on the investment has an important effect on the worth of the investment (asset), and the timing of debt repayments has an effect on the value of the commitment (liability). Business people have become acutely aware of this timing factor and invest and borrow only after carefully analysing the relative values of the cash outflows and inflows.

Accountants are expected to make and understand the implications of value measurements. To do so, they must understand and be able to measure the *present value* of future cash inflows and outflows. This measurement requires an understanding of compound interest, annuities, and present value concepts. Therefore, the basic objectives of this appendix are to discuss and illustrate the essentials of these concepts and provide some accounting and business-related examples in which they are applied.

APPLICATIONS OF TIME VALUE CONCEPTS

Objective 1

Identify accounting topics where time value of money is used.

Compound interest, annuities, and application of present value concepts are relevant to making measurements and disclosures when accounting for various financial statement elements. The following are some examples examined in this book and the chapters in which they appear:

[1] J. Alex Milburn, *Incorporating the Time Value of Money Within Financial Accounting* (Toronto: CICA, 1988), p. 1. This is an excellent study regarding financial accounting and present value measurements. Its objective is to "develop proposals for reflecting the time value of money more fully within the existing financial accounting framework so as to enable a substantive improvement in the usefulness and credibility of financial statements" (p. 1). While we, the authors, accept the basic premise of this study, it is not our intention to examine the model and suggested changes to current financial accounting that are presented. The purpose of this appendix is more basic— to examine the time value of money and show how it can be incorporated in making measurements.

[2] As another example of how interest can multiply dollars quickly, Sidney Homer (author of *A History of Interest Rates*) indicated, "$1,000 invested at a mere 8% for 400 years would grow to $23 quadrillion—$5 million for every human on earth." But, "the first 100 years are the hardest." (*Forbes*, July 14, 1986).

1. **Notes.** Valuing receivables and payables that carry no stated interest rate or a different than market interest rate (Chapters 7 and 14).
2. **Leases.** Valuing assets and obligations to be capitalized under long-term leases and measuring the amount of the lease payments and annual leasehold amortization (Chapter 21).
3. **Amortization of Premiums and Discounts.** Measuring amortization of premium or discount on both bond investments and bonds payable (Chapters 14 and 18).
4. **Pensions and Other Post-Retirement Benefits.** Measuring service cost components of employers' post-retirement benefits expense and benefit obligations (Chapter 20).
5. **Capital Assets.** Determining the value of assets acquired under deferred-payment contracts (Chapter 10).
6. **Sinking Funds.** Determining the contributions necessary to accumulate a fund for debt retirements (Chapter 14).
7. **Business Combinations.** Determining the value of receivables, payables, liabilities, accruals, and commitments acquired or assumed in a "purchase" (Chapter 18).
8. **Depreciation.** Measuring depreciation charges under the sinking fund and the annuity methods (Chapter 11).
9. **Instalment Contracts.** Measuring periodic payments on long-term sales or purchase contracts (Chapters 6 and 14).

In addition to accounting and business applications, compound interest, annuity, and present value concepts have applicability to personal finance and investment decisions. In purchasing a home, planning for retirement, and evaluating alternative investments, you need to understand time value of money concepts.

NATURE OF INTEREST

Interest ***is payment for the use of money.*** It is the excess cash received or paid over and above the amount lent or borrowed (**principal**). For example, if the Corner Bank lends you $1,000 with the understanding that you will repay $1,150, the excess over $1,000, or $150, represents interest expense to you and interest revenue to the bank.

The amount of interest to be paid is generally stated as a rate over a specific period of time. For example, if you use the $1,000 for one year before repaying $1,150, the rate of interest is 15% per year ($150/$1,000). The custom of expressing interest as a rate is an established business practice.[3] In fact, business managers make investing and borrowing decisions on the basis of the rate of interest involved rather than on the actual dollar amount of interest to be received or paid.

The rate of interest is commonly expressed as it is applied to a one-year time period. Interest of 12% represents a rate of 12% per year unless stipulated otherwise. The statement that a corporation will pay bond interest of 12%, payable semiannually, means a rate of 6% every six months, not 12% every six months.

How is the *rate* of interest determined? One of the most important factors is the level of **credit risk** (risk of nonpayment) involved. Other factors being equal, the higher the credit risk, the higher the interest rate. Every borrower's risk is evaluated by the lender. A low-risk borrower like Canadian Pacific Ltd. may obtain a loan at or slightly below the going market "prime" rate of interest. You or the neighbourhood delicatessen, however, will probably be charged several percentage points above the prime rate.

---

[3] Federal and provincial legislation requires the disclosure of the effective interest rate on an *annual basis* in contracts. That is, instead of or in addition to stating the rate as "1% per month," it must be stated as "12% per year" if it is simple interest or "12.68% per year" if it is compounded monthly.

Another important factor is **inflation** (change in the general purchasing power of the dollar). Lenders desire to protect the purchasing power of the future cash flows they will receive (interest payments and return of the principal). If inflation is expected to be significant in the future, lenders will require a higher number of dollars (i.e. a higher interest rate) in order to offset their anticipation that the purchasing power of these dollars will be reduced.

In addition to receiving compensation for risk and expected inflation, lenders also desire a **pure** or **real return** from letting someone else use their money. This real return reflects the amount the lender would charge if there were no possibility of default or expectation of inflation.

The *amount* of interest related to any financing transaction is a function of three variables:

1. **Principal**—the amount borrowed or invested.
2. **Interest Rate**—a percentage of the outstanding principal.
3. **Time**—the number of years or portion of a year that the principal is outstanding.

Simple Interest

Objective 2

Distinguish between simple and compound interest.

Simple interest *is computed on the amount of the principal only.* It is the return on (or growth of) the principal for one time period. Simple interest[4] is commonly expressed as:

$$\text{Interest} = p \times i \times n$$

Where

p = principal
i = rate of interest for a single period
n = number of periods

To illustrate, if you borrowed $1,000 for a three-year period, with a simple interest rate of 15% per year, the total interest you would pay would be $450, computed as follows:

$$\begin{aligned}\text{Interest} &= (p)\,(i)\,(n)\\ &= (\$1{,}000)\,(.15)\,(3)\\ &= \$450\end{aligned}$$

Compound Interest

John Maynard Keynes, the legendary English economist, supposedly called it magic. Mayer Rothschild, the founder of the famous European banking firm, is said to have proclaimed it the eighth wonder of the world. Today people continue to extol its wonder and its power.[5] The object of their affection is compound interest.

Compound interest *is computed on the principal* and *any interest earned that has not been paid.* To illustrate the difference between simple interest and compound interest, assume that you deposit $1,000 in the Last Canadian Bank where it earns simple interest of 9% per year, and you deposit another $1,000 in the First Canadian Bank where it earns annually compounded interest of 9%. Also assume that in both cases you do not withdraw any interest until three years from the date of deposit. The calculation of interest to be received is shown at the top of page A-4.

Note that simple interest uses the initial principal of $1,000 to compute the interest in all three years, while compound interest uses the accumulated balance (principal plus interest to date) at each year end to compute interest in the succeeding year. Obviously, if you had a choice between

---

[4] Simple interest is also expressed as i (interest) = P (principal) × R (rate) × T (time).

[5] Here is an illustration of the power of time and compounding interest on money. In 1626, Peter Minuit bought Manhattan Island from the Manhattoe Indians for $24 worth of trinkets and beads. If the Indians had taken a boat to Holland, invested the $24 in Dutch securities returning just 6% per year, and kept the money and interest invested at 6%, by 1971 they would have had $13 billion, enough to buy back all the land on the island and still have a couple of billion dollars left (*Forbes*, June 1, 1971). By 1988, 362 years after the trade, the $24 would have grown to approximately $34.6 billion—$29 trillion had the interest rate been 8%.

SIMPLE INTEREST VS. COMPOUND INTEREST

	Last Canadian Bank			First Canadian Bank		
	Simple Interest Calculation	Simple Interest	Accumulated Year-End Balance	**Compound** Interest Calculation	Compound Interest	Accumulated Year-End Balance
Year 1	$1,000.00 x 9%	$ 90.00	$1,090.00	$1,000.00 x 9%	$ 90.00	$1,090.00
Year 2	1,000.00 x 9%	90.00	1,180.00	1,090.00 x 9%	98.10	1,188.10
Year 3	1,000.00 x 9%	90.00	1,270.00	1,188.00 x 9%	106.93	1,295.03
		$270.00	**$25.03** Difference		$295.03	

investing at simple interest or at compound interest, you would choose compound interest, all other things—especially risk—being equal. In the example, compounding provides $25.03 of additional interest income.

Compound interest is generally applied in business situations. Financial managers view and evaluate their investment opportunities in terms of a series of periodic returns, each of which can be reinvested to yield additional returns. Simple interest is applicable only to short-term investments and debts that are due within one year.

Compound Interest Tables

Objective 3

Learn how to use appropriate compound interest tables.

Five different compound interest tables are presented at the end of this appendix (see pages A-25–A-29). These tables are the source for various "interest factors" used in solving problems involving interest illustrated in this appendix and throughout the book. The titles of these five tables and their contents are:

1. **Future Amount of 1**. Contains the amounts to which $1.00 will accumulate if deposited now at a specified rate and left for a specified number of periods. (Table A-1)

2. **Present Value of 1**. Contains the amounts that must be deposited now at a specified rate of interest to equal $1.00 at the end of a specified number of periods. (Table A-2)

3. **Future Amount of an Ordinary Annuity of 1**. Contains the amounts to which periodic rents of $1.00 will accumulate if the rents are invested at the *end* of each period at a specified rate of interest for a specified number of periods. (Table A-3)

4. **Present Value of an Ordinary Annuity of 1**. Contains the amounts that must be deposited now at a specified rate of interest to permit withdrawals of $1.00 at the *end* of regular periodic intervals for the specified number of periods. (Table A-4)

5. **Present Value of an Annuity Due of 1**. Contains the amounts that must be deposited now at a specified rate of interest to permit withdrawals of $1.00 at the *beginning* of regular periodic intervals for the specified number of periods. (Table A-5)

The excerpt at the top of page A-5 illustrates the general format and content of these tables. It is from Table A-1, "Future Amount of 1," which indicates the amount to which a dollar accumulates at the end of each of five periods at three different rates of compound interest.

Interpreting the table, if $1.00 is invested for three periods at a compound interest rate of 9% per period, it will amount to $1.30 (1.29503 × $1.00), the **compound future amount.** If $1.00 is invested at 11%, at the end of four periods it amounts to $1.52. If the investment is $1,000 instead of $1.00, it will amount to $1,295.03 ($1,000 × 1.29503) if invested at 9% for three periods or $1,518.07 if invested at 11% for four periods.

Throughout the foregoing discussion (and most of the discussion that follows) the use of the term *periods* instead of *years* is intentional. While interest is generally expressed as an annual rate, the compounding period is often shorter. Therefore, the annual interest rate must be converted to correspond to the length of the period. To convert the "annual interest rate" into the "compounding

Future Amount of 1 at Compound Interest
(Excerpt from Table A-1)

Period	9%	10%	11%
1	1.09000	1.10000	1.11000
2	1.18810	1.21000	1.23210
3	1.29503	1.33100	1.36763
4	1.41158	1.46410	1.51807
5	1.53862	1.61051	1.68506

period interest rate," ***divide the annual rate by the number of compounding periods per year.*** In addition, the number of periods is determined by ***multiplying the number of years involved by the number of compounding periods per year.***

To illustrate, assume that \$1.00 is invested for six years at 8% annual interest compounded quarterly. Using Table A-1, the amount to which this \$1.00 will accumulate is determined by reading the factor that appears in the 2% column (8% ÷ 4) on the 24th row (6 years × 4), namely 1.60844, or approximately \$1.61.

Because interest is theoretically earned (accruing) every second of every day, it is possible to calculate interest that is compounded continuously but, as a practical matter, most business transactions assume interest to be compounded no more frequently than daily.

How often interest is compounded can make a substantial difference in the rate of return achieved. For example, 9% interest compounded daily provides a 9.42% annual yield, or a difference of .42%. The 9.42% is referred to as the **effective yield** or **rate**[6] whereas the 9% annual interest rate is called the **stated, nominal, coupon,** or **face rate.** When the compounding frequency is greater than once a year, the effective interest rate is greater than the stated rate.

FUNDAMENTAL VARIABLES

The following four variables are fundamental to all compound interest problems:

1. **Rate of Interest**. This rate, unless otherwise stated, is an annual rate that must be adjusted to reflect the length of the compounding period less than a year.
2. **Number of Time Periods**. This is the number of compounding periods for which interest is to be computed.
3. **Future Amount**. The value at a future date of a given sum or sums invested assuming compound interest.
4. **Present Value**. The value now (present time) of a future sum or sums discounted assuming compound interest.

Objective 4

Identify variables fundamental to solving interest problems.

The relationship of these four variables is depicted in the ***time diagram*** on page A-6.

In some cases all four of these variables are known, but in many business situations at least one is unknown. Frequently, the accountant is expected to determine the unknown amount or amounts. To do this, a time diagram can be very helpful in understanding the nature of the problem and finding a solution.

---

[6] The formula for calculating the effective rate in situations where the compounding frequency (f) is more than once a year is as follows:

$$\text{Effective rate} = (1 + i)^f - 1$$

where i = the interest rate per compounding period.

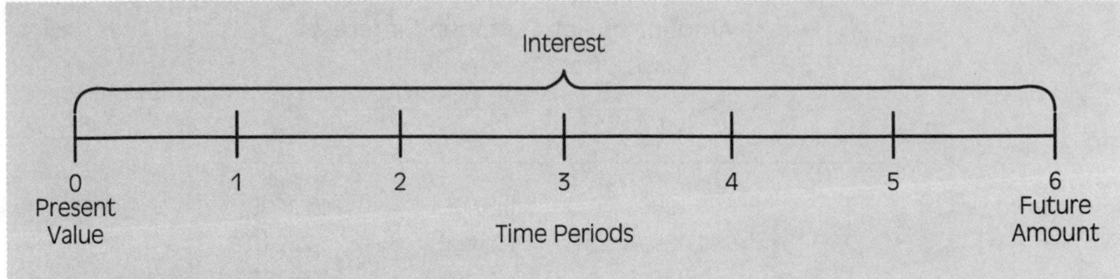

The remainder of the appendix covers the following six major time value of money concepts. Both formula and interest table approaches are used to illustrate how problems may be solved:

1. Future amount of a single sum.
2. Present value of a single sum.
3. Future amount of an ordinary annuity.
4. Future amount of an annuity due.
5. Present value of an ordinary annuity.
6. Present value of an annuity due.

SINGLE SUM PROBLEMS

Objective 5

Solve future and present value of single-sum problems.

Many business and investment decisions involve a single amount of money that either exists now or will exist in the future. Single sum problems can generally be classified into one of the following two categories:

1. Determining the *unknown future amount* of a known single sum of money that is invested for a specified number of periods at a specified interest rate.
2. Determining the *unknown present value* of a known single sum of money that is discounted for a specified number of periods at a specified interest rate.

Future Amount of a Single Sum

The "amount" of a sum of money is the future value of that sum when left to accumulate for a certain number of periods at a specified rate of interest per period.

The amount to which 1 (one) will accumulate may be expressed as a formula:

$$a_{\overline{n}|i} = (1 + i)^n$$

where

$a_{\overline{n}|i}$ = future amount of 1
i = rate of interest for a single period
n = number of periods

To illustrate, assume that $1.00 is invested at 9% interest compounded annually for three years. The amounts to which the $1.00 will accumulate at the end of each year are:

$a_{\overline{1}|9\%} = (1 + .09)^1$ for the end of the first year.
$a_{\overline{2}|9\%} = (1 + .09)^2$ for the end of the second year.
$a_{\overline{3}|9\%} = (1 + .09)^3$ for the end of the third year.

These compound amounts accumulate as follows.

Period	Beginning-of-Period Amount	×	Multiplier $(1 + i)$	=	End-of-Period Amount*	Formula $(1 + i)^n$
1	1.00000		1.09		1.09000	$(1.09)^1$
2	1.09000		1.09		1.18810	$(1.09)^2$
3	1.18810		1.09		1.29503	$(1.09)^3$

*These amounts appear in Table A-1 in the 9% column.

To calculate the *future value of any single amount,* multiply the future amount of 1 factor by that amount.

$$a = p(a_{\overline{n}|i})$$

where

a = future amount

p = beginning principal or sum (present value)

$a_{\overline{n}|i} = (1 + i)^n$ = future amount of 1 for n periods at i%

For example, what is the future amount of $50,000 invested for five years at 11% compounded annually? In time-diagram form, this investment situation is as follows.

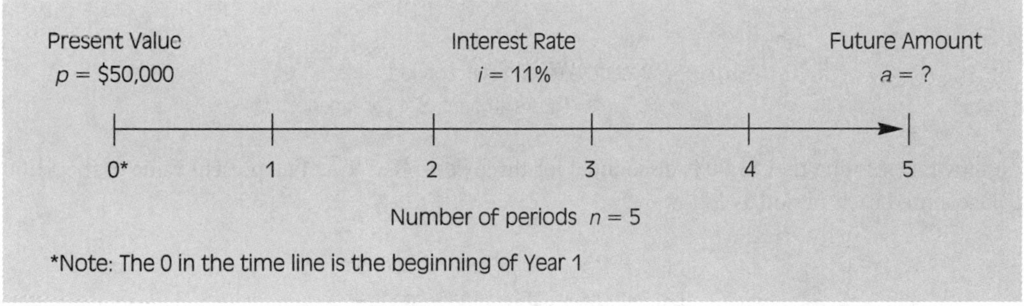

This investment problem is solved as follows:

$$\begin{aligned} a &= p(a_{\overline{n}|i}) \\ &= \$50{,}000(a_{\overline{5}|11\%}) \\ &= \$50{,}000\ (1.68506) \\ &= \$84{,}253. \end{aligned}$$

The future amount of 1 factor of 1.68506 is that which appears in Table A-1 in the 11% column and 5-period row.

To illustrate a more complex business situation, assume that at the beginning of 1994 Ontario Hydro Corp. deposits $250 million in an escrow account with Canada Trust Company as a commitment toward a small nuclear power plant to be completed December 31, 1997. How much will be on deposit at the end of four years if interest is compounded semiannually at 10%?

With a known present value of $250 million, a total of eight compounding periods (4 × 2), and an interest rate of 5% per compounding period (.10 ÷ 2), this problem can be time-diagrammed and the future amount determined as follows.

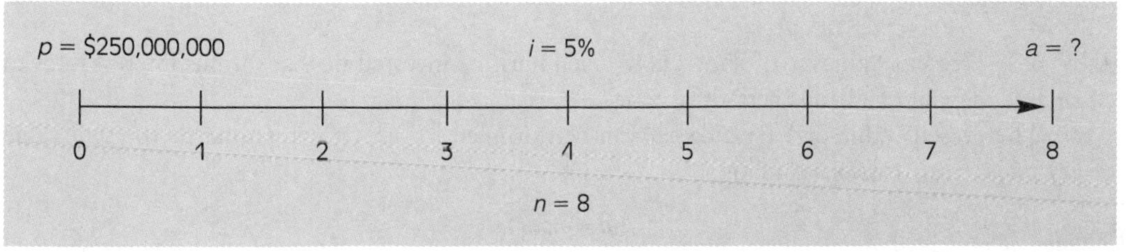

$$a = \$250{,}000{,}000\,(a_{\overline{8}|5\%})$$
$$= \$250{,}000{,}000\,(1.47746)$$
$$= \$369{,}365{,}000$$

The deposit of $250 million will accumulate to $369,365,000 by December 31, 1997. The future amount of 1 factor is found in Table A-1 (5% column and the 8-period row).

Present Value of a Single Sum

A previous example showed that $50,000 invested at an annually compounded interest rate of 11% will be worth $84,253 at the end of five years. It follows that $84,253 to be received five years from now is presently worth $50,000 given an 11% interest rate (i.e. $50,000 is the present value of this $84,253). The **present value** is the amount that must be invested now to produce a known future amount. The ***present value is always a smaller amount than the known future amount because interest is earned and accumulated on the present value to the future date.*** In determining the future amount we move forward in time using a process of **accumulation**, while in determining present value we move backward in time using the process of **discounting**.

The present value of 1 (one) may be expressed as a formula:

$$p_{\overline{n}|i} = 1 / a_{\overline{n}|i} = \frac{1}{(1 + i)^n}$$

where

$p_{\overline{n}|i}$ = present value of 1 for n periods at i%.

$a_{\overline{n}|i}$ = $(1 + i)^n$ = future amount of 1 for n periods at i%.

To illustrate, assume that $1.00 is discounted for three periods at 9%. The present value of the $1.00 is discounted each period as follows:

$p_{\overline{1}|9\%}$ = $1/(1 + .09)^1$ for the first period

$p_{\overline{2}|9\%}$ = $1/(1 + .09)^2$ for the second period

$p_{\overline{3}|9\%}$ = $1/(1 + .09)^3$ for the third period

Therefore, the $1.00 is discounted as follows.

Discount Periods	Future Amount	÷	Divisor $(1 + i)^n$	=	Present Value*	Formula $1/(1 + i)^n$
1	1.00000		1.09		.91743	$1/(1.09)^1$
2	1.00000		$(1.09)^2$		.84168	$1/(1.09)^2$
3	1.00000		$(1.09)^3$		.77218	$1/(1.09)^3$

*These amounts appear in Table A-2 in the 9% column.

Table A-2, "Present Value of 1," shows how much must be invested now at various interest rates to equal 1 at the end of various periods of time.

The present value of 1 formula $p_{\overline{n}|i}$ can be expanded for use in computing the present value of *any single future amount* as follows:

$$p = a(p_{\overline{n}|i})$$

where

p = present value of a single future amount

a = future amount

$$p_{\overline{n}|i} = \frac{1}{(1 + 1)^n} = \text{present value of 1 for } n \text{ periods at i\%}$$

To illustrate the use of this formula, assume that your favourite uncle proposes to give you $4,000 for a trip to Europe when you graduate three years from now. He will finance the trip by investing a sum of money now at 8% compound interest that will accumulate to $4,000 upon your graduation. The only conditions are that you graduate and that you tell him how much to invest now.

To impress your uncle you might set up the following time diagram and solve the problem as follows.

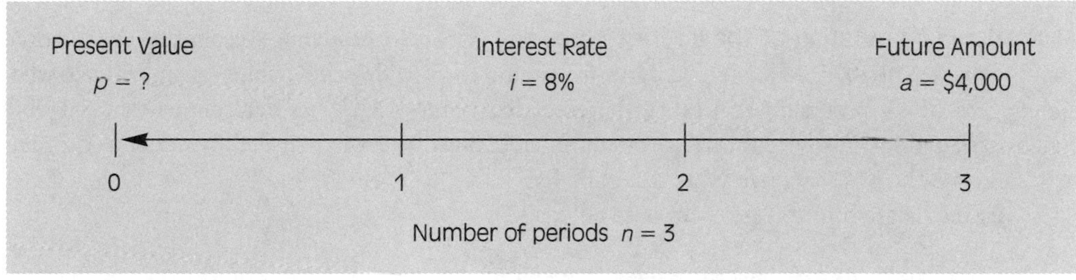

$$\begin{aligned} p &= \$4{,}000\ (p_{\overline{3}|8\%}) \\ &= \$4{,}000\ (.79383) \\ &= \$3{,}175.32 \end{aligned}$$

Advise your uncle to invest $3,175.32 now to provide you with $4,000 upon graduation. To satisfy your uncle's other condition, you must simply pass this course and many more. Note that the present value factor of .79383 is found in Table A-2 (8% column, 3-period row).

Single Sum Problems: Solving for Other Unknowns

In computing either the future amount or the present value in the previous single sum illustrations, both the number of periods and the interest rate were known. In business situations, both the future amount and the present value may be known and either the number of periods or the interest rate may be unknown. The following two illustrations demonstrate how to solve single sum problems when there is either an unknown number of periods (n) or an unknown interest rate (i). These illustrations show that if any three of the four values (future amount, a; present value, p; number of periods, n; interest rate, i) are known, the one unknown can be derived.

Illustration: Computation of the Number of Periods. The local Big Sisters and Big Brothers associations in Regina want to accumulate $70,000 for the construction of a day-care centre. If at the beginning of the current year the associations are able to deposit $47,811 in a building fund that earns 10% interest compounded annually, how many years will it take for the fund to accumulate to $70,000?

In this situation, the present value ($47,811), future amount ($70,000), and interest rate (10%) are known. A time diagram of this investment is as follows.

p = $47,811 i = 10% a = 70,000

n = ?

The unknown number of periods can be determined using either the future amount or present value approaches as shown below:

Future Amount Approach	Present Value Approach
$a = p(a_{\overline{n}\rvert 10\%})$	$p = a(p_{\overline{n}\rvert 10\%})$
$\$70{,}000 = \$47{,}811(a_{\overline{n}\rvert 10\%})$	$\$47{,}811 = \$70{,}000(p_{\overline{n}\rvert 10\%})$
$a_{\overline{n}\rvert 10\%} = \dfrac{\$70{,}000}{\$47{,}811} = 1.46410$	$p_{\overline{n}\rvert 10\%} = \dfrac{\$47{,}811}{\$70{,}000} = .68301$

Using the future amount of 1 factor of 1.46410, refer to Table A-1 and read down the 10% column to find that factor in the 4-period row. Thus, it will take four years for the \$47,811 to accumulate to \$70,000. Using the present value of 1 factor of .68301, refer to Table A-2 and read down the 10% column to also find that factor is in the 4-period row.

Illustration: Computation of the Interest Rate. The Canadian Academic Accounting Association wants to have \$141,000 available five years from now to provide scholarships to individuals who undertake a Ph.D. program. At present, the executive of the CAAA has determined that \$80,000 may be invested for this purpose. What rate of interest must be earned on the investments in order to accumulate the \$141,000 five years from now?

A time diagram of this problem is as follows.

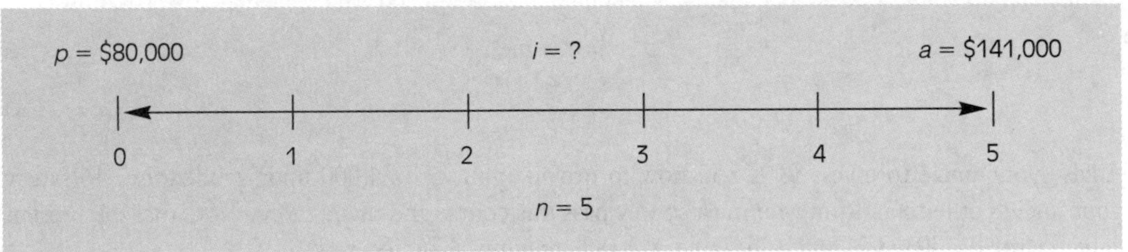

Given that the present value, future amount, and number of periods are known, the unknown interest rate can be determined using either the future amount or present value approaches as shown below:

Future Amount Approach	Present Value Approach
$a = p(a_{\overline{5}\rvert i})$	$p = a(p_{\overline{5}\rvert i})$
$\$141{,}000 = \$80{,}000\ (a_{\overline{5}\rvert i})$	$\$80{,}000 = \$141{,}000\ (p_{\overline{5}\rvert i})$
$a_{\overline{5}\rvert i} = \$141{,}000 / \$80{,}000$	$p_{\overline{5}\rvert i} = \$80{,}000 / \$141{,}000$
$= 1.7625$	$= 0.5674$

Using the future amount of 1 factor of 1.7625, refer to Table A-1 and read across the 5-period row to find a close match of this future amount factor in the 12% column. Thus, the \$80,000 must be invested at 12% to accumulate to \$141,000 at the end of five years. Using the present value of 1 factor of 0.5674 and Table A-2, reading across the 5-period row shows this factor in the 12% column.

ANNUITIES

The preceding discussion involved only the accumulation or discounting of a single principal sum. Accountants frequently encounter situations in which a series of amounts are to be paid or received over time (e.g., when loans or sales are paid in instalments, invested funds are partially recovered at regular intervals, and cost savings are realized repeatedly). When a commitment involves a series of equal payments made at equal intervals of time, it is called an annuity. By definition, an **annuity** requires that (1) the ***periodic payments or receipts*** (called **rents**) ***always be the same amount***, (2) the ***interval between such rents always be the same***, and (3) the ***interest be compounded once each interval.***

The **future amount of an annuity** ***is the sum of all the rents plus the accumulated compound interest on them.*** Rents may, however, occur at either the beginning or the end of the periods. To distinguish annuities under these two alternatives, an annuity is classified as an **ordinary annuity** ***if the rents occur at the end of each period***, and as an **annuity due** ***if the rents occur at the beginning of each period.***

Future Amount of an Ordinary Annuity

Objective 6

Solve future amount of ordinary and annuity due problems.

One approach to calculating the future amount of an annuity is to determine the future amount of each rent in the series and then aggregate these individual future amounts. For example, assume that \$1 is deposited at the *end* of each of five years (an ordinary annuity)and earns 12% interest compounded annually. The future amount can be computed as follows using the "Future Amount of 1," for each of the five \$1 rents.

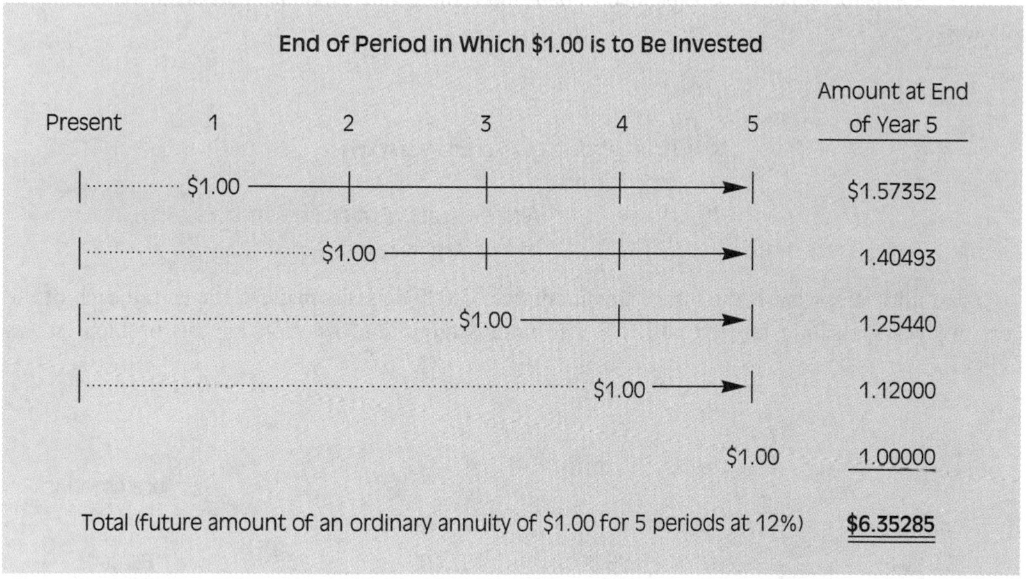

End of Period in Which \$1.00 is to Be Invested

Present	1	2	3	4	5	Amount at End of Year 5
	\$1.00					\$1.57352
		\$1.00				1.40493
			\$1.00			1.25440
				\$1.00		1.12000
					\$1.00	1.00000
Total (future amount of an ordinary annuity of \$1.00 for 5 periods at 12%)						**\$6.35285**

Although the foregoing procedure for computing the future amount of an ordinary annuity produces the correct answer, it is cumbersome if the number of rents is large. A more efficient way of determining the future amount of an ordinary annuity of 1 is by applying the following formula:

$$A_{\overline{n}|i} = \frac{(1+i)^n - 1}{i}$$

where

$A_{\overline{n}|i}$ = future amount of an ordinary annuity of 1 for n periods at i rate of interest

n = number of compounding periods

i = rate of interest per period

Using this formula, Table A-3 has been developed to show the "Future Amount of an Ordinary Annuity of 1" for various interest rates and investment periods. The top box on page A-12 is an excerpt from this table. Interpreting the table, if \$1.00 is invested at the end of each year for four years at 11% interest compounded annually, the amount of the annuity at the end of the fourth year will be \$4.71 (4.70973 × \$1.00). The \$4.71 is made up of \$4 of rent payments (\$1 at the end of each of the 4 years) and compound interest of \$0.71.

Future Amount of an Ordinary Annuity of 1
(Excerpt from Table A-3)

Period	10%	11%	12%
1	1.00000	1.00000	1.00000
2	2.10000	2.11000	2.12000
3	3.31000	3.34210	3.37440
4	4.64100	4.70973	4.77933
5	6.10510	6.22780	**6.35285***

*Note that this factor is the same as the sum of the future amounts of 1 factors shown in the previous schedule.

The $A_{\overline{n}|i}$ formula can be expanded to determine the future amount of an ordinary annuity as follows:

$$A = R\,(A_{\overline{n}|i})$$

where

A = future amount of an ordinary annuity
R = periodic rents

$$A_{\overline{n}|i} = \frac{(1+i)^n - 1}{i} = \text{future amount of an ordinary annuity of 1 for } n \text{ periods at } i\%$$

To illustrate, what is the future amount of five $5,000 deposits made at the end of each of the next five years, earning interest at 12%? The time diagram and solution for this problem are as follows.

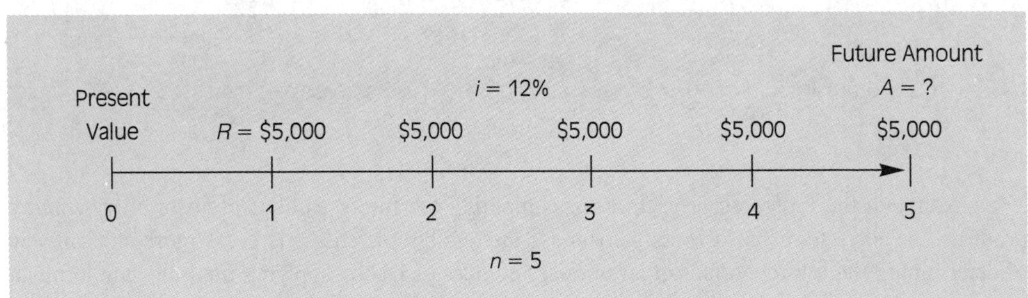

$$\begin{aligned} A &= R\,(A_{\overline{n}|i}) \\ &= \$5{,}000\,(A_{\overline{5}|12\%}) \\ &= \$5{,}000\,(6.35285) \\ &= \$31{,}764.25 \end{aligned}$$

The future amount of an ordinary annuity of 1 factor of 6.35285 is found in Table A-3 (12% column, 5-period row).

To illustrate these computations in a business situation, assume that Lightning Electronics Limited's management decides to deposit $75,000 at the end of each six-month period for the next three years for the purpose of accumulating enough money to meet debts that mature in three years. What is the future amount that will be on deposit at the end of three years if the annual interest rate is 10%? The time diagram and solution are as follows.

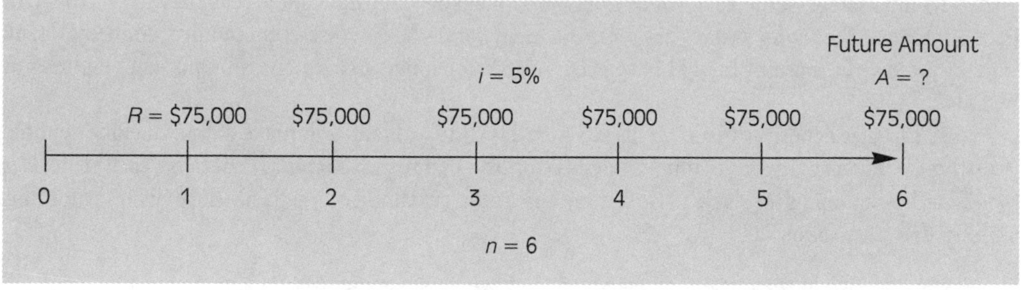

$$
\begin{aligned}
A &= R(A_{\overline{n}|i}) \\
&= \$75,000\,(A_{\overline{6}|5\%}) \\
&= \$75,000\,(6.80191) \\
&= \$510,143.25
\end{aligned}
$$

Thus, six deposits of $75,000 made at the end of every six months and earning 5% per period will grow to $510,143.25 at the time of the last deposit.

Future Amount of an Annuity Due

The preceding analysis of an *ordinary annuity* was based on the fact that the *periodic rents* occur at the *end* of each period. An **annuity due** is based on the fact that the *periodic rents* occur at the *beginning* of each period. This means an annuity due will accumulate interest during the first period whereas an ordinary annuity will not. Therefore, the significant difference between the two types of annuities is in the number of interest accumulation periods involved. The distinction is shown graphically below.

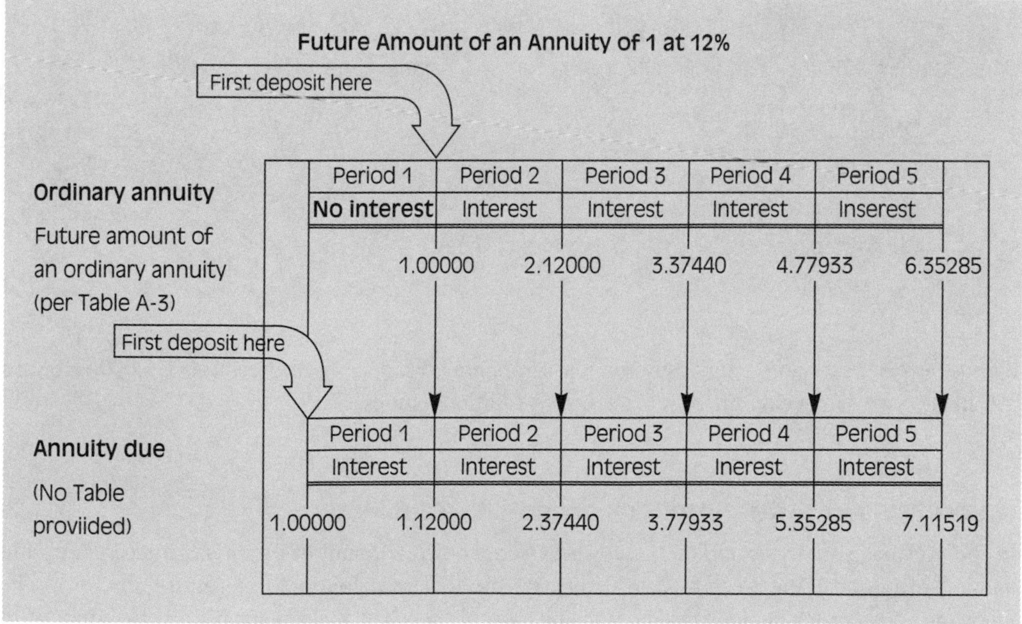

Because the cash flows from the annuity due come exactly one period earlier than for an ordinary annuity, the future value of the annuity due of 1 factor is exactly 12% higher than the ordinary annuity factor. Therefore, ***to determine the future value of an annuity due of 1 factor, multiply the corresponding future value of the ordinary annuity of 1 factor by one plus the interest rate.*** For example, to determine the future value of an annuity due of 1 factor for five periods at 12% compound interest, simply multiply the future value of an ordinary annuity of 1 factor for five periods (6.35285) by one plus the interest rate (1 + .12) to arrive at the future value of an annuity due of 1, 7.1159 (6.35285 × 1.12).

To illustrate, assume that Hank Lotadough plans to deposit $800 a year on each birthday of his son Howard, starting today, his tenth birthday, at 12% interest compounded annually. Hank wants to know the amount he will have accumulated for university expenses by his son's eighteenth birthday.

As the first deposit is made on his son's tenth birthday, Hank will make a total of eight deposits over the life of the annuity (assume no deposit on the eighteenth birthday). Because each deposit is made at the beginning of each period, they represent an annuity due. The time diagram for this annuity due is as follows.

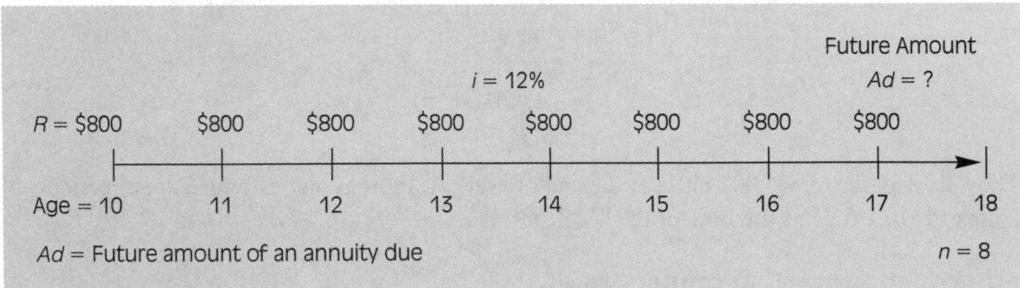

Referring to Table A-3, "Future Amount of an Ordinary Annuity of 1," for eight periods at 12%, a factor of 12.29969 is found. This factor is then multiplied by (1 + .12) to arrive at the future amount of an annuity due of 1 factor. As a result, the accumulated amount on his son's eighteenth birthday is computed as follows.

1.	Future amount of an ordinary annuity of 1 for 8 periods at 12% (Table A-3)	12.29969
2.	Factor (1 + .12)	× 1.12
3.	Future amount of an annuity due of 1 for 8 periods at 12%	13.77565
4.	Periodic deposit (rent)	× $800
5.	Accumulated amount on son's eighteenth birthday	$11,020.52

Because expenses to go to university for four years are considerably in excess of $11,000, Howard will likely have to develop his own plan to save additional funds.

Illustrations of Future Amount of Annuity Problems

In the previous annuity examples, three values were known (amount of each rent, interest rate, and number of periods) and were used to determine the unknown fourth value (future amount). The following illustrations demonstrate how to solve problems when the unknown is (1) the amount of the rents or (2) the number of rents in ordinary annuity situations.

Illustration: Computing the Amount of Each Rent. Assume that you wish to accumulate $14,000 for a down payment on a condominium apartment five years from now and that you can earn an annual return of 8% compounded semiannually during the next five years. How much should you deposit at the end of each six-month period?

The $14,000 is the future amount of ten (5 × 2) semiannual end-of-period payments of an unknown amount at an interest rate of 4% (8% ÷ 2). This problem is time-diagrammed as follows.

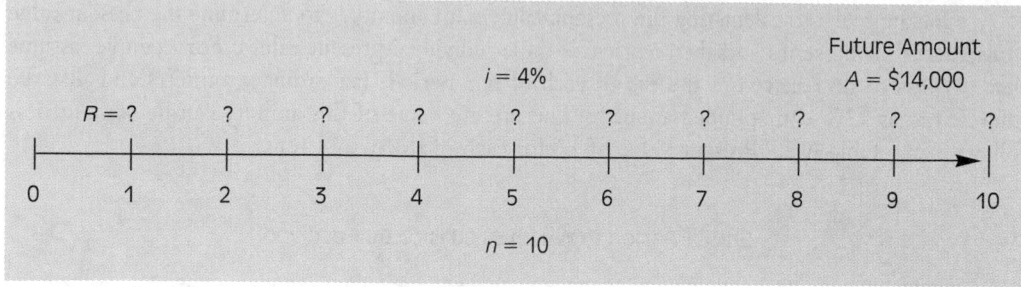

Using the formula for the future amount of an ordinary annuity, the amount of each rent is determined as follows:

$$A = R(A_{\overline{n}|i})$$
$$\$14,000 = R(A_{\overline{10}|4\%})$$
$$\$14,000 = R(12.00611)$$
$$\frac{\$14,000}{12.00611} = R$$
$$R = \$1,166.07$$

Thus, you must make 10 semi-annual deposits of $1,166.07 each in order to accumulate $14,000 for your down payment. The future amount of an ordinary annuity of 1 factor of 12.00611 is provided in Table A-3 (4% column, 10-period row).

Illustration: Computing the Number of Periodic Rents. Suppose that your company wants to accumulate $117,332 by making periodic deposits of $20,000 at the end of each year that will earn 8% compounded annually. How many deposits must be made?

The $117,332 represents the future amount of *n*(=?) $20,000 deposits at an 8% annual rate of interest. The time diagram for this problem is as follows.

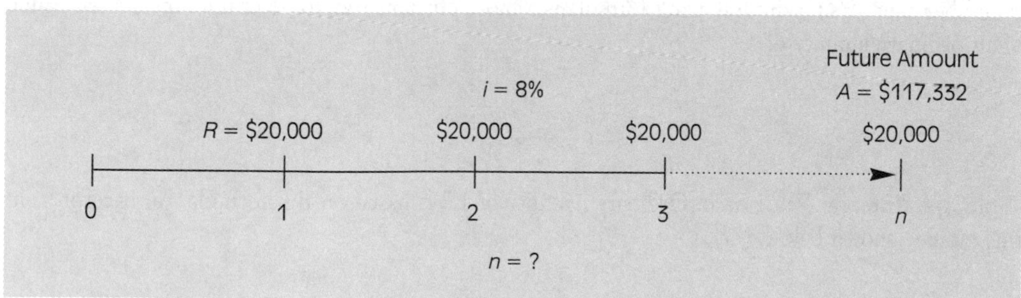

Using the future amount of an ordinary annuity formula, the factor of 1 is determined as follows:

$$A = R(A_{\overline{n}|i})$$
$$\$117,332 = \$20,000\ (A_{\overline{n}|8\%})$$
$$A_{\overline{n}|8\%} = \frac{\$117,332}{\$20,000} = 5.86660$$

Using Table A-3 and reading down the 8% column, 5.86660 is in the 5-period row. Thus, five deposits of $20,000 each must be made.

Objective 7

Solve present value of ordinary and annuity due problems.

Present Value of an Ordinary Annuity

The present value of an annuity may be viewed as the *single amount* that, if invested now at compound interest, would provide for a series of withdrawals of a certain amount per period for a specific number of future periods. In other words, the present value of an ordinary annuity is the present value of a series of rents to be withdrawn at the end of each equal interval.

One approach to calculating the present value of an annuity is to determine the present value of each rent in the series and then aggregate these individual present values. For example, assume that $1.00 is to be received at the *end* of each of five periods (an ordinary annuity) and that the interest rate is 12% compounded annually. The present value of this annuity can be computed as follows using Table A-2, "Present Value of 1," for each of the five $1 rents.

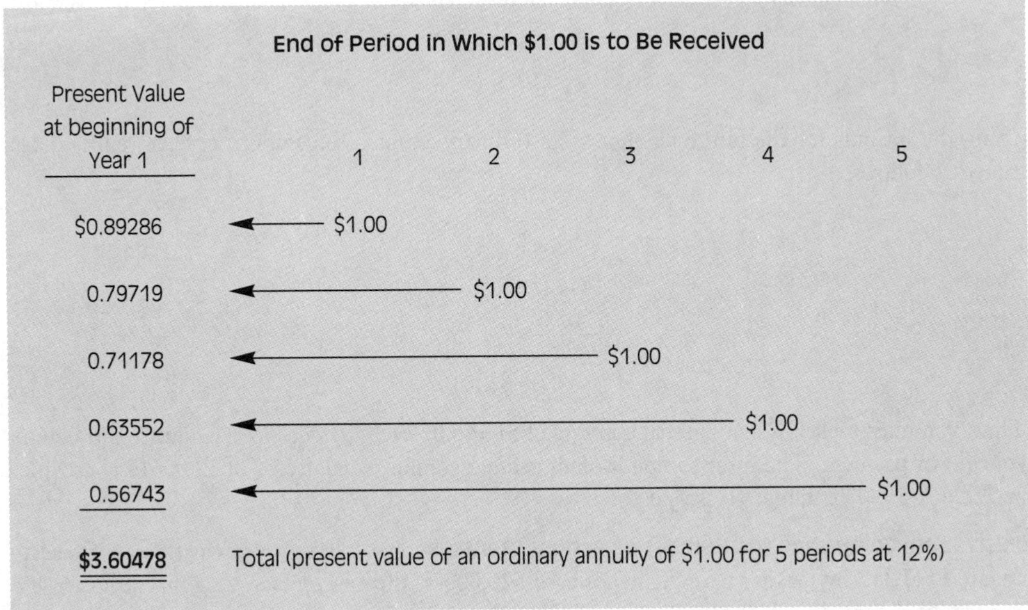

This computation indicates that if the single sum of $3.60 is invested today at 12% interest for five periods, $1.00 can be withdrawn at the end of each period for five periods. This procedure is cumbersome. Using the following formula is a more efficient way to determine the present value of an ordinary annuity of 1:

$$P_{\overline{n}|i} = \frac{1 - \frac{1}{(1+i)^n}}{i}$$

Table A-4, "Present Value of an Ordinary Annuity of 1," is based on this formula. An excerpt from this table is shown below.

Present Value of an Ordinary Annuity of 1
(Excerpt from Table A-4)

Period	10%	11%	12%
1	0.90909	0.90090	0.89286
2	1.73554	1.71252	1.69005
3	2.48685	2.44371	2.40183
4	3.16986	3.10245	3.03735
5	3.79079	3.69590	**3.60478***

*Note that this factor is equal to the sum of the present value of 1 factors shown in the previous schedule.

The formula for the present value of any ordinary annuity of any rent value is as follows:

$$P = R(P_{\overline{n}|i})$$

where

P = present value of an ordinary annuity
R = periodic rent (ordinary annuity)

$$P_{\overline{n}|} = \frac{1 - \frac{1}{(1+i)^n}}{i} = \text{present value of an ordinary annuity of 1 for } n \text{ periods at } i\%$$

To illustrate, what is the present value of rental receipts of $6,000 each to be received at the end of each of the next five years when discounted at 12%? This problem is time-diagrammed and solved as shown below. The present value of the five ordinary annuity rental receipts of $6,000 each is $21,628.68. The present value of the ordinary annuity of 1 factor, 3.60478, is from Table A-4 (12% column, 5-period row).

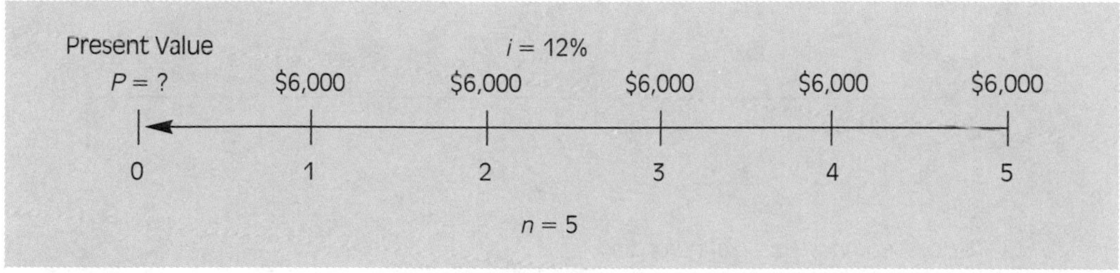

$$\begin{aligned} P &= R(P_{\overline{n}|i}) \\ &= \$6{,}000\,(P_{\overline{5}|12\%}) \\ &= \$6{,}000\,(3.60478) \\ &= \$21{,}628.68 \end{aligned}$$

Present Value of an Annuity Due

In the discussion of the present value of an ordinary annuity, the final rent was discounted back the same number of periods that there were rents. In determining the present value of an annuity due, there is always one fewer discount periods. This distinction is shown graphically below.

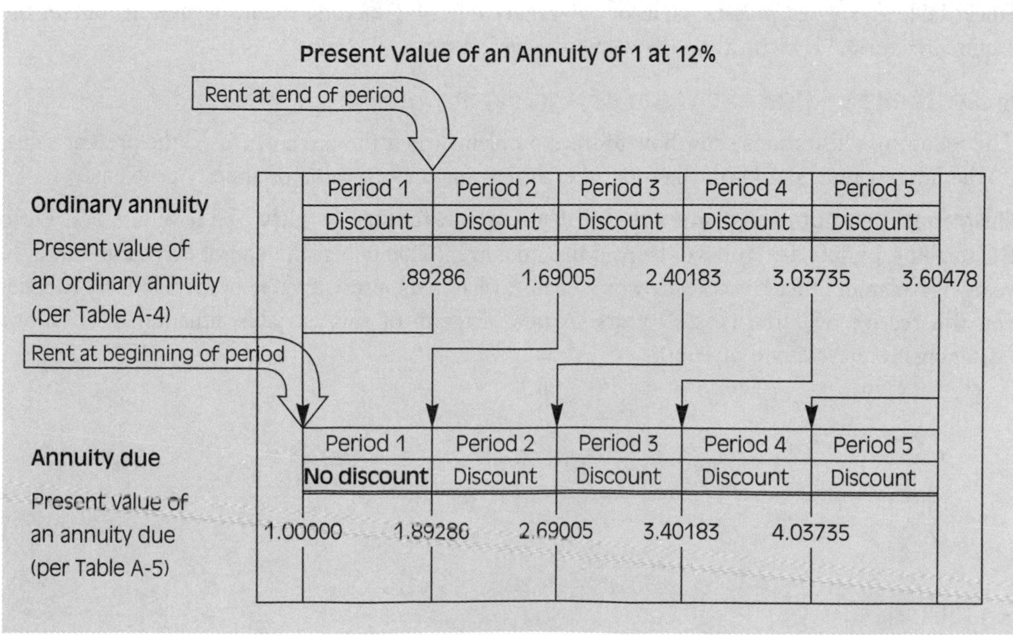

Because each cash flow (rent) comes exactly one period sooner in the present value of an annuity due, the present value of the cash flows is exactly 12% higher than the present value of an ordinary annuity. Thus, ***the present value of an annuity due of 1 factor can be found by multiplying the present value of an ordinary annuity of 1 by one plus the interest rate.*** For example, to determine the present value of an annuity due of 1 factor for five periods at 12% interest, take the present value of an ordinary annuity of 1 factor for five periods at 12% interest (3.60478) and multiply it by 1.12 to arrive at the present value of an annuity due of 1, 4.03735 (3.60478 × 1.12). Table A-5 provides present value of annuity due of 1 factors.

To illustrate, assume that Space Odyssey Inc. rents a communications satellite for four years with annual rental payments of $4.8 million to be made at the beginning of each year. Assuming an annual interest rate of 11%, what is the present value of the rental obligations?

This problem is time-diagrammed as follows.

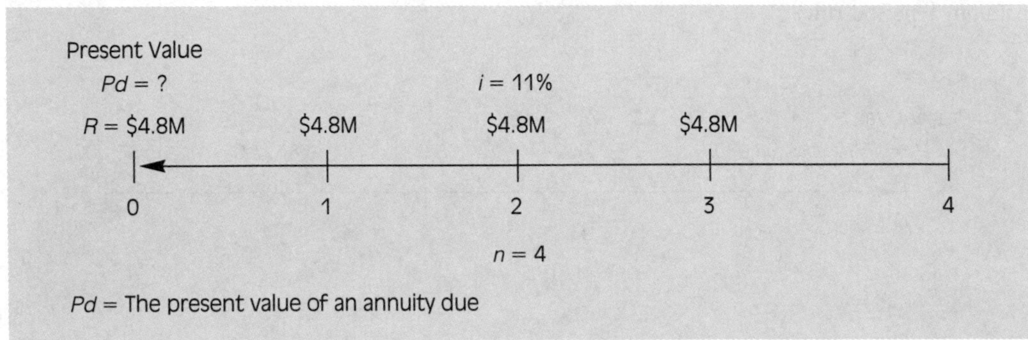

This problem can be solved in the following manner.

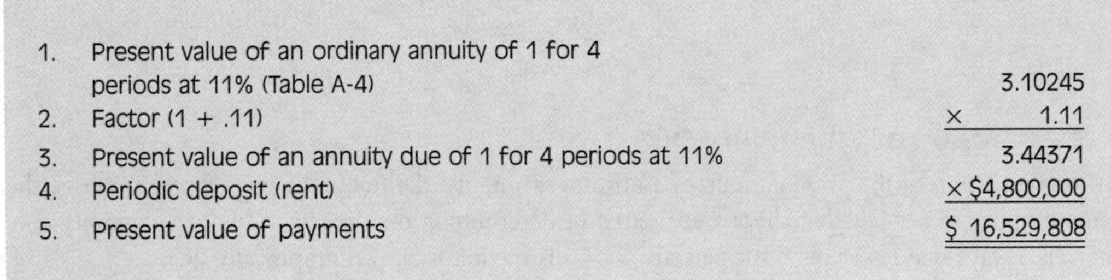

1.	Present value of an ordinary annuity of 1 for 4 periods at 11% (Table A-4)	3.10245
2.	Factor (1 + .11)	× 1.11
3.	Present value of an annuity due of 1 for 4 periods at 11%	3.44371
4.	Periodic deposit (rent)	× $4,800,000
5.	Present value of payments	$ 16,529,808

Since Table A-5 gives present value of an annuity due of 1 factors, it can be used to obtain the required factor 3.44371 (in the 11% column, 4-period row).

Illustrations of Present Value of Annuity Problems

The following illustrations show how to solve problems when the unknown is (1) the present value, (2) the interest rate, and (3) the amount of each rent for present value of annuity problems.

Illustration: Computation of the Present Value of an Ordinary Annuity. You have just won Lotto BC totalling $4,000,000. You will be paid the amount of $200,000 at the end of each of the next 20 years. What amount have you really won? That is, what is the present value of the $200,000 cheques you will receive over the next 20 years? A time diagram of this enviable situation is as follows (assuming an interest rate of 10%).

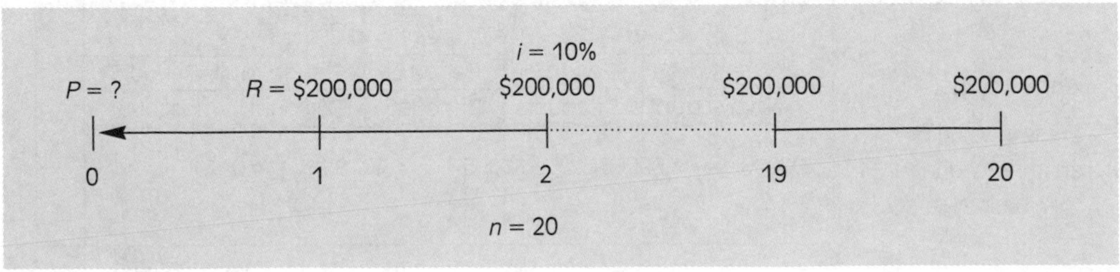

The present value is determined as follows:

$$\begin{aligned} P &= R(P_{\overline{n}|i}) \\ &= \$200{,}000\ (P_{\overline{20}|10\%}) \\ &= \$200{,}000\ (8.51356) \\ &= \$1{,}702{,}712 \end{aligned}$$

As a result, if Lotto BC deposits $1,702,712 now and earns 10% interest, it can draw $200,000 a year for twenty years to pay you the $4,000,000.

Illustration: Computation of the Interest Rate. Many shoppers make purchases by using a credit card. When you receive an invoice for payment, you may pay the total amount due or pay the balance in a certain number of payments. For example, if you receive an invoice from VISA with a balance due of $528.77 and are invited to pay it off in twelve equal monthly payments of $50.00 each with the first payment due one month from now, what rate of interest are you paying?

The $528.77 represents the present value of the twelve $50 payments at an unknown rate of interest. This situation is time diagrammed and the interest rate is determined as follows.

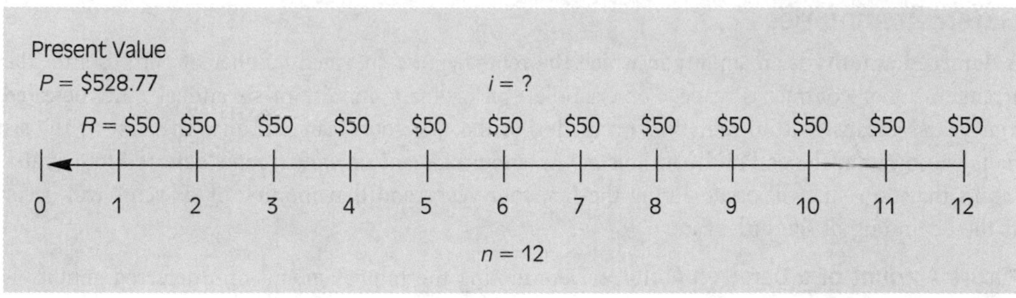

$$P = R(P_{\overline{n}|i})$$

$$\$528.77 = \$50\ (P_{\overline{12}|i})$$

$$P_{\overline{12}|i} = \frac{\$528.77}{\$50} = 10.5754$$

Referring to Table A-4 and reading across the 12-period row, the 10.57534 factor is in the 2% column. Since 2% is a monthly rate, the nominal annual rate of interest is 24% (12 × 2%) and the effective annual rate is 26.82413% $[(1 + .02)^{12} - 1]$. At such a high rate of interest, you are better off paying the entire bill now if possible.

Illustration: Computation of a Periodic Rent. Vern and Marilyn have saved $18,000 to finance their daughter Dawn's university education. The money has been deposited with the National Trust Company and is earning 10% interest compounded semiannually. What equal amounts can Dawn withdraw at the end of every six months during the next four years while she attends university and exhausts the fund with the last withdrawal? This problem is time-diagrammed as follows.

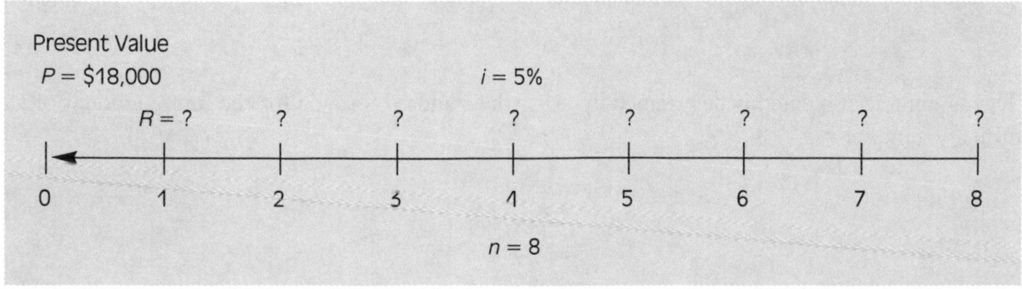

The answer is not determined simply by dividing $18,000 by 8 withdrawals because that ignores the interest earned on the money remaining on deposit. Given that interest is compounded semiannually at 5% (10% ÷ 2) for eight periods (4 years × 2) and using the present value of an ordinary annuity formula, the amount of each withdrawal is determined as follows:

$$P = R(P_{\overline{n}|i})$$
$$\$18{,}000 = R(P_{\overline{8}|5\%})$$
$$\$18{,}000 = R(6.46321)$$
$$R = \$2{,}784.99$$

COMPLEX SITUATIONS

It is often necessary to use more than one table to solve time-value problems. Two common situations will be illustrated to demonstrate this point:

1. Deferred annuities.
2. Bond problems.

Deferred Annuities

A **deferred annuity** is an annuity in which the rents begin a specified number of periods after the arrangement or contract is made. For example, "an ordinary annuity of six annual rents deferred four years" means that no rents will occur during the first four years and that the first of the six rents will occur at the end of the fifth year. "An annuity due of six annual rents deferred four years" means that no rents will occur during the first four years, and that the first of six rents will occur at the beginning of the fifth year.

Future Amount of a Deferred Annuity. Determining the future amount of a deferred annuity is relatively straightforward. Because there is no accumulation or investment on which interest accrues during the deferred periods, the future amount of a deferred annuity is the same as the future amount of an annuity not deferred.

To illustrate, assume that Sutton Co. Ltd. plans to purchase a land site in six years for the construction of its new corporate headquarters. Because of cash flow problems, Sutton is able to budget deposits of $80,000 only at the end of the fourth, fifth, and sixth years, which are expected to earn 12% annually. What future amount will Sutton have accumulated at the end of the sixth year?

A time diagram of this situation is as follows.

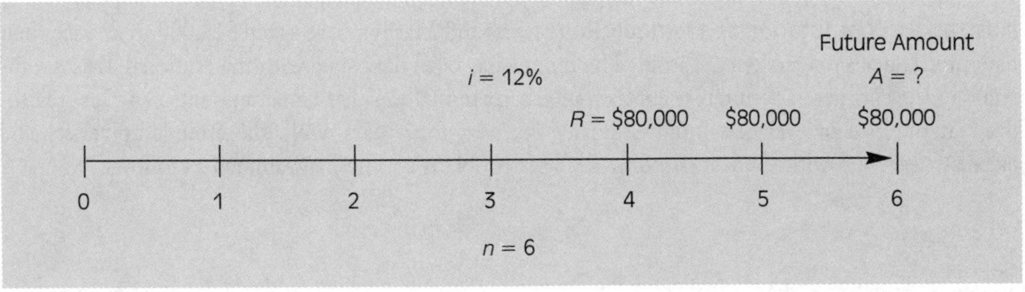

The amount accumulated is determined by using the standard formula for the future amount of an ordinary annuity:

$$A = R(A_{\overline{n}|i})$$
$$= \$80{,}000\ (A_{\overline{3}|12\%})$$
$$= \$80{,}000\ (3.37440)$$
$$= \$269{,}952$$

Present Value of a Deferred Annuity. In determining the present value of a deferred annuity, recognition must be given to the facts that no rents occur during the deferral period and that the future actual rents must be discounted for the entire period.

For example, Tom Whiz has developed and copyrighted a software computer program that is a tutorial for students in introductory accounting. He agrees to sell the copyright to Campus Micro Systems for six annual payments of $5,000 each, the payments to begin five years from today. The annual interest rate is 8%. What is the present value of the six payments?

This situation is an ordinary annuity of six payments deferred four periods and can be time-diagrammed as follows.

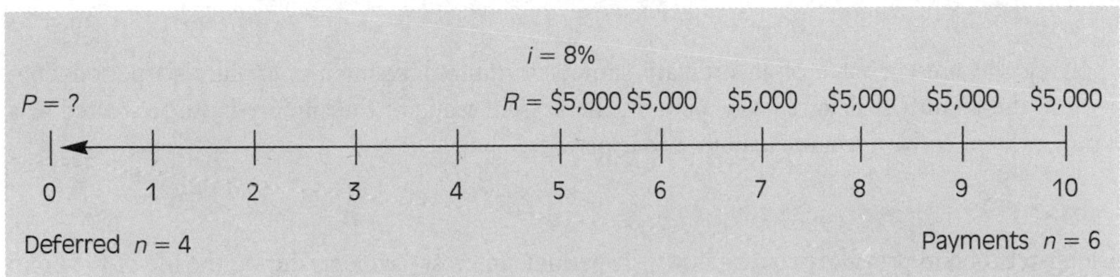

Two options are available to solve this problem. The first is to use only Table A-4 as follows.

1.	Each periodic rent		$5,000
2.	Present value of an ordinary annuity of 1 for total periods (10) [number of rents (6) plus number of deferred periods (4)], at 8%	6.71008	
3.	Less: Present value of an ordinary annuity of 1 for the number of deferred periods (4) at 8%	3.31213	
4.	Difference		× 3.39795
5.	Present value of 6 rents of $5,000 deferred 4 periods		$16,989.75

The subtraction of the present value of an ordinary annuity of 1 for the deferred periods eliminates the nonexistent rents during the deferral period and converts the present value of an ordinary annuity of 1 for 10 periods to the present value of 6 rents of 1, deferred 4 periods.

Alternatively, the present value of the six rents may be computed using both Tables A-2 and A-4. The first step is to determine the present value of an ordinary annuity for the number of rent payments involved using Table A-4. This step provides the present value of the ordinary annuity as at the beginning of the first payment period (this is the same as the present value at the end of the last deferral period). The second step is to discount the amount determined in step 1 for the number of deferral periods using Table A-2. Application of this approach is as follows:

Step 1: $P = R(P_{\overline{n}|i})$
$= \$5{,}000(P_{\overline{6}|8\%})$
$= \$5{,}000$ (4.62288) Table A-4 (Present Value of an Ordinary Annuity)
$= \$23{,}114.40$

Step 2: $p = a(p_{\overline{n}|i})$ ("a" is the amount "P" determined in Step 1)
$= \$23{,}114.40\ (p_{\overline{4}|8\%})$
$= \$23{,}114.40$ (.73503) Table A-2 (Present Value of a Single Sum)
$= \$16{,}989.77$

A time diagram reflecting the completion of this two-step approach is as follows.

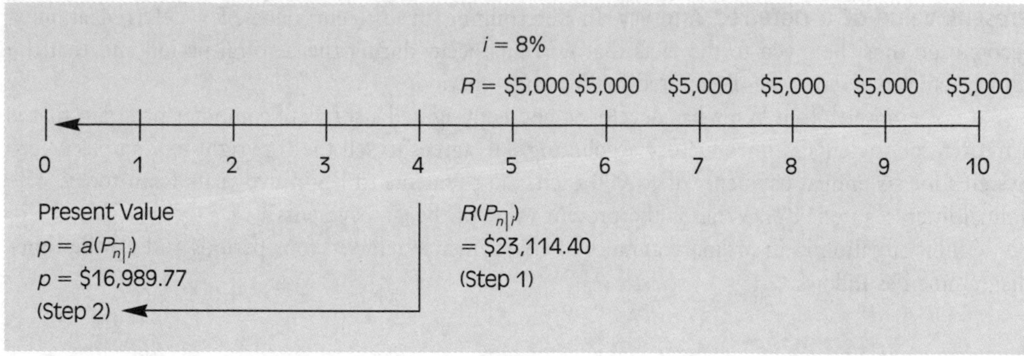

Applying the present value of an ordinary annuity formula discounts the annuity six periods, but because the annuity is deferred four periods, the present value of the annuity must be treated as a future amount to be discounted another four periods.[7]

Valuation of Long-Term Bonds

A long-term bond provides two cash flows: (1) periodic interest payments during the life of the bond and (2) the principal (face value) paid at maturity. At the date of issue, bond buyers determine the present value of these two cash flows using the market rate of interest.

The periodic interest payments represent an annuity while the principal represents a single sum. The current market value of the bonds is the combined present values of the interest annuity and the principal amount.

To illustrate, Servicemaster Inc. issues $100,000 of 9% bonds due in five years with interest payable annually at year end. The current market rate of interest for bonds of similar risk is 11%. What will the buyers pay for this bond issue?

The time diagram depicting both cash flows is shown below.

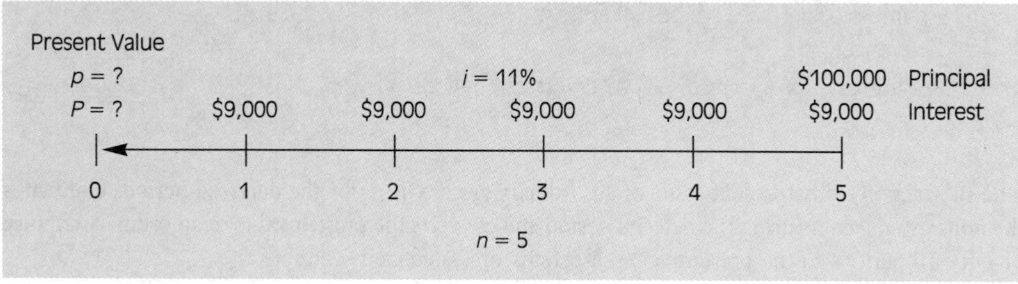

The present value of the two cash flows is computed as follows.

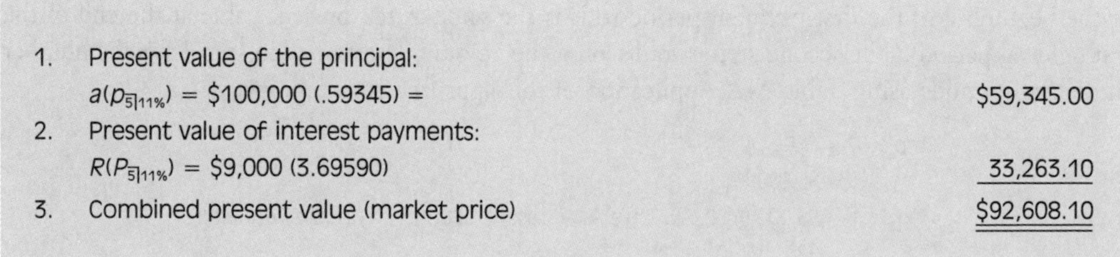

1.	Present value of the principal:	
	$a(p_{\overline{5}|11\%})$ = $100,000 (.59345) =	$59,345.00
2.	Present value of interest payments:	
	$R(P_{\overline{5}|11\%})$ = $9,000 (3.69590)	33,263.10
3.	Combined present value (market price)	$92,608.10

[7] Deferred annuity contracts are common in professional sports. For example, Rich Gossage's contract when he signed as a pitcher with the San Diego Padres was for him to be paid $240,000 a year from 1990 to 2006 and $125,000 from 2007 to 2016 in addition to salary and bonuses over the first five or six years. The deferred payouts from 1990 through 2016 total $5.33 million, but the present value of this deferred annuity was estimated at $1.5 million when the contract was signed.

By paying $92,608.10 at date of issue, the buyers of the bonds will realize an effective yield of 11% over the 5-year term of the bonds.

INTERPOLATION OF TABLES TO DERIVE INTEREST RATES

Throughout the previous discussion, the illustrations were designed to produce interest rates and factors that could be found in the tables. Frequently it is necessary to interpolate to derive the exact or required interest rate. **Interpolation** is used to calculate a particular unknown value that lies between two values given in a table. The following examples illustrate interpolation using Tables A-1 and A-4.

Example 1. If $2,000 accumulates to $5,900 after being invested for 20 years, what is the annual interest rate on the investment?

Dividing the future amount of $5,900 by the investment of $2,000 gives $2.95 which is the amount to which $1.00 will grow if invested for 20 years at the unknown interest rate. Using Table A-1 and reading across the 20-period line, the value 2.65330 is found in the 5% column and the value 3.20714 is in the 6% column. The factor 2.95 is between 5% and 6%, which means that the interest rate is also between 5% and 6%. By interpolation, the rate is determined to be 5.536% as follows (i = unknown rate and d = difference between 5% and i).

$$
\begin{array}{cccc}
 & & .05 = 2.65330 & \\
.01 & d & i = 2.95000 & .29670 \quad .55384 \\
 & & .06 = 3.20714 &
\end{array}
$$

$$\therefore \frac{d}{.01} = \frac{.29670}{.55384} \qquad d = \frac{.29670}{.55384}(.01) = .00536$$

$$\therefore i = .05 + .00536 = .05536$$

Example 2. You are offered an annuity of $1,000 a year beginning one year from now for 25 years for investing $7,000 cash today. What rate of interest is your investment earning?

Dividing the investment of $7,000 by the annuity of $1,000 gives a factor of 7, which is the "present value of an ordinary annuity of 1" for 25 years at an unknown interest rate. Using Table A-4 and reading across the 25-period line, the value 7.84314 in the 12% column and the value 6.46415 is in the 15% column. The factor 7 is between 12% and 15%, which means that the unknown interest rate is also between 12% and 15%. By interpolation, the rate is determined to be 13.834% as follows (i = unknown rate and d = difference between 12% and i).

$$
\begin{array}{cccc}
 & & .12 = 7.84314 & \\
.03 & d & i = 7.00000 & .84314 \quad 1.37899 \\
 & & .15 = 6.46415 &
\end{array}
$$

$$\therefore \frac{d}{.03} = \frac{.84314}{1.37899} \qquad d = \frac{.84314}{1.37899}(.03) = .01834$$

$$\therefore i = .12 + d = .12 + .01834 = .13834$$

Interpolation assumes that the change between any two values in a table is linear. Although such an assumption is incorrect, the margin of error is generally insignificant if the table value ranges are not too wide.

FUNDAMENTAL CONCEPTS

The following list of terms and their definitions is provided as a summarization and review of the essential items presented in this appendix:

1. **Simple Interest.** Interest is computed only on the principal, regardless of interest that may have accrued in the past.
2. **Compound Interest.** Interest is computed on the unpaid interest of past periods as well as on the principal.
3. **Rate of Interest.** Interest is usually expressed as an annual rate, but when the interest period is shorter than one year, the interest rate for the shorter period must be determined.
4. **Annuity.** A series of payments or receipts (called rents) which occur at equal intervals of time. The types of annuities are:

   (a) **Ordinary Annuity**. Each rent is payable (receivable) at the end of a period.

   (b) **Annuity Due**. Each rent is payable (receivable) at the beginning of a period.

5. **Future Amount**. Value at a later date of a given sum that is invested at compound interest.

   (a) **Future Amount of 1** (or amount of a given sum). The future value of $1.00 (or a single given sum) at the end of n periods at i compound interest rate (Table A-1).

   (b) **Future Amount of an Annuity.** The future value of a series of rents invested at compound interest; it is the accumulated total that results from a series of equal deposits at regular intervals invested at compound interest. Both deposits and interest increase the accumulation.

   (1) **Future Amount of an Ordinary Annuity.** The future value on the date of the last rent (Table A-3).

   (2) **Future Amount of an Annuity Due.** The future value one period after the date of the last rent. When an annuity due table is not available, use Table A-3 with the following formula:

$$\begin{array}{c}\text{Amount of annuity due} \\ \text{of 1 for } n \text{ rents}\end{array} = \begin{array}{c}\text{Amount of ordinary annuity of 1} \\ \text{for } n \text{ rents} \times (1 + \text{interest rate}).\end{array}$$

6. **Present Value**. The value at an earlier date (usually now) of a given sum discounted at compound interest.

   (a) **Present Value of 1** (or present value of a single sum). The present value (worth) of $1.00 due n periods hence, discounted at i compound interest (Table A-2).

   (b) **Present Value of an Annuity.** The present value (worth) of a series of rents discounted at compound interest; it is the present sum when invested at compound interest that will permit a series of equal withdrawals at regular intervals.

   (1) **Present Value of an Ordinary Annuity.** The value now of $1.00 to be received or paid each period (rents) for n periods, discounted at i compound interest (Table A-4).

   (2) **Present Value of an Annuity Due.** The value now of $1.00 to be received or paid at the beginning of each period (rents) for n periods, discounted at i compound interest (Table A-5). To use Table A-4 for an annuity due, apply this formula:

$$\begin{array}{c}\text{Present value of an annuity} \\ \text{annuity due of 1 for } n \text{ rents}\end{array} = \begin{array}{c}\text{Present value of ordinary annuity} \\ \text{of 1 for } n \text{ rents} \times (1 + \text{interest rate}).\end{array}$$

Table A-1 Future Amount of 1 (Future Amount of a Single Sum)

$$a_{\overline{n}|i} = (1 + i)^n$$

(n) periods	2%	2½%	3%	4%	5%	6%	8%	9%	10%	11%	12%	15%
1	1.02000	1.02500	1.03000	1.04000	1.05000	1.06000	1.08000	1.09000	1.10000	1.11000	1.12000	1.15000
2	1.04040	1.05063	1.06090	1.08160	1.10250	1.12360	1.16640	1.18810	1.21000	1.23210	1.25440	1.32250
3	1.06121	1.07689	1.09273	1.12486	1.15763	1.19102	1.25971	1.29503	1.33100	1.36763	1.40493	1.52088
4	1.08243	1.10381	1.12551	1.16986	1.21551	1.26248	1.36049	1.41158	1.46410	1.51807	1.57352	1.74901
5	1.10408	1.13141	1.15927	1.21665	1.27628	1.33823	1.46933	1.53862	1.61051	1.68506	1.76234	2.01136
6	1.12616	1.15969	1.19405	1.26532	1.34010	1.41852	1.58687	1.67710	1.77156	1.87041	1.97382	2.31306
7	1.14869	1.18869	1.22987	1.31593	1.40710	1.50363	1.71382	1.82804	1.94872	2.07616	2.21068	2.66002
8	1.17166	1.21840	1.26677	1.36857	1.47746	1.59385	1.85093	1.99256	2.14359	2.30454	2.47596	3.05902
9	1.19509	1.24886	1.30477	1.42331	1.55133	1.68948	1.99900	2.17189	2.35795	2.55803	2.77308	3.51788
10	1.21899	1.28008	1.34392	1.48024	1.62889	1.79085	2.15892	2.36736	2.59374	2.83942	3.10585	4.04556
11	1.24337	1.31209	1.38423	1.53945	1.71034	1.89830	2.33164	2.58043	2.85312	3.15176	3.47855	4.65239
12	1.26824	1.34489	1.42576	1.60103	1.79586	2.01220	2.51817	2.81267	3.13843	3.49845	3.89598	5.35025
13	1.29361	1.37851	1.46853	1.66507	1.88565	2.13293	2.71962	3.06581	3.45227	3.88328	4.36349	6.15279
14	1.31948	1.41297	1.51259	1.73168	1.97993	2.26090	2.93719	3.34173	3.79750	4.31044	4.88711	7.07571
15	1.34587	1.44830	1.55797	1.80094	2.07893	2.39656	3.17217	3.64248	4.17725	4.78459	5.47357	8.13706
16	1.37279	1.48451	1.60471	1.87298	2.18287	2.54035	3.42594	3.97031	4.59497	5.31089	6.13039	9.35762
17	1.40024	1.52162	1.65285	1.94790	2.29202	2.69277	3.70002	4.32763	5.05447	5.89509	6.86604	10.76126
18	1.42825	1.55966	1.70243	2.02582	2.40662	2.85434	3.99602	4.71712	5.55992	6.54355	7.68997	12.37545
19	1.45681	1.59865	1.75351	2.10685	2.52695	3.02560	4.31570	5.14166	6.11591	7.26334	8.61276	14.23177
20	1.48595	1.63862	1.80611	2.19112	2.65330	3.20714	4.66096	5.60441	6.72750	8.06231	9.64629	16.36654
21	1.51567	1.67958	1.86029	2.27877	2.78596	3.39956	5.03383	6.10881	7.40025	8.94917	10.80385	18.82152
22	1.54598	1.72157	1.91610	2.36992	2.92526	3.60354	5.43654	6.65860	8.14028	9.93357	12.10031	21.64475
23	1.57690	1.76461	1.97359	2.46472	3.07152	3.81975	5.87146	7.25787	8.95430	11.02627	13.55235	24.89146
24	1.60844	1.80873	2.03279	2.56330	3.22510	4.04893	6.34118	7.91108	9.84973	12.23916	15.17863	28.62518
25	1.64061	1.85394	2.09378	2.66584	3.38635	4.29187	6.84847	8.62308	10.83471	13.58546	17.00000	32.91895
26	1.67342	1.90029	2.15659	2.77247	3.55567	4.54938	7.39635	9.39916	11.91818	15.07986	19.04007	37.85680
27	1.70689	1.94780	2.22129	2.88337	3.73346	4.82235	7.98806	10.24508	13.10999	16.73865	21.32488	43.53532
28	1.74102	1.99650	2.28793	2.99870	3.92013	5.11169	8.62711	11.16714	14.42099	18.57990	23.88387	50.06561
29	1.77584	2.04641	2.35657	3.11865	4.11614	5.41839	9.31727	12.17218	15.86309	20.62369	26.74993	57.57545
30	1.81136	2.09757	2.42726	3.24340	4.32194	5.74349	10.06266	13.26768	17.44940	22.89230	29.95992	66.21177
31	1.84759	2.15001	2.50008	3.37313	4.53804	6.08810	10.86767	14.46177	19.19434	25.41045	33.55511	76.14354
32	1.88454	2.20376	2.57508	3.50806	4.76494	6.45339	11.73708	15.76333	21.11378	28.20560	37.58173	87.56507
33	1.92223	2.25885	2.65234	3.64838	5.00319	6.84059	12.67605	17.18203	23.22515	31.30821	42.09153	100.69983
34	1.96068	2.31532	2.73191	3.79432	5.25335	7.25103	13.69013	18.72841	25.54767	34.75212	47.14252	115.80480
35	1.99989	2.37321	2.81386	3.94609	5.51602	7.68609	14.78534	20.41397	28.10244	38.57485	52.79962	133.17552
36	2.03989	2.43254	2.88928	4.10393	5.79182	8.14725	15.96817	22.25123	30.91268	42.81808	59.13557	153.15185
37	2.08069	2.49335	2.98523	4.26809	6.08141	8.63609	17.24563	24.25384	34.00395	47.52807	66.23184	176.12463
38	2.12230	2.55568	3.07478	4.43881	6.38548	9.15425	18.62528	26.43668	37.40434	52.75616	74.17966	202.54332
39	2.16474	2.61957	3.16703	4.61637	6.70475	9.70351	20.11530	28.81598	41.14479	58.55934	83.08122	232.92482
40	2.20804	2.68506	3.26204	4.80102	7.03999	10.28572	21.72452	31.40942	45.25926	65.00087	93.05097	267.86355

Table A-2 Present Value of 1 (Present Value of a Single Sum)

$$P_{\overline{n}|i} = \frac{1}{(1+i)^n} = (1+i)^{-n}$$

(n) periods	2%	2½%	3%	4%	5%	6%	8%	9%	10%	11%	12%	15%
1	.98039	.97561	.97087	.96156	.95238	.94340	.92593	.91743	.90909	.90090	.89286	.86957
2	.96117	.95181	.94260	.92456	.90703	.89000	.85734	.84168	.82645	.81162	.79719	.75614
3	.94232	.92860	.91514	.88900	.86384	.83962	.79383	.77218	.75132	.73119	.71178	.65752
4	.92385	.90595	.88849	.85480	.82270	.79209	.73503	.70843	.68301	.65873	.63552	.57175
5	.90583	.88385	.86261	.82193	.78353	.74726	.68058	.64993	.62092	.59345	.56743	.49718
6	.88797	.86230	.83748	.79031	.74622	.70496	.63017	.59627	.56447	.53464	.50663	.43233
7	.87056	.84127	.81309	.75992	.71068	.66056	.58349	.54703	.51316	.48166	.45235	.37594
8	.85349	.82075	.78941	.73069	.67684	.62741	.54027	.50187	.46651	.43393	.40388	.32690
9	.83676	.80073	.76642	.70259	.64461	.59190	.50025	.46043	.42410	.39092	.36061	.28426
10	.82035	.78120	.74409	.67556	.61391	.55839	.46319	.42241	.38554	.35218	.32197	.24719
11	.80426	.76214	.72242	.64958	.58468	.52679	.42888	.38753	.35049	.31728	.28748	.21494
12	.78849	.74356	.70138	.62460	.55684	.49697	.39711	.35554	.31863	.28584	.25668	.18691
13	.77303	.72542	.68095	.60057	.53032	.46884	.36770	.32618	.28966	.25751	.22917	.16253
14	.75788	.70773	.66112	.57748	.50507	.44230	.34046	.29925	.26333	.23199	.20462	.14133
15	.74301	.69047	.64186	.55526	.48102	.41727	.31524	.27454	.23939	.20900	.18270	.12289
16	.72845	.67362	.62317	.53391	.45811	.39365	.29189	.25187	.21763	.18829	.16312	.10687
17	.71416	.65720	.60502	.51337	.43630	.37136	.27027	.23107	.19785	.16963	.14564	.09293
18	.70016	.64117	.58739	.49363	.41552	.35034	.25025	.21199	.17986	.15282	.13004	.08081
19	.68643	.62553	.57029	.47464	.39573	.33051	.23171	.19449	.16351	.13768	.11611	.07027
20	.67297	.61027	.55368	.45639	.37689	.31180	.21455	.17843	.14864	.12403	.10367	.06110
21	.65978	.59539	.53755	.43883	.35894	.29416	.19866	.16370	.13513	.11174	.09256	.05313
22	.64684	.58086	.52189	.42196	.34185	.27751	.18394	.15018	.12285	.10067	.08264	.04620
23	.63416	.56670	.50669	.40573	.32557	.26180	.17032	.13778	.11168	.09069	.07379	.04017
24	.62172	.55288	.49193	.39012	.31007	.24698	.15770	.12641	.10153	.08170	.06588	.03493
25	.60953	.53939	.47761	.37512	.29530	.23300	.14602	.11597	.09230	.07361	.05882	.03038
26	.59758	.52623	.46369	.36069	.28124	.21981	.13520	.10639	.08391	.06631	.05252	.02642
27	.58586	.51340	.45019	.34682	.26785	.20737	.12519	.09761	.07628	.05974	.04689	.02297
28	.57437	.50088	.43708	.33348	.25509	.19563	.11591	.08955	.06934	.05382	.04187	.01997
29	.56311	.48866	.42435	.32065	.24295	.18456	.10733	.08216	.06304	.04849	.03738	.01737
30	.55207	.47674	.41199	.30832	.23138	.17411	.09938	.07537	.05731	.04368	.03338	.01510
31	.54125	.46511	.39999	.29646	.22036	.16425	.09202	.06915	.05210	.03935	.02980	.01313
32	.53063	.45377	.38834	.28506	.20987	.15496	.08520	.06344	.04736	.03545	.02661	.01142
33	.52023	.44270	.37703	.27409	.19987	.14619	.07889	.05820	.04306	.03194	.02376	.00993
34	.51003	.43191	.36604	.26355	.19035	.13791	.07305	.05340	.03914	.02878	.02121	.00864
35	.50003	.42137	.35538	.25342	.18129	.13011	.06763	.04899	.03558	.02592	.01894	.00751
36	.49022	.41109	.34503	.24367	.17266	.12274	.06262	.04494	.03235	.02335	.01691	.00653
37	.48061	.40107	.33498	.23430	.16444	.11579	.05799	.04123	.02941	.02104	.01510	.00568
38	.47119	.39128	.32523	.22529	.15661	.10924	.05369	.03783	.02674	.01896	.01348	.00494
39	.46195	.38174	.31575	.21662	.14915	.10306	.04971	.03470	.02430	.01708	.01204	.00429
40	.45289	.37243	.30656	.20829	.14205	.09722	.04603	.03184	.02210	.01538	.01075	.00373

Table A-3 Future Amount of an Ordinary Annuity of 1

$$A_{\overline{n}|i} = \frac{(1+i)^n - 1}{i}$$

(n) periods	2%	$2\frac{1}{2}$%	3%	4%	5%	6%	8%	9%	10%	11%	12%	15%
1	1.00000	1.00000	1.00000	1.00000	1.00000	1.00000	1.00000	1.00000	1.00000	1.00000	1.00000	1.00000
2	2.02000	2.02500	2.03000	2.04000	2.05000	2.06000	2.08000	2.09000	2.10000	2.11000	2.12000	2.15000
3	3.06040	3.07563	3.09090	3.12160	3.15250	3.18360	3.24640	3.27810	3.31000	3.34210	3.37440	3.47250
4	4.12161	4.15252	4.18363	4.24646	4.31013	4.37462	4.50611	4.57313	4.64100	4.70973	4.77933	4.99338
5	5.20404	5.25633	5.30914	5.41632	5.52563	5.63709	5.86660	5.98471	6.10510	6.22780	6.35285	6.74238
6	6.30812	6.38774	6.46841	6.63298	6.80191	6.97532	7.33592	7.52334	7.71561	7.91286	8.11519	8.75374
7	7.43428	7.54743	7.66246	7.89829	8.14201	8.39384	8.92280	9.20044	9.48717	9.78327	10.08901	11.06680
8	8.58297	8.73612	8.89234	9.21423	9.54911	9.89747	10.63663	11.02847	11.43589	11.85943	12.29969	13.72682
9	9.75463	9.95452	10.15911	10.58280	11.02656	11.49132	12.48756	13.02104	13.57948	14.16397	14.77566	16.78584
10	10.94972	11.20338	11.46338	12.00611	12.57789	13.18079	14.48656	15.19293	15.93743	16.72201	17.54874	20.30372
11	12.16872	12.48347	12.80780	13.48635	14.20679	14.97164	16.64549	17.56029	18.53117	19.56143	20.65458	24.34928
12	13.41209	13.79555	14.19203	15.02581	15.91713	16.86994	18.97713	20.14072	21.38428	22.71319	24.13313	29.00167
13	14.68033	15.14044	15.61779	16.62684	17.71298	18.88214	21.49530	22.95339	24.52271	26.21164	28.02911	34.35192
14	15.97394	16.51895	17.08632	18.29191	19.59863	21.01507	24.21492	26.01919	27.97498	30.09492	32.39260	40.50471
15	17.29342	17.93193	18.59891	20.02359	21.57856	23.27597	27.15211	29.36092	31.77248	34.40536	37.27972	47.58041
16	18.63929	19.38022	20.15688	21.82453	23.65749	25.67253	30.32428	33.00340	35.94973	39.18995	42.75328	55.71747
17	20.01207	20.86473	21.76159	23.69751	25.84037	28.21288	33.75023	36.97371	40.54470	44.50084	48.88367	65.07509
18	21.41231	22.38635	23.41444	25.64541	28.13238	30.90565	37.45024	41.30134	45.59917	50.39593	55.74972	75.83636
19	22.84056	23.94601	25.11687	27.67123	30.53900	33.75999	41.44626	46.01846	51.15909	56.93949	63.43968	88.21181
20	24.29737	25.54466	26.87037	29.77808	33.06595	36.78559	45.76196	51.16012	57.27500	64.20283	72.05244	102.44358
21	25.78332	27.18327	28.67649	31.96920	35.71925	39.99273	50.42292	56.76453	64.00250	72.26514	81.69874	118.81012
22	27.29898	28.86286	30.53678	34.24797	38.50521	43.39229	55.45676	62.87334	71.40275	81.21431	92.50258	137.63164
23	28.84496	30.58443	32.45288	36.61789	41.43048	46.99583	60.89330	69.53194	79.54302	91.14788	104.60289	159.27638
24	30.42186	32.34904	34.42647	39.08260	44.50200	50.81558	66.76476	76.78981	88.49733	102.17415	118.15524	184.16784
25	32.03030	34.15776	36.45926	41.64591	47.72710	54.86451	73.10594	84.70090	98.34706	114.41331	133.33387	212.79302
26	33.67091	36.01171	38.55304	44.31174	51.11345	59.15638	79.95442	93.32398	109.18177	127.99877	150.33393	245.71197
27	35.34432	37.91200	40.70963	47.08421	54.66913	63.70577	87.35077	102.72314	121.09994	143.07864	169.37401	283.56877
28	37.05121	39.85990	42.93092	49.96758	58.40258	68.52811	95.33883	112.96822	134.20994	159.81729	190.69889	327.10408
29	38.79223	41.85630	45.21885	52.96629	62.32271	73.63980	103.96594	124.13536	148.63093	178.39719	214.58275	377.16969
30	40.56808	43.90270	47.57542	56.08494	66.43885	79.05819	113.28321	136.30754	164.49402	199.02088	241.33268	434.74515
31	42.37944	46.00027	50.00268	59.32834	70.76079	84.80168	123.34587	149.57522	181.94343	221.91317	271.29261	500.95692
32	44.22703	48.15028	52.50276	62.70147	75.29883	90.88978	134.21354	164.03699	201.13777	247.32362	304.84772	577.10046
33	46.11157	50.35403	55.07784	66.20953	80.06377	97.34316	145.95062	179.80032	222.25154	275.52922	342.42945	644.66553
34	48.03380	52.61289	57.73018	69.85791	85.06696	104.18376	158.62667	196.98234	245.47670	306.83744	384.52098	765.36535
35	49.99448	54.92821	60.46208	73.65222	90.32031	111.43478	172.31680	215.71076	271.02437	341.58955	431.66350	881.17016
36	51.99437	57.30141	63.27594	77.59831	95.83632	119.12087	187.10215	236.12472	299.12681	380.16441	484.46312	1014.34568
37	54.03425	59.73395	66.17422	81.70225	101.62814	127.26812	203.07032	258.37595	330.03949	422.98249	543.59869	1167.49753
38	56.11494	62.22730	69.15945	85.97034	107.70955	135.90421	220.31595	282.62978	364.04343	470.51056	609.83053	1343.62216
39	58.23724	64.78298	72.23423	90.40915	114.09502	145.05846	238.94122	309.06646	401.44778	523.26673	684.01020	1546.16549
40	60.40198	67.40255	75.40126	95.02552	120.79977	154.76197	259.05652	337.88245	442.59256	581.82607	767.09142	1779.09031

Table A-4 Present Value of an Ordinary Annuity of 1

$$P_{\overline{n}|i} = \frac{1 - \frac{1}{(1+i)^n}}{i} = \frac{1 - P_{\overline{n}|i}}{i}$$

(n) periods	2%	$2\frac{1}{2}$%	3%	4%	5%	6%	8%	9%	10%	11%	12%	15%
1	.98039	.97561	.97087	.96154	.95238	.94340	.92593	.91743	.90909	.90090	.89286	.86957
2	1.94156	1.92742	1.91347	1.88609	1.85941	1.83339	1.78326	1.75911	1.73554	1.71252	1.69005	1.62571
3	2.88388	2.85602	2.82861	2.77509	2.72325	2.67301	2.57710	2.53130	2.48685	2.44371	2.40183	2.28323
4	3.80773	3.76197	3.71710	3.62990	3.54595	3.46511	3.31213	3.23972	3.16986	3.10245	3.03735	2.85498
5	4.71346	4.64583	4.57971	4.45182	4.32948	4.21236	3.99271	3.88965	3.79079	3.69590	3.60478	3.35216
6	5.60143	5.50813	5.41719	5.24214	5.07569	4.91732	4.62288	4.48592	4.35526	4.23054	4.11141	3.78448
7	6.47199	6.34939	6.23028	6.00205	5.78637	5.58238	5.20637	5.03295	4.86842	4.71220	4.56376	4.16042
8	7.32548	7.17014	7.01969	6.73274	6.46321	6.20979	5.74664	5.53482	5.33493	5.14612	4.96764	4.48732
9	8.16224	7.97087	7.78611	7.43533	7.10782	6.80169	6.24689	5.99525	5.75902	5.53705	5.32825	4.77158
10	8.98259	8.75206	8.53020	8.11090	7.72173	7.36009	6.71008	6.41766	6.14457	5.88923	5.65022	5.01877
11	9.78685	9.51421	9.25262	8.76048	8.30641	7.88687	7.13896	6.80519	6.49506	6.20652	5.93770	5.23371
12	10.57534	10.25776	9.95400	9.38507	8.86325	8.38384	7.53608	7.16073	6.81369	6.49236	6.19437	5.42062
13	11.34837	10.98319	10.63496	9.98565	9.39357	8.85268	7.90378	7.48690	7.10336	6.74987	6.42355	5.58315
14	12.10625	11.69091	11.29607	10.56312	9.89864	9.29498	8.24424	7.78615	7.36669	6.98187	6.62817	5.72448
15	12.84926	12.38138	11.93794	11.11839	10.37966	9.71225	8.55948	8.06069	7.60608	7.19087	6.81086	5.84737
16	13.57771	13.05500	12.56110	11.65230	10.83777	10.10590	8.85137	8.31256	7.82371	7.37916	6.97399	5.95424
17	14.29187	13.71220	13.16612	12.16567	11.27407	10.47726	9.12164	8.54363	8.02155	7.54879	7.11963	6.04716
18	14.99203	14.35336	13.75351	12.65930	11.68959	10.82760	9.37189	8.75563	8.20141	7.70162	7.24967	6.12797
19	15.67846	14.97889	14.32380	13.13394	12.08532	11.15812	9.60360	8.95012	8.36492	7.83929	7.36578	6.19823
20	16.35143	15.58916	14.87747	13.59033	12.46221	11.46992	9.81815	9.12855	8.51356	7.96333	7.46944	6.25933
21	17.01121	16.18455	15.41502	14.02916	12.82115	11.76408	10.01680	9.29224	8.64869	8.07507	7.56200	6.31246
22	17.65805	16.76541	15.93692	14.45112	13.16800	12.04158	10.20074	9.44243	8.77154	8.17574	7.64465	6.35866
23	18.29220	17.33211	16.44361	14.85684	13.48857	12.30338	10.37106	9.58021	8.88322	8.26643	7.71843	6.39884
24	18.91393	17.88499	16.93554	15.24696	13.79864	12.55036	10.52876	9.70661	8.98474	8.34814	7.78432	6.43377
25	19.52346	18.42438	17.41315	15.62208	14.09394	12.78336	10.67478	9.82258	9.07704	8.42174	7.84314	6.46415
26	20.12104	18.95061	17.87684	15.98277	14.37519	13.00317	10.80998	9.92897	9.16095	8.48806	7.89566	6.49056
27	20.70690	19.46401	18.32703	16.32959	14.64303	13.21053	10.93516	10.02658	9.23722	8.45780	7.94255	6.51353
28	21.28127	19.96489	18.76411	16.66306	14.89813	13.40616	11.05108	10.11613	9.30657	8.60162	7.98442	6.53351
29	21.84438	20.45355	19.18845	16.98371	15.14107	13.59072	11.15841	10.19828	9.36961	8.65011	8.02181	6.55088
30	22.39646	20.93029	19.60044	17.29203	15.37245	13.76483	11.25778	10.27365	9.42691	8.69379	8.05518	6.56598
31	22.93770	21.39541	20.00043	17.58849	15.59281	13.92909	11.34980	10.34280	9.47901	8.73315	8.08499	6.57911
32	23.46833	21.84918	20.38877	17.87355	15.80268	14.08404	11.43500	10.40624	9.52638	8.76860	8.11159	6.59053
33	23.98856	22.29188	20.76579	18.14765	16.00255	14.23023	11.51389	10.46444	9.56943	8.80054	8.13535	6.60046
34	24.49859	22.72379	21.13184	18.41120	16.19290	14.36814	11.58693	10.51784	9.60858	8.82932	8.15656	6.60910
35	24.99862	23.14516	21.48722	18.66461	16.37419	14.49825	11.65457	10.56682	9.64416	8.85524	8.17550	6.61661
36	25.48884	23.55625	21.83225	18.90828	16.54685	14.62099	11.71719	10.61176	9.67651	8.87859	8.19241	6.62314
37	25.96945	23.95732	22.16724	19.14258	16.71129	14.73678	11.77518	10.65299	9.70592	8.89963	8.20751	6.62882
38	26.44064	24.34860	22.49246	19.36786	16.86789	14.84602	11.82887	10.69082	9.73265	8.91859	8.22099	6.63375
39	26.90259	24.73034	22.80822	19.58448	17.01704	14.94907	11.87858	10.72552	9.75697	8.93567	8.23303	6.63805
40	27.35548	25.10278	23.11477	19.79277	17.15909	15.04630	11.92461	10.75736	9.77905	8.95105	8.24378	6.64178

Table A-5 Present Value of an Annuity Due of 1

$$Pd_{\overline{n}|i} = \frac{1 - \dfrac{1}{(1+i)^{n-1}}}{i} = (1+i)\left(\frac{1 - P_{\overline{n}|i}}{i}\right) = (1+i)\,P_{\overline{n}|i}$$

(n) periods	2%	2½%	3%	4%	5%	6%	8%	9%	10%	11%	12%	15%
1	1.00000	1.00000	1.00000	1.00000	1.00000	1.00000	1.00000	1.00000	1.00000	1.00000	1.00000	1.00000
2	1.98039	1.97561	1.97087	1.96154	1.95238	1.94340	1.92593	1.91743	1.90909	1.90090	1.89286	1.86957
3	2.94156	2.92742	2.91347	2.88609	2.85941	2.83339	2.78326	2.75911	2.73554	2.71252	2.69005	2.62571
4	3.88388	3.85602	3.82861	3.77509	3.72325	3.67301	3.57710	3.53130	3.48685	3.44371	3.40183	3.28323
5	4.80773	4.76197	4.71710	4.62990	4.54595	4.46511	4.31213	4.23972	4.16986	4.10245	4.03735	3.85498
6	5.71346	5.64583	5.57971	5.45182	5.32948	5.21236	4.99271	4.88965	4.79079	4.69590	4.60478	4.35216
7	6.60143	6.50813	6.41719	6.24214	6.07569	5.91732	5.62288	5.48592	5.35526	5.23054	5.11141	4.78448
8	7.47199	7.34939	7.23028	7.00205	6.78637	6.58238	6.20637	6.03295	5.86842	5.71220	5.56376	5.16042
9	8.32548	8.17014	8.01969	7.73274	7.46321	7.20979	6.74664	6.53482	6.33493	6.14612	5.96764	5.48732
10	9.16224	8.97087	8.78611	8.43533	8.10782	7.80169	7.24689	6.99525	6.75902	6.53705	6.32825	5.77158
11	9.98259	9.75206	9.53020	9.11090	8.72173	8.36009	7.71008	7.41766	7.14457	6.88923	6.65022	6.01877
12	10.78685	10.51421	10.25262	9.76048	9.30641	8.88687	8.13896	7.80519	7.49506	7.20652	6.93770	6.23371
13	11.57534	11.25776	10.95400	10.38507	9.86325	9.38384	8.53608	8.16073	7.81369	7.49236	7.19437	6.42062
14	12.34837	11.98319	11.63496	10.98565	10.39357	9.85268	8.90378	8.48690	8.10336	7.74987	7.42355	6.58315
15	13.10625	12.69091	12.29607	11.56312	10.89864	10.29498	9.24424	8.78615	8.36669	7.98187	7.62817	6.72448
16	13.84926	13.38138	12.93794	12.11839	11.37966	10.71225	9.55948	9.06069	8.60608	8.19087	7.81086	6.84737
17	14.57771	14.05500	13.56110	12.65230	11.83777	11.10590	9.85137	9.31256	8.82371	8.37916	7.97399	6.95424
18	15.29187	14.71220	14.16612	13.16567	12.27407	11.47726	10.12164	9.54363	9.02155	8.54879	8.11963	7.04716
19	15.99203	15.35336	14.75351	13.65930	12.68959	11.82760	10.37189	9.75563	9.20141	8.70162	8.24967	7.12797
20	16.67846	15.97889	15.32380	14.13394	13.08532	12.15812	10.60360	9.95012	9.36492	8.83929	8.36578	7.19823
21	17.35143	16.58916	15.87747	14.59033	13.46221	12.46992	10.81815	10.12855	9.51356	8.96333	8.46944	7.25933
22	18.01121	17.18455	16.41502	15.02916	13.82115	12.76408	11.01680	10.29224	9.64869	9.07507	8.56200	7.31246
23	18.65805	17.76541	16.93692	15.45112	14.16300	13.04158	11.20074	10.44243	9.77154	9.17574	8.64465	7.35866
24	19.29220	18.33211	17.44361	15.85684	14.48857	13.30338	11.37106	10.58021	9.88322	9.26643	8.71843	7.39884
25	19.91393	18.88499	17.93554	16.24696	14.79864	13.55036	11.52876	10.70661	9.98474	9.34814	8.78432	7.43377
26	20.52346	19.42438	18.41315	16.62208	15.09394	13.78336	11.67478	10.82258	10.07704	9.42174	8.84314	7.46415
27	21.12104	19.95061	18.87684	16.98277	15.37519	14.00317	11.80998	10.92897	10.16095	9.48806	8.89566	7.49056
28	21.70690	20.46401	19.32703	17.32959	15.64303	14.21053	11.93518	11.02658	10.23722	9.54780	8.94255	7.51353
29	22.28127	20.96489	19.76411	17.66306	15.89813	14.40616	12.05108	11.11613	10.30657	9.60162	8.98442	7.53351
30	22.84438	21.45355	20.18845	17.98371	16.14107	14.59072	12.15841	11.19828	10.36961	9.65011	9.02181	7.55088
31	23.39646	21.93029	20.60044	18.29203	16.37245	14.76483	12.25778	11.27365	10.42691	9.69379	9.05518	7.56598
32	23.93770	22.39541	21.00043	18.58849	16.59281	14.92909	12.34980	11,34280	10.47901	9.73315	9.08499	7.57911
33	24.46833	22.84918	21.38877	18.87355	16.80268	15.08404	12.43500	11.40624	10.52638	9.76860	9.11159	7.59053
34	24.98856	23.29188	21.76579	19.14765	17.00255	15.23023	12.51389	11.46444	10.56943	9.80054	9.13535	7.60046
35	25.49859	23.72379	22.13184	19.41120	17.19290	15.36814	12.58693	11.51784	10.60858	9.82932	9.15656	7.60910
36	25.99862	24.14516	22.48722	19.66461	17.37419	15.49825	12.65457	11.56682	10.64416	9.85524	9.17550	7.61661
37	26.48884	24.55625	22.83225	19.90828	17.54685	15.62099	12.71719	11.61176	10.67651	9.87859	9.19241	7.62314
38	26.96945	24.95732	23.16724	20.14258	17.71129	15.73678	12.77518	11.65299	10.70592	9.89963	9.20751	7.62882
39	27.44064	25.34860	23.49246	20.36786	17.86789	15.84602	12.82887	11.69082	10.73265	9.91859	9.22099	7.63375
40	27.90259	25.73034	23.80822	20.58448	18.01704	15.94907	12.87858	11.72552	10.75697	9.93567	9.23303	7.63805

QUESTIONS

1. What is the time value of money? Why should accountants have an understanding of compound interest, annuities, and present value concepts?

2. What is the nature of interest? Distinguish between "simple interest" and "compound interest."

3. What are the components of an interest rate? Why is it important for accountants to understand these components?

4. Presented below are a number of values taken from compound interest tables involving the same number of periods and the same rate of interest. Indicate what each of these four values represent.
   (a) 7.36009
   (b) 1.79085
   (c) .55839
   (d) 13.18079

5. Harmon Co. deposits $18,000 in a money market certificate that provides interest of 12% compounded quarterly if the amount is maintained for three years. How much will Harmon have at the end of three years?

6. Phil Bayliss will receive $30,000 five years from today from a trust fund established by his mother. Assuming the interest rate is 12%, compounded semiannually, what is the present value of this amount today?

7. What are the primary characteristics of an annuity? Differentiate between an "ordinary annuity" and an "annuity due."

8. Norm Zelten Inc. owes $30,000 to Parton Company. How much would Zelten have to pay each year if the debt is to be retired through four equal payments made at the end of each year and the interest rate on the debt is 15%? (Round to two decimals.)

9. The Foxes are planning for a retirement home. They estimate they will need $130,000 four years from now to purchase this home. Assuming an interest rate of 10%, what amount must be deposited at the end of each of the four years to fund the home price? (Round to two decimal places.)

10. Assume the same situation as in question 9, except that the four equal amounts are deposited at the beginning of the period rather than at the end. In this case, what amount must be deposited at the beginning of each period? (Round to two decimals.)

11. Explain how the amount of an ordinary annuity interest table is converted to the amount of an annuity due interest table.

12. Explain how the present value of an ordinary annuity interest table is converted to the present value of an annuity due interest table.

13. In a book named *Treasure*, the reader has to figure out where a one kilogram, 24 kt gold horse has been buried. If the horse is found, a prize of $25,000 a year for twenty years is provided. The actual cost of the publisher to purchase an annuity to pay the prize is $210,000. What interest rate (to the nearest percent) was used to determine the amount of the annuity? (Assume end-of-year payments.)

14. Harried Enterprises leases property to Lia Inc. Because Lia Inc. is experiencing financial difficulty, Harried agrees to receive five rents of $8,000 at the end of each year, with the rents deferred three years. What is the present value of the five rents discounted at 12%?

15. Kell Inc. invests $20,000 initially, which accumulates to $38,000 at the end of five years. What is the annual interest rate earned on the investment? (**Hint**: Interpolation will be needed.)

16. Answer the following questions:
    (a) On May 1, 1994, Pat Company sold some machinery to Merlin Company on an installment contract basis. The contract required five equal annual payments, with the first payment due on May 1, 1994. What present value concept is appropriate for this situation?
    (b) On June 1, 1994, Struthers Inc. purchased a new machine that it did not have to pay for until May 1, 1996. The total payment on May 1, 1996 will include both principal and interest. Assuming an interest rate of 12%, the cost of the machine will be the total payment multiplied by what time value of money concept?
    (c) Koppel Inc. wishes to know how much money it will have available in five years if five equal amounts of $30,000 are invested, with the first amount invested immediately. What interest table is appropriate for this situation?
    (d) Burrows invests in a "jumbo" $100,000 three-year certificate of deposit. What table will be used to determine the amount accumulated at the end of three years?

17. Recently Sally Hogan was interested in purchasing a Honda Acura. The salesperson indicated that the price of the car was either $25,000 cash or $6,400 at the end of each of five years. Compute the effective interest rate to the nearest percent that Hogan would have to pay if she chose to make the five annual payments.

18. A football player was reported to have received an $11 million contract. The terms were a signing bonus of $500,000 in 1991 plus $500,000 in 2001 through the year 2004. In addition, he was to receive a base salary of $300,000 in 1991 which was to increase $100,000 a year to the year 1995; in 1996 he was to receive $1 million a year which would increase $100,000 per year to the year 2000. Assuming that the appropriate interest rate was 9% and that each payment occurred on December 31 of the respective year, compute the present value of this contract as of December 31, 1991.

EXERCISES

(Interest rates are per annum unless otherwise indicated.)

EA-1 **(FUTURE AMOUNT AND PRESENT VALUE PROBLEMS)** Presented below are three unrelated situations:

(a) Twig Company recently signed a 10-year lease for a new office building. Under the lease agreement, a security deposit of $10,000 was made which would be returned at the expiration of the lease with interest compounded at 6% per year. What amount will the company receive when the lease expires?

(b) Patterson Corporation, having recently issued a $10 million, 15-year bond issue, is committed to make annual sinking fund deposits of $300,000. The deposits are made on the last day of each year and yield a return of 10%. Will the fund at the end of 15 years be sufficient to retire the bonds? If not, what will the excess or deficiency be?

(c) Under the terms of his salary agreement, President Jed Sorensen has an option of receiving either an immediate bonus of $50,000 or a deferred bonus of $100,000, payable in 10 years. Ignoring tax considerations and assuming a relevant interest rate of 8%, which form of settlement should President Sorensen accept?

EA-2 **(COMPUTATION OF BOND PRICES)** What will you pay for a $50,000 debenture bond that matures in 15 years and pays $5,000 interest at the end of each year if you want to earn a yield of: (a) 8%; (b) 10%; (c) 12%?

EA-3 **(COMPUTATIONS FOR A RETIREMENT FUND)** Mr. Bud Light, a super salesman contemplating retirement on his fifty-fifth birthday, plans to create a fund which will earn 8% and enable him to withdraw $15,000 per year on June 30, beginning in 1998 and continuing through 2001. Bud intends to make equal contributions to this fund on June 30 of each of the years 1994–1997.

Instructions

(a) How much must the balance of the fund equal on June 30, 1997 in order for Bud Light to satisfy his objective?

(b) What is the required amount of each of Bud's contributions to the fund?

EA-4 **(UNKNOWN PERIODS AND UNKNOWN INTEREST RATE)**

(a) Ron Boyle wishes to become a millionaire. His money market fund has a balance of $83,905.43 and has a guaranteed interest rate of 10%.

Instructions

How many years must Ron leave the balance in the fund in order to get his desired $1,000,000?

(b) Lila Osage desires to accumulate $1,000,000 in 15 years using her money market fund balance of $122,894.51.

Instructions

At what interest rate must her investment compound annually?

EA-5 **(ANALYSIS OF ALTERNATIVES)** S.O. Easy, a manufacturer of low-sodium, low-cholesterol TV dinners, would like to increase its market share in Atlantic Canada. In order to do so, S.O. Easy has decided to locate a new factory in the Halifax area. S.O. Easy will either buy or lease a building depending upon which is more advantageous. The site location committee has narrowed down the options to the following three buildings:

Building A: Purchase for a cash price of $1,000,000, useful life 25 years.

Building B: Lease for 25 years with annual payments of $115,000 being made at the beginning of the year.

Building C: Purchase for $1,080,000 cash. This building is larger than needed; however, the excess space can be sublet for 25 years at a net annual rental of $12,000. Rental payments will be received at the end of each year. S.O. Easy has no aversion to being a landlord.

Instructions

In which building would you recommend that S.O. Easy locate assuming a 12% interest rate?

EA-6 **(FUTURE AMOUNT AND CHANGING INTEREST RATES)** Lisa Fleck intends to invest $10,000 in a trust on January 10 of every year, 1994 to 2008, inclusive. She anticipates that interest rates will change during that period of time as follows:

1/10/94–1/09/97	10%
1/10/97–1/09/04	11%
1/10/04–1/09/08	12%

How much will Lisa have in trust on January 10, 2008?

EA-7 **(AMOUNT NEEDED TO RETIRE SHARES)** Arrow Inc. is a computer software development company. In recent years, it has experienced significant growth in sales. As a result, the Board of Directors has decided to raise funds by issuing redeemable preferred shares to meet cash needs for expansion. On January 1, 1993, the company issued 100,000 redeemable preferred shares with the intent to redeem them on January 1, 2003. The redemption price per share is $25.

As the controller of the company, Dean Rask is asked to set up a plan to accumulate the funds that will be needed to retire the redeemable preferred shares in 2003. He expects that the company will have a surplus of funds of $120,000 each year for the next 10 years and decides to put these amounts into a sinking fund. Beginning January 1, 1994, the company will deposit $120,000 into the sinking fund annually for 10 years. The sinking fund is expected to earn 10% interest compounded annually. However, the sinking fund will not be sufficient for the redemption of the preferred shares. Therefore, Dean plans to deposit on January 1, 1998 a single amount into a savings account which is expected to earn 8% interest.

Instructions

What is the amount that must be deposited on January 1, 1998?

EA-8 **(COMPUTATION OF PENSION LIABILITY)** Homemaker Inc. is a furniture manufacturing company with 50 employees. Recently, after a long negotiation with the local union, the company decided to initiate a pension plan as a part of its compensation package. The plan will start on January 1, 1994. Each employee covered by the plan is entitled to a pension payment each year after retirement. As required by accounting standards, the controller of the company needs to report the projected pension obligation (liability). On the basis of a discussion with the supervisor of the Personnel Department and an actuary from an insurance company, the controller develops the following information related to the pension plan.

Average length of time to retirement	15 years
Expected life duration after retirement	10 years
Total pension payment expected each year for all retired employees.	
Payment made at the end of the year.	$700,000/year
The interest rate is 8%.	

Instructions

On the basis of the information given, determine the projected pension obligation.

(RETIREMENT OF DEBT) Mike Bone borrowed $100,000 on March 1, 1994. This amount plus accrued interest at 12% compounded semiannually is to be repaid March 1, 2004. To retire this debt, Mike plans to contribute to a debt retirement fund five equal amounts starting March 1, 1999 and for the next four years. The fund is expected to earn 10% per annum. **EA-9**

Instructions

How much must Mike Bone contribute each year to provide a fund sufficient to retire the debt on March 1, 2004?

(PRESENT VALUE OF A BOND) Your client, Wayne Inc., has acquired Housepent Manufacturing Company in a business combination that is to be accounted for as a purchase transaction (at fair market value). Along with the assets of Housepent, Wayne assumed an outstanding liability for a debenture bond issue having a principal amount of $7,500,000 with interest payable semiannually at a rate of 9%. Housepent received $6,800,000 in proceeds from the issuance five years ago. The bonds are currently 20 years from maturity. Equivalent securities command a 12% current market rate of interest. **EA-10**

Instructions

Your client requests your advice regarding the amount to record for the acquired bond issue.

(LEAST COSTLY PAYOFF: ORDINARY ANNUITY) Elliot Corporation has outstanding a contractual debt. The corporation has available two means of settlement: (1) it can make an immediate payment of $2,250,000 or (2) it can make annual payments of $250,000 for 15 years, each payment due on the last day of the year. **EA-11**

Instructions

Which method of payment do you recommend, assuming an expected effective interest rate of 8%?

(LEAST COSTLY PAYOFF: ANNUITY DUE) Assuming the same facts as those in EA-11 except that the payments must begin now and be made on the first day of each of the 15 years, what payment method would you recommend? **EA-12**

(INTERPOLATING THE INTEREST RATE) On July 17, 1994, Kris Blader borrowed $42,000 from his grandfather to open a clothing store. Starting July 17, 1995, Kris has to make 10 equal annual payments of $6,700 each to repay the loan. **EA-13**

Instructions

What interest rate is Kris Blader paying? (Interpolation is required.)

(INTERPOLATING THE INTEREST RATE) As the purchaser of a new house, Sandra Hofer signed a mortgage note to pay the Canadian Bank $16,000 every six months for 20 years, at the end of which time she **EA-14**

will own the house. At the date the mortgage was signed, the purchase price was $198,000 and Sandra made a down payment of $20,000. The first mortgage payment is to be made six months after the date the mortgage was signed.

Instructions

Compute the exact rate of interest earned by the bank on the mortgage. (Interpolate if necessary.)

PROBLEMS

PA-1 **(COMPUTATION OF PRESENT VALUE)** Answer each of these unrelated questions:

1. On January 1, 1994, Gizmo Corporation sold a building that cost $250,000 and that had accumulated depreciation of $100,000 on the date of sale. Gizmo received as consideration a $275,000 noninterest-bearing note due on January 1, 1997. There was no established exchange price for the building and the note had no ready market. The prevailing rate of interest for a note of this type on January 1, 1994 was 9%. At what amount should the gain from the sale of the building be reported?

2. On January 1, 1994, Gizmo Corporation purchased 100 of the $1,000 face value, 10% ten-year bonds of Heath Inc. The bonds mature on January 1, 2004 and pay interest annually beginning January 1, 1995. Gizmo Corporation purchased the bonds to yield 11%. How much did Gizmo pay for the bonds?

3. Gizmo Corporation bought a new machine and agreed to pay for it in equal annual instalments of $4,000 at the end of each of the next 10 years. Assuming an interest rate of 8% applies to this contract, how much should Gizmo record as the cost of the machine?

4. Gizmo Corporation purchased a tractor on December 31, 1994, paying $16,000 cash on that date and agreeing to pay $10,000 at the end of each of the next eight years. At what amount should the tractor be valued on December 31, 1994, assuming an interest rate of 12%?

5. Gizmo Corporation wants to withdraw $50,000 (including principal) from an investment fund at the end of each year for nine years. What is the required initial investment at the beginning of the first year if the fund earns 11%?

PA-2 **(FUTURE AMOUNTS OF ANNUITIES DUE)** Mack Aroni, a bank robber, is worried about his retirement. He decides to start a savings account. Mack deposits annually his net share of the "loot," which consists of $70,000 per year, for three years beginning January 1, 1992. Mack is arrested on January 4, 1994 (after making the third deposit) and spends the rest of 1994 and most of 1995 in jail. He escapes in September of 1995 and resumes his savings plan with semiannual deposits of $25,000 each beginning January 1, 1996. Assume that the bank's interest rate is 8% compounded annually from January 1, 1992 through January 1, 1995, and 10% compounded semiannually thereafter.

Instructions

When Mack retires on January 1, 1999 (six months after his last deposit), what will be the balance in his savings account?

PA-3 **(ANALYSIS OF ALTERNATIVES)** Cheapo Inc. has decided to surface and maintain for ten years a vacant lot next to one of its discount retail outlets to serve as a parking lot for customers. Management is considering the following bids involving two different qualities of surfacing for a parking area of 12,000 square metres:

Bid A. A surface that costs $8.25 per square metre. This surface will have to be replaced at the end of five years. The annual maintenance cost on this surface is estimated at 15 cents per square metre for each year except the last of its service. The replacement surface will be similar to the initial surface.

Bid B. A surface that costs $12.50 per square metre. This surface has a probable useful life of 10 years and will require annual maintenance in each year except the last year, at an estimated cost of 5 cents per square metre.

Instructions

Prepare computations showing which bid should be accepted by Cheapo Inc. You may assume that the cost of capital is 9%, that the annual maintenance expenditures are incurred at the end of each year, and that prices are not expected to change during the next ten years.

(ANALYSIS OF ALTERNATIVES) When James Baker died, he left his wife Tammy an insurance policy contract that permitted her to choose any one of the following four options: PA-4

(a) $55,000 immediate cash.

(b) $3,600 every three months payable at the end of each quarter for five years.

(c) $20,000 immediate cash and $1,500 every three months for 10 years, payable at the beginning of each three-month period.

(d) $4,000 every three months for three years and $1,000 each quarter for the following 25 quarters, all payments payable at the end of each quarter.

Instructions

If money is worth 2½% per quarter, compounded quarterly, which option will you recommend that Tammy choose?

(COMPUTATION OF UNKNOWN PAYMENTS) Provide a solution to each of the following situations by computing the unknowns (use the interest tables): PA-5

(a) Winona Potts invests in a $125,000 annuity insurance policy at 9% compounded annually on February 8, 1994. The first of 20 receipts from the annuity is payable to Winona 10 years after the annuity is purchased (February 8, 2004). What will be the amount of each of the 20 equal annual receipts?

(b) Bill Sullivan owes a debt of $40,000 from the purchase of his new sports car. The debt bears interest of 8% payable annually. Bill wishes to pay the debt and interest in eight annual instalments, beginning one year hence. What equal annual instalments will pay the debt and interest?

(c) On January 1, 1994, Bob Mackey offers to buy David Martin's used combine for $39,000, payable in 10 equal instalments, which are to include 9% interest on the unpaid balance and a portion of the principal, with the first payment to be made on January 1, 1994. How much will each payment be?

(PURCHASE PRICE OF A BUSINESS: DEFERRED ANNUITIES) During the past year, Shawna Leonard planted a new vineyard on 150 hectares of land which she leases for $30,000 a year. She has asked you to assist in determining the value of her vineyard operation. PA-6

The vineyard will bear no grapes for the first five years (1–5). In the next five years (6–10), Shawna estimates that the vines will bear grapes that can be sold for $60,000 each year. For the next 20 years (11–30), she expects the harvest will provide annual revenues of $110,000. During the last 10 years (31–40) of the vineyard's life, she estimates that revenues will decline to $80,000 per year.

During the first five years the annual cost of pruning, fertilizing, and caring for the vineyard is estimated at $10,000; during the years of production, 6–40, these costs will rise to $15,000 per year. The relevant market rate of interest for the entire period is 12%. Assume that all receipts and payments are made at the end of each year.

Instructions

Rob Bryshun has offered to buy Shawna's vineyard business. On the basis of the current value of the business, what is the minimum price Shawna should accept?

PA-7 **(TIME VALUE CONCEPTS APPLIED TO SOLVE BUSINESS PROBLEMS)** Answer the following questions related to Lazybones Inc.:

1. Lazybones Inc. has $114,400 to invest. The company is trying to decide between two alternative uses of the funds. One alternative provides $16,000 at the end of each year for 12 years, and the other is to receive a single lump sum payment of $380,000 at the end of 12 years. Which alternative should Lazybones select? Assume the interest rate is constant over the entire investment.

2. Lazybones Inc. has just purchased a new computer. The fair market value of the equipment is $717,750. The purchase agreement specified an immediate down payment of $100,000 and semiannual payments of $80,000 beginning at the end of six months for five years. What interest rate, to the nearest percent, was used in discounting this purchase transaction?

3. Lazybones Inc. loaned $300,000 to Wright Corporation. Lazybones accepted a note due in seven years at 8% compounded semiannually. After two years (and receipt of interest for two years), Lazybones needed money and therefore sold the note to Royal Canadian Bank, which required interest on the note of 12% compounded semiannually. What amount did Lazybones receive from the sale of the note?

4. Lazybones Inc. wishes to accumulate $700,000 by December 31, 2004 to retire outstanding bonds. The company deposits $150,000 on December 31, 1994, which will earn interest at 10% per year compounded quarterly, to help in the debt retirement. The company wants to know what additional equal amounts should be deposited at the end of each quarter for 10 years to ensure that $700,000 is available at the end of 2004. (The quarterly deposits will also earn interest at a rate of 10%, compounded quarterly.) Round to even dollars.

PA-8 **(ANALYSIS OF BUSINESS PROBLEMS)** Dave Analyst is a financial executive with Peanuts Company. Although Dave has not had any formal training in finance or accounting, he has a "good sense" for numbers and has helped the company grow from a very small company ($1,000,000 sales) to a large operation ($90 million sales). With the business growing steadily, however, the company needs to make a number of difficult financial decisions in which Dave feels a little "over his head." He therefore decided to hire a new employee with facility in "numbers" to help him. As a basis for determining who to employ, he asked each prospective employee to prepare answers to questions relating to the following situations he has encountered recently. Here are the questions which you are asked to answer:

1. In 1993 Peanuts Company negotiated and closed a long-term lease contract for newly constructed truck terminals and freight storage facilities. The buildings were constructed on land owned by the company. On January 1, 1994, Peanuts Company took possession of the leased property. The 20-year lease is effective for the period January 1, 1994 through December 31, 2013. Rental payments of $800,000 are payable to the lessor (owner of facilities) on January 1 of each of the first 10 years of the lease term. Payments of $300,000 are due on January 1 for each of the last 10 years of the lease term. Peanuts has an option to purchase all the leased facilities for $1.00 on December 31, 2013. At the time the lease was negotiated, the fair market of the truck terminals and freight storage facilities was approximately $6,500,000. If the company had borrowed the money to purchase the facilities, it would have to pay 10% interest. Should the company have purchased rather than leased the facilities?

2. Last year the company exchanged some land for a noninterest-bearing note. The note was to be paid at the rate of $20,000 per year for nine years, beginning one year from the date of the exchange. The interest rate for the note was 11%. At the time the land was originally purchased, it cost $90,000. What is the fair value of the note?

3. The company has always followed the policy to take any cash discounts offered on goods purchased. Recently the company purchased a large amount of raw materials at a price of $800,000 with terms 1/10, n/30 on which it took the discount. If Peanuts' cost of funds was 10%, should the policy of always taking cash discount be continued?

PA-9 **(ANALYSIS OF LEASE VS. PURCHASE)** Helpless Inc. owns and operates a number of hardware stores on the Prairies. Recently the company has decided to locate another store in a rapidly growing area of Manitoba; the company is trying to decide whether to purchase or lease the building and related facilities.

Purchase. The company can purchase the site, construct the building, and purchase all store fixtures. The cost would be $1,650,000. An immediate down payment of $400,000 is required, and the remaining $1,250,000 would be paid off over five years at $300,000 per year (including interest). The property is expected to have a useful life of 12 years and then it will be sold for $400,000. As the owner of the property, the company will have the following out-of-pocket expenses each period:

Property taxes (to be paid at the end of each year)	$48,000
Insurance (to be paid at the beginning of each year)	27,000
Other (maintenance which primarily occurs at the end of each year)	16,000
	$91,000

Lease. Strongman Corp. Ltd. has agreed to purchase the site, construct the building, and install the appropriate fixtures for Helpless Inc. if Helpless will lease the completed facility for 12 years. The annual costs for the lease will be $250,000. The lease would be a triple-net lease, which means that Helpless will have no responsibility related to the facility over the 12 years. The terms of the lease are that Helpless would be required to make 12 annual payments (the first payment to be made at the time the store opens and then each following year). In addition, a deposit of $125,000 is required when the store is opened, which will be returned at the end of the twelfth year, assuming no unusual damage to the building structure or fixtures.

Currently the cost of funds for Helpless Inc. is 10%.

Instructions

Which of the two approaches should Helpless Inc. follow?

(PRESENT VALUE BUSINESS PROBLEMS) Presented below are a series of time value of money problems. Solve each of them. **PA-10**

(a) Your client, Young Chen, wishes to provide for the payment of an obligation of $250,000 due on July 1, 2002. Chen plans to deposit $20,000 in a special fund each July 1 for eight years, starting July 1, 1995. She also wishes to make a deposit on July 1, 1994 of an amount that, with its accumulated interest, will bring the fund up to $250,000 at the maturity of the obligation. She expects that the fund will earn interest at the rate of 8% compounded annually. Compute the amount to be deposited on July 1, 1994.

(b) On January 1, 1994, Kap Inc. initiated a pension plan under which each of its employees will receive a pension annuity of $10,000 per year beginning one year after retirement and continuing until death. Employee A will retire at the end of 2000 and, according to mortality tables, is expected to live long enough to receive eight pension payments. What is the present value of Kap Inc.'s pension obligation for employee A at the beginning of 1994 if the interest rate is 10%?

(c) Yurie Company purchases bonds from Erica Inc. in the amount of $400,000. The bonds are 10-year, 13% bonds that pay interest semiannually. After three years (and receipt of interest for three years), Yurie needs money and, therefore, sells the bonds to Korea Company, which demands interest at 16% compounded semiannually. What is the amount that Yurie will receive on the sale of the bonds?

INDEX

WE WANT TO HEAR FROM YOU!

By sharing your opinions about Intermediate Accounting 4/E, you will help us ensure that you are getting the most value for your textbook dollars. After you have used the book for a while, please fill out this form. Either fold, tape, and mail, or fax us toll free @ 1(800)565-6802!

Course name: ______________________ School name: ______________________

Your name: ______________________

I am using: ❑ Volume 1 ❑ Volume 2

1) Did you purchase this book (check all that apply):
   ❑ From your campus bookstore
   ❑ From a bookstore off-campus
   ❑ New ❑ Used ❑ For yourself
   ❑ For yourself and at least one other student

2) Was this text available at the bookstore when you needed it?
   ❑ Yes ❑ No

3) Was the study guide available for purchase?
   ❑ Yes ❑ No ❑ Don't know
   If yes, did you purchase it?
   ❑ Yes ❑ No ❑ I intend to purchase it

4) How far along are you in this course (put an ✘ where you are now)?
   ❑ ____________ ❑ ____________ ❑
   Beginning Midway Completed

5) How much have you used this text (put an ✘ where appropriate)?
   ❑ ____________ ❑ ____________ ❑
   Skimmed Read Half Read entire book

6) Have you read the introductory material (i.e., the preface)?
   ❑ Yes ❑ No ❑ Parts of it

7) Even if you have only skimmed this text, please rate the following features:

Features:	Very valuable/effective	Somewhat valuable/effective	Not valuable/effective
Value as a reference			
Readability			
Design & illustrations			
Study & review material			
Problems & cases			
Relevant examples			
Overall perception			

8) What do you like most about this book?

____

____

____

What do you like least?

____

____

____

9) At the end of the semester, what do you intend to do with this text?
   ❑ Keep it ❑ Sell it ❑ Unsure

Thank you for your time and feedback!

WILEY

(fold here)

0108529899-M9W1L1-BR01

COLLEGE DIVISION
JOHN WILEY & SONS CANADA LTD
22 WORCESTER RD
PO BOX 56213 STN BRM B
TORONTO ON M7Y 9C1

(tape shut)